KLEPPNER'S
Advertising Procedure

Fourteenth Edition

KLEPPNER'S

Advertising Procedure

Fourteenth Edition

J. Thomas Russell
UNIVERSITY OF GEORGIA

W. Ronald Lane
UNIVERSITY OF GEORGIA

Prentice Hall, Upper Saddle River, New Jersey 07458

Acquisitions Editor: Whitney Blake
Editorial Assistant: Michele Foresta
Editor-in-Chief: Natalie Anderson
Marketing Manager: Shannon Moore
Production Editor: Aileen Mason
Permissions Coordinator: Monica Stipanov
Managing Editor: Dee Josephson
Associate Managing Editor: Linda DeLorenzo
Manufacturing Supervisor: Arnold Vila
Manufacturing Manager: Vincent Scelta
Designer: Ann France
Design Manager: Pat Smythe
Interior Design: Nicole Leong
Photo Research Supervisor: Melinda Lee Reo
Image Permission Supervisor: Kay Dellosa
Photo Researcher: Beth Boyd
Cover Design: Ann France
Illustrator (Interior): Electra Graphics, Inc.
Cover Illustration: Diana Ong/SuperStock, Inc.
Composition: York Production Services

Part and Chapter Opener Credits

1, 2: Library of Congress. **2:** Amazon.Com Books, Inc. **22:** Scott McKiernan/Zuma Press. **82:** Barbara Campbell/Gamma-Liaison, Inc. **112:** Ken Cavanagh/Photo Researchers, Inc. **140:** Courtesy of International Business Machines Corporation. Unauthorized use is not permitted. **168–169, 170:** Courtesy MTV. **198:** Robert E. Daemmrich/Tony Stone Images. **231:** Charles Gupton/Tony Stone Images. **255:** Courtesy Saturn Media Center. **288:** Dick Luria/FPG International. **330:** Hunter Freeman/Goodby, Silverstein & Partners. © California Milk Processor Board. **352:** Renee Lynn/Photo Researchers, Inc. **388:** Churchill & Klehr Photography. **420–421, 422:** Jeff Greenberg/Picture Cube, Inc. **446:** Chris Thomaidis/Tony Stone Images. **470:** Ronny Jaques/Photo Researchers, Inc. **490:** Macy's West. **521:** Goodby, Silverstein & Partners. **546:** Richard Hutchings/PhotoEdit. **562:** Daniel E. Wray/The Image Works. **587:** Paul Aresu/FPG International. **604–605, 606:** John Coletti. **628:** PhotoDisc, Inc. **652:** PhotoDisc, Inc. **675:** Michelle Bridwell/PhotoEdit.

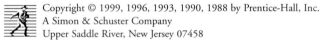
Library of Congress Cataloging-in-Publication Data
Russell, Thomas
    Kleppner's advertising procedure/J. Thomas Russell, W. Ronald
Lane. — 14th ed.
      p.   cm.
    Includes bibliographical references and index.
    ISBN 0-13-908575-0
    1. Advertising.   I. Lane, W. Ronald.   II. Kleppner,
Otto, 1899 –   Advertising procedure.   III. Title.
HF5823.K45   1998
659.1 — dc21   98-17851
                                          CIP

Prentice-Hall International (UK) Limited, London
Prentice-Hall of Australia Pty. Limited, Sydney
Prentice-Hall Canada, Inc., Toronto
Prentice-Hall Hispanoamericana, S.A., Mexico
Prentice-Hall of India Private Limited, New Delhi
Prentice-Hall of Japan, Inc., Tokyo
Simon & Schuster Asia Pte. Ltd., Singapore
Editora Prentice-Hall do Brasil, Ltda., Rio de Janeiro

Printed in the United States of America

10 9 8 7 6 5 4 3 2 1

BRIEF CONTENTS

Preface   xi
Instructor Support Material   xiii
Acknowledgments   xv
About the Authors   xvii

PART I   The Place of Advertising

Chapter 1   Background of Today's Advertising   2
Chapter 2   Roles of Advertising   22

PART II   Planning the Advertising   52

Chapter 3   The Advertising Spiral and Brand Planning   54
Chapter 4   Target Marketing   82

PART III   Managing the Advertising   110

Chapter 5   The Advertising Agency, Media Services, and Other Services   112
Chapter 6   The Advertiser's Marketing/Advertising Operation   140

PART IV   Media   168

Chapter 7   Basic Media Strategy   170
Chapter 8   Using Television   198
Chapter 9   Using Radio   229
Chapter 10 Using Newspapers   253
Chapter 11 Using Magazines   286
Chapter 12 Out-of-Home Advertising   330
Chapter 13 Direct-Response and Direct-Mail Advertising   352
Chapter 14 Sales Promotion   388

PART V   Creating the Advertising   420

Chapter 15 Research in Advertising   422
Chapter 16 Creating the Copy   446
Chapter 17 The Total Concept: Words and Visuals   470
Chapter 18 Print Production   490
Chapter 19 The Television Commercial   521
Chapter 20 The Radio Commercial   546
Chapter 21 Trademarks and Packaging   562
Chapter 22 The Complete Campaign   587

PART VI   Other Environments of Advertising   604

    Chapter 23 Retail Advertising   606
    Chapter 24 International Advertising   628
    Chapter 25 Legal and Other Restraints on Advertising   652
    Chapter 26 Economic and Social Effects of Advertising   675

Glossary   699
Index   706

CONTENTS

Preface   xi

Instructor Support Material   xiii

Acknowledgments   xv

About the Authors   xvii

PART I   The Place of Advertising

Chapter 1   Background of Today's Advertising   2
Beginnings   4
Origins of Newspaper Advertising   6
Three Momentous Decades: 1870–1900   6
America Enters the Twentieth Century   12
Advertising Comes of Age   13

Chapter 2   Roles of Advertising   22
Advertising, the Marketing Mix, and Integrated Marketing   25
CASE HISTORY: VISA'S "READ ME A STORY" PROGRAM TAKES TO THE ROAD: KETCHUM PUBLIC RELATIONS AND VISA U.S.A.   28
Advertising as an Institution   31
Advertising to Diverse Customer Interests   32
A Good Product that Meets a Perceived Need   35
Variations in the Importance of Advertising   40
The Place of Advertising in the Marketing Process   42
Advertising to the Consumer   43
Advertising to Business and Professions   46
Nonproduct Advertising   48

PART II   Planning the Advertising   52

Chapter 3   The Advertising Spiral and Brand Planning   54
Pioneering Stage   55
The Competitive Stage   59
The Retentive Stage   60
The Advertising Spiral   62

Chapter 4   Target Marketing   82
Defining Prime Prospects   83
Marketing Concept and Targeting   88
Planning the Advertising   92
Positioning   98
Profile of the Buyer   102
Beyond Demographics: Psychographics   103

PART III   Managing the Advertising   110

Chapter 5   The Advertising Agency, Media Services, and Other Services   112
The Agency   113
How Agencies Developed   113
CASE HISTORY: GENERATING NEW BUSINESS: GREG & GREG ADVERTISING   116
The Full-Service Agency   118
The Traditional Agency Organization   120
The Reengineering of the Agency   123
Global Agencies and Global Markets   126
Competing Accounts   128
Agency-Client Relationship Length   129
Agency of Record   129
Agency Multiple Offices   129
Agency Networks   130
Other Advertising Services   131
Forms of Agency Compensation   133
Other Services   135
CASE HISTORY: AMERICAN EXPRESS TRAVEL RELATED SERVICES COMPANY AND THE AMERICAN AUTOMOBILE ASSOCIATION PROMOTIONAL PROGRAM   138

Chapter 6   The Advertiser's Marketing/Advertising Operation   140
Marketing-Services System   141
Integrated Marketing Brand Management   143
Corporate Restructuring   147
Setting the Budget   148
The Changing Marketing Environment   152
Managing Brands   154
Agency-Client Relationships   156
Appraising National Advertising   160
Changes in Marketing   161
CASE HISTORY: SEA • DOO DIVISION, BARBARDIER MOTOR CORPORATION OF AMERICA   165

PART IV   Media   168

Chapter 7   Basic Media Strategy   170
Need for Greater Cost Efficiencies   172
CASE HISTORY: BRIDGESTONE SPORTS (U.S.A.) "PUT SOMETHING EXTRA . . .": PRECEPT EV EXTRA SPIN GOLF BALL   173
Achieving Minimum Waste Circulation   174
Consider New, Nontraditional Media Vehicles   175

Coordinate All Phases of Marketing
   Communication   176
Media Characteristics   177
The Components of the Media Plan   184
The Media Schedule   193
The Pressure of Competition   195
The Budget   195

Chapter 8   Using Television   198
Television as an Advertising Medium   199
The Rating-Point System   201
Share of Audience   203
The Many Faces of Television   204
CASE HISTORY: SIMMONS BEAUTYREST
   MATTRESS "DO-NOT-DISTURB"
   CAMPAIGN   205
Television Syndication   216
Cable Television   218
The Videocassette Recorder   222
Syndicated Rating Services   223
Sweeps   225
The Internet and the Electronic Superhighway   226

Chapter 9   Using Radio   229
Features and Advantages of Radio   230
CASE HISTORY: A FEW GOOD WOMEN,
   UNITED STATES MARINE CORPS   233
Limitations and Challenges of Radio   237
Technical Aspects of Radio   239
Selling Radio Commercial Time   240
Radio Ratings Services   245
Rate Classifications   246
Buying Radio   247
Using Radio Ratings   248

Chapter 10   Using Newspapers   253
The State of the Newspaper Industry:
   An Overview   254
CASE HISTORY: GEORGIA DOT EXPRESS
   LANES INTRODUCTION CAMPAIGN—
   CATEGORY: TRANSPORTATION   256
The National Newspaper   259
Marketing the Newspaper   260
Zoning, Total Market Coverage, and Newspaper
   Networks   264
Categories of Newspaper Advertising   266
Circulation Analysis   276
Technology and the Future of Newspapers   279
Newspaper-Distributed Magazine Supplements   280
The African American and Hispanic Press   281
Weekly Newspapers   283

Chapter 11   Using Magazines   286
Selectivity   287
CASE HISTORY: VOICE IT PERSONAL NOTE
   RECORDER   288
Costs and Revenues   290
Media Competition and Media Imperatives
   (Comparatives)   292
Cross-Media Buys   294
Magazines as an Advertising Medium   294
Features of Magazine Advertising   297
Magazine Elements   301
How Space Is Sold   306
Magazine Circulation   312
Measuring Magazine Audiences   314
Consumer Magazines—Summing Up   315
The Business Press and Business-to-Business
   Advertising   315
CASE HISTORY: ALCOA TRADE
   CAMPAIGN   320

Chapter 12   Out-of-Home
   Advertising   330
Out-of-Home Advertising   332
The Outdoor Industry: An Advertiser
   Perspective   333
Forms of Outdoor Advertising   337
The Elements of Outdoor   341
Measuring Outdoor Audiences   344
Transit Advertising   346
Shelter Advertising   349

Chapter 13   Direct-Response
   and Direct-Mail Advertising   352
Definition of Terms in Direct Response   353
The Modern Direct-Response Industry   354
Growth of Direct-Response Advertising   355
Database Marketing   358
Telemarketing   360
Radio and Direct Response   367
Magazines and Direct Response   368
Characteristics of Successful Direct-Response
   Advertising   369
Types of Direct-Response Offers   370
One-Step Purchase—Direct Sales   370
Two-Step Purchase—Getting Leads   374
Direct-Mail Advertising   376
The Mailing List   379
Planning and Producing the Direct-Mail Piece   382

Chapter 14　Sales Promotion　388
Promotion and Advertising　389
Forms of Sales Promotion　391
Point-of-Purchase Advertising　391
CASE HISTORY: KEEBLER SUMMER HANGOUT
　CAMPAIGN　396
Specialty Advertising　397
Coupons　400
Sampling　402
Event Marketing　406
Sweepstakes and Contests　408
CASE HISTORY: GOLD'N PLUMP POULTRY
　INSTANT WINNER SWEEPSTAKES　409
Cooperative Advertising　410
Trade Shows and Exhibits　413
Directories and Yellow Pages　414
Trade Incentives　417

**PART V　Creating the
　Advertising**　420

Chapter 15　Research in Advertising　422
Research Is an Informational Tool　423
The Right Kind of Research　424
Public Attitude Toward Survey Research　424
Advanced Analytics　424
Strategic or Account Planners　425
What Kind of Research Is Needed?　426
The Series of Research Steps in Advertising　435
Testing Creative Research　439

Chapter 16　Creating the Copy　446
Advertising's Challenge: A New Creative Vision　446
How Do We Create Great Advertising?　448
The Nature and Use of Appeals　448
Great Advertising Elements　451
Structure of an Advertisement　452
Copy Style　459
Slogans　462
The Creative Work Plan　464
Guidelines for Creating an Ad　464

**Chapter 17　The Total Concept:
　Words and Visuals**　470
Ideas Come from the Left and Right Brain　472
The Creative Team　472
The Idea　472
The Creative Leap　473

Chapter 18　Print Production　490
The Age of Digital Advertising and Production　491
Prepress Process　492
Print Production　493
Production Data　495
Production Planning and Scheduling　496
Selecting the Printing Process　497
Understanding Typography　500
Type and Reading　501
Typefaces　502
Type Fonts and Families　503
Typesetting　505
Electronic Mechanical and Artwork　505
Sending Duplicate Material　517
Other Production Advances　517

**Chapter 19　The Television
　Commercial**　521
Copy Development and Production Timetable　523
Creating the Television Commercial　523
Producing the TV Commercial　537
Role of the Producer　538
Controlling the Cost of Commercial Production　542

Chapter 20　The Radio Commercial　546
The Nature of the Medium　546
Radio Is the Great Equalizer　547
Creating the Commercial　548
Developing the Radio Script　549
Writing the Commercial　550
Timing of Commercials　554
Musical Commercials　556
Methods of Delivery　558
Producing the Radio Commercial　559

**Chapter 21　Trademarks
　and Packaging**　562
What Is a Trademark?　563
House Marks　573
Service Marks, Certification Marks　573
Company and Product Names　573
Packaging　577

Chapter 22　The Complete Campaign　587
Situation Analysis　589
Creative Objectives and Strategy　590
Media Objectives　596
Getting the Campaign Approved　597
Research—Posttests　597
CASE HISTORY: DUN & BRADSTREET
　SOFTWARE　602

PART VI Other Environments
of Advertising 604

Chapter 23   Retail Advertising 606
Retail Branding 608
Consumer Attitudes 612
Retailing in the Late 1990s 614
National and Retail Advertising 614
Types of Retail Advertising 614
The Retail Advertising Mix 616
CASE HISTORY: FOLKS RESTAURANT 625

**Chapter 24   International
Advertising** 628
Advertising, Marketing, and International Sales 630
Global Marketing and Advertising 631
Political and Economic Movements toward a World
Economy 634
The Multinational Advertising Agency 636
The Advertising Function in International
Advertising 639
Media Planning: A Global Perspective 642
International Advertising Legal and Regulatory
Prohibitions 645
Advertising Diversity in the United States 646

**Chapter 25   Legal and Other Restraints
on Advertising** 652
The Federal Trade Commission 654
The Robinson-Patman Act and Cooperative
Advertising 659
The Federal Food, Drug, and Cosmetic Act 660
Other Federal Controls of Advertising 660
Advertising and the First Amendment 661
Advertising of Professional Services 664
State and Local Laws Relating to Advertising 666
Comparative Advertising 667
The Advertising Clearance Process 668
Self-Regulation by Industrywide Groups 670

**Chapter 26   Economic and Social Effects
of Advertising** 675
The Economic Role of Advertising 676
The Social Role of Advertising 681
Types of Advertising Criticism 683
Inadvertent Social Implications of Advertising 689
Overt Use of Advertising for Social Causes 690
Advertising and Influence on Editorial
Considerations 695

Glossary 699
Index 706

In its fourteenth edition, *Kleppner's Advertising Procedure* continues to present the latest techniques, theories, and procedures common to the various elements of the advertising industry. Throughout the text, students are exposed to contemporary developments in marketing, advertising, and promotion. In keeping with the tradition of earlier editions, students will find that the text has been significantly updated to include industry practices about areas such as new media and Web site advertising, the move to digital graphics, and the latest developments in marketing and advertising research.

The current edition takes note of the interrelationships of the various fields of marketing communication. In text, cases, and exhibits, students are offered examples of the necessity of an integrated approach to marketing, advertising, and other business functions. Increasingly, companies are asking their marketing executives and agencies to utilize all facets of marketing communication in the most creative way possible. In this environment, it is crucial that students be conversant with all forms of promotion. The marketing executive of the twenty-first century will be required to be flexible and inventive in using an array of techniques that will be most successful in reaching audiences that are often fragmented both demographically and geographically.

Despite a more integrated approach to marketing communications, the major emphasis of the text continues to be the practice and philosophy of advertising. The text is not a marketing book, but rather an advertising text that places the advertising function within a marketing framework. The authors seek to show how the advertising function must be coordinated with all other aspects of marketing communications.

The authors recognize that the practice of advertising takes no single approach and that few fixed rules apply to every situation. Likewise, successful advertising is usually only one element within a complex matrix of product quality, consumer perception and preferences, pricing, distribution, and a number of other marketing, sociological, and psychological factors. Although bad advertising may doom a product to failure, the best advertising, in itself, will rarely achieve long-term sales success. The authors also seek to place advertising in historical, global, legal, and cultural perspectives.

In the past 50 years, as manufacturers find an increasing number of opportunities abroad, international advertising has become the norm for many companies. Similarly, the growing diversity of the U.S. population has required a greater knowledge and sensitivity of the culture, communication, and purchase habits of various segments of our domestic population. In the past two decades, advertising has begun to reflect more accurately and fairly the roles that women, minorities, and the increasingly large ethnic groups play in our multicultural society.

The fourteenth edition also explores the exciting technological developments that will play an even more important role in advertising over the next few years. In the near future, technology will provide speedier and more personal communication. It also will provide the public with the availability of two-way communication much more under the control of the audience. The transition from one-way to two-way communication offers a number of challenges and opportunities to advertisers. The text seeks to put these emerging media in a context of how they will affect advertising as well as those that seem to have the most practical applications in the coming years.

Kleppner's Advertising Procedure is divided into six parts that are organized according to the major topical areas of contemporary advertising. The first part deals with the historical development of advertising as it grew from the earliest exchange of goods to the modern era of the sophisticated buying of goods and services. Chapter 2 traces the many roles of advertising and promotion available to solve an array of marketing problems, and it includes a discussion of the limitation of advertising when used to address issues other than communications.

The second part of the text focuses on advertising planning and research. Successful advertising begins with the interpretation of reliable research that highlights consumer needs. It is said that product success is determined as much by consumer perceptions as any inherent characteristics of the product itself. Therefore, every aspect of product development and promotion must begin with a consumer perspective.

The third part of the text discusses the management and organization of the advertising function. Chapters 5 and 6 review the advertising management function from both the client and agency perspectives. In particular, issues such as brand management, marketing, and major changes in agency structure are outlined.

Part IV begins our discussion of the diverse media that advertisers utilize to carry the millions of promotional messages created each year. The assortment of media options is huge and growing larger each year. From network television to the Internet, media planners must choose the most efficient vehicles from both cost and communication perspectives. Chapter 7 introduces the media planning function. Chapters 8 to 14 offer a detailed discussion of each of the major media.

Part IV emphasizes the fact that there are no superior or inferior media. Rather, different communication vehicles are more suitable for solving certain types of problems. The media planner must be able to objectively judge all media and promotional vehicles to select the combination that will best serve the specific needs of particular marketing problems.

Part V begins our discussion of the creative function. Advertising creativity is purposely discussed in the later chapters of the text. Although it is true that most consumers consider the finished advertisements and commercials as defining the field, creative ideas are usually the result of research that offers insight into consumer, product selection, and media preferences. Chapters 15 to 23 seek to outline the many steps of planning, research, and production necessary to bring the rough idea to fruition as a finished ad. Contrary to popular opinion, great advertising is rarely the result of spontaneous ideas, but rather the fruit of long hours of hard work and study.

Part VI, a discussion of some specialized areas of advertising, concludes the text. Chapter 24 discusses the ever-changing face of international advertising and the unique skills necessary for its successful execution. Chapter 25 outlines the legal, regulatory, and public policy environment in which advertising operates. Chapter 26 focuses on an overview of ethical and economic aspects of advertising and brings together a number of issues discussed throughout the text.

Kleppner's Advertising Procedure is intended for three types of students. The first is planning a career in advertising and will go on to more advanced courses in the several areas covered by the text. The second group of students is majoring in related fields such as marketing or management. To those students, the text offers a foundation on which to understand the place of advertising in the general business environment. Finally, a number of students study advertising as an interesting elective area. Our hope is that the text provides this group with useful insights into becoming more sophisticated and intelligent consumers. To all, the authors hope that we have offered you insights into the profession and at the same time conveyed our sense of anticipation and enthusiasm over this ever-changing, but never dull business.

J. Thomas Russell

W. Ronald Lane

Since the publication of the thirteenth edition, we have gathered feedback on the various ancillary items that support *Kleppner's Advertising Procedure*. Through written reviews and focus groups, we have worked to refine and improve each item that is furnished to adopters and to provide direction on how all these materials can be used to create the best possible course. Your feedback on these support materials is very important to us, and we hope you will send us your comments and suggestions.

Instructor's Manual

Prepared by James V. Dupree of Grove City College, this manual contains (for each chapter)

> Learning Objectives
> Chapter Overview
> Lecture Outline
> Key Terms
> Answers to Case and End of Chapter questions
> Class Projects and Exercises including new Internet exercises
> Suggested video clips and commercials with a transcript of the video segment.

The manual also contains a section that describes the various video and Internet resources available to adopters of *Kleppner's Advertising Procedure* 14/E.

Test Item File

There are approximately 125 questions per chapter including true/false, multiple choice, application questions, and essay (for each chapter). In addition, the test file now includes some questions on the cases in the text.

PH Custom Test

The Prentice Hall Custom Test is available in both Windows and Mac versions.

PowerPoint Lecture Presentations

Prepared by Dynamic Presentations, these files include over 400 slides for use in preparing lecture presentations. The material presented enhances the text material, but does not duplicate the chapter material. Many of the key lecture slides are available in the package of overhead transparencies.

Color Acetate Transparencies

In addition to the PowerPoint resource, we have prepared a set of color acetates to enhance lectures. These transparencies include some of the PowerPoint files as well as a selection of print advertisements organized by general category/concept, and accompanied by brief lecture suggestions.

Advertising Video Library

New to the fourteenth edition, we are pleased to provide a comprehensive video library. These segments, ranging from eight to fifteen minutes, cover a wide range of concepts in the advertising course. They are company/campaign-based video segments, and many include broadcast commercials from the campaign or product. Examples include Got Milk?, Nike, Starbucks, Intel, Dupont, Nivea, Levi's Dockers, Lands' End, and many others.

In addition, the latest version of New York Festivals is included as a separate tape with the video library. This cassette features award-winning ads from 1996 and 1997. A new tape is available on an annual basis.

Web/Internet Resources

www.prenhall.com/phbusiness/phlip

New to the fourteenth edition, Prentice Hall is proud to offer the best Web resource in the industry for both professors and students. PHLIP is a comprehensive Web site that supports Prentice Hall Business Publishing. As one of the featured titles on PHLIP, *Kleppner's Advertising Procedure* offers bimonthly updates by chapter, which include timely readings and internet links. A password-protected Professor resource section allows adopters to download the *Instructor's Manual* and PowerPoint files, along with a set of video case/internet exercises that are supported in the video library. PHLIP also includes a feedback feature and bulletin board for professors teaching the introductory advertising course. Additional teaching resources are also available in the "faculty lounge" feature.

Student resources include updates, and access to study tips, software help, and related Web site links. PHLIP can be used to organize homework and out of class exercises and projects for students. PHLIP is developed and maintained by Dan Cooper of Marist College. Dan and his PHLIP team are improving the site every day and offering you more content, more suggestions, and more exciting resources for advertising. Visit the site now, and see what awaits you and your students!

ACKNOWLEDGMENTS

Over the years, *Kleppner's Advertising Procedure* has depended on the advice and expertise of hundreds of professional advertisers. Media planners, account executives, creative personnel, and marketing directors at numerous companies have combined their knowledge to offer students the latest information about the changing fields of advertising and promotion. Although the authors are solely responsible for the content of the text, we are indebted to the following people who have offered their counsel in the preparation of the fourteenth edition of the book.

John Adams, *Bozell, Jacobs, Kenyon & Eckhart*
Kimberly Alexander, *Siddall, Matus & Coughter Inc.*
Catherine L. Amann, *Inter-Act Promotion Network*
Jack Avrett, *Avrett, Free & Ginsberg*
Joanne Barthel, *Trade Fixtures*
Mike Bednarski, *Cramer-Krasselt*
Sheri Lane Bevil, *Folks Restaurant*
Carrie Bissell, *Technicolor Video Services*
John Bolton, *Bolton Group*
Edyie Brooks, *Healthtex, Inc.*
Tina Carlson, *Morton Vardeman & Assoc.*
Lynn Cass, Macon Magazine
Cathy Coffey, *Cox Newspapers*
Lynne Collins, *Council of Better Business Bureaus, Inc.*
Brett Compton, *Sawyer Riley Compton*
Phil Cuttino, *Cuttino Communications*
Tony Dieste, *Dieste & Partners*
Tim Duncan, *Advertiser Syndicated Television Association*
Chad Farmer, *Lambesis*
Amy Gard, *Direct Language Communications, Inc.*
Teresa Gay, *VISA*
Stephanie Glazer, *Fitzgerald & Co.*
Jeff Goodby, *Goodby, Silverstein & Partners*
Karen Gould, *Ketchum Public Relations*
Chris B. Hall, *J. Walter Thompson*
Joyce Harrington, *Periscope Marketing Communications*
Jackie Hathiramani, *Ogilvy & Mather–Singapore*
Sharon Hicks, *Aydlotte & Cartwright*
Dorothy Hughes-Shields, *Hughes Advertising*
Ben Icard, *Clear Choice Marketing*
David Dean Jacobs, *Eight-Sheet Outdoor Advertising Association, Inc.*
William Jelinek, *Verified Audit Circulation*
Shari Katz & Frances Seleh, *WebConnect*
Nicholas Keyes, *Key-Ads*
Jean Koelz, *Periscope Marketing Communications*
Jason Koertge, *Sprecher Bertalot & Co.*
Brian LaBadie, *Super Graphics, Inc.*
Russell N. Laczniak, *Iowa State University*
Bradford P. Majors, *Greg & Greg Advertising*
Rick Marks, *Newspaper National Network*
Chuck McBride, *Foote Cone & Belding/San Francisco*
Donald S. Morgan, *WestWayne*

Bill Morin, *Nabisco Foods*
Misti Morningstar, *Morning Star Design*
Terry O'Reilly, *Pirate Radio & Television*
Joe Ostrow, *Cabletelevision Advertising Bureau*
Shawn Parr, *Bulldog Drummond*
Janelle Pederson, *Transtop*
Don Perry, *Chick-fil-A, Inc.*
Richard Podolec, *Moot Wood Turnings*
Rick Radermacher, *Pollak Levitt Chaiet Advertising*
David C. Raines, *Coca-Cola (Japan) Co., Ltd.*
Julia Rallenby, *Waggener & Associates, Inc.*
Herman Ramsey, *WGNX-TV*
Richard Riley, *Sawyer Riley Compton*
Chris Robb, *BBDO West*
Philip Sawyer, *Roper Starch Worldwide*
Bruce K. Seidel, *Shelter Advertising Assoc.*
Jay Shields, *Austin Kelley Advertising Inc.*
Jane Shivers, *Ketchum Public Relations*
Lauren Slaff, *McCann-Erickson*
Rick Sullivan, *PS Promotions, Inc.*
David Swaebe, *Ingalls Advertising*
Lorraine Tao, *Leo Burnett Co. Ltd.*
Debbie Thornton, *Yellow Pages Publishers Association, Inc.*
John Tsao, *Magazine Publishers of America*
Paula A. Venle, *The Advertising Council*
Peter R. Viento, *J. Brown/LMC Group*
Ronald W. Waggener, *Waggener & Associates, Inc.*
Robert Shaw West, *West & Vaughan, Inc.*
Jeff White, *J. Walter Thompson*
James Wilson, The Atlanta Journal-Constitution
Mark Yearick, *Y Marketing & Design*
Ann Zeller, *Direct Marketing Association*
Curt Zimmerman, *The Zimmerman Agency*

Kleppner's Advertising Procedure has been one of the best-selling advertising books for many years. Each edition has benefited from valuable feedback from our adopters and students around the globe. We would like to thank a group of individuals who offered detailed comments during the process of developing this fourteenth edition. They are Bonnie Drewniany, University of South Carolina; Lee Wenthe, University of Georgia; Carolyn Stringer, Western Kentucky University; Howard S. Cogan, Ithaca College; and Jon Wardrip, University of South Carolina.

A book such as this could not be produced without the assistance of many people at Prentice Hall, especially Whitney Blake, our acquisitions editor, and Aileen Mason, our production editor. Nicole Leong, Ann France, and Pat Smythe created a wonderful design, and Jennifer Ballentine and Sandra Rush did a terrific job on the copyediting.

We would also like to thank Mary Jo Gregory and Gretchen Miller of York Production Services.

The authors would also like to take this opportunity to thank Ruhanna Neal and Donna LeBlond of the University of Georgia's College of Journalism staff for their invaluable help in the preparation of the manuscript.

OTTO KLEPPNER
(1899–1982)

A graduate of New York University, Otto Kleppner started out in advertising as a copy-writer. After several such jobs, he became advertising manager at Prentice Hall, where he began to think that he, too, "could write a book." Some years later, he also thought that he could run his own advertising agency, and both ideas materialized eminently. His highly successful agency handled advertising for leading accounts (Dewar's Scotch Whisky, I. W. Harper Bourbon and other Schenley brands, Saab Cars, Doubleday Book Clubs, and others). His book became a bible for advertising students, and his writings have been published in eight languages.

Active in the American Association of Advertising Agencies, Mr. Kleppner served as a director, a member of the Control Committee, chairman of the Committee of Government, Public and Educator Relations, and a governor of the New York Council. He was awarded the Nichols Cup (now the Crain Cup) for distinguished service to the teaching of advertising.

J. THOMAS RUSSELL

Thomas Russell is Professor of Advertising and Dean of the College of Journalism and Mass Communication at the University of Georgia. Tom received his Ph.D. in communications from the University of Illinois and has taught and conducted research in a number of areas of advertising and marketing. He was formerly editor of the *Journal of Advertising* and is the author of numerous articles and research papers in both academic and trade publications.

In addition to his academic endeavors, Tom has worked as a retail copywriter as well as principal in his own advertising agency. He is a member of a number of academic and professional organizations including the American Academy of Advertising, American Advertising Federation, and the Arthur W. Page Society. He has also served as a judge and faculty member for the Institute of Advanced Advertising Studies sponsored by the American Association of Advertising Agencies.

W. RONALD LANE

Ron has worked in most aspects of advertising. He began in advertising and promotion for a drug manufacturer. Ron has worked in creative and account services for clients including Coca-Cola, National Broiler Council, Minute-Maid, and Callaway Gardens Country Store.

He is a professor of advertising at the University of Georgia and has served as advertising manager of the *Journal of Advertising.* He was coordinator of the Institute of Advanced Advertising Studies sponsored by the American Association of Advertising Agencies for six years. He is also a partner in SLRS Communications, an advertising-marketing agency.

Currently, Ron is a member of the American Advertising Federation's (AAF) Academic Division, Executive Committee. He has been the AAF Academic Division Chair and served as a member of the AAF Board of Directors, Council of Governors, and Executive Committee. He has been an ADDY Awards judge numerous times and has been a member of the Advertising Age Creative Workshop faculty. He is a member of the Atlanta Advertising Club, American Academy of Advertising, American Marketing Association, and the ACEJMC Accrediting Council.

KLEPPNER'S

Advertising Procedure

Fourteenth Edition

The Place of Advertising

ADVERTISING IN THE UNITED STATES DID
not develop in a void. A number of other social, economic, and cultural
factors influenced the development of the industry. To appreciate
contemporary advertising, we must understand the events and colorful
practitioners that provided the foundation of this exciting field. Today,
advertising is among the most sophisticated business enterprises, with
every function researched with great care. Despite the dramatic changes
of the last 200 years, advertising remains a sales tool to bring buyers and
sellers together for the exchange of goods and services. The advent of
computers, advanced marketing research, and the application of the
disciplines of sociology and psychology have not changed the basic goals of
advertising since the clay tablets of ancient Babylonia or the tavern signs in

medieval England. Chapter 1 traces the development of advertising through the last 7,000 years.

Advertising is not a single function, but rather an umbrella term used to describe promotions as simple as a classified newspaper ad or as sophisticated as a Web site on the Internet. In chapter 2, we examine the wide variety of media, messages, and products that can successfully use advertising as a means of reaching prospective buyers. Advertising must be adapted to the consumer, the product, and the environment in which the sale takes place. A number of factors are discussed that can make advertising a profitable undertaking or result in a failed campaign and lost economic opportunities. The key to the study of advertising is to realize that it combines a number of elements and demands skills that are not always compatible. For example, the creativity demanded of the artist and copywriter are often different from the analytical expertise expected from the media planner or the attention to detail demanded of the account executive. As we see throughout the text, the successful advertising executive is often a person who is comfortable wearing a number of hats and carrying out diverse job responsibilities.

1

BACKGROUND OF
TODAY'S ADVERTISING

CHAPTER OBJECTIVES

MASS ADVERTISING REQUIRES A NUMBER OF
ECONOMIC AND SOCIAL FACTORS. IN THIS
CHAPTER, WE TRACE THE RELATIONSHIPS AMONG
ADVERTISING, DEVELOPMENT OF THE MASS MEDIA,
A RISING MIDDLE CLASS, EFFECTIVE
TRANSPORTATION, AND THE GROWTH OF MASS
PRODUCTION IN THE UNITED STATES. AFTER
READING THIS CHAPTER YOU WILL
UNDERSTAND

- the background of product exchange
- the early period of product promotion
- advertising and the American industrial revolution
- the fight for responsible advertising
- advertising growth during the post–World War II era
- global advertising and the twenty-first century.

From prehistoric times, there has been some form of communication concerning the availability and source of goods. Some of the earliest cave drawings refer to the makers of primitive objects. However, modern advertising can trace its roots to the United States of the late nineteenth and early twentieth centuries. To understand modern advertising, we must examine the conditions that made it possible.

As we see throughout this text, advertising does not function in a void. A host of economic and social requirements are necessary for successful advertising. Likewise, in its earliest days, many factors contributed to the growth of advertising. "Among these pre-conditions were a breakdown of localism, a collected audience and a concentrated market, an educated citizenry, an industrial structure characterized by oligopoly, the potential for mass production, a growth in per capita income, and a culture that valued consumption."[1]

Although it is difficult to make a judgment concerning the priority of these elements, it is clear that efficient transportation and the initiation of widely distributed branded goods of consistent quality set the stage for twentieth-century advertising. "National advertising developed when businesses in several important industries decided that branding and promoting their products would be profitable."[2]

During the period of the rise of commerce in the United States, most trade took place in a limited area through locally owned retailers receiving goods from local, or at most regional, producers. Manufacturers had little or no contact or relationship with their ultimate customers. They were totally dependent on local merchants for their sales.

Branded, nationally distributed goods radically changed this relationship. "Branding offered manufacturers a new kind of control when supported by effective advertising, by altering the balance of power in the traditional chain from manufacturer to . . . customer. No longer were customers to rely on the grocer's opinion about the best soap. . . . People asked for Ivory, which could only be obtained from Procter & Gamble."[3]

The convergence of the availability of branded products, the ability to provide national distribution, and a growing middle class as a market for these products had evolved sufficiently by 1920 to support the creation of an advertising industry that demonstrated most of the basic functions found among agencies and corporate advertising departments today.

The two elements missing in most advertising during the early years of this century were an ethical framework for judging promotional messages and research to measure the success of advertising. Despite efforts as early as 1890 to ensure honest advertising, it would be many years before the industry adopted effective means of self-regulation.

Likewise, the pioneering work of early advertising researchers such as Claude Hopkins would not gain widespread acceptance until the latter half of the twentieth century. "Several agencies boasted of . . . research into consumer attitudes in the late 1920s, but their crude, slapdash methods made these 'surveys' of questionable value in providing accurate feedback. One agency reported that it could obtain quick, inexpensive results . . . by having all members of the staff send questionnaires to their friends."[4] Generally, the advertisers of the period thought that an intuitive "feel" for the consumer was quite sufficient to produce effective advertising. Research opportunities did exist in the many mail-order ads of the day, which could measure results by coupon returns; however, pretesting of advertising was largely unknown.

Let us begin our survey of this exciting business enterprise by examining the history of advertising, which we divide into three broad periods:

1. *The **premarketing era.*** From the start of product exchange in prehistoric times to the middle of the eighteenth century, buyers and sellers communicated in very primitive ways. For most of this period, "media" such as clay tablets, town criers, and tavern signs were the best way to communicate a product or service. Only in the latter decades of this period did primitive printing appear.
2. *The **mass communication era.*** From the 1700s to the early decades of the twentieth century, advertisers were increasingly able to reach large segments of the population, first with faster presses and later through broadcast media.

<hr/>

[1]James D. Norris, *Advertising and the Transformation of American Society, 1865–1920* (New York: Greenwood Press, 1990), p. xiv.

[2]Daniel Pope, *The Making of Modern Advertising* (New York: Basic Books, 1983), p. 62.

[3]Susan Strasser, *Satisfaction Guaranteed* (New York: Pantheon Books, 1989), p. 30.

[4]Roland Marchand, *Advertising the American Dream* (Berkeley: University of California Press, 1985), p. 76.

Premarketing era
The period from prehistoric times to the eighteenth century. During this time, buyers and sellers communicated in very primitive ways.

Mass communication era
From the 1700s to the early decades of this century, advertisers were able to reach large segments of the population through the mass media.

3. *The **research era.*** During the last 50 years, advertisers have methodically improved the techniques of identifying and reaching narrowly targeted audiences with messages prepared specifically for each group or individual (in the case of direct mail). Modern communication technology has aided in this quest for the perfect advertising campaign.

In its evolution as a marketing power, advertising has become a major economic and social force. Advertising practitioners have come under close public scrutiny, and they find themselves working within a complex legal and regulatory framework. Perhaps the most important change in twentieth-century advertising is the sense of social responsibility of advertisers. Many advertising practices that were almost routine a century ago are universally condemned by the industry today. Advertisers realize that public trust is the key to successful advertising. Throughout the remainder of this chapter we discuss the forces that have shaped contemporary advertising.

BEGINNINGS

The urge to advertise seems to be a part of human nature, evidenced since ancient times. Of the 5,000-year recorded history of advertising right up to our present television satellite age, the part that is most significant begins when the United States emerged as a great manufacturing nation about 100 years ago. The early history of advertising, however, is far too fascinating to pass by without a glance.

It is not surprising that the people who gave the world the Tower of Babel also left the earliest known evidence of advertising. A Babylonian clay tablet of about 3000 B.C. bears inscriptions for an ointment dealer, a scribe, and a shoemaker. Papyri exhumed from the ruins of Thebes show that the ancient Egyptians had a better medium on which to write their messages. (Alas, the announcements preserved in papyrus offer rewards for the return of runaway slaves.) The Greeks were among those who relied on town criers to chant the arrival of ships with cargoes of wines, spices, and metals. Often a crier was accompanied by a musician who kept him in the right key. Town criers later became the earliest medium for public announcements in many European countries, and they continued to be used for centuries. (At this point, we must digress to tell about a promotion idea used by innkeepers in France around A.D. 1100 to tout their fine wines: They would have the town crier blow a horn, gather a group—and offer samples!)

Roman merchants, too, had a sense of advertising. The ruins of Pompeii contain signs in stone or terra-cotta, advertising what the shops were selling: a row of hams for a butcher shop (Exhibit 1.1), a cow for a dairy, a boot for a shoemaker.

Outdoor advertising has proved to be one of the most enduring forms of advertising. It survived the decline of the Roman Empire to become the decorative art of European inns in the seventeenth and eighteenth centuries. That was still an age of widespread illiteracy, so inns vied with one another in creating attractive signs that all could recognize. This accounts for the charming names of old inns, especially in England—such as the Three Squirrels, the Man in the Moon, and the Hole in the Wall (Exhibit

exhibit

1.1

This advertisement for a butcher shop in Pompeii is one of the oldest signs known.

Hog in Armour

Three Squirrels

King's Porter and Dwarf

Harrow and Doublet

The Ape

Hole in the Wall
"A Guide for Malt Worms"

Barley Mow

Bull and Mouth

Man in the Moon

Goose and Gridiron

exhibit

1.2

Signs outside
seventeenth-century
inns were easily
recognizable.

Hoarding
First printed outdoor
signs—the forerunner
of modern outdoor
advertising.

1.2). In 1614, England passed a law, probably the earliest on advertising, that prohibited signs from extending more than eight feet out from a building. (Longer signs pulled down too many house fronts.) Another law required signs to be high enough to give clearance to an armored man on horseback. In 1740, the first printed outdoor poster (referred to as a **"hoarding"**) appeared in London.

ORIGINS OF NEWSPAPER ADVERTISING

The next most enduring advertising medium, the newspaper, was the offspring of **Johann Gutenberg's** invention of printing from movable type (about 1438), which, of course, changed communication methods for the whole world. About 40 years after the invention, William Caxton of London printed the first ad in English—a handbill of the rules for the guidance of the clergy at Easter. This was tacked up on church doors. (It became the first printed outdoor ad in English.) But the printed newspaper was a long time coming. It really emerged from the newsletters, handwritten by professional writers, for nobles and others who wanted to be kept up to date on the news, especially of the court and important events—very much in the spirit of today's Washington newsletters.

The first ad in any language to be printed in a disseminated sheet appeared in a German news pamphlet in about 1525. And what do you think this ad was for? A book extolling the virtues of a mysterious drug. (The Food and Drug Administration did not exist in those days.) But news pamphlets did not come out regularly; one published in 1591 contained news of the previous three years. It was from such beginnings, however, that the printed newspaper emerged. The first printed English newspaper came out in 1622, the *Weekly Newes of London.* The first ad in an English newspaper appeared in 1625.

Siquis—Tack-Up Advertisements

The forerunner of our present want ads bore the strange name of **siquis.** The clergy were apparently the first to make use of the written word for the purpose of bringing together the forces of supply and demand. A candidate seeking a clerical position would post a notice setting forth his qualifications, or someone having an appointment to make would post a notice specifying the requirements. These early "want ads" were usually in Latin and began *si quis* ("if anybody"): hence the name siquis. The name continued, although soon these notices covered a variety of subjects, including lost-and-found objects, runaway apprentices, and so on.[5]

Advertising in the English newspapers continued to feature similar personal and local announcements. The British have, in fact, shown so much interest in classified ads that until a few years ago the *London Times* filled its first page with classified advertising.

Advertising Comes to America

The Pilgrims arrived on American shores before the *Weekly Newes of London* was first published, so they had had little chance to learn about newspapers. But later colonists acquainted them with the idea, and the first American newspaper to carry ads appeared in 1704, the *Boston Newsletter* (note the newsletter identification). It printed an ad offering a reward for the capture of a thief and the return of several sorts of men's apparel—more akin to the ad offering a reward for returned slaves written on Egyptian papyrus thousands of years before than to the advertising printed in the United States today. By the time the United States was formed, the colonies had 30 newspapers. Their advertising, like that of the English newspapers of the time, consisted mostly of ads we would describe today as classified and local.

THREE MOMENTOUS DECADES: 1870–1900

Neither those ads nor all the ads that appeared from ancient Egyptian days until the American industrial revolution explain the development of advertising in the United States. The history of advertising in the United States is unique because advertising took

---

[5]George Burton Hotchkiss, *An Outline of Advertising* (New York: Macmillan, 1957), p. 10.

hold just as the country was entering its era of greatest growth: Population was soaring, factories were springing up, railroads were opening the West. Advertising grew with the country and helped establish its marketing system. The United States entered the nineteenth century as an agricultural country, following European marketing traditions, and ended the century as a great industrial nation, creating its own patterns of distribution. A new age of advertising had begun.

We pick up the story in about 1870, when this era of transition was crystallizing. Among the major developments, transportation, population growth, invention, and manufacturing ranked high.

Transportation

Here was a country 3,000 miles wide. It had sweeping stretches of rich farmland. It had minerals and forests. It had factories within reach of the coal mines. It had a growing population. But its long-distance transportation was chiefly by rivers and canals.

Railroads today are fighting for survival, but 100 years ago they changed a sprawling continent into a land of spectacular economic growth. In 1865, there were 35,000 miles of railroad trackage in the United States. By 1900, this trackage was 190,000 miles. Three railroad lines crossed the Mississippi and ran from the Atlantic to the Pacific. Feeder lines and networks spread across the face of the land. Where railroads went, people went. No longer limited to the waterways, they established farms, settlements, and cities across the continent. The goods of the North and East could be exchanged for the farm and extractive products of the South and West. Never before had a country revealed such extensive and varied resources. Never since has so vast a market without a trade or language barrier been opened. This was an exciting prospect to manufacturers.

People

In 1870, the population of the United States was 38 million. By 1900, it had doubled. In no other period of American history has the population grown so fast. This growth, which included those recently freed from slavery, meant an expanding labor force in the fields, factories, and mines; it also meant a new consumer market. About 30 percent of the new population were immigrants. But all the settlers before them had been immigrants or descendants of immigrants who had had the courage to pull up stakes and venture to the New World, a land far away and strange to them, in search of a new and better life. The result was a people who were mobile, both in their readiness to move their homes and in their aspirations to move upward in lifestyle.

Inventions and Production

The end of the nineteenth century was marked by many notable inventions and advances in the manufacture of goods. Among these were the development of the electric motor and of alternating-current power transmission, which relieved factories of the need to locate next to waterpower sources, thus opening the hinterland to development and growth. The internal combustion engine was perfected in this period; the automobile age was soon to follow.

It was the age of fast communications; telephone (Exhibit 1.3, p. 8), telegraph, typewriter, **Mergenthaler linotype,** high-speed presses—all increased the ability of people to communicate with one another.

In 1860, there were 7,600 patent applications filed in Washington. By 1870, this number had more than doubled to 19,000; by 1900, it had more than doubled again, to 42,000.

Steel production has traditionally served as an index of industrial activity. Twenty *thousand* tons of steel were produced in 1867, but 10 *million* tons were produced in 1900. There is also a direct correlation between the power consumption of a country

Mergenthaler linotype
Ottmar Mergenthaler invented the linotype, which replaced hand-set type by automatically setting and distributing metal type.

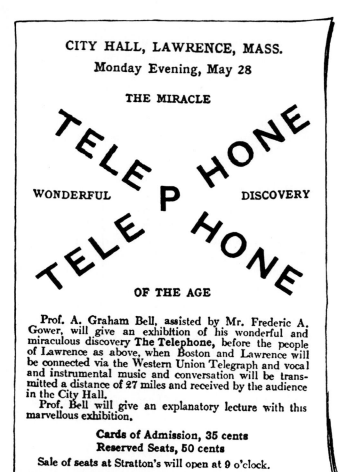

CITY HALL, LAWRENCE, MASS.
Monday Evening, May 28

THE MIRACLE

TELEPHONE

WONDERFUL   DISCOVERY

TELEPHONE

OF THE AGE

Prof. A. Graham Bell, assisted by Mr. Frederic A. Gower, will give an exhibition of his wonderful and miraculous discovery **The Telephone**, before the people of Lawrence as above, when Boston and Lawrence will be connected via the Western Union Telegraph and vocal and instrumental music and conversation will be transmitted a distance of 27 miles and received by the audience in the City Hall.

Prof. Bell will give an explanatory lecture with this marvellous exhibition.

Cards of Admission, 35 cents
Reserved Seats, 50 cents
Sale of seats at Stratton's will open at 9 o'clock.

exhibit

1.3

The first telephone ad was placed in 1877.

Penny press
Forerunner of the mass newspaper in the United States. First appeared in the 1830s.

and its standard of living. By 1870, only 3 million horsepower was available; by 1900, this capacity had risen to 10 million. More current means more goods being manufactured; it also means that more people are using it for their own household needs. Both types of use form a good economic index.

The phonograph and the motion-picture camera, invented at the turn of the twentieth century, enhanced the American lifestyle.

The Columbian Exhibition in Chicago in 1893 was attended by millions, who returned home to tell their friends breathlessly about the new products they had seen.

Media

Newspapers The first colonial newspaper, Benjamin Harris's *Publick Occurrences,* was published in Boston in 1690, and it was promptly banned by the governor after one issue. However, many newspapers followed over the next century, and by 1800 every major city in the United States had several newspapers. During the 1830s, the so-called **penny press** emerged. Combined with the introduction of Richard Hoe's rotary press, the public and advertisers could obtain inexpensive news on a regular basis.

In 1835, James Gordon Bennett founded the New York *Herald* and ushered in what many believe was the real beginnings of mass media. Bennett's *Herald* blended stories of sex, gore, and murder with political muckraking unheard of in its day. During the Civil War, the *Herald* achieved a circulation of 135,000 and became an extremely influential newspaper for both news and advertising. It also demonstrated the importance of mass media in molding public opinion. More important, the *Herald* and other papers of its day initiated the financial support from advertising for the media that would follow.

Religious Publications   Religious publications today represent a small part of the total media picture; but for a few decades after the Civil War, religious publications were the most influential medium. They were the forerunners of magazines. The post–Civil War period was a time of great religious revival, marking also the beginning of the temperance movement. Church groups issued their own publications, many with circulations of no more than 1,000; the biggest ran to 400,000. But the combined circulation of the 400 religious publications was estimated at about 5 million.

Religious publications had great influence among their readers, a fact that patent-medicine advertisers recognized to such an extent that 75 percent of all religious-publication advertising was for patent medicines. (Many of the temperance papers carried advertisements for preparations that proved to be 40 percent alcohol. Today we call that 80 proof whiskey.)

Magazines   Most of what were called magazines before the 1870s, including Ben Franklin's effort in 1741, lasted less than six months—and for good reason: They consisted mostly of extracts of books and pamphlets, essays, verse, and communications of dubious value. Magazines as we know them today were really born in the last three decades of the nineteenth century, at a time when many factors were in their favor. The rate of illiteracy in the country had been cut almost in half, from 20 percent in 1870 to a little over 10 percent in 1900. In 1875, railroads began carrying mail, including magazines, across the country. In 1879, Congress established the low second-class postal rate for publications, a subject of controversy to this day, but a boon to magazines even then. The Hoe high-speed rotary press began replacing the much slower flatbed press, speeding the printing of magazines. The halftone method of reproducing photographs as well as color artwork was invented in 1876, making magazines more enticing to the public. (*Godey's Lady's Book,* a popular fashion book of the age, had previously employed 150 women to hand-tint all of its illustrations.)

Literary magazines intended for the upper middle class now appeared—*Harper's Monthly, Atlantic Monthly, Century*—but their publishers did not view advertising kindly at first. Even when, at the turn of the century, Fletcher Harper condescended to "desecrate literature with the announcements of tradespeople," he placed all the advertising in the back of his magazine.

Inspired by the success of popular magazines in England, a new breed of publishers came forth in the 1890s to produce magazines of entertainment, fiction, and advice, forerunners of today's women's and general magazines. Magazines brought the works of Rudyard Kipling, H.G. Wells, Mark Twain, and Sir Arthur Conan Doyle to families across the face of the land. By 1902, *Munsey's* had a circulation of 600,000; *Cosmopolitan,* 700,000; *Delineator,* 960,000. The *Ladies' Home Journal* hit the million mark—a great feat for the age. The ten-cent magazine had arrived.

The amount of advertising that magazines carried was comparable to modern magazine advertising. *Harper's* published 75 pages of advertising per issue; *Cosmopolitan,* 103 pages; *McClure's,* 120 pages. Today a typical issue of the *Ladies' Home Journal* has 100 pages of advertising; *Reader's Digest,* 75; *Better Homes & Gardens,* 125. Magazines made possible the nationwide sale of products; they brought into being nationwide advertising.

Patent-Medicine Advertising

Patent-medicine advertisers had been around for a long time, and by the 1870s, they were the largest category of advertisers. After the Civil War, millions of men returned to their homes, North and South, many of them weak from wounds and exposure. The only kind of medical aid available to most of them was a bottle of patent medicine. As

exhibit

1.4

One of the More Restrained Ads in the Patent-Medicine Category

Electricity, the new, magic power of the 1890s, was offered in a curative belt.

a result, patent-medicine advertising dominated the media toward the end of the nineteenth century, its fraudulent claims giving all advertising a bad name (Exhibit 1.4).

National Advertising Emerges

Meanwhile, legitimate manufacturers saw a new world of opportunity opening before them in the growth of the country. They saw the market for consumer products spreading. Railroads could now transport their merchandise to all cities between the Atlantic and Pacific coasts. The idea of packaging their own products carrying their own trademarks was enticing, particularly to grocery manufacturers: it allowed them to build their businesses on their reputations with the consumer instead of being subject to the caprices and pressures of jobbers, who had previously been their sole distributors. Magazines provided the missing link in marketing—magazine advertising easily spread the word about manufacturers' products all over the country; Quaker Oats cereal was among the first to go this marketing route, followed soon by many others (Exhibit 1.5).

This was the development of national advertising, as we call it today, in its broadest sense, meaning the advertising by a producer of his or her trademarked product whether or not it has attained national distribution.

LEADERS IN NATIONAL ADVERTISING IN 1890'S

A. P. W. Paper	Gold Dust Washing Powder
Adams Tutti Frutti Gum	Gorham's Silver
Æolian Company	Gramophone
American Express Traveler's Cheques	Great Northern Railroad
Armour Beef Extract	H–O Breakfast Food
Autoharp	Hamburg American Line
Baker's Cocoa	Hammond Typewriter
Battle Ax Plug Tobacco	Hartford Bicycle
Beardsley's Shredded Codfish	Hartshorn's Shade Rollers
Beeman's Pepsin Gum	Heinz's Baked Beans
Bent's Crown Piano	Peter Henderson & Co.
Burlington Railroad	Hires' Root Beer
Burnett's Extracts	Hoffman House Cigars
California Fig Syrup	Huyler's Chocolates
Caligraph Typewriter	Hunyadi Janos
Castoria	Ingersoll Watches
A. B. Chase Piano	Ives & Pond Piano
Chicago Great Western	Ivory Soap
Chicago, Milwaukee & St. Paul Railroad	Jaeger Underwear
Chicago Great Western Railway	Kirk's American Family Soap
Chocolat-Menier	Kodak
Chickering Piano	Liebeg's Extract of Beef
Columbia Bicycles	Lipton's Teas
Cleveland Baking Powder	Lowney's Chocolates
Cottolene Shortening	Lundborg's Perfumes
Cook's Tours	James McCutcheon Linens
Crown Pianos	Dr. Lyon's Toothpowder
Crescent Bicycles	Mason & Hamlin Piano
Devoe & Raynolds Artist's Materials	Mellin's Food
Cuticura Soap	Mennen's Talcum Powder
Derby Desks	Michigan Central Railroad
De Long Hook and Eye	Monarch Bicycles
Diamond Dyes	J. L. Mott Indoor Plumbing
Dixon's Graphite Paint	Munsing Underwear
Dixon's Pencils	Murphy Varnish Company
W. L. Douglas Shoes	New England Mincemeat
Edison Mimeograph	New York Central Railroad
Earl & Wilson Collars	North German Lloyd
Elgin Watches	Old Dominion Line
Edison Phonograph	Oneita Knitted Goods
Everett Piano	Packer's Tar Soap
Epps's Cocoa	Pearline Soap Powder
Estey Organ	Peartltop Lamp Chimneys
Fall River Line	Pears' Soap
Felt & Tarrant Comptometer	Alfred Peats Wall Paper
Ferry's Seeds	Pettijohn's Breakfast Food
Fisher Piano	Pittsburgh Stogies
Fowler Bicycles	Pond's Extract
Franco American Soup	Postum Cereal
Garland Stoves	Prudential Insurance Co.
Gold Dust	Quaker Oats

Mass Production Appears

The words *chauffeur, limousine,* and *sedan* remind us that some of the earliest motor cars were made and publicized in France. In the United States, as in France, they were virtually handmade at first. But in 1913, Henry Ford decided that the way to build cars at low cost was to make them of standardized parts and bring the pieces to the worker on an assembly-line belt. He introduced to the world a mass-production technique and brought the price of a Ford down to $265 by 1925 (when a Hudson automobile cost $1,695 and the average weekly wage was $20). But in a free society, mass production is predicated upon mass selling, another name for advertising. Mass production makes possible countless products at a cost the mass of people can pay and about which they learn through advertising. America was quick to use both.

The Advertising Agency

We have been speaking of the various media and their advertising. The media got much of that advertising through the advertising agency, which started with people selling advertising space on a percentage basis for out-of-town newspapers. Later they also planned, prepared, and placed the ads and rendered further services. The story of the advertising agency is deeply rooted in the growth of American industry and advertising. Later in this book we devote a whole chapter (chapter 5) to the American agency, from its beginning to its latest patterns of operation. Until then, we need keep in mind only that the advertising agency has always been an active force in developing the use of advertising.

AMERICA ENTERS THE TWENTIETH CENTURY

The moral atmosphere of business as it developed after the Civil War reflected laissez-faire policy at its extreme. High government officials were corrupted by the railroads; the public was swindled by flagrant stock market manipulations; embalmed beef was shipped to soldiers in the Spanish-American War. Advertising contributed to the immorality of business, with its patent-medicine ads offering to cure all the real and imagined human ailments. There was a "pleasing medicine to cure cancer," another to cure cholera. No promise of a quick cure was too wild, no falsehood too monstrous.

The Pure Food and Drug Act (1906)

As early as 1865, the *New York Herald-Tribune* had a touch of conscience and eliminated "certain classes" of medical advertising, those that used "repellent" words. In 1892, the *Ladies Home Journal* was the first magazine to ban *all* medical advertising. The *Ladies' Home Journal* also came out with a blast by Mark Sullivan, revealing that codeine was being used in cold preparations and that a teething syrup had morphine as its base. Public outrage reached Congress, which in 1906 passed the Pure Food and Drug Act, the first federal law to protect the health of the public and the first to control advertising.

The Federal Trade Commission Act (1914)

In addition to passing laws protecting the public from unscrupulous business, Congress passed the Federal Trade Commission Act, protecting one business-owner from the unscrupulous behavior of another. The law said, in effect, "Unfair methods of doing business are hereby declared illegal." John D. Rockefeller, founder of the Standard Oil Company, got together with some other oilmen in the early days of his operation and worked out a deal with the railroads over which they shipped their oil. They arranged not only to get a secret rebate on the oil they shipped, but also to get a rebate on all the oil their *competitors* shipped. Result: They were able to undersell their competitors and drive them out of business. What was considered smart business in those days would be a violation of the antitrust laws today.

In time, the Federal Trade Commission (FTC) extended its province to protecting the public against misleading and deceptive advertising—as all who are responsible for advertising today are very much aware. Of this period of exposure and reform, the historian James Truslow Adams said, "America for the first time was taking stock of the morality of everyday life."

Yet, despite these praiseworthy efforts at self-regulation and many others in the years that followed, as well as general acceptance, the advertising industry was and continues

THE LONG, ADVENTUROUS ROAD . . .

● ●

. . . that *Kleppner's Advertising Procedure* has traveled. Starting with the eighth edition of *Advertising Procedure*, Tom Russell and Ron Lane have brought excitement, currency, and relevancy to each best-selling edition of the text.

Their combined teaching experience, together with a long list of friends, and contacts with top-notch advertisers and client companies, allows them to bring state-of-the-art information and examples to each edition of the text. The facilities at the University of Georgia provided a perfect laboratory for the authors to showcase topics that are most relevant to today's undergraduate students in advertising.

● ●

to be the target of criticism for its social effects. Chapter 26 in this book answers such criticism, and it has been placed at the end of the book so that in judging the criticisms you will have had the benefit of the advertising background that the intervening chapters provide.

ADVERTISING COMES OF AGE

In about 1905, there emerged a class of advertising executives who recognized that their future lay in advertising legitimate products and in earning the confidence of the public in advertising. They gathered with like-minded peers in their communities to form advertising clubs.

These clubs subsequently became the Associated Advertising Clubs of the World (now the American Advertising Federation). In 1911, they launched a campaign to promote truth in advertising. In 1916, they formed vigilance committees that developed into today's Council of Better Business Bureaus, which continues to deal with many problems of unfair and deceptive business practices. In 1971, the bureaus became a part of the National Advertising Review Council, an all-industry effort at curbing misleading advertising. The main constituency of the American Advertising Federation continues to be the local advertising clubs. On its board are also officers of the other advertising associations.

In 1910, the Association of National Advertising Managers was born. It is now known as the Association of National Advertisers (ANA) and has about 500 members, including the foremost advertisers. Its purpose is to improve the effectiveness of advertising from the viewpoint of the advertiser. In 1917, the American Association of Advertising Agencies was formed to improve the effectiveness of advertising and of the advertising agency operation. Over 75 percent of all national advertising today is placed by its members, both large and small.

In 1911, *Printers' Ink,* the leading advertising trade paper for many years, prepared a model statute for state regulation of advertising, designed to "punish untrue, deceptive or misleading advertising." The ***Printers' Ink* Model Statute** has been adopted in its original or modified form by a number of states, where it is still operative.

Up to 1914, many publishers were carefree in their claims to circulation. Advertisers had no way of verifying what they got for their money. However, in that year, a group of advertisers, agencies, and publishers established an independent auditing organization, the Audit Bureau of Circulations (ABC), which conducts its own audits and issues its own reports of circulation. Most major publications belong to the ABC, and an ABC circulation statement is highly regarded in media circles. The ABC reports of circulation are fully accredited in most areas. (Today, similar auditing organizations are operating in 25 countries throughout the world.)

In June 1916, President Woodrow Wilson, addressing the Associated Advertising Clubs of the World convention in Philadelphia, was the first president to give public recognition to the importance of advertising. Advertising had come of age!

Advertising in World War I

World War I marked the first time that advertising was used as an instrument of direct social action. Advertising agencies turned from selling consumer goods to arousing patriotic sentiment, selling government bonds, encouraging conservation, and promoting a number of other war-related activities. One of the largest agencies of the era, N.W. Ayer & Sons, prepared and placed ads for the first three Liberty Loan drives and donated much of its commission to the drive.[6]

---

[6]Ralph M. Hower, *The History of an Advertising Agency* (Cambridge, Mass.: Harvard University Press, 1949), p. 180.

Soon these efforts by individual agencies were coordinated by the Division of Advertising of the Committee of Public Information, a World War I government propaganda office. This wartime experience convinced people that advertising could be a useful tool in communicating ideas as well as in selling products.

The 1920s

The 1920s began with a minidepression and ended with a crash. When the war ended, makers of army trucks were able to convert quickly to commercial trucks. Firestone spent $2 million advertising "Ship by Truck." With the industry profiting by the good roads that had been built, truck production jumped from 92,000 in 1916 to 322,000 in 1920. Door-to-door delivery from manufacturer to retailer spurred the growth of chain stores, which led, in turn, to supermarkets and self-service stores.

The passenger car business boomed, too, and new products appeared in profusion: electric refrigerators, washing machines, electric shavers, and, most incredible of all, the radio. Installment selling made appliances available to all. And all the products needed advertising.

The Introduction of Radio   Radio was invented by Guglielmo Marconi in 1895 as a means for sending Morse code. The first voice transmission occurred in 1906. However, for the next 20 years radio was used largely by hobbyists, with few seeing any commercial potential for the device. In 1920, Westinghouse founded the first commercial radio station, KDKA in Pittsburgh. KDKA's first program was the Harding-Cox presidential debate on November 2, 1920. Westinghouse's primary goal for the station was to encourage more sales of its radio sets.[7]

Radio quickly caught the imagination of the public. Only five years after KDKA went on the air, the first network was founded by AT&T (with its sale a year later, it became NBC). Today, Americans average more than five radio sets per household, and it is difficult to find an automobile or workplace without a radio. From its noncommercial beginnings, advertisers now spend $11 billion each year in the medium.

The 1930s Depression

The stock market crash had a shattering effect on our entire economy: Millions of people were thrown out of work; business failures were widespread; banks were closing all over the country (there were no insured deposits in those days). There was no Social Security, no food stamps, no unemployment insurance. Who had ever heard of pensions for blue-collar workers? There were bread lines, long ones; and well-dressed men on street corners were selling apples off the tops of boxes for five cents (Exhibit 1.6). The Southwest was having its worst windstorms, which carried off the topsoil and killed livestock and crops. Farmers abandoned their farms, packed their families and furniture into old pickup trucks, and headed west. (John Steinbeck wrote his *Grapes of Wrath* around this experience.) The government finally launched the Works Progress Administration (WPA) for putting people to work on public-service projects, but the bread lines continued to be long.

Out of that catastrophe came three developments that affect advertising to this day:

1. Radio emerged as a major advertising medium. In March 1933, President Franklin D. Roosevelt made the first inaugural address ever to be broadcast by radio, giving heart and hope to a frightened people. His line "We have nothing to fear except fear itself," spoken to the largest audience that had ever at one time heard the voice of one man, became historic. In one broadcast, radio showed its power to move a nation. Radio had arrived as a major national advertising medium. It quickly be-

---

[7]Mitchell Stephens, "From Dots and Dashes to Rock and Larry King," *The New York Times,* November 20, 1996, p. C5.

exhibit

1.6

Chain-Store Ad, 1932

came part of the life of America. The 1930s began with 612 stations and 12 million sets and ended with 814 stations and 51 million sets.

2. The Robinson-Patman Act (1936) was passed to help protect the small merchant from the unfair competition of the big store with its huge buying power. This law is still operative today.

3. Congress passed the Wheeler-Lea Act (1938), giving the FTC more direct and sweeping powers over advertising, and the Federal Food, Drug and Cosmetic Act (1938), giving the administration authority over the labeling and packaging of these products. These laws, which we discuss in chapter 25, are a pervasive consideration in advertising today and a forerunner of the government's increasing interest in advertising.

Advertising during World War II

With World War II, industry turned to the production of war goods. Because all civilian material was severely rationed, many firms curtailed their advertising. Others felt that though they were out of merchandise, they were not out of business, and they wanted to keep the public's goodwill, so they applied their advertising efforts to rendering public service. The Goodyear Tire & Rubber Company's advice on how to take care of tires in days of product shortages was akin to ads that were to appear in 1974 and 1975 during the Arab oil embargo.

The War Advertising Council

With the inception of World War II, the advertising industry faced the prospects of a greatly diminished need for consumer advertising, and it turned its attention to the war effort. In 1942, business, media, and advertising leaders came together to found the War Advertising Council. Its mission was to build morale and communicate the necessity of civilian sacrifice.

War Advertising Council
Founded in 1942 to promote World War II mobilization. It later evolved into the Advertising Council.

Just four weeks after the bombing of Pearl Harbor, the **War Advertising Council** was founded as an adjunct to the U.S. Office of War Information. The aim of the organization was to work with the government to help mobilize the nation for victory. By coincidence, the advertising industry had not long before embarked on the idea of public service advertising to help in good causes, and by so doing to try to improve the public standing of business.

Among the themes and projects promoted by the council were conservation of items such as fuel, fat, and tires; planting victory gardens; buying war bonds; promoting rationing; and encouraging communications from home to our troops (see Exhibit 1.7). One of the most well-known campaigns was conducted by the J. Walter Thompson advertising agency to encourage women to fill in for the men who were at war. In the 1940s, many industries had never had women employees, and there existed entrenched biases, by both men and women, about the type of work in which women could, or should, engage. The "Rosie the Riveter" campaign was successful in overcoming these prejudices and brought millions of women to the workforce. Some credit these campaigns with beginning the process of bringing women into a number of industries after the war.[8]

By the end of the war, the War Advertising Council could report that advertisers and the media had contributed an estimated $1 billion worth of space and time for war-related messages. More than 800 million war bonds totaling $35 billion were sold; 50 million victory gardens were planted; and millions of pounds of rubber, tin, steel, and waste fats were salvaged. More than 60,000 nurses joined the Cadet Nurse Corps, and the Women's Army Corps recruiting increased 400 percent in one year.

The effort of the War Advertising Council was so successful that President Franklin Roosevelt urged that the Council be continued to promote peacetime projects. In 1945 the organization was renamed the Advertising Council, and, as we discuss in chapter 26, it continues to promote a number of social causes.[9]

---

[8]Mei-ling Yang, "Selling Patriotism: The Representation of Women in Magazine Advertising in World War II," *American Journalism,* Summer 1995, p. 309.

[9]Information in this section was provided by the Advertising Council.

exhibit

1.7

V-Mail was a way to speed up mail that went out to troops overseas. A letter written on a special form was photographed onto a film strip to save space and weight—one ad proclaimed that 1,700 letters could fit into a cigarette package—and once it reached its destination, the letter was transferred back onto paper, ensuring privacy.

Courtesy: The Advertising Council.

Advertising after World War II to 1975: The Word Was Growth

It is doubtful that any nation had ever experienced the rate of economic expansion the United States did during the postwar years. "Almost from the moment the hostilities ceased, America collectively became bent on speed-shifting into a postwar mode. Manufacturing facilities switched, almost overnight, from military production to consumer goods, and mustered-out troops re-entered the civilian world—a world joyful at their return yet not fully prepared to digest them—at a rate of hundreds of thousands every week."[10]

---

[10]Robert Goldsborough, "The Postwar Era 1945–1950," *Advertising Age,* July 31, 1995, p. 24.

Between 1940 and 1950, advertising expenditures more than doubled, and television captured the attention of millions of viewers as that medium evolved from a novelty to a social institution. Millions of viewers gave up playing bridge, going to the movies, and even social conversation to tune in to Milton Berle and *The $64,000 Question,* and advertising dollars soon followed.

By the 1960s, videotape, color programming, and better production techniques made television the major medium for national advertisers, forever changing magazines and network radio as advertising media. Television also altered both sports and politics. In its insatiable appetite for programming, television brought thousands of hours of sports into the living room. It was responsible for creating sports leagues such as the old American Football League and allowed mediocre players to become millionaires. But perhaps television of the period had its greatest impact on politics.

As television's popularity continued to grow, it soon became apparent to politicians that the same formula used so successfully in selling soap might be adapted to selling candidates. Rosser Reeves is generally credited with introducing the television spot to American politics during the 1960 election campaign of Dwight Eisenhower. In a series of one-minute spots, Reeves converted the reserved, rather stiff and awkward candidate into the personable "Man from Abilene." For better or worse, politics would never again be the same.

The Figures Also Said Growth   Between 1950 and 1973,[11] the population of the United States increased by 38 percent, whereas disposable personal income increased by 327 percent. New housing starts went up by 47 percent, energy consumption by 121 percent, college enrollments by 136 percent, automobile registrations by 151 percent, telephones in use by 221 percent, number of outboard motors sold by 242 percent, retail sales by 250 percent, families owning two or more cars by 300 percent, frozen-food production by 655 percent, number of airline passengers by 963 percent, homes with dishwashers by 1,043 percent, and homes with room air-conditioners by 3,662 percent.

Advertising not only contributed to the growth but was part of it, rising from an expenditure of $5.8 billion in 1950 to $28.3 billion in 1975—a growth of 490 percent. There were many developments in advertising during this time:

- In 1956, the Department of Justice ruled that advertising agencies could negotiate fees with clients rather than adhere to the then-required 15 percent commission on all media placed. This encouraged the growth of specialized companies, such as independent media-buying services, creative-only agencies, and in-house agencies owned by advertisers.
- The voice of the consumer became more powerful.
- Congress passed an act limiting outdoor advertising alongside interstate highways. Cigarette advertising was banned from television.
- The FTC introduced corrective advertising by those who had made false or misleading claims. Comparison advertising (mentioning competitors by name) was deemed an acceptable form of advertising.
- The magazine-publishing world saw the disappearance of the old dinosaurs—the *Saturday Evening Post, Collier's,* and *Women's Home Companion.* There was no vacuum at the newsstand, however, for there was an immediate upsurge in magazines devoted to special interests.
- Newspapers felt the effect of the shift of metropolitan populations to the suburbs. Freestanding inserts became an important part of newspaper billings.
- Radio took a dive when television came along. As discussed in chapter 9, the story of how it came out of that drastic decline is a good example of turning disadvantages into advantages.
- Direct-response advertising soared from $900 million in 1950 to $8 billion in 1980, reflecting the growth of direct marketing.

---

[11]We select 1973 as the last full year before the high inflation brought on by the oil embargo of 1974.

- The two biggest developments to emerge were television and electronic data processing. Television has changed America's lifestyle as well as the world of advertising. Data-processing systems have brought before the eyes of management a wealth of organized information. This, together with the syndicated research services, has revolutionized the entire marketing process and the advertising-media operation.

Advertising in the Fragmented 1980s

As we have seen in this chapter, advertising is rarely a stable business. It changes with business conditions, technology, and the social and cultural times. In some cases, it has a role in causing these changes; in others, it simply follows. The 1980s were a period of significant change in American society, and certainly advertising was affected by many of these changes.

Let us briefly discuss some of the major developments during this period:

1. *New technology.* Changes in technology and diversification of the communication system had profound effects on advertising during this period. Cable television, home video recorders, a proliferation of specialized magazines, the success of direct mail and home shopping techniques, and the growth of sales promotion changed the practice of advertising in fundamental ways. The advertising practitioners of today are much more likely than their predecessors to be marketing generalists, competent in evaluating research and understanding the psychology of consumer behavior.

2. *Audience fragmentation.* The 1980s may have marked the end of the traditional mass market. Advertisers no longer identified markets by households or size, but rather by demographics and number of heavy users of specific products. Television, which at one time offered three channels, now offered 50; newspapers, rather than appealing to a single homogeneous readership, were positioned more as cafeterias where readers choose only what they want to read; and the VCR and home computers began to let the audience control the media.

3. *Consolidation.* Paradoxically, as the media and audience proliferated, ownership of brands, ad agencies, and media was consolidated among a few giant companies. Firms such as Procter & Gamble, American Home Products, and Philip Morris provided corporate umbrellas for dozens, even hundreds, of separate brands. With their billion-dollar-plus budgets, they held tremendous control over the advertising agencies vying for their accounts. Like their clients, ad agencies also merged into so-called mega-agencies designed to offer greater service to these giant conglomerates. Often as not, these agency mergers led to as many headaches as benefits, starting with unmanageable client conflicts. Finally, the media were increasingly under the control of fewer and fewer communication companies. The Turner empire of cable networks, Time Warner's ownership of a bewildering array of media, and Gannett's interest in everything from newspapers to outdoor advertising to TV production were only a few examples of the changing media landscape during the 1980s.

4. *Credit.* Perhaps the greatest long-term legacy of the 1980s was the buy now, pay later mentality that pervaded every facet of American life from the federal government to the individual household budget. The leveraged buyouts of corporate America and the overuse of consumer credit created an atmosphere in which living within one's income was an illusion. By 1990, when companies and consumers began the slow process of paying for the excesses of the past decade, advertising was often the first victim of any cutbacks. Media saw advertising revenues fall; advertising was difficult to sell even with deep discounts; merchants began to deal with a reluctant consumer more interested in deals than fancy advertising; and some of the most famous names in American business faced serious trouble, if not outright bankruptcy.

Advertising and the Twenty-First Century

Although predicting the future is always undertaken at one's peril, there are two areas that most advertising executives agree will offer great potential for change and opportunities in the future.

1. *A locally oriented strategy for global marketing.* Mass marketers such as Coca-Cola, Sony, Ford, and Procter & Gamble will continue to increase their expansion on a worldwide basis. However, global strategies will increasingly be geared to a local country or region of the world. Instantaneous communication will allow centralization of management and localization of advertising.

2. *One-to-one communication.* Some form of one-to-one communication will be the norm. Technology will allow media, in whatever form they eventually take, to communicate personally with their audiences. Print media will be published according to the interests and tastes of individual readers, with each publication carrying editorial and advertising geared to the demographics and lifestyles of readers. The broadcast media will continue to fragment, with the audience expected to bear a greater burden of the cost. Totally free television will probably be discontinued in the next century. In exchange, viewers will have much more control over the content of that medium.

Already millions of Americans use their VCRs to control when they will watch previously broadcast programs, or they circumvent broadcasters altogether with rental movies. A number of cable systems offer movies-on-demand, interactive game shows, and other consumer services. The ongoing mergers among cable, telephone companies, and program services are an indication of the fact that these major corporations think interactivity is the wave of the future.

The Internet, providing personal conversations with individuals and groups with similar interests located around the globe, has already demonstrated the fragile nature of traditional mass communication. On-line computer links as well as television shopping networks are offering the first glimpse at the future of interactive communication by which consumers never have to leave their living rooms to conduct business or be entertained. Some people predict that even institutions such as the postal service will be made obsolete early in the next century.

The so-called electronic super highway offers the prospect of easy two-way access between buyers and sellers. It also makes inexpensive, readily available worldwide communication a reality. The global village, first suggested by Marshall McLuhan some 30 years ago, is fast becoming a technical reality. However, some observers question the more optimistic predictions of those who see an interactive world at our doorstep.

If there is one aspect of future advertising that is certain, it is that the cost of reaching potential buyers will continue to increase. Clients' demands for efficiency in the advertising function will continue to cause profit squeezes on agencies. Already we are seeing sometimes acrimonious negotiations between agencies and their clients over methods of compensation. Likewise, agencies are demanding concessions on media advertising rates. Many advertising executives on both the agency and corporate side wonder if advertising can be sustained at the same level as in past years in the face of these spiraling costs.

SUMMARY

As we write this text, the history of advertising is being written. The next decade will bring fundamental changes to mass communication not seen since the advent of high-speed presses and the introduction of broadcasting. In the current edition of this text, we explain the current practice of advertising while offering insights in this fast-changing field. In a real sense, you—as future advertising practitioners—will write the history of the industry. You will face a number of challenges unique to your generation. With these challenges will come opportunities, responsibilities, and rewards that advertisers of earlier periods could not have imagined.

REVIEW

1. What are some of the social and economic conditions necessary for advertising to be successful?
2. Briefly discuss the three broad periods of advertising development.
3. Define the following terms:
   a. Hoarding
   b. Siquis
   c. *Printers' Ink* Model Statute
   d. Audience fragmentation
4. Discuss the role of the emergence of the railroad in supporting advertising.
5. Briefly describe the development of the mass magazine during the nineteenth century.
6. What were some of the major changes in advertising resulting from the introduction of radio?
7. What was the purpose of the War Advertising Council?

TAKE IT TO THE NET

We invite you to visit the Russell/Lane page on the Prentice Hall Web site at **PHLIP** **http://www.prenhall.com/phbusiness** for the bimonthly Russell/Lane update and for this chapter's World Wide Web exercise.

chapter

2

ROLES OF ADVERTISING

CHAPTER OBJECTIVES

ADVERTISING IS AMONG THE MOST FLEXIBLE AND CREATIVE OF MARKETING COMMUNICATION TOOLS. IT IS USED BY VIRTUALLY EVERY COMPANY REGARDLESS OF WHETHER THEIR CUSTOMERS ARE INTERNATIONAL IN SCOPE OR CONFINED TO A FEW SQUARE BLOCKS. THE SPECIFIC GOALS OF ADVERTISING WILL VARY WIDELY; ADVERTISING CAN BE USED TO SOLVE A NUMBER OF MARKETING COMMUNICATION PROBLEMS. IT IS FOUND IN A WIDE ASSORTMENT OF FORMATS, CREATIVE STRATEGIES, AND MEDIA PLACEMENTS. AFTER READING THIS CHAPTER YOU WILL UNDERSTAND

- advertising as a marketing communication tool
- advertising and its role in the marketing mix
- the importance of strong brand identification
- marketing problems legitimately addressed by advertising
- advertising as both consumer and trade communication
- advertising of ideas and nonprofit organizations.

As we see in this chapter, advertising is used for a number of purposes by industrial giants, nonprofit organizations, and the smallest retail establishments. Modern advertising is undergoing a significant change from earlier years. The key to successful advertising can be summarized by answering two questions:

1. What marketing problems do I face that I can expect advertising to solve?
2. How can advertising fit into the overall marketing strategy of my firm?

These two simple questions have no easy answers. However, keeping these questions in mind will force you to position advertising in an overall marketing communication matrix, where it rightfully belongs. Advertising usually fails for two reasons:

1. bad advertising execution, that is, poor creativity, reaching nonprospects, and so forth
2. being asked to solve noncommunication problems; for example, advertising can rarely address issues such as poor product quality or service, inadequate distribution, or unreasonable pricing policies

Advertising is a *communication* tool. When we stray from this fundamental concept, we are placing unrealistic burdens on advertising and setting ourselves up for failure.

Once we have clearly defined the communication nature of advertising, we must then address the role of advertising in the overall marketing strategy of the firm. Properly executed, the advertising plan will flow directly from the marketing plan. Too often, advertisers confuse marketing goals and advertising goals and are then disappointed when advertising fails to solve these more general issues, which may have nothing to do with communication.

Let us first look at the components of a *marketing* plan:[1]

1. *Overall goal of the plan.* Usually, the goal is expressed in financial terms, such as expected sales revenues at the end of the first year or percent increases over previous years.
2. *Marketing objectives.* Here the objective and rationale of the plan are stated. For example, we may want to show a significant increase in market share relative to specific competitors.
3. *Marketing strategy.* The strategy outlines the steps to achieve our goals and objectives. We might suggest a greater investment in advertising or promotion or a switch in distribution outlets. The strategy offers only a general overview of primary marketing considerations.
4. *Situation analysis.* This analysis is a statement of the product benefits and the pertinent data available concerning sales trends, competitive environment, and industry trends.
5. *Problems and opportunities.* At this point, we outline the major problems and opportunities facing the brand. For example, a major manufacturer of lawn tools found that it was losing sales because its major competitors had signed exclusive contracts with major retail chains. However, the company soon found that there were numerous opportunities to sell through local, independent retailers who did not have access to several brands sold exclusively through chains.
6. *Financial plan.* The financial plan is an outline of the expected profit or loss that will be experienced over various time frames.
7. *Research.* Sometimes the marketing plan suggests that research is needed to answer questions for which there is no information available.

A number of studies have linked the contributions of advertising to the overall success of a firm. Basically, advertising contributions to the marketing strategy are to lower sales costs and thereby increase profits. Obviously, if a company can utilize a less-expensive sales tool, advertising will not be used. Ultimately, firms are seeking the highest possible return on their investment to maximize profits.

Research shows that, in most cases, return on investment (ROI) is directly related to share of market. That is, it is reasonable to assume that those companies with the greatest dominance of a market should expect to achieve economies of scale that will increase the ROI (see Exhibit 2.1, p. 24). In turn, it is clear that the share of market of a brand is determined by a number of factors: level of personal selling, product distribution, product quality, selling methods, and, of course, advertising and promotion.

---

[1]Adapted from David W. Schropher, *What Every Account Executive Should Know about a Marketing Plan* (New York: American Association of Advertising Agencies, 1990).

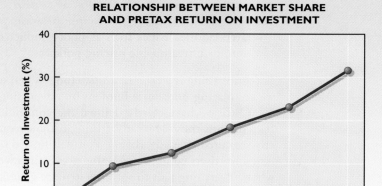

exhibit

2.1

Return on investment normally is enhanced as market share increases.

Courtesy: Cahners Publishing Co. Cahners Advertising Research Report No. 2000.1.

RELATIONSHIP BETWEEN MARKET SHARE AND PRETAX RETURN ON INVESTMENT

Brand preference
When all marketing conditions are equal, a consumer will choose a prefered brand over another.

Perhaps the most significant role that advertising plays is its contribution to the creation of **brand preference.** "In the competitive selling arena of American business, we compete for more than share of market. First we compete for share of mind [see Exhibit 2.2]. Gaining our share of the prospect's mind when he or she is ready to buy is a basic function of advertising. The objective is to increase brand preference for our product at the expense of our competition. When a person is ready to buy, it is advertising that helps pave the way to brand awareness and brand preference in our favor."[2]

Exhibit 2.3 shows the interrelationship among the various factors. Note that advertising is only one link in this chain and rarely can function successfully when other parts of the process are second rate. Likewise, when a firm is cursed with poor advertising it makes it that much more difficult for other areas of marketing.

Once we are satisfied that we have a clear picture of the role of advertising in the marketing function and its expected contribution to that process, we move ahead to begin our advertising planning. As mentioned previously, the advertising plan should flow easily and directly from the marketing plan. A typical advertising plan would include the following elements:

Advertising objectives
Those specific outcomes that are to be accomplished through advertising.

1. State the ***advertising objective(s)*** *in terms of the marketing goals and objectives.* There is a discipline in making yourself relate and justify the advertising objectives in marketing terms.

exhibit

2.2

Advertising of different brands competes for consumer share of mind.

Courtesy: Cahners Publishing Co. Cahners Advertising Research Report No. 2000.1.

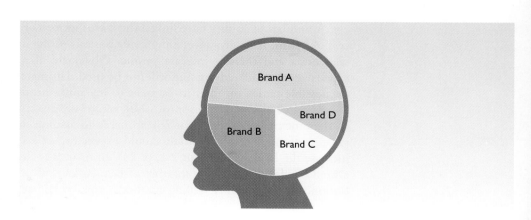

[2]*How Advertising Contributes to Return on Investment,* Cahners Advertising Research Report, No. 2000.1, Cahners Publishing Co.

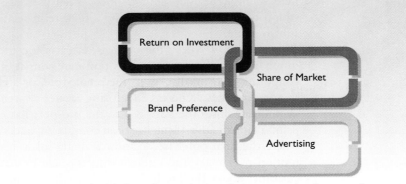

exhibit

2.3

Courtesy: Cahners Publishing Co. Cahners Advertising Research Report No. 2000.1.

Advertising is the final link in the marketing chain supporting increased return on investment. Advertising of the proper frequency and quality, concentrated to give maximum exposure to primary prospects (specialized business magazine advertising), dramatically increases brand preference. The results are seen in increased sales dollars per call. Share of market improves, and return on investment moves right up with it.

2. *Identify the target market.* Companies rarely advertise to everyone. Instead, they define a limited number of prospects (e.g., women, ages 18–35) and direct their marketing efforts to them. These customers are called target markets. As part of the marketing plan, advertisers define the target market in terms of potential sales and, if possible, the percent of product usage by the various subcategories of the total market. The market is often identified on the basis of demographic, geographic, and behavioral factors.

3. *Justify the budget.* The budget should be justified along with any changes from previous years. The budgeting process is discussed in chapter 6.

4. *Determine the value added.* How will advertising enhance the product and differentiate it from other products?

This general overview of the advertising plan is followed by more detailed creative and media plans. These are discussed in later chapters.

ADVERTISING, THE MARKETING MIX, AND INTEGRATED MARKETING

Marketing consists of four primary elements: product, price, distribution, and communication. Advertising's primary role is concerned with building brand awareness and product preference—both communication functions. Advertising is dependent on the other three areas of the "**marketing mix**"[3] for its success. Not only is advertising dependent on sound decisions in areas such as distribution and pricing, but, increasingly, it works in concert with other promotional and sales tools.

In recent years, companies have begun to use an arsenal of communication options to compete against other brands. In their quest to reach prospects, there are few communication vehicles that are not considered by agencies and their clients. To understand the complex relationships advertising has with other forms of marketing communications options, we need to briefly review the following four elements.

1. *Personal selling.* Personal communication is the most effective means of persuading someone. However, it is also the most expensive and is impractical as a means of

Marketing mix
Combination of marketing functions, including advertising, used to sell a product.

---

[3] A term coined in the early 1930s by Professor Neil H. Borden of the Harvard Business School to include in the marketing process such factors as distribution, advertising, personal selling, and pricing.

mass selling. Personal selling is most often used as a follow-up to mass communication to close the sale or develop a long-term relationship that will eventually result in a sale.

2. *Sales promotion.* Sales promotion is an extra incentive for a customer to make an immediate purchase. Sales promotion may consist of a special sale price, a cents-off coupon, a colorful display in the retail store, or a chance to win a trip to Hawaii in a sweepstakes. Whereas advertising creates awareness and brand preference, sales promotion closes the sale. "Once the prospect has entered the shopping state, the primary job of advertising has been completed, and sales promotion takes over. Even where the final purchase decision is made solely because of advertising, sales promotion may make the difference in the sale by having reminded the prospective customer about the product through a sales promotion activity."[4] Ideally advertising builds long-term brand loyalty, whereas sales promotion acts as a short-term boost to sales.

3. *Public relations.* According to the Public Relations Society of America, "**Public relations** helps an organization and its publics adapt mutually to each other." It is one of the most familiar forms of business communication, but only in recent years has it been fully integrated into the marketing communication plans of most companies. In the following Case History, note how Visa and Ketchum Public Relations use the techniques of public relations to increase credit card usage (see pp. 28–30). As one marketing executive pointed out, "Public relations is a partner with marketing, a key component. PR underscores our marketing messages. There are always opportunities to get those messages across, whether there's a story in a new marketing campaign, or a new product, or our annual sales report."[5] Public relations differs from advertising in that the advertiser directly pays for exposure of the message, controls in what medium and how often it will appear, and dictates exactly the message. The public relations communicator can influence all these elements, but has no direct control over them. However, public relations has the advantage of being presented as news rather than advertising and therefore often has more credibility with the audience.

4. *Advertising.* Advertising is a message paid for by an identified sponsor and usually delivered through some medium of mass communication. Advertising is persuasive communication. It is not neutral; it is not unbiased; it says, "I am going to sell you a product or an idea." Advertising is increasingly dealing with sophisticated consumers who understand the advertising process and its goals. And yet, even with the number of advertisements to which consumers are exposed each day, it remains the major promotional method that buyers cite as a motivation to try new brands (see Exhibit 2.4).

In the last decade, firms have endeavored to coordinate their sales messages to speak to consumers with a unified voice. As a result of this move to organize the total communication program, many advertisers have turned to **integrated marketing communication** (IMC).

This integrated perspective seeks to consolidate all forms of marketing communication.

> IMC is not about ads, or agencies, or direct mail pieces or PR projects, or the battle over who controls communication. It is about understanding the consumer and what the consumer actually responds to. The IMC process is a way of thinking and planning that aligns all of a company's commu-

Public relations
Communication with various internal and external publics to create an image for a product or corporation.

Integrated marketing communication (IMC)
The joint planning, execution, and coordination of all areas of marketing communication.

---

[4]Richard C. Ward, "Merchandising," in *What Every Account Executive Should Know about Merchandising and Sales Promotion,* a publication of the American Association of Advertising Agencies, 1990.
[5]Carolyn Shea, "Bang the Drum Loudly," *Promo,* June 1996, p. 117.

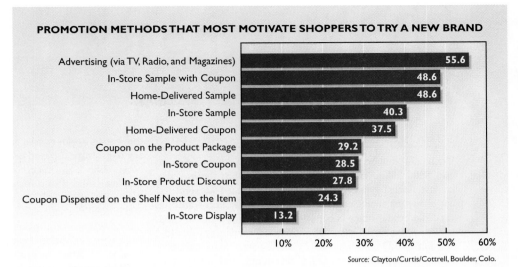

PROMOTION METHODS THAT MOST MOTIVATE SHOPPERS TO TRY A NEW BRAND

Method	Percentage
Advertising (via TV, Radio, and Magazines)	55.6
In-Store Sample with Coupon	48.6
Home-Delivered Sample	48.6
In-Store Sample	40.3
Home-Delivered Coupon	37.5
Coupon on the Product Package	29.2
In-Store Coupon	28.5
In-Store Product Discount	27.8
Coupon Dispensed on the Shelf Next to the Item	24.3
In-Store Display	13.2

Source: Clayton/Curtis/Cottrell, Boulder, Colo.

When choosing between two unfamiliar brands, 66.3 percent of respondents will choose the item that is advertised the most, according to a recent direct mail, personal interview, and focus group survey of 2,704 consumers. Of shoppers surveyed, 65.5 percent feel that a brand that is nationally advertised creates the perception that the item has better quality than the one that is not, up from 60.2 percent 1991.

exhibit

2.4

Advertising Makes the Difference

Adapted from "Numbers for the Nineties," *Advertising Age,* January 15, 1996, p. 30.

nications so that they are most effective and responsive to the consumer interest. IMC is driven by a philosophical shift from simply "moving products" to truly serving customer needs and building relationships with key publics.[6]

Although many marketing executives agree that the concept of IMC presents a realistic view of the relationship between a company and its customers, most firms have been reluctant to embrace the concept. In a 1995 study, less than one-third of companies had a marketing communication plan in place. The study found that, "IMC requires more intensive planning, intensive customer analysis and careful measurement of results."[7] The concept also requires a dramatic change in organization and culture for many companies. For example, IMC demands that departments and functions work together in roles that are unfamiliar to many executives. IMC also requires a level of communication coordination that some firms are not ready to adopt.

Obviously, agencies cannot operate in this new world of integrated marketing without significant adjustments. IMC is client driven, but agencies must adapt to service those companies that have adopted the IMC concept while still serving traditionally organized clients. One approach to integration used by some agencies is to create separate units to handle clients' needs beyond traditional advertising. These units will service clients in areas such as sales promotion, direct response, and product sampling as well as advertising.

As integration of the various promotional functions becomes more typical, the advertising person of the future will be required to make decisions about the role that advertising and other promotional tools will play in any particular campaign. This assessment will include an evaluation of marketing goals and strategies, identification of prime prospects, product characteristics, and the budget available for all areas of the communication mix.

---

[6]Newsletter of the Arthur W. Page Society.

[7]Kim Cleland, "Few Wed Marketing, Communications," *Advertising Age,* February 27, 1995, p. 10.

case
HISTORY

SITUATION OVERVIEW

With 271 million cards issued within the United States and $800 billion card charges annually, Visa is the world's largest, fastest growing brand of payment card. Despite its large market share, competition is especially fierce among card issuers who are competing for transactions and card loyalty. Historically, Visa has motivated card users in November and December with "Visa Rewards" national consumer sweepstakes, shopping discounts, and incentives. But, Visa wanted to create a motivating and extensive holiday campaign in 1996 that would work harder to build the brand's image and equity, increase holiday card usage, and involve and benefit member financial institutions and national merchants on the local level. Research showed cardholders responded very positively to cause-related marketing, so working with its sales promotion, advertising, and public relations agencies, Visa created its first fully integrated, national, cause-related marketing promotion, called "Read Me a Story" (RMaS). Reading was selected as its universally appealing cause, and Visa pledged to donate a minimum of $1 million to Reading Is Fundamental (RIF),

the nation's oldest and largest nonprofit children's literacy organization, based on Visa card usage volume between November 1 and December 31, 1996. Additionally, a goal was set to read one million stories to children. Ketchum Public Relations (KPR) was charged to develop a national public relations campaign that would dramatically leverage the news value and extend the impact of the advertising and sales promotional campaign on both the national and local levels. After extensive research on reading in America, KPR recommended bringing the Read Me a Story program "to life" by traveling a national "storybook" bus featuring 10 of America's favorite storybook characters performing an original musical score to 61 cities in 45 days.

RESEARCH

Besides Visa's in-depth consumer research into causes cardholders care about, KPR conducted extensive secondary research into the state of reading in homes across America to shed new light on important family lifestyle habits and to determine relevant newsworthy information validating the importance of a national reading awareness campaign. KPR investigated existing studies on reading and literacy in America from the Department of Education and International Reading Association, identified and contacted prominent reading and literary experts, and conducted vast database and Internet searches. KPR then commissioned a national family reading study with Yankelovich Partners. A national survey of 525 parents of children 2 to 8 years old was fielded to identify family reading practices and how families spend time with their children. Findings revealed that parents realize the importance of reading aloud and rank it as one of the most important activities that they can do to help their children's growth and development. It also revealed a gap between how much parents desire to read aloud versus how much they actually read to their children.

PLANNING

Objectives • maximize national and local grassroots awareness of Visa's "Read Me a Story" initiative to read one million stories to children and raise $1 million for Reading Is Fundamental
• increase Visa card usage during the fourth quarter
• gain involvement of Visa member financial institutions and merchants on a local grassroots level

Audiences
- Visa cardholders, Visa merchants, Visa member financial institutions, RIF volunteers, parents

Strategy
- obtain and shape new insights on reading practices in America to increase news interest in Visa's sales promotion
- leverage goal of reading one million stories to children as news-making vehicle to secure interest at grassroots level
- bring importance of reading to life with live performances and appearances by favorite children's storybook characters through national tour
- use performances to enhance local involvement/support among Visa's key member audiences

EXECUTION

Partnerships KPR worked with Reading Is Fundamental's extensive 200,000 volunteer network to help organize special events with local RIF chapters for RIF children in 61 cities along the bus tour route in November and December, as well as other U.S. markets. This involved

- leveraging Visa's National Football League sponsorship by arranging half-time shows at six NFL games nationwide
- coordinating distribution of "Reading Aloud" brochures (created with Scholastic, Inc.), which included a consumer sweepstakes and parent reading pledge form to count toward the million-story record

- negotiating with six of the nation's top children's book publishers to donate storybook character costumes and provide for licensed character appearances on the bus tour and in collateral materials
- working with celebrity ad star, Danny Glover, to extend awareness as national program spokesperson.

Bus Tour KPR identified and supervised professional children's songwriters, scriptwriters, recording artists, choreographer, set designer, costume designer, actors, sound technician, and stage crew to develop an original, fully portable and captivating 30-minute musical show promoting reading aloud with 10 of America's most popular storybook characters: Angelina Ballerina, Babar, Clifford the Big Red Dog, Jesse Bear, Little Red Riding Hood, Lyle the Crocodile, Mother Goose, Peter Pan, Pippi Longstocking, and Winnie-the-Pooh. KPR orchestrated the entire 15,000-mile tour, creating a colorful custom bus to travel across 36 states, to 61 cities in 45 days between November 7 and December 23, 1996. As many as four performances and media events were conducted each day for thousands of RIF children and adults at schools, libraries, hospitals, malls, and NFL games. Children received special Visa "RMaS" stickers, "Reading Aloud" brochures, bookmarks, candy canes, and books donated from local Visa member financial institutions to take home to their families. Mayoral and gubernatorial proclamations for "Read Me a Story" day were presented at 41 events in 67 percent of the bus tour markets across the country, and NFL players often made special cameo appearances.

National Launch The campaign was launched nationally at Town Hall theater in New York City, with a theater-style premiere of the "Read Me a Story" performance, starring Danny Glover, for 1,300 New York City–based RIF schoolchildren, national media, Visa VIPs, and program partners. Miss America Tara Holland, Visa president and CEO Carl Pascarella, RIF president Ruth Graves, and RIF chairman Lynda Johnson Robb, joined Glover. To extend grassroots awareness, Glover conducted a television satellite media tour, which aired in 29 markets. A video news release was distributed nationally. Yankelovich Partners survey results were released to national and local education press at the launch.

Merchant/Member Support Bus tour events created direct community tie-in opportunities for Visa member financial institutions to raise community awareness by donating books to children and cash to local RIF chapters at tour events. A colorful kiosk in the lobby of each performance venue acknowledged local bank and merchant support. Merchants displayed promotional signage and welcomed the storybook characters for a special in-store reading and "meet and greet" session with their customers on the tour.

Non–Bus Tour Support Comprehensive, turnkey "RMaS" event and publicity kits, including "Read Aloud" brochures, bookmarks, posters, stickers, and tally sheets to keep track of stories read, were created to enable RIF volunteers, financial institutions, and merchants to stage their own story-reading events in lieu of a bus tour visit to their city.

World Wide Web Weekly "Notes from the Road" were created for Visa's Web site, describing life on the "Read Me a Story" bus tour through character narrative. In addition, consumers could make story-reading pledges online and find out dates and locations of bus tour visits in their town.

Radio Promotions KPR leveraged Visa advertising merchandising dollars by partnering with 25 radio stations in nine markets for on-air promotional time to announce local bus tour visits and provide giveaways.

Hispanic Outreach Aggressive Hispanic media outreach was conducted in Miami, Houston, Chicago, Phoenix, Dallas, and Los Angeles to further extend grassroots awareness of the program. Spanish "Reading Aloud" brochures were distributed at these events.

Finale Event On the last day of the tour, Danny Glover and the storybook characters joined San Francisco 49ers mascot Sourdough Sam, the 49er Goldrush cheerleaders, and 1,000 local children on field for a "Read Me a Story" finale half-time performance at a sold-out 3Com Park stadium during the nationally televised Monday Night Football Game between the San Francisco 49ers and the Detroit Lions. During the performance Danny Glover led the stadium in America's largest-ever story-reading, and, with Visa's president and CEO, presented a check for $1 million to Reading Is Fundamental.

EVALUATION

Objective #1 *Maximize national and local grassroots awareness of Visa's "Read Me a Story" initiative to read one million stories to children and raise $1 million for Reading Is Fundamental.*

MEDIA RESULTS Reached more than 104 million consumers over a 2-month promotion through more than 400 local and national broadcast and print placements. Highlights included CNN, *The Today Show, USA Today, CBS This Morning, Fox After Breakfast, Extra;* local NBC, ABC, CBS, and Fox affiliates; and top daily metro newspapers throughout the bus tour. Publicity was generated beyond the bus tour in nearly 100 additional communities where local RIF chapters sponsored RMaS events.

ANALYSIS OF MEDIA RESULTS An average of three major stories appeared per bus tour market, and Visa was mentioned in every placement an average of 2.6 times. Publicity placements were evaluated based on three key messages (fundraising/card usage, bus tour/million story goal, Visa sponsorship mention). Overall 56 percent of placements contained two or more key messages and another 33 percent featured one brand message.

RADIO PROMOTION REACH Radio promotions and giveaways reached an estimated 11.1 million consumers. Stations aired a combined total of 290 prerecorded 30- and 60-second promotional spots including key program messages, 85 live on-air Visa mentions and calendar listings for public events, and 55 on-air Visa merchandise prize giveaways.

READING RESULTS Story-readings exceeded the program's one million story goal. More than 3,083,000 stories were read aloud to approximately 1.5 million children at 3,378 RIF sites. Nationwide consumer pledges have yet to be tallied.

Objective #2 *Increase Visa card usage during the fourth quarter.*

CARD USAGE In December, Visa card transactions increased by 20 percent over the previous year. Visa's donation to Reading Is Fundamental totaled more than the promised $1,000,000.

Objective #3 *Gain involvement of Visa member financial institutions and merchants on a local grassroots level.*

MEMBER/MERCHANT INVOLVEMENT Participation by Visa member financial institutions and merchants exceeded any previous holiday promotion by Visa. Forty member financial institutions, including 12 Visa board banks, donated more than 50,000 books (a $67,000 value) and $13,000 in cash to local RIF chapters. As many as five banks per market donated at least one book for each participating child. Nine national merchant partners also supported local bus tour events with monetary and in-kind donations to RIF.

Courtesy: © Visa U.S.A. Inc. All rights reserved. Reproduced with permission. Ketchum Public Relations Worldwide.

ADVERTISING AS AN INSTITUTION

Advertising is more than just a means of disseminating product information. It is a primary communications tool of our economic system and our culture. In many respects, advertising reflects the society and contemporary mores of a particular period. For example, 25 years ago, advertising portrayed a largely white, male, middle-class society while omitting most minorities and women or showing them in a secondary role. Today, advertising, like our society, is much more sensitive and realistic in its treatment of various people. It is not uncommon to see advertising in which a woman is portrayed as an executive, automobile buyer, or business traveler. Likewise, minorities are represented more often and in a more realistic and positive light than ever before. Advertising mirrors the society in which it functions and also brings about subtle changes in the mores and behavior of the public exposed to it. It is no wonder that advertising is one of the most scrutinized of all business practices.

Advertising has an ethical and moral responsibility to deal honestly with its portrayal of society, but it is also good business. Individual companies are judged by their own advertising, and the effectiveness of advertising is dependent on the overall attitude of consumers toward advertising generally. One study demonstrated that the extent to which individuals pay attention to particular advertising is influenced by their attitudes toward advertising as an institution. The value advertising has for specific brands is dependent on how informative and *truthful* a consumer thinks advertising is in general.[8]

Advertising's role as an institution has been studied for most of this century by critics as well as proponents. Perspectives about the roles of advertising generally fall into one of three categories: what advertising does for consumers, for business, or for society.

What Advertising Does for Consumers

One of the most important roles of advertising is showing people how to solve problems. Effective advertising must start from the premise, "Does my product help people?" Advertising should address the way in which a product relates to contemporary concerns. What are the customers for your product thinking about, worrying about, crusading for? "Some concerns, like health, money, raising children, and relationships with other people are always important. . . . Once you've identified the strongest contemporary concerns, you can ask how your product relates to them and what your product does to alleviate them."[9] Perhaps the major trend in modern advertising is making the consumer the focus of the marketing process. Companies find that starting with the consumer creates a relationship in which products are designed for the consumer rather than having to convince consumers that a preexisting product is the one they want. Obviously, this process also has made fundamental, extremely positive modifications in advertising.

What Advertising Does for Business

Chapter 1 discussed some of the reasons why advertising can fulfill its potential only in a reasonably developed society. Basically, advertising is most valuable in a prosperous society. "Advertising is not badly needed in an economy of scarcity, because total demand is usually equal to or in excess of total supply. . . . It is when potential supply outstrips demand—that is, when abundance prevails—that advertising begins to fulfill a

---

[8]Abhilasha Mehta and Scott C. Purvis, "When Attitudes Towards Advertising in General Influence Advertising Success," in Charles S. Madden, ed., *Proceedings of The American Academy of Advertising,* 1995, p. 192.

[9]Leonard V. Strong 3rd, *The How-to Book of Advertising* (Cambria, Calif.: Fairchild Publications, 1990), p. 10.

really essential economic function."[10] Without advertising, businesses would not be able to bring new products to the attention of enough consumers fast enough to make the enormous cost of creating, developing, manufacturing, and distributing these products practical. In other words, advertising is both a tool and a requirement of an abundant economy.

What Advertising Does for Society

Advertising has both intended and unintended results. Obviously, the intended result of most advertising is to contribute to the profitable sale of products. In addition to its economic role, advertising revenues support a diverse and independent press system protected from government and special interest control. As a key communication link in the marketing process, it also is a major stimulant to vigorous economic growth and stability.

However, there is a growing awareness that advertising must move beyond single-minded concerns with profitability. There is increasing agreement that advertising must be created in an atmosphere that considers a number of ethical factors. For example, a recent survey of advertising agency executives found that they faced six major ethical considerations in conducting business:

● treating clients fairly
● creating honest, nonmisleading, socially desirable ads
● representing unhealthy, useless, or unethical products
● representing clients whose products/services are unhealthy, unneeded, useless, or unethical
● treating suppliers, vendors, and media fairly
● treating other agencies fairly[11]

It is to the benefit of advertising and society in general that ethical issues are in the forefront of discussions concerning the practice of advertising.

ADVERTISING TO DIVERSE CUSTOMER INTERESTS

A particular advertisement simultaneously communicates its message to various groups and individuals who in turn interpret this message in the context of their own experience. When designing an advertisement or advertising campaign, firms must consider the many publics that will be reached by their messages and take into account the perception that advertising will have on each. Often an advertising campaign is intended to carry out several functions at once.

Some of the groups that might be considered are

1. *The distribution channel.* With the growth of huge national retailers such as Wal-Mart and Kmart, national advertisers must demonstrate to retailers that they are offering brands with high consumer demand and ones they are willing to support with significant advertising dollars.
2. *Employees.* A company's product advertising is a means of instilling pride and loyalty in its employees. Sometimes this is done overtly by mentioning the quality workmanship that goes into a product. More often, the message to employees is less overt, but nevertheless an important function of advertising.

---

[10]David Potter, "The Institution of Abundance: Advertising," in C. H. Sandage and Vernon Fryburger, *The Role of Advertising* (Homewood, Ill.: Richard D. Irwin, 1960), p. 22.

[11]Kineta Hung and Marshall Rice, "Ethical Problems of Canadian Advertising Agency Executives," in Karen Whitehill King, ed., *Proceedings of the American Academy of Advertising,* 1994, p. 215.

3. *Customers.* Present customers are a vital audience for any advertising. Current customers can be encouraged to use more of a product, not consider a competitor, and have previous purchase of the product reinforced as a good decision.

4. *Potential customers.* As discussed earlier, one of the primary objectives of advertising is to create awareness among those who are unfamiliar with a brand. Obviously, a person who doesn't know about a product will not buy it. For most products, advertising provides the lifeblood for continued success by encouraging prospects to become customers.

5. *Stockholders.* Most large national companies are publicly held and depend on stockholders as a major source of operating revenue. Studies have shown that high brand awareness and a company's positive reputation are contributing factors to keeping stock prices higher than they might otherwise be. Stockholders are a major reason companies such as airplane manufacturers and utilities advertise in consumer and business magazines.

6. *The community at large.* Many companies operate local plants throughout the country. Advertising is often used to influence public opinion so that when the inevitable disputes about local tax assessment, excessive noise, or zoning ordinances arise, the company is viewed as a good neighbor.

Advertising is only one of the many marketing communication tools available to a company. We must start by determining whether, and in what proportion, advertising can profitably be used. At this point, our marketing situation analysis will tell us if the marketing conditions are conducive to the use of advertising alone, or more likely in concert with other marketing communications tools.

Manufacturers, even those marketing similar products, demonstrate markedly different approaches to advertising. A particular advertisement should be designed to single out those consumers who are interested in the particular product features and benefits that you can offer. Successful advertising is built around a specific marketing plan. An advertisement is not created in a vacuum; rather, its message is intended to carry out the specific marketing goals and objectives of the firm. A company's advertising must be viewed as unique to each brand and product category.

Even with the most meticulous planning, advertising success is not guaranteed. If advertising could wield the influence ascribed to it by critics as well as proponents, we would not have seen some of the marketing failures of the last decade. When a product is introduced without a clear consumer benefit or differentiation from competing brands, even the most creative advertising usually fails.

Brand Name

Products are concrete objects; brands, on the other hand, represent attitudes and feelings about products. Branding allows companies to favorably position themselves and their products by creating unique identities. Brand identity is increasing in importance as companies try to differentiate their products in fields that have become increasingly crowded. Companies try to impart to their brands attributes such as instant recognition (McDonald's Golden Arches), trust, quality, and ultimately consumer loyalty.[12]

An established **brand name** is one of the most valuable assets that a company owns. A recent survey estimated that more than 75 brands—including such well-known names as Coca-Cola, McDonald's, and Sony—each had a value of at least $1 billion.[13] These brands give companies a worldwide presence.

In fact, it is only because of brands that advertising exists. Brands allow a consumer to buy a product with the assurance of consistency from one purchase to another.

Brand name
The written or spoken part of a trademark, in contrast to the pictorial mark; a trademark word.

---

[12]Radio Advertising Bureau, *Industry White Paper: Branding,* January 1997, pp. 1–2.
[13]Martin B. Rosen, "Changing a Brand? TLC Pays Dividends," *Advertising Age,* January 1, 1996, p. 10.

exhibit

2.5

Courtesy: Cahners Publishing Co. Cahners Advertising Research Report No. 101.1.

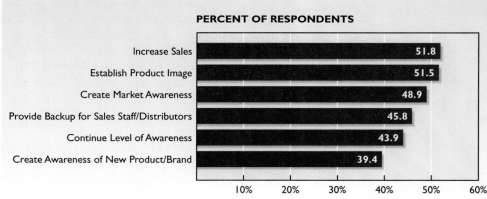

PERCENT OF RESPONDENTS

Increase Sales	51.8
Establish Product Image	51.5
Create Market Awareness	48.9
Provide Backup for Sales Staff/Distributors	45.8
Continue Level of Awareness	43.9
Create Awareness of New Product/Brand	39.4

Of the major goals of advertising programs, increasing sales is at the top of the list. Creating an image for a new product or brand is the lowest goal on the list.

Without brand identification, advertising could serve only a limited function in promoting generic goods.

The importance of brand image is so important that most companies see brand enhancement as a primary role of their advertising strategy (see Exhibit 2.5). In fact, only sales increases have a higher priority than increasing product image, and by a very narrow margin. In many respects, consumer opinions of specific brands create product value.

Because of the historical value of brands, a recent trend toward the purchase of store brands has many major companies concerned about the future value of their own brands. For example, one survey showed that only one in three consumers thought there was a great deal of difference between brands of running shoes or between domestic and imported cars. Only one in four saw differences between brands when considering hair care products, soft drinks, fast-food restaurants, or cosmetics.

Obviously, each firm must determine its own brand strategy, and no two companies face the same challenges from competitive pressure. However, one significant area of agreement among almost all brand managers is that price competition will undercut the value of a brand. A number of studies indicate that when marketing executives are asked how to build or maintain brand image, price cutting or price as a major consumer benefit consistently finishes at the bottom (see Exhibit 2.6). The problem with price competition is that it is the easiest benefit for competitors to match. In addition, because many consumers equate price and quality, a price-cutting strategy is diametrically opposed to the goal of enhancing brand image.

exhibit

2.6

Price cutting is a poor method of brand enhancement.

Courtesy: Bozell, Jacobs, Kenyon & Eckhart.
Source: American Advertising, Fall 1995, p. 21.

Priorities for Brand Enhancement

Improved customer service	73%
Improved quality	57
Significant innovative/technological changes	52
Better integration of marketing efforts	49
Improvement in marketing efforts	46
Global market expansion	43
Better corporate identity efforts	40
More database marketing	40
Increased brand or product advertising	31
Expanded distribution in existing markets	30
More public relations efforts	29
Increased corporate advertising	22
Changes in distribution in existing markets	15
More promotional spending	14
Lower prices	13

A GOOD PRODUCT THAT MEETS A PERCEIVED NEED

If the necessary ingredient for advertising is brand name, then the key to continued successful advertising is a good product. It goes without saying that no amount of advertising will persuade consumers to repeatedly buy a bad product. Movie producers learned years ago that their worst films should be introduced simultaneously in as many theaters as possible to keep bad word-of-mouth to a minimum. The strategy rarely works with bad movies and is even less likely to work with bad products.

The key to successful advertising is to view a product as a bundle of consumer benefits rather than a physical commodity. Consumer product usage and brand perception are crucial to determining advertising objectives. For example:

1. *Nature of the product.* A new product will require different strategies than will an established one. Likewise, an expensive product will require a different advertising approach than will an inexpensive one, just as a product with inherent consumer interest will have an advantage over more mundane items.
2. *Product purchase cycle.* Obviously, package goods bought on a biweekly cycle, such as groceries, will use different advertising compared to durable goods, such as appliances, which are purchased every five to ten years.
3. *Product awareness and market position.* Coca-Cola has a much different marketing strategy than does RC Cola, and it is reflected in both its advertising budget and its creative approach.
4. *Product seasonality.* Sun-tan lotion is marketed in a fundamentally different way than is toothpaste.
5. *Short-term advertising strategy.* Is a particular campaign designed to gain initial consumer trial, encourage higher purchase levels from current customers, or change established buying patterns?[14]

Product quality and consumer research go hand in hand. Product development is largely dependent on consumer research to determine the attributes most important in manufacturing a product. Likewise, research is crucial to determine which qualities are most important in influencing purchase behavior. For example, The Bolton Group conducted mall-intercept interviews for its client Bruce Hardwood Floors. The agency found that the product's target market of women home owners, 35 to 54 years old, with household incomes of $60,000 or more responsed to advertising that highlighted specific features of the flooring (see Exhibit 2.7, p. 36). The advertisement, with its combination of factual copy and product illustration, appeared in 17 magazines with outstanding results.

In another example, a survey of car buyers found the following product features were most important to the purchasers of the particular models:[15]

Model	Major Attribute	Percentage Citing Attribute
Hyundai	Price	62.4
Volvo	Safety	42.7
Honda	Manufacturer reputation	53.8
Cadillac	Size, style, color	32.4

It is obvious that any automobile must provide dependable transportation. However, it also is clear that drivers buy cars for vastly different reasons. The "bundle" of attributes that will move a person to purchase a Volvo are much different than those that appeal to a Cadillac buyer, even though the cars are similar in price.

---

[14] *Radio for the Advertiser,* a publication of the Radio Marketing Bureau, p. 4.

[15] *Auto Market Profiles,* a publication of the Radio Advertising Bureau.

exhibit

2.7

Advertising must speak to a targeted audience to be effective.

Courtesy: The Bolton Group.

Unfortunately, even the most focused and marketing-oriented company cannot guarantee success for all its products. The estimates for new product failures run as high as 90 percent. Behind each of these failures is a company that took a wrong turn. Sometimes the error was at the very beginning, by overestimating consumer demand; sometimes a good product idea is wrecked by inferior quality or service; sometimes an indifferent or untrained sales staff is the culprit; and sometimes unrealistic or poorly executed advertising must take the blame. Regardless of the reason for the failure of a particular product, some marketing mistake almost always plays a role. The concept of matching product quality with consumer demand is one that is fundamental to advertising and marketing.

Sales, Revenues, and Profit Potential

Throughout the text we discuss the need for marketing and advertising to satisfy consumer needs. However, a company can fulfill consumer needs only as long as it is doing so in a profitable manner. Advertising must address consumer preferences and be integrated into the overall marketing strategy. At the same time, it has an obligation to contribute to corporate profitability. Consequently, it is important that we continue to link the idea of sales, revenues, and, most important, profits with advertising.

The manner in which advertising contributes to profitability can take a number of forms. In some cases, it may create a favorable corporate image, it may complement short-term sales promotion, or it may introduce new products or improved features in place of old ones. However, in almost every case, advertising's role is relatively long term. Even in the case of retail advertising, its exact role is difficult to measure.

Regardless of the specific function a particular ad is assigned, it usually works in concert with other promotional elements and always within a broader marketing context. In the current environment of high costs and cutbacks by many firms, it is more incumbent than ever that advertisers be able to justify what they do in terms of their contributions to the bottom line.

The pressure to justify the advertising function has led to calls for more accountability. Because each company's advertising has unique objectives, it is difficult to judge advertising in a general way. However, advertisers are focusing increasingly on the role of advertising in maintaining sales and market share as a major goal. It is difficult to measure the value of advertising against sales not lost versus sales gained. However, the overall contributions to profitability may actually be greater in the former case.

Advertising tends to contribute most to sales and profits during the introduction and growth phase of a product. As advertising, promotion, and other forms of marketing communication become more intertwined, the difficulty of measuring the contribution to profits of any one element becomes more complex. Despite the difficulty of evaluating advertising on a long-term basis, its role must be determined for established products over extended periods. To measure a communications tool such as advertising solely against short-term sales is not only a mistake, but also shows an ignorance of the fundamental purposes of most advertising.

Finally, never make the mistake of viewing sales and revenues as substitutes for profits. A review of the last decade demonstrates that some of the largest U.S. companies (in terms of sales volume) experienced the largest financial losses. Anyone can devise a marketing plan that will result in greater sales if profits are not considered.

Product Timing

In comedy, it is said that timing is everything. In advertising it isn't everything, but success is often as much a matter of good timing as of a good product. Timing is a consideration for both product introduction and advertising. For example, many products have failed, only to see the same product succeed a few years later. By the same token, products that come into a market late often find it unprofitable to compete with established competitors.

Good timing, to paraphrase an advertising slogan, is being only slightly ahead of your time. Product innovations that capture a new trend or previously untapped need are those that are almost guaranteed success. For more than two decades, companies have been trying to introduce interactive technology that will allow consumers to conduct a wide array of business from a home computer. To date, these efforts have met with only limited success, but the popularity of the Internet and Web browsing offers the first realistic hope that average consumers will soon be "on-line."

A second element of advertising timing is determining the best opportunity to reach consumers for various products and services. The direct mail industry is astute in gathering information concerning the best time to launch a campaign for particular products. Even though no two advertisers face exactly the same problems, a general idea of when buyers are most likely to make certain purchases is valuable information to begin advertising planning. For example, according to the U.S. Department of Commerce, the best months for selling various product categories are

Product Category	Best Month	Percentage of Sales
All stores	December	10.4
Jewelry	December	23.0
Books	August	11.4
Lawn and garden	May	16.0
Tires	October	9.4
New homes	March	9.8

Although seasonality studies are helpful, they do not provide fail-safe solutions. They can provide only general guidelines and directions. Inventory clearances, unusual weather, general economic conditions, and a number of unpredictable factors can all affect the best time to advertise. In fact, off-timing from competitive advertising patterns is a method of differentiation if consumers will purchase during nontraditional periods. Still, it is rare for any product category to have consistent sales throughout the year, and advertisers are taking a major risk when they run counter to established consumer buying patterns and preferences.

Product Differentiation

Product differentiation is basically a process of giving prospective buyers a reason to purchase your brand rather than a competing one. The key to effective differentiation is exploiting those product benefits that are most important to consumers. Product improvement to meet the challenge of new competitors is a requirement for most companies if they are to survive. However, unless product improvements are effectively communicated to consumers, they are largely wasted as an effective marketing tactic.

Advertising's role in promoting product differentiation is to convey these improvements in a manner that makes product differential meaningful to consumers. The key element in successful product differentiation is consumer perception. If consumers *perceive* your product as differentiated from competitors, then it is.

Most advertising has at least some element of product differentiation as a primary theme. You only have to look at the headlines of most advertisements to determine the primary marketing strategy and the major sales differentiation from competing brands:

> *A desktop that's actually capable of telling you it's too hot.*
> *Compaq computers promoting its heat sensor and automatic cutoff feature.*

> *One of the coolest things about a York Peppermint Pattie is that it's low in fat.*
> *Candy enjoyment without the fat.*

> *It looks like shave gel. It feels like skin care.*
> *Gillette advertisement for shave gel with a skin care ingredient.*

> *Discover self-renewing color that wears on and on.*
> *Cover Girl lipstick that doesn't fade.*

> *Flonase gives you more days of nasal allergy relief than Claritin.*
> *In this case, the product differentiation is a direct comparison with the leading competitor.*

Product differentiation
Unique product attributes that set off one brand from another.

From these few examples, we can see the wide scope of possibilities for differentiating one product from another. In the case of Flonase, the strategy is a direct frontal assault on its competition. Gillette offers a differentiation through the introduction of a product line extension. Finally, York (Hershey) promotes a feature not new to the product but in line with current consumer concerns with high fat content. In each case, the basic tactic is to separate a brand from similar products and offer the consumer a unique reason to purchase the product.

Product differentiation is another method of target marketing. As we differentiate our product from similar brands, we are increasing our chances of selling to one market segment, but usually we are making it more difficult to reach other segments. For example, Pearl's toothpaste and drops have long appealed to consumers who are primarily interested in white teeth. A recent campaign had the slogan, "Put white in your bite."

By appealing to a narrow segment of the total dentrifrice market, Pearl's has captured a significant share of this segment. However, in doing so it has surrendered most of those consumers who are interested in features such as cavity control or better breath. Before embarking on a specific product differentiation strategy, you must make sure that it is a feature that is important to enough prospects that you will be able to sustain a profitable niche.

Advertisers also have a responsibility to promote meaningful product differences. Much of the criticism of modern advertising is that it tries to make obscure and inconsequential product differences important. There is no question that some advertising promotes inconsequential product features. However, the best and most successful products can demonstrate an obvious difference from their competitors.

Price

Product pricing is not only a means of recovering costs, executed properly, it is a fundamental element in basic marketing strategy. For most branded products, price is set in relation to competition, demand, or cost.

In Relation to Competition In this regard, pricing becomes an important tool of product differentiation. Because price implies value to many consumers, it becomes an important element in developing advertising messages. For example, the following automotive headlines convey markedly different points about the role of price as a marketing tool:

> *You've earned it. Now enjoy it.*
>
> *Buick Park Avenue*

> *It's friendly right down to its sticker.*
>
> *Dodge Neon*

In recent years, even the strongest brands have found that consumers have a growing interest in price and the perceived value they receive for their money. Consequently, we are seeing much more price-oriented advertising now than in previous years.

In Relation to Demand Obviously, those products with greatest demand are often better able to charge higher prices. In a sense, demand pricing is based on the value of a product to its customers and the competitive constraints of the marketplace. For example, AT&T, reacting to its cost-cutting rivals, advertises, "AT&T guarantees a competitive price."

Because demand is not constant over time or across market segments, sellers may adopt adjustable pricing strategies. The Hertz Corporation adjusts prices according to its periods of peak demand. Hertz knows, based on past performance and seasonal

Yield management
A product pricing strategy to control supply and demand.

changes, those times of strong and weak demand for car rentals. During peak demand seasons, Hertz raises prices and/or requires longer rental periods.

As a Hertz executive pointed out, "Price is a legitimate rationing device. What we're really talking about is efficient distribution, pricing, and response in the marketplace."[16] This strategy of using price to even out supply and demand is known as **yield management.**

In Relation to Cost   Obviously, the cost of producing and marketing a product has to play a major role in pricing strategy. The greater the gap between product cost and price, the greater the profit. However, a pricing strategy that concentrates solely on cost recovery and ignores consumer demand is overlooking an important element of the marketing process.

It also is important to note that in spite of the importance of pricing in current marketing, it would be a mistake to suggest that low price is necessarily a successful strategy. A number of prosperous companies have found that financially profitable niches can be found for higher price products if consumers perceive that the quality of the product is worth the higher price.

One important function of advertising is to create, or enhance, a positive gap between the price of a product and the value the average consumer ascribes to the product. The greater this "value gap," the more insulated the product is from competitive inroads into its market. The concept of the value gap underscores the notion that price is not a particularly safe means of establishing a long-term, competitive advantage (see Exhibit 2.8).

VARIATIONS IN THE IMPORTANCE OF ADVERTISING

To this point, we have discussed the many roles that advertising plays in the marketing plans of advertisers. Now we look at how diverse advertisers translate marketing goals into specific advertising plans and how different companies use advertising in markedly dissimilar ways. As companies increasingly look for synergism from the various elements of marketing communications, we inevitably see a great diversity in marketing communication plans. Companies with similar products use advertising in vastly different ways, and companies that have used certain sales techniques for years are looking for alternative communication mixes.

The determining factors that move a company or product category to a particular communication option are diverse and complex. However, four factors are paramount in determining to what degree advertising is used:

1. *Volume of sales.* In almost every case, as sales increase, the percentage of dollars spent on advertising decreases. This decrease is largely a matter of economies of scale—that is, regardless of a company's sales figures, there are only so many prospects to be reached with advertising. After sales reach a certain level, the ad budget may continue to rise, but at a slower rate.

2. *Competitive environment and profit margin.* The strength of competition will usually determine the size of the advertising budget. Companies facing intense competitive pressure are often forced to significantly increase their advertising. Beer and soft drinks are both in markets with high levels of competition and high profit margins, yet soft drinks spend almost 60 percent more on marketing as a percent of sales than beer. Why? Because beer companies, for social and political reasons, choose

---

[16]Ginger Conlon, "Making Sure the Price Is Right," *Sales & Marketing Management,* May 1996, p. 92.

ADVERTISING MAKES THINGS COST MORE, RIGHT?

We admit it. Advertising has a tremendous impact on prices. But you may be surprised by what *kind* of impact.

In addition to being informative, educational and sometimes entertaining, advertising can actually lower prices.

It works like this: Advertising spurs competition which holds down prices. And since advertising also creates a mass market for products, it can bring down the cost of producing each product, a savings that can be passed on to consumers.

Moreover, competition created by advertising provides an incentive for manufacturers to produce new and better products.

Which means advertising can not only reduce prices, but it can also help you avoid lemons.

ADVERTISING
ANOTHER WORD FOR FREEDOM OF CHOICE.
American Association of Advertising Agencies

exhibit

2.8

Properly executed advertising can contribute to lower prices.

Courtesy: American Association of Advertising Agencies.

to invest a greater percentage of their promotional dollars in event marketing (stock car races, rock concerts, and the like) than soft drinks, which are welcome sponsors in any medium.

3. *Overall management philosophy of advertising.* Obviously, the determining factor in the use of advertising is the management decision to use advertising versus some other promotional tool. For example, the Radio Advertising Bureau reported that Alamo Rent-A-Car was committed to television to overcome its reputation as an old, Florida-based firm. The company thought that television, targeted to upscale,

25 to 54 year olds would give the company a more dynamic image. On the other hand, Budget Rent-A-Car depends on trade promotion with corporate users and less dependence on advertising.

4. *New product introductions.* The greater the number of new products introduced and the higher the percentage of total revenues from new products, the greater the advertising budget. New product introductions are extremely expensive and usually require heavy advertising support. For example, Subway Sandwiches has developed a corporate strategy of rapid growth in stores during the 1990s. To support this growth. Subway increased its ad budget 32 percent in 1994 compared to a 4 percent growth for all restaurants. This strategy was in marked contrast to competitors such as McDonald's and Burger King, which spent a much higher level of funds on promotions at established units.[17]

We now move on to the next big step—to see how advertising fits into the marketing process.

THE PLACE OF ADVERTISING IN THE MARKETING PROCESS

As we have seen, the linkage among marketing, advertising, and other forms of promotion has never been greater than now. It is obvious that marketing decisions are not made in a void and that decisions in one area of marketing and promotion have an immediate and direct effect on others. Nowhere is this fact more apparent than in advertising.

For example, in the last few years a number of product categories have moved away from a dependence on couponing and other temporary promotions and have adopted across-the-board price cuts. This concept, known as **everyday low pricing** (EDLP), is a focused alternative to promotional spending.

Major brands of cigarettes, pet food, disposable diapers, and cereals are among the leaders in adopting this strategy. In each case, the price cuts were followed by significant decreases in promotional budgets and increases in advertising as consumers were informed of lower prices. In fact, it has been suggested that the continuing blurring of lines among marketing and various forms of marketing communications will soon require a new definition of advertising.

An examination of the wide variance in advertising-to-sales ratios across industries, or even among companies in the same product category, dramatically points out the different role that advertising plays among firms. For example, automobile dealers spend 1.2 percent of their sales on advertising; independent repair shops facing more competition, but with higher profit margins, spend almost three times more. Likewise radio stations, constantly fighting for listeners in a saturated field, spend 9.9 percent of sales on advertising, whereas television stations, with much less competition, spend only 3.2 percent.[18]

Marketing decisions not only determine the role of advertising, but often play a major role in the media that are used. Wal-Mart, one of the principal retail success stories of the last 25 years, is a case in point:

> Wal-Mart does extensive customer research. They know *price* is its shopper's first concern, before product selection or people oriented service. Wal-Mart focus group research shows their shoppers understand and respond to Wal-Mart's everyday low price policy. Wal-Mart aggressively protects and

Everyday low pricing (EDLP)
A marketing strategy that uses permanent price reductions instead of occasional sales promotion incentives.

---

[17]"Satellites, No-Frills, Tandems Feed Fast-Food," *Advertising Age,* September 27, 1995, p. 36.

[18]*Retail Ad Budget Guide,* a publication of the Radio Advertising Bureau.

promotes their low price marketing position. Wal-Mart's media decisions are driven by cost. Their biggest ad budget is dedicated to circulars (70% of which are delivered via newspapers; 30% via direct mail). Most of the remaining ad budget goes into spot TV (including cable), with network TV as a fill. Wal-Mart wants reach an extensive market penetration. They want it simple and they want it cheap. They dedicate only a small portion of sales to advertising (less than 1% of total sales); far less than competitors like Kmart and Sears. They believe that additional ad expenditures will not produce adequate sales increases to justify incremental investment.[19]

In the remainder of this chapter we examine some of the ways advertising functions in various industries and the stages of the marketing channel. Although you are most familiar with consumer advertising, it is only one of a number of categories that are used to bring products to market. Effective advertising must be successful on two levels: communication and carrying out marketing goals. Unfortunately, it is often the case that you can have successful communication on one level without accomplishing marketing goals (e.g., a humorous ad that everyone remembers but can't identify the brand).

Perhaps the easiest way to evaluate advertising's role in the marketing process is according to the directness of the intended communication effect and the anticipated time over which that effect is supposed to operate. In other words, how much of the total selling job should be accomplished by advertising and over what time frame should the job be accomplished?

Advertising designed to produce an immediate response in the form of product purchase is called direct-action, short-term advertising. Most retail advertising falls into this category. An ad that runs in the newspaper this morning should sell some jeans this afternoon. Advertising used as a direct sales tool, but designed to operate over a longer time frame, is called direct-action, long-term advertising. This advertising category is used with high ticket items (dishwashers and automobiles), for which the purchase decision is a result of many factors and the purchase cycle is relatively long.

Another category of advertising includes those advertisements that are used as an indirect sales tool. Such indirect advertising is intended to affect the sales of a product only over the long term, usually by promoting general attributes of the manufacturer rather than specific product characteristics. Included in this category are most institutional or public relations advertising. The exception would be remedial public relations advertising designed to overcome some negative publicity concerning product safety, labor problems, and so forth.

The aim of most advertising is to move a product or service through the various levels of the marketing channel. The objectives and execution of advertising will change from level to level. The intended target audience will result in markedly different advertising strategies. In the following sections we examine advertising to the consumer and to business.

ADVERTISING TO THE CONSUMER

National Advertising

The term **national advertising** has a special nongeographic meaning in advertising: It refers to advertising by the owner of a trademarked product (brand) or service sold through different distributors or stores, wherever they may be. It does not mean that the product is necessarily sold nationwide.

---

[19]From RAD National Marketing Update, September 1993.

National advertising
Advertising by a marketer of a trademarked product or service sold through different outlets, in contrast to *local advertising*.

Traditionally, national advertising has been the most general in terms of product information. Items such as price, retail availability, and even service and installation are often omitted from national advertising or mentioned in general terms. Instead, national advertising often identifies a specific target audience and creates an image for the product.

Although this general approach remains the norm, we are starting to see national advertisers take more regional (in a few cases even local) approaches to their advertising. As research allows national advertisers to more narrowly identify and reach specific market segments, we will see more regionalized advertising. When this occurs, national advertisers will be able to provide more information of interest to each segment, and national advertising executions will begin to approach local advertising in terms of content. However, in the short term, national advertising will continue to emphasize brand introductions of new products and greater brand loyalty for established products.

Retail (Local) Advertising

Retail advertising
Advertising by a merchant who sells directly to the consumer.

Usually **retail advertising** combines aspects of hard-sell messages with institutional advertising. On the one hand, retailers must compete in an extremely competitive business environment to move large volumes of merchandise. At the same time, their advertising must convey the image of the type of store with which consumers would like to do business.

To accomplish these dual tasks, retailers often include price information, service and return policies, location of their stores, and hours of operation—information that the national advertiser cannot provide. Often retail advertisements will include a number of products in a single advertisement, showing the range of merchandise available. Retail advertisements often are designed to feature sale merchandise that will build store traffic, with the hope that customers will buy other full-priced items once they are in the stores. Retail advertising is the unglamorous workhorse of the advertising industry.

End-Product Advertising

End-product advertising
Building consumer demand by promoting ingredients in a product. For example, Teflon and Nutrasweet.

What do products such as Intel computer chips, Lycra, Teflon, and Nutrasweet have in common? They are rarely purchased direct by consumers. Instead, they are bought as an ingredient in other products. The promotion of such products is called **end-product advertising** (or branded ingredient advertising). End-product advertising is most commonly used by manufacturers of ingredients used in consumer products. Successful end-product advertising builds a consumer demand for an ingredient that will help in the sale of a product. The knowledge that such a consumer demand exists will move companies to use these ingredients in their consumer products.

A number of companies have adopted aggressive end-product advertising campaigns. Long-time brands such as DuPont's Teflon (see Exhibit 2.9) and 3M's Scotchgard have successfully created consumer demand for these and other end products with creative advertising campaigns. Research indicates that end-product advertising is most effective when used as part of a multifaceted campaign coordinated among manufacturers of consumer products, retailers, and consumer end users. This strategy has the advantage of showing to the various elements of the trade channel that the end-product manufacturer is supporting them by building consumer demand.

Procter & Gamble engaged in an unusual form of end-product advertising when it introduced Fat-Free Pringles made with Olean, its fat-substitute product. The company ran two concurrent campaigns, one for the chips and another for the ingredient. The other unusual facet of the campaign is that the company was simultaneously conducting both primary and end-product advertising.

Building demand through end-product advertising is not easy. You must have an ingredient that both manufacturers and consumers recognize and believe will improve

a product. In addition, these ingredients usually are not obvious in the product, and therefore extensive advertising is required to make consumers aware of their advantages. End-product advertising is a variant of the more traditional national advertising that asks the consumer to buy a product by name. End-product advertising is an extremely small part of total advertising, but can be important to those companies that successfully use it.

Direct-Response Advertising

Direct-response advertising
Any form of advertising done in direct marketing. Uses all types of media: direct mail, TV, magazines, newspapers, radio. Term replaces *mail-order advertising.*

Direct marketing and **direct-response advertising** are not new. In this country, Ben Franklin is credited with the first direct-sales catalog, published in 1744 to sell scientific and academic books. The modern era of direct selling was ushered in with the publication of the Montgomery Ward catalog in 1872. Throughout the next century, direct selling was a popular method of reaching many consumers, especially those in rural areas without access to retail stores.

There is no question that direct marketing has become a major force in the promotional activities of most firms. Results from a recent study show that

- telephone marketing accounts for the majority of direct marketing expenditures. Telemarketing accounts for 40 percent of all expenditures, or $54 billion, followed by direct mail at $31.2 billion.
- the projected annual growth of direct marketing sales is 10.2 percent for business-to-business and 7.2 percent for consumers
- by the year 2000, the direct marketing job workforce will grow by 4 million jobs
- health, business, and financial services, in addition to computers, office equipment, and retailing, are the categories that show the most growth potential in terms of using and profiting from direct marketing activities.[20]

Direct response is becoming increasingly common in traditional advertising. Often companies offer toll-free numbers not only to sell a product, but also to allow customers to obtain information such as the location of local retailers or more detailed information about an item. In addition, cable television shopping channels and videocassettes give consumers the opportunity to see merchandise "live" before ordering it from their living rooms. The future holds great promise for various forms of interactive media that will provide even more innovative ways of communicating with prospects.

ADVERTISING TO BUSINESS AND PROFESSIONS

The average person doesn't see a very important portion of advertising because it is aimed at retail stores, doctors, home builders, wholesalers, and others who operate at various stages of the marketing channel. This type of advertising is done in addition to advertising products to consumers for their personal use.

Advertising to business takes several different forms: trade, industrial, professional, or corporate (institutional).

Trade Advertising

Before consumers have an opportunity to purchase a product, it must be available in retail stores. Manufacturers use trade advertising to promote their products to wholesalers and retailers. **Trade advertising** emphasizes product profitability to retailers as well as consumer advertising support provided by manufacturers. In addition, trade advertising also promotes products and services that retailers need to operate their businesses. Advertising for shelving, cleaning services, and cash registers are part of trade advertising.

Trade advertising can accomplish several goals:

1. *Gain additional distribution.* Manufacturers are interested in increasing the number of retail outlets that carry their brands. Trade advertising can create brand recognition for follow-up by personal salespersons or offer incentives to retailers who stock a product.
2. *Increase trade support.* Manufacturers compete for shelf space and dealer support with countless other brands. For example, the typical grocery store stocks more than 6,000 different items. Trade advertising can encourage retailers to give prominent position to products or to use a manufacturer's point-of-purchase material.

Trade advertising
Advertising directed to the wholesale or retail merchants or sales agencies through whom the product is sold.

---

[20]"Direct Marketing on a Fast Track," *Promo,* November 1995, p. 16.

3. *Announce consumer promotions.* Many trade advertisements offer a schedule of future consumer promotions. Manufacturers want to let dealers know that they are supporting retailers with advertising and encourage dealers to coordinate local promotions with national advertising efforts.

There are approximately 9,000 trade publications—several for virtually every category of retail business. The average consumer probably has not heard of most of these publications, but trade journals such as *Progressive Grocer* and *Drug Topics* play an important role in the advertising plans of most national advertisers.

Industrial Advertising

A manufacturer is a buyer of machinery, equipment, raw materials, and components used in producing the goods it sells. Companies selling to manufacturers most often address their advertising to them in appropriate industry publications, direct mail, telemarketing, and personal selling. This method is quite unlike consumer advertising and is referred to as **industrial advertising.**

Industrial advertising is directed at a very specialized and relatively small audience. The target audience of most industrial advertising is composed of relatively few buyers, each responsible for relatively large purchases. Industrial advertisements are written for experts, often containing product specifications and details that would be understood only by professionals in a particular manufacturing segment.

Industrial advertising rarely seeks to sell a product directly. The purchase of industrial equipment is usually a complex process that includes a number of decision makers. Often industrial advertising is a means of introducing a product or gaining brand name awareness to make it easier for follow-up from the company and sales representatives making personal calls to close sales.

Professional Advertising

Professional advertising is similar in intent to other types of trade advertising. That is, it is directed toward people who are not the actual users of a product, but influence the product decisions of ultimate consumers. The primary difference between professional advertising and other trade advertising is the degree of control exercised by professionals over the purchase decision of their clients.

A grocery store encourages consumer purchases of certain goods by the brands it stocks, but people can go to another store with more variety, lower prices, or better-quality merchandise. On the other hand, a person rarely will change doctors because a physician doesn't prescribe a certain brand of drugs; or change banks because the bank orders checks for its customers from a particular printer; or choose an architect based on how designs are reproduced. Consequently, professionals often make the final purchase decisions for their customers. In the case of professional products and services, customers probably are not aware of how professional advisers decide on the various brands they recommend.

Corporate (or Institutional) Advertising

Traditionally, **institutional advertising** has been viewed as a promotional technique intended to improve or maintain a corporate image, apart from selling the benefits of any single product. Although institutional advertising remains a long-term image-building technique, in recent years it has taken on a decided sales orientation in terms of the audiences reached and the intent of communication.

A review of corporate advertising indicates that the purpose of such advertising changes with the business climate. Like any advertising, corporate advertising reaches an identified target audience with a specific objective. Among the groups most often

---

Industrial advertising
Addressed to manufacturers who buy machinery, equipment, raw materials, and the components needed to produce goods they sell.

Professional advertising
Directed at those in professions such as medicine, law, or architecture, who are in a position to recommend the use of a particular product or service to their clients.

Institutional advertising
Advertising done by an organization speaking of its work, views, and problems as a whole, to gain public goodwill and support rather than to sell a specific product. Sometimes called *public-relations advertising.*

targeted for corporate advertising are ultimate customers, stockholders, the financial community, government leaders, and employees. Frequently cited objectives of corporate advertising are

- to establish a public identity
- to overcome negative attitudes toward a company
- to explain a company's diverse mission
- to boost corporate identity and image
- to overcome a negative image
- to persuade target audiences for later sales
- to associate a company with some worthwhile project.

These are only a few examples of possible corporate advertising objectives. The competitive environment of recent years has brought about dramatic changes in corporate advertising.

NONPRODUCT ADVERTISING

Idea Advertising

It is not surprising that the same marketing techniques so successful in selling products would be used to promote ideas (Exhibit 2.10). We are living in a period of conflicting ideas and special interest groups. It is understandable that the same advertising techniques that are used to solve marketing problems and sell products and services would be used to sway public opinion. As we saw in chapter 1, advertising propaganda is not a new phenomenon. What is new is the number of groups using advertising and the sophistication of the communication techniques being employed. Gun control, abortion, animal rights, and environmental issues are only a few of the topics that have used mass advertising in recent years.

Idea advertising is often controversial. Apart from the emotionalism of many of the topics being espoused, there are criticisms that advertising messages are too short and superficial to fully debate many of these issues. Proponents counter that advertising is the only practical way to get their message before a mass audience. They point out that idea advertising may be the most practical means for these groups to use their First Amendment privileges. Regardless of one's position on idea advertising, the increasing ability of media to narrowly target audiences, by ideology as well as product preference, will make this type of advertising more prevalent in the future.

Service Advertising

We are becoming a nation of specialists, with more and more Americans seeking advice and services for everything from financial planning to child care. On a broader scale, a complex society needs various financial, insurance, and medical services. The advertising of these services is much more difficult than that of most product advertising because what is being sold is essentially the expertise of a company. Hospitals such as St. Agnes offer medical information as value-added services to patients (Exhibit 2.11, p. 50). In turn, this information reinforces the expertise of the hospital and provides a differentiation from other institutions in an increasingly competitive field.

Because services are basically people enterprises, **service advertising** almost always has a strong institutional component. Often service companies keep the same slogan, theme, or identifying mark over long periods of time to increase consumer awareness. Because service industries are so similar (and often legally regulated), it is difficult to develop a distinct differentiation among competitors. Banks and insurance companies have a particularly difficult time in establishing an effective identity.

Idea advertising
Advertising used to promote an idea or cause rather than to sell a product or service.

Service advertising
Advertising that promotes a service rather than a product.

exhibit

2.10

Advertising effectively advocates a number of social issues.

Courtesy: Newspaper Association of America, the American Academy of Advertising, and Ronnie Couch and Carol Clements, Western Kentucky University.

Fundamentals of good advertising are the same regardless of whether a product or a service is being promoted. However, many marketing experts point out that differences between the two categories require some care in the manner in which service messages are handled. Some basic principles of service advertising include

1. *Featuring tangibles.* Because service advertising cannot feature a product in use, the service should be personalized in some way. For example, service ads often use testimonials. Service messages should show the benefits of the service, such as an on-time plane trip that results in closing a deal or an older couple contented as a result of good investment advice by their broker.

2. *Featuring employees.* Because the value of a service largely depends on the quality of a firm's employees, it is important to make them feel an important part of the service. Often service ads feature real employees in their ads. This approach has the advantage of personalizing the service to customers and building employee morale.

3. *Stressing quality.* Because services cannot be measured like products in terms of quality control, ads should feature consistency and high levels of services. Hospitals use terms such as "caring," "professional," and "convenience," in their advertising.

exhibit

2.11

Service advertising is
one of the fastest
growing advertising
segments.

Courtesy: Sprecher Bertalot
Company.

30 years ago, my grandfather
died of a heart attack.

10 years ago, my father
survived a heart attack.

Today, I'm avoiding one.

SUMMARY

From our discussion of the role of advertising, two major points should be emphasized:

1. Effective advertising can function only within the context of an organized marketing plan.
2. Advertising is a marketing communication tool and will be successful only if directed at communication problems. Advertising can rarely overcome deficiencies in the core marketing program.

An effective advertising plan is an extension of the marketing goals of a firm. Advertising, in addition to other functions, normally is asked to develop or maintain product awareness, build company and brand image, and provide product information that differentiates one brand from another. The execution of advertising will vary by the stage in the trade channel (e.g., retail, consumer, industrial, professional). It will adapt to the primary product benefits and how they are expressed (e.g., testimonials, demonstrations, long copy). Advertising will also be modified according to funds available as well as the corporate philosophy concerning the value of advertising within the marketing plan.

It is clear that advertising is only one of a number of possible sales tools. The advertising executive of the future will be a marketing communicator, able to utilize an array of marketing communication elements including promotion, public relations, and personal selling in a coordinated fashion to bring synergy and unity to the overall corporate message.

Although major changes in advertising are on the horizon, the specific role of advertising—the key to its success—will continue to be the ability to develop an interesting message that will reach potential customers in an appropriate environment at the proper time.

Planning is the foundation for successful advertising. During the remainder of the text we discuss the techniques of advertising against a backdrop of marketing, research, and planning.

REVIEW

1. Advertising is a tool of marketing communication. Discuss.
2. What are some of the primary differences between sales promotion and advertising?
3. Compare and contrast the marketing plan and the advertising plan of a company.

4. Creation of brand preference is one of the primary goals of most advertising. Discuss.
5. Discuss the role of advertising in the marketing mix.
6. Briefly describe integrated marketing communication. How does it differ from earlier types of marketing communication?
7. When a company engages in advertising, what groups might be considered as target audiences?
8. What is the role of branding in successful advertising?
9. Compare and contrast product differentiation and product pricing.
10. Define the following terms:
   a. National advertising
   b. Retail advertising
   c. End-product advertising
   d. Direct-response advertising
   e. Trade advertising

TAKE IT TO THE NET

We invite you to visit the Russell/Lane page on the Prentice Hall Web site at
PHLIP **http://www.prenhall.com/phbusiness** for the bimonthly Russell/Lane update and for this chapter's World Wide Web exercise.

Planning the Advertising

IT IS RARE THAT A GREAT CAMPAIGN IS simply the result of simple intuition. Most great advertising comes from hard work and research. Proper planning gives an advertiser the ability to better understand and reach prime prospects with the right message placed in the proper media environment. In fact, all integrated marketing communications requires careful planning.

Good advertising can rarely sell a bad product. The quality of a product, its competition, and its stage of development will affect advertising's role. Consumers are very perceptive about the products they buy. Chapter 3 traces the introduction, maturity, and eventual decline of products through the concept of the advertising spiral. The chapter also discusses the role of brands, brand equity, and integration of all forms of marketing communication.

In chapter 4, we consider the specific niche that a product occupies in the marketplace. Successful marketing depends on products that are narrowly targeted to a clearly defined group of consumers. Product success hinges on an advertiser's ability to target the right group effectively. Later, we'll use targeting information to help create the right message and make the appropriate media buys.

3

THE ADVERTISING SPIRAL
AND BRAND PLANNING

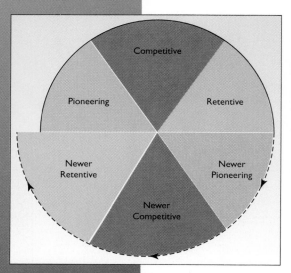

ONE OF THE CRITICAL ASPECTS OF
MARKETING COMMUNICATIONS DECISION
MAKING IS DEVELOPING A STRATEGY. IT HAS
BEEN SAID THAT STRATEGY IS EVERYTHING.
AFTER READING THIS CHAPTER YOU WILL
UNDERSTAND

- **the importance of understanding the product life cycle**
- **the relationship of the advertising spiral**
- **the birth and basics of branding**
- **brands and integrated marketing**
- **brand equity**
- **strategic planning methods.**

The 1990s have generated renewed interest on the part of marketers to protect their investment in their brands. In recent years, some marketers have been guilty of neglecting their brands in favor of short-term profit solutions—extensive couponing, pricing discounts, and so on—which weakened their product's value among consumers. As a result, more emphasis is being placed on ways to integrate marketing communications, build brand equity, and build better strategies for marketing that product. Great emphasis is now being placed on the development of product and its marketing objectives as part of a brand's *strategic plan* prior to creating ads. Here we examine several aspects important to creating the strategic plan and their advertising implications. Despite many marketing practices being challenged today, one of the constants is the need to have a clear understanding of the product and consumer wants and needs when making strategic advertising decisions.

The developmental stage of a product determines the advertising message. As products pass through a number of stages—from introduction to dominance to ultimate demise—the manner in which advertising presents the product to consumers depends largely upon the degree of acceptance the product has earned with consumers. The degree of acceptance can be identified as the product passes through its life cycle. It is this

exhibit

3.1

Primary Stages of the Life-Cycle Model

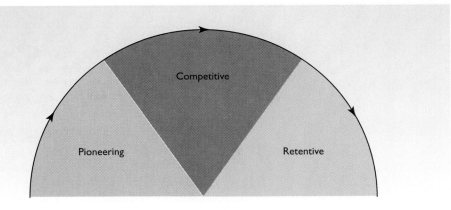

degree of acceptance that determines the advertising stage of the product. The life-cycle model discussed in this chapter consists of three primary stages (Exhibit 3.1):

- pioneering stage
- competitive stage
- retentive stage

The nature and extent of each stage are discussed in the following sections.

PIONEERING STAGE

When manufacturers create revolutionary new products they may think consumers will flock to buy them. Many times manufacturers have trouble accepting the fact that despite all the money spent in developing and then promoting their product, consumers pay little or no attention to it. There are no guarantees that consumers will see a need for the product. For one thing, it may never have occurred to consumers that they need or want the product, and as a result they don't feel compelled to buy it. Until people appreciate the fact that they need it, a product is in the **pioneering stage.**

Advertising in the pioneering stage introduces an idea that makes previous conceptions appear antiquated. It must show that methods once accepted as the only ones possible have been improved and that the limitations long tolerated as *normal* are now overcome. It may be difficult to believe, but consumers didn't rush out to buy the first deodorants. Many consumers who were concerned with body odor simply used baking soda under their arms. So we can't take for granted the fact that consumers will change their habits. Advertising in this stage must do more than simply present a product—it must implant a new custom, change habits, develop new usage, or cultivate new standards of living. In short, advertising in the pioneering stage of a product's life cycle must educate the consumer to the new product or service.

In 1973, Fleischmann's introduced Egg Beaters, a frozen egg alternative made from real eggs but without the yolk. The company had to convince consumers they needed an egg alternative—no easy task. They had to convert egg eaters into Egg Beaters customers. Their market was concerned about the high cholesterol and fat of egg yolks. Eggs represented 36 percent of dietary cholesterol for the average consumer. But to be successful, Fleischmann's had to change attitudes and habits. By accomplishing this, they became the dominating force in this new product segment. In the early 1990s, Egg Beaters tried to expand the market with an ad campaign built around the theme "When The Recipe Calls for Eggs" (Exhibit 3.2, p. 56). These ads tried to sell Egg Beaters as a substitute in cooking "because you're using the healthiest part of real eggs. No cholesterol. No fat."

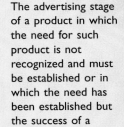

Pioneering stage
The advertising stage of a product in which the need for such product is not recognized and must be established or in which the need has been established but the success of a commodity in filling those requirements has to be established.

exhibit

3.2

Egg Beaters expands the market by trying to get the consumer to substitute Egg Beaters for eggs in cooking.

Courtesy: Fleischmann's Co., Division of Nabisco Foods.

The purpose of the pioneering stage of a product's life cycle, reduced to its simplest terms, is

- to educate consumers about the new product or service
- to show that people have a need they did not appreciate before and that the advertised product fulfills that need
- to show that a product now exists that is actually capable of meeting a need that already had been recognized but could not have been fulfilled before. Pioneering advertising generally stresses what the product can do, offer, or provide that could not have been done, offered, or provided by any product before.

A true pioneering product offers more than a minor improvement. It is important for the advertiser to remember that what determines the stage of the advertising is consumer perception of the product. In the pioneering stage, the consumer is trying to answer the question "What is the product for?" It does not really matter what the manufacturer thinks. Does the consumer think the improved changes in the product are significant? Or, is this really a better way of doing things?

Often the copy focuses on the generic aspect of the product category in an attempt to educate or inform the consumer. In the late 1980s, Interplak introduced a revolutionary new home dental product—an automatic instrument that removed plaque using two rows of counter-rotating oscillating brushes (see Exhibit 3.3). Interplak had to convince consumers that this product cleaned teeth better than any kind of toothbrush—electric or otherwise. This was no easy task because the product cost about $100 at introduction. The pioneering Interplak ads suggested that "Plaque is the real villain in oral hygiene. If not removed daily, its bacterial film can lead to early gum disease and tooth decay. But clinical studies have shown that manual brushing removes only some of the plaque buildup."

Consumer acceptance and understanding may take a long period of time—a few months, a number of years, perhaps never. The original idea behind Snapple was to create an all-natural juice drink line to be sold primarily in health-food stores. It was introduced in 1972, but didn't become a national beverage company until 1992. The idea of natural beverages, which is common today, wasn't an overnight success with the masses of beverage consumers. The same could be said of the fax machine, which was originated more than 50 years ago. Today, a large part of the population would love to own a fax machine—and may as prices continue to fall—unless the computer's ability to function as a fax machine clouds its future.

As with today's fax machines, manufacturers may produce a product that does something many consumers instantly desire—a VCR, a cellular phone, a laptop computer, or a home computer. For these products, advertising will not exhort consumers to raise their standards of acceptance, but rather will aim at convincing them that they can now accomplish something they couldn't before, through the use of the new product. For

instance, they can keep their personal finances or recipes or access the Web on a home computer. They can even fax Granny a message while she's at work. The cellular phone industry told businesswomen that the cellular phone could keep them in touch not only with their clients, but also the world, as a security device—especially if they had car trouble or were threatened in some way. Take the acceptance of computers in the home: in 1992 about 16 percent of U.S. households had a home computer, and that number is predicted to reach as high as 52 percent in 2010; among households with children younger than 18 years of age, it may reach more than 60 percent. Obviously, the concept of a computer in the home isn't a real hard sell. The deterrent to growth, which may continue to be a factor, is the cost to households. Many people want a home computer, but are delaying purchasing one because of cost or they are waiting for newer technology. Decades ago, it was predicted that every home would have a microwave in the kitchen. That number leveled off at around 72 percent. We are told that our CDs may soon be replaced by new technology. Are you willing to discard yours and start over with a new system?

Usually during the early introduction of a new product, heavy advertising and promotional expenses are required to create awareness and acquaint the target with the product's benefits. To expand, the manufacturer must gain new distribution, generate consumer trial, and increase geographical markets. At this stage, the product in the pioneering stage is not usually profitable. In other words, there can be a number of factors involved in the acceptance and purchase.

Purell Instant Hand Sanitizer was introduced in 1997 with a $15 million ad budget. Instant hand sanitizers require no soap, water, or towels and claim to be effective against 99.9 percent of all common germs. This was a new concept for consumers who may have used antibacterial soaps to kill germs. Purell was earlier marketed to only health-care and food-service workers, but the company wanted to grow the consumer market. Will consumers accept the idea of germ-free hands without washing? When a new pain product called Aleve, containing naproxen, was introduced, it created a new category in a very mature analgesic market. Consumers had many analgesic choices to fight pain: aspirin was the first major product (i.e., Bayer) to fight pain, then came aspirin compounds (Anacin, BC tablets, among others), then acetaminophen (Tylenol), then ibuprofen (Advil, Nuprin), and then naproxen. Aleve's advertising support for the introduction was about $50 million. As you can see, pioneering advertisers incur heavy expenses in the process of educating the public about the advantages of a new type of product. If the advertiser has some success with the new idea, one or more competitors will quickly jump into the market and try to grab share from the pioneer.

How do you get people to spend a lot of money on a new idea? That has been a challenge for General Motors' EV1, the first mass-produced electric car. General Motors invested about $350 million to develop this product. Being electric means it is silent. Being electric means you have to plug it in. So the intro ads played with the concepts "You will never again use the words 'Fill 'er up,' or 'Check the oil.' . . . You simply say, 'Unplug the car and let's go.'" "We didn't want to go into details because it would be judged in terms of conventional cars. *We're selling new technology, so the ads [had] to be disorienting, a little like sensory deprivation,* [italics added]" says Hal Riney & Partners' creative director. The car was introduced in some areas in late 1996, and by early 1997 General Motors had sold only 176 of the futuristic two-seater. Consumers don't always readily accept new improved ideas, especially those that are expensive.[1]

Usually the main advantage of being a pioneer is that you become the leader with a substantial head start over others. So a pioneering effort can secure customers before the competition can even get started. Then the trick is to hold onto your share.

---

[1]Ann Cooper, "Brave New World," *Adweek,* August 18, 1997, p. 30.

THE COMPETITIVE STAGE

Once a pioneering product becomes accepted by consumers, there is going to be competition. The consumer now knows what the product is and how it can be used. At this point, the main question the consumer asks is, "Which brand shall I buy?" When this happens, the product has entered the **competitive stage,** and the advertising for it is referred to as *competitive advertising.* (Note that this is a restrictive meaning of the term, not to be confused with the looser meaning that all ads are competitive with each other.)

In the short term, the pioneer usually has an advantage of leadership that can give dominance in the market. Snapple was the dominant leader in ready-to-drink iced tea, but Pepsi and Coke quickly became aggressive with their versions of ready-to-drink iced tea to get a piece of the action. In the rotisserie chicken market, there were many local or regional fast-food outlets selling the product. However, in 1993, KFC unleashed its Colonel's Rotisserie Gold chicken nationwide to the tune of about $55 million in advertising. The next year, America's Favorite Chickens, the parent of Popeye's Famous Fried Chicken & Biscuits and Church's Chicken, launched new products aimed at competing with KFC, along with new efforts from Boston Market. As a result, KFC later dropped their product in favor of a new baked chicken. Generally, in the early competitive stage, the combined impact of many competitors, each spending to gain a substantial market position, creates significant growth for the whole product category. If the pioneer can maintain market share during this initial period of competitors' growth, it can more than make up for the earlier expense associated with its pioneering efforts.

Among the many everyday products in the competitive stages are deodorants, soaps, toothpaste, cars, detergents, headache remedies, shaving creams, shampoos, televisions, VCRs, cat food, computers, and packaged foods. The *purpose* of competitive stage advertising is to communicate the product's position or differentiate it to the consumer; the advertising features the difference of the product.

Snap-on Tools Company (Exhibit 3.4) differentiates its wrench: "When we gave Flank Drive Plus wrenches up to 62% more torquing power, it marked the first significant improvement to open-end wrenches in over a hundred years." The Snap-on ad talks about the competition trying to copy their product's shape: "only Snap-on tools are pushed to the very limits in metallurgy, ergonomics and design. With over 350 patents and 15,000 products to prove it."

Competitive stage

The advertising stage a product reaches when its general usefulness is recognized but its superiority over similar brands has to be established in order to gain preference.

exhibit

3.4

Snap-on talks about their competition trying to copy their product's shape, price, and so forth.

Courtesy: Snap-on Tools Company and Sawyer Riley Compton.

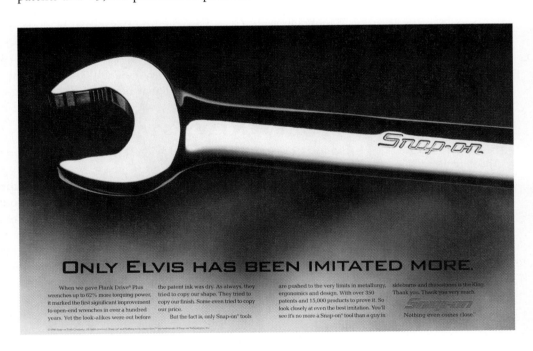

ONLY ELVIS HAS BEEN IMITATED MORE.

Competitive slogans and headlines include the following:

Every hand lotion stops dryness. This one stops germs.

Keri antibacterial hand lotion

Hill's Science Diet. A Whole New Look of Health.

Hill's cat food

You Want Your Money to Go Far, How About a Gazillion Miles.

Toyota Tercel

Dazzling White. Now a Bleach Gel and a Toothpaste in One.

Rembrandt toothpaste

Discover Breakthrough Relief That Lets You Stay Alert and Active.

Imitrex

Lumina Owners Have at Least One Reason to Drive a Car This Safe.

Lumina Chevrolet

Now, Getting On The Internet Is So Easy, Even An Adult Can Do It.

Philips Magnavox

Proud Winner of a Consumer's Digest Best Buy Award,
Car and Driver's Ten Best and Automobile Magazine's All-Stars.

Plymouth Voyager

There are tooth whiteners for people who care about their smiles.
What is there for people who care about their smiles and their teeth?
New Mentadent Advanced Whitening Toothpaste.

Mentadent Advanced Whitening toothpaste

West & Vaughan had to convey to consumers Visix Software's rapid Java programming and debugging features to separate it from the competition. "If you're gonna have the fastest, most powerful Java tool around, why not look like you do?" The speed decals (see Exhibit 3.5) suggest product benefits: "Control," "Visual Interface Developer," "Fast Foundation Class Libraries." For example, to the Web-site designer, "Springs & Struts," in the ad's upper center, are utilities that stretch and center on-screen graphics.

These one-liners don't educate you as to the product category advantages; that is taken for granted. Instead, each headline and the copy that follows set out to tell you why you should select that particular brand.

THE RETENTIVE STAGE

Products reaching maturity and wide-scale acceptance enter the **retentive stage,** or reminder stage, of advertising.

When a product is accepted and used by consumers, there may not be a need for competitive advertising. At this point, everybody knows about this product and likes or dislikes it—why advertise? Over the years, many manufacturers of successful products have stopped advertising and have seen the public quickly forget about them. Therefore, most astute advertisers try to retain their customers by keeping the brand name before them. The third stage through which a product *might* pass is called *reminder advertising*—it simply reminds consumers the brand exists. This kind of advertising is usually highly visual and is basically name advertising, meaning the ad gives little reason to buy the product. Most reminder ads look like posters—they have a dominant illustration of the product and a few words. Generally, there is little or no body copy because there is no need to give consumers this kind of information.

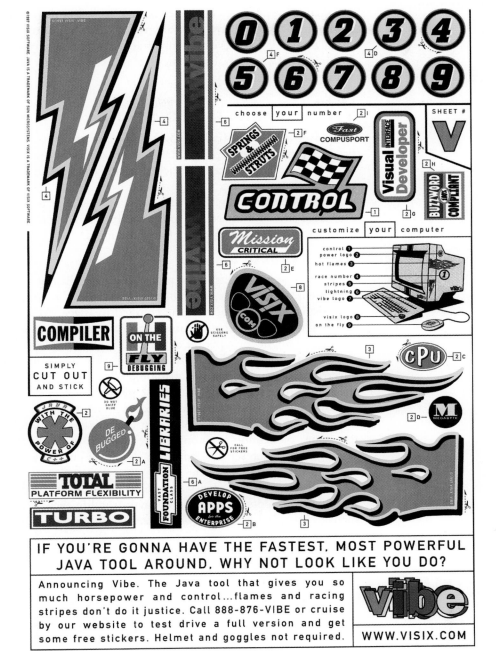

Very few advertisers reach the point where they can consider their product entirely in the reminder stage. There usually are other products in the pioneering and competitive stages challenging their leadership position. In fact, if your product is truly all alone in the retentive stage, that may be cause for alarm. It may mean the product category is in decline, and the competition sees little future in challenging you for consumers.

The advertiser's goal in the retentive stage is to maintain market share and ward off consumer trial of other products. Products in the retentive stage do not necessarily cut back on their advertising expenditures, but they adopt different marketing and promotional strategies than those used in the pioneering and competitive stages. When a brand is used by a large portion of the market, its advertising is intended to keep present customers and increase the total market, on the assumption that the most prominent brand will get the largest share of the increase.

Generally, products in the retentive stage are at their most profitable levels because developmental costs have been amortized, distribution channels established, and sales contacts made. The development of advertising and promotion may often be routine at this stage. Obviously, companies like to maintain their products in the retentive stage as long as possible.

THE ADVERTISING SPIRAL

The advertising spiral (Exhibit 3.6) is an expanded version of the advertising stages of products just discussed. The spiral provides a point of reference for determining which stage or stages a product has reached at a given time in a given market and what the thrust of the advertising message should be. This can be important information for deciding on strategy and giving the creative team a clear perspective on what information they need to communicate to prospects. In many respects, the advertising spiral parallels the life cycle of the product (see Exhibit 3.1).

Comparison of Stages

There are fewer products in the pioneering stage than in the competitive stage. The development of new types of products or categories does not take place frequently. Most advertising is for products in the competitive stage. As already pointed out, such advertising often introduces features of a new product that is in the pioneering stage and gets the spotlight for a period of time.

In using the advertising spiral, we deal with one group of consumers at a time. The advertising depends upon the attitude of *that* group toward the product. A product in the competitive stage may have to use pioneering advertising aimed at other groups of consumers to expand its markets. Fax machines are in the competitive stage with businesses, where their use is accepted, but they are largely in the pioneering stage for home use. Thus, pioneering and competitive advertising will be going on simultaneously for fax machines. Each series of ads, or each part of one ad, will be aimed at a different audience for this same product.

Products in the retentive stage usually get the least amount of advertising. This stage, however, represents a critical moment in the life cycle of a product, when important management decisions must be made. Hence it is important to create effective advertising in this stage.

exhibit

3.6

The Advertising Spiral

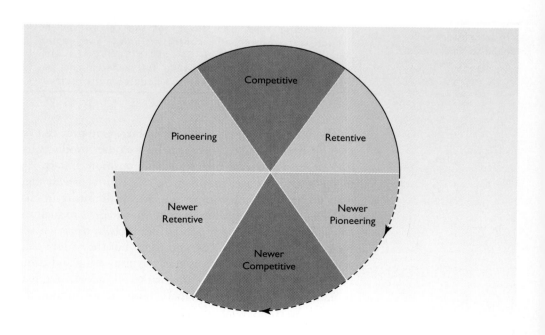

Product in Competitive Stage, Improvement in Pioneering Stage   It is not unusual for a new brand to enter the competitive stage without doing any pioneering advertising. A new product entering an established product category must hit the ground running to differentiate itself from the competition. Every new brand thus enjoys whatever pioneering advertising has already been done in the product category.

Change is a continuum: As long as the operation of a competitive product does not change, the product continues to be in the competitive stage, despite any pioneering improvements. Once the principle of its operation changes, however, the product itself enters the pioneering stage. Think about the change from the needle record player to compact disc technology. When a product begins to move into more than one stage, the changes are not always easy to categorize.

Whenever a brand in the competitive stage is revitalized with a new feature aimed at differentiating it, pioneering advertising may be needed to make consumers appreciate the new feature. Huggies diapers added a soft elastic band. If this advantage had not been advertised, consumers might have ignored the improvement.

In 1992, Scramblers and Better'n Eggs, Healthy Choice eggs, and Simply Eggs created nonfrozen egg substitutes to compete with Egg Beaters' frozen product. Egg Beaters developed a refrigerated version to go with its frozen product. Exhibit 3.7 shows the

television commercial for the new product, telling consumers they can find Egg Beaters either in the freezer or in the egg section of their grocery. Exhibit 3.8 shows a free-standing insert emphasizing the health benefits and the availability of both refrigerated and frozen products with a coupon. Is the new Egg Beaters in the competitive stage, the pioneering stage, or both?

After the Retentive Stage

The life of a product does not cease when it reaches the retentive stage. In fact, it may then be at the height of its popularity, and its manufacturer may feel it can just coast along. But a product can coast for only a short time before declining. No business can rely only on its old customers over a period of time and survive.

As noted earlier, the retentive stage is the most profitable one for the product. But all good things must come to an end. A manufacturer has a choice between two strategies when the product nears the end of the retentive stage.

In the first strategy, the manufacturer determines that the product has outlived its effective market life and should be allowed to die. In most cases, the product is not immediately pulled from the market. Rather, the manufacturer simply quits advertising it and withdraws other types of support. During this period, the product gradually loses market share but remains profitable because expenses have been sharply curtailed. This strategy is the one typically presented in textbook descriptions of the product life cycle, but not necessarily the one that corresponds to actual product development.

The problem with the life-cycle model in Exhibit 3.9 is that it portrays an inevitable decline in the product life cycle, whereas most long-term products go through a number of cycles of varying peaks and duration before they are finally taken off the market. The advertising spiral depicted in Exhibit 3.6 shows these cycles. The advertising spiral—the second strategy available to the manufacturer of a product nearing the end of the retentive stage—does not accept the fact that a product must decline. Instead, it seeks to expand the market into a newer pioneering stage. General Mill's CEO's advice is, "Do not believe in the product life cycle. Innovate constantly. Take risks with the brand. Do not live and die on consumer research. Reward everyone in the process for his or her ideas."

As a product approaches the retentive stage, management must make some important decisions:

- Can it make some significant improvements in the present product so that it virtually represents a new type of product or category (e.g., Clorox Cleaner)?
- Is there a possibility for line extensions (e.g., Diet Coke)?

As we have seen, the life cycle of a product can be affected by many conditions. If, however, the product is to continue to be marketed, its own advertising stage should be identified before its advertising goals are set.

The three basic stages of the spiral shown in the top half of Exhibit 3.6 (pioneering, competitive, and retentive) are straightforward and easy to understand. However, the stages in the bottom half (newer pioneering, newer competitive, and newer retentive) are trickier. To continue to market an established product successfully and profitably, creative marketing is necessary.

The newer pioneering stage attempts to get more people to use the product. Basically, there are two ways to enter this new stage. The first is by product modification. This can be minor, such as adding a new ingredient to a detergent or a deodorant to a

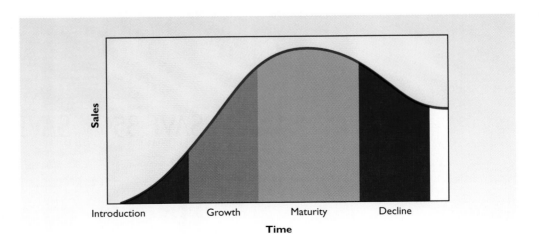

exhibit

3.9

A Typical Product Life-Cycle Model

bar of soap, or—in the other direction—taking caffeine or sodium out of a soft drink or fat out of a food product. Alternatively, it may entail a complete overhaul of a product, such as a radical model change for an automobile. In some cases, advertising alone may be enough to get consumers to look at the product in a new light.

Advertisers cannot afford to simply rely on old customers because they die off, are lured away by the competition, or change their lifestyles. Smart advertisers will initiate a change in direction of their advertising when their product is enjoying great success. They will show new ways of using the product and give reasons for using it more often. For instance, if you are a successful soup company and your customers are eating your canned soup with every meal, you have reached a saturation point. How can you increase sales? Simply by encouraging people to use soup in new ways. You create recipe advertising that shows new food dishes and casseroles that require several cans of your product. You now have your customers eating your soup as soup, along with making casseroles from your soup. Of course, this means more sales and a new way of thinking about soup. That's exactly what Egg Beaters did once they got consumers to switch from eggs to Egg Beaters for breakfast. Exhibit 3.10 tries to get cooks to use Egg Beaters in their next recipe and emphasizes taste. The ad even guarantees, "you'll love the taste, or your money back." Exhibit 3.11 shows how they tried to educate the consumer as to the quality and taste prior to the recipe ads with "Real eggs. Real healthy. Real delicious. Egg Beaters. We're good eggs."

exhibit

3.10

In 1997, Egg Beaters was still challenging consumers to use it instead of eggs in their recipes, this time with a lemon cake recipe.

Courtesy: Fleischmann's Co., Division of Nabisco Foods.

exhibit

3.11

This 15-second TV commercial ran for two years reinforcing that Egg Beaters are made from real eggs.

Courtesy: Fleischmann's Co., Division of Nabisco Foods.

New Pioneering Stage and Beyond

A product entering the new pioneering stage is actually in different stages in different markets. Long-time consumers will perceive the product as in the competitive or retentive stage. New consumers will perceive it as being a pioneer. For instance, the personal computer (PC) is in the competitive stage (more than 150 PC manufacturers were at a recent computer show) for most large and many medium-sized businesses, but in the pioneering stage for small businesses and home users. Hence the dual nature of computer advertising. Some advertising focuses on a number of users and the sophistication of the computer, assuming that the firm has already bought a computer system. Other computer ads are clearly trying to sell the value of having a computer. We will soon see computers becoming pioneers in other markets. Think about the opportunities for expanding the market for desktop publishing as prices fall on hardware and software becomes easier to use. At this point the advertising spiral will have entered still another cycle (Exhibit 3.12, p. 68), which we call the *newest pioneering stage,* where the focus is on getting more people to use this type of product.

The product in this stage is faced with new problems and opportunities. Can you convince segments of your market not using your product that they should? Obviously, you have to understand why they were not interested in the product earlier. Creative marketing and a flexible product help this process.

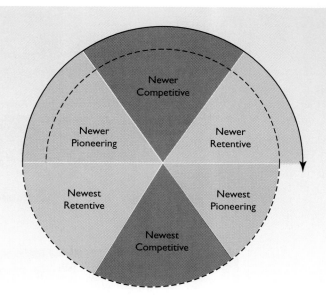

exhibit

3.12

**The Expanded
Advertising Spiral**

Nike, Jell-O, Pepsi-Cola, Mountain Dew, Budweiser, Miller High Life, and Gillette are a few of the brands that reached the retentive stage and began to look for ways to move beyond it. All of these companies moved into new pioneering with product innovations. Hence, products such as Diet Coke, Cherry Coke, Diet Pepsi, Diet Dr. Pepper, Diet Mountain Dew, Miller Genuine Draft, and Bud Light were born. New pioneering can be the result of reworking the original product or a line extension—with a new formula and name—that is related to the original version of the product.

Christian Dior had been selling mascara for years. Then in 1997, they introduced Mascara Flash, which instantly highlights hair instead of eyelashes. Originally intended as just a fun summer promotion, Dior recast Mascara Flash within a few days of its being on the market as a permanent addition to its cosmetic lineup. This product created a new cosmetic category—makeup for the hair. In this case, the product was an instant hit. Sales were phenomenal, with most stores selling out quickly. Dior's ads encouraged consumers to add a touch of color to their hair with Mascara Flash. The ad read, "New from Dior, Mascara Flash highlights for the hair." The copy told consumers that it was "instant makeup for the hair that lets you play it your way: tone-on-tone for natural highlights—or contrasting shades for even more daring effects. Stroke it on in a 'flash'—shampoo it out with the greatest of ease." The product looked like the eye mascara that they had sold for years and years, but the marketers at Dior found a new use. Within a month on the market, competitors were already looking to market similar products. Is this simply pioneering advertising in a new product category, or is it new pioneering because they are using the basic mascara product with a new twist for hair? You might be able to argue both ways. Again, we would have to see how consumers perceive the product. But we know that consumers have to be told there is now instant makeup for their hair. Does the Egg Beater's dairy section product belong in this stage? Again, consumer attitude decides.

Creating product innovation does not always translate into brand share. Royal Crown Cola has been an industry innovator—first with national distribution of soft drinks in cans (1954), a low-calorie diet cola (1962), a caffeine-free diet cola (1980), and a sodium-free diet cola (1983).[2] They had the innovation but didn't effectively manage their advertising against the larger companies of Coca-Cola and Pepsi, nor did they effectively communicate with consumers.

---

[2]"Royal Crown Plotting a Comeback with New Owners' Financial Support," *The Atlanta Journal and The Atlanta Constitution,* March 6, 1994, p. C8.

The advertising focus in *newer pioneering* must be on getting consumers to understand what the product is about. Michelob's research found that consumers had absolutely no idea what *dry* meant when it came to beer. Or ice in relationship to beer brands—basically the same problem. Advertising in the newer competitive stage aims at getting more people to buy the brand. The newer retentive stage relies on existing prestige to keep customers. Diet Pepsi and Diet Coke are looking for ways to enter the newer pioneering stage. If Pepsi discovered that its product would remove warts, they might consider this new market potential and create appropriate advertising. Of course, this is an extreme example, but it illustrates how the spiral can continue (see Exhibit 3.12).

Moving through these stages—newer pioneering, newer competitive, newer retentive—is not easy. It requires the manufacturer to develop either product innovations or advertising positioning strategies that make the product different in consumers' eyes. Also, as we move to the newer stages of the spiral, there are usually fewer prospects for the product. Therefore, a company must become most efficient at targeting smaller groups of prospects.

The Advertising Spiral as a Management Decision Tool

A product may try to hold on to its consumers in one competitive area while it seeks new markets with pioneering advertising aimed at other groups. We must remember that products do not move through each stage at the same speed. In some instances, a product may go quickly from one stage in one cycle to a newer stage in another cycle. This change may also be a matter of corporate strategy. A company may believe it can obtain a greater share of business at less cost by utilizing pioneering advertising that promotes new uses for the product. It is possible that the same results could be obtained by continuing to battle at a small profit margin in a highly competitive market. A retentive advertiser may suddenly find its market slipping and plunge into a new competitive war without any new pioneering work. Like a compass, the spiral indicates direction; it does not dictate management decisions.

Before attempting to create new ideas for advertising a product, the advertiser should use the spiral to answer the following questions:

- In which stage is the product?
- Should we use pioneering advertising to attract new users to this type of product?
- Should we work harder at competitive advertising to obtain a larger share of the existing market?
- What portion of our advertising should be pioneering? What portion competitive?
- Are we simply coasting in the retentive stage? If so, should we be more aggressive?

So far this chapter has shown how the life cycle of a product or brand may be affected by many conditions. If the brand is to continue to be marketed, its advertising stage must be identified before its advertising goals can be set. Next, we examine how to expand on what we have learned to develop a strategic plan for a brand.

Building Strong Brands and Equity

Every product, service, or company with a recognized brand name stands for something slightly different from anything else in the same product category. If the difference is a desirable one, and is known and understood by consumers, the brand will be the category leader. Today, more than ever before, the perception of a quality difference is essential for survival in the marketplace.[3]

The Birth of Branding   In the mid-1880s, there were no **brands** and little quality control by manufacturers. Wholesalers held power over both manufacturers and retailers.

Brand
A name, term, sign, design, or a unifying combination of them, intended to identify and distinguish the product or service from competing products or services.

---

[3]David Martin, *Romancing the Brand* (New York: Amacon, 1989), p. xiv.

Manufacturers had to offer the best deals to wholesalers to get their products distributed. This created a squeeze of profits. As a result of this profit squeeze, some manufacturers decided to differentiate their products from the competition. They gave their products names, obtained patents to protect their exclusivity, and used advertising to take the news about them to customers over the heads of the wholesalers and retailers. Thus the concept of branding was born. Among the early brands still viable today are Levi's (1873), Maxwell House Coffee (1873), Budweiser (1876), Ivory (1879), Coca-Cola (1886), Campbell Soup (1893), and Hershey's Chocolate (1900).[4] In 1923, a study showed that brands with "mental dominance" with consumers included Ivory (soaps), Gold Medal (flour), Coca-Cola (soft drinks), B.V.D. (underwear), Kellogg's Cornflakes (breakfast food), Ford (automobiles), Del Monte (canned fruit), and Goodyear (tires).[5]

Accelerated Life Cycle   The competition for shelf space has made marketing efforts fierce. Many brands with 40-, 50-, and 60-year histories have lost their prominence. There are many reasons: the company has been sold, there is a different focus, or new competitors have reduced their market share. Stores have been overrun with brands looking for niches as well as a flood of discount brands and house brands cramping available shelf space. As a result, many companies have killed off weak brands in their restructuring of priorities and resources. A major cause of the accelerated death rate is the UPC, the universal product code that is scanned at the checkout counter. In today's competitive environment, even large manufacturers are having difficulty providing advertising and marketing resources for dynamic and weak brands.[6] Many old friends of consumers will die in the life cycle of brands—from introduction to dominance to decline or replacement. Yet smart managers can defy this situation.

Consumer Environment

The brand environment also has changed because consumers have changed. Today, consumers set the terms of their marketplace relationships because they have more access to information than ever before, and marketers seek to meet terms set by consumers. Advertisers talk in terms of direct response. Database marketers talk in terms of customer satisfaction. Information specialists talk in terms of smart systems. This is a new era for brands. It is about consumers telling marketers what they want and marketers responding. It is about interactive, continuous, real-time dialogue replacing traditional models of advertising and consumer communication. Yet consumers have consistently said year after year in Yankelovich's MONITOR research that once they find a brand they like, "it is difficult to get them to change." Earlier in this chapter, we talked about trying to change consumer's habits—it is difficult to do. The challenge to marketers is to offer consumers brands they will like well enough to stay loyal.[7]

People's past experiences with a brand are consistently the most important factors in their future choices. Despite all the talk about quality, *past experiences* followed by *price, quality,* and *recommendations from other people* lead the reasons people buy a brand. These factors haven't significantly changed over the past two decades; however, price has become more important. Yes, psychological motivations are important, but a brand's most powerful advantage is rooted in the human tendency to form habits and stick to routines. Most people will buy the same brand over and over again if it continues to satisfy their needs.

For marketers to succeed, they must answer three questions: Who buys the brand? What do they want from it? Why do they keep coming back? Healthtex understands

---

[4]Norman Berry, "Revitalizing Brands," *Viewpoint,* July–August 1987, p. 18.

[5]Martin, *Romancing the Brand,* p. xiv.

[6]Stuart Elliott, "The Famous Brands on Death Row," *The New York Times,* November 7, 1993, p. 3-1.

[7]J. Walker Smith and Ann Clurman, *Rocking the Ages* (New York: Harper Business, 1997), pp. 276–286.

their products, but also knows how to talk to moms in both beneficial and emotional terms (Exhibits 3.13 and 3.14). According to the Roper Organization, many people buy familiar brands even if they believe the product does not have an actual advantage. Only half of Americans think that a specific brand of mayonnaise is different or better than others and worth a higher price. However, 62 percent know what brand of mayonnaise they want when they walk into the store. Another 22 percent look around for the best price on a well-known brand. *Brand behavior is complex.* Not everyone is brand conscious, and not all brand-conscious people are truly brand driven.[8]

---

[8]Diane Crispell and Kathleen Brandenburg, "What's in a Brand?" *American Demographics,* May 1993, pp. 26–28.

Marketers need to be aware that as consumers' needs change, their purchase behaviors also may change. It is not unusual for needs to change when life stage changes. For example, a couple may trade in their sports car for a van when they have a child. A recently divorced parent may be forced to change buying patterns due to less income. Interestingly, 40 percent of the people who move to a new address change their toothpaste. Yes, we need to understand consumers and their relationship to brands.

Brands and Integrated Communication

In the past, many marketing functions—advertising, promotion, packaging, direct marketing, public relations, events—were created and managed independently in most organizations. The economic pressures facing companies in the 1990s has created the need to manage these activities more efficiently and to ensure they all reinforce each other. Today a brand's equity is best strengthened through the integrated use of all marketing communication tools. It is imperative to project a single, cohesive brand image into the marketplace and into the consumer's mind. The result has been what is labeled *integrated marketing communications.*

Integrated communications refers to all the messages directed to a consumer on behalf of the brand: media advertising, promotion, public relations, direct response, events, packaging, and so forth. Each message must be integrated or dovetailed in order to support all the other messages or impressions about the brand. If this process is successful, it will build a brand's equity by communicating the same brand message to consumers. Egg Beaters packaging tells the same story as the ad copy. Exhibit 3.15 is communicating the same message in a cross-promotion communication.

Let us look at other definitions.[9] Integrated marketing communications is

A concept of marketing communications planning that recognizes the added value of a comprehensive plan that evaluates the strategic roles of a variety of communications disciplines and combines these disciplines to provide clarity, consistency, and maximum communication impact.

Integrated direct marketing is

the art and science of managing a diverse marketing media as a cohesive whole. These interrelationships are catalysts for response. The resulting media synergy generates response rates higher than could be achieved by individual media efforts.

There are those who say integration has been around for 20 years, but it wasn't as important an issue as it is today. (We discuss aspects of integrated communication throughout this text, and its organization in chapters 5 and 6.)

During the 1980s, too many marketers milked their brands for short-term profits instead of protecting and nurturing their brands. In the 1990s, brand building has become fashionable again. Marketers realize the brand is their most important asset. Because integrated programs and brand building are so important, we discuss a system of integrated communications that builds brand equity. The most important factor in determining the actual value of a brand is its equity in the market. We can define **brand equity** as the value of how people such as consumers, distributors, and salespeople think and feel about a brand relative to its competition. Let us look at how Young & Rubicam assesses brand equity's value.

Young & Rubicam's Brand Asset Valuator

Young & Rubicam (Y & R) has a procedure to evaluate a brand's value called the brand asset valuator (BAV), which explains the strengths and weaknesses of brands on measures

Brand equity
The value of how such people as consumers, distributors, and salespeople think and feel about a brand relative to its competition over a period of time.

---

[9]Neil M. Brown, *Marketing News,* March 19, 1993, p. 4.

of stature and vitality. It believes the relationship between these two factors tells the true story about the health of brand equity and can help diagnose the problems and solutions.

According to Y & R, a brand's vitality lies in a combination of differentiation and relevance. A brand must be distinct, or it simply isn't a brand. But the fact that a brand is highly differentiated doesn't necessarily mean consumers have the desire or means to buy it. Unless a brand is also relevant, the consumer has no reason to select it. One of their studies revealed that U.S. brands with high differentiation are Disney, Dr Pepper, Jaguar, Snapple, and Victoria's Secret. Brands with high relevance include AT&T, Kodak, Campbell's, and the U.S. Post Office.

The two components of brand stature are esteem and familiarity, that is, whether people know and understand your brand and whether they like it. A brand that more consumers know than like is a clear warning signal. Similarly, a brand that is held in high esteem but ranks lower in familiarity suggests that increasing awareness is an appropriate objective. Brands with high familiarity include Coca-Cola, Jell-O, McDonald's, and Kellogg. Among the brands with high esteem are Rubbermaid, Philadelphia brand cream cheese, Reynolds Wrap, and Band-Aid.

Sharon Slade of Marketing Corporation of America says, "Where many people go wrong is to assume there is one answer to evaluating brand equity. Having worked across a variety of categories, I can tell you that you need a variety of tools in your tool box.

One of the keys to understanding brand equity is to recognize that there are differences between product categories. People buy computers differently from the way they buy soft drinks. Their relationship to that category is different, so the way you diagnose the health of a brand will be different as well."[10]

Hopefully, you are getting the sense that the development of advertising strategy and building brand equity deals with many complex issues. This discussion has been a little deep, but it has given you a feel for the many issues and terms advertising practitioners face daily. Despite this complexity, the development of advertising isn't brain surgery. It is understanding all the ramifications in the market and the consumer's mind, so we can integrate better, so we build brand equity better.

Brand Equity and Developing Integrated Marketing Communications Strategic Plans

Before you start to think about creating ads for a brand, you need a strategic plan. Before you can develop a strategy, you need an understanding of the marketing situation and a clear understanding of the brand's equity. There are four logical steps in this process resulting in the creative brief or plan:

● brand equity audit analysis
● strategic options and recommendations
● brand equity research
● creative brief

Of course, these generally would be followed by evaluation or assessment of some nature. An outline of a strategic planning process is presented next to give you insight into what is required. Some of the concepts and terms are discussed in more detail throughout the text.

Brand Equity Audit Analysis

There are a number of areas to examine in the first step, brand equity audit analysis. For instance, the context of the market, strengths and weaknesses, consumer attitude descriptions, and competitive strategies and tactics are of importance here.

Market Context   We begin by examining the existing situation of both the market and the consumer. What we are looking for are clues and factors that positively or negatively affect brand equity. The whole purpose is to set the scene. The types of questions that are asked include the following:

● What is our market and with whom do we compete?
● What are other brands and product categories?
● What makes the market tick?
● How is the market structured?
● Is the market segmented? If so, how? What segment are we in?
● What is the status of store and generic brands?
● Are products highly differentiated?
● What kind of person buys products in this category?
● In the minds of these consumers, what drives the market or holds it back (needs, obstacles, and so forth)? What are the key motivators?
● Do consumers perceive the brands as very much alike or different?
● Is the product bought on impulse?
● How interested are consumers in the product?
● Do consumers tend to be **brand loyal?**

Brand loyalty
Degree to which a consumer purchases a certain brand without considering alternatives.

[10]Chip Walker, "How Strong Is Your Brand?" *Marketing Tools,* January/February 1995, pp. 46–53.

These questions should help us understand the status and role of brands in a given market. For example, when the market is made up of a few brands, the consumer will likely be more brand sensitive than if the market is split up into many brands.

Palmas Del Mar is a resort, not something a consumer picks up off a shelf, but the analysis process is the same (Exhibit 3.16). What kind of people would prefer a Caribbean luxury resort without the crowds of typical resorts? Product or service—we must look at the market from varying angles, and select only the relevant ones, so that we can set the scene for understanding and building brand equity.

Brand Equity Weaknesses and Strengths Now we have a better understanding of the market context and are ready to examine the current brand equity—how strong or weak consumer bias is toward our brand relative to other brands. The following is a list of weakness and strength indicators often used.

- brand awareness—top of mind is best
- market share, price elasticity, share of voice, and similar factors
- brand sensitivity—the relative importance of the brand to other factors involved in the purchase, such as price, pack size, model
- consistency of the brand's communication over time
- image attribute ratings, or ranking attributes
- distribution, pricing, product quality, and product information
- brand loyalty—the strength of a brand lies in the customers who buy it as a brand rather than just as a product

Once the key weakness and strength indicators have been identified, they are used for future tracking purposes.

Consumer Attitude Descriptions After we understand the **market** in which our brand operates and have a clear understanding of the strengths and weaknesses of our brand equity, we need to identify and describe the consumer's thoughts and feelings that result in their bias toward our brand relative to other brands. This personal relationship between the consumer and the brand provides the most meaningful description of brand equity. To accomplish this, we need to analyze from two points of view.

Market
A group of people who can be identified by some common characteristic, interest, or problem; use a certain product to advantage; afford to buy it; and be reached through some medium.

exhibit

3.16

It is important to understand the marketing context and the target.

Courtesy: Hughes Advertising, Atlanta.

This isn't the resort everyone's talking about. It's the one everyone's dreaming about.

Before you go to the resort everyone else goes to, there's something you should consider. "Everyone" is a lot of people. Fortunately, there is a place where crowds won't crush your Caribbean fantasy. Palmas del Mar in Puerto Rico. Imagine riding horseback on a lonely, breezy beach. Or lining up your putt on our championship golf course then pausing to gaze at the ocean. Here, you'll find the best tennis center in the Caribbean. Fine restaurants. And coral reefs so unique, they attract divers and snorkelers from around the world. We're certain you've never seen a place like Palmas del Mar. At least, not with your eyes open.

PALMAS DEL MAR RESORT
800 ~ 468 ~ 3331

First, we need to review all the available research to get as close a feeling as possible on how consumers view the brand and how they feel about it. Second, we must analyze in depth our brand's and its competitors' communications over a period of time. It is from these communications that most of the consumer's feelings (emotional elements) and opinions (rational elements) about the brand are derived (see Exhibit 3.17).

A brand equity description for the Golf GTI automobile might be as follows:

Emotional Elements	Rational Elements
My little sports car	Inexpensive
Sets me free	High gas mileage
It makes me feel and look good	Retains value
Simple	Durable
It's there when I want it	Dependable
I'm in control	Handles well
	Easy to park—small

Competitive Strategies and Tactics   This area of the analysis is designed to provide a clear summary of the current communication strategies and tactics of our brand and of key competitors. It should include an analysis of all integrated communications in relation to brand equity. Is the strategy designed to reinforce current brand equity? Who is the target audience? Are there different target audiences? What are the themes and executional approach? How are the marketing funds being spent (consumer pull versus trade push, advertising, promotions, direct marketing, others)? An assessment of problems and opportunities is also in order here.

Strategic Options and Recommendations   The second step draws on the conclusions from the analysis to develop a viable recommendation plan. The strategic options include

- *Communication objectives.* What is the primary goal the message aims to achieve?
- *Audience.* To whom are we speaking?
- *Source of business.* Where are the customers going to come from—brand(s) or product categories?
- *Brand positioning and benefits.* How are we to position the brand, and what are the benefits that will build brand equity?
- *Marketing mix.* What is the recommended mix of advertising, public relations, promotion, direct response, and so on?
- *Rationale.* How does the recommended strategy relate to, and what effect is it expected to have on, brand equity?

Brand positioning Consumers' perceptions of specific brands relative to the various brands of goods or services currently available to them.

Brand Equity Research

The third step is where we do the proprietary, qualitative research. It is exploratory and task oriented. Here we need to determine which element(s) of brand equity must be created, altered, or reinforced to achieve our recommended strategy and how far we can stretch each of these components without risking the brand's credibility. This may give us a revised list of rational and emotional elements that describe how we want consumers to think and feel about our brand in the future.

Creative Brief

The final step is a written *creative brief* (or *work plan*) for all communications. We synthesize all the information and understanding into an action plan for the development of all communications for the brand: advertising, public relations, promotion, and so forth. The creative work plan or brief is illustrated in chapter 16.

The creative strategy (brief or work plan) is a one-page statement that clearly defines our audience; how consumers think or feel and behave; what communication is intended to achieve; and the promise that will create a bond between the consumer and the brand. A typical strategy would include

- *Key observations*—the most important market/consumer factor that dictates the strategy
- *Communication objective*—the primary goal the advertising/communication aims to achieve
- *Consumer insight*—the consumer "hot button" our communication will trigger
- *Promise*—what the brand should represent in the consumer's mind; what the brand is promising the consumer
- *Support*—the reason the promise is true
- *Audience*—to whom we are speaking and how they feel about the brand.

There may be a need for an additional element:

- *Mandatories*—items used as compulsory constraints; for example, if there is a specific legal requirement or corporate policy that impacts the direction of the strategy

Other Examples of Strategic Planning

It is important to understand that there isn't just one approach to developing an integrated strategic plan for a brand. The basic steps are similar, but each agency approaches the process with a little different wrinkle. Let us take a look at the basics of how J. Walter Thompson (JWT) approaches what the firm calls *Thompson Total Branding*.

J. Walter Thompson began a series of organizational changes in 1996 to deliver a broader range of agency services to clients. "More and more clients were coming to us and saying, 'How can we revitalize our brand?' not 'We need a new campaign for this spring,'" according to the New York general manager of JWT. The changes were part of a program the agency calls Thompson Total Branding, a worldwide effort to shift the company's focus from simply creating advertising to broader marketing issues.

Thompson T-Plan

Part of JWT's strategic planning process includes the Thompson T-Plan (see Exhibit 3.18, p. 78). This planning cycle includes answering five basic questions about the brand: Where are we now? Why are we there? Where could we be? How can we get there? Are we getting there? Let us take a brief look at each step:

- *Where are we now?* Here the brand is examined in the marketplace, in consumers' minds, in relation to its competitors, and in the client's mind. This enables JWT to evaluate and determine the brand's overall appeal.

exhibit

3.18

Thompson T-Plan

Courtesy: J. Walter
Thompson/Atlanta.

- *Why are we there?* The agency uses a series of tools designed to help them develop insights into the reasons behind a brand's current position. They use *Key Discoveries* about the brand, the category, the consumer, and the communication. These discoveries and the client's attitude and resources all lay the groundwork for identifying what JWT calls the *Brand Vision,* which serves as a strategic focus for all the brand's communication activities.
- *Where could we be?* Using *Key Discoveries* as a foundation, the JWT brand team puts itself in the consumer's shoes to identify the most powerful connection between the brand and the consumer. The end product is the *Brand Vision.*
- *How can we get there?* The next step is identifying the *Brand Idea,* which is the creative expression of the *Brand Vision.* This idea becomes the foundation of all communication briefs. Upon this *Branding Idea,* JWT builds a communication plan, in which they determine how to reach the consumer target where and when they will be most receptive to the message.
- *Are we getting there?* An essential aspect of communications planning is accountability. JWT needs to know how well it has accomplished its objectives, and how to improve next time. Thompson Total Branding provides proprietary tools to evaluate and learn from its performance.

Avrett Free & Ginsberg's Planning Cycle

Jack Avrett, former chairman of Avrett Free & Ginsberg (AFG), describes the basics of his firm's brand planning process. They have a seven-step planning cycle that helps create strategic advertising. They use the discipline of account planning at each stage of developing strategy. Briefly, the framework for their strategic planning cycle (see Exhibit 3.19) involves the following steps:

- *Brand/market status.* AFG evaluates where the brand is in its marketplace and determines strengths, weaknesses, opportunities, and threats.
- *Brand mission.* After determining brand status, AFG proposes and agrees upon brand goals, that is, where they can take the brand.

exhibit

3.19

AFG Planning Cycle

Courtesy: Avrett, Free &
Ginsberg.

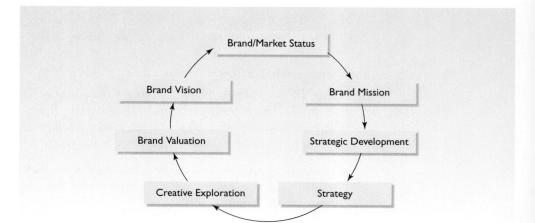

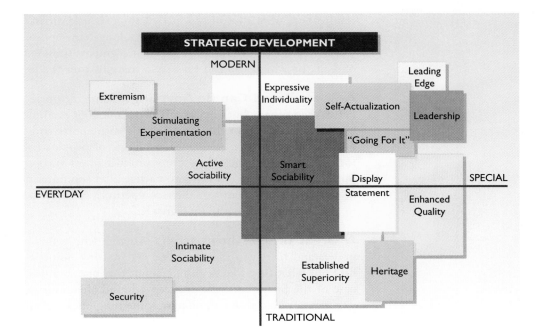

exhibit

3.20

The AFG Needs-Mapping Process

Courtesy: Avrett, Free & Ginsberg.

- *Strategic development.* Here they explore various options to determine which of several strategies will empower the brand to achieve the mission. AFG uses a process called *needs mapping* (Exhibit 3.20). The basic principle is that people respond or bond to products based on a wide range of psychological and rational needs. This process is loosely based on Maslow's Hierarchy of Needs.
- *Strategy.* AFG formulates a tight strategy to be used in developing a fully integrated marketing communication program.
- *Creative exploration.* AFG develops, explores, and evaluates a range of executions to ensure that they maximize the relevancy, distinctiveness, and persuasiveness of the strategy and final execution.
- *Brand valuation.* AFG tracks marketplace performance and progress because it believes it must be accountable for the results its work generates. AFG constantly fine-tunes and improves communications in response to changing market conditions.
- *Brand vision.* In building equities for a brand through effective communications, AFG plots long-range expansion plans for the base brand. AFG determines if the emerging brand equities can be line extended or translated to serve needs in other related categories.

These seven steps are constantly pursued in the evaluation of a brand's life cycle to ensure long-term growth and brand equity.

What Great Brands Do

Scott Bedbury, senior vice president of marketing at Starbucks Coffee, said, "I walked through a hardware store last night and I came across 50 brands I didn't know existed. They may be great products, but they're not great brands." Scott should know brands. He's the man who gave the world "Just Do It," Nike's branding campaign. A few of Bedbury's brand-building principles are examined here:[11]

A Great Brand Is in It for the Long Haul   For decades there were brands based upon solid value propositions—they had established their worth in the consumers' minds. Then, in the 1980s and 1990s, companies focused on short-term economic returns and diminished their investment in long-term brand-building programs. As a

---

[11]Alan M. Webber, "What Great Brands Do," *Fast Company,* August–September 1997, pp. 96–100.

result, there were a lot of products with very little differentiation. Today a great brand is a necessity, not a luxury. By using a long-term approach, a great brand can travel worldwide, speak to multiple consumer segments simultaneously, and create economies of scale, by which you can earn solid margins over the long term.

A Great Brand Can Be Anything   Some categories lend themselves to branding better than others, but anything is brandable. For example, Nike is leveraging the deep emotional connection that people have with sports and fitness. Starbucks focuses on how coffee has woven itself into the fabric of people's lives, and that's an opportunity for emotional leverage. Almost any product offers an opportunity to create a frame of mind that is unique. Do you know what Intel computer processors do, how they work, or why they are superior to their competitor? All most people know is that they want to own a computer with "Intel Inside."

A Great Brand Knows Itself   Anyone who wants to build a great brand has to understand first who they are. The real starting point is to go out to consumers and find out what they like or dislike about this brand and what they associate as the very core of the brand concept. To keep a brand alive over the long haul, to keep it vital, you have got to do something new, something unexpected. It has to relate to the brand's core position.

A Great Brand Invents or Reinvents an Entire Category   The common ground that you find among brands such as Disney, Apple, Nike, and Starbucks is that these companies made it an explicit goal to be the protagonists for each of their entire categories. Disney is the protagonist for fun family entertainment and family values. Nike transcends simply building shoes or making apparel; it has an informed opinion on where sports is going, how athletes think, how we think about athletics, and how we each think about ourselves as we aim for our personal best. A great brand raises the bar—it adds a greater sense of purpose to the experience.

A Great Brand Taps into Emotions   The common ground among companies that have built great brands is not just performance. They realize consumers live in an emotional world. Emotions drive most, if not all, of our decisions. It is an emotional connection that transcends the product. And transcending the product is the brand.

A Great Brand Is a Story That's Never Completely Told   A brand is a metaphorical story that is evolving all the time. This connects with something very deep. People have always needed to make sense of things at a higher level. Look at Hewlett-Packard and the "HP Way." That's a form of company mythology. It gives employees a way to understand that they are part of a larger mission. It is a company rich in history, a dynamic present, and a bright future.

Levi's has a story that goes all the way back to the gold rush. They have photos of miners wearing Levi's dungarees. Stories create connections for people. Stories create the emotional context people need to locate themselves in a larger experience.

A Great Brand Has Design Consistency   Successful brands have a consistent look and feel and a high level of design integrity. Nike employs more than 350 designers to keep close watch over the visual expression of the brand.

A Great Brand Is Relevant   A lot of brands are trying to position themselves as "cool," but most of them fail. The larger idea is to be relevant. It meets what people want; it performs the way people want it to. In the past couple of decades a lot of brands promised consumers things they couldn't deliver. Consumers are looking for something that has lasting value. There is a quest for quality, not quantity.

Products pass through a number of stages from introduction to ultimate demise, known as the *product life cycle*. Advertising plays a different role in each stage of product development. Until consumers appreciate the fact that they need a product, that product is in the pioneering stage of advertising. In the competitive stage, an advertiser tries to differentiate its product from that of the competition. The retentive stage calls for reminder advertising.

A product's age has little to do with the stage it is in at any given time. Rather, consumer attitude or perception determines the stage of a product. As consumer perception changes, moving it from one stage to another, the advertising message should also change. In fact, the advertising may be in more than one stage at any given time. Creative marketing may propel a product through new pioneering, new competitive, and new retentive stages. And it is even possible for a product to continue on into the newest pioneering, newest competitive, and newest retentive stages. As a product ages, so do its users, which is why no product can survive without attracting new customers. Long-term success depends on keeping current customers while constantly attracting new ones.

In the mid-1880s there were no brands. Manufacturers differentiated their products and gave them names as the concept of branding was born. Brands are now among the most valuable assets a marketer owns. The product is not the brand. A product is manufactured; a brand is created and is made up of both rational and emotional elements. In today's marketing environment, it is essential that every communication reinforces brand personality in the same manner: advertising, public relations, promotion, packaging, direct marketing, and so forth. The most important factor in determining the actual value of a brand is its equity in the market: how consumers think and feel about the brand.

Advertising agencies have their own unique systems to develop strategic planning for a brand. J. Walter Thompson uses Total Branding, which includes the Thompson T-Plan, to answer five key questions: Where are we now? Why are we there? Where could we be? How can we get there? Are we getting there?

REVIEW

1. What is the pioneering stage?
2. What determines the stage of a product?
3. What is the essence of the advertising message in each stage of the spiral?
4. What is brand equity?
5. What are the elements of the creative brief?
6. What are the key elements in Avrett Free & Ginsberg's planning cycle?

TAKE IT TO THE NET

We invite you to visit the Russell/Lane page on the Prentice Hall Web site at
PHLIP **http://www.prenhall.com/phbusiness** for the bimonthly Russell/Lane update and for this chapter's World Wide Web exercise.

4

TARGET MARKETING

IT IS CRITICAL FOR MARKETERS TO UNDERSTAND
WHO THEIR PRIME PROSPECTS ARE. FOR A BUSINESS
OR BRAND TO SURVIVE, THE MARKETERS MUST
UNDERSTAND THE IMPACT OF THE CHANGING
WORLD. AFTER READING THIS CHAPTER YOU WILL
UNDERSTAND

● prime prospect definition
● importance of target marketing information
● marketing concept and targeting
● niche marketing and positioning
● beyond demographics: psychographics.

In the last chapter we examined the existing state of the brand in the context of market and consumers. As we have seen, a lot of questions have to be answered. There are numerous types and sources of information to help us make strong strategic decisions about potential markets and consumers. As you answer these questions, you have to determine which segments of this information are really important to your decision making.

Who do we think is going to buy our product? Men? Women? Men and women? 25- to 49-year-olds? Seniors? Hispanics? Affluents? A lot of possibilities. Obviously, we need to know the answer so we can aim our advertising, promotion, and other integrated marketing communications in their direction. Does that mean we don't aim at everybody that has money? We know that won't work—that's a shotgun approach. We need to be focused and direct, like a rifle shot, to hit our target.

As we have just indicated, the monolithic mass market of the mid-twentieth century has long been laid to rest, and smaller mass markets have taken its place. As we discuss many factors and groups used by marketers, a word of caution. Marketers have a tendency to generalize. We talk about baby boomers, seniors, generation X, or limit discussions to demographics (age, income, sex) as if each is a uniform group of people who live, think, and act exactly the same. Do all 20-year-olds think and act alike? Virtually no generalization encompasses an entire consumer segment, especially age groups. If we stop to think about it, we know better than to generalize. Consider that seniors or matures can be wealthy or not, love the outdoors or not, be inclined to travel or be homebodies, own a vacation home or live in a mobile home. Or that generation Xers are all cyberheads. The same considerations apply to virtually each of these catch-all categories. Of course, these groupings or segments can be very useful in assessing potential markets; after all, they do group behavior and lifestyle commonalities. These segments should be considered, but remember they stereotype groups of people. We all know that all Russians drink vodka, Germans drink beer, and the French drink wine, right? Or that all Southerners eat grits? It is okay to start with a premise in narrowing to one of these groups, but it is important to dig deeper. A cardinal rule in marketing has always been to know your market. That doesn't mean segmenting young and old or rich and poor. It means defining your target in such detail that circumstances allow and necessity requires. There is a reason that reliable market research looks at multiple factors such as age, gender, income, net worth, ethnicity, geography, lifestyle, and family status. It is very appropriate to use "families" as a partial descriptor of a given market, as long as it doesn't become a synonym for the market itself.[1] Now that we have sent up a red flag, let us look at some factors and segments used in target marketing.

Once you ask the obvious questions, you must determine which answers are critical to your decision making. Do you need more information to reach your prospects successfully? Do you understand their problems? Have you thought about what you want people to think and feel about your brand as a result of being exposed to your advertising?

DEFINING PRIME PROSPECTS

One of the keys to success is defining the prime prospects so you do not waste time and money advertising your product to people unlikely to buy it or people you can't make a profit by attracting. This search for the best prospects among all consumers is called **target marketing.**

The process of finding prime prospects can be very complex because there are numerous ways of looking at consumers, many different kinds of information to consider, and a constantly changing consumer environment.

The ad for Yamaha golf cars (Exhibit 4.1, p. 84) is obviously designed for a segment of the golfing market, but is it aimed at every golfer? Who are they? Where are they? Does income matter? How about age? What about gender? How often do they play?

Where Do We Start?

Different agencies and companies approach the process a little differently, as we saw in the last chapter but all have to answer the same important questions before advertising can be created. Brand equity research, for instance, seeks to answer a number of questions and examine the existing state of the brand in the context of market and consumers. Today, marketers have a host of informational sources to help plan integrated marketing programs aimed at individual users or groups. Let us look at some of the information sources and trends in America and their implications for advertising planning.

Census Data

Census data offer marketers a wealth of information about people and how they live in the United States. Much of the database is on-line. The *Topologically Integrated Geographic Encoding and Referencing* system, known as TIGER, is one of the more sophisticated tools. This coding of the country's natural, political, and statistical boundaries includes every street, road, and subdivision. TIGER provides the data for computer

Target marketing
Identifying and communicating with groups of prime prospects.

---

[1]Joe Marconi, "Targets Big Enough to Miss," *American Demographics,* October 1996, pp. 51–52.

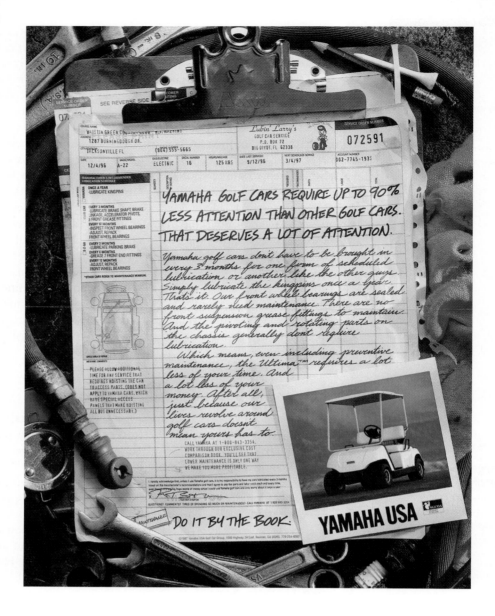

maps to plan sales territories and pinpoint direct-marketing prospects. This information can be linked to a number of relevant characteristics, such as age, income, and race. Custom research companies using these data have developed software for marketers to access geodemographic databases.

Population   In the United States, marketers have always had to deal with population growth and shifts that influence advertisers' markets in some way. Obviously, we need to know who is out there in the marketplace. How many of them? Where and how they live? What they need? What buying patterns? We can't easily reach people if we don't know where they are. But population is more than simple numbers of people. Society tends to group people by age or ethnicity or generation or some factor to help better understand some or all of the people. For instance, there are the *matures,* born before 1946, who total 68.3 million. And the *boomers* born between 1946 and 1964—77.6 million of them. How they think, act, and spend influences marketers. Or *generation Xers,* born after 1964—44.6 million—who think, act, and buy differently in many ways. An advertiser must understand these people.

exhibit

4.2

Selected Census
State Population
Projections,
1995–2025

State	1995 Population	2025 Population	Change 1995–2025 (%)
California	31,590,000	49,290,000	56
Texas	18,720,000	27,190,000	45
Florida	14,170,000	20,710,000	46
New York	18,140,000	19,830,000	9
Illinois	11,830,000	13,440,000	14
Ohio	11,150,000	11,740,000	5
Georgia	7,200,000	9,870,000	37
North Carolina	7,200,000	9,350,000	30
Arizona	4,220,000	6,410,000	52
West Virginia	1,830,000	1,850,000	1

Source: U.S. Census Bureau.

The millennium will bring with it major *population changes.* "By the year 2000, everyone in California will be a minority in the literal sense of the word," says Peter Morrison, demographer at the Rand Corporation, a think tank. "And that reflects what will happen to the rest of the country decades from now."[2]

The U.S. Census Bureau data projections indicate that by the year 2025, 70 percent of the growth will take place in the South and West. By 2025, there will be moderate growth for New York, New Jersey, Pennsylvania, Ohio, and Michigan. California will double its population from 1990 to 2040. But that is only part of the story. California gained 1.3 million immigrants while losing 1.5 million natives to surrounding states. So numbers alone don't tell the picture. But the numbers themselves indicate change. Exhibit 4.2 shows population projections for selected states.

Minority Markets

African Americans   The Census Bureau's statistical profile of African Americans released in 1997 indicated a population of 33.9 million, or 12.8 percent of the nation's total. The black population is younger and faster-growing than the white population. The median income of all black families was $25,970 compared to that of white families at $45,020. However, married-couple black families' median income was similar to the income of white families, $49,752 versus $59,025. Census data indicate areas of the country where large concentrations of African Americans live and don't live.

Hispanics   Census projections call for Hispanics to overtake blacks as the nation's largest minority in 2009. By 2050, Hispanics will make up a quarter of the U.S. population and blacks less than a sixth. In 1995, there were about 26.5 million Hispanics in this country, or 10 percent of the population. In perspective, this market is comparable to the entire population of Canada. By 2010, the Hispanic population is projected to increase by 8.3 million, which parallels the current populations of Wisconsin, Iowa, and Wyoming combined. Keep in mind there isn't a single Hispanic market because of cultural differences from their countries of origin.

Asians   The 1990 census counted 7.2 million Asians and Pacific Islanders living in the United States. This marked a 108 percent increase over 1980 data, and thus the highest growth rate for any group in the country. Their population is projected at 12 million by the year 2000, 17 million by 2010, and 41 million by 2050. Asians also cannot be lumped together into a single group. There are separate communities to consider: Japanese Americans, Chinese Americans, Filipino Americans, Asian Indians, and others.

---

[2]Haya El Nasser, "Immigration to Lead Population Boom in West," *USA Today,* October 23, 1996, p. 7A.

Households

Income   The Bureau of Labor Statistics' Consumer Expenditure Survey produces annual estimates of household spending on hundreds of items, cross-tabulated by demographic characteristics. As with most data, you need to use these data wisely. In addition to looking at household income, advertisers often look at disposable and discretionary income. *Disposable income* is the after-tax income. *Discretionary income* is the amount of money consumers have after paying taxes and buying necessities such as food and housing. In 1995, 8.0 percent of all U.S. households earned between $50,000 and $74,000 and accounted for 17.8 percent of the country's total income.

Spending   *American Demographics* found that the average U.S. metropolitan household devotes 16 percent of its spending for shelter, 17 percent for transportation, 14 percent for food, 6 percent for utilities, 6 percent for apparel, 5 percent for entertainment, 3 percent for household operations, and 11 percent for personal insurance. Average household spending in Nassau-Suffolk, New York, was $44,220 compared to the U.S. metro average of $33,410. Other findings were that Long Island is one of America's best places to own a grocery store, an insurance agency, or another business that appeals to middle-aged homeowners. If you are in the health-care business, a place like Sarasota, Florida, is a good market (average health-care spending is $2,230 versus the U.S. average of $1,800). Spending patterns depend strongly on the unique age and income characteristics of individual markets.[3]

Marrieds   The U.S. Census Bureau reported in 1997 the continued decline of married households. In 1996, of the 99.6 million households in this country, married couples with or without children accounted for 53.7 percent. In 1990, married households accounted for 56 percent; in 1980, they made up 60.8 percent; and in 1970, they comprised 70.5 percent. Clearly, this decline has had social and marketing ramifications.

Numbers   It is also estimated that by the year 2000, couples without children under age 18 will outnumber those with children by about 6.1 million. Household projections for 2000 include couples with children, 24 percent of households; couples without children, 30 percent; single parents with children, 8 percent; other families, 7 percent; men living alone, 11 percent; women living alone, 15 percent; and other nonfamilies, 5 percent. In the mid-1990s, the Census Bureau made its first effort to forecast the number of Americans who live alone, as well as the number of families without children. The bureau also reported that the number of households consisting of one person has grown from 6.8 percent in 1970 to 24.9 percent in 1995.

Birth Rate   The birth rate in the United States has been in decline for decades. In 1960, the rate was 23.7 per 1,000 population, and it is projected to be 14.2 per thousand in 2000. The Census Bureau reports children are geographically concentrated today. Increasingly, they are in neighborhoods dominated by young adults. Other factors important to marketers include the following: Between 1995 and 2001, there will be slightly fewer than 4 million babies a year; about one-third of children in 1997 were ethnic minorities, and roughly 62 percent of married mothers with preschoolers were in the workforce (in 1965 only 23 percent of married mothers worked). Times continue to change.

We are not going to attempt to cover all the demographics that may be important, but these items should give you something to think about, keeping in mind that these may or may not be important to a specific marketing situation. It is very necessary to get a handle on what data are important.

---

[3]Marcia Mogelonsky, "America's Hottest Markets," *American Demographics,* January 1996, pp. 20–27.

Generations

The consumer society is really a twentieth-century phenomenon, and for the past 98 years or so, many businesses have made decisions based on the assumptions that one generation will grow up and make the same kinds of choices made by the group that went before them at the same stages of life.

Researchers have concentrated on three generations mentioned earlier: *matures, boomers,* and *generation X* (also Gen X or Xers). There are distinct differences in how each generation thinks and buys.

The values of matures are close to what are considered classic American values: They favored a kind of puritan work ethic, with plenty of self-sacrifice, teamwork, conformity for the common good, and so forth.

The boomers, on the other hand, are self-assured and self-absorbed. They are much better educated than any generation before them, and they are aware of this. They think they are more sophisticated and believe they know better than their predecessors. They are very self-conscious about changing the world and fixing things.

Generation X got a bad rap from people indicating they were slackers, which was wrong. Their values are simply different in that they don't want to work as participants in a vast cooperative enterprise, as matures did. Now, for the first time in years, most college graduates say they are looking to small businesses or entrepreneurial ventures, rather than large corporations. Keep in mind that many of them will work for large corporations. Their skepticism is a positive characteristic. They are comfortable with risk. They lived with all the excesses of the boomer generation. Xers are the generational cohort that has never been able to presume success.[4]

Why is all this important to advertising people? Without an accurate view of generations, you are likely to misinterpret what you see in the marketplace. Marketers need to know all about generations. The consumer marketplace is no longer the homogeneous marketplace of the 1950s and early 1960s that was dominated by matures. The Xers' view of convenience has moved from the matures' "do it quickly" and the boomers' "do it efficiently" to their own "eliminate the task." No longer would consumers buy a different sneaker for every sport. Out of this shift in generationally driven values was born cross-trainer athletic footwear.[5]

In 1991, the media defined Generation X as 18- to 29-year-olds. In 1997, the business world continued to define Xers as 18- to 29-year olds. The popular definition of Gen X is gradually becoming a dinosaur. The president of Collegiate Marketing reminds us to be wary of stereotyping as we segment. He points out that Generation X is not a lifestage; it is a birth group ultimately moving through stages of life, Clearly, a generation—usually defined as 30 years—extends past a single decade. Demographers are beginning to agree that Gen Xers were born between 1964 and 1984. The bottom line is that Xers extend well beyond 18- to 29-year-olds, and in 1997 that range is from 14 to 34 years. This group has been broken into subsets by some marketers—Xoomers to describe 29- to 34-year-olds because this subset closely resembles the baby boomers.[6]

Compared to boomers, Xers are more marketing savvy, media saturated, outwardly cynical (but with underlying optimism), and technologically sophisticated, being by-products of the Information Age. Some of the perceptions about being body-piercing slackers represents a small subset, again an example of the characteristics of the few being mistakenly applied to the many. The stereotypes can work, but they must be used with caution. Mountain Dew's "Dew Dudes" television campaign ("Been There. Done That.") artfully tapped a topic that universally appeals to adrenaline junkies as well as

---

[4]Catherine Calhoun and Frederic Smoler, "Generation X," *Audacity,* Spring 1997, pp. 44–49.

[5]J. Walker Smith and Ann Clurman, *Rocking the Ages* (New York: HarperCollins, 1997), p. 16.

[6]David Ashley Morrison, "Beyond the Gen X Label," *Brandweek,* March 17, 1997, pp. 23–25.

exhibit

4.3

ATI Grips make fun of generation differences.

Courtesy: Bulldog Drummond.

Marketing concept
A management orientation that views the needs of consumers as primary to the success of a firm.

couch potatoes. The stereotype succeeds because it does not pigeonhole the target. The tongue-in-cheek communication simply speaks to one facet of a complex market psyche. ATI Grips (bike handlebar grips) use visual irreverence and "Just one more thing your parents won't understand" to attract their target (Exhibit 4.3).

MARKETING CONCEPT AND TARGETING

Companies cannot operate in every market and satisfy every consumer need. They generally find that it is necessary to divide the market into major market segments, evaluate them, and then target those segments it can best serve. This focus on specific groups of buyers is called *market segmentation.* It is an extension of the **marketing concept,** defined by Philip Kotler, that achieving organizational goals depends on determining the needs and wants of target markets and delivering the desired satisfactions more effectively and efficiently than competitors. This idea has been stated as "find a need and fill it" or "make what you sell instead of trying to sell what you can make." Advertisers have expressed this concept in colorful ways; for example, Burger King said, "Have It Your Way," and United Airlines said, "You're the Boss."[7]

Frederick E. Webster Jr., however, says the old marketing concept—the management philosophy first articulated in the 1950s—is a relic of an earlier period of economic history. Most of its assumptions are no longer appropriate in the competitive global markets of the 1990s. Today the world is rapidly moving toward a pattern of economic activity based on long-term relationships and partnerships among economic actors in the loose coalition frameworks of *network* organizations. The concept of *customer value* is at the heart of the new marketing concept and must be the central element of all business strategy.

As we look at the differences, the old marketing concept had the objective of making a sale, whereas under the new marketing concept, the objective is to develop a customer relationship in which the sale is only the beginning. Under both marketing concepts, market segmentation, marketing targeting, and positioning are *essential* re-

---

[7]Philip Kotler, *Marketing Management,* 8th ed. (Upper Saddle River, N.J.: Prentice Hall, 1994), pp. 18–21.

quirements for effective strategic planning. In the new marketing concept, the focus is sharpened by adding the idea of the value proposition.[8]

Market-driven companies need to understand how customer needs and company capabilities converge to form the customer's definition of value. This is more than a philosophy; it is a way of doing business. It includes customer orientation, market intelligence, distinctive competencies, value delivery, market targeting and the value proposition, customer-defined total quality management, profitability rather than sales volume, relationship management, continuous improvement, and a customer-focused organizational structure.[9]

Marketing databases are helping companies deliver one-to-one relationships not previously available. They include comprehensive data about individual customers' and prospects' sales histories, as well as demographics and psychographics. Interest by marketers has changed from simply getting people to switch brands to figuring ways to keep from losing current customers by continually trying to meet their needs.

What Is a Product?

Seems like a silly question, doesn't it? Let us define it as a bundle of ingredients put together for sale as something useful to a consumer. You don't go into a store to buy water, hydrofluorocarbon 152A, isobutane, polyquaternium-11, DEA-methoxycinnamate, sodium cocoyl isethionate, panthenol, fragrance, isosteareth-10, dimethicone copolyol, lauramide dea, methylparaben, DMDM hydantoin. Many do, however, go into a store and buy Condition by Clairol 3-in-1 Mousse. It is more than a physical object. It represents a bundle of satisfactions—hair that holds, is conditioned and shines, is protected against the sun's damage, is protected against dryness, imparts self-esteem—that are considered more or less important by each consumer.

Some of these satisfactions are purely functional—a watch to tell time or a car for transportation. Some of the satisfactions are psychological—a car may represent status and a watch may represent a piece of beautiful jewelry. Different people have different ideas about which satisfactions are important. Products are often designed with satisfactions to match the interests of a particular group of consumers. Within the product class of cameras, there is equipment that is simple to operate and geared to no-mistake photography, and there is also sophisticated equipment for the serious photographer, or now even digital cameras. We are also judged in large measure by our physical possessions—think of your attitude toward Mercedes, Jaguars, beepers, cellular phones, and so on. The products that we purchase say something about us and group us with people who seek similar satisfactions from life and products. As we match people and benefits, we create product loyalty that insulates us against competitive attack.

New products have a difficult time finding a place in the market. The manufacturer must be selective in defining the most profitable market segments because the cost of introducing a new product can be expensive. There are numerous ways to estimate the chances of getting a heavy user of another brand to try a new brand. One technique is to define market segments according to their brand loyalty and preference for national over private brands. Studies of packaged goods brand loyalty found six such segments:[10]

1. *National-brand loyal.* Members of this segment buy primarily a single national brand at its regular price.

---

[8]Frederick E. Webster Jr., "Defining the New Marketing Concept," *Marketing Management,* 2, no. 4. pp. 23–31.

[9]Frederick E. Webster Jr., "Executing the New Marketing Concept," *Marketing Management,* 3, no. 1, pp. 9–16.

[10]Robert C. Blattberg, Thomas Buesing, and Subrata K. Sen, "Segmentation Strategies for New National Brands," *Journal of Marketing,* Fall 1980, p. 60. (*Courtesy: Journal of Marketing,* a publication of the American Marketing Association.)

2. *National-brand deal.* This segment is similar to the national-brand-loyal segment, except that most of its purchases are made on deal (that is, the consumer is loyal to only national brands but chooses the least expensive one). To buy the preferred national brand on deal, the consumer engages in considerable store switching.
3. *Private-label loyal.* Consumers in this segment primarily buy the private label offered by the store in which they shop (for example, Eckerds, A&P, and other store brands).
4. *Private-label deal.* This segment shops at many stores and buys the private label of each store, usually on deal.
5. *National-brand switcher.* Members of this segment tend not to buy private labels. Instead, they switch regularly among the various national brands on the market.
6. *Private-label switcher.* This segment is similar to the private-label-deal segment, except that the members are not very deal prone and purchase the private labels at their regular price.

Price, product distribution, and promotion also affect the share of market coming from each competing brand. However, a new national brand would expect to gain most of its initial sales from segments 2 and 5, whereas segments 1 and 3 would normally be poor prospects to try a new brand. There are many factors to consider. But remember a camera is not just a camera; markets change with the product, and products change with the market.

What Is a Market?

All advertising and marketing people could easily answer this question, but you might get different answers, depending on their perspectives. For our purposes, a *market* can be defined as a group of people

- who can be identified by some common characteristic, interest, or problem
- who could use our product to advantage
- who could afford to buy it
- who can be reached through some medium.

Examples of potential markets are mothers of young children, singles, matures, newly marrieds, skiers, tennis players, Hispanic teens, do-it-yourselfers, runners, and tourists. Yamaha USA (Exhibit 4.4) obviously aims at country club and golf course fleet buyers. Electra's Gamma Knife radiosurgery software (Exhibit 4.5, p. 92) is aimed directly at a narrow portion of the medical community.

The *majority fallacy* is a term applied to the assumption, once frequently made, that every product should be aimed at, and acceptable to, a majority of all consumers. Research tells us that brands aimed at the majority of consumers in a given market will tend to have rather similar characteristics and will neglect an opportunity to serve the needs of consumer minorities. Take, for example, chocolate cake mixes. A good-sized group of consumers would prefer a light chocolate cake or a very dark chocolate cake, but the majority choice is a medium chocolate cake. So although several initial cake mix products would do best to market a medium-chocolate cake to appeal to the broadest group of consumers, later entrants might gain a larger share by supplying the smaller, but significant group with their preference.

What Is Competition?

Wander through a pharmacy or grocery store and look at the toothpaste choices. There are many kinds—brighteners, abrasives, fresh breath, fluoride, paste, gels, peroxides, and so on. Or in the analgesic section, look at the pain killers. You will find many brands competing for your attention: Bayer, Aleve, Advil, Tylenol, Aspirin-Free Anacin, Empirin, Vanquish, Motrin IB, Goody's, BC, Excedrin IB, Cope, Bufferin, Nuprin, and

the list goes on. Why does one consumer choose one brand and another consumer something else? How does one even get on the shelf to compete? These are very important questions to the makers of these products.

We speak of competition in the broadest sense to include all the forces that are inhibiting the sales of a product. They may be products in the same subclass as your product, or in the same product class, or forces outside the category of your product. Our list of analgesics included products in different subcategories: Bayer, Tylenol, Aleve, and Nuprin are each in different analgesic categories, such as aspirin, acetaminophen, naproxen, and ibuprofen. Advil and Nuprin are in the same subcategory. Does that mean they compete with only themselves? The answer is generally no. Many consumers don't even consider the subclasses, they only think in terms of pain relief. If consumers are considering only the benefits of an ibuprofen, then the answer is yes. Advil, Motrin IB, Excedrin IB, and Nuprin would all compete. The point is that advertisers and marketers need to try to find the answers as to which products in what categories compete for the consumer's attention and dollar. It may sound confusing because you don't know

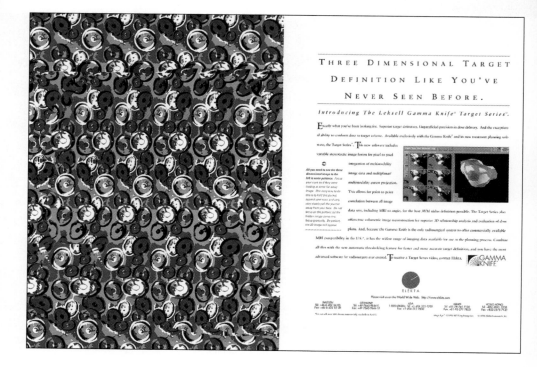

the category, but the seasoned marketer for these products knows its category and the products and the reasons people buy.

Marketers for all kinds of products and services must answer: Who are our competitors? What brands? What other product categories? Are there many brands or only a few? Which are strong? Which are vulnerable? What impact, if any, do store brands and generics have? Are there any strong, long-established brands, or is the market volatile? In this context, how would you define the competition for Mountain Dew? Is it Surge? 7-Up? Mellow Yellow? All Sport? Colas? Milk? Iced tea? Again, the answer could be all of these. A major purpose of target marketing is to position a brand effectively within a product category (soft drinks) or subcategory (lemon-lime soft drinks).

PLANNING THE ADVERTISING

Market Segmentation

Market segmentation
The division of an entire market of consumers into groups whose similarity makes them a market for products serving their special needs.

Today, you can't efficiently reach every person who has a dollar to spend. It is just too broad a goal, so in most cases we simply don't and shouldn't try. As a result, most marketers develop target segments or groups. The division of an entire market of consumers into groups whose similarity makes them a market for products servicing their special needs is called **market segmentation.**

This classifying of consumers is generally one of the tasks of a marketing plan's **situation analysis** section. It has been said, "One size does not fit all"—the premise behind segmentation marketing. It's about maximizing your potential in the marketplace by targeting your product to certain segments of the population with similar behaviors, such as people of the same age, gender, ethnic background, or lifestyle. From a communication standpoint, it is more difficult than you may think. You must understand each segment's cultural nuances and choose the right message, so you don't stereotype the service or product you are selling as one designed for only them.

Situation analysis
The part of the advertising plan that answers the questions: Where are we today and how did we get here? It deals with the past and present.

Power Master malt liquor was introduced to target African Americans, but the campaign backfired. Many blacks got angry because they felt stereotyped as socially irre-

exhibit

4.6

Palmas Del Mar
Resort appeals to the
readers lifestyle.

Courtesy: Hughes Advertising,
Atlanta.

sponsible. The company did the right thing the wrong way. They identified a segment but came up with the wrong ideas for marketing them. The ads used people from the target they were selling, but the *in-group bias* theory didn't work. It's not just about including people from certain groups in ads, but how they are portrayed.[11]

There are a number of factors to be considered in planning advertising to take advantage of market segmentation. The first step is to determine the variable to use for dividing a market. In addition to demographics, the major means of market segmentation are geographical, product user, and lifestyle segmentation. Palmas Del Mar Resort (Exhibit 4.6) targets couples who want to get away and share their time.

Geographical Segmentation   Geographical segmentation, the oldest form of segmentation, designates customers by geographical area. It dates back to earlier days when distribution was the primary concern of manufacturers. Today geomarketing is of particular importance to media planners in deciding on national, regional, and local ad campaigns. It is only recently that geomarketing has been elevated to a marketing discipline the way demographics was in the 1950s and psychographics was in the 1970s. In this instance, consumers haven't changed but marketers' awareness of regional and global marketing has. Geodemographical marketing is just another way of segmenting the market for companies in search of growth.

Recently, there has been a "data explosion" on local markets. Some of the information comes from an abundant number of research services for use on merchandising and buying decisions. Many retail companies such as supermarkets practice micromarketing—treating each individual store as its own market and trading area. Often this approach translates into different ads for different markets. When thinking about geographic segmentation, advertisers have a number of categories to explore:

- census trace data
- zip codes
- counties
- metropolitan statistical areas

- areas of dominant influence (ADI)
- states
- census regions
- total United States

---

[11]Mary Hardie, "On Target Segmentation Marketing Latest Technique," *Gannetteer,* July–August 1994, pp. 8–9.

Companies that lack national distribution may consider geographical segmentation. Pro Balanced dog food is distributed basically in the South, but has to compete against national brands to survive. There are many local or regional brands that must be successful in their geographical areas to survive. Cheerwine is a cherry cola–like soft drink that is strong in its home area, but would have problems in areas where its history and tradition were unknown. As a matter of fact, in the mid-1990s, Cheerwine used a slogan that said, "It's a Carolina Thing." In New England, Cains' Mayonnaise and Country Salad Dressings have been sold since 1914 (Exhibit 4.7). In these examples, geographical segmentation is a distribution strategy rather than a promotional one.

It is not unusual for national companies to divide their advertising and marketing efforts into regional units to respond better to the competition. McDonald's uses a major advertising agency to handle its national advertising and numerous (generally smaller)

Cains. Keeping stockboys off the streets since 1914.

For over 80 years, grocers everywhere have been stocking up on Cains® as a proven way to bolster business. And thanks to a line of products ranging from Reduced Fat Mayonnaise to Country Salad Dressings, Cains plans to carry on the New England tradition of wholesome quality, as well as uphold the work ethic of stockboys. So stock up now on Cains' entire family of fine foods. Call Buckley Thorne Messina Pierce at (800) 394-2200 or (508) 653-6000.

agencies to handle franchise and regional efforts supplementing the national effort. This gives McDonald's the ability to react to the marketplace by cities, regions, or individual stores.

Product user segmentation
Identifying consumers by the amount of product usage.

Product User Segmentation   User segmentation is a strategy based on the amount and/or consumption patterns of a brand or category. The advertiser is interested in product usage rather than consumer characteristics. As a practical matter, most user segmentation methods are combined with demographic or lifestyle consumer identification. Here the advertiser is interested in market segments that have the highest sales potential. Typically, a market segment is first divided into all users and then subdivided into heavy, medium, and light users. For example, let us look at the frequency of weekly use of fast foods:

Frequency	Adults	Men	Women
Heavy (4 plus visits)	11.4%	14.8%	8.3%
Medium (1–3 visits)	44.9	46.5	43.3
Light (less than weekly)	22.8	20.6	24.8

The definition of usage varies with the product category. For example, heavy fast-food use may be defined as 4+ times per week; heavy luxury-restaurant use as once a week; and heavy seafood-restaurant use as once a week. As you can see, product user segmentation can get quite complex, but this kind of data allows marketers to use a rifle instead of a shotgun.

Lifestyle segmentation
Identifying consumers by combining several demographics and lifestyles.

Lifestyle Segmentation   **Lifestyle segmentation** makes the assumption that if you live a certain way, so do your neighbors, and therefore any smart marketer would want to target clusters filled with these clones. Lifestyle clusters are more accurate characterizations of people than any single variable would be.

The concept of lifestyle segmentation is a viable one; however, researchers are having to adjust to a sea of changes taking place among America's shopping public. For example, old attitudes toward work and leisure or fitness don't fit today's realities. As a result, segmentation researchers are changing how they view many of the new lifestyle characteristics driving this new era.[12]

Values and lifestyles system (VALS)
Developed by SRI International to cluster consumers according to several variables in order to predict consumer behavior.

Each research company has its own terminology for the various clusters it identifies. For example, SRI International developed the **values and lifestyles system** (VALS), which classifies people according to their values and lifestyles. Some advertisers had difficulties applying the clusters to their problems, so SRI refined the research as VALS 2, which puts less emphasis on values and more on the psychological underpinnings of behavior (see chapter 15 for a description of VALS 2). VALS 2 recently has been reengineered and repositioned as a tool for understanding new product acceptance and innovation. The new version divides people into three groups (people who are principle-oriented, status-oriented, or action-oriented) and subdivides these into eight segments. SRI recently launched iVALS, a project that focuses on the attitudes, preferences, and behaviors of on-line service and Internet users. Early results of iVALS indicate that there is a dual-tiered society based on knowledge, not income. Researchers Kevin Clancy and Robert Shulman argue that "off-the shelf segmentation studies cannot be as good as customized segmentation done with a specific product or service in mind. VALS will help break up the world into pieces, but the pieces may or may not have any relevance for any one brand."[13] Another example of syndicated segmentation research is the Upper Deck survey, with its clusters of affluent investors whose incomes are in the top 10 percent, available from Mediamark Research.

---

[12]Rebecca Piirto Heath, "The Frontier of Psychographics," *American Demographics,* July 1996, p. 40.

[13]Kevin J. Clancy and Robert S. Shulman, *The Marketing Revolution* (New York: Harper Business, 1991), p. 63.

exhibit

4.8

Demographically
identical consumers
can be very different
people.

Consumer A	Demographic Profile	Lifestyle Profile
	Age: 36; Sex: male; Race: white; Occupation: managerial; Income: $55,000; Married, two children	Republican; President of Lions Club; Member of Kids Soccer Association, Town and Gown Theater, and the Rolling Hills Tennis Club
Consumer B	Age: 36; Sex: male; Race: white; Occupation: managerial; Income: $55,000; Married, two children	Libertarian; President of Classic Computer Club; President of Green Preservation Society; Vice President of People's Rights Group

One approach to determining lifestyle characteristics is to identify consumers' activities, interests, and opinions (AIO). Typical AIO measures are

Activities: leisure time preferences, community involvement, and preferences for social events
Interests: family orientation, sports interest, and media usage
Opinions: political preferences and views on various social issues.

Exhibit 4.8 shows that consumers A and B are identical demographically, but an advertiser would detect important differences by examining their lifestyles.

Benefits and Attitude Segmentation   Not everyone wants the same thing from a product. You don't have just a single toothpaste, because some people are interested in taste, or fresh breath, or whiteness of their teeth, or decay prevention, or tartar control for gums, or value, and so on. The basis here is to cluster people into groups based upon what they want in a product.

Segmentation Risks   Although segmentation is very important to successful advertising it isn't without risks. One problem is that once the outer limits of the niche are reached, sales growth will be limited unless the company can expand beyond its niche. By too narrowly defining your market—that is, by excessive segmenting—you can become inefficient in media buying, creating different ads, and obtaining alternative distribution channels. A few years ago, Taco Bell was the first fast-food chain to target people with their Value Menu. They were so successful that most other fast-food companies followed with their own Value Menus. As a result of this competition, the pool of value-conscious consumers was split among numerous companies, diluting the profit.

Niche marketing can serve at least two purposes. It can gain a product entry into a larger market by attacking a small part of it not being served by the competition. It can also cater to latent needs that existing products do not adequately satisfy.

Niche Marketing

Niche marketing
A combination of
product and target
market strategy. It is
a flanking strategy
that focuses on niches
or comparatively
narrow windows of
opportunity within a
broad product market
or industry. Its guiding
principle is to pit your
strength against their
weakness.

Niche marketing is not another buzzword for marketing segmentation, says Alvin Achenbaum.[14] It is essentially a flanking strategy, the essence of which is to engage competitors in those product markets where they are weak or, preferably, have little or no presence. The guiding principle of niche marketing is to pit your strength against the competitor's weakness. No-frill motels did not exist for many years, but they were logical means of competing against other motel segments. Red Roof Inn opened their motels with an ad claiming "Sleep Cheap," and positioned themselves to value consumers not wanting to pay high prices for a place to sleep. Later they even made fun of hotels placing a chocolate mint on your pillow for an extra $30 or $40. Today, Holiday Inn and Ramada have moved into that niche with their own no-frills *Express* motels.

---

[14]Alvin Achenbaum, "Understanding Niche Marketing," *Adweek,* December 1, 1986, p. 62.

In the very turbulent airline market, Southwest Airlines has shown that niche marketing can be very profitable. With careful control of costs, astute selection of short-haul routes, inexpensive fares, and no-frills service, it became a thorn in the side of the major air carriers. Its advertising hammered home its policy of low fares for all seats on all flights against their competitions' many restrictions surrounding their low fares. How many other airlines have copied their model?

The major growth segments in the United States for the future are in the minority population, as indicated earlier in this chapter. Commonalties can be found among the three major ethnic groups, Hispanic, African American, and Asian. Each is also quite diverse and contains many subsets with different buying habits and preferences. African American consumers differ by age, geographic region, income, and education. Additionally, Caribbean- and African-born Americans have mindsets different from African Americans raised in the United States. Hispanic consumers differ by language preference, birthplace (U.S.-born versus foreign-born), and nationality (Mexican, Puerto Rican, Cuban, or other Latin countries). There is no Asian market per se; Japanese, Chinese, Korean, Filipino, and Vietnamese Americans differ in language, history, and culture. Each factor drives what will be the most effective channel for reaching these consumers, whose combined spending power is estimated to be in excess of $600 billion.

Hispanic & Asian Marketing Research substantiated the claim that ads that address Hispanics in Spanish are more effective. Half of those questioned in a recent survey said they bought something they saw on Spanish TV, whereas only one-quarter bought something advertised during English programming.[15]

Beware of literal translations. Expressions in one language may be out of context when translated into another language. A ballpoint pen manufacturer once translated the word *embarrass* to *embarazar,* a message that suggested the pen wouldn't leak in your pocket and make you pregnant. The word *light* in English generally connotes something positive. In Spanish, it suggests something insubstantial. The bottom line is to create appropriate messages that will be familiar to the target audience and add value to their lives.

Many marketers think their general-market advertising efforts are effective in reaching ethnic groups; other marketing researchers argue that generic efforts miss the mark. Black people are not dark-skinned white people, says a Burrell Communications Group head. Blacks are significantly different in terms of approach and history. There is a significant difference in behavior, and that manifests itself all the way to the marketplace.[16] One of Burrell's ads for McDonald's takes place in an African art store. When black people saw the ad showcasing African art, which was timely because of the black consumer's Afrocentric interest, there was depth to the response. White people didn't get that kind of meaning, but they did get a very interesting and entertaining spot.

Each niche offers challenges for advertisers. When trying to develop niche marketing to Asians and Latinos, understanding of cultural and language issues is required, as we have indicated. From another perspective, Kraft found that America's Jewish population offers a niche that is mainstream, upscale, educated, and affluent. The purchase patterns of this niche are similar to those of average Americans with a little different twist. Traditionally, grocery shopping is heaviest around holiday time. Christmas generates the most volume in the overall food category, but Passover now has become the second most prosperous season in supermarkets, not surprisingly because more than 40 percent of kosher food sales occur during the week prior to the holiday. To top this market, Kraft's Philadelphia brand cream cheese promoted specific Passover ads in Jewish magazines and newspapers throughout the country.

---

[15]Esther Novak, "Honoring Traditions," *Brandweek,* May 19, 1997, pp. 32–34.

[16]Christie Fisher, "Ethnics Gain Market Clout," *Advertising Age,* August 5, 1991, p. 3.

Almost 40 percent of the U.S. Jewish population lives in metro New York, 15 percent in Los Angeles, with other large concentrations in Chicago and southern Florida. Nearly 200 Jewish-targeted publications reach more than 4 million readers monthly. Because the average Orthodox Jewish household has an average of 4.8 children, Beech-Nut baby foods has had kosher certification on their foods for many years. The headline for one of their ads aimed at this niche read, "Feeding your baby kosher is as simple as choosing Beech-Nut."[17]

Companies can build growth out of finding small niches to serve consumers' needs. For example, Kimberly-Clark launched Huggies Pull-Ups training pants in 1989. In 1994, it launched Goodnites for older children who wet the bed. In 1997, it introduced Huggies Little Swimmers designed to survive swimming. The niche for Huggies Little Swimmers is a very narrow category segment. Originally, Procter & Gamble said the training pants niche was too small, but it grew to a $400 million segment within the disposable diaper category. Kimberly-Clark has a 41.6 percent share of the total disposable diaper category.[18]

POSITIONING

Positioning has to be done with a target in mind. You position a product in the mind of a specific prospect. Positioning is another term for fitting the product into the lifestyle of the buyer. It refers to segmenting a market by either or both of two ways: (1) creating a product to meet the needs of a specialized group, and/or (2) identifying and advertising a feature of an existing product that meets the needs of a specialized group.

Estrovite vitamins recognized a potential problem among women on birth control pills and created a product positioned to fulfill that need. Their headline read, "Your birth control pills could be robbing you of essential vitamins and minerals." The copy explained why.

The purpose of positioning is giving a product a meaning that distinguishes it from other products and induces people to want to buy it. *Positioning is what you do to the mind of the consumer.* Specifically, you position the product in the mind of the prospect. You want your positioning to be in harmony with the lifestyles and values we have discussed. It is necessary to understand what motivates people to buy in the product category—what explains their behavior. It is also necessary to understand the degree to which the product satisfies the target's needs.[19] One automobile may be positioned as a sports car, another as a luxury sports car, another as the safest family car, and still another as a high-performance vehicle.

It is possible for some products to successfully hold different positions at the same time. Arm & Hammer baking soda has been positioned as a deodorizer for refrigerators, an antacid, a freezer deodorizer, and a bath skin cleanser without losing its original market as a cooking ingredient.

You might try to get the following reactions from consumers to a new line of frozen entrees that are low in calories, sodium, and fat, and have larger servings than the competition's. Before seeing your advertising, the consumer thinks:

> I like the convenience and taste of today's frozen foods but I don't usually get enough of the main course to eat. I would like to try a brand that gives me plenty to eat but is still light and healthy—and, most important, it has to taste great.

---

[17]Elie Rosenfeld, "Kosher Consumers," *Brandweek,* May 19, 1997, pp. 29–31.

[18]Jeff Neff, "Huggies Little Swimmers Tests Out a New Niche," *Advertising Age,* August 25, 1997, p. 8.

[19]Kevin J. Clancy and Robert S. Shulman, *The Marketing Revolution* (New York: Harper Business, 1991), pp. 84–87.

After being exposed to your advertising, the consumer thinks:

> I may buy Ru's Frozen Food entrees. They taste great and I get plenty to eat, and they are still low enough in calories that I don't feel I'm overeating. They're better for me because they have less sodium and fat than others. Also, there is enough variety so that I can eat the foods I like without getting bored by the same old thing.

Creating a Product for Selected Markets

One of the ways that marketers attract a focused consumer group is through variations on a conventional product. A new variation looks for a group with needs not fully met by existing products. In addition, marketers or products in the retentive stage may see variations as a means of rejuvenating a product whose sales have gone flat.

Bayer aspirin created an adult low strength for aspirin regimen users. Research indicated that second heart attacks were greatly reduced by simply taking an aspirin daily. The only problem was that regular use of aspirin by some people resulted in stomach problems. A regular aspirin tablet consisted of 325 milligrams. The doctor-recommended daily therapy for patients having suffered an initial heart attack was 81 milligrams. Adults started taking children's aspirin, which was 81 milligrams, to prevent stomach problems and yet get the advantage of heart attack protection. As a result of this consumer action, Bayer introduced Bayer enteric aspirin, which was 81 milligrams and protects the stomach.

Positioning to Expand Brand Share

Positioning—or, more accurately, repositioning—can be an effective method of increasing brand share when a company already has a high percentage of the market for a type of product. Let us assume our company, Acme Widgets, has 80 percent of the widget market. Two strategies that the company might adopt are shown in the following tables.

Strategy I: Traditional Brand Promotion (No Brand Repositioning)

1996 Brand Share (%)		1997 Advertising	1998 Brand Share (%)	
A	10	$10 million spent	A	9.9
B	5	against brands	B	5.0
C	5	A, B, and C	C	5.0
Acme	80		Acme	80.1
Total	100		Total	100.0

Strategy II: Acme Widget's Brand Repositioning

1996 Brand Share (%)		1997 Advertising	1998 Brand Share (%) Primary Market	
A	10	$6 million spent	A	10
B	5	to keep present	B	5
C	5	market share	C	5
Acme	80		Acme	80
Total	100		Total	100
			Alternative Market	
		$4 million spent	Other brands	
		to promote repositioned	and brands already	
		Acme Widget to	in market	85
		new market	A, B, C	5
			Acme	10
			Total	100

In Strategy I, Acme, by engaging in direct brand competition, has increased its market share very slightly. However, it is extremely doubtful that further sales can be profitably taken from the competition. Increased advertising expenditures to make inroads into brands A, B, and C will probably cost proportionally more than the revenues realized.

The repositioning strategy depicted in Strategy II has allowed Acme to keep its overwhelming share. At the same time, by spending 40 percent ($4 million of its $10 million advertising allowance) of its budget to position the company in a new market, Acme gained 10 percent of this formerly untapped market segment rather than the 0.1 percent of the primary market it achieved with the first strategy. In this example, no physical changes were made in the product—only different appeals were used. This is the basis for positioning by choice of appeal.

How to Approach a Positioning Problem

As you would expect, not all products lend themselves to the type of positioning discussed here. The advertiser must be careful not to damage current product image by changing appeals and prematurely expanding into new markets. Jack Trout and Al Ries, who have written about positioning for several decades, say that the advertiser who is thinking about positioning should ask the following questions:[20]

What position, if any, do we already own in the prospect's mind?
What position do we want to own?
What companies must be outgunned if we are to establish that position?
Do we have enough marketing money to occupy and hold that position?
Do we have the guts to stick with one consistent positioning concept?
Does our creative approach match our positioning strategy?

David Aaker says the most used positioning strategy is to associate an object with a product attribute or characteristic. Developing such associations is effective because when the attribute is meaningful, the association can directly translate into reasons to buy the brand. Crest toothpaste became the leader by building a strong association with cavity control in part created by an endorsement of the American Dental Association. BMW has talked about performance with its tag line: "The Ultimate Driving Machine." Mercedes, "The Ultimate Engineered Car." Hyundai, "Cars that Make Sense." The positioning problem is usually finding an attribute important to a major segment and not already claimed by a competitor.[21] For example: Chase developed a new position statement that augmented its "The Right Relationship Is Everything" tag that had been used, by pounding home "The Relationship Company." Chase's object was to ground the notion of *the relationship bank* in consumers' minds and link every product and service under the Chase brand name to that positioning. Chase and Chemical Bank had recently merged. Chemical was better known for customer service. The new bank hoped to establish its brand name among consumers, but once it was established it had to stand for something. "We hope the take-away is an emotional one," claimed a Chase spokesperson. "If you can build relationships and offer those customers mortgages and auto financing, it would give us a tremendous advantage as far as leveraging our size. And that's what the merger is supposed to be about."[22]

Positioning Examples

Dove is positioned as a moisturizing beauty bar.
Whirlpool appliances make your world a little easier.
Cheer is the detergent for all temperatures.

---

[20]Jack Trout and Al Ries, *The Positioning Era* (New York: Ries Cappiello Colwell, 1973), pp. 38–41.
[21]David A. Aaker, *Managing Brand Equity* (New York: The Free Press, 1991), pp. 114–115.
[22]"Chase Softens via $45–65M Ad Blitz," *Brandweek*, March 31, 1997, p. 6.

Intel is the computer inside.
Lever 2000 is the deodorant soap that's better for your skin.
Saturn is a different kind of company, a different kind of car.
Milk-Bone dog biscuits clean teeth and freshen breath.
Wrangler is the Western original.
Jenn-Air appliances are the sign of a great cook.
Advil is the advanced medicine for pain.
Fujitsu builds electronics for humans.
Ford is the best-built, best-selling American truck.

Some marketers frequently alter a brand's positioning for the sake of change. This is especially unfortunate for those brands that are firmly entrenched and successful because their reason for being is widely accepted. In the past, a number of positioning statements were successful, but were dropped; "Good to the Last Drop," "Pepperidge Farm Remembers," and "Two Mints in One," are examples. These campaigns were revised long after they were discontinued because they truly represented the consumer end benefit and character of the brand.[23]

Profile of the Market

Market profile
A demographic and psychographic description of the people or the households of a product's market. It may also include economic and retailing information about a territory.

Up to this point, we have discussed market segments. Now we examine the overall **market profile** for a product. First, we determine the overall usage of the product type. This is usually defined in terms of dollars, sales, number of units sold, or percentage of households that use such a product. Then we determine if the category is growing, stagnant, or declining. We compare our share of the market to the competition (see Exhibit 4.9). Next we ask what the share trends have been over the past several years. Finally, we want to know the chief product advantage featured by each brand.

During the last 52 weeks, Crest lost share and Colgate sales were flat in the $1.45 billion toothpaste market.

When you look at market share, beware as to whether you are looking at a *brand's share* (Resolve carpet cleaner, 19.3 percent) or a *company's share*. For example, in the hot dog market, Oscar Mayer as a company has a 19 percent share; Sara Lee is second with its Hygrade, Ball Park, Best's, and Bryan Foods brands, which total a 15.2 percent share; ConAgra, which markets Healthy Choice, Hebrew National, and Armour brands, has a 13.2 percent share. Nabisco's Ritz brand is a leader in the cracker category with a 9.6 percent share. Goldfish brand crackers ranks seventh in the category with a 3.7 percent share. In the facial skin-care category, Oil of Olay commands a 24.2 percent share, Plénitude a 17.1 percent share, and Pond's a 14.7 percent share; these three brands control more than 56 percent of the category. A marketer with a leading share in a product category and a marketer with a very small share will probably approach advertising in very different ways.

It is important for the advertiser to know not only the characteristics of the product's market, but also similar information about media alternatives. Most major

e x h i b i t

4.9

Every share point may be worth millions of dollars in sales.

Dentifrice Brand	Sales (millions)	$ Share (%)
Crest	$395.8	27.2
Colgate	$276.4	19.0
Mentadent	$163.5	11.3
Aquafresh	$156.3	10.8
Arm & Hammer	$106.0	7.3
Total Market	**$1,453.1**	

Source: Advertising Age, April 21, 1997, p. 16.

---

[23]Lewis Brosowksy, "Ad Themes that Last," *Advertising Age,* February 28, 1994, p. 26.

newspapers, magazines, and broadcast media provide demographic and product-user data for numerous product categories. Database marketing is giving the marketer an abundance of information upon which to base integrated promotional decisions.

PROFILE OF THE BUYER

Earlier in this chapter we highlighted ethnic groups (Hispanics, African Americans, and Asians) who were largely ignored by advertisers in the past, but their increasing numbers demand attention in today's marketplace. The Xers, boomers, teenagers, college students, and the 50-plus markets all are studied by smart advertisers to understand their potential for specific products and services. As indicated, these groups of consumers are not necessarily easy to understand or reach with effective integrated programs. Not all boomers act the same, and all Xers don't respond to messages in the same manner. Advertisers have to look at demographics and lifestyles, for starters, to understand any market.

Demography is the study of vital economic and sociological statistics about people. In advertising, demographic reports refer to those facts relevant to a person's use of a product. Exhibit 4.10 presents a snippet of average weekly regular and diet soft-drink demographics.

The selected soft-drink demographics probably offer few surprises to you. However, be sure to examine the differences in regular and diet consumption between males and females, or between age 18 to 24 and older consumers; and compare regional differences for starters. You can begin to understand how demographic differences could be important factors in advertising strategy and expenditure decisions.

Heavy Users

Take any product category and you will find a small percentage of users are responsible for a disproportionately large share of sales. The principle of heavy usage is sometimes referred to as the 80/20 rule—that is, 80 percent of the units sold are purchased by only 20 percent of the consumers. Few products meet this exactly, but Kraft's Miracle Whip does. And the most avid Miracle Whip customers live in the Midwest. So Kraft knows who buys the most and where they live. Of course, the exact figure varies with each product and product category, but the 80/20 rule is representative of most product sales. In the case of Diet Coke, 8 percent of the households account for 84 percent of the volume—rather significant information. Keeping that small segment loyal to Diet Coke is smart marketing, pure and simple. Heavy users are identified not only by who they are, but also by when they buy and where they are located. Of course, an-

<table>
<tr><td></td><td></td><td colspan="2">Regular</td><td colspan="2">Diet</td></tr>
<tr><td colspan="2">Demographic</td><td>Cola</td><td>Other</td><td>Cola</td><td>Other</td></tr>
<tr><td colspan="2">Total 18+</td><td>60.3</td><td>43.3</td><td>42.2</td><td>29.2</td></tr>
<tr><td>Sex:</td><td>Male</td><td>65.5</td><td>46.1</td><td>38.6</td><td>27.8</td></tr>
<tr><td></td><td>Female</td><td>55.5</td><td>40.5</td><td>45.6</td><td>30.4</td></tr>
<tr><td>Age:</td><td>18–24</td><td>72.5</td><td>50.4</td><td>32.7</td><td>24.4</td></tr>
<tr><td></td><td>25–34</td><td>67.6</td><td>48.8</td><td>42.5</td><td>30.1</td></tr>
<tr><td></td><td>35–44</td><td>62.6</td><td>45.1</td><td>45.2</td><td>29.3</td></tr>
<tr><td></td><td>65+</td><td>46.3</td><td>34.5</td><td>41.2</td><td>29.2</td></tr>
<tr><td>Region:</td><td>Northeast</td><td>59.8</td><td>45.3</td><td>37.6</td><td>27.7</td></tr>
<tr><td></td><td>Midwest</td><td>56.6</td><td>42.6</td><td>46.8</td><td>31.6</td></tr>
<tr><td></td><td>South</td><td>65.0</td><td>42.2</td><td>41.8</td><td>26.9</td></tr>
<tr><td></td><td>West</td><td>57.2</td><td>43.4</td><td>42.2</td><td>31.5</td></tr>
<tr><td>Race:</td><td>White</td><td>58.9</td><td>41.1</td><td>43.5</td><td>29.1</td></tr>
<tr><td></td><td>Black</td><td>69.3</td><td>55.4</td><td>35.7</td><td>27.2</td></tr>
</table>

Source: Radio Advertising Bureau.

exhibit

4.10

Selected Demographics of Regular and Diet Soft Drink Average Weekly Consumption for Specific Types (in percentages)

other issue for marketers is not only how to reach these consumers, but what to say or do once you have made contact.

The following table shows that the heavy users of brand X are women aged 55 and older. In addition, the most effective selling is done from January through June in the East Central and Pacific regions. Obviously, heavy users are an important part of the market; however, they are also the group most advertisers are trying to target, and therefore the competition can be fierce and expensive. Some advertisers find that aiming for a less lucrative segment—medium or light users—may offer more reasonable expectations. A marketer cannot just assume the best prospects are 18- to 49-year-old women, heavy users, or people similar to current customers. Instead, marketers need to carefully study their target audience in great depth. In defining your market, then, you must determine who the heavy users are and identify their similarities, which would define your marketing goal (see Exhibit 4.11, pp. 104–105).

Users of Brand X

1. Target Audience: Current Consumers			
Women	Pop. (%)	Consumption (%)	Index (100 = national average)
18–24	17.5	5.0	29
25–34	21.9	10.1	46
35–54	30.1	24.0	80
55+	30.5	61.0	200
Total	100.0	100.0	

2. Geography: Current Sales			
Area	Pop. (%)	Consumption (%)	Index
Northeast	24	22	92
East Central	15	18	120
West Central	17	16	94
South	27	24	89
Pacific	17	20	118
Total	100	200	

3. Seasonality				
Period	Jan.–Mar.	Apr.–Jun.	Jul.–Sept.	Oct.–Nov.
Consumption (%)	30	36	20	14
Index	120	144	80	56

BEYOND DEMOGRAPHICS: PSYCHOGRAPHICS

When driving through any suburban area past modest-sized yards of middle-class homes, one is struck first by their similarity. But a harder look is more illuminating, for behind the similarities lie differences that reflect the interests, personalities, and family situations of those who live in such homes. One yard has been transformed into a carefully manicured garden. Another includes some shrubs and bushes, but most of the yard serves as a relaxation area, with outdoor barbecue equipment and the like. A third yard is almost entirely a playground, with swings, trapezes, and slides. A swimming pool occupies almost all the space in another yard. A tennis court occupies yet another. Still another has simply been allowed to go to seed and is overgrown and untended by its obviously indoor-oriented owners.

Although the neighborhood consists of homes of similar style, age, and value, the people are not all the same. If you want to advertise to this neighborhood, you would be speaking to people with different interests and different tastes. There may be a big difference in the nature and extent of purchases between any two groups of buyers who

Data to Be Gathered and Reported (If Possible, to Be Directly Accessible)

Characteristic	Minimum Basic Data to Be Reported	Additional Data— Highly Valued
I. Persons Characteristics		
A. Household Relationship	Principal Wage Earner in HH (defines HH head)	
	Principal Shopper in HH (defines homemaker)	
	Spouse	
	Child	
	Other Relative	
	Partner/Roommate	
	Other Non-Relative	
B. Age	Under 6	2–5
	6–11	6–8
	12–15	35–49
	16–20	25–49
	18–20	
	16 or older	
	18 or older	
	18–24	
	25–34	
	35–44	
	45–49	
	50–54	
	55–64	
	65–74	
	75 or older	
C. Sex	Male	
	Female	
D. Education	Last Grade Attended:	
	Grade School or Less (Grade 1–8)	
	Some High School	
	Graduated High School	
	Some College (at least 1 year)	
	Graduated College	any postgraduate work
	If currently attending school . .	—(If pertinent to study)—
		Live home
		Live away
		—Live in student housing
		—Live off campus
	Full-Time Student	
	Part-Time Student	
E. Marital Status	Married	Spouse Present
		Spouse Absent
	Widowed	
	Divorced or Separated	Spouse working
	Single (never married)	
	Parent	Engaged
	Pregnant	
	'Living together'	
F. Religion—Political		Protestant — Active (Practicing)
		Catholic — Inactive
		Jewish — (Non-Practicing)
		Other
		None
		Political—Conservative
		—Liberal
		—Moderate

exhibit
4.11

Data to Be Gathered and Reported (If Possible, to Be Directly Accessible)		
Characteristic	Minimum Basic Data to Be Reported	Additional Data—Highly Valued
G. Race	White Black Other	
H. Principal Language Spoken at Home	English Spanish Other	
H1. Other Languages Spoken at Home	English Spanish Other	
I. Individual Employment Income	Under $10,000 $10,000–14,999 $15,000–19,999 $20,000–24,999 $25,000–29,999 $30,000–39,999 $40,000–49,999 $50,000–74,999 $75,000 and over	$75,000–99,000 $100,000 and over IEI Income by Quintile as Determined by the Survey Ziptiles. Other Income

IEI by Quintile
Income Interval

Quintile	% Adults	Low	High	Median Income
1	20	—	10,156	6,391
2	20	10,757	19,999	13,959
3	20	20,000	29,999	24,953
4	20	30,000	43,243	34,967
5	20	43,244	—	60,150

exhibit

4.11

(continued)

Psychographics
A description of a market based on factors such as attitudes, opinions, interests, perceptions, and lifestyles of consumers comprising that market.

have the same demographic characteristics. The attempt to explain the significance of such differences has led to an inquiry beyond demographics into psychographics. **Psychographics**—studying lifestyles—sharpens the search for prospects beyond demographic data. It has been said that lifestyle information gives the soul of the person. Good creative people can devise copy that appeals to a specific segment's lifestyle interest. Exhibit 4.12 (p. 106) illustrates how lifestyle can help differentiate the product or services—"The Romans had lions. We've got hockey." The body copy says, "It's ugly out there. All the more reason to wear AIR II shoulder pads." The media are then selected, and advertising is directed to that special target group or groups. Put very simply, lifestyle information gives the soul of a person, demographics alone gives only a skeleton and not a whole person.

Target Audience: Beyond Demographics

Let us look at an example of a travel advertiser's defined target. This profile is based upon the advertiser's research that helped define those people *most likely* to visit the area.

Research indicated that the basic demographic guideline for the consumer target is households with a combined household income of $35,000 or more. Households with less than $35,000 simply do not have the discretionary income necessary for vacation travel.

The other qualifiers in defining a consumer **target audience** are lifestyle and geography:

Target audience
That group that composes the present and potential prospects for a product or service.

● *Primary vacation travelers*—vacation travelers who take a one-week plus vacation during the primary season (summer)

exhibit

4.12

Easton appeals to
hockey players. The ad
copy focuses on
reasons to wear AIR II
shoulder pads.

Courtesy: Bulldog Drummond.

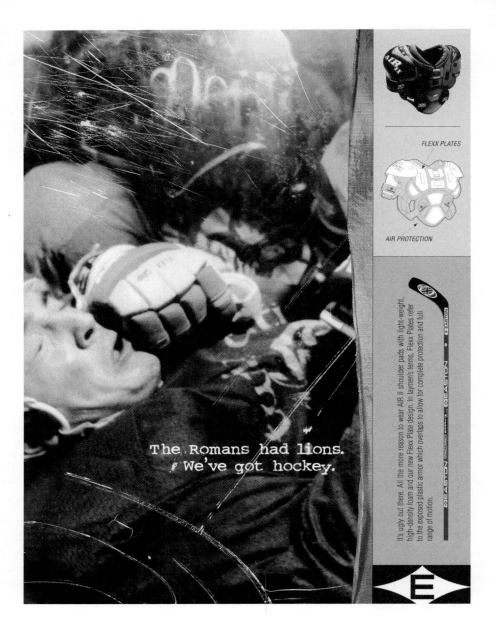

The Romans had lions.
We've got hockey.

It's ugly out there. All the more reason to wear AIR II shoulder pads with light-weight, high-density foam and our new Flexx Plate design. In laymen's terms, Flexx Plates refer to the exposed plastic armor which overlaps to allow for complete protection and full range of motion.

FLEXX PLATES

AIR PROTECTION

- *Weekend travelers*—those people living in states within close proximity who can be attracted during the fall, winter, and spring seasons
- *Mature market (50+)*—people who have both the discretionary income and available time to travel
- *Business travelers*—business people coming to an area on business who can be encouraged to either extend their stay for pleasure travel purposes or to bring their spouse and family along
- *International travelers*—Canada provides an enormous influx of visitors. Also, the increasing number of international flights to and from the area provide increasing opportunities

Exhibits 4.13 and 4.14 (p. 108) are aimed at two different targets. Palmas Del Mar Resort in Puerto Rico says, "Out of 5 billion people you found the right one. Now, how do you get away from the other 4,999,999,999?" Is this aimed at any of the segments just listed? They are obviously not targeting households with kids for a family vacation. Florida's Space Coast, on the other hand, is trying to target people from the North who are heading to Orlando to visit the coast only 35 miles away. The ad tells of sites of in-

exhibit

4.13

Palmas Del Mar targets people that want luxury but not the crowds.

Courtesy: Hughes Advertising, Atlanta.

terest for families. These are two tourism ads with different targets. Today there is much more refined information available. Agency research information includes syndicated research from outside sources, client's research, and the agency's own resources.

Syndicated research services specialize in different types of information on what types of products people buy and which brands, who buys them and their demographic and psychographic distinctions, a comparison of heavy and light users, how people react to products and to ads, and people's styles of buying and what media reach them.

Lifestyle categories are numerous. Data categories are available through syndicated research to advertisers and their agencies to help them select the target market. This information is available on a market-by-market basis defining both demographic and lifestyle information. Some of the categories, indicating the percent of household activities include

- *credit card usage* for travel and entertainment, bank cards, gas and department store usage
- *good life activities,* which include such activities as attending cultural or arts events, foreign travel, gourmet cooking and fine food interests, stock investments, antique interest, wines
- *high-tech activities and usage,* which involve home computers, watching cable TV, VCR recording and viewing, photography interests
- *sports and leisure activities* by households, which include bicycling, boating, golf, bowling, tennis, jogging
- *outdoor activities,* which include the number of households in a specific market involved in camping, fishing, motorcycles, environmental interests
- *domestic activities* such as gardening, Bible and devotional reading, coin collecting, pets, sewing, crafts, reading.

Test Marketing

Although extremely helpful, psychographic research cannot replace market testing as the ultimate guide to successful advertising and marketing. Manufacturers seldom introduce

One small step from Orlando,
One giant leap from Toledo.

new products without doing some prior testing. This kind of testing helps determine if consumers will really purchase a product or react to specific advertising and promotional activities. Recently, Huggies Little Swimmers swim pants for toddlers were tested by Kimberly-Clark with TV, magazine and newspaper ads in Tucson, Ariz.; Evansville, Ind.; Charleston, S.C.; Peoria, Ill.; and Savannah, Ga. AccuPOLL Precision Research, a concept testing service, gave Little Swimmers a high purchase probability grade.

It is difficult to say which cities are best for testing. Ira Weinblatt, a Saatchi & Saatchi senior vice president, says, "You can't say one place represents everything because there are so many different lifestyles." Some cities are historically popular for test marketing. The Midwest has been popular because, geographically, it was the heartland of America. Each test market represents a kind of microcosm of America. Saatchi & Saatchi ranks the top performing test markets. To make the list,

- a city's demographics must fall within 20 percent of the national average
- the city should be somewhat isolated
- local media should be relatively inexpensive
- citizens should not be extremely loyal to any particular brand
- supermarkets should be impartial enough to give new products good display on their shelves.

Milwaukee, one of the test market cities that historically makes the list, is popular because the newspapers offer marketers the flexibility to split production runs. This allows advertisers to test up to four ads at a time and to experiment with run-of-the-paper color or free-standing inserts. Typically, researchers examine purchases for a number of weeks before ads run, during the period of the test, and afterward.

Procter & Gamble has tested Tide Mountain Spring laundry detergent, a heavier-scented version of the original, since September 1996. It was test marketed in Los Angeles, San Diego, Phoenix, and Tucson. P&G's research found that people wanted more scents in products. They also determined that fragrance-free laundry products have become a slow mover and specialized niche products. The perils of introducing a product nationally without test marketing include results similar to the new-formula Coke failure. Failure can be extremely expensive, and most marketers are not willing to take that risk without some type of testing.

SUMMARY

The accurate identification of current and prospective users of a product will often mean the difference between success and failure. The targeting of advertising to these prospects in an efficient media plan with appropriate creativity is critical.

This chapter has concentrated on fundamentals: Who are the prospects? What is a market? What about competition? Positioning? Numerous methods of examining segmentation and other important considerations in planning integrated marketing programs have been discussed. Understanding these basic concerns through research is part of the process. Research is the key to successful target marketing. Market research to define prime market segments, product research to meet the needs of these segments, and advertising research to devise the most appropriate messages are mandatory for success of a firm in a competitive environment. Also, we need to be familiar with the multitude of research services providing data for aiding our planning.

Ads are aimed at consumers with a rifle instead of a shotgun approach. It is becoming easier to tailor messages through a variety of special-interest media vehicles.

Advertisers place more importance on lifestyle characteristics than on demographic factors. Advertisers recognize that purchase behavior is the result of a number of complex psychological and sociological factors that cannot be explained by a superficial list of age, sex, income, or occupational characteristics.

Finally, we need to keep abreast of changes in population and better understand such important segments as Hispanics, Asians, and African Americans as well as generational groups. This kind of knowledge will lead to better communications and targeting. We need to know more than simply numbers and location. We need to understand consumer lifestyles, identities, and motivations.

REVIEW

1. What is target marketing?
2. What is a market?
3. Name key demographic characteristics used by advertisers.
4. What is positioning?
5. What is the 80/20 rule as it relates to target marketing?
6. Why are boomers important to some marketers?

TAKE IT TO THE NET

We invite you to visit the Russell/Lane page on the Prentice Hall Web site at
PHLIP **http://www.prenhall.com/phbusiness** for the bimonthly Russell/Lane update and for this chapter's World Wide Web exercise.

part

III

Managing the Advertising

WE ALWAYS HAVE TO REMEMBER NOT TO
lose sight of the fact that advertising is a business. It has structure,
organization, and must be managed, as with any business. It is more than
just creating ads. In many respects, success in advertising depends on using
the same sound business practices that apply to other fields. In other
respects, the advertising business is different from other business
enterprises.

Chapter 5 concentrates on advertising agencies. Advertising agencies'
main assets are people. These assets go down the elevator at the end of
the day. Agencies are, in fact, little more than office furniture and the ideas
of their employees. They also differ from other companies in that they are
organized largely according to the needs of their clients. There are

specialized advertising agencies that concentrate on specific advertising niches—among them consumer, health care, business-to-business, Hispanic, pharmaceutical, high technology, and financial. Each agency serves a select few clients, satisfying their marketing and advertising needs. Advertising, after all, is a service business.

Chapter 6 views the advertising process from the client's perspective. Advertisers may choose to use or not use an advertising agency. If they do so, the agency works as a team with the company's advertising department. It is crucial that this teamwork operate efficiently. Often this teamwork involves being a partner in the total integrated marketing communication program of the company. The choosing of an agency or agencies, and managing them, can be one of the most important decisions a corporation can make.

5

THE ADVERTISING AGENCY, MEDIA SERVICES, AND OTHER SERVICES

CHAPTER OBJECTIVES

ADVERTISING AGENCIES CREATE MOST OF THE NATIONAL AND INTERNATIONAL ADVERTISING. THEIR ROLE AND RELATIONSHIP WITH MARKETERS IS CHANGING. AFTER READING THIS CHAPTER YOU WILL UNDERSTAND

- the agency
- the history of the agency business
- the full-service agency
- global advertising agencies
- agency and client relationships
- forms of agency compensation
- other advertising services.

The 1990s have been a period of business turmoil—mergers, partnerships, short-term pressures on the bottom line, employee cutbacks, management reorganizations, and an increasing emphasis on global marketing, and so forth—at companies across the country and globe. The editor of *Fast Company* magazine characterizes the times, "We're living through the most radical business revolution in the last 100 years."[1] When you have new corporate structure and new managers, you also affect the marketing process and the advertising agencies involved. Agencies have undergone their own reengineering, adapting to the environment within which they operate and to the clients they serve. Not only have agencies changed their structures, many have gobbled up specialty firms such as health-care, on-line, mail-order, and promotion companies, and other units involved in integrated communication. *Make no mistake about it, it's not business as usual. Roles and relationships are changing.* Despite all these changes, "In 1997, the U.S. advertising industry is in better shape than it's been for 30 years," says a Prudential Security analyst.[2]

---

[1]John Carroll, "Young Bucks," *Adweek,* March 3, 1997, pp. 36–37.
[2]Yumiko Ono, "Acquisitions Are Expected to Help Agencies Post Earning Increases," *The Wall Street Journal,* July 17, 1997, p. B7.

The agency remains in transition. However, despite all the changes, advertising agencies continue to be the most significant companies in the development of advertising and marketing in the world.

THE AGENCY

An *advertising agency*, as defined by the American Association of Advertising Agencies, is an independent business, composed of creative and businesspeople, who develop, prepare, and place advertising in advertising media for sellers seeking to find customers for their goods or services. West & Vaughan, a $30 million agency in Durham, N.C., created Exhibit 5.1 to inform consumers about Central Carolina Bank's tele-banking services.

According to the U.S. Census Bureau, there are more than 10,000 agencies in operation in this country. The *Standard Directory of Advertising Agencies* (also known as the *Agency Red Book*) lists 8,700 agency profiles, including full-service agencies, house agencies, media-buying services, sales-promotion agencies, and public relations firms. The *Adweek Agency Directory* lists more than 4,300 agencies and media-buying services. There are about 2,000 agencies listed in the *New York Yellow Pages* alone. Unfortunately, there isn't a single directory that lists every agency throughout the country. The majority of agencies are small one- to ten-person shops (we talk about size and services later in this chapter). You will see ads for many specialized products and services throughout this text—from consumer, medical software, and industrial products and services to candy—in which the ad agency had to become an expert in the marketing as well as the writing of the ad (for example, Exhibit 5.2, p. 114, which promotes the Electric Cooking Council).

HOW AGENCIES DEVELOPED

Before we discuss present-day agencies further, let us take a look at how advertising agencies got started and how they developed into large worldwide organizations that play such a prominent role in the marketing and advertising process.

The Early Age (Colonial Times to 1917)

It is not generally known that the first Americans to act as advertising agents were colonial postmasters:

> In many localities advertisements for Colonial papers might be left at the post offices. In some instances, the local post office would accept advertising copy for publications in papers in other places; it did so with the permission of the postal authorities. . . . William Bradford, publisher of the

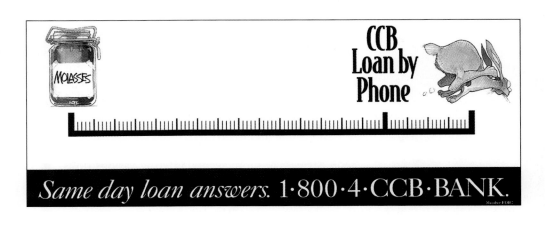

first Colonial weekly in New York, made an arrangement with Richard Nichols, postmaster in 1727, whereby the latter accepted advertisements for the New York Gazette at regular rates.[3]

Space Salesmen Volney B. Palmer is the first person known to have worked on a commission basis. In the 1840s, he solicited ads for newspapers that had difficulty getting out-of-town advertising. Palmer contacted publishers and offered to get them business for a 50 percent commission, but he often settled for less. There was no such thing as a rate card or a fixed price for space or commission in those days. A first demand for $500 by the papers might be reduced, before the bargain was struck, to $50. (Today we call that negotiation.) Palmer opened offices in Philadelphia, New York, and Boston. Soon there were more agents, offering various deals.

---

[3]James Melvin Lee, *History of American Journalism,* rev. ed. (Boston: Houghton Mifflin, 1933), p. 74.

Space Wholesalers   During the 1850s in Philadelphia, George P. Rowell bought large blocks of space for cash (most welcome) from publishers at very low rates, less agents' commissions. He would sell the space in small "squares"—one-column wide—at his own retail rate. Rowell next contracted with 100 newspapers to buy one column of space a month and sold the space in his total list at a fixed rate per line for the whole list: "An inch of space a month in one hundred papers for one hundred dollars." Selling by list became widespread. Each wholesaler's list was his private stock in trade. (This was the original media package deal.)

The First Rate Directory   In 1869 Rowell shocked the advertising world by publishing a directory of newspapers with their card rates and his own estimates of their circulation. Other agents accused him of giving away their trade secrets; publishers howled too because his estimates of circulation were lower than their claims. Nevertheless, Rowell persisted in offering advertisers an estimate of space costs based on those published rates for whatever markets they wanted. This was the beginning of the media estimate.

The Agency Becomes a Creative Center   In the early 1870s, Charles Austin Bates, a writer, began writing ads and selling his services to whoever wanted them, whether advertisers or agents. Among his employees were Earnest Elmo Calkins and Ralph Holden, who in the 1890s founded their own agency, famous for 50 years under the name of Calkins and Holden. These men did more than write ads. They brought together planning, copy, and art, showing the way to combine all three into effective advertising. Not only was their agency one of the most successful for half a century, but the influence of their work helped establish the advertising agency as the creative center for advertising ideas. Many of the names on the list of firms advertising in 1890 (see chapter 1) are still familiar today; their longevity can be attributed to the effectiveness of that generation of agency people who developed the new power of advertising agency services. The business had changed from one of salesmen going out to sell advertising space to one of agencies that created the plan, the ideas, the copy, and the artwork, produced the plates, and then placed the advertising in publications from which they received a commission.

To this day, the unique contribution to business for which agencies are most respected is their ability to create effective ads.

Agency-Client Relationship Established   In 1875, Francis Ayer established N.W. Ayer & Son (one of the larger advertising agencies today). Ayer proposed to bill advertisers for what he actually paid the publishers (that is, the rate paid the publisher less the commission), adding a fixed charge in lieu of a commission. In exchange, advertisers would agree to place all their advertising through Ayer's agents. This innovation established the relationship of advertisers as clients of agencies rather than as customers who might give their business to various salespeople, never knowing whether they were paying the best price.

The Curtis No-Rebating Rule   In 1891, the Curtis Publishing Company announced that it would pay commissions to agencies only if they agreed to collect the full price from advertisers, a rule later adopted by the Magazine Publishers of America. This was the forerunner of no-rebating agreements, which were an important part of the agency business for more than 50 years. (Agency commissions, however, ranged from 10 to 25 percent in both magazines and newspapers.)

Standard Commissions for Recognized Agencies Established   In 1917, newspaper publishers, through their associations, set 15 percent as the standard agency commission, a percentage that remains in effect for all media to this day (except local advertising, for which the media deal directly with the stores and pay no commission).

case HISTORY

Greg & Greg Advertising, Greensville, S.C., wrote a children's story to recruit prospective clients, "Digging to Reach the Top"—a story with a message (their symbol is a star over a shovel). Greg & Greg's seasoned strategy and development executive, Brad Majors, says he has never seen such a response to their simple story for creating new business interest. The story starts:

> *Beyond your knees, past your feet,*
> *Just below your toes,*
> *Digging in the fresh, brown dirt*
> *Where the green grass grows,*
>
> *Lived persistent little Doodle*
> *Whose love it was to dig,*
> *And digging he did daily*
> *With hopes of something big.*

The last page raises the question: What can we learn from Doodle? They continue: "We think two important 'surprising truths' emerge from "Digging to Reach the Top."

1. *Those who succeed don't have to be the most beautiful, the smartest, or the most talented. They just have to work with faith and 'purposeful diligence' to meet their objectives.*
2. *Sometimes the best results are achieved from an approach that may, at first, seem quite unconventional.*

"At Greg & Greg Advertising, you'll find a group of smart talented, and (some say) attractive professionals who are persistent in their mission. . . . Need some help digging to reach your star?"

Courtesy: Greg & Greg Advertising.

The commission would be granted, however, only to agencies that the publishers' associations "recognized." One of the important conditions for recognition was an agency's agreement to charge the client the full rate (no rebating). Other criteria for recognition were that the agency must have business to place, must have shown competence in handling advertising, and must be financially sound. These three conditions are still in effect. Anyone may claim to be an agency, but only agencies that are recognized are allowed to charge a commission.

Today's agencies still receive commissions from the media for space they buy for clients. However, artwork and the cost of production are generally billed by the agency to the advertiser, plus a service charge—usually 17.65 percent of the net, which is equivalent to 15 percent of the gross. By preagreement, a charge is made for other services.

The American Association of Advertising Agencies The most important agency association is the **American Association of Advertising Agencies** (sometimes known as AAAA or 4As), established in 1917. This organization has continuously acted as a great force in improving the standards of agency business and advertising practice. Its members, large and small, place more than 80 percent of all national advertising today.

The No-Rebate Age (1918–1956)

The events of this era that left their mark on today's agency world are summarized here.

Radio One of the main events of 1925 was the notorious Scopes trial, and the main advent was radio. They did a lot for each other. Radio dramatized evolution-on-trial in Tennessee; it brought the issue of teaching scientific evolution home to Americans and it brought people closer to their radios. Tuning in to radio soon became a major part of American life, especially during the Great Depression and World War II. Radio established itself as a prime news vehicle. It also gave advertising a vital new medium and helped pull agencies through those troubled years. A number of agencies handled the entire production of a radio program as well as its commercials. By 1942, agencies were billing more for radio advertising ($188 million) than they were for newspaper advertising ($144 million). The radio boom lasted until television came along.

Television Television became popular after 1952, when nationwide network broadcasts began. Between 1950 and 1956, television was the fastest-growing medium. It became the major medium for many agencies. National advertisers spent more on television than they did on any other medium. TV expenditures grew from $171 million in 1950 to $1,225 million in 1956.

Electronic Data Processing The computer entered advertising through the accounting department. By 1956, it was already changing the lives of the media department, the marketing department, and the research department—all having grown in competence with the increasing number of syndicated research services. Agencies prided themselves on their research knowledge and were spending hundreds of thousands of dollars for research every year to service their clients better.

Business was good, and American consumers were attaining a better standard of living than they had ever enjoyed. The period from 1950 to 1956 proved to be the beginning of the biggest boom advertising ever had. Total expenditures jumped from $4.5 billion in 1950 to $9.9 billion in 1956. More than 60 percent of this spending was national advertising placed by advertising agencies. And the agency business was good, too.

The Age of Negotiation (1956–1990)

Consent Decrees In 1956, a change occurred in the advertiser-agency relationship. The U.S. Department of Justice held that the no-rebating provision between media associations and agencies limited the ability to negotiate between buyer and seller and therefore was in restraint of trade and a violation of antitrust laws. Consent decrees to stop no-rebating provisions were entered into by all media associations on behalf of their members.

Although the Justice Department's ruling in no way affected the 15 percent that commission agencies were accustomed to getting from the media, it opened the way to review the total compensation an agency should receive for its services, with the 15 percent commission a basic part of the negotiations. Later we look at the effects this has had on the agency-client relationship.

The Reengineering Age

Integrated Services The 1990s has been about agencies reevaluating how they operate. Integrated services has been a buzzword relating to efforts to coordinate a client's entire marketing mix, including public relations, promotion, direct marketing, package design, and so on. Some agencies have expanded their communication services to clients by expanding departments or buying or creating subsidiary companies that enable them to offer sales promotion, public relations, direct marketing, logo and packaging design, and even television programming. One of the reasons is financial—clients have been moving dollars from advertising to promotion, and clients want their communications integrated. Agencies are trying to change to supply those needs.

Interactive Communications As cable, computers, satellite communication, video technologies, and the like become global, agencies are having to learn how to use this technology for their clients. This involves understanding the hardware of how interactive services are delivered; the message development, which will be different from traditional advertising; and the interactive consumer. The future will be different.

THE FULL-SERVICE AGENCY

Full-service agency
One that handles planning, creation, production, and placement of advertising for advertising clients. May also handle sales promotion and other related services as needed by client.

In the simplest terms, the **full-service agency** offers clients all the services necessary to handle the total advertising function—planning, creation, production, placement, and evaluation. Many have expanded this to include the management of all integrated marketing communications. Today, integrated marketing makes it possible to manage the product's message through a variety of disciplines—advertising, promotion, direct marketing, public relations, and so forth—with a tight strategic marketing focus so that the brand image is reinforced every time the consumer is exposed to a communication.

Many agencies have concluded that the next generation of advertising requires a new concept of the role and responsibilities of an advertising agency. A new mission demands a different organization. As we have said, many agencies have undergone a restructuring or reengineering in recent years. Most believe that brand building is impossible without creative, persuasive advertising, which is with few exceptions the most potent component in the marketing communication mix. Despite the restructuring, most marketers will find familiar unit names: account management, creative, media, research or account planning, and administration. But many of these agencies have changed how they operationalize the work. It still isn't brain surgery, but it does require a managed process.

First, there isn't a universal model, but let us take a look at the functions full-service agencies perform. When a new account or a new product is assigned to a full-service agency, work on it will generally proceed along the following lines.

Diagnosing the Marketing and Brand Problem

The process begins with the collection of all that you know about the product category, the brand, and its competitors. Research takes the lead, looking at consumer attitudes to develop penetrating insights into the prospects and defining the brand's core: Who

exhibit

5.3

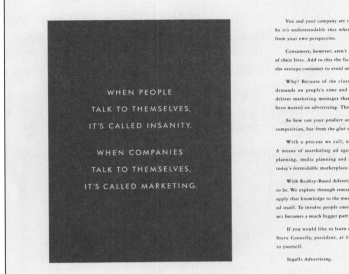

Ingalls promotes their reality-based advertising, which is based on their research abilities, to potential clients.

Courtesy: Ingalls Advertising.

are the prime prospects? Where are they? What are their demographics and psychographic characteristics? How does the product fit into their lifestyles? How do they regard this type of product? This particular brand? Competitive products? What one benefit do consumers seek from this product? This particular brand? In what distinctive way can the product solve the prime prospects' problems? What media will best reach your market? Some ad agencies sell their research capability to attract clients. An Ingalls Advertising ad (Exhibit 5.3) says: "When people talk to themselves, it's called insanity. When companies talk to themselves, it's called marketing." A sampling of their body copy states:

> You and your company are close to your product. You live it every day. So it's understandable that when you advertise that product, you tend to do it from your own perspective. . . . With Reality-Based Advertising, we don't promote who you think you want to be. We explore through research who consumers will let you become. Then we apply that knowledge to the most important part of any communication plan, the ad itself. To involve people emotionally and credibly. And the result? Your product becomes a bigger part of consumers' lives.

Setting Objectives and Developing Strategy

Using the answers to these questions, a strategy is formulated that positions the product in relation to the prime-prospect customer and emphasizes the attribute that will appeal to the prime prospect. Account management is responsible for leading this phase. Here you define what is to be accomplished strategically, such as intensifying brand imagery and recapturing prior users, and plan how to carry it out. These strategic dialogues involve teams of account, creative, media, and research people.

Creating the Communication

Once the overall strategy is determined, you decide on the creative strategy, write copy, and prepare rough layouts and storyboards. In advertising, the creative impulse is always disciplined—an imaginative and persuasive expression of the selling strategy and the character of the brand.

The Media Plan   You define media strategy, checking objectives to ensure that they parallel your marketing objectives. Then you select media. All traditional and nontraditional options are explored, the goal being to avoid mere execution and add value instead. Media schedules are prepared with costs. At this stage, you seek to coordinate all elements of the marketing communication mix to ensure maximum exposure. Media leads the process by developing an environment that multiplies the impact of the creative team.

The Total Plan   You present roughs of the copy, layouts, and production costs, along with the media schedules and costs—all leading to the total cost.

Evaluation Plan   The evaluation step in the process is both the end and the beginning. It is the moment of reckoning for the creative work, based on the objectives set in the beginning, and provides the evidence needed to refine and advance future efforts. As such, it is an accountable system.

Notify Trade of Forthcoming Campaign

For many product categories you would inform dealers and retailers of the campaign details early enough so that they can get ready to take advantage of the ad campaign.

Billing and Payments

When ads are run, you take care of the billing to client and payment of bills to media and production vendors. As an example of the billing procedure, let us say that through your agency an advertiser has ordered an ad in *Leisure Gourmet* magazine for one page costing $10,000. When the ad appears, the bill your agency gets from the publisher will read something like this:

1 page, August *Leisure Gourmet* magazine	$10,000
Agency commission @ 15% (cash discount omitted for convenience)	1,500
Balance Due	$ 8,500

Your agency will then bill the advertiser for $10,000, retain the $1,500 as its compensation, and pay the publisher $8,500.

The agency commission applies only to the cost of space or time. In addition, as mentioned earlier, your agency will send the advertiser a bill for production costs for such items as

- finished artwork
- typography (typesetting)
- photography
- retouching

- reproduction prints/films
- recording studios
- broadcast production

The items are billed at actual cost plus a service charge, usually 17.65 percent (which is equivalent to 15 percent of the net).

THE TRADITIONAL AGENCY ORGANIZATION

In this section, we first examine the traditional approach to the full-service agency structure, and then we look at the reengineering of this process.

Advertising agencies come in all sizes and shapes. The largest employ hundreds of people and bill thousands of millions of dollars every year. The smallest are one- or two-person operations (usually a creative person and an account manager). As they grow, they generally must add to their organizational structure to handle all the functions of a full-service agency.

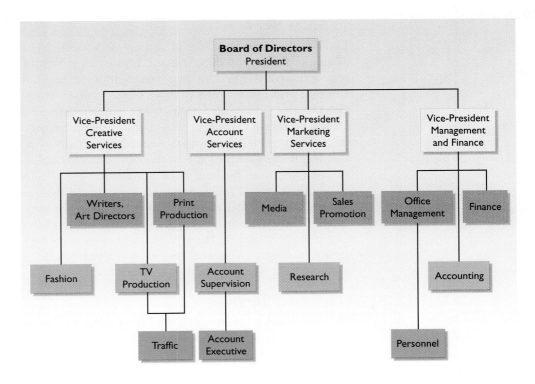

exhibit

5.4

Organization of a Typical Full-Service Agency

All agencies do not structure themselves in exactly the same manner. For discussion purposes, we have chosen a typical organizational structure under the command of major executives: the vice presidents of (1) the creative department, (2) account services, (3) marketing services, and (4) management and finance (Exhibit 5.4). We discuss briefly how each department is organized.

Creative Department

The agency creative director is almost a mythical, often legendary creature positioned near the top of the agency totem pole. The creative director is considered to be responsible for the care and feeding of its most prized possession—the creative product. Today, more than ever before, success is measured by the client's results. The creative director is expected to have an opinion on everything from sales promotion to public relations. In addition to den mother, psychologist, cheerleader, arbiter of taste, basketball coach, team player, historian, jack-of-all-trades, showman, social convener, architect, designer, and Renaissance person, today's more evolved species is also required to be a strategist, businessperson, planner, financier, and new product developer. Bill Westbrook, upon taking over as creative head of Fallon McElligott, stressed the importance of strategy: "If it's not a great strategy, it isn't a great campaign." Lee Chow, chairman and chief creative officer of TBWA/Chiat Day, says, "Managing an integrated campaign is different from doing just ads, as creative directors we've become joined at the hip with account planners."[4]

At first, all writers and artists will work right under one creative director; but as the business grows, various creative directors will take over the writing and art activities of different brands. A traffic department will be set up to keep the work flowing on schedule.

The print production director and the TV manager also report to the creative director, who is ultimately responsible for the finished product—ads and commercials.

---

[4]Ann Cooper, "Bernbach's Children Come of Age," *Adweek,* March 25, 1996, pp. 33–36.

Account Services

The vice president in charge of account services is responsible for the relationship between the agency and the client and is indeed a person of two worlds: the client's business and advertising. This vice president must be knowledgeable about the client's business, profit goals, marketing problems, and advertising objectives. He or she is responsible for helping to formulate the basic advertising strategy recommended by the agency, for seeing that the proposed advertising prepared by the agency is on target, and for presenting the total proposal—media schedules, budget, and rough ads or storyboards—to the client for approval. Then comes the task of making sure that the agency produces the work to the client's satisfaction.

As the business grows and takes on many clients, an account supervisor will appoint account executives to serve as the individual contacts with the various accounts. Account executives must be skillful at both communications and follow-up. Their biggest contribution is keeping the agency ahead of its client's needs. But the account supervisor will continue the overall review of account handling, maintaining contacts with a counterpart at the client's office (Exhibit 5.5).

Marketing Services

The vice president in charge of marketing services is responsible for media planning and buying, for research, and for sales promotion. The marketing vice president will appoint a media director, who is responsible for the philosophy and planning of the use of media, for the selection of specific media, and for buying space and time. As the agency grows, there will be a staff of media buyers, grouped according to media (print, TV, or radio), accounts, or territory. The media staff will include an estimating department and an ordering department, as well as a department to handle residual payments due performers. The media head may use independent media services, especially in the purchase of TV and radio time.

The research director will help define marketing and copy goals. Agencies usually use outside research organizations for field work, but in some agencies, research and

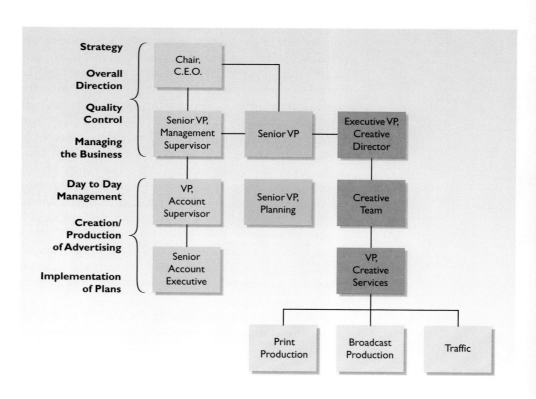

exhibit
5.5

Typical Team Responsibilities

In some agencies, the account planner works directly with creative to provide research and consumer viewpoints.

media planning are coordinated under one person. The division of work among the executives may vary with the agency.

The sales-promotion director takes care of premiums, coupons, and other dealer aids and promotions.

Management and Finance

Like all businesses, an advertising agency needs an administrative head to take charge of financial and accounting control, office management, and personnel (including trainees).

THE REENGINEERING OF THE AGENCY

During the past decade a number of attempts have been made to reengineer the agency. At this time, there isn't a standard structure brought about by reengineering or even a desire by most agencies to radically restructure. Some of the efforts have been successful and others have been questionable. For example, D'Arcy Masius Benton & Bowles several years ago restructured around brand teams; although they later decided to return to a more traditional pyramid structure, which better served clients such as Procter & Gamble. However, the driving force behind any reengineering is the desire to meet the wants and needs of clients cheaper, faster, and better.

A few years ago, Jay Chiat, a pioneer in agency reengineering, said:

> We believe the hierarchical structure [of the traditional agency], if not obsolete at present, is on its way. The traditional pyramid is about personal power and focuses on how to run a business. Therefore most decisions are about the organization's needs, concentrating on fiscal and administrative issues. An agency is a service organization whose sole existence depends on satisfying client needs.[5]

What Does Reengineering Do?

It sets up a process whereby the top management of agencies is in direct contact with clients instead of functioning only as administrators. In traditional agencies, senior managers spend 15 to 20 percent of their time on client business. In reengineered agencies, they spend about 60 percent of their time in the trenches working on client business. Middle managers in reengineered agencies act as coaches, team leaders, and quality control managers. One of the significant changes is that creative staff, account managers, and media planners must work together as a *team*—a team of people working together to rapidly solve problems. Most agency reengineers say their teams consist of 8 to 12 people, although Sawyer Riley Compton uses teams called *account circles* of about 20. Most agencies' reengineered structure is somewhat similar to traditional structure. It is how business works that is different. People don't do their thing in isolation; they approach problem solving together. The team concept often helps younger people because it allows them to work side by side with senior people.

Leo Burnett, with billings of almost $6 billion, and 83 full-service offices in 72 international markets, announced a reorganization into "miniagencies" built around brand teams. Each miniagency has its own management and will be staffed with personnel from client services, planning, creative, and production; it also includes specialists from the media division. The groups no longer are housed in their respective departments on different floors, but are grouped together and dedicated to a single piece of business.[6]

---

[5]Jeff Weiner, "Anxious Ranks," *Agency,* Spring 1994, p. 42.
[6]"CEO Fizdale Outlines Plan at Gathering," *Advertising Age,* September 2, 1997, p. 10.

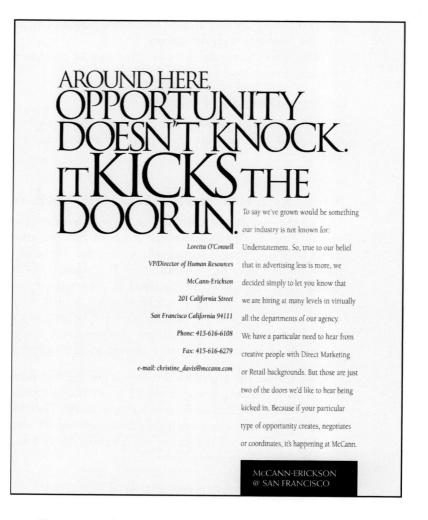

Changing technology also plays an important part in most restructuring efforts. The linking of teams and clients electronically and the reduction of the time and cost of producing advertising is part of the effort to use technology effectively. McCann-Erickson Worldwide began a program to electronically link its offices in 117 countries to give the agency and its clients quick access to information. Prior to this effort, it had more than 70 separate computer systems operating around the globe.[7] Exhibit 5.6 illustrates how agencies seek good people in many areas to build their teams. The McCann-Erickson San Francisco ad says, "we decided simply to let you know that we are hiring at many levels in virtually all the departments of our agency. We have a particular need to hear from creative people with Direct Marketing or Retail backgrounds. But those are just two of the doors we'd like to hear being kicked in."

As with any new management trend, traditional agencies will copy and modify those reengineering structures that have been successful to meet their specific needs. There is little doubt that the agency structure in the future will not be a copy of today's.

How Is Reengineering Different?

The job function doesn't radically change in the reengineered agency. There is a significant shift, however, in how that job function relates to others in the process. For example, under the traditional structure, an account person may meet regularly with creative people to discuss strategy and ad copy, or with media people to review scheduling,

---

[7]Bradley Johnson, "McCann to Link Computers via IBM," *Advertising Age,* September 15, 1997, p. 32.

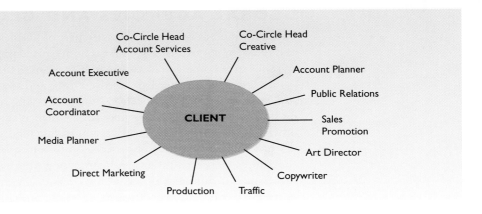

exhibit

5.7

Sawyer Riley Compton Account Circle Approach

or separately with the public relations person. In some cases, there might be a meeting where specific players in the process meet to discuss a problem or progress. In most reengineered operations, on the other hand, the key people on the team meet on a regular basis so that everyone knows what is going on in every aspect of the account. Richard Riley says the account circle at Sawyer Riley Compton meets every Monday morning to review the week's work—and meets again when necessary. This means the sales promotion person knows about the public relations work, and the art director knows about media planning. If necessary, the client participates in the review. Exhibit 5.7 shows the players on a typical account circle team. One of the pluses in this process is that everyone on the team—senior or junior staffer—understands every function in the process and how their work relates to everyone else's work. In theory, a client could call anyone on the team to get an answer. Sawyer Riley Compton specializes in business-to-business marketing, which may involve ads (see Exhibit 5.8), public relations, direct response, promotion, or other functions. The team circle keeps everyone involved and in the know. Exhibit 5.8 shows an example of Sawyer Riley Compton's work. This ad for Snap-on Industrial tools focuses on the Snap-on rep: "Because your Snap-on rep is a problem-solver with years of experience. Not an order-taker."

exhibit

5.8

This *Business-to-Business* ad creatively tells readers that Snap-on Industrial's reps solve problems. "The right people. The right tools. The right answer."

Courtesy: Sawyer Riley Compton and Snap-on Tools.

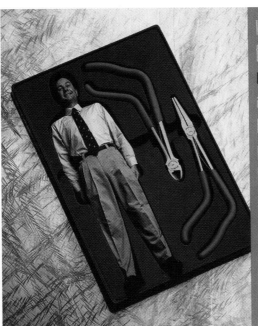

GLOBAL AGENCIES AND GLOBAL MARKETS

Globalization has become a necessary part of business and advertising. The demands on marketers to survive in a global economy place pressures on large and medium-sized agencies to become global partners. It is more than simply a language problem. Companies and agencies need to learn cultural and market patterns and understand consumers from a global perspective. Someone trying to sell burgers, fries, and soft drinks outside of the United States may think there is no competition because there are no other burger outlets. The local version of fast food may not include hamburgers at all; the real competition may be a rice shop or a tacqueria.

Unless marketers understand competing sources for that same dollar, they won't be successful.[8] It can be complex. Many small to medium agencies who don't have the resources for international offices have made affiliations with agencies or independent agency networks throughout the world to service clients and give advice. If an agency doesn't have the resources to help clients engage in international marketing, then the client is likely to turn to other agencies that do have the resources and knowledge, or the client may seek a local agency in the country where they are doing business. Major agencies have been global in nature for decades, if not longer, to service their clients' international needs.

J. Walter Thompson opened its first office outside the United States in 1891 in London. It now has 206 offices in 78 countries. They have developed international offices and a system to manage a client's global business that includes

1. *global teams.* JWT can help clients achieve their communications objectives virtually anywhere in the world.
2. *director-in-charge system.* JWT uses an account director, who is the director-in-charge (DIC) on a global scale. These people operate as heads of an "agency within the agency," working with all offices to service global clients. The DICs work closely with their regional directors, local office CEOs, and account directors in each country to make sure the agency's network comes together seamlessly to execute a multinational advertiser's global communications efforts to build its business.
3. *regional directors.* The JWT regional directors have the responsibility for a specific group of countries. The CEOs of JWT's offices in that region report to the regional director.
4. *global directors.* Each worldwide client is represented by a global business director, who sits on the JWT worldwide executive group. The DIC reports to the global business director, whose role is to ensure that the full resources of the JWT global network are brought to bear in servicing multinational accounts.

In chapter 24, we deal extensively with international operations.

The leading international advertising centers ranked in terms of local advertising billings are New York and Tokyo—fighting neck and neck for world leadership. These two advertising giants are followed by London, Paris, Chicago, Los Angeles, Detroit, San Francisco, Minneapolis, Frankfurt, São Paulo, Düsseldorf, Madrid, and Seoul. Almost every country has an advertising agency center. For U.S. agencies, setting up a foreign office can be very complex. Each country is a different market, with its own language, buying habits, ways of living, mores, business methods, marketing traditions, and laws. So instead of trying to organize new agencies with American personnel, most U.S. agencies purchase a majority or minority interest in a successful foreign agency. They usually have a top management person as head of an overseas office. Key members of the international offices regularly meet for intensive seminars on the philosophy and operation of the agency, and share success stories. Remember, good marketing ideas can come from any place. The United States doesn't have a lock on great ideas.

---

[8]Jan Larson, "It's a Small World, After All," *Marketing Tools,* September 1997, pp. 47–51.

Cost efficiencies in production of global advertising motivate advertisers to seek a single world execution. A single execution also helps build the same global brand equity. However, "every international brand starts out as a successful local brand . . . reproduced many times."[9] Being a global advertiser and having one global campaign sounds easy. But it is not. Despite being a global advertiser for many decades, it was only in 1992 that Coca-Cola launched its first global advertising campaign—*all the ads being similar in each country.* Exhibit 5.9 shows an ad developed by the Coca-Cola Company–Japan. In 1994, Chanel No. 5 (perfume) was having problems with its global advertising campaign because they were taking a manufacturer approach instead of a consumer approach. A brand and its advertising must be presented in relevant and meaningful ways in the context of local environments, or consumers won't care. As many experienced multinational marketers such as Unilever, Gillette, and Nestlé know, for any given brand, advertising that elicits the same response from consumers across borders matters much more than running the same advertising across borders. That may mean using the same brand concept or advertising concept and similar production format

---

[9]Ashish Banerjee, "Global Campaigns Don't Work; Multinationals Do," *Advertising Age,* April 18, 1994, p. 23.

across borders, but the executions need to be customized to local markets so the consumers can relate to and empathize with the advertising. Simply translating American ads into foreign languages has proved dangerous. Perdue's (Chicken) Spanish translation of "It takes a tough man to make a tender chicken," actually said, "It takes a sexually excited man to make a chick affectionate."

It is only logical that multinational clients want their agencies to know how to develop great advertising campaigns that can run across all the principal markets of the world. As the chairperson of Leo Burnett International said, "As the world gets smaller, there needs to be brand consistency so people don't get confused as they move from market [country] to market."[10] The result of this need is pressure on U.S. agencies to produce, place, and research global advertising. A sampling of BBDO Worldwide's offices that enable them to service marketers across the globe is shown in the following table.

BBDO Worldwide Sampling of Domestic and International Offices and Affiliates

United States	Africa	Asia	Europe	Latin America	Canada
Atlanta	Johannesburg	Beijing	Oslo	Buenos Aires	Toronto
Chicago		Sydney	Vienna	Caracus	
Los Angeles		Hong Kong	Brussels	Santiago	
Miami		Bangkok	Budapest	Bogota	
Minneapolis		Jakarta	Copenhagen	Mexico City	
New York		Kuala Lumpur	Moscow	San Jose	
Southfield, Mich.		Singapore	Prague	Lima	
		Taipei	Stockholm	San Salvador	
			London	San Juan	
			Lisbon	Guatemala City	
			Paris	Managua	

COMPETING ACCOUNTS

The client-agency relationship is a professional one. It may involve new product strategies, new promotions, sales data, profit or loss information, and new marketing strategies—information that is sensitive and confidential. As a result, most clients will not generally approve of an agency's handling companies or products in direct competition; Coca-Cola isn't going to allow their agencies to handle Pepsi products. In some cases, agencies will handle accounts for the same type of product or service if they do not compete directly—for example, banks that do not compete in the same market. Many agency-client conflicts result from mergers in which one merger partner handles an account for a product that competes with a product being handled by the other merger partner. When agencies consider merging, the first question is, "Will any of our accounts conflict?" The recent merger of True North Communications and Bozell, Jacobs, Kenyon & Eckhardt forced True North's Foote, Cone & Belding (FCB) agency to resign the $240 million Mazda Motor of North America account. Bozell's key account was Chrysler Corporation. Chrysler objected to a linkup with an agency holding company involved with Ford Motor Company. Likewise, Ford, which owns 33 percent of Mazda, also raised concerns about seeing FCB even indirectly connected to Chrysler. Sounds complicated and it is. There are a number of large national agencies with independent offices around the country that hope clients will not view the same type of account in another office as a conflict; in the case of Chrysler and Ford, that didn't work.

---

[10]"Coke Seeks Ad Formula with Global Appeal," *Atlanta Journal-Constitution,* November 18, 1991, p. A5.

AGENCY-CLIENT RELATIONSHIP LENGTH

Clients generally keep agencies as long as the relationship seems to be working. However, most contracts allow for a 90-day cancellation by either party if the relationship goes sour. At the same time, agencies can resign an account if they differ with the client's goals and the account isn't profitable. American Association of Advertising Agencies research has indicated that the average tenure of client-agency relationships has declined from 7.2 years to 5.3 years since 1984. Yet in 1997, advertising's oldest continuing client relationships included the following:

Oldest Continuing Client–Agency Relationships (as of 1997)

Marketer	Agency	Duration (years)
Unilever	J. Walter Thompson Co.	95
Sunkist	Foote, Cone & Belding	90
Exxon	McCann-Erickson Worldwide	85
Del Monte	McCann-Erickson Worldwide	80
Armstrong World Industries	BBDO Worldwide	80
Other Selected Long-Term Relationships		
General Electric	BBDO Worldwide	77
Levi's	Foote, Cone & Belding	67
Kellogg	J. Walter Thompson Co.	67
Kodak	J. Walter Thompson Co.	43
McDonald's	DDB Needham Worldwide	27

Source: Advertising Age, January 27, 1997, pp. 3, 42.

AGENCY OF RECORD

In some instances, large advertisers may employ a number of agencies to handle their advertising for various divisions and products. To coordinate the total media buy and the programming of products in a network buy, the advertiser will appoint one agency as the agency of record. This lead agency will make the corporate contracts under which other agencies will issue their orders, keep a record of all the advertising placed, and communicate management's decisions on the allotment of time and space in a schedule. On the McDonald's fast-food account, DDB Needham is the lead agency, with about 66 percent of the business, and Leo Burnett handles about 33 percent. For this service, the other agencies pay a small part of their commissions (usually 15 percent of 15 percent) to the agency of record.

AGENCY MULTIPLE OFFICES

Many major agencies have agency offices in cities throughout the United States. Foote Cone & Belding is typical, with major offices in New York, Chicago, and San Francisco. Ogilvy & Mather has offices in New York, Chicago, Detroit, Atlanta, Houston, and Los Angeles. For the most part, each office functions as an autonomous agency that serves different clients and is able to draw on the talents and services of the other offices. As a rule, these offices don't normally work on the same project for the same client. Whereas the parent organizations are busily marketing themselves as global networks, each local office fiercely tries to protect its unique culture. As Foote, Cone & Belding's CEO puts it, "We have a very New York agency; a very Chicago agency; and a very San Francisco agency. When agencies succeed in putting two or more offices together on a project, a New York office is usually involved." This most commonly occurs on the media side. In fact, some offices will make media buys in their region of the country for all of the agency's offices. BBDO's chairman says, "It's no secret that BBDO in Los Angeles is our best agency in terms of print creative. Why shouldn't we make that expertise available to clients from other offices?"[11] It may be said that because each office handles different kinds of accounts, each office probably has different specialties that could be leveraged on behalf of all clients. But as a general rule, each office works primarily on its own accounts.

A few agencies recently created new West Coast offices to take advantage of the many talents that exist there. These offices are evolving as creative idea centers to help clients in any of the agency brand's offices develop stronger creative products.

AGENCY NETWORKS

In general, the agency networks consist primarily of small and medium-sized agencies that have working agreements with each other to help with information gathering and sharing. Usually there is only one network member in each market or region. The Leading Independent Agency Network is an organization of independent agencies that bills at least $50 million. Only one member is allowed per region of the country. The Mutual Advertising Agency Network provides a way for member agencies to share experience, knowledge, and other ideas with agencies in other parts of the country and the world. They provide a network of information and financial skills used to enhance agency operations.

The Mega-Agency Networks

Mega-agencies have offices or networks of their offices around the world to serve clients. It all started in 1986, when a small London agency, Saatchi & Saatchi PLC, systematically grew over a two-year period to become a mega-agency network with capitalized billings of more than $13.5 billion. This was a significant change in the advertising business as it became the world's largest advertising organization for a brief period and truly changed gobal advertising. Today, the largest organizations are WWP Group (London), Omnicom Group (New York), and Dentsu (Tokyo). These and other mega-advertising organizations own many advertising agencies throughout the world. Some of the holdings of the Interpublic Group of Companies and Omnicom Group are listed here:

Interpublic Group	**Omnicom Group**
Ammirati Puris Lintas	Baxter, Gurian & Mazzei
Dailey & Associates	BBDO Worldwide
Long Haymes Carr	Goodby Silverstein & Partners
The Lowe Group	Bernard Hodes Advertising
The Martin Agency	Merkley Newman Harty
McCann-Erickson Worldwide	TBWA/Chiat Day

Mega-agencies offer several advantages to their clients other than sheer size. Among the most important are a greater reservoir of talent and an ability to shift portions of accounts from one agency to another without going through the time-consuming, and often confusing, agency review. (Coca-Cola has switched assignments for its brands among several Interpublic agencies and given new product assignments to others.) There are also some disadvantages for clients, the most important of which is conflicts with competing accounts.

Size, in itself, doesn't have significant advantages or disadvantages in developing the ads themselves. All agencies—large or small—consist of small units or teams that work on an assigned account or group of accounts. The ability of the team and the dedication

---

[11]Mark Gleason, "Agency Nets Puzzle over Brand Identity," *Advertising Age,* May 6, 1996, p. 15.

to creative and professional excellence are dictated by the talent and innovative abilities of individuals, not the size of their company. Obviously, size and structure of an agency will attract or repel clients, depending on what level and quality of services they are seeking. The agency business is simply mirroring business in general by diversifying, economizing, and becoming more efficient and profitable.

OTHER ADVERTISING SERVICES

New services are continually springing up in competition with advertising agencies. Each new service is designed to serve clients' needs a little differently. This competition has impacted agency structure and operations.

Talent and Production Agencies Creating Creative

A hot new wrinkle in the melding of talent sources to develop ad concepts began about a decade ago and since then has cooled somewhat as major competition to agencies. Creative Artists Agency (CAA), a production and talent agency involving entertainment stars, writers, directors, and others made inroads with Coca-Cola as a working partner with Coke's advertising agencies, in some cases independently developing advertising concepts and commercials. CAA usurped McCann-Erickson Worldwide's creative stronghold on the Coca-Cola Classic account. McCann had been totally responsible for developing Coca-Cola Classic's creative. The 1993 Coke-guzzling polar bears were created by both Coke's agency and CAA. A number of other talent agencies have had working agreements with marketers and their advertising agencies to provide creative and talent services. CAA as it was created does not exist today. Some industry insiders believe such talent agency relationships can add another dimension to the advertising agency and client resources.

Independent Creative Services

Some advertisers seek top creative talent on a freelance, per-job basis. Many creative people do freelance work in their off hours. Some make it a full-time job and open their own *creative shop* or *creative boutique*. In general, the creative boutique has no media department, no researchers, and no account executives. The purpose is strictly to develop creative ideas for their clients.

À La Carte Agency

Today, many agencies offer for a fee just the part of their total services that advertisers want. The à la carte arrangement is used mostly for creative services and for media planning and placement. Many agencies are spinning off their media departments into independent divisions to seek clients interested only in media handling. Handling only the media portion of an account typically brings commissions that range from 3 to 5 percent.

In-House Agency

In-house agency
An arrangement whereby the advertiser handles the total agency function by buying individually, on a fee basis, the needed services (for example, creative, media services, and placement) under the direction of an assigned advertising director.

When advertisers found that all the services an agency could offer were purchasable on a piecemeal fee basis, they began setting up their own internal agencies, referred to as *in-house agencies*. The **in-house agency** can employ a creative service to originate advertising for a fee or markup. They can buy the space or time themselves or employ a media-buying service to buy time or space and place the ads. As a rule, the in-house agency is an administrative center that gathers and directs varying outside services for its operation and has a minimum staff.

Folks, Inc., an Atlanta restaurant company with two different restaurant concepts, had an agency. Then it created an in-house agency, which developed all creative

concepts, copy, layout ideas, radio scripts, and so forth (Exhibit 5.10). It used art studios and graphic computer services to produce the finished art, and broadcast production companies for its broadcasts. It bought all print media in-house and used a media-buying service to place its broadcast buys. It also developed all direct mail, store marketing, public relations, and promotion. Recently Folks found a need for strategic marketing services and hired an advertising agency to assist in strategic development for one of its restaurant concepts. The agency then created advertisements, produced advertising, and bought media.

In-house agencies are generally created to save money or give advertisers more control over every aspect of their business. Many industrial companies have highly technical products that constantly undergo technological changes and advances; it may well be more efficient to have in-house technical people prepare ads. This saves endless briefings that would be necessary if outside industrial writers were used. But the companies place their ads through an agency of their choice, at a negotiated commission.

Rolodex Agency

An agency run by several advertising specialists, usually account and/or creative people, that has no basic staff is called a *Rolodex agency.* It hires specialists—in marketing, media planning, creative strategy, writing, art direction, whatever—who work on a project basis. The concept is similar to hiring freelance creative people to execute ads, except that the experts are hired as needed. The Rolodex agency claims to be able to give advertisers expertise that small full-service agencies cannot match.

Media-Buying Services

There has been significant growth of independent media services outside traditional advertising agencies in recent years. These services developed with the rapid growth of television in the 1960s and put pressure on agency media directors for the best deal. They handle such tasks as media planning and buying. These services promote themselves as specialists in that the media are their business, and their only business. By one estimate, outside media services will handle media buys representing 10 to 12 percent of all domestic advertising billings by the year 2000.[12]

Agency media directors have been under great pressure to make the most effective use of their budgets by planning, placing, and negotiating the best deal for a media schedule. Negotiations have become such an art that many agency media directors have left their agencies to form media-buying services.

In-House Services

A few large advertisers have taken the media buying function in-house so they will have more control over the buying operation. However, this doesn't appear to be a trend. It is more likely that advertisers will keep a seasoned media consultant on staff to ride herd on their agency or media service's performance.

Agency Media Groups

It is fairly common in Europe for agencies to jointly buy media through a combined media buying group. The combined efforts give the agencies more media-buying clout, resulting in media savings for their clients. If this concept is to be successful, it must overcome client conflicts from within the participating agencies.

FORMS OF AGENCY COMPENSATION

Historically, agency compensation has been fairly standardized since the 1930s. An agency received a commission from the media for advertising placed by the agency. The commission would cover the agency's copywriting and account services charges. This method of compensation has been unsatisfactory during recent years due to the changing nature of business. The straight 15 percent remains, but in some instances there are fixed commissions less than 15 percent (some large advertisers have negotiated a rate closer to 10 percent), sliding scales based upon client expenditures, flat-fee arrangements agreed upon by clients and agency, performance-based systems, and labor-based

---

[12]Stuart Elliott, "A Tug-of-War between Traditional Agencies and New Media Services," *The New York Times,* January 21, 1993, p. C18.

fee-plus-profit arrangements. In other words, compensation arrangements now take many forms. Despite this change, there are only two basic forms of advertising agency compensation: *commissions* and *fees.*

● *Media commissions.* The traditional 15 percent commission remains a form of agency income, especially for modestly budgeted accounts. Clients and agency may agree to a relationship in which the rate is fixed at less than 15 percent. This generally applies to large budget accounts—the larger the budget, the lower the rate for the agency. With a sliding-scale commission agreement, the agency receives a fixed commission based upon a certain expenditure. After that level of spending, the commission is reduced (there may be a 14 percent commission for the first $20 million spent by the client and a 7 percent commission on the next $15 million). The combinations are endless.

● *Production commissions or markups.* As indicated earlier, agencies subcontract production work (all outside purchases such as type, photography, illustrators) and charge the client the cost plus a commission—17.65 percent is the norm.

● *Fee arrangements.* At times, the 15 percent commission is not enough for agencies to make a fair profit. For example, it may cost an agency more to serve a small client than a large one. The agency and client may negotiate a fee arrangement. In some cases it is a commission plus a fee. There are a number of options: A *cost-based fee* includes the agency's cost for servicing the account plus a markup, a *cost-plus fee* covers the agency cost and a fixed profit; a *fixed fee* is an agreed-upon payment based on the type of work being done (for example, copywriting at hourly fixed rates, artwork charges based on the salary of the involved personnel); and a *sliding fee* is based on a number of agreed-upon parameters. Again, there are many possibilities based on agency and client needs.

● *Performance fee.* A predetermined performance goal may determine the compensation fee. For example, ad recall scores, unit sales, or market share may determine the level of compensation. If the agency meets the goals, compensation may be at the 15 percent level; if it exceeds them, a bonus could give the agency a 20 percent level; if it fails to meet the goals, compensation could be much less than 15 percent.

All Coca-Cola agencies are on fees plus bonuses. This payment system allows the agencies not to worry if Coke cuts their advertising budget; it is designed to give the agency the best return on investment they get. An example of a commission plus a fee is described in the following agency contract copy:

> Internal creative services provided by [agency] shall be applied against the monthly agency fee at the prevailing hourly rates [as distinguished from services bought outside our organization]. Such services include preparation of print, radio, television production, storyboards, special comprehensive layouts, booklets, catalogues, direct mail, sales representations, extraordinary research, package design, collateral materials, etc.

Schedule of Agency Hourly Rates

Creative director	$150
Copywriter	100
Art director	100
Production supervisor	95
Computer design	130
Type and composition	130
Computer artwork	130
Research/planning	130

Most agencies aim for a 20 percent profit on each account to cover personnel and overhead costs plus a profit. The president of Campbell-Mithun-Esty says, "There's a broad acceptance among clients that it's in their best interest that their account be profitable for their agency. The smarter client understands that's what gets it the best people on their account. That's what gets it the best service."[13]

An advertising management consultant suggests the key flaw of compensation based on the price of traditional media is the lack of a consistent relationship between income generated and the cost of providing services required by the clients. This will continue to be a problem as new media techniques are developed. He suggests agencies align their compensation with their roles as salespeople, not buyers of media, and to link agency profit goals to agreed-upon performance standards.[14]

OTHER SERVICES

Barter

Barter
Acquisition of broadcast time by an advertiser or an agency in exchange for operating capital or merchandise. No cash is involved.

One way for an advertiser or agency to buy media below the rate card price, especially in radio or television, is **barter.** For example, a barter company, Media Store, placed all the radio time for Lufthansa Airlines in return for a six-year lease on its Manhattan ticket office. The airline had too many ticket offices, and the original lease was extremely high per square foot. So the Media Store took over the lease on barter and sublet it. They then paid Lufthansa with radio time for the regular schedules they run.

The International Reciprocal Trade Association indicates there is a fast-growing trend among advertisers to barter, particularly through three-way alliances among barter companies, advertisers, and their ad agencies.

Barter houses often become brokers or wholesalers of broadcast time. They build inventories of time accumulated in various barter deals. These inventories are called *time banks,* which are made available to advertisers or agencies seeking to stretch their broadcast dollars.

One of the drawbacks of barter is that the weaker stations in a market are more apt to use it the most. Some stations will not accept barter business from advertisers already on the air in the market. Generally, the air time is poor time, although it is generally a good value at the low rate paid.

Research Services

The advertiser, the agency, or an independent research firm can conduct any needed original research. Large agencies may have substantial in-house research departments. In some, the research title has been replaced by the account planner. Account planning has a crucial role during strategy development, driving it from the consumer's point of view. The account planners are responsible for all research, including quantitative research (usage and attitude studies, tracking studies, ad testing, and sales data) as well as qualitative research (talking face-to-face to their target). On the other hand, many smaller agencies offer little in-house research staffing, although many agencies have moved to add account planners.

In addition to the syndicated research previously discussed, which regularly reports the latest findings on buyers of a product—who and where they are, how they live and buy, and what media they read, watch, and listen to—these research companies offer many custom-made research reports to advertisers and their agencies, answering their questions about their own products and advertising. Studies cover such subjects as advertising effectiveness, advertising testing, customer satisfaction, concept and product testing, premium or package design testing, image and positioning, brand equity measurement, market segmentation, strategic research, media preferences, purchasing patterns, and similar problems affecting product and advertising decisions. Exhibit 5.11 (p. 136) talks to potential clients about Ingalls' consumer research in developing a creative strategy and resulting interpretation of the ad's role in the process.

---

[13]Terrence Poltrack, "Pay Dirt," *Agency,* July/August 1991, pp. 20–25.
[14]Stan Beals, "Fresh Approaches to Agency Compensation," *Advertising Age,* August 29, 1994, p. 20.

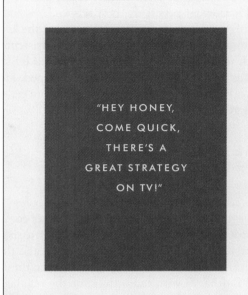

A fascinating variety of techniques is available to gather such information. They include consumer field surveys (using personal or telephone interviews or self-administered questionnaires), focus groups, consumer panels, continuous tracking studies, cable testing of commercials, image studies, electronic questionnaires, opinion surveys, shopping center intercepts, and media-mix tests. (Research techniques are discussed in chapter 15.) Regardless of the technique used in collecting data for a research report, its real value lies in the creative interpretation and use made of its findings.

Managing Integrated Brands

A brand needs a single architect, someone who will implement and coordinate a cohesive strategy across multiple media and markets. According to David Aaker, the advertising agency is often a strong candidate for this role.[15] It regularly develops brand strategy and gains insights due to exposure to different brand contexts. An advertising agency inherently provides a strong link between strategy and executions, because both functions are housed under the same roof. Strategy development in an agency is more likely to include issues of implementation. On the down side, many agencies still have a bias toward media advertising, and their experience at managing event sponsorships, direct marketing, or interactive advertising may be limited.

The challenge for today's agency is to be able to develop an integrated program that accesses and employs a wide range of communication vehicles. There are several approaches to managing this.

Agency Conglomerate Many agencies have approached the integrated communication program by acquiring companies with complementary capabilities. The usual mix includes promotions, corporate design, direct marketing, marketing research, package design, public relations, trade shows, and even event marketing. The hope is that advertisers will buy one-stop coordinated communications. The general consensus is that this approach doesn't work well, because the units that make up the conglomerate often don't blend well with each other and are rivals for the advertiser's budget, and each unit within the conglomerate isn't necessarily best suited to solve the problem at hand.

---

[15]David Aaker, "The Agency as Brand Architect," *American Advertising,* Spring 1996, pp. 18–21.

In-House Generalist Agency   Another option is to expand the agency's capabilities to include such functions as promotions and public relations. Brand teams spanning communication vehicles can then deal with the coordination issue. Hal Riney & Partners exemplified this approach with its set of promotional programs designed for Saturn. Riney was named guardian of the Saturn brand, and created ads, promotions, and a Web site, and even helped design a retail concept. This concept works if the agency has the talent to handle the new services or has the clients or revenues to support such a diverse staff.

Service Cluster   A service cluster team is a group of people drawn together from all the agency affiliate organizations. Strategically, the cluster's purpose is to service client needs, and the cluster has the flexibility to change with the needs of the client. A key characteristic of the service-cluster team is that it focuses on creating *ideas* rather than ads.

Communication Integrator   In this approach the agency draws from sources outside the agency and integrates these services for the brands.

Brand Strategy In-House

Many advertisers choose not to rely on the agency at all for managing brand strategy. Their view may be that agencies may be great at creating ads, but brand strategy may be better planned by the brand management team. If outside help is needed, their view may be that the agency may not be the best source—particularly if it has limited research resources. Some clients have found it beneficial to employ a team of specialized communication firms that each are the best in what they do. The advertiser may develop specialized expertise—including research, media buying, and strategy consulting.

SUMMARY

The advertising agency is in a period of transition. It is being reevaluated and reengineered to be more responsive to clients' needs.

A full-service agency works on many aspects of a client's marketing problems: strategy, creative response, media planning, and trade campaigns. Many agencies are organized into four divisions: account services, marketing services, creative services, and management and finance. Some agencies have a domestic network of offices or affiliates to service their large accounts better. The growing importance of global marketing to some clients has led agencies to expand internationally. Clients usually pay agencies by commission, fees, or a combination of the two.

There are other types of advertising services beside the traditional advertising agency: in-house agencies, à la carte agencies, creative boutiques, Rolodex agencies, and media-buying services. Agencies usually cannot and will not handle two accounts that compete in the same market.

REVIEW

1. What is a full-service agency?
2. What is the normal media commission?
3. What is an "agency of record"?

TAKE IT TO THE NET

We invite you to visit the Russell/Lane page on the Prentice Hall Web site at **PHLIP**   **http://www.prenhall.com/phbusiness** for the bimonthly Russell/Lane update and for this chapter's World Wide Web exercise.

case
HISTORY

Today, agencies may be asked to create ad campaigns or buy media or other services an advertiser seeks. They may not necessarily handle the national advertising campaign or be responsible for the client's total integrated marketing communication program, or they may be the main agency. Their job may be to develop a portion of the marketing communication plan, whether it be large or small. A small agency, McRae Communications located in suburban Atlanta (Fayetteville) was asked to create a special program for a major client—in this case, a joint total communications program for two companies.

CLIENT

American Express Travel Related Services Company, Inc., and the American Automobile Association (AAA), including its Canadian division, CAA.

PURPOSE/OPPORTUNITY/PROBLEM

To create an international sweepstakes involving 1,200 AAA/CAA offices in the United States and Canada.

GOALS/OBJECTIVES

- to increase total sales of American Express Travelers Cheques at AAA/CAA offices
- to promote the availability of all types of American Express Travelers Cheques and to encourage people at the offices to buy the cheques as part of their travel preparations
- to initiate interest so all branches will participate

TARGET AUDIENCES

All AAA and CAA members, especially those visiting their local branches to plan summer travel. Median age of members is 49. Median income is $42,000 to $50,000.

HOW AND WHERE USED

Point-of-sale (POS) displays were placed in the lobbies of AAA/CAA offices. Ads and press releases were supplied to each branch for use at their discretion. Seller posters (for the AAA and CAA staffs) were supplied to be displayed in break rooms and offices.

IMPLEMENTATION

McRae developed the travel-oriented Cheque, Mate! Australian theme, which then led to the development of prizes. The POS display and seller poster tout the prizes and show enticing photographs of Australia, as well as a rendering of an Australian adventurer signing an American Express Travelers Cheque. Amy Lokken wrote the copy to convey a great deal of necessary information in an engaging, easy-to-read manner, which plays on the theme. The POS display was designed as a stand-alone piece for the lobby to help cut through the clutter of posters that typically fill the walls of AAA/CAA offices. Due to the international nature of the promotion, the sales pieces were produced in three different dialects—American English, Canadian English, and French Canadian. The external promotion naturally supported an internal promotion for the travel counselors and sellers. Other pieces and items produced included a structure sheet, letters to the branches, T-shirts, pens, buttons, stickers, and entry forms.

RESULTS

The response was overwhelming. The previous year's promotion had 65 percent of the branches participating. This program had 99 percent participation. The previous year, 50,000 entries were received. This promotion generated more than 350,000 entries.

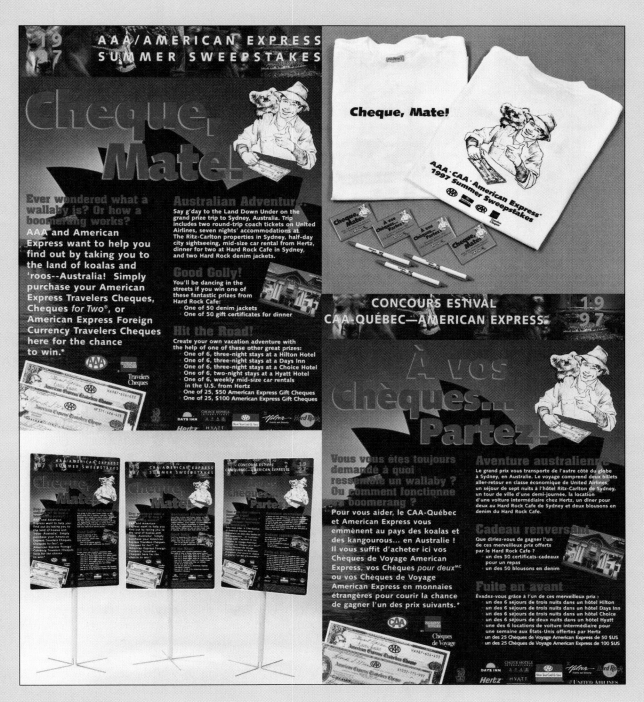

Courtesy: American Express.

6

THE ADVERTISER'S MARKETING/ADVERTISING OPERATION

CHAPTER OBJECTIVES

MARKETERS HAVE BEEN RESTRUCTURING THEIR OPERATIONS TO BE MORE COMPETITIVE. DESPITE THESE CHANGES, THE GOALS AND FUNCTIONS REMAIN ESSENTIALLY THE SAME. HERE WE LEARN ABOUT SOME FUNDAMENTALS. AFTER READING THIS CHAPTER YOU WILL UNDERSTAND

- **the marketing-service system**
- **integrated marketing brand management**
- **how advertising budgets are set**
- **advertising goals versus marketing goals**
- **agency-client relationships.**

Marketers in the 1990s have been preoccupied with competition, price pressure, and promotion, and have lost touch with consumers. Paul Higham, senior vice president–marketing and communications at Wal-Mart Stores, says, "Perhaps we should think less about our brands and more about our consumers." A Procter & Gamble (P&G) executive has said, "We've become our own worst enemy by creating a system whereby 75 percent of our dollars are trying to win the loyalty of brand switchers." P&G is returning to the tried-and-true practices of hard-sell, demographic advertising, and heavy focus on product innovation.

The 1980s and 1990s have brought all kinds of pressures to corporations. Downsizing, cost cutting, mergers, and partnerships, both domestic and foreign, have been common. The same kind of pressures have affected the marketing and advertising departments. Marketers have struggled with price wars, recession, and the growing strength of private labels. It seems no company—successful or not—has been untouched by these pressures to be more competitive. Companies have restructured and reorganized divisions and departments. Obviously, when restructuring takes place there will be changes in how they manage or handle marketing and advertising. For example, Ford now has three group managers with a number of brand managers under them: Crown Victoria brand manager, Taurus brand manager, Contour brand manager, Escort brand manager, Mustang/Thunderbird brand manager, Explorer brand manager, and Expedition brand manager. Then there is the Windstar brand manager, Ranger brand manager, F150/F250 brand manager, Econoline brand manager, F-superduty brand manager, and medium truck brand manager, as well as the tactical marketing manager and cross-vehicle strategy manager.

Prior to this system, the Ford brand managers had names such as family brand merchandise manager, sporting brand marketing plans manager, toughbrand merchandising and communication manager, and so forth.

Today everyone wants to be more efficient and competitive. For some companies it is simply a case of survival. The advertising and marketing departments control the dollars and decide on the need for an advertising agency, or in some case agencies, for different products. At times they may hire an agency to handle only creative or to place the ads in the media. They may choose to use freelancers or creative boutiques or to use a media-buying service or combine their media-buying strength for all their products with one agency. They may decide to staff an in-house agency to develop ads, as discussed in chapter 5. It is their ball game. They call the shots.

Because companies vary in size and structure, it only makes sense that advertising and marketing staffs also differ from organization to organization. They may have a large department controlling all marketing activities, or they may have limited personnel in marketing, or they may rely on operation managers or the president to make the marketing decisions. Before we complicate the process of integrated marketing structure, let us examine the typical structure.

MARKETING-SERVICES SYSTEM

With increasing structural and organizational changes in business, the results are being felt in the advertising and marketing function. The advertising department structure—the traditional system—worked well for most companies. Exhibit 6.1 illustrates this organizational structure.

However, as companies such as Procter & Gamble grew with a number of brands, this structure needed to change to solve their marketing problems. The result was a new organizational concept called the *marketing services system.* This concept has been widely adopted, especially in the package goods fields and by a number of service-oriented companies.

Under this concept, developed in 1931, each brand manager is, in essence, president of his or her own corporation-within-the-corporation. The brand manager is charged with developing, manufacturing, marketing, promoting, integrating, and selling the brand.

exhibit

6.1

Simple Organization Chart of an Advertising Department

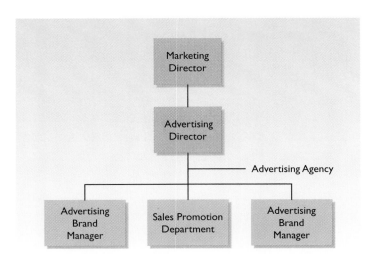

The marketing services system has two parts (Exhibit 6.2). One is the marketing activity, which begins with the product manager assigned to different brands. The other part of the structure is a structure of marketing services, which represents all the technical talent involved in implementing a marketing plan, including creative services, promotion services, media services, advertising controls, and marketing research services. All of these services are available to the product manager, as is the help from the ad-

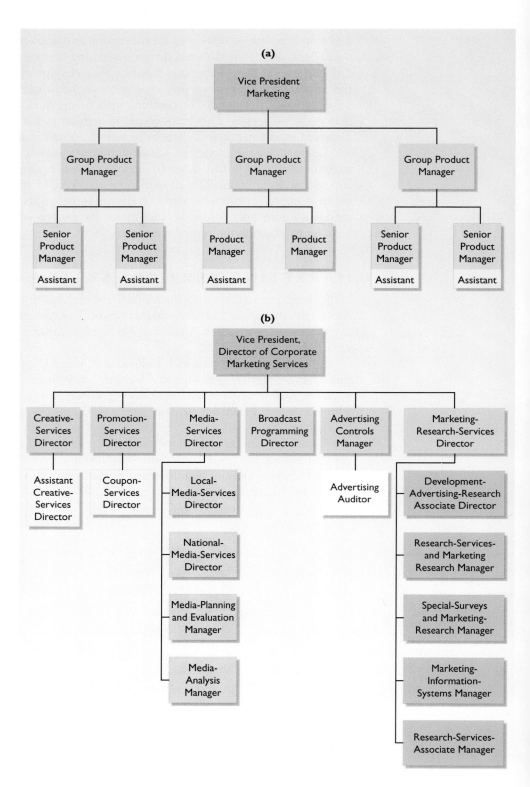

exhibit

6.2

A large company with a marketing services division may be organized into (a) a marketing department; and (b) a marketing services department, where specialists in creative, media, and research advise product managers and consult with counterparts in the agency.

vertising agency assigned to that manager's brand. The product manager can bring together the agency personnel and his or her counterpart in the marketing services division, giving the company the benefit of the best thinking of both groups—internal and external. Each group has a group product manager, who supervises the individual product managers.

The **product manager** is responsible for planning strategy and objectives, obtaining relevant brand information, managing budget and controls, and getting agency recommendations, and is the primary liaison between the marketing department and all other departments. The product manager's plans must be approved by the group product manager, who then submits the plans for approval of the vice president for marketing and finally of the executive vice president.

P&G has approximately 80 brand managers. In 1997, they lost the media planning responsibility when the company centralized print advertising planning and buying at Leo Burnett Co. According to a former P&G category manager, today's brand managers are still strong, but they do have to share more power with more people than in the past. The brand managers still have responsibility for the positioning of brands based on consumer needs, and for developing broad media strategy—deciding, for example, what media mix is best to reach target consumers. They are charged with managing and further developing brand equity.[1]

The advertising department is a branch of the *marketing services division.* The vice president for advertising, responsible for the review and evaluation of brand media plans, attends all creative presentations to act as an adviser and consultant on all aspects of advertising. The vice president for advertising reports to the senior vice president, director of marketing.

Under this system, the advertising does not all come through one huge funnel, with one person in charge of all brands. The advantage to the corporation is that each brand gets the full marketing attention of its own group, and all brands get the full benefit of all the company's special marketing services and the accumulated corporate wisdom. The more important the decision, the higher up the ladder it goes for final approval.

Large companies with many categories of products, such as Procter & Gamble or Lever Brothers, may have another layer of management called the category manager. All disciplines—research, manufacturing, engineering, sales, advertising, and so on—report to the **category manager.** The category manager follows the product line he or she is in charge of and decides how to coordinate each brand in that line. The category manager decides how to position brands in each category. For example, the category manager for laundry products decides how to position and advertise Tide and Cheer detergents to avoid conflicts and overlap (Exhibit 6.3, p. 144).

Today at Procter & Gamble, *global strategic teams* made up of brand and category managers worldwide identify "global success models" in areas such as ad copy and product development. For instance, the tag "Makes hair so healthy it shines" has become a staple of global advertising for Pantene Pro-V.

INTEGRATED MARKETING BRAND MANAGEMENT

Previously, we discussed integrated marketing, or one-voice marketing, from the agency perspective. There has been debate about whether agencies can effectively implement this concept because of their structure. One of the major problems is that agencies are set up as separate profit centers, which results in competition among their own units for a strong bottom-line showing.

---

[1]Jack Neff, "P&G Redefines the Brand Manager," *Advertising Age,* October 13, 1997, p. 1.

Product manager
In package goods, the person responsible for the profitability of a product (brand) or product line, including advertising decisions. Also called a brand manager.

Category manager
A relatively new corporate position. This manager is responsible for all aspects of the brands in a specific product category for a company including research, manufacturing, sales, and advertising. Each product's advertising manager reports to the category manager. Example: Procter & Gamble's Tide and Cheer detergent report to a single category manager.

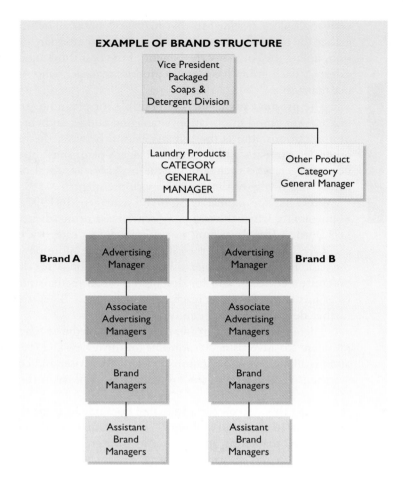

EXAMPLE OF BRAND STRUCTURE

Vice President Packaged Soaps & Detergent Division

Laundry Products CATEGORY GENERAL MANAGER

Other Product Category General Manager

Brand A — Advertising Manager | Advertising Manager — Brand B

Associate Advertising Managers | Associate Advertising Managers

Brand Managers | Brand Managers

Assistant Brand Managers | Assistant Brand Managers

Research involving marketing executives indicates that integration of advertising, promotion, public relations, and all other forms of marketing communications is the most important factor influencing how strategies will be set. Larry Light, the former chairman of the international division of Bates Worldwide, says, "The reason integrated marketing is important is consumers integrate your messages whether you like it or not. The messages cannot be kept separate. All marketing is integrated in the mind of consumers. Your only choice is how that message is integrated."[2]

An *Advertising Age* survey found major disagreement between agencies and advertisers in terms of whether integration should be managed inside the corporation or by the agency; 82.9 percent of marketers say integration is their responsibility in terms of setting strategy for and coordination of integration, and 63 percent of agencies said that's their domain.[3] Advertisers feel they can put in place, or already have in place, ad agencies, public relation firms, promotion agencies, direct-marketing companies, and design firms—all outside communication specialists needed to accomplish its integrated goals.

Integrated Functions

Integrated marketing communication (IMC) can function in the marketing services system if there is management of this process among all the departments involved— advertising, sales promotion, public relations, and other existing departments. Radical

---

[2]Scott Hume, "Integrated Marketing: Who's in Charge Here?" *Advertising Age,* March 23, 1993, p. 3.

[3]Adrienne Ward Fawcett, "Marketers Convinced: Its Time Has Arrived," *Advertising Age,* November 8, 1993, p. S-1.

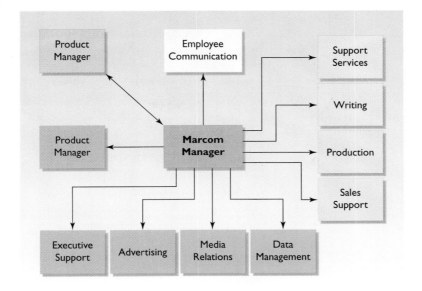
organizational changes don't seem to work well with regard to implementation. Many organizations have found that integrated functions become evolutionary. However, there are marketers that feel this kind of management isn't practical because the resistance to change by managers is just too great. Don Schultz, author of *Integrated Marketing Communications* and president of Agora Inc., suggests that reengineering the communications function and structure within the company is sometimes necessary. He suggests the following functions:

● Start with the customer or prospect and work back toward the brand or organization. That's the outside-in approach. Most organizations are structured to deliver inside-out communications, which allows the budget cycle to dictate when communications can be delivered.

● Good communications require knowledge of customers and prospects. Without specific customer information, the marketing organization will continue to send out the wrong message and information to the wrong people at the wrong time at an exorbitant cost. A database is critical to carry out the IMC communication task.

● Brand contacts—all the ways the customer comes in contact with the organization—are the proper way to think about communications programs. This goes beyond traditional media. It includes managing the impact and influence of packaging, employees, in-store displays, sales literature, and even the design of the product so that the brand clearly or concisely communicates with the right person, at the right time, in the right way, with the right message or incentive through the right delivery channel.

There are three forms of adaptation to integrated marketing within corporate structures:[4]

● *Marcom (marketing communications) manager.* Adapting a business-to-business organizational structure called marcom management centralizes all the communication activities under one person or office (see Exhibit 6.4). Under this structure, all communication is centralized. Product managers request communication programs for their products through a marcom manager. The manager develops the strategy and then directs the communication programs either internally or externally.

---

[4]Don E. Schultz, "Managers Still Face Substantial IMC Questions," *Marketing News,* September 27, 1993, p. 10.

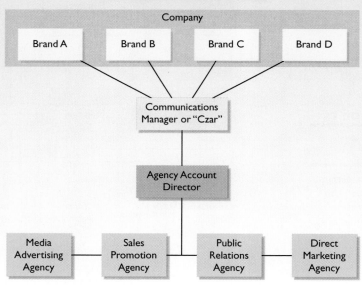

COMMUNICATIONS MANAGER

exhibit

6.5

The communication manager approves or coordinates all communications programs for the entire organization.

- *Restructured brand management approach.* This approach reduces the layers previously involved in the process. All sales and marketing activities for the brand, category, or organization are reduced to three groups, all reporting to the CEO, and all are on the same organizational level. They are marketing services/communications (MSC), marketing operations, and sales. Marketing operations is responsible for developing and delivering the product to the MSC, which works with sales to develop and implement all sales and marketing programs (including advertising).
- *Communications manager.* This approach names a communication manager who is responsible for approving or coordinating all communications programs for the entire organization. The various brands develop their own communication programs as they have traditionally done. These plans go to the communications manager, who is responsible for coordinating, consolidating, and integrating the programs, messages, and media for the organization (see Exhibit 6.5).

IMC Goals

Using IMC to coordinate all messages a company communicates through advertising, direct marketing, public relations, promotion, and so on helps to create a unified image and support relationship building with customers. The key, however, is to determine exactly what your IMC strategy should achieve.

One of the first steps is to identify the specific target (such as users or influencers) and understand what each needs from your IMC campaign. To sharpen the focus, concentrate on one or two goals to avoid stretching the strategy or budget. Three such possible goals are the following:[5]

- *Build brand equity.* By using IMC to reinforce your brand's unique value and identity, you increase awareness and encourage stronger preference among customers and prospects. The business-to-business ads for Scotchgard, the stain protector, aimed at the textile and garment industry, for example, tell them the product keeps apparel in good shape by adding stain-shedding qualities.

---

[5]Marian Burk Wood, "Clear IMC Goals Build Strong Relationships," *Marketing News,* June 23, 1997, p. 11.

- *Provide information.* Business customers need a lot of information. Differentiate products or features if applicable.
- *Communicate differentiation/positioning.* What does the product stand for and how is it better than competitors'? IMC helps convey your most significant points. For instance, a UPS ad stressed the range of guaranteed "urgent delivery" choices. These choices differentiated it from its competition while positioning it as able to meet virtually any deadline.

CORPORATE RESTRUCTURING

New Corporate Attitude

There has been a recent trend among leading marketers to dump their marginal brands and focus on the top performers in their portfolios. Many marketers are selling or spinning off divisions or brands that haven't lived up to expectations in their categories. PepsiCo spun off its restaurant operations. Campbell's Soup Company unloaded Swanson frozen foods. This trend is a move by marketers to focus on their core brands and an unwillingness to support those that don't offer large-scale manufacturing, distribution, and advertising synergies. A Reach Marketing executive says, "Retail chains are carrying only the top brands and once you've hit No. 3, media buying efficiency and marketing spending drop." Swanson had dropped to fifth place in its category. Tom Lawson of Arnold Communications says, "Second-tier brands become milked by their owners, then they stop being brands and become products."[6]

Marketing Structure Changes

Recently, Quaker Oats restructured and said if a function does not provide a competitive advantage and does not represent a clear cost savings compared to using an outside specialist service, then the role or function will be outsourced. An analyst cited this as Quaker's movement beyond cost savings and into their pursuit of brand building so they could focus on spreading their equity across product lines and in new channels of distribution. Five major divisions were to be restructured with changes in job descriptions. It is fair to say that marketing and related advertising organizational structures have been and are in flux.

Over a period of nine months in late 1996, Coca-Cola Company changed how it tried to sell soft drinks to minorities by essentially disbanding its ethnic marketing department and rolling those responsibilities under the brand managers of its different beverages.

The brand managers and their marketing teams became responsible for developing advertising, promotions, and other marketing tactics to attract *all consumers.* "Today, each of our brand groups has the responsibility for reaching the Latino consumer," said the late CEO Roberto Goizuita, "Just as each of our brand groups has the responsibility for reaching young consumers, African American consumers, blue-collar consumers." The change in structure was termed a "philosophical change," but under each brand there still is a person whose responsibility is targeting African American consumers. Coca-Cola realized that some past advertising geared toward ethnic markets appeals to mainstream audiences. One popular television spot called "Pied Piper" depicted young black singer Tyrese Gibson. Domestically, Coke sells about 183 million cases of Coke Classic and 110 million cases of Sprite to African Americans, and 325 million Classic cases and 40 million Sprite cases to Hispanics. The latest independent soft drink market share figures gave Pepsi a lead among both ethnic groups.[7]

---

[6]Judann Pollack and Jack Neff, "Marketer Decree: Be a Top Brand or Begone," *Advertising Age,* September 15, 1997, p. 1.

[7]Chris Roush, "Marketing Shift," *Atlanta Journal-Constitution,* January 19, 1997, p. D-1.

Many other large consumer marketers, such as Anheuser-Busch and Kraft, maintain large ethnic departments. Each marketer perceives the market and how to organize to reach market differently.

SETTING THE BUDGET

Advertising is supposed to accomplish some objective. It is a business decision. The three ads in Exhibit 6.6 (a, b, and c, p. 150) are for three totally different kinds of advertisers, each with a different reason for being. What is the ad or campaign supposed to accomplish? Launch a new product? Increase a brand's awareness level? Neutralize the competition's advertising? A key question is how much money is it going to take to accomplish the objective? Even if we have been successful with the product, do we know whether we are spending too much on advertising—or not enough? Despite all the technology available to help us to determine how much should be spent, the final decision

exhibit

6.6a

Illinois Power tries to attract industry and business to Downstate Illinois.

Courtesy: Aydlotte & Cartwright.

is a judgment call by corporate management. The person responsible for the budget decision varies across companies and according to objectives. In general, a Gallagher Report says, the vice president of marketing and the vice president of advertising are the people most responsible for setting the ad budget (see Exhibit 6.7, p. 150). Two-thirds of advertising budgets are submitted for approval in September or October; almost 80 percent are approved during the period September to November. As you might expect for such an important decision, most presidents or chief operating officers strongly influence the approval process.

Budgets are usually drawn up using one of four approaches: percentage of sales, payout plan, competitive budgeting, and the task method.

Percentage of Sales

The percentage of sales method simply means the advertising budget is based upon a percentage of the company's sales. For instance, a family restaurant chain might budget 5 percent of their sales for advertising. A company using this method to determine their

exhibit

6.6c

Custom X bodyboards
are completely
symmetrical and
seamless.

Courtesy: Bulldog Drummond.

advertising budget will not spend beyond its means because the ad budget will increase only when sales increase. If sales decrease, so will its advertising; however, if competitive pressures are severe, it may have to maintain or increase the budget to retain market share, even though there is no prospect of increased profit. This method can actually reverse the assumed cause-and-effect relationship between advertising and sales. That is, because the budgeting is based either on the previous year's sales—usually with some percentage of increase added—or next year's anticipated sales, then it can be said that the sales are causing the advertising rather than advertising causing the sales.

A Gallagher Report indicates that about 9 percent of companies surveyed take a percentage of last year's sales.[8] Roughly 35 percent use a percentage of anticipated sales, 30 percent combine needed tasks with percent of anticipated sales, 13 percent outline needed tasks and fund them, 13 percent set arbitrary amounts based on general fiscal

exhibit

6.7

Who Prepares Clients' Ad Budgets[a]	
VP Marketing	63.2%
VP Advertising	31.6
Ad manager	22.2
Brand manager	16.3
Ad agency	21.7
Sales promotion	5.6
Who Approves Client's Ad Budgets[a]	
President or CEO	68.5%
VP Marketing	37.3
Executive VP	20.9
Division manager	17.2
VP Advertising	14.4
Treasurer or controller	8.6

[a]Totals more than 100% due to multiple responses.

Source: 26th Gallagher Report Consumer Advertising Survey.

---

[8]26th Gallagher Report Consumer Advertising Survey.

		Year 1		Year 2		Year 3
Sales		$84,854,000		$218,737,000		$356,248,000
Food cost	34%	28,850,000	34%	74,371,000	34%	121,124,000
Paper cost	5	4,245,000	5	10,937,000	5	17,812,000
Labor	22	18,668,000	20	43,747,000	20	71,250,000
Overhead	21	17,819,000	19	41,560,000	18	64,125,000
Total op. exp.	82	69,580,000	78	170,615,000	77	274,511,000
Gross profit	18	15,274,000	22	48,122,000	25	81,937,000
Advertising/Promo		$15,274,000		$48,122,000	13	$46,312,000
Store profit		0		0	10	35,625,000
Corp. invest.		10,300,000		0		0
Corp. profit		(10,300,000)		0		35,625,000
Cumulative		(10,300,000)		(10,300,000)		25,625,000

exhibit

6.8

Fast-Food Payout Plan

outlook of the company, and 9 percent calculate a medium between last year's actual sales and anticipated sales for the coming year. In any method, a change in sales changes the amount of advertising expenditure.

Payout Plan

The payout plan looks at advertising as an investment rather than an expenditure. It recognizes that it may take several years before the company can recover start-up costs and begin taking profits.

Exhibits 6.8 and 6.9 are examples of typical payout plans. Let us go briefly through Exhibit 6.8, a payout plan for a new fast-food operation. In the first year of operation, the company spent the entire gross profits ($15,274,000) on advertising. In addition, the company invested $10,300,000 in store development, for a first-year operating loss.

In the second year, the company again invested gross profits ($48,122,000) in advertising and carried over the $10,300,000 debt from the first year. By the third year, sales had increased to the point where advertising as a percentage of gross sales had dropped to 13 percent, or $46,312,000, leaving a profit of $35,625,000. After covering the first-year debt of $10,300,000, the payout was $25,625,000.

If the company had demanded a 10 percent profit in the first year (0.10 × $84,854,000 = $8,485,400), it would have had to curtail advertising drastically, reduce

exhibit

6.9

Package Goods Product Payout Plan

Investment Introduction—36-Month Payout

	Year 1	Year 2	Year 3	3-Year Total	Year 4
Size of market (MM cases)	8	10	11		12
Share goal:					
Average	$12\frac{1}{2}$%	25%	30%		30%
Year end	20	30	30		30
Consumer movement (MM Cases)	1.0	2.5	3.3	6.8	3.6
Pipeline (MM Cases)	.3	.2	.1	.6	—
Total shipments (MM Cases)	1.3	2.7	3.4	7.4	3.6
Factory income (@ $9)	$11.7	$24.3	$30.6	$66.6	$32.4
Less costs (@ $5)	6.5	13.5	17.0	37.0	18.0
Available P/A (@ $4)	$ 5.2	$10.8	$13.6	$29.6	$14.4
Spending (normal $2)	$12.8	$10.0	$ 6.8	$29.6	$ 7.2
Advertising	10.5	8.5	5.4	24.4	5.7
Promotion	2.3	1.5	1.4	5.2	1.5
Profit (Loss):					
Annual	($ 7.6)	$ 0.8	$ 6.8	—	$ 7.2
Cumulative	($ 7.6)	($ 6.8)	—	—	$ 7.2

corporate store investment, or do some combination of both. In that case, the company would have made a profit the first year but risked future profits and perhaps its own long-term survival.

Competitive Budgeting

Another approach to budgeting is to base it on the competitive spending environment. In competitive budgeting, the level of spending relates to percent of sales and other factors: whether the advertiser is on the offensive or defensive, media strategies chosen (for example, desire to dominate a medium), or answers to questions such as, "Is it a new brand or an existing one?" The problem here is that competition dictates the spending allocation (and the competing companies may have different marketing objectives).

The Task Method

The task method of budgeting is possibly the most difficult to implement, but it may also be the most logical budgeting method. The method calls for marketing and advertising managers to determine what task or objective the advertising will fulfill over the budgetary period and then calls for a determination of how much money will be needed to complete the task. Under this method, the company sets a specific sales target for a given time to attain a given goal. Then it decides to spend whatever money is necessary to meet that quota. The task method might be called the "let's spend all we can afford" approach, especially when launching a new product. Many big businesses today started that way. Many businesses that are not here today did too.

The approach can be complex. It involves several important considerations: brand loyalty factors, geographic factors, product penetration. Advertisers who use this method need accurate and reliable research, experience, and models for setting goals and measuring results.

The task method is used most widely in a highly competitive environment. Budgets are under constant scrutiny in relation to sales and usually are formally reviewed every quarter. Moreover, they are subject to cancellation at any time (except for noncancelable commitments) because sales have not met a minimum quota, money is being shifted to a more promising brand, or management wants to hold back money to make a better showing on its next quarterly statement.

No one approach to budgeting is always best for all companies.

THE CHANGING MARKETING ENVIRONMENT

The changes that have taken place over the past few years in advertiser organizations have not been a result of business cycles. Marketers are in an irreversible restructuring in the way businesses operate—one that may require a major rethinking of the agency-client relationship in the late 1990s and beyond. Some of the factors driving the change at companies include the following:[9]

- *Fragmented consumer target.* Consumer groups are more fragmented than ever before by demographics, age, ethnicity, family type, geographic location, and media usage.
- *Parity performance.* The importance of value, convenience, and service in influencing preference is increasing, and the impact of low-priced, satisfactorily performing private brands is growing.
- *Cost control.* Marketers must remain price competitive and must develop new strategies for offsetting internal cost increases.

---

[9]Robert M. Viney, "Solving the Agency-Client Mismatch," *Advertising Age,* May 24, 1993, p. 20.

- *Erosion of advertising effectiveness.* Advertisers have settled for advertising that doesn't present a compelling basis for consumer preference and fails to effectively reinforce relevant brand equity in other marketing activities.
- *Strengthened retailer influence.* Retailers are equipped with detailed data on consumer purchase behavior, which gives them leverage against marketers.

Changes in the National Mood

Over the past 15 years, Roper research says there have been three distinct national moods, each lasting about five years. The United States is now beginning a new period. These emerging social, economic, and political environments in which business will operate to the end of the twentieth century are significant departures in the way people look at their lives—and the brands they buy, the services they use, the work they do, and the major issues that concern them. Among the trends are the following:[10]

- *Moderation.* Americans are seeking greater balance in nearly all aspects of their lives. A new sense of moderation and realism is changing people's perspectives and choices as they seek a satisfying lifestyle that is not too exhausting. Perhaps most important, the public's approach to the traditional work ethic has fundamentally changed: Work has lost ground as a basic priority, and leisure has gained.
- *Time control.* In a growing number of upscale and even luxury markets, consumers are placing ever higher premiums on their time and seeking more control over how it is used. They are segmenting their time, allocating it more efficiently, and looking for more ways to stretch their leisure hours. Consumers simply have come to *expect* time-saving features in products and services.
- *Tactical consumerism.* Price cuts, private labels, generous promotions, and the "deep discounted" retail landscape came of age in the 1980s. Today a new breed of shopper regularly expects and gets high quality without a high price. When choosing among brands, more people than at any time in the past 20 years now say a *reasonable* price is their top purchase criteria, rivaling even quality. Manufacturers must establish a clear and justifiable reason for higher prices.
- *Eye-catching information.* Americans are becoming more discriminating about the ads they choose to view. Ad messages need to be more memorable and attractive to the eye without detracting from useful consumer information. Visual recall is half the challenge. Creative efforts should turn increasingly to dramatic staging, exciting images, and bold graphics. In print, copy should strive to be more inviting to the eye and easier to read. Creating strong images that also draw the eye to informational text emphasizing product benefits is the goal.
- *Personal responsibility.* As disenchantment with the nation's elites grows, people are increasingly looking inward for the solutions to the country's problems. There is growing evidence of an emerging ethos of personal responsibility among Americans (see Exhibit 6.10, p. 154).
- *Environment movement matures.* In keeping with the growing sense of personal responsibility, individuals are admitting to their own shortcomings with respect to environmental protection. The best opportunity for business may be advertising and communications that encourage and help individuals to take action while reaping the benefits of national leadership.
- *The family.* Despite overwhelmingly pessimistic rhetoric, the evidence suggests the future vitality of the American family. The nature of the modern family is different from the traditional family. First, most families will have both parents working. Second, the average size of the family will be smaller. Third, the number of nontraditional family structures—

---

[10]"25 Major Trends Shaping the Future of American Business," *The Public Pulse,* Vol. 5, No. 5, 1994.

single parents, stepfamilies, unmarried couples with children, grandparents with children, and so on—will continue to rise.

- *Women's shift priorities.* Now a majority of women say they would rather stay home to care for a house and family than be employed. However, this attitude shift does not mean there will be a mass exodus of women from the workplace. The reality is that most working women say they simply cannot give up their jobs. Whereas the average working woman has grown disillusioned with the workplace, increasing numbers of female executives and professionals report being satisfied with their working situations.

MANAGING BRANDS

Efficient Consumer Response

In 1993, the grocery industry launched its efficient consumer response (ECR) initiative designed to make the industry more efficient. This initiative includes using technology in purchasing, distribution, promotion, reducing inventories, and other aspects of the business, including marketing. It is another attempt by business to prepare for the future by eliminating the inefficient parts of the system of selling grocery products by changing the approach to creating, selling, and distributing those products. In the process, ECR is forcing marketers and retailers to rethink new products, pricing, in-store merchandising, and the division of dollars between trade promotion and consumer marketing.

Slotting Allowances

Every square foot of a supermarket costs money and needs to pay for itself by moving products and brands quickly. There is only so much shelf space for the category manager to obtain from grocers. Because grocers control the space, many charge *slotting allowances* for shelf space. This admission fee, which comes primarily from the marketer's trade promotion funds, ensures space for a period of about three to six months. Supermarkets use the slotting allowance to pay for slow-moving products and for administrative overhead for placing a new product into their system, including warehouse space, computer input, communications to individual stores about the product's availability, and the redesign of shelf space. The frozen food section has only a finite amount of space and almost always demands slotting allowances.

Retailer Control

There is no doubt about the control of shelf space and entry into supermarkets, discounters, and mass merchandise stores today. The marketer is at the mercy of the retailer. As a result, category managers must learn the following:[11]

- Marketplace leverage is at the local level. As consumers' tastes, needs, and wants continue to expand and fragment, leverage can be achieved only by delivering relevant products, services, messages, and promotions to consumers as individuals.
- Building brand equity among retailers should become as important as building brands among consumers.
- Marketing decisions must shift to the sales level. Manufacturers' marketing and promotion programs must eventually become store-specific to succeed.
- Information is the most important asset you have. Only the first company to use information wins. As brand building moves from national media to the supermarket shelf, marketing and merchandising executions must be adapted to the needs of each consumer market and store franchise.

Experimentation and Risk

Marketers are forced to find the right formula and be innovative in marketing new products today. Old marketing rules don't necessarily work in today's environment. For example, BellSouth, a telecommunications giant that primarily provides local phone service in the southeast, tested putting phone service on retail store shelves. The first product, Teen Line Pack, was placed in Kroger, Office Depot, and Target Stores, among others. In addition to a second phone line, the package included a number of services aimed at the demographic group. Although the idea of selling phone services like cereal off the grocery shelf seems odd, it fits with the changes taking place in the telecommunications area. Retail sales are one of the growing ways telecom service providers are trying to grab market share.

Bill Borders, president of Borders, Perrin & Norrander, says, "risk taking is the lifeblood of an agency." However, a former director of creative at Pepsi-Cola says, "the problem with most clients is that they are not willing to join the agency in the risk. Through the years Pepsi-Cola has told BBDO to take the risk. If you miss, we

---

[11]Spencer Hapoienu, "Supermarketing's New Frontier," *Advertising Age,* April 14, 1988, p. 18.

understand that not everything is going to be a home run. But it could be a single. Occasionally, we have burned the film knowing that we tried and it just didn't work."[12] Unfortunately, most clients can't find the courage to join Pepsi in taking chances or risk to seek cutting-edge advertising.

When meeting with agencies, Paul Michaels, vice president marketing of M&M/Mars, carries a cardboard contraption that he calls the "Excite-O-Meter," making a point about the candymaker's advertising. Dave Gulick, account director at DMB&B, says Michaels has redefined risk. He wants cutting-edge creative. In the past, many of their ads were described by Michaels as lacking emotional topspin. The ads were wallpaperish and very safe. According to Michaels, the difference in creative came when Mars relaxed its attitude and encouraged its agencies to think creatively. Of course, it has to be on strategy, not just for the sake of being funny.[13]

AGENCY-CLIENT RELATIONSHIPS

It has been said that agency-client relationships are much like interpersonal relationships: if you don't like each other, you move apart. If you like each other, you gravitate toward each other and great stuff gets produced. The agency should be trusted as an employee—they are in business with the client. The relationship between the agency and the client is a partnership.

A study conducted by the North American Advertising Agency Network suggests agency professionalism, strategic planning, and cost efficiency beat leading-edge creative and integrated communications capabilities when marketers select an advertising agency. The study suggests that some clients were willing to accept mediocre work delivered on time and on budget. Other factors revealed a degree of importance to integrated communications capabilities: agency experience on a similar account and longevity of client relationships were more important than account rosters with big-name or blue-chip clients.[14] Agencies have always prided themselves on selling the creative product; however, many people feel today's agencies are not producing the strongest creative product.

Why do clients hire agencies? Tom Patty, executive vice president of TBWA/Chiat Day says, "in essence, clients hire ad agencies because they believe they can help them persuade customers to *do* or *think something*." Clients select an agency based on the agency's ability to be persuasive. The real task is to become a persuasion partner.[15]

When advertisers develop a new product or become disenchanted with their existing advertising, they will conduct advertising reviews in which their current agency and others can compete for the account. This review process may take several months. The advertiser will evaluate which agencies it wants to participate in the review. Keep in mind that there are agencies that specialize in certain types of accounts. For example, Leo Burnett or Ammariti Puris Lintas are considered giant consumer agencies; Longwater specializes in shipping and transportation; Fair Riley Call/Bozell in health care; Sawyer Riley Compton in business-to-business (see Exhibit 6.11); Dieste & Partners in the Hispanic market (Exhibit 6.12); Ogilvy & Mather Direct in direct response; and Burrell Advertising in the African American market. All of the mentioned agencies may have other expertise to sell clients, so advertisers would evaluate their needs and seek agencies to match those needs.

[12]Joe Mandee, "How Far Is Too Far?" *Agency,* May/June 1991, p. 39.

[13]Judann Pollack, "Engaging Creative Concept Re-emerges as Weapon," *Advertising Age,* October 20, 1997, p. s/4.

[14]Melanie Wells, "Many Clients Prize Agency Efficiency over Creativity," *Advertising Age,* May 16, 1994, p. 28.

[15]Tom Patty, "Clients Today Need Partners in Persuasion, Not Agencies," *Advertising Age,* January 24, 1994, p. 26.

exhibit
6.11

Sawyer Riley Compton specializes in business-to-business marketing. Their Cutler-Hammer ad touts their IQ Analyzer, which has an easy-to-use meter.

Courtesy: Sawyer Riley Compton and Cutler-Hammer.

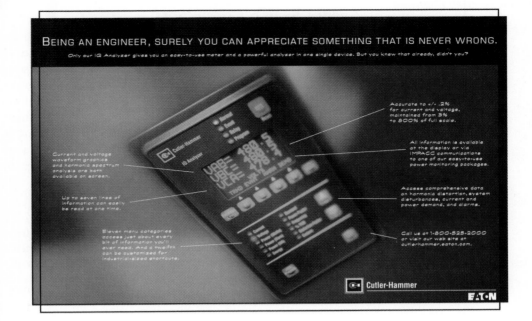

exhibit
6.12

"Lo que siempre ha usado el vaquero Wranger." This Hispanic ad for Wrangler jeans was created by Dieste & Partners.

Courtesy: Dieste & Partners.

Agency Search Consultants

Today more and more clients hire consultants to help them seek out the best agency to handle their accounts. An estimated 60 percent of recent account reviews for major advertisers involved consultants, whose job is to do the initial screening, manage the search process, and in some cases negotiate compensation agreements. This may cost a client between $35,000 and $100,000. In the past, clients relied more heavily on their own marketing departments to conduct searches. Consultants have been hired more in recent years because fewer clients find they are qualified to do it themselves and because there have been so many changes in the agency landscape, according to an agency principal.[16] The consultant has been characterized as a "marriage broker" between client and agency.

Selecting an Agency

Choosing an agency can be a complicated matter. Do you need a full-service agency, one with integrated services, one with strong media departments, or a specialized agency? After deciding whether you want a large, medium, or small, specialized, full-service, domestic, or global agency, the following points may help you in evaluating specific agencies:

1. Determine what types of service you need from an agency, and then list them in order of their importance to you. For instance: (a) marketing expertise in strategy, planning, and execution; (b) creative performance in TV, print, radio, or outdoor; (c) media knowledge and clout; (d) sales-promotion and/or trade relations help; (e) public relations and corporate- or image-building ability; (f) market research strength; (g) fashion or beauty sense; (h) agency size; (i) location in relation to your office. Your special needs will dictate others.

2. Establish a five-point scale to rate each agency's attributes. A typical five-point scale would be: (1) outstanding, (2) very good, (3) good, (4) satisfactory, (5) unsatisfactory. Of course, you should give different values or weights to the more important agency attributes.

3. Check published sources and select a group of agencies that seem to fit your requirements. Use your own knowledge or the knowledge of your industry peers to find agencies responsible for successful campaigns or products that have most impressed you. Published sources include the annual issue of *Advertising Age,* which lists agencies and their accounts by agency size, and the "Red Book" (*Standard Advertising Register*), which lists agencies and accounts both alphabetically and geographically. In case of further doubt, write to the American Association of Advertising Agencies, 666 Third Avenue, New York, NY 10017, for a roster of members.

4. Check whether there are any apparent conflicts with accounts already at the agency. When agencies consider a new account, that is the first question they ask (along with the amount of the potential billings).

5. Now start preliminary discussions with the agencies that rate best on your initial evaluation. This can be started with a letter asking if they are interested or a telephone call to set up an appointment for them to visit you or for you to visit the agency. Start at the top. Call the president or the operating head of the agency or office in your area, who will appoint someone to follow up on the opportunity you are offering.

6. Reduce your original list of potential agencies after the first contact. A manageable number is usually no more than three.

7. Again prepare an evaluation list for rating the agencies on the same five-point scale. This list will be a lot more specific. It should cover personnel. Who will supervise

---

[16]Jennifer Comiteau, "Power Play," *Adweek,* June 10, 1996, pp. 33–38.

your account and how will the account be staffed? Who are the creative people who will work on your business? Similarly, who will service your needs in media, production (TV) research, and sales promotion, and how will they do it? What is the agency's track record in getting and holding on to business and in keeping personnel teams together? What is the agency's record with media, with payments? Make sure again to assign a weighted value to each service aspect. If TV is most important to you and public relations aid least, be sure to reflect this in your evaluation.

8. Discuss financial arrangements. Will your account be a straight 15 percent commission account, a fee account, or a combination of both? What services will the commission or fee cover, and what additional charges will the agency demand? How will new-product work be handled from both a financial and an organizational point of view? What peripheral service does the agency offer, and for how much?

9. Do you feel comfortable with them?

10. If your company is an international one, can the agency handle all of your nondomestic business, and if so, how will they do it?

Some industry observers believe there are currently more reviews of their agencies by marketers than in recent years. Part of this is a result of the restructuring of businesses. When marketing departments get restructured and people change jobs, there is a tendency to start from scratch and this includes reviewing or changing advertising agencies. In addition, one of the driving forces on account reviews is pressure on advertiser's marketing departments to sell more units and a fixation on quarterly financial results. That position deemphasizes the importance of long-standing relationships and puts the spotlight on how well agencies can deliver quick fixes to sales problems. Because marketers have already done as much downsizing as practical, increases now have to be achieved through "real unit growth."[17] This creates pressure on both clients and agencies.

Multiple Agency Strategy   Many clients are now hiring several agencies and giving them different assignments for the same product. In some cases, this is changing the agency-client relationship by treating agencies as vendors and not as full marketing partners. One of the reasons for this change is that new marketing executives are under pressures from their CEOs. The message is, "I don't care about your situation. I need an idea and people who are passionate about my business."

In the 1950s, the agency-client relationship was defined in *The Encyclopedia of Advertising:*

An advertising agency is an organization which provides advertising, merchandising and other services and counsel related to the sale of a client's goods or services. It is understood that the client agrees not to engage a second agency to handle part of the advertising of the product without the consent of the first agency.

Many clients today are looking for home runs or a bailout to pick up their business fortunes. Many company marketing executives are in power an average of 18 months. They care about what's happening *now*. According to Larry Light, a marketing consultant, the current brand management system prevents failure by depending totally on research and testing. Brand managers often are promoted if they don't make mistakes as well as if they hit a home run. This creates brand managers who play it safe and won't take risks, according to Light.[18]

Coca-Cola decided that its agency of many years wasn't creating enough big ideas. As a result, it took the freelance route for a while and then hired about 40 agencies and

[17]Laura Petrecca, "The Year in Review: Is It a Record Pace?" *Advertising Age,* June 2, 1997, p. 1.
[18]Keith Gould, "Limited Partners," *Adweek,* July 22, 1996, pp. 21–22.

boutiques over time to create ads. Coke's contention was: We know and understand our strategy better than our agencies do. So their job is to do the best execution of the strategy they can. Chrysler, on the other hand, feels they are partners with their agencies. Their agencies understand their history from the beginning. They understand the selling attributes. They have the luxury of time to get into Chrysler's business. Chrysler contends there is a direct correlation between sales success and continuing brand advertising over a period of time. In today's changing marketplace, the view of what the agency-client relationship should be is varied.

What's fueling this boom in clients using more than one agency is the same thing that fostered the recent reverse trends in consolidations: Marketers want a creative edge and are changing the nature of their agency relationships. In the end, successful advertising has more to do with the quality of the advertiser's agency relationship than with the quantity of them. Big advertisers from AT&T to Sears have trusted their brand images to teams of agencies. "The size of our business is such that it demands the expertise and attention of a number of agencies," said the national director of marketing communications at AT&T. "There are so many projects and assignments to be handled that one agency couldn't do it all. But using multiple agencies puts the onus on us to make sure all the messages are coordinated and represent one consistent voice coming from the company." Some advertisers, such as Boston Market, divide the workload pie according to functions: They have used one agency for the core dinnertime business, another for Boston Carver sandwiches, and yet another for Hearth Honey Ham and holiday and seasonal lines. These needs are different from a client having one agency partner to handle everything.

The ad business is famously cyclical, so it remains to be seen whether this multiple agency trend is a permanent shift or a temporary blip. Right now, advertisers are looking for the best custom-made solutions to their marketing problems.[19]

APPRAISING NATIONAL ADVERTISING

The big questions that national advertising and marketing management must answer are: How well is our advertising working? How well is our investment paying off? How do you measure national advertising, whose results cannot be traced as easily as those of direct-response advertising?

Advertising Goals versus Marketing Goals

Advertising goals
The communication objectives designed to accomplish certain tasks within the total marketing program.

The answer is not simple. Much of the discussion on the subject centers around a report Russell H. Colley prepared for the Association of National Advertisers.[20] The thesis of this study is that it is virtually impossible to measure the results of advertising unless and until the specific results sought by advertising have been defined. When asked exactly what their advertising is supposed to do, most companies have a ready answer: Increase their dollar sales or increase their share of the market. However, these are not advertising goals, Colley holds; they are total **marketing goals.**

Marketing goals
The overall objectives that a company wishes to accomplish through its marketing program.

National advertising alone cannot accomplish this task. It should be used as part of the total marketing effort. The first step in appraising the results of advertising, therefore, is to define specifically what the company expects to accomplish through advertising. The Colley report defines an advertising goal as "a specific communications task, to be accomplished among a defined audience to a given degree in a given period of time."

[19]Alice Z. Cuneo, " 'Split Decisions' a Growing Trend," *Advertising Age,* November 11, 1996, p. 20.

[20]Russell H. Colley, *Defining Advertising Goals for Measured Effectiveness* (New York: Association of National Advertisers, 1961).

As an example, the report cites the case of a branded detergent. The marketing goal is to increase market share from 10 to 15 percent, and the advertising goal is set as increasing, among the 50 million housewives who own automatic washers, the number who identify brand X as a low-sudsing detergent that gets clothes clean. This represents a specific communications task that can be performed by advertising, independent of other marketing forces.

The Colley report speaks of a marketing-communication spectrum ranging from unawareness of the product to comprehension to conviction to action. According to this view, the way to appraise advertising is through its effectiveness in the communication spectrum, leading to sales.

Researchers disagree on whether the effectiveness of national advertising—or, for that matter, of any advertising—should be judged by a communication yardstick rather than by sales. As a matter of fact, in chapter 15 we discuss whether an ad's effectiveness should be measured by some research testing score.

CHANGES IN MARKETING

Clearly we are in the midst of a revolution. This period of change has been compared to the French and Russian revolutions. The truth is we are in the midst of several revolutions at once, including globalization, technology, management, and economic. We are in competition with everyone, everywhere in the world. Computers and electronics have altered the way we do everything. Word processing replaced the typewriter, ATM machines have replaced bank tellers, and voice mail and E-mail have given us the ability to communicate 24 hours a day. Today's management buzz words are reengineering, downsizing, and eliminating hierarchy. Small flexible organizations have the advantage in today's world. Finally, we are undergoing a revolution in our business structure.

The Traditional Five Ps of Marketing

The traditional five Ps of marketing consist of the elements product, price, place, packaging, and promotion (which includes positioning, advertising, sales promotion, public relations, and so forth). With a strategy in each of these areas, a person can put together an effective marketing plan. In the package goods category, the general belief is that promotion accounts for about 90 percent of the marketing equation. Each product category may be different, as seen with automobiles, where price and product are key, with promotion being a small percentage. So the advertiser must understand what is important.

The New Five Ps of Marketing

Tom Patty of TBWA/Chiat Day says the old five Ps served us well in a world dominated by stability and a growing economy with much less competitive pressures than we have today. Patty's new five Ps are aimed at helping us succeed in a world where chaos has replaced stability, where the fast-growing economy has slowed, and where global competition demands even greater levels of effectiveness and efficiency. The new five Ps are more abstract and conceptual than the traditional ones. They include paradox, perspective, paradigm, persuasion, and passion.[21]

Paradox   A paradox is a statement or proposition that, on the face of it, seems self-contradictory. Example: "All cars are the same; all cars are different." The paradox always contains within it an opportunity. An advertiser must exploit the differentiation. Miller used the paradox of "lite" beer to help them focus on the dual benefits of the

---

[21]Tom Patty, "Mastering the New Five P's of Marketing," TBWA/Chiat Day Web site, www.TBWAchiatday.com, 1997.

lite paradox, "Tastes Great, Less Filling." Everyone knows what a sports car is, but Nissan created a new category of sports cars in which it was first—the four-door sports car. To master the paradox, you first have to find or identify this opportunity and then exploit the changes. One way to create this unique identity is to be the first *something*. For years, advertising told us that trucks are tough and rugged and durable, whereas cars are comfortable, luxurious, and safe. The new Dodge Ram exploits the paradox of combining many car-type features with the rugged look and performance of a Mack truck.

Perspective   Perspective is the ability to see things in relationship to each other. The manufacturer's perspective isn't the proper perspective. Advertisers must look at every issue—whether it's a product issue, a pricing issue, or a distribution issue—from the consumer perspective. The only perspective is the consumer's perspective. Here several questions need answers: What consumer need does my product or service satisfy? How does it satisfy differently and better than competitors? Similarly, as it relates to advertising, are we in the advertising business or are we in the persuasion business? We should be in the business of persuading consumers to think or to do something.

Paradigm   Here we need a pattern example, a model way of doing things. We need to understand that we may not need to do business the "old" way. Certainly, the marketing bundle of Saturn reflects a new automotive paradigm. Instead of believing that product and price are the main ingredients of the marketing equation, Saturn believes that the major components are issues such as the experience of buying and owning a Saturn. They place much less emphasis on the product and much greater emphasis on the experiential component. There are also different advertising paradigms. In the model advertising paradigm, advertising has a simple task: "Show the product and communicate the product features and benefits." A very different paradigm is called the brand advertising paradigm, for which Saturn again is a good example. In this paradigm the task is to communicate who and what you are.

Persuasion   Here we attempt to induce someone to do or think something. All marketing and sales jobs are in the business of persuasion. The advertising agency's role is to help the client persuade potential consumer audiences either to do or to think something. To be persuasive, you have to understand three essential components: the credibility of the speaker, the content of the message, and the involvement of the audience. This is a problem for advertisers. According to Yankelovich Monitor, only 8 percent of people believe advertising. Credibility and trust are emotional, not rational. You can't make someone trust you. You have to earn it over time. The Honda brand has credibility. Consequently, the advertising tends to be simple and sparse. For a brand with less credibility you need to provide more content, more information to be persuasive. The content includes the position of the brand. It needs to address the consumer need or desire this product satisfies. Remember, consumers do not buy products; they buy solutions to their problems. They buy holes, not drill bits; they buy hope, not perfume. The third and final element in any attempt to persuade is you must understand the motivation of your customer so you can create an emotional connection with them. You also need to select the right persuasion tool. For example, if the brand has a credibility problem, the most persuasive tool might be public relations, although it is more difficult to control the content of the message in public relations. In advertising, you get complete control of content.

Passion   Passion is an aim or object pursued with zeal or enthusiasm. We no longer have products for the masses. Instead, products are designed for specific needs and wants. Marketers are moving into a new paradigm in which advertising creates exciting, stimulating dialogues with consumers designed not just to make a sale but to create a relationship. In this new marketing environment, you need passion (see Exhibit 6.13).

exhibit

6.13

Coca-Cola (Japan) Co., Ltd., tries to create a dialogue with young consumers in an attempt to develop a lasting relationship between the brand and the reader.

Courtesy: Coca-Cola (Japan) Company, Limited.

SUMMARY

Procter & Gamble first developed the marketing service system. Today it has two parts: (1) brand management, under a brand manager, who is assigned a brand, and (2) marketing services, comprised of the technical talent involved in implementing the marketing plan, including creative services, promotion services, media services, advertising controls, and marketing research.

As companies consider implementing integrated marketing communications into their firms, there are three basic structures available: a centralized communication function under a marcom manager, a restructured brand manager approach, and the structure involving a communication manager who is responsible for approving and coordinating all communication programs.

Advertising budgets are usually drawn up using the task method, the payout plan, competitive budgeting, and the most commonly used percent-of-sales method.

Advertisers are seeing the advantage of allowing their agencies more creative freedom and encouraging them to take more creative risk as long as it is on strategy. As Bill Borders said, "Risk taking is the lifeblood of an agency."

Agency search consultants are sometimes hired to help find the best agency for their company. The consultant has been characterized as a marriage broker between client and agency. Many clients hire several agencies for multiple products or for the same product. Many senior company marketing executives are in their positions an average of 18 months.

The traditional five Ps of marketing consist of product, price, place, packaging, and promotion. Tom Patty says the new five Ps are paradox, perspective, paradigm, persuasion, and passion.

REVIEW

1. What is the marketing-services system?
2. What is a category manager?

3. What are the major methods of developing an advertising budget?
4. Who in the corporation prepares most of the advertising budgets?
5. What is a slotting allowance?

TAKE IT TO THE NET

We invite you to visit the Russell/Lane page on the Prentice Hall Web site at
PHLIP **http://www.prenhall.com/phbusiness** for the bimonthly
Russell/Lane update and for this chapter's World Wide Web exercise.

case
HISTORY

BACKGROUND

Sales of personal watercraft, although introduced in 1968, did not take off until the mid-1980s. SEA•DOO watercraft became the market leader soon thereafter. SEA•DOO wanted to consolidate its market share to diffuse two threats: an increasingly saturated market and the misperception that watercraft were unsafe. Overcoming these marketing hurdles called for a dramatic escalation in brand awareness outside the core market of enthusiasts while maintaining brand position within the enthusiast market. In an attempt to curb the perceptions of watercraft as unsafe equipment, SEA•DOO was also committed to taking a responsible leadership role in providing solutions to the safety issues. Ketchum Public Relations–Atlanta devised a three-pronged approach to maintain enthusiast loyalty, excite the nontraditional consumer, and dispose of negative stigmas attached to watercraft riding.

RESEARCH

- audited enthusiast and general media to gauge the volume and tone of previous coverage in each category
- compared watercraft core consumer profile with profiles of newly predisposed consumer groups to identify ways to broaden visibility and reinforce brand identity
- evaluated competitor communications for messages and the image they deliver

PLANNING

Objectives

COMMUNICATIONS

1. reinforce SEA•DOO brand identity and encourage brand loyalty with watercraft devotees
2. romance the nontraditional consumer with the SEA•DOO brand—broaden market beyond traditional enthusiasts
3. establish SEA•DOO as the leader in watercraft safety

BUSINESS

4. raise their market share from 41 percent to 50 percent within 2 years

Strategies

THREE-PRONGED APPROACH

- legitimize SEA•DOO dominance to the enthusiast media through a concentrated blitz of timely, accurate, and accessible information
- invade the general media, emphasizing that "SEA•DOO spells fun on the water" by focusing on the owners' Club SEA•DOO events and sporting events to portray new, fun ways for enjoying craft and to leverage advertising campaign
- thread safety messages throughout all communications and generate publicity on SEA•DOO as preeminent in emphasizing responsible watercraft operation

BUDGET March–August average: $67,000/month

EXECUTION

The Ketchum blitz further positioned SEA•DOO as the market leader, introduced the general media and consumers to the allure of SEA•DOO, and bombarded the public with SEA•DOO safety messages.

- *SEA•DOO press kits.* Distributed press kits with complete information on the company and products to targeted media.
- *IJSBA (International Jet Sports Boating Association) Bud Jet Sports Tour.* Created national public relations campaigns to leverage SEA•DOO participation in 10 cities. Created the following collateral to entice the media.

- *Team SEA•DOO media guide.* Created the first-ever media guide to acquaint enthusiast media with all members of Team SEA•DOO, the professional racers sponsored by SEA•DOO.
- *Team SEA•DOO posters.* Created Team SEA•DOO poster to distribute to the general public and media.
- *Club SEA•DOO.* Launched the owners' club with Club SEA•DOO membership kit. Coordinated a number of Club SEA•DOO events throughout the country that brought SEA•DOO owners together to have fun on the water with SEA•DOO watercraft.
- *On Board (owners' video and print newsletter).* Revamped owners' newsletter to create a more professional, seductive look and provide more substantive interesting information.
- *SEA•DOO Wakeboard Series.* Leveraged the first-ever national title sponsorship of SEA•DOO Wakeboard Series in four major markets. By linking SEA•DOO with various sponsorships, the company was able to blanket a much larger, broader audience.
- *SEA•DOO Indy Lights Sponsorship.* Created North American public relations campaign for the sponsorship of the SEA•DOO/SKI•DOO Pole Award in 10 markets in the United States and Canada.
- *SEA•DOO Celebrity Challenge.* As part of Jet Jam '96, SEA•DOO sponsored this first-ever celebrity competition, creating and developing a national public relations campaign.
- *SEA•DOO "Ride Smart from the Start" program/public service announcements with Jeff Gordon and Dennis Scott.* To address safety concerns, produced two public service announcements: one with NASCAR Winston

Cup champion Jeff Gordon and the other with NBA three-point star Dennis Scott of the Orlando Magic. Both announcements focused on the importance of safe, responsible operation and offered evidence to the general public of SEA•DOO's initiatives regarding safe riding.

EVALUATION

Here is how the Ketchum program met the goals:

1. Enthusiast Media Maintenance:

   • The efforts of Ketchum and SEA•DOO resulted in nearly 80 million print impressions in 6 months.
   • SEA•DOO is *now* positioned as the market leader in all trade publications with numerous cover stories and award winners.

2. General Media Introduction:

   • The national media invasion resulted in nearly 40 million print impressions and set the standard for excitement in general interest publications and papers with stories ranging from sports to science, lifestyle, technology, and design.
   • Relentless pursuit of product coverage resulted in exposure for SEA•DOO in such unexplored media as *People* magazine, the *Los Angeles Times, Popular Mechanics, Men's Journal,* and *Wired* magazine, to name a few. These are publications that have never covered personal watercraft.

• Electronic outreach resulted in unprecedented SEA•DOO coverage—more than 60 television placements, including ABC's *Good Morning America,* NBC's *Today* and "NBA Inside Stuff," ESPN's "Inside NASCAR" and "The Extreme Scene," the Sports Channel, NBC's "Extra," *E! News Daily,* and an array of regional morning shows.

3. Safety Message Delivery:

   • Reached 15 of the top 25 ADI (Arbitron's Area of Dominant Influence) markets with the "Ride Smart from the Start" message points.
   • Resulted in 25 television placements including ESPN, the Nashville Network, and the Sports Channel, all of which refer to the "Ride Smart from the Start" program, which is specific to SEA•DOO.

4. Market Share Increase:

   • In 1996, SEA•DOO had climbed from holding a 41 percent market share of the watercraft industry to a late summer tally of 48 percent—and the season was not over yet. It was anticipated that mid-summer sales tallies would reach the goal of 50 percent market share—reaching the primary business goal ahead of schedule.

Courtesy: Ketchum Public Relations.

Media

CREATIVE COMMERCIALS, COLORFUL
magazine advertisements, and larger-than-life outdoor signs are the elements of advertising that most people consider when they think of advertising. However, it is the *media function*—the decision of where to buy time and space for the millions of advertisements that we see each year—that is taking on more and more importance to cost-oriented advertisers. In recent years, the cost of media placement has far exceeded the expense of producing advertisements and commercials. In addition, the explosion of media outlets, including dozens of new cable outlets, Web sites, and numerous newcomers within traditional media categories, has placed even more demands on media planners. Finally, a fragmented

audience looking to more specialized media vehicles is making it even more difficult to devise an efficient media schedule.

In this section, we discuss each of the major media and the manner in which they are used to reach selective prospects for a number of advertisers. The complexities of the media function are demanding that media planners be generalists in understanding the wide array of media opportunities. The term "creative" usually refers to the creation of ads, but it is being used more and more when we speak of the media planner attempting to devise strategies to reach an elusive audience with limited funds. In addition, we will soon be dealing with an audience that controls the communication process to an unprecedented degree. The advent of two-way communication systems that allow the audience to deal on an interactive basis with the media will make the media planner's job even more difficult and demand greater expertise as we move into the twenty-first century.

Today, it is not enough for the media planner to simply understand individual media. Rather, he or she must be able to make decisions based on the synergistic effects of audience, media, and products. The contemporary media executive will be required to be well versed in the fundamentals of marketing, research, psychology, and the effects of the mass media. For those who can meet the challenge, the media function offers great opportunities. The need for professionally trained media personnel has never been greater.

BASIC MEDIA STRATEGY

IN AN INCREASINGLY COMPETITIVE ENVIRONMENT, ADVERTISERS RELY ON EFFICIENT MEDIA PLANNING TO DELIVER THEIR MESSAGES TO THE BEST PROSPECTS FOR THEIR PRODUCTS AND SERVICES. AFTER READING THIS CHAPTER YOU WILL UNDERSTAND

- **the importance of efficiency and effectiveness in the media planning function**
- **diversity of media vehicles and the communication process**
- **the relationship between media and target marketing**
- **individual characteristics of the various media**
- **the distinct components of the media plan.**

Media planners
Media planners are responsible for the overall strategy of the media component of an advertising campaign.

As discussed in chapter 5, most national advertising is bought by advertising agencies or through independent media buyer organizations. Regardless of the method of buying media, the basic media function is similar. The key to the media function is the **media planner.** The media planner generally determines the strategy of the media portion of the advertising campaign. The planner must determine the overall marketing goals of the client, consider creative themes and the media that will best convey them, analyze current product and media research, as well as supervise the tactical buying function.

The role of the media planner is to supervise all areas of the advertising campaign as it relates to the media function. For example:

- *Planners make sure media buys are targeted to primary prospects.* In the upcoming Bridgestone Sports case history (pp. 173–174), note how its advertising agency uses only two media vehicles to reach the potential buyers of its golf ball.
- *Planners target the season.* It makes sense for suntan lotion advertisements to run in the summer and hot cereal ads in the winter. Likewise, watch companies advertise in the spring for graduation and after Thanksgiving for Christmas buying.

● *Planners target the message.* Demonstration ads work on television and not on radio. Coupons are better suited to print, and direct mail is extremely efficient in delivering detailed or complex product information.

Contemporary media planners have added the role of marketing specialist to their other duties.

> For media planners, knowing product marketing increasingly is part of the job description. . . . The forte of the new breed of planner is not merely creating low-cost, high-reach media plans but investigating and using the proper media—traditional and/or unconventional—needed to reach a marketing objective.[1]

The media planner also must be creative in developing plans that utilize the fast-growing number of media options with limited budgets.

> Traditionally, creative has described an offbeat way of making an advertiser's message successfully cut through competitive clutter. Yet today, that phrase has evolved to not only reflect the use of various media alternatives, but—perhaps more significantly—the pressure to create big breakthroughs with smaller budgets.[2]

In the future, the media professional will become an even more vital part of the advertising team. The input of media professionals in the advertising process has become increasingly important in recent years. The media environment is changing so rapidly that it is part of the media planner's job to anticipate future trends in communications and keep agency management and clients abreast of major changes. In such an atmosphere, media planners will occupy a pivotal position in the advertising process.

The media planning process has become so specialized that it is increasingly being concentrated among a few large agencies and independent media-buying companies. Large advertisers such as Procter & Gamble often negotiate the media-buying function separate from other aspects of their advertising. For example, Leo Burnett USA buys all P&G print advertising for the nine agencies that work on the account.[3] Increasingly, major agencies view their media departments as stand-alone units that sell their services to other companies or agencies as a function separate from the agency's other operations.

Effective media planning is a requirement for successful advertising. The average consumer is bombarded with hundreds of advertising messages daily, and it takes a combination of creative communication, correct timing, and imaginative media placement to make advertising rise above the crowd.

The advent of new technology is dramatically changing the media environment. Exhibit 7.1 (p. 172) demonstrates some of the anticipated changes facing the advertiser of the twenty-first century. Note that the key to these changes is a growing awareness that advertising and promotion must be customized to the individual consumer. The mass media of the past are not only cost inefficient, but, compared to new technology, ineffective as a means of reaching selective audiences.

Given the number and extent of these changes, long-term predictions concerning the advertising media function are difficult, and uncertainty is the norm. However, there are some general principles that we should examine as we attempt to track the future

---

[1] Jane Hodges, "Say Hello to New Breed of Planner," *Advertising Age,* July 24, 1996, p. S-12.

[2] William Spain, "Creative Media Make Pennies Work Like Dollars," *Advertising Age,* July 22, 1996, p. S-10.

[3] Mark Gleason and Chuck Ross, "P&G Plans to Review TV Buying," *Advertising Age,* March 17, 1997, p. 1.

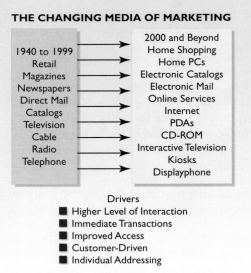

THE CHANGING MEDIA OF MARKETING

1940 to 1999	2000 and Beyond
Retail	Home Shopping
Magazines	Home PCs
Newspapers	Electronic Catalogs
Direct Mail	Electronic Mail
Catalogs	Online Services
Television	Internet
Cable	PDAs
Radio	CD-ROM
Telephone	Interactive Television
	Kiosks
	Displayphone

Drivers
- Higher Level of Interaction
- Immediate Transactions
- Improved Access
- Customer-Driven
- Individual Addressing

Source: Gartner Groups, *Marketing Knowledge & Technology Research Note K-EMM-005,* September 27, 1995.

of advertising media. Media planners and marketing communication executives will increasingly

1. strive for greater cost efficiencies in media selection
2. attempt to achieve minimum waste circulation by reaching only prime prospects and current customers
3. consider new media outlets to supplement or replace traditional media vehicles
4. coordinate media buys with all phases of the advertising and marketing goals of a firm.

To better understand this new media environment, let us take a moment to discuss each of these changes and their implications for the future.

NEED FOR GREATER COST EFFICIENCIES

Media cost represents the major expenditure for most advertisers (see Exhibit 7.2). In recent years, advertisers and their agencies have spent a great deal of time dealing with the spiraling cost of media. Although media inflation decreased significantly during the 1990s, the cost of time and space are enormous and continue to rise at the rate of 5 to 6 percent annually. Added to the overall increase in media prices is the greater difficulty (and expense) of reaching an increasingly fragmented audience.

Media planners examine factors such as circulation and costs to ensure the best media buys for their clients. The search for media efficiencies has created a competitive—some would call it cutthroat—atmosphere of rate negotiation. Advertisers, with the leverage of an expanded number of media alternatives, are demanding price concessions from the media.

exhibit

7.2

1997 Estimated Media Expenditures (billions)

Direct response	$85.05
Television	51.05
Newspapers	45.90
Radio	17.35
Magazines	14.34
Out-of-home	3.50

INDUSTRY RELEVANCE

• •

If you study from Kleppner's Advertising Procedure, recruiters want you.

Throughout the Fourteenth Edition, new and updated examples show students
how the industry really works — and what to expect when they start looking
for a career in advertising.

• •

case HISTORY

MARKETING SITUATION

The Precept EV Extra Spin golf ball was entering its second year on the market at the beginning of 1995. The brand had enjoyed very encouraging success in its first year: 200,000 dozen sold to just over 5,100 accounts (out of a universe of about 12,000 "quality" accounts). These initial results were even more impressive in light of the fact that the top-grade golf ball market is a very mature one, with category growth of about 1 to 2 percent annually, and is filled with excellent, well-entrenched brands such as Titleist, Top Flite, and Maxfli.

Precept EV Extra Spin is one of the first "two-piece" constructed (solid center plus the cover) golf balls to combine the distance advantage of a traditional two-piece ball with the feel and spin characteristics of a wound ball. In fact, the ball accomplished that job so well that Nick Price, the PGA Player of the Year in both 1993 and 1994, and arguably the top PGA Senior Tour player, Raymond Floyd, both play the ball in competition. Prior to the introduction of Extra Spin, it was unprecedented for a touring professional to play a two-piece ball.

The second year of Extra Spins's life cycle was critical to establishing the brand for long-term growth. Two marketing challenges had to be addressed:

1. Sustain the early momentum to (a) continue the brand's growth, and (b) reinforce the trade's decision to stock it, for the sake of Precept EV Extra Spin and future brands to be introduced by Bridgestone.
2. Prosper in the face of new, well-supported competition in the high spin two-piece category from leaders Titleist and Top Flite.

CAMPAIGN OBJECTIVES

1. Sell 400,000 dozen Precept EV Extra Spin golf balls in calendar year 1995.
2. Sell the brand to a minimum of 5,500 accounts (on-course golf pro shops and off-course golf specialty shops).
3. Increase market share to an average of 3.0 percent (average of on-course and off-course).

TARGET AUDIENCE

Men
Age: 25 to 54
Household income: $50,000+
Play golf a minimum 20+ times/year
This profile defines the frequent and serious golfers in the United States, the ones who play the majority of rounds and purchase the bulk of equipment. These players were the company's best chance of success for a still new product, primarily because they would be rabid enough about the game to at least entertain something new. In addition, this group knows that a touring professional *simply does not play a two-piece ball,* so this is where the company's creative strategy would have the most impact.

CREATIVE STRATEGY

Bridgestone continued a very simple but impactful strategy of using two very well-known personalities, Price and Floyd. To serious golfers, the idea that two of the best players in the world would play a two-piece ball is cause for them to sit up and take notice.

The simple message was that Nick Price and Raymond Floyd have switched to Precept EV Extra Spin because it is the only ball that gives them the distance of a two-piece with the feel and spin a world-class player demands.

MEDIA STRATEGY

In 1995, Bridgestone continued to be outspent by its major competitors by as much as 6 to 1. For example, based on 1994 total-year spending and year-to-date data available through June 1995, competitive spending for the category leaders for calendar 1995 was projected to finish the year at: Titleist $12,500,000; TopFlite $12,300,000.

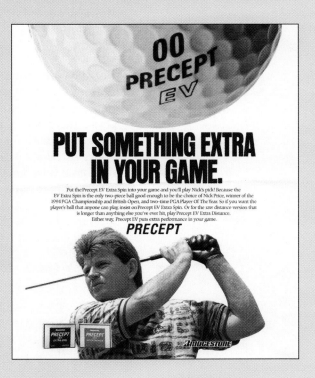

By comparison, Bridgestone will have spent less than $1,700,000 behind the Precept EV Extra Spin campaign in 1994.

The media strategy was to attack the "core" golfer, the one most active and influential, using two media, both highly targeted at the intended audience: a national golf enthusiast publication (*Golf* magazine) and ESPN golf tournament telecasts.

The decision to use ESPN, as opposed to broader over-the-air networks, was a tactical one born out of an inferior budget, and came down to a choice of "frequency" versus "reach." The choice was made to have more frequency with true golf fanatics, the ones who will watch anything and everything about the game, and are hopefully influential over their peers. That job was done well on ESPN with a limited budget. Over-the-air networks would have reached more consumers, but not have been able to have enough frequency to have much impact.

EVIDENCE OF RESULTS

Goal:	400,000 dozen sold for calendar year 1995
Results:	776,000* dozen sold through November 15, 1995
Goal:	5,500 accounts sold Precept EV Extra Spin in calendar year 1995

Results:	6,119 accounts sold Precept EV Extra Spin through November 15, 1995
Goal:	3.0% share-of-market by end of calendar year 1995
Results:	3.4% share* in on-course pro shops
	5.2% share* in off-course stores
	4.3% average share (on-course and off-course outlets each represent approximately 50% of total market)

Source: Audits & Surveys, sales for peak golf season of June through September 1995.

SUMMARY

Existing in a highly competitive parity marketplace, Precept EV Extra Spin faced the difficult task of taking share away from firmly entrenched brands. By using the unexpected creative direction of employing very successful touring professionals as spokesmen for a product they would not normally play, Precept EV Extra Spin exceeded goals for both sales and distribution, and more than doubled its share-of-market from the previous year.

Courtesy: Austin Kelley Advertising, Inc.

The primary problem of achieving media cost efficiencies is that the goal of low cost is largely contradictory to the current move toward specialized media. Until a few years ago, advertisers were faced with a limited number of media choices. In an environment controlled by a few mass circulation magazines, dominance by three major TV networks, and largely monopolistic daily newspapers, advertisers sought to reach as many people as possible, mostly ignoring who constituted these media audiences.

In today's world of fragmented media with much smaller, but homogeneous audiences, advertisers are routinely paying much more for each person reached than they did only a few years ago.

> But the continuing splintering of the audience . . . will lead to great opportunities for target marketing. Media departments will collect and combine measured media ranging from ads on the back of highway toll tickets to the Internet to billboards and Yellow Pages—and even delve into marketing disciplines such as public relations and direct response—in the hopes of coming close to reaching the numbers the network buys alone once could. Because media planners will be savvier and better trained than ever, and have superior technology and research at their fingertips, the advertising messages also should reach consumers who are more engaged and receptive.[4]

ACHIEVING MINIMUM WASTE CIRCULATION

Media plan
The complete analysis and execution of the media component of a campaign.

One of the primary measures of the success of a **media plan** is the degree to which it targets prime prospects. Given the rising cost of advertising, clients cannot tolerate high levels of nonprospects in a media schedule. Media planners are asked to build a plan

---

[4]Tom Forbes, "The Media Monsoon," *Agency,* Winter 1997, p. 22.

that will reach prospects with a frequency that rises above the clutter of competing messages. Moreover, this efficiency must be achieved in a communications atmosphere conductive to the product or service being offered—no small order!

One of the major tools for achieving efficiency is well-designed research. Media research serves two primary functions. First, it provides both primary and secondary information about audience characteristics, which allows buyers to most efficiently develop a schedule. Second, it meets the growing demands of clients for advertising accountability. As clients have become more sophisticated, media planners have had to increasingly justify their schedules and the results obtained by the media advertising they place.

The media researcher's primary function is to support both **media buyers** and planners by providing information on which they can make their decisions. Another role of the media researcher is to keep planners and clients aware of changes and trends relating to media. The research department of most agencies is very small, with the director acting as a coordinator and much of the actual research done on a contract basis with private firms or through secondary syndicated research services.

In an era of specialized media and smaller, but discrete, audience segments, sophisticated media research has never been more important. As one media vice president pointed out, "As clients, products, and services become more personalized and aimed at specific target market groups, we'll get better at identifying these people. For us, media has become more personalized and we're finally able to match the media target to the message. We're moving to a marketing environment where, ultimately, you speak to a target audience of one."[5]

Media buyers
Execute and monitor the media schedule developed by media planners.

CONSIDER NEW, NONTRADITIONAL MEDIA VEHICLES

Most media planners use a **building block strategy** in developing a media schedule. They start with the medium that reaches the most prospects and work down to those that reach the smallest portion of the audience. Normally, the first or second "building blocks" are relatively easy to determine. Most national advertisers use network television or magazines as the dominant medium. The media planner will then consider those vehicles that best reach smaller audience niches. For example, Cadillac is a heavy user of magazines and television, but uses direct mail to reach Lincoln drivers whose leases are ending.

In the last few years, the media options available to supplement an advertiser's primary vehicles have grown dramatically. The introduction of vehicles such as the World Wide Web, video catalogs, and interactive television has brought major changes to the job of the media planner. For example:

Building block strategy
A media concept that buys the medium that reaches the most prospects first and works down to those that reach the smallest number of prospects.

1. Media planners are forced to go beyond costs in developing plans. When dealing with these specialized media, planners must consider factors such as additional weight against prime prospects, ability to deliver a communication message in a unique manner, and the prestige of a medium that may outweigh low audience delivery.

   The media planner must also consider the **synergistic effect** of the plan. That is, the ability of a combination of media to deliver a message more effectively than the sum of each individual medium. For example, radio advertising is often enhanced by the visualization that comes from television commercials using the same product message. Listeners are able to envision a product from the television commercial and yet the advertiser can save a great deal of money by using radio in combination with television.

Synergistic effect
In media buying, combining a number of complementary media that create advertising awareness greater than the sum of each.

---

[5]Jack Klues, "Forum," *Mediaweek,* February 20, 1995, p. 14.

2. Technology is changing the fundamental relationships among media, audiences, and advertisers. Media technology is creating an environment where distinctions among media are fading. For example, is the delivery of newspaper content via computer still a "print" medium? Likewise, are text messages available through television still "broadcast" signals?

New interactive media will demand that consumers carry a higher share of editorial costs. In return, consumers can expect to enjoy a greater number of media options.

3. Advertisers and the media are taking a more realistic view of what can be accomplished by a single medium. Media salespeople are attempting to place various media in a total campaign context using the concepts of the building-block media plans and media synergism. It is common for a salesperson for radio to develop an advertising plan that shows potential clients how the medium can complement television or newspapers.

The campaign approach to selling media is a more efficient approach for the advertiser. Moreover, it is good business for the media. For one thing, such an approach adds credibility to a sales pitch when a media representative acknowledges the need for a variety of media. In addition, the campaign sales approach is the only practical means for media such as outdoor or radio that usually occupy a supplemental medium position (a secondary building block) to gain advertising sales.

Although outdoor may have little chance of becoming a dominant medium in a national advertising schedule, if it can move from a 2 percent share of a national campaign to 5 percent, it would realize a significant increase in ad dollars. Multiply this seemingly small increase across hundreds or even thousands of campaigns, and you can see why this more realistic approach to selling media is growing in popularity.

COORDINATE ALL PHASES OF MARKETING COMMUNICATION

Changes in media buying and scheduling are putting pressure on media planners to become more knowledgeable in areas that were not part of their responsibility only a few years ago. In the near future, job functions such as media planners and media buyers will be replaced by more inclusive terms such as marketing communication specialists. The change in terminology is more than semantic; rather, it more accurately reflects both the job function and the expectations of the advertising media executive of the future.

As discussed in chapter 2, advertising professionals, including media planners, must become experts in integrated marketing.

It is currently and will continue to be even more critical to make every element of a brand's communication mix work as synergistically as possible. To help achieve this objective, the planner must understand the role of media and its implications on a brand's promotional efforts, direct marketing activities, public relations actions, etc., since integrated planning is a future necessity and the media planner is uniquely able, because of his or her training and analytical skills, to evaluate communications delivery from a variety of sources.[6]

The need for expertise across advertising and promotional vehicles is underscored by the forecast of continuing growth in all areas of promotion. Most advertising executives predict that measured media (broadcast, magazines, newspapers, and so forth)

---

[6]Jay B. Schoenfeld, "Beyond the Numbers," *Journal of Media Planning,* Spring 1991, p. 28.

will demonstrate slower growth than nonmeasured media (Yellow Pages, direct mail, interactive media) and sales promotion in all its forms will show significant dollar increases into the next century.

Many advertisers predict that in the near future we will not be dealing with distinct media vehicles. Rather, through the use of in-home fiber optics, there will be a convergence of media into a single multimedia source where telephones, interactive computers, movies on demand, and laser printers make obsolete the notion of competing media. Consumers will have much greater control over communication outlets, selecting only those entertainment, information, and advertising messages they want. Waste circulation will be limited; by definition, self-selected communication will go only to prospects. The organizations we view as media today will be information sources, and the carriers of this information will be limited to a few cable outlets, telephone companies, or other common carriers.

MEDIA CHARACTERISTICS

Faced with a multitude of media choices, one of the most important attributes of a media planner is an open mind. From established media such as network television to the newly emerging Internet, media planners must be able to sort out those media with features that best fit the marketing and promotional goals of individual clients and efficiently utilize them.

As one business executive pointed out, "Each medium has its own advantages. It's up to us to sort out the possibilities of each and then exploit their advantages."[7] The experienced media buyer must be able to look beyond personal media preferences and determine the media vehicles that will best reach prospects. It may be that a network television spot is needed, or the best ad placement may be a stock car carrying a sponsor's logo. In many case, media planners must be able to step away from their personal biases and put themselves in the place of a client's prime prospects.

As indicated earlier, media planners must be experts in the marketing plans, advertising goals, and creative strategy of their clients. However, one of the primary tasks of the media planner is to determine those vehicles that will best communicate the message of the advertiser at the most efficient cost. Media planners must keep up with basic media characteristics and latest trends in each of the media, as well as new technology that may have long-range effects on advertising media. To set the stage for our examination of basic media strategy, it will be helpful to briefly outline their major characteristics.[8]

Newspapers

As Exhibit 7.2 showed, newspapers rank just behind television as the major recipient of advertising dollars. Although television has recently overtaken newspapers as the number one advertising medium, newspapers will remain the primary local medium, with almost 90 percent of newspaper advertising revenues accounted for by local and classified categories. However, for the last decade, newspapers have faced declining advertising shares as new competitors have taken ad dollars and many retailers have cut advertising budgets or moved to direct mail.

Pros
1. Newspapers have wide exposure, especially to an upscale audience of age 35 and older adults.

---

[7]Stuart Elliott, "Advertising," *The New York Times,* April 26, 1996, p. C17.

[8]Portions of this section were adapted from *Media Facts: A Comprehensive Media Guide,* a publication of the Radio Advertising Bureau, 1996.

2. Newspaper advertising is extremely flexible, with opportunities for color, large and small ads, timely insertion schedules, coupons, and some selectivity through special sections and targeted editions.
3. Newspapers are timely, reach their audiences at the convenience of the reader, and maintain high credibility as an advertising medium.
4. With a variety of ad sizes and prices available, newspapers can fit the advertising budgets of virtually any advertiser.

Cons

1. Most newspapers have more than 60 percent advertising content. This high ratio of advertising, combined with average newspaper reading time of less than 30 minutes, means few ads are read.
2. Overall newspaper circulation has fallen far behind population and household growth. In many markets, total newspaper penetration is below 30 percent. In addition, readership among a number of key demographics such as teens and young adults has not kept pace with population growth.
3. Advertising costs have risen much more sharply than circulation in recent years.
4. Newspapers face growing competition from television as a primary source of news.

Television

Television is more than a medium of entertainment, information, and advertising. It has become part of the social and cultural lives of most adults and children. It reaches every demographic category and achieves creative impact with both color and motion. For example, the top 100 national advertisers place approximately $17 billion in television or some 40 percent of the total advertising expenditure of these major firms (see Exhibit 7.3).

Pros

1. Television reaches 98 percent of all U.S. households with average daily viewing of approximately 8 hours.
2. Television is an extremely creative and flexible medium, which can be used for virtually any product message.
3. Despite recent cost increases, it remains extremely efficient for large advertisers needing to reach a mass audience. By utilizing selected cable outlets and local broadcast stations, advertisers are able to provide a local or regional component to their national television schedules.

e x h i b i t

7.3

Television is by far the major medium for leading advertisers.

Courtesy: Advertising Age.
Source: "100 Leading National Advertisers," *Advertising Age,* September 30, 1996, p. s54.

National Ad Spending by Media (100 Leading National Advertisers)

Media	Advertising Expenditures			Media as % of Total	
	1995	1994	% chg	1995	1994
Magazines	$4,416.5	$3,884.0	13.7	9.3	9.0
Sunday magazines	398.6	415.6	−4.1	0.8	1.0
Newspapers	3,031.5	2,603.0	16.5	6.4	6.0
National newspapers	262.4	266.6	−1.6	0.6	0.6
Outdoor	350.4	284.5	23.2	0.7	0.7
Network TV	9,709.3	9,085.0	6.9	20.5	21.0
Spot TV	4,903.5	4,893.6	0.2	10.4	11.3
Syndicated TV	1,652.1	1,573.3	5.0	3.5	3.6
Cable TV networks	1,931.8	1,694.8	14.0	4.1	3.9
Network radio	450.3	340.5	32.2	1.0	0.8
National spot radio	425.5	339.6	25.3	0.9	0.8
Yellow Pages	109.5	96.9	13.0	0.2	0.2
Measured	27,641.4	25,477.4	8.5	58.4	58.9
Unmeasured	19,662.3	17,799.5	10.5	41.6	41.1
Total	47,303.7	43,277.0	9.3	100.0	100.0

Note: Dollars are in millions. Measured media for 100 leaders and all advertisers from Competitive Media Reporting.

4. Television offers advertisers the prestige and influence lacking in most other media. For example, 61 percent of women report getting political campaign information from television, as contrasted to only 16 percent from newspapers.

Cons

1. The television message is perishable and easily forgotten without expensive repetition.
2. The television audience is fragmented, with alternatives such as cable, independent stations, VCRs, and on-line computer services vying for limited viewing time. The potential of 500 channel systems combined with interactive technology will make fragmentation even more of a problem in the future.
3. Shorter spots, some as short as 15 seconds, have contributed to confusing commercial clutter.
4. The introduction of the remote control and channel surfing by viewers have greatly restricted the time spent with commercials by the average television user.

Radio

Radio is a personal medium that takes advantage of its many stations and formats to direct advertising to extremely well-defined audience segments. The medium can be heard in the home, at work, in the car, and during most leisure activities. More important, radio is listened to in the marketplace as prospective buyers go to their favorite shopping locations. Radio has high weekly coverage and station loyalty by the audience; still it maintains the lowest costs of all major media.

Pros

1. With the exception of direct response, radio is the primary media for targeting narrow audience segments, many of whom are not heavy users of other media. For example, radio is particularly popular with teenagers.
2. Radio is a mobile medium, going with listeners into the marketplace and giving advertisers proximity to the sale (see Exhibit 7.4, p. 180).
3. Radio, with its relatively low production costs and immediacy, can react quickly to changing market conditions.
4. Radio has a personal relationship with its audience unmatched by other media. This affinity with listeners carries over to the credibility it has for many of the products advertised.
5. Radio, with its low cost and targeted formats, is an excellent supplemental medium for secondary building blocks to increase reach and frequency to specific target markets.

Cons

1. Without a visual component, radio often lacks the impact of other media. Also many listeners use radio as "background noise" and don't pay full attention.
2. The low average audience of most radio stations requires high frequency to achieve acceptable reach and frequency.
3. Adequate audience research is not always available, especially in the important drive-time and out-of-home listener categories. Many small market stations have no audience research available.

Direct Response

Direct response advertising, with its ability to reach prospects with pinpoint precision, is among the fastest growing media categories. With sophisticated computer-generated programs, direct response advertisers can accurately reach virtually any demographic, product-user, or even lifestyle segment. It is a medium particularly attuned to the target marketing philosophy of the 1990s and gives every indication of remaining a major element in the advertising plans of national as well as local advertisers.

exhibit

7.4

Radio is an effective
marketplace medium.

Courtesy: Radio Advertising
Bureau.
*Source: Media Facts: A
Comprehensive Media Guide,* a
publication of the Radio
Advertising Bureau, 1996, p. 12.

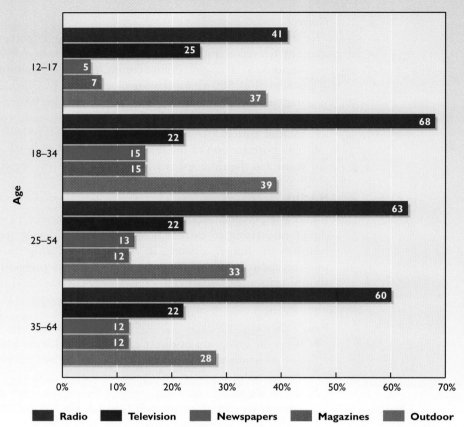

**PERSONS REACHED BY MEDIUM WITHIN ONE HOUR
OF LARGEST PURCHASE**

Source: *Media Targeting 2000,* xvii.

Telemarketing
Contacting
prospective buyers
over the telephone. A
major area of direct
marketing.

Pros
1. Direct response has the ability to target even the most narrowly defined audiences on a geographical, product-usage, or demographic basis.
2. Research is an important element of direct response. It allows advertisers instant feedback to an advertising message using virtually any medium as well as telemarketing, coupons, and so forth.
3. Direct response allows advertisers to personalize their messages and thus build a closer relationship to target audiences than is possible in traditional mass media vehicles.

Cons
1. High cost per contact is a major problem with many forms of direct response. Expenses for printing, production, and personnel have all increased significantly in recent years.
2. Prospect lists must be constantly updated at considerable expense to the advertiser.
3. Direct response, especially direct mail and **telemarketing,** has an image problem among many consumers and lacks the credibility of other major media.
4. Couponing, long one of the fundamental techniques of direct response, is demonstrating a significant decrease in redemption levels, reducing the impact and tracking of many direct response campaigns.

Magazines

Magazines, like their newspaper counterparts, have seen circulation lag behind population and household growth as people continue to read less and depend more on television for information. Offsetting this trend is the ability of magazines to offer advertisers a number of specialized titles as well as geographic and demographic editions to reach narrowly defined audience segments. Virtually every potential consumer interest is represented by at least one magazine.

Pros

1. Like radio and cable television, the number and range of specialized magazines provide advertisers with an opportunity for narrowly targeted audiences. Magazines can effectively use messages that reach these audiences with creative themes (see Exhibit 7.5).
2. Studies indicate that magazines are among the most prestigious media and consequently provide a prestige, quality environment for advertisers.
3. Magazine advertising has a long life and is often passed along to several readers. Business publications are especially useful as reference tools and are routinely passed along and kept for long periods of time.

Cons

1. In recent years, magazine audience growth has not kept up with increases in advertising rates. Magazines are among the most expensive media on a per-prospect basis.
2. Most magazines have relatively long advertising deadlines, reducing flexibility and the ability of advertisers to react to fast-changing market conditions.

e x h i b i t

7.5

Magazines are effective in reaching narrowly targeted audiences.

Courtesy: Bulldog Drummond.

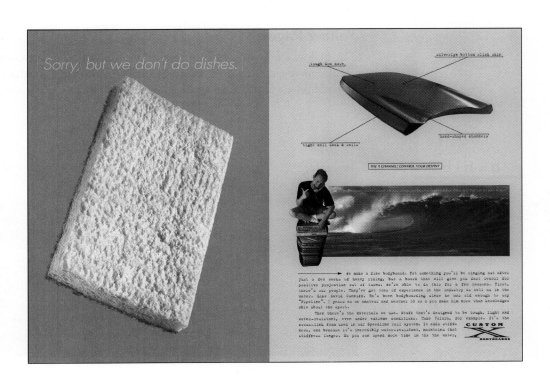

3. Despite the obvious advantages of magazine specialization, a single magazine rarely reaches the majority of a market segment. Therefore, several magazines must be used or alternative media must supplement the magazine schedule. With more than 1,000 consumer magazines, advertisers have difficulty in choosing the correct vehicle.

Out-of-Home

Out-of-home
Outdoor and transportation advertising.

Spectacular
Outdoor sign built to order, designed to be conspicuous for its location, size, lights, motion, or action. The costliest form of outdoor advertising.

In an era of target marketing and increased emphasis on finely tuned media strategies, outdoor and **out-of-home** are among the few media that reach largely undifferentiated audiences. Outdoor advertising is a visual medium intended for brand-name reinforcement. It also can be effective as a supplemental medium in introducing new products and brands. From the familiar highway billboard to the one-of-a-kind **spectacular** to transit advertising (see Exhibit 7.6), out-of-home is impossible to ignore.

Pros

1. Outdoor can reach most of the population in a market with high frequency at a very low cost per exposure.

2. It is an excellent means of supplementing other media advertising for product introduction or building brand-name recognition.

3. With the use of color and lighting, outdoor is a medium that gains immediate audience attention.

4. The outdoor industry has diversified the product categories that use the medium in an attempt to lose its image as a "beer and cigarette" medium.

Cons

1. Outdoor is rarely able to communicate detailed sales messages. Copy is usually limited to seven to ten words.

2. The impact of outdoor advertising is extremely difficult to measure, making audience comparisons with other media almost impossible.

3. Outdoor has been attacked in many communities as a visual pollutant, which has made it the topic of some controversy and legal restrictions. A few state and local governments have banned the medium altogether. This negative image may discourage some advertisers from using outdoor.

Yellow Pages

The Yellow Pages are excellent reference sources that direct consumers to a specific company. However, they do little to create demand for a product or service. Yellow Pages provide an easy means of finding a company once the decision to buy has been made.

e x h i b i t

7.6

Out-of-home advertising reaches a mobile population.

Courtesy: SuperGraphics.

exhibit

7.7

Yellow Pages provide a constant advertising reference.

Courtesy: Yellow Pages Publishers Association.
Source: Yellow Pages Industry Facts & Media Guide, 1995–1996 Edition, p. 21.

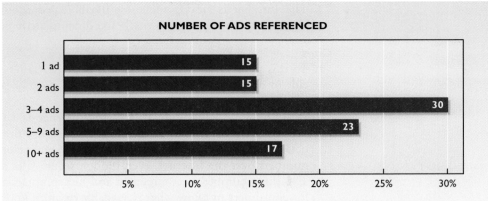

NUMBER OF ADS REFERENCED

Ads	%
1 ad	15
2 ads	15
3–4 ads	30
5–9 ads	23
10+ ads	17

Sixty-two percent of Yellow Pages references are to ads, and an average of 5.4 ads are considered. In 53 percent of references, consumers have no name, or two or more store or business names in mind and can be influenced by what they see in the Yellow Pages. Eighty-eight percent of references result in a contact, and 44 percent of those are from new customers. Ninety percent of references result in a purchase (52%) or an intended purchase (38%); of the 52 percent of references where a purchase was made, 46 percent are from new customers. Seventy-six percent of references are for home or personal reasons. Twenty-four percent of references are for business reasons. Sixty-six percent of references are made from home. Thirty-one percent of references are made from work.

Pros

1. Yellow Pages are used by a large segment of the population on a regular basis. More than 50 percent of adults use the Yellow Pages weekly.
2. Yellow Pages appeal to a self-selected consumer already in the market for a specific product or service, but still deciding on a particular business from which to purchase (see Exhibit 7.7).
3. Yellow Pages consumers are looking for a place to spend their money. They normally do not know from whom they will make a purchase prior to using the Yellow Pages.

Cons

1. The Yellow Pages offer limited promotional opportunities. They cannot create an image, build demand, or promote a special sale.
2. Yellow Pages cannot protect an advertiser from clutter. Virtually every major competitor will be competing for consumer time with your ad.
3. Yellow Pages are inflexible. If a company changes its product line, hours of operation, prices, or address, it may be months before these adjustments are reflected in the company's advertising.

Internet

Internet
A worldwide system of computer links that provide instantaneous communication.

The **Internet** is a medium with vast potential, but very few companies have been able to successfully adapt the technology to a practical or profitable sales tool. The primary attraction of the Internet is its ability to deal one-to-one with consumers. In theory, business and consumers can buy products, exchange product information, and acquire valuable research with the touch of a computer key. In practice, the Internet remains an experimental medium with vast underutilized potential.

Pros

1. The Internet offers an inexpensive, quick, and easily available response medium.
2. The Internet is the ultimate research tool, with its ability to measure exactly how many people used the medium and/or purchased a product.

3. The Internet is among the most flexible media, with an ability to immediately change copy in reaction to market and competitive conditions.

Cons

1. To this point, the Internet is mostly promise rather than performance. It is difficult to determine the effectiveness of the service because it is largely experimental in a commercial sense.

2. Despite the growing popularity of the Internet as a means of informal communication, many consumers are still reluctant to use the service for purchasing products and services. In particular, consumers seem reluctant to give their credit card numbers over the Internet, even though secure sites are available.

3. The sheer number of commercial and noncommercial Web sites makes it difficult for consumers to know what is available or, once known, have much time to spend with any single site.

THE COMPONENTS OF THE MEDIA PLAN

Knowing the characteristics of the various media is only the first step in designing a media plan. The media planner must be able to use these media characteristics as part of a sophisticated analysis that leads to a complete media plan for an advertising campaign. Although there is no standard format, the following elements are found in most plans:

- a description of the target audience
- communication requirements and creative elements
- geography—where is the product distributed?
- the efficiency/effectiveness balance—shall we emphasize reach, frequency, or continuity?
- the pressure of competition
- the budget

The Target Audience

As mentioned earlier in this chapter, the media planner cannot develop a media plan without a thorough knowledge of the prime prospects of a product or service and the media most likely to economically and efficiently reach them. Media buying is undergoing fundamental changes because new technology and sophisticated consumers require major modifications in media planning. For the most part, these changes are directed at identifying consumer groups, their needs, and the product benefits that meet these needs.

One approach is the so-called *target market incentive statement,* which summarizes four important means of reaching consumers. In one sentence the statement recaps the target audience's relationship to the product: "To *(user group), (name of brand)* is the *(product category)* that *(benefit of brand).*"[9] For example, To "*young marrieds, Honda Civic* is the *automobile* that *delivers the greatest dependability at the lowest cost.*"

Such a statement keeps the media planner broadly focused on the total picture of consumer, product, and benefit rather than more narrowly considering only reaching the target market at the lowest cost. Advertising researchers are constantly seeking more sophisticated tools to get a clear picture of consumers and the ways in which they interact with media and advertising messages. Audience profiles are constantly changing, and advertisers must track these fluctuations.

Media planners must balance cost efficiency against reaching more narrowly defined audiences. Cost considerations require that media plans maximize delivery of prospects as opposed to people or households. Not too many years ago, media planners used very

---

[9]Don E. Schultz, Stanley I. Tannenbaum, and Anne Allison, *Essentials of Advertising Strategy,* 3rd ed. (Lincolnwood, Ill.: NTC Business Books, 1996), p. 57.

rough measures of cost efficiency. The most common, and one still widely used, is the **cost per thousand** (*CPM*).

The *CPM* is a means of comparing media costs among vehicles with different circulations. The formula is stated as:

$$CPM = \frac{\text{ad cost} \times 1,000}{\text{circulation}}$$

McCall's magazine has a circulation of 4.2 million and a four-color page rate of $115,000. Its *CPM* is thus calculated as:

$$McCall's\ CPM = \frac{\$115,000 \times 1,000}{4.200.000} = \$27.38$$

Obviously, no medium provides an audience where every member is of equal benefit to a specific advertiser. Let us assume that our client is a diaper manufacturer and wants to reach only women with children two years old or younger. To measure the efficiency of *McCall's* against this audience, we might use some variation of the *weighted* or *demographic CPM*. Let us look at an example of the weighted *CPM*.

In this case, we find that of *McCall's* 4.2 million readers, 600,000 have children age two and younger. Here we calculate the weighted *CPM* using only our target audience rather than the total circulation of the magazine.

$$\text{Weighted } CPM = \frac{\$115,000 \times 1,000}{600.000} = \$191.66$$

In using a weighted *CPM*, a media planner can substitute any number of lifestyle, product user, or psychographic data for the demographic category we used in the *McCall's* example. Chapter 4 discussed a number of different means of identifying target markets. It is important to note that *CPM* figures are important only as comparisons with those of other media. *McCall's CPM* of $27.38 is of interest only to the extent that it might be compared to *Redbook's CPM* of $36.90.

Media planners are constantly attempting to fine-tune cost efficiencies against more useful and targeted client prospects. Another version of the weighted *CPM* combines cost comparisons with communication involvement of the audience. This approach seeks to find a media plan that features high audience involvement with individual programs or publications.

Research has shown that high levels of audience involvement with a medium is positively related to advertising response. This relationship is particularly true with television, where a large portion of the audience for many programs is paying only minimal attention. The greater the involvement with a program, the more effective the advertising. Using logic similar to the weighted *CPM*, some media researchers have developed a cost comparison called the Cost Per Thousand Involved *(CPMI)*.

Without going into the research methodology, the *CPMI* computes an involvement index by comparing audience involvement (on a four-point scale) for a program. For example:

Assume that program A has an involvement score of 3.20 compared to an involvement score of 2.80 for all programs considered. Program A's involvement index is 1.14 (3.20/2.80).

Again, assuming that the *CPM* for program A is $11.30, we divide it by 1.14 to calculate the *CPMI*. In this case, it is $9.91 ($11.30/1.14). In other words, because program A has higher audience involvement, it is a better buy than its *CPM* would indicate.[10]

---

[10]David W. Lloyd and Kevin J. Clancy, "CPMs versus CPMIs: Implications for Media Planning," *Journal of Advertising Research,* August/September 1991, p. 34.

Cost per thousand (CPM) A method of comparing the cost for media of different circulations. Also weighted or demographic cost per thousand calculates the *CPM* using only that portion of a medium's audience falling into a prime-prospect category.

The weighted *CPM* and the *CPMI* are only two of a number of techniques that media planners use to refine their audience analyses. The important point in all these techniques is that the media planner can no longer deal only with total circulation of a medium. Prospects may account for a small portion of the audience for any medium, and this must be reflected in its cost efficiency.

Claritas's Potential Rating Index by ZIP Market (PRIZM)

A shortcoming of many audience analysis methods is that they consider only a single variable. The earlier *McCall's* example designated women with children age two and younger as the target market for diapers. However, we know that within this broad category there are a number of differences. For example, a working woman might purchase diapers from a day-care center without making a brand decision. Some women may use a diaper service rather than purchase disposable diapers. Likewise, income, education, and other factors might change the purchase behavior of a woman in this general category. Media planners realize that a multivariable approach is often needed to correctly identify a particular target segment.

One of the most innovative methods of segmenting markets on a multivariable basis is the **potential rating index by ZIP market** (PRIZM) system developed by the Claritas Corporation. PRIZM divides the population into 15 social groups (see Exhibit 7.8a) and further subdivides these large segments into 62 subcategories (see Exhibit 7.8b). The primary variables for determining these social groups are urbanization and social class.

The PRIZM categories are arranged in descending order of affluence from the "blue-blood estates," who reside in the elite suburban social group, to "hard scrabble," whose residents live in the most rural and lowest social class areas of the country. The value of PRIZM groups is that these general categories can be matched with those products and media that members of a particular group are most likely to use. For example, inhabitants of the "elite suburbs" are likely to drive luxury cars and be among the heavi-

Potential rating index by ZIP market (PRIZM)
A method of audience segmentation developed by the Claritas Corporation.

exhibit

7.8a

PRIZM allows marketers to target customers by geography and lifestyle.

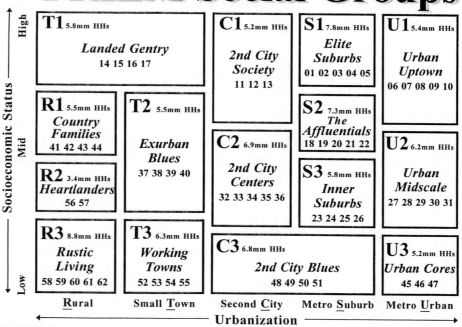

Copyright 1994, Claritas Inc.

PRIZM by Claritas
Demographic Reference Chart

Race/Ethnicity
W-White, B-Black, A-Asian
H-Hispanic, F-Foreign Born
□ Prevelent • Above Avg

PREDOMINANT CHARACTERISTICS

Grp	Clstr	Nickname	Income Level	Family Type	Age	Education	Occup	Housing	W	B	A	H	F
S1	01	Blue Blood Estates	Elite	Family	35-54	College	Exec	Single	□		•		•
	02	Cashmere & Country Clubs	Wealthy	Family	35-54	College	Exec	Single	□		•		•
	03	Executive Suites	Affluent	Couples	25-34	College	WC/Exec	Single			•		•
	04	Pools & Patios	Affluent	Couples	55-64	College	Exec	Single			•		•
	05	Kids & Cul-de-Sacs	Affluent	Family	35-54	College	WC/Exec	Single	•		•		•
U1	06	Urban Gold Coast	Affluent	Singles	25-34	College	Exec	Hi-Rise	□		•		•
	07	Money & Brains	Affluent	Couples	55-64	College	Exec	Hi-Rise	□		•		•
	08	Young Literati	Upper Mid	Sgl/Cpl	25-34	College	Exec	Hi-Rise	•		•		•
	09	American Dreams	Upper Mid	Family	35-54	College	WC	Single		•	•	•	•
	10	Bohemian Mix	Middle	Singles	< 24	College	WC	Hi-Rise		•	•	•	•
C1	11	Second City Elite	Affluent	Couples	35-64	College	WC/Exec	Single	□				
	12	Upward Bound	Upper Mid	Family	25-54	College	WC/Exec	Single	□				
	13	Gray Power	Middle	Sgl/Cpl	65+	College	WC	Single					•
T1	14	Country Squires	Wealthy	Fam/Cpl	35-64	College	Exec	Single	□				
	15	God's Country	Affluent	Family	35-54	College	WC	Single	□				
	16	Big Fish Small Pond	Upper Mid	Family	35-54	HS/College	WC	Single	□				
	17	Greenbelt Families	Upper Mid	Family	25-54	College	WC	Single	□				
S2	18	Young Influentials	Upper Mid	Sgl/Cpl	< 35	College	WC/Exec	Multi	•		•		
	19	New Empty Nests	Upper Mid	Couples	35-64	College	WC/Exec	Single	•				
	20	Boomers & Babies	Upper Mid	Family	25-54	College	WC/Exec	Single	•		•		•
	21	Suburban Sprawl	Middle	Fam/Cpl	< 35	College	WC	Mixed	•		•	•	•
	22	Blue-Chip Blues	Middle	Family	35-54	HS/College	WC/BC	Single	•				
S3	23	Upstarts & Seniors	Middle	Cpl/Sgl	Mix	College	WC/Exec	Multi	□				
	24	New Beginnings	Middle	Sgl/Cpl	< 35	College	WC/Exec	Multi	•		•	•	•
	25	Mobility Blues	Middle	Fam/Cpl	< 35	HS/College	BC/Serv	Mixed		•		□	•
	26	Gray Collars	Middle	Couples	> 55	HS	BC/Serv	Single	•				
U2	27	Urban Achievers	Middle	Cpl/Sgl	Mix	College	WC/Exec	Hi-Rise	□		•	•	•
	28	Big City Blend	Middle	Family	35-54	HS	WC/BC	Single		•		□	•
	29	Old Yankee Rows	Middle	Couples	55+	HS	WC	Multi	•		•		•
	30	Middle Minorities	Middle	Fam/Cpl	35-54	HS/College	WC/Serv	Multi		□			•
	31	Latino America	Middle	Family	25-34	< HS	BC/Serv	Multi				□	•
C2	32	Middleburg Managers	Middle	Couples	> 55	College	WC/Exec	Single	□				
	33	Boomtown Singles	Middle	Sgl/Cpl	< 34	College	WC/Exec	Multi	□				
	34	Starter Families	Middle	Family	25-34	HS	BC	Mixed	•			•	
	35	Sunset City Blues	Lower Mid	Couples	> 55	HS	BC/Serv	Single	•				
	36	Towns & Gowns	Lower Mid	Singles	< 35	College	WC/Serv	Hi-Rise	•		•		
T2	37	New Homesteaders	Middle	Family	35-54	College	WC	Single	□				
	38	Middle America	Middle	Family	25-44	HS	BC	Single	□				
	39	Red, White & Blue-Collar	Middle	Family	35-64	HS	BC	Single	□				
	40	Military Quarters	Lower Mid	Family	25-54	College	WC/Serv	Multi		•	•		•

PRIZM by Claritas
Demographic Reference Chart

Race/Ethnicity
W-White, B-Black, A-Asian
H-Hispanic, F-Foreign Born
□ Prevelent • Above Avg

PREDOMINANT CHARACTERISTICS

Grp	Clstr	Nickname	Income Level	Family Type	Age	Education	Occup	Housing	W	B	A	H	F
R1	41	Big Sky Families	Upper Mid	Family	35-44	HS/College	BC/Farm	Single	□				
	42	New Ecotopia	Middle	Fam/Cpl	35-54	College	WC/BC	Single	□				
	43	River City, USA	Middle	Family	35-64	HS	BC/Farm	Single	□				
	44	Shotguns & Pickups	Middle	Family	35-64	HS	BC/Farm	Single	□				
U3	45	Single City Blues	Lower Mid	Singles	Mix	Mix	WC/Serv	Multi		•	•	•	•
	46	Hispanic Mix	Poor	Family	< 35	< HS	BC	Hi-Rise			□	•	□
	47	Inner Cities	Poor	Sgl/Fam	Mix	< HS	BC/Serv	Multi		□		•	•
C3	48	Smalltown Downtown	Lower Mid	Sgl/Fam	< 35	HS/College	BC/Serv	Multi		•		•	
	49	Hometown Retired	Lower Mid	Sgl/Cpl	65+	< HS	Service	Mixed	□			□	•
	50	Family Scramble	Lower Mid	Family	< 35	< HS	BC	Mixed		•		□	•
	51	Southside City	Poor	Sgl/Fam	Mix	< HS	BC/Serv	Multi		□			
T3	52	Golden Ponds	Lower Mid	Couples	65+	HS	BC/Serv	Single	□				
	53	Rural Industria	Lower Mid	Family	< 35	HS	BC	Single	□				
	54	Norma Rae-Ville	Poor	Sgl/Fam	Mix	< HS	BC/Serv	Single	□	□			
	55	Mines & Mills	Poor	Sgl/Cpl	55+	< HS	BC/Serv	Single	□				
R2	56	Agri-Business	Middle	Family	35+	HS	Farm	Single	□			•	
	57	Grain Belt	Lower Mid	Family	55+	HS	Farm	Single	□			•	
R3	58	Blue Highways	Lower Mid	Family	35-54	HS	BC/Farm	Single	□				
	59	Rustic Elders	Lower Mid	Couples	55+	HS	BC/Serv	Single	□				
	60	Back Country Folks	Lower Mid	Couples	35+	HS	BC/Farm	Single	□				
	61	Scrub Pine Flats	Poor	Family	35+	< HS	BC/Farm	Single	□	□			
	62	Hard Scrabble	Poor	Family	35+	< HS	BC/Farm	Single	□				

Income Level	Avg Annual HH Income
Elite/Wealthy	$65,000 and over
Affluent	$50,000 - $64,500
Upper Mid	$37,000 - $49,500
Middle	$28,000 - $36,500
Lower Mid	$20,000 - $27,500
Poor	under $20,000

Education	
< HS	Grade School
HS	High School / Technical School
HS/College	High School / Some College
College	College Graduates

Family Type	
Family	Married Couples w/Children or, Single Parents w/Children
Couples	Married Couples (few children)
Singles	Singles / Unmarried Couples
Fam/Cpl	Mix of Married Couples with/without Children
Sgl/Cpl	Mix of Married Couples and Singles

Occupation	
Exec	Executive, managerial & professionals (teachers, doctors, etc.)
WC	Other White-Collar (technical, sales, admin/clerical support)
BC	Blue-Collar (assembly, trades & repair, operators, laborers, etc.)
WC/BC	Mix of White-Collar & Upper-Level Blue Collar
Service	Service (hospitality, food prep, protective & health services, etc)
WC/Serv	Mix of Other White-Collar & Service
BC/Serv	Mix of Blue-Collar & Service
Farm	Farming, Mining & Ranching (farm operators, forestry, etc.)
BC/Farm	Mix of Blue-Collar and Farming

exhibit

7.8b

est readers of magazines. By identifying theses groups geographically, companies can develop efficient marketing and advertising plans without the waste circulation of a less targeted campaign.

In the future, the computer and more sophisticated research methodology will make even more finely tuned audience identification possible. In fact, we may be approaching a time when audience segmentation techniques will be able to target prospects more precisely than media vehicles will be able to practically or efficiently reach them. Even the most thoroughly researched media plan will reach some nonbuyers. The job of the media planner is to keep waste circulation to a minimum while achieving maximum cost efficiencies. A media schedule with zero nonprospects would be not only theoretically impossible to achieve, but prohibitively expensive.

Communication Requirements and Creative Elements

The media planner does not have responsibility for the creative elements of a campaign. However, media planners consider the creative goals, the message themes, and the creative execution in developing a media plan. Due to the cost of time and space, there is a tendency to become so concerned with media cost analyses that we forget effective advertising must communicate to our listeners and readers.

Media planners must make a distinction between exposure to advertising and advertising communication. It also is important to consider differences between purchase decisions and actual purchases. For example, children have a significant influence on restaurant choices of adults, and the media plan must consider the relationship of children and parents. McDonald's advertising is a prime example of how children are brought into the advertising mix.

In the past, a major criticism of advertising was that media and creative functions were not coordinated closely enough. The result, according to critics, was advertising that did not fully utilize the communicative strengths of the various media vehicles. Fortunately, the separation between the creative and media functions seems to have diminished in recent years. Among major advertising agencies, there seems to be a heightened sensitivity that creative/media cooperation is necessary for effective advertising.

Among the primary **communication components** for the media planner are the following:

> **Communication components**
> That portion of the media plan that considers the effectiveness of message delivery as contrasted to the efficiency of audience delivery.

1. *Creative predispositions of the audience.* For example, teens are predisposed to radio in a different way than they are to print.
2. *Qualitative environment for the message.* *Golf* magazine reaches readers who are in the proper frame of mind for ads for golf balls and golf clubs.
3. *The synergistic effect.* Advertisers seek a combination of media for a communicative effect that is greater than the sum of each medium. For example, automobile manufacturers use outdoor to gain brand recognition, magazines for detailed product information, newspapers for dealer location and price, and television for demonstration and image. The net effect is greater than any single medium used alone.
4. *The creative approach.* Does the need for long copy or quality reproduction require print, even if other media might be more cost efficient?

In the future, interactive media will require even closer coordination between media placement and the communication environment. However, the specific role between media planning and the new media, particularly the use of client Web sites, is still to be determined. Clearly, the relationship will be much different from traditional media buys and demand more involvement by the media planner to make the new media an effective advertising force.

> Like everything else on the Internet, Web directories require entirely new thinking. Competition for readers will be on the basis of content and con-

exhibit

7.9

In addition to company identifiers such as name and logo, advertisers anticipate including company history, listings of office locations, product, catalog, and ordering information in a majority of Web sites.

Source: Cahners Advertising Research Report, No. 812.0.

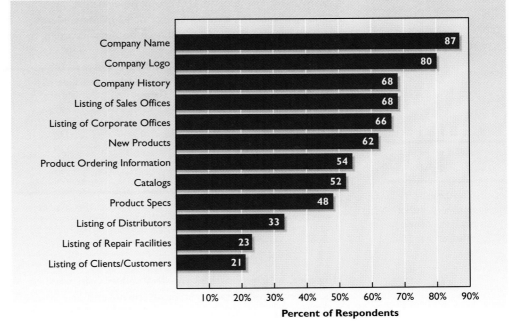

	Percent of Respondents
Company Name	87
Company Logo	80
Company History	68
Listing of Sales Offices	68
Listing of Corporate Offices	66
New Products	62
Product Ordering Information	54
Catalogs	52
Product Specs	48
Listing of Distributors	33
Listing of Repair Facilities	23
Listing of Clients/Customers	21

venience of use. Who has the most up-to-date listings? What format is easiest to use? The annual [Web site] publication is history—weekly or even daily updates will become the norm. The Web directory publisher has to invest in building readership, but usage will eventually translate into ad dollars for links, boldface and display ad, and opportunities to provide Web presence for marketers.[11]

Obviously, media planners are going to have to become familiar with a number of factors before they can utilize the new media. Exhibit 7.9 shows some of the basic information that business-to-business advertisers anticipate providing on their Web sites. Obviously, reaching a general consumer audience will present different, and more difficult, decisions for both clients and planners.

Geography—Where Is the Product Distributed?

Geographical considerations are among the oldest factors in buying media. Long before advertisers were knowledgeable about the importance of demographics and target markets, they knew the area in which their products were distributed and sought those promotional vehicles that best reached those areas. Even in an era of narrowly defined audiences, geography remains a primary consideration of the planner.

Obviously, areas with the greatest population also offer the highest potential for sales of most products. However, the media planner must also relate population to prospects for a particular product and allocate the budget to different areas in the most efficient manner. One method of relating sales, advertising budgets, and geography is the **brand development index** (BDI). An example of the BDI is shown in Exhibit 7.10 (p. 190).

Geographical considerations are becoming more important as advertisers find that consumers in different parts of the country demonstrate markedly different attitudes and opinions concerning various product categories. These differences have to be reflected in regional advertising that supplements national media plans. For example, Cavalier is the mainstay volume seller for Chevrolet dealers in most of the country.

Brand development index (BDI)
A method of allocating advertising budgets to those geographic areas that have the greatest sales potential.

---

[11]Bernard Schnoll, "The Freshest Information Is Key to Web Success," *Direct Marketing,* July 22, 1996, p. 22.

Computing the Brand Development Index

ACME Appliance has a media budget of $2 million and sells in 20 markets. The media planner wants to allocate the budget in the 20 markets according to the sales potential of each market.

exhibit

7.10

The brand development index emphasizes prime sales areas.

Market	Population (%)	ACME Sales (%)	Budget by Population (000)	BDI (Sales/ Population)	Budget by BDI
1	8	12	$ 160	150	$ 240,000
2	12	8	240	67	160,800
3	6	6	120	100	120,000
etc.					
20	100%	100%	$2,000	—	$2,000,000

Example: Market 2, based on its population, should have an advertising allocation of $240,000 (0.12 × $2,000,000). However, the sales potential of market 2 is only 67 percent as great as its population would indicate (sales/population or 8/12). Therefore, the media planner reduces the allocation to market 2 to $160,800 ($240,000 × 0.67) and reallocates funds to markets with greater potential such as market 1.

However, in Oregon they are slow sellers compared to pickups and sport utility vehicles. Likewise, Toyota has strongly promoted the "Buy American" theme, emphasizing its Kentucky assembly plant, yet in California it makes little difference to buyers where a car is built.[12]

Regional differences in product usage require many firms to develop a secondary localized media plan to supplement their national media schedule. National advertisers are increasingly using local advertising options, such as local cable, and specialized product-specific publications, such as restaurant guides. Studies indicate that more than 60 percent of national advertisers plan to use localized media, with local cable television being the most popular media choice, followed by regional editions of national magazines.

The Efficiency/Effectiveness Balance: Should Reach, Frequency, or Continuity Be Emphasized?

At this stage, the media planner is moving into the specific tactics of the media schedule. The first step is consideration of audience reach, frequency, and continuity. Reach refers to the total number of people to whom you deliver a message; **frequency** refers to the number of times it is delivered within a given period (usually figured on a weekly basis for ease in schedule planning); and continuity refers to the length of time a schedule runs. Only the biggest advertisers can emphasize all three factors at once, and even they seek to spread their money most efficiently.

Frequency
Of media exposure the number of times an individual or household is exposed to a medium within a given period of time.

Reach, frequency, and continuity must be balanced against the demands of a fixed budget. However, the media planner must also consider the balance between the least expensive media (efficiency) and those most able to communicate the message and reach the best prospects (effectiveness). Exhibit 7.11 shows the relationship among the three elements in some typical media strategies.

In reality, the media planner's primary considerations are reach and frequency. Normally, the budget is predetermined, and the planner functions within fairly strict guidelines as to the continuity of the campaign. In other words, the media planner rarely has the option of reducing a year-long campaign to six months in order to fulfill reach or frequency goals.

Most media planners start with frequency as the first building block. A determination is made as to the minimum exposures required to make an impact on the prospect

---

[12]"Media Options Drive Cars into Strong Region Spending," *Advertising Age,* September 27, 1995, p. 4.

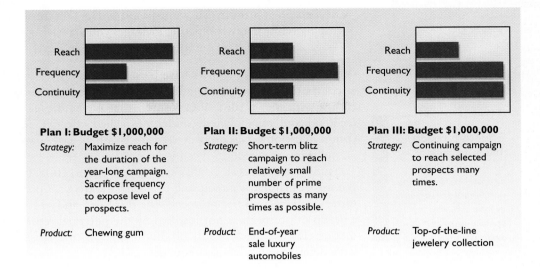

Plan I: Budget $1,000,000

Strategy: Maximize reach for the duration of the year-long campaign. Sacrifice frequency to expose level of prospects.

Product: Chewing gum

Plan II: Budget $1,000,000

Strategy: Short-term blitz campaign to reach relatively small number of prime prospects as many times as possible.

Product: End-of-year sale luxury automobiles

Plan III: Budget $1,000,000

Strategy: Continuing campaign to reach selected prospects many times.

Product: Top-of-the-line jewelery collection

during some buying cycle. We might look at the reach/frequency question in terms of total exposures that can be purchased with our ad budget.

Let us say our budget will purchase 2 million exposures. These exposures can be bought in a number of ways as long as they total 2 million. However, each time we increase the number of exposures per prospect, we reduce the number of prospects we can reach:

$$5 \text{ exposures} \times 400{,}000 \text{ prospects} = 2{,}000{,}000$$

$$10 \text{ exposures} \times 200{,}000 \text{ prospects} = 2{,}000{,}000$$

$$2 \text{ exposures} \times 1{,}000{,}000 \text{ prospects} = 2{,}000{,}000$$

As you can see, if we decide to increase the number of exposures per prospect, we risk failing to reach other prospects at all. Yet we must be careful to break the communications barrier, or else our ad message will be totally ineffective.

A continuing problem facing all media planners is maximizing frequency. Too little frequency prevents a message from penetrating the market and too much wastes valuable resources by continuing to expose an audience to a saturated message. Many factors will determine the frequency allocation in a media plan; some of the primary considerations include the following:

1. *Audience motivation.* Does the consumer have to be motivated to consider the product class before buying a brand? Do you first have to persuade consumers to exercise and then move them to buy a HealthRider or Nordic Track?
2. *Purchase cycle.* How often does the typical consumer purchase the product? A seldom purchased high-ticket item may require less frequency than a product bought on a regular basis.
3. *Message complexity.* Products with a complex story to tell or products using long, reason-why copy will probably demand more frequency to acquaint consumers with the benefits of the product.
4. *Advertising effectiveness.* The strength of the creative message may require less frequency. It is obvious that the higher the interest and recall of a commercial, the less frequently consumers will have to be exposed.
5. *Time of day/attention level.* Generally, attention levels are higher at night for television commercials. A daytime or combination daytime/prime-time schedule may require more frequency than a prime-time only schedule.

6. *Competitive pressure.* Most media plans have to consider what the competition is doing. How many competing messages you are having to overcome to get your message across will have an effect on the frequency level.[13]

In recent years, planners have been concerned with the effectiveness of advertising as contrasted to simply generating exposure levels. Increasingly, media planners are concerned with the "quality of exposure," that is, the degree to which the message is understood and remembered (sometimes called effective communication). To measure communication versus exposures, media planners have adapted the terms **effective reach** and effective frequency.

Effective reach is an extension of targeting marketing. In determining effective reach, the media planner is attempting to determine the core prospects (and best current customers), the second tier prospects, the third tier, and so forth until the cost of reaching a group of prospects is not justified by the potential return from sales. Accurately estimating effective reach is difficult, but it pales in comparison to the problems associated with determining effective frequency.

Chapter 2 discussed the emerging concept of integrated marketing in which all forms of marketing communications are developed in a systematic manner to complement each other. The growing popularity of integrated marketing places even more pressure on media researchers to develop a frequency model that will measure advertising and its relationship to word-of-mouth, public relations, sales promotion, and other marketing communication techniques.

The problem of measuring frequency is that there is no universal agreement on exactly how it works. Let us examine a few of the major theories of advertising frequency:[14]

1. *Positive message synergy.* Virtually all theories of effective frequency suggest that consumers must be exposed more than once for advertising to be effective. Each subsequent exposure increases audience awareness and communication up to some point of diminishing return. This theory demands multiexposures to a point where saturation has been reached.

2. *Learning theories of advertising frequency.* Learning theory assumes that consumers acquire the most information from the first exposure, and each subsequent exposure creates less learning until a point where each additional exposure creates only reinforcement. Obviously, a planner operating under this theory is less compelled to provide heavy frequency because each exposure is providing less benefit than the one before.

3. *Message interaction theory.* Message interaction theory takes the position that the most effective frequency occurs when consumers are exposed to similar messages from different sources. For example, consumers might be more receptive to word-of-mouth if they had previously been exposed to advertising that provided some knowledge of the product. This theory is the strongest support for an integrated marketing approach to promotion, but it also is the most difficult theory in which to measure the effectiveness of individual communication sources.

4. *Message composition theory.* Message composition theory assumes that consumers learn different product information from different sources. This theory requires high frequency because a consumer must be exposed to multiple messages *and* multiple promotional outlets to gain the full message.

---

[13]Jim Surmanek, "One-Hit or Miss: Is a Frequency of One Frequently Wrong?" *Advertising Age,* November 27, 1995, p. 17.

[14]Hugh M. Cannon and Edward A. Riordan, "Beyond Effective Frequency: Advertising Media Planning in an Era of Integrated Marketing Communication," *Proceedings of the 1996 Conference of the American Academy of Advertising,* p. 28.

Effective reach
The percentage of an audience that is exposed to a certain number of messages or has achieved a specific level of awareness.

Recency   Another view of advertising frequency is that it is not the number of times a consumer is exposed, but the timing of the exposure. In this view, a single advertising message can influence the consumer who is ready to purchase. The concept of *recency* takes the approach that a consumer who is ready to buy a product will be most affected by ads promoting a brand. The closer to the point of sale that a consumer is exposed to advertising, the more receptive the person will be to the message. The motivating force of an ad is greatly determined by timing—how close to the purchase decision exposure occurs.[15]

Proponents of recency would emphasize vehicles such as radio, outdoor, Yellow Pages, and point-of-purchase to provide advertising for consumers actively in the marketplace. They also would likely stress a consistent advertising schedule to ensure that consumers are exposed to messages as they begin the purchase process.

No single theory of frequency will totally explain the communication process. Consumers viewing the same advertisements will learn different information at different rates and act on information in various ways. Despite the difficulty of measuring levels of frequency, it remains one of the key decisions that any media planner has to make.

THE MEDIA SCHEDULE

Media schedule
The detailed plan or calendar showing when ads and commercials will be distributed and in what media vehicles they will appear.

Once the media planner has determined the best target audience, the media building blocks, and a general strategy regarding reach and frequency, it is time to prepare the **media schedule.** A media schedule is a calendar or blueprint of the advertising plan. The schedule must offer in specific detail exactly what media will be bought, when they will be purchased, and how much time or space will be used for each advertisement or commercial. For example, if we decide to purchase ad space in *Sports Illustrated,* will we use four-color or black-and-white insertions; will we place a full-page or half-page advertisement; will we use the entire circulation of the publication or one of the numerous geographic editions offered; which of the 52 issues will we use?

Remember that we must make similar decisions for each of the media vehicles that we purchase. For a national advertiser, a media schedule might encompass dozens or even hundreds of stations, networks, magazines, and out-of-home opportunities. In addition, many of these buys must be negotiated and availabilities determined. As we discuss in chapter 8, just because you want to buy a spot on *Frazier,* or *Home Improvement* doesn't mean that it will be available. It is not unusual for a media-buying group to spend several days on a single network buy. At this stage, the media planner turns over much of the day-to-day execution of the schedule to media buyers and the planner functions in a supervisory role, making sure the buys follow the overall strategy of the media plan.

The tactics of buying media have improved in recent years through the introduction of electronic data interchange (EDI). Basically, EDI is a means of connecting the agencies, clients, and media involved in the media-buying process in a paperless system that allows the exchange of insertion orders and invoices electronically. Not only is the system more efficient than former approaches to media buying, but it significantly reduces errors by decreasing the number of people involved in the buying and billing process.

The development of the media schedule and the media buys themselves must be done in terms of the overall advertising and marketing goals of the client. The experienced media planner will combine reach and frequency goals with the buying pattern most conducive to reaching the maximum prospects. It might be instructive now to review some of the most used scheduling patterns.

---

[15]"Recency," *Industry White Paper,* March 1997, a publication of the Radio Advertising Bureau.

Flighting

One of the most used advertising scheduling techniques is **flighting.** Flighting consists of relatively short bursts of advertising followed by periods of total or relative inactivity. For example, Taster's Choice coffee runs a segment of its continuing advertising drama and then backs off before another flight begins with the next segment. The idea is to build audience perception for your product so that brand awareness carries over these periods of inactivity. Done correctly, the advertiser achieves the same brand awareness at a cost greatly reduced compared to a steady advertising schedule.

The concept is obviously appealing to advertisers who rarely think they have enough funds to reach all their prospects with a consistent advertising program. The problem facing the advertiser is that available research on flighting cannot precisely predict the awareness levels needed to achieve any particular flighting strategy. One thing is certain, advertisers must guard against significant erosion of brand awareness during breaks between flights. Exhibit 7.12 demonstrates the ideal outcome of a properly executed flighting strategy compared to a steady schedule, both using the same advertising budget.

In the steady schedule, audience awareness peaks fairly quickly (after about 20 weeks) and afterward shows little, if any, increase. The flighting schedule grows much more slowly, but because of budget savings it is able to reach more prospects and therefore actually achieve higher levels of brand awareness. As we cautioned earlier, an advertiser must be careful to consider the communication component of the media plan. Some media planners think that a flighting plan may sacrifice depth of communication even through minimal awareness may be achieved.

Regardless of the flighting schedule used, the following factors should be considered:

1. *Competitive spending.* How does your plan coincide with that of primary competitors? Are you vulnerable to competition between flights?
2. *Timing of flights.* Does the schedule go contrary to any seasonal features found in the product-purchase cycle?
3. *Advertising decay.* Are you spending enough in peak periods to remain visible between flights?
4. *Secondary media.* Should secondary or trade media be used between flights to maintain minimal visibility?

A less extreme form of flighting is called *pulsing.* Pulsing schedules use advertising more or less continuously throughout the year, but with peaks during certain periods of the year. These peaks coincide with primary sales periods or special promotion during contests or sweepstakes.

exhibit

7.12

Steady Versus Flighting Media Schedules

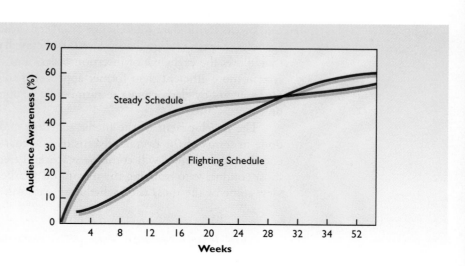

THE PRESSURE OF COMPETITION

Advertising operates in a competitive environment, usually with a number of companies vying for the same consumers. Advertisers must constantly be aware of competitors' advertising strategy, product development, pricing tactics, and other marketing and promotional maneuvers. The media planner not only must develop an effective campaign for a product, but must do so in a way that distinguishes one product from another.

The media planner also must walk a tightrope between a healthy respect for competitors' actions and blindly reacting to every competitive twist and turn. Rather than operating from a defensive mentality, advertisers should take a practical stance in determining what their marketing and advertising plans can reasonably accomplish and how they meet the inroads of competing brands.

One of the most difficult attributes for advertisers to develop is how to objectively analyze the market. One of the primary functions of an advertising agency is to bring an objective voice to the table. Companies sometimes unrealistically judge the value and quality of their products, but it is important to reach only those consumers who represent authentic (and profitable) prospects. One of the factors determining the level of awareness of your advertising is the degree with which consumers are satisfied with the alternative brands they are currently using.

For example, consumers who are aware of our brand but have never used it are probably satisfied with the product they are currently buying. Both the creative and media plans will have to work hard to give these consumers a reason to switch. In fact, we may have to recognize that some market segments cannot be captured regardless of the quality of our advertising. In such a case, brand switching would be an inappropriate strategy and we instead might target another market segment with new advertising appeals, creatively positioned products, or both.

A competitive analysis also must consider the various media alternatives and how they are reacting to their own competitive situation. For example, a smaller company in a product category may find that television is impractical if it is dominated by advertisers with budgets that are beyond its reach. Likewise, we might find that certain media are so saturated with competitors' advertising that it will be difficult to make a unique statement in the midst of the clutter. Or we may find that competition among media, particularly during economic slowdowns, will determine in large measure how receptive the media are to making price concessions for their time and space. Media buyers must be aware of a number of variables in preparing the plan. The key point is that advertisers should undertake a thorough and candid appraisal of all aspects of the competitive situation. In doing so, a media buyer becomes an integral member of the campaign team.

THE BUDGET

If there is any advertising axiom, it is that no budget is ever large enough to accomplish the task. With the spiraling cost of media over the last several years, media planners view the budget with a growing sense of frustration. In addition, media planners are constantly caught between large media (especially the major TV networks) demanding higher and higher advertising rates and clients demanding more efficiency for their advertising dollars. Because the media budget is by far the largest portion of the advertising allocation, it is the media planner who is expected to make the greatest cost savings.

Advertisers and their agencies have reacted to this cost squeeze by instituting more stringent cost controls and accountability for their advertising dollars. In addition to these stricter controls on media costs, we will see advertisers looking for alternative methods of promotion and advertising in the future. Already, consumer sales promotions (sweepstakes, coupons, price-off sales, and so forth) have passed advertising in terms of total share of promotional dollars. Advertisers also are using media such as cable and first-run syndicated programming to circumvent the high cost of network television. As the media continue to fragment, we will probably see even more experimentation with nontraditional media vehicles, many which did not exist only a few years ago.

If there is any encouraging sign for advertisers, it is that the increases in media costs of past years seem to have moderated. Instead of double digit increases, media costs are being held to levels more in line with the overall **consumer price index.** In response to these increases, advertisers are more precisely defining their prospects to cut down on waste circulation and are negotiating more aggressively with media salespeople. With the proliferation of media options and new technology, it is doubtful that we will see significant increases in advertising costs in the near future. However, the fragmentation of media and audiences is driving up the *CPM* levels to a point that it is costing more and more to reach selected target audiences.

SUMMARY

The media-buying process has become one of the most complex and exciting areas of advertising in recent years. For those people with quantitative proficiency, it can be an excellent entry level to the advertising business and an area where there will always be a need for highly trained experts.

The complexity and proliferation of new technology, target marketing techniques, and the sheer number of media options has fundamentally changed the advertising media function in recent years. With *CPM* levels continuing to climb, clients are demanding more and more expertise and accountability from media planners. Advertising efficiency and cost controls are increasingly the responsibility of media planners and buyers. With as much as 90 percent of the typical advertising budget allocated to the purchase of time and space, this pressure on media departments will only grow.

The media-planning function will continue to occupy a primary role in the advertising function. The tension, due to higher media costs, between planners and their clients seeking increasingly efficient media will result in even more experimentation with new media or spinoffs of existing media. If there is one sure factor in an otherwise unpredictable area, it is that the advertising media function will continue to look for narrowly defined markets and, with few exceptions, disregard those media vehicles that promise substantial, but largely undefined audiences.

Accompanying the increasing complexity of the media function will be a greater financial risk to the advertiser. Agencies will be asked to justify their media plans in more detail than ever before. In the following chapters, we examine each of the media available to the media planner as well as some promotional techniques associated with advertising. As you will see, the nature of the media function will require a media planner who is well versed in quantitative skills, marketing strategy, and, of course, all aspects of advertising.

REVIEW

1. Discuss some of the primary functions of the media planner.
2. Why is cost efficiency so important in media planning?
3. Describe the *building block* strategy of media buying.
4. Discuss the primary advantages and disadvantages of the following media:
   a. Television
   b. Out-of-home
   c. Newspapers
   d. Radio
   e. Magazines

5. Why is target audience identification usually the first step in building a media plan?
6. How do creative considerations interact with media planning?
7. How is the Brand Development Index used in geographic advertising budgeting?
8. What are some of the factors that must be considered in developing a flighting media schedule?

TAKE IT TO THE NET

We invite you to visit the Russell/Lane page on the Prentice Hall Web site at
PHLIP **http://www.prenhall.com/phbusiness** for the bimonthly Russell/Lane update and for this chapter's World Wide Web exercise.

8

USING TELEVISION

TELEVISION IS NO LONGER A UNIFIED MEDIUM; RATHER, IT COMPRISES A NUMBER OF RELATED BROADCAST AND CABLE ENTITIES THAT EXHIBIT SIGNIFICANT CONTRASTS FROM THE STARS OF NETWORK PRIME TIME TO THE LARGELY UNKNOWN PERSONALITIES OF LOCAL CABLE PROGRAMS. WITH THE ADVENT OF NEW TECHNOLOGY AND INTERACTIVE POSSIBILITIES, THE SPLINTERING OF TELEVISION PROGRAMMING SHOWS NO INDICATION OF ABATING. AFTER READING THIS CHAPTER YOU WILL UNDERSTAND

- **the diversified nature of the television industry**
- **the power of television as an advertising medium**
- **the growing competition for traditional TV network dominance**
- **changes in the rating services and methodology**
- **the VCR and television viewing.**

Television had its debut more than 50 years ago. Many businesses and institutions have long since become mature and stale; however, television viewing levels and advertising dollars have never been higher, and technological innovation is the norm. Even people who do not watch television are strongly influenced by it. Television news sets the political agenda, entertainment programming creates fads from hairstyles to the end-zone antics of professional football players, and TV advertising slogans have become part of our everyday vocabulary.

In a recent poll conducted by Roper Starch Worldwide:

over half of the public (53%) considers television to be the most credible news source, more than double that of the number two source, newspapers (23%), and far outdistancing radio (7%), magazine (4%) and on-line news (1%). Furthermore, television commercials were described as the most persuasive among the major media, cited by 70% compared to 14% for newspaper ads, 7% for magazine ads, 4% for radio commercials, and 1% for Internet/on-line sources.[1]

Over the years, the complexion of television has changed dramatically. Television is moving from a mass medium to a niche medium similar in many respects to radio and magazines. Certainly the level of network dominance enjoyed in television's early years is now part of television history. Network viewing during the last 15 years is estimated to have declined almost one-third. The majority of this lost network viewership has gone to **cable networks,** which in the aggregate represent a continuing threat to network audience levels.

Beginning with the VCR and moving toward the inevitable introduction of a number of interactive formats, the audiences have become active participants in the communication process rather than passive receivers. One catalyst for the introduction of two-way television communication is the Internet. Studies show that households using the Internet demonstrate lower levels of television viewing. Most predictions see Internet household penetration increasing significantly in the next several years. Consequently, it will be imperative for television to continue to move toward interactivity, which can combat this move away from the medium. The concern is all the more important because research indicates that most adopters of new technology are concentrated among upscale consumers—prime targets for television advertisers.

In the era of integrated marketing, television will follow the lead of newspapers and radio in showing advertisers how the medium can function as part of a broadened media mix. Continuing a trend of recent years, television advertising revenues will grow fastest at the local level. Television's growing popularity among local advertisers will offer the medium a broader base of advertisers, and television's fragmented audience offers advertisers tremendous opportunities to reach narrowly defined prospects.

TELEVISION AS AN ADVERTISING MEDIUM

Advantages

In the fall of 1996, *Seinfeld* and *ER* became the first regularly scheduled network series in which advertising sold for $1 million per minute. Previously, only a few special programs, such as the Super Bowl, sold at that level. Given the investment in all forms of television advertising, it is difficult to imagine the medium without commercials. However, in the earliest days of experimental television, commercials were actually illegal.

It wasn't until May 2, 1941, that the **Federal Communications Commission** (FCC) granted 10 commercial television licenses and allowed the sale of commercial time. The first commercial aired on July 1, 1941, during a Dodgers–Phillies baseball game. It was sponsored by Bulova watches and cost $4 for air time and $5 for station charges. It was seen by an estimated 4,000 people.[2]

Television rates are driven by ratings, demographics, and advertiser demand. Those programs most popular among choice audience segments, such as 18- to 34-year-olds, command the highest prices. Whereas *NFL Monday Night Football,* with its high ratings and favorable demographics, can command premium prices for commercial spots, the bottom tier of shows is lucky to sell out its commercial inventory. As one network television buyer pointed out, "there is significant stratification of demand and pricing in the marketplace. Although the highest-demand shows are getting ever more

Cable networks
Networks available only to cable subscribers. They are transmitted via satellite to local cable operators for redistribution either as part of basic service or at an extra cost charged to subscribers.

Federal Communications Commission (FCC)
The federal authority empowered to license radio and TV stations and to assign wavelengths to stations "in the public interest."

---

[1] "TV Remains Dominant News and Product Information Source, New Poll Reveals," *The PointCast Network,* May 28, 1997, p. 1.

[2] Jane Dalzell, "Who's on First," *Advertising Age, 50 Years of TV Advertising,* Spring 1995, p. 8.

expensive, the lower-end shows are declining in price."[3] It is important to remember that, like all media, commercial television's primary marketing goal is to deliver prime target audiences to advertisers.

There is no advertising medium that approaches the popularity of television. Whereas 62 million Americans see a newspaper each day for an average of 20 minutes, U.S. households average almost 7.5 hours daily television viewing. For many years, television has been the primary medium for national advertisers. With the growth of local TV advertising and cable, television has passed newspapers as the principal advertising media in terms of overall billings.

As newspapers and magazines struggle to maintain circulation, television adds niche cable networks such as the History Channel and the Golf Channel to compete with up-scale magazines and light viewers of standard television fare. Although these specialized outlets individually reach small audiences, in the aggregate they are siphoning significant advertising dollars from other media. In fact, the primary advantage of television as an advertising medium is that it reaches virtually everyone.

From General Motors, Procter & Gamble, and Philip Morris, with their multimillion dollar television advertising budgets, to a local restaurant spending a few dollars a week on the local cable outlet, television is a valuable marketing tool for selling virtually any product or service. With the growth of local television and cable advertising, there has been a significant redistribution of advertising dollars. However, even with the growing competition for television advertising, all segments of the industry continue to demonstrate healthy growth.

In addition to its high household penetration, television offers creative flexibility not found in any other medium. With its combination of sight, sound, color, and motion, television is equally adept at communicating humorous, serious, or tongue-in-cheek commercials. Television is a 24-hour medium with an ability to reach viewers of every lifestyle from housewives to third-shift workers. Television also offers a number of advertising formats from the 15-second announcement to the 30-minute program-length commercial.

Although television will face a number of challenges in the coming years, there is no question that it will remain the major advertising medium for national advertisers and provide significant competition for newspapers and other media for local dollars.

Limitations of Television

Cost Household television viewing has been relatively flat for the last decade. After all, it's difficult to squeeze in more than seven hours a day of viewing! Nevertheless, the growing number of options for television audiences has created an extremely fragmented audience and generally lower ratings for all segments of the industry. Despite the generally lower per-channel audiences, television rate increases are averaging 5 to 7 percent per year. The result is spiraling *CPM* increases.

Network advertisers, in particular, are concerned about these increases. However, major manufacturers of products such as package goods, automobiles, and other broadly based consumer products see little choice but to continue investing in the medium. The demand for television's limited time has created a seller's market, especially at the network level. Procter & Gamble was the first company to pass the $1 billion mark in yearly TV expenditures, and it will be joined shortly by a number of others.

Advertisers know that, despite high *CPM* costs and continuing commercial rate increases, there is still no more efficient method of reaching a broadly based consumer market than through television. It is important to consider not only the cost of televi-

[3]Joe Mandese, "NBC's 'Seinfeld,' 'ER' Hit Record $1 Million Minute," *Advertising Age*, September 16, 1996, p. 52.

sion time, but also the cost of producing commercials. In chapter 19 we discuss in detail the process of television production. However, with some network television commercials routinely costing as much as $1 million, production expense is another important cost consideration for any television advertiser.

Clutter   Television **clutter** is defined as any nonprogram material carried during or between shows. Commercials account for more than 80 percent of this material, with the other time devoted to public service announcements and program promotional spots. The average prime-time network hour contains eight minutes of commercials (13 percent) with non–prime-time accounting for approximately 25 percent commercial time. Many newspapers and magazines contain 50 to 60 percent advertisements, radio commonly has more commercials than programming, and most direct mail and out-of-home is 100 percent advertising. Yet, interestingly enough, it is television that is usually criticized for clutter and overcommercialization. The reasons are twofold:

- Unlike other media, television commercials are intrusive and out of the control of the viewer. Even radio commercials normally don't interrupt the flow of a program because most radio formats are music and talk. Television commercials are seen by many members of the audience as an imposition.
- Over the years the number of shorter, less than one-minute commercials, has given the perception that more commercials are being run than are actually aired. More than 90 percent of all commercials last either 30 or 15 seconds and some promote more than one product, which also gives an impression that more commercials are being run. The continuing demand for commercial time means that clutter will continue to be a problem with no short-term solution.

THE RATING-POINT SYSTEM

TV advertisers evaluate the medium according to the delivery of certain target audiences. In the case of networks and large affiliates, advertisers tend to look for exposure to fairly broad audience segments, such as women aged 18 to 49. Cable networks and some independent stations are evaluated by their ability to deliver more narrowly defined audiences that are both smaller in size and more expensive to reach on a *CPM* basis but have less waste circulation.

The basic measure of television is the **rating point.** The rating, expressed as a percentage of some population (usually TV households), gives the advertiser a measure of coverage based on the potential of the market. The rating is usually calculated as follows:

Rating = program audience/total TV households

When ratings are expressed as percentages of individuals, the same formula is used, but the population is some target segment rather than households. For example, if we are interested only in 18- to 34-year-old males, the formula would be:

Rating = 18–34 males viewing program/total 18–34 males in population

A household rating of 12 for a program means that 12 percent of all households in a particular area tuned their sets in to that station. Prime-time network programs usually achieve a rating of between 9 and 25, with the average being around 15.

As we discuss later in this chapter, TV advertising is rarely bought on a program-by-program basis. Instead, advertisers schedule a package of spots that are placed in a number of programs and dayparts. The weight of a schedule is measured in terms of the total ratings for all commercial spots bought (the **gross rating points,** or *GRP*s).

*GRP*s were calculated by multiplying the insertions times the rating. In the case of *All My Children,* the rating was 8.6 × 25 (the number of insertions) = 215 *GRP*s (see Exhibit 8.1).

Sidebar definitions

Clutter
Refers to a proliferation of commercials (in a medium) that reduces the impact of any single message.

Rating point (TV)
(1) The percentage of TV households in a market a TV station reaches with a program. The percentage varies with the time of day. A station may have a 10 rating between 6:00 and 6:30 P.M., and a 20 rating between 9:00 and 9:30.

Gross rating points (GRP)
Each rating point represents 1 percent of the universe being measured for the market. In TV it is 1 percent of the households having TV sets in that area.

exhibit

8.1

Vehicle	Rating	Cost	Spots	GRPs
All My Children	8.6	$15,950	25	215.0
General Hospital	8.7	15,950	25	217.5
Guiding Light	7.4	15,950	19	140.6
One Life to Live	7.4	15,950	14	103.6
Total GRPs				676.7

Reach = 99.9.
Frequency = 6.77.

Advertisers also use *GRP*s as the basis for examining the relationship between reach and frequency. These relationships can be expressed mathematically:

$$R \times F = GRP$$

$$\frac{GRP}{R} = F \quad \text{and} \quad \frac{GRP}{F} = R$$

where R = reach and F = frequency.

To use these relationships, you must know (or be able to estimate) the unduplicated audience. In the TV schedule in Exhibit 8.1, we estimate that we have reached virtually the entire target market (reach = 99.9 percent) and that the average number of times we reached each person in the audience was 6.77. We can check the formulas using the solutions previously calculated:

$$R \times F = GRP \quad \text{or} \quad 99.9 \times 6.77 = 676$$

$$\frac{GRP}{F} = R \quad \text{or} \quad \frac{676}{6.77} = 99.9$$

$$\frac{GRP}{R} = F \quad \text{or} \quad \frac{676}{99.9} = 6.77$$

One of the principal merits of the *GRP* system is that it provides a common base that proportionately accommodates markets of all sizes. One *GRP* in New York has exactly the same relative weight as one *GRP* in Salt Lake City. *GRP*s cannot be compared from one market to another unless the markets are of identical size. However, Exhibit 8.2 shows that the cost of TV commercial time varies by city size. Here is an idea of the use of *GRP*s in two markets, Los Angeles and Boston:

exhibit

8.2

Market	TV Homes (THOUSANDS)	Avg. Cost per Spot	Avg. Prime Time Rating
Los Angeles	4,241	$2,800	18
Boston	1,930	2,200	18

The advertiser has to decide how much weight (how many *GRP*s) to place in his or her markets and for how long a period. This is a matter of experience and of watching what the competition is doing. Suppose the advertiser selects 100 to 150 per week as the *GRP* figure (considered a good working base). Within this figure, the advertiser has great discretion in each market. How shall the time be allocated: Put it all on one station? Divide it among all the stations? Use what yardstick to decide? The answers depend on whether the goal is reach or frequency.

Look again at the hypothetical pricing structure in Exhibit 8.2.

If we buy three prime-time spots in these markets, we would expect to receive 54 *GRP*s (3 spots × 18 average rating). However, it would be a serious mistake to equate a 54-*GRP* buy in Los Angeles with the same level in Boston. In Los Angeles, 54 *GRP*s would deliver 2,290,140 household impressions (0.54 × 4,241,000 HH, or households) at a cost of $8,400 (3 spots × $2,800 per spot). On the other hand, a 54-*GRP* buy in Boston would deliver 1,042,200 household impressions at a cost of $6,600. To estimate buys, advertisers often use the **cost per rating point** (*CPP*) calculation:

$$CPP = \frac{\text{cost of schedule}}{GRPs}$$

In this case:

Boston: $$CPP = \frac{\$6,600}{54} = \$122.22$$

Los Angeles: $$CPP = \frac{\$8,400}{54} = \$155.55$$

If we make the mistake of comparing *GRP*s from markets of different sizes, it would appear that a rating point costs 27 percent more in Los Angeles than in Boston. However, a rating point represents 42,410 households (1 percent of 4,241,000) in Los Angeles versus only 19,300 in Boston. A rating point in Boston costs $33.33 less than in Los Angeles. However, the advertiser is actually getting 219 percent more households for only a 27 percent higher cost in Los Angeles. So Boston is hardly a bargain.

In addition to the problem of intermarket comparisons, the *GRP* has other limitations. It does not tell us the number of *prospects* for the product who are being reached by a program. Still, the *GRP* concept does provide a unified dimension for making scheduling judgments.

It must also be remembered that *GRP*s alone cannot tell how effectively a broadcast schedule is performing. If an advertiser's target audience is women aged 18 to 49, for example, 5 *GRP*s will often deliver more women in that group than 10 *GRP*s will. This, as you would expect, is a function of where the *GRP*s are scheduled. Five *GRP*s during a Sunday night movie will almost always deliver many times more women aged 18 to 49 than will 10 *GRP*s scheduled on a Saturday morning.

SHARE OF AUDIENCE

Although the rating is the basic audience-measurement statistic for TV, another measure, the **share of audience** (or simply, share), is often used to determine the success of a show. The share is defined as the percentage of households using television that are watching a particular show. It is used by advertisers to determine how a show is doing against its direct competition.

Let us assume that the *Today Show* has 5,000 households watching it in a market with 50,000 households. In this case we know that the rating for the *Today Show* would be 10.

$$\text{Rating} = \frac{Today \text{ viewers}}{\text{total TV households}} \times 100 = \frac{5,000}{50,000} \times 100 = 10$$

The share calculates the percentage of households using television (*HUT*) that are tuned to the program. Let us assume that of the 50,000 households, 25,000 are watching television. In this case, the share for the *Today Show* would be 20:

$$\text{Share} = \frac{Today \text{ viewers}}{HUT} \times 100 = \frac{5,000}{25,000} \times 100 = 20$$

It is understood that both the ratings and share of audience are expressed as percentages (hence the factor of 100 in the equations). Therefore, we do not use decimal points to refer to the measures in the example as "10 percent" and "20 percent." Instead, we say that the rating is 10 and the share is 20.

THE MANY FACES OF TELEVISION

Instead of a single mass medium dominated by three networks, television has become a group of related but distinctly different media. Except for the fact that they appear on the TV screen, there is little similarity between The Travel Channel and the Cartoon Channel or Home Shopping Network and MTV. Television serves vastly different advertisers, reaches a variety of demographic audience segments, and accomplishes a number of promotional objectives. Media buyers, while continuing to look to television to deliver high audience levels, primarily judge the success of the medium in terms of demographic reach as opposed to total households. Television is exhibiting the characteristics of an individual-user medium, with the majority of the audience viewing alone during most dayparts. The use of television as a personal medium is further demonstrated by the number of multiset households.

Contemporary television, with its diverse programming and fragmented audience, is evolving in a number of ways and is being perceived differently by its various audiences. To some viewers, television is a constant companion; to others it is an occasional diversion or only a source of news; and to many it is basically a conduit for their favorite video game. In this section, we examine the many aspects of this extremely complex medium, which occupies so much of our time and advertisers' dollars.

Network Television

In recent years, much has been written about the declining influence of the major television **networks.** However, network television advertising continues to be the primary recipient of national advertising dollars. Only network television can provide the combination of efficient distribution to virtually every household, high penetration levels within major demographic and lifestyle categories, and a choice of program content suitable for even the most discerning advertiser. For example, when Simmons mattresses wanted to achieve high awareness throughout the country, network television became the medium of choice. However, changes in television networks that effect viewers, advertisers, and programmers have transformed the medium in a number of ways during the last decade.

In this section, we discuss some of the major elements necessary to understand television networks as an advertising medium.

Clearance and Affiliate Compensation
When advertisers purchase network advertising, they are buying a group of independent stations that have agreed to join a network and carry its programming. The exceptions are a relatively few major market stations that are owned by the networks. These are known as O & O (owned and operated) stations. The three major networks have approximately 220 affiliates usually comprising the strongest stations in the various markets. The Fox Network has been aggressive in courting major affiliates of the other networks and it has been successful in markets such as Atlanta in inducing long-time major network affiliates into their lineup. The newest networks, WB and UPN, have affiliations with smaller stations in most markets. In fact, some of the WB and UPN affiliates are *secondary* affiliates, which means they belong to another network and air WB or UPN shows on a delayed basis, usually during non–prime-time hours.

Networks sell national advertising on the basis of station **clearance.** Network clearance is expressed as the percentage of the network's lineup that has agreed to clear their schedules for network programming. In the case of the top four networks, clearances normally run close to 100 percent. The new networks often express their clearance rates as a percentage of the U.S. population that is potentially reached. For example, if a network fails to get clearance in New York City, it immediately loses the potential to reach approximately 10 percent of the total national audience. Until a network or other program source reaches 70 percent potential coverage, it is usually not considered a national program.

Networks
Interconnecting stations for the simultaneous transmission of TV or radio broadcasts.

Clearance
The percentage of network affiliates that carry a particular network program.

case
HISTORY

MARKETING SITUATION

Simmons sells in a highly fragmented, extremely competitive market of more than 700 mattress manufacturers. The top five firms comprise 60 percent of the total U.S. market share:

Sealy	17 percent
Simmons	15
Serta	13
Spring Air	9
Stearns and Foster	2

In this competitive market environment, achieving product differentiation among mattresses is difficult due to:

1. Infrequent purchase patterns—only 10 percent of U.S. households buy a mattress in a given year, and the average life of a mattress is more than 10 years.
2. On the surface, all mattresses look alike. Because the basic construction of a mattress is covered by the ticking, consumers often make decisions based on aesthetics and a limited "trial" (less than five minutes of lying on the bed in the showroom).
3. A confused brand situation—all the major brands begin with "S"—make it difficult for consumers to remember and separate features of different brands. As a result, brand decisions are most often driven by the retail salesperson or price.

The primary challenge for Simmons is to communicate its distinctive construction, which is a major advantage over competing brands. The patented Simmons Pocketed Coil allows each individual coil to move independently from the coils that surround it. Thus, if weight is placed on one coil, the coils that surround it will not move. All other mattresses use a construction called "wire-tied," in which helical coils are interlaced across all coils to "tie" them together. In this type of construction, when weight is placed on one coil, all other coils surrounding that coil also move.

For the past few years, Simmons had been promoting the independent coil movement benefit by featuring the "contouring" effect the Simmons Pocketed Coil construction allows. This contouring benefit also has been featured in mattress advertising from competitors; however, the Simmons Beautyrest construction gives it an advantage over conventional "wire-tied" competitors.

CAMPAIGN OBJECTIVES

The Simmons Beautyrest "Do-Not-Disturb" campaign had four specific marketing goals:

1. to create a distinct positioning identity for Beautyrest that would make it the preferred brand for consumers to buy

2. to provide the retail salesperson with a positioning that would make Beautyrest an easier product to sell to consumers
3. to leverage this distinct positioning to gain additional floor space among existing accounts and to gain new distribution
4. to achieve sales growth of 10 percent over the previous year, especially among higher priced and higher margin mattresses

TARGET AUDIENCE

Adults 25 to 49 years old have traditionally been the primary target for all mattress advertising. Research indicates that more than 70 percent of higher priced and higher margin bedding is purchased by married adults, with the female being the primary brand decision maker. Simmons's advertising agency, WestWayne, decided to direct Simmons Beautyrest advertising to adults 25 to 54 who sleep with a partner.

CREATIVE STRATEGY

The creative strategy was to position Simmons Beautyrest as the "Do-Not-Disturb" mattress by creating a dramatic demonstration of the unique construction and benefit of the Simmons Pocketed Coil. Creative research revealed that many wives complain that their husbands wake them up in the middle of the night by tossing and turning or by getting up. As the U.S. population continues to age, the problem of waking in the middle of the night will continue to grow, as sleep researchers have shown that older adults are lighter sleepers than their younger counterparts.

The "Do-Not-Disturb" strategy was adopted for three reasons:

1. It allows Simmons to exploit the unique construction difference of the Simmons Beautyrest mattress in a way that could not be preempted by competitors.
2. It speaks to a very real problem for many adults—being awakened by their partners during the night.
3. It has long-term potential in that the problem of having sleep disturbed by a partner increases with age.

The resulting "bowling ball" commercial and accompanying point-of-purchase material used a dramatic demonstration to illustrate that the unique construction of the Beautyrest mattress offers a significant advantage over all competitive mattresses—less transfer of motion across the coil construction and therefore less disturbance, so "when your partner moves, you don't." The theme was carried out in an integrated campaign utilizing sales promotion, public relations, and direct mail.

MEDIA STRATEGY

Network television was chosen as the primary medium due to the need to introduce this campaign across all regions of the country. Because Sealy outspends Simmons by a 4-to-1 margin ($40 million versus $10 million), the media strategy was to concentrate the spending during two key selling periods—April/May and August/September. These times are traditionally when major furniture retailers run aggressive local promotions. Simmons advertising was timed to immediately precede the sales periods so local retailers could supplement Simmons national advertising with their own local promotions.

The media mix included all dayparts—prime (20%), late night (30%), daytime (30%), and early fringe (20%). A special effort to place Simmons advertising in high-interest, special-event programming was made, and Beautyrest advertising was seen in such high-profile programming as the Country Music Awards, Daytime Emmy Awards, and the Barbara Streisand Special. A national cable buy was used to supplement the network buy, with a clustering strategy to gain greater dominance during the advertising period.

EVIDENCE OF RESULTS

The campaign met or exceeded all major campaign objectives:

1. Consumer research confirmed that the "Do-Not-Disturb" positioning gives Beautyrest a unique situation in the marketplace. Consumer research indicated that 82 percent of respondents acknowledge that being disturbed is a problem that Beautyrest solves better than competitors.
2. Retail salespersons gave high marks to the campaign because it offered them a feature that could easily be demonstrated on the sales floor. Beautyrest offers customers a real and provable benefit.
3. After the introduction of the "Do-Not-Disturb" campaign in April, Beautyrest gained 154 new accounts during 1995 with sales potential of $7.3 million per year.
4. Importantly, sales are up dramatically as a result of this campaign:

Month to Month Comparison Following Campaign Launch

Month	Beautyrest Sales	Total Simmons Sales
June	+ 9.0%	+10.9%
July	+28.8	+19.6
August	+15.9	+15.9

Overall, the campaign had an impact on every aspect of the company's business. It also contributed significantly to sales increases for other Simmons products.

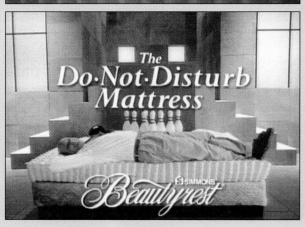

Courtesy: Simmons and WestWayne.

Compensation
The payment of clearance fees by a TV network to local stations carrying its shows.

Related to clearance is network **compensation** to its affiliates. The most valuable commodity that stations have is their time. When they clear their schedules to carry network programming, they expect to be compensated for the time they are giving to the networks. In recent years, the rate of compensation has been a point of major contention between networks and their affiliates.

During the last 20 years, the rate of network compensation has fallen dramatically. The networks argue that the quality programming they provide allows local stations to gain higher prices for their local commercials placed at network breaks and during locally produced shows, especially the news. Stations, on the other hand, contend that without station clearances there would be no networks. Compensation has become a competitive issue in recent years with the start-up networks paying compensation premiums to entice local stations to change affiliation. Assuming the WB and UPN networks are as successful as Fox, we will doubtless see competitive pressure to increase compensation fees for affiliates. The ultimate threats for a station to gain higher compensation threat is to refuse to clear the weaker shows in a network's schedule or to consider affiliation with another network.

Network Ownership   At one time, the major networks were independent companies. Their primary business was news and entertainment, and the people who occupied the executive suites had spent their entire careers in the business of broadcasting. Today, each of the networks is a relatively small part of a major conglomerate. Disney owns ABC, Westinghouse holds CBS, General Electric controls NBC, and Murdoch's News Corp began Fox. In no case is a network the largest business within its parent company. Some argue that the change in ownership has brought a bottom-line mentality to the networks that is reflected in the quality of programming and, in some cases, the reduced investment in news and public service.

Declining Shares of Network Audiences   In 1974, 90 percent of primetime television viewers were watching one of the three networks. Even with the addition of the Fox network, the figure had fallen to 64 percent by 1994. With a total of six networks, it is predicted that the audience share will be 57 percent in 2000.[4]

One problem facing the networks is that first one audience segment and then another has turned to cable channels that indulge their particular viewing tastes. Cable viewing that begins as an experiment becomes a habit—one that is very difficult for the networks to break. As one network executive said, "Viewers still check out the network channels first. But if they don't find what they want there, they know they can check out TNT, or Discovery, or somewhere else down the dial and find something that will make them comfortable. We have to find a way to make them comfortable with us again."[5]

There is no question that the days of 80 and 90 network shares are over. However, even with three additional networks, the slide continues. There are simply too many cable, independent station, and public broadcast options to expect the major networks to maintain their audience dominance. However, despite their decline in viewers, it is important to remember that the television networks still command an overwhelming percentage of the audience, with millions of households viewing them on any given evening. By contrast, the average viewership of most cable networks remains under one percent of the total television audience.

> The network side [as compared to cable] gets an extra bump by remaining the primary TV home of quality original programming. The broadcast networks are still the only outlets able to spend millions of dollars on

---

[4]Veronis, Suhler & Associates Communications Industry Forecast, 1996, p. 92.
[5]Bill Carter, "CBS Counterattacks the Cable Networks, Hoping to Reclaim Its Old Loyalists," *The New York Times,* September 16, 1996, p. C8.

programming day after day. Network-quality programming draws huge numbers of viewers, an attraction that no other medium can currently replicate and no major advertiser can avoid. The truth is, network TV still delivers the biggest and broadest audiences.[6]

Block Programming

Network executives have to choose programs that will appeal to a large segment of households and at least a handful of major advertisers, and their work is made even more difficult by the fickle audience. Over many years, the networks have found that shows do not stand on their own, but are greatly influenced by the programs directly before, called the *lead-in,* and the total daypart schedule, called a *block.*

The importance of lead-ins can be seen in the investment local stations make to get the strongest syndicated programming to run prior to their early evening news shows. The demand for strong news lead-ins is in large measure responsible for the enormous prices paid for off-network syndicated programs. The same principle is at work in building a network schedule. Programmers strive to make sure that individual programs will attain high ratings, and just as important, that the block will work together throughout the evening to attract a similar audience.

Network programmers are very aware of the ebb and flow of audiences as they move from one program to another. For example, each fall, new shows are judged as much in terms of how they maintain audience levels from their lead-ins as the actual ratings. For example, in 1996, *Suddenly Susan* starring Brooke Shields premiered after months of publicity. The show was rated second among all prime-time programs during its debut week, and yet NBC was concerned with the loss of audience from *Seinfeld,* its immediate lead-in. Although the show eventually met network expectations, NBC's initial concern demonstrates the way in which networks evaluate the contributions of shows to a program block rather than just the rating for a particular show.

Network Television Advertising Criteria

Clients and their advertising agencies apply a variety of criteria in determining if, and to what extent, they will use network television. However, buying decisions are largely determined by three factors: demos, *CPM,* and demand.[7]

Demos   Whereas at one time households were the unit of purchase, today most advertisers place major emphasis on the demographics of individual viewers. This change in criteria has altered the manner in which networks choose shows and the pricing structure for advertisers. For many advertisers, the makeup of the audience of potential network buys has become more important than the size of the audience. Of course, advertisers as well as the networks demand that a show attain a certain minimum rating, but the price for shows with favorable demographics usually exceeds what their ratings alone would bring.

For example, shows such as *Friends* and *Spin City,* as popular as they are, command even higher commercial prices than their rating alone would indicate because of the composition of their audiences. During the 1997 television season, the average *CPM* for viewers in the 18- to 34-year-old category was $23, whereas those in the 35 and older age group had a *CPM* of just $9. It is no surprise, given this pricing structure, that networks try to program shows that appeal to younger audiences.

CPMs   Although most advertisers are seeking favorable demographics and are willing to pay a premium to get them, there are other advertisers who are driven primarily by cost considerations. Of course, no advertiser ignores the audience profile of its adver-

---

[6]Scotty Dupree, "Struggling for Hits in a Strong Market," *Adweek,* September 9, 1996, p. 11.
[7]"Mil-a-Minute TV Not All Bad," *Advertising Age,* September 23, 1996, p. 28.

tising buys. However, there are a number of advertisers who emphasize cost efficiencies and *CPM* levels, regardless of the premium nature of the audience.

Broadly based package goods advertisers are more likely to take this approach than advertisers of a more narrowly distributed product. These companies take the position that, within certain broad audience criteria, they gain a benefit from virtually any audience because their product usage is so universal. Campbell's is a company that is noted for bottom-line considerations in its media buys. The company demands competitive pricing from the media it buys, and it has the budget clout to deal from a position of strength with media.

Demand   The third criterion that determines the advertising buying relationship between networks and advertisers is the demand for certain programs. Of course, demand is a function of both demographics and *CPM*s, but there are also qualitative factors, such as association with a special event such as the Miss America Pageant or with a star that has unique appeal to a particular target market such as Oprah Winfrey, that create a pricing structure over and above the objective numbers.

Avails   The combination of high demand and finite network commercial time creates a situation in which there are not enough choice time slots to go around. Networks attempt to ration the prime commercial spots among their major advertisers. The availability (called *avails* in network jargon) problem is solved, in part, by combining top-rated avails with less popular ones as advertisers buy packages of commercial time from each network. The availability of a top-rated show to a particular advertiser will depend as much on the company's total advertising investment on that network as the price it is willing to pay for a specific program. Package plans allow the networks to work with agencies to place commercials across their entire schedule, with the understanding that each advertiser will have to accept some lower rated (but demographically acceptable) spots in order to obtain some "jewels."

Up-Front and Scatter Buys   The network buying season is divided into two categories. The first is the **up-front buy** period in May. At one time, the up-front period consisted primarily of negotiations between major agencies and the three major networks. Today, up-front buyers are looking beyond the major networks to Fox, UPN, and WB, as well as a host of syndicated shows and, of course, the cable networks, with their growing audiences and original programming. The first step after the networks announce their fall schedule is for agencies and clients to screen the programs and estimate potential audience shares and *CPM*s and conduct preliminary negotiating sessions with program suppliers.

After these meetings, the actual buying period begins. It may last only a week or 10 days because agencies move quickly to prevent being left out as prime commercial slots are committed by the networks. During the up-front buying period, the major agencies and their clients buy the majority of their network advertising. It is a period of intense negotiation, representing buyers from the largest agencies, brands, and networks. It is not a time for the fainthearted or for small players. Several top advertising agencies, representing a platinum roster of clients, spend close to $1 billion each in television, with as much as half expended during the up-front period. Overall, the up-front season accounts for more than $6 *billion* in commercial buys.

The second wave of buying is known as the **scatter plan** buying sessions.[8] Scatter plans are usually bought on a quarterly basis throughout the year. They are designed for larger advertisers who want to take advantage of changing marketing conditions or, more often, for smaller advertisers who are shut out of the up-front buys. Generally,

Up-front buy
Purchase of network TV time by national advertisers during the first offering by networks. Most expensive network advertising.

Scatter plan
The use of announcements, over a varying of network programs and stations, to reach as many people as possible in a market.

---

[8]The term "scatter plan" has two definitions. The first refers to buying a group of spots across a number of programs. The second meaning refers to those spots that are still available after the up-front buying season is completed.

scatter plans will sell at a higher *CPM* because there is less time inventory, and smaller advertisers don't have the leverage to negotiate the *CPM* levels of huge network advertisers.

Alternatives to the scatter market are cable networks and syndicated buys. At one time, cable networks were bought in a second wave after the up-front buying season. However, because audiences and program quality have increased dramatically on many cable networks, many advertisers are looking at cable simultaneously with the up-front market. In effect, an up-front market has been created for the major cable networks.

There also are up-front markets for other dayparts. Buyers interested in late night will fight for slots on the *Tonight Show with Jay Leno,* the *Late Show with David Letterman,* or the upscale audience of Ted Koppel's *Nightline* as well as other after-midnight programs. Similarly, early morning and midday programming each have their own up-front season, special advertising categories, and pricing structure. It is important to understand that network avails are largely filled through the up-front seasons in each daypart.

Negotiation   As mentioned in the last section, negotiation is the key to network buying. Because each advertising package is unique to a particular advertiser, there are no rate cards for network television advertising. Instead, agencies determine what they are willing to pay per rating point and the networks arrive at the bargaining table with some gross dollar figure in mind for their upcoming schedule. Each knows that there will be some give and take, and generally these experienced negotiators know the parameters within which the final deal will be made. However, an extremely small difference in the cost of a rating point has great significance when an agency is buying hundreds of commercials.

Make-Goods   One of the major elements of network negotiation concerns **make-goods.** As the name implies, make-goods are concessions to advertisers for a failure to achieve some guaranteed rating level. Make-goods are normally offered on the basis of total *GRP*s for an advertiser's television advertising schedule. That is, when the advertiser fails to achieve a certain agreed-upon cost per point, the make-good provisions are initiated. At one time, make-goods were part of most advertising negotiations—they were always part of the up-front market. Make-goods usually take the form of future commercials to make up for a shortfall in ratings. Refunds are virtually never given as part of a make-good plan.

Only in the last several years have make-goods become a major point of contention between networks and agencies. Prior to that time, the networks were so dominant that it was rare for an advertiser to qualify for a make-good. Each network could reasonably expect to get a 25 to 35 share of the total prime-time schedule. Consequently, a make-good was a relatively risk-free incentive offered by networks to agencies and their clients.

The new competitive environment has changed the make-good situation dramatically. With some network shows achieving sub-10 ratings, the make-good has become a major negotiating point with agencies and a high-risk endeavor for networks. If a prime-time network schedule includes a number of low-rated or canceled shows, it may well mean the network will give up a significant portion of its inventory during the winter and spring to accommodate make-goods. In part because of make-goods, networks are very reluctant to support low-rated shows. Each season there are a few shows that are canceled after one or two airings to prevent a significant demand for make-goods.

The importance and potential financial risk of make-goods have brought even greater focus to the significance of reliable ratings. Nielsen estimated that fall 1996 network viewership among 18- to 34-year-olds had decreased some 1.2 million compared to the year before. "As a result, the six commercial-broadcast networks could wind up

Make-goods
When a medium falls short of some audience guarantee, advertisers are provided concessions in the form of make-goods. Most commonly used in television and magazines.

owing advertisers $100 million in airtime in the fourth quarter alone for not delivering the viewership they had pledged."[9] The networks argue with Nielsen over the reliability of the ratings, but that just underscores the importance of ratings to the financial well-being of the industry.

Spot Television

Spot television
Purchase of time from a local station, in contrast to purchasing from a network.

When national advertisers buy local stations the practice is known as **spot television** or spot buys. The term comes from the fact that advertisers are spotting their advertising in certain markets, as contrasted to the blanket coverage offered by network schedules. The primary disadvantages of spot television are (1) that it requires a great deal more planning and paperwork than network because each market must be bought on a one-to-one basis, and (2) it is more costly on a *CPM* basis.

Spot advertising is an extremely competitive market, with almost 1,000 local stations vying for national dollars. Networks are constantly demonstrating to advertisers that their stations will deliver a narrow target audience of prime prospects (see Exhibit 8.3, p. 212). Overall, network affiliates have an advantage in selling spot time because they can piggyback on the greater popularity of most network programs, compared to independent stations where programming tends to be more inconsistent.

Representative (rep)
An individual or organization representing a medium selling time or space outside the city or origin.

Most spot advertising is placed through station **representatives** called reps. The rep is paid a commission by the station based on the time sold. The commission is negotiable, but it usually ranges from 5 to 10 percent, depending on the size of the station. The good sales rep is both a salesperson and a marketing specialist for advertisers. The rep must be able to show a national advertiser how a schedule on WAWS-TV in Jacksonville or KDKA-TV in Pittsburgh will meet a national company's advertising objectives.

Rep firms may have 100 or more station clients on a noncompetitive basis. Reps go to agencies and advertisers and attempt to convince them that the markets in which these stations broadcast have important prospects for specific brands. To make the purchase of spot buys more efficient, a rep will allow advertisers to buy all or any number of stations that it represents. Because the idea is to provide one order and one invoice, it is similar to a network buy. However, the stations sold through a rep are not linked in any way other than being a client of a particular rep. These station groups are called **nonwired networks.** The commercials bought on a nonwired network, unlike a real network, are not broadcast at the same time. The nonnwired concept is simply a means of providing buying efficiency for spot advertisers.

Nonwired networks
Groups of radio and TV stations whose advertising is sold simultaneously by station representatives.

In recent years, the role of reps and their place in the spot television market has begun to change. At one time, a single owner could hold only seven television licenses. Today, the rules allow a person or corporation to control stations with total TV household coverage of up to 35 percent of the U.S. population. With this loosening of ownership rules have come a number of station groups, some with dozens of outlets. Some of the groups are large enough to support their own national salesforce.

Group owners making direct deals with advertising agencies have created a potential conflict with their reps because most rep firms have contracts with their station clients calling for a rep commission on all sales regardless of how the sale is made. In addition, a few advertising agencies have indicated their intention to deal directly with major stations and groups and bypass reps. These agencies think that they can negotiate more favorable buys directly rather than through a rep.

If this trend of direct station deals expands, there is a real question about the future of the station-rep relationship. Obviously, stations will not continue to pay a rep

---

[9]Elizabeth Jensen, "Networks Blast Nielsen, Blame Faulty Ratings for Drop in Viewership," *The Wall Street Journal,* November 22, 1996, p. A1.

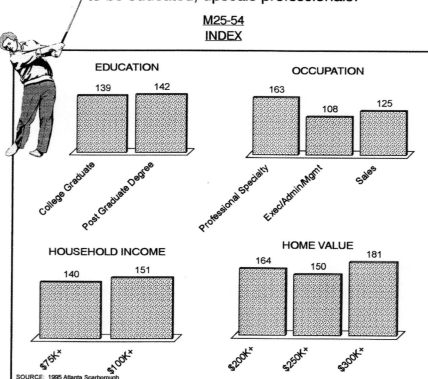

commission for sales that are generated at the local level. As one TV station general manager said,

> You'll find no stronger supporter of our rep . . . than us and I will fight tooth and nail to get agencies to deal with them. But when push comes to shove, and I'm going to lose business if I don't deal direct, then I'll deal direct. And I don't want to pay my rep if he or she's just standing there while my people are doing the deal.[10]

Why Buy Spot?

Regardless of the procedure for buying spot television, the market is growing for a number of reasons. Basically there are two types of spot advertisers. The first are those that use spot exclusively. The second category are advertisers who use spot advertising as a

---

[10]Chuck Ross, "Rep Firms Alarmed by BJK&E's Going Direct to TV Stations," *Advertising Age,* April 29, 1996, p. 4.

complement to their network buys. Spot advertising offers a number of advantages for national advertisers. The following are the primary reasons for entering the spot advertising market:

1. *Uneven product distribution or inadequate budgets for network.* Many products have distribution patterns that are so irregular that network coverage would create unacceptable waste circulation. By the same token, many national companies simply lack the funds to purchase adequate time on a national television basis. However, by judiciously buying in markets where they have strong sales or sales potential, these companies can compete in selected areas.

2. *Geographic targeting.* Few brands, even those with strong national distribution, have consistent sales patterns in every market. Spot offers a method of building local television weight in those markets with the greatest potential while still taking advantage of the lower *CPM*s of network for national exposure. By combining spot and network, a company can take advantage of the sales potential of its best markets while providing adequate exposure to all markets through network advertising.

3. *Local identity.* By using spot advertising, a national advertiser can more closely identify with the local market and its retailers. In addition, different markets have unique viewing habits, which networks cannot accommodate. For example, spot advertising can buy strong local news shows and other locally produced programming that fit the demographics of prime prospects in that market. Spot also offers opportunities for local cooperative promotions with retailers, which would be impossible in network. Finally, spot buys can be made on independent stations that are not network affiliated but might have special strengths such as sports programming.

4. *Flexibility.* Unlike network advertising, in which commitments are made several weeks or months in advance, spot buys allow an advertiser to immediately react to changing market conditions. Assuming commercials are ready, an advertiser can be on-air in as little as 48 hours.

Defining the Television Coverage Area

Before the advent of television, companies generally established sales and advertising territories by state boundaries and arbitrary geographical areas within them. However, television transmissions go in many directions for varying distances; they are no respecter of maps. Television research uses three levels of signal coverage to designate potential station coverage of a market area.

Total survey area
The maximum coverage of a radio or television station's signal.

1. *Total survey area.* This survey area is the largest area over which a station's coverage extends.

2. *Designated market area.*[11] A term used by the Nielsen Media Research to identify those countries in which home market stations receive a preponderance of viewers.

3. *Metro rating area.* This rating area corresponds to the standard metropolitan area served by a station.

Local television stations also provide advertisers with signal coverage maps to show the *potential* audience reach of the station (see Exhibit 8.4, p. 214). The signal coverage designations have become less important in recent years because cable has greatly extended the area over which a television station can be viewed.

An interesting battle over the spot market has surfaced between local network affiliates and satellite companies. Once an insignificant portion of the local viewing audience, satellite penetration is growing rapidly. Most local affiliates find that satellite network feeds to households in their coverage area come from other areas. Therefore, local stations are deprived of those households in selling local and national spot time.

---

[11]The Arbitron Company used a similar designation known as *area of dominant influence.* Even though Arbitron no longer conducts TV ratings, the term is still used by many advertisers.

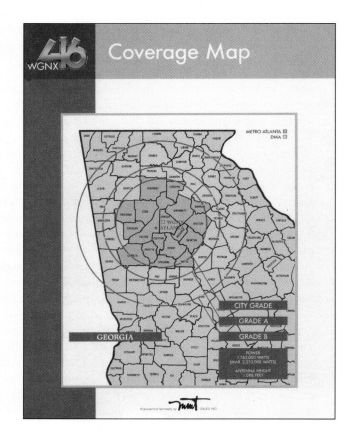

exhibit

8.4

The power of a local station's broadcast signal has been greatly extended by the growth of cable.

Courtesy: WGNX-TV, Atlanta, Ga.

Currently, the FCC requires that satellite companies can carry network programming only into areas without an available network signal. However, in those cases where network programming has been denied to local dish owners, the public relations problem for the local station has been significant. Nationally, the number of dish owners has not reached the level where it presents a major problem to any single-market stations. However, it emphasizes again the changing landscape of television and advertising.

Local Television Advertising

Television advertising is increasingly purchased by local advertisers. Businesses as diverse as record stores and banks place advertising on local stations. However, a significant portion of the approximately $18 billion invested in local television is placed by local franchise outlets of national companies. For example, PepsiCo has sold its fast food outlets. McDonald's is the largest local advertiser.

Local television advertising expenditures are slightly ahead of spot and could challenge network revenues by the end of the decade. Advertisers spend more than $33 billion on spot and local television combined, approximately 50 percent more than the amount invested in network. The growth in local station advertising is indicative of three factors:

● the effective marketing promotions by local stations and the television industry to show how television can effectively be used by local retail outlets
● the increased number of local television outlets, which has created a competitive environment that has kept prices down, bringing the medium within the budget of more local advertisers

- the trend by national marketers to move to local strategies, which, in many cases, has been reflected by greater advertising allowances and control of budgets by local or regional advertisers

Local television advertising is an important source of revenue for most stations. A decade ago, local advertising accounted for a minor portion of the total revenues of most network affiliates. Profitability was assured from network compensation and national spot accounts. However, strong independent stations in many markets showed that aggressive selling could substantially increase local advertising. Soon, affiliates were creating local advertising departments, promoting television as a viable local medium, and playing catch-up with their independent counterparts.

Local TV stations also realized that they could not expect to garner the majority of local retail advertising dollars and adopted the familiar stance of selling television as a *complement* to other local media. It is much easier to convince local advertisers to convert 5 percent of their budgets to television than 95 percent. Once stations were successful in getting retailers to give television a try, it was much easier to compete for more dollars and approach other retailers.

Buying and Scheduling Spot and Local TV Time Because advertisers have shifted more of their budgets to local markets, media buyers must be familiar with the specifics of buying spot and local TV time.

The TV Day Spot and local TV advertising are often purchased by daypart rather than by specific program. Each daypart varies by audience size and demographic profile. Media planners must be familiar with the audience makeup of various dayparts. Some typical daypart designations are

1. morning: 7:00–9:00 A.M. Monday through Friday
2. daytime: 9:00 A.M.–4:30 P.M. Monday through Friday
3. early fringe: 4:30–7:30 P.M. Monday through Friday
4. prime-time access: 7:30–8:00 P.M. Monday through Saturday
5. prime time: 8:00–11:00 P.M. Monday through Saturday and 7:00–11:00 P.M. Sunday. These are East and West Coast Time Zone designations; Central and Mountain Time Zones are 7:00–10:00 P.M. Monday through Saturday and 6:00–10:00 P.M. Sunday.
6. late news: 11:00–11:30 P.M. Monday through Friday
7. late fringe: 11:30 P.M.–1:00 A.M. Monday through Friday

Preemption Rate A considerable portion of spot TV advertising time is sold on a preemptible (lower-rate) basis, whereby the advertiser gives the station the right to sell a time slot to another advertiser that may pay a better rate for it or that has a package deal for which that particular spot is needed. Whereas some stations offer only two choices, nonpreemptible and preemptible advertising, others allow advertisers to choose between two kinds of preemptible rates. When the station has the right to sell a spot to another advertiser any time up until the time of the telecast, the rate is called the *immediately preemptible* (IP) rate (the lowest rate). When the station can preempt only if it gives the original advertiser two weeks' notice, the rate is designated *preemptible with two weeks' notice* and is sold at a higher rate. The highest rate is charged for a non-preemptible time slot, the two-week preemptible rate is the next highest, and the immediately preemptible rate is the lowest.

The following table is an excerpt from a rate card.

	I	II	III
Tues., 8–9 A.M.	$135	$125	$115

Column I is the nonpreemptible rate; column II, the rate for preemption on two weeks' notice; and column III, the rate for preemption without notice. Notice how the rate goes down.

Special Features News telecasts, weather reports, sports news and commentary, stock market reports, and similar programming are called *special features.* Time in connection with special features is sold at a premium price.

Run of Schedule (ROS) An advertiser can earn a lower rate by permitting a station to run commercials at its convenience whenever time is available rather than in a specified position. (This is comparable to run of paper in newspaper advertising; see chapter 10.)

Package Rates Every station sets up its own assortment of time slots at different periods of the day, which it sells as a package. The station creates its own name for such packages and charges less for them than for the same slots sold individually. The package rate is one of the elements in negotiation for time.

Product Protection Every advertiser wants to keep the advertising of competitive products as far away from its commercials as possible. This brings up the question of what protection against competition an ad will get. Although some stations say that they will try to keep competing commercials 5 to 10 minutes apart, most say that although they will do everything possible to separate competing ads, they guarantee only that they will not run them back to back.

Scheduling Spot and Local Time *Rotation of a schedule* refers to the placement of commercials within a schedule to get the greatest possible showing. If you bought two spots a week for four weeks on a Monday-to-Friday basis, but all the spots were aired only on Monday and Tuesday, your rotation would be poor. You would miss all the people who turn to the station only on Wednesday, Thursday, or Friday. Your *horizontal rotation* should be increased. *Vertical rotation* assures there will be differences in the time at which a commercial is shown within the time bracket purchased. If you bought three spots on the *Tonight Show,* which runs from 11:30 P.M. to 12:30 A.M., but all your spots were shown at 12:15 A.M., you would be missing all the people who go to sleep earlier than that. To avoid this situation, you would schedule one spot in each half hour of the program, vertically rotating your commercial to reach the largest possible audience.

TELEVISION SYNDICATION

Television syndication is the sale of television programming on a station-by-station, market-by-market basis. Syndication companies seek to sell individual programs to one station in every market. Most major **syndicated TV programs** are sold on an advertiser-supported or barter basis. **Barter syndication** refers to the practice of selling shows to stations in return for a portion of the commercial time in the show rather than (or in addition to) cash. A majority of the commercial time is packaged into national units and sold to national advertisers. The typical syndicated show comes with spots presold on a national basis, and the station sells the remaining time to local and spot advertisers.

Syndication began when producers sold their canceled network shows to stations for inexpensive "fillers" during late afternoon or other time periods not programmed by the networks. During the early days of syndication, no one thought that it was anything but a method for producers to pick up a few extra dollars by selling to local stations a program that had completed its network run. During this period, syndication was a minor portion of television advertising.

Syndication has become a primary advertising vehicle. Currently, syndication accounts for more than $2 billion in advertising revenues and an equal amount from sta-

Syndicated TV program
A program that is sold or distributed to more than one local station by an independent organization outside the national network standard.

Barter syndication
Station obtains a program at no charge. The program has presold national commercials and time is available for local station spots.

exhibit

8.5

Syndication accounts for a significant percent of television audience share.

Courtesy: Advertiser Syndicated Television Associations.
Source: "ASTA 1997 Guide to Advertiser-Supported Syndication," p. a-6.

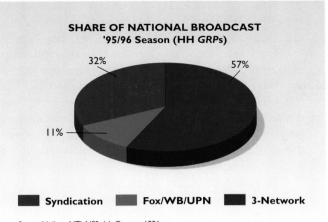

SHARE OF NATIONAL BROADCAST
'95/96 Season (HH *GRP*s)

32%   57%

11%

■ Syndication   ■ Fox/WB/UPN   ■ 3-Network

Source: Neilson NTI, NSS, 4th Quarter 1996.

tion program fees. Overall, more than 16,000 hours of television programming time is filled with syndicated shows; almost one-third of the national television audience share is accounted for by syndication (see Exhibit 8.5).

The average viewer seldom knows or cares whether a particular show is distributed through syndication. All they know is that syndicated shows such as *Rosie O'Donnell, Hercules, Baywatch,* and *Bob Vila's Home Again* provide hours of entertainment. These shows, and dozens more, are produced exclusively for the syndicated market and are known as first-run syndication, as contrasted to network reruns such as *I Love Lucy* or *In the Heat of the Night,* which are known as **off-network syndication.** Occasionally, long-running network shows such as *Home Improvement* go into syndication while they are still on a network schedule.

As is the case with any television programming, syndication commercial costs vary with the ratings of a show. *Seinfeld* and first-run syndicated hits such as *Entertainment Tonight* will offer 30-second barter commercials for more than $100,000, whereas lower-rated daytime talk shows typically will charge in the $15,000 to $20,000 range. Off-network shows will usually command a higher price because they have a proven track record and high audience recognition; compared to buying first-run syndication, there is less risk in buying off-network shows.[12]

Several circumstances have changed the syndicated market in recent years:

1. *Repeal of the Primetime Access Rule.* In a decision that many think planted the seeds for syndication as a major advertising vehicle, the FCC passed the Primetime Access Rule in 1971. The rule limited the amount of time that local network affiliates could broadcast network-supplied programs during prime time. This limitation was intended to provide prime-time access to program suppliers other than the networks and diversify programming at the local station level.

    Under the rule, the Commission also forbid top-50 market affiliates from using off-network syndicated reruns during the access period. Because few local stations could afford to produce local programming, the rule opened the market for first-run syndication. In 1996, the FCC repealed the rule, and now these large stations can bid on a number of shows formerly banned from a major portion of their lineups. There is little question that the influx of these stations bidding for shows such as *Cheers, Home Improvement,* and *Roseanne* will drive up prices that already are running as much as $750,000 *per episode* (usually shows can be run 7 to 10 times under these contracts).

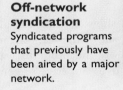

Off-network syndication
Syndicated programs that previously have been aired by a major network.

---

[12]Joe Mandese, "Off-Network Hits Dominate Barter Ad Price Survey," *Advertising Age,* January 13, 1997, p. s5.

2. *The growth of cable networks.* The creation of dozens of cable networks, most operating on a 24-hour basis, has created an insatiable appetite for all forms of programming. Nickelodeon, Lifetime, TNT, The Family Channel, and a host of other cable networks are buying a number of off-network programs from the syndication market and driving up the prices of those that remain.

3. *Advertising agency participation in syndication.* Normally, advertisers and their agencies select syndicated buys (either barter or spot) from what is available in the syndicated market. However, sometimes there is no program available that provides a good "fit" between a particular brand and the content or potential audience of the shows offered. In addition, a particular syndicated show might not be aired in a prime market for an advertiser.

To gain control and accessibility over the syndication market, some large advertising agencies have actively entered the market. In some cases, agencies have helped syndicators sell shows in certain markets. A large agency has the influence through its spot buying power to persuade stations to clear these programs. Agencies also agree to place clients' advertising on shows they pitch to producers. In effect, they are underwriting a portion of the show and, in return, designing its content. For example, "for advertisers in the hotly competitive kids' market, these alliances ensure the appropriate programming will be there to meet the advertising needs of their product lines. Marketers of kids' products, such as sweetened cereals and toys, really need kids' TV programming to sell their products."[13]

4. *Syndication as a spot advertising vehicle.* Many advertisers use syndicated programming as a means to extend reach on a demographic and/or geographic basis. For those advertisers pursuing higher reach, broadcast syndication normally surpasses cable networks.

5. *Profitability of syndication to stations.* In the typical network show, stations are allowed to sell 1 minute of commercial time. In a syndicated show, the station can sell from 6 to 12 minutes of commercials depending on how the program was bartered to the station. Consequently, a syndicated program does not have to generate huge ratings to be a financial success for a station.

Because local stations find syndication profitable, and the demand for new syndicated programming continues to grow, there is every reason to believe that syndication will be a major advertising vehicle into the next decade. If anything, syndication will be an even stronger competitor to the traditional networks, and the relationship between syndicators and stations may become more formal.

Stripping

Most local stations schedule syndicated shows on a five-night-a-week basis. That is, they will run *Jeopardy* or *Inside Edition* Monday through Friday in the same time slot. This practice is called **stripping** because the show is stripped across a time period. It is cost efficient to buy fewer shows for multiple showings, and it allows a station to build a consistent audience for selling commercials to potential advertisers. Because most syndication is used as a lead-in either for early news or prime time, stations don't want huge rating or audience composition differences from one day to another.

CABLE TELEVISION

The earliest cable systems were established in the late 1940s to import television signals into rural areas. These early systems, known as community antenna television (CATV), marked the start of a multibillion industry. Today, **cable television** household penetra-

---

Stripping
Scheduling a syndicated program on a five-day-per-week basis.

Cable television
TV signals that are carried to households by cable. Programs originate with cable operators through high antennas, satellite disks, or operator-initiated programming.

[13]Laurie Freeman, "For Hungry Syndicators, Agencies Fill the Plate," *Advertising Age,* January 15, 1996, p. 26.

Viewers to Basic Cable Programming Are Upscale

Cable offers advertisers the opportunity to reach young, educated, and affluent households, which also exhibit high levels of employment.

Household Income	Total U.S.	Cable* Network	Prime-Time TV	Radio	Newspaper	Magazine
$75,000+	100	123	85	108	125	106
$50,000–$75,000	100	116	91	107	115	106
$25,000–$50,000	100	102	99	103	101	102
Under $25,000	100	80	112	90	81	92
Education						
College graduate	100	109	88	106	124	107
Attended college	100	106	93	106	104	107
HS graduate	100	102	106	100	99	101
Not HS graduate	100	80	110	86	73	83
Occupation						
Executive/managerial/ administrative	100	119	85	109	122	107
Professional	100	106	84	109	118	107
Employed full-time	100	106	94	108	103	103
Not employed	100	91	113	87	96	94
Household Size						
3+ persons	100	104	96	105	97	102
2	100	102	105	96	108	99
1	100	80	104	88	93	93
Age						
18–49	100	101	94	108	92	103
25–54	100	103	97	107	98	103
55+	100	95	115	81	115	92

*Any viewing past week

Source: MRI, Doublebase 1995.

Source: 1996 Cable TV Facts, a publication of the Cabletelevision Advertising Bureau, p. 39.

exhibit

8.6

tion is slightly more than 70 percent. In addition, cable programming reaches a more upscale audience than most other media (see Exhibit 8.6). More important, viewers in cable households spend a significant amount of time with cable. In fact, those households with pay cable view cable programming 51 percent of the time, according to the Cabletelevision Advertising Bureau (CAB).

Unlike over-the-air broadcasters, who receive their total revenue from advertising, the cable industry receives the majority of its income from basic cable fees, with advertising providing slightly less than 25 percent of total revenues. The CAB projects that by 2002, 42 percent of all entertainment dollars will be spent in some form of pay video service.

Although cable television accounts for a sizable portion of the total audience, individual cable networks generate relatively small ratings. For example, of the more than 50 cable channels, only one, the USA Network, has an average rating of 2.0. Beyond the major networks such as ESPN, TBS, CNN, and two or three others, most cable networks have average ratings of less than 1.0. Cable networks have begun to make significant investments in original programming to increase ratings. In the past 10 years, program investment by cable has increased 500 percent to more than $4 billion.

Advertisers are drawn to cable because of the variety of programming and audience targeting opportunities it presents. As one agency media director observed, "The nice thing about cable is that there are networks that focus their content toward specific audiences. For an advertiser with an upscale demo, you can find those people in greater concentration on these networks."[14] In many respects, cable duplicates many of the marketing characteristics of selective magazines.

Because of the nature of cable programming, advertisers are more particularly interested in the lifestyles and preferences of cable audiences. For example, the Discover Channel stresses the fact that many of its viewers are upscale intellectuals who seek knowledge for its own sake and are very active and well read.[15] Similar studies have been conducted for other cable networks to gain more in-depth knowledge of these small, but important audiences.

Buying Cable Advertising

Historically, television has been considered by advertisers to be a mass media. However, as cable becomes more established, advertisers are using a combination of cable and broadcast television to reach both mass and niche audiences. For example, Procter & Gamble, General Motors, and AT&T are major advertisers in both cable and broadcast. Still cable and broadcast are used for different purposes by advertisers. From a marketing perspective, cable is comparable to radio and magazines as a medium to reach narrowly defined audiences, but one that requires numerous spots on several networks to achieve adequate levels of reach or frequency. In fact, advertisers often buy a combination of specific radio formats and niche cable as a method of extending reach. Cable also reinforces media synergism, which is becoming an integral part of selling many media.

Cable is often used to deliver audience reach. Alone, or more likely in combination with other media, cable can achieve high levels of unduplicated audiences. Cable has the capability of targeting audiences on a demographic, geographic, or lifestyle basis. A selective mix of cable channels can reach viewers that are light or nonviewers of most other television outlets. As Exhibit 8.7 demonstrates, basic cable is extremely efficient in attaining high reach levels among prime advertising prospects.

There are a number of factors that make cable television an attractive medium for advertisers:

1. *Ability to target audiences.* When advertisers consider cable television, its targetability is almost always the prime consideration.
2. *Low cost.* The cable industry is faced with a competitive environment that prevents significant increases in *CPM*s. With an abundance of cable channels, many trying to prove themselves to advertisers, it is very unlikely that we will see the type of advertising increases that have been so prevalent among the major broadcast networks recently.
3. *A strong summer season.* In recent years, cable has counterprogrammed the networks by presenting some of their strongest programs against network summer reruns. Many advertisers have taken advantage of the audience shifts inherent in this strategy to move dollars into cable during what is typically a down viewing time for networks.
4. *Opportunity for local and spot cable advertising.* Approximately 65 percent of cable advertising dollars are spent at the network level. However, local cable advertising is growing at a rate slightly higher than network expenditures. Local cable spending comes from national spot buyers looking to enhance advertising weight in specific markets and a wide variety of local firms such as restaurants, video stores, and small retailers.

---

[14]"Niche-Drive or Mass Appeal, Cable Readies a Powerful Programming Mix for '96/'97," *1996 Cable Programming Guide,* in *Advertising Age,* May 20, 1996, p. A3.
[15]"New Markets for Cable TV," *American Demographics,* June 1995, p. 43.

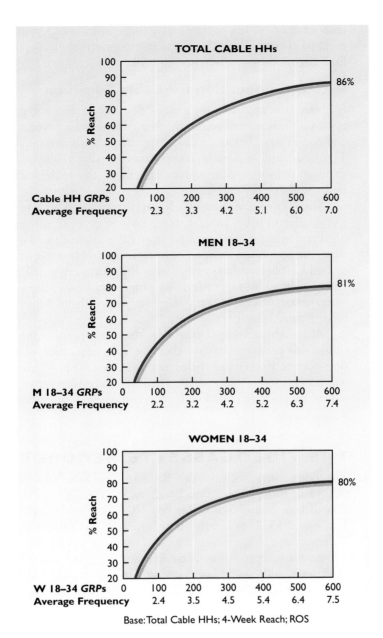

TOTAL CABLE HHs

Cable HH GRPs	0	100	200	300	400	500	600
Average Frequency		2.3	3.3	4.2	5.1	6.0	7.0

86%

MEN 18–34

M 18–34 GRPs	0	100	200	300	400	500	600
Average Frequency		2.2	3.2	4.2	5.2	6.3	7.4

81%

WOMEN 18–34

W 18–34 GRPs	0	100	200	300	400	500	600
Average Frequency		2.4	3.5	4.5	5.4	6.4	7.5

80%

Base: Total Cable HHs; 4-Week Reach; ROS

exhibit

8.7

Cable television is an excellent means of increasing reach.

Courtesy: Cabletelevision Advertising Bureau.
Source: 1996 Cable TV Facts, a publication of the Cabletelevision Advertising Bureau, p. 37.

Two innovations in local cable advertising have greatly enhanced the importance of this segment. First is the use of *cut-ins* on network cable programs. Cable networks, like their broadcast counterparts, turn back some advertising spots to local system operators to sell to local advertisers. Rather than having a spot appear on a largely unwatched local channel, commercials for the local pizza shop now can air on CNN's *Larry King Live* or ESPN's *Sports Center.*

A further strengthening of local cable advertising comes from the use of **interconnects.** "An interconnect exists where two or more cable systems [in the same market] link themselves together to distribute a commercial advertising schedule simultaneously."[16] In Chicago, an advertiser can simultaneously air up to five different commercials in various

Interconnects
A joint buying opportunity between two or more cable systems in the same market.

---

[16] *1995 Cable TV Facts,* a publication of the Cabletelevision Advertising Bureau, p. 72.

areas of the city. The agency gets a single bill with all brand information to facilitate individual client billing. The use of interconnects should greatly enhance the prospects for bringing more spot advertisers to cable.

Future Competition for Cable Television

It is rare that any industry grosses $50 billion without gaining some serious competition. Cable is no exception. With a reduction in government regulation, a number of companies have begun to compete with cable operators for the lucrative cable dollars. The two most important competitors are direct broadcast satellite (DBS) companies that can deliver satellite signals directly to the individual household and the regional Bell telephone companies.

Small satellite dishes, which can be purchased for less than $300 and have monthly fees similar to cable charges, receive a vast array of movies, sporting events, and other news and information programs from cable channels and over-the-air broadcasters. Likewise, the telephone companies hope to use their presence in virtually every household to build a fiber optic system that will provide expanded services, such as banking and Internet, in addition to television programming. We are already seeing many cross-over agreements with cable companies merging with broadcasters and telephone companies buying cable systems.

Although cable operators view these competitive intrusions with some apprehension, cable programmers are glad to see the expansion of a new generation of distribution outlets. Rather than being confined to a 30 to 50 channel system, new technology will provide for as many as 500 channels. Expanded systems will allow second-tier channels to increase their national reach and compete for advertising dollars with the major networks.[17]

THE VIDEOCASSETTE RECORDER

The videocassette recorder (VCR) has moved from an upscale novelty to a common appliance in most households. By the year 2000, it is estimated that more than 95 percent of U.S. households will have a VCR—virtually matching television-set ownership. The use of VCRs is clearly contributing to the further fragmentation of the television audience.

At one time, it was anticipated that the primary use of VCRs would be to record regular television shows for later viewing. This off-air recording for later viewing is called **time-shift viewing.** However, studies show that more than half of recorded shows are never watched, the audiences for time-shift viewing tend to be demographically different than original audiences, and the VCR allows viewers to fast-forward through commercials.

In recent years, the major usage of VCRs has been for prerecorded tapes, especially theatrically released movies. The preference for taped movies, as contrasted to time-shift viewing, has created two major approaches to the marketing of tapes:

1. *A move to sell tapes directly to consumers.* At one time, movie producers believed that the consumer tape market was relatively small and confined to a few hard-core movie connoisseurs. However, led by a number of children's titles such as *The Lion King* and *The Little Mermaid,* consumers have begun to get into the habit of buying movies. In fact, the large children's market has shown a rise in multi-VCR households corresponding to the earlier growth in multi–television set households. Adult movies such as *Forrest Gump* have sold 10 million copies and they have provided a major source of additional income to film producers.

2. *Tapes as promotional tie-ins.* The high level of VCR household penetration has created a number of promotional opportunities. Many companies, such as fast-food

[17]Michael Burgi, "Learning to Live with Its Success," *Adweek,* September 9, 1996, p. 12.

Time-shift viewing
Recording programs on a VCR for viewing at a later time.

outlets, have marketed tapes as promotional tie-ins. In other cases, advertisers have provided coupons in the video sleeves that offer brand discounts or rebates on the purchase of a product. The advantage of such promotions is that they are relatively inexpensive and, because advertisers know with some certainty the audience for a particular film, they can be targeted with the precision of direct mail.

In the future, many executives within the television industry predict that pay-per-view (PPV) movies will provide competition for both prerecorded tapes and television viewing in general. However, despite the fact that some 30 million homes have PPV capability, the segment has been used more for special events, such as prize fights or rock concerts, than for regular movie viewing.

Another growing use of videocassettes is for direct response. Companies such as Nissan and Nordic Track have been extremely successful in having consumers call in for a tape demonstration of their products. Not only does the tape provide a more in-depth and realistic demonstration of the product, but the process also provides a database of potential consumers, which allows companies to follow up with telemarketing.

The television industry is well aware that each hour spent watching these prerecorded tapes is time not available for regular television viewing. Of particular concern to both broadcasters and advertisers is the demographic makeup of heavy VCR users. For example, young affluent adults, prime prospects for many television advertisers, are the most likely to rent videotapes. This audience is then unavailable for exposure to traditional broadcast and cable outlets and their advertisers.

SYNDICATED RATING SERVICES

The television industry provides viewers with a wealth of information, entertainment, and advertising. However, for advertisers, the medium is a delivery system for current and potential customers. The price these advertisers pay networks and stations for commercial time is determined by the size and demographic composition of the audience. Needless to say, it is crucial for advertisers and their agencies to have reliable data on which to make buying decisions and to determine if they are paying a fair price.

In recent years, the problem of accurately accounting for the fragmented television audience has become more and more difficult. At the same time, as audiences for each television outlet decrease, the magnitude of any error increases as a percentage of the total viewing audience. For example, a one-rating-point error for a program with a 20 rating is 5 percent; the same error for a program with a 5 rating is 20 percent. Because advertising rates are directly determined by ratings, these errors are a cause for considerable concern among advertisers.

Committee on Nationwide Television Audience Measurement

Committee on Nationwide Television Audience Measurement (CONTAM)
Industry-wide organization to improve the accuracy and reliability of television ratings.

The **Committee on Nationwide Television Audience Measurement** (CONTAM) was established in 1963 as a joint effort by the three networks and the National Association of Broadcasters (NAB). Its purpose was to improve the accuracy and reliability of ratings research. Currently, CONTAM is working to provide an accurate and reliable reflection of a television audience that is constantly changing. The problems associated with accurately measuring the fragmented viewership of television are immense.

Television technology that was unknown two decades ago is now a reality. This reality is creating tremendous methodological problems for rating services. For example, how do you count viewers watching a picture-in-picture screen? Do you double count them (certainly unfair to competing shows)? Do you half them? Do you give more weight to the picture on the larger portion of the screen?

Television time buyers are demanding that ratings methodology and technology deal with these and a multitude of other questions. For example, buyers need to know if a VCR viewer is watching a prerecorded tape or an off-the-air program and, if off-the-air, which program? How do you measure children who are too young to use rating devices? How do you account for the large out-of-home viewership of some late-night shows and sporting events? Advertisers also are demanding instantaneous ratings, with household rating mechanisms wired directly to client computers.

The Rating Services   When the Arbitron Company dropped its local television measuring service in 1994, it left only Nielsen Media Research as the major supplier of syndicated television ratings. Network ratings are provided through the Nielsen Television Index (NTI) and local market ratings through the Nielsen Station Index (NSI). Nielsen produces numerous individual reports—some on a 24-hour basis for network prime-time programming.

The television industry has been understandably concerned by the lack of a competing rating supplier. There have been a number of potential challenges to Nielsen. One with significant advertising industry support is Statistical Research, Inc. (SRI), a company with extensive experience in radio measurement. The company is attempting to provide ratings information within 30 minutes through a system called System for Measuring And Reporting Television (SMART).

SMART allows viewers to click on a remote control to indicate they are watching. Signals are collected by a sensor on the screen and transmitted to SRI's mainframe computer. "Data can be sorted by daypart, sex, age, socio-economic identifiers, individual person and even pairs of persons—as when . . . siblings watch the same show."[18] SRI began testing the system in 1997 in Philadelphia. Major advertisers, such as AT&T, General Motors, and Procter & Gamble, as well as some large advertising agencies gave their support to the initial effort.

Rating Methodologies

As audience researchers grapple with the growing problems of measuring the fragmented audience for television, they constantly review and refine their research methodologies. The methods used to measure the television audience continue to evolve as new technology becomes available. Rating methods have gone through several phases over the years:

1. *The telephone.* The first rating service, the Cooperative Analyses of Broadcasting, began in 1930. Arch Crossley used the telephone recall method to determine listening behavior during the previous 24 hours. Telephone research is still used for special research projects, but not on a regular basis for syndicated TV ratings.
2. *The diary.* The diary method requires that all persons in a household keep a record of their viewing habits. For many years, the diary has been the mainstay for TV ratings. It is still used for smaller-market local ratings. However, the multichannel television of the 1990s cannot be adequately measured by research methods of the 1950s. It is clear that the diary, as a primary source of research data, is being phased out.
3. *The household meter.* The next development in the quest to provide better ratings information was the metered household. Since 1950, when Nielsen introduced the Nielsen Storage Instantaneous Audimeter (referred to as either SIA or simply Audimeter), metered audience measurement has been the principal method of obtaining national ratings. The meters give an accurate profile of the programs to which the TV set is tuned. However, they do not measure who, if anyone, is watching and are significantly more expensive than diaries.

---

[18]David J. Wallace, "High Hopes for Smart Ratings Service, but Promises Need to Be Fulfilled," *Advertising Age,* July 22, 1996, p. S16.

People meter
Device that measures TV set usage by individuals rather than by households.

4. *People meters.* A new era in TV ratings was initiated in 1987 when Nielsen introduced the so-called **people meter.** It attempted to overcome the problems of both diaries and set meters. Ideally, people meters combine the accuracy of set meters with the diary's ability to gather demographic information, for it not only records what is being watched, but by whom. When the people meter expanded to its present sample of 4,000 households in 1988, the major beneficiaries were the cable networks. The smaller, but more homogeneous audiences of these networks could now be sold to advertisers with some certainty as to what they were buying.

5. *People meters—The next generation.*

Passive people meters. A problem with the people meter is that viewers have to remember to program them as they begin watching. Much like the diary, there is nothing wrong with the methodology except human nature. The rating services are testing the so-called **passive meter.** One technique would have a meter programmed through a sensor in the television set that is unique to each member of the household. When that person enters the room where the television set is turned on, the sensor will automatically begin to record that person's viewing. One problem is that a person may be in a room with the television tuned in but not be watching, and erroneously be recorded as a member of the audience. However, the method still overcomes major shortcomings of both the diary and people meter.

Passive meter
Unobtrusive device that measures individual viewing habits through sensors keyed to household members.

The pocket people meter. A method that many think is more practical than the sensor-activated passive people meter is the pocket people meter that an individual would carry and record any viewing during a rating period. Questions about the pocket people meter center around the willingness of people to carry them and also the concerns about out-of-home viewing discussed earlier.

The practical application of the passive and pocket people meters is in the future. They do demonstrate the problems of measuring a mobile, segmented audience in the current television environment. It is imperative that the television industry deliver credible ratings to advertisers in exchange for their multibillion-dollar advertising investments.

SWEEPS

Because of the expense of obtaining rating information, daily measures are conducted only in the top 34 markets. Nielsen uses set meters to provide overnight ratings in these markets. The remaining 177 television markets are measured by Nielsen with diaries four times a year. During February, May, July, and November, the entire television audience, including metered markets, is measured, or swept, hence the term **sweep weeks.**

Sweep weeks
During these periods, ratings are taken for all television markets.

In each market, between 300 and 400 households keep a viewing diary for three or four weeks. The diaries provide information about basic viewer demographics as well as viewing habits. For the local television stations, the sweeps set advertising rates for the coming quarter. May sweeps are used for the fall season; November for the following spring; and February for late spring and early summer. The July book is used for late summer and is considered the least important measure because the audience is smaller and reruns are more likely to be aired.[19]

In recent years sweep periods have become very controversial for advertisers. It is obvious that stations and networks save their best programming for the sweeps and artificially inflate ratings (and ad rates) for the rest of the year. There is no question that programming changes during the sweeps. In 1997, the Television Advertising Bureau, which represents local stations, began to explore the possibility of continuous ratings at the local level. Whether this is financially or logistically possible remains to be seen. However, the current abuses of sweep week ratings make such a proposal long overdue.

---

[19]Laura Dalton, "The Scoop on the 'Sweeps,'" *Gannetteer,* November/December 1996, p. 18.

Qualitative Ratings

In our discussion of cable television, we commented on the need for cable networks to sell the quality and lifestyle of their audiences in contrast to the basic numbers reported by most major rating reports. Another type of qualitative audience measure seeks to offer insight into audience involvement or degree of preference for particular television shows or personalities. These measures can be used to determine if a person can be successfully used as a testimonial spokesperson or to see if a popular show is beginning to wear out.

The best-known qualitative research service is Marketing Evaluations, which compiles a number of "popularity" surveys called "Q" reports. The most familiar of these are the **TvQ** and Performer Q.

Let us assume that a TV show, *Big Bob Monday Night Circus,* is familiar to 50 percent of the population, and 30 percent of the people rank it as one of their favorite shows. The *Q* score would be calculated as follows:

$$Q = \frac{FAV}{FAM} \text{ or } \frac{30}{50} = 60$$

Q ratings will not take the place of traditional audience ratings. However, they can provide evidence of which personalities and programs might benefit from more promotion or a change to a higher-profile time slot. It is important to note that a *Q* score is not a substitute for minimum ratings. Regardless of how well liked a show or a performer may be, there has to be a minimum audience for the show to remain on the air.

Ratings for Program Content

Reacting to pressure from Congress and a number of public interest groups, the networks introduced a system of program content ratings in 1996. The system, modeled after movie ratings, rated programs from TV-Y (suitable for all ages) to TV-M (suitable only for mature audiences). The long-term effect of these content ratings is still being determined. However, some television program executives think that adult-oriented programming may be hurt as advertisers resist being identified with programs that have been identified as having sexual or violent content. In any case, advertisers, programmers, and viewers are now subject to one more analysis of the television landscape.

THE INTERNET AND THE ELECTRONIC SUPERHIGHWAY

The Internet is a communications phenomenon. Every day, millions of messages, including personal notes, business correspondence, and advertising, are transmitted around the world. However, few of the people that use the Internet have the vaguest idea of how it works. Many more users are predicting great potential for the many Web sites that populate the Internet, but few commercial users have been able to make them profitable. Even optimistic estimates of future Web advertising predict that it will account for no more than 2 percent of all advertising revenues by the year 2000.

Most commercial Web site users and providers encounter three major obstacles:

1. *Buying commercial spots.* A major problem in the early days of Web site expansion was that the builders of the sites were technical experts with little understanding of marketing their sites. On the other hand, the companies and advertisers making advertising decisions were interested in using the Web as any other media, and the two parties often had little in common.

   In recent years, a number of rep firms have begun to represent Web sites in much the same way they sell spot television time. In fact, Katz Media Group and other major television reps were among the first companies to begin the process of

TvQ

A service of Marketing Evaluations that measures the popularity (opinion of audience rather than size of audience) of shows and personalities.

representing Web sites. As the president of one rep firm said, "Part of our strategy for the company overall is to create an infrastructure where advertisers can buy interactive media as easily as other media."[20]

2. *Audience measures.* If Web site owners are going to sell advertising space, they have to expect that potential advertisers will request audience measures. To this point, advertisers complain that it is a very cumbersome process to determine exactly when their advertising ran and how many contacts (or *hits*) were totaled. There is even a debate about what constitutes an impression on the Web. Is it the total of duplicated contacts or is it when a potential consumer makes some interactive contact with the Web? For example, some sites require some consumer information before a person can go beyond a certain point in a site.

3. *Results.* The ultimate decision to buy any medium is usually its contribution to sales and profits. Because the Internet is such a new medium, it is very difficult to determine with any certainty what it offers to a company's overall marketing strategy. To date, a diverse group of advertisers have tested the use of Web advertising. AT&T, MasterCard, and American Airlines are among the largest Web advertisers.

At least one preliminary study by Nielsen indicated that homes that subscribe to America Online watch 15 percent less television.[21] As one advertising executive pointed out, **on-line services,** although not supplanting television, might provide reach to light users of the medium. Most observers think that on-line services will continue to grow and at some point provide significant competition to television viewing at least among some audience segments.

The new age of television and related information systems is often referred to as the *electronic superhighway,* a road over which we will buy, sell, laugh, and be informed. The electronic highway will not only change the way we use television and other media, but according to its most optimistic proponents, it will change the way we live and work. In fact, many executives in the communications industry think that business applications, from telecommuting to home banking, will be the first general uses of the technology. However, to make any such system economically viable, it must appeal to the general public.

On-line services
Refers to computer-accessed databases and information services for business and home use.

SUMMARY

The nature of mass communication is changing rapidly, and nowhere is the change more apparent than in television. Television will soon be more than a medium of entertainment and news. Already, in a number of markets, telecommunication providers are establishing revolutionary interactive systems that allow viewers to pay bills, make airline reservations, receive pay-per-view programming on demand, and even play computer games with other viewers. How long it will be before these systems are generally available and what their final form will take are still very much in question. However, programmers, advertisers, and the general public will be dealing with a dramatically changed television medium in the not-too-distant future.

Regardless of the specific form that future television takes, it is clear that the relationship between the medium and its audience is changing rapidly. Television is entering a period of *narrowcasting.* Although the major networks continue to be the dominant source of programming for most viewers, an erosion of network shares will continue into the next century. This erosion will be brought about by niche services that appeal to fewer viewers than the networks can profitably reach. Already the first move toward interactive television can be seen in the home shopping networks where viewers call in, comment about merchandise, and place orders.

[20]Ed Caldwell, "The Repping of the Web," *Adweek,* January 26, 1996, p. 21.

[21]Bill Carter, "Does More Time On Line Mean Reduced TV Time?" *The New York Times,* January 31, 1997, p. C5.

Television in the next century faces an uncertain existence. However, the opportunities for a two-way flow of information and advertising offers advantages to viewers and advertisers alike.

The tremendous acceleration already evident in the demassification process, along with the formation of what futurist Murray Hillman calls "global societies"—people with common interests, residing in different nations, maintaining "live" online contact with each other—and the well-documented efforts to target and personalize sales messages, may prove to be a boon to future network programmers and sales departments.[22]

REVIEW

1. Define the following terms:
   a. Clutter
   b. Share-of-audience
   c. Ratings
   d. Network
   e. Block programming
   f. Make-goods
   g. Syndicated television
   h. Sweeps
2. Why is it unwise to use cost-per-point comparisons in markets of significantly different sizes?
3. Briefly discuss the importance of clearance rates for networks.
4. What are some of the reasons for falling audience share levels among major television networks?
5. What role does negotiation play in setting television advertising rates?
6. What is the difference between a wired and nonwired network?
7. What are the prospects for growth in the local television advertising segment?
8. What are the primary means of collecting ratings data?
9. Briefly discuss the concept of narrowcasting and its importance for the future of television.

TAKE IT TO THE NET

We invite you to visit the Russell/Lane page on the Prentice Hall Web site at **PHLIP** **http://www.prenhall.com/phbusiness** for the bimonthly Russell/Lane update and for this chapter's World Wide Web exercise.

---

[22]Fred Danzig, "No Longer 'Licenses to Make Money,' Nets Are Still Resilient, So Don't Count 'em Out," *Advertising Age, 50 Years of TV Advertising,* Spring 1995, p. 54.

9

USING RADIO

RADIO'S PRIMARY STRENGTH AS A MARKETING TOOL IS ITS ABILITY TO TARGET VARIOUS AUDIENCE SEGMENTS. THE NUMBER OF STATIONS ALLOWS THE MEDIUM TO PROGRAM DIVERSE AND ECLECTIC FORMATS THAT REACH VERY NARROW SEGMENTS OF THE LISTENING AUDIENCE. AFTER READING THIS CHAPTER YOU WILL UNDERSTAND

- radio's transition from a mass to a selective medium
- radio's strength as an out-of-home medium
- radio's ability to reach audiences at a low cost
- the lack of a visual element in radio
- dominance of FM
- the rating system in radio.

At one time radio was the premier mass medium for audiences and advertisers. From 1926, when the first network, the National Broadcasting Company, was formed until the mid-1950s, radio was the most prestigious of the national media. During those golden years of radio the family gathered around the living room radio set to listen to Jack Benny, Fred Allen, and Bob Hope entertain them while news personalities such as Edward R. Murrow enlightened them. All of this programming was brought to the audience by the major advertisers of the day.

However, starting in the late 1940s a number of factors, many beyond the control of the radio industry, were coming on the horizon to make radical changes in radio. The primary challenge to radio was television. In 1951, the advent of coast-to-coast television broadcasts and the introduction of instant hits such as *I Love Lucy* and *The $64,000 Question* marked the decline of radio as a national medium. Despite the problems facing radio, its critics underestimated the public demand and the management skills and creativity of radio executives. Without dismissing the rough times that radio has had over the last 30 years, the medium is anything but forgotten.

With more than $13 billion in annual billings, radio is the fourth largest advertising medium in the United States. In the last 25 years, radio has consistently accounted for 6 to 7 percent of total advertising dollars. Radio permeates American society with a daily reach of approximately 77 percent and a weekly reach of some 95 percent of the population, with automobile listenership achieving 80 percent reach levels. On a given weekday, adults average almost three and a half hours with their radios. In addition, 36 percent of the radio audience listens at work. Unlike other media, radio is truly an "all-day" advertising vehicle.[1]

Radio is used as either a primary or a secondary advertising medium, depending on the needs of specific advertisers. Radio also is an excellent medium for reaching audiences such as teens, who are light users of other media. In addition, radio's portability makes it the preferred medium for out-of-home audiences both in cars and in the workplace. Radio also allows advertisers to reach audiences while they are in the marketplace. Only point of purchase is able to reach prospects closer to the time of purchase. Finally, radio is inexpensive, both on a *CPM* basis and from a production standpoint. Although the average cost of a network television commercial is approximately $250,000, the typical radio commercial is very inexpensive, some as little as a few hundred dollars. In fact, some local stations will produce commercials at no cost to an advertiser. As we see in this chapter, radio's success as an advertising medium is a result of the medium matching the marketing goals of advertisers in a way that other media find difficult to duplicate.

FEATURES AND ADVANTAGES OF RADIO

In many respects, radio has led the way toward a more segmented media environment during the last 20 years. Radio's localized, fragmented strategy, born out of necessity in the 1950s, has been adopted by more and more media. With the advent of cable, even television has become a niche medium in many respects. MTV, the Weather Channel, Headline News, and ESPN all have their roots in the segmented climate begun by radio. In this section, we discuss some of the primary advantages of the medium from an advertiser's perspective.

A Personal Medium

The human voice is the most personal means of communication. Radio gives the advertiser the opportunity to take advantage of the right combination of words, voices, music, and sound effects to establish a unique "one-on-one" connection with prospects that lets you grab their attention, evoke their emotions, and persuade them to respond.

Advertisers now are looking at radio differently than in recent years. Radio "can be targeted by lifestyle formats and is more efficient than other media from a cost and production standpoint. As a result many advertising agencies are moving more of their budgets into radio. Radio's strong local bond with its listeners bodes well for advertisers that have seen other media become more distanced from their audience."[2]

Broadly Selective

Radio is the most pervasive of all advertising media. The average household owns almost six radios, and virtually every new car comes with a radio as standard equipment. More important than set ownership is the fact that radio is listened to by practically everyone at some time during the day. Radio has the unique ability to deliver both high levels of

---

[1]Unless otherwise noted, the information in this chapter comes from the Radio Advertising Bureau.

[2]B. Eric Rhoads, "Looking Back at Radio's Future," *Media Studies Journal,* Summer 1993, p. 20.

**Radio Reaches 77% of All Consumers
Every Day . . . and 95% Every Week**

	Demo	Average Daily Reach	Average Weekly Reach
Persons	12+	76.5%	95.1%
Teens	12–17	79.5	95.6
Adults	18+	76.1	95.1
Men	18+	78.0	95.2
	18–34	80.5	96.3
	25–54	81.0	96.3
	35–64	79.4	95.7
	65+	65.5	90.1
Women	18+	74.4	95.0
	18–34	78.2	97.4
	25–54	78.1	96.9
	35–64	76.5	96.0
	65+	61.2	88.1

Sources: Average daily reach: RADAR ® 53, Spring 1996,
© Copyright Statistical Research, Inc. (Monday–Sunday, 24
hours, based on daily cume); Average weekly reach: Spring
1996 Arbitron National Database Cume PUR Estimates,
based on Arbitron's 94 Continuous Measurement Markets.

reach and frequency as well as narrowly targeted market segments. As shown in Exhibit 9.1, radio has extremely high reach in all dayparts and across every major demographic category. Overall, radio reaches 95 percent of all adults on a weekly basis.

Radio's high overall reach and its ability to provide numerous formats makes it a multifaceted medium. In some sense, each programming category, whether country, classical, all-talk, or rhythm and blues, can be treated as a distinct medium for marketing purposes. From a marketing perspective, radio has the ability to reach prospects by sex, age, or interest with a format that adds an even greater dimension to its already strong personal communication environment.

Because of the relatively low cost of production, advertisers are able to adapt commercials to the various stations they buy, a strategy that would normally be prohibitively expensive in television. Coca-Cola has long been a pioneer in developing commercials for the diverse radio station formats that it buys. Many radio advertisers, to provide an even closer association between commercials and formats, elect to have local station talent announce their commercials rather than having them preproduced. We discuss the creative approaches to radio in more detail in chapter 20.

As a Complement to Other Media

In some cases, radio is the primary medium for local advertisers. However, for national advertisers and most large local and regional firms, radio is most often used as a complementary medium to extend the reach and frequency of primary vehicles in their advertising schedules. When the Marine Corps wanted to increase the number of women in both enlisted and officer categories, it turned to a combination of magazines and radio to reach a targeted audience of women who might be interested in a career in the Marines. In the accompanying case, we see how radio not only reached these women, but reinforced *"The Few. The Proud. The Marines."* theme from the print ads.

For many years, a fundamental marketing strategy for radio has been its ability to successfully work with other media to increase reach and frequency or to reach nonusers or light users of other media. The radio industry realizes that the bulk of its revenues come from advertisers who use radio as a secondary medium. Exhibit 9.2 (p. 232) shows the high listenership of radio compared with other media.

exhibit

9.2

Radio listenership is number one.

Courtesy: Radio Advertising Bureau.
Source: 1997 Radio Marketing Guide and Fact Book for Advertisers, a publication of the Radio Advertising Bureau, p. 2.

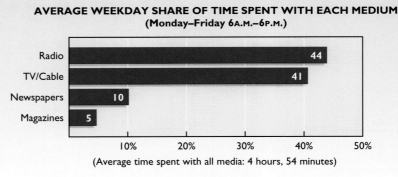

AVERAGE WEEKDAY SHARE OF TIME SPENT WITH EACH MEDIUM
(Monday–Friday 6 A.M.–6 P.M.)

(Average time spent with all media: 4 hours, 54 minutes)

Source: Media Targeting 2000: The Arbitron/RAB Consumer Study, 1995.

Low *CPM*

Advertisers are giving increasingly more attention to cost efficiencies. Radio delivers its audience at a *CPM* level below that of virtually any other medium. Not only are the *CPM* levels low, but radio's recent increases also have been below that of its major competitors. As demonstrated in Exhibit 9.3, radio *CPM* increases have been approximately half of all media increases and, with the exception of outdoor, radio is the only medium with rate increases lower than the CPI.

When Congress passed the Telecommunications Act of 1996, the ensuing deregulation allowed mergers and acquisitions that created a number of huge radio conglomerates. In addition to larger group ownership, the legislation also permitted local marketing agreements (LMA) by which one station owner operates one or several stations in a market for another owner.

exhibit

9.3

Radio is among the least expensive media.

Courtesy: Radio Advertising Bureau.
Source: 1997 Radio Marketing Guide and Fact Book for Advertisers, a publication of the Radio Advertising Bureau, p. 26.

Radio Is Cost-Effective

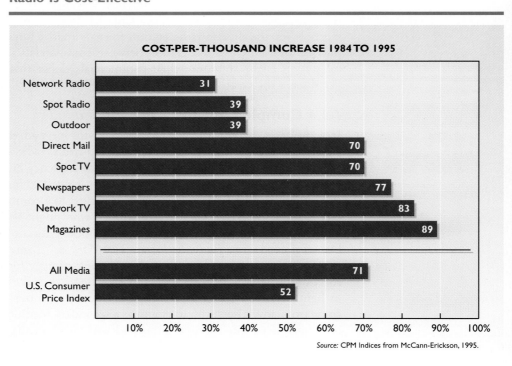

COST-PER-THOUSAND INCREASE 1984 TO 1995

Source: CPM Indices from McCann-Erickson, 1995.

MARKETING SITUATION

Give a description of the competitive environment.

Recruiting Women to a *Male* Brand

Without question, the Marine Corps is perceived as a "male" brand. Although the theme line "We're looking for a few good men" has not been used in six years, it still defines who the Marine Corps is and consequently whom it recruits. The Marines are the military branch to which our nation has bestowed the unenviable responsibility to be the first into combat. However, by law, women are still *not* permitted into combat. Nevertheless, women have indeed served our nation proudly in the Marine Corps since World War I. Currently, they make up approximately 5 percent of the Marine Corps, and long-term goals will bring this composition up dramatically over the next five years.

In recent years, the Marine Corps has increased its recruiting efforts to women. In the process, however, the drop-out rates at boot camp have also increased, indicating that in many cases either the "wrong" type of women were joining, they were joining for the wrong reasons, or they were not adequately prepared for the rigorous training they were about to receive.

get a make-over that's more than skin deep.

CAMPAIGN OBJECTIVES

Give specific goals for your campaign.

Looking for a "Few Good Women," Too

Within the boundaries of the distinctively male brand, the Marine Corps set out to increase the number of women recruits and women officer candidates. The key was to increase the number of women in the Marine Corps without distorting the Corps persona to a point where *consideration* among all prospects would drop off.

1. Specifically, the recruiting mission (sales goal) for women was up for both enlisted and officer ranks:

	FY95
Enlisted	1,966 + 16.8%
Officer	75 + 15 %

2. A secondary objective was to design a communications program that would appeal to the right kind of woman and to accurately set her expectations of boot camp. This would be demonstrated in a reduction in the attrition rate (which identifies how many women drop out of boot camp).

TARGET AUDIENCE

Provide a detailed target audience definition.

Women Who Want to Rekindle the Feeling that Anything Can Be Accomplished

In their preadolescent years, many women believe they can accomplish anything. The possibilities are endless. Through adolescence, however, this world all changes. Society places great pressures on them that distract from their belief that they can accomplish anything. Instead of being encouraged to reach for the stars, they are repeatedly told what they are not permitted to do, what they cannot accomplish. At the age of 13 to 15 they perceive that they are living in a world built for men. Suddenly the options to excel may seem limited.

Against this backdrop the Marines set out to recruit not only more women, but women who had the ability to pass the Corps' rigorous tests. They wanted women who would succeed. To find these unique individuals, all materials were designed to appeal to certain characteristics that were consistent with successful women Marines:

- women who had *something to prove to themselves* and everyone else
- women who were *looking deep inside* for improvement

- women who wanted to *recapture a feeling of limitless opportunities*
- women who were looking for *real change rather than superficial change*

CREATIVE STRATEGY

Describe strategy upon which you based your creative approach.

Challenge Women to Rediscover Themselves and Find Success in the Marine Corps

Unlike other brands or products that can be conveniently repackaged to suit their many prospective buyers, the Marine Corps has neither the inclination nor the ability to do this.

The challenge in recruiting women was to present the Marine Corps for what it is (its goals, history, values, and its challenges) in a relevant way to this unique audience. To accomplish this, the Marine Corps had to be positioned as the vehicle that would help these women rediscover that lost feeling from preadolescence. It had to convince women that only through a meaningful endeavor could they recapture the sense that they could accomplish anything. The communications had to challenge and inspire them. It had to position the Marine Corps as

- the place where women rediscover their potential
- the toughest, yet most rewarding, challenge they can meet
- a place for substantial vs. superficial improvements.

you can look at models, or you can be one.

MEDIA STRATEGY

Describe media strategies and rationale.

Targeted Magazines and Radio to Reach Our Prospect

Two primary vehicles were used to reach these young women. With the objective of reaching high school juniors and seniors, a print schedule in *Teen* and *Seventeen* magazines was selected. As a secondary medium, radio spots were distributed to youth networks and local stations.

Client:	USMC
Campaign:	National Paid Radio
Title:	"Proudest Moment/Paid"
Media:	Radio
Length:	:60

ELEMENTS	AUDIO
Music	
SFX:	(Up & Under)
Buscaglia:	I had no direction. I did not know where I was going.
Esparza:	I didn't see my life really going anywhere.
Graves:	I was working at an endless job making five dollars an hour.
Kerley:	I just wanted to do something with my life.
SFX:	(Recruits: "Yes Ma'am!")
Beattie:	I got off that bus, and I was scared to death.
Gabbert:	I've never worked so hard for something in my life.
Derisio:	I did things that I thought I couldn't do.
Keeling:	You have to put all your heart and your soul into what you're doing at boot camp.
Campbell:	After the weeks were over you were like "Wow! Look, I'm awesome now too!"
Esparza:	I am a Marine.
Thwing:	You feel like you conquered the world.
SFX:	(DI at graduation: "Platoon four thousand, fifteen . . . dismissed!" Graduates: "Aye Ma'am!")
Derisio:	That day that they say, "Dismissed," you *know* that you are a Marine . . . that you *are* one of the elite.
Anncr:	Maybe you can be one of us. The Few. The Proud. The Marines. Call 1-800-MARINES.
Koon:	When I crossed that parade deck and they played the Marine Hymn . . . that was the proudest moment in my life.
"Paid" Tag:	Paid for by the Marines.

OTHER COMMUNICATION PROGRAMS

Describe other programs implemented with this campaign.

Integrated Communications Designed to Appeal to Prospective Women Marines at Several Levels
- posters and folders for distribution at high schools and in one-on-one interviews with recruiters designed to bring prospects into the decision mode
- a film designed for use by recruiters during one-on-one interviews

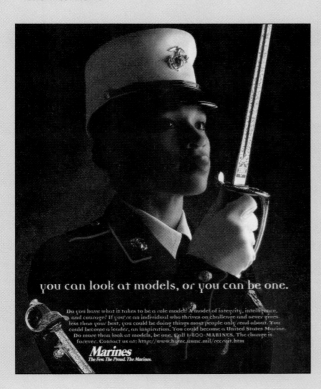

you can look at models, or you can be one.

Do you have what it takes to be a role model? A model of integrity, intelligence, and courage? If you're an individual who thrives on challenge and never gives less than your best, you could be doing things most people only read about. You could become a leader, an inspiration. You could become a United States Marine. Do more than look at models, be one. Call 1-800-MARINES. The change is forever. Contact us at: http://www.hqmc.usmc.mil/recruit.htm

Marines
The Few. The Proud. The Marines.

EVIDENCE OF RESULTS

Must relate directly in campaign objectives.

1. *Recruiting to Women Successful at Every Level*

NUMBER OF WOMEN RECRUITED

	FY95 Goal	FY95 Actual
Enlisted	1,966	2,119 + 18% (vs. FY95 goal)
Officer	75	80 + 23% (vs. FY95 goal)

Through the implementation of this program, recruitment improved for both enlisted and officer women prospects. In fact, in FY95 the Marine Corps achieved double digit improvement in female recruiting, while having no adverse effect on male recruiting.

2. *Boot Camp Attrition Down 46 Percent*
   Not only did the Marine Corps attract substantially more women as a result of this program, but they were the right kind of women. Attrition for women Marines at boot camp dropped by 46 percent versus previous years.

Courtesy: J. Walter Thompson–Atlanta.

Under these agreements, some companies control as many as eight stations in a market and more than 40 percent of total radio revenues. This added bargaining power has made some advertisers and agencies nervous about the future of inexpensive radio advertising spots.[3] In late 1996, the U.S. Justice Department put broadcasters on notice that mergers that give a single broadcaster more than 40 percent of the radio advertising in a particular market would come under close scrutiny. The American Association of Advertising Agencies (4As) expressed concern that even the so-called 40 percent rule still had the potential of giving a single station group enormous leverage in a market.[4]

---

[3]Steven W. Colford, "Who's Making Radio Waves?" *American Advertising,* Fall 1996, p. 30.

[4]Ira Teinowitz and Michael Wilke, "Justice Dept. Sets 40% as Guide on Radio Mergers," *Advertising Age,* November 18, 1996, p. 65.

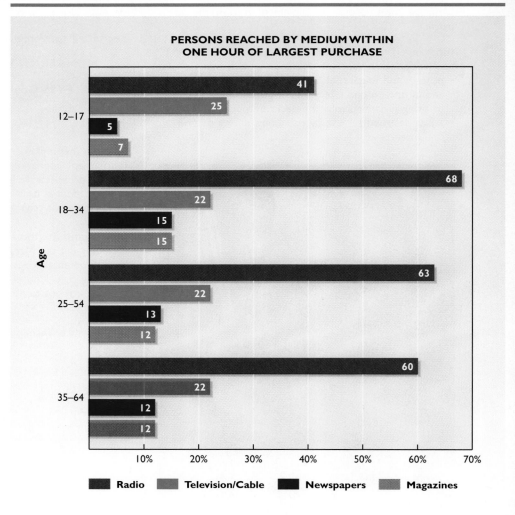

PERSONS REACHED BY MEDIUM WITHIN ONE HOUR OF LARGEST PURCHASE

■ Radio ■ Television/Cable ■ Newspapers ■ Magazines

exhibit

9.4

Radio is in the marketplace with consumers.

Courtesy: Radio Advertising Bureau.
Source: 1997 Radio Marketing Guide and Fact Book for Advertisers, a publication of the Radio Advertising Bureau, p. 10.

Proximity to Purchase

The mobility of radio and its huge out-of-home audience gives the medium an advantage enjoyed by few other advertising vehicles. In the competitive environment facing most companies, it is imperative that brands achieve consumer reinforcement as near as possible to the purchase decision. Only point-of-purchase and outdoor can compete with radio for the out-of-home audience, and radio has the advantage of being able to deliver a personal sales message created specifically for a particular target segment.

"Marketing has shifted to the point where the concept of advertising now is simply one element of the overall picture. Today's retailers and manufacturers are faced with the monumental challenge of effectively reaching the American consumer, and marketing provides the link between them and their customers."[5] Radio allows advertisers to meet this challenge by complementing other media to extend reach and frequency and by functioning as one of the last opportunities to deliver a sales message to a motivated consumer. This close proximity to sale is one of radio's primary strengths (see Exhibit 9.4).

---

[5]Gary Fries, *The State of the Radio Industry,* a publication of the Radio Advertising Bureau, June 1996, p. 1.

Creativity and Flexibility

Production costs of a typical network television commercial may be $250,000, with more elaborate productions costing two or three times that amount. Even the most complex radio commercials, on the other hand, usually are produced for only a few thousand dollars. In addition to the cost advantages of radio commercials, simple formats such as voice-only can be created almost immediately to reflect changing market conditions or new competition.

The personal nature of radio, combined with its flexibility and creativity, makes radio the choice for numerous product categories. Copy changes can be made very quickly. The short lead time in radio ad production is an enormous benefit to advertisers who must react quickly to changing marketing conditions.[6]

The ability to anticipate or react to changing conditions cannot be underestimated. For example, when the Indianapolis 500 ends on Memorial Day afternoon, radio commercials touting tire and oil companies begin running that evening. The simplicity of radio can be a major advantage in making tactical marketing decisions. Radio's sense of immediacy and flexibility, all at a cost within the budget of even the smallest advertiser, has made it an important part of the advertising strategy of many advertisers.

LIMITATIONS AND CHALLENGES OF RADIO

As discussed in chapter 7, every advertising medium has special strengths and weaknesses that makes it more or less suited to special marketing problems of specific advertising. There is no one medium ideal for every advertiser in every situation. Like all advertising media, radio has both advantages and disadvantages and is not suitable to address every marketing or advertising goal. Radio has a number of characteristics that make it an ideal vehicle for numerous advertisers as either a primary or secondary medium. By the same token, advertisers need to consider some of the major disadvantages of radio. Two of the major problems facing advertisers using radio are the sheer number of stations that create a very fragmented environment, especially for those advertisers needing to reach a general audience, and the medium's lack of a visual element.

Audience fragmentation
The segmenting of mass-media audiences into smaller groups because of diversity of media outlets.

Audience Fragmentation

As noted earlier, no medium reaches more diverse audience segments than radio. Its wide variety of stations and programming formats allow advertisers to reach virtually any marketing niche. However, in radio's quest to continue to fine-tune its reach, some advertisers wonder if radio is offering too many narrowly defined options. To put the situation in perspective, there are more than twice as many radio stations as television stations, consumer magazines, and daily newspapers combined!

Some media buyers think that segmentation may have been carried too far. For those product categories with broad appeal, it is difficult to gain effective reach and frequency without buying several radio stations or networks. Radio executives respond that even though there are a few major markets where competition has forced stations into continually narrowing their program formats, for the most part radio remains among the most effective means of achieving the target marketing desired by the majority of advertisers.

One relatively small, but growing radio audience that formerly has been beyond the reach of advertisers has been the affluent listeners of public radio. National Public Radio (NPR) went on the air in 1971. Today, through a network of more than 500 stations, it serves 12 million listeners each week with programs as diverse as *All Things*

---

[6]*Why Radio?* a publication of the Radio Advertising Bureau.

Considered, Car Talk, and classical music. Public radio listeners are significantly upscale. The NPR audience is twice as likely as the average American to be college educated; one-third hold managerial or professional positions; and more than 70 percent own their own home.

In 1995, NPR began allowing corporate underwriters to broadcast slogans promoting their companies and organizations. Some critics bemoan what they see as an encroachment by advertisers, but the current money problems faced by NPR make the continuance of such announcements a certainty. Although it is unlikely that true commercials will come to NPR, advertisers do have limited access to this audience through these announcements.[7]

Regardless of an advertiser's opinion of radio's fragmentation, it is clear that the number of stations and program options present special problems for advertising agencies buying for national clients. First, because radio spots are relatively inexpensive, agencies earn a lower per spot commission than if they were placing the same number of advertising insertions in other media. Second, the audience research available in radio, especially in measuring out-of-home listeners, is often difficult to evaluate and compare to that of other media. Consequently, the agency media planner may have to work harder for less profit. Sometimes it is the path of least resistance simply to exclude radio as a major part of a client's media plan.

Lack of a Visual Element

A fundamental problem for advertisers is radio's lack of a visual element. At a time when advertisers are attempting to enhance brand image and build consumer awareness, many advertisers find radio's lack of visualization a difficult problem to overcome. With the growth of self-service retailing and competitive brand promotions, package identification is crucial for many advertisers.

Radio has long used a number of creative techniques to substitute the ear for the eye and attempt to overcome the lack of visuals. Sound effects; jingles; short, choppy copy; and vivid descriptions attempt to create a mental picture. In recent years, radio has attempted to show that images familiar to consumers from television commercials can be transferred to consumers through radio.

Indeed, a major research study by Statistical Research, Inc. demonstrated that listeners are able to effectively develop "mental pictures" as a result of radio commercials. Using **imagery transfer research,** SRI showed that a majority of listeners correctly described the prime visual element of television commercials when listening to radio commercials for the same products.

The study found that imagery transfer is most effective when the same, or similar, audio tracks are used in both television and radio commercials. Data show that 75 percent of all consumers who see a television commercial will mentally "replay" the visual images when exposed to a corresponding radio commercial.

This research reinforces the value of radio as a cost-efficient complement to other media and shows that radio can provide a visual image for multimedia campaigns. This research therefore has major implications for creative approaches to radio and media buying. For example, advertisers who plan for and use radio as an integral part of their television campaigns can

1. extend campaign reach
2. substantially increase message frequency
3. improve awareness during and between television flights
4. maximize advertising investments
5. reach out-of-home consumers.

Imagery transfer research
A technique that measures the ability of radio listeners to correctly describe the primary visual elements of related television commercials.

---

[7]Tibbett L. Speer, "Public Radio: Marketing without Commercials," *American Demographics,* September 1996, p. 63.

exhibit

9.5

(a)

(b)

In amplitude modulation (a) waves vary in height (amplitude): frequency is constant. Frequency modulation (b) varies the frequency but keeps the height constant. These drawings, however, are not made to scale, which would reveal that width is the significant difference between AM and FM. The FM wave is 20 times wider than the AM wave. This fact helps to explain how FM captures its fine tones.

Amplitude modulation (AM) Method of transmitting electromagnetic signals by varying the *amplitude* (size) of the electromagnetic wave, in contrast to varying its *frequency*. Quality is not as good as frequency modulation, but can be heard further, especially at night.

Frequency modulation (FM) A radio transmission wave that transmits by the variation in the frequency of its wave, rather than its size (as in AM modulation). An FM wave is 20 times the width of an AM wave, which is the source of its fine tone. To transmit such a wave, it has to be placed high on the electromagnetic spectrum, far from AM waves with their interference and static, hence its outstanding tone.

If used properly, the concept of imagery transfer allows television advertisers to enhance their campaigns. "It keeps images fresh in consumers' minds and increases product awareness. It allows advertisers to create a marketing synergy that results in maximum cost efficiency and increased sales."[8]

TECHNICAL ASPECTS OF RADIO

The Signal

The electrical impulses that are broadcast by radio are called the *signal*. If a certain station has a good signal in a given territory, its programs and commercials come over clearly in that area.

Frequency

All signals are transmitted by electromagnetic waves, sometimes called *radio waves*. These waves differ from one another in *frequency* (the number of waves that pass a given point in a given period of time).

Amplitude

All electromagnetic waves have height, called the *amplitude*, whose range resembles the difference between an ocean wave and a ripple in a pond, and speed, measured by the frequency with which a succession of waves passes a given point per minute. If, for example, a radio station operates on a frequency of 1,580 kHz, 1,580,000 of its waves pass a given point per second.

AM and FM Radio

On the basis of these two dimensions—amplitude and frequency—two separate systems have been developed for carrying radio waves. The first system carries the variations in a sound wave by corresponding variations in its amplitude; the frequency remains constant. This is the principle of **amplitude modulation** (AM; Exhibit 9.5a). The second system carries the variation in a sound wave by corresponding variations in its frequency; the amplitude remains constant. This is the principle of **frequency modulation** (FM; Exhibit 9.5b).

---

[8]*If You Think They're Seeing Your TV Ad Now . . . Wait 'Til They See It on the Radio!,* a publication of the Radio Advertising Bureau, 1996.

Frequencies for AM stations are measured in kilohertz (kHz), and FM stations frequencies are measured in megahertz (MHz). The FCC has assigned the following frequencies to all radio stations.

AM: 540 to 1700 kHz

FM: 88.1 to 107.9 MHz

The technical structure of AM and FM radio has created, in effect, two distinct media, each offering a different value to the listener and the advertiser. AM signals carry farther but are susceptible to interference. FM has a fine tonal quality, but its signal distances are limited. Any particular station's quality of reception is determined by atmospheric conditions and station power (broadcast frequency).

SELLING RADIO COMMERCIAL TIME

Radio is very much a local medium. Unlike television, network radio remains a very minor advertising vehicle in terms of total advertising expenditures. With estimated radio advertising revenues of more than $17 billion, radio has experienced healthy increases throughout the 1990s. Although both network and spot radio sales have increased, they continue to lag far behind local advertising, as a percent of total revenues:

Local   78.6%
Spot   17.5
National   3.8

Selling radio advertising involves a number of steps, many of which are unique to the medium. Many radio advertising terminology and audience definitions are distinctive to the medium. Likewise, the pricing structure, which often involves a number of dayparts, is also different from other media. Most important, the radio salesperson must

> be aware that everyone involved in the transaction is looking for different results. The media buyer is looking for efficient cost per point, while the client's goal is to move product. . . . Clients generally view all radio stations from the same perspective: the station has something for sale, and they may or may not buy it from you. Because of this, it is important for you to build value into your station by offering credible benefits that produce results and solutions for your clients.[9]

The biggest mistake radio salespeople can make in attempting to sell advertising is to assume they are selling time. Radio commercial time is simply the unit of sale. What is being sold is an audience that is in the market for a specific product and can provide profits to a company more efficiently than if the company does not use radio.

The astute radio salesperson must begin with the client's needs and marketing goals. The first step in this process is to meet with the client to gain as much information as possible about the client and his or her business. After the salesperson has a firm grasp of the advertising problem, the next step is to prepare a proposal. Although there is no set format for a radio sales proposal, the successful ones begin with the clients' problems and sales objectives and move systematically to a solution.

Often the job of the radio salesperson must be conducted on a number of levels. First, an advertiser who is not currently scheduling radio may have to be convinced that the medium in general is suitable for a particular product. Second, the salesperson must move from the general advantages of radio to the advantages of the specific station.

---

[9]Roger Dodson, *5 Steps to Stronger Negotiating*, a publication of the Radio Advertising Bureau, 1996.

Third, the radio representative may have to show how radio fits into the media mix currently being used by the advertiser.

Radio advertising faces challenges both from within the industry and from other media as it competes for advertising dollars. First, it must compete with selective media, especially those such as Yellow Pages and direct response, which also reach targeted audiences. Of equal concern is competition from other radio stations in a particular market. Whereas a typical city usually has one major daily newspaper and a few suburban weeklies, three network affiliates and a couple of independent television stations, and perhaps two out-of-home media companies, there may be 30 or more radio stations in the metropolitan area. Although radio advertising, like television, is made up of network, local, and spot advertising, the similarity ends there.

Although local radio advertising is the largest category of radio revenues, both network and spot advertising are important components of the industry. In the next sections we discuss these categories of radio advertising.

Network Radio

Network radio has very little in common with its television counterpart. Even with the inroads of cable television and independent stations, the four major television networks control the majority of viewers and dominate national advertising. Network radio has revenues of less than $500 million, or about 3.8 percent of total radio billings of some $13 billion. But it is not just the relatively low revenues that separate network radio from television networks.

The demise of network radio as a major national medium and the beginning of local radio began in 1948 with the introduction of television. Bob Hope's radio show rating dropped from 23.8 in 1948 to 5.4 in 1953. Soap operas left radio for television throughout the 1950s until "Ma Perkins," the last survivor, went off the air in 1960. The last major radio dramas, "Suspense" and "Have Gun Will Travel" ended in 1962, and the era of network radio was essentially over. For the next decade, network programs were largely confined to news and features.

In recent years, network radio has made a comeback through the miracle of satellite technology. Satellites made instant national program syndication possible. It also made overnight celebrities of personalities such as Larry King and Rush Limbaugh. Today, there are approximately 40 radio networks, which function primarily as program suppliers.

However, defining a network is not always easy. For example, although the Rush Limbaugh program has many characteristics of a network—that is, a daily, live satellite hookup—it is not considered a network in terms of a lineup of affiliated stations. Instead, the industry considers the satellite as a distribution tool, "no different in principle from the mailbox in the days when programs were syndicated on transcriptions and tape. The cost of the program to a local station may be free or it may be expensive, depending [on] whether the syndicator is more anxious to offer national coverage to advertisers or collect revenue selling a program."[10] Regardless of the definition, these satellite-distributed shows function in the same way as traditional network programming, and serve the identical function for national advertisers.

Unlike television stations, a single radio station may belong to several radio networks simultaneously. For example, a station might get sports reports from one network, personality profiles and news from another, and entertainment fare from yet another. Whereas in television local stations sell advertising time on the basis of the strength of the network programming, in radio the networks must depend on local ratings to garner national advertising support.

---

[10]John McDonough, "Radio: A 75-year Roller-coaster Ride," *Advertising Age,* September 4, 1995, p. 24.

Another major difference between television and radio networks is that although TV networks dominate the media schedules of most national advertisers, network radio is a secondary medium to virtually every advertiser who uses it. For example, Sears Roebuck & Co. has been the consistent leader in network radio advertising during the last several years. However, the radio budget for Sears accounts for less than 4 percent of the company's total advertising expenditure. This pattern is consistent with almost all radio network advertisers.

Despite the many differences with television, radio networks do offer some of the same advantages as their television counterparts. For example, an advertiser prepares one insertion order for multiple stations, pays one invoice, and is guaranteed uniform production quality for the commercial on on all stations. Radio networks also provide economical reach and, like all radio, are able to target special audience segments who may be light users of other media.

The emergence of satellite links for national radio programming offers a number of advantages for their local station affiliates:

1. Stations are guaranteed quality programming based on the latest audience research for a particular format.
2. Radio networks bring celebrities to the medium that local stations could not afford.
3. Even the smallest stations can obtain national advertising dollars as part of a network. Stations that would not be considered by national advertisers as part of a local spot buy may now be included in a network radio schedule.
4. The cost efficiencies of sharing programming with several hundred other affiliates keeps both personnel and programming costs to a minimum.

Network radio will never return to its former status as a primary medium for national advertisers. However, as a source of program services, with its ability to target narrow audience segments, it will continue to play an important role for a number of national advertisers.

Spot Radio

You will recall from the discussion in chapter 8, spot advertising is the buying of time on local stations by national advertisers. Heavy users of spot radio tend to fall into one of two categories. The first are those companies with a national presence who have widely differentiated market potential from one location to another and who face a number of competitors. Firms that fall into this group are telecommunications companies such as MCI, US West, AT&T, as well as a number of the larger so-called "baby bells." Spot radio offers these advertisers an opportunity to react quickly to changing competitive challenges and hit narrowly segmented markets with little waste circulation.

A second group of heavy spot radio users are national companies with extensive retail outlets. Spot radio commercials allow these companies to build on their national brand awareness with localized spots directed at the local community. Sears, Office Depot, and Tandy (Radio Shack) are all advertisers that use spot radio to augment their national advertising.

Although spot radio may be a useful piece in the total advertising puzzle, it constitutes a very small portion of national advertising plans. For example, Procter & Gamble, a major player in spot radio, spends a small percentage of its total advertising budget in the medium. From these figures, it is clear that national advertisers use spot just as they use local and network radio. That is, they reach small demographic niches such as Hispanic, farm, or older audiences as well as add weight to those audiences that constitute the best potential for sales and profits.

As discussed in chapter 8, most spot broadcast purchases are made through reps. In principle, radio reps serve the same function as those in TV. The best reps are those that serve as marketing consultants for their client stations. They work with agencies to match target audiences with the appropriate stations in their client list. Sometimes this is done on a market-by-market basis. In other cases, buys are made through nonwired networks in the same manner as TV nonwired networks, which was discussed in the previous chapter. In fact, radio reps initiated the nonwired network, which has been adopted by TV. In both radio and TV, these "networks" offer advertisers the ability to buy many markets with one insertion order and one bill. This greatly simplifies the media planner's job and helps to increase spot buying, especially among smaller stations.

AM versus FM as an Advertising Medium

Currently, there are more than 10,000 radio stations with almost 9,500 commercial outlets. Among the commercial stations, approximately 5,000 are FM and the others AM. However, despite the number of stations in each category, FM dominates the listening audience overall and in most formats. In some major markets, as much as 80 percent of the audience is normally listening to FM and typically most AM stations are far down the list of stations in terms of ratings and audience share. In fact, AM stations tend to reach an older audience with talk, news, and specialty formats such as gospel and nostalgia.

The growth of FM radio audiences and advertising revenues during the last 20 years is the most important trend in the industry in recent years. In many respects the development of FM resulted in the revitalization of radio as a medium. In 1960 there were only 815 commercial FM stations, 19 percent of total stations. Since then FM has grown dramatically in terms of stations, audiences, and advertising revenues.

In the foreseeable future, FM will continue to dominate radio. There are several reasons for the emergence of FM, including the following:

1. In 1972 the Federal Communication Commission ruled that joint owners of both AM and FM stations in the same market had to program different formats. This ruling opened the way for FM as a separate medium.
2. The sound quality of FM is markedly better than AM. Because music formats dominate radio, FM has steadily gained audience share at the expense of AM.
3. The decline in the cost of FM sets coincided with the popularity of the medium. Thirty years ago radio sets with an FM band were much more expensive than AM-only sets. Also, few cars were equipped with FM radio. Currently, 88 percent of car radios are AM/FM and virtually all radio sets are equipped with both AM and FM bands.
4. As radio audiences turned to FM for the most popular music formats, AM was left with an audience skewed to older listeners, a less than prime market segment for most advertisers. Therefore, the switch to FM by audiences was quickly followed by an increase in advertising dollars.

It is clear that FM will continue to be the dominant radio medium as AM stations search for a niche to ensure their survival. We can expect AM stations to continue to appeal to an older audience. AM stations are also attempting to develop more creative programming to this older audience. For example, some stations offer financial, health, and other specialized programming that appeals to the majority of the upscale segment of the talk radio audience.

Time Classifications—Dayparts

The broadcast day is divided into time periods called dayparts as follows:

Daypart	Characteristics
6 A.M.–10 A.M.	Drive time, breakfast audience, interested chiefly in news
10 A.M.–3 P.M.	Daytime, programs characteristic of station, talk, music, or all-news
3 P.M.–7 P.M.	Afternoon, drive time; radio prime time and same as morning drive time
7 P.M.–12 A.M.	News, music, talk shows
12 A.M.–6 A.M.	Music, talk shows

Weekends are regarded as a separate time classification. Most radio spot time is sold in 60-second units. The cost varies with the daypart.

The size of radio audiences varies widely from daypart to daypart. The peak listening period is from 7 A.M. to 10 A.M., with an average of 31 to 24.5 percent of the audience tuning in during subsequent quarter hours. TV viewing, of course, peaks between 8 and 10 P.M., with average quarter-hour audiences in the 50 percent range. Radio also differs from television in seasonality of audience levels. Radio listening is remarkably stable throughout the year, whereas TV audiences fluctuate as much as 25 percent from fall to summer.

Types of Programming

Given the current structure of the radio industry, there is little traditional programming. Instead, radio stations appeal to audiences with general formats. Unlike television viewers, who tune to a certain program for a half hour or hour and then move to another station for another show, radio audiences tend to demonstrate loyalty to a station because of the *type* of music, sports, or information it programs. Currently, the most popular radio format is country music, carried by more than 2,300 stations; in second place is adult contemporary music, programmed by some 1,500 stations, followed by talk (1,354) and news (1,124). At the other extreme are six formats programmed by 25 or fewer stations. These include new age music, bluegrass, and children's programs.[11]

Each of the more than 40 formats appeals to a certain group of the larger listening audience (see Exhibit 9.6). Although every station would like to be the leader in a popular format, radio executives know that it is extremely difficult for more than one or two stations in a market to be financially successful in any particular format. Why would an advertiser buy the third- or fourth-rated country station?

Consequently, second- and third-tier stations are constantly searching for niche formats that will allow them to be the leader among some audience segment that is of value to advertisers. Specialty formats, such as classical music or jazz, usually depend on an upscale audience that is difficult for advertisers to reach in other media. However, with as many as 50 stations in some large market listening areas, selling formats is not only cutthroat, but often a little silly. For instance, stations without impressive total numbers may resort to calling themselves the number one station in a particular daypart (e.g., midnight to 6 A.M.) or developing subcategories of a format to differentiate themselves from other stations (easy listening country).

The bottom line for a successful radio station is the same as most commercial media. That is, stations must deliver a homogeneous audience that represents a major target segment for some group of advertisers. Without such an audience, no amount of selling or research data is going to convince an advertiser to buy time on a station. Radio stations are continually fine-tuning their formats to differentiate themselves from competing stations to maximize advertising revenues. However, those stations that are

---

[11]*Bacon's Radio Directory* (Chicago: Bacon's Information, 1996), p. 2.

Radio Offers the Ultimate in Targetability via a Host of Programming and Format Options

	Average Audience Composition (%)					
	Adults 18–24	Adults 25–34	Adults 35–44	Adults 45–54	Adults 55–64	Adults 65+
Adult contemp.	17.0	30.8	25.4	14.4	6.5	5.9
All news	2.6	18.7	24.2	20.6	12.7	21.2
Album rock	26.8	41.8	20.3	8.3	1.8	1.0
Alternative	34.9	41.2	16.9	5.0	1.0	1.0
Classical	10.9	17.9	23.6	20.5	10.9	16.2
Classic rock	21.2	36.4	32.3	7.7	1.3	1.1
Contemp. hits (CHR)	35.5	34.4	19.0	6.7	1.4	3.0
Country	14.8	25.8	22.5	17.3	10.0	9.6
Easy listening	12.4	17.0	16.6	17.7	16.0	20.3
Full service	8.6	9.4	17.8	6.9	32.1	25.1
Jazz	13.1	22.6	39.6	14.7	5.0	5.0
Modern rock/new age	27.0	33.8	21.1	11.7	3.5	2.9
News/talk	5.7	17.8	24.6	18.5	12.3	21.1
Nostalgia	6.2	6.1	10.0	14.7	21.2	41.8
Oldies	12.5	24.6	30.1	21.9	5.8	5.1
Religious	10.2	24.1	27.7	14.8	11.0	12.2
R&B	13.4	25.8	30.3	14.6	7.1	8.8
Soft contemp.	10.4	26.6	30.8	15.6	7.1	9.5
Spanish	26.3	26.9	23.8	10.9	6.2	5.9
Urban contemp.	30.7	30.1	22.7	10.3	2.5	3.7

Source: Simmons, 1996.

exhibit

9.6

Radio targets listeners with a number of distinctive formats.

Courtesy: Radio Advertising Bureau.
Source: Sound Solutions, a publication of the Radio Advertising Bureau, p. 5.

constantly changing or tinkering with their formats are virtually always the weaker stations in a market.

Occasionally, these format changes result in "lightning striking," and a station moves dramatically ahead in ratings. More often, it is seen by advertisers as an admission that the station couldn't compete in a particular niche. One factor that works in the favor of stations trying to make changes to enhance their audiences is the relatively low ratings achieved by radio stations.

Radio should be considered a quasi-mass medium. Despite its generally high aggregate audiences, the number of people listening to any particular station at a given time is very small. Even the top stations in a market will be lucky to achieve ratings of 8 or 10; a rating of 1 to 3 is more common. Consequently, an audience increase that would be insignificant in other media might make a major difference in the financial health of a radio station. For example, a change of one rating point for a station with an average rating of 3 is an increase of 33 percent, a figure that often will move a station significantly up the rankings in a market.

RADIO RATINGS SERVICES

Because of the number of stations, the diversity of formats, and the relatively small listenership per station, radio ratings are much more difficult to obtain than those for television. For one thing, most radio listeners, unlike television viewers, do not have the advantage of regularly scheduled programs to recall their listening habits. Therefore, recall of listening behavior is very difficult. Added to the lack of specific programming is the fact that radio is increasingly an out-of-home medium. It is impossible to measure current listenership in cars and impractical to survey respondents in the workplace. Consequently, a large portion of the radio audience is missed, miscounted, or dependent on recall to give their responses.

Local radio station ratings are obtained largely through **The Arbitron Company.** The basic tool for gaining radio ratings information is Arbitron's self-administered

The Arbitron Company
Syndicated radio ratings company.

diary. Despite the widespread use of these diaries, there are two primary problems with their methodology. The first difficulty is not actually the methodology, but human nature. Diaries can be put aside and either not returned or filled in all at once, which creates a recall problem.

The diary is also a less than adequate means of measuring the increasing out-of-home audience. The same problem occurs in connection with television ratings, as discussed in the previous chapter. However, except for a few categories of shows such as sports and late night, the out-of-home television audience remains relatively small. In radio, the out-of-home audience is large and growing. It is estimated that only 45 percent of the total radio audience listens at home. Out-of-home listeners are neither inclined nor able to fill out diaries.

As discussed in chapter 8, the portable people meter offers some promise for more accurate out-of-home ratings. Another device aimed at measuring this elusive audience is the actual radio measurement (ARM). A suitcase-sized instrument placed along a road automatically identifies the radio stations to which passing cars are tuned. With approximately 30 percent of all radio listening done in automobiles, the device offers substantial potential in the race to provide more accurate ratings.[12]

Because of the local nature of radio, station ratings are much more critical than network ratings for most advertisers. However, as discussed earlier, network radio is an important medium to a number of advertisers. For many years the only major source of radio network ratings has been **Radio All Dimension Audience Research** (RADAR), a service of Statistical Research, Inc. Data used in RADAR reports are collected through telephone recall interviews. In summer 1996, Arbitron and RADAR agreed to explore the possibility of a joint rating service for network radio based on Arbitron's diary methodology.

Although advertising executives were generally supportive of a joint venture, they continue to express misgivings about the shortcomings of the diary method. In fact, media discussions between the two ratings services came to an end over the issue of methodological differences between the two companies. As one media researcher commented, "We have no problem with the two radio ratings agencies joining. However, we believe the larger issue is to get advertisers more involved in the process so the numbers more accurately reflect buyers' needs, unlike the current situation where sellers [stations and network] pay most of the research cost and influence its design and implementation."[13]

Radio All Dimension Audience Research (RADAR)
Service of Statistical Research, Inc., major source of network radio ratings.

RATE CLASSIFICATIONS

Every station establishes its own classifications and publishes them on its rate card. The negotiated cost of time depends on those classifications, which are typically the following:

- *Drive time.* **Drive time** is the most desired and costly time on radio; it varies by the community and usually has the highest ratings.
- *Run-of-station.* The station has a choice of moving the commercial at will, wherever it is most convenient. Preemptible run-of-station is the least costly time on the rate card.
- *Special features.* Time adjacent to weather signals, news reports, time signals, traffic, or stock market reports usually carries a premium charge.

Package Plans

Most spot time is sold in terms of a weekly package plan, usually called *total audience plans,* or TAP. A station offers a special flat rate for a number of time slots divided in

Drive time (radio)
A term used to designate the time of day when people are going to, or coming from, work. Usually 6 A.M. to 10 A.M. and 3 P.M. to 7 P.M., but this varies from one community to another. The most costly time on the rate card.

---

[12]Michael Wilke, "ARM to Expand in Radio Research," *Advertising Age,* October 14, 1996, p. 6.

[13]Michael Wilke, "Radio Ratings Rivals to Offer Joint Service," *Advertising Age,* July 8, 1996, p. 2.

different proportions over the broadcast day. A typical TAP plan distributes time equally through the broadcast day.

An advertiser can buy the total plan or parts of it. In all instances, there is a quantity- or dollar-discount plan, depending upon the total number of spots run during a given period of time:

Number of Times*	8	12	20	32	40
1 minute, $	110	100	92	86	79
30 seconds, $	88	80	74	69	63

*Per week $\left(\frac{1}{4} \text{ A.M.,} \ \frac{1}{4} \text{ P.M.,} \ \frac{1}{4} \text{ housewife,} \ \frac{1}{4} \text{ night} \right)$.

BUYING RADIO

As an advertising medium, radio is unusual in several respects:

1. *Advertising inventory is inflexible.* When a spot goes unsold, revenue is permanently lost.
2. *Radio is normally used as a supplement to other media.* Therefore, coordination with a client's total advertising plan is crucial for most radio sales.
3. *Every radio buy is unique.* Almost all radio advertising is sold in packages of spots that are unique, to some degree, to each advertiser.
4. *A fixed rate card rarely exists for radio advertising.* Because of the unique nature of each buy, pricing is largely the result of negotiation between media buyers and radio salespersons.

Given the nature of radio buys, it is imperative that both buyer and seller understand the relationship involved in the process. This starts with credibility. One of the primary ways a radio salesperson gains trust is to position radio as a part of the marketing plan. This entails walking a fine line between aggressively selling the medium and a particular station, and at the same time, acknowledging the strengths and contributions of other media. For example, rather than trying to convince heavy newspaper advertisers to move out of the medium, show them how radio can make newspaper advertising more effective.

Advertisers are not interested in buying time; they are interested in meeting some need. Therefore, the key to successful selling is identifying with the problems of the clients. To do this, the salesperson needs to show the advertisers that radio can solve an immediate problem, and needs answers to questions such as

- What is the biggest problem you face?
- What do you like most and least about the advertising you are currently doing?
- What makes your company and your advertising different from the competition?
- Why do you think customers buy from you?[14]

This type of exchange not only allows the salesperson to find out a great deal of information about the client, but, just as important, it creates an atmosphere in which clients know there is a genuine interest in their problems.

Radio selling has never been more competitive. The radio salesperson finds that the media landscape is full of new competitors, each claiming to accomplish many of the same tasks as radio. As national advertisers have increasingly adopted a localized strategy, media such as television have seen the advantages of competing for local advertisers as well as selling added local weight to national advertisers.

---

[14]Pam Lontos, *Marketing Skills Workbook,* a publication of the Radio Advertising Bureau, July 1996, p. 2.

At one time, radio competed only with newspapers for local dollars. Today, radio finds Yellow Pages, local cable outlets, broadcast stations, free shoppers and specialty books for real estate and automobiles, outdoor, and direct mail all trying to get a share of the local advertising dollar. All of these competitors have a visual element that radio lacks. It has never been more important for radio to develop creative strategies to overcome this major disadvantage. Radio reps have become marketing consultants, a partner with the client in showing how radio can solve specific advertising problems.

It is clear that clients buy radio as part of an overall media strategy. Radio—or for that matter any medium—is rarely purchased on an individual basis. The client and the media salesperson must view the media plan as a synergistic one in which each medium complements others. Unless radio can create a value to other media, it is unlikely it will be part of a media schedule. Fortunately, radio offers unique characteristics that will allow it to be considered for at least a secondary role in the advertising plans of virtually all advertisers.

USING RADIO RATINGS

TV ratings and share of audience were defined in chapter 8. Radio also uses ratings and shares, and calculates them in the same way. However, the audiences and programming of radio mandate that ratings be used in ways much different from the way ratings are used in television. In this section, we discuss some uses of ratings that are unique to radio.

Among the primary differences between the use of ratings in television and radio are the following:

1. Radio advertisers are interested in broad formats rather than programs or more narrowly defined television scatter plans.
2. Radio ratings tend to measure audience accumulation over relatively long periods of time or several dayparts. Most TV ratings are for individual programs.
3. The audiences for individual radio stations are much smaller than television, making radio ratings less reliable.
4. Because most radio stations reach only a small segment of the market at a given time, there is a need for much higher levels of advertising frequency compared to other media. Consequently, it is extremely difficult to track accurate ratings information for national radio plans that include a large number of stations.

Let us begin our discussion by examining several definitions used in radio ratings analyses.

Geographical Patterns of Radio Ratings

Radio audience ratings use two geographic boundaries to report audiences: metro survey area (MSA) and total survey area (TSA). Typically, the majority of a station's audience comes from within the MSA.

Metro Survey Area   An MSA always includes a city or cities whose population is specified as that of the central city together with the county (or counties) in which it is located.

Total Survey Area   The TSA is a geographic area that encompasses the MSA and certain counties located outside the MSA, and also meets certain listening criteria.

Definitions of the Radio Audience

The basic audience measures for television are the ratings and share of audience for a particular show. Some media planners mistakenly buy radio and television on the same basis without considering major differences between the two media. In radio, audience measurements are usually given by either **average quarter-hour estimates** (AQHE) or

Average quarter-hour estimates (AQHE)
Manner in which radio ratings are presented. Estimates include average number of people listening, rating, and metro share of audience.

by cumulative, or unduplicated, estimates, called *cume estimates*, of audience listening to a station over several quarter-hours or dayparts.

1. Average Quarter-Hour Estimates *(AQHE)*
   a. Average Quarter-Hour Persons
      The *AQH* persons are the estimated number of people listening to a station for at least 5 minutes during a 15-minute period.
   b. Average Quarter-Hour Rating
      The *AQH* rating calculates the *AQH* persons as a percentage of the population being measured:

$$\frac{AQH \text{ persons}}{\text{Population}} \times 100 = AQH \text{ rating}$$

   c. Average Quarter-Hour Share
      The *AQH* share determines what portion of the average radio audience is listening to a particular station:

$$\frac{AQH \text{ persons to a station}}{AQH \text{ persons to all stations}} \times 100 = AQH \text{ share}$$

2. Cume Estimates
   Cume estimates are used to determine the number or percentage of different people who listen to a station during several quarter-hours or dayparts.
   a. Cume persons is a measure of the number of *different* people who tune to a radio station for at least 5 minutes.
   b. Cume rating is the percentage of different people listening to a station during several quarter-hours or dayparts.

$$\frac{\text{Cume persons}}{\text{Population}} \times 100 = \text{Cume rating}$$

   Let us look at a typical station's audience and calculate these formulas. For station XYYY, Monday–Friday, 10 A.M.–3 P.M., adults age 12+

$$AQH \text{ persons} = 20,000$$

$$\text{Cume persons} = 60,000$$

$$\text{MSA population} = 500,000$$

$$\text{MSA } AQH \text{ persons} = 200,000$$

   For station XYYY:[15]

$$AQH \text{ rating} = (20,000/500,000) = 4$$

$$\text{Cume rating} = (60,000/500,000) = 12$$

$$AQH \text{ share} = (20,000/200,000) = 10$$

3. Using our XYYY example, we can also calculate the following:
   a. Gross impressions (GI) = *AQH* persons × number of commercials
      If we buy six commercials on XYYY, we have purchased 120,000 impressions (20,000 *AQH* persons × 6 spots).
      Remember, these are *impressions*, not people.
   b. Gross rating points = *AQH* rating × number of commercials
      Again, six commercials would deliver 24 *GRP*s (4 *AQH* rating × 6 spots).
   c. Listeners per dollar (LPD) = *AQH* persons/spot cost
      If a spot of XYYY costs $500, then the LPD is 40 (20,000 *AQH* persons/$500).

---

[15]It is understood that decimals are not used in reporting ratings and share figures.

The media planner must be able to manipulate the various radio data to develop a plan most suited to any particular client. Although the computer makes these manipulations quickly, it does not substitute for a basic understanding of the process. The same budget, and even the same number of spots, used in different dayparts and across multiple stations can deliver vastly different results. As few as 12 spots bought on two stations in the same market result in major differences in cume, reach, and frequency, as shown in the following comparison:

Lower *GRP*s May Give Equal or Greater Reach

Station	# of Spots	AQH Rating	Cume	GRPs	Reach	Frequency
WCCC	12	1.8	130,300	87.0	11.7	7.5
WDDD	12	1.5	159,600	72.8	13.4	5.4

Station WDDD delivers 16% fewer *GRP*s but delivers 15% more reach than station WCCC.

Courtesy: Radio Advertising Bureau.

The Radio Buy

To this point, we have examined the stations, formats, and costs of the radio stations in the markets we wish to consider. We have evaluated radio as a medium, and the available stations in light of other media alternatives, marketing strategy (both quantitative and qualitative factors), and advertising requirements such as compensating for the medium's lack of a visual element. It is now time to discuss scheduling radio spots.

Scheduling for Radio   The first step in buying a radio schedule is to rank the stations in each market against the previously defined target market for our product. In the past, stations would be ranked according to standard demographic data. Let us assume that we are selling luxury cars and we know that our target market is men aged 35 to 64. Using Arbitron ratings, we rank the following stations against this group of prospects:

Market Population = 445,900
Monday–Friday, 6–10 A.M.
Men 35–64

Station	AQH (00)	Average Rating	Market Rank
WXXX	252	5.5	1
WAAA	211	4.6	2
WYYY	190	4.1	3
WZZZ	129	2.8	4

Remember, the media planner of the 1990s has much more powerful marketing tools than were available in previous decades. As shown in chapter 7, the use of lifestyle data such as PRIZM allows us to identify market segments more narrowly. Let us assume that our prime prospects for luxury cars are in two particular upscale categories. Our computer model now ranks our stations on the basis of cluster ratings rather than demographic ratings, with the following results:

Station	Demographics Average			Cluster Ratings		
	AQH (00)	Average Rating	Rank	AQH (00)	Average Rating	Rank
WXXX	252	5.5	1	101	2.2	2
WAAA	211	4.6	2	96	2.1	3
WYYY	190	4.1	3	109	2.4	1
WZZZ	129	2.8	4	88	1.9	4

exhibit

9.7

Newspaper/radio mix
by market size (adults
18+) shows favorable
results compared to
newspaper alone.

Courtesy: Radio Advertising
Bureau.

	Full-Page Ad Reach × Freq. = GRPs	$\frac{1}{2}$-Page + Station A Reach × Freq. = GRPs
Top 10 markets	18 × 1.0 = 18	29 × 2.3 = 66
Markets 26–50	20 × 1.0 = 20	30 × 2.5 = 75
Markets 101–150	11 × 1.0 = 11	32 × 3.6 = 115
Markets 151–200	20 × 2.0 = 40	31 × 2.2 = 68
Markets 201–250	28 × 1.0 = 28	63 × 3.3 = 208

*A single selected market was used for purposes of comparison from each of the above groups.
(AM/FM combination shown as one station.)*

Source: Arbitron, Metro Area, Spring 1984.

By using lifestyle measures, we are able to identify those stations that best reach more narrowly targeted markets of upscale men. The next step is the actual scheduling of the spots on each station. Computer technology and statistical estimates make these calculations fairly routine.

Intermedia Scheduling in a Market   Because radio listeners are often light users of other media, radio is an excellent means of extending both reach and frequency of an advertising schedule. As already discussed, radio is most often used as a supplemental medium. The media planner is frequently asked to schedule radio in combination with other media in a manner that yields the best results per dollar.

For several years now, the **Radio Advertising Bureau** (RAB) has studied the role of radio combined with other advertising media. As Exhibit 9.7 shows, radio in combination with newspapers is much more effective than either medium alone.

**Radio Advertising
Bureau (RAB)**
Association to
promote the use of
radio as an advertising
medium.

SUMMARY

With its many stations and formats, radio offers a number of opportunities for advertisers seeking to reach narrowly defined markets. Not only does radio offer high levels of reach and frequency, but it delivers impressive audience levels at a *CPM* that is among the lowest of all major media. In addition, radio has high penetration among light users or nonusers of other media. For example, many teens use radio almost exclusively as a means of entertainment and information. Given the current demand by advertisers for narrowly defined audience segments, radio is increasingly becoming a major factor in virtually every media plan.

Despite the opportunities for radio to become more important in the advertising plans of both large and small advertisers, the medium faces two major problems. First, the medium lacks the type of research data enjoyed by most other media. A mobile, out-of-home audience makes it very difficult to reach a large majority of radio listeners. In addition, the lack of traditional programming makes recall more complicated than similar audience research in television. Promising research innovations, such as battery-operated people meters, offer hope for future improvement in radio research, but to date the technology has not been perfected to make this practical.

A second major problem with radio is the lack of a visual element. Many advertisers think that without strong visual brand identification the medium can play little or no role in their advertising plans. The industry has sponsored a number of research studies to show that radio can work effectively with television to remind consumers of the commercials they have previously seen. This process is called imagery transfer and offers radio advertisers a strong selling point to national advertisers seeking an inexpensive supplement to their television schedules.

To further emphasize the importance and effectiveness of radio advertising, the radio industry has created the Radio Mercury Awards to recognize the most creative efforts in radio advertising. Clearly, the industry is moving to improve both the perception and the fact of utilizing the medium in a more creative manner.

Radio also is providing national advertisers with a number of opportunities through satellite-distributed, syndicated programming. Technological advances and decreases in the cost of satellite time and equipment have made it easier, cheaper, and less risky to launch national syndicated shows. Shows such as Rush Limbaugh demonstrate that properly packaged syndicated radio can deliver significant advertising impact to advertisers on both a local and national basis.

There is an irony that radio, once the major national medium, may be returning to its roots. Obviously, national syndication alone cannot bring radio back into the media spotlight. However, its newfound success coupled with radio's inherent strengths as a vehicle to deliver narrowly targeted audiences bodes well for the future.

REVIEW

1. Briefly discuss the evolution of radio from the 1920s to the present.
2. Discuss the use of imagery transfer research by advertisers.
3. Radio has been described as being broadly selective. Discuss.
4. How does radio function as a complement to other media?
5. What are some of the major factors that keep radio *CPM*s low compared to other media?
6. What do the terms AM and FM mean?
7. Compare and contrast network radio and network television.
8. Define the following terms:
    a. Drive time
    b. Run-of-station
    c. Package plans
    d. Cume
    e. Average quarter-hour ratings

TAKE IT TO THE NET

We invite you to visit the Russell/Lane page on the Prentice Hall Web site at
PHLIP **http://www.prenhall.com/phbusiness** for the bimonthly
Russell/Lane update and for this chapter's World Wide Web exercise.

10

USING NEWSPAPERS

NEWSPAPERS ARE A MAJOR FORCE IN ADVERTISING, ESPECIALLY AMONG LOCAL RETAILERS, NATIONAL FRANCHISES, AND A DIVERSE GROUP OF ADVERTISERS SEEKING A REGIONAL OR LOCAL AUDIENCE. NEWSPAPERS ARE AMONG THE MOST CREDITABLE OF THE MASS MEDIA, AND THEY ARE A SOURCE OF INFORMATION, ENTERTAINMENT, AND ADVERTISING FOR MILLIONS OF HOUSEHOLDS EACH DAY. AFTER READING THIS CHAPTER YOU WILL UNDERSTAND

- **the place of newspapers in the marketing mix**
- **how newspapers are marketed to both readers and advertisers**
- **advertising formats and geographical options available**
- **the national and local characteristics of newspapers**
- **the significance of weeklies and ethnic publications.**

As advertisers increasingly include some regional and/or local strategy in their advertising plans, newspapers face growing competition in an area where they have long been dominant. In the most dramatic development for newspapers, television passed newspapers in terms of overall advertising revenues in 1996 to become the leading advertising medium.

Given the huge budgets of national advertisers and the concentration of their budgets in television, this situation should come as no surprise.

The ascendancy of television reflects the extraordinary degree to which national advertisers, especially packaged-goods advertisers, have become dependent upon it. This can be seen in the supply-and-demand situation for the network prime time slots that generate the biggest audiences and the biggest bucks. . . . National advertisers feel they have no alternatives; they *must* be on TV.[1]

At the same time that newspapers are fighting a battle to gain a respectable share of national advertising dollars, they face growing competition from media as diverse as direct mail and cable television for the local advertising budget. Even **classified advertising,** long a profitable mainstay of the newspaper industry, is nervous over the potential for on-line services offering similar information.

Although newspapers have every reason to be concerned, they still offer one of the most valuable advertising and informational vehicles. The following are among the significant strengths newspapers provide advertisers:[2]

1. Newspapers offer flexibility of advertising formats and audience coverage. Advertisers can choose from a variety of formats from a full-page, color advertisement down to a one-inch classified notice. In addition, most major dailies offer advertisers the full circulation plus total market coverage alternatives or specialized editions that reach only a small segment of the market. There is a newspaper advertising option for all advertisers, regardless of the size of their budgets. For example, as shown by this chapter's case history (pp. 256–258), when the Georgia Department of Transportation had to quickly inform drivers of changes in the Atlanta expressway system, newspapers were the only logical medium to accomplish the task.

2. Newspapers reach a majority of adults each day, and they are especially useful in reaching upscale readers. Note in Exhibit 10.1 how the readers of the *Atlanta Journal* and *Constitution* skew toward upper income and educational groups. Even among younger age groups, stereotyped as being nonreaders, more than half of adults in the 18 to 34 age category read the newspaper.

3. Newspapers are able to offer advertisers a number of creative options. In recent years, newspapers have greatly improved their color capability to provide a local option for advertisers needing quality color to enhance their advertising. Newspapers also compete effectively with direct mail by carrying preprinted inserts, many on a less-than-full-circulation basis.

4. Newspapers provide qualitative advantages lacking in other media. Newspapers have "formed a strong relationship with consumers, anchored by two attributes: credibility and reliability. Consumers have a comfort level with newspapers as the source. The source for accuracy, for details, and for analysis. Newspapers' relationship with consumers extends into advertising as well."[3]

THE STATE OF THE NEWSPAPER INDUSTRY: AN OVERVIEW

Currently, there are 1,532 daily newspapers with a total circulation of approximately 58 million readers. In addition, there are almost 900 Sunday newspapers with a total circulation of 62 million. During the last 25 years, two trends have become obvious. First, newspaper circulation has lagged far behind both population growth and new household formation. Overall, newspaper circulation has increased only 10 percent since 1950; during the same period the U.S. population grew by almost 90 percent.

The second trend is the move toward consolidation. Consolidation is evident on the national level by the increasing dominance of relatively few newspaper chains. For

---

Classified advertising
Found in columns so labeled, published in sections of a newspaper or magazine set aside for certain classes of goods or services—for example, Help Wanted, Positions Wanted, Houses for Sale, Cars for Sale. The ads are limited in size and generally are without illustration.

---

[1]Leo Bogart, "On Being Number 1," *Presstime,* January 1996, p. 28.

[2]Information in this section comes from *Facts about Newspapers, 1996,* published by the Newspaper Association of America.

[3]John Sturm, speech delivered to the Media Institute, Washington, D.C., January 16, 1996.

	Projected Adults		Atlanta Journal and Constitution Sunday Readers			
	Number	Percent	Number	Composition (%)	Coverage (%)	Index
Demographics Total	2,554,661	100	1,683,570	100	66	100
Gender						
Male	1,227,909	48	797,601	47	65	98
Female	1,326,752	52	885,969	53	67	101
Age						
18–24	329,348	13	179,228	11	54	82
25–34	621,663	24	403,851	24	65	98
35–44	646,991	25	446,526	27	69	104
45–54	450,435	18	325,945	19	72	109
55–64	228,913	9	155,933	9	68	103
65+	277,311	11	172,087	10	62	94
Household income						
<$24,999	290,932	11	141,050	8	48	73
$25,000–$34,999	390,396	15	221,343	13	57	86
$35,000–$49,999	721,362	28	456,698	27	63	96
$50,000–$74,999	651,317	25	459,287	27	71	107
$75,000+	500,654	20	405,192	24	81	122
$35,000+	1,873,333	73	1,321,177	78	71	107
$50,000+	1,151,971	45	864,479	51	75	113
Education						
Less than high school	238,486	9	96,156	6	40	61
High school graduate	757,156	30	449,544	27	59	90
College (some)	614,423	24	422,466	25	69	104
College graduate	651,667	26	494,178	29	76	115
Advanced college degree	282,376	11	216,994	13	77	116
Race						
White (Caucasian)	1,835,836	72	1,227,933	73	67	101
Black/African American	632,255	25	405,083	24	64	97
Other	100,580	4	59,621	4	59	89
Ages of children						
5 or younger	495,775	19	325,745	19	66	99
Age 6–12	587,388	23	383,244	23	65	99
Age 13–17	406,144	16	272,959	16	67	101
Age 18+	310,288	12	222,124	13	72	108
Marital status						
Married	1,448,401	57	1,008,985	60	70	105
Single	1,086,709	43	660,744	39	61	92
Occupation						
Professional/managerial	820,818	32	601,910	36	73	111
Sales	77,224	3	59,518	4	77	116
Clerical	426,189	17	293,371	17	69	104
Blue collar	501,146	20	261,555	16	52	79
Home ownership						
Own	1,791,439	70	1,223,044	73	68	103
Rent	728,502	29	432,388	26	59	90
Type of dwelling						
Single family	1,915,040	75	1,296,362	77	68	102
Multi-family	624,880	24	380,481	23	61	92
Years at address						
<5 years	918,085	36	598,085	36	65	98
5–9 years	515,470	20	351,998	21	68	103
10–14 years	287,706	11	190,350	11	66	100
15–19 years	171,735	7	124,071	7	72	109
20+ years	356,301	14	214,119	13	60	91

Prepared by: The Atlanta Journal-Constitution Marketing Research Dept.

exhibit

10.1

Reader demographics are very important to newspaper advertisers.

Courtesy: Atlanta Journal-Constitution.

case HISTORY

MARKETING SITUATION

The Georgia Department of Transportation (DOT) is responsible for constructing and maintaining the state and federal roadways within Georgia. Working with the Federal Highway Administration in the 1970s, the Georgia DOT accepted federal funds to build interstates through Atlanta, with the understanding that the Georgia DOT would add high-occupancy vehicle (HOV) lanes, known as express lanes, to these interstates when traffic volume warranted this additional construction.

In 1992, the Georgia DOT determined that it was time to explore adding HOV lanes to the area's interstates. Preliminary plans were developed internally during the next two years. As a first step in the process, HOV lanes were added to a new, short interstate section already under construction (Interstate 20, east of Atlanta), which was scheduled to open in December 1994.

More important, plans were developed to implement HOV lanes on more than 78 miles of existing roadway within Atlanta's perimeter (beltway). These interstates serve the vast majority of Atlanta's commuting population, more than 300,000 cars each day. It was agreed that the lanes would be constructed prior to the 1996 Summer Olympic Games, even though the Georgia DOT estimated that this timetable would require contractors to begin work by June 1995 and to work around the clock, seven days a week. It was further agreed that this project would take place only if the Georgia DOT received acceptable construction bids from contractors. Otherwise, construction would be delayed until after the Olympics.

Requests for proposals were distributed to qualified contractors in April, with a proposal due date of April 21, 1995. In March 1995, the Georgia DOT hired Siddall, Matus & Coughter to assist with a public information campaign to announce the construction project and to promote its benefits. However, the information campaign would be undertaken only if the Georgia DOT received an acceptable bid.

The Georgia DOT received the construction bids on April 21, 1995, and determined that they were too high. It asked the contractors to recalculate costs and to submit lower bids by mid-May.

Finally, on Wednesday, May 17, the Georgia DOT received an acceptable construction bid and decided to proceed with the project. It was agreed that the media campaign would launch on Sunday, May 21, and that a press conference would be held on Monday, May 22. This would be the first communication to the public that Atlanta's interstates were about to be transformed. And there were only three weeks to make sure that Atlanta's commuters knew about the project and how much it would affect their lives during the coming year.

CAMPAIGN OBJECTIVES

1. to create awareness for the project by announcing that the Georgia Department of Transportation would construct express lanes on Atlanta's major interstates during the period from June 12, 1995, to July 1, 1996
2. to create awareness among the driving public that this project was so large that it would adversely affect the lives of every person and every business in the metropolitan Atlanta region
3. to create public support for the project (thereby reducing potential opposition and reducing or preventing criticism of the Georgia DOT) by creating awareness of the project's long-term benefits (namely, improved traffic management for the region and both cost and time savings for commuters using express lanes)

TARGET AUDIENCE

The campaign had three targets, defined in order of their importance:

1. people who drive on Atlanta's interstates within the perimeter for their work commutes
2. the remaining people and business in the Atlanta region
3. market influencers, especially the local media, community organizations, and elected officials

CREATIVE STRATEGY

The Georgia DOT decided to take an aggressive, preemptive approach in communications with its target audiences. Specifically, the Georgia DOT used an aggressive media campaign in local newspapers and on local radio stations, coupled with an aggressive public relations effort to inform and influence opinions among local media, community organizations, and elected officials.

A series of four newspaper advertisements explained the project's scope, in terms of the project's specific details (that is, when construction would begin, which roads and ramps would be affected, when construction crews would be working) and how much the project would inconvenience local commuters (especially because speed limits on the interstates would be lowered to 40 miles per hour during the construction period), as well as promoting the benefits of the future express lane system. A series of four radio commercials and a Metro Traffic sponsorship (including 10- and 15-second tags) also were used to reinforce the overall messages of the construction project's scope and benefits.

A straightforward, honest approach was used in each of the communications elements. Anticipating future criticism for the project, communications elements promised that the project would "make driving so unpleasant for the next 12 months, you may just want to stay at home." The communications materials were designed to establish a market expectation that the construction period would be difficult, but that the project was worthwhile.

The series of radio commercials also featured a humorous fictional Georgia DOT employee ("Ed") who had been given the unfortunate assignment of alerting Atlanta residents of the construction project.

OTHER COMMUNICATIONS PROGRAMS

An aggressive public relations program complemented the express lanes introduction communications plan. This program was designed both to help inform the general public through media relations and media events, as well as to show how much community organizations supported the construction project.

Two press events were used during the introductory campaign. First, a press conference was conducted at the Georgia DOT headquarters on Monday, May 22, immediately following distribution of the press release, and the second event was a groundbreaking ceremony on June 12.

During these events, Georgia DOT Commissioner Wayne Shackelford explained the project, and representatives from the Atlanta Committee for the Olympic Games, governmental agencies (the Federal Highway Administration, the Environmental Protection Agency), community organizations (the Atlanta Regional Commission, the Atlanta Chamber of Commerce) and mass transit/rideshare organizations (Cobb County Transit, Metropolitan Atlanta Rapid Transit Authority) showed their support for the express lane construction project, even though the project's construction period would be a major short-term disruption.

In conjunction with the two events, the commissioner sent personal letters, with background information and fact sheets, to Atlanta's political leaders to ensure that legislators and other elected officials were informed and educated about the project. Finally, Georgia DOT officials conducted one-on-one information meetings with key officials and the media to brief them on the project and its importance.

MEDIA STRATEGY

Mass media was used to achieve the campaign objective of informing every driver in Atlanta about the project. A spread advertisement was used in the *Atlanta Journal and Constitution* on the Sunday immediately following the Friday press release. The major unit specifically addressed the inconvenience the project would cause. Subsequent advertisements appeared in the *Atlanta Journal and Constitution* over the next three weeks to remind drivers about the project and to encourage them to plan alternate commuting routes.

Newspaper advertising was complemented with an aggressive radio campaign. With the specific goal of reaching people who commute, the radio campaign consisted

of spots running exclusively during commuting periods. The majority of the campaign's commercials were further targeted to run in metro traffic reports, ensuring that commuting motorists would learn that construction would begin in mid-June.

In total $331,236 was invested in paid media communications.

EVIDENCE OF RESULTS

The nature of the construction project caused significant coverage by Atlanta's local media. However, the two press events helped position the project as a necessity to help manage Atlanta's traffic. During the three-week introductory period, more than 50 newspaper articles and 40 television reports appeared, most in support of the project.

To measure the campaign's effectiveness, 302 commuter interviews were conducted by North American Research. Interviews were conducted from June 13 (the day after groundbreaking) to June 19. These interviews were conducted among people who fit the Georgia DOT's primary communications target: people who personally drive on the affected interstates at least three days each week for their work commutes. This survey found the following:

93 percent of the target market was aware of the project. On an unaided basis, 67 percent of the primary target knew that the Georgia DOT was beginning to construct the express lane system on interstates within the perimeter. (Question: "Are you aware of any construction projects taking place within the perimeter? (If yes) Which ones?") On an aided basis, another 26 percent of the primary target said that they were aware of the project. **Three out of four commuters (77 percent) said they supported the project.** Even after respondents had been told that the project would last for a year and that it would affect every interstate within the perimeter, two out of five commuters (40 percent) said they were strongly in favor of the construction project, and an additional 37 percent were somewhat in favor of the project.

Four out of five commuters (79 percent) were in favor of car pools and van pools as a way for people to get to work. Almost 60 percent of the primary target said they supported carpools and vanpools, which would use the Express Lanes, "a lot," and an additional 20 percent said they supported these alternate transportation modes "a little."

85.6 percent of the target market could remember seeing advertisements or hearing commercials announcing the project. Three out of five commuters (60 percent) could recall hearing a radio commercial or a metro traffic report announcement, and 40 percent remembered seeing a newspaper advertisement.

By all measures, the Georgia DOT express lane announcement campaign was a success. Commuters were informed of this major construction project in such a way that they understood how massive the project was and how much it would inconvenience their lives. However, the project was also explained in such a way, through advertising and public relations, that residents, commuters, and local organizations remained supportive of the construction project's overall mission: helping Atlanta manage its traffic.

Courtesy: Siddall, Matus & Coughter, Inc.

example, the seven largest newspaper companies control more than one-third of daily circulation. Events of the last couple of years indicate that independent dailies, if they exist at all, will be confined to the smallest markets. As we discuss later, this consolidation offers many benefits for national advertisers looking for more efficient placement in a number of newspapers.

If chain ownership is the harbinger of national consolidation, the decline of the evening newspaper represents local consolidation. Although evening newspapers still outnumber morning papers (see Exhibit 10.2), their numbers have decreased significantly in the last 20 years. However, the typical evening newspaper is found in smaller communities. In fact, the average daily circulation of all evening newspapers is only 16,000.

One newspaper executive pointed out that the evening paper does not meet the demands of the majority of readers or advertisers. "Their [evening papers'] main competition is not other media, but the whole range of human activity that kicks in about the time the papers are delivered. Our research shows a p.m. paper has a shorter window to be read."[4]

In addition to lifestyle considerations, the evening paper also is more difficult to deliver. A morning paper is easily distributed at 5 A.M., but getting around a major city at 5 P.M. is an entirely different matter. Also, the number of evening papers has declined as publishers have found it much more profitable to publish a single newspaper in a market rather than to offer both morning and evening editions. Finally, and perhaps most important, retailers want immediate results from their advertising. The morning paper offers a full day for potential sales, whereas the evening paper is something to "sleep on"—hardly an advantage to a retailer wanting prompt returns.

[4]Barbara Z. Gyles, "PM: Is the Sun Setting on Evening Dailies?" *Presstime,* April 1996, p. 44.

exhibit

10.2

Newspapers have responded to shifting consumer preference for morning and Sunday reading.

Courtesy: Newspaper Association of America. Source: NAA Facts About Newspapers 1996, p. 21.

Number of U.S. Daily Newspapers				
Year	Morning	Evening	Total M&E[1]	Sunday
1946	334	1,429	1,763	497
1950	322	1,450	1,772	549
1955	316	1,454	1,760	541
1960	312	1,459	1,763	563
1965	320	1,444	1,751	562
1970	334	1,429	1,748	586
1975	339	1,436	1,756	639
1980	387	1,388	1,745	735
1985	482	1,220	1,676	798
1987	511	1,166	1,645	820
1988	529	1,141	1,642	840
1989	530	1,125	1,626	847
1990	559	1,084	1,611	863
1991	571	1,042	1,586	874
1992	596	995	1,570	891
1993	607	966	1,552	888
1994	611	947	1,538	889
1995[2]	621	928	1,532	894

[1]*"All-day" newspapers publish several editions throughout the day. There were 17 all-day newspapers in 1995. They are listed in both morning and evening columns but only once in the total.*

[2]*Preliminary data. The number of newspapers is calculated through March 1, 1996. Sources: Editor & Publisher 1946–1992, NAA 1993–1995.*

The newspaper industry faces both problems and opportunities as we approach the next century. However, it is obvious that long-term trends will continue to endanger the basic foundation of newspaper readership and advertising. As we see throughout the remainder of this chapter, newspapers are more than up to the task of meeting these challenges as they take innovative initiatives to function successfully in a competitive environment.

THE NATIONAL NEWSPAPER

For many years, the United States was one of the few developed countries without a true national newspaper. *The New York Times* and *The Los Angeles Times,* both with more than 1 million circulation, and the *Washington Post,* with some 800,000 circulation, have national influence and some national distribution, but are basically local papers. Perhaps the closest to a national newspaper is *The Wall Street Journal.* It is an upscale, specialized paper with an emphasis on financial news, but with great influence in politics and public policy issues. In fact, with a circulation of more than 1.7 million, it is the highest circulation newspaper in the country.

In 1982, the Gannett Company made a commitment to develop *USA Today* as a general readership national newspaper. In recent years, Gannett has largely accomplished its goal, but not without some financial risk. Indeed, few corporations would have had either the resources or management support to invest in such an endeavor. It is estimated that before *USA Today* had its first profitable year in 1993, it had lost more than $250 million. This loss was not the result of a lack of readers. The paper averages 1.6 million readers daily and generally passes the 2 million mark on Friday with its weekend edition.

USA Today was popular with readers from the beginning, with its mix of bright colors, short articles, and wide distribution, especially bulk sales to hotels and airlines. Although newspaper purists often criticize the paper's lack of depth, it has been a favorite of travelers from its introduction.

Despite its popularity with readers, *USA Today* continues to cope with advertiser resistance to the publication. A national newspaper is a hybrid vehicle for most advertisers. Unlike other newspapers, national papers are unlikely to gain advertising from grocery stores, department stores, and other local product categories that have traditionally used newspapers as their major medium. Instead, *USA Today* depends on national automotive and computer companies and financial services for much of its advertising revenue.

In addition, the fact that a high percentage of *USA Today*'s circulation is transient presents a major problem for media planners. As one media executive pointed out, "when you buy media you want not only to buy reach. You also want to insure that you will gain some degree of measurable frequency for your message. It takes a reasonable number of exposures to gain total readership and total penetration of the ad message."[5]

To build a base of repeat readers, *USA Today* has recently made some subtle changes in its editorial approach. Although the hallmark of the paper continues to be relatively short articles, it has begun to include more features and occasional in-depth pieces on major topics. Like any product, the paper must be careful not to lose its base readership as it attempts to increase its audience.

Whatever problems the newspaper may have, the popularity and influence of *USA Today* are evident in the design of other newspapers. In the last decade, newspapers throughout the world have added color, maps, and charts, as well as the short story format that appeals to the TV generation and drives newspaper purists crazy. The *USA Today* style and format also have created profitable spinoffs, most notably *USA Today Baseball Weekly*, which takes advantage of the popular sports section of the core newspaper.

After a long struggle, it appears that *USA Today* has turned the corner on profitability. It has taken a long time for the advertising community to embrace the notion of a national paper. Now that the publication is increasingly being considered as a part of the plans of many advertisers, its future seems secure.

MARKETING THE NEWSPAPER

Despite their well-deserved reputation as a bulwark for democracy, newspapers also are a product to be marketed to both readers and advertisers. In recent years, newspapers have faced unprecedented competition for both advertising dollars and readers' time. Not long ago, newspapers were virtually assured of high household penetration and excellent advertising support. However, in the last two decades newspapers have had to adopt sophisticated marketing research techniques and a consumer orientation to combat competing media. Newspapers understand that they must aggressively fight to maintain both readership and advertising dollars.

Overall newspaper advertising revenues are nearly $40 billion. In addition, American newspaper readers spend $10 billion on subscriptions and newsstand sales. Because significant newspaper revenues come from both advertisers and readers, the industry must be aware of marketing strategies directed to both groups. In the last 20 years, newspapers have taken a number of steps to identify their customers and advertisers, and the preferences of both. This process starts with marketing research. It is rare for any newspaper not to conduct at least one readership or market survey each year. Large newspapers annually conduct several studies of their markets.

Several factors have become apparent as a result of these studies. One newspaper circulation director summarized the most important findings:[6]

> The most disturbing trend . . . is that many average citizens have discovered that they won't actually die if they don't read a newspaper. We are now

---

[5]Iver Peterson, "*USA Today*, the Fast Food of Dailies, Is Expanding Menu," *The New York Times,* August 19, 1996, p. C1.

[6]Chuck Downing, *Readership in the 90's,* Associated Press Managing Editors Association 1995 Readership Committee Report.

in the infancy of the information age and many people feel they're already on "overload."

Meanwhile, advertisers . . . are getting more demanding. And, why not? They have stiffer competition and often a slimmer profit margin than we [newspapers] do. They know that we continually increase advertising and circulation rates and subscriber penetration is flat. We may still be the best way to reach the buying public on a mass-medium basis now, but will we still be the best deal in three to five years? Competition among advertisers [has] forced many to seek niche marketing strategies rather than putting their message out to the masses. Targeted mail, alternate delivery companies, the Internet, fax mail, E-mail and cable are eating away at our once-solid foundations.

Although newspapers face some formidable challenges, there is no question that they will remain a major advertising medium in the foreseeable future as the contemporary newspaper offers unique advantages to both readers and advertisers. However, because newspapers dominated the local market for so long they did not develop a marketing mentality. Unfortunately, the industry is now playing catch-up with its more aggressive media competitors. In the next sections, we discuss how newspaper publishers are successfully selling the medium to both readers and advertisers. We examine some of the approaches that newspaper marketers are using to protect and extend their turf with both sources of revenue.

Marketing to Readers

From a marketing and advertising standpoint, media are basically prospect delivery systems. Therefore, the advertising success of newspapers, or any medium, must begin with the proposition that they can deliver prospects more efficiently than competing media. It is for this reason that newspapers have devoted significant dollars for reader research and are constantly searching for ways to keep current readers and attract new ones.

Although newspapers have shown an overall decrease in readership, they also find that many advertisers are shifting from a strategy of mass marketing to one of a more customized approach to reach their audiences. To meet this demand, publishers are designing the newspaper with various sections that cater to a host of different tastes. The modern newspaper is more a cafeteria than a full meal. Most of the audience reads only certain sections of a paper and spends differential amounts of time with those sections that they do read. For example, the editorial page is read almost equally by men and women, but only 65 percent of women read the sport pages, compared to 84 percent of men.[7] Knowing readers' preferences among the different sections of a newspaper is a great advantage in selling advertisers who wish to reach specific prospects.

Although maintaining overall readership remains the most important area for newspapers, publishers are particularly concerned about bringing in younger readers, most of whom are not presently heavy newspaper users. Newspaper publishers fear that once media habits are established that exclude newspapers, it will be very difficult to reach these people as older adults. Newspaper reading habits are formed by about age 30 and tend to change very little after that.

In the past, most efforts to reach young readers concentrated on the 18 to 24 age group. However, in the last few years, a significant effort has been made to interest younger teens in reading the newspaper and to develop cooperative programs to encourage the use of newspapers in middle and lower schools to reach younger children.

Many newspapers print special teen sections, and others include stories in each section with graphics and headlines designed to appeal to teens. For example, each

---

[7] *Understanding and Working with the Local Newspaper,* a publication of the Radio Advertising Bureau, January 1995.

Monday, the *Atlanta Journal* and *Constitution* includes a "News For Kids" feature in each section of the newspaper. In this way, children can read about sports, business, and local and world news on a level specifically targeted for them.

Research also is finding that newspapers continue to be an extremely popular medium with prospective customers. For example, one study found that newspapers

- best help consumers decide where to shop
- are most often used when people are ready to make a purchase
- are most effective in accomplishing advertising objectives
- are the most credible medium.[8]

Needless to say, all these characteristics are welcomed by advertisers as they consider media placement.

Despite the medium's many strengths, newspapers will continue to see a need to aggressively market the medium to readers. One editor remarked that the way newspapers maintain readership is by providing something of value. Readers want information about things to do and places to go, self-help articles, local news of personal interest, and national and international news that has an effect on their lives. Valuable information consists of "usually things not found in other media. Interestingly enough, they're also things that newspapers large and small have been doing for years. The sophistication level, in some cases, may be greater these days. The fundamental reader interest, though, is the same."[9] In today's diverse, multicultural society, appealing to readers is extremely difficult compared to earlier times when the population was much more homogeneous, but it is a necessary task if newspapers are to maintain their prominent position.

Marketing to Advertisers

As noted earlier, about 75 percent of all newspaper revenues comes from advertising. In fact, among newspapers with circulations of more than 81,000, advertising comprises the majority of the space.[10]

Circulation	% Advertising	% News
17,200–18,400	42.7	57.2
81,000–101,000	51.1	48.8
244,800–346,100	57.0	42.9

Therefore, to remain fiscally sound, it is imperative that newspapers continue to convince advertisers that they are an efficient means of meeting a variety of marketing and advertising objectives. To accomplish this goal, newspapers must develop a plan that shows a diverse group of current and potential advertisers that newspapers should be a part of their media plans.

The marketing task for newspapers is a twofold undertaking: (1) deliver the audience and (2) compete for advertisers. The newspaper industry must convince advertisers that it represents the best local medium and should constitute an important element in national advertising strategy. For example, Exhibit 10.3 shows that readers prefer newspaper advertising as a source of information for a number of major product categories. To accomplish these goals means that newspapers must retain the local retailers

---

[8] *Significant Findings from the Newspaper Perceptual Study,* a publication of the Radio Advertising Bureau, April 1997.

[9] Rich Farrant, *Keeping the Basics in Mind,* Associated Press Managing Editors Association 1995 Readership Committee Report.

[10] Nancy M. Davis, "News Hole, Inch by Inch," *Presstime,* April 1996, p. 26.

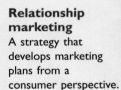

exhibit

10.3

Daily newspapers are the preferred medium in all 14 categories in which respondents were asked to select their primary source for advertising information.

Courtesy: Gannetteer, Gannett Co., Inc.
Source: Gannetteer,
September/October 1996, p. 5.

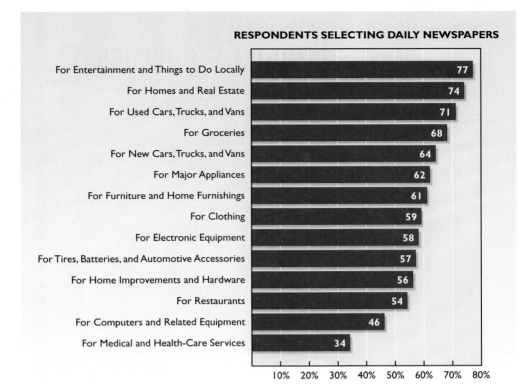

RESPONDENTS SELECTING DAILY NEWSPAPERS

Category	Percent
For Entertainment and Things to Do Locally	77
For Homes and Real Estate	74
For Used Cars, Trucks, and Vans	71
For Groceries	68
For New Cars, Trucks, and Vans	64
For Major Appliances	62
For Furniture and Home Furnishings	61
For Clothing	59
For Electronic Equipment	58
For Tires, Batteries, and Automotive Accessories	57
For Home Improvements and Hardware	56
For Restaurants	54
For Computers and Related Equipment	46
For Medical and Health-Care Services	34

Relationship marketing
A strategy that develops marketing plans from a consumer perspective.

who have traditionally comprised the bulk of newspaper revenues and bring in national advertisers who have not used newspapers to any great extent. In the current media climate, neither job will be easy. However, newspapers have a tremendous advantage in providing readers with localized, in-depth information concerning products and services in their communities. For categories such as real estate, newspapers are an indispensable advertising vehicle (see Exhibit 10.4, p. 264).

Whether marketing to readers or advertisers, newspapers have found that they are most successful when they develop a consumer-oriented perspective. Rather than attempting to sell an array of services to advertising clients, many newspapers are training their salespeople in **relationship marketing.** This concept attempts to develop a team approach between the newspaper and the advertiser to work with clients as partners to solve problems rather than operating on a salesperson/customer basis.

Newspapers are also developing a number of strategies and products to bring new advertisers into the medium. These new tactics encompass a host of elements, including some as sophisticated as electronic communication and others as simple as promotional tie-ins between the newspaper and advertisers.

Newspapers also are approaching major advertising agency media buyers on a personal basis to demonstrate the utility of newspaper advertising in national media schedules. Many of the complaints of media buyers center around the difficulty of buying local newspapers on a market-by-market basis. This is a particular problem for media buyers who are accustomed to the relative ease of buying national broadcast spots and magazines. In a later section, we discuss some of the steps being taken by newspapers to make the buying process more efficient.

Despite the difficult competitive environment in which newspapers must operate, they will remain a major advertising medium for both local and national advertisers. However, newspapers will change. Their survival in the long run depends on their ability to react to market conditions as they are delineated by readers and advertisers. It appears that newspapers are well prepared to meet this challenge into the next century.

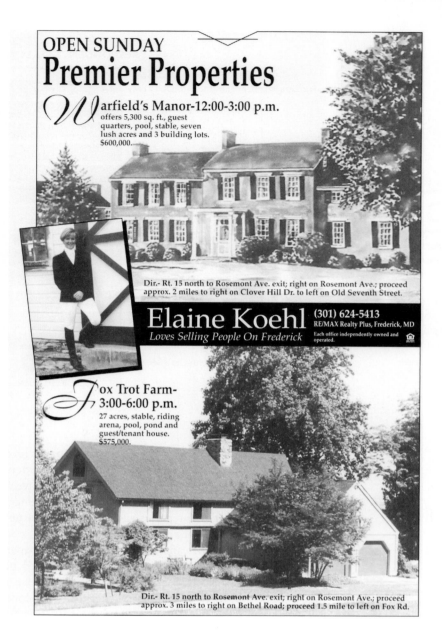

ZONING, TOTAL MARKET COVERAGE, AND NEWSPAPER NETWORKS

A diversity of companies use newspaper advertising, and the industry is constantly developing a number of different advertising products to serve them. Unlike most other media, which have a core of homogeneous advertising clients, newspapers have virtually every advertising category as a potential customer. A single edition of a newspaper is not suitable for the advertising objectives of all its advertisers nor the reading preferences of all its readers. In recent years, newspapers have begun to offer a number of services that recognize the diverse needs of their advertising and reading audiences. The fine-tuning of newspaper delivery systems has long been one of the core goals of newspaper marketing. Newspapers, armed with computer technology and more sophisticated means of audience identification, will offer even more circulation breakouts in the future.

Zoned Editions

As we discuss in chapter 13, direct mail has become a major advertising media and a primary competitor for newspaper advertising dollars. By allowing advertisers to pinpoint audiences on both a demographic and geographic basis, direct mailers have captured more than 20 percent of total advertising expenditures, only a couple of percentage points behind newspapers. Newspapers have had to recognize that a number of their primary accounts, especially small- and medium-sized retailers, have no use for full-run advertising. The corner dry cleaner and local pizza parlor are not going to attract customers from across town. Buying the entire circulation of the newspaper is a huge waste of money to them. By the same token, some national advertisers also may identify some sections of a city as being more valuable than others and prefer zoned coverage.

Direct mail offers an obvious alternative to newspapers because it can reach only those customers who live in a store's trade zone. For a number of years, most major newspapers have offered some form of **zoning** for newspaper inserts. For example, the *Atlanta Journal* and *Constitution,* through its Zoned Area Preprints (ZAP) program to subscribers, offers 162 zones (see Exhibit 10.5), which allows advertisers to use only those areas that reach their prospects. This paper also provides mail service to nonsubscribers in the same area through its ZIP program editions. These zones are, for the most part, broken out on a zip code basis and usually allow advertisers to distribute

Zoning
Newspaper practice of offering advertisers partial coverage of a market, often accomplished with weekly inserts distributed to certain sections of that market.

e x h i b i t

10.5

Newspapers offer a number of zoned editions.

Courtesy: Atlanta Journal and Constitution.

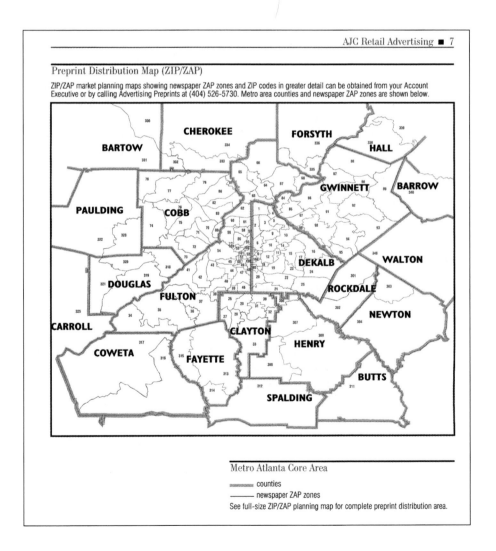

Preprint Distribution Map (ZIP/ZAP)

AJC Retail Advertising ■ 7

ZIP/ZAP market planning maps showing newspaper ZAP zones and ZIP codes in greater detail can be obtained from your Account Executive or by calling Advertising Preprints at (404) 526-5730. Metro area counties and newspaper ZAP zones are shown below.

Metro Atlanta Core Area

counties
newspaper ZAP zones
See full-size ZIP/ZAP planning map for complete preprint distribution area.

preprinted inserts to residences with selected zip codes. In addition to zoned zip code distribution of preprinted material, some newspapers publish extra weekly tabloids, which are delivered to targeted households.

In addition to preprint zoning, many metropolitan newspapers are providing suburban weekly or even daily sections in the newspaper to serve reader and advertiser demands for information about their section of the city. In the past, many newspapers devoted limited resources to these editions. Today, most newspapers are making meaningful investments in their zoned editions, and, in many cities, publishers have been rewarded with significant readership and advertising increases.

Zoning by zip code has been a major source of additional advertising revenue for newspapers, and in many markets has slowed the erosion of dollars to direct mail. However, some newspapers are finding that even zip code breakouts are too broad for many advertising accounts. A number of major newspapers are further fine-tuning their distribution into *microzone* systems. For example, the *Daily Oklahoman* of Oklahoma City offers 271 zones.[11]

Microzoning can take a number of forms, but at a minimum it means that a newspaper can deliver preprinted inserts to advertising zones below the zip code level. In most cases, microzoning allows an advertiser to identify specific carrier routes, but it may also mean that distribution can be address-specific. In other words, if you were a customer of the local video store, your newspaper would have an insert with a movie rental coupon, whereas the paper delivered to your next-door neighbor, who has never rented a movie from the store, would not.

Total Market Coverage

Ironically, as newspapers seek to serve those advertisers who are interested in a narrowly defined group of readers, they also find that a number of advertisers are seeking total penetration of a market. Because no newspaper has complete coverage of its market (in many markets it as low as 30 percent), other means must be used to augment regular circulation and achieve **total market coverage** (TMC). Total market coverage may be accomplished in a number of ways:

- weekly delivery of a nonsubscriber supplement that carries mostly advertisements
- using direct mail to nonsubscribers
- free newspaper delivery to all households once a week

Regardless of the method used to achieve total market coverage, the aim is the same—to reach all the households in a market whether they are newspaper readers or not. The aim is to combine the regular daily paper with a supplemental TMC product and thus allow advertisers to reach virtually 100 percent of the households in a market.

CATEGORIES OF NEWSPAPER ADVERTISING

Newspaper advertising revenues come from a number of sources, and like almost all media these revenues constitute the majority of financial support for the medium. Circulation accounts for approximately 25 percent of total newspaper revenues, and more than 70 percent of these come from subscriptions. Of the more than $50 billion spent in newspaper advertising, approximately half comes from local retail advertisers.

Newspaper advertising comprises several categories and subcategories. The two major types of newspaper advertising are display and classified. Within the display cate-

Total market coverage (TMC) Where newspapers augment their circulation with direct mail or shoppers to deliver all households in a market.

---

[11]Ann Lallande, "Navigating the Microzone Maze," *Presstime,* January 1996, p. 29.

gory there are local (also called retail) and national advertisers. The breakout of these categories according to advertising expenditures are

	$ (billions)	%
Classified	17.9	40.7
Local	20.4	46.4
National	5.6	12.7

Classified Advertising

Classified advertising, the common "want ads," for years has been the most profitable source of revenue for newspapers. Not only does classified advertising account for a huge share of total newspaper revenue, it is much more profitable than either local or national advertising. In the past, classified advertising sales consisted mainly of order taking with little or no selling required. However, in recent years, the almost monopolistic situation that newspapers enjoyed with classified advertising has changed dramatically. In particular, telephone companies have been aggressive in developing on-line interactive systems that provide constantly updated consumer information and advertising (see Exhibit 10.6).

Newspapers also carry advertisements with illustrations in the classified section. These are known as *classified display* advertisements and normally are run in the automotive and real-estate sections. All fall under the heading of classified advertising, which has its own rate card and is usually operated as a separate department.

Of the more than $15 billion invested in classified advertising, three categories—employment (40 percent), automotive (28.5 percent), and real estate (17.1 percent)—constitute more than 75 percent of all classified dollars.[12] The concentration of classified advertising in so few categories makes it relatively easy for competitors to identify and move against these profitable areas. "While 88 percent of companies still use newspapers to attract workers, they spend 79.8 percent of their recruitment dollars elsewhere. In automotive sales, other media [attract] 63.4 percent of car dollars. In real estate, 57.6 percent of ad dollars go to non-newspaper options."[13]

Although classified revenues continue to grow, publishers are increasingly worried about the extent of competition vying for these dollars. For example, from 1988 to 1994

exhibit

10.6

Yellow Pages aggressively compete for classified advertisers.

Courtesy: Bell South Advertising & Publishing.

[12]Rebecca Ross Albers, "Classified: Countering the Crisis," *Presstime,* May 1997, p. 69.

[13]Elsie Burroughs, "Crisis in Classifieds," *Presstime,* May 1996, p. 40.

newspapers lost nearly $1 *billion* in rental classified advertising to niche publications, and they saw a decrease of 33 percent in rental linkage during the same period. If the trend of recent years continues, newspapers stand to lose 50 percent of their classified dollars in the next decade.

Obviously, newspapers are not passively allowing these attacks on their classified franchise to go unchallenged. Major newspapers throughout the country are establishing telephone lines, World Wide Web sites, fax connections, and computer classified databases that can be reached 24 hours a day. On an industry-wide basis, newspapers are looking to services sponsored by the **Newspaper Association of America** (NAA) such as RealFind USA, which provides a national real estate relocation service for newspaper advertising. People moving to a new city can call a toll-free number, and RealFind USA will provide real estate material provided by the newspaper in that area. The service provides a value added for local newspaper real estate advertisers and it provides the local newspaper with the names of those people moving into its city who become prospective readers of the newspaper.[14]

In the fight for the classified dollar, newspapers have a number of advantages over their rivals. First, people associate classified advertising with newspapers and will have to be convinced to go to another source. Second, newspapers are challenging these new competitors by adding classified services. Third, newspapers have huge cash flows from classified to invest in marketing to prospective classified customers. Fourth, newspapers have the largest databases of classified products for sale.

With the potential revenues involved and the relative ease of selling and producing classified ads, many advertising executives predict that classified advertising will be one of the first major battlefields for the electronic information highway of the future. However, for now, the traditional newspaper classified sections will be the primary source of these notices for most customers. Moreover, newspapers are well positioned to maintain their dominance in this category, albeit with greater competition and expenses than in the past.

Display Advertising

With the possible exception of legal advertising and public notices, most nonclassified newspaper advertising is display advertising, which has two categories: local and national.

Local Advertising Local advertising is the foundation of newspaper revenues. No other medium has the loyalty or strength among retailers enjoyed by newspapers. Local advertising refers to all nonclassified advertising placed by local businesses, organizations, and individuals. Major local newspaper advertisers constitute a retail "who's who," with virtually every major retail chain such as Federated and May Department Stores, Circuit City, Kmart, and Sears spending hundreds of millions of dollars in newspapers. In fact, only two nonretailers are among the top 10 local newspaper advertisers.[15] There is every expectation that newspapers will continue to be the dominant local advertising medium. However, the share of advertising dollars will be reduced by the many options now available to retail advertisers.

Newspapers also are moving to make buying newspaper advertising space a simpler process. For example, in 1993 the NAA introduced the standard advertising invoice (SAI), which standardizes the local advertising invoice and statement. The SAI consolidates 29 elements into a single form and makes it especially efficient for retailers who purchase space in more than one newspaper.

Newspaper Association of America (NAA)
The marketing and trade organization for the newspaper industry.

---

[14]RealFind USA Seeks Members," *Presstime,* October 1996, p. 13.

[15]"Top 25 Local Newspaper Advertisers," *Advertising Age,* September 27, 1995, p. 52.

Direct mail represents the other major competitor for local advertising dollars. As discussed earlier, newspapers realize that they must offer advertisers more narrowly targeted audience segments to compete with direct mail. Although steps are being taken to counter the threat of direct mail, it remains to be seen if the newspaper industry can effectively develop services that meet the growing challenge of direct mailers.

A major characteristic of retail newspaper advertising is its emphasis on price competition. Compared to other media, local newspaper advertising is much more likely to emphasize short-term sales. It features price, place, and product with few advertising frills. Most local newspaper advertising attempts to create immediate results that the retailer can see within 24 hours.

National Advertising   In its quest to increase overall advertising revenues, the newspaper industry faces its most perplexing problem—how to bring more national advertising dollars to the medium. As the competition heats up at the local level, newspapers have tried to offset losses in local advertising share with increased national dollars. However, national newspapers expenditures remain relatively small compared to other media, and in the last decade national newspaper advertising as a percentage of all national advertising has dropped a half percent to 2.5 percent.

Clearly, the newspaper industry is concerned about the declining share of national advertising. As one newspaper executive stated,

> No area cries out for attention quite as loudly as the need to transform ourselves into a stronger national medium for advertisers. Many national advertisers have stayed away from newspapers because we were committing the cardinal sin in the decade of the consumer. We were tough to do business with. We have a fantastic connection with our readers, closer and more personal than just about any other medium. But for years, we had been wasting it. In the eyes of the customer, we were fragmented, we were inconsistent, we seemed to some to be more trouble than we were worth.[16]

Despite efforts of the newspaper industry to increase national advertising dollars, many national advertisers and their agencies remain unconvinced that newspapers are a viable national medium. In a survey of major advertising agency media planners, "newspapers failed to make an appearance in first- or second-placed rankings of effective vehicles for national advertising. Overall, only billboards and [out-of-home] media ranked lower than newspapers in relative effectiveness for national advertising accounts."[17]

Although there are a number of points of disagreement between national advertisers and newspapers, one of the most serious is the continuing debate over the so-called local/national **rate differential.** Most newspapers charge a substantial premium to national advertisers. In the most recent figures released by the American Association of Advertising Agencies, national advertisers were charged an average of almost 75 percent more than local advertisers for the same space. On some large papers this differential is close to 100 percent. Newspapers defend the difference on the basis that they must pay an agency commission for national advertising, and many of these advertisers are only occasional users of their papers, unlike retailers with whom they enjoy continuing support.

A second major area of concern for national advertisers is the generally cumbersome system of buying space. In recent years, newspapers have introduced networks where a number of papers can be purchased with one insertion order and a single invoice. Currently, there are approximately 250 networks. Some are set up like the

Rate differential
The controversial practice of newspapers charging significantly higher rates to national advertisers as compared to local accounts.

---

[16]John F. Strum, speech to the American Forest and Paper Association Industry, New York, March 12, 1996.

[17]Karen Whitehill King, "Why Buyers Aren't Buying," *Presstime*, October, 1995, p. 19.

Georgia Network, which covers Georgia's primary metropolitan areas outside of Atlanta by allowing advertisers to purchase newspapers in Athens, Augusta, Savannah, Columbus, and Macon.

Georgia Network, which covers Georgia's primary metropolitan areas outside of Atlanta by allowing advertisers to purchase newspapers in Athens, Augusta, Savannah, Columbus, and Macon. An advertiser buying the Georgia Network will cover approximately 300,000 households within these five markets with one insertion and one bill. Other networks may be part of a large national newspaper chain and operate in a number of states. Regardless of the size of the network, the basic strategy is to simplify the buying process for advertising's needing to buy a number of papers. Most networks offer advertisers customized plans involving numerous combinations of these publications.

Newspaper networks are much more than several papers offering space to advertisers on a joint basis. Many advertisers want to use preprinted inserts, so the distribution of these pieces must be coordinated among the network papers. Also, some advertisers will demand that a newspaper network provide TMC capability in each market. Because newspapers solve their TMC problem in a number of different ways, this adds to the complexity of newspaper networks.

Advertisers are not interested in the problems newspapers face in developing their networks, they are only interested in results. Unfortunately, newspapers were late to develop formal networks, and there is still a lack of national coordination for such buys. The NAA, the marketing arm of the newspaper industry, is currently moving to develop standard procedures that should make newspaper network buying easier in the future.

The most significant move to a simplified system of buying national advertising space is the Newspaper National Network (NNN) established by the newspaper industry in 1995 (see Exhibit 10.7).

The purpose of the NNN is to streamline the buying process for national advertisers, convince advertisers that newspapers are a cost-efficient national medium, and offer marketing counsel to national advertisers contemplating newspaper buys. Individual newspapers permit the NNN to negotiate on their behalf with national advertisers at a cost below what each newspaper charges individually. The NNN emphasizes that ease of buying alone will not gain, or keep, national advertisers. Instead, the pricing policies and buying procedures are simply part of the marketing and sales package to encourage national advertisers to consider newspapers as part of their media schedules.

In 1997 NNN placed more than $80 million in national advertising in 860 newspapers. The NNN accepts advertising for a limited number of product categories: computers and software, automotive, beverages, cosmetics, drugs and remedies, food, and household products. Because of restraint-of-trade implications, each category must be approved by the Justice Department.[18]

The NNN also provides national advertisers with **Standard Advertising Units** (SAUs) from one newspaper to another (Exhibit 10.8, p. 272). Space standardization allows national advertisers to purchase space in virtually every major U.S. newspaper and prepare one advertisement that will be accepted by each of them. As you can see, NNN formats are flexible enough to provide virtually every advertiser a design that will fit any creative execution.

Newspapers must overcome several obstacles if they are to increase their national advertising share. Given the tight retail market and the potential for growth in the national sector, newspapers must settle many of the long-standing rifts with potential national clients. An effective system of national newspaper advertising will take time. However, it is encouraging that both advertisers and newspapers are addressing their problems. The ultimate catalyst to finding solutions to the problems of national advertisers will be the self-interest of both groups.

---

[18]Jane Hodges, "National Network Looking More Computer Friendly," *Advertising Age,* April 28, 1997, p. s4.

Newspaper networks
Groups of newspapers that allow advertisers to buy several papers simultaneously with one insertion order and one invoice.

Standard Advertising Unit (SAU)
Allows national advertisers to purchase newspaper advertising in standard units from one paper to another.

exhibit

10.7

Newspapers are
working to increase
national advertising.

Courtesy: Newspaper National
Network.

**Cooperative
advertising**

Joint promotion of a
national advertiser
(manufacturer) and
local retail outlet on
behalf of the
manufacturer's
product on sale in the
retail store.

Cooperative Advertising

One of the historical outgrowths of the newspaper local/national rate differential was
the development of a relationship between national advertisers and their retail distributors called **cooperative (co-op) advertising.** We discuss cooperative advertising more
fully in chapter 14 along with other sales promotion techniques, but it is such an important part of newspaper advertising that we need to mention it here.

Co-op advertising is placed by a local advertiser, but paid for, all or in part, by a
national advertiser. The national manufacturer usually provides the ad, allowing space
for the retailer's logo. The original reason for the development of co-op advertising was
that it allowed national advertisers to place ads at the local rate.

Today, co-op is a huge source of advertising funds. It is estimated that approximately $24 billion are available for co-op in virtually all media including television, ra-
dio, outdoor, and direct mail. Co-op also is a source of building goodwill with distributors and retailers and exercising some creative control over local advertising as well as
saving money.

Because national advertisers pay anywhere from 50 to 100 percent of the cost of
locally placed co-op, it extends the budgets of local advertisers as it saves money for

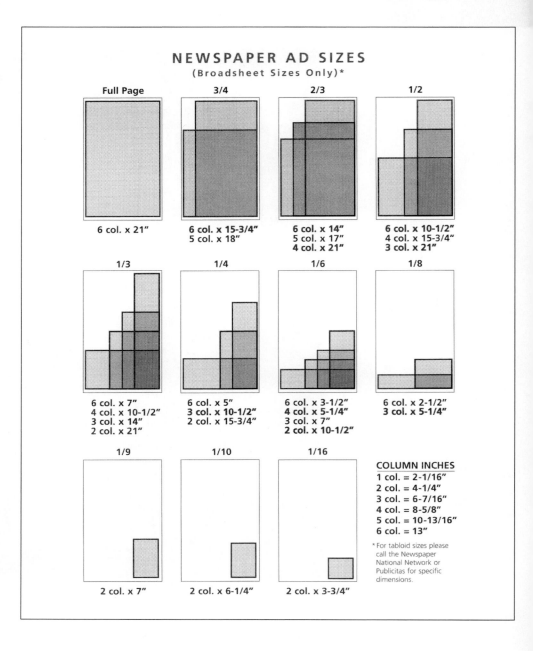

NEWSPAPER AD SIZES
(Broadsheet Sizes Only)*

Full Page
6 col. x 21"

3/4
6 col. x 15-3/4"
5 col. x 18"

2/3
6 col. x 14"
5 col. x 17"
4 col. x 21"

1/2
6 col. x 10-1/2"
4 col. x 15-3/4"
3 col. x 21"

1/3
6 col. x 7"
4 col. x 10-1/2"
3 col. x 14"
2 col. x 21"

1/4
6 col. x 5"
3 col. x 10-1/2"
2 col. x 15-3/4"

1/6
6 col. x 3-1/2"
4 col. x 5-1/4"
3 col. x 7"
2 col. x 10-1/2"

1/8
6 col. x 2-1/2"
3 col. x 5-1/4"

1/9
2 col. x 7"

1/10
2 col. x 6-1/4"

1/16
2 col. x 3-3/4"

COLUMN INCHES
1 col. = 2-1/16"
2 col. = 4-1/4"
3 col. = 6-7/16"
4 col. = 8-5/8"
5 col. = 10-13/16"
6 col. = 13"

* For tabloid sizes please call the Newspaper National Network or Publicitas for specific dimensions.

exhibit

10.8

Standardized ad formats are crucial to national newspaper advertisers.

Courtesy: Newspaper National Network.

national firms. It is ironic that a system that was developed largely to circumvent the national/local newspaper rate differential is strongly supported by the newspaper industry. Because newspapers receive more than half of all co-op dollars placed, their sales staffs are extremely aggressive in helping retail accounts find and use co-op money.

The Rate Structure

The local advertiser, dealing with one or two newspapers, has a fairly easy job buying newspaper space. The rate structure and discounts for any one newspaper are usually straightforward. However, as we have seen, the national advertiser has a much more difficult time. An advertiser buying space in a number of newspapers confronts an unlimited set of options and price structures, including discounts, premium charges for color, special sections, preferred positions, and zoned editions. In the following discussion, we look at some of the primary options and rate decisions that an advertiser must make.

Discounts Newspapers are divided into two categories: those with a uniform **flat rate** that offers no discounts, and those with an **open rate** that provides some discount structure. The open rate also refers to the highest rate against which all discounts are applied. The most common discounts are based on *frequency* or *bulk* purchases of space. A bulk discount means there is a sliding scale so that the advertiser is charged proportionally less as more advertising is purchased. A frequency discount usually requires some unit or pattern of purchase in addition to total amount of space.

Frequency Within 52-Week Contract Period Full-Page Contract		Bulk Within 52-Week Contract Period	
Open Rate	$2.50/Column Inch	No. of Column Inches	Rate
10 insertions	2.20	500	2.40
15 insertions	2.20	1,500	2.30
20 insertions	2.10	3,000	2.20
30 insertions	2.00	5,000	2.10
40 insertions	1.90	10,000	2.00
50 insertions	1.80	15,000	1.90

ROP and Preferred-Position Rates The basic rates quoted by a newspaper entitle the ad to a run-of-paper (abbreviated ROP) position anywhere in the paper that the publisher chooses to place it, although the paper will be mindful of the advertiser's request and interest in getting a good position. An advertiser may buy a choice position by paying a higher, preferred-position rate, which is similar to paying for a box seat in a stadium instead of general admission. A cigar advertiser, for example, may elect to pay a preferred-position rate to ensure getting on the sports page. A cosmetic advertiser may buy a preferred position on the women's page. There are also preferred positions on individual pages. An advertiser may pay for the top of a column or the top of a column next to news reading matter (called *full position*).

Each newspaper specifies its preferred-position rates; there is no consistency in this practice. Preferred-position rates are not as common as they once were. Now many papers simply attempt to accommodate advertisers that request a position, such as "above fold urgently requested."

Combination Rates A number of combinations are available to advertisers. What they all have in common is the advantage of greatly reduced rates for purchasing several papers as a group. The most frequently seen combination rate occurs when the same publisher issues both a morning and an evening paper. By buying both papers, the advertiser can pay as little as one-third to one-half for the second paper. This type of combination may involve as few as two papers in a single metropolitan market or many papers bought on a national basis. In either case, the advertiser has to deal with only one group and pays a single bill.

The Rate Card

For most media, the advertising rate card, if it exists at all, is simply a starting point for negotiation. As discussed earlier, most radio and television stations don't publish formal rate cards because rates are determined by negotiated scatter plans that are unique to each advertiser. During the 1980s, many consumer magazines also began to negotiate their rates with individual advertisers. Today, newspapers are one of the few media to maintain rate integrity by offering all advertisers the same rates and discounts.

Of course, newspapers have a major advantage over their broadcast counterparts in maintaining rates. In a real sense the size of the newspaper is determined by the amount of advertising. Nonadvertising space in a newspaper is called the *news hole,* and, although averages are hard to come by, most major dailies have a news hole of approximately

25 percent. It is obvious that advertising determines the size of a paper by comparing bulky Sunday or Thursday (typically the day grocery stores run most of their advertising) papers with the much smaller Saturday edition.

Although newspapers have a more fixed rate card than other media, we should not leave the impression that they do not accommodate advertisers with flexible rates in the face of competitive pressure. Examples of such alternative rate structures include the following:

- *Multiple rate cards.* Many newspapers offer a number of rate cards for different categories of advertisers. For example, package goods, travel, business, and retail stores may all qualify for different rates. Even the NNN provides buying opportunities for only six categories of products including automotive, drugs, and beverages. Some critics charge that by offering an array of different rates, newspapers are making the buying process unnecessarily complex, and still maintaining a type of discrimination from one group of advertisers to another that has the same intent as individual rate negotiation.
- *Newspaper merchandising programs.* Many newspapers refuse to directly negotiate rates but are willing to make other types of merchandising concessions. These programs, also known as *value-added programs,* may include sharing detailed audience research and providing free creative or copy assistance to advertisers.
- *Pick-up rates.* An advertiser that agrees to rerun an ad may receive a lower rate. This encourages return business and passes along some of the savings that the newspaper enjoys from not having to produce a new ad.

Because of the tradition of the newspaper rate card, it is unlikely that we will see the type of rate negotiation that has become so prevalent in other media. However, newspapers recognize that they will have to meet the competitive pressure. Consequently, we will see even more creative value-added programs offered by newspapers in the future.

Comparing Newspaper Advertising Costs

National advertisers, many of whom consider hundreds of newspapers in a single media plan, want to make cost comparisons among their potential newspaper buys. For many years, the standard measure for comparing the cost of newspaper space was the milline rate.[19] The milline rate has been replaced in recent years by the *CPM* comparison discussed earlier.

Using the *CPM* for newspaper rate comparisons has two advantages:

1. It reflects the move to page and fractional-page space buys. Media planners are much more comfortable using the standardized space units of the NNN than lines or column inches in space buys.
2. Comparisons among media are more easily calculated using a standard benchmark such as the *CPM*. Although qualitative differences among newspapers and other media must still be considered, the *CPM* does offer a consistent means of comparison:

Newspaper	Open-Rate Page Cost	Circulation	CPM
A	$5,400	165,000	$32.72
B	3,300	116,000	28.45

Example: $\dfrac{\$5,400 \times 1000}{165,000} = \$32.72$

---

[19]The milline rate is a hypothetical figure that measures what it would cost per agate line to reach a million circulation of a paper, based on the actual line rate and circulation. The formula is:

$$\text{Milline} = \frac{1,000,000 \times \text{rate per line}}{\text{circulation}}$$

(There are 14 agate lines per column inch.)

The Space Contract, the Short Rate

If a paper has a flat rate, obviously there is no problem with calculating costs—all space is billed at the same price regardless of how much is used. However, space contracts in open-rate papers must have flexibility to allow advertisers to use more or less space than originally contracted. Normally, an advertiser will sign a *space contract* estimating the amount of space to be used during the next 12 months. Such a space contract is not a guarantee of the amount of space an advertiser will run, but rather an agreement on the rate the advertiser will pay for any space run during the year in question.

The space contract involves two steps: First, advertisers estimate the amount of space they think they will run and agree with the newspaper on how to handle any rate adjustments needed at the end of the year; they are then billed during the year at the selected rate. Second, at the end of the year, the total linage is added, and if advertisers ran the amount of space they had estimated, no adjustment is necessary; but if they failed to run enough space to earn that rate, they have to pay at the higher rate charged for the number of lines they actually ran. That amount is called the **short rate.**

The Newsplan contract outlines the arrangement as follows:

> Advertiser will be billed monthly at applicable contract rate for entire contract year. At end of contract year advertiser will be refunded if a lower rate is earned or rebilled at a higher applicable rate if contract is not fulfilled.

As an example, let us assume that a national advertiser plans to run advertising in a paper with the following rates:

- open rate, $5.00 per column inch
- 1,000 column inches, $4.50/column inch
- 5,000 column inches, $4.00/column inch
- 10,000 column inches, $3.50/column inch

The advertiser expects to run at least 5,000 column inches and signs the contract at the $4.00 (5,000 column-inch) rate (subject to end-of-year adjustment). At the end of 12 months, however, only 4,100 column inches have been run; therefore, the bill at the end of the contract year is as follows:

Earned rate: 4,100 column inches @ $4.50 per column inch = $18,450

Paid rate: 4,100 column inches @ $4.00 per column inch =   16,400

                                           Short rate due = $ 2,050

or

Column inches run $\times$ difference in earned and billed rates

$$= 4,100 \text{ column inches} \times 0.50$$

$$= \$2,050$$

If the space purchased had qualified for the 10,000 column-inch rate ($3.50), the advertiser would have received a **rebate** of $5,000. The calculation then would be:

Paid rate: 10,000 column inches @ $4.00 per column inch = $40,000

Earned rate: 10,000 column inches @ $3.50 per column inch = $35,000

                                           Rebate due = $ 5,000

Newspapers will credit a rebate against future advertising rather than actually paying the advertiser. Some papers charge the full rate and allow credit for a better rate when earned.

Short rate
The balance advertisers have to pay if they estimated that they would run more ads in a year than they did and entered a contract to pay at a favorable rate. The short rate is figured at the end of the year or sooner if advertisers fall behind schedule. It is calculated at a higher rate for the fewer insertions.

Rebate
The amount owed to an advertiser by a medium when the advertiser qualifies for a higher space discount.

CIRCULATION ANALYSIS

The Audit Bureau of Circulations

Prior to the founding of the **Audit Bureau of Circulations** (ABC) in 1914, those newspaper publishers that bothered to provide circulation figures at all used self-reported numbers. Obviously, many publishers grossly inflated their circulation and created an adversarial relationship among newspapers, advertising agencies, and clients.[20]

The ABC serves advertisers, agencies, and publishers. It is a self-regulating and self-supporting cooperative body. Revenues for the ABC come from annual dues paid by all members and auditing fees paid by publishers.

The verification process involves three reports: two publisher's statements and the ABC audit. The publisher's statements are issued for six-month periods ending March 31 and September 30. The ABC audit is conducted annually for 12-month periods ending either March 31 or September 30. Advertisers can also get summary information in reports called FAS-FAX, which are available more quickly than the full reports. Exhibits 10.9 and 10.10 (p. 278) are portions of an ABC audit report. It should be noted that the information in ABC reports is constantly changing in response to subscribers' needs.

The ABC report includes the following primary information:

1. Total paid circulation.
2. Amount of circulation in the city zone, retail trading zone, and all other areas. (*Note:* The city zone is a market made up of the city of publication and contiguous built-up areas similar in character to the central city. The retail trading zone is a market area outside the city zone whose residents regularly trade with merchants doing business within the city zone.)
3. The number of papers sold at newsstands.

The ABC reports have nothing to do with a newspaper's rates. They deal with circulation statistics only. Publishers have always been glad to supply demographic data on their readers, but the ABC now has its own division for gathering demographic data for many of the markets in the United States. All data are computerized and quickly available.

In recent years, newspapers have been particularly concerned about the use of circulation rather than readership as a measure. They point to the fact that national advertisers and their agencies have become accustomed to using readership figures when buying consumer magazines. Obviously, this places newspapers in a competitive disadvantage in attempting to encourage more consideration by national clients.

Most studies show that pass-along newspaper readership is significant. Major market surveys show readers per copy (or RPC) are often double or triple circulation figures. For example, estimated readership of the combined *San Francisco Chronicle* and *San Francisco Examiner* (circulation 551,127) was 1.808 million, an RPC of 3.0. Similar situations exist at the *Chicago Tribune* (624,237 versus 1.829 million, or an RPC of 2.9), and the combined *Arizona Republic* and the *Phoenix Gazette* (445,356 versus 1.138 million, or an RPC of 2.6).[21]

Newspaper publishers know that circulation figures are an important consideration in the decision to buy newspaper advertising. However, they feel that it is important for competitive reasons also to report their total readership. The ABC has indicated that they will investigate the feasibility of developing a system of reporting readership, but audited circulation continues to be the major concern of that organization.

---

[20]*Academic Casebook,* a publication of the Audit Bureau of Circulations.
[21]Barbara Z. Gyles, "Bowing to Audience Requests," *Presstime,* February 1997, p. 29.

AUDIT REPORT:

THE TRIBUNE (Evening)
Anytown (Red County), Illinois

TOTAL AVERAGE PAID CIRCULATION FOR 12 MONTHS ENDED SEPTEMBER 30, 19--:

			Evening
1A. TOTAL AVERAGE PAID CIRCULATION (BY INDIVIDUALS AND FOR DESIGNATED RECIPIENTS):			41,315

1B. TOTAL AVERAGE PAID CIRCULATION (BY INDIVIDUALS AND FOR DESIGNATED RECIPIENTS) BY ZONES:
(See Par. 1E for description of area)

CITY ZONE

	Population	Occupied Households	
1980 Census:	80,109	29,143	
#12-31-87 Estimate:	80,500	30,000	

Carrier Delivery office collect system, See Pars. 11(b) & (c).....	1,875
Carriers not filing lists with publisher........................	18,649
Single Copy Sales.......................................	2,168
Mail Subscriptions	47
School-Single Copy/Subscriptions, See Par. 11(d)	50
Employee Copies, See Par. 11(e)	100
Group (Subscriptions by Businesses for Designated Employees), See Par. 11(f)	50
TOTAL CITY ZONE	22,939

RETAIL TRADING ZONE

	Population	Occupied Households	
1980 Census:	268,491	75,140	
#12-31-87 Estimate	272,000	79,000	

Carriers not filing lists with publisher	15,138
Single Copy Sales.......................................	1,549
Mail Subscriptions	908
School-Single Copy/Subscriptions, See Par. 11(d)	25
Employee Copies, See Par. 11(e)	25
Group (Subscriptions by Businesses for Designated Employees), See Par. 11(f)	50
TOTAL RETAIL TRADING ZONE	17,695
TOTAL CITY & RETAIL TRADING ZONES	40,634

	Population	Occupied Households	
1980 Census:	348,600	104,283	
#12-31-87 Estimate:	352,500	109,000	

ALL OTHER

Single Copy Sales & Carriers not filing lists with publisher	256
Mail Subscriptions	375
School-Single Copy/Subscriptions, See Par. 11(d)	20
Employee Copies, See Par. 11(e)	20
Group (Subscriptions by Businesses for Designated Employees), See Par. 11(f)	10
TOTAL ALL OTHER	681
TOTAL PAID CIRCULATION (BY INDIVIDUALS AND FOR DESIGNATED RECIPIENTS)	41,315

1C. THIRD PARTY (BULK) SALES:

Airlines — Available for passengers	1,000
Hotels, Motels — Available for guests	500
Restaurants — Available for patrons	500
Businesses — Available for employees.......................	50
Other	600
TOTAL THIRD PARTY (BULK) SALES.....................	2,650

#S&MM Estimate. See Par. 11(a).

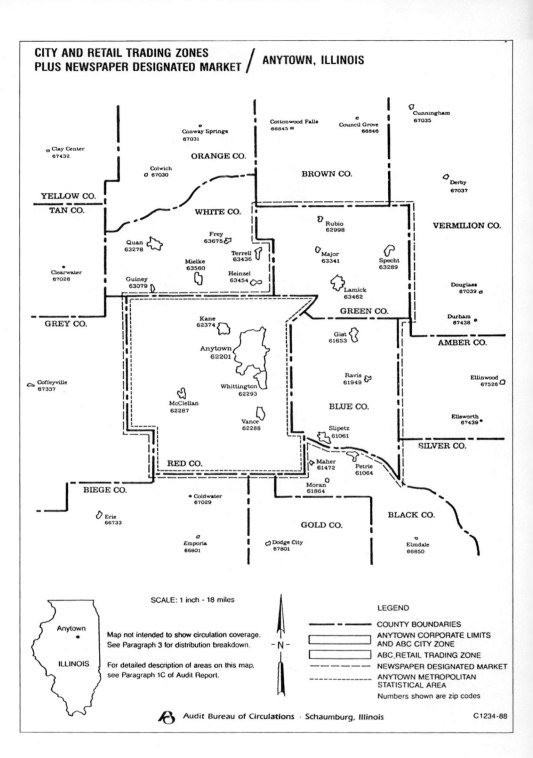

CITY AND RETAIL TRADING ZONES PLUS NEWSPAPER DESIGNATED MARKET / ANYTOWN, ILLINOIS

SCALE: 1 inch - 18 miles

Map not intended to show circulation coverage. See Paragraph 3 for distribution breakdown.

For detailed description of areas on this map, see Paragraph 1C of Audit Report.

-N-

LEGEND

COUNTY BOUNDARIES

ANYTOWN CORPORATE LIMITS AND ABC CITY ZONE

ABC, RETAIL TRADING ZONE

NEWSPAPER DESIGNATED MARKET

ANYTOWN METROPOLITAN STATISTICAL AREA

Numbers shown are zip codes

Audit Bureau of Circulations · Schaumburg, Illinois

C1234-88

Anytown

ILLINOIS

exhibit

10.10

Courtesy: Audit Bureau of Circulations.

TECHNOLOGY AND THE FUTURE OF NEWSPAPERS

After a number of false starts during the last two decades, a new age of information technology is upon us. Newspapers, as is the case with all media, are having to rethink traditional methods of doing business and, in some cases, redefine their businesses. Although we are still some years away from the fulfillment of the most optimistic predictions of the electronic superhighway, it is clear that new technology must be an immediate consideration of any media company.

In the near future, newspaper executives may come to view themselves as information providers, not newspaper editors and publishers. This distinction is not one of simple semantics. Rather, it allows people to think beyond the newspaper as a print-on-paper product and consider alternative delivery systems as well as the type of information that is provided and to which customers it is disseminated.

More and more newspapers are going on-line with their Web sites. At the simplest level, these sites provide the same information that is in the paper. Other Web sites have additional information or even interactive systems so that the audience can "talk" to editors or reporters. Many predict that the classified advertising section will be the first practical battlefield for the new technology. As discussed earlier, it is mandatory that newspapers maintain their franchise among classified users, and on-line technology must be developed to serve this audience.

To date, household penetration of on-line information systems has been relatively low. However, the introduction of the Internet and the decreasing cost of most on-line services such as America Online have significantly increased the number of households and businesses with this capability. In addition, the numbers themselves do not tell the full story. Most studies indicate that use of on-line services is concentrated among the young, the well-educated, and the affluent. Obviously, this is a group of great interest to newspapers and their advertisers.

Newspapers also are providing fax editions and telephone databases. For example, the *Atlanta Journal* and *Constitution* provided a Web-site view of traffic during the Olympics that was updated every 5 minutes, another site offered restaurant guides, and continuing sites gave news about the Braves and Falcons and other topics of interest. Recognizing that the majority of its readers do not have access to a computer, the newspaper has long used the telephone for interactive communication with readers.

By dialing 511, callers can access tomorrow's classified ads by fax over the phone. The newspaper provides a Yellow-Pages-Now service to locate specific businesses; a Movies-Now service that offers titles, times, and ratings; and answers to questions about the news in the paper.

To date, most of the new technology, particularly Web sites, has not been profitable. However, recent research shows that readers are adapting to the Web. For example, 60 percent of Web users frequently read newspapers on-line. Respondents indicate that although they continue to read print newspapers, they view the Web version as a more current and available source of information. Research also indicates that most Web users would be reluctant to pay extra for access to on-line newspapers. It seems that in the short term, advertising is the only practical source of revenue for supporting these vehicles.[22]

On the other hand, advertisers will invest in on-line services only when they are convinced they offer a viable means to economically reach prospects. The media have to understand that advertisers don't care how they reach their audiences, as long as *prospects* are reached as economically as possible. In this sense, advertisers are not partners with the media in paying to develop new technology. Newspapers have the

---

[22]"NPD Survey Shows Six Out of Ten Web Users Frequently Read Online Publications," *PR Newswire*, April 8, 1997.

responsibility of delivering an audience that advertisers think is more valuable than those provided by competing media. The technology used to reach this audience is not the problem of the advertiser.

NEWSPAPER-DISTRIBUTED MAGAZINE SUPPLEMENTS

Sunday Supplements

Sunday supplements generally fall into two categories: locally produced supplements and syndicated national Sunday magazines. The first category comprises less than 30 major market supplements such as *The New York Times, The Los Angeles Times,* and *Washington Post* magazines. These publications are sold as upscale publications and carry advertising from advertisers such as Christian Dior and Estee Lauder. The magazines are designed and marketed as specialty magazines and compete with city and specialty publications for advertisers.

Apart from these few metropolitan newspapers that produce their own Sunday publications, most newspapers subscribe to either *USA Weekend* or *Parade,* the two major syndicated supplements. Both magazines deliver huge readership at a cost to newspapers and advertisers that is less than most independent supplements. *Parade* tends to be more popular at larger-circulation newspapers, with a circulation of 36.4 million in 335 papers. *USA Weekend* is distributed by 486 newspapers, but has a lower circulation of 20 million. *Parade* is the largest circulation consumer magazine by a wide margin. Both publications offer numerous opportunities for regional buys. In fact, with the exception of a few very large investors in Sunday supplements such as Procter & Gamble, General Motors, and Campbell Soup, some form of less-than-full-run buy is the norm in both supplements.

From a marketing perspective, the supplements sell the idea that advertisers get network buying efficiency, a magazine format, consistent quality reproduction, and a *CPM* lower than both newspapers and most magazines. As the publisher of *USA Weekend* has pointed out, "We've grown ad revenue by positioning ourselves as one of the few national places where you can find an attentive mass audience at a specific period of time."[23] Despite favorable *CPM*s, neither publication is inexpensive. The base full-page, 4-color cost for *Parade* is approximately $600,000, and the cost for *USA Weekend* is more than $350,000.

With the exception of a few large markets, most newspapers find that it is not cost efficient to produce their own Sunday supplements, and there is probably going to be a further consolidation among marginal Sunday publications. However, it is clear that the features, entertainment news, and opportunities for advertisers to buy Sunday newspaper circulation in a magazine format will make the supplement a continuing part of our Sunday reading ritual.

There is one other national supplement of note, *Vista,* which is directed to a Hispanic audience. It is an English-language monthly publication distributed in some 25 newspapers in metropolitan areas with large Hispanic populations. Since its start in 1985, *Vista* has shown remarkable growth in an extremely competitive market, with total circulation of more than a million.

Comics

Any discussion of newspaper special features would have to include a mention of the comics. The newspaper comic traces its origins to 1889, when the New York *World* used newly installed color presses to build circulation with a comic section. The importance of comic strips became obvious in 1895 when two titans of journalism, Joseph Pulitzer

---

[23]"*USA Weekend* Tops 10 Years," *Gannetteer,* January/February 1996, p. 16.

and William Randolph Hearst, waged a fierce battle over ownership of the most popular cartoon of the day, "The Yellow Kid."

Although not a major advertising vehicle, comics are a major source of readership and a feature that editors are constantly evaluating as they choose among the hundreds of available strips. The most recent research indicates that 73 percent of newspaper readers turn to the comic section each day.[24] For those advertisers who want to use the comic sections, there are networks similar to those discussed earlier that sell the comic sections in a number of combinations so that advertisers can place advertisement simultaneously in a number of papers.

THE AFRICAN AMERICAN AND HISPANIC PRESS

At one time, many major metropolitan newspapers did not print birth, wedding, or funeral notices for African Americans. Unfortunately, most news of the black community also was largely ignored. In this environment, it was understandable that a number of African American leaders started newspapers directed specifically at African American readers. In fact, the black press has a distinguished history since the early nineteenth century.

The black press was at its height during the 1960s, with almost 300 papers and total circulation of 4 million. These newspapers were sources of news, political agitation, and advertising. They contributed to much of the social progress made during this period. One of their significant legacies was their drive for passage of the Voting Rights Act and other civil rights legislation during the term of President Lyndon Johnson.

Ironically, the black press has suffered financially as opportunities have opened to African American citizens. During the 1960s and 1970s, the majority press began to incorporate coverage of black readers into their papers. As time went on, it was less important to have separate newspapers to cover news of black readers.

Today, there are still a number of newspapers directed primarily to the African American audience. Virtually every major metropolitan center has at least one newspaper published for this audience. With the exception of the *Atlanta Daily World,* the *Chicago Daily Defender,* and the *New York Daily Challenge,* all are weeklies or biweeklies. During the last two decades, most black-oriented newspapers have lost both circulation and advertising revenue. However, several newspapers directed at the black community still maintain significant levels of circulation and advertising support. Among the most important are the *Washington Informer,* the *Michigan Chronicle,* and the *Houston Forward Times,* all with circulations in the 35,000 to 50,000 range.

Advertisers, particularly major national companies, have shifted significant dollars into television, radio, and magazines with high African American audiences. For example, *Soul Train, Jet, Black Enterprise,* and *Essence* have all enjoyed notable support from corporations seeking to reach the lucrative African American market.

In the future, it appears that all but the strongest members of the black press will continue to struggle. Research indicates that African American adults prefer television and magazines to newspapers. Black teens, like their white counterparts, overwhelmingly use radio as their medium of preference. In one sense, the current troubles of the black press are a tribute to the job it did in bringing fairness and equity to the African American community.

There are approximately 30 million Hispanics in the United States, more than 10 percent of the total population. It is estimated that by the year 2010 they will be the largest minority in this country. More important, Hispanics constitute a major economic force. In the last 20 years, the number of Hispanic households with incomes of more than $50,000 has increased by almost 200 percent. In many markets, it is not

---

[24]Rolf Rykken, "Funny Business," *Presstime Planner,* April 1995, p. S2.

unusual to find Spanish-language media and advertising in both specialized and some mainstream media (see Exhibit 10.11).

As the Hispanic population grows in size, influence, and economic power, the Hispanic press continues to enjoy major growth in a number of cities. In Los Angeles and Miami, the Hispanic population is more than one-third of the total. In San Antonio, more than half the population is Hispanic. In these and similar markets, Hispanic-oriented media are among the mainstream media. In Los Angeles alone, there are 23 radio stations and 16 newspapers directed primarily at the Hispanic audience.

Newspapers such as *La Opinion* in Los Angeles, *El Neuvo Herald* in Miami, and El Paso's *Diario de Juarez* all have daily circulations in excess of 100,000. Overall, an estimated 1,500 media outlets target the Hispanic market, and radio is the most widespread and popular media outlet for this group.

Reaching the Hispanic market is not an easy task, and the advertiser that treats this audience segment as a homogeneous group is making a major error. For example, although approximately half of all Hispanic Americans are of Mexican heritage, the remainder identify with a number of South American, Central American, and Caribbean countries, each with its own unique culture and product preferences.

exhibit

10.11

It is imperative to reach an increasingly diverse population.

Courtesy: Advertising Council.

TRANSLATION:
THE ONLY THING WORSE THAN LOSING A SON THROUGH AIDS, IS TO FIND OUT THAT THIS COULD HAVE BEEN AVOIDED.

Thousands of women will lose children through AIDs, especially during pregnancy because they did not have an examination for immune-deficiency virus. They did not know that they were being infected, and could not apply the new treatments that can contribute to stopping the passage of the virus from mother to child. If you are pregnant, please be examined for immune-deficiency virus detection. To receive confidential information regarding immune-deficiency virus and AIDs, call the 24-hour phone line at 1-800 344-7432.

Miles de mujeres perderán hijos por el SIDA, únicamente porque durante el embarazo no se someten a un examen de detección del VIH. No sabían que estaban infectadas, y no pudieron aprovechar los nuevos tratamientos que pueden contribuir a detener la propagación del virus de la madre al niño.
Si está embarazada, por favor, sométase a un examen de detección del VIH.
Para recibir información confidencial respecto al VIH y el SIDA, durante las 24 horas del día, llame al 1 800 344-7432.

Pediatric AIDS Foundation

Even the language preference of the Hispanic market varies widely. For example, studies show that a majority of the Hispanic market prefers to speak Spanish or both Spanish and English at home, but Hispanic populations in Texas are more likely to prefer English. A large majority of the Hispanic population prefers English-language media, but this preference is very much related to age. "Advertisers who want to target Hispanics between the ages of 18–34 should consider English language radio and television as primary media. The 35 and older market may require a mix of English and Spanish language broadcast media [for effective reach]."[25]

Beginning in 1732 when Benjamin Franklin published *Philadelphische Zeitung* (*Philadelphia Newspaper*), the foreign-language press has played a major role in this country. The Spanish-language press is the largest category of foreign-language newspapers, and the increasingly multicultural nature of the United States is reflected in a growing number of newspapers available in more than 40 languages. Virtually every language is represented by at least one newspaper. From French, Italian, and Czech to Vietnamese, Chinese, and Arabic, every part of the world is represented by a publication unique to some ethnic group.

The success of the ethnic press is largely determined by the same formula used by mainstream media—advertising support.

> Traditionally, the ethnic press survived on classified advertising and ads from local auto repair stores, grocers, and travel agents though a few well-established black and Hispanic newspapers have always attracted some mainstream advertisers. But now relatively large billings are going to publications that serve smaller and diverse communities. . . . Ethnic publications are key to tapping that market; they hone right in.[26]

WEEKLY NEWSPAPERS

Weekly newspapers fall into a number of categories: suburban papers covering events within some portion of a larger metropolitan area, traditional rural weeklies providing local coverage, specialty weeklies covering politics or the arts, and free shoppers with little editorial content. During the last 30 years, the complexion of the weekly newspaper field has changed dramatically. Far from its rural, small-town roots, the typical weekly is more likely to be located in a growing suburb, and rather than covering weddings and family reunions its major topics are probably zoning disputes, overcrowded schools, crime, and how to control future growth while increasing the industrial tax base.

After a 20-year period of decline, weeklies have grown dramatically in both numbers and circulation in recent years.

Weekly Circulation and Numbers

Year	Circulation per Paper	Number of Weeklies
1960	2,566	8,174
1970	3,660	7,612
1980	5,324	7,954
1990	7,309	7,550
1995	9,425	8,453

Source: *Facts About Newspapers 1996*, a publication of the Newspaper Association of America, p. 25.

[25]Wayne W. Melanson and Jerry C. Hudson, "Survey Results of Hispanic Media Usage, Language Preferences, and Perceptions of Advertising," in Gary B. Wilcox, ed., *Proceedings of the American Academy of Advertising, 1996,* p. 200.

[26]Sreenath Sreenivasan, "As Mainstream Papers Struggle, the Ethnic Press Is Thriving," *The New York Times,* July 22, 1996, p. C7.

Weekly growth will be concentrated in suburban and urban areas for the remainder of the 1990s and into the next century. Weeklies will occupy a separate niche for small retailers who cannot afford major dailies or who have a limited distribution area. These weeklies rarely are considered by large metro retailers or national advertisers. Consequently, there is little direct competition for either readers or advertisers between weeklies and dailies. The weekly battlefield is largely between traditional small-town, paid-circulation papers and the free circulation publications that have moved into many of these communities.

SUMMARY

There is no question that the daily newspaper remains a major advertising medium as well as the medium of choice for millions of households. However, in the future, newspaper executives face a number of challenges as they enter a period of transition and changing methods of doing business. A recent survey asked newspaper publishers to identify the major threat they perceived to the future well-being of the industry. Those most mentioned (and the percentage of respondents naming them) were

- increased competition from other media for readers' time (78 percent)
- increased competition from other traditional media for advertising dollars (58 percent)
- readers bypassing newspapers in favor of nontraditional competitors (56 percent).

Although these areas cover a multitude of specific problems, the common thread is that newspaper publishers know that marketing the medium to both advertisers and readers is going to be at the top of their agenda for years to come. The newspaper industry must find ways to reach nonreaders and occasional readers. The fact that many young adults do not read the newspaper with any regularity is an especially acute problem for the industry.

Given the growing competition for local advertising budgets, newspapers must develop ways of accommodating national advertisers if they are to significantly increase expenditures from advertising agencies. Newspapers must standardize all aspects of the buying and placing of ads. The NNN's attempt to build a national newspaper network is the latest hope for a move in that direction.

However, no amount of standardization will outweigh the perception by national advertisers that newspapers are unfairly priced. The huge local and national rate differentials are a primary impediment to increased national advertising investment. In addition, newspapers must be prepared to offer national discounts and value-added programs on an equal basis with their retail clients.

Compounding the difficulty of increasing national dollars is the defection of many local advertisers to other media. The newspaper no longer has a stranglehold on the local advertising dollar. Today's retailer can choose from a media menu of everything from direct mail to cable TV. The loss of readers and growing competition comes at a time when publishing costs and accompanying advertising rate increases are continuing to increase CPMs to unacceptable levels for some advertisers.

At the same time, newspapers must continue to experiment with alternative methods of reaching audiences to prepare for the electronic superhighway of the future. Larger newspapers have already made a number of strides in the area of technology. However, the major challenge for the future is how to make these alternative delivery systems widely accepted and profitable.

Despite these problems, it would be wrong to suggest that newspapers will not continue to be a viable medium in the future. However, newspapers will increasingly be forced to devote time and money to marketing themselves to readers and advertisers. This marketing orientation will mean new formats and designs, including color. It will also mean that the newspaper will have to appeal to specific audiences with editorial matter directed especially to them. Some editors worry that newspapers in the future will be edited according to readership surveys.

In terms of advertisers, newspapers must diversify the categories of products and services that use the paper. They can no longer depend solely on retail stores to provide the majority of their advertising. Total market coverage must be offered on an easy-to-buy basis for both local and national advertisers. We will continue to see consolidation of information companies where newspapers, cable and broadcast TV, city magazines, direct-mail firms, and virtually all other media will be owned by single conglomerates. Advertising will increasingly be sold on a cross-media basis, with newspapers being part of an overall communication package for advertisers.

REVIEW

1. How have regional advertising strategies by national advertisers impacted newspapers?
2. What are some of the primary problems with evening newspaper circulation?
3. Discuss the strategies involved in marketing newspapers to (a) readers and (b) advertisers.
4. What are the primary categories of newspaper advertising?
5. Contrast zoned editions with total market coverage plans in newspaper advertising.
6. What is the role of newspaper networks in advertising?
7. What are the three major categories of classified advertising?
8. What are some of the traditional impediments to the growth of national advertising?
9. What is the role of the National Newspaper Network?
10. Define the following terms:
    a. Short rate
    b. Rebate
    c. Value-added programs
    d. Combination rates
    e. Standard Advertising Unit (SAU)
11. What is the role of the electronic newspaper in the future?

TAKE IT TO THE NET

We invite you to visit the Russell/Lane page on the Prentice Hall Web site at
PHLIP **http://www.prenhall.com/phbusiness** for the bimonthly Russell/Lane update and for this chapter's World Wide Web exercise.

11

USING MAGAZINES

IN THE LAST **20** YEARS, MAGAZINES HAVE INCREASINGLY APPEALED TO THE SPECIALIZED TASTES OF A NUMBER OF DIVERSE AUDIENCES. THE MAGAZINE SUCCESS STORIES OF RECENT YEARS HAVE BEEN LARGELY THOSE PUBLICATIONS THAT IDENTIFY A NARROWLY DEFINED NICHE AND HOLD A LEADERSHIP POSITION AMONG BOTH READERS AND ADVERTISERS. BOTH CONSUMER AND TRADE PUBLICATIONS MUST BE SELECTIVE IN THE WAY THEY APPEAL TO THEIR AUDIENCES. AFTER READING THIS CHAPTER YOU WILL UNDERSTAND

- the evolution of magazines from a mass to a class medium
- financial support from both readers and advertisers
- characteristics of the successful magazine
- magazine options available to advertisers
- paid and controlled circulation
- differences between business and consumer magazines.

The magazine industry is undergoing dramatic changes in all aspects of the way it does business. "While the nature of magazines may remain constant, the industry which supports it and gives it life will always be fluid. Shifts in circulation patterns, growth in magazine advertising pages and revenue, and further advances in technological innovations are indicative of this dynamic magazine environment."[1]

There is little in the way of magazine production, distribution, circulation, or advertising that is not undergoing some type of innovation. From a marketing perspec-

---

[1] *The Magazine Handbook, 1994–95,* a publication of the Magazine Publishers of America (MPA), p. 1. Unless otherwise noted, information in this chapter is provided by the MPA.

tive, magazines exhibit many of the characteristics of radio. With many titles directly competing with each other, only a few in each category are successful. For example, although there are dozens of magazines directed toward women, five publications hold 43 percent of total advertising revenues (*McCall's, Good Housekeeping, Family Circle, Ladies' Home Journal, Woman's Day*).[2] Advertisers and audiences are being courted through growing fragmentation of formats and themes.

Although magazine advertising pages and circulation are at or near an all-time high, the combination of hefty increases in postage costs, dealer fees for newsstand sales, and increasing competition from other media for advertising dollars have eroded publishers' profits. Magazines have had to reposition themselves in the face of new competition, a fickle reading audience, and most of all, the marketing needs of national advertisers.

Consumer magazines do not represent a single unified medium with common strengths and weaknesses. Instead, there are simultaneous successes and failures among different categories of publications. For example, one list of 200 major magazines showed a range in annual circulation growth from a high of 46.8 percent to a low of −20.9 percent.[3] In a similar list of 50 major publications, annual percentage growth in advertising pages varied from a maximum of 74.7 percent to −14.0.[4] Throughout this chapter, we need to keep in mind that generalities about consumer magazines invariably encounter a number of exceptions.

To understand the contemporary consumer magazine industry, we have to examine two primary factors: (1) selectivity and (2) cost versus revenue considerations.

SELECTIVITY

A quick glance at those magazines with double-digit and even triple-digit growth in circulation and ad revenues gives an idea why selectivity is so important to magazine publishers. The successes of *Cigar Aficionado, Family PC, Fitness, Soap Opera Update,* and *Martha Stewart Living* give ample testimony to the importance of a well-defined editorial approach. Virtually without exception, the successful titles are those that offer readers and advertisers a narrowly focused editorial product in an environment suited to selling specific product categories. Not only are these publications targeted to identified audience segments, but their high-interest readers are usually willing to pay a premium for the magazines. In the Voice It Personal Note Recorder case history (pp. 288–289), note how specialized magazines were used to narrowly target prime prospects in the successful introduction of the product.

Today, publishers, like their radio counterparts, continue to fine-tune formats, seeking narrower and narrower audiences. For example, the general parenting magazine category has been joined by such subcategory publications as *Modern Dad, Black Child, Hip Mama,* and *Jewish Family & Life!* as publications that address special interests within the family setting. The American multicultural society is being reached by a number of publications, including *People en Español,* published by Time, Inc., and *Latina,* a publication supported in part by Essence Communications.[5]

The Evolution of the Modern Magazine

Although selectivity is one of the keys to contemporary magazine success, audience and editorial selectivity is actually rooted in the historical development of magazines. The magazines of the mid-nineteenth century were targeted to audiences of special interests,

---

[2]R. Craig Endicott, "Ad Age 300," *Advertising Age,* June 17, 1996, p. S1.

[3]Keith J. Kelly, "Magazines Stay on Downward Course in First Half," *Advertising Age,* August 26, 1996, p. 25.

[4]Keith J. Kelly, "Bytes, Bites Fuel Magazines' 5.1% Growth in '95 Ad Pages," *Advertising Age,* January 22, 1996, p. 33.

[5]Jeff Garigliano, "Is *Oneworld* Enough for Everyone?" *Folio,* September 1, 1996, p. 20.

case HISTORY

MARKETING SITUATION

The Voice It Personal Note Recorder was conceived and developed in 1994 as an easy-to-use, yet sophisticated, battery-operated digital note recorder. As the first product of its kind, the Voice It Personal Note Recorder was positioned as a better way to communicate personal thoughts or notes versus the old-fashioned handwritten method. The introduction of the new Voice It Personal Note Recorder, at a $79.00 retail price point, in effect created a new category (digital note recorders).

Based on advanced digital technology, the Voice It Personal Note Recorder stores information on a digital chip and does not require traditional magnetic tape, making it especially convenient, both in size and ease-of-use.

Business conditions made it imperative that Voice It Worldwide, a small start-up company, generate at least $7 million in sales in its first full year of business. Obstacles to accomplishing the sales goal were similar to those faced by other new product/category introductions:

• Small marketing budget
• Low brand awareness
• Limited retail distribution
• Under-staffed national sales force

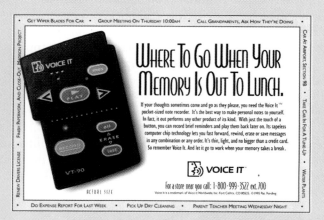

CAMPAIGN OBJECTIVES

Sales

• Achieve $7 million in sales in 1995 versus $2 million in second half 1994; representing a highly aggressive goal increase of 350%.

Distribution

• Increase retail outlets from 2,000 to 3,000 units; a 50% growth goal. Target efforts to office superstores,

department stores, electronic specialty outlets, catalog showrooms, and selected high-end mass merchants.

TARGET AUDIENCE

Voice It targeted adults, 25–54 (with a male skew), college graduates who were current "technology users."

The target audience selection was driven by syndicated research, which defined technology users as consumers indexing 120+ against use of computers, cellular phones, and personal recorders. Technology users were shown to be early adopters of new electronic/technologically advanced products, such as the Voice It digital note recorder. Additionally, this consumer was well educated and watched, listened to, and read news-based programs/publications. This consumer was employed primarily in white-collar professions, and was mobile, traveling often for business.

• Position Voice It Personal Note Recorders as an easy-to-use recording device that enhances one's personal communication and efficiency.

To help achieve Voice It's aggressive sales and distribution goals, advertising provided compelling product information to motivate interested readers/listeners to respond via a toll-free number designed to identify local retailers stocking Voice It products.

Four-color, half-page print ads featured actual-size product photography (reinforcing convenient size), arresting headlines and copy communicating Voice It's advanced technology and ease-of-use. Each ad's border copy contained example messages to magnify the volume of information each consumer must process and remember every day—reinforcing Voice It's benefit as a personal communication tool.

MEDIA STRATEGY

• Obtain 60%+ coverage of Voice It's target audience utilizing national consumer magazines. Newsweeklies and in-flight magazines were selected because they indexed extremely well (120+) against Voice It's target.

The introductory media program utilized two half-page, four-color ads, each containing its own coded 800 telephone number (directing callers to retail outlets in their area by zip code) to track responses by ad, by publication, by week for guidance in determining future media vehicles and creative executions. Employment of half-page ads resulted in greater media cost efficiency, and encouraged greater ad readership due to same-page editorial placement.

- Obtain 80%+ coverage of target audience utilizing spot radio in Voice It's top sales distribution markets. 60 radio (including 10 retailer tags) aired on top news talk formats in each market. Local retailer tags enhanced Voice It Worldwide's retailer support as part of its effort to expand distribution.

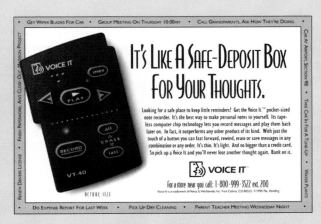

OTHER COMMUNICATIONS PROGRAMS

- Fitzgerald & Company developed a comprehensive public relations program to help build awareness, create demand, and gain support from industry spokespersons and syndicated consumer electronic columnists—both influential audiences critical to consumer education.
- To further enhance advertising and retail efforts, a Web site was designed and implemented

(http://www.voiceit.com) to merchandise Voice It products and to reinforce Voice It as a technologically advanced corporation. The site offers an on-line dealer locator, which directs consumers to all retail locations within 60 miles of their zip code. Secondary goal of the Web site was to provide a media tracking and demographic collection vehicle via an on-line contest featuring Voice It products as prizes.

- Point-of-purchase materials were developed and made available to key retail accounts, enabling consumers to see the actual size of the product and hear its remarkable sound reproduction capability.

EVIDENCE OF RESULTS

Sales

- Total 1995 sales of $13.5 million were achieved, exceeding Voice It's aggressive $7 million goal by 93%. Sales of $13.5 million represented a 675% increase over year ago gross sales.

Distribution

- Voice It retail distribution grew to 4,000 outlets, representing a 100% increase (versus a goal of +50%).

  Voice It obtained 100% saturation of the office superstore channel, 100% distribution in catalog showrooms, and a major presence in key upscale department stores nationally. Distribution expanded by June 1995 to include national distribution in Target, chain-wide distribution in May Company stores, and the two largest electronic specialty chains (Circuit City and Best Buy).

Courtesy: Voice It Worldwide, Inc. and Fitzgerald & Company.

sold at a high cost, and carried little advertising. Most magazines were literary, political, or religious in content and depended on readers or special interest groups to provide most of their financial support.

In the later years of the nineteenth century, a rising middle class, mass production, and national transportation combined to provide the opportunity for nationally distributed branded goods. The opportunities offered by national brands could be exploited only with the efficiencies of mass promotion. During the 1890s, a trio of publishers provided the beginnings for the ad-supported, mass-circulation magazine. Frank Munsey *(Munsey's)*, S. S. McClure *(McClure's)*, and Edward Bok *(Ladies' Home Journal)* brought low-cost magazines to an enthusiastic public.

Until the advent of radio in the 1920s, magazines were the only national advertising medium. Even after the introduction of radio, magazines were still the only *visual* medium available to national manufacturers. However, when television came on the scene in the 1950s, people's reading habits became viewing habits, and national magazines had to change to survive.

Magazines found themselves in a difficult situation. As a mass medium they could not compete with television's low *CPM*s. On the other hand, the mass magazines of the 1950s, such as *Life*, were not selective enough to reach narrowly defined target audiences demanded by many advertisers. Clearly, after more than 50 years of unchallenged success as a mass medium, magazines had to make some radical changes. In the future, only those magazines with a clear editorial focus will survive.

It is extremely difficult for general magazines to be successful. Even the largest circulation publications tend to appeal to a fairly narrowly defined market segment. For example, *Sports Illustrated, Time, Consumer Reports,* and *Modern Maturity,* all among the circulation leaders, would not be classified as general editorial magazines. Only newspaper-distributed *Parade* and *USA Weekend* have both huge circulations and general appeal. However, as discussed in chapter 10, they are hybrid publications, which many consider more newspapers than magazines.

COSTS AND REVENUES

Magazine publishers are faced with a number of costs that are largely out of their control. Postage and printing expenses continue to increase at a rate higher than advertising prices. In addition, magazines find that costs to maintain and increase circulation are a major expense. From 1980 to the present, marketing costs have risen almost 25 percent, reflecting the keen competition from hundreds of magazines fighting for readers' time and money.

Another problem magazines face is the concentration of magazine advertising dollars among a relatively few product categories. The top five advertising categories (automotive, direct response, cosmetics, computers, and business and consumer services) account for more than 48 percent of all revenues. Even more alarming for publishers is the fact that of the top six brands in terms of magazine spending, five are automobiles (see Exhibit 11.1).

In dealing with advertisers, magazines face two major problems: dependence on a thin advertising base and a constant need for rate hikes.

Dependence on a Thin Advertising Base

The concentration of advertising dollars in so few industries means that magazines are vulnerable to substantial decreases in revenue when these companies face an economic downturn or if they change their media strategy. Throughout the past 20 years magazines have tried to insulate themselves from the vagaries of advertising by shifting a disproportionate percent of the cost of magazines to readers.

Magazines passed a major milestone in 1985 when, for the first time, advertisers contributed less than half of total magazine revenues. That percentage has fallen steadily

Top 25 Magazine Advertisers

Rank	Advertiser	Advertising Spending		
		1995	1994	% Change
1	General Motors Corp.	$412.0	$378.0	9.0
2	Philip Morris Cos.	373.8	294.1	27.1
3	Ford Motor Co.	254.3	241.9	5.1
4	Procter & Gamble Co.	251.5	196.4	28.0
5	Chrysler Corp.	231.1	148.9	55.2
6	Toyota Motor Corp.	121.1	128.2	−5.5
7	Time Warner	119.9	110.1	8.9
8	Unilever NV	109.5	113.4	−3.5
9	IBM Corp.	109.2	60.4	80.7
10	L'Oreal	98.4	125.4	−21.5
11	Johnson & Johnson	85.3	82.8	3.0
12	Joh. A. Benckiser GmbH	77.8	71.5	8.9
13	Walt Disney Co.	76.7	76.2	0.6
14	Sony Corp.	73.3	75.3	−2.6
15	B.A.T. Industries	70.4	63.8	10.3
16	Microsoft Corp.	69.7	32.6	114.0
17	Seagram Co.	65.7	50.6	29.8
18	Bertelsmann AG	64.5	58.6	10.1
19	Honda Motor Co.	62.6	63.0	−0.6
20	Estee Lauder Inc.	57.3	48.6	17.9
21	Nestle SA	54.7	39.9	37.2
22	Milk Industry Foundation	53.6	0.0	NA
23	RJR Nabisco	52.7	54.8	−3.7
24	AT&T Corp.	52.6	35.3	48.9
25	Roll International	52.4	60.4	−13.2

Note: Dollars are in millions.

Source: Competitive Media Reporting; Ad Age's 100 Leading National Advertisers (*Advertising Age*, September 30).

exhibit

11.1

Magazine advertising is concentrated in a relatively few industries.

Courtesy: Advertising Age.
Source: Advertising Age, October 14, 1996, p. S14.

to the point that readers now account for 70 percent of total revenues, and the costs of single copies and subscriptions continue to rise. Interestingly, both publishers and advertisers are happy with the change.

Advertisers view readers who are willing to pay a premium for a publication as being more interested in a magazine and its advertising than are pass-along readers or those subscribers enticed with deep discount prices. Publishers, for their part, see a shift to reader support as a method of protecting their publications during periods of economic downturn. As one publisher observed, "Attending to reader-driven markets means we can better control our destiny, especially in the face of advertisers with changeable marketing plans. And by charging the prices we do—and delivering a quality product—we're able to be very profitable."[6]

Constant Need for Rate Hikes

Because of the high fixed cost of magazine publishing, magazines have had to raise advertising rates on a continuing basis, even when circulation did not seem to warrant an increase. Exhibit 11.2 (p. 292) shows the long-term effect of these increases on *CPM* levels compared to other major media. One might expect the competitive nature of the magazine industry to restrain rate increases, but in fact the trend is just the opposite.

These increases in advertising rates have created a somewhat contentious environment between advertisers and publishers. Commenting on magazine rate increases, one advertising executive commented, "advertisers don't want to pick up the full tab for magazines' rising paper, postage and ink costs. It's time for publishers to show faith in

---

[6]Leah Rosch, "Gray Matters," *Folio,* June 1, 1996, p. 67.

Media Cost-Per-Thousand Trends 1983–1996

	Magazines	Network TV	Cable TV	Spot TV	Newspapers	Network Radio	Spot Radio	Outdoor
1983	100	99	100	99	100	101	99	100
1984	108	111	89	109	109	107	108	108
1985	116	120	87	116	116	116	115	116
1986	122	126	87	123	124	123	121	119
1987	126	135	92	128	131	119	126	123
1988	134	144	102	132	140	115	134	127
1989	141	151	107	136	148	127	123	132
1990	150	161	109	147	154	129	127	136
1991	161	154	112	141	158	132	124	135
1992	166	152	115	148	160	119	119	131
1993	174	157	120	152	163	125	127	131
1994	182	164	122	162	168	123	135	133
1995	192	176	129	173	178	126	143	135
1996	205	188	138	185	189	129	151	139

Source: McCann-Erickson, Robert J. Coen.

Between 1993 and 1996, network and spot TV as well as spot radio *CPMs* have been increasing faster than all other media including magazines. Network radio and outdoor have had the smallest cost increases and are up only 29 percent and 39 percent, respectively, since 1983.

exhibit

11.2

Courtesy: Magazine Publishers of America.
Source: The Magazine Handbook, 1996–97, a publication of the Magazine Publishers of America, p. 24.

their products by asking readers to pay a fair share. Which only can make advertisers more willing to pick up their own part of the tab."[7]

As if they did not have enough problems, magazines also face the loss of millions of dollars in cigarette advertising if suggested U.S. Food and Drug Administration (FDA) guidelines are implemented. One of the FDA proposals would limit cigarette advertising to black and white, text-only ads in magazines with significant numbers of readers under 18 years old. Some magazines in that category receive as much as 6 to 10 percent of their revenues from cigarettes. Regardless of whether these specific rules are implemented, it seems obvious that the current climate is working against significant investments by cigarette advertisers in traditional media in the foreseeable future.

Magazine publishers are finding that some of their costs in printing and paper have risen less rapidly than in earlier years. Furthermore, many magazines are experimenting with desktop publishing systems designed to save on typesetting and design. However, because visual quality is one of the major advantages of magazines, they must take care not to cut costs to the point that they sacrifice quality.

Finally, publishers have begun to experiment with alternative methods of distribution. A number of alternative delivery companies that can distribute magazines have been established. A major problem with some of these organizations is that it is cost effective only in areas with high circulation density. Readers for many small circulation specialty publications are so widely dispersed that these delivery systems are not cost effective. Currently, less than 1 percent of magazines are delivered by alternative systems.

Media imperatives
Based on research by Simmons Media Studies, showed the importance of using both TV and magazines for full market coverage.

MEDIA COMPETITION AND MEDIA IMPERATIVES (COMPARATIVES)

Whereas television, magazines' major competitor for national advertising dollars, continues to market itself by outlining its strengths relative to other media, magazine marketing strategy has largely been a matter of pitting one publication against another. Consequently, magazines tend to expend their energy fighting each other and at the same time providing ammunition for their media rivals.

---

[7]"Mag Prices Must Get Real," *Advertising Age,* August 19, 1996, p. 16.

Of course, publishers are aware of the long-term damage done to their industry and are taking steps to correct the situation. Working with the Magazine Publishers of America, the leading trade association, individual magazines have supported a number of research projects to sell the value of magazine advertising. One of the most effective approaches is to show that certain audiences can be reached effectively only through magazines.

This study divides the U.S. population into five groups, or quintiles, according to their degree of magazine usage. These groups are called *magazine imperatives,* or comparatives, because they are heavy users of magazines (who are also light users of TV) who can be reached only through magazines. There are other groups that are television comparatives, that is, heavy TV viewers (and light magazine users) who can be effectively reached only using television.

The importance of this research to magazines is that it shows an inverse relationship between heavy television viewers and heavy magazine readers. Consequently, most large national advertisers cannot reach a mass audience by using only television. In addition, the magazine comparative audience represents much better prospects for a number of product categories than television. In recent years, magazines have taken this research one step further and developed a concept called *Media QuadMaps,* which offer a two-dimensional presentation of television and magazine usage by consumer segments or product usage.

Exhibit 11.3 demonstrates how household income is related to media usage. Households with incomes between $40,000 and $49,999 are likely to share their magazine and television usage very evenly (the midpoint of the *x* and *y* axes would mean a person was exactly average in magazines and television usage). Brands seeking to reach households with less than $20,000 income would virtually exclude magazines from the schedule, and those seeking to reach high-income families would depend heavily on magazines.

Magazine executives applaud this type of research. It favorably positions magazines in relation to television and it also demonstrates the power of magazines as a targeted marketing tool. It does not remove the problems of magazine-against-magazine competition, but it is a beneficial first step in that direction.

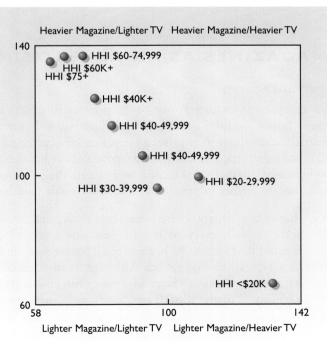

exhibit

11.3

Magazine readers are affluent and have household incomes (HHI) of $40,000 or more per year. Those living in less affluent households, with incomes less than $40,000 a year, watch more television than the average U.S. adult.

Data are based on total number of adults; scale shows percent from average.

Courtesy: Magazine Publishers of America.

Source: The Magazine Handbook, 1996–97, a publication of the Magazine Publishers of America, p. 53.

Source: *MRI Spring 1996 Report* © 1996, MRI. All rights reserved.

CROSS-MEDIA BUYS

Magazines, with their high credibility as a source of information and advertising, are an ideal element in the total marketing mix. Exploiting these strengths, magazines have moved to sell themselves as part of a synergistic approach to an overall media plan. Today more magazine advertising is sold as part of a buying concept known as **cross-media buys.**

In the past, most cross-media buys were put together by multimedia companies that offered special advertising programs and discounts that involved a number of their properties. For example, major media conglomerates such as the Hearst Corporation not only offer cross-media buys from among their many holdings, but will tailor package buys for individual advertisers. As they state, "Hearst offers advertisers a range of media and marketing options, including broadcast and cable television, videos, radio, newspapers, in-store promotions, custom publishing, data-base management, and product sampling opportunities."[8]

Magazine publishers have been prime movers in developing cross-media vehicles that take advantage of the equity of their publications. Often, these magazine-initiated cross-media projects involve broadcast vehicles. As early as 1931, *Time* magazine produced a radio series called "The March of Time," which featured enactments of current news stories. Likewise, since the 1960s, *National Geographic* television documentaries have been among the most popular and they are a regular television feature.

As cable outlets demand more programming, we will see magazines develop more broadcast properties. Some of these, such as CNN/SI, a cooperative effort between the Cable News Network and *Sports Illustrated* magazine, constitute entirely new networks. In other cases, a magazine might be a spin-off of a television property. For example, the highly successful *ESPN, The Magazine* was introduced in March 1998.

Magazine cross-media developments fit in perfectly with the current emphasis on the media mix and segmented audience identification. By using an established magazine, an advertiser is guaranteed high name recognition and credibility with that portion of a publication's audience that is interested in some activity or topic. There is little question that the cross-media market will become a normal extension of the business of virtually every major publisher. An indirect benefit of cross-media selling is that it further emphasizes the media synergism gained through a combination of magazines and television.

MAGAZINES AS AN ADVERTISING MEDIUM

Advantages

As discussed in chapter 7, one of the primary functions of a media planner is to determine how a medium or individual vehicle will enhance the advertising objectives of a particular company. It requires an experienced planner to sort through the numerous titles, formats, rates, and editorial viewpoints of the hundreds of consumer magazines available to advertisers. In this section we examine the primary considerations that determine whether magazines in general, or a particular title, will be included in a media plan.

1. *Audience selectivity.* There is a magazine targeted for virtually every market segment, and essentially everyone reads at least one magazine during a given month. It is estimated that almost 90 percent of all adults read an average of 11.8 different issues in a typical 30-day period. Although total readership is important, the primary strength of magazines as an advertising medium is reaching specific audience niches. Recently, 7 of the top 10 magazines in terms of total circulation lost readers. Al-

---

Cross-media buys
Several media, or several vehicles within one medium, package themselves to be sold to advertisers to gain a synergistic communication effect and efficiencies in purchasing time or space.

---

[8] *Standard Rate and Data Consumer Magazine & Agri-Media Source,* a publication of SRDS, May 1994, p. 297.

though many high-profile magazines search for a market in a world of instant communication, publications targeted at hobbies and other diversions are having great success. "Niche magazines are very, very valuable and it is clearly the most important development in print publishing. We like to think that more people are interested in the news of the world than in basement handicrafts, but that isn't necessarily the case."[9]

2. *Exposure to a company's primary target audiences.* Magazines can reach narrowly defined audience segments as defined by demographics, product usage, or readers' lifestyles. Rhino Records has developed a strong following among serious music listeners who are interested in pop albums from past decades. Magazine advertising for the company has created a host of pop-culture allusions from the past (see Exhibit 11.4). The ads invite readers to study the illustration to find various personalities and symbols from the past.

3. *Long life and creative options.* Unlike a perishable broadcast message or the daily newspaper, many magazines are kept and referred to for a long period of time, and others are passed along to other readers. MRI, a leading magazine research firm, suggests that the average magazine has more than four readers per copy and is accessible for approximately 28 weeks. In addition, magazines are portable; readers report that approximately 60 percent of their reading is done out of home. In this disposable media world, magazines are alone as a tangible vehicle. Magazines are

exhibit

11.4

There is a magazine for every target market.

Courtesy: BBDO West.

[9]William Spain, "In General, Where Are the Readers?" *Advertising Age,* October 14, 1996, p. S6.

often used as reference sources—articles are clipped, back issues are filed, and readers may go back to a favorite magazine numerous times before finally discarding it. Advertisers potentially benefit from each of these exposures.

The magazine is also a visual medium with a number of creative options. Magazines offer advertisers a wide range of flexible formats such as double-page spreads, bright colors, and even product sampling. Magazines are particularly suited to long copy. Discussions of detailed product attributes for automobiles and appliances as well as advertising for financial services all lend themselves to magazines.

4. *Availability of demographic and geographic editions.* Chapter 10 discussed newspaper zoning as a reaction to advertiser demand for selected segments of a publication's circulation. On a national scale, magazine demographic and geographic editions meet the same demands of large advertisers. National magazines generally offer some type of regional or demographic breakout of their total circulation. These special editions are called **partial runs** and are so common and important to magazine advertising that they are discussed separately in a later section of this chapter.

5. *Qualitative factors.* One of the most important elements of magazines is their credibility with readers. Advertisers buy magazines based on their ability to deliver a particular audience at a reasonable cost. However, more than any other medium, magazines depend on less easily measured, qualitative factors for their success.

Exhibit 11.5 shows that readers overwhelmingly regard magazines as the most effective medium for gaining new ideas and information. The targeted content of most magazines allows them to become leading authorities in their field. Car owners look to *Road & Track,* hunters to *Sports Afield,* stockholders to *Fortune,* and gardeners to *Southern Living* as sources of reliable information. As discussed earlier, the positioning of magazines as authoritative sources has led to so many cross-media spinoffs into other media. Sometimes the relationship between media credibility and advertising is direct. For example, the Good Housekeeping Seal has been used by *Good Housekeeping* magazine for more than 50 years as a method of endorsing products that are advertised in the publication. In other cases, the connection is less obvious, but nevertheless an important part of the qualitative selling environment of magazine advertising.

The niche character of most magazines offers advertisers a compatible editorial environment for their messages. When a person picks up *Golf Digest, Money, Glamour,* or *PC Computing,* there is little doubt about their interests. These same readers also watch prime-time television, listen to the radio on the way home from work, and see numerous billboards each day. However, it is difficult to anticipate what they are thinking

Partial runs
When magazines offer less than their entire circulation to advertisers. Partial runs include demographic, geographic, and split-run editions.

e x h i b i t

11.5

Courtesy: Magazine Publishers of America.
Source: The Magazine Handbook, 1996–97, a publication of the Magazine Publishers of America, p. 45.

Magazines Are the Most Effective Medium for Knowledge and Usable Ideas

Medium	U.S. Adults (%)
Magazines	95
Newspapers	74
Television	72
Radio	9
Total	**100**

Source: Study of Media Involvement VII 1996, conducted by Beta Research, Inc. Based on net of 12 measured product categories.

The *Study of Media Involvement VII* revealed that of four media, magazines were, by far, the medium that consumers most counted on for their main source of knowledge, information, and usable ideas. This was true across the board for all the major areas of their lives, from cars to financial issues to health.

about at these moments. On the other hand, specialized magazines can practically guarantee a synergism between reader and editorial content.

Despite the recent attention given to the qualitative nature of magazines, the ultimate measure of magazines as an advertising vehicle will be determined by their ability to deliver prime prospects at a competitive cost. Media planners will continue to judge magazines on a cost-efficiency basis using criteria such as *CPMs* and reach and frequency. The ultimate evaluation of magazines, as with any medium, is whether they can deliver the right audience, at the right price, and in the right environment.

Disadvantages

Despite the many advantages that magazines offer advertisers, there are several problems that must be considered before buying magazine advertising.

1. *High cost.* Magazines generally are the most expensive media on a *CPM* basis. It is not unusual for specialized magazines to have *CPM* levels of more than $100 compared to $10 to $20 for even relatively low-rated television shows. Of course, magazines point out that these high costs are tempered by very selective audiences. Ironically, as magazines have refined their audiences, they find that many advertisers are complaining about reach levels. Major advertisers find that in order to reach a majority of their prospects they may have to buy several magazines and then risk some unacceptable overlap in readership.

2. *Long **closing dates**.* Because of the printing process, most magazine advertisements must be prepared well ahead of publication. Unlike the spontaneity of radio and newspapers, magazines tend to be inflexible in reacting to changing market conditions. For example, a magazine advertisement may not run until 8 to 10 weeks after an advertiser submits it. This long lead time makes it difficult for advertisers to react to current marketing conditions either in scheduling space or developing competitive copy. The long closing dates are one reason why most magazine copy is very general.

   Many magazines have one date for space reservations and a later date for material submitted. Normally, the space contract is noncancelable. It is not unusual for a magazine to require that space be reserved two months prior to publication and material sent six weeks before publication. Some publications require that material be submitted with the order.

   Many magazines have sought to overcome the competitive disadvantage of long closing dates by providing **fast-close advertising.** As the name implies, fast-close allows advertisers to submit ads much closer to publication dates than standard closing dates allow. At one time, fast-close was very expensive and carried a significant premium compared to other advertising. However, competitive pressure has forced many publications to offer fast-close at little or no extra expense.

   The use of computer technology and satellite transmission has allowed magazines to offer major advertisers fast-close services that would have been impossible a few years ago. In some cases, advertisers can submit an advertisement as little as two days before the close date. However, although fast close insertion costs have been reduced, it still is an added expense for advertisers.

The remaining sections of this chapter examine some specific features and techniques involved in buying advertising in magazines.

FEATURES OF MAGAZINE ADVERTISING

Partial-Run Magazine Editions

Earlier in this chapter, we mentioned that demographic and geographic editions are a major feature that magazines provide to advertisers. Partial-run editions allow an

Closing date
Date when all advertising material must be submitted to a publication.

Fast-close advertising
Some magazines offer short-notice ad deadlines, sometimes at a premium cost.

advertiser to buy some segment of the total circulation, which is known as the **full-run edition** of a publication. Partial-run editions give advertisers with less than national product distribution or with regional marketing requirements an opportunity to use magazines. In addition, partial-runs allow advertisers to reach prime prospects among a magazine's readers without the waste circulation of full-run advertising.

There are approximately 200 magazines that offer some form of partial-run editions. Magazines receive almost 12 percent of total advertising revenues from these editions. The most common type of partial-run editions are geographical. In some smaller circulation magazines, the circulation may be broadly divided into areas of the country. However, for some major magazines, advertisers can choose from more than 100 circulation options.

Time magazine sells advertising space in state editions and top-50 metropolitan editions as well as 11 regional editions. In addition, advertisers are permitted to tailor their advertising buys from among the various regional editions. Many advertisers want to move beyond simple geographical circulation breakouts and reach target segments according to demographic or lifestyle characteristics.

Again, a major publication such as *Time* will provide advertisers with editions that reach readers with certain attributes, regardless of the area of the country in which they live. For example, "*Time* Top Management" reaches only executives at the president or CEO level, "*Time* Women Select" is distributed to women in management positions or living in high-income households, and "*Time* Campus" encompasses the college market.

As advertiser demand to reach narrow target audiences increases and the techniques honed by direct response and other direct marketing strategies become more prevalent, we will see most magazines offering some form of partial-run circulation. Computer technology and advances in high-speed printing are allowing magazines to meet these advertiser requirements.

Split-Run Editions A special form of the partial-run edition is the split-run. Whereas most partial-run editions are intended to meet special marketing requirements of advertisers, split-run editions normally are used by advertisers and publishers for testing purposes. The simplest form of split-run test involves an advertiser buying a regional edition (a full run is usually not bought because of the expense) and running different advertisements in every other issue.

Each advertisement is the same size and runs in the same position in the publication. The only difference is the element being tested. It may be a different headline, illustration, product benefit, or even price. A coupon is normally included, and the advertiser can then determine which version of the advertisement drew the highest response. This split-run technique is called an A/B split. Half of the audience gets version A and half version B.

As the competition for readers has grown, so has the use of split-run tests by magazines themselves. Magazines sometimes experiment with different covers for the same issue. The split-run technique has been instrumental in providing publishers and advertisers with insight into how magazine advertising can be most effective. Partial-run and split-run editions offer a number of benefits to advertisers (and in some cases to publishers):

1. Geographic editions allow advertisers to offer products only in areas where they are sold. For example, snow tires can be promoted in one area, regular tires in another.
2. Partial-runs can localize advertising and support dealers or special offers from one region to another. As advertisers increasingly adopt local and regional strategies, the partial-run advantages will become even more apparent.
3. Split-run advertising allows advertisers to test various elements of a campaign in a realistic environment before embarking on a national roll out.

4. Regional editions allow national advertisers to develop closer ties with their retailers by listing regional outlets. This strategy also provides helpful information to consumers for products that lack widespread distribution.

Partial-run editions also have some disadvantages that make them less than ideal for all advertising situations:

1. *CPM* levels are usually much more expensive than full-run advertising in the same publication, and closing dates can be as much as a month earlier than other advertising.

2. In the case of demographic editions, the lack of newsstand distribution for these advertisements can be a major disadvantage if single-copy sales are significant for the publication.

3. Some publications run their partial-run advertising in a special section set aside for such material (this is called banking). There also may be special restrictions placed on partial-run advertising. For example, such advertising often must be full-page, and only four-color will be accepted by some publications.

Selective binding
Binding different material directed to various reader segments in a single issue of a magazine.

Selective Binding **Selective binding** attempts to make the customization of partial-run editions even more sophisticated. Although the concept of selective binding is essentially the same as that of partial-run advertising, it is usually used to refer to different editorial material or large advertising sections that are placed in less than the full-run of a publication. Using computer technology and sophisticated printing techniques, advertisers and publishers can develop advertising and editorial material specifically for one group or even for individual readers.

For example, *Money* magazine includes in each edition a listing of the best credit lenders in the geographical area of the subscriber. The subscriber's name is printed in the heading of the list. The technique personalizes each issue for the individual reader. Because *Money* offers ideas on money management, the individualization offered by selective binding gives readers a feeling that they are being served on a personal basis.

Selective binding first gained popularity among major farm publications. Articles and advertisements were published in editions delivered to farmers that raised only certain types of crops or livestock. In recent years, selective binding has been offered to advertisers by consumer magazines on a limited basis.

Selective binding is most useful when there are significant subcategories of larger target markets. Occasionally, a magazine will offer selective binding that is fully integrated into the editorial format of a magazine. More commonly, the technique is used with multipage advertising inserts distributed to a select audience segment identified by age, income, or other factors.

Selective binding is an example of a technology that, to be successful, must be advertiser driven. That is, advertisers must be convinced that selective binding offers enough value to justify the additional expense. Many advertising executives think that the practical applications of selective binding are more apparent for business and farm publications than for consumer magazines for which there are a number of selective publications. Like interactive television, selective binding is a technology that is readily available but widespread demand by either advertisers or consumers is not yet apparent.

Obviously, the widespread use of selective binding has major implications for direct mail. If the technique becomes widely used, advertisers could combine the individual characteristics of direct mail with the credible environment of the magazine. Just as important, selective binding costs the advertiser about double what a normal magazine ad costs, whereas direct mail *CPM*s generally cost five times those of consumer magazines. Like most partial-run techniques, a major drawback of selective binding is that it can be used only for subscribers.

Because selective binding adopts some of the techniques of direct response, it also raises the same questions of readers' concerns with invasion of privacy. If subscribers are targeted by anything more than name and address, they may regard selective binding as inappropriate, with negative ramifications to both the advertiser and magazine. Still, a custom-made magazine, including both editorial and advertising material of specific interest to an individual reader, is an intriguing concept.

City Magazines

Magazines directed to readers within a particular city are not a new idea. *Town Topics* was published in New York City in the late nineteenth century, but most observers credit *San Diego* magazine, first published in the 1940s, as being the forerunner of the modern city magazine. Today, city magazines are available in virtually every major city.

Two major trends in recent years have characterized the growth of the city magazine:

1. A number of magazines have been introduced into smaller communities. Whereas the city magazine was formerly a domain of metropolitan communities, we now find successful publication in cities with populations of less than 100,000, such as Athens and Macon, Georgia (see Exhibit 11.6).
2. Like the general magazine industry, city magazines have undergone a period of specialization. During its earlier years, the typical city magazine was a general publi-

exhibit

11.6

City magazines are popular in markets of any size.

Courtesy: Macon Magazine.

It's Not Just Advertising

● ●

Increasingly, companies are asking their marketing executives and agencies to utilize all facets of marketing communication in the most creative way possible.

The interrelationships of the various fields of marketing communication are highlighted throughout text and examples in the Fourtheenth Edition.

● ●

INTEGRATED
MARKETING

cation about the entertainment, personalities, and culture of a metropolitan area. However, in recent years we have seen local publications dealing with relatively narrow segments of the life of a community. For example, many publishers are combining the traditional strengths of the city magazines with specialized publication content, and initiating such titles as *Chicago Bride* and *Atlanta Home*.

The financial health of city magazines tends to be cyclical. During the economic downturn of the early 1990s many city magazines experienced significant decreases in advertising pages. A soft economy tends to be seen first in areas such as retailing and automobile sales, two prime categories of city magazine advertising. In addition, city magazines are normally a supplement to mainline advertising for many of the magazines' clients. Consequently, when advertising is decreased, they are often among the first to be excluded.

Despite being regarded as a niche medium, city magazines are an important medium to a number of advertisers and product categories. Advertisers find these publications ideal to reach an affluent, urban audience. In fact, readership studies show that city magazines appeal to a significantly higher education and income group than any but the most selective national publications.

City publications are in some ways a hybrid between small circulation specialty publications and the partial-run editions of national magazines. They have an advantage over both in reaching upscale local audiences with editorial and advertising content specifically directed to their interests.

Magazines and Psychographic Research

As mentioned earlier, magazines cannot effectively compete with other media on a cost basis because advertisers can usually find less expensive media. However, magazines offer an environment that projects a style of living to both advertisers and readers. Advertisers are interested in the demographics of the audience, and they are also interested in how the readers think of themselves when they read a particular publication. The *Playboy* man and the *Cosmopolitan* woman are as much a matter of readers' perception as reality.

Chapter 7 discussed the PRIZM system of categorizing people by their lifestyle characteristics. Increasingly, magazines use psychographic and lifestyle research to sell advertisers on the qualitative aspects of their audiences. Unlike many other media, magazines offer advertisers relatively high levels of audience involvement. Consequently, magazine advertisers are more apt to use understated creative approaches as contrasted to the hard-sell advertising found in so many other media.

MAGAZINE ELEMENTS

Once an advertiser has made the difficult choice of which magazine to select among the hundreds of options, the job is not over. Now the media buyer must decide the size, color, placement, and format that will best serve the advertiser's marketing goals and the creative message.

Page Size

The page size of a magazine is the type area, not the size of the actual page. For convenience, the size of most magazines is characterized as *standard size* (about 8 by 10 inches, such as *Time*) or *small* (about $4\frac{3}{8}$ by $6\frac{1}{2}$ inches, such as *Reader's Digest*). There also are a few oversized publications, such as *Rolling Stone*, but they tend to be the exception. When ready to order printing plates, the media buyer must get the exact sizes from the publisher's latest rate card, because sizes may change.

Position and Space-Buying Designations

Space in magazines is generally sold in terms of full pages and fractions thereof (half pages, quarter pages, three columns or one column; see Exhibit 11.7). The small ads in the shopping pages of many magazines are generally sold by the line. Most magazines are flexible about allowing one page or double page ads to be broken up into separate units. Advertisers are constantly trying to determine optimum ad placement, and for many years they have conducted research to determine the best position for their advertisements. Traditionally, advertisers have regarded right-hand pages at the front of the magazine, preferably near related editorial matter, as the ideal ad placement. "FFRHPOE," or "far forward, right-hand page opposite editorial," is routinely stamped on many insertion orders delivered to magazines.

Publishers, faced with growing placement requests, are in an impossible situation trying to accommodate too many advertisers in too few spaces. Publishers are particularly frustrated because most research shows that position tends to add little to the efficiency of most advertising (see Exhibit 11.8).

Magazine covers are the positions that consistently produce significantly elevated readership levels. The front cover of a magazine is called the *first cover,* which is seldom, if ever, sold in American consumer magazines (although it is sold in business publications). The inside of the front cover is called the *second cover,* the inside of the back cover is the *third cover,* and the back cover the *fourth cover.* Normally, advertisers pay a premium for a cover position.

Studies show that the second cover achieves almost 30 percent more attention than an inside page; the third cover, 22 percent; and the fourth cover 22 percent.[10] Although

exhibit

11.7

Various Ways of Using Magazine Space

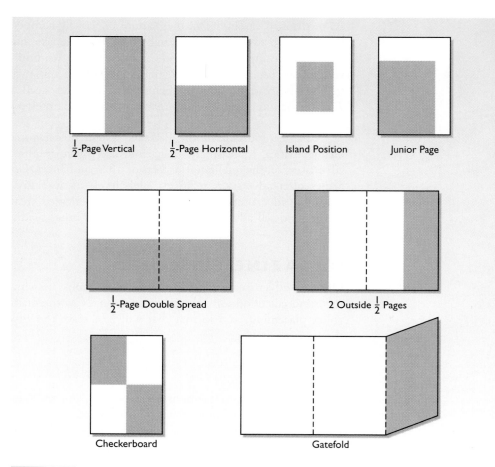

$\frac{1}{2}$-Page Vertical $\frac{1}{2}$-Page Horizontal   Island Position   Junior Page

$\frac{1}{2}$-Page Double Spread   2 Outside $\frac{1}{2}$ Pages

Checkerboard   Gatefold

[10] *The Magazine Handbook, 1994–95,* a publication of the Magazine Publishers of America, p. 29.

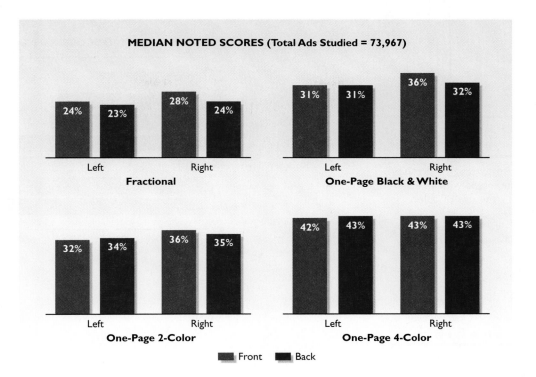
cover positions almost always result in higher readership, they also cost significantly more than inside pages. Therefore, cover *CPM*s may be higher than those for inside pages, even with the covers' increased attention scores.

Research seems to overwhelmingly support the contention that "In general, position alone does not affect readership of an ad or increase awareness for a brand. A strong creative execution will perform well regardless of its placement in the magazine. A 'bad ad' will not perform well even if it is in the front of the book."[11]

Ad Color and Size

The ability to present products in realistic color has long been a major sales advantage for magazines. In fact, until the advent of color television in the 1960s and high-speed printing for direct mail, color was a unique advantage for magazines for most of this century. Unlike ad positioning, there is irrefutable evidence that color significantly increases the interest and readership of magazine advertising (see Exhibit 11.9, p. 304). The specific ad size and use of color add dramatically to the value of advertising. Exhibit 11.10 (p. 304) demonstrates the benefits of combining size and color in various advertising formats. Notice that the two elements go hand in hand, with both color and size increasing readership.

An interesting feature concerning advertising color is that most research indicates that four-color has much more impact than two-color. The increase in readership for two-color versus black-and-white is negligible. However, four-color advertising has a marked effect on readership. Because adding color and/or increasing size adds significantly to the cost of advertising, it is important to use these elements as efficiently as possible.

As advertising space increases, the size of the audience does not grow proportionately (nor does the cost). For example, a full-page advertisement may be seen by 40 percent of a magazine's readers. If we double the space to a two-page spread, we can reasonably expect to increase readership by 33 to 50 percent (even though we have increased the space

---

[11] *The Magazine Handbook, 1994–95,* a publication of the Magazine Publishers of America, p. 27.

exhibit

11.9

Advertising readership
increases with size and
the use of color.

Courtesy: Cahners Publishing
Co., Cahners Advertising
Research Report No. 105.1B.

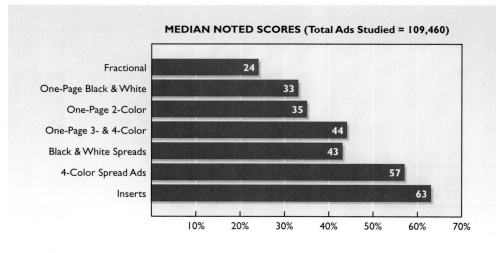

MEDIAN NOTED SCORES (Total Ads Studied = 109,460)

Fractional	24
One-Page Black & White	33
One-Page 2-Color	35
One-Page 3- & 4-Color	44
Black & White Spreads	43
4-Color Spread Ads	57
Inserts	63

exhibit

11.10

Magazine advertising
allows a variety of
creative executions.

Courtesy: Cramer-Krasselt.

*N*othing dresses up your traditional holiday
desserts like the original taste of Reddi-wip whipped cream.

by 100 percent). The reason, of course, is that as size increases there are not enough non-exposed readers remaining to continue to increase readership at the same rate.

Even though the increase in audience exposures is not proportionate to increases in magazine ad size, larger space allows more creative flexibility. Advertising objectives that require long copy can be much more effectively presented in a larger space. It also is important to remember that averages do not hold for every circumstance. For example, Magazine Publishers of America research shows that two-page spreads add virtually nothing to the readership of floor covering, wine, or tanning lotion advertising. On the other hand, advertisements for import cars, traveler's checks, and major appliances increased readership by as much as 50 percent with two-page spreads. These findings point out again that the specific objectives and creative approach must be considered in designing magazine advertising.

Bleed Pages

Bleed
Printed matter that runs over the edges of an outdoor board or of a page, leaving no margin.

Magazine advertising is able to use a number of formats and designs unavailable or impractical in other media. A common technique is bleed advertising, in which the ad runs all the way to the edge of the page with no border. **Bleed** ads are used to gain attention and use all the space available. Without a border, the advertisement does not have the appearance of being confined to a particular space. Typically, bleed advertising will be seen by 10 to 15 percent more readers than nonbleed advertising.

There is no particular pattern for premium charges for bleed advertising. For example, *TV Guide* and *Reader's Digest* have no extra charge for bleed advertising, *Newsweek* and *Rolling Stone* each have a 5 percent surcharge, and *People* magazine has a levy of 15 percent. In the competitive marketplace for magazine advertising, a number of publications offer bleed advertising at no extra charge as a value-added or extra incentive for advertisers. Even when a magazine has a standard charge for bleed advertising, large advertisers often make these charges a point of negotiation with publishers.

Inserts and Multiple-Page Units

Multiple-page advertising covers a broad spectrum of insertions. The most common form of multipage advertising is the facing, two-page spread. Among the most frequent users of multipage inserts and spreads are automobile manufacturers. They face an extremely competitive environment; they need to show their cars in the most favorable, bigger-than-life fashion; and they often have an in-depth story to tell about the features of their brands—all reasons to use large space advertising. A spread increases the impact of the message and eliminates any competition for the consumer's attention. Some spreads come off the front cover and normally are either two or three pages. These advertisements are known as *gatefolds*.

More elaborate forms of multipage advertisements consist of bound-in booklets. Advertisers often use these booklets as both multipage advertisements as well as point-of-purchase collateral material for dealers. Normally, the advertiser takes responsibility for printing the insert, and the magazine simply binds it into the magazine. Compared to equivalent space bought from the magazine, preprinted inserts are much less expensive. Inserts also allow more creativity to the advertiser. For example, Calvin Klein had a fold-out poster bound into an issue of *Rolling Stone*.

Not all inserts are large size. Many advertisers use insert cards. These are often combined with a full-page advertisement to offer readers a convenient method of responding to a direct-mail offer or to obtain information without having to cut out a page from the magazine. Most magazines have their own insert cards in each edition for subscribing to the magazine. *Money* magazine will allow advertisers to use insert cards only if the wraparound portion contains a *Money* circulation offer.

Cost is a major consideration when planning inserts. Although inserts will be less expensive than run-of-publication advertising, the advertiser is still concentrating significant dollars in the publications that carry the inserts. This expense will reduce the number of media vehicles that can be included in a media schedule. Because an advertiser is putting a disproportionate share of advertising into one or a few vehicles, the likely result is a reduction in reach and frequency compared to a more traditional media plan.

Cost is a primary consideration in using multiple-page advertisements, but especially so in considering inserts. There is no question that inserts gain readership, but their use can rarely be justified solely on a cost basis, in the absence of a specific marketing objective. Although the advertiser will probably save on space costs, responsibility for the cost of design, printing, and paper will more than offset these savings. As discussed earlier, it is rare for the increase in audience awareness to match the added cost of advertising. Therefore, the *CPM* of an insert is significantly higher than for the magazine as a whole.

Finally, one of the problems with the growing use of multiple-page advertising is that it has lost much of its novelty to consumers. Readers can turn to practically any consumer magazine and find numerous examples of such advertising, so inserts have come to be taken for granted even by serious prospects. It is important to consider the qualitative environment of the publication before budgeting a multiple-page advertisement. It is equally important to work closely with the creative team to make sure that such expensive space is going to be fully utilized with a meaningful message. The most effective multiple-page units are for advertisers with an interesting product, a new story to tell, and a relatively select group of prospects.

HOW SPACE IS SOLD

Advertising Rates, Negotiation, and Merchandising

Buying full-run magazine advertising was at one time the easiest function for the media planner. Clients usually bought full-page advertisements, circulations were audited, discounts for frequent usage were obtained from straightforward rate cards, and rates were consistent for every advertiser who qualified for available discounts. In addition, most advertisers would buy only a few high-circulation publications.

This situation began to change when magazine advertising experienced a downturn in advertising revenues during the 1980s. The number of new titles coming on the market made the situation even worse as more magazines competed for shrinking advertising dollars. As the advertising market diminished, magazines began to negotiate with individual advertisers for special rates. This practice of one-to-one negotiation is called *going-off-the-card*. Prior to the 1980s, it was regarded as a last-ditch effort for failing magazines to survive. It also was generally viewed as an unethical practice, because one advertiser might pay more than another using the same space.

It is generally conceded that the women's service magazines were the first to use general advertising negotiation, but such negotiation soon spread to a number of other categories. As we entered the 1990s, negotiation had become a common practice among magazines. Many advertisers regarded the rate card as simply a point to start negotiation, and magazines were caught in another profit squeeze as they negotiated with more and more advertisers for lower and lower advertising rates.

Today, many publishers are desperately trying to reverse the widespread discounting. However, once started, going-off-the-card is a difficult cycle to break. Agencies are trying to get the lowest possible rates for their clients, and they have no incentive to cooperate with publishers to stop rate negotiation. In this environment, publishers find it very difficult to convince advertisers that they should not negotiate rates.

Basically, publishers have adopted a two-pronged approach to the problem. First, they are raising their rates to a level that accepts negotiation as a fact of life. In other words, instead of raising rates 4 percent, a magazine will raise rates 8 percent with the hope that they can negotiate for the 4 percent. This does nothing to change the industry mind-set that magazines are really worth less than they are asking. In addition, it assumes that experienced media planners don't know what is happening and won't negotiate away the entire 8 percent increase.

A second approach to maintaining rate integrity and still being competitive for advertising dollars is the development of extensive merchandising programs that extend the value of advertising in a particular publication. These merchandising initiatives often have two purposes: (1) to provide additional incentives for advertisers, and (2) to give the magazine additional revenue streams.

Magazine merchandising services take numerous forms and they are used by virtually every major magazine. *Better Homes & Gardens* produces greeting cards, provides real estate services, and franchises garden centers. Meanwhile, consumers can buy *Family Circle* classical CDs, *Field & Stream* bass lures, and *Popular Mechanics* work boots. It is estimated that ancillary services account for 10 percent of magazine revenues, and this is expected to rise to 20 percent in the next decade. As one magazine publisher put it, "Such ventures are not only potentially profitable in and of themselves, but they can make a magazine more visible and attractive to its traditional sources of revenue: readers and advertisers. You're putting a halo around the brand."[12]

The key to merchandising programs is to coordinate a magazine's reputation and expertise with marketing techniques that help advertisers sell their products. Among the more traditional merchandising programs are trade shows, conferences, newsletters, database services, and copromotions, such as point-of-purchase that highlights certain advertisers who are using a publication. For example, a women's magazine may cosponsor a fashion show with an advertiser or promote a recipe contest in which ingredients from an advertiser must be used. All of these techniques allow advertisers to extend the message of their advertising into related areas.

The key to successful merchandising programs is that they truly differentiate a publication from its competitors and provide a perceived value to advertisers. In recent years, one of the most common merchandising vehicles has been magazine Web sites. One study indicated that Web sites provide publishers with

- a progressive image to advertisers and readers
- immediate reader feedback
- advertising sale opportunities
- expanded geographic, even international, reach
- more specific reader demographics.[13]

Obviously, each of these characteristics is important to publishers and advertisers. The Hearst Corporation has developed an on-line service called HomeArts. The intent is to bring the Hearst Corporation, its advertisers, and the audiences for its diverse media holdings together in an interactive medium. For example,

> A consumer logs on to the HomeArts site and clicks on "Fresh Today." She finds a short news item discussing the benefits of using salted vs. unsalted butter for holiday baking. The news bite then links her to the Land O'Lakes Web site, where she finds related recipes and baking tips.[14]

To most executives, interactive media will soon become a regular part of the sales package of every publisher. Although in the short run such systems may not be profitable or add significantly to the audience or advertising base of a publication, advertisers

---

[12] Robin Pogrebin, "Extending the Brand," *The New York Times,* November 18, 1996, p. C1.

[13] Jenna Schnuer, "Making Sense of New Media," *Folio,* July 1, 1996, p. 26.

[14] Susan C. Russo, "A Natural Synergy," *American Advertising,* Winter 1995–96, p. 24.

will soon expect some form of interactivity as a normal merchandising tool. As one sales consultant observed, publishers must "sell auxiliary products in a way that help customers do their jobs better. The success of [merchandising programs] is based on recognizing the strengths of your magazine and leveraging those assets into a series of win/win scenarios."[15]

Despite the advantages of value-added programs, these programs are not inexpensive. In some respects, publishers may have substituted one form of profit reduction for another. Whether a publisher decreases profits by cutting ad rates or by increasing merchandising expenditures, the end result may be the same. It is clear that advertisers have come to expect at least some of these services as part of doing business with magazines.

Another problem with value-added programs is how to evaluate them as part of a media schedule. Although media planners may be able to place a cost value on a particular merchandising program, they will unlikely be able to determine how this program improves the utility of the advertising for their clients or differentiates one publication from another.

The rest of this section outlines the basics of buying magazine space. Remember, however, that these steps represent only the starting point for a magazine buy. The experienced media buyer will always probe the market to come up with additional efficiencies for a client.

Magazine Rate Structure

In the examples that follow, we assume the advertiser is making a full-run magazine buy; that is, the entire circulation of the publication is being purchased. An advertiser buying a partial-run edition will consider a number of other options. A typical rate card for a weekly publication might look like this:

Living World Bulletin **Color Rates (4-color)**

Space	1 ti	6 ti	12 ti	26 ti
1 page	32,800	29,750	28,150	26,675
$\frac{2}{3}$ page	24,210	22,950	21,740	20,630
$\frac{1}{2}$ page	22,880	18,430	20,615	19,510
$\frac{1}{4}$ page	11,800	11,050	10,550	9,860

An advertiser buying this publication will pay $32,800 for a one-time, four-color, full-page insert. The advertiser who buys at least 26 inserts in the publication will pay only $26,675 per ad for the same space.

Before placing a magazine on its advertising schedule, the advertiser will compute the cost efficiency of that publication against others being considered. Let us assume that *Living World Bulletin (LWB)* has an average circulation of 660,132. Using the *CPM* formula discussed earlier, we can calculate the efficiency of the publication as follows:

$$CPM = \frac{\text{cost/page}}{\text{circulation (000)}} = \frac{\$32,800}{660} = \$49.69$$

Discounts

Frequency and Volume Discounts   The one-time, full-page rate of a publication is referred to as its *basic,* or *open, rate.* In the case of *LWB,* its open rate is $32,800. All discounts are computed from that rate. Most publications present their discounts on a

---

[15]Kathi Simonsen, "How to Sell Auxiliary Products," *Folio: Special Sourcebook Issue, 1996,* p. 266.

Frequency discounts
Discounts based on total time or space bought, usually within a year. Also called *bulk discounts*.

per-page basis in which rates vary according to frequency of insertion during a 12-month period, as we have done here. However, some publications use either **frequency discounts** or *volume discounts* based on the number of pages run. For instance:

Frequency (Pages)	Discount (%)
13 or more	7
26 or more	12
39 or more	16
52 or more	20

In a similar fashion, the volume discount gives a larger percentage discount based on the total dollar volume spent for advertising during a year. The volume discount is convenient for advertisers that are combining a number of insertions of different space units or are using a number of partial-run insertions. A volume discount might be offered as follows:

Volume ($)	Discount (%)
83,000 or more	8
125,000 or more	11
180,000 or more	17
260,000 or more	20

Other Discounts In addition to discounts for volume and frequency, individual magazines offer a number of specialized discounts, usually for their largest advertisers. Among the more common discounts in this category is a lower per-page price for advertisers who combine buys with other publications owned by the same magazine group. These discounts are similar to volume discounts except advertisers accumulate credit across a number of titles. In addition, some magazines offer discounts called *continuity* discounts for advertisers who agree to advertise at a certain rate over a period of time, usually two years. These discounts are designed to guarantee the magazine a certain level of inserts in the future in exchange for a lower cost to the advertiser.

Remnant Space A number of publishers, especially those with geographic or demographic editions, often have unsold space in one or more editions. This space, also called *standby space,* is sold at a deep discount. For advertisers whose products or advertising messages are not time or location sensitive, **remnant space** can be a great bargain. However, it is strictly a take-it-or-leave-it proposition. Magazines will not allow any position requests, and normally advertisers must take whatever partial-run editions are available.

Remnant space
Unsold advertising space in geographic or demographic editions. It is offered to advertisers at a significant discount.

The Magazine Short Rate

As we have seen, most magazine discounts are based on the amount of space bought within a year. However, the publisher normally requires that payment be made within 30 days of billing. Therefore, an advertiser and a publisher sign a space contract at the beginning of the year and agree to make adjustments at the end of the year if the space usage estimates are incorrect. If the advertiser uses less space than estimated, the publisher adjusts by using a higher-than-contracted rate. If more space is used, the publisher adjusts by using a lower rate.

Let us look at a typical short rate, using the rate card for *Living World Bulletin.*

Acme Widgets contracted with *LWB* to run eight pages of advertising during the coming year. At the end of the year, Acme had run only five pages. Therefore, it was short the rate for which it had contracted and an adjustment had to be made, as follows:

$$\begin{aligned}
\text{Ran 5 times. Paid the 6-time rate of \$29,750 per page} &= (5 \times \$29,750) \\
&= \$148,750 \\
\text{Earned only the 1-time rate of \$32,800 per page} &= (5 \times \$32,800) \\
&= \$164,000 \\
\text{Short rate due } (\$164,000 - \$148,750) &= \$15,250
\end{aligned}$$

Some publishers charge the top (basic) rate throughout the year but state in the contract, "Rate credit when earned." If the advertiser earns a better rate, the publisher gives a refund. If the publisher sees that an advertiser is not running sufficient pages during the year to earn the low rate on which the contract was based, the publisher sends a bill at the short rate for space already used and bills further ads at the higher rate earned. Failure to keep short rates in mind when you are reducing your original schedule can lead to unwelcome surprises.

Placing the Order

Placing magazine advertising is a two-step process. The first step is the *space contract,* which tells the magazine the total number of pages that an advertiser will use during the coming year. It enables the publisher and advertiser to establish a basic rate for billing and is considered a binding contract. The space contract does not commit an advertiser to specific ad placement, but it allows both parties to agree on the cost of future advertising.

The second step is the *space order* (also called an insertion order). The space order commits the advertiser to a particular issue and is usually accompanied by production materials for the ad. Exhibit 11.11 shows an example of the 4As publication order blank. Note that the form includes both the space contract and insertion order, depending on which box is checked. In fact, an advertiser can also use the form to cancel or change ad requirements, if such changes are permitted by the magazine.

Magazine Dates

There are three sets of dates to be aware of in planning and buying magazine space:

1. *cover date:* the date appearing on the cover
2. *on-sale date:* the date on which the magazine is issued (the January issue of a magazine may come out on December 5, which is important to know if you are planning a Christmas ad)
3. *closing date:* the date when the print or plates needed to print the ad must be in the publisher's hands to make a particular issue deadline

Dates are figured from the cover date and are expressed in terms of "days or weeks preceding," as in the following example:

New Yorker
- published weekly, dated Monday
- issued Wednesday preceding
- closes 25th of 3rd month preceding

Magazine Networks

The term network, of course, comes from broadcast in which affiliated stations cooperated to bring audiences national programming as early as the 1920s. In recent years, a special adaptation of the network concept has been employed by virtually every medium as a means of offering advertisers a convenient and efficient means of buying multiple vehicles. There are newspaper networks, outdoor networks, and even networks for direct-mail inserts and comic strips. Magazines are no exception.

As mentioned earlier, one of the problems of the growing specialization in magazines is that advertisers increasingly need to buy more titles to achieve reach and fre-

Magazine networks
Groups of magazines that can be purchased together using one insertion order and paying a single invoice.

quency goals. Another consequence of smaller circulations among magazines is that *CPM* levels have increased. Many large national advertisers have complained about the difficulty of buying numerous magazines as well as the higher *CPM*s. To accommodate these advertisers, a number of publishers have established **magazine networks.** As with networks in other media, their intent is to make it possible for an advertiser to purchase several publications simultaneously with one insertion order, one bill, and often significant savings compared to buying the same magazines individually.

Currently, there are more than 100 magazine networks, some representing dozens of different titles. The network concept allows several magazines to compete for advertisers by offering lower *CPM*s and delivering a larger audience than any single publication. Networks must be carefully tailored to reach a particular audience segment with little waste circulation. Otherwise, the network provides advertisers with nothing more than the audience of a general circulation magazine with all the pitfalls previously discussed.

Although there are a number of magazine networks, they generally fall into only two categories, single publisher or independent networks.

Single Publisher Networks Here a network is offered by a single publisher who owns several magazines and will allow advertisers to buy all or any number of these publications as a group. For example, Hearst Magazine Group publishes 15 magazines and allows advertisers who use at least three titles to build network discounts.

The publisher network can be especially effective in encouraging a media buyer to choose among similar magazines. For example, let us assume a media buyer has decided to purchase space in *Cosmopolitan* and *Town and Country,* both Hearst magazines. A third option is to purchase either *Redbook,* another Hearst magazine, or *Ladies' Home Journal.* Assuming the two magazines meet the advertising criteria of a particular client, the discounts available from buying *Redbook* as part of the Hearst network may well sway the media buyer in that direction.

Independent Networks   The second type of magazine network is made up of different publishers who edit magazines with similar audience appeals. These networks are usually offered by a rep firm, which contracts individually with each publisher and then sells advertising in the group. The concept is similar to the space wholesaling that George Rowell began in the 1850s, as discussed in chapter 5. Media Networks, the largest independent network firm, offers six networks, each geared to a specific audience. For example, the Media Networks Business Network consists of seven magazines including *Money, Financial World,* and *Time.* Even though these magazines are owned by different publishers, they know that there are advantages to cooperating in selling space to large advertisers.

Magazine networks are not confined to major national publishers. A number of regional and city publications have joined together to offer network buys. For example, the Public Broadcasting Magazine Network allows advertisers to buy magazines published by local public television stations. The magazine network concept is ideal for publications to offer advertisers a larger audience and a lower cost than any one magazine could provide and, at the same time, maintain a targeted audience.

MAGAZINE CIRCULATION

As with any medium, accurate readership measurement of a magazine is extremely important to advertisers. Media planners don't buy magazines, television spots, or outdoor signs; they buy people. More specifically, they buy certain groups of people who are presently or prospectively customers for their products. Publishers have two distinct methods of determining their audiences: paid circulation or readership.

Paid Circulation and the Rate Base

The first, most objective method of audience measurement is paid circulation. Most major consumer magazines have their circulation audited by an outside company. As with other media, magazine rates are based on the circulation that a publisher promises to deliver to advertisers, referred to as the *guaranteed circulation.* Because the guaranteed circulation is the number of readers advertisers purchase, it is also known as the **rate base.**

One of the most dramatic trends of the last several years is the number of magazines that have reduced their rate base through a planned program of circulation decreases. It is estimated that as many as 50 percent of magazines have adjusted their circulation downward in the last eight years.

At one time, if a magazine decreased its rate base the advertising community saw it as a sign that the magazine was in trouble.

> Throughout the late seventies and early eighties, the trend was to pump up rate bases, usually to demonstrate a magazine's vitality and to justify increases in ad rates. Also, many publishers believed magazines were competing against television for advertisers, and that they needed huge readerships in order to stack up competitively.[16]

Rate base
The circulation that magazines guarantee advertisers in computing advertising costs.

---

[16]Cris Beam, "The Overbuilt Ratebase," *Folio,* July 1, 1996, p. 80.

Two changes in the magazine business have combined to change the perception of a lowered rate base. First, publishers realize that the cost of maintaining marginal circulation is becoming prohibitively expensive. With readers carrying the majority of costs for most magazines, publishers would rather concentrate on a core of loyal readers than spend excessive promotional dollars on readers who come on board only for the deep discounted subscription, never to be heard from again.

By the same token, advertisers would rather buy space in magazines with a quality readership, that is, those who are interested in both the magazine and its advertising. Rather than viewing magazines cutting their base as a sign of trouble, advertisers think it is positive evidence that a magazine is getting its house in order to the benefit of both the publisher and advertisers.

Adjusting a magazine's rate base has become more or less accepted by advertisers. Missing a rate base is an entirely different problem. Magazines may overcome the problems in a number of different ways. Because the rate base is figured on six-month average circulation, a magazine that is falling short of its circulation numbers may use a number of techniques to increase its numbers in the short term. For example, it may continue to send copies to subscribers whose subscriptions have expired. Under auditing rules, a magazine can do this for three months after expiration. In addition, the magazine may use public placement firms in hotels or doctors' offices. Of course, if the circulation shortfall is something other than a temporary blip, the publication will have to reduce its rate base.[17]

A magazine does not necessarily offer a rate base to advertisers. In fact, a number of audited publications do not make a specific guaranteed circulation claim. These publishers provide advertisers with accurate circulation for past issues, but they don't take any risk for circulation shortfalls in the future. In the volatile world of magazine advertising, many smaller magazines do not want to deal with the financial problems involved with a short-term drop in audience. A few large-circulation publications do not offer a guaranteed circulation, but this is unusual.

It is important that we not confuse an unaudited publication with one that does not offer a rate base. A rate base is an additional inducement to assure advertisers that they will obtain a certain level of audience if they buy space in a publication or they will be compensated for a failure to meet the magazine's guarantee. An audit, on the other hand, guarantees that over some period of time (usually a year or six months) the publication has achieved some circulation level. An audit makes no promises for future circulation.

Readership

In magazine terminology, "readership" usually combines paid circulation (subscribers and newsstand purchasers) with pass-along readers. For example, according to Mediamark Research, *Family Circle* has a paid circulation of 4.97 million, but with 4.85 readers per copy (RPC), more than 20 million people see each issue. The more general the publication's editorial, the more likely it is to have significant pass-along readership.

Many advertisers and even magazine publishers are concerned about the use of readership as a substitute for paid circulation. Historically, the use of readership is rooted in the magazine's industry competition with television. As discussed in the last section, magazines are retrenching somewhat from a "numbers at any cost" circulation mentality and again selling quality of readership. Nevertheless, publishers want to keep readership surveys to fairly take into account their total readers.

It would seem that total readership, accurately measured, would be a reasonable approach to measuring magazine audiences. The problem arises from the fact that many media buyers regard pass-along readers of consumer magazines as inherently inferior to paid circulation. Between those advertisers who see no value in readership and those who view it as equal to paid circulation, there is probably a middle ground. As in most

---

[17] E. Daniel Capell, "Trimming the Ratebase," *Folio: Special Sourcebook Issue, 1996,* p. 185.

marketing and advertising questions, the real answer is determined by the specific objectives of the publication and its readers. However, regardless of the value that one places on readership, most acknowledge that it is different from paid circulation.

MEASURING MAGAZINE AUDIENCES

We now turn to the issue of how publishers verify the circulation and readership of their magazines. Advertisers normally will not purchase a magazine unless its publisher can provide independent verification of the magazine's readership. In magazine terminology, *readership* has two distinct meanings. One refers to the time spent with a publication. The other, and the one we discuss here, includes all readers of a magazine as contrasted to only those who buy a publication.

The Audit Bureau of Circulations

The Audit Bureau of Circulations (ABC) is the largest of several auditing organizations that verify magazine circulation. The ABC provides two basic services: the publisher's statements, which report six-month periods ending June 30 and December 31; and the ABC audit, which annually audits the data provided in the publisher's statements. The ABC reports total circulation, as well as circulation figures by state, by county size, and per issue during each six-month period. The ABC reports also state the manner in which circulation was obtained—for example, by subscription, newsstand sales—and any discounts or premiums provided to subscribers. Exhibit 11.12 is a sample of the ABC publisher's statement.

exhibit

11.12

ABC offers total circulation analyses for publications.

Courtesy: Audit Bureau of Circulations.

PROTOTYPE

CLASS, INDUSTRY OR FIELD SERVED: Travel, customs of people, products and related human interest, subject to geographical and sociological nature.

1. AVERAGE PAID CIRCULATION FOR 6 MONTHS ENDED DECEMBER 31, (YEAR)

Subscriptions:	295,069
Single Copy Sales:	109,721
AVERAGE TOTAL PAID CIRCULATION	404,790
Advertising Rate Base and/or Circulation Guarantee Paid Circulation:	
Average Total Analyzed Non-Paid Circulation	10,000
Average Total Non-Analyzed Non-Paid Circulation	2,050

NOTE: THIS PUBLICATION ALSO PROVIDES AN ABC PUBLISHER'S STATEMENT ANALYZING ITS NON-PAID CIRCULATION

1a. AVERAGE PAID CIRCULATION of Regional, Metro and Demographic Editions

Edition & number of issues		Edition & number of issues		Edition & number of issues	
Eastern (6)	149,772	Central (6)	161,916	Western (6)	93,102

2. PAID CIRCULATION by Issues

Issue	Subscriptions	Single Copy Sales	Total Paid	Issue	Subscriptions	Single Copy Sales	Total Paid
July	285,960	116,637	402,597	Oct.	301,738	105,764	407,502
Aug.	297,181	107,749	404,930	Nov.	290,590	109,495	400,085
Sept.	300,315	102,700	403,015	Dec.	294,630	115,979	410,609

ANALYSIS OF TOTAL NEW AND RENEWAL SUBSCRIPTIONS

Sold during 6 Month Period Ended December 31, (Year)

3. AUTHORIZED PRICES

(a) Basic Prices: Single Copy: $1.50.	
Subscriptions: 1 yr. $12.00; 2 yrs. $22.00; 3 yrs. $30.00	19,431
(b) Higher than basic prices:	None
(c) Lower than basic prices: 1 yr. $7.00, $8.00, $8.99; 2 yrs. $13.99	78,924
(d) Association subscription prices	None
Total Subscriptions Sold in Period	98,355

4. DURATION OF SUBSCRIPTIONS SOLD:

(a) One to six months (1 to 6 issues)	660
(b) Seven to twelve months (7 to 12 issues)	85,669
(c) Thirteen to twenty-four months	1,021
(d) Twenty-five to thirty-six months	143
(e) Thirty-seven to forty-eight months	9,100
(f) Forty-nine months and more	1,822
Total Subscriptions Sold in Period	98,355

5. CHANNELS OF SUBSCRIPTION SALES:

(a) Ordered by mail and/or direct request	68,501
(b) Ordered through salespeople:	
1. Catalog agencies and individual agents	8,644
2. Publisher's own and other publisher's salespeople	590
3. Independent agencies' salespeople	14,100
4. Newspaper agencies	None
5. Members of schools, churches, fraternal and similar organizations	6,317
(c) Association memberships	None
(d) All other channels, See Par. 11(a)	203
Total Subscriptions Sold in Period.	98,355

The ABC reports are very matter-of-fact documents that deal only with primary readers. They do not offer information about product usage, demographic characteristics of readers, or pass-along readership.

Syndicated Magazine Readership Research

Advertisers are, of course, interested in the primary readers of magazines, but they are also interested in who these readers are and what they buy—as well as in pass-along readers who are given the publications. Currently, there are two principal sources of syndicated magazine readership research: A&S/Simmons Magazine Metrics and Mediamark Research, Inc. (MRI).

MRI methodology consists of selecting a sample of approximately 20,000 households and eliciting media usage, demographic characteristics, and product purchase information. Using personal interviews, respondents are prompted by logo cards (magazine titles printed as they appear on publications) of the various magazines being tested and asked how recently they read a particular publication. This technique is called the *recent reading method.* The recent reading method provides estimates of readership and product usage.

A&S/Simmons is a joint venture between Audit and Surveys Worldwide and Kantar Media Research, parent company of **Simmons Market Research Bureau** (SMRB). Its study uses mailed questionnaires and measures some 600 magazines with an emphasis on audience information.[18]

Simmons Market Research Bureau (SMRB)
Firm that provides audience data for several media. Best known for magazine research.

CONSUMER MAGAZINES—SUMMING UP

Like so many other media, magazines are facing a number of challenges in the coming years. Perhaps most important, they are having to reposition themselves to compete in a changing marketing environment. In recent years, the growing use and respectability of direct response advertising have made serious inroads into the audience selectivity that has long been a unique advantage for magazines.

Despite the competitive atmosphere of magazine marketing, magazines remain well positioned as an important marketing tool. They can play a role as either the primary medium for a national advertiser or as a niche medium to reach prime prospects. Magazines will continue to be a major source of news, information, and entertainment for millions of prime prospects. It is the combination of prestige and segmentation that gives magazines a major qualitative advantage over most other media. The fact that magazines are asking readers to carry a major share of their financial support also has enhanced their value to advertisers.

In the future, it is probable that qualitative factors will continue to vie with cost efficiencies in judging the value of an advertising medium. There is no medium that provides the combination of selective audiences, targeted advertising, and editorial involvement to the degree provided by consumer magazines. Another primary benefit of consumer magazines is their ability to appeal to upscale audiences. Magazines rank as the favorite medium among most high income, highly educated audience segments. This appeal to upscale prospects makes the higher cost of magazines a profitable investment in the marketing communication programs of most companies.

THE BUSINESS PRESS AND BUSINESS-TO-BUSINESS ADVERTISING

Business-to-business advertising
Advertising that promotes goods through trade and industrial journals that are used in the manufacturing, distributing, or marketing of goods to the public.

To this point, we have discussed magazines directed primarily at consumers. The remainder of this chapter is devoted to the business press and **business-to-business advertising.** In terms of the number of titles, specialization of content, industry economics,

---

[18]Ann Marie Kerwin, "Joint Venture to Expand A&S Study," *Advertising Age,* January 26, 1998, p. 51.

and the competitive environment, the business press has a number of characteristics that differ from consumer publications.

Prospects for most business advertisers are fewer and more concentrated, they tend to be experts concerning the products they purchase, and audience selectivity is much more important than *CPM*s or reach measures used in consumer media. Another feature of business publications is their low cost compared to consumer magazines (see Exhibit 11.13). Given the specialized audience of these publications and their moderate cost, the business magazine continues to be a bargain.

Both the tone and advertising of business publications differ significantly from those of consumer magazines.

> As a general rule, the more expensive the product, the more serious the message. . . . When people buy "big ticket" items, they tend to shop and compare products, prices, and features. They take their time and are receptive to facts. Your advertising message should be consistent with the seriousness of the purchase.[19]

The level of communication with a business audience has a different tone than with consumers. More than 70 percent of business magazine readers report they see these publications at work or while commuting. The business press is a medium of reference and commerce, whereas consumer magazines are vehicles of entertainment, news, and leisure reading. Many business publications are used on a regular basis to keep up with the latest industry trends, competitive activity, and product category marketing strategy.

Promotion and marketing activities directed to a business audience must consider different objectives than those aimed at consumers. "The fundamental rule in consumer marketing is to know the customer. Business-to-business firms must follow a slightly more complicated rule: they must know the customer *and* the customer's customer."[20]

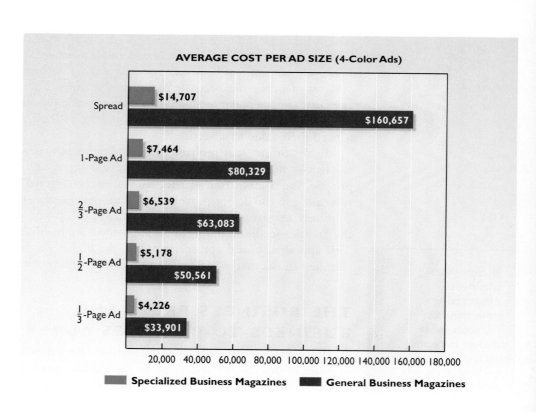

exhibit

11.13

General business magazine rates are 10 times higher than specialized business magazine rates.

Courtesy: Cahners Publishing Co., Cahners Advertising Research Report No. 540.2D.

AVERAGE COST PER AD SIZE (4-Color Ads)

Spread	$14,707 / $160,657
1-Page Ad	$7,464 / $80,329
$\frac{2}{3}$-Page Ad	$6,539 / $63,083
$\frac{1}{2}$-Page Ad	$5,178 / $50,561
$\frac{1}{3}$-Page Ad	$4,226 / $33,901

20,000 40,000 60,000 80,000 100,000 120,000 140,000 160,000 180,000

■ **Specialized Business Magazines**   ■ **General Business Magazines**

[19]Al Ries, "One and the Same," *Sales & Marketing Management,* February 1996, p. 23.
[20]"Know the Customer's Customer," *American Demographics,* March 1996, p. 2.

exhibit

11.14

Business-to-business advertising must be as attention-getting as its consumer counterpart.

Courtesy: J. Walter Thompson–Atlanta.

On the other hand, business advertising has the same demands for attention-getting creative messages as its consumer counterparts (see Exhibit 11.14).

In this section, we examine the business-to-business sector and look at the differences and similarities with consumer advertising. We begin by discussing some major techniques and goals of business-to-business advertisers.

Characteristics of the Business Press

Audiences   The relationship between readers and their business publications is much different than that of readers and typical consumer magazines. The readers of a trade publication are reading it as part of their business. The utility of the magazine is determined by how well it improves their ability to do their jobs, market their products, and improve their profits. Consequently, business magazines must develop a depth of understanding of their readers that is typically not required in the consumer press.

A primary difference between consumer and business advertising is their respective objectives. In the Alcoa case history (pp. 320–321), notice how the company and its agency cite research, production data, and graphic design advantages to convince manufacturers that aluminum cans are competitive with glass and plastic containers.

Recognizing that business advertising can carry out only part of the sales job, trade magazines need to develop a problem-solving partnership with their readers. For successful business publications and the advertisers using them, this relationship involves three steps:

1. *Identify the special problems and opportunities faced by readers and their industry.* For example, what are the primary competitors; what are the short- and long-term trends

in the industry; and what social, legal, or technical elements are likely to play a role in the success or failure of companies within the industry?

2. *Identify specific solutions to the primary problems facing readers of the publication.* Both editorial and advertising in business publications present detailed material and technical, industry-oriented information to their readers.

3. *Create a long-term profitable relationship by treating audiences as clients rather than just readers.* The success of a trade publication is largely dependent on the success of the industry it covers.

Competition   Nowhere is the concept of integrated marketing more apparent than in business-to-business selling. At one time, the business press had a virtual monopoly on business-to-business advertising. Today, business publications still occupy the primary role in the advertising plans of most business-to-business advertisers. However, a recent study indicated that the typical business-to-business seller uses an average of seven different media or promotional techniques.

Business professionals increasingly are using on-line services in their jobs. A study by Cahners Publishing Company indicated that 88 percent of manufacturing executives used the Internet at least weekly. On average, these professionals spent more than one hour per day on the Internet. More important, for business-to-business media, the majority of this time was spent obtaining product information and evaluations (see Exhibit 11.15). With its capability of providing immediate, up-to-date information, the Internet may one day be the major source of competition for all business-to-business media.

Exhibit 11.16 shows a breakdown of the marketing communication budget for business-to-business firms. Apart from salesforce management—that is, the cost of meetings and training for the personal salesforce—advertising is the largest communication expenditure by a wide margin, with business publications constituting 52.9 percent of the total advertising allocation. Television and newspapers each account for approximately 10 percent of business advertising. Of the dollars spent in magazines, the computer software industry is the largest contributor, with more than $600 million, or approximately 5 percent of the total.[21]

exhibit

11.15

Seven in 10 of manufacturing professionals are using the World Wide Web for product information and evaluation.

Courtesy: Cahners Publishing Co., Cahners Advertising Research Report No. 824.0.

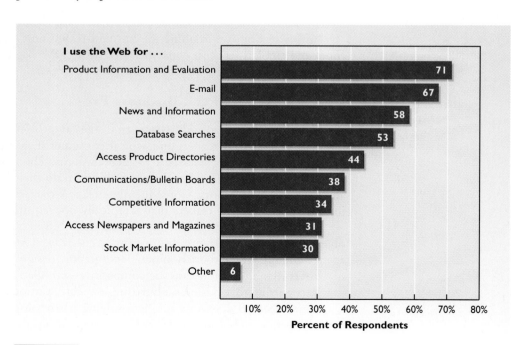

I use the Web for ...

Category	Percent of Respondents
Product Information and Evaluation	71
E-mail	67
News and Information	58
Database Searches	53
Access Product Directories	44
Communications/Bulletin Boards	38
Competitive Information	34
Access Newspapers and Magazines	31
Stock Market Information	30
Other	6

Percent of Respondents

[21]Char Kosek, "Business-to-Business Grabs $51.7 Billion," from *The Business-to-Business Census,* a supplement to *Advertising Age,* June 1996, p. S-3.

Business-to-Business Category Spending

	1995	
	$ billions	%
Salesforce management[a]	11.9	22.9
Advertising	11.3	21.9
Direct marketing	6.3	12.3
Sales promotions	6.3	12.2
Trade shows	5.5	10.7
Public relations	2.6	5.1
Market research	2.5	4.7
Other	2.0	3.9
Premiums/Incentives	1.9	3.7
On-line	1.4	2.6
Total	51.7	100.0

[a]*Excludes compensation and commissions.*

Source: OutFront Marketing study.

The array of business titles available to an advertiser is huge. For example, whereas there are approximately 900 consumer magazines, estimates place the number of business publications at more than 4,500. In fact, only radio has more individual media vehicles than the business press. Much like its radio and consumer magazine counterparts, the business press has seen a recent growth in even more specialized editorial formats. For example, publications such as *Packaging World* and *Packaging Digest* offer broad-based information on the industrial packaging industry. However, in 1993, *Pharmaceutical & Medical Packaging News* was launched to cover packaging concerns in a single industry. Building on its success, the company then introduced *Cosmetic/Personal Care Packaging.*

Because of the affinity readers have with business publications, companies are finding that magazines provide the best introduction for products and companies. However, once advertising gains customers' attention, other means of contact take over. Virtually every business ad includes a toll-free number, fax number, E-mail address, Web site, and/or reader service card. In this sense, business advertising introduces the company and its salespersons so that the final sales job can begin.

Another role that business magazines play is providing regular contact with customers whose accounts don't warrant regular personal sales contacts. As shown in Exhibit 11.17, less than 60 percent of customers receive one sales call per year. Trade

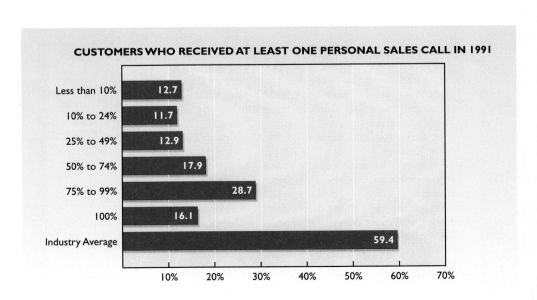

CUSTOMERS WHO RECEIVED AT LEAST ONE PERSONAL SALES CALL IN 1991

Less than 10%	12.7
10% to 24%	11.7
25% to 49%	12.9
50% to 74%	17.9
75% to 99%	28.7
100%	16.1
Industry Average	59.4

case HISTORY

SITUATION

A lack of can innovation and a lack of an effective pro-aluminum message had resulted in a utilitarian image for the aluminum can at every level of the beverage integration chain. This commodity image resulted in lost opportunity in the juice and soft drink markets and loss of can share in the beer market, and it served as a barrier to entry and success in the "other beverage" (i.e., new age, teas, coffees, sparkling waters, isotonics) segment.

Alcoa, the industry leader, mounted a trade advertising program to tout the significant benefits of, rejuvenate interest in, and build preference for the aluminum beverage can. The print and direct-mail campaign was targeted at the beverage (marketing VPs, brand managers, and product managers), packaging (package development managers, packaging engineers, directors of packaging, consultants, and design firms), and can manufacturing industries.

While leading the charge for the aluminum industry in general, Alcoa also wanted the campaign to position Alcoa as the proactive, innovative category leader.

SOLUTION

Alcoa's agency, Pollak Levitt Chaiet, developed a trade advertising campaign that used bold headlines, bright colors, and striking can designs to position the aluminum can as anything but utilitarian. To maximize the impact of the ads, and to showcase the product (the aluminum can), the agency developed original beverage brand names and label designs. Names such as "Cranberry Cola," "FruitFace Funky Citrus," and "E. Gadd's Amazingly Good Ginger Ale" were trademark searched, cleared, and ultimately trademarked themselves.

With these unique can designs as a base, the decidedly "untrade" trade ad campaign was strategically designed to

- begin to secure the future of the aluminum beverage can by addressing serious generational perception, and reposition the can as young, fresh, and preferred
- show how the aluminum can could be designed and decorated to project a unique, high-quality, contemporary image
- introduce new sizes, particularly the Alcoa-designed 8-oz. SlimCan
- reclaim the aluminum can's positioning as the environmentally superior, environmentally smart package
- trumpet the can's ability to provide the freshest, best-tasting, and most convenient product in the most recyclable package.

The five-ad campaign used intriguing headlines such as: "You Can Actually See More of Your Product in an Alu-minum Can" (graphic design capabilities); "How Can the Same Package That Makes Things Last Longer on the Shelf Also Make Them Practically Fly Off It?" (freshness/shelf life); "You Wouldn't Want to Put Your Hot, New, Cutting-Edge, Youth-Oriented Beverage in a Square Package, Would You?" (SlimCan), and "Shhh! Don't Bother the Andersons. Can't You See They're Busy Saving the Planet?" (environmental).

In addition, Alcoa put decorated SlimCans in the hands of key decision makers. An actual kids' lunch box was delivered to 500 people at the top U.S. juice companies. The lid invited recipients to "Look What Happens Once You Start Thinking Outside the Box." Inside was a SlimCan and the headline, "You Get a Product That Kids Think Is Anything But Square."

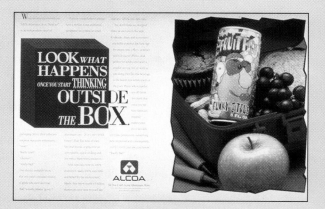

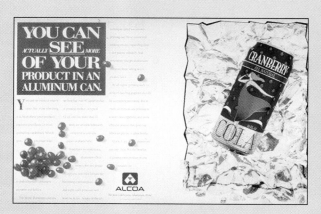

RESULTS

The campaign opened many eyes and many doors at the leading beverage companies.

Alcoa conducted a pre- and postwave telephone research survey to judge the effectiveness of the campaign. After one year, Alcoa's awareness rose more than 20 percent, a steep increase for just one year of advertising in only five trade magazines. Awareness increased despite the fact that fewer respondents in the postwave indicated that they were actually working directly in aluminum packaging.

In addition, the advertising campaign was honored by the Business Marketing Association with a Best of Division Creative Award.

Courtesy: Pollak Levitt Chaiet Advertising.

advertising and other forms of direct marketing, such as telemarketing, can augment these infrequent personal calls and make what would otherwise be an unprofitable account worthwhile.

Marketing synergism among a number of promotional and sales methods is a given in most business advertising. Because of the relatively small prospect pool for most business products, business-to-business marketing allows the use of innovative technology and experimentation that would often be cost prohibitive in consumer advertising. On the other hand, given the high dollar value of a typical business-to-business sale, the constraints of *CPM*s found in the consumer sector are rarely a factor in business marketing.

Business Publication Expansion of Services

We discussed the fact that many consumer magazines have introduced a number of merchandising and ancillary services. Likewise, business-to-business publications have long engaged in expanding their communication efforts to a number of related fields. Trade shows cosponsored by magazines and their major advertisers have long been popular as a business merchandising venture.

In recent years, some innovative publishing programs have been introduced to increase the profits of business publications as well as to provide a value-added service to their advertisers. For example, *National Jeweler* magazine sells a newsletter called "Your Jeweler and You" to local jewelers, who in turn send it to their best customers under their own logos. The customer receives a four-color newsletter, the local jeweler is able to provide its patrons with a mailing piece far beyond the budget or expertise of one done on an individual basis, and the newsletter requires little additional expense for *National Jeweler* because the magazine's staff prepares the newsletter using information they have at hand.[22]

Another major development in the magazine business is the development of custom publishing. A custom publication, a hybrid between consumer and business publications, takes two primary forms:

1. *Event-related publications.* As an example, during the Atlanta Olympics, *Sports Illustrated Olympic Daily* was published each morning and distributed only in Atlanta. In some cases, these temporary magazines double as programs for sporting events. The U.S. Open Golf Championship program is 200 pages with almost half advertising.[23]
2. *Custom advertiser publications.* Generally, these publications are produced by major publishers for a single advertiser. The content is appropriate to the company and the lifestyle of its customers. Distribution is usually to a select segment of a company's best customers. An example of a custom publication is *Living Healthy,* sponsored by Massachusetts Blue Cross and Blue Shield, which promotes a healthy

---

[22]"Spin Off a Newsletter for Your Customers," *Folio,* February 1996, p. 10.

[23]Stacy Lu, "Magazines You Won't Find in Publishers Clearinghouse," *The New York Times,* July 22, 1996, p. C7.

lifestyle and general wellness programs. Another custom magazine is *Access,* sponsored by NYNEX, a telecommunications company, which is sent to telecommunications professionals and deals with various problem areas in the field.[24]

In a number of cases, a custom publication is issued on a regular basis. *Sony Style* is distributed twice a year and recently began selling advertising to noncompeting companies. Overall, custom publishing is a $3 billion industry and is growing at a rate equal to magazines in general. Virtually all major magazine publishers are engaged to some degree in custom publishing. Financial services, the consumer health industry, and high-tech companies are the largest users of custom publishing. The growth of custom publishing has been driven by marketers shifting dollars from media to database-driven promotions. In effect, it combines many of the advantages of direct response target marketing with the editorial environment of a magazine.[25]

Entry into ancillary services usually is more successful for established magazines than for their smaller, less well known competitors. Magazines provide credibility and high visibility to these ancillary events, which would be lacking without the tie-in to a major publication. Seeing the growth of promotional techniques in business-to-business advertising, many magazine publishers employ ancillary vehicles to add to their overall profitability and decrease their dependence on advertising from their publications.

Regardless of their format, ancillary activities offer a number of advantages to a publisher. First, they utilize the publisher's knowledge of a particular industry to help clients develop a coordinated promotional and advertising campaign. Second, they gain revenue from companies who do not use advertising as a primary business-to-business marketing tool. Finally, they increase a magazine's credibility by demonstrating far-reaching expertise in a number of promotional areas. In the future, we will see publishers developing a variety of information services and promotional techniques in addition to their basic magazines.

Types of Business-to-Business Publications

Despite their wide array, business publications can generally be placed in one of four categories:

● Distributive trades (trade)
● Manufacturers and builders (industrial)
● Top officers of other corporations (management)
● Physicians, dentists, architects, and other professional people (professional)

Trade paper
A business publication directed to those who buy products for resale (wholesalers, jobbers, retailers).

Trade Papers Because most nationally advertised products depend upon dealers for their sales, we discuss advertising in **trade papers** first. Usually, this advertising is prepared by the agency that handles the consumer advertising, and in any new campaign both are prepared at the same time. The term *trade papers* is applied particularly to business publications directed at those who buy products for resale, such as wholesalers, jobbers, and retailers. Typical trade papers are *American Druggist, Supermarket News, Chain Store Age, Hardware Retailer, Modern Tire Dealer, Women's Wear Daily,* and *Home Furnishings.*

Almost every business engaged in distributing goods has a trade paper to discuss its problems. Trade papers are a great medium for reporting merchandising news about the products, packaging, prices, deals, and promotions of the manufacturers that cater to the particular industry. The chain-store field alone has more than 20 such publications. Druggists have a choice of more than 30, and more than 60 different publications are

---

[24]Blair R. Fischer, "Message and Medium," *Promo,* November 1995, p. 107.
[25]Alicia Lasek, "'No Backing Out' Now for Custom Publishing," *Advertising Age,* November 6, 1996, p. S-14.

issued for grocers. There are many localized journals, such as *Texas Food Merchant, Michigan Beverage News, Southern Hardware, California Apparel News,* and *Illinois Building News.*

Industrial Publications   As we move into the category in which a company in one industry sells its materials, machinery, tools, parts, and equipment to another company for use in making a product or conducting operations, we are entering an altogether different ballpark—the industrial-marketing arena.

There are fewer customers in the arena than in the consumer market, and they can be more easily identified. The amount of money involved in a sale may be large—hundreds of thousands, perhaps even millions, of dollars—and nothing is bought on impulse. Many knowledgeable executives with technical skills often share in the buying decision. The sales representative has to have a high degree of professional competence to deal with the industrial market, in which personal selling is the biggest factor in making a sale. Advertising is only a collateral aid used to pave the way for or support the salesperson; hence, it receives a smaller share of the marketplace budget.

Advertising addressed to people responsible for buying goods needed to make products is called industrial advertising. It is designed to reach purchasing agents, plant managers, engineers, controllers, and others who have a voice in spending the firm's money.

Management Publications   The most difficult group for a publication to reach is managers. After all, even the largest companies have only a relatively few decision makers. When these decision makers are widely dispersed across a number of industries and job descriptions, publications must be extremely creative to reach them.

The management category is one that straddles a gray area between consumer and business-to-business publications. Magazines such as *Business Week, Fortune,* and *Nation's Business* have characteristics that would place them in either the business or the consumer category. Even magazines such as *Time* have at least some of their partial-run editions listed in the *Business Publications* of the Standard Rate and Data Service (SRDS).

Professional Publications   The **Standard Rate and Data Service** (SRDS), in its special business publication edition, includes journals addressed to physicians, surgeons, dentists, lawyers, architects, and other professionals who depend upon these publications to keep abreast of their professions. The editorial content of such journals ranges from reportage about new technical developments to discussions on how to meet client or patient problems better and how to conduct offices more efficiently and profitably. Professional people often recommend or specify the products their patients or clients should order. Therefore, much advertising of a high technical caliber is addressed to them.

Some Special Features of Business Publication Advertising

Business publications exhibit several differences from consumer magazines. This section briefly discusses the more important ones.

Pass-along Readership   A significant number of readers of business publications receive their magazines on a pass-along basis. We earlier noted that such readership among consumer magazines is generally regarded as inferior to paid circulation. However, one of the notable differences between business and consumer publications is the way advertisers view **pass-along readership.** The typical consumer medium has a relatively short life and low pass-along readership. Occasionally, a recipe will be clipped or a magazine will be passed on to a neighbor, but consumer magazines are largely read for pleasure and tossed aside. In any case, advertisers view pass-along readership of consumer magazines as vastly inferior to primary readership.

Business publication advertisers, in contrast, view pass-along readership as quite valuable. For one thing, readers don't normally browse through *Electronic Design* or

Standard Rate and Data Service (SRDS)
SRDS publishes a number of directories giving media and production information.

Pass-along readership
Readers who receive a publication from a primary buyer. In consumer publications, pass-along readers are considered inferior to the primary audience, but this is usually not the case with business publications.

Concrete Construction; they pay close attention to copy. For another, some business publications limit their circulation in a way that forces pass-along readership.

Controlled Circulation   Magazines are sometimes distributed free to selective readers. Free circulation is known as **controlled circulation.** The term "controlled" refers to the fact that publishers distribute only to a carefully selected list of people who are influential in making purchase decisions for their industry. They use the same database techniques that direct mailers use in building their mailing lists. Controlled circulation makes sense when dealing with an easily defined audience of decision makers. To some media planners, the logic of controlled circulation is little different from that of direct mail except the ad is delivered in an editorial environment. Despite the fact that controlled circulation is widely used in the trade press, it is not universally embraced. In the past, most research has indicated that a high percentage of clients and media directors prefer the reader commitment inherent in paid circulation.

The number of controlled publications in the business field plays a major role in their share of advertising-to-circulation revenues compared to consumer magazines. On average, approximately two-thirds of trade publication circulation is controlled. A number of publications use a mix of controlled and paid in which qualified readers receive the magazine free and others can buy it if they wish.

Controlled circulation creates a significant dependence on advertising support. Unlike consumer magazines, business publications have been largely unsuccessful in shifting to a reader-driven revenue stream. This dependency on advertising is another reason why business publications suffer so much during economic downturns.

Vertical and Horizontal Publications   Industrial publications are usually considered either *horizontal* or *vertical.* A **vertical publication** is one that covers an entire industry. An example is *Baking Industry,* which contains information concerning product quality, marketing, plant efficiency, and packaging.

Horizontal publications are edited for people who are engaged in a single function that cuts across many industries. An example is *Purchasing* magazine, which is circulated to purchasing managers. It discusses trends and forecasts applicable to all industries.

North American Industrial Classification   For many years, industrial marketers used a U.S. government numbering system known as the standard industrial classification (SIC). The SIC was a four-digit system that classified manufacturing firms into 10 major categories with subcategories within each. In 1997, the government moved to replace the SIC code with a new, 20-sector, six-digit classification called the **North American Industrial Classification System** (NAICS). The advantages of the new system are (1) after 60 years, the SIC was not able to categorize many specialized areas of technology and service industries, and (2) the new system is consistent in both Canada and Mexico, giving a single North American industrial code. Like the SIC designation, the NAICS will be used by marketers and business-to-business media to identify and reach various segments of industrial corporations.

Circulation Audits   Business-to-business advertisers are keenly interested in the circulation of the publications in which they advertise. In some respects, the readership numbers are more important than those in general consumer magazines. The total audience is smaller, the *CPM* for most publications is significantly higher than for consumer magazines, and the competition makes it imperative that business-to-business marketers reach their target audience in a timely fashion.

Because of the number and diversity of audiences contacted by the trade and business press, a number of auditing organizations are used by business publishers and advertisers. More than 1,000 trade and industrial magazines are audited by the Business

---

Controlled circulation magazines
Sent without cost to people responsible for making buying decisions. To get on such lists, people must state their positions in companies; to stay on it, they must request it annually. Also known as *qualified-circulation publications.*

Vertical publications
Business publications dealing with the problems of a specific industry: for example, *Chain Store Age, National Petroleum News, Textile World.*

North American Industrial Classification System (NAICS)
System that uses six-digit identification numbers for classifying manufacturing firms.

exhibit

11.18

Most business-to-business magazines prefer to be audited, indicating that an audit remains a tool in the fight to gain advertising. Generally, advertisers ask to see the audit and it does help, according to respondents to this poll.

Courtesy: Julie McWilliams.
Source: Lambeth Hochwald, "Circulators Stick with What Works," *Folio,* May 1, 1996, p. 44.

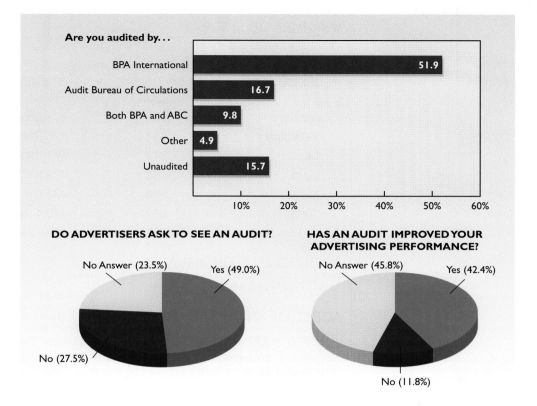

Are you audited by...

BPA International	51.9
Audit Bureau of Circulations	16.7
Both BPA and ABC	9.8
Other	4.9
Unaudited	15.7

DO ADVERTISERS ASK TO SEE AN AUDIT?

No Answer (23.5%)   Yes (49.0%)   No (27.5%)

HAS AN AUDIT IMPROVED YOUR ADVERTISING PERFORMANCE?

No Answer (45.8%)   Yes (42.4%)   No (11.8%)

Publications Audit (BPA) of Circulation International, the leading business auditor (see Exhibit 11.18). Because many business publications are circulated to a general business audience, the Audit Bureau of Circulations is used for publications such as *Business Week,* and a few publications use both auditing firms.

A third auditing organization is the Verified Audit Circulation (VAC). Founded in 1951, VAC provides circulation audits for a wide variety of newspapers, shoppers, magazines, and even Yellow Pages directories. Exhibit 11.19 (p. 326) shows a portion of the audit for *Better Nutrition for Today's Living* magazine. There are a number of publications in the business area that are not audited. Although an unaudited publication can survive, there are a number of business-to-business advertisers and agencies that, as a matter of policy, will not consider an unaudited publication.

Agribusiness Advertising

At one time, farm media, both print and broadcast, were largely geared to the millions of families who lived and worked on small farms. In recent years, the farm press has had to adapt to dramatic changes in the way agriculture is conducted in this country. Between 1940 and 1991, the number of farm workers declined by almost 70 percent. During that same period, the number of farm residents dropped from 31 million to 5 million.[26]

Contemporary agribusiness media and advertisers are tailoring their messages to a concentrated industry of huge farm cooperatives and farm managers with income and educational levels that rival those of the CEOs of any major business. Weather and crop prices are still major topics of the farm press, but these publications are just as likely to

---

[26]Marc Spiegler, "Hot Media Buy: The Farm Report," *American Demographics,* October 1995, p. 18.

Magazine Audit Report — 1994

QUALIFIED CIRCULATION BY ISSUE

ISSUE 1994	# OF STORE ACCOUNTS	TOTAL PAID
January	830	471,665
February	831	475,390
March	842	474,290
April	856	473,890
May	860	474,015
June	862	473,115
AVERAGE	847	473,728

ADDITIONS & REMOVALS

NOT APPLICABLE

AUDIT OF INTERNAL RECORDS

VERIFIED AUDIT CIRCULATION examined Publishers Printing Company invoices and certifies that an average of 489,336 copies of *BETTER NUTRITION For Today's Living* were printed for the 6 issues covered by this report. Canceled checks affirm payment for the services rendered by Publishers Printing Company. Invoices from Delta Mailing and UPS distribution records verified bulk shipments to the various store locations. Argus Business' canceled checks confirm payment for the services rendered by Delta Mailing.

Records for the period covered by this report were reviewed in order to verify payment status of store accounts. Using standard methods of sample selection, VAC determined that data presented in the report is fully supported by the audit findings.

AFFIDAVIT

Verified Audit Circulation swears to the best of its knowledge, all data contained in this report is accurate.

August 1994

---

be discussing the weather in Russia and price controls and export policies as opposed to what is happening in a local community.

The farm press is facing many of the problems of the business press in general. A number of media competitors have come on the scene in recent years to take advertising dollars from the print media. Unlike business-to-business advertising, for which television and radio have only recently been used by advertisers, farm broadcasting has a long history of serving the farm community.

There are a number of local and regional farm broadcasters, but on a national level the primary sources of agribusiness news and advertising are

- *AgDay,* a daily syndicated television show that reaches 130 markets and is supported by a number of national advertisers such as DuPont and Chevrolet
- the weekly *U.S. Farm Report,* which is syndicated to approximately 93 percent of the nation's television households
- *National Farm Report,* which is syndicated to some 350 radio stations
- the *Agri-Voice Network,* a network of 90 smaller Midwestern radio stations broadcasting daily farm reports.

In addition, a number of Web sites have been established by the farm media and agribusiness advertisers. It is estimated that some 33 percent of farmers are actively using the Internet for information and exchanging views on farm issues.[27]

Advertising products to the agribusiness community uses many of the same techniques demonstrated by other sectors of business marketing. However, agribusiness promotional techniques are even more specialized than those of traditional business-to-business selling. The relatively small agribusiness population makes sophisticated information readily available. Agribusiness advertising can target audiences and deliver a message that solves specific problems of the farm industry.

The business of farming has been hit hard during recent years with an uncertain farm economy, high prices for feed and other supplies, and the ravages of the great Midwestern flood of 1993. These factors have combined to make it very difficult for farm magazines and agribusiness advertising in general. A continuing consolidation of farms has reduced the number of farmers and companies involved in agribusiness. This trend toward consolidation has been reflected in the farm press by lower circulation and fewer advertising dollars during the last two decades.

Ironically, as the number of farms and major agribusiness suppliers have decreased, the number and diversity of media competing for advertising dollars in the sector has grown dramatically. To compete in this environment, farm publications have utilized many of the techniques of the business press in expanding the means they use to reach their audiences. For example, these magazines have accumulated sophisticated databases to develop subscriber list rentals, do their own direct mail to nonsubscribers, and publish special catalogs and other material. Like the business press, farm magazines will probably see more revenue coming from nonpublishing sources as they become more successful in promoting these ventures.

The Organization of the Farm Press

Farm magazines fall into three classifications: general farm magazines, regional farm magazines, and vocational farm magazines.

General Farm Magazines   The three major publications in the category are *Farm Journal, Successful Farming,* and *Progressive Farmer.* In recent years, each of these publications has experienced circulation decreases reflecting the consolidation of the farming industry. The general farm publications are designed to address all aspects of farm life, but with a clear emphasis on business. For instance, the SRDS "Publisher's Editorial Profile" for *Successful Farming* reads as follows:

> *Successful farming* editorial is designed as management guidance for business farmers and their families. Articles are written as practical help in making those decisions which directly affect the profitability of the business, and the welfare of the family. Editors seek their information from those in the forefront of farm change, and much editorial is case history reporting of successful innovation. There are also monthly reports on developments in government, finance, equipment, etc. Editorial is 100% business of farming and farm family management.

Regional Farm Magazines   A number of farm publications are directed to farmers in a particular region. These publications tend to be general in nature, but they contain little of the family-oriented topics found in the large-circulation farm magazines. They address issues of crops, livestock, and government farm policy unique to a particular region. Among the publications in this category are the *Prairie Farmer,* the

---

[27]Barnaby J. Feder, "Getting Personal and Global in Farm Broadcasting," *The New York Times,* December 18, 1995, p. C5.

majority of whose readers live in Indiana and Illinois; the *Oregon Farmer-Stockman;* and the *Nebraska Farmer.*

Vocational Farm Magazines   The last category of farm publications comprises those devoted to certain types of farming or livestock raising. Typical of these publications are *Soybean Digest, The Dairyman, American Fruit Grower,* and *Tobacco.* Many of the vocational magazines combine elements of both regional and vocational publications—for instance, *The Kansas Stockman* and *Missouri Pork Producer.*

Whatever a farmer's interests may be, a number of publications are edited to cater to them. Many farm homes take several publications.

SUMMARY

Business-to-business publications are facing a number of challenges in the coming years. Among the most obvious are the consolidation of many industries into fewer and fewer firms. This merging of firms has resulted in a decrease in both the number of potential advertisers to support the business press and the number of companies that are being reached with advertising.

A second major trend in the business press has been the growth of competition for advertising dollars. At one time, trade and business publications had a virtual monopoly in the business sector and the farm press had only radio as a major competitor. Today, that situation has changed dramatically. Business advertisers are putting their marketing communication dollars in numerous vehicles and utilizing sophisticated database technology to demand immediate and measurable results from their advertising.

Because of the relatively low price of trade magazine advertising, it is possible to appeal to specialized job interests with different messages in a variety of publications. The messages of these publications are also specialized. Factual copy with product information is presented to a knowledgeable audience in a manner that would be impractical in most consumer magazines.

Business publications are an ideal medium for reaching the targeted audience segments that advertisers seek in any environment suited to the mood of that audience. Business magazines also provide audience involvement to a degree impossible in most of other media, and the affinity for these magazines carries over to the advertising messages (see Exhibit 11.20).

exhibit
11.20

The more intense the relationship a reader has with a publication, the more likely the reader is to read, believe, and act on information in the ads.

Courtesy: Cahners Publishing Co., Cahners Advertising Research Report No. 120.1.

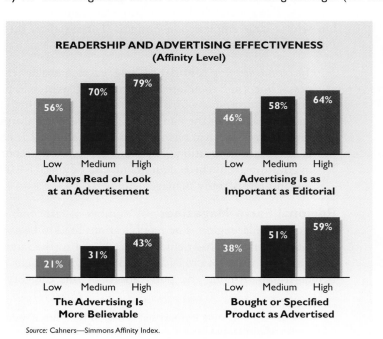

READERSHIP AND ADVERTISING EFFECTIVENESS
(Affinity Level)

Always Read or Look at an Advertisement
Low 56% | Medium 70% | High 79%

Advertising Is as Important as Editorial
Low 46% | Medium 58% | High 64%

The Advertising Is More Believable
Low 21% | Medium 31% | High 43%

Bought or Specified Product as Advertised
Low 38% | Medium 51% | High 59%

Source: Cahners—Simmons Affinity Index.

With the ability of computers to track employment demographics and new technology to reach them through partial-run editions and selected binding, business magazines can compete in an increasingly competitive media environment. On the negative side, business magazines face the same problems of rising costs of postage, printing, and marketing as their consumer counterparts. Quality, credibility, believability, and audience selectivity are the elements that will continue to make the business press a primary choice of business-to-business advertisers.

REVIEW

1. Discuss the importance of audience selectivity as it relates to the success of magazines.
2. What were the contributions of publishers such as Frank Munsey and Edward Bok to the development of the modern magazine?
3. What are some of the factors that have moved magazines to shift a larger portion of costs to readers?
4. Discuss the importance of qualitative audience considerations to magazines.
5. Define the following terms:
    a. Cross-media buys
    b. Media imperatives
    c. Partial-run editions
    d. Fast-close advertising
    e. Split-run editions
    f. Selective binding
    g. Third cover
    h. Bleed pages
    i. Controlled publications
6. Discuss the role of the city magazine as an advertising vehicle.
7. Take a moment to review the various PRIZM categories in Exhibit 7.8 and try to match these audiences with the primary readers of some major magazines.
8. How does the closing date for a magazine differ from the cover date?
9. Why is the rate base so important to the credibility of a magazine's advertising?
10. Compare and contrast the competition for advertisers between trade and consumer publications.
11. What are the primary differences between a vertical and horizontal publication?

TAKE IT TO THE NET

We invite you to visit the Russell/Lane page on the Prentice Hall Web site at **PHLIP** **http://www.prenhall.com/phbusiness** for the bimonthly Russell/Lane update and for this chapter's World Wide Web exercise.

OUT-OF-HOME ADVERTISING

got milk?

CHAPTER OBJECTIVES

OUTDOOR SIGNS PROMOTING GOODS AND SERVICES ARE THE
OLDEST FORM OF ADVERTISING AND DATE TO PREHISTORIC
TIMES. TODAY, AN INCREASINGLY MOBILE AND OUT-OF-HOME
POPULATION IS REACHED WITH A NUMBER OF PROMOTIONAL
MESSAGES IN A WIDE ARRAY OF FORMATS. THE TRADITIONAL
OUTDOOR BILLBOARD IS STILL THE PRIMARY COMPONENT OF
THE INDUSTRY, BUT IT HAS BEEN JOINED BY A NUMBER OF
OTHER PROMOTIONAL FORMATS IN EVERY IMAGINABLE SHAPE
AND SIZE. AFTER READING THIS CHAPTER YOU WILL
UNDERSTAND

- the diverse formats of the out-of-home industry
- outdoor's role as a supplement to other media
- primary advertising goals of out-of-home ads
- overcoming image problems of outdoor advertising
- creative uses of out-of-home, transit, and shelter posters
- measurement of the outdoor audience.

Outdoor is the oldest form of promotion. Evidence of outdoor messages can be found in prehistoric carvings on bronze and stone tablets in the Middle East. In Egypt, outdoor was a popular means of posting public notices as well as sales messages. These were placed on well-traveled roads and are the forerunner of the modern highway billboard. Painted advertising dates to Pompeii, where elaborately decorated walls promoted local businesses.

In this country, outdoor "broadsides" announced the Boston Tea Party and reported the Boston Massacre, and posters publicized the presidential campaign of Andrew Jackson. The first American commercial billboard was a poster by Jared Bell for the 1835 circus season. Throughout the 1800s, posters promoted a number of products and political causes.

The modern era of outdoor advertising was introduced when the automobile created a mobile society in the early years of the twentieth century. In addition, outdoor benefited from new printing techniques and a growing advertising industry that was looking for effective means of reaching prospective customers. During this period, the industry adopted standardized signs; formed the forerunner of its national trade association, the **Outdoor Advertising Association of America** (OAAA); established what is now the Traffic Audit Bureau for Media Measurement to authenticate audience data; and initiated a national marketing organization, OAAA Marketing.[1]

In recent years, outdoor advertising has experienced unprecedented growth in terms of numbers of advertisers as well as total revenues. It is estimated that some $3.5 billion is spent annually on all forms of out-of-home, with outdoor posters accounting for more than $2 billion of this total. Currently, outdoor is growing faster than the rate of total advertising as new advertisers representing categories such as package goods, insurance, and apparel come into the medium and traditional outdoor users such as automobiles increase their investment in outdoor.

There are a number of reasons for the growth of outdoor advertising. One factor has been the expanded assortment of creative options offered the advertisers. Overall, the OAAA estimates that there are more than 30 types of out-of-home media, including everything from the largest outdoor signs, to airport and shopping mall kiosks, to stadium signs, to airplanes towing banners. Among the more common forms of outdoor are

Medium	Number
Posters	350,000
Bulletins	55,000
Bus shelters	35,000
Buses	40,000

In the future, these forms will be joined by a number of digital formats that will duplicate television capability on a poster size screen and provide instant message rotation.

As one outdoor advertising executive observed, "There are a number of reasons for this growth—including innovative creative, fragmentation of broadcast and print, advertiser/agencies looking for better media efficiencies, more complete geo-demographic data, technological breakthroughs in production techniques, and new outdoor products."[2]

The variety of outdoor advertising vehicles has even resulted in the term out-of-home advertising replacing the more familiar term outdoor advertising in recent years to more fully reflect the scope of this industry. Today, outdoor normally has a more narrow meaning, referring only to highway posters and large signs. The change is more than just a difference in terminology. It reflects the diversity of the industry and its marketing strategy. As we see in this chapter, out-of-home advertisers are using a number of different media, more narrowly pinpointing and identifying their target markets, and appealing to a broader spectrum of advertisers than in previous years.

The out-of-home medium comprises a number of advertising vehicles with a common marketing objective. That is, all out-of-home advertising seeks to reach consumers who are in the marketplace, many with the intention to purchase. It does so with colorful, spectacular messages that are difficult to ignore (see Exhibit 12.1, p. 332). The two primary categories of out-of-home advertising are outdoor and transit.

---

[1]Unless otherwise noted, material for this section was provided by the Outdoor Advertising Association of America.

[2]Robert M. Nyland, "The Numbers Tell the Story in the Out-of-Home Medium," a special advertising section of the Outdoor Advertising Association of America, p. A-4.

Outdoor Advertising Association of America (OAAA) Primary trade and lobbying organization for the outdoor industry.

exhibit

12.1

Out-of-home
advertising takes many
forms.

Courtesy: SuperGraphics.

OUT-OF-HOME ADVERTISING

Out-of-home advertising is a relatively small medium, with expenditures of approximately $3.5 billion. However, the diversification of out-of-home has made it difficult to categorize the various options, much less keep track of their revenues. For instance, out-of-home encompasses a host of media including posters, transit, one-of-a-kind spectaculars, computer painting and laser light shows, and bus shelters (see Exhibit 12.2). For simplicity, we confine most of our discussion in this section to standardized outdoor posters.

exhibit

12.2

Out-of-home
messages are difficult
to ignore.

Courtesy: TranStop and Shelter
Advertising Association.

THE OUTDOOR INDUSTRY:
AN ADVERTISER PERSPECTIVE

Advantages of Outdoor Advertising

Outdoor is a dominant medium that combines high levels of reach and frequency, a colorful presentation of products, and low *CPM,* while reaching an audience already in the marketplace. Outdoor is one of the last opportunities to reach consumers prior to purchase. In this regard, it combines the best features of radio and point-of-purchase.

With its ability to command attention, outdoor also is well suited to enhance the effectiveness of other advertising media. It can function as an economical supplement to a media plan or stand alone as a primary medium. Outdoor advertising has a number of characteristics that sets it apart from other media vehicles. Ironically, in this era of segmented marketing, in which seemingly every medium is trying to outdo every other one with claims that it can reach more narrowly defined markets, outdoor stands alone as a truly "mass medium." Outdoor provides opportunities to reach particular portions of a geographic or demographic market, but its major strength is its ability to reach the entire mobile population quickly and cheaply. Let us briefly discuss several other important characteristics of the outdoor industry that have contributed to its recent popularity with advertisers.

Outdoor is an excellent secondary medium to increase reach and frequency and support the primary media of a campaign. Outdoor can complement virtually any medium:

- Outdoor reinforces a television campaign with strong visuals, which extend broadcast imagery and enhance the overall reach and frequency of television.
- Outdoor provides the graphic, visual association missing with radio.
- Outdoor can increase frequency missing in many magazine campaigns.
- The graphic imagery of outdoor, combined with newspapers, provides bold visual impact. Outdoor also extends the life of newspaper advertising.[3]

Product categories using outdoor have grown significantly in the last decade. According to the OAAA, the five major categories of outdoor advertising are entertainment and amusements, tobacco, retail, business and consumer services, and automotive.

Although relatively few industries still account for a disproportionate share of advertising dollars, the outdoor industry has been successful in attracting companies such as Kellogg's Nutri-Grain cereal and McDonald's. It is notable that beer and wine are no longer in the top five advertising categories for the medium.

Demographic trends seem to favor future outdoor growth. According to the OAAA, outdoor advertising offers advertisers a way to reach a growing, mobile population in a much more efficient manner than other media.[4] From 1970 to 1995, the average time spent with traditional media showed little change:

Television	+12%
Radio	+14
Newspapers	−8
Magazines	−4

At the same time, media choices grew at astounding rates:

Cable households	+1,542%
TV channels per household	+680
Total radio stations	+45
Magazines	+144

---

[3]University of Texas, Outdoor Archive.

[4]From "Facts & Figures," Outdoor Advertising Association of America Web site (www.OAAA.org).

During this period, the prime audience for outdoor—the mobile adult population—kept growing:

Total population	+23%
Cars per household	+49
Daily car trips	+82
Daily car miles	+82
Number of vehicles on road	+128

Not only has overall automotive travel increased, but business travel by car also has shown significant growth. Approximately 60 percent of all business travel is done by car, with some 700 million person-days traveled each year. These business automobile travelers spend an average of $80 per day, and they have an average personal income of $50,000. As one writer pointed out, "Hotels, restaurants, business copying services, gasoline stations, credit cards, and long-distance telephone calling cards all should pay attention."[5] They not only represent a major market, but, with the exception of radio, one that is virtually impossible to reach with traditional media.

Outdoor is a valuable tool for supporting primary media in a campaign. In addition, some advertisers are finding that outdoor can be a major means of reaching those segments of the population that are generally light users of other vehicles. Young consumers, both adults and teens, tend to be light users of print media and are often out of the home during a good portion of the day. Therefore, although outdoor may be at a disadvantage in presenting a complete sales message, it can at least maintain some level of brand awareness to these hard-to-reach groups.

Most outdoor advertising provides continuous 24-hour coverage of a market. Whereas other media can be ignored, or their exposure is dependent on the habits of the audience, outdoor cannot be turned off, fast-forwarded, put aside, or left unopened. The outdoor message is always working to increase purchases and profits. In a society in which the labor force increasingly works nontraditional hours, continuity becomes a major advantage of outdoor advertising.

Outdoor advertising is the most cost efficient of the major media categories. Outdoor advertising consistently generates the lowest *CPM* media figures. There is no major media vehicle that can challenge outdoor from a cost standpoint. According to figures compiled by the OAAA, outdoor is much less expensive than other media in reaching adults 18 years and older:

Media Category	CPM	% Over Outdoor
Outdoor posters	$ 1.39	—
Radio (top 100 markets)	4.70	338
Spot television	15.20	1,093
Magazines (4-color ad)	7.65	550
Newspapers (top 100 markets)	9.30	669

Although outdoor can achieve a number of advertising goals, it is not suitable for every advertiser or every advertising or marketing situation. Like each advertising medium we have discussed, outdoor is most successful when it is used in accordance with narrowly defined marketing objectives that utilize the strengths of the medium.

In almost every case, advertisers who take full advantage of outdoor observe one of the following advertising strategies:

- Companies are introducing a new product and want immediate brand name recognition to complement other forms of advertising.
- Firms are marketing established, well-known, and recognized brands and want to provide reminder advertising to consumers in the marketplace.

---

[5]Christy Fisher, "King of the Road," *American Demographics,* August 1995, p. 55.

Disadvantages of Outdoor Advertising

When considering outdoor advertising, a firm must carefully consider the weaknesses inherent in the medium and how these may influence a particular marketing, media, or creative strategy. The problems advertisers have identified in using outdoor include the following:

1. *Creative limitations and low attention levels.* Because exposure to outdoor is both involuntary and brief, there is little depth of exposure, even among a product's most loyal customers. It is estimated that most signs are seen for less than 10 seconds by the average person. In addition, the average outdoor "copy" is 7 to 10 words.

2. *Little audience selectivity.* For the most part, the medium offers little selectivity among demographic groups and is more a shotgun than a rifle. However, national, regional, and local advertisers can tailor their messages to reach specific audiences by pinpointing certain neighborhoods or specific streets, such as roads that lead to stadiums or shopping malls.

3. *Availability problems.* In some communities, demand for premium outdoor sites means some advertisers cannot be served with their first-choice locations.

Despite these disadvantages, properly executed outdoor advertising can be an inexpensive method of gaining immediate product visibility.

The Image of Outdoor

During the last 30 years, outdoor advertising has become "embroiled in disputes over issues such as its dependence on revenue from marketers of alcoholic beverages and cigarettes, the clustering of signs for products such as fortified wines and malt liquor in inner-city neighborhoods, and the eye pollution caused by signs that obscure landmarks and scenic attractions."[6]

Unlike most other media, which readers and viewers choose to use or ignore, outdoor cannot be overlooked. Among its primary characteristics is the fact that outdoor is a big, intrusive medium that cannot be disregarded. Although this may be a characteristic with great appeal for the advertising community, it is source of significant criticism among environmentalists and other public activists, who have long lobbied Congress, state legislatures, and city councils to ban or severely restrict the outdoor industry. Outdoor executives are frustrated by the fact that many of the examples of irresponsible outdoor signs are not part of the regulated, standardized medium. Instead, they are often on-premise signs, which, ironically, are often specifically excluded from legislation against outdoor in order to protect local merchants.

Highway Beautification Act of 1965
Federal law that controls outdoor signs in noncommercial, nonindustrial areas.

Federal control of outdoor advertising began in earnest with the **Highway Beautification Act of 1965** (known as the "Lady Bird bill" after Lady Bird Johnson, who lobbied for the legislation). The act restricted the placement of outdoor signs along interstate highways and provided stiff penalties for states that failed to control signs within 660 feet of interstate roads. Since passage of the legislation, the number of outdoor signs has been reduced from 1.2 million to less than 400,000. Most of those that remain are concentrated in commercially zoned areas.

Today, the degree of outdoor control varies tremendously from one locale to another. The most extreme cases are the outright bans in Alaska, Hawaii, Maine, and Vermont. During recent years hundreds of local communities have enacted laws limiting or eliminating outdoor posters. In many cases, these state and local laws have provided for a phase-out period, many of which are now coming due. Throughout the country,

---

[6]Stuart Elliott, "Big, Bold, Outside and in Fashion," *The New York Times,* July 11, 1996, p. C1.

outdoor companies are filing suits against various restrictions. These suits tend to take one of two approaches:

1. *It is a violation of free speech to limit outdoor advertising.* Most legal scholars predict that this stance has little chance of success. Although, as we discuss in chapter 25, the Supreme Court has recently relaxed many of the distinctions between commercial speech and other communication protected by the First Amendment, local ordinances against outdoor placement usually survive court tests.

2. *Outdoor companies must be reimbursed for loss of property.* Whether local governments must compensate outdoor companies has not been settled by the courts. However, many attorneys think that there is precedent for requiring such payment by local governments. Everyone agrees that few cities will move ahead with such restrictions if taxpayer funds would be required for compensation.

The outdoor industry also is dealing with the loss of tobacco advertising. As part of a sweeping agreement, tobacco companies and Congress agreed that outdoor and transit tobacco advertising would be prohibited. At the time of the ban, tobacco advertising constituted approximately 10 percent of all out-of-home revenues. However, the industry had seen some form of regulation on the horizon and had steadily decreased its dependence on tobacco advertising during the last several years. For example, in the 1960s, tobacco accounted for some 25 percent of total outdoor revenues.

In addition to diversifying its advertising base, the outdoor industry has moved on a number of fronts to improve its image and create positive public relations in the communities it serves. One step to counteract negative publicity toward the industry has been the enactment of a voluntary Code of Advertising Practice by the OAAA. As part of this code, outdoor companies are asked to limit the number of billboards in a market that carry messages about products that cannot be sold to minors. Specifically, the code asks that member companies "establish **exclusionary zones** which prohibit advertisements of all products illegal for sale to minors which are either intended to be read from, or within 500 feet of, established places of worship, primary and secondary schools and hospitals." Furthermore, such "off-limit" boards will carry a decal featuring the symbol of a child (see Exhibit 12.3).

The Outdoor Advertising Plan

As with any advertising situation, we must start with the role that we expect outdoor to play in the overall marketing and advertising strategy. Most outdoor advertising is used either as an introduction of a new product or event (such as a sale) or as a re-

Exclusionary zones (outdoor)
Industry code of conduct that prohibits the advertising of products within 500 feet of churches, schools, or hospitals of any products that cannot be used legally by children.

exhibit

12.3

The international children's symbol was adopted by the OAAA to mark billboards that are "off-limits" to alcohol and tobacco ads.

Courtesy: Outdoor Advertising Association of America.

minder to keep consumers continually aware of a brand. With its headline format, outdoor is rarely suited to offer a complete sales message.

As already mentioned, national advertisers rarely use outdoor as their primary medium. Consequently, it is extremely important to plan the outdoor portion of the total advertising campaign in a manner that will assure maximum efficiency and support to other advertising and promotional vehicles. Planning and execution of outdoor follow many of the basic rules of advertising in other media. However, there are a number of unique features of outdoor that an advertiser and its agency must consider:[7]

1. *Know your geography.* The out-of-home population universe differs from both broadcast and print media. In outdoor advertising, areas are usually defined by the counties or zip codes to be covered.

2. *Define your target audience.* Many outdoor companies employ sophisticated geo-demographic mapping to more accurately target an audience as they travel.

3. *Plan in advance.* With today's tight marketplace, it is more important than ever to plan in advance in order to achieve your media objectives. Ideally, space should be purchased at least four months in advance; some markets require even more time. Like spot television and radio, out-of-home is a supply-and-demand business.

4. *Make arrangements.* The next step in outdoor planning is to contact the local outdoor company to make arrangements for production and posting of signs. The basic business unit of the outdoor industry is the local outdoor company, known as a **plant.** Its primary assets are the locations it has leased or bought under local zoning regulations permitting the erection of signs. Having acquired a location, the plant builds a structure at its own expense, leases advertising space, posts or paints the advertiser's message, and is responsible for maintaining the board and the ad in good condition during the life of the advertiser's contract. As we discuss later in this chapter, most major market outdoor plants are part of large national outdoor companies that allow an advertiser to place outdoor advertising in a number of cities without going through individual offices.

5. *Do a postbuy inspection.* After the posters are up, an in-market check of poster locations should be made. This inspection determines if proper locations were used and that the signs were posted or painted properly.

The fact that national outdoor is not a primary medium should not suggest that fundamental principles of advertising planning do not apply. In some respects, planning in outdoor is even more complex than in other media. As a supplement to other media, planners must make certain that the characteristics and objectives of outdoor mesh properly with those of more dominant media. The complementary nature of outdoor is an overriding concern in most outdoor schedules. The planner must be certain that outdoor can, in fact, reinforce the media schedule in a cost-efficient manner.

FORMS OF OUTDOOR ADVERTISING

As mentioned at the outset of this chapter, outdoor is only one of several categories of out-of-home advertising. In terms of revenues, public familiarity, and long-term usage, the two basic forms of outdoor are *posters* and painted bulletins (see Exhibit 12.4, p. 338). In both vehicles, the message is designed by the advertising agency. The design is then reproduced on paper and posted on panels. The larger painted bulletins are prepared by outdoor company artists either in a studio or on-site.

Plant
In outdoor advertising, the local company which arranges to lease, and to sell the advertising space on it.

---

[7]"The Key Ingredients to a Successful Out-of-Home Program Revolve around Strategic Planning of Your Campaign," a special out-of-home advertising section, p. A-4.

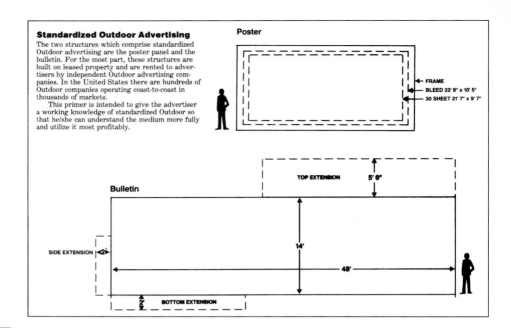

Standardized Outdoor Advertising

The two structures which comprise standardized Outdoor advertising are the poster panel and the bulletin. For the most part, these structures are built on leased property and are rented to advertisers by independent Outdoor advertising companies. In the United States there are hundreds of Outdoor companies operating coast-to-coast in thousands of markets.

This primer is intended to give the advertiser a working knowledge of standardized Outdoor so that he/she can understand the medium more fully and utilize it most profitably.

exhibit

12.4

Posters and bulletins make up the standardized outdoor industry.

Courtesy: Outdoor Advertising Association of America.

Poster panel
A standard surface on which outdoor posters are placed. The posting surface is of sheet metal. An ornamental molding of standard green forms the frame. The standard poster panel is 12 feet high and 25 feet long (outside dimensions).

Illuminated posters
Seventy to 80 percent of all outdoor posters are illuminated for 24-hour exposure.

Eight-sheet poster
Outdoor poster used in urban areas, about one-fourth the size of the standard 30-sheet poster. Also called *junior poster.*

Poster Panels

The most common type of poster is really two posters in one. Bleed and 30-sheet posters, the most widely used form of outdoor advertising, use the same frame and constitute the typical highway billboard. These posters are available in some 9,000 communities. Poster buys can be made for a single location or total national coverage.

The primary use of most posters is to reach the majority of a market quickly and inexpensively. However, 30-sheet posters also can be used to reach targeted demographic groups. For example, posters placed in financial districts or on routes to and from upscale residential neighborhoods reach more affluent customers, and those near colleges communicate with a younger audience.[8]

The standard poster panel measures 12 feet by 25 feet. The bleed poster either prints to the edge of the frame or uses blanking paper matching the background of the poster. The term "bleed" is, of course, borrowed from the bleed magazine ad, which has no border. The term "sheet" originated in the days when presses were much smaller and it took many sheets to cover a poster panel. Today, presses can print much larger sheets, and in many cases single vinyl surfaces are used, but space is still measured in terms of sheets.

Poster displays are sold on the basis of **illuminated** and nonilluminated panels. Normally, poster contracts are for 30 days with discounts for longer periods. Those panels in locations with high traffic volume are normally illuminated for 24-hour exposure. A typical poster showing will consist of 70 percent to 80 percent illuminated posters. When buying an outdoor showing, the advertiser is provided information about the number of displays, the number that are illuminated and nonilluminated, the monthly and per-panel cost, and total circulation or exposure.

The Eight-Sheet Poster[9]

One of the fastest growing types of outdoor advertising is the eight-sheet poster. **Eight-sheet posters** measure 5 feet by 11 feet, slightly less than one-third the size of 30-sheet posters (see Exhibit 12.5). The posters, sometimes called *junior posters,* were originally

---

[8] *30-Sheet Poster Buyers Guide, 1997,* a publication of Waggener & Associates, Inc., p. 19.

[9] Unless otherwise noted, material in this section is provided by the Eight-Sheet Outdoor Advertising Association.

exhibit

12.5

**Eight-Sheet
Outdoor
Specifications**

Courtesy: Eight-Sheet Outdoor
Advertising Association.

developed to provide small, local businesses with affordable outdoor advertising, but
when the Eight-Sheet Outdoor Advertising Association established a standard poster
size, it enabled national and regional advertisers to use the medium throughout the
country. Research shows that eight-sheet displays, placed low and close to the street, deliver dramatic advertising visibility and impact at a reasonable cost. The average *CPM*
of eight-sheet posters is approximately half that of 30-sheets.

In most markets, zoning regulations are more favorable for the smaller eight-sheet
posters. Therefore, they can be used in a most cost-effective way to reach various target audiences, such as shoppers, without expensive waste circulation. Sales increase when
products are advertised near their point of sale. Whether it is food product advertising
placed near fast-food restaurants (see Exhibit 12.6) or soft-drink advertisements near

exhibit

12.6

Eight-sheet posters
can be displayed in
areas of high
pedestrian traffic.

Courtesy: Eight-Sheet Outdoor
Advertising Association.

convenience stores, eight-sheet represents the last mass advertising opportunity before a consumer's purchase.

Ethnic Targeting   Eight-sheet can effectively target various ethnic communities. Hispanic and Asian consumers are being reached in their own languages (see Exhibit 12.7).

Economic or Age Group Targeting   With creative location selection, eight-sheet advertising can be aimed at a wide variety of age, income, and lifestyle segments.

Eight-sheet posters are handled by special poster plants, but frequently appear concurrently with 30-sheet showings in a market. The Eight-Sheet Outdoor Advertising Association (ESOAA) was founded to promote the interests of the eight-sheet poster medium. Currently these posters are available in some 2,500 markets.

Painted Bulletins

Painted bulletins are the largest and most prominent type of outdoor advertising. Painted bulletins are of two types: *permanent* and the more popular *rotary.* The permanent bulletin remains at a fixed location and size is flexible because it is never moved. The **rotary bulletin** is a standardized sign that is three times larger (14 feet by 48 feet) than the standard poster and provides greater impact than traditional posters. It can be moved from site to site to ensure maximum coverage of a market over a period of months. Both types of bulletins are located at choice sites along heavily traveled thoroughfares. They are almost always illuminated.

Bulletins are approximately four times more expensive than posters. In recent years, the basic bulletin has been augmented with special embellishments, such as cutouts, freestanding letters, special lighting effects, fiber optics, and inflatables. Painted bulletin contracts usually are for a minimum of one year; however, short-term contracts are available at a higher monthly rate.

The rotary bulletin gives the advertiser the advantages of the greater impact of the painted bulletin along with more coverage and penetration than a single site could deliver. The rotary bulletin can be moved every 30, 60, or 90 days, so that during a 12-month period consumers throughout the market will have seen the advertiser's message.

Spectaculars

As the name implies, outdoor spectaculars are large, usually unique displays designed for maximum attention in high traffic areas. They may consist of special lighting or other types of ingenious material and innovations. In some cases they utilize a building

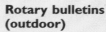

**Rotary bulletins
(outdoor)**
Movable painted
bulletins that are
moved from one fixed
location to another
one in the market at
regular intervals. The
locations are viewed
and approved in
advance by the
advertiser.

as the canvas for the message. The cost of spectaculars is very expensive, and both production and space rentals are normally negotiated on a one-time basis. However, the minimum contract period for most spectaculars is usually a year.

With the advent of new technology in outdoor advertising, what was once a spectacular may soon be the norm. The outdoor industry is currently using a variety of digital and laser technology for computerized painting and printing systems. Often printed on flexible vinyl, these systems provide consistent, magazine-quality reproduction in all markets. In the future, outdoor planners envision the ability to provide satellite-distributed video images, similar to giant television screens, where messages can be changed immediately. Regardless of what new technology comes to outdoor, it is obvious that the static, paper poster soon may be history.

THE ELEMENTS OF OUTDOOR

Once the objectives of an outdoor advertising buy have been established, the media planner begins the job of executing the campaign. The outdoor campaign combines three elements: designing, buying, and verifying. In this section, we examine the basic guidelines that will ensure that your outdoor messages have the greatest chance of achieving the desired marketing objectives.

Designing

Designing an outdoor display is among the most difficult tasks for a creative team. Creating a picture and a few words to be seen by fast-moving traffic at distances ranging up to 500 feet is difficult enough—to do so in a manner that moves customers to buy a product adds an obstacle not found in other media. However, outdoor also is one of the most enjoyable media to work with from a creative standpoint. Its size and color allow maximum creativity without the constraints of other advertising vehicles.

Copy   Outdoor allows only a headline, usually no more than seven words. Unlike copy in traditional media, there is no theme development or copy amplification. Conciseness is not only a virtue, it is a necessity. Advertisers have learned to work with these constraints to make outdoor among the most creative contemporary advertising.

Color   Color is one of the primary advantages of outdoor. However, color must be chosen carefully to create easy readability. Outdoor designers use colors that create high contrast in both *hue* (red, green, etc.) and *value* (a measure of lightness or darkness). For example, Exhibit 12.8 demonstrates 18 combinations of colors, with 1 being the most visible and 18 the least visible.

Type Typefaces in outdoor should be simple, clear, and easy to read. Some of the basic rules of outdoor type and lettering include

- the use of capitals should be kept to a minimum
- considerable care should be given to spacing between letters and between words
- whatever typeface is selected, the ultra-bold and ultra-thin versions should be avoided
- a simple typeface is better for outdoor.

In a major study sponsored by Gannett Outdoor and the University of Alberta, researchers found that effective outdoor followed a number of guidelines. Among the most important were (1) the greater the clarity of the type, the higher the recall; (2) the more intriguing or humorous the message, the higher the recall; and, perhaps most important, (3) out-of-home messages with fewer concepts have more impact.[10]

Although outdoor presents a number of challenges to the design team, when all elements come together it offers a marvelous message. Chick-fil-A outdoor boards present one of the great campaigns of recent years (Exhibit 12.9). The three-dimensional cows immediately gain attention. The humor is whimsical and, best of all, it gets across a strong sales message promoting the chicken entrees of the chain.

Buying Outdoor

Both the methods and terminology used in buying outdoor advertising are different in a number of ways from those used in other media. Poster advertising is purchased on the basis of *gross rating points* (*GRP*s) or **showings.** As for television, one *GRP* is equal to 1 percent of the population. Showings normally are bought in units of 50 or 100 and measure the *duplicated* audience reached by a poster *allotment.* An allotment is the number of posters in a market. A 50 showing in a market means that we will have daily exposures to our outdoor messages equal to 50 percent of the adult population of the market.

The audience for an outdoor showing is called the *daily effective circulation* (*DEC*) and is calculated as in the following example. Let us assume the 24-hour traffic count is 36,000. For nonilluminated posters, the traffic count factor is .45; therefore,

$$.45 \times 36{,}000 = 16{,}200 \text{ adult } DEC$$

For illuminated posters the traffic count factor is .64; therefore,

$$.64 \times 36{,}000 = 23{,}040 \text{ adult } DEC$$

---

[10]Riccardo A. Davis, "Outdoor Ad Creativity Is Focus of Gannett Study," *Advertising Age,* October 18, 1993, p. 12.

Let us examine a market and work through these calculations:

Market: Metropolis
Population: 800,000
Audience level purchased: 50 *GRPs* (showings)
Allotment: 26 posters (20 illuminated; 6 nonilluminated)
Explanation: Our 26-poster allotment generated a *DEC* of 400,000. We calculate this by the following formula:

$$DEC = GRP \times \text{market population}$$
$$= 50\% \times 800,000$$
$$= 400,000$$

You may not compare *GRP* levels in markets of different sizes, except as a measure of advertising weight and intensity. A 50 *GRP* might require an allotment of 50 or 100 posters in a larger market. For example, in a market of 2 million population, a 50 *GRP* buy would generate a *DEC* of 1 million, not 400,000. One final difference in buying outdoor compared to other media is that the agency commission in outdoor is 16.67 percent rather than the standard 15 percent.

Verifying

The final part of the planning process for outdoor advertising is verification of the buy. This procedure involves both pre- and postbuy factors. The most important considerations are the following:[11]

1. *Audit circulation.* National advertisers hire audit firms that specialize in outdoor advertising to conduct an audit of the outdoor showing in each market. Verification assures the advertiser that the posting was done properly and according to agreed-upon specifications. When there is some discrepancy, an audit allows the advertiser to obtain make-goods from the plant operator.
2. *Check market coverage.* The advertiser should request location maps and review major routes to determine traffic flow along its poster locations. If there are weaknesses in coverage, the advertiser may work with the outdoor plant to make adjustments in poster locations.
3. *Pre-ride the showing.* Visibility and traffic patterns change from month to month because of road construction, new building construction, vegetation growth from season to season, among other factors.
4. *Ride the showing.* After posting, a review of the total marketing postings should be conducted. This process of **"riding the boards"** is crucial to making sure that the proper number of posters are up, the correct proportion of illuminated and non-illuminated posters have been used, and the posters are properly maintained with no flags or tears in the paper. This process is similar to the submission of tearsheets in print advertising or verification forms in broadcast.
5. *Establish maintenance and "make-good" policies before the fact.* Any number of unavoidable occurrences might affect a showing—storm damage, electrical outages, or strikes. The advertiser should know the compensation policy for any lost showing days.
6. *Obtain a "postbuy analysis" report.* At the conclusion of the posting, the advertiser should request a report stating the actual posting dates, current circulation, and any lost showing days and make-goods.

Riding the boards
Inspecting an outdoor showing after posting.

[11] *30-Sheet Poster Buyers Guide, 1997,* a publication of Waggener & Associates, Inc., p. 8.

Outdoor Networks

For most of its history, outdoor has been a local business with a number of outdoor plants doing business on a local or regional basis. National advertisers and their agencies often found buying outdoor a major problem. Because outdoor constituted a relatively minor share of total billings, only the largest agencies had full-time outdoor buying units. Not only were the terminology and units of sale unique to the outdoor industry, but a national advertiser often had to deal with a multitude of local plants to complete a schedule.

In the mid-1990s this situation changed dramatically. During this period, the outdoor industry underwent unprecedented consolidation of ownership. In 1995, Eller Media, a major national plant operator, bought Patrick Media, creating the largest plant operation, with billings of more than 20 percent of total outdoor sales. However, in recent years, Outdoor Systems, a Phoenix-based outdoor plant operator, has become the largest outdoor company, with almost 100,000 billboards in 40 states.

The creation of large national companies has made it much easier for advertisers to create national outdoor plans. As one outdoor executive observed, "The recent consolidation has helped elevate outdoor advertising to the status of a true national medium, like network television or magazines."[12] Outdoor consolidation has provided added efficiency for agencies and advertisers wanting to buy outdoor on a national basis. However, advertisers still find that a single outdoor company may not operate in all the markets they want to buy. Small agencies sometimes contract with independent outdoor media experts who put together "network" deals among a number of plants. This process is similar to radio's nonwired networks discussed earlier.

MEASURING OUTDOOR AUDIENCES

A major problem for outdoor advertising is providing accurate audience measurement. Trying to determine audience estimates for a mobile population is extremely demanding, as we saw with the difficulty experienced by radio in gathering ratings information. Outdoor faces the problem that national advertisers increasingly demand better data. However, because these advertisers generally place a small portion of their total advertising budget in outdoor, they are unwilling to support the expenditure of significant dollars in outdoor audience research.

Despite these problems, the outdoor industry has made progress in providing sophisticated research and standardized policies to advertisers. There are a number of companies providing a variety of data and audience measures for the industry. The most important are

Traffic Audit Bureau for Media Measurement (TAB)
An organization designed to investigate how many people pass and may see a given outdoor sign, to establish a method of evaluating traffic measuring a market.

- *Traffic Audit Bureau for Media Measurement.* The **Traffic Audit Bureau** (TAB) is an independent, nonprofit organization that provides circulation verification for the out-of-home industry. TAB not only measures outdoor audiences, but also establishes standards for visibility of outdoor signs.
- *Simmons Market Research Bureau.* The Simmons Market Research Bureau is a national consumer study conducted annually with more than 19,000 respondents. SMRB data provide analyses of target audiences, media usage habits, and outdoor delivery for 750 consumer products and services.
- *The Harris Donovan Model for Outdoor Planning.* One of the newest tools for planning outdoor media is the Harris Donovan Model. Available for personal computers, the Harris Donovan Model measures the potential audience exposed to an outdoor campaign. The model combines cost and audience information to determine if specific campaign objectives have been met with a particular outdoor campaign.

---

[12]Mark Hudis, "All the Signs Point Up," *Mediaweek,* July 15, 1996, p. 6.

- *Buyer's Guides.* Waggener & Associates publishes a number of rate guides for 30- and 8-sheet posters and bulletins. The *Buyers Guide* provides information concerning costs, number of panels in a showing, and market population (see Exhibit 12.10).

As the outdoor industry seeks to encourage more advertising from package goods and retail advertisers, it must adopt practices similar to those of other media. One of the potential benefits of consolidation of the outdoor industry may be industrywide support for a number of research and audience measurement studies. As outdoor aims to become a true national medium, it will continue to provide reliable and credible audience data and research.

Trends in Outdoor Advertising

Outdoor advertising is growing at a faster rate than advertising in general. Furthermore, it is appealing to a number of new product categories as advertisers look for cost-efficient means of gaining brand awareness and supporting primary media buys. There are a number of positive trends that bode well for outdoor as a growing medium into the next century.

Bakersfield   CA   MMA **84**

MARTIN OUTDOOR ADVERTISING
3101 Sillect   Suite 106
Bakersfield, CA 93308

Todd E. Hansen
(805) 324-8031
FAX: (805) 324-8031

Ship to:
Same

Counties Served: Kern

18+ Population: 453,407
Total Panels Available: 310/178
TAB DEC: Illum.: 16,600   Non-Ill.: 6,700

	Market Coverage	No. of Panels Ill./Non-Ill	One Month Rate	Total per Month	12* Month Rate	Total per Month
General Coverage	100	32/16	633.00	30,400.00	633.00	30,400.00
	75	24/12	633.00	22,800.00	633.00	22,800.00
	50	16/8	633.00	15,200.00	633.00	15,200.00
	25	8/4	633.00	7,600.00	633.00	7,600.00
Hispanic Market Coverage	100	16/8	633.00	15,200.00	633.00	15,200.00
	75	12/6	633.00	11,400.00	633.00	11,400.00
	50	8/4	633.00	7,600.00	633.00	7,600.00
	25	4/2	633.00	3,800.00	633.00	3,800.00

Adjacent Markets Sold Separately:

Arvin, CA	Buttonwillow, CA
Delano, CA	Lake Isabella, CA
Lamont, CA	Mojave, CA
Shaffer, CA	Taft, CA
Tehachapi, CA	Wasco, CA

Palm Springs   CA   MMA **63**

HEYWOOD COMPANY
1948 N. "E" Street
San Bernardino, CA 92405

Hal R. Heywood/Dori Niessen
(909) 886-5244
FAX: (909) 881-2307

Ship to:
462 E. Ramsey
Banning, CA 92220

Counties Served: San Bernardino, Riverside

18+ Population: 658,307
Total Panels Available: 90/48
TAB DEC: Illum.: 23,180   Non-Ill.: 7,950

	Market Coverage	No. of Panels Ill./Non-Ill	One Month Rate	Total per Month	12* Month Rate	Total per Month
General Coverage	100	22/22	496.00	21,824.00	446.00	19,624.00
	75	18/18	496.00	17,856.00	446.00	16,056.00
	50	12/12	496.00	11,904.00	446.00	10,704.00
	25	6/6	532.00	6,384.00	479.00	5,748.00
Hispanic Market Coverage	100	4/4	496.00	3,968.00	446.00	3,568.00
	75	3/3	496.00	2,976.00	446.00	2,676.00
	50	2/2	496.00	1,984.00	446.00	1,784.00
	25	1/1	532.00	1,064.00	479.00	958.00

Special Notes and Additional Discounts: Agency Commission: 16-2/3% to recognized agencies.
*Reflects 10% continuity discount for 12-month consecutive month showing.

Adjacent Markets Sold Separately:

Hemet, CA	Yucca Valley, CA

Adjacent Markets $448.00/Panel

(continued)

exhibit

12.10

(continued)

Sacramento   CA   MMA 34

JACOBS BILLBOARD COMPANY
P.O. Box 15098
Sacramento, CA 95853

David Jacobs
(360) 377-9867
FAX: (360) 377-9870

Ship to:
2338 LaLima Way
Sacramento, CA 95833

Counties Served: Sacramento

18+ Population: 1,142,000
Total Panels Available: 2/28

TAB DEC: Illum.: 144,000 Non-Ill.: 12,500

	Market Coverage	No. of Panels Ill./Non-Ill	One Month Rate	Total per Month	12* Month Rate	Total per Month
General Coverage	100					
	75					
	50	2/26	450.00	12,600.00	400.00	11,200.00
	25	1/13	450.00	6,300.00	400.00	5,600.00
Hispanic Market Coverage	100	1/15	450.00	7,200.00	400.00	6,400.00
	75	1/11	450.00	5,400.00	400.00	4,800.00
	50	1/7	450.00	3,600.00	400.00	3,200.00
	25	0/4	450.00	1,800.00	400.00	1,600.00

Special Notes and Additional Discounts:
Single permanent panel = $650.00/month.
Custom showings and permanent directional locations available.

- *The rate of outdoor cost increases have been far below those of other media.* Regardless of the method of comparison with other media, outdoor provides audience delivery at bargain prices. The *CPM* for outdoor is the lowest of any print or broadcast medium, cost increases during the last decade have been minimal, and reach and frequency levels are unsurpassed by other advertising vehicles.
- *Outdoor continues to diversify the categories of advertisers using the medium.* Although tobacco and alcohol remain major clients for outdoor, the influx of retail, automotive, and package-goods advertisers in recent years has been encouraging. Entertainment-related advertisers currently constitute the largest group of outdoor users.
- *Creativity in outdoor has never been stronger.* The future offers the prospect of computerized displays, satellite transmission to outdoor displays, and the use of fiber optics. When these systems are in place, advertisers will be able to create a limitless array of creative messages and do so with an immediacy that will allow them to react to any changes in market conditions.
- *Research data are improved.* Outdoor is providing much improved audience information and providing demographic and geographic data that allow advertisers to pinpoint audiences in a manner never before possible.
- *Outdoor meets the public relations challenge.* Outdoor must continue to improve its public image as well as market the medium to advertisers. The industry needs to find areas of accommodation with environmentalists and other critics. Outdoor also must get the message out to the general public that it is a responsible member of the community. For example, the majority of outdoor plants provide free space for public service advertising (see Exhibit 12.11).

TRANSIT ADVERTISING

Transit advertising encompasses a number of formats and distinctly different advertising vehicles. According to the Transit Advertising Association, the major forms of transit advertising are

- bus exteriors
- taxi exteriors
- bus and commuter rail interiors
- commuter station posters
- miscellaneous displays, such as terminal clocks and air terminal posters.

Transit advertising provides a low-cost option for reaching a mobile, urban audience. Total revenues are estimated at approximately $350 million, and it is likely that mass transit will become more popular in the coming years. Transit advertising is extremely inexpensive, with *CPM* figures in the $1 range. Like outdoor, it reaches a mobile population already in the marketplace.

With the purchase of Transportation Displays Inc. (TDI), the largest transit advertising firm, by Infinity Broadcasting, transit became part of a national multimedia company with additional resources and capability to serve national advertisers. Advertisers now enjoy some of the same national buying capability earlier resulting from consolidation within the outdoor industry.

In addition, a number of municipal governments that formerly banned advertising on municipal transit systems are now looking to such advertising as a means of additional revenue. For example, in 1996, Atlanta's MARTA transit system began allowing exterior transit advertising on its buses the same day it approved a fare increase. The transit system expects to receive $1 million from advertisements annually to defray operational costs.[13]

Exhibit 12.12 (p. 348) offers a summary of several of the primary forms of interior and exterior bus displays. The king-size posters have traditionally dominated bus advertising space and are the most used format for both national and local transit advertisers. However, in recent years, advertisers have begun to look for new ways to gain audience attention with transit advertising.

One of these concepts is the *brand train,* by which advertisers purchase all or half of the interior space on a subway car or bus. The additional space allows much more flexibility for an advertising message and it reduces advertising clutter, allowing advertisers to make great audience impact. When the brand train idea was introduced on New York subway cars, major advertisers such as Nike, Levi Strauss, Heineken, and Sony saw it as an ideal way to reach a significant number of the 3.5 million daily passengers.[14]

Now new technology has allowed transit systems to offer even greater dominance of the market through the introduction of exterior bus *wraps,* which turn vehicles into mobile murals. The wraps can be used on any commercial vehicle. Companies such as

---

[13]"Q&A," *Atlanta Journal,* August 16, 1996, p. A2.

[14]John Nichols, "Outdoor New York Tops Ideas," *Gannetteer,* September 1995, p. 8.

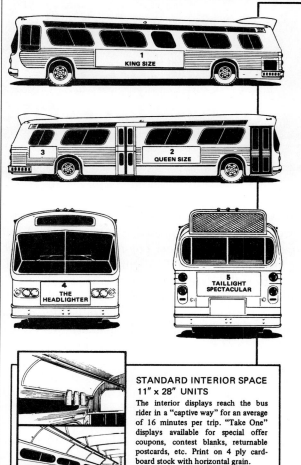

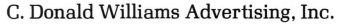

C. Donald Williams Advertising, Inc.

SUITE 200   342 SOUTH SALINA ST.   SYRACUSE, NY 13202
CALL COLLECT (315) 422-2213

SPECIFICATIONS
Bus Advertising Displays

1 KING SIZE

30" x 144"
Street Side or Curb Side of Bus

The largest poster on the bus—a moving billboard at eye level—carrying its sales message daily to people downtown, in plants or offices, in suburbs or shopping centers.

2 QUEEN SIZE

30" x 88"
Curb Side of Bus

The Queen is located on the curb side of the bus between the entrance and exit doors. The Queen reaches people on the move whether walking, riding or boarding a bus. Sometimes used in conjunction with Kings to cover both sides of the street.

3 TRAVELING DISPLAY

21" x 44"
Curb Side or Street Side of Bus

The Traveling Display is our baby billboard used when high frequency and high reach is the priority but budget is tight. Can be used in conjunction with Fronts and Rears for outstanding results.

4 THE HEADLIGHTER

21" x 40"
Front of Bus

The front display is called the Headlighter. Visible in any kind of weather, the Headlighter reaches pedestrians, bus riders and drivers or passengers of other vehicles.

5 TAILLIGHT SPECTACULAR

21" x 70"
Rear of Bus

The rear spectacular offers high visibility and readability. Especially high impact and readership from auto drivers and passengers who follow immediately behind the bus. Highest exposure at traffic lights and intersections.

STANDARD INTERIOR SPACE
11" x 28" UNITS

The interior displays reach the bus rider in a "captive way" for an average of 16 minutes per trip. "Take One" displays available for special offer coupons, contest blanks, returnable postcards, etc. Print on 4 ply cardboard stock with horizontal grain.

UP FRONT SALES LIGHTER
14" x 20"

Special space behind driver.

SuperGraphics prepare total bus advertising on 50 lines/inch vinyl screen. The process allows riders to see out, but from the outside it creates a moving billboard. Exhibit 12.13 shows examples of various wraps.

Transit provides a number of advantages to advertisers and, although still a small medium by total advertising standards, has grown at a significant rate in the last several years. Transit reaches prospects in the marketplace and is attracting an increasingly upscale audience as public transportation becomes more popular in many cities. In the case of interior signs, advertisers are reaching a captive audience of riders who average almost 20 minutes per trip. The nature of the transit audience allows somewhat longer messages than outdoor signs. In the case of exterior transit signs, the repetitive nature of the message quickly builds high levels of frequency over relatively short periods.

exhibit

12.13

New materials and technology offer more creative options in transit advertising.

Courtesy: SuperGraphics.

SHELTER ADVERTISING

An important category of transit is shelter advertising. With traditional out-of-home facing a number of environmental, legal, and zoning challenges, shelter advertising has become a fast-growing sector of the out-of-home industry. Currently, there are some 26,000 shelter panels, mostly in high-traffic metropolitan markets. They have the advantage of being seen by transit riders, pedestrians, and vehicular traffic.

Shelter advertising has several major advantages for both national and local advertisers:

1. *It is an extremely inexpensive medium. CPM* levels for shelter advertising are among the lowest of any advertising medium. It also is similar to other out-of-home media in that it generates high reach and frequency in a short time. Rates are available from the Shelter Advertising Association's *Buyers Guide.*
2. *Advertisers can use shelter advertising to target specific markets.* For example, a packaged good may use shelters in front of supermarkets or jeanswear on the college campus.
3. *Shelter advertising is illuminated for 24-hour reach and provides maximum exposure and awareness.* With 4 × 6 signs, shelter advertising provides stopping power for both pedestrian and vehicular traffic. Unlike other media, it rarely suffers from clutter from other competing messages. Exhibit 12.14 (p. 350) shows some examples of outstanding shelter advertising.

Shelter advertising is used by a number of major advertisers, and it has been a leader in developing the type of diverse advertising support sought by other forms of out-of-home. Shelter advertising, although accounting for a small portion of total advertising,

exhibit

12.14

Shelter advertising reaches an audience on the move.

Courtesy: TranStop and Shelter Advertising Association.

will continue to grow at a faster rate than overall advertising. As new product categories come into the medium, we may even see larger increases in the shelter sector. Finally, rather than facing the regulatory problems of outdoor, the revenues generated by shelter posters are often shared with municipal transit companies, making the medium a revenue producer for many cities facing tight budgets.

SUMMARY

Out-of-home advertising is growing at a faster rate than most other advertising media as advertisers search for affordable alternatives to traditional media. Out-of-home media are able to remind, introduce, and increase brand awareness of products. Out-of-home functions in much the same way as point-of-purchase advertising to reach consumers immediately before purchase. With the options available from the various formats of out-of-home, there is a format for almost every advertising objective.

In recent years, the various components of the outdoor industry have moved to accommodate national advertisers. For one thing, there is much more standardization from one market to another. In addition, industry consolidation has created efficient means of buying multiple markets and has changed the complexion of the industry from one dominated by local firms to more national media. Out-of-home media also are enjoying the benefits of more sophisticated research concerning both audience levels and effects of the medium. As new national advertisers begin to consider out-of-home advertising, it will be necessary for the industry to provide research similar to what is available from other media competitors.

If there is a problem with out-of-home, it is that it is a victim of its own success. As more companies begin to offer out-of-home alternatives, it becomes more difficult to control the quality of the medium. The established organizations such as the OAAA and the Transit Advertising Association are constantly working with their members and advertisers to ensure that the industry meets the highest standards possible. However, as noted in the case of nonstandardized outdoor signs, it is extremely difficult to deal with nonmember companies or those who don't have the social responsibility of these major out-of-home organizations.

REVIEW

1. What are some of the primary marketing considerations in using out-of-home advertising?
2. What are some of the primary reasons for the recent growth of out-of-home advertising?
3. Why has the out-of-home industry actively sought to diversify the types of advertisers using the medium?
4. Briefly discuss the public image of outdoor advertising.
5. Briefly discuss the three primary forms of outdoor advertising.
6. Compare and contrast the advantages of eight-sheet outdoor with traditional forms of the medium.
7. Define the following terms:
   a. Gross rating points (outdoor)
   b. Daily effective circulation
   c. Illuminated posters
   d. Rotary bulletins
   e. Bus wraps

TAKE IT TO THE NET

We invite you to visit the Russell/Lane page on the Prentice Hall Web site at
PHLIP **http://www.prenhall.com/phbusiness** for the bimonthly Russell/Lane update and for this chapter's World Wide Web exercise.

13

DIRECT-RESPONSE AND DIRECT-MAIL ADVERTISING

CHAPTER OBJECTIVES

DIRECT-MAIL AND DIRECT-RESPONSE MARKETING ARE NOT NEW METHODS OF SELLING. BENJAMIN FRANKLIN SOLD SCIENTIFIC BOOKS BY MAIL IN THE 1740S, AND MORE THAN 100 YEARS AGO, MONTGOMERY WARD HAD A THRIVING MAIL-ORDER BUSINESS THROUGH HIS CATALOG. TODAY, VIRTUALLY EVERY MEDIUM, AS WELL AS DIRECT MAIL, COMPETES FOR CUSTOMERS THROUGH DIRECT-RESPONSE OFFERS. AFTER READING THIS CHAPTER YOU WILL UNDERSTAND

- **the size and scope of direct marketing**
- **societal factors encouraging the growth of direct response**
- **computer technology and database marketing**
- **diverse formats of direct response including telemarketing and home shopping**
- **specialized techniques of direct mail.**

Direct-response marketing and advertising have moved from minor segments in the sales plans of most companies to primary means of promoting and selling goods and services. In fact, the emergence of direct response advertising is one of the primary changes in marketing and promotion during the last 30 years. Only a few years ago direct-response advertising consisted primarily of direct mail and was regarded as a minor medium by most national firms. Today, direct marketing will account for a significant share of all advertising expenditures and generates more than 7 percent of all sales.

The contribution of direct response to both media revenues and sales is enormous. Exhibit 13.1 shows projected direct-response expenditures through the year 2000. Both consumer and business-to-business direct response have performed better than almost all other media, with business-to-business spending outpacing consumer expenditures. Most advertising executives predict that direct response will continue to outperform traditional media for the foreseeable future.

Direct-response marketing also has had a number of significant effects on all forms of advertising. Many of the concepts of direct marketing and direct-response advertis-

Direct Marketing Advertising Expenditures by Medium and Market (Billions of Dollars)

Telemarketing is the lead category of all direct marketing media expenditures—followed by direct mail and television direct response.

	1991	1995	1996	1997	2001	Compound Annual Growth 1991–1996	1996–2001
Direct Mail	24.5	32.9	34.6	36.5	46.9	7.1	6.3
Consumer	15.2	19.6	20.3	21.3	25.8	6.0	4.9
Business-to-Business	9.3	13.3	14.2	15.2	21.1	8.8	8.2
Telephone Marketing	42.4	54.1	57.8	62.1	84.4	6.4	7.9
Consumer	15.2	18.3	19.3	20.6	26.7	4.9	6.7
Business-to-Business	27.2	35.8	38.5	41.5	57.7	7.2	8.4
Newspaper	10.5	13.1	13.9	14.6	18.9	5.8	6.3
Consumer	6.4	7.6	8.0	8.3	10.3	4.6	5.2
Business-to-Business	4.1	5.5	5.9	6.3	8.6	7.6	7.8
Magazine	5.1	6.8	7.2	7.6	10.1	7.1	7.0
Consumer	2.5	3.1	3.2	3.4	4.3	5.1	6.1
Business-to-Business	2.6	3.7	4.0	4.3	5.8	9.0	7.7
Television	10.0	14.3	15.5	16.7	23.9	9.2	9.0
Consumer	5.4	7.3	7.8	8.3	11.5	7.6	8.1
Business-to-Business	4.6	7.0	7.7	8.4	12.3	10.9	9.8
Radio	3.1	4.4	4.7	5.1	6.8	8.7	7.7
Consumer	1.5	2.0	2.1	2.2	2.9	7.0	6.7
Business-to-Business	1.6	2.5	2.6	2.8	3.9	10.2	8.4
Other	8.0	10.3	10.9	11.4	14.0	6.4	5.1
Consumer	4.5	5.6	5.8	6.0	7.1	5.2	4.1
Business-to-Business	3.5	4.8	5.1	5.3	7.0	7.8	6.5
Total	103.6	136.0	144.5	154.0	205.0	6.9	7.2
Consumer	50.7	63.3	66.5	70.2	88.6	5.6	5.9
Business-to-Business	52.9	72.7	78.0	83.8	116.4	8.1	8.3

Note: These numbers have not been inflation adjusted—they represent current (nominal) dollars. Due to rounding totals may not exactly equal the sum of each column.

exhibit

13.1

Direct response has become a leading means of reaching consumers.

Courtesy: Direct Marketing Association.
Source: U.S. Direct Marketing Today, a publication of the Direct Marketing Association.

Direct marketing
Selling goods and services without the aid of wholesaler or retailer. Includes direct-response advertising and advertising for leads for sales people. Also direct door-to-door selling. Uses many media: direct mail, publications, TV, radio.

ing, such as audience segmentation, testing consumer response, and more individualized creative and media placement, have been adopted by virtually all advertisers, agencies, and media. In addition, both broadcast and print media are finding that direct response constitutes a significant percentage of their clients' advertising.

Direct marketing has three primary objectives:

1. *Direct orders* include all direct-response advertising that is designed to solicit and close a sale. All the information necessary for the prospective buyer to make a decision and complete a transaction is provided in the offer.
2. *Lead generation* includes all direct-response advertising that is designed to generate interest in a product and provide the prospective buyer with a means to request additional information about the item or qualify as a sales lead for future follow-up.
3. *Traffic generation* includes all direct-response advertising conducted to motivate buyers to visit a business to make a purchase. The advertisement provides detailed information about the product, but usually no order form.[1]

DEFINITION OF TERMS IN DIRECT RESPONSE
Direct Marketing

Direct marketing is a general term that encompasses direct-response and direct-mail advertising as well as their research and support activities. The term direct marketing is

---

[1] *Direct Marketing Course Rationale,* a publication of the Direct Marketing Educational Foundation, p. 1.

used when sellers and/or customers deal directly with each other rather than through a retailer or medium. Direct advertising, for example, distinguishes direct-response messages from those that utilize some form of mass media. In direct-mail advertising the advertiser has greater control over the communication process than traditional forms of media advertising. The advertiser determines the audience, timing, and production techniques, rather than having these dictated by a medium.

The term *direct marketing* is supplanting the term *mail order* because today so much of the business uses means other than mail. Later in this chapter, we devote our attention to two of these techniques—telemarketing and broadcast in-home shopping services.

Direct-Response Advertising

Many people confuse the terms *direct mail* and *direct response,* sometimes considering them synonymous. In fact, direct response is any advertising used in selling goods directly to consumers. The message doesn't have to come through the mail (although it often does); it can be a direct advertisement in a newspaper, a telephone solicitation, or a magazine ad featuring a toll-free number.

THE MODERN DIRECT-RESPONSE INDUSTRY

In part, the growth of direct response advertising is directly attributable to a changing marketplace. We have moved from a manufacturer-driven economy to one that is dominated by huge retailers. As we enter the twenty-first century, consumers are increasingly taking charge. Home computers and fiber-optic technology are making it practical for consumers to avoid traditional media and make purchasing decisions on a one-to-one basis with sellers. Soon consumers will no longer be limited by traditional market channels, but rather—whether they live in a major city or a remote village—they will have immediate availability to goods and services. This is the marketing environment in which direct response will continue to prosper.

As mentioned in earlier chapters, belt-tightening has become a way of corporate life. Companies are demanding accountability and proven results from their advertising investment. In this atmosphere, advertisers are finding that direct response can provide a number of benefits:

1. *It is targeted communication.* Unlike most mass media, the advertiser determines exactly who will be reached by the sales message. The copy can be tailored to the demographic, psychographic, and consumption profile of the audience. In addition, both the timing and production of advertising are totally under the control of the advertiser.
2. *Direct response is measurable.* One of the disadvantages of most traditional advertising is that the results can only be estimated. However, in many forms of direct response the results can be computed to the penny. Furthermore, the advertiser is able to measure precisely various messages and other creative alternatives.
3. *The message of direct response is personal.* With new high-speed printing methods and computer technology, we can address our audience by name. In other cases, the direct-response medium is so targeted that we know the interests and buying behavior of the audience and can make the message relevant to their needs in a way that other forms of marketing communication cannot. A number of companies provide services to advertisers that allow them to greatly enhance their ability to reach a targeted audience.

It is imperative for most direct-response offers to reach a narrowly targeted audience. Many direct-response formats, such as mail catalogs, mail-distributed product samples, and so forth, can be extremely expensive if directed at nonprospects. On a *CPM* basis, most direct-response advertising is much more costly than traditional media exposure. However, a properly executed direct-response campaign will reach a significantly higher percentage of prospects with much less waste circulation than mass advertising. In addition, a major portion of the investment in direct response is intended to create an immediate sale, whereas advertising investment is usually only one step in a process of building awareness and brand equity to lead to a sale sometime in the future.

Although direct-response advertising can be both profitable and efficient in many circumstances, it is most successful when building on other elements of the marketing mix. Just as mass advertising often must depend on public relations, sales promotion, and other marketing elements, direct response is dependent on complementary factors. Direct response is most successful in selling products for which there is already positive brand awareness. A strong brand image is a major asset for direct marketing. Consequently, we are seeing major direct-marketing firms working to build brand equity, often through traditional media advertising. For example, both L.L. Bean and Lands' End invest significant funds in magazine advertising to introduce their catalogs, and from time to time television to build brand awareness.

As we see in this chapter, direct-response advertising takes many forms and is expected to accomplish a number of marketing objectives. In the future, even more companies will opt for direct marketing as a part of their total sales and communication strategy.

GROWTH OF DIRECT-RESPONSE ADVERTISING

There are a number of reasons why experts predict direct response will continue to expand. The most important are the following:

1. *The demographic composition of the general public is becoming more favorable for direct marketing.* In the near future, there will be even more two-earner families, time will be at a premium, and people will want to set their own pace and time for shopping. In addition, future generations will be more comfortable with direct marketing as it becomes more common as a sales method for leading brands. Research also shows that the main audience for direct marketing comprises better-educated and high-income individuals, a prime market for many brands.

2. *Direct marketers will continue to improve the quality and diversity of their offers.* In addition, consumer guarantees concerning product satisfaction and returns will continue to build the sense of security essential to the success of direct marketing.

3. *The newest communications technologies will enhance rather than diminish direct marketing's ability to sell goods and services.* Whether the Internet, interactive television, or a combination of television and computers will be the next major marketing breakthrough, direct marketing can take full advantage of these systems.[2]

A number of direct-response providers have entered the market for Web advertising. Because they have experience in reaching targeted audiences in nontraditional media, it is only logical that these companies can provide similar services to advertisers using Web sites. Exhibit 13.2 (p. 356) shows the services that can be provided through WebConnect, a joint venture of CMP Media and Worldata, a leading list brokerage and database marketing company.

A combination of younger buyers fully comfortable with buying through direct response and an aging population favoring in-home shopping will fuel significant growth in direct response during the next decade. It is estimated that some 100 million Americans will make at least one purchase from a direct-response offer during the coming year.

---

[2]Richard A. Barton, "The Vision Thing," *DM News,* August 26, 1996, p. 52.

exhibit

13.2

Direct response is increasingly using new technology.

Courtesy: Worldata, WebConnect, and CMP Media. Graphic artist: Shari Katz; copywriter: Frances Saleh.

Direct Marketing Association (DMA)
Organization to promote direct-mail and direct-response advertising.

The Image of Direct Response

If there is a cloud over the optimistic predictions about the future growth of direct marketing, it concerns the image problems surrounding the industry. Specifically, direct marketing has been plagued by concerns over privacy, intrusive selling practices, and consumer complaints about unscrupulous sellers, particularly in telemarketing. The direct marketing industry, through its trade association, the **Direct Marketing Association** (DMA), has initiated a number of measures to attempt to protect customers from deceptive practices. The DMA has moved aggressively to initiate a number of steps for better self-regulation of the industry, although there is still room for improvement.

Let us briefly discuss some of the major areas of consumer complaints with direct response marketing.

Fraudulent Sales Offers   The DMA, the Federal Trade Commission (FTC), and the U.S. Postal Service are the primary organizations attempting to deal with consumer fraud in direct response. To alert the public to the types of common deceptive practices, the DMA has provided the media with guidelines to identify the most prevalent types of scams. The areas most likely to be used by illegal operators are the following:

- *Get rich quick.* Offers for "work at home," loan offers to finance new businesses, guarantees of return on investment, and ads implying some connection with the U.S. government are among the most common propositions.
- *Health fraud.* Overnight cures, guaranteed weight loss, and offers of mail-order medical preparations from little-known laboratories and companies should be investigated.
- *Credit repair.* Offers to wipe out bad credit history or guaranteed credit card offers for people with poor credit should be viewed with suspicion.
- *Product misrepresentations.* Merchandise offered at well below market value, off-brand products with names similar to national brands, and vague product descriptions might be a warning of fraudulent advertising.
- *Travel fraud.* Low-cost travel, particularly requiring prepaid membership in travel clubs, should be fully investigated.[3]

Despite constant warnings by industry and government groups, it is estimated that consumers lose billions of dollars each year, most for offers similar to the ones outlined here.

Concerns over Invasion of Privacy   One of the major debates over direct response marketing is the privacy issue. Both Congress and the courts have taken up the issue to determine where the legitimate gathering of marketing information ends and encroachment on consumer rights begins. As one marketing executive pointed out, "Direct marketers . . . are interested in knowing if you play tennis so that we can offer you a great new tennis racquet, a video on how to improve your groundstrokes or a subscription to a tennis magazine. We have no interest in creating dossiers."[4]

There is no question that virtually all marketers are interested in consumer information only to the extent that they can better serve their customers by knowing more about their individual tastes and brand preferences. However, many consumers fear that companies simply know too much about them and that the use of the information is not subject to adequate controls. As a survey on direct-response marketing by Yankelovich Partners demonstrates, direct marketers must address the privacy issue aggressively and quickly:[5]

Issue	% Agree
It is a serious violation of privacy for a company to sell a mailing list without the permission of those on the list	66
Unsolicited phone calls for fund-raising are a serious violation of privacy	55
There should be more legislation to safeguard consumer privacy	45

Consumer Avoidance of Unwanted Solicitations   One of the most difficult and potentially damaging problems for direct marketers is how to deal with those consumers who want no unsolicited offers. Many people find both mail and telephone solicitations helpful, and, indeed, billions of dollars worth of merchandise are sold by these methods each year. However, other consumers view direct sales contacts as an intrusion and want to avoid them. The industry recognizes that reaching uninterested prospects not only is a public relations problem, but is costly to the advertiser. Therefore, the direct marketers support efforts to allow consumers to eliminate unwanted solicitations.

---

[3] *Misleading Advertisements Media Guidelines,* a publication of the Direct Marketing Association.
[4] "The Experts Predict," *Target Marketing,* January 1996, p. 20.
[5] "Consumers Want Privacy," *Advertising Age,* October 30, 1995, p. 38.

The DMA acts as a clearinghouse for consumers who do not wish to be contacted by direct marketers. The DMA has established a telephone preference service (TPS) as well as a mail preference service (MPS). The TPS and MPS are designed to allow customers to place their names in a delete file that is sent to direct marketers on a monthly basis. Although the services will eliminate a number of calls or mailings, it will not eliminate local solicitations nor advertising from organizations that are not members of DMA.

In addition to industry attempts to address the problem, in 1995 the FTC implemented its *telemarketing sales rule,* intended to allow consumers to choose whether telemarketers can continue to call them. The rule requires that telemarketers promptly disclose to consumers that they are making a sales call, the identity of the seller, the nature of the goods or services being offered, and, if it is a prize promotion, the fact that no purchase is necessary to win. In addition to the disclosure provisions of the rule, it also includes broad prohibitions about misrepresentations.[6]

The FTC rule concerning telemarketing is a classic example of how government inevitably moves in to areas where there is no industry self-regulation or the regulation is regarded by the public to be inadequate to address the problem. For example, despite the DMA's best efforts, one survey indicated that 85 percent of businesses reported that they had been approached by an illegitimate telemarketer.[7]

Despite the problems facing the industry, direct response has made great strides in recent years. Major national advertisers are routinely using direct response methods to reach important audience segments, and many business-to-business firms are routinely using some form of direct response. In the remainder of this chapter, we examine the strategies and techniques currently used by companies large and small.

DATABASE MARKETING

It is estimated that 60 percent of the information that a business has about its customers changes each year.[8] As customers move, have children, divorce, or, in the case of business-to-business clients, change purchasing agents or product lines, their purchasing behavior may demonstrate major adjustments. The purpose of a database is to provide up-to-date information on current and prospective customers. Without a current source of customer information, a company will soon lose touch with this evolving consumer environment.

Database marketing
A process of continually updating information about individual consumers. Popular techniques with direct-response sellers.

The key to successful **database marketing** is the ability to use information to predict trends. If the database is only a repository of information, its value is limited. However, to the extent that these data are used creatively to predict future purchase behavior and product trends, the database is among the most valuable tools in a marketer's arsenal. "Direct marketers make their living anticipating trends, dividing the population into ever more refined targets, predicting buying habits and cashing in on them."[9]

As computer technology has become more sophisticated, database managers have moved from a focus on past transactions and updating consumer demographics to an emphasis on relationships that forecast trends and discover patterns. The next generation of databases are called *data warehouses.* Whereas databases are storage and retrieval systems, data warehouses are comprehensive systems that link every department within a company. Information from sales, accounting, and distribution are stored and networked so that employees throughout the organization can have access to a comprehensive view of customers. The data warehouse makes decisions easier because they are based on fact rather than opinion.[10]

---

[6]*Advertising Topics,* August 1995, p. 3, Supplement 549, a publication of the Council of Better Business Bureaus.

[7]*The Boiler-Room Blues,* a publication of the Specialty Advertising Association International.

[8]"16 Techniques That Work," *Target Marketing,* February 1996, p. 16.

[9]"Brave New Selects," *DM News,* August 12, 1996, p. 44.

[10]Ginger Conlon, *Sales & Marketing Management,* April 1997, p. 41.

The high cost of waste circulation and the need for maintaining customer loyalty and repeat sales have made database technology extremely important. One of the extravagances that companies can ill afford is the cost of reaching nonprospects. Accumulating exposures through mass advertising with no clear idea of the potential payout for each of these exposures is no longer cost effective. The cost of media advertising cannot be justified without an identification of the customers being reached. In recent years, list companies have been able to provide custom-tailored lists for a number of advertising categories (see Exhibit 13.3).

Advertisers also rely on database marketing to build and maintain customer loyalty. Marketing executives refer to their continuing attempts to relate to their customers as *relationship marketing*. "Relationship marketing is the eliciting of information from existing customers on an ongoing basis, and using the data to improve customer service and build meaningful relationships."[11] A prime motivation for relationship marketing is that the expense of keeping a current customer is minimal compared to gaining a new one.

---

[11]Jean Halliday, "Cars Put New Faith in Relationships," *Advertising Age,* December 2, 1996, p. 24.

Let us examine a very simple example of database marketing. The ACME Catalog Company has the following information on a customer:

Jane I. Buyer, married, 32, two children: boy 7, boy 9
Lives in an affluent zip code

Address: 677 Brookhaven Dr., Evanston—June 1996–present
101 Sunny Lane, Chicago—April 1992–June 1996
44 Olive Blvd., Miami—May 1989–March 1992
777 Main St., St. Louis—September 1987–May 1989

Purchases from ACME:			
	Woman's sweater	$99	4/5/98
	Snow skis	233	3/25/98
	Desk set	49	12/10/96
	Dressing gown	98	12/10/95
	Perfume	124	10/4/95
	Diamond locket	566	8/3/95
	Crystal glasses	210	5/12/94

From this very simple database example, you can tell several things about the customer. Most important, Jane is a regular customer of ACME. She comes from an upwardly mobile household and, judging by the items she purchases, has reasonably high levels of discretionary income. From a marketing standpoint, she does not purchase children's items from ACME (is she a potential customer for these items?). Because of her purchase history she will be on the "A" list for frequency of catalog mailings and will be contacted by special telemarketing efforts aimed at the company's best customers.

Database marketing also allows direct marketers to compute the **lifetime value** of a customer. Because initial contact through direct response is often more expensive than through other media, it is important to determine those customers who are most likely to create long-term revenues. The concept of lifetime value is related to relationship marketing and is used to increase inactive accounts, retain current customers, and identify any unmet customer service requirements. Database marketing is about gaining and reinforcing sales and being customer driven rather than sales driven.

Although the advantages of database marketing are obvious for many advertisers, it is an expensive endeavor and should be initiated only if it is right for an individual firm. The characteristics that must be considered before engaging in database marketing are the following:

1. Relatively frequent and/or high dollar volume of purchases by consumers.
2. A diverse market in which the marketing effort would benefit from segmenting it into subgroups.
3. A customer list that represents opportunities for higher volume of purchases.

If these three factors are not present, then it may indicate that the expense of establishing and maintaining a database is not worthwhile. However, when market characteristics are positive for such efforts, database techniques can greatly expand the profitability of a firm.

TELEMARKETING

At a time when telemarketing has never been more popular, it finds itself in a legal and regulatory environment that has become a management nightmare. As mentioned earlier in this chapter, concerns over consumer privacy and phone scams have moved the FTC to initiate strict regulations covering telephone selling.

Despite the problems associated with telemarketing, all evidence points to continuing growth in what has become the major promotional and sales tool for many busi-

Lifetime value
An estimate of the long-term revenue that can be expected from a particular prospect.

nesses. As Exhibit 13.1 shows, telephone marketing is particularly valuable in business-to-business sales. From an already strong base, telemarketing should outpace virtually every other sales and promotional vehicle over the next several years. In less than two decades, telemarketing has moved from an infrequently used sales supplement to a key ingredient in the marketing plans of many companies.

It is rare that a major national company does not engage in some form of telemarketing. Telemarketing is so important that toll-free numbers are included on product labels to allow consumers to obtain more information or register a complaint. In addition to their use as a direct sales tool, toll-free numbers have become a familiar part of many advertisements, and research shows that they aid in gaining higher consumer awareness for advertising.

There are a number of techniques and definitions used in telemarketing. Some examples follow.

Outbound and Inbound Telemarketing

There are two forms of telemarketing, **outbound** and inbound. Outbound telemarketing occurs when the seller calls prospects to make a sale, to determine interest by offering catalogs or other sales material, or to pave the way for a personal sales call. Market research is another use of outbound telemarketing.

Outbound telephone solicitations have several advantages over other techniques. Telemarketing is immediate; the offer and consumer response are practically instantaneous. In addition, telephone solicitations are flexible: sales messages can be adapted to the individual buyer as the conversation develops. Telephone offers can be tested quickly and inexpensively.

Like other forms of direct marketing, the key to telemarketing is a good list of prospects and a well-honed script. In the same way advertising copywriters test their copy, headlines, and slogans, the telemarketer thoroughly researches the sales message.

> There's an art and science to any script. The science part is the introduction and legalese. The art is capturing someone's attention in a short period of time. After all, they weren't waiting for your call, and it's likely you interrupted whatever they were doing. Try to get them to refocus. . . . You don't want your script to confuse someone with any other facts that will cloud the issue.[12]

Inbound telemarketing is most often used with some other medium and is usually an order-taking operation. The familiar mail-order catalog is the largest user of inbound telemarketing. Inbound telemarketing has been made possible largely through the creation of the toll-free number. Since their introduction in 1967, toll-free numbers have grown to the point that they are a part of our daily routine.

A recent survey indicated that 90 percent of respondents indicated they used toll-free numbers. Approximately one-third of users dial toll-free numbers 60 or more times per year. More important from a marketing perspective, 86 percent of consumers prefer to deal with companies that provide toll-free numbers for customer service, and 63 percent indicate they would more likely buy products from companies that offer toll-free service.[13]

The toll-free number is used for a variety of functions including sales calls to customers, placing orders by customers, and offering product information both before and after purchase. The Sherwin-Williams 800 service offers consumers a convenient way of ordering wallpaper, receiving advice, or finding the location of the nearest dealer (see

---

[12]Lambeth Hochwald, "High-Stakes Scripts," *Folio,* May 15, 1996, p. 39.
[13]"800/900 Number," *Target Marketing,* December 1995, p. 58.

exhibit

13.4

Advertisers often provide direct means of communication with customers.

Courtesy: Sherwin-Williams.

Up-selling
A telemarketing technique designed to sell additional merchandise to callers.

Exhibit 13.4). Some form of toll-free service is a tool that most businesses cannot do without. In fact, the popularity of 800-prefix numbers resulted in the system reaching capacity in 1995. To meet the demand for toll-free service, AT&T introduced the 888 prefix in 1996 and 877 prefix in 1997.

Catalog sales, magazine ads that encourage customers to call for addresses of nearby retailers or more information, and product hotlines set up to give consumers help or to process their complaints are all examples of inbound telemarketing that depend on toll-free numbers for their existence. However, inbound telemarketing should not be viewed as a passive one-way process. Savvy telemarketers train their operators to use inbound calls as a platform to sell additional merchandise. This technique is called **up-selling.**

A major innovation in inbound telemarketing is the development of interactive voice response (IVR). IVR systems combine the technology of computers with telephones to provide a system that handles many more consumer calls at a fraction of operator exchanges. When accessing the service, callers are asked a series of questions and given an opportunity to use their push-button phones to respond until they get the automated answer they are seeking, or in special cases a representative will come on the line. Companies using the system can greatly decrease the need (and expense) of online service personnel. Furthermore, information is available during nonbusiness hours.

If there is a downside to the service, it is the loss of personal contact between companies and their customers. However, many customers seeking basic information such as bank balances prefer the speed and convenience of automated services. Virtually all companies provide service representatives for those customers wanting them, many on a 24-hour basis.

900-Telemarketing

If the toll-free number represented a positive breakthrough in telemarketing and customer service, the 900/976-prefix number was often the black sheep of the telemarketing family. Unfortunately for the growth of 900-prefix numbers, a disproportionate number of early users of the service were sex lines and other unsavory, and sometimes illegal, companies. Its early history made the public wary of using any form of 900 service.

The original promise of the 900-prefix, that is, to provide valuable information to consumers in exchange for a nominal fee, was quickly tainted by every imaginable charlatan and scam artist. The situation reached a point where 900 was almost interchangeable with phone sex, and legitimate companies dropped the service in droves.

In recent years, regulations aimed at weeding out illegitimate businesses, and the use of the service by well-known and reputable companies, has helped establish the service as an appropriate marketing and information medium. The primary use of the service remains as an information source. Using a push-button phone, callers can get the latest forecast from the Weather Channel or current scores from ESPN. It is estimated that 900-prefix numbers grossed almost $1 billion in 1997, and revenue growth is approximately 10 percent annually.

Despite the renewed respectability and growth of 900 prefixes, a number of consumers still view 900 services critically. With the availability of toll-free services, companies may find resistance from customers when asked to pay for a service when similar ones are available at no cost. Successful 900 calling depends on providing callers with a clearly defined service and value for their money.

Automatic Dialing Systems

As we saw in the case of IVR, computer technology has made a dramatic change in telemarketing, but it is a change unwelcome in some quarters. There are two major systems of computerized telemarketing. One, called automatic dialing recorded message programs (ADRMP), can dial hundreds of numbers a day and deliver a prerecorded sales message. The major complaints concerning ADRMP come from people with unlisted numbers and others who think indiscriminate random dialing is an invasion of privacy. These systems also tie up the line until the message is complete.

Another, more recent innovation in automatic dialing is *predictive dialing*. The predictive dialing system, like the ADRMP, automatically reaches potential customers. However, instead of delivering an impersonal sales message, a short recorded message tells the prospect what the call is about and asks that the listener remain on the line until a salesperson is available. The advantage of this system is that it combines the advantages of random computer dialing with personal contact.

Telemarketing Regulation

As discussed earlier in this chapter, telemarketing has been a major target of government regulation as public complaints mounted over its abuses. Telephone fraud costs the public an estimated $40 billion each year. When President Clinton signed the

Telemarketing and Consumer Fraud and Abuse Act, the telemarketing industry was put on notice that many telephone sellers were going to have to clean up their acts.

Moving under the provisions of the act, the FTC developed a number of rules addressing practices of telemarketers. Several dealt with routine practices such as prohibiting solicitations before 8 A.M. or after 9 P.M. and requiring full disclosure that the call was a sales offer. In other cases, the FTC addressed the more serious problem of misrepresentation. Moving quickly to underscore that it meant business, the Commission fined one telemarketer $1.2 million for misrepresenting the value of artwork as an investment, and an office supply business was fined $2.425 million and barred from selling similar products in the future.

Although many marketers think that some of the rules are unnecessarily harsh, honest telemarketers applaud the move to rid the industry of its "bad apples." However, the act deals not only with sellers, but also with advertising agencies. One of its stipulations holds agencies liable if they "know or consciously avoid knowing" that a client intends to engage in telemarketing fraud. The FTC has made it very clear—by bringing more than 200 cases of telemarketing fraud to the federal courts—that dishonest business practices in the $240 billion industry will not be tolerated.[14]

Television and Direct Response Advertising

Television direct response has long been the butt of many jokes about its methods and merchandise. However, in recent years television direct response has moved out of the back room and become a billion-dollar industry. Although television direct response uses a number of formats, three categories constitute the majority of such offers.

Traditional 30-Second Commercial   A number of companies rely on the 30-second format with a tag line allowing consumers to order merchandise by phone. This method is the least expensive, but has the major disadvantage of trying to get a sales message and ordering instructions in a very short time frame. This format is more successful when dealing with well-known products and brands with established demand, in which the selling job can be kept to a minimum.

Two-Minute Commercial   The long-form spot often has problems gaining station and network availabilities and consequently most often is scheduled in fringe-time programming such as late-night movies. The format has the advantage of allowing more sales time and an opportunity for information about ordering the product.

Infomercial   In the last decade the infomercial has become a multibillion dollar advertising format. By utilizing well-known personalities, slick production techniques, and blanket coverage during certain dayparts, the **infomercial** has created a number of legendary product success stories. Because of the importance of the infomercial in terms of time allotted and sales produced, the following section is devoted primarily to this format.

Several factors have contributed to the success of the television infomercial:

1. *Consumers' comfort level with purchasing through television offers.* A combination of familiarity, use by well-known brands, and consumer protection through credit-card purchases has provided consumers with more confidence that television sales are a legitimate and convenient method of purchasing good and services.
2. *Production quality of infomercials.* There is no question that products are judged by the production quality of the commercials that promote them. If a commercial looks like it was taped in someone's garage, that is the image potential customers have of the product. Today, the typical infomercial often has the same production values that viewers normally see on network shows.

Infomercial
Long form television advertising that promotes products within the context of a program-length commercial.

---

[14]Robyn Griggs, "Working Out Their Differences in D.C.," *Agency,* Fall 1995, p. 12.

3. *The segmented television audience.* The fragmentation of television audiences has made it an ideal medium for direct response. With the Nashville Network appealing to country music buffs, ESPN programming a 24-hour sports format, and Lifetime staking out a position among women, the niche audiences that direct response advertisers seek are available. In addition to the audiences they deliver, the sheer number of channels and networks provided by cable make time available at a reasonable cost, another advantage for infomercial sponsors.

4. *Better understanding of the infomercial.* In recent years, advertisers and their agencies have come to understand how to use the infomercial. As already mentioned, the quality of production had to improve significantly before the public would take infomercials seriously. In addition, firms recognized that research was important in determining the success of infomercials as is the case with any marketing plan. For example, Stilson & Stilson, a major infomercial producer, offers advertisers a service called MarketSearch whereby, for as little as $35,000, products and creative themes can be given on-air tests to see if they are viable for direct-response television or if other market strategies would be more appropriate.[15]

5. *Global potential for infomercials.* In a global environment with a potential market of some 800 million households, sellers are finding that infomercials that are successful in this country tend to achieve excellent sales results in the international arena. As one direct marketer commented, "Infomercials represent a powerful marketing vehicle that is not limited by geographic borders. U.S. manufacturers are in a fierce competition to create brands and infomercials that can create shelf space for products in consumer homes on a global basis."[16]

The most successful infomercial products tend to be clustered in a relatively small number of categories—health and beauty products, financial products and services, kitchen and small household appliances, and lifestyle services, including everything from psychic readings to advice for personal development. A typical week will find the most advertised products to be a mix of the Psychic Friends Network; the Power Rider, HealthRider, and Abflex; and Victoria Jackson Cosmetics.

Although these products appeal to diverse market segments, they have several characteristics in common:

● They lend themselves to demonstration and/or testimonial endorsements.
● They normally are not readily available at traditional retail outlets.
● They have relatively high profit margins, which support the frequency needed to sell the products.

Methods of Buying Time

In a given year, some 750 infomercials are produced, an average of two every day of the year. The popularity of infomercials is a result of television's ability to combine personal selling with the efficiency of mass-media advertising. Television offers a number of opportunities for direct-response advertisers. However, the increasing cost of time to run infomercials is a growing problem for infomercial marketers.

In 1991, infomercial sales were $881.1 million and media expenditures were $251.8 million, a media-to-sales ratio of 28 percent. Currently, the ratio is 58 percent, a 107 percent increase. Television is well aware of the success and popularity of infomercial selling and has adjusted its rates accordingly. The rising time cost will no doubt result in a decline of some small and marginal infomercial sellers, which may be a positive step for the credibility of the industry.[17]

---

[15] *It's No Fluke,* promotional flyer from Stilson & Stilson Direct.

[16] Kim Cleland, "Infomercial Audience Crosses Over Cultures," *Advertising Age International,* January 15, 1996, p. 18.

[17] Si Sanders, "What Price DRTV?" *DM News,* November 11, 1996, p. 44.

Per inquiry (PI)
Advertising time or space where medium is paid on a per response received basis.

Direct response advertising is sold both on a paid and **per inquiry (PI)** basis. PI advertising is more common in television than in magazines. Basically, PI advertisers share their risk with a television station or cable channel. There are no up-front costs for time, but the television outlet will divide the profits (if any) when the orders come in. On the surface, PI advertising is very beneficial, especially to companies with good products but little capital. However, PI advertising entails a number of features that are significantly different from paid television advertising.

One of the most difficult aspects of PI is determining a fair percentage for all parties. A company considering PI advertising must estimate all the costs involved, including the product itself, inbound telemarketing, fulfillment of orders, and commercial production and fees associated with getting the commercial on the air. A company contemplating PI advertising has to be fair to television stations or they will not carry its spots. On the other hand, if the product is a huge hit, the firm doesn't want to be locked into an agreement that provides windfall profits to stations. PI advertising has grown so large and is so particular that it is usually handled by companies specializing in PI sales.

As large national companies increasingly use the format, we will see continued growth of infomercial selling. As is the case with most promotional techniques, the infomercial is being used more as a complement to other forms of advertising and marketing. Many companies use a combination of television spots and infomercials just as other companies use advertising and sales promotion. That is, they build brand awareness and brand equity with advertising and use the infomercial to close the sale. Exhibit 13.5 shows the benefits of 30-second spots and long-form infomercials.

TV Shopping Networks

The logical extension of long-form infomercials is an entire network devoted to selling. Home shopping channels are coming into their own as a major source of product sales. It is not unusual to see name-brand merchandise being sold on QVC or the Home

exhibit

13.5

Short spots and long infomercials both offer benefits.

Source: Target Marketing, February 1996, p. 20.

30 Minutes	vs.	30 Seconds
Most *effective* selling medium		Most *efficient* reach medium
Attracts an interested audience from a huge channel surfing universe		Intrudes on viewers' awareness watching program content; no accounting for viewers' interest
Free-standing sponsored programming		Dependent upon host program for audience
Creative focuses on all product benefits		Creative focuses on one feature or benefit
Each rating point equals interested prospects		No correlation between ratings and interested prospects; ratings reflect only the program's audience
Infomerical show ratings are a true measurement of interested prospects		Rating points erode due to approximately 39 percent of viewers zapping and channel surfing
Direct correlation to direct and retail sales		Weak measurable connection to sales
Half-hour theater		30-second "blur"
Content-rich product information through entertaining format		Little content, mostly imagery based on fantasy-world presentation
Due to duration, maximum impact		Due to brevity, minimum impact
20 to 25 minutes of audience viewing time (new breed of infomerical)		15 to 30 seconds of average viewing time
With 800-number respondents, 50-percent average recall up to 6 weeks later		12- to 15-percent next day unaided recall
Unique—only a $750 million media market		Clutter crisis—a $35 billion media market
Production budget range between $250K and $750K for a half-hour		Production budget range between $250K and $770K for only 30 seconds
Creative breakthrough opportunity unlimited		Tough breakthrough potential; 170 million spots aired this year

Shopping Network, and celebrities as diverse as Cal Ripkin and Joan Rivers appear to sell sports memorabilia and jewelry. A number of major retailers and designers already are using TV shopping networks to sell their products to a variety of consumers.

Although home shopping has grown significantly in recent years, many observers see the real potential for home shopping in interactive systems. The most optimistic proponents of shopping networks predict that they will fundamentally change retailing in the next two decades. Some experts estimate that sometime in the next century traditional retailing will all but be replaced by interactive home shopping.

A study of home shopping channel buyers by the Aragon Consulting Group found that approximately 16 percent of adults have purchased from a home shopping channel. The typical home shopper is between 35 and 54 years old, married, with household of income between $50,000 and $75,000. Viewership of these channels follows the pattern of traditional television, with the audience peaking between 9 P.M. and midnight.[18]

Video Direct Marketing

With VCR household penetration surpassing 90 percent, a number of advertisers are looking to Video Direct Mail or *V-mail* as a means of reaching selected target markets. Both videocassettes and CD-ROM formats are increasingly used to reach consumers with not only advertising messages, but also product demonstrations that can be provided with high impact and low cost. With available technology, tapes and CDs can be provided at a cost less than a printed catalog or other mailing piece.

Companies such as Technicolor can provide full-service creative and production functions for advertisers (see Exhibit 13.6, p. 368). The firm also can personalize each tape with custom audio messages. V-mail can be used for direct mailings, sales promotion, in-package premiums, and trade show giveaways. The primary advantage of V-mail is that it combines the targeting of direct mail, product demonstration, and impact of television, and the low cost of traditional media.

RADIO AND DIRECT RESPONSE

Radio, with its niche programming, provides a ready-made medium for direct response. At a reasonable cost, commercials can be tailored to the particular listening preferences of the audiences of the various formats. In addition, the low time charges make possible high frequency to saturate prime prospects.

The primary disadvantage of direct response radio is its lack of visualization. Radio is deficient in many of the elements so familiar to direct response in other media. Radio cannot show a product, no coupons can be provided, and a toll-free number cannot be flashed on a screen. Radio is often used to supplement other forms of direct response. For example, publishers use radio to alert people that a sweepstakes mailing is beginning and to encourage their participation. Radio will never be a primary direct-response medium. However, radio will continue to be of great value as a secondary support medium to targeted audience segments.

Per-inquiry advertising is a growing area of radio direct response. Many radio stations find that per-inquiry advertising is a means of using unsold commercial spots for a number of direct-response products and services. With the number of stations and commercial spots available, it is almost impossible for even the most prosperous station to sell all its time. Unsold inventory can be especially acute during certain months, such as January. Rather than using this time for public service announcements or station promotions, the sales manager may be willing to run per-inquiry spots at significant discounts.

---

[18]"Home Shopping Watched More at Night," *Target Marketing,* January 1997, p. 22.

MAGAZINES AND DIRECT RESPONSE

Magazines garner more than half of all direct-response media advertising (see Exhibit 13.7). Magazines provide direct-response advertising with an ideal combination of characteristics. Many consumer magazines have special sections for small direct-response advertisers. In magazine direct response, like its counterparts in other media, success is not measured in terms of the *CPM*s, but rather its cost per order or cost per inquiry.

Magazines have several advantages for the direct-response advertiser:

1. *Audience selectivity.* Magazines are able to attract an audience with common interests and characteristics. More important, specialized publications offer an editorial environment compatible with the advertising messages they carry, ensuring that the reader is in the proper "mood" for an advertisement.

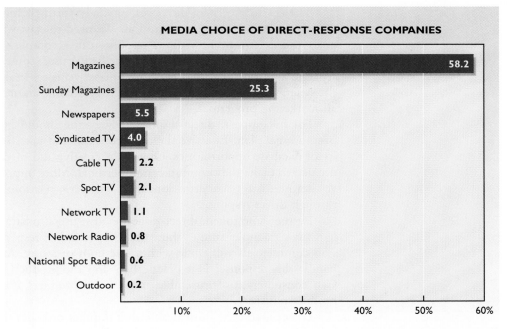

MEDIA CHOICE OF DIRECT-RESPONSE COMPANIES

Medium	Percent
Magazines	58.2
Sunday Magazines	25.3
Newspapers	5.5
Syndicated TV	4.0
Cable TV	2.2
Spot TV	2.1
Network TV	1.1
Network Radio	0.8
National Spot Radio	0.6
Outdoor	0.2

Source: Magazine Publishers of America.

2. *Magazine audiences often are distinct from other media.* Magazine readers tend to include light users of other media. Consequently, magazine direct response can reach an audience that would normally be excluded by other media vehicles.
3. *Long life.* Magazines have a long life, which allows coupons to be clipped and responses made to offers days or weeks after the magazine is received. The long life of magazines also makes pass-along readership possible, thereby expanding the potential audience.
4. *Size and color.* The typical magazine advertisement offers enough space to allow for coupons and detailed product information. In addition, excellent quality reproduction presents products to their best advantage.
5. *Prestige.* Magazines offer many of the advantages of direct mail, but with added prestige to the advertiser.

Magazine audience selectivity also allows advertisers to be creative in reaching special audiences. Advertisers know that certain magazines not only will reach an audience of prime prospects, but will do so in an environment that makes direct response action more likely. For example, a woman's magazine may carry an advertisement with a mail-in offer for a recipe book, or a sports magazine may run an ad for a high-performance automobile with a toll-free number for additional information.

CHARACTERISTICS OF SUCCESSFUL DIRECT-RESPONSE ADVERTISING

A number of factors contribute to the success of direct-response advertising. The most important are the following:

1. It is targeted to specific consumers who are current or potential users of a particular product or service.
2. Copy is written in a personal, one-to-one conversational style.
3. Products offered through direct response usually are unavailable in traditional retail outlets or have some particular differentiation such as price, style, or convenience over competing brands.

The key to successful direct-response advertising is fundamentally the same as with any type of advertising or promotion. We need to start with clearly defined marketing goals and determine how direct response can accomplish its role in the total promotional plan. Unfortunately, inexperienced advertisers sometimes treat direct response as separate and unrelated to other promotional vehicles. In doing so, direct response loses the synergy with other promotions and may become an inefficient stepsister to the overall marketing program.

For full impact, direct-response advertising should be viewed as part of the total promotional plan. Effective direct response should take full advantage of the availability of database opportunities. Obviously, creative and media functions should be coordinated to make the communication personal. More important, the direct-response advertiser needs to make provisions for a long-term relationship with consumers available through direct response.

By the same token, direct-response advertisers must anticipate some unique problems. For example, studies show that 85 percent of responses to direct-response television commercials will come within one hour of airing. Are there enough operators to handle this response? Is it practical to ship the product, or is it too heavy or fragile? Can consumers easily assemble and use the product? What is the anticipated rate of product returns?

Direct marketers must deal with a number of issues that traditional retailers rarely face. Direct response offers a number of exciting alternatives to traditional media advertising. However, unless direct response is used properly, it can become a time-consuming, inefficient, and tremendously costly enterprise.

TYPES OF DIRECT-RESPONSE OFFERS

Direct-response offers fall into two general categories:

- direct sales solicitations, known as *one-step offers*
- intermediate contacts designed to gather leads, answer consumer questions, or set up appointments when purchase offers can be made, known as *two-step offers*

Although a number of products use both types of direct response, high ticket items, especially those sold on a business-to-business basis, are more likely to use the two-step process. Relatively low priced consumer items are more likely to use the one-step sales process, in which an offer is made and the sale completed with one request.

Regardless of the type of offer, successful direct response is characterized by flexibility in formats, media, and types of offers. The common thread in most direct response is its ability to target audiences and communicate in a personal manner. In this section, we discuss some of the primary means by which marketers move goods and services through the direct-marketing channel.

ONE-STEP PURCHASE—DIRECT SALES

As the name implies, the direct-sale offer is straightforward, presenting a product and asking consumers if they want to buy it. A straight sales offer may take the form of a telephone solicitation for a magazine subscription or an elaborate brochure for a cruise. Regardless of the simplicity or complexity of the offer, the intent of the promotional effort is to close a sale.

The simplest examples of this type of direct-response advertising are the small ads in the back of the shopping section of many magazines or in a Sunday newspaper supplement. Whoever responds to a mail-order ad will probably receive a package containing the product ordered plus one or more circulars offering other merchandise of related interest. **Bounce-back circulars,** as these are called, can produce as much as 20

Bounce-back circular
An enclosure in the package of a product that has been ordered by mail. It offers other products of the same company and is effective in getting more business.

to 40 percent additional sales from the same customers and often launch a one-time customer on the path to becoming a steady buyer. The key to the one-step approach is pinpointing the prime prospects because this approach cannot depend on follow-ups to complete the sale.

Catalogs

By far the most popular form of mail order is the catalog. In terms of sales produced and dollars invested, it trails only telemarketing among the many forms of direct marketing. The use of catalogs dates at least to 1498, when Aldus Manutius published his book catalog containing 15 titles. Since its humble beginnings, the catalog has become a keystone of direct marketing. As early as 1830, New England companies were selling fishing and camping supplies by mail. By the end of the 1800s, both Sears Roebuck & Co. and Montgomery Ward brought retail merchandise to every household in the country through their catalogs. However, not until the 1970s was there a major growth period of catalog selling.

As Americans continue to be pressed for time, catalog marketing shows significant annual growth. It is estimated that consumer and business-to-business catalog purchases will increase 100 percent from $53 billion in 1992 to $106 billion in 2002.[19] Consumer sales will constitute approximately 60 percent of the total, although business-to-business will grow at about the same rate as consumer purchases. Catalog buying has become an accepted method of purchasing products, especially from catalogs that have long traditions of providing quality products at a fair price with superior customer service.

In the early days of catalog selling, catalogs were primarily directed to low- and middle-income families outside of major cities. Today, the catalog business is increasingly directed toward an upscale audience with an interest in specialty merchandise not readily available in retail stores. The general sales catalog has just about disappeared. The future of the catalog, like radio and magazines, is in narrowly defined, targeted books (catalogs are called *books* in the direct-response industry).

Today, catalogs offer an array of merchandise from ties to works of art. However, six product categories annually accumulate more than 10 million buyers each:[20]

Product	Customers (in millions)
Clothing	47.8
Home furnishings	32.4
Books	31.6
Music and videos	21.9
Toys/games	14.1
Gardening	11.5

The selection of merchandise is one of the most crucial aspects of catalog selling. The catalog marketer must be in the mainstream of consumer taste, yet offer distinctive merchandise that is not readily available at local stores. In addition, unlike the local department store, which regularly offers slow-moving items at a discount, catalog sellers are locked into their price schedules.

Trends in Catalog Marketing   Although catalog marketing has been hugely successful in recent years, it faces a number of problems, which are moving the industry toward some major changes:

1. *Higher expenses.* Costs of paper, printing, and mailing have skyrocketed in the past decade. Catalog marketers have found that they must be more selective about which

---

[19]Renee Wijnen, "Catalog Sales Will Surge into Millennium," *DM News,* July 14, 1997, p. 3.
[20]"Ordering for Christmas," *Atlanta Journal,* December 7, 1995, p. E3.

prospects receive a catalog and how many times catalogs will be mailed to certain segments of customers. Estimates indicate that mailers are sending fewer catalogs and being more selective about the demographics of those who receive them. In addition, some mailers are more restrictive about keeping customers on their list. For example, a catalog company may have a formula requiring so many purchases or a certain dollar amount or a customer will be dropped.

Likewise, catalogers are being creative in gaining new customers. They may ask for referrals from present customers, or mailers may use selective advertising vehicles to build their lists. Direct mailers do have a major advantage over retailers in that they can closely monitor the value of their customers in a precise manner based on sales versus the expense of creating those sales.

2. *Catalogs as part of the marketing mix.* More marketers are beginning to regard catalog selling as another retail option rather than a stand-alone distribution channel. As more retailers have realized that a large portion of their customers prefer home shopping, they have moved into the catalog arena. Victoria's Secret, Tiffany, Brooks Brothers, and Sharper Image are only a few of the well-known retailers who have their own catalog sales operations.

3. *Creativity.* In the competitive environment of catalogs, mailers find that state-of-the-art graphics are a necessity to set themselves off from the crowd. In addition to quality color, plentiful pictures and graphics, and catchy text, catalogs are increasingly turning to personalization to gain customers. With the introduction of high-speed jet printing, many catalogs are providing personalized messages within the text of the catalog. Some even vary their messages from one catalog to another, depending on the audience segment receiving them. For example, catalogs to recent customers will have one message, whereas catalogs going to first-time prospects will have different copy.[21]

The Future of the Catalog   Despite the success of catalog selling, the industry faces a number of challenges in the coming years. In some respects, catalogs are becoming victims of their own success. As more catalogs are printed, it becomes difficult to distinguish one from another and to keep profitability up. The major problems facing catalog marketers are the following:[22]

1. *Dealing with weaker customer loyalty.* A trend toward price-driven retailing and the sheer number of catalogs have encouraged a number of consumers to shop for the lowest prices rather than to display high loyalty to a particular catalog.

2. *Making more use of databases to better target and personalize communications with customers.* By tracking customers' purchase histories, direct marketers can mail smarter and track response to predict buying activity better. Almost every improvement in merchandising and marketing will be driven by database research.

3. *Working in a cost-conscious environment.* With cost increases coming in virtually every area of the catalog business, managers will have to be proactive in holding costs down. Technology will have to be refined to identify prospects, product quality and prices will have to be a paramount concern, and more efficient means of catalog distribution and production will have to be explored.

4. *Making it easier for customers to shop through catalogs.* Customer service will be a key to future success. In addition, catalogers will have to make it more convenient to shop. Using the Internet, fax, and overnight delivery systems will become standard in the industry.

---

[21]Jack Schmid, Lois Boyle, and Cindy Holter, "Personalized Catalogs Get Opened," *Target Marketing,* August 1996, p. 46.

[22]Adapted from Jack Schmid, "Challenges for All," *Target Marketing,* April 1996, p. 18.

e x h i b i t

13.8

American catalogers
seek sales in
international markets.

Courtesy: L.L. Bean.

5. *Expanding the market.* Currently, 45 percent of households and businesses are not regular catalog users. It has been suggested that an industry-wide public relations campaign to sell the benefits of mail order would significantly boost the percentage of usage.

Although the catalog found its initial success in the United States, it has become an international phenomenon. A number of major U.S. catalogers have moved aggressively into international markets. For example, L.L. Bean merchandise has become something of a fad among younger Japanese buyers and has achieved annual sales in Japan approaching $200 million since 1990 (see Exhibit 13.8).

Negative Option Direct Response

Continuing relationships with loyal customers is a key to successful and efficient marketing. The **negative option** technique is designed to initiate and maintain just such an association. Rather than selling a single item, it provides consumers with a subscription for the purchase of future merchandise.

The Book-of-the-Month Club is credited with introducing this method of "one-package-a-month" selling. Today we see records and CDs, as well as miniature cars, porcelain figurines, and a host of other merchandise offered on a negative option basis. The idea is that the buyers must notify the company in order *not* to have an item sent.

The consumer appeal of negative options is that companies make the initial offer ridiculously inexpensive in order to encourage consumers to sign up. For example, BMG Music Service offered buyers 11 CDs for the price of one as an introductory offer. The advantage to sellers is that once customers join the plan, the company hopes to maintain them for some period of time. Consequently, sales costs are virtually nonexistent for continuing customers.

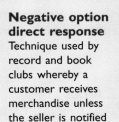

Negative option direct response
Technique used by record and book clubs whereby a customer receives merchandise unless the seller is notified not to send it.

Fulfillment

The primary goal of product **fulfillment** is customer service. The fulfillment center makes sure that orders are filled correctly and merchandise is sent within the time promised. However, companies that view their fulfillment operation only as a "pack and send" transaction are missing a valuable opportunity for what some call *back in* marketing.

Firms should never miss an opportunity to build a stronger relationship with a customer. The roles of a full-service fulfillment center include the following:

1. *Customer service.* This includes fast and accurate sending of merchandise to customers. When problems and complaints arise they should be handled professionally and every effort should be made to have a dissatisfied customer feel good about the company when the problem is settled.
2. *Customer communication.* Inbound calls should be taken by people who are knowledgeable about merchandise and have complete information about models, sizes, guarantees, and so forth. When merchandise cannot be sent on time, customers should be notified and given an option to reorder or cancel.
3. *Cross-selling opportunities.* Database technology allows you to immediately "connect" with former customers to know what they have ordered in the past and their general preferences. Cross selling can be as simple as asking the caller, "What is the next item you would like to order?" or it may involve actively suggesting other merchandise that would complement past or current purchases.
4. *Practice retention marketing.* Marketers realize that there is nothing more valuable than a current customer and few things more difficult than gaining a new one. Taking steps to make customers feel good about their orders and their association with your company is a key to retention marketing. Many companies will offer premiums to their best customers or communicate with their best buyers on a regular basis rather than waiting for inbound calls.

At one time, complaints about order fulfillment were almost standard in the direct-marketing industry. It became so bad that the FTC adopted special guidelines concerning the prompt shipping of merchandise. Although fulfillment is still a major problem in the industry, leading marketers know that professional fulfillment operations are a point of differentiation between them and their competitors. L.L. Bean, for one, has established much of its outstanding reputation on its fulfillment operation. In the competitive environment facing direct marketing, companies know that many customers will not tolerate even one mistake before taking their business elsewhere.

At one time, the fulfillment function was regarded as a shipping service and one that, sometimes grudgingly, handled complaints. Today, fulfillment operations are total customer service departments, which include a multitude of services. Because of the complexity of the fulfillment process, many smaller companies contract out the fulfillment function. Independent fulfillment houses are most commonly used for one-time promotions such as a sweepstakes or premium offers. These types of fulfillment operations are discussed in chapter 14.

TWO-STEP PURCHASE—GETTING LEADS

Although sales are the ultimate goal of virtually all direct-response marketing, as in the case with advertising, sales are sometimes accomplished through intermediate communication. Companies that sell very expensive merchandise, especially business-to-business items, often are dealing with a small universe of potential buyers. In addition, it is rare that a single contact within a company makes the entire purchase decision. Exhibit 13.9 shows the way in which advertising, direct sales, and inside sales (usually telephone contact from someone within the selling company) are used to reach decision

exhibit

13.9

Courtesy: Cahners Publishing Co., Cahners Advertising Research Report No. 544.5.

Percentage of Total Expenses Directed to Reaching People at Each Step of the Buying Process

Buying Steps	Advertising	Direct Sales	Inside Sales
Determine the need	37	22	20
Set specifications	14	16	12
Evaluate suppliers	14	13	7
Select supplier	12	17	9
Approve spending	7	13	14
Place order	16	19	38

Advertising is heavily targeted to people who "determine the need" at the front end of the buying process. Inside sales is heavily targeted to those who "place orders," the last step of the buying process.

makers at various levels. Note that advertising is the most used vehicle (37 percent), and the inside salesforce deals primarily with the person responsible for placing the order (38 percent). Because direct salespersons are more flexible in whom they can see, their effort is spread more evenly across all levels of decision makers.

Lead getting is much more than just obtaining a list of names of potential prospects. Remember, your customers are busy people and they have no inclination to explain their businesses to a salesperson. Sophisticated lead getting will attempt to fill in the blanks. What are the prospects for the product category? How does this company rank in the industry? Does the firm face special problems that you can solve? Selling is basically problem solving, and effective two-step direct marketing is a method of determining specific problems.

Because of the expense of personal selling, some companies actually resort to a three-step process. Instead of going directly to a personal sales call when they get a response, companies may choose instead to send more detailed literature or even a product sample. Exhibit 13.10 indicates the importance of having sales literature in the hands of buyers because more than half refer to such material when making purchase decisions. The key is to generate leads from the most profitable customers. Cost per order (CPO) is a major way of measuring the success of straight sales direct response. In two-step operations, we often see the term *cost per lead* (CPL). The CPL measure recognizes that the first step in a two-step direct response is intended only to generate prospects, not to make final sales.

exhibit

13.10

A majority of all buyers consult their literature files at least once a month.

Courtesy: Cahners Publishing Co., Cahners Advertising Research Report No. 550.21.

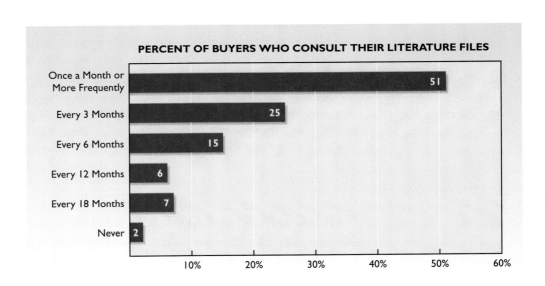

PERCENT OF BUYERS WHO CONSULT THEIR LITERATURE FILES

Once a Month or More Frequently	51
Every 3 Months	25
Every 6 Months	15
Every 12 Months	6
Every 18 Months	7
Never	2

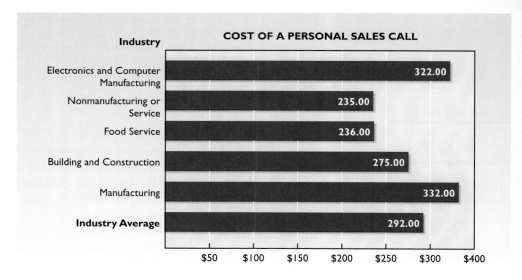

COST OF A PERSONAL SALES CALL

Industry

Industry	Cost
Electronics and Computer Manufacturing	322.00
Nonmanufacturing or Service	235.00
Food Service	236.00
Building and Construction	275.00
Manufacturing	332.00
Industry Average	292.00

Business-to-Business Direct Marketing

The majority of the users of lead-getting direct response are business-to-business sellers. The target marketing characteristics of direct-response are ideal for business-to-business marketing. As discussed earlier in this chapter, the leading business-to-business direct-marketing technique in terms of sales revenue and expenditures is telemarketing, and direct mail is a distant second. The most important features of business-to-business marketing are the following:

1. *A relatively small market.* Compared to the typical consumer market, the number of businesses in any industry is quite small. For example, in the industrial sector it is common for fewer than five firms to account for 80 percent or more of total sales.
2. *Concentrated buying decisions.* The number of purchasing decision makers on the business side is very small compared to consumer marketing. It is practical to spend a great deal of money to reach each of these decision makers and still keep the total promotional budget at a reasonable level.
3. *High average per purchase expenditures.* Business-to-business advertisers are playing for big stakes. Whereas a consumer may buy a $3,000 personal computer, a purchasing agent may buy a multimillion dollar computer system. Factors such as *CPMs,* so important in consumer promotions, have little relevance to business marketers.
4. *Flexibility.* Business-to-business direct response must be flexible and adapt to the needs of different industries or even individuals in a way that consumer advertising does not.

Another factor in the growth of the business-to-business advertising segment of direct response is the cost of personal selling. The cost of a typical sales call is now close to $300, and these costs have risen sharply in recent years (see Exhibit 13.11). Increasingly, we are going to see the frequency of personal sales calls concentrated on large customers, leaving smaller clients with infrequent sales calls. However, these customers will be reached with both direct-response and traditional business-to-business advertising.

DIRECT-MAIL ADVERTISING

We discuss direct mail as a separate category of direct marketing because it has a number of features that are unique to the medium. Successful direct-mail advertising is determined by four basic elements: product, offer, list, and timing.

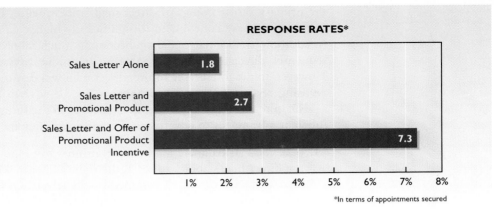

RESPONSE RATES*

- Sales Letter Alone — 1.8
- Sales Letter and Promotional Product — 2.7
- Sales Letter and Offer of Promotional Product Incentive — 7.3

(Scale: 1% 2% 3% 4% 5% 6% 7% 8%)

*In terms of appointments secured

1. *The product.* A quality product at a fair price that offers consumers differentiation from competing brands is the key to all sales. Products are most effectively sold through direct mail if they are not available in most retail outlets.

2. *The offer.* Direct mail offers unlimited space for a detailed sales message. The serious prospect can be given much more information than would be practical in media advertising with little or no increase in cost. Because sales can be tracked precisely, the copy in direct mail can be tested and fine-tuned in a way that is very difficult in other media. In addition, databases combined with high-speed printing technology can personalize direct mail similar to a personal sales call. The offer is made in an uncluttered environment. In the case of stand-alone direct mail offers, there is no editorial material or advertisements competing for the reader's attention.

   It has been found that response rates to direct mail can be enhanced with the use of specialties and other promotional products. For example, Exhibit 13.12 shows how response rates were enhanced when mailers used incentives with letters asking for appointments for its representatives. Because of the number of direct-mail offers, it is sometimes difficult to get the recipient's attention. It is estimated that the average consumer decides in 3.5 seconds whether to open a mailing piece.

3. *The mailing list.* The key to productive direct-mail advertising is an up-to-date mailing list. Some direct mailers believe that as much as half of the value of a direct-mail offer is determined by the accuracy of the mailing list. An excellent product and compelling copy will be wasted if delivered to nonprospects. The mailing list is the equivalent of media scheduling in traditional advertising.

4. *Timing.* Correct timing of a direct-mail offer has been demonstrated to play a major role in its success. Direct mailers are extremely cognizant of the importance of timing. The Kleid Company, a major list provider, has done extensive tracking of the best selling months for a variety of products. For example, fund raising solicitations do best in August, November, and October, whereas self-improvement products sell best in July, September, and December.

   A more sophisticated approach to timing is called *synchographics.* It tracks dramatic changes in people's lives where purchases will always take place. For example, marriage, birth of a baby, move to a new home, and retirement will result in the purchase of certain products or services. Computer databases allow marketers to reach people in these circumstances at the precise moment of change.[23]

Characteristics of Direct Mail

Direct mail is the oldest form of direct-response advertising and is second only to telemarketing in terms of sales produced. It has many unique advantages as a marketing tool. However, it also faces a number of challenges in the twenty-first century. One of

---

[23]Denny Hatch, "Joe Montana Marketing," *Target Marketing,* October 1996, p. 96.

the primary shortcomings of direct mail is its expense. Rising costs of postage, paper, and printing have contributed to significantly higher *CPM*s for direct-mail advertisers. In addition, traditional media are becoming much more specialized and targeted. Consequently, direct mail has lost some of its unique advantage as *the* targeted medium. However, in the foreseeable future, direct mail will continue to be a major source of advertising revenue and an important part of the advertising plans of many advertisers.

Despite the prospect of serious challenges in the future, direct mail still offers many inherent advantages to advertisers. The primary ones are the following:

1. *Selectivity.* As database marketing continues to pinpoint consumers, advertisers will use direct mail's ability to reach the right audience with the most appropriate message, and with timing determined by the advertiser. Direct mail is especially useful for promoting special products and services that appeal to a limited number of people.

2. *Personalized selling.* Because a direct mailer is addressing a homogeneous audience, a firm can personalize the sales message in a manner that would be impractical in most general advertising. At one time, personalization was confined to having the customer's name in a message that was otherwise the same for all recipients. However, direct mailers now have the capability of altering the message for various segments within a mailing list. This technique, called **message management,** allows direct mail to fully utilize extensive databases to make an offer specific to each individual receiving it. For example, note how the various lists from BMG Music allow advertisers to target diverse groups (see Exhibit 13.13). Different listening preference groups possess different age and gender demographics besides the obvious differences in lifestyles. Each group represents a distinct target audience for mail-order offers, magazines, catalogs, and so on. Some credit card companies make offers in their bills based on spending habits of individual customers. A cardholder who spends $3,000 a year on airline tickets may be offered discounts by a rental car company.

3. *Copy can be longer and more informative.* Because direct mail is sent to a select audience, copy can go into more detail about product benefits. Unlike media advertising, the longer copy in direct mail is more likely to be read by this interested audience. Also, within reason, long direct-mail copy does not add to the expense of the advertising.

4. *Results are often immediate and measurable.* Advertisers are able to measure results and test various copy approaches in a way that would be impossible with most other forms of advertising. Usually a mailing is thoroughly tested with mailings to a sample of the target audience before the entire mailing is conducted.

Testing Direct-Mail Advertising

The key to successful direct mail is testing. Most direct mail campaigns are extremely expensive on a *CPM* basis ($1,000 or more per 1,000 exposures is not uncommon). It is rare for a national mailing to be initiated without extensive testing of every aspect of the program. One of the major advantages of direct mail advertising is that it is relatively easy and inexpensive to test the various components of a mailing. The mailing list, the primary offer, the creative presentation, even the method of reply can all be tested.

The key to testing direct mail is to concentrate on major elements that normally determine the success or failure of a mail campaign. It is extremely important to test only one element at a time. Too many mailers try to cut corners by testing several items in a single mailing. Obviously, if you change the format, the mailing list, and the offer, it is impossible to determine what factor created any changes in test results. In the following section we examine some methods of testing major direct-mail elements.

Message management
Utilizes database information to offer different message to various consumer categories.

THE MAILING LIST

The mailing list is so important to the accomplishment of the goals of direct mail that an entire industry has developed to provide mailers with targeted lists. It has been said that the mailing list is the glue that holds the direct-mail industry together. "A mailing list consists of the names and addresses of a group of people or companies all having one or more things in common. The list represents a meaningful grouping. Direct marketing companies do not have a single mailing list. They have many . . . opportunities to segment the customer file into marketing units with purchasing behavior characteristics [that] are vast."[24]

Without an up-to-date and properly maintained mailing list, successful direct-mail advertising is impossible. Direct mail is the only medium for which the advertiser determines the circulation. The list is the media plan of direct mail. Just as the media buyer must carefully analyze the audiences of the various vehicles that will make up the final media schedule, the advertiser must carefully choose the list(s) that will provide

---

[24]Rose Harper, "Rose Harper on Lists," *Target Marketing,* September 1995, p. 26.

the greatest number of prospects at the lowest cost. Most list are *compiled lists;* that is, they are developed from a number of existing sources and names are compiled into a single list.

As we see in the remainder of this section, names and prospects are easily available. The problem for the direct-mail advertiser is developing these names into a single list and then fine-tuning it for accuracy, duplication, and so forth.

Organizations Involved in the Direct Mail Process

List Brokers   Among the key figures in direct mail are **list brokers.** Brokers function as liaisons between mailers who need lists of particular target prospects and sources with lists to rent. Some of the primary functions of list brokers include the following:

- *Research available lists.* It is imperative to find a broker with expertise in the particular product category. With thousands of lists on the market, no one individual can be an expert in all areas. Larger list broker firms assign different people to specific categories to allow them to be experts in narrow areas.
- *Negotiate for the client.* Often a broker will be dealing with a number of list sources. The broker can negotiate not only price, but also special arrangements such as allowances for testing the list, various methods of payment, and a number of discounts.
- *Research.* The list broker is an expert in the field who not only knows about existing lists, but also may be able to approach list owners who have never rented their customer's names. In addition, the broker should be able to advise you on which lists would be best for a particular marketing situation.
- *General marketing advice.* List brokers are in the marketplace all the time. They are aware of innovations in list usage and other aspects of direct mail. A list broker can provide objective advice similar to that given by an advertising agency to its clients.
- *Back-end analysis.* List brokers are interested in a long-term relationship. Consequently, they can be invaluable in analyzing results from past mailings to see how improvements in the marketing plan can bring even better results in the future.

As one direct mailer said, "I think of my broker as another member of my staff—a person with highly specialized knowledge, assigned to a task which would otherwise consume the precious hours in my week."[25]

The list broker is paid a commission by the list owner, usually 20 percent, each time a list is rented. The broker represents the mailer, not the list owner. The relationship between the mailer and the list broker is similar to that of an advertising agency and its clients, in which the media pay a commission based on media placement. Obviously, the list broker is a marketing consultant, not just a source of list rentals.

Mailing lists vary widely in cost. The two factors most important in determining price are the selectivity of the names and their potential value. For example, a list of automobile owners, which is easily obtained through public records, might cost as little as $35 for 1,000 names. On the other hand, a list of health-care specialists, particularly those who have responded to other direct-mail offers, might be $125 per 1,000.

List Compilers   The list compiler is usually a broker who rents a number of lists from published sources and combines them into a single list and then rents them to advertisers. List compilers date to the nineteenth century. For example, Charles Groves, superintendent of Michigan City schools in the late 1800s, compiled lists of teachers by writing other school superintendents around the country. He then sold the lists to textbook publishers and other companies who wanted to reach teachers.[26] Compilers tend to specialize in either consumer or business lists, although a few do both.

List broker
In direct-mail advertising an agent who rents the prospect lists of one advertiser to another advertiser. The broker receives a commission from the seller for this service.

---

[25]Cheryl Bagdan, "Why & How to Hire a Broker," *Target Marketing,* August 1996, p. 30.

[26]Lewis Rashmir, "The First Compiler Was Charles Groves," *DM News,* February 15, 1993, p. 35.

List manager
Promotes client's lists to potential renters and buyers.

Merge/purge (merge & purge)
A system used to eliminate duplication by direct response advertisers who use different mailing lists for the same mailing. Mail merge/purge office that electronically picks out duplicate names. Saves mailing costs, especially important to firms that send out a million pieces in one mailing. Also avoids damage to the goodwill of the public.

Response lists
In direct mail, prospects who have previously responded to a direct mail offer.

Lettershop
A firm that not only addresses the mailing envelope but also is mechanically equipped to insert material, seal and stamp envelopes, and deliver them to the post office according to mailing requirements.

List Managers The **list manager** represents the *list owner* just as the broker is the agency for the mailer. The primary job of the list manager is to maximize income for the list owner by promoting the list to as many advertisers as possible. List managers are usually outside consultants, but some large companies have in-house list managers. Most national magazines offer their lists for rent. These lists are ideal direct-response vehicles because most magazines appeal to a narrowly defined, specialized audience. Another benefit of magazine lists is that magazine subscribers often buy through direct-mail offers, so they are proven direct-mail prospects.

Service Bureaus Service bureaus provide a number of functions. One of the primary jobs of the service bureau is to constantly improve lists. This function is called *list enhancement.* List enhancement includes a number of steps, one of the most important of which is known as **merge/purge.** Basically merge/purge systems eliminate duplicate names from a list. Such duplication is costly to the advertiser and annoying to the customer. Duplication also offsets any personal contact with the customer by portraying the message as a mass mailing—and one done with little care. Merge/purge is accomplished by computers that are so sophisticated that names are cross-checked against the same addresses and similar spellings.

Lettershop The **lettershop** is in reality a mailing house. These companies coordinate the job of mailing millions of pieces of mail from printing the labels to keeping abreast of the latest postal regulations. Large lettershops may even have a representative of the U.S. Postal Service on the premises to work with every aspect of the delivery of mail in a timely fashion.

Response Lists As discussed earlier, the great majority of mailing lists are compiled. However, many mailing-list houses sell or rent lists of people who have previously responded to a direct-mail offer or demonstrated some interest in doing so. People on **response lists** are those who are prone to order by mail; therefore, these lists are more productive than compiled lists.

Generally, response lists are more expensive than compiled lists. Compiled lists are regarded as less valuable than response lists by direct mailers. The biggest drawback cited for compiled lists is that many compiled lists don't offer a previous record of direct-response purchases. Direct-response advertisers often use compiled lists as supplements to response lists. By combining response and compiled lists, a mailer can reach previous customers as well as a larger pool of prospective customers.

Response lists are often obtained from previous customers of a company. These are called *house lists* and are among the most valuable commodities of a direct mailer. From time to time, owners of house lists will use rental response lists from noncompeting companies. The source and number of rental lists is almost endless. Advertisers can buy lists of people who have gone on cruises, who hunt specific animals, or who have bought books on psychoanalysis in the past six months. One list offered the names of people who had ordered false teeth adhesive by mail!

List Protection Because mailing lists are so valuable, companies go to great lengths to protect them from misuse. The most common list abuse is multimailings beyond an agreed-upon limit. For example, one direct mailer reported that a company rented his list on a one-time basis and used it 13 times.

The traditional protection for such misuse is to include a number of fictitious names so that the list owner can trace the number of mailings. This is known as *list decoying.* In addition to protecting the list itself, list renters should also ask for a sample of the mailing material. Occasionally, a mailing may be in bad taste or contain a deceptive offer. However, the much greater problem is that the mailing may be too closely competitive with the list owner's products. Renting a list should provide additional profit, not additional competition!

Other Direct-Mail Techniques

The format and execution of direct-mail campaigns can take many forms. In this section we briefly discuss a few of the primary ones.

Package Inserts   For many years, direct marketers have used package inserts to promote additional purchases of products sent to customers or other items in their product lines. As mentioned earlier in this chapter, these bounce-back circulars are very inexpensive because there are no additional postage costs, but, more important, they are directed at proven customers who have just made a direct-mail purchase.

Today, many direct marketers are negotiating with other companies to use inserts in their packages much as you would buy space in a magazine. These inserts are called **ride-alongs,** and can be sent at a fraction of the cost of an independent mailing. Typical ride-along *CPM*s are in the $40 to $50 range compared to $200 to $300 for the simplest direct-mail piece.

Beside their low cost, inserts allow an advertiser to gain an implied endorsement from the distributing company. Also the number of ride-along programs available offers a degree of target marketing that approaches an independent mailing. It is estimated that there are as many as 20,000 programs available to advertisers. A number of companies use package inserts for product sampling as well as advertising notices. This method of sampling guarantees a logical product tie-in with what is already being purchased. Just as important, it provides the sample at a fraction of the cost of mailing the sample alone.

Ticket Jackets   A popular form of ride-alongs involves promotions on airline, bus line, or train ticket jackets. Companies such as car rental firms find that they are ideal to reach the prime target audience. Because ticket stuffers are a high-volume medium, the *CPM* is in the neighborhood of $20.

Cooperative (Joint) Mail Advertising   With the cost of postage continuing to increase, direct mailers often attempt to share expenses through cooperative mailings. There are a number of firms that specialize in joint mailings. These mailings may include 20 or more different advertising offers in one envelope. Each advertiser provides a coupon or other short message, and the joint mailer handles the mailing and divides the cost among the advertisers.

Cooperative mailings have two major drawbacks. First, they are extremely impersonal because each advertiser's message must be very short. Second, it is difficult to reach your specific customers through joint mailings with the precision you would have with your own list. The dilemma of joint mailings is that as the number of participating advertisers increases, the cost per advertiser goes down, but, likewise, the unique feature of the mailing decreases.

Statement Stuffers   Few companies miss an opportunity to include a message with your monthly statement. These messages are similar to ride-alongs and have several advantages. First, they cost nothing to deliver because the mailing expense is going to be incurred in any case. Second, they are at least seen, because everyone eventually gets around to opening their bills. Finally, most recipients are credit qualified and have already dealt with the company before or they would not be getting a statement. The disadvantage is that some consumers may not be in the mood for another purchase while paying for their last one.

PLANNING AND PRODUCING THE DIRECT-MAIL PIECE

The first step in planning a direct-mail piece is to study the overall marketing and advertising program. Direct marketing is not separate from the firm's other marketing efforts, but is an integrated part of the system. The first question a direct marketer should

---

Ride-alongs
Direct-mail pieces that are sent with other mailings, such as bills.

ask is, "How will my direct marketing efforts complement the total marketing program of my company?"

To answer this question you might ask yourself the following:

- Will the direct-mail effort be supported with media advertising? Before, during, or after the mailing?
- Is the direct-mail message aimed at present or potential customers, or both?
- Am I attempting a straight sale or building leads for future follow-up? If the latter, does our salesforce know about and understand the purpose of the mailing?

Other questions you ask will, of course, be determined by the specific marketing problem you are trying to solve. However, only after you have approached the direct-mail promotion from the perspective of your marketing goals and objectives are you ready to begin production of your mailing piece.

The creator of direct mail has a wide latitude in format: It may be a single card encompassing a coupon, or it may be a letter with a return card, a small folder, a brochure, or a folded broadside with an order form and return envelope. Each format has a different function and use, depending on the cost of the product being sold, the importance of pictures, and the nature and length of the copy. As a rule, a warm letter, even if not personalized, should accompany any request for the order. This letter should stress the product's benefits, describe its key features and their importance, and ask for the order. No matter what kind of material is being sent, it is always possible to present it in an interesting form (within postal limitations).

What a different world direct-mail production is, compared to magazine ad production! With magazine ads, the publisher is responsible for the total printing and delivery of the publication. In direct mail, the advertiser undertakes the complete burden of having all the material printed, which involves selecting the paper and the type, establishing prices, and selecting the printer. It also involves selecting a lettershop, whose functions we discussed earlier.

A Mail-Production Program

Perhaps the clearest way to see what is involved is to work through a schedule and touch on some of the key points.

Checking Weight and Size with Post Office   Everything begins on receipt of a layout of the mailing unit, including copy and artwork from the creative department, along with quantities and mailing dates. The first—and most important—thing to do is to check with the post office on weight and size.

Selecting the Printing Process   In chapter 18 we discuss the three major types of printing: letterpress, offset, and gravure. For the time being, we can say that most direct-mail advertising is printed by the offset method, except very large runs, which may use rotogravure.

Selecting the Paper   Here we have to pause to become familiar with some important elements in the choice of paper, as this is not covered elsewhere in the book. The three chief categories of paper ("stocks") used in advertising are writing stocks, book stocks, and cover stocks. The printer will submit samples of paper suitable for a given job.

Writing Stocks   This class comprises the whole range of paper meant to be written or typed on. Quality varies from ledger stock, used to keep records; to bond stock, for top-level office stationery; to utility office paper, used to keep records; to memorandum paper. If you wanted to include a letter in a mailing, you would find a paper in this class.

Book Stocks   Book stocks are the widest classification of papers used in advertising. Chief among the many variations of book stocks are the following:

- *News stock.* This is the least costly book paper, built for a short life and porous so that it can dry quickly. It takes line plates well. It is used for free-standing inserts in magazines, but it is not very good for offset.
- *Antique finish.* A soft paper with a mildly rough finish, antique finish is used for offset. Among the antique classifications are eggshell antique, a very serviceable offset paper; and text, a high-grade antique used for quality offset books, booklets, and brochures (it is often watermarked and deckle-edged or irregular).
- *Machine finish.* Most books and publications are printed on machine-finish paper. It is the workhorse of the paper family.
- *English finish.* This paper has a roughened nonglare surface. Widely accepted for direct-mail and sales-promotion printing, it is especially good for offset lithography and gravure.
- *Coated.* This is a paper given a special coat of clay and then ironed. The result is a heavier, smoother paper. Coated paper is not usually used for offset. It can take 150-screen halftones very well for letterpress printing and is therefore frequently used in industrial catalogs, where fine, sharp reproduction is important and where there will be continuous usage over a period of time.

Cover Stocks   These are strong papers, highly resistant to rough handling. Cover stock is used not only for the covers of booklets, but also sometimes by itself in direct-mail work. Although it has many finishes and textures, it is not adaptable for half-tone printing by letterpress but reproduces tones very well in offset.

Basic Weights and Sizes   Paper comes off the machine in large rolls. It is then cut into large sheets in a number of different sizes. In that way, many pages can be printed at one time. Paper is sold by 500-sheet reams, and its grade is determined by weight. To meet the problem of comparing the weight of paper cut to different sizes, certain sizes have been established for each class as basic for weighing purposes:

- For writing paper: 17 by 22 inches
- For book paper: 25 by 38 inches
- For cover stock: 20 by 26 inches

Hence, no matter how large the sheet into which the paper has been cut may be, its weight is always given in terms of the weight of that paper when cut to its basic size. Thus, one hears a writing paper referred to as a "20-pound writing paper," a book paper referred to as a "70-pound paper," and a cover stock identified as a "100-pound cover."

Paper, which has to be selected in relation to the printing process and the plates to be used, is usually procured by the printer after a specific choice has been made by the advertiser. In large cities, it may also be bought directly from paper jobbers. Both printers and jobbers will be glad to submit samples. Before you give the final order for paper, you should check once more with the post office for weight, shape, and size of envelope. Check the total package.

In planning direct mail, you must know basic paper sizes and plan all pieces so that they may be cut from a standard sheet size without waste. Before ordering envelopes, check with the post office to learn the latest size restrictions, which are subject to change.

Selecting the Printer   The problem in selecting a printer is, first of all, to find those printers who have the type of presses and the capacity to handle the operation that you have in mind. They may not be located near you. In any case, experience has

exhibit

13.14

Reverse production timetables are used to schedule direct-mail campaigns.

Courtesy: Direct Mail/Marketing Association, New York. Source: The Direct Mail Marketing Manual, Release 4005, July 1976.

Description of item or project: _____

REVERSE TIMETABLE

(The purpose of which is to work backward to make sure enough time is allowed for proper completion.)

Final Date Due in Hands of Recipients _____ — This is when you expect the mailing to reach the people who are going to read it and act upon it.

Mailing Date _____ — When you must release it to get it there on time. Avoid disappointment by allowing enough time for the P.O.

Assembly Date _____ — All material must be in on this date to allow sufficient time for the mailing operations.

Printing Completion Date _____ — This could be same as the assembly date except where time is required for shipment to an out-of-town point.

Final Artwork Approval Date _____ — This is the date the artwork must be ready to turn over to the printer.

Artwork Completion Date _____ — Although most details should have been okayed before work actually began, quite often several people must approve the finished artwork. Allow enough time for this approval.

Finished Artwork Assignment Date _____ — This is the day the artist or art department gets the job. Allow at least a week. If no type has to be set, the interval can be cut short.

Consideration and Approval Date _____ — Allow four or five days for staff members, including legal department if necessary, to see finished copy and layout.

Copy and Layout Assignment Date _____ — Allow a week or more to give the copy and layout people time to do their jobs. Give more time when you can; they will more readily come through for you when a rush job is really critical.

Starting Date _____ — You need some time to think about the job and draw up a set of instructions.

Reverse production timetable

Used in direct mail to schedule a job. The schedule starts with the date it is to reach customers and works backward to a starting date.

shown that it is always best to get three estimates. Of course, the reputation of the firm for prompt delivery is important.

Finished mechanicals with type and illustrations or photographic negatives should be made ready to turn over to the printer. Proofs should be checked carefully and returned promptly to the printer.

Production Schedule for Direct Mail

The planning and execution of a direct-mail campaign is not an overnight operation. The advertiser must work backward from the target date for the customer to receive the mailing piece to determine the necessary lead time. A **reverse production timetable** can be helpful in planning each step of a project (see Exhibit 13.14).

Direct-response marketing has moved into center stage as a means of reaching and selling a diverse universe of consumers. In terms of sales produced and expenditures for the medium, it represents more dollars than all other forms of advertising combined. It is rare for a company not to include direct marketing and direct-response advertising as a major element in its marketing mix. Companies have come to realize that the ability to combine personal messages with highly selective audience segmentation gives direct response advantages seen in few other media. The tremendous strides in computer technology have made the future of direct response both exciting and uncertain.

Interactive television and other methods of home shopping will be a major threat to traditional retailing in the near future. As we examine both the number of consumers using home shopping and the dollars spent, it is obvious that buyers are becoming more comfortable with the diverse world of direct response.

The flexibility of direct response makes it practical for virtually every advertiser. In addition, the ability to test and verify direct marketing is vitally important in the current era of accountability. The ability to precisely measure many types of direct response is a major advantage to advertisers and provides the audience research increasingly demanded by companies.

Regardless of the format of future direct response, there is little question that it will continue to grow, probably at a faster rate than media advertising. Not only will direct response become more important in the marketing plans of many companies, but we will see the concept of audience segmentation adopted by all media. History will probably mark the 1990s as the end of the era of mass media and mass audience delivery. In the future, audience segmentation will be even more refined. More important, one-way communication will slowly give way to some form of interactive media. There is little question that direct response will play a major role in this transition.

In addition to the technological advances of direct-response advertising, societal changes also are working in its favor. For example, the two-income family, working mothers, an aging population, and less leisure time are only a few of the factors leading people to favor in-home buying. Greater demand and customer acceptability of direct response are pushing more companies to enter the field.

Perhaps the greatest challenge facing direct marketing is public skepticism, especially concerns over privacy issues. However, industry-wide efforts sponsored by the Direct Marketing Association and other organizations have made great strides in improving the industry's image. The fact that most Fortune 500 companies routinely include some form of direct marketing in their promotional plans is testimony to its growing respectability among advertisers and improved credibility among consumers. Nevertheless, the industry is aware that legislation affecting its operation is constantly being introduced and presents a threat to future growth.

REVIEW

1. What are some of the primary reasons for the growth in direct-response advertising during the last 25 years?
2. What are some of the major public concerns about direct-response marketing?
3. Discuss the role of database marketing in direct-response advertising.
4. Define the following terms:
   a. Lifetime value
   b. Inbound telemarketing
   c. Up-selling
   d. Bounce-back circulars

  e. List protection

  f. Reverse timetable

5. Discuss some of the characteristics of a successful infomerical product.

6. What are some of the primary advantages and disadvantages of catalog selling?

7. Discuss the importance of the fulfillment function in successful direct-response marketing.

8. Compare and contrast business-to-business and consumer direct-response marketing.

9. Discuss the role of list brokers in direct-mail advertising.

TAKE IT TO THE NET

We invite you to visit the Russell/Lane page on the Prentice Hall Web site at

PHLIP **http://www.prenhall.com/phbusiness** for the bimonthly Russell/Lane update and for this chapter's World Wide Web exercise.

SALES PROMOTION

CHAPTER OBJECTIVES

FOR A NUMBER OF YEARS, TOTAL SPENDING IN ALL FORMS OF SALES PROMOTION HAS OUTPACED INVESTMENTS IN ADVERTISING. PROMOTION SPENDING CONTINUES TO GROW FASTER THAN ADVERTISING, AND THE TREND SHOWS NO SIGN OF DIMINISHING. AFTER READING THIS CHAPTER YOU WILL UNDERSTAND

- the role of sales promotion in short-term sales
- coordination between advertising and promotional activities
- the numerous promotional formats
- national companies' participation in cooperative advertising
- trade incentives versus consumer sales promotion.

Sales promotion
(1) Sales activities that supplement both personal selling and marketing, coordinate the two, and help to make them effective. For example, displays are sales promotions. (2) More loosely, the combination of personal selling, advertising, and all supplementary selling activities.

Each day, even if we don't realize it, we come into contact with numerous examples of sales promotion. In fact, the techniques of **sales promotion** are so diverse and widely used that it would be almost impossible not to be involved in some form of sales promotion. The T-shirt from the local automobile dealer, the holiday calendar from the insurance agent, and the newspaper coupon for the local grocery store are all examples of the far-flung world of promotions.

Sales promotion is directed to a number of different target markets and comes in an array of formats. However, they all have in common the goal of creating short-term sales. In recent years, sales promotion and advertising have been increasingly used in an integrated effort to build brand loyalty and long-term sales (advertising) and create an incentive to push the consumer toward an immediate purchase (sales promotion).

When advertising and sales promotion efforts are not coordinated properly, there is a danger of sacrificing long-term buyer loyalty for short-term sales. In their search for new customers, companies sometimes forget to reward their continuing faithful buyers and instead place a disproportionate share of their budget in efforts to give preferential treatment to new or occasional customers. It is particularly aggravating for a long-time customer to find that promotions such as free checking, half-price service calls, or promotional premiums are offered only to new customers.

To provide a better balance between advertising and sales promotion, we are finding that a number of companies are consolidating overall responsibility for advertising and promotion under a single corporate executive. Despite the fact that advertising and sales promotion are different in many respects, there must be some level of coordination. For example, whereas promotions at one time were short-term in duration, we now see a number of programs, such as Candice Bergen's "Dime Lady" campaign for Sprint, combine a discount promotion with advertising for an extended run.

Despite the merging of advertising and sales promotion in terms of both management responsibility and creative execution, we should be aware that advertising and sales promotion are different in terms of execution and objectives. It is impossible to be successful as a client, advertising agency, marketing manager, or promotion manager without a knowledge of the broad concepts involved in the total system of **marketing communication.**

In this chapter, we discuss the primary types of sales promotion and how they complement media advertising. As with advertising, the opportunities for successful execution of sales promotion programs depend on an understanding of the marketing objectives of a particular firm or individual brand. As in the case of advertising, sales promotion failures are most often a direct result of poor planning and a lack of integration with the total marketing mix.

PROMOTION AND ADVERTISING

Effective sales promotion has two basic functions: (1) to inform and (2) to motivate. Normally, sales promotion is most effective when its message is closely coordinated to advertising themes. Point-of-purchase displays may feature a testimonial spokesperson appearing in television commercials, counter displays often use the same headlines and copy style as print advertisements, and product sampling will offer miniature packages to enhance brand identification promoted in the company's advertising. Even though the means of communication may be different than in advertising, information is a key to successful promotions and, in this respect, promotions are closely related to advertising.

The second feature of promotions—motivation—differs in some major respects from that of advertising. Motivation, in a marketing sense, is the means used to move a customer to purchase a brand. This process usually moves across a continuum from awareness (initially hearing about a product) to purchase. Exhibit 14.1 shows that advertising and sales promotion have markedly different responsibilities in the communication and purchase processes.

Recognizing that in a totally integrated marketing program, advertising and sales promotion may be adapted to somewhat different functions, let us look at the purposes and objectives normally associated with sales promotion and advertising.[1]

Marketing communication
The communication components of marketing, which include public relations, advertising, personal selling, and sales promotion.

exhibit

14.1

Advertising and sales promotion should function in a complementary fashion.

THE CONSUMER COMMUNICATION AND PURCHASE PROCESS

Awareness	Positioning	Consideration	Preference	Shopping	Purchase

Primarily the Role
of Advertising

Primarily the Role
of Sales Promotion

---

[1] *Advertising and Sales Promotion: An Overview,* a publication of the Television Advertising Bureau.

Promotion Industry Gross Revenues ($ millions)

	1995	1994	% Change
Premium incentives	$20,800.0	$20,000.0	+4.0%
P-O-P displays	12,024.0	11,098.0*	+8.3
Advertising specialties	8,037.0	7,008.0*	+14.7
Couponing	6,950.0	6,995.0	−0.6
Specialty printing	5,250.0	4,870.0*	+7.8
Promotional licensing	4,850.0	4,900.0	−1.0
Sponsored events	4,700.0	4,250.0	+10.6
Promotion fulfillment	2,160.0	2,180.0	−0.9
Interactive	1,540.0	1,126.0*	+36.8
Research	941.0	856.8	+9.8
Promotion agencies	999.9	833.0	+20.0
In-store marketing	990.4	828.8	+19.5
Product sampling	774.0	703.9	+10.0
	$70,016.3	$65,649.5	6.7%

*Adjusted figure

exhibit

14.2

Most areas of promotion are growing at a significant pace.

Courtesy: Promo.

Sales promotion is best suited for

● short-term product movement
● measurable, immediate results
● encouraging consumers to try new products
● selling undifferentiated products using price appeals
● gaining trade awareness and acceptance

Advertising is best suited for

● long-term image and building brand equity
● cumulative effects over time
● communication of product features and benefits
● gaining consumer awareness and acceptance

It is evident that advertising and promotion serve distinct, but complementary roles in achieving the objectives and goals of a marketing program. In most instances, successful sales promotion depends on strong consumer identity with a brand. In this respect, advertising "sets the table" for sales promotion to close the deal. The parallel functions of promotion and advertising make it imperative that "the entire effort . . . use[s] a common theme, common visuals, and common communications messages for maximum effectiveness."[2]

Promotional expenditures cover a wide range of programs. Exhibit 14.2 shows some of the major categories of spending in promotions. It is interesting to note that the largest percentage increase is in the area of interactive promotions. Like their advertising counterparts, promotional spenders are experimenting with various means of using new technology in the marketing process.

Total promotion budgets are generally divided into three categories: consumer advertising, consumer promotion (usually referred to as either sales promotion or simply promotion), and trade promotion (known as dealer promotion or merchandising). Although close coordination among these promotional classifications is important, they each serve a distinct purpose. Let us examine the place of each in the marketing mix and the share of budgets spent in these promotional categories.

---

[2] *What Every Account Executive Should Know about Merchandising and Sales Promotion,* a publication of the American Association of Advertising Agencies, p. 18.

Consumer advertising
Directed to people who will use the product themselves, in contrast to trade advertising, industrial advertising, or professional advertising.

1. ***Consumer advertising.*** The role of measured media advertising vehicles is to build long-term brand equity and promote basic product attributes, location of dealers, and/or comparisons with other products. The percent of total promotional budgets spent on advertising has declined steadily over the last decade. Approximately 25 percent of promotional dollars are currently spent in advertising.

2. *Consumer sales promotion.* These are sales-promotional incentives directed to the consumer. Cents-off coupons are the most common consumer promotion, but premiums, rebates, and sweepstakes also are used frequently. Driven primarily by a decrease in the use of coupons, consumer sales promotion has fallen slightly to 25 percent of spending.

3. *Trade promotions.* Accounting for about half of the promotional budget, trade incentives are designed to encourage a company's salesforce or retail outlets to push its products more aggressively. These are the most expensive types of promotion on a per-person basis. Winning dealers or retailers may get a trip to Hawaii, a new car, or a cash bonus. Behind the significant increase in trade promotions is the fact that companies think they get more immediate payout for their spending in this sector and that they have more control over expenditures than in other forms of promotion.

Despite some movement of dollars among the three categories, the long-term trend seems to be a ratio of 75 percent of promotional dollars in trade and sales promotion and 25 percent in advertising. The relatively low figure for advertising might be even further depressed if we had an accurate measure of the advertising dollars that are allocated to support major promotions such as sweepstakes, rebates, or sales. Most marketing executives predict minimal future increases in advertising's share of total promotion budgets.

FORMS OF SALES PROMOTION

In the remainder of this chapter, we discuss the primary types of sales promotion. Priority is given to those techniques most associated with advertising, especially at the consumer level. However, we also briefly discuss trade-oriented promotions. In all cases, we need to keep in mind the complementary functions of advertising and promotion. The most frequently used forms of sales promotion are the following:

- point-of-purchase advertising
- premiums
- specialty advertising
- coupons
- sampling
- deals
- event marketing
- sweepstakes and contests
- cooperative advertising
- trade shows and exhibits
- directories and yellow pages
- trade incentives

POINT-OF-PURCHASE ADVERTISING

Point-of-purchase advertising
Displays prepared by the manufacturer for use where the product is sold.

Point-of-purchase displays date to the earliest shopkeepers, who probably placed a crude sign on some slow-moving merchandise. However, from its humble beginnings, **point-of-purchase** (P-O-P) has become one of the most prevalent and fastest-growing segments of sales promotion. Notice the effective and eye-catching display for Crayola, which quickly builds interest with children as well as parents (see Exhibit 14.3, p. 392). Today, P-O-P displays provide effective in-store reminders. In fact, if P-O-P were treated as a separate medium, it would rank behind only television and newspapers, with almost $20 billion invested in all forms of displays. P-O-P has several primary advantages as a sales promotion technique:

1. *Remind consumers about brands and products.* One of the major roles of P-O-P is to remind consumers about product categories and brands that they might overlook. In

exhibit

14.3

Point-of-purchase is an
effective means of
reaching consumers.

Courtesy: Conocraft.

this role, P-O-P often complements traditional advertising by reminding consumers of brands they have previously been positively inclined toward through advertising. Because shelf space is the most valuable commodity of most retailers, many P-O-P displays double as product shelving to overcome space problems (see Exhibit 14.4).

2. *Motivate unplanned shopping.* Studies consistently show that the majority of grocery shoppers make a number of unplanned purchases. According to the Point-of-Purchase Advertising Institute, 60 percent of supermarket purchases are unplanned. For some categories, in-store decisions make up more than 90 percent of all purchases. It is no wonder that supermarket shelves, ceilings, counters, and floors are filled with last-ditch attempts to gain the attention of wavering consumers.

3. *Influence brand switching.* Consumers show remarkably low levels of brand loyalty in food categories. In a study by the Meyers Research Center, "more than half of grocery shoppers would switch brands if their preferred item were not available, compared to only a third of shoppers who would do the same if their favorite non-food item were unavailable."[3] This research not only shows the need for P-O-P, but also indicates that the use of such displays will be an ongoing necessity to contact an unpredictable market.

[3]"Out of Sight, Out of Mind," *Promo,* March 1996, p. 16.

At one time, P-O-P was simply placed by manufacturers' reps in those stores that would give them space. Now, in-store displays are a much more sophisticated process and highly coordinated at both the local and national level.

> Today's consumer is one with media savvy—no messages exist in isolation. For this reason, media today are complementary, not competitive—carrying consistent ad messages from storyboard through to the store aisle. From this need to integrate, we are seeing partnering like never before among brand marketers, retailers, P-O-P suppliers and ad agencies—all striving to carry messages through to the ultimate moment when all the elements of a purchase meet—the consumer, the product and the dollar.[4]

Given the range of display and other P-O-P techniques, it is important to choose those displays and placements that will best catch the attention of shoppers. Exhibit 14.5 is an example of new technology that allows signs to be placed on windows without blocking the view from inside stores. Remember, P-O-P is much like outdoor in that customer traffic passes it very quickly, so the message must grab the audience in three to five seconds.

In the future, we will see even more sophisticated uses of P-O-P. The P-O-P industry is also moving into electronic, interactive, and broadcast media. Grocery store checkout-line computers will allow more finely tuned identification of local store customers, which, in turn, will allow targeted in-store messages. Video and audio displays will increase and provide immediacy to react to changing marketing conditions in the local area. In addition, new technology such as holograms will soon provide even more eye-catching store displays.

P-O-P will increase in both cost and the time devoted to service and local store coordination. Retail space is the most valuable commodity that local merchants have, and they will allocate P-O-P spots only to those companies and brands that provide the highest-quality displays, greatest merchandising and advertising support, and, most important, the most significant profit potential.

---

[4]"Dick Blatt, *Increasing Sales Is the Point,* a publication of the Point-of-Purchase Advertising Institute in conjunction with *Brandweek,* p. 3.

Not only are these innovations in point-of-purchase interesting in themselves, they point up once again that advertising, promotion, and marketing are increasingly becoming interrelated to the point that it is difficult to tell when one stops and the other begins. Rather than trying to decide in what category a technique belongs, managers are becoming more concerned with using whatever techniques work.

Premiums

Premiums are items given to purchasers as an inducement to buy a product. Premiums, such as toys in cereal, have been offered for more than a century. In fact, some major products actually began as premiums. In 1892, William Wrigley began giving two packs of chewing gum with each can of baking soda he sold. He found that the gum was more popular than the baking soda, and soon Wrigley's chewing gum was available throughout the world. Likewise, David McConnell, a door-to-door book salesman, gave small vials of cologne with each purchase in the 1880s. By the 1930s, from its humble beginnings as an advertising premium, Avon had become one of the world's largest cosmetic companies.[5]

Premiums are among the oldest and most popular forms of sales promotion. In terms of billings, they are the largest segment of the promotional industry, with more than $20 billion in total investment. Even though coupons are the most widely distributed sales promotion component, nothing approaches the dollar volume of premiums. Like most forms of sales promotion, premiums are designed to encourage customers to make an immediate purchase. Premiums come in an infinite number of formats and are often used in connection with other forms of advertising or promotion.

Many premium offers are promoted through advertising. Strictly speaking, many well-known forms of sales promotion are, in fact, premiums. For example, an on-pack coupon is a type of premium. Premiums are limited only by the imagination of the companies offering them. Most premiums are offered at the time of purchase. However, other premiums—known as **traffic-building premiums**—are given merely for visiting a retailer, a real-estate development, or an automobile dealer.

Despite the huge expenditures in premiums, the industry has experienced slow growth during the last five years. The rate of growth of premium offers has declined as some formerly large users of premiums have moved to everyday low pricing strategies. Premium marketers also are being asked to integrate these promotions to contribute more directly to brand enhancement.

One of the most significant changes in the way premiums are viewed is the development of integrated marketing programs by a number of companies. "Incentives [premiums] are being fitted into overall strategies that are linked to other objectives, rather than as stand-alones. There's been an explosion of loyalty marketing at all levels. . . . With the proliferation of value-added promotion offers, the continuity program concept is growing."[6]

It is important to note that premiums, like many other forms of sales promotion, are being asked to take on an additional role to their traditional function as immediate sales motivators and begin to contribute to brand growth. In some cases, this dual function is accomplished by *continuity* plans in which the premium builds in value as consumers continue to purchase the product. For example, Merit cigarettes provide customers with a gift catalog. As they accumulate proofs of purchase from packages, they can send in for a variety of merchandise—40 proofs of purchase for a lighter, 80 for sunglasses, 450 for a radio, and so on.

There are a number of types of premiums, with the most common being those offered with the product (*in-* or *on-pack*), also called **direct premiums** and mail-in offers.

---

[5]Maurice Baren, *How It All Began* (West Yorkshire: Smith Settle Ltd., 1992), pp. 7, 120.
[6]"Premium Incentives: $20.8 Billion," *Promo,* July 1996, p. 37.

Premium
An item, other than the product itself, given to purchasers of a product as an inducement to buy. Can be free with a purchase (for example, on the package, in the package, or the container itself) or available upon proof of purchase and a payment (self-liquidating premium).

Traffic-building premium
A sales incentive to encourage customers to come to a store where a sale can be closed.

Direct premium
A sales incentive given to customers at the time of purchase.

case HISTORY

Keebler sought to increase sales and brand awareness during the important summer season. The company wanted to entice nonusers to try the brand, increase repeat purchases, and maintain summer-long merchandising support. The instant-win games in 25 million packages of cookies allowed customers to win Koosh balls or a free copy of *Zig Zag* magazine. One of six different free temporary tattoos was included in every package. To spur multiple sales, Keebler offered free or discount tickets to local attractions with two proofs of purchase. In addition to the in-pack offers, the campaign included discounts to local family attractions, local radio and television advertising, and shopping cart signs.

Courtesy: J. Brown/LMC Group.

Marketers also are looking for creative tie-ins to hold down costs of premiums. In most cases, package premiums are part of a total promotion program including advertising support. For example, the "Keebler Summer Hangout" campaign (as described above) used numerous advertising and promotional tactics including package premiums.

Regardless of the method of distributing the premium, the most popular type of premium is **self-liquidating.** As the name implies, these premiums are designed to have customers pay all or a major portion of their cost. On average, customers are required to pay approximately 75 percent of the cost. It is not surprising in this era of tight budgets that self-liquidating premiums are the most popular and the fastest-growing category.

In some cases, the premiums have become so popular that they have actually become major profit centers for a company. Coca-Cola and Harley-Davidson are but two of the many examples for which branded merchandise is so popular that it is sold as "stand alone" stock. This merchandise is no longer a premium, but it shows the popularity that some brands (and their premiums) have achieved.

Before engaging in premium marketing, companies must be sure that the relatively high investment in such an endeavor will be worthwhile. The primary considerations that a marketer would want to contemplate before moving to a premium campaign are the following:

Self-liquidating premium
A premium offered to consumers for a fee that covers its cost plus handling.

1. *Exclusivity.* Make sure that your premium will be unique in its product category. Survey the competition and determine what premiums they are using.
2. *Quality.* If you cannot afford quality merchandise, don't bother. Remember, your brand is associated with the quality of the premium.
3. *Popularity.* What is hot now may be passé in a few months. Trying to ride a fad with your premium can be risky unless you have a short timeline for execution.
4. *Research.* Match the premium with your customer's demographic profile. It is not uncommon for premium companies to offer clients general advice on the best products.
5. *Fit the customer.* Make sure you are rewarding the decision maker rather than the purchaser. Cereal makers have long directed their premiums to children, who are the major decision makers in the category.

6. *Price.* If at all possible, you need to test to see what the optimum premium cost should be. Although quality counts, you don't want to overspend if a less expensive premium will do the job.

7. *Profits.* Although profits from a self-liquidating offer should be secondary to marketing considerations, don't overlook the potential for money-making offers.

Premiums, like other sales promotions, are most effective when supported and coordinated with a strong advertising campaign. Most research shows that premiums almost always do better when combined with advertising.[7]

Fulfillment

Fulfillment firm
Company that handles the couponing process including receiving, verification, and payment. It also handles contests and sweepstake responses.

As discussed in chapter 13, the physical work of opening, organizing, and responding to requests for merchandise is normally handled by **fulfillment firms.** The fulfillment function is extremely important to companies using mail-in premiums, especially in the case of self-liquidators. Fulfillment firms usually operate on a fee basis according to the number of requests. Their work is crucial to the success of any mail-in promotion. Sloppy fulfillment services can virtually guarantee an unsuccessful promotion as well as long-term damage to customer goodwill. Before contracting with a fullfillment firm, it is important to determine if the company is experienced in handling the type of promotion you are planning. Fulfillment is an extension of customer service, and it is your company, not the fulfillment firm, that will be blamed if something goes wrong.

SPECIALTY ADVERTISING[8]

Specialty advertising
A gift given to a consumer to encourage a purchase.

Specialty advertising is related to premiums, but differs in a major respect. Whereas premiums are offered in return for a purchase or other consumer action, specialties are free gifts given for past purchases or in the hope that the recipient will make a purchase in the future based on the goodwill created by the specialty. Specialty advertising employs a wide array of merchandise imprinted with the advertiser's name, logo, or a short message (see Exhibit 14.6, p. 398). Specialty advertising dates to 1845 when a New York insurance salesman gave out calendars imprinted with his name.

The basic premise of the specialty industry is that everyone likes a gift. As one marketing executive observed, "No other medium [specialty] lasts as long as this in this marketplace. A good $2 pen I give to the chairman of a large company builds good will and creates an impression. How long will a print ad last?"[9] It is estimated that specialties will account for some $9 billion this year, and this investment is increasing at a rate of more than 10 percent annually.

The uses and formats of advertising specialties are interminable, with more than 15,000 items available to carry out virtually any marketing objective. Specialties also complement other media and can be targeted to prime prospects with little waste circulation. The ideal specialty is one that is used on a continuing basis, thereby creating continuing frequency with no additional cost.

The disadvantages of specialties include their significant expense on a *CPM* basis and, like outdoor, they offer little opportunity for a lengthy sales message. In addition, there is no natural distribution system for specialties and, depending on the item selected, production time may take up to six weeks.

Although there are numerous opportunities for creative use of specialties, a few categories of gifts make up the majority of those given. According to the Promotional

---

[7]"Key to Premium Marketing," *Promo,* May 1996, p. P6.

[8]Unless otherwise noted, material in this section was provided by the Promotional Products Association International.

[9]"No End in Sight for 'Trinket' Popularity," *Promo,* July 1996, p. 38.

Products Association International (PPAI), the leading trade group for the industry, the following are the primary categories of specialties:[10]

Wearables	23.4%
Writing instruments	12.0%
Glassware	10.0%
Calendars	8.9%

Advertising specialties are used to accomplish a number of marketing objectives. However, the key to the successful use of specialties, as is the case with any advertising medium, is determining their place in the overall marketing strategy. Rather than just picking a product, a specialty advertiser should do the following:

1. *Define a specific objective.* For example, building brand recognition by consumers, encouraging retail distribution, or enhancing goodwill for a company's salesforce.

---

[10]"Sales by Product Category," *DM News,* July 15, 1996, p. 51.

2. *Identify the audience to be reached.* Is the specialty to be a mass distributed item for past customers, new prospects, or a specific segment within the total market? Obviously, these factors will affect the specialty advertising budget.
3. *Determine a workable distribution plan.* Similar to direct mail, specialty advertisers have responsibility for the dissemination of their messages.
4. *Create a central theme for the promotion.* As in any advertising, there must be some overriding creative approach to specialty advertising. Often specialties adapt the theme of the company's media campaign to offer an integrated communication approach to consumers.
5. *Develop a message to support the theme.* The message is confined to the equivalent of a headline, logo, or slogan in most cases.
6. *Select an appropriate promotional product.* The product should preferably be one that bears a natural relationship to the advertiser or theme.[11]

According to a survey conducted by Southern Methodist University for the PPAI, there are six major reasons companies use promotional items in their marketing strategy (respondents could give multiple reasons):[12]

1.	to enhance a company's image and build goodwill	72.0%
2.	to promote a product or service	50.2
3.	as trade show giveaways	39.6
4.	in customer retention programs	37.0
5.	in award programs	34.6
6.	in sales contests	20.0

Business Gifts

Chapter 11 discussed the growing diversity of business-to-business media. Specialty advertising has become such a major participant in business-to-business promotions that a special category known as business gifts is considered a separate industry. Latest figures indicate that approximately half of all companies give gifts on a regular basis to principal customers.

Although, from a marketing perspective, specialties and business gifts serve many of the same functions, there are notable differences. The most significant contrast between business gifts and specialties is that business gifts normally do not carry the advertiser's logo, although sometimes the items will be imprinted with the logo of the firm to whom the gift is given.

Business gifts must be chosen with a great deal of care. For one thing they are costly compared to specialties. However, most marketers advise against very expensive gifts. An overly generous gift may offend some recipients, who might view it as an obligation. In some cases, businesses with relatively few clients select individual gifts such as books on a topic of interest to the person. This personal touch will probably mean more than a more expensive gift chosen with little thought for the receiver.

There are other factors that should be considered before a gift is given. For example, does the client company have policies that would prevent a person from accepting the gift? Normally, companies will allow executives to accept relatively inexpensive gifts—another reason to keep the price low. Be very careful to consider cultural, gender, and religious etiquette in choosing a gift. Finally, because the majority of business gifts are given at the end of the year, some companies choose other times for gift giving to gain a degree of exclusivity, such as the Fourth of July, Halloween, or some date of significance to the recipient such as the date of the founding of the company.

---

[11]Adapted from *What Every Marketing Major Should Know about Promotional Products,* a publication of the Promotional Products Association International.

[12]"The Popularity of Promotional Items," *Sales & Marketing Management,* December 1996, p. 58.

Organization of the Specialty Advertising Industry

Suppliers   The thousands of keychains, balloons, and pens that constitute advertising specialties are manufactured and imprinted by about 1,000 firms.

Distributors   Most specialty merchandise is sold to advertisers by distributors. Distributors contract with one supplier—or, more commonly, a number of suppliers—to provide merchandise to advertisers. There are perhaps 5,000 distributors, ranging from one-person operations to large companies with regional branch offices.

Direct Houses   Among the largest firms in the specialty industry are **direct houses.** A direct house combines the functions of the supplier and the distributor. It manufactures its own line of merchandise and maintains a salesforce to contact advertisers.

The Advertiser   The key to the success of any specialty advertising program is the advertiser. Responsibility for the distribution, timing, and compatibility of the merchandise with the total marketing program largely rests with the advertiser. However, in recent years, distributors have been offering marketing services to advertisers rather than just selling them merchandise.

COUPONS

There is some debate among marketing historians as to whether the first **coupon** was issued by C. W. Post for his Grape Nuts Flakes or by Coca-Cola for fountain drinks. Regardless of who should get credit for their introduction, in the last century coupons have become the most pervasive of all sales promotion techniques. Accurate estimates are difficult to determine, but approximately 275 *billion* coupons will be distributed this year.

In terms of usage and popularity, coupons are without question the most familiar form of sales promotion. However, after decades of spectacular growth—1,000 percent from 1970 to 1994—the use of coupons as a core marketing strategy is increasingly being questioned by manufacturers. In fact, 1996 saw a decline of some 8 percent compared to 1995, the first annual drop in more than three decades. A number of reasons for the lagging growth of coupons have been suggested:

1. *Coupon glut.* With the annual number of coupons distributed per household approaching 1,500, they no longer represent a distinctive value-added for customers. Rather, they are an easily matched form of price cutting, which only encourages customers to reject brand loyalty for price considerations.
2. *Value-pricing.* A number of manufacturers, notably Procter & Gamble, have experimented with the elimination of coupons in favor of everyday low pricing (EDLP) and shifting dollars to brand building. The no-coupon marketing strategy by P&G and major cereal companies accounted for 50 percent of the total decline in coupons.[13]
3. *Corporate cost cutting.* Coupon redemption rates, depending on method of distribution, generally are between 2 and 5 percent. Some manufacturers are questioning whether this level of redemption is worth the effort and expense of distributing and redeeming billions of coupons. Exhibit 14.7 shows the manufacturer's cost of redeeming a 55-cent coupon.

Despite the changing environment of couponing, it would be a mistake to write off coupons as a marketing force. For example, a study by Promotion Decisions indicated that more than half of redeemed coupons are used by new or lapsed buyers of a brand. In addition, almost 65 percent of repeat purchases are made without a coupon.

---

[13]"Companies Clip Coupon Use," *Presstime,* March 1997, p. 14.

exhibit

14.7

Coupon promotions include a number of expenses to the manufacturer.

Courtesy: Promo.
Source: Promo/Progressive Grocer Special Report, February 1995, p. 8.

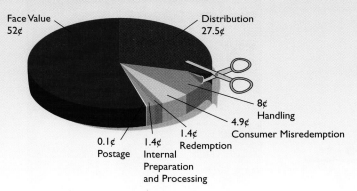

COUPON COST ANALYSIS
Marketers Pay $.95 per Redeemed Coupon

Face Value 52¢ — Distribution 27.5¢ — 8¢ Handling — 4.9¢ Consumer Misredemption — 1.4¢ Redemption — 1.4¢ Internal Preparation and Processing — 0.1¢ Postage

The study indicated that coupons produce favorable return on investment for manufacturers and promote brand loyalty.[14]

Coupon Distribution

There are a number of methods used to distribute coupons. As Exhibit 14.8 shows, the different methods show a wide variance in the rate of redemption for each method. Although the majority of coupons are distributed as newspaper **free-standing inserts** (FSI), the trend is toward more targeted approaches of coupon delivery. The search for more precise methods of couponing has resulted in a number of means of distribution including in-store, bounce-back circulars, in- and on-pack, and the second most used method, direct mail. The two largest mail distribution companies are Cox Direct's Carol Wright program and Larry Tucker, Inc. In co-op mailing, a number of noncompeting companies will share the cost of a single mailing containing up to 30 coupon offers.

Many executives think that in-store couponing is the wave of the future. In-store promotions of all types are growing in popularity because they reach a targeted segment in the marketplace. For example, the Inter•Act Promotion Network (IPN; see Exhibit 14.9, p. 402) uses individual store cards that provide a database of purchases at checkout. When inserted in the touch screen terminal, coupon offers are tailored to the previous purchase history of the shopper. The IPN system overcomes waste circulation, eliminates coupon clutter, and targets known prospects in a shopping environment.

exhibit

14.8

Coupon redemption rates vary widely according to distribution method.

Courtesy: Promo.
Source: Promo, April 1996, p. 86.

Free-standing inserts (FSI)

Preprinted inserts distributed to newspaper publishers, where they are inserted and delivered with the newspaper.

Coupon Redemption Rates by Method

Method	1990	1991	1992	1993	1994	1995
Bounceback	36.4%	28.4%	27.5%	30.7%	23.2%	21.0%
Direct mail	6.3	6.8	5.2	4.8	5.7	5.7
Direct mail co-op	3.5	2.8	2.6	2.3	2.2	1.8
Electronic checkout	7.6	7.9	7.9	8.5	8.8	9.0
Electronic shelf			10.1	13.0	11.5	11.1
Free-standing insert	2.3	2.3	2.3	2.1	1.9	1.8
Handout	3.8	4.0	4.1	4.2	3.5	3.9
In-pack	6.0	5.4	5.0	5.8	5.7	6.0
Instant redeemable	28.8	29.8	29.7	30.6	29.4	29.5
Magazine on-page	.6	.7	.6	.6	.5	.5
Newspaper ROP	.9	.9	.8	.7	.6	.6
On-pack	5.9	5.9	4.7	5.4	5.0	4.8

Source: CMS.

---

[14]"New Research Shows FSI Coupons Contribute to Brand Loyalty, According to Promotion Decisions, Inc.," from *PR Newswire,* March 17, 1997.

exhibit

14.9

In-store couponing is increasingly popular.

Courtesy: Systems. Inter•Act

Coupon Redemption Fraud

When we redeem our 50-cent coupons, we give little thought to the significant investment for manufacturers offering them. Unfortunately, those interested in defrauding manufacturers through the illegal redemption of coupons are very much aware of their value. The most common type of fraud occurs when a person sends in coupons for which no product purchase has been made. There have been instances in which criminals have obtained millions of coupons and sent them to manufacturers using the name of supermarkets and other retailers. In some cases, manufacturers have spent millions of dollars on redemptions for fraudulent claims.

In recent years, the U.S. Postal Service has made a number of arrests for mail fraud in connection with coupon misredemption (the mails are generally used to send coupons to fulfillment houses). Postal authorities have had some success in stopping this type of coupon fraud by publishing coupons for nonexistent products. Because no product could have been purchased, any coupon redemption request constitutes fraud. This approach has been tried a number of times and has led to the successful prosecution of many retailers and coupon thieves.

The newspaper industry is particularly concerned about the problem because 90 percent of coupons are distributed by newspapers. Obviously, if manufacturers reduce newspaper coupon distribution because of misredemption fears, it would mean a decline in newspaper advertising. In 1981, the Audit Bureau of Circulations established the ABC Coupon Distribution Verification Service, which is basically an audit of publishers' practices concerning security and verification of distributed preprinted coupons (see Exhibit 14.10).

SAMPLING

Sampling
The method of introducing and promoting merchandise by distributing a miniature or full-size trial package of the product free or at a reduced price.

We have emphasized throughout the text that, regardless of the quality of the advertising and promotion, ultimately the product must sell itself. This is the philosophy behind product **sampling.** Sampling is the free distribution of a product to a prospect market. In recent years, the use of product sampling has grown significantly, and in many cases it has replaced coupons as a manufacturer's primary method of gaining product trial. The total cost of sampling, including products and distribution, is almost $800 million.

exhibit

14.10

The ABC Coupon
Verification Service
audits publishers'
coupon distribution
practices.

Courtesy: Audit Bureau of
Circulations.

I. Security/Storage of Preprinted Coupon Sections:

(a) Publisher's Practices:

It is the publisher's practice to verify the number of free standing coupon inserts at the time of receipt. Records are maintained of differences between the number claimed to have been shipped and the number received. Any differences noted are reported to the printer and advertiser. Run of press coupon sections are printed in advance of issue date and are accounted for by the publisher.

Run of press coupon sections are stored at company owned and independently owned distribution agencies. Free standing coupon inserts are stored at the publisher's mailroom. All storage areas are restricted and accessible only to qualified publishing personnel.

Free standing coupon inserts are inserted into pre-run sections at the publisher's plant. These pre-run sections and run of press coupon sections are inserted into the complete newspaper by carriers and newsdealers at various locations. All leftover pre-printed coupon material is baled with other newsprint waste and sold to a local recycling company.

(b) Auditor's Findings:

Publisher's practices were in accord with established guidelines.

II. Unsold Copies Returned to Publisher:

(a) Publisher's Practices:

It is the publisher's policy that all unsold copies of the newspaper are fully returnable from distributors and single copy sales accounts in the City Zone, Balance in Newspaper Designated Market, and Outside Newspaper Designated Market. Whole copy returns and unsold copies from newsdealers in the City Zone are brought back to the publisher's plant, where personnel make spot checks to determine that free standing coupon inserts and/or run of press coupon sections are included. Returned copies are sold to a wastepaper company for recycling.

(b) Auditor's Findings:

Publisher's practices were in accord with established guidelines.

III. Unsold Copies Not Returned to Publisher:

(a) Publisher's Practices:

It is the publisher's policy to require mastheads only for credit from dealers in the Balance in Newspaper Designated Market and Outside Newspaper Designated Market. The publisher requires these dealers to have on file a written statement attesting to the manner in which unsold copies are disposed of to render advertiser coupons unusable.

(b) Auditor's Findings:

Publisher's practices were in accord with established guidelines.

IV. Newspaper Distribution Procedure:

(a) Publisher's Practices:

Distribution of the newspaper is made through employees to single copy sales accounts, independent carriers, independent distributors, and company owned and operated agencies for home delivery and single copy sales. This practice is applicable in the City Zone, Balance in Newspaper Designated Market, and Outside Newspaper Designated Market.

The number of copies to be served to independent carriers, independent newsdealers, and independent distributors is not limited; however, it is the publisher's practice to monitor draw increases.

It is the publisher's practice not to have newsdealers for the Thursday only (coupon) issue. Sunday only newsdealers are permitted.

(b) Auditor's Findings:

Publisher's practices were in accord with established guidelines.

The records maintained by this publication pertaining to data reported for the period covered have been examined in accord with established guidelines. Tests of records and other verification procedures considered necessary were conducted. Based on ABC's examination, the information in this report presents fairly the data verified by Bureau auditors.

(Chicago Tribune, Chicago, Illinois   October, 1985   CV#590, 591   AR#140777, 140778   RWM-KSK   01-1110-0)

Research shows that sampling is the most popular means of in-store promotion.[15] More important than consumer preference for sampling are the proven sales results. For example, one research study showed that "Among those who had previously purchased the test product, one-half indicated that receiving the free sample had positively influenced their decision to buy it again. Among those who had never before purchased the product, 86 percent indicated that the free sample was an important element in their decision to buy the tested product for the first time."[16]

exhibit

14.11

County Seat Cafe combines sampling and a deal to encourage patronage.

Courtesy: County Seat Cafe.

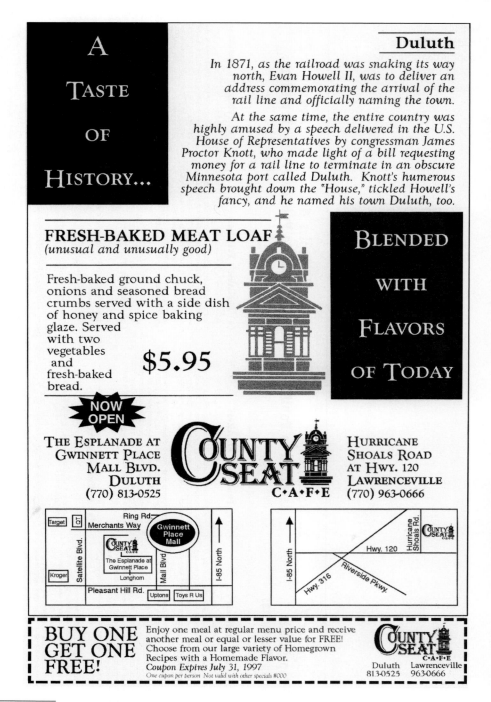

[15]"Effectiveness of Selected In-Store Advertising Techniques," *Promo,* April 1997, p. 163.

[16]Thomas O. Mooney, "The Proving Ground," *Special Sampling Report,* a publication of the PMAA Product Sampling Council, p. 17.

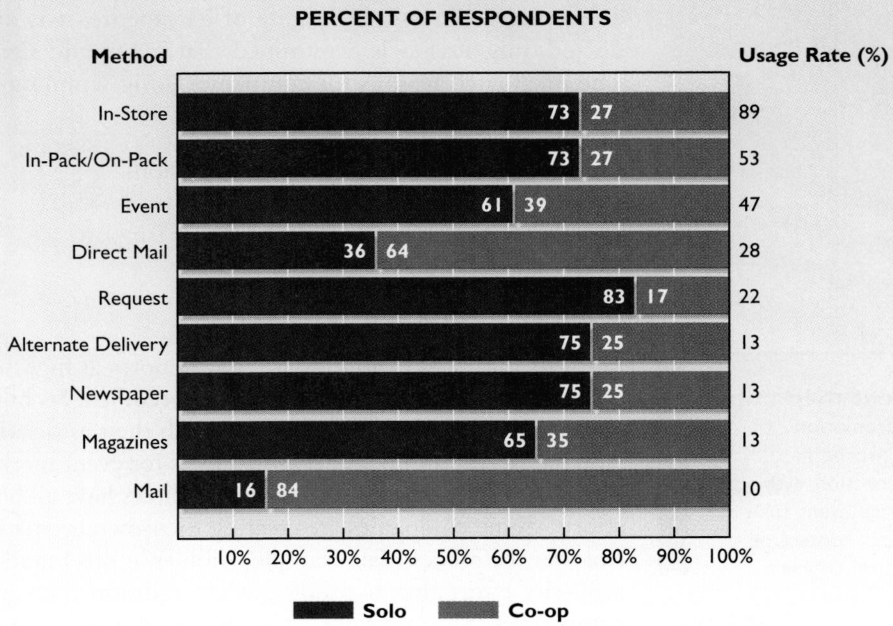

PERCENT OF RESPONDENTS

Method		Usage Rate (%)
In-Store	73 / 27	89
In-Pack/On-Pack	73 / 27	53
Event	61 / 39	47
Direct Mail	36 / 64	28
Request	83 / 17	22
Alternate Delivery	75 / 25	13
Newspaper	75 / 25	13
Magazines	65 / 35	13
Mail	16 / 84	10

10% 20% 30% 40% 50% 60% 70% 80% 90% 100%

■ Solo   ■ Co-op

Source: Donnelley Marketing.

exhibit

14.12

Getting Them Out

Source: Trial and Conversion, a publication of the PMAA Product Sampling Council, p. 11.

Four out of five manufacturers use product sampling in their marketing mix, according to Donnelley Marketing's 17th Annual Survey of Promotional Practices. Of those that offer samples, 70 percent use solo programs and 30 percent use co-ops to deliver them.

This chart shows the usage of different sample distribution vehicles and the relative share allocation to solo and co-op.

Another version of sampling is a type of deal that offers a "free" product with purchase of a product. For example, in Exhibit 14.11, the County Seat Cafe offers a free meal with the purchase of a regular price meal. The combination of a deal and sampling reduces the expense of a straight sample offer, and the combination of advertising and product sampling has the advantage of building long-term brand equity while simultaneously creating short-term product trial.

At one time, sampling was viewed as a mass distribution technique with little means of reaching specialized target markets. However, in recent years, the same techniques used by direct-response marketers to reach selective markets are being employed to reach prime prospects. The most popular means of sample distribution are the following:

● In-store demonstration and distribution. Getting the customer, the product, and the place of purchase together has obvious advantages. The benefits of in-store sampling make it by far the most used distribution method (see Exhibit 14.12).
● On-pack and in-pack distribution. Washing machines often are delivered with a box of detergent, or shaving cream might come with a disposable razor attached.
● Special events and venue sampling. When special markets are sought, ice cream might be sampled at theme parks to reach teens and children. Hospitals often give new mothers a "kit" of baby products as they leave the maternity ward.
● Door-to-door and newspaper delivery. More and more, sampling programs are conducted on a co-op basis by having products delivered with telephone directories, newspapers, or with other noncompeting products.[17]

---

[17] *Free for All,* a publication of the PMAA Product Sampling Council, p. 7.

As is the case with any marketing strategy, sampling must be conducted with a specific objective in mind. Because of its expense, it is imperative that sampling be conducted only after it is determined that it can add significantly to the marketing mix. The most cited reasons for companies using sampling are

1. introducing new products
2. gaining trial for product line extensions
3. building consumer goodwill
4. demonstrating retail merchandising support.

EVENT MARKETING

From its humble beginnings as radio remotes at high school dances and live broadcasts at local retailers, **event marketing** has become a $6 billion business. Increasingly, companies are promoting themselves through their association with some event. Sports provide the largest number of opportunities for event marketing. Events as diverse as sporting contests, rock concerts, and flower shows have all been the scene of major marketing efforts. Some companies are creating their own events so that they can have better control over the process. For example, Kibbles 'n Bits brand dog food was promoted through a 33-city effort that had dog owners audition their pets for the next Kibbles 'n Bits commercial. The auditions were supported with consumer broadcast advertising brand support, trade promotion (see Exhibit 14.13) and local public relations to promote the

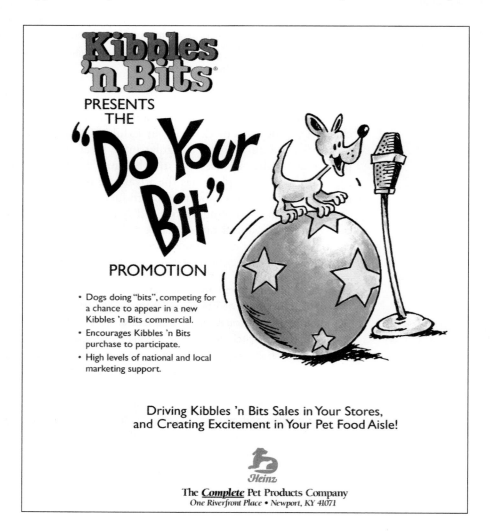

event. More than 11,000 people came to the tryouts, and the brand increased its market share from one to four points in major markets.[18]

Event marketing is most effective when it involves long-term relationships that offer advertisers a chance to develop a continuing connection with a loyal audience. For example, research indicates that 72 percent of stock car racing fans report that they buy the products promoted at races. Racing sponsors promote products as diverse as Kellogg's Corn Flakes, Tide detergent, and General Motors' Mr. Goodwrench.[19]

Regardless of the event being sponsored, the key to event marketing is fundamentally no different from any other promotion. The following are the primary considerations for investing in event marketing:

- *Audience composition.* A prime consideration is whether the event will reach the market for your product.
- *Image compatibility.* Will the event convey the type of image with which you and your brands want to be associated?
- *Exclusivity.* Will you have exclusive association with the event or at least be guaranteed that no competing brands will be promoted?
- *Media coverage and recognition.* A major consideration for event marketing is the degree to which an event will be covered by the media and any opportunities for related public relations associated with the event.
- *Measurability.* One of the major problems with event marketing is that it rarely allows the type of audience measurement demanded from other media.
- *Continuity.* Is this a one-event program or is there an opportunity for a long-term relationship?
- *Trade opportunities.* Even event marketing programs designed for consumer audiences offer trade possibilities. For example, at sporting events, major retail clients might be given special seats or invited to pre- or postgame gatherings.[20]

Effective event marketing requires that the association between the event and the advertising be unambiguous. During the Atlanta Olympic Games, the fear of unauthorized use of the Olympic name and symbol was a primary concern for both sponsors and the Olympics. The intentional attempt to deceive the public into thinking a company has an association with an event such as the Olympics is called *ambush marketing.* Because companies were paying up to $50 million for sponsorships, they had every right to expect that they would have exclusive rights to their product category.

Product Placement

A marketing practice related to event marketing is product placement in movies and television shows. The popularity of such product placement has grown to the point that a number of companies have been started to act as liaisons between corporations hoping for product placement and film and television studios.

Although a direct cause-and-effect relationship between movie placement and sales is tenuous, there seem to be a number of examples in which such placements have boosted sales dramatically. For example, when Tom Cruise wore his Ray-Ban sunglasses in both *Risky Business* and *Top Gun,* sales of the glasses achieved an all-time high. Likewise, sales of Nike sneakers and apparel soared after Tom Hanks's Forrest Gump character was portrayed wearing the products.

Some placements are more complicated than simply gaining screen time. For example, when James Bond switched from his Aston-Martin to a BMW Z3, BMW agreed

---

[18]Wayne D'Orio, "The Main Event," *Promo,* March 1997, p. 19.
[19]Brian Trusdell, "Life in the Fast Lane," *Sales & Marketing Management,* February 1997, p. 74.
[20]Adapted from "10 Steps to Evaluating an Event," *Promo,* November 1995, p. 61.

to an extensive media blitz to support the change. During the first two weeks of the promotion, BMW logged 3,000 preorders for the car, which was not yet available, and the movie *Golden Eye* became the top-grossing Bond film of all time.[21]

Both event marketing and product placement differ from other forms of promotion in two major ways. First, they are often used to build brand equity. In this respect, they are much like advertising. Second, the value of event marketing and product placement can be very difficult to measure. Both the immediate value, including public relations associated with the sponsorship, and the meeting of long-term goals must be considered. However, reducing these outcomes to traditional *CPM* or sales measures is very difficult.

As investment in event marketing has grown, advertisers increasingly seek to quantify the exposures from such events. A number of companies have been established to help event marketers estimate the return on their dollars. Companies such as the Bonham Group evaluate exposures to advertising signage at an event as well as television coverage that includes an advertiser's logo and any public relations or news coverage. Nevertheless, event marketing and product placement are growing in popularity. It is estimated that event marketing will produce revenues of more than $5 billion, so it is understandable that advertisers want to have some measure of results.[22]

Deals

Deals are a catch-all category of promotional techniques designed to save the customer money. The most common deal is a temporary price reduction, or "sale." The cents-off coupon is also a consumer deal because it lowers the price during some limited period. A deal also may involve merchandising. For example, a manufacturer may offer three bars of soap wrapped together and sold at a reduced price. Another deal possibility is attaching a new product to a package of another established product at little or no extra cost—an effective way of new product sampling.

Among the most familiar deals are rebates toward the purchase of a product. Among the most frequent rebates are those for automobiles. Rebates gained popularity during the oil embargo of the early 1970s, but trace their roots to 1914 when Henry Ford offered a rebate of $40 to $60 toward the purchase of a Model T.[23] Sometimes a deal lets the consumer save money on another product or an additional purchase of the same product. A two-for-one sale offers a free product after the consumer buys the first one. Cash rebates are among the most common deals offered by manufacturers.

The downside of offering frequent deals is that a promotion may start off as a temporary incentive and become, to some buyers, an expectation. The automotive rebate is an excellent example of such an expectation. These promotions have worked so well and have become so popular with buyers that today many potential car purchasers simply wait for the next rebate plan before purchasing a car. Deals can be extremely effective in building sales at the trade level. Trade deals offered to retailers and wholesales and others in the trade channel are discussed later in this chapter as a type of trade incentive.

SWEEPSTAKES AND CONTESTS

The goal of sales promotion is to gain immediate sales and consumer involvement. Two primary techniques to accomplish both these goals are sweepstakes and contests. Although the strategies of both are similar, there are significant differences in the two types

---

[21]Blair R. Fischer, "Making Your Product the Star Attraction," *Promo,* January 1996, p. 88.

[22]David Barboza, "Research Firms Say They Can Tell Companies If Sponsoring an Event Is Worth the Money," *The New York Times,* November 18, 1996, p. C11.

[23]"100 Years of Auto Ads," *Advertising Age,* January 8, 1996, p. S6.

case
HISTORY

Gold'n Plump Poultry sought to increase sales and brand loyalty during the fall season, a typically slow time for poultry sales. The company ran a match-and-win game for five weeks in October, offering customers a chance to win from $1 to $50,000 by matching two halves of bills. Outdoor, television, and radio spots supported the game; newspaper advertisements offered coupons; and P-O-P included in-store posters. A toll-free number offered recipes, brand information, and store locations. Results exceeded goals in key markets of Minneapolis/St. Paul and Milwaukee, toll-free number call volume exceeded previous programs, and the sales increase lasted into the next year.

Courtesy: Option One, Minneapolis.

of promotions. Sweepstakes are much more popular than contests and are based solely on chance. Contests, on the other hand, must contain some element of skill, such as writing a jingle or completing a puzzle.

Sweepstakes

Sweepstakes
A promotion in which prize winners are determined on the basis of chance alone. Not legal if purchaser must risk money to enter.

Sweepstakes usually depend on some form of random drawing, but many sweepstakes use a continuity format, such as having consumers find bottle caps that spell out a word or phrase. The primary advantage of sweepstakes is that the rules are relatively simple and there is little or no judgment involved in choosing winners. In addition, the Gold'n Plump Poultry case history demonstrates the so-called "instant winners" sweepstakes, which heightens the anticipation and consumer involvement. Fast-food chains and soft-drink companies are among the primary users of instant winners. It is estimated that almost $2.5 billion will be spent on sweepstakes this year.

One problem faced by sweepstakes is the necessity for bigger and bigger prizes to make an impact with consumers. One factor in the larger payouts is the growing popularity of state lotteries. As one promotion executive observed, "Jackpot inflation is the consequence of lottery fever. Now 39 states have lotteries, their prizes have gotten huger and huger, and promotions have had to follow suit."[24]

---

[24]Glenn Collins, "Promotional Sweepstakes Are Winning the Day, and the Payouts Are Now Bigger and Bigger," *The New York Times,* May 30, 1996, p. C5.

Another problem with sweepstakes is that so many companies have used them over the years that it is becoming more difficult to capture consumers' attention as they lose their novelty. Marketers must also take care that the sweepstakes do not make the product secondary to the game. Many contests and sweepstakes are often entered by professional game players who have no interest in the product and will not become regular users once the contest or sweepstakes is completed. On the other hand, a major sweepstakes may generate a great deal of publicity beyond the paid advertising used to promote it. Most people are familiar with the Publishers Clearing House because of its annual sweepstakes.

Contests

As mentioned earlier, **contests** are not nearly as popular as sweepstakes. Advertisers conduct roughly five times as many sweepstakes as contests. Because contests call for some element of skill, there must be a plan for judging and making certain all legal requirements have been met. The typical contest is also much more expensive than a sweepstakes. When millions of entries are anticipated, even the smallest overlooked detail can be a nightmare for the contest sponsor.

Another limitation of contests is the time (and skill) required of participants. The majority of consumers are not going to devote the time necessary to complete a contest. Therefore, if the intent of the promotion is to gain maximum interest and participation, a sweepstakes will probably be better suited to the objective. On the other hand, a cleverly devised contest that complements the product and appeals to the skills of prime prospects can be extremely beneficial and more efficient than a sweepstakes.

Marketing Objectives

In recent years, we have seen a more sophisticated approach to sweepstakes and contests as a marketing tool. At one time, companies often launched such promotions with little thought to the marketing ramifications. Today, there is a greater understanding of how to use sweepstakes and contests as marketing tools. "We're seeing more of a focus on trying to use sweepstakes effectively to make something happen. There is more interest in having the promotions tie back in with marketers' objectives rather than just throwing a sweepstakes out there. Marketers are becoming more sophisticated in how to use them."[25]

Although sweepstakes and contests are similar in terms of many of the marketing objectives they seek to fulfill, they do differ in their basic strategies. Marketers should be clear about the goal of sweepstakes or contests.

Contest Goals	Sweepstakes Goals
Involve existing customers	Enhance image
Reward loyal users	Build consumer database
Reinforce use of product or service	Gain retail support
	Encourage extensive consumer involvement

COOPERATIVE ADVERTISING

Cooperative advertising (or *co-op*) is a category of trade promotion in which national manufacturers reimburse retailers for placing local advertising to promote national brands. Co-op advertising has several purposes for both the retailer and the manufacturer:

1. *It benefits retailers by allowing them to stretch their advertising budgets.* Most co-op is offered on a 50 percent basis; that is, the national firm pays half of the local ad-

[25]Carolyn Shea, "Playing to Win," *Promo,* August 1996, p. 53.

Contest
A promotion in which consumers compete for prizes and the winners are selected strictly on the basis of skill.

vertising costs. However, a number of co-op plans will reimburse retailers at 100 percent. In other cases, a manufacturer will place some limit on the amount of reimbursement according to a formula based on sales of the product by the retailer. As we discuss in chapter 25, federal law requires that regardless of the formula of reimbursement, manufacturers must treat all retailers proportionately the same.

2. *National manufacturers build goodwill with retailers, encourage local support of their brands, and, by having the retailer place the advertising, qualify for lower local rates, especially in newspapers.* Manufacturers also gain a positive association between local retailers and their products, thus enhancing the brand equity among customers of specific retailers. Many co-op advertisements are prepared by national advertisers and require only that retailers add their logo.

3. *The media are among the strongest supporters of co-op.* Co-op allows current advertisers to place more advertising and at the same time brings new advertisers into the marketplace. Because co-op involves local advertising, it is not surprising that the majority of co-op dollars are spent in newspapers. However, in recent years co-op has reflected the diversity of local media. Currently, more than 60 percent of co-op budgets are spent in newspapers, followed by direct mail, television, and radio, each with approximately 10 percent. In the future, we will see significant dollars going into local cable co-op programs, and this will increase the share of television co-op.

One of the surprising aspects of co-op advertising is the money that is available, but goes unspent. It is estimated that as much as one-fourth of the $20 billion allocated for co-op is not used. The primary reasons for the failure to fully use co-op are primarily a result of a lack of knowledge on the part of retailers as to how to use co-op and an unwillingness to meet the restrictions placed on their expenditures by manufacturers.

Special Forms of Co-op

Vendor program
Special form of co-op advertising in which a retailer designs the program and approaches advertisers for support.

Vendor Programs A special form of co-op normally used by large retailers is the **vendor program.** The primary difference between vendor programs and other forms of co-op is that vendor programs are initiated by retailers. They are custom programs designed by retailers (often in cooperation with local media). In vendor programs, manufacturers are approached by retailers to pay all or a share of the program.

For example, a department store might plan a summer "beach party" promotion. The store would then approach manufacturers of swimwear, sunglasses, suntan preparations, and so forth and request funds to support the advertising and promotion of the event. Often manufacturers can fund vendor programs from their unspent co-op money.

Ingredient Manufacturer Co-op Most co-op programs are set up between manufacturers and retailers. However, as discussed in chapter 2, many companies make ingredients that they sell to other manufacturers for inclusion in finished products. This strategy is called end-product advertising and represents another opportunity for co-op. Often the ingredient manufacturer will contract with finished product manufacturers to co-op with retail outlets or even to co-op on a national basis to promote the ingredient.

Manufacturer to Wholesaler Co-op Occasionally, distribution in an industry is organized through a relatively few wholesale outlets, and manufacturers have little direct relationship with retailers. In this situation, it often is more practical to have co-op dollars allocated to wholesalers who then make co-op arrangements with individual retailers. Most manufacturers avoid going through wholesalers because they lose much of the goodwill aspect engendered by direct allocation of co-op dollars by the national company.

Controlling Co-op Dollars

Retailers are paid for advertising when they submit documentation or proof of performance. For print inserts, they show tear sheets giving the name of the publication and the date it ran. These advertisements can be matched with the media invoice. For radio and television cooperative ads, proof of performance was a perennial problem until the Association of National Advertisers (ANA), and the Radio Advertising Bureau (RAB) developed an affidavit of performance (see Exhibit 14.14), which documents in detail the content, cost, and timing of commercials. The Television Bureau of Advertising (TvB) has a similar document. The adoption of stricter controls in broadcast co-op has been a major contributing factor in the growth of co-op dollars for both radio and television.

Despite attempts to improve the process, expenditures of co-op dollars still are allocated improperly out of neglect or inexperience by retailers. In a few cases, there is

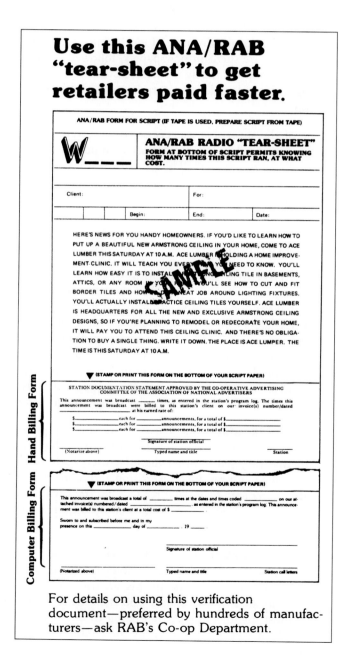

exhibit

14.14

Affidavit of Performance

Courtesy: Radio Advertising Bureau.

evidence of outright fraud. Co-op fraud usually takes one of two forms. In the first, retailers bill manufacturers for ads that never ran, using fake invoices and tear sheets. The second type of fraud, called *double billing*, occurs when manufacturers are overcharged for the cost of advertising. Basically, retailers pay one price to the medium and bill the manufacturer for a higher price by using a phony (double) bill. It should be noted that double billing is regarded as an unethical (in many circumstances illegal) practice, and only a small minority of retailers and media engage in it.

TRADE SHOWS AND EXHIBITS

It is estimated that almost 100 million people attend more than 5,000 trade and consumer shows each year. Products as diverse as boats and cosmetics are promoted through these shows. In some cases, the shows are open to the trade and public and will be visited by more than 100,000 buyers. In other cases, the shows are extremely selective and open by invitation only to a few dozen prospects.

Trade shows provide a number of advantages for both buyers and sellers. They allow face-to-face selling at a cost much lower than personal sales calls. In addition, trade shows are a self-selecting process because only prospects generally take the time to attend. Although some sales take place at these exhibits, they are more likely to provide leads for future sales calls or introduce new product lines to prospective customers.

The major objectives of trade shows are[26]

- generating new sales
- generating sales leads
- introducing new products and building company awareness
- gaining additional sales from current customers
- surveying competition
- finding new distributors.

Trade exhibits are necessary in many industries to maintain competitive parity, but they are also a very expensive means of reaching customers. However, one survey indicated that 91 percent of participants said trade shows were "extremely useful."[27] In fact, trade shows are now the second largest category of the total promotion budget of business-to-business marketers (see Exhibit 14.15).

exhibit

14.15

Trade shows are an important communications tool in business marketing.

Source: Cahners Advertising Research Report No. 510.1C.

Percentage of Business Marketing Budgets

Allocated For	%
Specialized business publication advertising	22
Trade shows	18
Promotion/market support	10
Dealer/distributor materials	13
Telemarketing/telecommunications	6
Direct mail	11
General magazine advertising	2
Publicity/public relations	5
Market research	5
Directories	6
Other	2

---

[26]Jeff Tanner, *Curriculum Guide to Trade Show Marketing,* a publication of the Center for Exhibition Industry Research, p. T35.

[27]Jeff Tanner, *Curriculum Guide to Trade Show Marketing,* a publication of the Center for Exhibition Industry Research, p. T17.

To fully utilize the strengths of trade shows, manufacturers must do more than just show up. Successful trade shows require participants to engage in extensive pre- and postplanning. Furthermore, the trade show must be part of an overall marketing plan. They should be regarded as a hybrid sales technique between business-to-business advertising and personal selling.

Like most of the promotional techniques discussed in this chapter, trade shows are an important complement to media advertising. The more consumers know about your product and the higher name recognition your brand enjoys, the greater the chances that trade show participants will stop by your booth.

DIRECTORIES AND YELLOW PAGES

Although often given little attention, one of the most important advertising vehicles for local businesses is the Yellow Pages and other business and consumer directories. Directories are a cost-efficient medium that reaches serious prospects who are in the marketplace and in the mood to purchase. It is estimated that there are more than 10,000 directories aimed at both consumers and trade buyers. Because directory advertising is available when the purchase decision is being made, there are few companies that do not include at least some directory advertising in their marketing plans. Many retailers, particularly service businesses such as plumbers, rely on directories as their only type of promotion.

In fact, Yellow Pages subject headings can trace changes in consumer lifestyles. For instance, the increase in listings for daycare centers, elderly care, divorce lawyers, moving companies, and truck rentals indicate a society that is increasingly mobile while we pursue careers and end marriages.[28] Without much thought, we make tremendous use of the Yellow Pages on a daily basis.

Directory advertising has many of the characteristics of the more expensive direct-response media with none of their obtrusiveness. It also offers advertisers a continuing presence and high-frequency use without continuing advertising expenditures. Specialized directories are a major medium for business-to-business advertising and frequent reference sources for business buyers.

Yellow Pages

Since its beginning in New Haven, Connecticut, in 1878, the Yellow Pages have become a major advertising medium. Today, it is estimated that more than 19 billion annual references are made to the Yellow Pages, with 60 percent of the population referring to them on a weekly basis. Many Yellow Pages directories offer a number of advertising formats from simple one line listings to four-color ads (see Exhibit 14.16).

The Yellow Pages Industry   The Yellow Pages industry is not a unified medium. Instead, it comprises some 250 publishers who produce more than 6,000 separate directories. Overall, $11 billion will be spent in Yellow Pages this year, a figure larger than expenditures for all consumer magazines. The Yellow Pages are an important complement to other forms of advertising and promotion. In many cases, the medium is the last chance to reach the prospect at the time a purchase decision is being made. In fact, more than half of Yellow Pages users have not made a purchase decision when they turn to the Yellow Pages. More important, research shows that 84 percent of

---

[28]John Hess, "Yellow Pages Offer Insight into Trends," *Advertising Age,* November 18, 1996, p. 38.

exhibit

14.16

Yellow Pages offer advertisers creative flexibility.

Courtesy: Yellow Pages Publishers Association.

Yellow Pages references result in a contact, and more than half of those result in a sale.

According to the Yellow Pages Publishers Association, more than 1.3 *billion* references are made each year to the physician and surgeon category alone. Twelve business categories each spend in excess of $100 million in the Yellow Pages. The five largest categories of Yellow Pages in terms of dollars invested are[29]

Rank	Expenditures (millions)
1. Attorneys	$578
2. Physicians	510
3. Insurance	261
4. Dentists	215
5. Auto repair	143

More important than the size of the Yellow Pages audience is the quality. Research shows that heaviest users of Yellow Pages are concentrated among higher income and educational groups (see Exhibit 14.17, p. 416). More important, because Yellow Pages users are already in the market for the products and services advertised, this finding is of particular significance.

The Yellow Pages are a prime example of integrated marketing in action. They are rarely intended to work alone. Rather than being a competitor to traditional advertising media, the Yellow Pages are *designed* to increase the effectiveness of other advertising vehicles. Research shows that by combining the Yellow Pages with another medium,

---

[29]"Marketing Insights," *Link,* July/August 1996, p. 8.

exhibit

14.17

		Weekly Usage (Reach)	Average Frequency (Total Pop.)	% of Uses (Total Pop.)	% of U.S. Population	Usage Index
Total	Adults 18+	58	1.9	100	100	100
Sex	Males	58	1.9	48	48	100
	Females	59	1.9	52	52	100
Age	18–24	58	2.3	15	12	125
	25–34	66	2.3	26	22	118
	35–49	66	2.3	37	31	119
	50–64	58	1.6	15	18	83
	65+	36	0.9	7	17	41
Education	<H.S. Grad.	36	1.1	8	14	57
	H.S. Grad.	55	1.7	32	36	89
	Some College	66	2.4	28	23	122
	College Grad.+	69	2.3	32	27	119
Household Income	Under $10,000	42	1.4	6	10	60
	$10-$24.9	54	1.9	20	23	87
	$25-$39.9	65	2.1	23	23	100
	$40-$59.9	69	2.4	27	24	113
	$60,000 or more	71	2.5	24	20	120
Census Region	Northeast	54	1.9	20	21	95
	Midwest	59	1.9	24	24	100
	South	58	1.9	35	35	100
	West	62	2.0	21	20	105

Column 3   The average weekly usage or "reach" by the demographic subgroup.
Column 4   The average number of uses per week for each demographic subgroup.
Column 5   The distribution of uses in a typical week within each subgroup.
Column 6   The distribution of adult population within each subgroup.
Column 7   The result of dividing column 5 by 6. As an index, it is used to compare strength of Yellow Pages usage by demographic subgroup.

Among users of the Yellow Pages, heavy users are defined as those who made five or more references in the past seven days. They are more likely to be males under 50 years old, who make $40,000–$60,000, have at least some college education, and live in a household of three or more adults. Heavy users are less likely to live in one of the 21 largest metropolitan areas.

the proportion of purchasers influenced increases from 30 percent (with newspapers) to as much as 300 percent (with radio) compared to using these media alone. It also is true that the stronger the brand equity and awareness of a product, the more likely the customer will associate the Yellow Pages listing with positive images of the product.

Yellow Pages and New Technology   One of the primary disadvantages of directory advertising is its inflexibility. Most directories are issued annually and changes in company or product information or advertising copy is impossible in the interim. However, some Yellow Pages advertisers are beginning to augment the directories with interactive technology called *audiotex* to overcome this problem. There are three systems of audiotex:

1. *Voice information services.* These allow the caller to be connected to a service to provide information on products, consumer tips, health news, weather, and so forth (see Exhibit 14.18). The message in these systems can be immediately updated.
2. *Consumer tips.* A directory will offer a four-digit number by which callers can gain additional information concerning a particular directory category. For example, a number might be given at the beginning of the directory heading Carpet and Rug Cleaners. The caller will hear information about carpet maintenance or how to dye a carpet. The recording will usually be sponsored by one of the businesses in the directory listing.
3. *Talking ads.* Talking ads are four-digit numbers given in the directory listing of individual firms. A caller can obtain additional information about the advertiser's busi-

ness. The primary advantage of all of these systems is that the messages can be changed and basic directory information can be supplemented.

A decade ago, audiotex was viewed as a major breakthrough to provide interactivity between companies and their customers. Today, the system is a relatively small business, accounting for $50 to $70 million in advertising revenues, or less than 5 percent of total Yellow Pages revenues. Many companies that in earlier years would have been prime prospects for audiotex have instead moved into Internet and Web site systems to reach customers less expensively. Most Yellow Pages marketers view videotex as more a value-added for the print directory than a stand alone medium.

TRADE INCENTIVES

Whereas deals are designed to encourage consumer sales, trade incentives are used to motivate those in the marketing channel to support a brand or company. Such incentives are directed at wholesalers, retailers, and a firm's internal sales staff. Companies use the same basic short-term reward system as consumer sales promotion to accomplish their objectives. However, there are a number of differences between consumer and trade promotions.

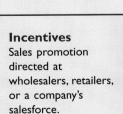

Incentives
Sales promotion
directed at
wholesalers, retailers,
or a company's
salesforce.

Sales promotions directed to the trade channel are called **incentives.** There are two types of incentives: *dealer incentives,* which are directed to retailers and wholesalers; and *sales incentives,* which are directed to the company's salespeople. Almost 80 percent of incentives are offered to direct salespeople. The most common incentives to wholesalers or retailers are price reductions in the form of promotional allowances. In effect, these incentives are comparable to cents-off promotions at the consumer level. In addition, sweepstakes, contests, and continuity promotions (some with prize catalogs) based on sales volume are all used at the trade level.

Cash and travel are the most popular incentives for the internal sales staff. Travel incentives account for more than $4 billion in total expenditures. The major recipients of incentive travel are company sales personnel, with more than 78 percent of travel incentives directed to this group.[30] Retailers and distributors also are offered travel incentives, but at a significantly lower rate than salespersons.

The key to successful incentive programs is to have them complement overall business strategy. The goals that the incentive program are intended to address should be very specific. For example, a company may use incentives to gain support for a new product line, motivate salespersons to open new accounts, or expand distribution to new retailers or in new territories.

There is no question that trade incentives can be extremely effective in increasing sales, productivity, and morale. However, regulatory agencies are increasingly questioning the ethics of some trade incentives that do not provide full disclosure to customers. For example, in a retail store consumers may seek objective information from a salesperson about one brand over another. How objective can retailers be if they are receiving significant rewards for promoting a particular brand? Currently, there is no effective system of providing consumer disclosure for trade incentives. However, as competition in many industries grows more intense and the financial value of incentives increases, we may see both state and federal regulators take a new look at the entire system of trade incentives.

SUMMARY

In the contemporary environment of integrated marketing communication, the separation between sales promotion and advertising is growing less important. Both promotion and advertising are designed to ultimately lead consumers to the purchase of a product or service. The element that separates sales promotion from advertising is that promotions provide a direct, usually short-term, device to encourage sales. As in the case with advertising, sales promotion should reinforce a positive product image. Because of the higher *CPM*s of most sales promotions, cost efficiency is extremely important.

Despite their differences, it is rare that advertising or promotion is used alone. Virtually all marketing programs depend on all aspects of marketing communication working together to present a consistent message to consumers. The target audience for a product rarely makes a distinction regarding the communication channels through which it hears messages about the product. Consequently, it is essential that companies develop an understanding of the relationship between promotion and advertising. Not only must there be coordination between the two, but it also is crucial that promotion be used in a manner that will enhance, rather than erode, brand equity.

In addition to consumer sales promotion, companies normally use some combination of trade and retail promotions as well as advertising to carry out overall marketing objectives. In fact, by far the largest segment of marketing communication involves trade promotions. To a large degree, the increase in trade promotions reflects the growth of large retail chains, which require national manufacturers to compete for shelf space and divert funds from promotions and advertising that encourage consumer loyalty. The consequence of this action is that customers are waiting for the next sale, or rebate, or coupon offer instead of purchasing on the basis of product quality and differentiation.

---

[30]Blair R. Fischer, "Travel Is Tops," *Promo*, May 1996, p. 68.

R E V I E W

1. Discuss the role of brand loyalty and sales promotion.
2. What are some of the primary marketing functions most suited to being addressed by sales promotion?
3. Compare and contrast consumer and trade promotions.
4. What are some of the major differences between premiums and specialties? Similarities?
5. Why are self-liquidating premiums so popular?
6. Why have coupon offers declined in recent years?
7. What are some of the primary strengths of sampling as a marketing tool?
8. Compare and contrast sweepstakes and contests. Why are sweepstakes so much more popular than contests?
9. What are the major advantages of co-op advertisers to both retailers and national advertisers?
10. Discuss the role of the Yellow Pages in the marketing mix of a national advertiser.

T A K E   I T   T O   T H E   N E T

We invite you to visit the Russell/Lane page on the Prentice Hall Web site at **PHLIP** **http://www.prenhall.com/phbusiness** for the bimonthly Russell/Lane update and for this chapter's World Wide Web exercise.

part V

Creating the Advertising

YOU HAVE IDENTIFIED YOUR PRIME
prospect, the marketing, and advertising goals are clearly stated, media planning is beginning—it's time now to create exciting communication, especially the ads. The advertising process moves from ideas to executions to final production.

Chapters 15 and 16 present the kinds of research used to give insight into consumers' problems. These chapters show how to develop appeals and structure the ads. The process starts with the isolation of a product attribute, which the creative team can translate into a benefit that the consumer considers significant.

Chapter 17 discusses the role of the creative team—writer and artist—in developing concepts. We see that having an idea is only part of the process. Chapters 18, 19, and 20 show that preparing the ad for reproduction is equally important. How can you get the final ad to look like the vision in your head? The creative team must understand the medium. These chapters examine the differences in production for print and broadcast.

Chapter 21 addresses the important role of packaging and naming of products in the branding process as it fits into an integrated marketing program. Chapter 22 teaches how ads fit together into a complete advertising plan—the development of advertising campaigns.

15

RESEARCH IN ADVERTISING

CHAPTER OBJECTIVES

ADVERTISERS NEED TO UNDERSTAND WHAT MOTIVATES CONSUMERS IN THE MARKETPLACE. RESEARCH HELPS THEM ACCOMPLISH THAT. RESEARCH IS A CRITICAL INFORMATIONAL TOOL THAT CAN HELP THE ADVERTISER UNDERSTAND HOW CONSUMERS REACT TO THEIR MESSAGES. AFTER READING THIS CHAPTER YOU WILL UNDERSTAND

- how advertisers use research
- the role of the account planner
- anthropology, sociology, and psychology, in relation to advertising
- values and lifestyle and life-stage research
- research steps in advertising
- types of advertising research.

To be successful, an advertiser needs to know what motivates consumers. There are many questions to be answered. What consumer need does my product or service satisfy? How does it satisfy differently and better than competitors? How can I reach consumers? In this chapter, we look at various types of research available—product, market, consumer, advertising strategy, and message research—to answer the advertiser's questions. We also examine ways to judge whether an ad will communicate effectively before we spend the money to run it in the media.

You cannot build strong campaigns without knowing the motivations, attitudes, and perceptions behind consumers' choices. The failure for not understanding the consumer may be failure for the product or service. Remember Howard Johnson's restaurants—with their orange roofs, they dominated the restaurant business for about 20 years. In fact, in the mid-1960s, their sales were more than McDonald's, Burger King, and Kentucky Fried Chicken combined. But what about Howard Johnson's restaurants today? If it were so easy to be successful, new products wouldn't have such a high failure rate, and established brands might not get into trouble. Advertisers would simply plug in the magic formulas. But there are no formulas to guarantee success.

Think about why you choose a laundry detergent brand. Why do you buy the products you put in your shopping cart? Think about the items in your bathroom that you have bought. Why did you buy that toothpaste? Deodorant? Shampoo? Soap? Hair spray? Why did you purchase those specific products? Was it the brand? Was it the price? Quality? Package? Do you really know? Could you explain your reasons for your preferences to a marketing researcher? Use the same thought pattern to items you buy at the supermarket. For that matter, why do you choose the supermarket? Location? Image? Prices? Service? Fresh vegetables? Chances are you may consider as many as three options. Those options make up your *competitive set*. These brands immediately come to mind when you think about buying a product or service. How did they get to be the top-of-mind brands in your brain?

What kind of advertising motivates you to buy something? As a marketer, how do I reach you? What was the last ad that made you go out and buy anything?

RESEARCH IS AN INFORMATIONAL TOOL

Research is and should be used to help improve an advertiser's effectiveness and profitability by staying in touch with the consumer. More specifically, research is used most often in the following ways:

- to help identify consumers
- to help look for new ideas in products or services
- to help improve what is offered in product or services
- to help pinpoint causes of special problems
- to monitor activities
- to help in communications development
- to study promotional tools

A little later we talk specifically about advertising research (see Exhibit 15.1).

exhibit

15.1

What is the message readers will take away from being exposed to this ad?

Courtesy: Lambesis.

You walk tightropes.
You walk daisies.
You walk fencepoles.
You walk long,
long dirt roads.

charles david *by Nathalie M*

THE RIGHT KIND OF RESEARCH

What kind of research and how much research are always legitimate questions. And there are dangers. Former chairman of Roper Starch Worldwide's Roper division commented on a classic failure—Ford's Edsel—and the misuse of research. In the case of the Edsel automobile, the research was used to make people believe something that wasn't true, not to design a product to meet consumers' tastes. Ford designed a powerful, flashy car with a horse-collar grille *before* doing any consumer research. After the car was designed, research found consumers wanted a quietly styled, conservative, American-made, Mercedes-Benz–like vehicle. Ford then tried to make consumers fit the car by marketing Edsel as a conservatively styled automobile. It generated interest, but when consumers saw the car they were disappointed.

On the other hand, Roper cited new Coke as an example of research overkill and overreliance. In several taste tests, new Coke beat Pepsi. But other studies have shown that sweeter products often are preferred initially. In-house and outside research for Coca-Cola failed because it didn't run normal usage taste tests on consumers. If Coke had given consumers a case of new Coke and came back in two or three weeks and asked them what they thought, a more accurate response would have been generated. Roper's conclusions are that people shouldn't always follow the findings of a research study, whether it be a consumer products study or a political campaign. There are dangers as well as potential rewards.

PUBLIC ATTITUDE TOWARD SURVEY RESEARCH

Research on research shows that although refusals to cooperate in survey research are on the rise, respondents believe that research surveys serve a useful purpose. The Council for Marketing and Opinion Research (CMOR) Respondent Cooperative Study clearly shows that respondents think surveys provide an opportunity for feedback on products and services. In four years the refusal rate increased by 5 percent. Some 37 percent of the CMOR survey indicated that they had refused to participate in at least one study during the past year. The study confirmed that shorter interviews are better and that incentives possibly help. Eighty percent of those who were given an incentive said they would be willing to participate again, compared with 70 percent who received no incentive. Disclosing the length of the survey up front actually hurts and has no effect on future willingness to participate.

According to CMOR, 80 percent reported receiving telemarketing calls in the past year, which competes for time with research calls. One study found an average of 28.3 telemarketing calls and 4.2 marketing calls per year. Some 56 percent said they screen calls on answering machines because they get too many telemarketing calls, and another 36 percent screen because they get too many market research calls. Refusal rates are higher among African Americans and Hispanics.[1]

ADVANCED ANALYTICS

Some researchers can now study the impact of advertising by directly measuring sales tied to each available element of the marketing mix through what is called *advanced analytics,* a mathematical modeling system. Joe Plummer, noted researcher at McCann-Erickson, says, "With larger data sets and analytic software, the modeling can deliver." Advanced analytics isn't new; its principle began with retail scanner data. Advances in computer technology and software now allow researchers to manipulate large amounts

---

[1]"Public Believes Research Is Useful," *The Frame,* a publication of Survey Sampling, Inc., June 1996.

of data, and they have refined the modeling and research process. "It will definitely change the way we do business," says Lewis Cashman, VP–global research at Campbell Soup Co. "We have more insight into how our dollars are being spent."

At present, only a small portion of advertisers is measured this way. Advanced analytics isn't considered a breakthrough, but its use is expanding among research firms, clients, and agencies. The 1980s saw dollars shift from advertising to promotions. In the companies that use advanced analytics, and use it well, the emphasis on advertising is much stronger than it has been in years, according to Simon Dratfield, ASI Market Research.

STRATEGIC OR ACCOUNT PLANNERS

In the 1980s, some U.S. agencies moved toward copying the British restructuring of the research department. British agencies found clients doing much of their own research, yet the agency research function remained necessary to understand the information on consumers and the marketplace. The agencies restructured their research departments by adding **account planners,** sometimes called *strategic* or *marketing planners.* Their task was to discern not just who buys specific brands but why. The account planners are usually responsible for all research including quantitative research (usage and attitude studies, tracking studies, ad testing, and sales data) as well as quantitative research (talking face-to-face to their targets).

Account planning is based on a simple premise. A client hires an advertising agency to interpret its brand to its target audience. The account planner is charged with understanding the target audience and then representing it throughout the entire advertising development process, thereby ensuring that the advertising is both strategically and executionally relevant to the defined target. Planners provide insight and clarity that move discussion from *I think* to *I know.* It sorts through the multilayers that develop around marketing a brand, eliminating the irrelevant and highlighting the relevant. It is more productive and more focused than traditional research, according to Jane Newman, partner of Merkley Newman Harty.[2]

Account planning has a crucial role during strategy development, driving it from the consumer's point of view. During creative development, account planners act as sounding boards for the creative team. They are responsible for researching the advertising before production to make sure it is as relevant as it can be, and finally, once the work runs, they monitor its effect in depth with a view to improving it the next time around.

The key benefit to the creative teams is usable research—someone who explains and communicates, giving them useful insights.

Because many marketers direct much of the needed research themselves, the agency is not necessarily a partner in planning the type and direction of research studies conducted for a specific brand or company, but the agency researchers or planners are available to the account groups to help them get the needed information and may be involved in all kinds of advertising research.

The planner works with both account management and creative, covering most research functions. The planner is more a partner to the account team than a traditional researcher, who would basically supply information. The planner is considered the team's spokesperson for the consumer and an interpreter of available research. To work, advertising must deeply understand, empathize with, and speak the same language as the consumer. Leading-edge advertising must be on the leading edge of social change (see Exhibit 15.2, p. 426).

Account planner
An outgrowth of British agency structure where a planner initiates and reviews research and participates in the creative process. In some agencies, the planner is considered a spokesperson for the consumer.

---

[2]Jane Newman, "What Is the Client Relationship to Account Planning?" Essays on Account Planning, World Wide Web (www.apgus.org/2_2a.html), 1997.

exhibit

15.2

The planner's job is to understand how consumers view a product and the context of the message. Here, the true test is the bagel expert New Yorker.

Courtesy: Dieste & Partners and Mrs. Baird's Bagels.

Secondary research
Research or data that is already gathered by someone else for another purpose.

WHAT KIND OF RESEARCH IS NEEDED?

Now that we have a better understanding of the research structure, let us look at the kinds of research available and some specific examples. Keep in mind that marketing has become far more complex than in the past because of the tremendous increase in new products, the high cost of shelf space, the expansion of retailer control over the distribution system, changing media habits, overload of information, and the bewildering array of communication choices.

As a general rule, no research project should be undertaken without a search of **secondary research** sources (i.e., data already gathered by someone else for another purpose). Of course, this would include looking at any syndicated studies that were available. This is a logical part of any investigation and should be done early in the process and before collecting any primary data.

Marketing research—*up-front* research—tells us about the product, the market, the consumer, and the competition. There are four basic considerations in any market research undertaking: (1) maintaining a consumer-behavior perspective, (2) being sure the right questions are being asked, (3) using appropriate research techniques and controls, and (4) presenting the research findings in a clear, comprehensible format that leads to action. After completing market research, we do advertising research—principally pretesting of ads and campaign evaluation—to get the data we need to develop and refine an advertising strategy and message.

The behavioral sciences—anthropology, sociology, and psychology—have had a strong influence on up-front research.

Anthropology and Advertising

Today, marketers employ anthropologists who use direct observation to understand consumer behavior. They study the emotional connection between products and consumer values. When Warner-Lambert wanted to find out what consumers thought of Fresh Burst Listerine, a mint-flavored product designed to compete with Scope, they paid families to set up cameras in their bathrooms and film their routines around the sink. Users of both brands said they used mouthwash to make their breath smell good, but they treated their products differently. Users of Scope typically swished and spat it out. Devotees of the new Listerine felt obliged to keep the mouthwash in their mouths longer; one went so far as to keep it in his mouth until he got to his car.

Honda and Toyota have sent staff to live with families to observe how they use their vehicles—a tactic that Honda says confirmed they needed to add back-seat room to the 1998 Accord. BBDO West sent its account executive on Pioneer Stereo to Austin, Texas, to drive around with the kind of guys Pioneer hoped would buy its car stereo. They incorporated their lingo, "My car is my holy temple, my love shack, my donut maker, my drag race of doom," into an ad campaign that helped moved Pioneer ahead of rival Sony.[3]

Whirlpool appliances enlisted an anthropologist to tap into consumer's feelings about, and interactions with, their appliances. They visited people's homes to observe how they used their appliances and talked to all the household members. Usage patterns and behavior emerged that helped Whirlpool gain insight into the flow of household activities and how tasks got accomplished. For instance, after finding that in busy families women aren't the only ones doing the laundry, Whirlpool came up with color-coded laundry controls that children and husbands can understand.[4]

Anthropologists have found that certain needs and activities are common to people the world over. Bodily adornment, cooking, courtship, food taboos, gift giving, language, marriage, status, sex, and superstition are present in all societies, although each society attaches its own values and traditions to them. Anthropologists see the United States as a pluralistic society made up of an array of subcultures. In each subculture lives a different group of people who share its values, customs, and traditions. Think about the cultural differences among Italians, Poles, African Americans, and Hispanics, as a starting point.

We are all aware of regional differences in the American language. For example, a sandwich made of several ingredients in a small loaf of bread is a "poor boy" in New Orleans, a "submarine" in Boston, a "hoagie" in Philadelphia, and a "grinder" in upstate New York. Geomarketing allows advertisers to use these cultural differences in food preferences, terminology, and subgroup identities when they advertise their products.

Sociology and Advertising

Sociology examines the structure and function of organized behavior systems. The sociologist studies groups and their influence on, and interaction with, the individual. Advertisers recognize group influences on the adoption of new ideas, media use, and consumer purchase behavior. They use sociological research to predict the profitability of a product purchase by various consumer groups.

---

[3]Leslie Kaufman, "Enough Talk," *Newsweek,* August 18, 1997, pp. 48–49.
[4]Tobi Elkin, "Product Pampering," *BrandWeek,* June 16, 1997, pp. 28–40.

Social Class and Stratification   We are a society that is clustered into classes determined by such criteria as wealth, income, occupation, education, achievement, and seniority. We sense where we fit into this pattern. We identify with others in our class ("these are my kind of people"), and we generally conform to the standards of our class. Experienced advertisers have recognized that people's aspirations usually take on the flavor of the social class immediately above their own.

Social-class structure helps explain why demographic categories sometimes fail to provide helpful information about consumers. A professional person and a factory worker may have the same income, but that doesn't mean their interests in products will coincide. In today's marketing environment, research has shown that no single variable, such as age, income, or sex, will accurately predict consumer purchases. We have discovered that using several variables gives a more accurate prediction of consumer behavior. Think of the differences between homemakers and working women of the same age, income, and education in their food preferences for themselves and their families, usage of convenience goods, child care, and media habits.

Trend Watching   Quantitative research is as important as ever, but there seems to be a new premium on nuggets of more attitudinal, psychographic market smarts with which marketers hope to base the creative approach to their communication.

Trends come from all forms of media and advertising. They come from music, from politics, from travel, and from the Internet. They develop everywhere. Fads, on the other hand, are like crushes; they burn fast and hot, but die quickly and often leave a bitter taste. The macarena and platform shoes came and went quickly. Trends are a product of society. They reflect our changing attitudes, behaviors, and values. They are the most obvious and most concrete signs of the times. Trends can be two sizes: macro and micro.

Macro trends are about the "big issues"—our definitions of happiness, success, fulfillment. Macro trends come from the way people think. They emerge when people feel a dissatisfaction with the status quo, in their own lives and in society. They announce our new definitions of happiness. Some of the neotraditionalism is reflected in the return to traditions with a 1990s spin—people setting new priorities in the balance among work, family, and friends.

Micro trends are the detail in the bigger picture. They are the tangible manifestations of the macro trends in fashion, music, and sports activities. For example, the macro trend of neotraditionalism will foster micro trends such as cooking schools cropping up as the microwave generation tries to behave like their grandparents and throw dinner parties.

Generally, young people set trends, but not every young person is a trendsetter. Those most comfortable on the cutting edge are the ones called *early adopters, alphas, trendsetters, leading edgers, innovators*—all these terms mean the same thing. These are the people who are willing to experiment. Not all trends will work for a brand. Yet, look at what Mountain Dew did by using extreme sports and over-the-top imagery, not to mention using Mel Torme in juxtaposition, to become the extreme brand.[5] Many companies spend much money trying to track trends. Coffeehouses and teahouses—are they fads or trends?

Cohort Analysis   Using a research technique called cohort analysis, marketers can access consumers' lifelong values and preferences, and develop strategies now for products they will use later in life. Cohorts are generations of people with the same birth years and core values. According to Natalie Perkins of Trone Advertising, these values are formed by significant events between the ages of 13 and 20 and endure throughout one's life. For example, such events as the Great Depression, the Korean War, McCarthyism, the Vietnam War, the sexual revolution, and the Gulf War, or the in-

---

[5]Jane Rinzler, "Trendspotting for Profit and Fun," *Adweek,* April 28, 1997, pp. 23–25.

fluence of Martin Luther King, television, computers, divorced and single families, and environmental crisis can form a value system.

Generally, we study consumers using demographics, psychographics, lifestyles, and behaviors. Cohort analysis combines these data and adds to the consumer profile by examining the past as well as the present. Four cohort groups exist: traditionalists, transitioners, challengers, and space-agers. Each group is unique, evolving, and maturing.

1. *Traditionalists.* In their 60s and 70s, traditionalists are enjoying retirement and leisure time and are in declining health. They are being cared for, or are making plans for when they will need care. Traditionalists are powerful financially and politically. Many feel guilty for no longer working and are anxious to remove financial responsibility from their children; they are determined to care for themselves as they grow older. They use wisdom and experience in making decisions.

2. *Transitioners.* Born in the 1930s and 1940s, transitioners are caring for aging parents, enjoying prosperity and high incomes, and facing retirement. Many have empty nests and boomering kids, and are in long-term or second marriages. They are brand loyal and value-oriented, and they don't make impulsive decisions. They value convenience and comfort, and are beginning to spend money on themselves now that their children have gone.

3. *Challengers.* In their 30s and 40s, many challengers are in unconventional households: single parents, working women. They have high incomes, high debt, and have started later than their cohorts before them to raise a family. They idolize youth but are becoming middle-aged, and they don't like it. Highly educated, they are concerned about retirement but are financially unable to plan for it. They are obsessed with reducing stress and guilt. They still believe in having it all. They seek information before they buy. They are caught between reality and their black-and-white morality and have difficulty dealing with the world of gray. They are still concerned with what others think, but they haven't abandoned the self-indulgent lifestyle.

4. *Space-agers.* Space-agers are in their 20s, completing education, starting careers, and developing lasting relationships. They are financially unstable and have a lower standard of living since moving from their parents' home. In general, they think they have inherited an unsound system. They are skeptical. They are concerned their future will not be as good as or better than their parents'. They are economically liberal but politically conservative. This group has the *just do it* attitude, believes in unrestricted equality, and is more materialistic than it admits. Space-agers resent challengers. They missed *open sex, drugs, and rock 'n' roll,* and, instead have been repeatedly told to say no to drugs and practice safe sex. They value products developed for them, not for challengers. Most important to marketers, they are street-smart consumers. Motivated by money for security, they look for lasting values, tangible benefits, and instant gratification. They make emotional purchases and require less information. They don't just talk action, they act.

By identifying a generation's collective hot buttons, mores, and memories, advertisers can hone messages and create persuasive icons to better attract them.[6] This kind of research can aid in developing a product marketing plan that follows the lifetime of a consumer.

Life-Stage Research Advertisers have traditionally considered the family as the basic unit of buying behavior. Most traditional households pass through an orderly progression of stages, and each stage has special significance for buying behavior.

---

[6]Natalie Perkins, "Zeroing in on Consumer Values," *Advertising Age,* March 22, 1993, p. 23.

Knowledge of the **family life cycle** allows a company to segment the market and the advertising appeal according to specific consumption patterns and groups. Of course, the concept of the family has significantly changed over the past decades. Yet there are still crucial points in the lives of consumers—they leave home, get married or unmarried, bear children, raise children, and send adult children into lives of their own. As a result of these life transitions, people suddenly or gradually go from one stage of life to another (see Exhibit 15.3).

According to census data, the nature of the traditional family life cycle has changed in the past 30 years. For example, people are waiting longer to get married, women are postponing childbearing, the incidence of divorce has almost tripled, the proportion of single-parent households has significantly increased, and more young adults are living with their parents than in the past. As a result, some advertisers have reevaluated the way they look at the family life cycle. By examining these segments' subgroups, adver-

tisers begin to get a clearer picture of buying behavior and lifestyles. Researchers refer to these subgroup studies as life-stage research. As with the family life cycle, life-stage research looks at the crucial points in consumers' lives. Advertisers can find syndicated research services that analyze young singles, newlyweds, young couples, mature couples, and teenage households. As we approach the millennium, advertisers need knowledge of the life stages to help them develop and understand the changes taking place so they can create more effective integrated marketing communications.

Pychology and Advertising

Psychology is the study of human behavior and its causes. Three psychological concepts of importance to consumer behavior are motivation, cognition, and learning. *Motivation* refers to the drives, urges, wishes or desires that initiate the sequence of events known as "behavior." *Cognition* is the area in which all the mental phenomena (perception, memory, judging, thinking, and so on) are grouped. *Learning* refers to those changes in behavior relative to external stimulus conditions that occur over time.[7] These three factors, working within the framework of the societal environment, create the psychological basis for consumer behavior. Advertising research is interested in cognitive elements to learn how consumers react to different stimuli, and research finds learning especially important in determining factors such as advertising frequency. However, in recent years, the major application of psychology to advertising has been the attempt to understand the underlying motives that initiate consumer behavior.

Values and Lifestyles   The research company that popularized the lifestyle approach to psychographic segmentation developed Values and Life Style 2 (VALS 2). SRI International's VALS 2 is designed to predict consumer behavior by profiling attitudes of American consumers. It segments respondents into eight clusters of consumers, each with distinct behavioral and decision-making patterns that reflect different self-orientations and available psychological and material resources (see Exhibit 15.4, p. 432).

VALS 2 classifies consumers along two key dimensions: *self-orientation*—the fundamental human need to define a social self-image and create a world in which it can thrive—and *resources*—the range of psychological and material resources available to sustain that self-concept.

This concept takes into account personal or psychological orientations such as principle, status, and action. Consumers with the principle orientation look inside themselves to make choices, rather than to physical experience or social pressure. Those with status orientation make choices in relation to the anticipated reactions and concerns of others in the group to which they belong or aspire to belong. Action-oriented consumers base their choices on consideration related to activity. They value feelings only when they result from action.

Resources, on the other hand, include both material and acquired attributes (e.g., money, position, education) and psychological qualities (e.g., inventiveness, interpersonal skills, intelligence, energy).

According to VALS 2, an individual purchases certain products and services because he or she is a specific type of person. The purchase is related to lifestyle, which in turn is a function of self-orientation and available resources. VALS 2 is a network of interconnected segments. Neighboring types have similar characteristics and can be combined in varying ways to suit particular marketing purposes.

Advertisers can use the VALS 2 typology to segment particular markets, develop marketing strategies, refine product concepts, position products and services, develop advertising and media campaigns, and guide long-range planning.

---

[7]James A. Bayton, "Motivation, Cognition, Learning—Basic Factors in Consumer Behavior," *Journal of Marketing*, January 1958, p. 282.

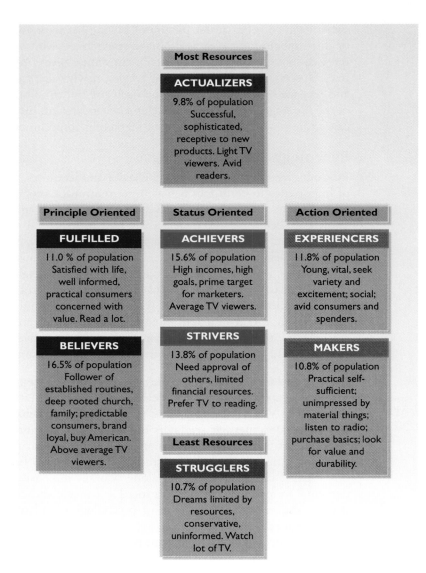

exhibit

15.4

VALS 2 American Lifestyle Categories

Source: Compiled from data from SRI international, Menlo Park, California.

The characteristics of eight VALS lifestyle categories shown in Exhibit 15.4 are discussed next, along with index values for their interests (general population = 100), where a high index indicates more involvement and a low index indicates less involvement.

Actualizers Actualizers are successful, sophisticated, active, "take-charge" people with high self-esteem and abundant resources. They are interested in growth and seek to develop, explore, and express themselves in a variety of ways—sometimes guided by principle and sometimes by a desire to have an effect, to make a change.

Image is important to actualizers, not as evidence of status or power but as an expression of their taste, independence, and character. Actualizers are among the established and emerging leaders in business and social issues and are open to change. Their lives are characterized by richness and diversity. Their possessions and recreation reflect a cultivated taste for the finer things in life.

Index values of consumer activities that involve actualizers include membership in an arts association, with an index of 382, and owning a motorcycle, with an index of 44.

Principle Oriented: Fullfilleds and Believers Principle-oriented consumers seek to make their behavior consistent with their views of how the world is or should be.

Fulfilleds Fulfilleds are mature, satisfied, comfortable, reflective people who value order, knowledge, and responsibility. Most are well educated and in (or recently retired from) professional occupations. They are well informed about world and national events and are alert to opportunities to broaden their knowledge. Content with their career, families, and stations in life, their leisure activities tend to center around the home.

Fulfilleds have a moderate respect for the status quo institutions of authority and social decorum, but are open minded to new ideas and social change. Fulfilleds tend to base their decisions of firmly held principles and consequently appear clam and self-assured. Although their incomes allow them many choices, fulfilleds are conservative, practical consumers; they look for durability, functionality, and value in the products they buy.

Index values of consumer activities that involve fulfilleds include a swimming pool/in-ground index of 197 and a drink malt liquor index of 48.

Believers Believers are conservative, conventional people with concrete beliefs based on traditional, established codes: family, church, community, and the nation. Many believers express moral codes that are deeply rooted and literally interpreted. They follow established routines, organized in large part around home, family, and social or religious organizations to which they belong.

As consumers, believers are conservative and predictable, favoring American products and established brands. Their income, education, and energy are modest but sufficient to meet their needs.

Index values of consumer activities that involve believers include an own organ index of 141, a buy packaged moist dog food index of 127, a use mesquite charcoal for barbecue index of 59, and a drive car with 5-speed manual transmission index of 44.

Status Oriented: Achievers and Strivers
Status-oriented consumers have or seek a secure place in a valued social setting. They make choices to enhance their position or to facilitate their move to another, more desirable group. Strivers look to others to indicate what they should be and do, whereas achievers, who are more resourceful and active, seek recognition and self-definition through achievements at work and in their personal lives.

Achievers Achievers are successful career- and work-oriented people who like to, and generally do, feel in control of their lives. They value consensus, predictability, and stability over risk, intimacy, and self-discovery. They are deeply committed to work and family. Work provides them with a sense of duty, material rewards, and prestige. Their social lives reflect the focus and are structured around family, church, and career.

Achievers live conventional lives, are politically conservative, and respect authority and the status quo. Image is important to them; they favor established, prestige products and services that demonstrate success to their peers.

Index values of consumer activities that involve achievers include a swimming pool/in-ground index of 192, an own a snow blower index of 184, and an attended classical concert past year index of 55.

Strivers Strivers seek motivation, self-definition, and approval from the world around them. They are striving to find a secure place in life. Unsure of themselves and low on economic, social, and psychological resources, strivers are concerned about the opinions and approval of others.

Money defines success for strivers, who don't have enough of it and often feel that life has given them a raw deal. Strivers are impulsive and easily bored. Many of them seek to be stylish. They emulate those who own more impressive possessions, but what they wish to obtain is often beyond their reach.

Index values of consumer activities that involve strivers include an enrolled in frequent flyer program index of 44.

Action Oriented: Experiencers and Makers Action-oriented consumers like to affect their environment in tangible ways. Makers do so primarily at home and at work; experiencers in the wider world. Both types are intensely involved.

Experiencers Experiencers are young, vital, enthusiastic, impulsive, and rebellious. They seek variety and excitement, savoring the new, the offbeat, and the risky. Still in the process of formulation of life values and patterns of behavior, they quickly become enthusiastic about new possibilities but are equally quick to cool. At this stage in their lives, they are politically uncommitted, uninformed, and highly ambivalent about what they believe.

Experiencers combine an abstract disdain for conformity with an outsider's awe of other's wealth, prestige, and power. Their energy finds an outlet in exercise, sports, outdoor recreation, and social activities. Experiencers are avid consumers and spend much of their income on clothing, fast food, music, movies, and video.

Index values of consumer activities that include experiencers include an attend rock/pop concert in past year index of 260, own small sporty foreign car index of 177, and own city/municipal or state bonds index of 17.

Makers Makers are practical people who have constructive skills and value self-sufficiency. They live within a traditional context of family, practical work, and physical recreation, and have little interest in what lies outside that context. Makers experience the world by working on it—building a house, raising children, fixing a car, or canning vegetables—and have enough skill, income, and energy to carry out their projects successfully.

Makers are politically conservative, suspicious of new ideas, respectful of government authority and organized labor, but resentful of government intrusion on individual rights. They are unimpressed by material possessions other than those with a practical or functional purpose (such as tools, utility vehicles, and fishing equipment.)

Strugglers Strugglers lives are constricted. Chronically poor, ill-educated, low-skilled, without strong social bonds, elderly, and concerned about their health, they are often resigned and passive. Because they are limited by meeting the urgent needs of the present moment, they do not show a strong self-orientation. Their chief concerns are for security and safety.

Strugglers are cautious consumers. They represent a very modest market for most products and services, but are loyal to favorite brands.

Personal Drive Analysis

> **Personal drive analysis (PDA)**
> A technique used to uncover a consumer's individual psychological drives.

BBDO has used the **personal drive analysis** (PDA) technique to uncover a consumer's individual psychological drives toward indulgence, ambition, or individuality, which play a role in his or her brand choices. BBDO found that people are often attracted to brands because of their psychological reward. It is important for marketers to identify this reward if they are to understand the equity of their brands and successfully sell their products. When the agency applied PDA to athletic shoes, Nike emerged as the brand a person would buy if motivated by such drives as status or winning. Reebok was the brand for those who desired comfort and stability. Results indicated that Reebok represents the athletic shoe you can count on; Nike represents the athlete you want to be.[8]

Marketing Environment

Companies and agencies want to accumulate as much information about their markets as possible before making crucial integrated marketing decisions. Technology has been assisting marketers in getting more information faster.

---

[8]Cyndee Miller, "Spaghetti Sauce Preference Based on Whether You're in the Mood for Love," *Marketing News*, August 31, 1992, p. 5.

Universal Product Code   Universal product code (UPC) information has greatly enhanced the process of tracking product sales. When the grocer scans a price into the register at checkout, that information is instantly available to the retailer. Scanner reporting systems have allowed marketers to track their performance quickly, rather than monthly or bimonthly, and at local levels. UPC information allows marketers to determine what their share of market is, if one kind of packaging sells better, and which retailers sell the most units. Cash-checking cards can be scanned into the system to keep a record of what kind of products consumers buy. This offers the retailer and manufacturer the opportunity to target promotions directly to people who have used the product in the past. This information can contribute to any database marketing effort by the retailer.

Single-Source Data   For single-source data, retail tracking scanner data are integrated with household panel data on purchase patterns and ad exposure. The information comes from one supplier and is extracted from a single group of consumers. These data can be combined with other research sources to supply micromarketers with a wealth of information on who, what, and how. Despite these new micromarketing capabilities, research firms are far more adept at generating data than most clients are at using the information.

Databases   Marketers use sweepstakes entries, rebate information, merchandise orders, free product offers, requests for new-product information, and purchase information to build consumer databases telling them a great deal about how consumers live. This information offers many opportunities for database marketing.

Future Trends   "With all the technology available," says Gian Fulgoni, CEO of IRI, the leading U.S. provider of electronic point-of-purchase purchase data, "someone has to translate the scanner readouts to action solutions." The best way to get from a simple count to a broader meaning, Fulgoni believes, is to metamorphose from sample to census—not just counting a few out of the many but counting all. He believes that the census will replace the sample of sales transactions, which will give a better look at store-by-store business activity.[9]

THE SERIES OF RESEARCH STEPS IN ADVERTISING

The term "advertising research" is broadly defined. It includes research that contributes to all four stages of the advertising process:

1. *Advertising strategy development.* Research tries to answer many questions: Who is the market and what do they want? What is the competition we are specifying? What communication do we want our selected market to get from our advertising? How will we reach the persons selected as our market?
2. *Advertising execution development.* There are two kinds of research used at the execution stage of advertising. The first is exploratory research to stimulate the creative people and to help them know and understand the language used by consumers. The other is research to study proposed creative concepts, ideas, rough, visuals, headlines, words, presenters, and so forth, to see whether they can do what the creative strategy expects of them.
3. *Evaluating pretesting executions.* Pretesting is the stage of advertising research at which advertising ideas are tested. Partly because of the finality of much pretesting, it is the most controversial kind of advertising research.

---

[9]Kenneth Wylie, "Specialized Services Making a Splash," *Advertising Age,* May 19, 1997, pp. 47–48.

4. *Campaign evaluation.* Campaign evaluation usually involves a tracking study to measure the performance of a campaign.

The primary goal of advertising research is to help in the process of creative development. Before we examine the research process advertisers would use in developing advertising strategy for campaigns, let us get a better perspective on using research information.

Translating Information into Strategy

A few years ago the brilliant McCann-Erickson researcher, Jack Dempsey, said, "By itself information has no value." It acquires value only when the strategist takes "a point of view" about what the information means—a point of view that is relevant to the marketing and advertising issues. You have to get involved in all the data at your disposal and, if necessary, fill in some gaps by acquiring more information. But then you have to step back from it. The secret of effective strategy formation lies in deciding which data are important and which are not. It is a process of organizing simplicity out of complexity, for the best strategic insights are usually the very simple ones.

Take the consumer's point of view. Ask yourself what the consumer is really buying. Is he or she buying the product because of its functional benefits? How important are the psychological benefits? The corporate landscape is littered with examples of companies and industries that failed to appreciate what their consumers were really purchasing. Because of this, they defined their markets inappropriately and often disastrously. Begin with an analysis of how people *behave* rather than an analysis of how they feel or what they believe. You will probably get into these issues, but behavior is the foundation from which you build. And, above all, try to see the world with the consumers' eyes.

Think about the question, "How many pairs of shoes do you buy in a year?" Now, if you disregard such factors as style and fashion, the number of shoes bought in a year depends largely on how much walking is done, not on age, sex, or social class. These may be associated variables, but less determinant than the amount of walking the individual does. You see, information by itself has no value.

Market, Product, Competitive, and Consumer Research

Basic information is gathered and analyzed to determine the marketing strategy for a product or service, projected sales, the source of business, pricing and distribution factors, geographic information, and how to develop data to identify the size and nature of the product category. This kind of research includes data on competitors, sales trends, packaging, advertising expenditures, and future trends. *Situation analysis* helps to define clearly the market in which the product or service competes (see Exhibit 15.5).

Prospect research is critical to define clearly who is expected to buy the product or service. Studies may identify users, attitudes, lifestyles, and consumption patterns—all of which identify the prime project.

e x h i b i t

15.5

Situation Analysis

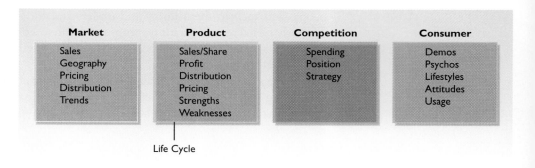

Market	Product	Competition	Consumer
Sales	Sales/Share	Spending	Demos
Geography	Profit	Position	Psychos
Pricing	Distribution	Strategy	Lifestyles
Distribution	Pricing		Attitudes
Trends	Strengths		Usage
	Weaknesses		

Life Cycle

exhibit

15.6

Brand
Trial/Awareness
Ratios: Strategic
Options

	Awareness–High	Awareness–Low	
Trial–High	• Increase Frequency of Purchase • Expand Number of Product Uses	• Increase Awareness so as to Broaden Trial Base	Trial–High
Trial–Low	• Reposition Brand	• Increase Awareness • Make Sure Positioning Is Sound	Trial–Low
	Awareness–High	Awareness–Low	

The amounts and kinds of information required will vary according to the product category and marketing situation. Exhibit 15.6 outlines strategy choices indicated by different levels of brand trial and awareness. It is difficult to talk about strategy until you have information on awareness levels for each brand in the market. "Brand trial" will occur if what consumers know about the brand fits in with their needs and is sufficiently important or motivating. The relationship between a brand's level of awareness and its trials may be expressed as a ratio. A high ratio will suggest one strategy option, a low ratio another. For example, high awareness and low trial (lower left-hand box of Exhibit 15.6) clearly indicates that what people know about the brand is not sufficiently motivating or relevant, and the brand may need repositioning.

Product research can give creative teams inspiration. Research showed that Penn tennis balls needed to be more consistent in weight and bounce than the competition, giving them a highly marketable uniformity. Penn created a TV spot called the "bounce test," in which tennis balls were dropped from the Chrysler building in New York City. Each Penn tennis ball bounced to the same height and inspired the copy tag "Penn tennis balls. You've seen one, you've seen them all."

Research does not always tell us what we want to hear, which can create problems if we think an advertising idea is really strong. Take the classic, "Avis. We try harder," campaign. It tested poorly in research. Consumers said the "We're number two" concept meant Avis was second-rate. Research was against running it, but creative genious Bill Bernbach fervently believed in the idea and convinced Avis to take a chance with it. Today, the Avis campaign is considered one of the most powerful, memorable ad campaigns in history.

Advertising Strategy or Message Research

Message research is used to identify the most relevant and competitive advertising sales message. It may take many forms: focus groups, brand mapping, usage studies, motivation studies, or benefit segmentation.

Focus Group Research   **Focus groups** have become most marketers' main method of **qualitative research** to find out why consumers behave as they do. The focus group offers a means of obtaining in-depth information through a discussion-group atmosphere. This process is designed to probe into the behavior and thinking of individual group members. The focus group can elicit spontaneous reactions to products or ads. A trained moderator leads a group of 8 to 12 consumers, usually prime prospects. The

Focus group
A qualitative research interviewing method using indepth interviews with a group rather than with an individual.

Qualitative research
This involves finding out what people say they think or feel. It is usually exploratory or diagnostic in nature.

typical focus group interviews last one-and-a-half to two hours. The number of different group sessions vary from advertiser to advertiser based somewhat on expense, topic being discussed, and time considerations. Most clients conduct five or six focus groups around the country. The client usually watches the interview from behind a one-way mirror so as not to disrupt the normal function of the group.

Quaker State new-product testing in focus groups revealed that consumers were confused by traditional motor oil labels. The marketers had invited some of the engineers to watch the focus groups from behind one-way mirrors. One of the engineers emerged from a session, stunned that no one in the group could define synthetic oil. You've got to pick smarter focus groups, he declared. A new campaign was designed so that even the oil-illiterate could recognize and focus on the product.

Videoconferencing links, television monitors, remote-control cameras, and digital transmission technology allow focus group research to be accomplished over long-distance lines. There are about 150,000 videoconferencing focus groups a year. Many advertising agencies believe videoconferencing enriches the creative process because it gives more people input. "Now we have up to 14 agency and client people watching groups, including the CEO and executive creative director. That wouldn't happen if they had to travel," says Susan Eisler, executive vice president and director of strategic planning for Lintas.[10]

A typical videoconference uses two cameras focused on the group of participants, controlled by the client (agency or advertiser) who holds a remote keypad. Executives in a far-off boardroom can zoom in on faces and pan the focus group room as they wish for about $1,500 per session for the transmission of signals. A two-way sound system connects viewers to the boardroom, focus group room, and directly to the moderator's earpiece. Typically, the moderator, renting of facilities, microphones, special video set-ups to record the focus group, and the recruiting and paying of respondents can cost anywhere from $2,500 to $4,000 per group.

There are critics of the overemphasis on focus groups. They point to the fact that many good ideas—whether a 30-second commercial or a new product or concept—often get killed prematurely because they did not do well with a focus group. Most account planners agree that focus groups should never be used as a replacement for quantitative research. But these groups are useful to determine consumer reaction to certain language in a TV commercial or in the development process for creative.

Pretest Research   The client wants assurances that the advertising proposed will be effective. In pretesting, a particular ad passes or fails, or selects one offering as better than all the others. The only alternative is for the client to depend solely on the judgment of the agency or their own personnel.

In general, there are two levels of research aimed at helping advertisers determine how well an ad will perform. **Copy testing** is done in two stages:

Copy testing
Measuring the
effectiveness of ads.

1. Rough copy research is needed to determine if the copy is effectively achieving its goals in terms of both message communication and attitude effects.
2. Finished copy research is done on the final form of the copy to evaluate how well the production process has achieved communication and attitude effects.

Pretesting is the stage of advertising research in which a complete ad or commercial is tested. It is important that the objectives of pretesting research relate back to the agreed advertising strategy. It would be wasted effort to test for some characteristic not related to the goal of the advertising.

A number of variables can be evaluated in pretesting, including the ability of the ad to attract attention, comprehension by the reader/viewer, playback of copy points

---

[10]Rebecca Piirto, "Future Focus Groups," *American Demographics,* January 1994, p. 6.

(recall), persuasion (the probability that the consumer will buy the brand), attitude toward the brand, credibility, and irritation level.

Pretests should be used as guides and not as absolute predictors of winners or losers. In copy testing, a higher score for one ad over another does not guarantee a better ad. As Bill Bernbach once said, "Research is very important, but I think it is the beginning of the ad." And Norm Grey, creative director, once commented on creative testing, "If you don't like the score an ad gets, demand another test. The only thing that's certain is that you'll get another score." These comments do not imply that creative testing is bad. They simply point to the fact that it is controversial and simply another tool for the advertiser. There have been arguments about the value of testing ads for years. In general, clients demand them and agency creatives are suspect of the process. Ed McCabe, chairman of McCabe & Company, makes a distinction between *research* and *testing:* "Without great research, you can't make great advertising. However, testing is the idiocy that keeps greatness from happening. Testing is a crutch the one-eyed use to beat up the blind." He points to his Hebrew National hot dog campaign in which an actor portraying Uncle Sam is brought up short by the company's insistence on exceeding federal regulations because its products are kosher and must "answer to a higher authority." The ads did not test well, and the client was reluctant to run them. After much discussion, the ads ran. Some 20 years later, the ads are still running. The point is that testing can be useful, but it is not a foolproof science. If you were spending millions of dollars on a creative idea, wouldn't you do everything possible to reduce the risk—or, to put it another way, "to better guarantee" a chance for success?

Campaign Evaluation Research   In evaluating advertising, within the total marketing effort, an advertiser should analyze the market and competitive activity and look at advertising as a campaign—not as individual ads. This information can help determine whether changes in the advertising strategy are needed to accomplish the objectives established for the campaign or to deal with a changed situation (Exhibit 15.7).

Advertisers frequently conduct tracking studies to measure trends, brand awareness, and interest in purchasing, as well as advertising factors. The research at the end of one campaign becomes part of the background research for selecting the next campaign strategy.

TESTING CREATIVE RESEARCH

Creative research takes place within the context of the preceding research stages. This kind of research aids in the development of what to say to the target audience and how to say it. Copy development research attempts to help advertisers decide how to execute approaches and elements. Copy testing is undertaken to aid them in determining whether to run the advertising in the marketplace.

exhibit

15.7

Effectiveness Measures by Type of Consumer Response for Copy Research

Response Criterion	Measurement
Cognitive (Think)	
Attention	Eye camera
Awareness	Day-after recall
Affective (Feel)	
Attitude	Persuasion
Feelings	Physiological response
Conative (Do)	
Purchase intent	Simulated shopping
Sales	Split cable/scanner

Adapted from John Leckency. "Current Issues in the Measurement of Advertising."

1. A good copy-testing system provides measurements that are relevant to the objectives of the advertising. Of course, different advertisements have different objectives (for example, encouraging trial of a product).

2. A primary purpose of copy testing is to help advertisers decide whether to run the advertising in the marketplace. A useful approach is to specify *action standards* before the results are in. Examples of action standards are:
   - Significantly improves perceptions of the brands as measured by _____.
   - Achieves an attention level no lower than _____ percent as measured by _____.

3. A good copy-testing system is based on the following model of human response to communications; the reception of a stimulus, the comprehension of the stimulus, and the response to the stimulus. In short, to succeed, an ad must have an effect.
   - On the eye and the ear—that is, it must be received *(reception)*
   - On the mind—that is, it must be understood *(comprehension)*
   - On the heart—that is, it must make an impression *(response)*

4. Experience has shown that test results often vary according to the degree of finish of the test. Thus, careful judgment should be exercised when using a less-than-finished version of a test. Sometimes what is lost is inconsequential, at other times it is critical.[11]

Forms of Testing

Each advertiser and agency uses similar but modified steps in the testing of creative research. The following are examples of this process.

Concept Testing   **Concept testing** may be an integral part of creative planning and is undertaken for most clients as a matter of course. Creative concept testing can be defined as the target audience evaluation of (alternative) creative strategy. Specifically, concept testing attempts to separate the "good" ideas from the "bad," to indicate differing degrees of acceptance, and to provide insight into factors motivating acceptance or rejection.

There are a number of possible concept tests:

1. *Card concept test.* Creative strategies are presented to respondents in the form of a headline, followed by a paragraph of body copy, on a plain white card. Each concept is on a separate card. Some concepts cannot be tested in card form (for example, those requiring a high degree of mood, such as concepts based on humor or personalities).

2. *Poster test.* This is similar to a card test except that small posters containing simplified illustrations and short copy are used rather than plain cards without illustrations.

3. *Layout test.* A layout test involves showing a rough copy of a print ad (or artwork of a TV commercial with accompanying copy) to respondents. Layout tests are more finished than poster tests in that they use the total copy and illustration as they will appear in the finished ad. Additionally, whereas a card or poster test measures the appeal of the basic concept, the purpose of the layout test may be to measure more subtle effects such as communication, understanding, and confusion.

Finished Print Tests   This testing procedure can take many forms of measuring the finished ad as it would appear in print.

Print Testing Example   The Video Storyboard Test tests television and print ads. Its ad promoting the testing of *rough print* ads says "develop testing procedures which allow you to compare alternative executions without spending the time and money to finish an ad." Its procedure goes something like this: Test ads, finished or unfinished,

[11]PACT—Positioning Advertising Copy Testing, *The PACT Agencies Report 1982,* pp. 6–25.

Concept testing
The target audience evaluation of (alternative) creative strategy. Testing attempts to separate good and bad ideas and provide insight into factors motivating acceptance or rejection.

are inserted into a 20-page magazine-in-a-folder containing both editorial and control ads. Prospects preview the magazine in one-on-one interviews in high-traffic malls. Respondents are questioned regarding unaided, aided, and related recall of the test ad. Next they are asked to focus on the test ad only and are probed for reactions. Agencies are furnished with diagnostic data to improve the ad. The ads are measured for stopping power, communication, relevance, and persuasion. They also provide likes and dislikes about the ad. All of this costs about $3,500 for each test execution per 100 respondents. Results take about 12 days (see Exhibit 15.8).

Test Commercials   Generally, commercial testing on film or videotape falls into one of four categories:

1. *Animatics.* This is artwork, either cartoons or realistic drawings. Some animatics show limited movement; those that do not are usually called *video storyboards.*

Animatics cost from about $1,500 to $4,000 plus artists' fees, although the simplest nonmovement video storyboard may cost as little as $750.

2. *Photomatics.* These are photographs shot in sequence on film. The photos may be stock (from a photo library) or shot on location. Photomatics cost about $10,000 to produce.

3. *Liveamatics.* This involves filming or taping live talent and is very close to the finished commercial. A liveamatic commercial test costs $10,000 to $20,000 to produce.

4. *Ripamatics.* The commercial is made of footage from other commercials, often taken from ad agency promotion reels. Ripamatics are used many times for experimentation on visual techniques.

Finished Commercial Testing   TV testing techniques can generally be classified into two categories:

1. those that attempt to evaluate a commercial's effectiveness in terms of viewers' recall of a certain aspect of the commercial
2. those that attempt to evaluate a commercial's effectiveness in terms of what it motivates a viewer to say or do

Recent advances in production technology are helping the testing process. The more closely the test spot resembles the finished commercial, the more accurate the test results will be. Computer animation has become less expensive, and so there is more computer-generated artwork in commercial testing.

BBDO's Emotional Testing   According to BBDO, traditional copy tests have failed to measure emotional response accurately. The techniques tend to measure thoughts rather than feelings. Instead of asking consumers to choose from a list or write in their own words, the agency has devised a deck of 53 photos representing the universe of emotion. Each features one of six photos with different expressions ranging from happy/playful to disgusted/revolted. There are a total of 26 categories of emotions expressed. Here is how it works:

● As with most copy testing, consumers are shown a single commercial or group of spots. Then they are given a questionnaire to test whether brand names and copy points are remembered.
● Photos are given to the participants. They are asked to sort through the photos quickly, setting aside any or all that reflect how they feel after viewing the commercial.
● A researcher tabulates how often a particular photo is chosen by the 150 to 600 participating consumers. In the system, the expressions are plotted on a "perceptual map" to determine whether the response is positive or negative, active or passive.

Agency researchers can compare a spot's effect on different groups: women versus men, teenagers versus adults. They cannot tell whether consumers will buy one brand or another, but they can say whether the ad has generated the intended emotion.

According to BBDO, the main advantage to this system is that it can be used to validate creative approaches and ensure that "we're punching the right buttons." When testing Gillette's Atra Plus razor campaign, "The best a man can get," the agency wanted to know whether the male-targeted campaign would alienate women. Men were more likely than women to feel "proud and confident" after watching the spot, but more women than men felt "happy and joyful." The vice president of marketing for Wm. Wrigley Jr. Co. put it this way, "We've always known there's been an emotional component to advertising, but when you try to put it into measurable terms, it goes touchy-feely." This system is one of the first to test feedback on whether a commercial did elicit a response on the emotional level. However, there is a great distance between measuring emotional response and manipulating it.[12]

Who Sees and Reads Your Ad?

Today when advertisers face mounting competition both in the market and on the printed page, the ability to determine if an advertisement is being seen is more important than ever before. One such readership service that supplies this kind of information is the Starch Readership Service from Roper Starch.

The Starch Readership Service is designed to measure the extent to which advertisements are being seen and read and the level of interest they arouse. Starch interviews more than 75,000 consumers each year to determine their responses to more than 50,000 print ads. Starch uses the *recognition* method of interviewing. With the publication open, the respondent explains the extent to which he or she had read each ad prior to the interview. For each ad, respondents are asked, "Did you see or read any part of this ad?" If *yes,* a prescribed questioning procedure is followed to determine the observation and reading of each component part of each ad—illustration, headline, signature, and copy blocks. After these questions are asked, each respondent is classified as follows:

- *Noted reader.* A person who remembers having previously seen the advertisement in the issue being studied.
- *Associated reader.* A reader who not only *noted* the advertisement, but also saw or read some part of it that clearly indicated the brand or advertiser.
- *Read most.* A person who read half or more of the written material in the ad.

Clients receive *Adnorm* data with the Starch Readership Reports. Adnorms enable advertisers to compare readership data of their ad in a given magazine issue to the norm for ads of the same size and color in the same product category. These data can help advertisers identify the types of layouts that attract and retain the highest readership. They can also compare current ads against those of competitors, compare the current campaign against previous campaigns, compare the current campaign against a competitor's previous campaign, and compare current ads against the Adnorm tables.

Exhibit 15.9 shows a Starch ad. The sticker indicates the noted scores.

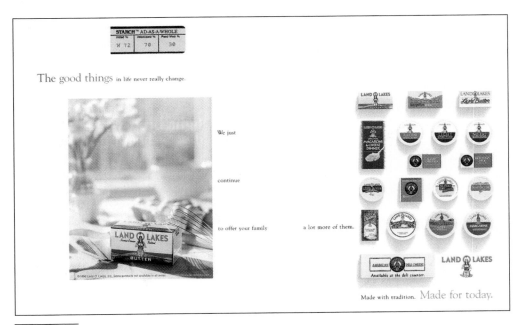

exhibit

15.9

The label represents the Starch scores for this ad.

Courtesy: Land O' Lakes.

---

[12]Rebecca Piirto, "Future Focus Groups," *American Demographics,* January 1994, p. 6.

exhibit

15.10

Central Carolina Bank (CCB) could test text size, illustration position, or what the consumer recalls.

Courtesy: West & Vaughan and Central Carolina Bank.

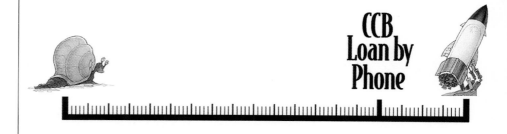

Need to Sell Benefits Philip Sawyer of Starch Research points out that few advertisers seem to be able to solve the riddle of how to communicate effectively to consumers precisely or concisely what they stand to gain from the product or service being advertised. In the advertising created in the 1980s, consumers aspired to the brand; in the 1990s, the brand and the advertising promoting it needs to aspire to fit the consumer's lifestyle. Most advertising is decidedly "me oriented" when it should be "you oriented" about consumers' wishes, dreams, and desires. If an advertisement does not answer the very basic question, "What's in it for me?" it is an unlikely candidate to be read or watched.

Consumer Outdoor Recognition Study (CORS)

To conduct CORS research, interviewers visit three or four locations, mostly malls, in designated markets for person-to-person interviews. Participants are asked if they can remember particular outdoor campaigns. Then they are shown 30 to 50 different recent advertising campaigns run in the area and quizzed about those that they recall. Besides demographics, the survey is tracking other variables, including text size and picture placement, that make outdoor advertising effective. The average recognition score is 30 and the range of scores is between 5 percent and 75 percent (see Exhibit 15.10).

SUMMARY

Advertising is a people business. Successful advertisers know who their prospects are and—to whatever extent is practical—their needs and motives, which result in the purchase of one product or service and the rejection of another. Consumer behavior is usually the result of a complex network of influences based upon the psychological, sociological, and anthropological makeup of the individual.

Advertising rarely, if ever, changes these influences, but rather channels needs and wants of consumers toward specific products and brands. Advertising is a mirror of society. The advertiser influences people by offering solutions to their needs and problems, not by creating these needs. The role of the advertiser is to act as a monitor of the changing face of society.

Advertisers pay special attention to what we call up-front research or market research that reflects the market, the consumer, and the competition. Such information as cohort analysis and VALS can help us understand consumer lifestyles and values, which aids in developing strategies.

Once all of this information is digested, it is used in the four stages of advertising development: strategy development, execution development, pretesting of executions, and campaign evaluation. *By itself, information has no value.* It aquires value only when we take a point of view about what the information means.

There are a number of stages of testing available in creative research ranging from concept testing and commercial testing techniques to finished print and commercial tests. It is much less expensive to test concepts and ads prior to buying expensive media schedules.

REVIEW

1. Why are sociology, psychology, and anthropology important to advertising?
2. What kind of people are *achievers?*
3. What kind of research is used in advertising *execution* development?
4. What is the role of the animatic commercial?
5. What is qualitative research?

TAKE IT TO THE NET

We invite you to visit the Russell/Lane page on the Prentice Hall Web site at **PHLIP** **http://www.prenhall.com/phbusiness** for the bimonthly Russell/Lane update and for this chapter's World Wide Web exercise.

16

CREATING THE COPY

GREAT ADVERTISING COPY IS ESSENTIAL TO GREAT ADVERTISING. UNDERSTANDING CONSUMERS AND WHAT APPEALS TO THEM IS PART OF THE DEVELOPMENTAL PROCESS NEEDED TO CREATE GREAT COPY. AFTER READING THIS CHAPTER YOU WILL UNDERSTAND

● the nature and the use of appeals
● elements of an ad
● structure of an ad
● copy styles
● slogans
● the creative work plan.

Up to this point we have laid the foundation for you to develop advertising. Now it is time to discuss the creation of the ad itself. But before we get to the details let us put today's and tomorrow's advertising into perspective. Let us see what challenge lies ahead for us in creating effective ads and examine ad copy's role.

ADVERTISING'S CHALLENGE: A NEW CREATIVE VISION

To say we are living in the information age is somewhat stating the obvious. It is also true to say that knowledge is power, and the speed with which marketers utilize that knowledge in the future will determine success or failure. Because advertising is, in its most basic form, a conveyor of information, it will be at the center of this revolution. But there are a number of factors working against that happening.

According to John Hegarty, creative director at Bartle Bogle Hegarty, London, we are already having to deal with a major communication problem. It's called time famine. How do consumers assimilate this ever-growing mass of messages that is being directed at them? How do they cope with the volume of traffic going through their brains? How do they process this valuable information as opposed to allowing it to pass straight through unnoticed? Another related issue that has been debated for years is media clutter. Are consumers reaching the point of "overchoice," as futurist Alvin Toffer predicted? "We are racing against overchoice—the point at which the advantages of choice and individualization are canceled by the complexity of the buyer's decision-making process."

Yet another issue is our audience's ability to turn us off. Advertisers interrupt viewing and listening, or we sit alongside printed material shouting for attention. As electronic media take a greater hold on the distribution of information, our audience will have great control over turning us off, unless we are compelling and necessary. Unless we recognize the change in the balance of power and take into account our consumers' aspirations, we will be cut out of the loop and become irrelevant. What can we do as communicators?

Strategy and Great Writing

The typical ad for *The Economist* (a British publication read in more than 140 countries) has been three columns of copy talking about the benefits of reading the publication—much information aimed at a sophisticated, well-educated target. Yet a simple poster says,

> *I've never read* The Economist.
>
> *Signed, Management Trainee, aged 42*

There is a valuable message in this example for those creating advertising. The lesson is, the faster ideas get across, the more powerful they become. As you reduce the idea down, as you hone it to its essential structure, its power increases. The faster it penetrates the thinking the longer it stays there. You aren't trying to buy newspaper or magazine space or time in a commercial break. The space you are trying to buy is in the consumer's head. That is the most valuable space. That is what you are trying to influence.

Was it Oscar Wilde—it doesn't really matter—who understood that an idea got better as it got faster? How do we do that? *The brilliance of our craft is to reduce, to distill messages down, not to elongate.* Remember Abraham Lincoln's quote, "You can fool all the people some of the time, and some of the people all the time, but you cannot fool all the people all of the time." He captured the essence of modern politics in one sentence, and most of us remember it. Great writing is about using fewer words to be more compelling. When you do that, you liberate your ideas to become more powerful, more involving, and hopefully more memorable. Brevity not only allows us to become more powerful, it allows us to become more stimulating. If you are more stimulating, there is a good chance you are becoming more relevant. We have to change because our audience is demanding it.

The Greeks said that information is taken through the heart. As we have moved from the unique selling proposition (USP) to the emotional selling proposition, we need to understand that the way we talk to consumers must also change. Advertising still needs to be based upon the foundation of product or corporate attributes. But we must remember that it may no longer be unique, nor will it necessarily be obvious.

Creative Vision

Creativity isn't just about putting a strategy down on a piece of paper but about capturing the essence of that strategy and giving it a creative vision. That is both compelling and competitive. What worked yesterday isn't necessarily going to work today or tomorrow. The consumer has not only less time to listen to us, but also less inclination.[1]

---

[1] John Hegarty, "My Apologies for This Letter Being So Long. Had I More Time It Would Have Been Shorter," *Creativity*, March 1997, p. 12.

HOW DO WE CREATE GREAT ADVERTISING?

Ron Huey, award-winning creative director, says, "Simplicity is the key to great advertising. Take the single most salient feature of your product or service and communicate that in a simple, thought provoking or entertaining way. Good copy speaks to the common man. It should be smart, entertaining and conversational, not fancy or frilly. Today's best creative people are resilient. Great ideas are killed every day for sometimes stupid reasons. The best creatives accept that and come back with something even better." Huey's thoughts on advertising through the years: "The great ads from Bernbach in the '60s, Fallon McElligott in the '80s, Wieden [Wieden & Kennedy], Goodby [Goodby, Silverstein & Partners] and The Martin Agency today, all have a common thread—The headline, visual and logo communicate the idea immediately." He also believes, "Three quarters of today's best ads use humor. But it's wry humor. Not a bathroom joke or humor that's intended to shock people."[2]

Good Copy's Importance

Procter & Gamble's president said, "I have seen through 25 years that the correlation between profitable business growth on our brands and having great copy on our brands isn't 25 percent, it's not 50 percent. It is 100 percent. I have not seen a single P&G brand sustain profitable volume growth for more than a couple of years without having great advertising." Lou Centlivre, formerly of Foote, Cone & Belding, said: "The days are gone of left-brained reason-why messages; so insignificant and strained and boring and unbelievable they fall on deaf ears. The creative people who can get into the heart—not just the brain—and make people cry or laugh or silently say, 'Yeah, that's how I really feel' will be the superstars."

THE NATURE AND USE OF APPEALS

Advertising motivates people by appealing to their problems, desires, and goals, and by offering a means of solving their problems. Let us look at the value of using a psychological **appeal** in advertising. David Martin, founder of The Martin Agency, points to decades of research indicating the relative strengths of motives and appeals in advertising. He believes human desires are woven into our basic nature. They do not change with lifestyles or external environmental stimuli. Consumers will always have a desire for food and drink; for rest, comfort, and security; and for a sense of social worth, independence, power, and success. Parental feelings to protect and provide are basic. Human nature is a constant. Humans are born with certain instincts: fear (self-preservation), hunger (need for food and drink), sex (love), and rage (anger). People also have five senses: sight, touch, smell, hearing, and taste. The instincts and senses are often a starting point for advertising appeals.[3]

The creative genius of the late 1960s, the late Bill Bernbach, put it this way:

> There may be changes in our society. But learning about those changes is not the answer. For you are not appealing to society. You are appealing to individuals, each with an ego, each with the dignity of his or her being, each like no one else in the world, each a separate miracle. The societal appeals are merely fashionable, current, cultural appeals which make nice garments for the real motivations that stem from the unchanging instincts, and emotions of people—from nature's indomitable programming in their genes. It is unchanging person that is the proper study of the communicator.[4]

Appeal
The motive to which an ad is directed, it is designed to stir a person toward a goal the advertiser has set.

---

[2]Ron Huey, interviews by W. Ronald Lane, September 1994 and September 1997.
[3]David Martin, *Romancing the Brand* (New York: Amacom, 1989), pp. 134–136.
[4]From an American Association of Advertising Agencies speech, May 17, 1980.

Why are babies so hard to dress? Put your toes in your mouth and try to put your pants on.

Tasty toes. Reason number 128,965 we make playwear easy to put on and take off. Generous neck and arm openings, big snaps down each leg and around the crotch. All to make dressing your little pretzel easier. *Healthtex* 1-800-554-7637

Call us toll-free at 1-800-554-7637 for the store nearest you, or if you simply have questions.

exhibit

16.1

Wry humor and illustration appeal to parental feelings.

Courtesy: Healthtex.

Jo Alexander, who writes Healthtex ads for The Martin Agency, found that mothers are information sponges, willing to read anything and everything about babies. Hence, the copy for Healthtex ads creates a bond with its bond-minded audience, to have an intimate conversation and establish an unmistakable tone of voice.[5] Specifically, let us look at parental feelings, and also what Ron Huey said about using wry humor, in the Healthex ads (see Exhibit 16.1). "Why are babies so hard to dress? Put your toes in your mouth and try to put your pants on." The head and the illustration work at appealing to you in a humorous way. And the body copy continues the tone: "Tasty toes. Reason number 128,965 we make playwear easy to put on and take off. Generous neck and arm openings, big snaps down each leg and around the crotch. All to make dressing your little pretzel easier."

Selecting the Appeal

Most products have a number of positive appeals that could be successfully promoted, so how do we go about making the decision as to which direction to go with an ad or appeal? The idea is to choose the one that is most important to the majority of our

[5]Cathy Madison, "Bye, Bye, Wordy?" *Creativity*, September 1995, pp. 16–19.

target. Because selecting the primary appeal is the key to any advertising campaign, many research techniques have been developed to find which appeal to use. In chapter 15, we discussed some of the aspects of advertising research that help us make strategic and creative decisions. Here we limit the discussion to three techniques that may help us decide on appeals: concept testing, focus groups, and motivational research.

Concept Testing   Concept testing is a method to determine the best of a number of possible appeals to use in your advertising. A creative concept is defined as a simple explanation or description of the advertising idea behind the product.

A tourism association developed several appeals that might motivate prime prospects to drive two hours to the mountains from a large metro area in another state:

1. only two hours to relaxation
2. mountain fun in your own backyard
3. the family playground in the mountains
4. escape to white water rafting, fishing, and the great outdoors
5. weekend vacation planner package

By using cards with the theme statement and/or rough layouts, the advertiser tries to obtain a rank order of consumer appeal of the various concepts and diagnostic data explaining why the concepts were ranked as they were.

The tourism group found that targets had not realized they were so close to these mountain areas. As a result, they had not been considered in their vacation or recreation plans.

In the case of a car rental company, a test of vacation travelers found that one benefit stood out: the lowest-priced full-size car. The second most important benefit was no hidden extras.

One drawback of concept testing is that consumers can react only to the themes presented to them. You may find that they have chosen the best of several bad concepts.

Focus Groups   In chapter 15, we discussed the nature, cost, and typical procedure of focus group research. Here we examine the role of focus groups in selecting the primary appeal. Generally, the interviewer starts by discussing the product category, then proceeds to products within the category, and finally brings up past or current ads for a product or products. And, of course, the focus group can be used to test several new ad concepts of the appeal of print, storyboard, or more finished ad forms. The creative team watching from behind the one-way mirror has the opportunity to hear how participants perceive its products, ads, and ideas.

The leader of the group directs the conversation to determine what problems or "hang-ups" the prime prospects associate with the product. Thus, the answers are not predetermined by the advertiser or the researcher. Rather, they are direct responses to the product and the benefits and problems these prime prospects see in it. Further, because the research is done in a group, people feel less inhibited than they do in one-on-one interviews. The result is usually a good evaluation of the problems, attributes, and particular strengths and weaknesses of the product from the consumer's point of view.

One example of this type of research was conducted by the Atlanta Symphony Orchestra. Its agency interviewed two groups of prime prospects: attendees at regular-season symphony concerts and pop concert goers. The symphony's management wanted to discover prospects' attitudes about programming, length of concerts, and types of soloists. In this case, the results were not surprising. They confirmed management's original perceptions but provided a more tangible basis for arriving at strategic marketing decisions.

Motivational Research   Motivational research has its foundation in the psychoanalytic techniques of Sigmund Freud. Popularized by Ernst Dichter during the 1950s as a marketing tool, this type of research seeks to find the underlying reasons for consumer behavior. Its value rests on the premise that consumers are motivated by emotions they may not be aware of consciously.

Motivational research uses unstructured techniques to elicit open-ended responses that are recorded verbatim. The idea is that among these responses there will be the kernel of an unanticipated consumer motivation that can be translated into a unique advertising appeal. Although motivational research has lost some of its glamour, it still has its advocates in the advertising community.

All research data must be interpreted. In fact, data interpretation may be the most critical step in effective advertising research. It requires insight and skill. We also must remember that many advertising appeals result from intuition and personal observation.

Whether created by research or in other ways, the appeal provides the basis of the advertising structure. This appeal can be expressed in many ways. Here we discuss how to make use of words, called *copy,* in presenting the appeal.[6]

GREAT ADVERTISING ELEMENTS

The Creative Council of Ogilvy & Mather Worldwide found that examples of great advertising have certain elements in common (the same fundamental principles apply to direct response and sales promotion):[7]

- *Potent strategy.* The strategy is the heart of advertising. It is impossible to do great advertising if the strategy is weak or does not exist at all.
- *A strong selling idea.* Great advertising promises a benefit to the consumer. The idea must be simple, and it must be clear. The brand must be integrated into the selling idea.
- *Stands out.* A great ad is memorable, even when competing for attention with news and entertainment. Exhibit 16.2, which ran in *Parents* magazine, definitely gets your attention. The

exhibit

16.2

This ad will stand out in a parenting magazine. The headline and main illustration attract attention and compel the reader to relate.

Courtesy: Healthtex.

"Mom, Amanda said I looked like I dressed in the dark. I did not. I had the light on."

Healthtex

---

[6]The term *copy* is a carryover from the days in printing when a compositor, given a manuscript to set in type, was told to copy it. Before long, the manuscript itself became known as copy. In the *creation* of a printed ad, copy refers to all the reading matter in the ad. However, in the *production* of print ads, copy refers to the entire subject being reproduced—words and pictures alike. This is one of those instances in advertising when the same word is used in different senses, a practice that all professions and crafts seem to enjoy because it bewilders the uninitiated.

[7]Luis Bassar, "Creative Paths to Great Advertising," *Viewpoint,* September/October 1991, pp. 23–24.

headline and the main illustration appeal to your humor and humanity and truth: "Mom, Amanda said I looked like I dressed in the dark. I did not. I had the light on." The body doesn't get boring but is informative: "We admit putting the wrong shirt with the wrong pants and the wrong headband with the wrong socks is cute. The first time. And maybe the second day. But not every morning. So here at Healthtex we make clothes even circus clowns or five-year-olds can coordinate. With skirts, pants, and socks and shoes that mix effortlessly. Check them out. And introduce the word ensemble to her vocabulary."

- *Always relevant.* Prospects can easily relate the advertising to their experience and to the role of the product in their lives.
- *Can be built into campaigns.* No matter how clever one idea may be, if you cannot make it into a campaign, it is not a great idea.

STRUCTURE OF AN ADVERTISEMENT

In some instances, the promise is the whole advertisement.

Surf Removes Dirt and Odor

Usually, however, a fuller exposition is required, in which case the promise can act as the headline—the first step in the structure of the advertisement. Most ads are presented in this order:

- promise of benefit (the headline)
- spelling out of promise (the subheadline, optional)
- amplification of story (as needed)
- proof of claim (as needed)
- action to take (if not obvious)

People tend to scan print ads in the following manner: illustration first, followed by the headline, first line of the body copy, and then the logo. If they are still interested, they will go back and read the rest of the copy. Yes, you can get people to read the copy, but the first sentence and first paragraph are extremely important in keeping readers. As a matter of fact, the drop-off rate of readers is pretty significant during the first 50 words, but not so great between 50 and 500 words.

The Headline

The headline is the most important part of an ad. It is the first thing read, and it should arouse interest so the consumer wants to keep on reading and get to know more about the product being sold. If the headline does not excite the interest of the particular group of prime prospects the advertiser wants to reach, the rest of the ad will probably go unread.

The Zimmerman Agency created an ad to reassure parents that Columbia Plantation General Hospital offers the security of serving their needs in an emergency (see Exhibit 16.3). The headline reads: "Our Pediatric ER Is Like Most Things In Life. You May Not Need It, But It's Good To Know It's There." The copy says: "If your kids go bump in the night, remember Columbia Plantation General Hospital's 24-hour Pediatric Emergency Room. Unlike a lot of hospitals, out pediatricians aren't on call. They're actually at the hospital around the clock. So, you won't ever have to wait for a doctor to scramble out of bed and find the coat and keys." The structure of the ad works; if you have children, the headline gets the process started and compels you to read more.

No formula can be given for writing a good headline. However, there are several factors that should be considered in evaluating an effective headline:

- It should use short, simple words, usually no more than 10.
- It should include an invitation to the prospect, primary product benefits, name of the brand, and an interest-provoking idea to gain readership of the rest of the ad.

- The words should be selective, appealing only to prime prospects.
- It should contain an action verb.
- It should give enough information so that the consumer who reads only the headline learns something about the product and its benefit.

The Sweet Factory headline in Exhibit 16.4 (p. 454) says all that needs to be communicated: "Our Milk Chocolate Covered Raisins Are Always Double Layered So There's Nary A Wrinkle To Be Seen."

Not every headline is going to adhere to these guidelines. However, when you write a headline that excludes any of these points, ask yourself: Would this headline be more effective if it did adhere to the guidelines? You want to be sure you have thought through the process.

Many headlines fall into one of four categories:

1. *Headlines that present a new benefit.* The moment of peak interest in a product is when it offers a new benefit. That is why, in our innovative society, you often see headlines such as these:

> *Now there's a boil-in-bag rice that's perfect in only 5 minutes.*
> > *Minute Rice*

> *Now there's more fruit in Quaker Instant Oatmeal.*
> > *Quaker Oatmeal*

> *ZIPLOC introduces the only color seal you can feel.*
> > *ZIPLOC storage bags*

> *Introducing a new way to lower your cholesterol.*
> > *Cholestin*

> *Now, getting on the Internet is so easy, even an adult can do it.*
> > *Philips Magnavox*

exhibit

16.4

This headline is the copy. It tells the reader the product is milk chocolate covered raisins and is double layered.

Courtesy: Bulldog Drummond.

2. *Headlines that directly promise an existing benefit.* Products cannot be offering new benefits all the time, of course, so headlines often remind consumers of a product's existing features:

> *Some things scratch. Some don't.*
>
> *Soft Scrub*

> *Adults who eat cereal consume less fat each day.*
>
> *Kellogg*

> *Heavy isn't healthy.*
>
> *Purina Fit & Trim*

> *Depression hurts. Prozac can help.*
>
> *Prozac*

Navigator from Lincoln. What a luxury should be.

Lincoln

The National Osteoporosis Foundation recommends a diet rich in calcium from broccoli, salmon, milk and Tums.

Tums

3. *Curiosity-invoking and provocative headlines.* By invoking curiosity, an advertiser may grab attention from an otherwise disinterested audience by challenging the curiosity of the readers, thereby prompting them to read further and leading them into the key message. David Ogilvy warned against using heads that don't communicate the benefits because of the large numbers of readers that don't read the body copy. It can work, but the writer must be careful to build a strong relationship between the curiosity point and the brand. North Broward Medical Center's Memory Disorder Center tries to get people into the copy by being provocative and making the head work with the illustration (Exhibit 16.5). Here are some more curiosity-invoking headlines:

How do you feed a 100,000 hungry hairs?

Nioxin

Chips & Dips

South Padre Island

15 seconds to heaven

Cool Whip

exhibit

16.5

A brush and a toothbrush: which one goes into your mouth evokes curiosity.

Courtesy: The Zimmerman Agency and North Broward Medical Center.

Imagine not knowing which one goes in your mouth.

Memory Disorder Center. It's the little things. How to brush their teeth, tie their shoes and get out of bed that they forget. If someone you love suffers from a memory disorder, you already know this. What you may not know is that there's help. Our Center specializes in proper diagnosis and research. Our staff is specially trained to help you cope. Call the Center at 786-7392, or the District Health Line at 355-4888, ask for code #29-040, for more information. Imagine the difference one call can make.

North Broward Medical Center

201 EAST SAMPLE ROAD·POMPANO BEACH, FL 33064
NORTH BROWARD MEDICAL CENTER IS A FACILITY OF THE NORTH BROWARD HOSPITAL DISTRICT AND IS AN EQUAL OPPORTUNITY EMPLOYER AND AFFIRMATIVE ACTION PROCURER OF GOODS AND SERVICES

ecnalg

Ginkoba

Introducing forgiveness in a bottle.

409 carpet cleaner

I scream. You scream. We all scream.

Breyers Smooth & Creamy Yogurt

What the best dressed chickens will be wearing this year.

Kraft Parm Plus herbs

The question headline that works best is the kind that arouses curiosity so the reader will read the body copy to find the answer. Readers do not like being tricked. They want a strong relationship between the curiosity and the product.

4. *Selective headlines.* Readers looking through a magazine or newspaper are more likely to read an ad they think concerns them personally than one that talks to a broad audience. The selective headline aimed at a particular prime prospect who would be more interested in the product is often used. If the head says, "Condominium owners," and you don't own a condominium, you probably won't pay attention; conversely, if you do own a condo, you might read it. A Pampers ad head reads, "Babies absorb everything around them. Wetness doesn't have to be one of them." Obviously, if you don't have a baby in your life, you probably aren't going to read this ad. However, if you do have a baby you may be attracted to the copy. Four such headlines that specifically reach out to special groups are

To All Men and Women
To All Young Men and Women
To All College Men and Women
To All College Seniors

The first headline is addressed to the greatest number of readers, but it would be of the least interest to any one of them. Each succeeding headline reduces the size of the audience it addresses and improves the chances of attracting that particular group. What about "All College Seniors Who Need Jobs"? You get the idea!

Besides addressing a particular group directly, headlines can appeal to people by mentioning a problem they have in common:

Most baby bottoms stink. (And their tops aren't great, either.)

Healthtex

Urinary discomfort shouldn't be a burning issue.

AZO-Standard

Another vital quality in headlines is specificity. Remember, consumers are more interested in the specific than the general. Therefore, the more specific you can be in the headline, the better: "A Peppermint Peroxide Toothpaste That Will Help Kill Bacteria and Keep Tartar From Your Teeth" is better than "A Nice Tasting Toothpaste That Cleans Your Teeth."

The Subheadline

A headline must say something important to the reader. The actual number of words is not the deciding factor; long or short headlines may work well. A headline sometimes can be more than one sentence.

The tides are treacherous.
The wind sometimes fierce.

It's hard to get here.
When can we expect you?

North Carolina

If the message is long, it can be conveyed with a main headline (with large type) and a subheadline (with smaller type but larger than the body copy). The subheadline can spell out the promise presented in the headline. It can be longer than the headline; it can invite further reading; and it serves as a transition to the opening paragraph of the copy.

Headline

Lamb & Rice & Less Fat.

Subhead

Low fat, healthy foods are good for all pets, not just overweight ones.

Waltham Formula

Headline

There's something new in the air.

Subhead

Introducing Mountain Spring Scented Tide.

Mountain Spring Tide

Amplification

The headline and, if used, the subheadline are followed by the body copy of the ad. It is here that you present your case for the product and explain how the promise in the headline will be fulfilled. In other words, the body copy amplifies what was hinted in the headline or subheadline. What you say and how deep you go depend on the amount of information your prime prospect needs at this point in the buying process. A high-cost laptop computer probably calls for more explanation than a low-cost product, such as a barbecue sauce with a new flavor. If a product has many technical advances, such as digital videorecording discs, there probably is not sufficient room to detail all the features. In this case, the objective is to create enough interest to get the prime prospect to the store for a demonstration and more information.

Amplification should emphasize those product or service features that are of primary importance but cannot be included in the headline. Take, for example, how much the Marines (Exhibit 16.6, p. 458) can tell you in a headline:

You can go anywhere if you've got the right make-up.

and then the amplification:

There are those that think make-up is something that makes you look good on the outside. And there are those who know about another kind of make-up, the kind that's found on the inside. It consists of characteristics like honor, courage, and commitment. The qualities you'll find in every woman who becomes a United States Marine. Qualities that can take you anywhere.

Proof

The body copy does amplify what the headline promised. At times the process acts to reassure the consumer that the product will perform as promised. Consumers may look for proof in an ad, and proof is particularly important for high-priced products, health, and new products with special features. Here are a few ways in which proof can be offered to the reader.

exhibit

16.6

The body copy gives details to support the headline.

Courtesy: Marines and J. Walter Thomspon USA/Atlanta.

Seals of Approval   Seals of approval from such accredited sources as *Good Housekeeping* and *Parents* magazines, the American Dental Association, the American Medical Association, and Underwriter's Laboratories allay consumers' fears about product quality. An Ayer senior vice president of planning says that it gives a product a difference and that the seal can give a new product an edge of credibility in the market. Niagara spray starch advertises the Good Housekeeping seal.

Guarantees   Wendy's, Arby's, and Mrs. Winner's have offered consumers money-back guarantees for trying specific products to reduce the risk and get trial by consumers. Products such as Silent Floor systems guarantee their floors will be free from warping or defects. Hartz Control Pet Care System will refund your money if you don't see an improvement in 30 days.

Trial Offers and Samples   BMG Music offers any eight CDs for the price of one with their 10-day risk-free trial. Proctor & Gamble offered free industrial-strength Spic and Span liquid samples to consumers who called a toll-free telephone number, to reduce the risk and get trial.

Warranties Sherwin-Williams SuperPaint is advertised with a 20-year warranty against peeling. James Hardie Building Products touts its 50-year warranty for its siding. Maytag water heating appliances are covered by a 10-year tank warranty.

Reputation Copy for Woolite says, "It's recommended by the makers of more than 350 million garments."

Demonstrations "Before" and "after" demonstrations are used to show how a product works. Starch Research says showing models to demonstrate cosmetic products is powerful. In one ad, Almay showed a supermodel from the neck up, making it easy to see her facial imperfections—or lack thereof after using Almay's line of hypoallergenic cosmetics. Find a way to tell consumers a benefit, and you will do well; find a way to *show* them, and you will fare even better.

Testimonials The ability to attract attention to ads and offer a credible source has made testimonials a popular device. Testimonials should come from persons viewed by consumers as competent to make judgments on the products they are endorsing.

COPY STYLE

As with a novel or a play, good ad copy has a beginning, a middle, and an ending. And, like a novel, the transition must be smooth from one part to another. Up to this point, we have discussed how the building blocks of copy are put together. Now we need to think about what it takes to create special attention and persuasion. It takes style—the ability to create fresh, charming, witty, human advertising that compels people to read. Remember what Ron Huey said: "Take the single most salient feature of your product or service and communicate it in a simple, thought provoking or entertaining way." See the product in a fresh way, explore its possible effects on the reader, or explain the product's advantages in a manner that causes the reader to view the product with a new understanding and appreciation.

Most ads end with a close by asking or suggesting that the reader buy the product. The difference between a lively ad and a dull one lies in the approach to the message at the outset.

The lens through which a writer sees a product may be the magnifying glass of the technician, who perceives every nut and bolt and can explain why each is important, or it may be the rose-colored glasses of the romanticist, who sees how a person's life may be affected by the product. That is why we speak of **copy approaches** rather than types of ads. The chief approaches in describing a product are the factual, the imaginative, and the emotional.

Factual Approach

In the factual approach, we deal with reality—that which actually exists. We talk about the product or service—what it is, how it is made, what it does. Focusing on the facts about the product that are most important to the reader, we explain the product's advantages.

One of the interesting things about a fact, however, is that it can be interpreted in different ways, each accurate but each launching different lines of thinking. Remember the classic example of an eight-ounce glass holding four ounces of water, of which can be said: "This glass is half full" or "This glass is half empty." As you know, both are correct and factual. The difference is in the interpretation of reality, as the Mitsui O.S.K. ad headline for shipping seafood says, "We cater to the best schools." Their copy talks facts: "MOL takes a great deal of pride in catering to the needs of the world's most discriminating shippers. Salmon, shrimp, crabs, mussels and other gourmet seafood, for example, are delivered in 40′ high-cube reefer containers so that they arrive fresh and

Copy approach
The method of opening the text of an ad. Chief forms: factual approach, imaginative approach, emotional approach.

delectable in Asian and American markets." Skill in presenting a fact consists of projecting it in a way that means the most to the reader.

The factual approach can be used to sell more than products or services. Facts about ideas, places—anything for which an ad can be written—can be presented with a fresh point of view.

Imaginative Approach

There is nothing wrong with presenting a fact imaginatively. The art of creating copy lies in saying a familiar thing in an unexpected way. Thomas Howell Group, one of the world's largest loss adjustment firms, could have simply said, "We can help you and your insurer save." How much more interesting the approach in Exhibit 16.7 is. "We See What Others Don't." The illustration and head work together. The copy says, "The potential for loss is often difficult to see, or predict. Nevertheless, very real. . . . we can identify what our competitors are more likely to miss."

As with the other Healthtex ads we have seen in this text, Exhibit 16.8 creatively talks about fabric size and shape and comfort. "He's not going to start shrinking until he's 80. Why should his clothes?"

We See What Others Don't.

Risk is often hidden. There nevertheless, poised to strike.

At Thomas Howell Group, we can identify what our competitors are more likely to miss. And ultimately, our precision will reduce your cost.

Your risk management deserves a closer look from experts with a keen eye and a thorough understanding of your business.

That's why we place such a high priority on our staff. And why top international companies have learned to expect prompt, tailored service from the experienced professionals at Thomas Howell Group.

We're one of the world's largest adjustment firms, and we provide a complete range of risk-related services around the globe. To learn how we can provide you with clear

solutions, contact Thomas Howell Group (Americas) at Six Concourse Parkway, Suite 3100, Atlanta, GA 30328. Or call 1-800-554-8697, ext. 6724. You'll find that when it comes to expertise, the differences at Thomas Howell Group are easy to see.

THOMAS HOWELL GROUP (AMERICAS) INC.

AWARD-WINNING COMMERCIALS AND RADIO ADS

● ●

Continuing a popular tradition with an added twist, Prentice Hall makes available a new videotape of award-winning commercials from New York Festivals, together with an audiotape of radio commercials.

Notes for each commercial are included with the Instructor's Manual.

● ●

Emotional Approach

Emotion can be a powerful communicator. The feelings about your product or company can be an important plus or minus. Copy using psychological appeals to love, hate, or fear has great impact. The illustration and headline in Exhibit 16.9 show not only sensitivity, warmth, maternal instincts, but also emotion—every parent can identify with the feeling. "If Just Looking at This Has a Profound Effect on You, Imagine What It's Doing for This Three Pound Baby." Often the copy will continue the emotional appeal, although at times it will take a factual direction to inform the reader about

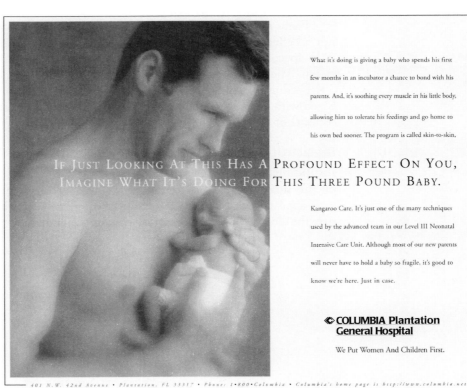

specific features of the product to convince the reader of its value. The Columbia Hospital copy starts: "What it's doing is giving a baby who spends his first few months in an incubator a chance to bond with his parents. And it's soothing every muscle in his little body, allowing him to tolerate his feedings and go home to his own bed sooner. This program is called skin-to-skin, Kangaroo Care."

Research indicates emotion can create positive feelings, such as warmth, happiness, and delight, which work best for low-involvement goods. For high involvement, higher-ticket items, such as CD players or automobiles, emotions must be unique and mesh with the brand. Kodak has produced ads so emotional they bring tears to your eyes.

Comparative Advertising

Comparative advertising
It directly contrasts an advertiser's product with other named or identified products.

Comparing your product directly with one or more competitors is called **comparative advertising.** It is actually encouraged by the Federal Trade Commission, but it has risks. Some advertisers think it isn't smart to spend money to publicize your competition. Others think it creates a bad atmosphere for the company that demeans all advertising. Pepsi has frequently run ads in *Nation's Restaurant News* featuring "Coke and Pepsi View Your Business Two Different Ways," and the copy talks about how they do business differently.

Despite each comparative ad being different, there are certain rules of thumb that can be applied: (1) The leader in the field never starts a comparative campaign. (2) The most successful comparison ads are those comparing the product with products identical in every respect except for the special differential featured in the ad. The stronger the proof that the products are identical, the better. (3) The different features should be of importance to the consumer.

SLOGANS

Originally derived from the Gaelic *slugh gairm,* meaning "battle cry," the word *slogan* has an appropriate background. A slogan sums up the theme for a product's benefits to deliver an easily remembered message in a few words.

There have been many very memorable slogans in advertising over the years. Yet, not all effective slogans are etched in every consumer's mind. Many slogans, however, do help communicate the essence of the product position. For example, "Rosemary Beach. The new traditional town on the gulf."

Used even more often on television and radio than in print, slogans may be combined with a catchy tune to make a jingle. Slogans are broadly classified as either institutional or hard-sell.

Institutional Slogans

Institutional slogans are created to establish a prestigious image for a company. Relying on this image to enhance their products and services, many firms insist that their slogans appear in all of their advertising and on their letterheads. An entire ad may feature the slogan. Some institutional slogans are familiar:

You're in Good Hands With Allstate

Allstate Insurance

The Document Company

Xerox

Just Imagine

NEC Multimedia

America's Supermarket

Winn Dixie

Hard-Sell Slogans

These capsules of advertising change with campaigns. They epitomize the special significant features of the product or service being advertised, and their claims are strongly competitive.

Get Met. It Pays

MetLife

Where To Get It.

Sherwin-Williams

Eat What You Like.

Healthy Choice

A Different Kind of Company. A Different Kind of Car.

Saturn

M&M's. The Milk Chocolate Melts in Your Mouth—Not In Your Hands.

M&M's

Slogans are widely used to advertise groceries, drugs, beauty aids, and liquor. These are products that are bought repeatedly at a comparatively low price. They are sold to consumers in direct competition on the shelves of supermarkets, drugstores, and department stores. If a slogan can remind a shopper in one of those stores of a special feature of the product, it certainly has served its purpose. Slogans can also remind shoppers of the name of a product from a company they respect. Not all advertising needs slogans. One-shot announcements—sale ads for which price is the overriding consideration—usually do not use slogans. Creating a slogan is one of the fine arts of copywriting.

Elements of a Good Slogan

A slogan differs from most other forms of writing because it is designed to be remembered and repeated word for word to impress a brand and its message on the consumer. Ideally, the slogan should be short, clear, and easy to remember.

Nobody Can Eat Just One.

Lays Baked potato chips

Nationwide Is On Your Side.

Nationwide Insurance

There's Only One.

Jeep

Where Shopping Is a Pleasure

Publix supermarket

Generation Next

Pepsi

There Isn't a Business We Can't Help.

Ernst & Young

Aptness helps:

Feel the Hyatt Touch.

Hyatt hotels

Trusted By More Women Than Any Other Brand.

Massengill

Solutions for a Small Planet.

IBM

It is an advantage to have the name of the product in the slogan:

Delta.

Delta Air Lines

Kroger. For Goodness Sake.

Kroger

THE CREATIVE WORK PLAN

Before most agencies start creating an ad, they develop a creative work plan to guide them in the right direction. You will recall from chapter 3 the Lintas:Link creative brief consisting of the following elements:

- key observation
- communication objective
- consumer insight
- promise
- support
- audience
- mandatories

The purpose of the work plan is to provide proper direction for the creative team prior to developing ideas, heads, and copy. Exhibit 16.10 shows a work plan format originally developed by Young & Rubicam that is widely used by a number of agencies and is different from the Lintas approach. Note that the work plan emphasizes factual information and research data. The creative process is not a "shot in the dark" but rather depends on knowing as much as possible about the product, the consumer, and the expected benefits. The advertising professional is able to channel objective information into a creative and attention-getting sales message. Many agencies and clients have their own format and style for specific information they think necessary for creative strategy development.

GUIDELINES FOR CREATING AN AD

The following was written by Philip W. Sawyer, editor, Starch Tested Copy, after years of studying Starch Advertisement Readership Studies. Here he offers some specific rules and thoughts on developing effective advertising:[8]

What follows are 10 guidelines that we believe advertisers should keep in mind whenever they sit down to create an ad. As we offer these, we are well aware that any number of ads ignore these guidelines yet are very successful. That's fine. Mark Twain broke almost every rule of grammar when he wrote *The Adventures of Huckleberry Finn.* But he had to know the rules before he could break them effectively.

1. Keep It Simple, Stupid The KISS principle, as this is called, has no better application than in advertising, yet it is probably the most abused principle of all. Here is the best argument for simplicity: a great many magazine readers do not read maga-

---

[8] *Starch Tested Copy,* a publication of Roper Starch Worldwide.

exhibit

16.10

**A Creative Work
Plan**

CREATIVE WORK PLAN

PRODUCT: NEW ORLEANS

KEY FACT
Bevil Foods is a 30 year old New Orleans' based frozen
food company. In 1993, Bevil Foods will introduce a new
line of premium frozen entrees to be distributed nationally.

PROBLEM THE ADVERTISING MUST SOLVE
Currently there is **NO Awareness** of the New OrLEANS Product
among potential consumers.

ADVERTISING OBJECTIVE
To achieve 70% awareness of the product at end of year one.
To communicate the taste and low-calories-fat benefits of the
product.

CREATIVE STRATEGY

PROSPECT DEFINITION
1. Women 25-54, professional/managerial, with household
   incomes of $25,000 plus.
2. Adults 25+ professional/managerial, with household incomes
   of $25,000.

   Psychographically, these people tend to be active, concerned
   with their health, and "on the go" a lot.

PRINCIPAL COMPETITION
Lean Cuisine, Weight Watchers, Healthy Choice.

KEY PROMISE
New OrLeans are lite entrees with the great taste of New Orleans.

REASON WHY
Less than 300 calories; low fat, great tasting, original New Orleans
recipes, served in fine restaurants for 30 years.

MANDATORIES
Must use logo, calorie and fat information, and original New Orleans
recipes in each ad.

---

zines to look at the ads. Therefore, advertising needs to catch the eye quickly, deliver its message quickly, and allow the reader to leave as quickly as possible (Exhibit 16.11, p. 466). Ads that clutter the page with multiple illustrations and varied sizes and styles of type offer no central focus for the eye, no resting place. Because of these visual disincentives for staying with "busy" ads, readers naturally move on, having spent little or no time with them.

2. You're Not Selling the Product; You're Selling the Benefits of the Product An old *New Yorker* cartoon depicts a pompous-looking young man at a party, talking to a young woman. "Well, that's enough about me," he says. "Now, what do you think about me?" Most advertisements suffer from the same kind of egotism. They assume that the reader is as interested in the product as is the advertiser. In reality, most readers do not enter the advertiser's realm readily. They do so only when convinced that the product will do something for them. If an advertiser does not answer the reader's implicit question—What's in it for me?—the ad is unlikely to attract any real interest.

Most ads are simply descriptive; they explain what the product or service is. The worst ads give you a long history about the company, its values, commitments, and size —as if anyone really cares. But the best ads directly address the problems that the product or service solves and suggest how that solution makes life better for the potential consumer.

3. When Appropriate, Spice It Up with Sex Psychologist Joyce Brothers once predicted that "the days of sexy advertising are numbered. The reason is that within five years, the number of marriageable women will be greater than the number of

by giving her red tulips,

you've just declared your hopeless and undying love.

a little strong for a first date, don't you think?

at the corner of fifth and washington. 619/293-7200 | THE FLORAL EMPORIUM

exhibit

16.11

The simple illustration, color, and copy communicate effectively.

Courtesy: Bulldog Drummond.

marriageable men. This will be the beginning of the 'she' generation, which will be a generation unimpressed with sex as a selling point."

Dr. Brothers makes the common (and, it could be argued, sexist) mistake of assuming that men are interested in sex and women are not. In truth, the publications that carry the sexiest advertising today are women's publications. And that kind of advertising attracts considerable notice and readership and will continue to do so until human beings reproduce exclusively by parthenogenesis.

At the same time, it should be emphasized that sexy ads tend to be simple ads—perfectly reasonable because clutter and salaciousness are not really compatible. The best ads of this type may feature nudity, but are not explicitly erotic.

To the politically correct, we say: Sex sells. Get used to it.

4. Use Celebrities   Opinion surveys indicate that Americans do not believe an ad simply because it features a well-known person hawking the product. However, according to our data, ads with celebrities earn "noted" scores that are 13 percent higher than average. They are particularly effective with women readers, scoring 15 percent higher than average, compared with 10 percent higher for men. Overall, ads with testimonials from celebrities score 11 percent above the average, whereas testimonials from noncelebrities actually earn below-average scores. Celebrities may not be believable, but they are very effective at attracting reader attention, the first job of any advertisement.

5. Exploit the Potential of Color   Print advertising has potential to contend with television. The moving image is a profoundly effective means of communication, and anyone who has ever tried to amuse a baby knows that the eye has an inherent attraction to motion. At the same time, the eye is also attracted to bold, bright, and beautiful color. Our data indicate that one-page color ads earn "noted" scores that are 45 percent higher on average than comparable black and white ads; two-page color ads earn scores that are 53 percent higher than similar black and white ads. Generally, the more colorful, the better (as long as the advertiser keeps in mind the other nine principles).

Television has a lock on the moving image, but print's ability to generate astonishing, eye-catching colors is substantial, and publications should do everything possible to stay current with new advances in color technology.

6. Go with the Flow   Every ad has flow to it, and the flow is determined by the positioning of the various creative elements. Ads with good flow send the reader's eye around the page to take in all the important elements: the illustration, headline, body copy, and brand name. Ads with bad flow may attract a fair amount of attention at first, but send the reader off the page. For example, a number of advertisers make the mistake of placing a flashy illustration toward the bottom of the page and the copy and headline at the top. In such cases, the most powerful element of an ad can turn out to be the most detrimental, because that alluring illustration steals attention away from the copy.

For another example, consider the automobile industry and the way some advertisers position the automobile on the page. The eye, our data indicate, tends to follow the car from back to front. Thus, if the car is facing to the right on the page and is positioned above the body copy, the eye, moving back to front, ends up over the beginning of the copy, exactly the right place if you want to have your copy read. But consider how many advertisers position their cars facing left to right, thus "leading" the reader to the right side of the page, the point at which the reader is most likely to continue on to the next page without studying the rest of the ad.

7. Avoid Ambiguity   Although it appears that Europeans accept, if not welcome, ambiguous themes and symbols, we have found that Americans have little tolerance for advertising that does not offer a clear and distinct message. Several years ago, Benson & Hedges attracted a great deal of attention with an ad featuring a man clad only in pajama bottoms and a bewildered expression, standing in a dining room in the middle of what appears to be a brunch party. The trade press evidently was far more attracted to the ad than were readers, who, our data indicated, were as nonplused by the ad as its star was by his predicament, and reacted with considerable hostility to the advertiser who dared to confuse them.

Americans like it straight. They choose not to spend a great deal of time thinking about the messages in their advertising. If the point of the ad is not clear, the typical American reader will move on to the next page.

8. Heighten the Contrast   We live in a visual culture, and one thing that delights the eye is contrast. So advertisers would do well to employ what might be called "visual irony" in their advertising. One suggestion: contrast the content of the ads.

American Express produced one of the best ads of 1988 by featuring the diminutive Willie Shoemaker standing back to back with the altitudinous Wilt Chamberlain. The contrast was humorous and eye-catching. Another way to fullfill this principle is to contrast the elements constituting the form of the ad—color, for example. Our data indicate that using black as a background makes elements in the foreground pop off the page. Stolichnaya earned average scores with a horizontal shot of the product against a white background. When the same layout was produced with a change only in the background, from white to black, the scores increased by 50 percent, on average.

9. Use Children and Animals   Almost any advertising can succeed with an appeal to the emotions, and children and animals appeal to all but the most hard-hearted. It is logical, of course, to use a close-up of a child when selling toys. (Yet flip through an issue of a magazine for parents and notice how many products for children's clothing, for example, do not use children—a missed opportunity if there ever was one.) And pets, of course, are naturals for pet food.

The trick is to find an excuse to use a child or furry little beast when your product is not even remotely connected to those models. Hewlett-Packard pulled this off beautifully by featuring a Dalmatian and the headline, "Now the HP LaserJet IIP is even more irresistible." The ad won the highest scores in the computer and data equipment product category for the 1990 Starch Readership Award. Hitachi has used the double lure of celebrity Jamie Lee Curtis and various animals–cats and parrots primarily—to hawk the company's televisions in a campaign that has consistently garnered the highest "noted" scores for the category.

10. When an Ad Has a Good Deal of Copy, Make It as Inviting as Possible   A source of never-ending astonishment to us is the advertiser who insists on shrinking and squeezing copy into a tight corner of an ad in order to maximize "white space"—a triumph of style over common sense. Others present copy over a mottled background, making it almost impossible to read easily. Two other common problems are reverse print over a light background, offering too little contrast, and centered copy (i.e., unjustified right and left margins), which forces the reader to work too hard to find the beginning of each line. An advertiser who includes a fair amount of copy obviously hopes that it will be read. Relatively few readers choose to spend the time to read most of the copy of any advertisement; if you get 20 percent of magazine readers to delve into your copy, you are doing very well. So the challenge is to make the whole process as easy for the reader as possible. Good content alone will not attract readers. The best-written, wittiest, and most powerful copy will be overlooked unless it is well spaced and sufficiently large and clear to invite the reader.

SUMMARY

Simplicity is the key to great advertising. Good copy speaks to the common man. The great creative shops of today have a common thread running through their advertising—the headline, visual, and logo communicate the idea immediately.

Advertising motivates people by appealing to their problems, desires, and goals, and offering them a solution to their problems, satisfactions of their desires, and a means of achieving their goals.

In general, ads have a definite structure consisting of a promise of benefit in the headline (and maybe the spelling out of the promise in a subheadline), amplification of the story or facts, proof of claim, and action to take. Effective heads can be long or short, but they need to clearly communicate the message. The subheadline can expand on the promise presented in the headline and can provide transition between the headline and the first sentence of the body copy. The body copy is where you build your case with consumers for the product and support the promise in the head or subhead. The details about the product or service are presented here, along with support for your claim.

The creative essence of copywriting is to see a product in a fresh unique way. The chief approaches used to describe products are the factual, the imaginative, and the emotional. A slogan sums up the theme for a product's benefits. It needs to be a memorable message with few words.

Slogans can be developed from several points of view; the institutional and hard-sell viewpoints are the most common.

The place to start planning an ad is the creative work plan or the creative brief. If written properly, the creative work plan will tell you what the message should be in the ad and what the ad is to accomplish. It tells you the ad's specific purpose. However, no work plan will tell you how to execute the copy—that's part of the creative process.

REVIEW

1. What is time famine?
2. How can advertisers use psychological appeals?
3. What are Ogilvy's great advertising elements?
4. What's the purpose of the headline?
5. What is the purpose of amplification?
6. What is meant by "copy style?"
7. What are the characteristics of an effective slogan?

TAKE IT TO THE NET

We invite you to visit the Russell/Lane page on the Prentice Hall Web site at **PHLIP** **http://www.prenhall.com/phbusiness** for the bimonthly Russell/Lane update and for this chapter's World Wide Web exercise.

17

THE TOTAL CONCEPT: WORDS AND VISUALS

IDEAS AND ADS. HOW DOES A CREATIVE TEAM GET FROM AN IDEA TO A FINISHED AD? WHAT KIND OF VISUALS ARE BEST? HOW DO WE GENERATE FRESH IDEAS? AFTER READING THIS CHAPTER YOU WILL UNDERSTAND

- **concepts and executional ideas**
- **left- and right-brain ideas**
- **how a creative team works**
- **visualizing the idea**
- **principles of design**
- **kinds of visuals.**

What are some of the great ads you remember from your growing-up years? Why do you remember them? There probably was an idea that was relevant or entertaining to you. Our minds work in mysterious ways. We have to learn to take the reader or viewer beyond the strategy. We also need to go beyond style into a magical dimension. Classic campaigns did this: Brylcream's *Greasy Kid Stuff,* Avis's *We're Only No. 2,* Volkswagen's *Lemon,* Wendy's *Where's the Beef,* and AT&T's *Reach Out and Touch Someone.* Before we can create this kind of advertising, we have to learn to develop the idea behind the strategy.

George Lois, the outrageous art director, was once asked, "What is advertising?" He answered, "Advertising is poison gas. It should bring tears to your eyes, and it should unhinge your nervous system. It should knock you out." He admitted that his description is probably excessive but regards it as a forgivable hyperbole because it certainly describes the powerful *possibilities* of advertising. Great advertising should have the impact of a punch in the mouth. Great advertising should ask, without asking literally, "Do you get the message?" And the viewer should answer, without literally answering, "Yeah, I got it!" Lois says all of this can be accomplished with the "big idea."

The creative process can be broken down into four basic areas: concepts, words, pictures, and the medium or vehicle used to present them. The dictionary defines a concept as a general notion or idea, an idea of something formed by mentally combining all its characteristics or particulars. In advertising, the **total concept** is a fresh way of looking at something—a novel way of talking about a product or service, a dramatic new dimension that gives the observer a new perspective. A concept is an *idea*. Many in advertising, including Lois, call it the big idea—one that is expressed clearly and combines words and visuals. The words describe what the basic idea is, and the visuals repeat what the words say or, even better, reinforce what the words say or provide a setting that makes the words more powerful.

Your creative concept must not only grab attention, it must also get across the main selling point and the brand name. How often has someone seen a compelling ad only to later say, "I don't remember the brand name or product." The Pepto-Bismol ad created by Leo Burnett–Toronto (see Exhibit 17.1) combines the head and visuals to communicate a single thought.

Total concept
The combining of all elements of an ad—copy, headline, and illustrations—into a single idea.

e x h i b i t

17.1

Copy and visual work together in this Pepto-Bismol ad.

Courtesy: Leo Burnett—Toronto and Pepto-Bismol.

LETS YOU STOMACH IT.

IDEAS COME FROM THE LEFT AND RIGHT BRAIN

The left hemisphere of the brain provides reasoning, controls verbal skills, and processes information (characteristics of copywriters). The right side provides intuition, processes information, controls the creative process, thinks nonverbally, responds to color, and is artistic (characteristics of art directors). So we are talking about a left-brain person and a right-brain person working together to develop a concept. Each comes to the table with a different point of view.

Having created a host of memorable campaigns—"Millertime," "Soup Is Good Food," "Things Go Better With Coke," "Tastes Great, Less Filling"—Bill Backer, in his *The Care and Feeding of Ideas,* defines a *basic idea* or concept as an abstract answer to a perceived desire or need. And an **executional idea** is a rendering in words, symbols, sounds, colors, shapes, forms, or any combination thereof, of an abstract answer to a perceived desire or need. We use *execute* in ad development. It is a schizophrenic verb. It means to complete or put into effect or to use according to a pattern—as a work of art. Of course, it also means "to put to death."

THE CREATIVE TEAM

In general, the responsibility for the visual, layout, and graphics is that of the art director. The copywriter has the job of creating the words for the ad, and maybe the ad concept. We say "maybe" because where creative teams are used it is the responsibility of the team to develop a concept. The copywriter needs to understand art direction and the art director needs to appreciate the impact of words. Together they need to have a rapport to be successful. Both are concept thinkers. Both think in terms of words and pictures, after the team arms themselves with all the information they need. When they have settled on a target audience and a creative strategy, these left- and right-brain people begin to create.

This relationship between copywriter and art director is almost like a marriage. You spend an average of 8 hours a day with your partner—that's 40 hours a week, or 2,080 hours a year. The truth is, better teams feed off each other. Each has their own method of developing big ideas. But there probably isn't a single method. Dick Lord, chairman of The Lord Group, says, "I get my biggest drawing pad and I'll draw little thumbnails and I'll just do headlines or visual ideas. I'll brainstorm myself. I'll sit by myself and do 60, 70—I don't edit them. And then you go over them a little later and you find that maybe 10 or 12 that you could look at again. Then, you get with your art director partner, and say, 'Well, what have you got? I have this.'"

THE IDEA

Strong ideas may be difficult to develop but are worth fighting for when you find one. Strong ideas are simple ideas. People do not remember details as clearly as they recall concepts. In advertising, simple concepts become great ads through attention to detail—the words, typestyle, photography, and layout. A great advertising concept might survive poor execution, but the better crafted the ad, the better the chances that prospects will become customers.

We are not necessarily talking about hitting home runs with breakthrough advertising. We are not talking about Nike, Coke, or Pepsi, or glamorous products. We are talking about ideas that solve problems and communicate to consumers. Ogilvy & Mather took the declining Lever Brothers' Surf detergent brand and increased their sales by more than 20 percent by telling it like it is—doing laundry is a drag and there's no point in trying to deny it. Research showed that 45 percent of all laundry-doers do laundry only as a last resort. Lever's even has a name for them—the un-laundry peo-

---

Executional idea
It is a rendering in words, symbols, sounds, colors, shapes, forms, or any combination thereof, of an abstract answer to a perceived desire or need.

ple. The campaign's idea was to accentuate the negative by playing up the drudgery of doing laundry in a light-hearted way.

The idea must come alive, leap off the page, or grab your senses while you watch television. In addition, creative ideas do two important things: (1) They make the prime prospect consider your product first. (2) They implant your brand name indelibly in the prospect's mind and connect it to the positive attributes of your products.

Visualizing the Idea

At this stage of the process, the creative team forms mental pictures of how the basic appeal can be translated into a selling message. It is time to execute the big idea. Just as a good novel has various subplots that are brought together in a creative and interesting, cohesive story line, a good ad has a well-coordinated layout that flows well to create a compelling message about the product and its benefits.[1] You might visualize a sports car as speeding on a mountain road and around hairpin curves. You might see a sedan of understated luxury in front of a country club.

These mental pictures can be shown in words or in the crudest sketches. The crucial thing is to imagine the kind of mental picture that best expresses your idea. While thinking in the visual form, find the words that work with the visual for the most powerful effect. Make as many versions of the basic idea as you can. Stretch your idea to the limit. Remember, Dick Lord said he sketched 70 rough ideas with heads. There is no magic number, some creative teams may do twice that number. Try every possibility, but remember your end result must deliver the basic message and the brand name. Does the illustration and copy deliver the creative work plan promise?

Marketing Approach to Visualization

We know that ads are not created for the sake of creativity. Each ad is created for a specific marketing purpose. All ads for a product should conform to the same set of objectives, even though some ads may not appear to be related, and usually they use the same theme or slogan in each ad.

Using all the information you have about the product or service, write a statement of the one thing you need to say about the product to the prime prospect. This is your promise, or the basic theme. A family restaurant might shift to low-fat menu items and promise, "We offer you all the things you like about family-style restaurants—convenience, great tasting foods, and reasonable prices, with the added benefit of fitting into your lifestyle since you want food that is nutritious and good for you." The illustrations must reflect these marketing concepts.

The promise is a consumer benefit statement that tells the prospect what the product will do for them.

THE CREATIVE LEAP

Are we about ready to begin to create an ad? Yes, if we have done our homework. Joseph Wallas, a creative theorist, said creativity is the product of four developmental stages: preparation, incubation, illumination, and verification or evaluation. A Leo Burnett creative director has said, "The best creative comes from an understanding of what people are thinking and feeling. Creativity is a sensitivity to human nature and the ability to communicate it." Starch Research suggests that we have to evaluate the consumer, address the consumer's needs, and suggest the clear benefit of using the product: "Tell her how her life will change for the better if she uses the product, and she'll pay close attention."

---

[1]Roper Starch Worldwide, Inc., *Starch Tested Copy,* Vol. 5, No. 3, p. 4.

Where does the inspiration come from? Some think brainstorming or free association is the answer to creative inspiration, but others say very few ideas come from these techniques. A crazy idea may be the spark for a great campaign. The idea usually comes when you are not looking. The process is one part reason, one part heart, and one big part simple intuition, say others. So the creative leap is not necessarily the same for everyone. There may be truth that you spend more time on the logical process, and then the emotional part comes easier. Once you get the idea—the concept and visual and words that work together—you've made the creative leap. Leonard Monahan developed a visual idea for North protective work gloves that got right to the point of product advantage by using a wet sponge cut out in the shape of a hand as the illustration. The headline read, "This is what your hand looks like to most toxic chemicals." The headline and visual spoke to the reader as one. A mundane product became the most talked-about ad in its industry.

Everyone's Racquet shows the Extender Series racquet. The headline says, "The politically correct way to humiliate and degrade another human being." The body copy says, "The Extender Series isn't about playing fair. It's about making opponents question their very existence." The visual and copy work well together, but the important thing is that it reflects the idea of how tennis players think and are competitive. The benefit is wrapped in wry humor. The ad is creative, yet it communicates the benefits (see Exhibit 17.2).

Layout

The creative leap is only the first step in ad making. The ad itself has a variety of elements: headlines, illustration, copy, logotype, maybe a subheadline, several other illustrations of varying importance, a coupon—the number of components varies tremendously from ad to ad. Putting them all together in an orderly form is called making up the layout of the ad. **Layout** is another of those advertising terms that is used in two senses: It means the total appearance of the ad—its overall design, the composition of its elements; it also means the physical rendering of the design of the ad—a blueprint for production purposes. You will hear some say: "Here's the layout," while handing another person a typed or keyboarded copy and a drawing. Right now, we are talking about the layout as the overall design of the ad.

Layout
A working drawing (may be computer developed) showing how an ad is to look. A printer's layout is a set of instructions accompanying a piece of copy showing how it is to be set up. There are also rough layouts, finished layouts, and mechanical layouts, representing various degrees of finish. The term *layout* is also used for the total design of an ad.

Layout Person as Editor

Although the person who creates the visual idea may be the same as the one who makes the layout, the two functions are different. The visualizer translates an idea into visual form; a layout person uses that illustration and all the other elements to make an orderly, attractive arrangement.

Before putting pencil to paper, however, the layout person—usually an art director—and the writer review all of the elements. The first task is to decide what is most important. Is it the headline? The picture? The copy? How important is the package? Should the product itself be shown, and if so, should it be shown in some special environment or in use? Is this ad to tell a fast story with a picture and headline, or is it a long-copy ad in which illustration is only an incidental feature? The importance of the element determines its size and placement within the ad.

Working Hard to Get Noticed

Attracting attention. Getting noticed. High visibility. No matter how you say it, this is the primary creative objective of an ad. Today's advertising has to work very hard to get noticed. You cannot rely on strategy alone—the positioning, the product appeals, the demographic and psychographic data that tell you what wavelength the consumer is on—to sell the consumer. Obvious as it sounds, you cannot sell people until you attract their attention. Put another way, people are not going to read the ad if they do not see it. Remember, your ad is competing with all the advertising clutter and editorial matter in a publication. Unfortunately, most ads in most publications are invisible.

All the creative elements—the visual, the headline, the copy—must be strongly executed if the ad is to succeed (Exhibit 17.3, p. 476). Research cannot tell us which creative techniques will work best because creative is not that scientific. Research generally tells us what has been successful, but there are no yardsticks to measure breakthrough advertising ideas. The basic guidelines for writing and designing ads are helpful, but there are not really any rules. How do you get an ad to stand out? The illustration is usually the key. Either an ad grabs people or it does not, and most often it is the illustration that gets them. Of course, many illustrations cannot tell the story alone—they require a headline to complete the communication. So the headline is extremely important to keep people's interest.

A picture is worth a thousand words, but we do not use illustrations solely to attract attention. They must have a strong relationship to the selling concept. Using a shock visual merely to gain attention is generally a mistake. If you are selling a hammer and your dominant visual is a woman in a bikini, you are using sexist imagery that has no relationship to the product. You are duping people. *Now that we have your attention, buy our hammer.* And because most people dislike being duped, they will resent your ad—and often your product as well. Yet, powerful images can demand your attention. The frog in the RemoteWare ad is a compelling visual. The product provides the foundation of remote and mobile computer users to communicate with the office and each other fast (see Exhibit 17.4, p. 476).

There are three basic means of attracting attention:

1. using the visual alone
2. using the headline alone
3. using a combination of the visual and headline

See how the illustration and the copy balloon attract attention in Exhibit 17.5 (p. 477). This is a very simple visual concept that works.

Do not assume that because we listed the visual first that the art director is more important than the copywriter. Remember, they are a team working together on both visual and language ideas.

---

exhibit

17.3

How do you communicate about vein grafts for coronary bypass or transplants? CryoVein illustrates through the visual, headline, or copy.

Courtesy: Aydlotte & Cartwright.

exhibit

17.4

The size and color of this frog asks for the reader's attention. Generally, large interesting illustrations attract attention.

Courtesy: The Zimmerman Agency and RemoteWare.

Basic Design Principles

There are some general principles that guide the design of advertising and promotional layouts. Some art directors may use different terminology from that used here, but the basic assumptions are the same.

The following design principles, properly employed, will attract the reader and enhance the chances that the message is read.

Unity   All creative advertising has a unified design. The layout must be conceived in its entirety, with all its parts (copy, art, head, logo, and so forth) related to one another to give one overall, unified effect. If the ad does not have unity, it falls apart and becomes visual confusion. Perhaps unity is the most important design principle, but they are all necessary for an effective ad.

Harmony   Closely related to unity is the idea that all elements of the layout must be compatible. The art director achieves harmony by choosing elements that go together.

This process is similar to dressing in the morning. Some items of clothing go together better than others—for example, stripes, plaids, or paisleys with solid colors. The layout needs harmonious elements to be effective; there should not be too many different type faces or sizes, illustrations, and so on.

Sequence   The ad should be arranged in an orderly manner so it can be read from left to right and top to bottom. The sequence of elements can help direct the eye in a structural or gaze motion. Place the elements so that the eye starts where you want it to start and travels a desired path throughout the ad. "Z" and "S" arrangements are common.

Emphasis   Emphasis is accenting or focusing on an element (or group of elements) to make it stand out. Decide whether you want to stress the illustration, the headline, the logo, or the copy. If you give all of these elements equal emphasis, your ad will end up with no emphasis at all.

Contrast   You need differences in sizes, shapes, and tones to add sparkle so the ad will not be visually dull. Altering type to bold or italic or using extended typefaces brings

exhibit

17.6

Formal design makes
this ad communicate
sophistication.

Courtesy: McCann-Erickson
Worldwide and Gillette
Stationery Products Group.

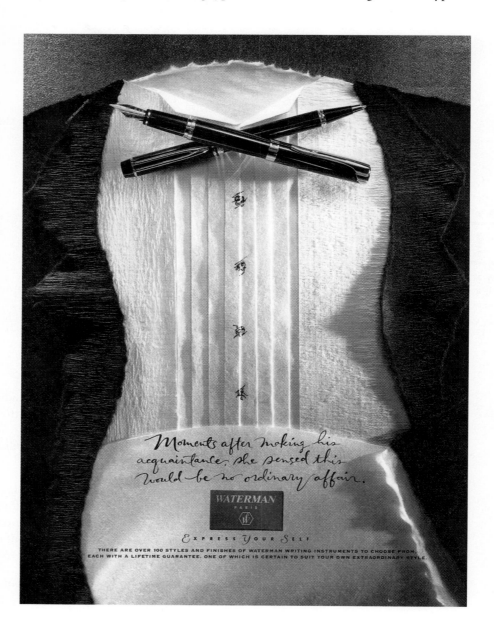

attention to a word or phrase and creates contrast between type elements. Contrast makes the layout more interesting.

Balance By balance, we mean controlling the size, tone, weight, and position of the elements in the ad. Balanced elements look secure and natural to the eye. You test for balance by examining the relationship between the right and left halves of the ad. There are basically two forms of balance: formal and informal.

Formal Balance The Waterman ad (Exhibit 17.6) signals sophistication and graphically has elements of equal weights, sizes, and shapes on the left and right sides of an imaginary vertical line drawn down the center of the ad. Such symmetrical ads give an impression of stability and conservatism. For example, Central Carolina Bank wants to show the stability of their telebanking in Exhibit 17.7.

Informal Balance The optical center of a page, measured from top to bottom, is five-eighths of the way up the page; thus, it differs from the mathematical center. (To test this, take a blank piece of paper, close your eyes, then open them, and quickly place a dot at what you think is the center of the page. The chances are that it will be above the mathematical center.) Imagine that a seesaw is balanced on the optical center. We know that a lighter weight on the seesaw can easily balance a heavier one by being

1 · 8 0 0 · 4 · C C B · B A N K CCB telebanking

farther away from the fulcrum. (The "weight" of an element in an ad may be gauged by its size, its degree of blackness, its color, or its shape.) In informal balance, objects are placed seemingly at random on the page, but in such relation to one another that the page as a whole seems in balance. This type of arrangement requires more thought than the simple bisymmetric formal balance, but the effects can be imaginative and distinctive, as illustrated by Exhibit 17.8.

Other Composing Elements

Color   One of the most versatile elements of an ad is color. It can attract attention and help create a mood. Depending on the product and the advertising appeal, color can be used for a number of reasons.

exhibit

17.8

This informal balance ad for animals & things expresses visual freedom.

Courtesy: West & Vaughan and animals & things.

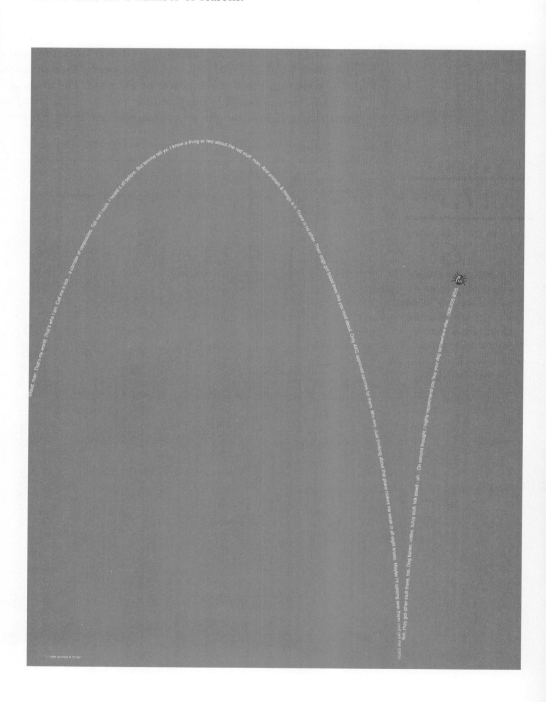

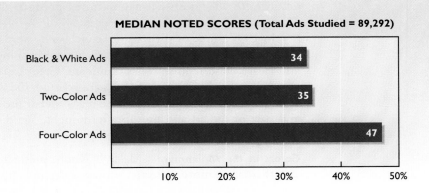
MEDIAN NOTED SCORES (Total Ads Studied = 89,292)

Black & White Ads	34
Two-Color Ads	35
Four-Color Ads	47

10% 20% 30% 40% 50%

A classic example of a product using color to differentiate itself was Nuprin analgesic tablets. It increased its share of the ibuprofen market by using a superficial product difference—the yellow tablet. Nuprin's ads that simply said research showed two Nuprins gave more headache relief than Extra Strength Tylenol did not advance its share. Grey Advertising's Herb Lieberman said, "You have to convince consumers that your product is different before they will believe the product is better." The color idea happened when their group creative director emptied a whole bunch of pain relievers on his desk and found Nuprin was the only yellow tablet there. Color was a way to dramatically and graphically show that Nuprin was different. Thus, the yellow-tablet campaign was born, showing a black-and-white photo of hands holding two yellow tablets. The tagline explained that Nuprin is *for your worst pain.*

Color can be extremely important in everything from ad layouts, products, and packaging to the psychological messages consumers perceive. Starch Advertisement Readership Service has over the years consistently found that color—bold colors and contrast—adds to an ad's pulling power.

Color Is an Attention-Getting Device   With few exceptions, people notice a color ad more readily than one in black and white. Exhibit 17.9 illustrates that the addition of four-color (using color photographs, for example) significantly increases the average advertising readership score beyond both two-color and black-and-white ads.

Some products can be presented realistically only in color. Household furnishings, food, many clothing and fashion accessories, and cosmetics would lose most of their appeal if advertised in black and white. Studies have been done to find the best consumer color or colors. For instance, the Pantone Color Institute asked consumers to select their current and future color preferences in specific product categories. In addition, a questionnaire collected data on demographics and placed the respondents into five lifestyle categories: prudent, impulsive, pessimistic, traditional, and confident. Advertisers found significant differences for such products as luxury cars versus economy cars. Leatrice Eisman, executive director of the Pantone Color Institute, says, "The impact of color can be used to gain attention to an ad or product. If used out of context, mustard yellow can get enormous attention on the printed page. Use a color out of context so that it is totally obnoxious, for example, a green hot dog. There is no way anybody is ever going to ignore looking at the page."[2]

Predicting Popular Colors   The Pantone Color Institute conducts color research on color psychology, preferences, and professional color applications. Another organization that predicts colors is the Color Association of America, which forecasts color trends for products and fashion. Another group, the Color Marketing Group (CMG), is a not-for-profit association of some 1,500 designers that forecasts trends one to three years in

---

[2]Anne Telford, *Communication Arts,* January/February 1977, pp. 84–89.

advance for all industries, manufactured products, and services. Obviously, these predictions have an impact on advertisers.

In 1997, some of the research conclusions were that dark tones have been replaced by colors touched by the sun. Greens are diminishing in influence; blue remains strong and clearer; and reddish tones dominate. Color can highlight specific elements within an ad, but should be carefully built into the ad. Occasionally, an advertiser will use spot color for a product in an otherwise black-and-white ad. Any color needs to be an integral part of the ad and not an afterthought. We discuss the techniques of color production in chapter 18 and packaging in chapter 21.

Colors in the Millennium   Melanie Wood, president of the Color Marketing Group, says that as we move collectively toward the millennium, colors used in industry, interiors, fashion services, and communication will become brighter, happier, livelier, and more fun—in keeping with the general optimism generated by the event. There is a sense that things are definitely on the upswing, and color choices are being affected by it. Most of the colors you see in today's marketplace are the results of forecasts by the group several years ago.

Wood sees a particular manifestation of livelier colors in the growing popularity of retro colors and styles of the 1930s, '40s, and '50s. She says, for example, that "people will take wonderful, bright colors, combined with a surface coating or veiling, or iridescence . . . what we're seeing is veiled colors—orange tones, sheer coverings, an almost sherbety feeling, or combinations of spice tones, reds, metallics." She says, "Color surrounds us, it is involved in every facet of graphics, of communication, of emotion, and psychology. It is vital that the designers are aware of the impact of various colors, of the nuances, of how they move audiences, since color is, in the end, communication." The CMG Contract Palette Forecast includes

- *Rose Tattoo:* the new coral, a shifting of red-off-center
- *Blue Moon:* a watercolor blue, tranquil and softened, but not too sweet; a twinkle of lavender in the pool of pale blue
- *Back to the Fuschia:* rich, regal, opulent blued-red that complements neutrals, blues, and greens
- *Orange A-Peel:* a citrus trend, clean and usable as an accent or attention-getter; a subdued orange-earth inspired by techno-connected.

Sandra Imre, cochair of the CMC Contract Color Directions says, "We are becoming bolder with color and we are determined to pull our comfort zones from ethnic roots, from nature, from different cultures and create a bridge to a balanced globalized environment." Marketers are taking note.[3]

White Space   Some layout and designers become so preoccupied with the illustration that they forget that white space or blank space is a very significant design tool. The basic rule for using white space is to keep it to the outside of the ad. Too much white space in the middle of an ad can destroy unity by pushing the eye in several directions and confusing the reader.

Preparing the Layout

The layout is the orderly arrangement of all the copy elements in a print ad. It is basically a blueprint that the production people will follow to complete the finished ad. An ad may go through different levels of roughness as it is developed. These different types of layouts represent different stages of conventional, i.e., not electronic, development of the ad.

- *Thumbnail sketches:* miniature drawings trying out different arrangements of the layout elements. The best of these will be selected for the next step.

---

[3]"Millennium Promises Brighter Colors," *Graphic Design: USA,* June 1997, pp. 81–96.

- *Rough layouts:* drawings that are equivalent to the actual size of the ad. All elements are presented more clearly to simulate the way the ad is to look. The best of these will be chosen for the next step.
- The **comprehensive,** *or mechanical, layout* (often just called the *comp* or the *mechanical*): all the type set and placed exactly as it is to appear in the printed ad. Artwork is drawn one and a half times the actual size it will be in the ad (to be reduced by one-third for sharper reproduction) and is prepared separately; therefore, it is precisely indicated on the comprehensive by blank boxes or electronically scanned into position for a computer comp. This layout will be used for client approval.

The rough layout in Exhibit 17.10 uses markers, whereas the comprehensive (Exhibit 17.11, p. 484), uses computer-generated type and illustration. Exhibit 17.12 (p. 485) is the finished color ad as it appeared in the publications.

Once the basic ad for a campaign has been approved, layouts for subsequent ads usually consist of just a rough and finished layout.

Computer Design

The computer serves as a word processor and a typographer, producing heads, text, and even the development design, illustration, and finished layout. Computer software makes it easy to see alternatives to typefaces, illustration size, inexpensive layout modifications, and color changes.

We define *computer graphics* as the ability to draw or display visual information on a video terminal. *Raster scan graphics* is the most common computer display. Each spot on the screen, called a **pixel,** represents a location in the computer's memory. The number of individual pixels will determine the resolution of the image—this is the difference between poor-quality computer-set type or visuals and good reproduction-quality images. The more pixels, the higher the resolution and the smoother the image. The resolution of a screen controls its clarity and sharpness.

Comprehensive
A layout accurate in size, color, scheme, and other necessary details to show how a final ad will look. For presentation only, never for reproduction.

Pixel
The smallest element of a computer image that can be separately addressed. It is an individual picture element.

e x h i b i t
17.10

An Example of a Rough Marker Layout

Courtesy: Folks Restaurant Management Group.

One of the keys of computer design's growth has been the proliferation and sophistication of the software that tells the computer how to operate. Quark XPress and Aldus Pagemaker offer designers professional layout and editing software that have allowed Macintosh and Windows users acute text and graphic handling, and image-creation programs such as Photoshop have increased the designer's productivity. Then there is the dazzling Silicon Graphics (SGI) hardware that allows three-dimensional design graphics high-speed RIP (raster image processing) functions to go on simultaneously. The SGI machines use a UNIX-based language, which makes for faster image processing. We won't get into the specifics here because the technology is changing so rapidly.

Computer design and image manipulation are highly complex because you have to learn the software, and that continues to be a problem, considering all the changes and upgrades. It is difficult for the advertising layout artist to be an expert in all of the software possibilities.

The computer allows development of every phase of creation and production, blurring the distinction between these phases of the process. We talk more about the meshing of computer design functions with production in chapter 18. Here we need to get an appreciation of the role of the computer in the creative process.

Today most agencies do some, if not all, of the layout function in-house on their own computers. However, there are independent graphic computer service houses that are specialists and have the expertise to operate their expensive and highly sophisticated hardware and software for a reasonable fee.

In the past, the creation and production processes have been separate and distinct. Because of the advances in computer hardware and software, it is possible for one person to do both layout and production, although software expertise may continue to

exhibit

17.12

This is the way the ad shown in Exhibits 17.10 and 17.11 looks when it is finished.

Courtesy: Folks Restaurant Management Group.

keep these functions specialized. Today, mastery of layout demands a knowledge of art, type, design, and also photography, computers, and electronic imaging.

The Visual

Research indicates that 98 percent of the top-scoring ads contain a photograph or illustration, proving that human beings are highly visual creatures, according to Cahners Advertising Performance Studies. In most ads, the photograph or illustration takes between 25 and 67 percent of the layout space (see Exhibit 17.13).[4]

exhibit

17.13

The majority of top-scoring ads contain a photograph or illustration.

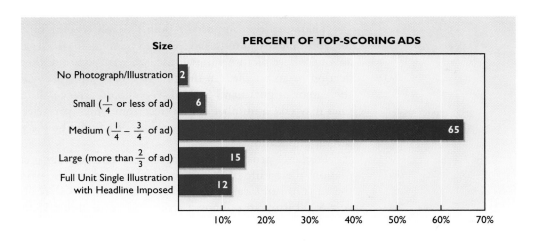

[4]Cahner's Publishing Co., *CARR Report* No. 118.5, p. 4.

Art Directing Photography

Art directing and photography are twin disciplines—each, in theory raises the other up a notch. Having a great photo in the wrong layout makes for bad advertising. Betsy Zimmerman, art director at Goodby, Silverstein & Partners, says, "The layout's gotta come first. I'll bring a Xerox of the layout to the shoot, and we try to do Polaroids to size, so I can put the two together. The key is to shoot a million Polaroids so I can iron out all the idiosyncrasies rather than be surprised on film." It might look great as a photo, but once you put it in its environment it is totally different. Jeff Weiss of Margeotes/Fertitta & Weiss says every ad contains two things: what you want to say and how you want to say it. What art directing can do is deliver things emotionally, not intellectually. Great art direction takes the selling idea and furthers it without your even knowing it. Take Saks, for example. Their ads cannot just say Saks is glamorous in words —it has to *feel* glamorous and sophisticated.[5]

Photography can be very expensive. A photo for use in an ad may cost between $700 and $10,000, depending on the photographer's reputation and the advertiser's willingness to pay.

The Artist's Medium

The tool or material used to render an illustration is called the *artist's medium,* the term *medium* being used in a different sense than it is in the phrase *advertising medium* (for example, television or magazines). The most popular artist's medium in advertising is photography. Other popular ones are pen and ink, pencil, and crayon. Perhaps a photograph will be used as the main illustration for an ad, but pen and ink will be used for the smaller, secondary illustration. The choice of the artist's medium depends on the effect desired, the paper on which the ad is to be printed, the printing process to be used, and, most important, the availability of an artist who is effective in the desired medium.

Trade Practice in Buying Commercial Art

Creating an ad usually requires two types of artistic talent: the imaginative person, who thinks up the visual idea with a copywriter or alone and makes the master layout; and an artist, who does the finished art of the illustrations. Large agencies have staff art directors and layout people to visualize and create original layouts, as well as studios and artists to handle routine work.

In the largest advertising centers, a host of freelance artists and photographers specialize in certain fields for preparing the final art. In fact, agencies in some cities go to one of the major art centers to buy their graphic artwork for special assignments.

There are two important points to observe in buying artwork, especially photographs. First, you must have written permission or a legal release (Exhibit 17.14) from anyone whose picture you will use, whether you took the picture or got it from a publication or an art file. (In the case of a child's picture, you must obtain a release from the parent or guardian.) Second, you should arrange all terms in advance. A photographer may take a number of pictures, from which you select one. What will be the price if you wish to use more than one shot? What will be the price if you use the picture in several publications?

Freelance artists' and photographers' charges vary greatly, depending on their reputation, the nature of the work, in what medium the work is being used, and whether the ad is to run locally, regionally, or nationally. An art illustration for a magazine may cost $200 if by an unknown artist and up to about $5,000 if by an established artist.

---

[5]"Art Directing Photography," *Art Direction,* March 1993, pp. 42–54.

MODEL/PERFORMANCE RELEASE

For value received and without further consideration, **I HEREBY CONSENT** that all pictures/photographs taken of me and/or recordings made of my voice or musical or video performances, may be used for advertising purposes, by **SLRS Advertising, Inc.,** and by advertisers SLRS Advertising, Inc., may authorize or represent, in any manner. I understand that illustrations/ performances may be edited, changed or reproduced in any manner without my approval. I agree that all reproductions thereof and plates, films, and tapes shall remain the property of SLRS Advertising, Inc., or of advertisers represented by SLRS Advertising, Inc.

WITNESS _____   SIGNED _____

SOC. SEC. NO. _____

IF SUBJECT IS A MINOR UNDER LAWS OF STATE OF PERFORMANCE.

GUARDIAN_____

WITNESS_____   DATE_____

SLRS COMMUNICATIONS, INC. / P.O. BOX 5488 / ATHENS, GA 30604-5488 / (706) 549-2664

---

exhibit

17.14

Typical Model Release Used by Agencies

Courtesy: SLRS Advertising.

A photography session may cost $200 a day for an unknown to about $2,500 for an established photographer. People charge what they think the art or photography is worth or what the client can or is willing to pay. As a result, the better the reputation of the artist or photographer, the more expensive the final product will likely be.

Other Sources of Art and Photography

Clients will not always be able to afford the money or time for original advertising art or photography. There are three basic sources of ready-made images: clip art, computer clip art, and stock photos.

Clip Art and Computer Clip Art Ready-to-use copyright-free images are available from clip-art services. The art may be available on CD-ROM or from printed services in which the illustrations are in black and white on glossy paper, ready to use. All you have to do is cut it out or print it off your computer. Almost any kind of image is available from clip-art services: families, men, women, children, business scenes, locations (e.g., farm, beach), and special events. The disadvantage to using clip art is that you have to match your idea to available images, and many of the illustrations are rather average. The advantages are the very reasonable costs and extensive choice of images.

Some clip-art services offer a monthly book or computer disk (or on-line service) with a wide variety of images; others offer specialized volumes—restaurant art, supermarket art, or medical art, for example. Once you purchase the clip-art service, the art is yours to use as you see fit.

Stock Photos There are hundreds of stock-photo libraries available to art directors and advertisers. Each maintains thousands of photographs classified according to the subject categories, including children, animals, lifestyle situations, city landscapes, sports, and models. A photographer submits photos to the stock company, which will publish some photos in their catalog (or on a CD-ROM). The photographer pays for the space occupied by the photos. Clients then browse through the stock company's catalog to research its files for a suitable photo. The art director or advertiser then leases or contracts for use of the selected photo to use in an ad. The fee is based on the intended use of the photo.

Comstock's Encyclopedia of Stock Photography has an on-line access service, which is a computer bulletin board that lets you access and preview your images from one of their catalogs 24 hours a day. They add new images daily. Comstock says, "Stock photo pricing isn't based on the known cost of producing the photo: It's based on exactly how you will use it. The more modest your project, the less an image will cost." Their on-line service is described as: "Your selection, hand picked from our library of more than 5 million images, will be fully digitized and accessible via modem for you to download and review in 4 hours." In the past, the delivered image was in the form of a transparency or chrome image. Many on-line capabilities have been around since 1994 featuring stock-photo agencies that allow ad agencies to select images from an on-line network from numerous stock-photo sources. The agency can select images and then instantly download low-resolution *thumbnail* images for inspection. The image may also be marketed and delivered by means of CD-ROM. Images are scanned, stored, digitized, and reproduced on a CD-ROM.

Other companies offer a whole disc of images—ranging from about 300 to 500 digitized picture files—on a CD-ROM for a single purchase price. The CD technology offers individual photographers the opportunity to market their images on their own CDs. When a user decides to order an image, the computer will notify the company and negotiate fees.

SUMMARY

We have now made the transition from thinking of ideas to making ads. We have started with the primary consumer benefit, the most important thing we can say about the product.

In advertising, the *total concept* is a fresh way of looking at something. A *concept* is an idea. A *big idea* is one that expresses clearly and combines words and visuals. Another way of looking at it is that a basic idea is an abstract answer to a perceived desire or need.

The creative team—an art director and a copywriter—next develops the best approach to presenting the *executional idea*—a rendering in words, symbols, sounds, shapes, and so forth, of an abstract answer to a perceived desire or need. Then comes layout preparation (usually done by an art director), in which the various elements of the ad are composed into a unified whole. Creating an ad that will attract attention is one of the art director's primary concerns. When arranging the elements of an ad, the layout artist has to consider the principles of design: unity, harmony, sequence, emphasis, contrast, and balance.

Ads usually begin as thumbnail sketches. Subsequent steps are rough layout, the finished layout, and the comps. The computer simplifies this process: In computer design, the roughs are no longer rough, and the comprehensives are better because the layout and typography are exact.

In most cases, art and photography are original executions of the art director's ideas, illustrated or shot according to his or her specifications by freelance artists or photographers. When time or money is short, clip-art or computer-art services or stock photography may be used.

REVIEW

1. What is the big idea?
2. What is the executional idea?
3. What do art directors and copywriters do?
4. What are the basic means of attracting attention?
5. What is the difference between a thumbnail and a rough layout?
6. What are stock photos?

TAKE IT TO THE NET

We invite you to visit the Russell/Lane page on the Prentice Hall Web site at **PHLIP** **http://www.prenhall.com/phbusiness** for the bimonthly Russell/Lane update and for this chapter's World Wide Web exercise.

18

PRINT PRODUCTION

CHAPTER OBJECTIVES

THE AGE OF DIGITAL PRODUCTION IS ALMOST COMPLETE. MANY PUBLICATIONS AND PRINTERS HAVE INSTITUTED COMPUTER-TO-PLATE PRODUCTION SYSTEMS OVER THE PAST FEW YEARS; HOWEVER, ADVERTISING PRODUCTION HAS BEEN BEHIND THE CURVE. TODAY, BOTH TRADITIONAL AND DIGITAL PRODUCTION EXIST. AFTER READING THIS CHAPTER YOU WILL UNDERSTAND

- production department
- digital and traditional production processes
- mechanical and artwork
- proofing.

It is important for advertising and marketing people to understand what happens after a print ad, collateral, or promotion has been written, the layout prepared, and the illustrations completed. What is the next step? What do we need to send to the publication so they can print the piece? What are the preparation steps and printing procedures for the brochure or insert? Do I need to use traditional or digital methods of production? How long will this take?

Advertising and marketing people need to have a working knowledge of production because it involves quality, cost, and time issues. This conversion process, going from the original layout to a finished piece (see Exhibit 18.1), is the responsibility of the advertiser or agency, and is called *print production.* Production requirements differ from ad to ad. Advertising and marketing staff may be producing magazine or newspaper ads, collateral brochures, direct response, outdoor, and transit. They need a working knowledge of all these production processes, as well as publication mechanical specifications. The planning process may involve a great deal of money and people. Before we get into the organization, let us look at some important issues.

exhibit

18.1

A Finished Ad

Courtesy: Ingalls Advertising.

THE AGE OF DIGITAL ADVERTISING AND PRODUCTION

You might think the age of digital advertising is upon us—creating the ad on a computer and going directly from computer files to making printing plates. The situation is not quite as clear as you might think, however. The more appropriate scenario is that we are almost in the digital age of advertising. Yes, most ads are created on a computer, but much of the production still involves converting the ad from the computer screen to film for the publication or printer. To some extent, the advertising industry controls only a portion of their production efforts. If you have a print ad going into a publication, the publication sets its own specifications standards of how ads are to be produced and presented. Today, some publication production is primarily traditional; however, many publications are attempting to use only digital, with others using varying degrees of both traditional and digital. Traditional production requires converting all of the ad elements to film and then to plates. Total digital production is converting the computer images to plates, bypassing any film.

In this chapter we are forced to think in terms of both—traditional printing and digital production. It may be some time before *all* ads and printing are produced totally in digital formats in all publications. But there is no doubt we are entering the age of digital advertising. Publishers have been ahead of advertisers in converting to this technology.

For the most part, the creation of an ad is primarily digital. Publication's prepress operations may be a combination of digital and traditional. Once the press has a plate made from either technology, the printing process is generally traditional.

In 1997, only 10 percent of advertisers using *Scientific American* magazine supplied ads in digital files. The publication itself has been using computer-to-plate (CTP) printing technology since 1996. The publication has to scan any films submitted by advertisers in order to deliver a digital datastream to their printer. The magazine requests digital ads from advertisers, but still accepts film. That appears to be the norm.

Many publishers are trying to educate their salespeople, advertisers, media buyers, and ad production departments about the direct financial benefits of an all-digital workflow. Until the concept is sold, however, production will involve both film and digital ads.

Time, Inc. has moved all of its publications to 100 percent CTP. They want all ads to be digital. However, in reality they too are receiving a relatively low percentage of their advertising in digital format. Peter Miers, director of imaging and transmission systems at *Time,* explains that the publisher is working with specific ad agencies in a digital partnership to develop procedures for sending and receiving digital ad files. At this point, *Time* prefers digital ads but doesn't require them. They may charge agencies for film scanning. *Time* sends agencies and advertisers a digital ad kit with complete instructions for sending files in two formats: TIFF/IT (tagged image file format/image technology) for color electronic prepress system files; or PostScript for desktop publishing files. Meridith Corp. (*Ladies Home Journal, Better Homes and Gardens,* among others) takes a similar stance in preferring digital ads. Their director of production quality says, "We will continue to do conversion works—how long, I wish I knew." Alan Darling, chief operating officer at Western Laser Graphics, says, "Everyone thinks taking ads digital is about technology, but monetary considerations play an important part as well."[1] The agency production people use what they are convinced is the best method to control the quality of a job for their clients. For many production directors, the digital process has many potential problems that have not been totally resolved despite the promise of speed, economy, and good quality.

Experimenting with Digital Ads

TV Guide has developed a lab to experiment with digital ads. Teleflora first participated in a 1996 November issue of *TV Guide* by creating an electronic computer ad (designed and produced digitally). After the ad was created, both the printer and advertiser okayed the digital proofs (using the Kodak Approval proofing device), and the files then were sent to *TV Guide*'s production facility (in TIFF/IT/P1 format), where they were processed for both gravure and offset printing of the different editions of the magazine. Teleflora saved more than 50 percent in film and conventional proofing costs over what the advertiser typically pays, and reduced the production schedule by three to four days. The quality was good. This can be typical; however, obviously it isn't this simple or everyone would be doing it. Problems with digital advertising are often attributed to technology issues, and there can be many of these, as well as financial issues.

Industry Standards

It appears that digital file transmission formats such as TIFF/IT and Adobe's PDF (portable document format) are close to becoming industry standards, and proofing devices such as Kodak Approval, the Iris, and the Rainbow are becoming more acceptable. Many believe that the real issues aren't technological, but rather financial. The investment can be huge.

PREPRESS PROCESS

What has to be done to the layout design before it can be printed involves the preparation for the act of printing. Here we outline the major steps for the traditional and digital methods.

Traditional: Ad concept: copy, layout, and approvals
                Typesetting
                Electronic color separations
                Layout
                Film preparation
                Platemaking
                Printing

---

[1] Pat Soberanis, "The Wall Came Down," *Folio,* March 1, 1997, pp. 44–46.

Digital: Ad concept: copy, layout, and approvals
                      Scanning
                      Layout
                      Proofing
                      Film preparation (if not CTP)
                      Platemaking
                      Printing

Robert Hannan, director of operations and quality control at Emmerling Post Advertising, looks at some of the processes that have recently changed: comprehensives, type, artwork, and publication material.

Comprehensives, or Comps

In the initial stages, a comp is created digitally by an art director or designer. There are very few "loose" comps (hand- or marker-drawn) today. The comp presented to the client *appears* to be finished. Costs for type, cellos, paper, and studio labor have all been eliminated, leaving only color-output charges for presentation comps.

Type

Typography, photostats, and mechanicals rarely exist. These are subsumed in the digital studio, under the heading of *electronic type/mechanical.* The material costs for typesetting, film, stats, mechanical boards, and studio labor have basically vanished.

Artwork

Art in various forms, such as dye-sublimation prints, is no longer submitted for reproduction. These prints, too, are being replaced by digital processes. The turnaround time for production has significantly decreased, for example, to produce a rush newspaper ad, once the idea is created, the agency sets it in the desktop (several hours), pulls stock photos off the Internet (several hours), then digitally transmits the execution to six daily newspapers (one hour). The total cost of materials to the client is the stock-photo charge plus digital transmission: $550 to $1,200. The material costs are a fraction of what they were 10 years ago, and the turnaround time is slashed from days to hours.

Publication Material

Material for publication used to be manufactured in the photoengraving process. Now, photoengraving charges have been replaced by *separation/composition,* and the average turnaround time has been reduced from eight to one or two working days for the first submission. In addition, the average cost for separations and composition has been cut in half. The cost reductions are due to the advances in desktop publishing and telecommunications, which allow agencies to produce work more efficiently at a fraction of the cost.[2]

PRINT PRODUCTION

The agency's print production group performs that transformation process from the original creative concept to the client's printed communication; this may include magazines, newspapers, outdoor and transit, point-of-purchase, collateral brochures, and direct response. This group must have a working knowledge of all these production processes, as well as publication mechanical specifications, budgetary considerations, and quality requirements. Last but not least, they must understand the time span available for the execution. All of these factors may be interrelated in a complicated manner (see Exhibit 18.2, p. 494).

---

[2]Robert Hannan, "Better, Faster, Cheaper," *Agency,* Fall 1997, pp. 42–43.

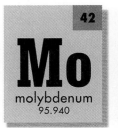

exhibit

18.2

The Zimmerman Agency production people needed to know publication deadlines and basics such as page size and color specifications, to prepare this ad for publication.

Courtesy: The Zimmerman Agency and Capital Culture Center.

These print production people are not merely technical purchasing agents who are knowledgeable and assigned to buying typesetting, printing image carriers, paper, and other graphic arts services. They are graphic arts consultants, production planners, and production liaison people. They function both internally, with the creative, traffic, media, and account management areas, and externally, with graphic arts vendors and the print media.

The size of a print production group is related to the billing size of the agency. A very small agency may employ a single print production expert. In a very large agency, the print production staff, headed by a print production manager, may consist of a considerable number of people with very specialized expertise.

The print operations area encompasses the following:

- *Illustration buyers* are versed in various forms of photographic and illustrative techniques. They know the available talent and make all contracts with photographers, illustrators, digital artists, and others, in coordination with art directors.
- *Typography experts* are trained in the creative as well as technical aspects of typography. They select and specify type, working with the art directors. Of course, in some agencies the art director may create the final type on his or her computer. Or the type director may send the disk to a supplier for final output.
- *Print producers* coordinate all print production activities with the traffic, account management, and creative groups.

exhibit

18.3

These posters were created digitally. Then the agency had to decide how to print them. The print buyer had to be knowledgeable about printers, processes, paper, and so forth.

Courtesy: Greg & Greg Advertising.

● *Printing buyers* specialize in the production planning and buying of outdoor and transit advertising, newspaper and magazine inserts, as well as collateral printed material from brochures to elaborately die-cut direct-mail pieces. A printing buyer's knowledge reaches into properties of paper and ink, and into the capabilities of printing, binding, and finishing equipment (see Exhibit 18.3).

In addition to those functions already mentioned, a large production department may include estimators and proofreaders. Generally, clients require an agency to submit a production budget on work to be done. As a rule, a total yearly campaign production budget is estimated to give the client an understanding of approximately how much ads and/or collateral will cost to produce. Clients must sign off on each project's production cost in advance of the work being prepared. It is important for the production department to supply accurate production cost estimates.

The production department works closely with the traffic department, which sets and monitors schedules of the operation from creative through final production.

PRODUCTION DATA

Production people need to be well versed in the technical aspects of art and type processes, printing methods, and duplicate plates, which we discuss later in the chapter. Let us look first at sources of information for print media. The production person will usually reach for the Standard Rate and Data Service (SRDS) production source—*SRDS Print Media Production Data*—which carries essential production information for major national and regional publications. The SRDS publications for other media (e.g., newspapers, consumer, business) carry closing dates and basic mechanical production requirements, but not in as complete detail as *Print Media Production Data.* Production people must directly contact publications that are not included in the SRDS publications to obtain their production requirements. Of course, each publication determines its own advertising due dates and mechanical specifications based upon printing requirements. Exhibit 18.4 (p. 496) shows some of the specifications for a typical publication.

Mechanical Specification

All national editions are printed offset. The SWOP standards for proofing should be followed

Proofs

Black and white—10 complete proofs.
2-color and 4-color—10 complete proofs and 10 sets of progressives.

Bleed Sizes

Page 8-1/4″ × 11-1/8″

2 pages facing—16-1/2″ × 11-1/8″

For bleed pages keep essential matter 1/2″ from top, bottom and sides of all film, and at least 11/16″ from front bleed edge on both pages of facing page spread.

Live matter in facing pages should not be closer than 1/8″ to center fold.

Publication reserves the right to crop up to 3/16″ from either side of full page film to compensate for variations in trim page size.

Columns	Column Width in Picas	Minimum Depth in Agate Lines
1	13 picas and 9 points	14
2	28 picas and 2 points	28
6	85 picas and 10 points	148

Due Dates

Issue	Color	Black & White
August 9	June 19	July 3
23	July 4	July 11
September 6	July 25	August 7
20	August 8	August 21
October 10	August 15	August 28
24	September 4	September 18
November 8	September 18	October 2
21	October 2	October 16
December 6	October 16	October 30
27	October 30	November 12

Page Makeup

All run-of-paper advertising units are measured in terms of agate lines and number of columns. The width of a single column is 13 picas and 9 points (2 9/32″). Each additional column is 14 picas and 5 points (2 3/8″).

Advertisements exceeding 270 agate lines line depth must occupy full columns (296 agate lines).

exhibit

18.4

1999 Mechanical and Due Date Requirements

PRODUCTION PLANNING AND SCHEDULING

To ensure that the creative and production work moves along with the necessary precision, a time schedule is planned at the outset. The closing date is the date or time when all material must arrive at the publication. Once this is known, the advertiser works backward along the calendar to determine when work must begin to meet the date.

Now that we better understand the production environment, let us take a look at the key considerations in a number of production steps.

Computer Production

Before desktop computers were available, most art directors had only to design, create accurate mechanicals, and specify color breaks or other information on tissues. Now many art directors and/or studio designers working on their computers perform many production steps.

Digital Studios   Some agencies call their computer area an image studio or digital imaging studio, where art directors work on computers to develop the visuals and layout. In some agencies (especially in small or medium-sized shops) art directors take on part of the production. They can design, typeset, do layouts, create tints, scan, separate, produce final film, and in some cases, transmit the job directly to the press or service bureau. The fact is that many of these people haven't mastered all of the complicated steps or haven't been trained to do so. In general, most production jobs will require the services of outside vendors. Most agencies rely on outside services for imagesetting, high-resolution scanning, and printing. There are *output service bureaus,* which offer high-quality PostScript imagesetter output and scanning primarily for those companies or agencies. Then there are electronic prepress shops, which offer imagesetting for computer-generated files. If asked to do so, they will use their expertise in taking care of trapping and other operations necessary to prepare the files for film output. Suppliers can be found for almost every stage of the prepress operation.

Foote, Cone & Belding, San Francisco, established a Digital Imaging Studio in 1989. An outgrowth of having art directors use computers to create their work was that they started doing production instead of working on their next project. FCB's solution was to hire more computer-literate specialists to handle the mechanical art rather than have the ill-prepared art directors perform such tasks. Now, production tasks have been transferred from all their art directors. Graphic people now can use one tool at every step of design and production to develop an entire project. Yes, the concept of one person being the artist, typesetter, copy editor, proofreader, color separator, filmmaker, computer expert, production guru, and so on sounds good; but as FCB found out—it does not quite work in reality. As software gets more sophisticated, it requires an expert to produce the degree of *quality* required by advertising clients.

The future of computer production lies in both the knowledge of the people involved and the sophistication of the hardware and software to perform quicker, less-expensive, quality, computer-generated design and production.

As we have said, most agencies use computers for producing layouts, typesetting, and creating comps and maybe proofs. The sophisticated hardware and software required to equal the quality of traditional production methods have been expensive, although this is changing somewhat. As a result, most major agencies still rely heavily on traditional production methods.

SELECTING THE PRINTING PROCESS

In most cases, the printing process used depends on the medium in which the ad is running, not on the advertiser or the agency. However, in some areas, such as sales promotion, ad inserts, direct mail, and point-of-sale, the advertiser must make the final decision regarding print production. To deal effectively with printers, the advertiser must have some knowledge of the basic production techniques and which is the most appropriate for the job at hand.

If the printing process is not predetermined, the first step in production is to decide which process is most suitable. There are three major printing processes:

- letterpress printing (from a raised surface)
- offset lithography (from a flat surface)
- rotogravure (from an etched surface)

Each of these printing processes has certain advantages and disadvantages, and one process may be more efficient than another for a particular job. Once the printing process has been established, the production process has been dictated, for all production work depends on the type of printing used.

As we have indicated, the prepress operation is in transition from traditional to digital operations. Once the ad, collateral advertising, or promotion has been created and converted to a printing plate, the printing process is very similar to what it has been for many decades. The presses are more efficient now than ever before, but the printing concept is not new.

Letterpress Printing

Letterpress printing isn't as popular as it once was in printing publications; however, advertisers have many uses for this printing process, and you should know the basics. In its simplest form, think of the concept of **letterpress** as follows: If you have ever used a rubber ink stamp (with name, address, etc.), you've applied the principle of letterpress printing. You press the rubber stamp against an ink pad. Then, as you press the stamp against paper, the ink is transferred from the stamp to the paper, and the message is reproduced.

In letterpress printing, the area to be printed is raised and inked. The inked plate is pressed against the paper and the result is a printed impression (see Exhibit 18.5).

Your artwork, photographs, type, and so forth must be converted to a photoengraving (a process of making the plate a raised surface) before printing can occur. The advertiser or agency must supply the photoengraving or duplicates of such plates to the newspaper, magazine, or letterpress printer. In general, this process doesn't reproduce photos as well as offset or gravure. Each of the printing processes has advantages and disadvantages that the advertising person needs to learn over time.

Offset Lithography

In its basic description, **offset lithography** is a photochemical process based upon the principle that grease and water will not mix. In theory, offset can print anything that can be photographed. In reality, there are some things that will not print very well by offset.

Offset lithography is a planographic (flat-surface) process using a thin, flat aluminum plate that is wrapped around a cylinder on a rotary press. The plate is coated with a continuous flow of liquid solution from dampening rollers that repel ink. The inked plate comes in contact with a rubber blanket on another cylinder. The inked impression goes from the plate to the rubber blanket. The inked blanket then transfers or offsets the inked image to the paper, which is on a delivery cylinder. The plate does not come in direct contact with the paper (Exhibit 18.6).

Because offset is a photographic process, it is very efficient and is the most popular printing process in this country. It is used to reproduce books (including this text), catalogs, periodicals, direct mail pieces, outdoor and transit posters, point-of-sale, and most newspapers.

Advertisers or their agencies must supply the artwork and electronic-mechanicals or films from which offset plates can be made.

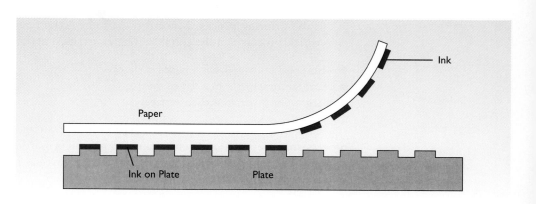

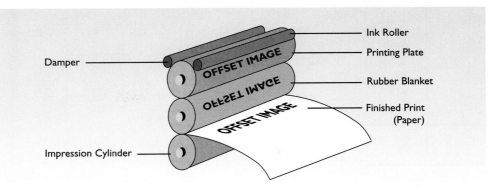

Rotogravure

The image in **rotogravure** printing is etched below the surface of the copper printing plate—the direct opposite from letterpress printing—creating tiny ink wells (tiny depressed printing areas made by means of a screen). The gravure plate is inked on the press and wiped so that only the tiny ink wells contain ink. The plate is then pressed against the paper, causing suction that pulls the ink out of the wells and onto the paper (see Exhibit 18.7).

Gravure is used to print all or parts of many publications, including national and local Sunday newspaper supplements, mail-order catalogs, packaging, and newspaper inserts. The gravure plate is capable of printing millions of copies very efficiently; however, it is not economical for short-run printing. Rotogravure becomes competitive with offset when printing exceeds about 100,000 copies. When printing exceeds a million copies, gravure tends to be more efficient than offset.

Rotogravure prints excellent color quality on relatively inexpensive paper, but the preparatory costs are comparatively high, and it is expensive to make major corrections on the press.

Sheet-Fed versus Web-Fed Presses

Letterpress, offset, and gravure printing processes can all utilize sheet-fed or web-fed presses.

- *Sheet-fed presses* feed sheets of paper through the press one at a time. The conventional sheet-fed press prints about 6,000 to 7,000 "sheets" per hour.
- *Web-fed presses* feed paper from a continuous roll, and the printing is rapid—about 1,000 feet per minute. Most major promotional printing utilizes web-feb presses.

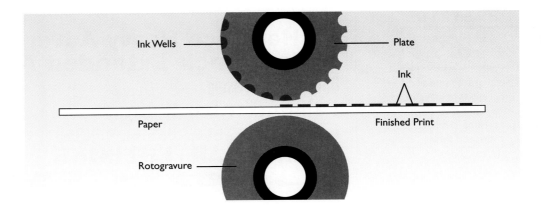

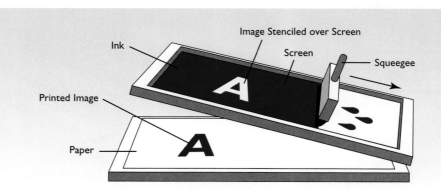

Image Stenciled over Screen

Ink

Screen

Squeegee

Printed Image

Paper

A

A

exhibit

18.8

Screen Printing

Screen Printing

Another printing process, **screen printing,** which is based on a different principal than letterpress, offset, and rotogravure, is especially good for short runs. This simple process uses a stencil. The stencil of a design (art, type, photograph) can be manually or photographically produced and then placed over a textile (usually silk) or metallic-mesh screen (it actually looks like a window screen). Ink or paint is spread over the stencil and, by means of a squeegee, is pushed through the stencil and screen onto the paper (or other surface), as illustrated in Exhibit 18.8.

Screen printing is economical, especially for work in broad, flat colors, as in car cards, posters, and point-of-sale displays. It can be done on almost any surface: wallpaper, bricks, bottles, T-shirts, and so on. Basically, screen printing is a slow short-run process (from one copy to 100 or 1,000 or so copies), although sophisticated presses can print about 6,000 impressions per hour. This expanding printing process is becoming more useful to advertisers.

UNDERSTANDING TYPOGRAPHY

Type has always been an important part of ad design. It creates moods, enhances or retards readability, and gives your communication an image (Exhibit 18.9). It is now more important than ever before for advertising people to understand how to use type because so much of it is being created in-house on the agency or client computer. Before the computer explosion, art directors would use specialists—typesetters or typographers—for type. Most agree that few art directors or designers have as good an understanding of type use as the typesetters or typographers. Getting type up on the screen does not mean that it is typeset effectively. We talk about this again after we learn some of the fundamentals.

exhibit

18.9

85 Helvetica Heavy Adverting
Swiss Black Extended Advertising
Onyx BT Advertising
Palatino Advertising
Caslon Openface Advertising
STENCIL ADVERTISING
Latin Wide

Typography
The art of using type effectively.

The art of using type effectively is called **typography.** It entails a number of issues: choosing the typeface and size of type; deciding on the amount of space between letters, words, and lines; determining hyphenation use; and preparing type specifications for all the ad copy. Notice the differences in type styles, line lengths, and sizes in Exhibits 18.9, 18.10, and 18.11 (p. 502).

TYPE AND READING

The objective of text typography is to provide quick and easy communication. Display headlines are supposed to attract the reader's attention and encourage reading of the body copy. Using uppercase (all-cap) typography does not generally accomplish these objectives.

More than 95 percent of text is set in lowercase letters. Research has shown that readers are more comfortable reading lowercase letters than all caps. Studies have also proved that the varying heights of lowercase letters forming words create an outline shape that is stored in the reader's mind, which aids in recalling the words when they are seen. Words comprised of lowercase characters can be read faster than words set in all caps.

The ideal reading process occurs when the eye is able to scan across a line of copy, grasp groups of three or four words at a time, and then jump to another set of words, then another. The separate stops, or fixational pauses, take about one-quarter of a second each. Words in lowercase letters allow this process to take place. On the other hand,

words set in all caps force the reader to read individual letters and mentally combine the letters into words, and the words into phrases and sentences. The results is a 10 to 25 percent slowdown in reading speed and comprehension.

There are times when all-cap headlines or subheadlines are, graphically, the right thing to use. Design may take precedence over the "rules of communication," or you may not be able to convince a client or art director that lowercase is a better idea. In these instances, words and lines should be held to a minimum. More than four or five words on a line and more than a couple of lines of all caps become difficult to read.[3]

TYPEFACES

The typeface selected for a particular ad is very important. Exhibit 18.12 illustrates the major classifications of type: text, old Roman, modern Roman, square serif, sans serif, and decorative.

exhibit

18.12

Examples of Families of Type

Text	Old English
Old Roman	Garamond
Modern Roman	Century
Square Serif	Lubalin
Sans Serif	Avant Garde
Decorative	Ransom

[3]Allan Haley, "Using All Capitals Is a Graphic Oxymoron," *U & lc,* Fall 1991, pp. 14–15.

Bookman
abcdefghijklmnopqrstuvwxyz
ABCDEFGHIJKLMNOPQRSTU
1234567890$(&?!%',:;)* VWXYZ

Bookman Bold
abcdefghijklmnopqrstuvwxyz
ABCDEFGHIJKLMNOPQRSTU
1234567890$(&?!%',:;)* VWXYZ

TYPE FONTS AND FAMILIES

A *type font* is all the lowercase and capital characters, numbers, and punctuation marks in one size and face (Exhibit 18.13). A font may be roman or italic. Roman (with a lowercase "r") type refers to the upright letter form, as distinguished from the italic form, which is oblique. Roman (capital "R") denotes a group of serifed typeface styles.

Type family is the name given to two or more series of types that are variants of one design (Exhibit 18.14). Each one, however, retains the essential characteristics of the

Helvetica Thin
Helvetica Light
Helvetica Light Italic
Helvetica
Helvetica Italic
Helvetica Italic Outline
Helvetica Regular Condensed
Helvetica Regular Extended
Helvetica Medium
Helvetica Medium Italic
Helvetica Medium Outline
Helvetica Bold
Helvetica Bold Compact Italic
Helvetica Bold Outline
Helvetica Bold Condensed
Helvetica Bold Condensed Outline
Helvetica Bold Extended
Helvetica Extrabold Condensed
Helvetica Extrabold Condensed Outline
Helvetica Extrabold Ext.
Helvetica Compressed
Helvetica Extra Compressed
Helvetica Ultra Compressed

exhibit

18.15

**Major Terms for
Type Height**

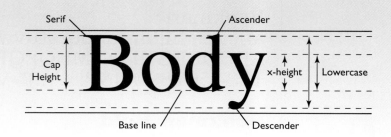

basic letter form. The series may include italic, thin, light, semibold, bold, medium, condensed, extended, outline, and so forth. Some type families have only a few of these options, whereas others offer a number of styles. The family of type may provide a harmonious variety of typefaces for use within an ad.

Measurement of Type

Typographers have unique units of measurement. It is essential to learn the fundamental units of measure if you are going to interact with production people. The *point* and *pica* are two units of measure used in print production in all English-speaking countries. Let us take a closer look at these two units of measure.

Point   A **point (pt)** is used to measure the size of type (heights of letters). There are 72 points to an inch. It is useful to know that 36-point type is about $\frac{1}{2}$ inch high and 18-point type is about $\frac{1}{4}$ inch high. Exhibit 18.15 illustrates the major terms used in discussing the height of type. Type can be set from about 6 points to 120 points. Body copy is generally in the range of 6 to 14 points; most publications use type of 9, 10, or 11 points. Type sizes above 14 points are referred to as *displays* or *headline type*. However, these ranges are simply labels—in many newspaper ads, the body copy is 18 points or so, and there have been ads in which the headline was in the body-copy size range. Exhibit 18.16 provides a visual perspective on basic type sizes.

Points also are used to measure the height of space between lines, rules, and borders, as well as the height of the type.

Pica   A **pica** is a linear unit of measure. A pica equals 12 points of space, and there are 6 picas to an inch. Picas are used to indicate width or depth and length of line.

Em   An em is a square of space of the type size and is commonly used for indentation of copy blocks and paragraphs. Traditionally, it is as wide as the height of the capital M in any type font.

Point (pt)
The unit of measurement of type, about $\frac{1}{72}$ inch in depth. Type is specified by its point size, as 8 pt., 12 pt., 24 pt., 48 pt. The unit for measuring thickness of paper, 0.001 inch.

Pica
The unit for measuring width in printing. There are 6 picas to an inch. A page of type 24 picas wide is 4 inches wide.

exhibit

18.16

**A Visual
Perspective on
Basic Type Sizes**

Advertising (8 Point)
Advertising (10 Point)
Advertising (12 Point)
Advertising (18 Point)
Adverti (36 Point)
Ad (48 Point)

Every Year
We Invest In
Miles Of Line,
Tons Of
Equipment,
And
Thousands
Of These.

Our best investments aren't made in technology or machines: they're made in people.

More specifically, they're made in students. At Illinois Power, we provide scholarships, classroom grants and sponsor various educational programs. Including CHOICES, a program to help young people realize the importance of staying in school.

Because at Illinois Power, we never underestimate the power of a good education.

To learn more about these and the many other ways we're serving the community, stop by an area office, or give us a call.

ILLIN☀IS P*WER
Service You Can See.

Agate Line   Most newspapers (and some small magazines) sell advertising space in column inches or by the agate line, a measure of the depth of space. There are 14 agate lines to a column inch, regardless of the width of the column. Newspaper space is referred to by *depth* (agate lines) and *width* (number of columns); for "100 × 2," read "one hundred lines deep by two columns wide."

Line Spacing   Also called *leading*, line spacing is the vertical space between lines of type and is measured in points from baseline to baseline of type. Lines are said to be set solid when no additional line spacing has been added. Space is added to make type more readable. The rule of thumb is that the extra space should be no more than 20 percent of the type size. Thus, if you are using 10-point type, the maximum extra space between the lines is 2 points, for a 12-point leading.

TYPESETTING

Earlier in this chapter we said that almost all typesetting is performed on a desktop computer. The typographer of the future is an art director or designer—maybe even a copywriter—for whom type is more a means than an end.

Many agencies use low-end laser printers (usually 300 dots per inch [dpi]), which is not high enough resolution for reproduction. However, it is fine for doing layout comps. To achieve high-resolution type, it is not unusual for the computer operator to "dump" the file into a high-quality imagesetter, often at an electronic type house or typographer. There the more sophisticated typesetter (about 3,600 dpi) prints type of reproduction quality. In addition, the typographer's more expensive high-end computers and printers offer more type fonts than the agency generally has on its computer.

ELECTRONIC MECHANICAL AND ARTWORK

After the copy has been approved and placed in the ad on the desktop system with the rest of the ad's material (e.g., illustrations, logos), the advertiser will approve the electronic comp or rough. After approval, the digital file is sent to prepress.

There are several types of art that the production people have to deal with, including line art and halftones in both black and white and color.

Line Art

Any art, type, or image that is made up of a solid color (and has no tonal value) is called *line art*. If you set type on your computer, it is line art (if it is in solid form). Artwork drawn in pen and ink is line art because the ink has no tonal value. Generally, such art is drawn larger than needed for the mechanical so as to minimize the art's imperfections when it is reduced and printed. Exhibit 18.17 contains an example of line art.

Linetint   You can give line art some variation in shades by breaking up the solid color with *screen tints* or *benday screens*. Exhibit 18.18 (p. 506) uses a screen tint to give the illusion of gray and contrast.

exhibit

18.18

Advertising
Advertising
Advertising

The top word *Advertising* is solid cyan color. The second is screened at 50 percent. The lowest word is set at 25 percent of the cyan color. The background is 25 percent black. Creating tints, as done here, can change the look and feel of a word or shape.

This may be done on the computer layout, or the platemaker adds the screens during the film-stripping stage just prior to platemaking.

Line Color Artwork does not need to be in color to produce line plates, in two, three, or more flat colors. Instead, each extra color is marked on a separate tissue or acetate overlay on the base art as a guide for the platemaker, who then makes a separate plate for each color. Line color provides a comparatively inexpensive method of printing in color with effective results (see Exhibit 18.19).

exhibit

18.19

This is an example of using three flat color inks. This line color was created on the computer. The printed matter bleeds on four sides—the printed image extends to the edge of the page.

Courtesy: Folks Restaurant Management Group.

A solid color (flat or match color) is printed with the actual color. The color is specified with a Pantone Matching System (PMS) color reference number, and the printer mixes an ink that is literally that color. It is like going into a paint store and choosing a color swatch and having the clerk mix the paint to match your color. The ink is applied to the paper through printing, and the specified color is obtained.

Halftones

At the end of this chapter we discuss some of the new production technology (including stochastic screening), which may eventually change the way photos are reproduced. At present, the 100-year-old technology does the job reasonably well.

If you look at black-and-white photographs you recognize they are different from line art—they have tonal value. Such photos have a range of tonal value between pure blacks and pure whites and are called **continuous-tone** artwork.

To reproduce the range of tones in continuous-tone art, the art (photo) must be broken up into dots. The art is then called a *halftone*. Halftones may be reproduced either with a printer's camera or digitally; either way breaks the image into dots. Exhibit 18.20 shows the reproduction of a black-and-white halftone. Remember that black ink is black ink and not shades of gray, so the production process must create an optical illusion by converting the tonal areas to different-size halftone dots on the printed paper that the eye perceives as gray. If you look at the printed halftone gray areas with a

Continuous tone
An unscreened photographic picture or image, on paper or film, that contains all gradations of tonal values from white to black.

exhibit

18.20

The halftone is broken into dots to give the illusion of tonal value.

Courtesy: Aydlotte & Cartwright.

THE COLD WAR ISN'T OVER YET.

And there are all kinds of casualties. Unemployment. A family crisis. Or a long-term illness. It could happen to anyone. Add to that the normal increase in energy cost that's needed for heat during the winter months and you're fighting a losing battle.

Warm Neighbors can save the day. Administered by the Energy Assistance Foundation, Warm Neighbors is a non-profit organization founded in 1982 with a $250,000 donation from Illinois Power. When you give to Warm Neighbors, Illinois Power gives too. Dollar for dollar up to $100,000. Thanks to your generosity, nearly 2,000 needy families were sheltered from last winter's chill.

We're always looking for recruits to join our cause. Won't you sign the Warm Neighbors Pledge included in your next energy bill? Or call us at 1-800-755-5000. And help us call an end to the cold war.

WARM NEIGHBORS
FOUNDED BY ILLINOIS POWER

exhibit

18.21

**Magnification of
Exhibit 18.20**

magnifying glass, you will see little black dots and not gray (Exhibit 18.21 shows a magnification). In the traditional process, the dots are formed on the negative during the camera exposure when a screen is placed between the film and photograph (or other kinds of continuous-tone copy). As the film is exposed, light passes through the screen's 50 to 200 hairlines per square inch, and the image reaching the film is in dot form. The size of the dots will vary according to the contrast of tone in the original; this simply means that dark areas in the original photo will give one size dot, medium tones another size dot, and lighter tones still another size dot. The result is a film negative with dots of varying sizes, depending on the tonal variations in the original.

After the halftone negative is made, it is placed on a metallic plate and is exposed to the plate. In letterpress printing, the engraving is splashed with acid that eats away the metal, leaving the dots as raised surfaces. In offset printing, the dots are transferred to the smooth flat plate photographically.

Halftone screens come in a variety of standard sizes. Each publication has its own requirement for the screen size, dictated somewhat by the printing process and paper being used. Newspapers, magazines, and promotional materials printed by offset use screens that generally range from 110 to 133 lines per square inch. In other words, a 133-line screen produces 133 dots to an inch. The more dots per inch, the greater the quality of detail reproduced from the original. The quality of the paper must also increase to accommodate the higher dot levels, which drives up paper costs.

The Halftone Finish If you want to make a halftone of a photograph, the platemaker can treat the background in a number of ways; that treatment is called its *finish*. A few of the techniques that can be applied to halftones include

- *square halftone*. The halftone's background has been retained.
- *silhouette*. The background in the photograph has been removed by the photo-platemaker or the computer operator (Exhibit 18.22).
- *surprint*. This is a combination plate made by exposing line and halftone negatives in succession on the same plate.
- *mortise*. An area of a halftone is cut out to permit the insertion of type or other matter.

Line Conversion A line conversion transforms a continuous-tone original into a high-contrast image of only black-and-white tones similar to line art. The conversion transfers the image into a pattern of some kind: mezzotint, wavy line, straight line, or concentric circle.

Two-Color Halftone Plates A two-color reproduction can be made from mono-chrome artwork in two ways. A screen tint in a second color can be printed over (or

e x h i b i t

18.22

An Example of a Silhouette

Courtesy: Ogilvy & Mather Advertising, Singapore.

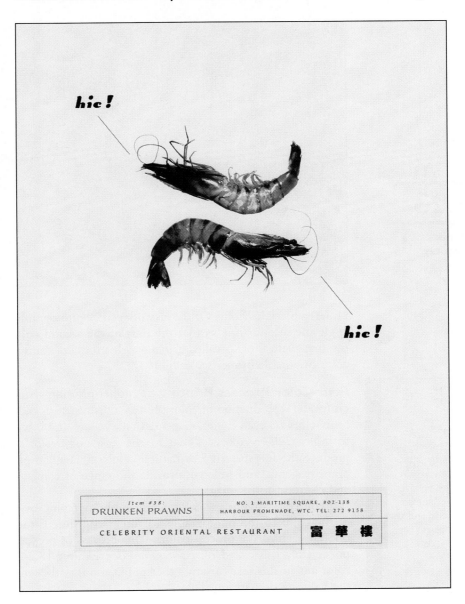

under) a black halftone. Or the artwork can be photographed twice, changing the screen angle the second time so that the dots of the second color plate fall between those of the first plate. This is called a *duotone*. It produces contrast in both colors of the one-color original halftone (see Exhibit 18.23).

Four-Color Process Printing   Another printing system is needed when the job requires the reproduction of color photos. This system is called a **four-color process.** The four colors are cyan (blue), magenta (red), yellow, and black. (CMYK are the letters used to indicate these colors.) These are the least number of colors that can adequately reproduce the full spectrum of natural colors inherent in photography. The first three—cyan, magenta, and yellow—provide the range of colors; the black provides definition and contrast in the image.

Full-color or process color requires photographic or electronic scanner separation of the color in the photographs (or other continuous-tone copy) into four negatives, one for each of the process colors. This process of preparing plates of the various colors and black is called *color separation* (see Exhibit 18.24). If you examine any of the color ads in this text (or any other publication) with a magnifying glass, you will find the halftone dots in four colors.

Four-color process
The process for reproducing color illustrations by a set of plates, one which prints all the yellows, another the blues, a third the reds, and the fourth the blacks (sequence variable). The plates are referred to as *process plates.*

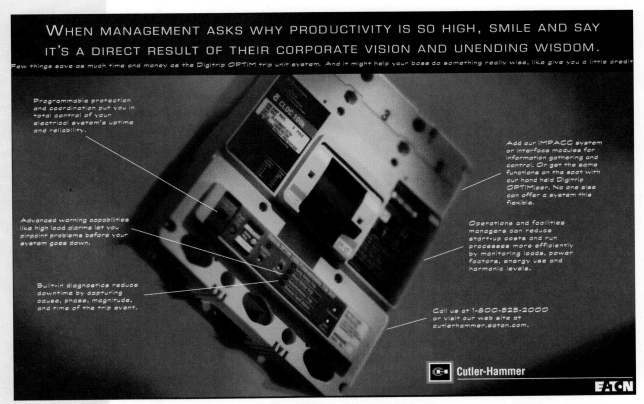

exhibit

18.24

Four-color process printing involves combining four plates—blue (cyan), red (magenta), yellow, and black—to produce the desired colors and contrasts.

Courtesy: Sawyer Riley Compton and Eaton.

Digital Scanners Transforming a photograph into a digital file is done by a device called a scanner. There are two basic types: flatbed and drum scanners. You probably have either seen or used a *flatbed scanner.* These require little training and their quality varies. Printers or agencies use professional scanners that are capable of creating high-quality images. In general, a *drum scanner,* in which the original photo or image wraps around a drum that rotates next to a light source, is capable of producing very high quality results. They are the most expensive image-capturing device on the market. These machines digitally scan the photos to be used in ads. They create the dot pattern used in making a halftone by the traditional method. The important thing to remember is that photographs (whether color or black and white) must be broken up into a dot pattern to print.

Color Proofing

Achieving color reproduction that satisfies ad agencies and advertisers is one of the most crucial roles of the magazine production manager. Agencies generally demand to see a proof before the job is printed. In today's *electronic* color production, traditional proofing systems seem to have taken a back seat to digital color proofers, color printers, networked color copiers, and short-run color production devices.

For the most accurate contract proofs—those requiring the best match to jobs printed by conventional offset lithography—nothing beats a film-based laminated, or single-sheet, off-press proof. An off-press proof ensures the separator that color separations have been made according to customer expectations.[4]

yellow, red, blue, and black plates

(continued)

[4]Richard M. Adams II, "Color-Proofing Systems," *Pre,* March/April 1994, pp. 55–59.

Exhibit 18.24 *(continued)*

yellow plate

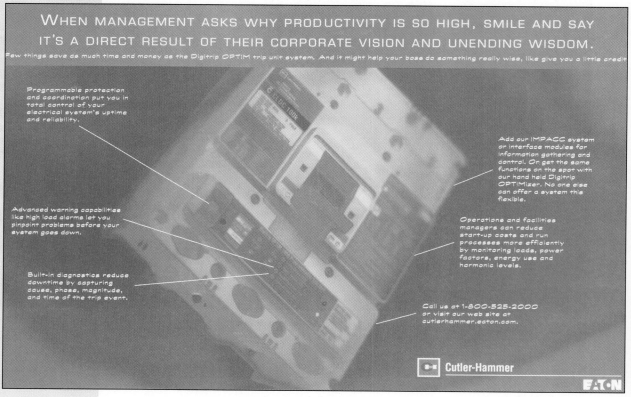

red plate

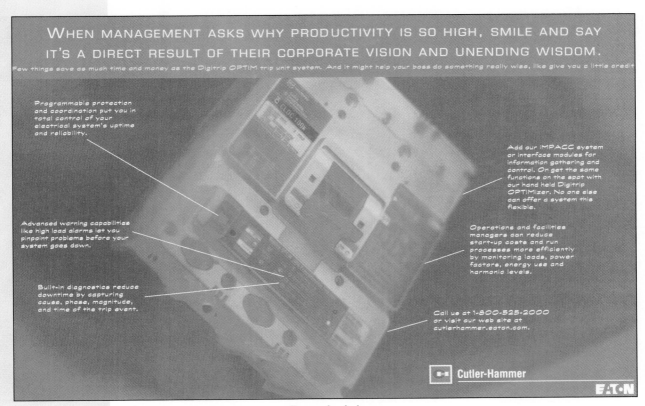

yellow and red plates

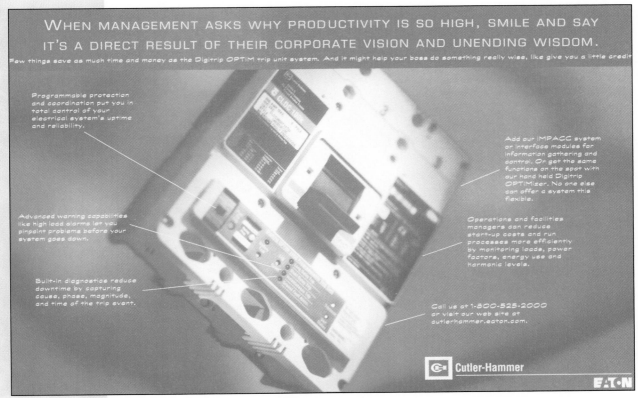

blue plate

Exhibit 18.24 *(continued)*

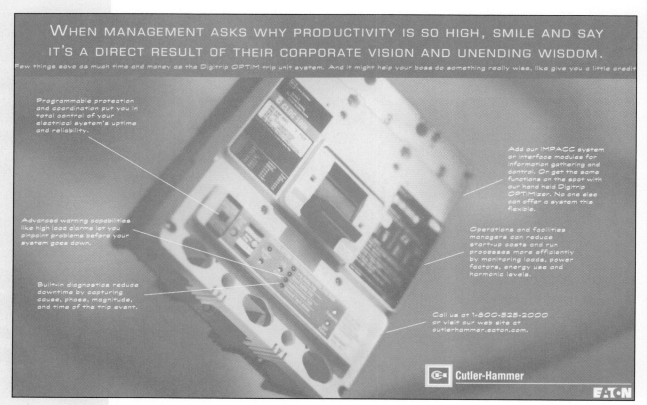

blue and yellow plates

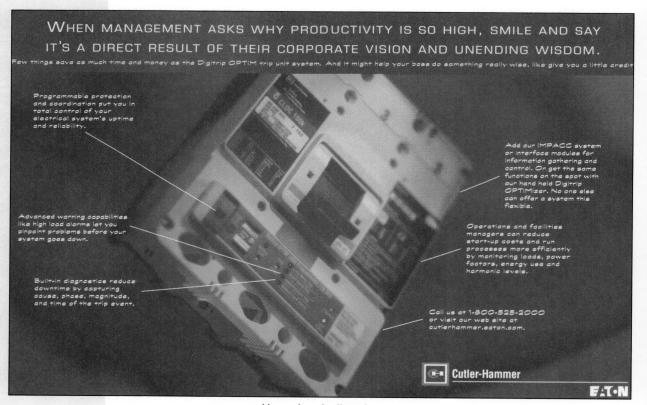

blue, red, and yellow plates

black plate

Press Proofs

For years, press proofs, or progressives, usually made on special proofing presses, were the standard proofs sent to agencies for checking. Prior to the development of off-press proofs, color separators used press proofs. Making a press proof involved stripping the separations on film, making plates, mounting the plates on a proof press, and printing the desired number of proofs. Press proofs are made with ink on paper—often the same paper that will be used for the job—rather than with a photographic simulation process of off-press systems. Today press proofs are still used by many ad agencies who are willing to pay the steep price for what they believe is the most accurate proof. In theory, press proofs provide a virtually exact representation of the final project.

Progressive Proofs (Progs)   These proofs give the advertiser a separate proof for each color (red, yellow, blue, and black), as indicated in Exhibit 18.24, as well as a proof for each color combination (red and yellow, red and blue, blue and yellow)—seven printings in all. After approval by the advertiser and agency, the proofs are sent to the printer to use as guides in duplicating the densities for each color.

Off-Press Proofs

These proofs are made from film negatives generated from the electronic file. The same films will be used to make printing plates. These proofs are less expensive and faster than press proofs, and they are adequate in most cases. Off-press proofs are the typical color proof today. No plate or printing is involved. There are numerous types of off-press (prepress) proofing systems. The most popular are overlay and adhesive proofs.

Overlay Proofs   The development of overlay proofing enabled color proofs to be made from film without using a proof press. The overlay proofs consist of four exposed sheets containing the cyan (blue), magenta (red), yellow, and black process colors, overlaid on a backing sheet. The four overlays (yellow, red, blue, and black) are then stacked to produce a composite image. Because they use multiple, separate, plastic layers, overlay proofs cannot be expected to accurately predict color on press; but they are still used today for checking color break, or general color appearance and position.

Adhesive or Laminate Proof   In 1972, DuPont introduced the first off-press proofing system that closely resembled printed images, the Cromalin system. *Cromalin* is a laminated or single-sheet proof, in which four (or more) layers are exposed separately and laminated together to reproduce the image of cyan, magenta, yellow, and black separations. Cromalins use dry pigments to produce images on photosensitive adhesive polymers or pretreated carrier sheets. Cromalin is generally considered the superior adhesive process. The proofs are keyed to SWOP (Specifications for Web Offset Publications)/GAA (Gravure Association of America) guidelines, which set standards for inks, density of tones, reverses, and other technical matters. Among the highest fidelity four-color proofs are the **MatchPrint** and the Signature proof, both very similar but from different suppliers. Campbell-Mithun-Esty says the Kodak Signature system has enabled their supplier to eliminate one or perhaps two rounds of press proofs, saving them money. These proofs can be made on the actual paper stock chosen by the agency and advertiser. Among the popular adhesive brands are the 3M MatchPrint, Agfa Agfaproof, Hoechst-Celanese PressMatch, and Fuji Color-Art.

There are digital hard and soft copy systems that eliminate film to produce continuous-tone proofs. The soft proofing systems allow production and design people to call up a digitized color image and evaluate it before separations are made for an intermediate or position proof. D'Arcy Masius Benton & Bowles (St. Louis) was the first agency to employ an interactive system that allows artists to make on-screen adjustments to the agency and instantly relay the changes to the printer to be incorporated into the final proof. The interactive system gives the agency more flexibility with deadlines and saves time and money for clients.

Types of Proofs   The choices of types of proof are numerous. Production managers need to decide how accurate a proof is needed, or to put it another way, how much quality they need to pay for. Obviously, they don't want expensive proofs if they are not needed. Here are a number of proof types:

Proof Type	Color Accuracy	Cost
Black-and-white laser	Prints can show color breaks but no color. 300–600 dpi.	Inexpensive
Bluelines	Proofs made from exposing film to light-sensitive paper. They show only a single color image. Uses halftone film.	Inexpensive
Velox	Simple black-and-white proofs made from film on photographic paper. Uses halftone film.	Moderate
Digital high-end	Proofs made from an electronic file. Made by Kodak, 3M, among others. Several processes all meet industry standards. 1800 dpi and higher. Cannot proof actual film.	Moderate
Desktop digital	Usually use ink jet or thermal wax and gives fairly accurate approximation of color. 300 dpi. Needs color management system to give close approximation of color.	Inexpensive

MatchPrint
A high-quality color proof used for approvals prior to printing. Similar to a Signature print.

Laminate/adhesive	Composite proofs are created by exposing the color separations in contact to proofing film and laminating the results. Uses halftone film. Very accurate in color match.	Moderate+
Overlay	Made up of layers of acetate attached to a backing substrate. Each overlay film has an image from each separation color. Colors indicate color breaks, not very accurate. Uses halftone film.	Moderate
Press	Proof run on printing press. Uses halftone film. Uses actual printing inks to give most accurate proof.	Expensive

SENDING DUPLICATE MATERIAL

Most print ads run in more than one publication. Frequently, advertisers have different publications on their schedules, or they need to issue reprints of their ads or send material to dealers for cooperative advertising. There are various means of producing duplicate material of magazine or newspaper ads. Keep in mind that this process in some cases can be done by sending a digital file to the publication. A brief summary of the traditional processes still used by a number of publications follows.

Letterpress Duplicates

There are several kinds of letterpress duplicate plates because publishers may require a specific type of duplicate plate. Stereotypes are still used to duplicate ads for some newspapers. This process makes a paper or plastic mold or mat, which is sent to the paper. The paper then pours hot molten lead into the mat, converting it into a metal stereotype plate. This process is being replaced by photopolymer plates, which are produced on photosensitive plastic. Electrotype is another duplicate plate produced from a plastic mold using a combination of metals; it is very durable and is capable of printing millions of impressions. Cronapress plates (called *Cronars*) can be made with a pressure-sensitive material capable of duplicating the original impression exactly.

Offset and Gravure Duplicates

Duplicate material for offset publication can consist of repro proofs (reproduction proofs) or 3M Scotchprints (a plasticized repro proofing material). Usually, photoprints or reproduction proofs are preferred for partial-page newspaper ads; film is often required for full-page newspaper insertions. Duplicate films can also be made from the original artwork or mechanicals. For color gravure magazines or Sunday supplements, duplicate positive films are usually supplied. For black-and-white offset or gravure ads, photographic prints are often substituted for films.

A number of newspapers use satellite transmission systems to send a facsimile of each page of the newspaper to a reception station, where it is recorded on page-size photofilm. The film is then used to make offset plates, which are placed on the presses to reproduce the newspaper in the usual way. This system permits the papers to run different regional editions utilizing the main news items from headquarters while allowing for variations in advertising content within each regional edition. There are services that can transmit an advertiser's ad by satellite to publications with reception stations in much the same way.

OTHER PRODUCTION ADVANCES

The rapid changes in technology during the past few years have been changing the prepress and printing processes. In the near future, production managers and art directors will have many new options for handling their projects. In all cases, the new technologies are beginning to make an impact on the production and printing processes as we know them. These new techniques range from color separation, color management, and proofing to printing. The following techniques are of particular interest.[5]

Stochastic Screening and Color Separations

Stochastic screening, or frequency modulation screening, is a process for producing incredible tone and detail that approximates photographic quality. With conventional screens, the dots are spaced equally on a grid (e.g., 110 or 133 lines per inch) and the tonal value is achieved by increasing or decreasing the size of the dots. On the other hand, stochastic screening has very tiny dots all of the same size, and their numbers vary according to the tonal value. Used by a quality printer, the image appears to be continuous tone or photographic quality and much better than any traditional process. At this time, few companies produce this process: Linotype-Hell with their Diamond screening, Agfa with CristalRaster, Scitex with FULLtone, and Black Box of Chicago. Agfa and Linotype are processed from a Macintosh platform. These companies offer an advertiser the ability to produce higher-quality color separations, which in turn allows them to print sharper color ads.

HiFi Color   High-fidelity color is expanding what we know and can do with print reproduction techniques and processes. HiFi color was born out of the limitations of the conventional color printing gamut, which are only a fraction of what the human visual system can see. It is a group of emerging technologies that will expand this printed gamut and extend control by improving and increasing tone, dynamic range, detail, spatial frequency modulation, and other appearance factors of print and other visual media.

HiFi color comprises the technologies of stochastic, or frequency modulation screening, four-plus color process and waterless printing methods, specialty papers, films, coatings, and laminates, proofing systems, color management systems, software and hardware.

Color Management Systems (CMS)   The ideal—and we haven't yet gotten to this point in technology—is seeing an image on a screen and getting an exact printed image, or, as it is touted, *what you see is what you get.* This is very important in terms of quality control and design. As images go through the production process, the information is transformed in different ways; for example, as photographic data in the original; as pixels of red, green, and blue on the computer screen; as dots of cyan, magenta, yellow, and black on paper. Software color management systems can bring more consistency to this process, but designers need to know what they can and cannot control. It can be complex even with a color management system.

Waterless Printing   The new technology of waterless printing is gaining popularity; however, the explanation here is kept simple. Most offset presses use a dampening system of water to cover the plate. Offset is based upon the fact that water and grease (ink) don't mix. In waterless printing, a silicone-coated plate is used that rejects ink in the nonimage areas. The result is spectacular detail, high-line screens, richer densities, and consistent quality throughout the press run; in short, great quality.

Other Developments   *Gamut color,* in simplified terms, adds the computer pixel colors of red, green, and blue (actually closer to orange, green, and purple) to the process colors (magenta, cyan, yellow, and black) giving a much wider range of hues for printing. This system may offer expanded color options and quality.

---

[5]Kurt Klein and Daniel Dejan, "New Printing Technology," *Communication Arts,* Design Annual 1993, pp. 283–290.

In *direct-digital printing,* printers are connected to workstations, which take and send files to the press. Film is not used, and in some cases neither are plates. Digital information is transferred onto electrophotographic cylinders instead of plates, and these cylinders use toner to print process color. There are other presses that receive digitized pages onto special plates, often used where the printing runs are short. Presstek/Heidelberg created another waterless printing process that uses no film, no stripping, and no plate processing; has recyclable plates, faster make-ready, and no ink/water balance problems; and is time saving and boasts a reduction in production costs. It has some problems, though; it is basically designed to run good short-run color for jobs in the 500 to 5,000 impression range.

The computer and digitization are spawning most of this advancement in printing and production technology. The day is not far off when the printing and production industry will have a completely filmless, digital process.

The student of advertising production will have to learn these advances in the field, many of which will be both revolutionary and evolutionary, complicating the decision as to which system to use.

SUMMARY

All advertising people need to understand the basics of production. The production terms, concepts, and processes are not easy to learn but are essential to know because they affect budgets, time, and efficiency issues.

Publishers set mechanical requirements for their publications. Advertising production people need to be familiar with sources of information pertaining to print production requirements.

Today most ads are created on the computer (digital). The comps presented to clients appear to be finished. The process from the computer screen to a finished ad in a publication may be completed in a digital or traditional fashion, or a mix of the two processes. The future will involve more computer-to-plate digital production.

There are three basic kinds of printing processes: letterpress (printing from a raised surface), offset lithography (printing from a flat surface), and gravure (printing from a depressed surface). In addition, silk screen or screen printing offers advertisers additional production applications. The form of printing may affect the type of material sent to the publication to reproduce the ad.

Advertisers may use new prepress digital technology or traditional means to prepare ads for production. The publication tells the advertiser what type of material is required or accepted. Each method of prepress has advantages and disadvantages, depending on the degree of quality desired. Typography concerns the style (or face) of type and the way the copy is set. Typefaces come in styles called *families.* The size is specified in *points* (72 points per inch). The width of typeset lines is measured in *picas* (6 picas to an inch). The depth of newspaper space is measured in lines. The space between the lines of type is called *leading* or *line spacing.*

The graphics and production processes can be complex because what you *see* isn't always what really *is.* Continuous-tone art (a photograph) must be converted into halftone dots (may be scanned or use traditional printer's darkroom procedure) so that the tonal values of the original can be reproduced. Line art has no tonal value; it is drawn in black ink on white paper using lines and solid black areas.

Production technology is constantly changing to produce printed materials faster, cheaper, and more efficiently. Achieving color reproduction that satisfies ad agencies and advertisers is one of the most crucial roles of the magazine production manager. There are a multitude of proofs for the production manager to choose from dictated by the need to match colors exactly and the expense involved. "How much quality do we need?" is an often-asked question in terms of which proof to use. Color management systems help advertisers *get what you see.*

REVIEW

1. Differentiate among the three basic printing processes.
2. What is a digital file?
3. What is continuous-tone copy?
4. What is line art?
5. What are color separations?
6. What are the colors used in printing press or four-color?
7. When is a laminate/adhesive proof used?

TAKE IT TO THE NET

We invite you to visit the Russell/Lane page on the Prentice Hall Web site at
PHLIP **http://www.prenhall.com/phbusiness** for the bimonthly
Russell/Lane update and for this chapter's World Wide Web exercise.

THE TELEVISION COMMERCIAL

CHAPTER OBJECTIVES

IT IS ESTIMATED THE AVERAGE PERSON SPENDS MORE THAN 1,500 HOURS EACH YEAR WATCHING TELEVISION PROGRAMS. TELEVISION ADVERTISING IS POWERFUL AND EXPENSIVE. IT IS COMPLICATED BY THE FACT THAT EVERY VIEWER IS A TELEVISION ADVERTISING EXPERT. EVERYONE KNOWS WHAT HE OR SHE LIKES AND DISLIKES ABOUT TV SPOTS. THIS CREATES A CHALLENGE FOR ADVERTISERS. AFTER READING THIS CHAPTER YOU WILL UNDERSTAND

- copy development
- creating the commercial
- producing the commercial
- controling the cost.

Television is the most powerful advertising medium because it blends sight, sound, and motion that can create emotional reactions. Still it poses some problems: commercial clutter that leaves viewers confused about advertisers, loss of audiences, high production costs, and zapping. For example, according to Roper Reports, 38 percent of viewers say they often switch to another channel when ads come on, up 24 percent from 1985.[1] These problems are constant reminders to advertisers of the need to plan their messages very carefully. But it is precisely this adversity that breeds innovation—and creative innovation. Today, 31 percent of viewers say they are often amused by funny or clever commercials (up 5 percent from 1993); about 70 percent agree advertising is often fun or interesting to watch.

In an Ingalls Advertising self-promotion ad, the copy says, "there are a select few advertisements which cut through, appealing to consumers with humor, intelligence, charm and emotion. Yes, there are ads people actually like. Chances are, you like them

---

[1]"Entertained by Commercials," *American Demographics,* November 1997, p. 41.

too. Why? Because goods ads are like good people. They're smart, funny, and engaging. You tend to remember them long after they're gone. . . . Don't even think about getting into consumers' wallets unless you first get into their lives (see Exhibit 19.1). If you knew how to do this, you wouldn't have to read the rest of this chapter. On the other hand, many people who are supposed to know this don't practice it.

One of the things advertisers have to be aware of is that solutions to grab a viewer's attention come and go. Remember the shaky camera, Claymation, morphing an object into another object, or using the oldies film footage? There is a continuing search for some new way to wake up an audience. Simply having a sound strategy isn't enough to make a viewer watch. There must be a sound strategy wrapped in a strong creative idea. We're back to the big idea concept. We take the big idea and blend visuals, words, motion, and technology to create emotional reactions—done properly, this is what makes television the most powerful advertising medium.

AS A CONSUMER, NAME YOUR FAVORITE TV COMMERCIAL.

AS A DIRECTOR OF MARKETING, WOULD YOU EVER APPROVE IT?

There are few things in life the average person loves to hate more than advertising. It's not only because the vast majority of ads talk down to people. Or at people. Or fail to engage them with a single, coherent thought or emotion.

It's that even the best ads are essentially intrusions by somebody who wants to sell you something. With annoying frequency, ads interrupt your favorite television shows, your radio programs, your magazines and newspapers. Worst of all, ads invade your leisure time.

Yet given all this, there are a select few advertisements which cut through, appealing to consumers with humor, intelligence, charm and emotion. Yes, there are ads people actually like. Chances are, you like them too.

Why? Because good ads are like good people. They're smart, funny and engaging. You tend to remember them long after they're gone. That's reality.

It's also one of the seven principles of a process we call Reality-Based Advertising. A principle which proposes this to advertisers: Don't even think about getting into consumers' wallets unless you first get into their lives.

Reality-Based Advertising doesn't promote who you think you want to be. We find out who consumers will let you become. Then we apply those findings to the most important part of any communications plan, the ad itself. To involve people emotionally and credibly so that your product becomes a bigger part of their lives.

If you'd like to learn more about Reality-Based Advertising, talk to Steve Connelly, president, at 617-295-7985. We think you'd approve of the result.

Ingalls Advertising.

COPY DEVELOPMENT AND PRODUCTION TIMETABLE

The creative process is difficult to predict. It isn't always easy to develop new break-through copy within the planned timetable or guess the client's reaction to the copy. The agency may love it; the client may hate it. It may take time to develop the right ideas. However, it is important to develop a reasonable timetable for copy development and production. A typical copy/development timetable sequence might include

- copy exploratory
- present ideas to client
- revisions to client for approval to produce
- circulate copy for clearance (legal, R&D, management)
- on-air clearance (network/local stations)
- prebid meeting (specifications/sets)
- bid review/award job
- preproduction meeting
- shoot
- postproduction
- rough cut to client for approval
- revisions
- final to client
- ship date.

The responsibility for such a timetable is shared by the advertising agency and the client. How long does it take for a one- to five-day shoot with 2 to 10 actors to clear this process? Anywhere from 11 to 43 days. This range illustrates the complexity of the process. It isn't easy to generalize.

CREATING THE TELEVISION COMMERCIAL

Many creative people believe it is easier to create a good television commercial than it is to create a good print ad. After all, the TV creative person has motion to command more attention, sound, professional actors, producers, directors, and editors. They should be able to communicate with all that support if there is a grain of an idea.

The TV commercial has two basic segments: the *video* (the sight or visual part) and the *audio* (spoken words, music, or other sounds). The creation process begins with the video because television is generally better at showing than telling; however, the impact of the words and sounds must be considered.

Visual Techniques

Testimonials Testimonials can be delivered by known or unknown individuals. Viewers are fascinated with celebrities. A celebrity personality (Cindy Crawford, Tim Allen, Michael Jordon, Tiger Woods, for example) will grab a viewer's attention. About 20 percent of all TV commercials feature a celebrity. Athletes have outdistanced entertainers in the celebrity endorsement area since 1989.[2] There is always a risk with some celebrities getting into trouble or publicly saying the wrong thing or supporting the wrong cause, but it is worth it because of all the attention they get and the impact they have, says a vice president for Total Research Corp.[3] It costs an advertiser about $20,000 to research a celebrity to get diagnostic information of not only the personality, but whether the personality fits their product or service.

---

[2]Colin Bessonette, "Q&A on the News," *The Atlanta Journal,* January 1, 1996, p. A2.
[3]Cyndee Miller, "Celebrities Hot Despite Scandals," *Marketing News,* March 28, 1994, pp. 1–2.

Serials   Serials are commercials created in groups or campaigns; each commercial continues the previous story. MCI's serial campaign about a fictional publishing house, Gramercy Press, was a takeoff on the technique made popular by the Taster's Choice couple. MCI developed a 12-part series of commercials, which communicated a lot of information about products. Several beer companies have also tried the serial approach, as have Pacific Bell telephone, Ragu spaghetti sauce, and Energizer batteries.

The Taster's Choice serial of its romantic couple was first run in November 1990. Consumers became intrigued by the couple's romance from their first meeting as new neighbors. In 1997, even Taster's Choice print ads read, "Andrew or Michael? Who will win her undying love? Is it Andrew or is it Michael? Their destiny is in your hands." The reader could vote on a coupon. The results were announced in *Soap Opera Digest* in 1998. The product moved from the third largest-selling instant coffee to surpass Folger's and Maxwell House in less than three years after the commercials started.

Oldies Footage   Classic television and film sequences are now easily manipulated to create ads that target media-savvy viewers. Audiences have recently seen John Wayne selling Coors beer, Ed Sullivan introducing the Mercedes M-class sport-utility vehicle, Fred Astaire sweeping with a Dirt Devil, and Lucy Ricardo and Fred Mertz pushing tickets for the California lottery.

The Lucy ad features Lucy and Fred in her kitchen discussing what to buy Ethel for her birthday. Much to the duo's surprise, in walks a scrappy frat boy look-alike, who raids the refrigerator and shares his opinions on why a California "Birthday Scratch" lottery ticket would be a perfect gift. The creative team, wanting a look similar to the original *I Love Lucy* clip, filmed the visitor on 35-mm film before transferring it. Postproduction was completed in three days using Quantel's Henry and Discreet Logic's Flame and Inferno (software). The visitor was originally shot in color and then transferred to black and white.[4]

Spokesperson   This technique features a "presenter" who stands in front of the camera and delivers the copy directly to the viewer. The spokesperson may display and perhaps demonstrate the product. He or she may be in a set (a living room, kitchen, factory, office, or out of doors) appropriate to the product and product story, or in limbo (plain background with no set). The spokesperson should be someone who is likable and believable but not so powerful as to overwhelm the product. The product should be the hero.

Demonstration   This technique is popular for some types of products because television is the ideal medium for demonstrating to the consumer how the product works: how a bug spray kills, how to apply eye pencils in gorgeous silky colors, or how easy it is to use a microwave to cook a whole meal quickly. When making a demonstration commercial, use close shots so the viewer can see clearly what is happening. You may choose a subjective camera view (which shows a procedure as if the viewer were actually doing whatever the product does), using the camera as the viewer's eyes. Make the demonstration relevant and as involving as possible. Do not try to fool the viewer for two important reasons: (1) Your message must be believable; and (2) legally, the demonstration must correspond to actual usage—most agencies make participants in the commercial production sign affidavits signifying that the events took place as they appeared on the TV screen.

Close-Ups   Television is basically a medium of close-ups. The largest TV screen is too small for extraneous details in the scenes of a commercial. A fast-food chain may use close-ups to show hamburgers cooking or the appetizing finished product ready to

---

[4]Michael Speier, "I Love Lucy," *Millimeter,* June 1997, p. 19.

be consumed. With this technique, the audio is generally delivered offscreen (the voice-over costs less than a presentation by someone on the screen).

Story Line   The story-line technique is similar to making a miniature movie (with a definite beginning, middle, and end in 30 seconds), except that the narration is done offscreen. A typical scene may show a family trying to paint their large house with typical paint and brush. The camera shifts to the house next door, where a teenage female is easily spray-painting the house, the garage, and the fence in rapid fashion. During the scenes, the announcer explains the advantages of the spray painter.

Comparisons   Their soft drink has sodium. Our brand is sodium-free. Comparing one product with another can answer questions for the viewer. Usually, the comparison is against the leader in the product category. You could do a *user* lifestyle comparison between your brand and a competitive brand. In direct product comparisons, you must be prepared to prove in court that your product is significantly superior, as stated, and you must be credible in the way you make your claim, or the commercial may induce sympathy for the competitor.

Still Photographs and Artwork   By using still photographs and/or artwork, including cartoon drawings and lettering, you can structure a well-placed commercial. The required material may already exist, to be supplied at modest cost, or it can be photographed or drawn specifically for your use. Skillful use of the TV camera can give static visual material a surprising amount of movement. Zoom lenses provide an inward or outward motion, and panning the camera across the photographs or artwork can give the commercial motion (*panning* means changing the viewpoint of the camera without moving the dolly it stands on).

Slice-of-Life   Slice-of-life is an old dramatic technique where actors tell a story in an attempt to involve people with the brand. It is a short miniplay in which the brand is the hero. Most slice-of-life commercials open with a problem, and the brand becomes the solution.

The viewer must see the problem as real, and the reward must fit the problem. Because problem solving is a useful format in almost any commercial, slice-of-life is widely used.

Customer Interview   Most people who appear in TV commercials are professional actors, but customer interviews involve nonprofessionals. An interviewer or offscreen voice may ask a housewife, who is usually identified by name, to compare the advertised kitchen cleanser with her own brand by removing two identical spots in her sink. She finds that the advertised product does a better job.

Vignettes and Situations   Advertisers of soft drinks, beer, candy, and other widely consumed products find this technique useful in creating excitement and motivation. The commercial usually consists of a series of fast-paced scenes showing people enjoying the product as they enjoy life. The audio over these scenes is often a jingle or song with lyrics based on the situation we see and the satisfaction the product offers.

Humor   Humor has long been a popular technique with both copywriters and consumers because it makes the commercial more interesting. The dangers are that the humorous aspects of the commercial will get in the way of the sell and that the viewer will remember the humor rather than the product or the benefit. The challenge is to make the humorous copy relevant to the product or benefit.

Animation   **Animation** consists of artists' inanimate drawings, which are photographed on motion-picture film one frame at a time and brought to life with movement as the film is projected. The most common form of animation is the cartoon. A

Animation (TV)
Making inanimate objects appear alive and moving by setting them before an animation camera and filming one frame at a time.

favorite among children but popular with all ages, the cartoon is capable of creating a warm, friendly atmosphere both for the product and for the message. Animation can also be used to simplify technical product demonstrations. In a razor commercial, the actual product may be shown as it shaves a man's face, and an animated sequence may then explain how the blades of the razor remove whisker after whisker. The cost of animation depends on its style: With limited movement, few characters, and few or no backgrounds, the price can be low.

Stop Motion When a package or other object is photographed in a series of different positions, movement can be stimulated as the single frames are projected in sequence. Stop motion is similar to artwork photographed in animation. With it, the package can "walk," "dance," and move as if it had come to life.

Rotoscope In the rotoscope technique, animated and live-action sequences are produced separately and then optically combined. A live boy may be eating breakfast food while a cartoon animal trademark character jumps up and down on his shoulder and speaks to him.

Problem Solution This technique has been around since the beginning of television. The purpose of many products is to solve the prime prospect's problem—a headache, poor communication, or plaque. You get the idea. The product is selling the solution. Problem solution is similar to slice-of-life, but lacks the depth of story line or plot development.

Mood Imagery This technique is expensive and difficult. If often combines several techniques. The main objective is to set a certain mood and image for the product you are trying to sell. An example of this technique is the GE "We bring good things to life" campaign.

Split and Bookend Spots A variation on the serial commercial is the split spot: Two related (usually 15-second) spots run with a completely unrelated spot between them. For example, Post Grape-Nuts ran a split spot in which a woman asks a man how long the cereal stays crunchy in milk. The man does not want to find out, but she insists, and viewers are left hanging. Next is an unrelated 30-second commercial for another product. The couple then comes back, and she says, "After all this time it's still crunchy."

The theory behind split and bookend commercials is that breaking out of the expected format will get your product remembered.

Infomercials As discussed in chapter 8, the infomercial is a commercial that looks like a program. These commercials sell everything from woks to make-a-million-in-real-estate programs, and usually run for 30 minutes. The National Infomercial Marketing Association recommends that every infomercial begin and end with a "paid advertisement" announcement so that consumers understand what they are watching. The obvious advantage is that the advertiser has an entire program about its product.

Combination Most commercials combine techniques. A speaker may begin and conclude the message, but there will be close-ups in between. In fact, every commercial should contain at least one or two close-ups to show package and logo. Humor is adaptable to most techniques. Animation and live action make an effective mixture in many commercials, and side-by-side comparisons may be combined with almost any other technique.

Chuck McBride, group creative director and copywriter/director of Foote, Cone & Belding–San Francisco, developed several themeless spots for Levi's Wide Leg jeans. One featured Richard being rushed into a hospital emergency room with a bloody face, wear-

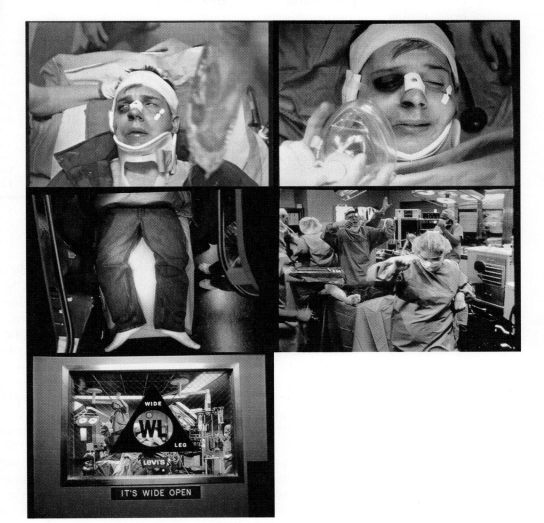

exhibit

19.2

A Creative Commercial

Courtesy: Levi's and Foote, Cone & Belding–San Francisco.

ing a neck brace and regulation jeans and a plaid shirt. As Richard is rushed into surgery he seems to be passing through a white-light experience on the surgical table (see Exhibit 19.2). He's twitching to the beat of the 1980s dance number, "Tainted Love." He's really into his out-of-body experience as he takes the mask off and says, "I've got to get away from the pain you drive into the heart of me." The surgeon and staff begin to sing. This is followed by Richard's heartbeat flatlining and then being shocked; then a moment of silence until the heart monitor spikes and everyone continues singing "Tainted Love." Reactions of viewers ranged from hilarious to horrified. The commercial was aimed at 18- to 24-year-olds, who accepted the commercial better than their parents did. One of the other commercials was about a romantic elevator fantasy. The only tie between the commercials was the tagline, "It's wide open."

Video Influence

Many techniques used in commercials that were once unique to MTV have become the visual rules of today. These include hyperkinetic imagery, visual speed, and sophistication; ironic, wise-guy attitudes; unexpected humor; quick, suggestive cuts rather than slow segues; narrative implications rather than whole stories; attitudes, not explanations; tightly cropped, partial images instead of whole ones; mixtures of live action, newsreel footage, animation, typography, film speeds, and film quality; and unexpected soundtrack/audio relationships to video.

Video Storyboard Persuasion Results

	Women	Men	18–34	34–49	50+
Commercials with **humor**	57	**68**	58	63	64
Commercials with **children**	**61**	44	52	56	52
Commercials with **celebrities**	39	34	44	34	30
Real-life situations	34	30	**39**	33	24
Brand **comparisons**	32	23	**35**	31	20
Musical commercials	**29**	18	27	23	20
Product **demonstrations**	17	**26**	19	24	21
Endorsements from experts	**17**	13	16	16	14
Hidden-camera testimonials	12	10	**14**	10	9
Company **presidents**	6	**12**	**12**	9	7

Source: Adweek, August 15, 1994, p. 17.

exhibit

19.3

Which Technique?

There have been a number of studies to help advertisers make up their minds as to what kind of commercials to run. None provides all the answers, however. Ogilvy & Mather found that people who liked a commercial were twice as likely to be persuaded by it compared to people who felt neutral toward the advertising. Perhaps the single most striking finding was the fact that commercial liking went far beyond mere entertainment. People like commercials they feel are relevant and worth remembering, which could have an impact on greater persuasion. Original or novel approaches by themselves seem to have little to do with how well a commercial is liked. They also found that liking was a function of product category. A lively, energetic execution also contributed to liking, but was less important than relevance.

In other research findings, Video Storyboard tests reinforce that consumers like commercials with celebrities. In fact, consumer preference for this type of commercial has risen in the past 10 years. Such commercials are more persuasive than slice-of-life vignettes or product demonstrations. Exhibit 19.3 shows that celebrities are bested only by humor and kids as executional elements that characterize persuasive commercials.

"To me, technique has never been as interesting as ideas," says director Bob Giraldi, "and now that we're in this time when technique is as important if not more important than anything, I keep thinking how I can come up with techniques that are interesting."[5]

A year ago Diet Rite Cola put a modern couple in absurd situations to help sell the drink. "The 15-second spots were about entertaining people," said director Steve Wax. "It was a conscious decision not to sell a distinctive attribute of the drink." In the "bungee" spot, the husband attempts an indoor bungee jump, suspending himself from the ceiling, as wife and dog look on. In "golf," a lone golf ball sails through the living room. The walls shake as the husband drives a golf cart through the room. A voice-over warns people not to try these stunts in their homes. Using a lock-off camera angle, the director built the spots with only two shots. However, timing the action became critical. The voice-over was loaded into the computer, and then timed out exactly where the action was to happen. The noted cue point was programmed into the computer and copy was handed out to everyone on the set. It was almost as if the computer was directing the commercial.

Planning the Commercial

In planning the TV commercial, there are many considerations: cost, medium (videotape or film), casting of talent, use of music, special techniques, time, location, and the big idea and its relationship to the advertising and marketing objectives and, of course, to the entire campaign.

---

[5]Anthony Vagnoni, "Back to the Future," *Creativity,* June 1996, pp. 19–20.

Let us review some of the basic principles of writing the commercial script or thinking the idea through:

- You are dealing with sight, sound, and motion. Each of these elements has its own requirements and uses. There should be a relationship among them so that the viewer perceives the desired message. Make certain that when you are demonstrating a sales feature, the audio is talking about that same feature.
- Your audio should be relevant to your video, but there is no need to describe what is obvious in the picture. Where possible, you should see that the words interpret the picture and advance the thought.
- Television generally is more effective at showing than telling; therefore, more than half of the success burden rests on the ability of the video to communicate.
- The number of scenes should be planned carefully. You do not want too many scenes (unless you are simply trying to give an overall impression) because this tends to confuse the viewer. Yet you do not want scenes to become static (unless planned so for a reason). Study TV commercials and time the scene changes to determine what you personally find effective. If you do this, you will discover the importance of pacing the message—if a scene is too long, you will find yourself impatiently waiting for the next one.
- It is important to conceive the commercial as a flowing progression so that the viewer will be able to follow it easily. You do not have time for a three-act play whose unrelated acts can be tied together at the end. A viewer who cannot follow your thought may well tune you out. The proper use of opticals or transitions can add motion and smoothness to scene transitions.
- Television is basically a medium of close-ups. The largest TV screen is too small for extraneous detail in the scenes of a commercial. Long shots can be effective in establishing a setting, but not for showing product features.
- The action of the commercial takes more time than a straight announcer's reading of copy. A good rule is to purposely time the commercial a second or two short. Generally, the action will eat up this time, so do not just read your script. Act it out.
- You will want to consider the use of supers (words on the screen) of the basic theme so that the viewer can see, as well as hear, the important sales feature. Many times, the last scene will feature product identification and the theme line.
- If possible, show the brand name. If it is prominent, give a shot of the package; otherwise, flash its logotype. It is vital to establish brand identification.
- Generally, try to communicate one basic idea; avoid running in fringe benefits. Be certain that your words as well as your pictures emphasize your promise. State it, support it, and, if possible, demonstrate it. Repeat your basic promise near the end of the commercial; that is the story you want viewers to carry away with them.
- Read the audio aloud to catch tongue twisters.
- As in most other advertising writing, the sentences should usually be short and their structure uncomplicated. Use everyday words. It is not necessary to have something said every second. The copy should round out the thought conveyed by the picture.
- In writing your video description, describe the scene and action as completely as possible: "Open on husband and wife in living room" is not enough. Indicate where each is placed, whether they are standing or sitting, and generally how the room is furnished.

Exhibit 19.4 (p. 530) is a 30-second spot that takes into account these basic principles.

Writing the Script

Writing a TV commercial is very different from writing print advertising. First, you must use simple, easy-to-pronounce, easy-to-remember words. And you must be brief. The 30-second commercial has only 28 seconds of audio. In 28 seconds, you must solve your prime prospect's problems by demonstrating your product's superiority. If the product is too big to show in use, be certain to show the logo or company name at least

California Milk Processor Advisory Board
"Aaron Burr" ZGRE 4309
As Produced
:30 TV

Video	Audio
OPEN INSIDE LARGE STUDIO AS MAN IS SITTING AT TABLE, SURROUNDED BY ANTIQUES.	(SFX: Radio playing Viennese classical music. Music fades out)
CUT TO ANTIQUE RADIO.	RADIO DJ: "And now let's make that . . . random call with today's $10,000 question . . .
CUT TO CU OF MAN SLOWLY AND METHODICALLY SPREADING A THICK COAT OF PEANUT BUTTER ON A PIECE OF BREAD THAT HE HOLDS DIRECTLY IN FRONT OF HIS FACE.	
CUT TO WALL FEATURING SEVERAL PAINTINGS AND SCULPTURES OF ALEXANDER HAMILTON. A "HAMILTON" NAME PLATE IS MOUNTED TO THE WALL. SLOW ZOOM IN.	who shot . . .
CUT TO MAN STUFFING HIS MOUTH FULL WITH THE FOLDED, PEANUT BUTTER PIECE OF BREAD.	Alexander Hamilton in that famous duel?"
CUT TO TWO ANTIQUE GUNS, PRESUMABLY USED IN THE FAMOUS DUEL.	
CUT TO A SHOWCASED BULLET UNDER WHICH A SIGN READS "THE BULLET."	(SFX: Gunfire)
QUICK CUT TO CU OF MAN'S RIGHT EYE SHIFTING TO THE OTHER SIDE OF THE ROOM.	
CUT TO ANOTHER PAINTING OF THE FAMOUS DUEL BETWEEN AARON BURR AND ALEXANDER HAMILTON, BOTH OF WHOM HAVE NAME PLATES UNDERNEATH. ZOOM IN ON PICTURE TO CU OF AARON BURR. PAN DOWN TO HIS NAMEPLATE, "A. BURR."	
CUT BACK TO MAN SITTING AT TABLE. HIS EYES LIGHT UP AS HE STARES AT PHONE RINGING.	(SFX: Phone ringing)
CUT TO CU OF MAN'S FACE AS HE PICKS UP PHONE AND BEGINS SPEAKING WITH HIS MOUTH STILL FULL OF PEANUT-BUTTERED BREAD.	MAN: "Hewo?!?" RADIO DJ: "Hello, for $10,000 . . .
CUT TO FULL SHOT OF MAN AT TABLE, SITTING UP, EXCITED NEXT TO PEANUT BUTTER AND MILK. HE INTERRUPTS THE DJ.	who shot—" MAN: "Arwoon Boor!"
CUT BACK TO CU OF MAN ON PHONE. HE LOOKS VERY PROUD AND PLEASED.	RADIO DJ: "Excuse me?"
UPON HEARING THE DJ'S RESPONSE, HE TENSES UP.	MAN: "Arwoon Burr. Whai, hold on, lemme . . .

exhibit

19.4

Example of a TV Script

Courtesy: California Fluid Milk Advisory Board/Goodby, Silverstein & Partners.

CUT TO MAN'S FACE AS VIEWED
THROUGH AN EMPTY, CLEAR DRINKING
GLASS, HE PICKS UP CARTON OF MILK
AND POURS IT IN THE GLASS. ONLY A
SMALL SPLASH OF MILK DRIPS OUT OF
THE CARTON. HE SITS FORWARD,
SHAKING THE CARTON FRANTICALLY,
YELLING.

dring some milk . . .

Milk!!!!!"

CUT BACK TO OPEN SHOT OF MAN AS
HE SLAMS THE CARTON DOWN.

RADIO DJ: "I'm sorry, your time is up."
(SFX: Phone hang up. Dial tone.)

AFTER DJ HANGS UP, HE HOLDS THE
PHONE STILL, AND QUIETLY,
PATHETICALLY MUMBLES TO HIMSELF.

MAN: "Arwoon Boor."

FADE TO BLACK TITLE CARD. WHITE
SUPER: "GOT MILK?"

(SFX: Dial tone continues)

twice during the commercial. Think of words and pictures simultaneously. You usually
divide your script paper into two columns. On the left, you describe the video action,
and on the right you write the audio portion, including sound effects and music. Corresponding video and audio elements go right next to each other, panel by panel. Some
agencies use specially designed sheets of paper $8\frac{1}{2}$ by 11 inches, with boxes down the
center for rough sketches of the video portion (Exhibit 19.5a). For presentations, most
agencies use full-size TV storyboards. Write copy in a friendly, conversational style. If
you use an off-camera announcer, make certain that his or her dialogue is keyed to the

exhibit

19.5a

This photoscript
combines both the
storyboard and script
on to one easy-to-
handle few pages. It
allows everybody to
have their own copy.

Courtesy: Leo Burnett Co. Ltd.,
Toronto and Fruit of the
Loom.

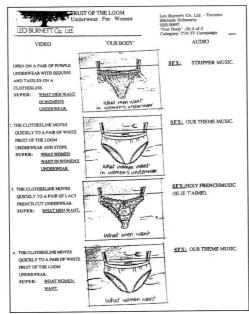

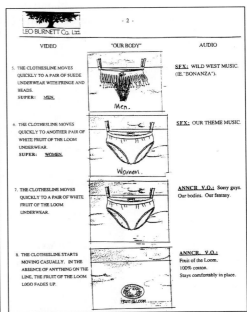

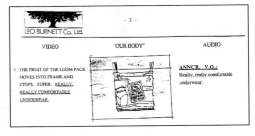

scenes in your video portion. Although it is not always possible, matching the audio with the video makes a commercial cohesive and more effective. The audio—words, sound effects, or music—in a script is as important as the video portion. They must work together to bring the viewer the message. You need strong copy and sound and strong visuals. All are vital for an effective commercial.

Developing the Storyboard

Once the creative art and copy team has developed a script, the next step is to create a **storyboard**, which consists of a series of sketches showing key scenes developed in the script. It is a helpful tool for discussing the concept with other agency or client personnel, who may not know the background or who may not be able to visualize a script accurately. Without a storyboard, each individual may interpret the script's visuals differently.

Storyboard versus Finished Look   It is extremely difficult, if not impossible, to visualize the look of a finished commercial from the storyboard. Director Jim Edwards says, "The hardest thing to do in directing is to make someone understand your vision before you actually make the pictures and then it's too late. Most people [clients, account people] are very literal minded and don't work well with their imaginations"— and that's what a storyboard is supposed to help you do. Of course, the quality of the storyboards varies from virtual stick figures in limbo to full-color drawings. Keep in mind, using this limited medium, it is a difficult task to show all the details that are necessary to understand for production purposes.

Storyboards consist of two frames for each scene. The top frame represents the TV screen (visual). The bottom frame carries a description of the video (as per script) and the audio for that sequence (some storyboards carry only the audio portion). The number of sets of frames varies from commercial to commercial and is not necessarily dictated by the length of the commercial. There may be 4 to 12 or more sets of frames, depending on the nature of the commercial and the demands of the client for detail.

The ratio of width to depth on the TV screen is 4 by 3. There is no standard-size storyboard frame, although a common size is 4 inches by 3 inches.

The storyboard is a practical step between the raw script and actual production. It gives the agency, client, and production house personnel a common visual starting point for their discussion. Upon client approval, the storyboard goes into production.

Exhibit 19.5b is an example of a photoboard. It is basically similar to the storyboard, but shows the actual frames that were shot. It is frequently used by companies as a sales tool to show merchants and dealers exactly what kind of advertising support they will be given.

Other Elements of the Commercial

Opticals   Most commercials contain more than a single scene. Optical devices or effects between scenes are necessary to provide smooth visual continuity from scene to scene. They are inserted during the final editing stage. The actual opticals may be one of the director's functions. However, these are used to aid in the transition of getting from one scene to the next scene or establishing a visual. Sometimes which technique depends on the importance of a particular scene or the detail that needs to be seen. Exhibit 19.6 (p. 534) illustrates some very basic optical decisions. Among the most common are the following.

CUT. One scene simply cuts into the next. It is the fastest scene change because it indicates no time lapse whatsoever. A cut is used to indicate simultaneous action, to speed up action, and for variety. It keeps one scene from appearing on the screen too long.

Storyboard
Series of drawings used to present a proposed commercial. Consists of illustrations of key action (video), accompanied by the audio part. Used for getting advertiser approval and as a production guide.

Opticals
Visual effects that are put on a TV film in a laboratory, in contrast to those that are included as part of the original photography.

exhibit

19.5b

This is an example of the finished commercial shown on this photoboard.

Courtesy: Leo Burnett Co. Ltd., Toronto and Fruit of the Loom.

DISSOLVE. An overlapping effect in which one scene fades out while the following scene simultaneously fades in. Dissolves are slower than cuts. There are fast dissolves and slow dissolves. Dissolves are used to indicate a short lapse of time in a given scene, or to move from one scene to another where the action is either simultaneous with the action in the first scene or occurring very soon after the preceding action.

FADE-IN. An effect in which the scene actually "fades" into vision from total black (black screen).

FADE-OUT. This is opposite of a fade-in. The scene "fades" into total black. If days, months, or years elapse between one sequence of action and the next, indicate "Fade out . . . fade in."

MATTE. Part of one scene is placed over another so that the same narrator, for example, is shown in front of different backgrounds.

exhibit

19.6

**Examples of
Camera Directions**

ECU - An Extreme Close Up shows, for example, person's lips, nose, eyes.

CU - The Close Up is a tight shot, but showing face on entire package for emphasis.

MCU - The Medium Close Up cuts to person about chest, usually showing some background.

MS - The Medium Shot shows the person from the waist up. Commonly used shot. Shows much more detail of setting or background than MCU.

LS - The Long Shot shows the scene from a distance. Used to establish location.

SUPER. The superimposition of one scene or object over another. The title or product can be "supered" over the scene.

WIPE. The new scene "wipes" off the previous scene from top or bottom or side to side with a geometric pattern (Exhibit 19.7). A wipe is faster than a dissolve but not as fast as a cut. A wipe does not usually connote lapse of time, as a dissolve or fade-out does. There are several types of wipes: *flip* (the entire scene turns over like the front and back of a postcard), *horizontal* (left to right or right to left), *vertical* (top to bottom or bottom to top), *diagonal, closing door* (in from both sides), *bombshell* (a burst into the next scene), *iris* (a circle that grows bigger is an *iris out*), *fan* (fans out from center screen), *circular* (sweeps around the screen—also called *clock wipe*). Wipes are most effective when a rapid succession of short or quick scenes is desired, or to separate impressionistic shots when these are grouped together to produce a montage effect.

ZOOM. A smooth, sometimes rapid move from a long shot to a close-up or from a close-up to a long shot.

Soundtrack   The audio portion of the commercial may be recorded either during the film or videotape shooting or at an earlier or later time in a recording studio. When

exhibit

19.7

Example of Wipe

the soundtrack is recorded during the shooting, the actual voices of the people speaking on camera are used in the commercial. If the soundtrack is recorded in advance, the film or videotape scenes can be shot to fit the copy points as they occur; or if music is part of the track, visual action can be matched to a specific beat. If shooting and editing take place before the soundtrack is recorded, the track can be tailored to synchronize with the various scenes (see sound studio in Exhibit 19.8).

Music   Music has the ability to communicate feelings and moods in a unique way. As a result, the use of music can make or break a TV commercial. In some commercials, it is every bit as important as the copy or visuals. It is often used as background to the announcer's copy or as a song or jingle that is integral to the ad.

exhibit

19.8

Modern Sound Studio

Courtesy: Bob Green Productions.

Here are some ways you can put music to work:[6]

- *Backgrounds.* In many commercials, background music is used primarily to contribute to the mood. Appropriate music can be used to establish the setting; then it can fade and become soft in the background.
- *Transitions.* Music can be an effective transition device to carry viewers from one setting to another. For example, the music may start out being sedate as the scene is peaceful. As it switches to the product being used, the music changes to rock and the tempo builds, marking the transition from place to place.
- *Movement.* Sound effects (SFX), natural sounds, and music can contribute to movement. Music that moves up the scale, or down, supports something or someone moving up or down.
- *Accents.* Music can punctuate points or actions. The "beat" of the music and visuals can match to hold viewers' attention and drive the commercial. Musical sounds—as little as a single note—can attract attention.

Using Classic Rock Oldies   Although it is almost always expensive, the licensing of an old song can be effective. When a great song is part of the creative equation, audiences can't get enough of it. When "Don't Fence Me In" accompanied all those MCI Gramercy Press sagas, that didn't stop Mercedes-Benz from using the same tune two years later. "Night and Day" has been reborn and reborn again for Air France, Audi, Ford, and Maxwell House, as was "Stand by Me" for Buick, after years at Citibank. "Wild Thing" simply has too many credits to mention. What "Wild Thing" tells us is that classic songs gain, rather than lose, creative impact with multiple uses; and that they do so not only via network commercials but also via local ones; all of which reinforce one another in a seemingly endless cycle. Rick Lyon of Rick Lyon Music says, "In a certain sense, a song like 'Wild Thing' belongs to all of us. Maybe that's why audiences not only accept but enjoy its repeated use as they've enjoyed other visual advertising cons." It is similar to using the Statue of Liberty or the Mona Lisa.

Licensed music gains instant access to the listener's subconscious. It lets a brand such as Buick communicate trust and reliability when its "Stand by Me" had just done the same for Citibank. Or it lets McDonald's promote a folksiness with Randy Newman's "You've Got a Friend in Me," only months after it had gained fame in the popular family hit movie *Toy Story.*[7]

American music tastes are broadening, according to a poll by the National Endowment of the Arts and Census Bureau data. When people were asked to name the kind of music they liked best, country/western music ranked first by 21 percent of adults, followed by rock (14 percent), gospel/hymns (9 percent), mood/easy listening (9 percent), classical (6 percent), and jazz (5 percent). Yet, one-third of adults, about 60 million people, said they liked classical and jazz artists. The top five musical genres are liked by 40 to 50 percent of the adult population, or between 72 and 96 million people.[8]

The most evident trend in America's musical tastes is a hefty increase in the popularity of blues, rhythm and blues, and soul music. Rock music has also increased in popularity over the past 10 years.

Whatever the tone of the music, it can help transfer drama, love, happiness, or other feelings to the viewer. It is a tool to cue the viewer's feelings. Original music can be written and scored for the commercial, or licensing of old or popular songs can be obtained, which can be very expensive. The least expensive music is stock music sold by stock music companies. It is cheap because it is not exclusive.

---

[6] *Music—How to Use It for Commercial Production,* a publication of the Television Bureau of Advertising, New York.

[7] Rick Lyon, "The Circle Game," *Creativity,* September 1997, p. 18.

[8] Nicholas Zill and John Robinson, "Name That Tune," *American Demographics,* August 1994, pp. 22–27.

PRODUCING THE TV COMMERCIAL

The job of converting the approved storyboard is done by TV production. There are three distinct stages to this process:

- *Preproduction* includes casting, wardrobing, designing sets or building props, finding a location or studio, and meeting with agency, client, and production house personnel.
- *Shooting* encompasses the work of filming or videotaping all scenes in the commercial. In fact, several takes are made of each scene.
- *Postproduction,* also known as editing, completion, or finishing, includes selecting scenes from among those shots, arranging them in the proper order, inserting transitional effects, adding titles, combining sound with picture, and delivering the finished commercial.

In charge of production is the producer, who combines the talents of coordinator, diplomat, watchdog, and businessperson. Some producers are on the staffs of large agencies or advertisers. Many work on a freelance basis. The work of a producer is so all-embracing that the best way to describe it is to live through the entire production process. Let us do that first and pick up the details of the producer's job in the section headed "Role of the Producer."

Let us begin with the problems of shooting the spot, for which a director is appointed by the producer.

The Director's Function

The key person in the shooting, the **director** takes part in casting and directing the talent, directs the cameraperson in composing each picture, assumes responsibility for the setting, and puts the whole show together. A director of a regional commercial will earn about $7,500 per day, and national commercial directors average about $13,000 per commercial; however, better-known directors may demand $25,000 to $35,000 per spot.

The Bidding Process

There is only one way to provide specifications for a commercial shoot when you are seeking bids from production companies, and that is in writing. There is an industry-accepted form (AICP Bid and Specification Form). Information for this form is provided by the agency and client. The use of this form ensures that all production companies are provided with identical job specifications for estimating production costs. It ensures that all bids are based on the same information.

The Preproduction Process

A preproduction meeting must be held prior to every production. The agency producer is expected to chair this meeting. The following agency, client, and production company personnel usually attend:

Agency: producer, creative team, account supervisor
Client: brand manager or advertising manager
Production company: director, producer, others as needed

The following points should be covered at every preproduction meeting: direction, casting, locations, and/or sets, wardrobe and props, product, special requirements, final script, legal claims/contingencies, timetable update.

In addition to covering the points just listed, the creative team and the director will likely present shooting boards and the production thinking behind the commercial. The shooting boards should be used for the following purposes:

- to determine camera angles
- to determine best product angles

- to project camera and cast movement and help determine talent status (extra versus principal)
- to determine number of scenes to be shot
- to determine timing of each scene

ROLE OF THE PRODUCER

Agency Producer

The producer's role begins before the approval of the storyboard. Conferring with the copywriter and/or art director, the producer becomes thoroughly familiar with every frame of the storyboard.

1. The producer prepares the "specs," or specifications—the physical production requirements of the commercial—to provide the production studios with the precise information they require to compute realistic bids. Every agency prepares its own estimate form. In addition, many advertisers request a further breakdown of the cost of items such as preproduction, shooting, crew, labor, studio, location travel and expenses, equipment, film, props and wardrobe, payroll taxes, studio makeup, direction, insurance, editing.

2. The producer contacts the studios that have been invited to submit bids based on their specialties, experience, and reputation; meets with them either separately or in one common "bid session"; and explains the storyboard and the specs in detail.

3. The production house estimates expenses after studying specs, production timetable, and storyboard. Generally, a 35 percent markup is added to the estimated out-of-pocket expenses to cover overhead and studio profit. Usually, the production company adds a 10 percent contingency fee to the bid for unforeseen problems. The bids are submitted. The producer analyzes the bids and recommends the studio to the client.

4. The producer arranges for equipment. The studio may own equipment, such as cameras and lights, but more often it rents all equipment for a job. The crew is also freelance, hired by the day. Although the studio's primary job is to shoot the commercial, it can also take responsibility for editorial work. For videotape, a few studios own their own cameras and production units; others rent these facilities.

5. Working through a talent agency, the producer arranges, or has the production company arrange, auditions. Associates also attend auditions, at which they and the director make their final choices of performers. The client may also be asked to pass on the final selection.

6. The producer then participates in the preproduction meeting. At this meeting the producer, creative associates, account executive, and client, together with studio representatives and director, lay final plans for production.

7. During the shooting, the producer usually represents both the agency and the client as the communicator with the director. On the set or location, the creative people and client channel any comments and suggestions through the producer to avoid confusion.

8. It is the producer's responsibility to arrange for the recording session. Either before or after shooting and editing, he or she arranges for the soundtrack, which may call for an announcer, actors, singers, and musicians. If music is to be recorded, the producer will have had preliminary meetings with the music contractor.

9. The producer participates in the editing along with the creative team. Editing begins after viewing the dailies and selecting the best takes.

10. The producer arranges screenings for agency associates and clients to view and approve the commercials at various editing stages and after completion of the answer print.

11. Finally, the producer handles the billings and approves studio and other invoices for shooting, editing, and payment to talent.

The "Outside" Producer

An **outside producer** is the person representing a production company whose entire business is filmmaking. He or she is hired by the agency producer to create the TV commercial according to agency specifications.

Shooting

Most productions consist of the following steps:

1. *Prelight.* This is simply the day (or days) used to set the lighting for specific scenes. To do this exclusively on shoot days would tie up the entire crew.
2. *Shooting.* This phase of the production process is the filming (or taping) of the approved scenes for the commercial. These scenes are then "screened" the next day (dailies) to ensure that the scene was captured as planned.
3. *Wrap.* This signals the completion of production. It is at this stage that most of the crew is released.
4. *Editing.* This takes place after the shoot is completed. Scenes are screened and selected for use in the commercial. The scenes are then merged with a sound track, titles, and opticals, composing a completed or finished commercial.

The role of the client and account service at the shoot is one of advisor. It is really the creative's day and it is their responsibility to deliver the spot. In situations where the client needs to provide input on the set, the prime contact is the account representative or agency producer. The producer is generally the liaison between the agency and the director. This chain of command is simple and direct and eliminates confusion on the set, which is an absolute necessity when shooting.

Postproduction Process

Postproduction begins after a production company exposes the film in the camera at the "shoot." The film that comes out of the camera must be developed in a chemical bath and then printed onto a new strip of positive film called the "dailies." The editor then screens these "dailies" and selects the good takes from the day's shooting.

The editor then physically splices the takes selected from each scene together with the next to create a "rough cut," which is a rough rendition of the finished commercial. Once the editor has cut this film and the agency and client approve the cut, the editor takes the original film that was shot and developed and pulls the takes from that film that matches his selected workprint takes.

Today, virtually all final edits, effects, and opticals are done on videotape. The original camera film takes (35 mm motion picture film) are transferred electronically to one-inch videotape. During this transfer of film to videotape, the color is corrected.

The editor then takes this material into a video edit, where each take is run on videotape and the "cut-in" through "cut-out" points for each take are laid down in sequence, from the first frame of the first scene to the end frame of that scene (to match the workprint), until the entire commercial is laid down from the color-corrected videotape matter (called the "unedited tape master"). Titles and other special effects are added during this final unedited-tape-to-edited-tape session. The sound (which the editor and agency had worked on along with the picture) is then electronically relayed onto the video-edited master, and the spot is finished. Sound complicated? It is.

Postdirectors are independent contractors in the production mix. They are in the business of cutting film and creatively supervising videotape transfers from film; supervising video edits and special effects; recording narration, sound, music, and sound effects; mixing these sounds together; relaying them onto the picture; and delivering a finished product to the agency.

Computer Postproduction Technology

The computer is, and has been, revolutionizing some aspects of print production and prepress activities and is also active in revolutionizing TV postproduction. Advances in hardware and software are continuing to change the creation and production of TV commercials. Names such as Silicon Graphics, Avid, Wavefront, Flame, and Quantel's Henry and Harry have been mainstays for a number of years. Terms such as 3-D animation, compositing, morphing, 2-D animation, nonlinear editing, live-action compositing, and real-time are common among the professionals who generate visual images and special effects. The systems used in the early 1990s to produce the video magic could cost $25,000 to $250,000. Today, Macintosh offers many of the same video effects to more producers of commercials at lower costs. As usual, when discussing computer hardware and software, each system has a plus and a minus; but the availability offers more creative and production people more options to create unique visuals and commercials.

It is safe to say that today's **computer-generated imagery** (CGI) offers creative minds great new opportunities in production and postproduction. This technology allows creative people to squash, squeeze, stretch, and morph objects in less time than ever before. Computers are turning live action into cartoon action. At production facilities, creative talents can use digital-graphics/animation-compositing systems to top four or five layers of live action with five or six layers of graphics, all simultaneously, allowing the finished visual composite to be seen as it develops.

CGI Wizardry Remember the Budweiser Clydesdale who held the pigskin for the point-after attempt in the Super Bowl? Or the beer-slurpin' frogs? These are largely computer generated (CG) or a mix of special techniques. The ability of animators and software engineers to imbue their characters with a greater sense of charm and warmth has made skeptics become computer converts. It doesn't hurt that the work from *Toy Story* to Coca-Cola polar bears has been embraced by audiences. Computer-animation people have been preoccupied with technical issues in the past. Technology has changed that. Now we have the ability to make photorealistic animals, for example. They look real, for the most part, only now they can do things no animal could be trained to do. Lowe came up with the idea of illustrating side-impact air bags by placing a new Mercedes in a herd of lumbering rhinos on New York streets. The digital crew worked with stock film footage to study how rhinos move.

CGI and cel animation both play big roles in television commercial production. Costs of both are dropping, software is improving, and the proliferation of computer-generated graphics has created a growing reservoir of artists, techniques, and trends. The classic Coca-Cola polar bears could exist only in CGI. Cost, however, is still a major factor in using CGI and is considerably higher than live action budgets. "National spots are rarely budgeted below $250,000 for a 30-second commercial; they can easily reach $1 to 2 million on the high end for clients like Coca-Cola, Intel, auto companies, and other large corporations," says executive producer Paul Golubovich.[9]

Recently, we have seen in television production an awareness that CGI can be used to help create things that couldn't otherwise be created. Taking different techniques and marrying them into one cohesive unit is difficult, but with developing software, and more skilled people, the process becomes easier and more creative.

The combination of elements from two or more photographic sources often produces a striking effect. With the advent of computers, the process of combining different layers became much easier, but at the same time it is more complex because the variety of combinations are now seemingly limitless. Filmed images can now be scanned

---

Computer-generated imagery (CGI)
Technology allowing computer operators to create multitudes of electronic effects for TV—to squash, stretch or squeeze objects—much more quickly than earlier tools could. It can add layers of visuals simultaneously.

---

[9]Michael Spier, "Why CGI?" *Millimeter*, May 1997, pp. 93–100.

into the computer by running compositing software, enabling the digital blending of several—or, literally hundreds—of layers of imagery.

You may have heard of some of the following electronic production tools and techniques:

- *Compositing.* In the digital realm, compositing is the umbrella term for many processes required to technically accomplish image combination in the computer.
- *Matte.* Essentially a silhouette in black and white, matte is the necessary signal for the computer to cut out the part of the image intended to be visible. It can also exist in many other physical forms, such as a painting on glass or a masked-off camera composition.
- *Keying.* Keying is electronically composing one picture over another. The two types of keying are luminance and chroma-keying. This term came from the word "keyhole" and is interpreted by the computer as a signal enabling a hole to be cut in a clip layer.
- *Chroma-keying.* This is another matte derivation method in which the computer sources a specific color (usually green, blue, or red) to create a key signal. This is a way of performing automatic matte extraction, using the colored background. In a weather program that has a map and the weatherperson in front of the map, the map is an electronic image chroma-keyed off of a green screen. The weatherperson can't actually see the map without looking at a monitor. All that is actually behind them is a color screen. It is interpreted by the computer as a hole and is replaced with the layer behind, in this case a map.
- *Keyer.* A keyer is simply an electronic composer.

Morphing
An electronic technique that allows you to transform one object into another object.

- *Morphing.* **Morphing** is an industry term for metamorphosing, which means transforming from one object to another. For example, in a Schick shaving spot, a man's head is turned into a 3-D cube, and for Exxon a car turns into a tiger. This computer graphics technique allows its operator to move between the real world and computer graphics by electronically layering visual transitions between live action.

  The cost of morphs varies. They can range from $5,000 for a "garage" job using a PC up to $70,000, depending on the complexity. But meticulous advance planning remains the key to a successful job. A Schick shaving heads commercial, which morphed a series of six talking shaving heads and upper torsos, required a two-day blue-screen shoot, composited over a bathroom background.[10]

- *Harry.* The Quantel Henry/Harry on-line system is an editing device with an optical device tied to it. It allows computer composites to mix with live video. Ninety percent of Harry work can be created on a Macintosh. The Harry is faster and much more expensive, but the Mac appears to be closing the gap quickly with its Apple RISC-based PowerPC.
- *Flame.* On the other hand, Flame is an optical device with an editing device tied to it. It functions as a high-capacity, random-access, multilayer compositing system, with video editing/effects/digital-audio capacity. So you can see that you have to have the right technology for the right job. And, yes, it can be confusing to the nonproduction person in the advertising industry.
- *In-House Desktop.* During the early 1990s, agencies could use their in-house Macintosh computers to interface with video composers. This made video editing, long the domain of highly trained specialists, a viable in-house option. This allowed the agency personnel to cut and paste video images just as desktop computers cut and paste print graphics. The quality isn't quite the level of the production houses' hardware/software, but it is getting closer and allows agencies to cut costs and use them for producing the storyboard, the animatic for testing, and rough cuts, and then send the disc to the production company, where the spot is polished into a final commercial of broadcast quality. Those clients that do not need top-quality images can complete the entire commercial postproduction process on the system.

---

[10]Beth Jacques, "The Do's and Don'ts of Mixing Animation and Live Action," *Millimeter,* April 1994, pp. 77–82.

CONTROLLING THE COST OF COMMERCIAL PRODUCTION

The cost of producing a TV commercial is of deep concern to both the agency and the advertiser. The chief reason that money is wasted in commercials is inadequate preplanning. In production, the two major cost items are labor and equipment. Labor—the production crew, director, and performers—is hired by the day, and equipment is rented by the day. If a particular demonstration was improperly rehearsed, if a particular prop was not delivered, or if the location site was not scouted ahead of time, the shooting planned for one day may be forced into expensive overtime or into a second day. These costly mistakes can be avoided by careful planning.

Cost Relationship

Several areas that can have a dramatic impact on TV production costs are

● *Location or studio.* Is the commercial planned for studio or location? Location shoots (Exhibit 19.9), outside geographic zones, mean travel time and overnight accommodations for the crew, adding a minimum average cost of $7,500 per away day.

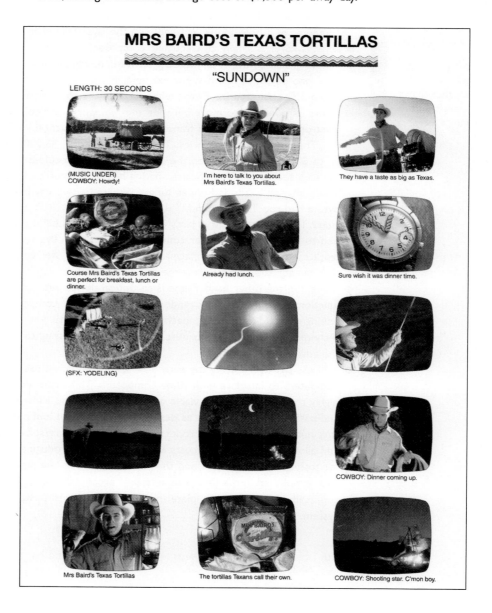

- *Talent.* The number of principals on the storyboard is important and can be expensive. The more people on-camera in your commercials, the higher the talent residual bill. The rates for talent are based on the Screen Actors Guild (SAG) union contract. For national commercials, you can roughly estimate your talent cost per on-camera principal as .0015 of your media budget for the spot. That is, $15,000 per person per $10 million in exposure. If 20 on-camera people are involved in your spot, expect a $300,000 bill. That chunk of your budget may exceed the entire net cost of production. So it is important to discuss how many on-camera principals are planned for the spot and how many are absolutely necessary.

- *Residuals.* Another major expense is the **residual**, or reuse fee, paid to performers—announcers, narrators, actors, and singers—in addition to their initial session fees. Under union rules, performers are paid every time the commercial is aired on the networks, the amount of the fee depending upon their scale and the number of cities involved. If a commercial is aired with great frequency, a national advertiser may end up paying more in residuals than for the production of the commercial itself. This problem is less severe for the local advertiser because local rates are cheaper than national rates. The moral is: Cast only the number of performers necessary to the commercial and not one performer more.

  The use of extras presents less of a cost issue. The first 30 extras in a spot must be paid a session fee ($232/day) and are not entitled to residuals. Rates for use of extras beyond the first 30 can be negotiated.

- *Special effects.* If the board indicated the use of special effects or animation (either computer-generated or cel), ask how the special effect will be achieved. It is not unusual for complicated computer-generated effects to cost $6,000 to $12,000 per second and more! To prevent surprises, ask questions. What may appear to be a simple execution on the surface may in fact contain extremely expensive elements. Neither the agency nor client should be satisfied until everyone understands the project. Anything short of this can result in surprise creative and expenditures.

- *Estimate costs.* Given the potential complexity of shooting commercials due to a wide range of factors (location, special rigs, special effects, talent, set construction), it is not uncommon to believe a relatively "simple" looking spot presented in storyboard form will be "relatively" inexpensive. This is simply not the case. Both the client and the agency must always, always require a rough cost for each spot recommended. The number provided will help put the project into focus relative to the planned media support for the commercials. Generally, it is not uncommon for clients to spend 10 percent of their planned media budget in production. As this percentage escalates, the production decision becomes more difficult, particularly in today's economic climate.

- *Editorial fee cost.* There is a creative labor fee for the editor's service. This charge is for the editor's and assistant editor's time. Depending on the editor and the difficulty of the edit, a creative free can range from $400 to $500 (to supervise sound only, for example, on a single-scene commercial) to more than $9,000 to cut a multi-image, complex spot with special effects manipulations and music.

- *The cost of film transfer and videotape conform or edit and finishing.* This cost can range from about $1,000 for this work, including tape stock and finished materials, to $7,500 for expansive and difficult treatments.

- *Special effects and titling.* This cost can range from $100 to make a title art card and include it in the edit session, to $10,000 to $30,000 for heavy design, frame-by-frame, picture manipulations.

- *Recording and mixing.* The cost of recording and mixing a voice-over, music, and sound effects together can range from $450 to $4,000 or more.

If you total all of these possibilities, from the combined lowest to the combined highest, the cost can be $2,136 to $67,100 to edit a 30-second commercial!

Residual
A sum paid to certain talent on a TV or radio commercial every time the commercial is run after 13 weeks, for the life of the commercial.

TV Cost Average

An American Association of Advertising Agencies' study indicates that the average national commercial rose to $222,000 to produce. Obviously, there is great variation in producing commercials: interviews/testimonials averaged $249,000; animation, $210,000; and tabletop/products, food averaged $111,000. These figures indicate the importance of producing a TV spot that is on target because the investment simply to get the idea on film or tape is significant.[11] Historically, location shoots take more time than studio shoots; and in 1993, for the first time, more location shoots were done than studio shoots.

Digital Links and Post Production

No sooner than we could send a voice from room to room, we wanted to send it from continent to continent. And if we could beam a voice, why not a piece of paper? And if paper works, well, why not commercials in progress? Long-distance transmissions and manipulation of commercials are becoming a reality. Agencies, production houses, and directors are using various forms of digital links. Of course, the purpose is for people in one location to communicate about the creative process and maintain control over the process without having to travel.

To understand how this works, consider telephone lines first. For this we need to understand the technology. There are four basic types of phone lines. The standard phone line carries a voice, sending it at 56 to 64 kilobits per second—too slow to send commercial clips. Next is the ISDN (Integrated Services Digital Network) line, which is twice as big, at 112 kb a second. If you bundle 24 ISDN lines, you have what is called a T-1 line. Now you can transmit at 1.5 megabits a second. When you put 28 T-1 lines together, you have a T-3 line, which is capable of transmitting broadcast-quality video. Now you can send commercial cuts from one location to another. Of course, the fee for this line can cost $2,000 per month, not including the equipment on each end to make it work.

Let us look at some examples of how the technology is being used. BBDO/Detroit used a Macintosh environment to connect to a postproduction house, where it pulls dailies for their Dodge account. The impetus for such a link is driven by the volume of work for a single client and the need for heavy posttelevision production. Director Henry Sandbank used this technology on a Coca-Cola project that involved 40 scenes and took weeks to complete in postproduction; he could check in several times every day with the San Francisco effects production house from his New York office. The agency creatives didn't have to travel or hang around, either. Everyone could keep tabs on the special-effects progress whenever they desired. Another example of technology and producing commercials from two locations is the videofax. Here a black box with a keyboard connected to an ISDN line compresses and digitizes the video, then outputs to a desk on the other end. The best quality takes about 30 minutes for a 30-second commercial, but often is used for shorter cuts. The videofax costs about $65, not including about $500 a month for the equipment.[12]

In the case of Mercedes-Benz, technicians at Digital Domain animated the late Ed Sullivan's jaw from the original television clips so that it appeared that he was introducing the Mercedes M-class. A voice impersonator said the words. The graphic artists also altered Sullivan's appearance from the original clips, removing sideburns and smoothing wrinkles so that the images taken from different programs would look alike. The *Ed Sullivan Show* aired for 23 years, ending in 1971.

Uses of this technology include accessing film and photo libraries, video and audio production facilities, and such services as image rendering, compression, and data conversion.

---

[11]Joe Mandese, "Study Shows Cost of TV Spots," *Advertising Age,* August 1, 1994, p. 32.
[12]Cathy Madison, "The Mod Couple," *Creativity,* September 1995, pp. 26–30.

Television remains the most powerful advertising medium because of its ability to blend sight, sound, and motion to create emotional reactions. The time to communicate is very short—usually 15 to 30 seconds—and creates a challenge for communicating the product story or position.

There are numerous creative techniques available to the creative team: testimonials, demonstrations, slice-of-life, interviews, humor, animation, serials, infomercials, and so forth. Research can aid the creative decision process in terms of which technique is appropriate for the strategy.

Storyboards are usually created to help communicate the idea to the advertiser and the production company. It is important that everyone clearly visualize the same commercial before time and money are invested in the idea.

Developing commercials requires some understanding of production terminology such as wipes, dissolves, and close-ups that help communicate the nature of a particular visual or transition from one scene to the next. Writing and visualizing the commercial in simple and easy-to-understand terms is essential to success—it is, after all, a visual medium. Because a good idea can be destroyed by bad production, producing the finished commercial is just as important as conceiving the "big idea."

Producing the commercial involves three distinct stages: preproduction, shooting, and post-production. Computer-generated imagery allows creative people to do almost anything they can imagine—but at a high cost.

REVIEW

1. What is ad retention? What is the retention range for TV commercials?
2. What cost-relationship factors are involved in the making of a TV commercial?
3. John Wayne selling Coors beer is an example of which technique?
4. Who attends the preproduction meeting?
5. What is a *Harry*?

TAKE IT TO THE NET

We invite you to visit the Russell/Lane page on the Prentice Hall Web site at

PHLIP **http://www.prenhall.com/phbusiness** for the bimonthly Russell/Lane update and for this chapter's World Wide Web exercise.

20

THE RADIO COMMERCIAL

CHAPTER OBJECTIVES

IN PRINT AND TELEVISION, VISUALS ARE AN INTEGRAL PART OF COMMUNICATION. RADIO IS A DIFFERENT MEDIUM, ONE FOR EARS ALONE. AFTER READING THIS CHAPTER YOU WILL UNDERSTAND

- the nature of the medium
- how to create from a strategy
- structuring the commercial
- writing the commercial
- musical commercials
- producing radio commercials
- unions and talent.

The writing of radio advertising should be easy. All you have to do is talk to someone about the product. Right? Well, maybe. Great radio advertising is very difficult. You need to be able to awaken images in the listeners' minds by using sound, music, and voices. You have the opportunity to play with their imagination in what is referred to as "the theater of the mind."

THE NATURE OF THE MEDIUM

Phil Cuttino, president of Cuttino Communications, often refers to "watching radio—the most misunderstood medium." He should know, he's an expert. Let us take a closer look at the nature of the medium.

Before the beginning of widespread viewing of television in the mid-1950s, families used to "watch" the radio. We have all heard excerpts from radio's **"theater of the mind"**—*Superman, The Lone Ranger, Bulldog Drummon, Inner Sanctum,* and Orson Welles's fabulous spoof, *War of the Worlds.* People watched the radio because the mental imagery that came with every episode was breathtaking or scary or beautiful or just plain funny. However, television's combination of audio and visuals was very compelling and certainly effective as a storyteller and theater. TV also was, and is, a dynamic advertising medium. Unfortunately, radio was subordinated to the position of music man, talk, and other audio-oriented programming.

Theater of the mind
In radio, a writer paints pictures in the mind of the listener through the use of sound.

Today TV is the darling of the airwaves. Even television advertising has taken on a star quality. In major publications, there are commentaries on TV commercials, as well as an objective and subjective rating. TV is the closest that ad people come to "show biz." Another contributing factor to radio's lowly position in the creative pecking order is the fact that most creative teams consist of art directors, designers, and copywriters. Because radio has no material visuals, the visual arts people are out of business when it comes to radio. This tends to lead the creative team to either print or television advertising.

Over time, a new type of radio commercial has emerged, which Phil Cuttino calls "print radio." When radio is needed, some copywriters, who are experienced in print advertising but know little about radio, tend to fall back on a familiar copy format. As a result, we hear "print radio" all the time. There is a headline, a subhead, body copy, a logo, and a slogan—an audio newspaper ad.

To understand the importance of radio, you need to understand the cynical nature of the American consumer.

No one believes anyone anymore. American consumers are searching for an excuse to disbelieve what you are saying. All they need is a cue that you are trying to sell them something, and they will blank you out mentally. They may not change the dial; this is a case of "The lights are on, but nobody's home." Before you can tell the consumer your story, you must disarm him, entertain him, amuse him, get him on your side.

Radio, like magazines, is a very personal medium. Almost everyone has a favorite radio station. Consumers get to know the radio personalities; they attend events sponsored by their radio station. It is this kind of listener allegiance, this nonhostile environment, that makes it easier for marketers to approach the listenership. Remember, consumers are not waiting to hear your commercial. They are listening to the radio to be entertained, so entertain them, then sell them. Entertainment is your admission ticket to their consciousness.

RADIO IS THE GREAT EQUALIZER

In chapter 9, radio was said to offer more than other advertising media. It has the flexibility, the marketability, the promotionability, and the price to fit advertisers' needs to reach their targets—if they choose the right stations and use the right message.

- *You have 60 seconds all to yourself.* Print ads have to fight for attention with other ads on the page. TV has to contend with channel surfers because viewers have favorite TV *programs,* whereas radio listeners have favorite radio *stations.* In the time span of a 60-second radio commercial, no other advertising can interfere with your message. The main equalizer in radio is the ability of a locally produced radio spot to be on a level playing field with any national spot. The power of a radio commercial is the idea, the imagery. Unlike TV, national-quality production can be easily created for a reasonable cost. Your advertiser can be as big as any other marketer for 60 seconds.
- *Radio has the most captive audience of any media.* The advent of mass transit has not changed the fact that in most cities, to get from point A to point B, you still have to get in your car and drive. The heaviest radio listenership occurs in the morning and afternoon drive times. During that time, listeners cannot go to the kitchen for a beer, answer the door, or pick up a magazine. They are trapped in their cars, listening to the traffic report, the news, and, of course, your radio commercial.
- *Listeners and advertisers have many programming formats to choose from:* country, adult contemporary, news/talk/sports/business, oldies, top 40, religion, classic rock, urban rhythm and blues, easy listening, alternative rock, variety, ethnic, classical, gospel, jazz, new age, and preteen. This makes radio a highly selective medium for the advertiser. Reflecting the ethnic multinational nature of our society, there also are foreign-language stations in many markets available to advertisers.

CREATING THE COMMERCIAL

Even though radio requires a different style of advertising, ads are developed through a thought process similar to that used in other media. You have to understand your target. As Tom Little, award-winning creative director, once said, "People don't buy products. They buy solutions to problems." Last year people bought about 350,000 $\frac{1}{4}$-inch drill bits in this country. People didn't want $\frac{1}{4}$-inch drill bits. They wanted $\frac{1}{4}$-inch holes. The radio creative writer has to refer back to the objectives and strategy and describe the target in both demographic and psychographic terms before beginning the creative process. The writer needs to be sure the message is going to be believed—that it says the right things to the right people—and needs to ask if the copy strengthens the brand position, the place you want to occupy in the consumer's mind. Is it credible? Do you have all the copy points that your research indicates is needed? Is it human? Is it believable communication? Do people really talk like that? Or is it simply copy lingo? These are some of the things the radio copywriter must think about when sitting down to the blank page or the computer screen.

The writer for radio has the opportunity to develop an entire commercial alone (although in some agencies a creative team may work on a project). That means writing the script, picking the talent, and producing the commercial. In radio, the copywriter enjoys the freedom to create scenes in the theater of the listener's imagination by painting pictures in sound—a car starting or stopping, a phone ringing, water running, ice cubes falling into a glass, crowds roaring, a camera clicking. Remember, sound alone has an extraordinary ability to enter people's minds.

Let us look at the three elements the copywriter uses to create mental pictures, memorability, and emotion: words, sound, and music.

Words

Words are the basic building blocks of effective radio commercials. They are used to describe the product, grab attention, create interest, build desire, and evoke a response from the listener. The warmth of the human voice may be all that is needed to communicate your message.

Sound

Used properly, sound can unlock the listener's imagination and create feelings. Any sound effect used should be necessary and recognizable; you should never have to explain it for the audience.

The sound has to convey a special message or purpose; it has to attract attention and complement the words. Sound can be used to underscore a point; create feelings of suspense, excitement, or anger; and invoke almost any mood you desire.

There are three basic sources of sound effects: manual, recorded, and electronic. *Manual effects* are those that are produced live, either with live subjects or with studio props; opening doors, footsteps, and blowing horns are examples. *Recorded effects* are available from records, tapes, or professional sound libraries. They offer the copywriter almost every conceivable sound—dogs barking, cats meowing, leaves blowing, thunder crashing, cars racing. *Electronic effects* are sounds that are produced electronically on special studio equipment. Any sound created by using a device that generates an electrical impulse or other electronic sound is an electrical effect.

Music

Music can be very powerful in catching the listener's attention and evoking feelings. Thus music has been called the "universal language." Different kinds of music appeal to different emotions: A minor key is sadder than a major key; an increased tempo creates a sense of anticipation.

Commercials are often set to music especially composed for them or adapted from a familiar song. A few bars of distinctive music played often enough may serve to identify the product instantly. Such a musical logotype usually lasts from 4 to 10 seconds. **Jingles** are a popular means of making a slogan memorable—think of the music for Coca-Cola, Pepsi, Chevrolet, Oldsmobile, and McDonald's over the years.

Create from Strategy

What's brown, fuzzy, round on the outside, green on the inside, and tastes good? The California Kiwifruit Commission set an objective to increase awareness of their ugly little product. Their strategy was built around "Kiwifruit Is Fun." The commission understands people's perception of the California kiwifruit and gave us permission to have fun with its outward appearance . . . knowing that it's what's inside that counts," says Christine Coyle, creative director of Dick Orkin's Radio Ranch. The spots humorously played out two situations: a recognizable school food pageant and a California Kiwifruit audition. The ads were able to convince consumers who were suspect of the funny looking fruit to go ahead and give it a try. The vertical integrated program combined radio with some print and some in-store services that helped educate grocery produce managers. Unit sales the first year of the campaign went up 67 percent, or an increase of about 5 million new households purchasing the product. The strategy worked.

DEVELOPING THE RADIO SCRIPT

You will find some differences in the formats used in the script examples in this chapter. This is because most agencies have their own format sheets for copywriters. Formats also vary according to how the script will be used: If you are going to be in the studio with the producers and talents, you can verbally explain how the script is to be read or answer any questions that come up. If, however, you are going to mail the script to DJs to be read live, you need to be certain that anyone reading it will understand exactly what you want. The guidelines shown in Exhibit 20.1 illustrate explicit script directions.

Client: Wild Corporation
Length: :60
Job No. 3364

LEFT SECTION OF PAGE IS FOR INFORMATION RELATING TO VOICES, ANNOUNCER, MUSIC, SOUND, USUALLY IN CAPS.	The right section of the script consists of copy and directions. It should be typed double-spaced. Pause is indicated by dots (. . .) or double dash (——). <u>Underline</u> or use CAPS for emphasis.
MUSIC:	Music is usually indicated by all caps. WILLIAM TELL OVERTURE ESTABLISH AND FADE UNDER. In some cases, music is underlined. Directions may be indicated by parentheses ( ).
VOICE #1	(LAUGHING LOUDLY) Excuse me sir . . .
OLD MAN	Yes . . . (RAISING VOICE) What do you *want?*
SFX:	SUPERMARKET NOISES, CRASHING NOISES AS SHOPPING CARTS CRASH. Sound effects indicated by SFX: (:08) BUZZER
SINGERS:	He's bright-eyed and bushy-tailed . . .
ANNCR:	This indicates announcer talking.
VO:	Voice Over.

Radio, Theater of the Mind

According to Cuttino, one of the biggest mistakes you can make in creating radio is the failure to recognize the fact that everyone has mental images of sounds that they hear. When no material images exist, sound creates an image in the mind's eye. It is the duty of the radio writer/producer to take control of the listener's imagery and guide it to a positive reaction that seeds the memory with the targeted message and leads to the proper response. For instance, a writer creates a commercial featuring a car dealer who is screaming about a sale, assuming that the tactic will get the listener's attention and will eventually lead the consumer to the dealership because of the "incredible savings." Unfortunately, the mind's eye of the listener doesn't see a sleek new car or the money he is saving; he sees a middle-aged man in a garish plaid suit yelling at him. In communications, it is important to be concerned about what people *feel* about your advertisement.

The Elements of a Good Radio Commercial

- *Be single-minded, focused.* Don't ask the consumer to take on too much information at one time. Prioritize your copy points. Think of your commercial as a model of our solar system. The major copy point is the sun and all the other copy points are planets of varying degrees of importance, but they all revolve around and support the central idea.
- *Research your product or service.* Many clients keep tabs on their competition, but they rarely relate their features and benefits to factual data. Meaningful statistics can give substantial support to your message.
- *Relate to the consumer.* When you tell consumers your story, always relate the brand to their wants and needs. Do not assume they will come to the right conclusion.
- *Generate extension.* You can multiply the effect of your commercial many times over by achieving extension . . . consumers picking up phrases from the spot and using them. A clever phrase or execution can have consumers asking other people if they have heard the spot, people requesting the spot to be played on the radio, even getting mentions by DJs.
- *Produce an immediate physical, emotional, or mental response.* Laughter, a tug on the heart strings, or mental exercises of a consumer during a radio spot help seed the memory and aid message retention.
- *Use plain, conversational English.* Be a clear communicator. Don't force your characters to make unnatural statements. This is not the board room . . . no "execubabble," just clear, plain, and simple English.

Folks Restaurants created a commercial, "couscous" (Exhibit 20.2), which played off their southern roots. The commercial uses banter between a waitress with a Southern drawl and a prissy guy who wants prissy food. The commercial sets the stage for letting people know that Folks is the restaurant with "real food for real people." The commercial used three different tags to promote specific entree specials: (1) pork porterhouse; (2) chicken pot pie in a bread bowl, pork porterhouse, and savory new recipe for meatloaf; and (3) a holiday catering special at different times.

WRITING THE COMMERCIAL

Some agencies have a special creative director in charge of radio advertising. For years, the feeling has been that agencies have assigned junior talent to write radio commercials. It is now hoped that having a specific person in charge of radio will generate enthusiasm for doing great radio. Others hire the expertise of people like Phil Cuttino of Cuttino Communications to generate strategic radio advertising.

There are radio boutiques that have been used for many years by clients and agencies to help create and produce radio commercials. Some of the most popular boutiques include Dick Orkin's Radio Ranch, BarzRadio, The Chuck Blore Company, World Wide Wadio, Radioland, Hungarian Radio, and Sarley, Bigg & Bedder.

Client: Folks
Job Number: FOLKS-7Y-1281
Description: "couscous" :60 Radio (:40 spot, :20 tag)

SFX:	(casual, family-style restaurant sounds)
NILES:	(in a voice like Niles on Frasier) Miss. Yoo-hoo, miss.
WAITRESS:	(syrupy, Southern drawl) Watchu need, darlin?
NILES:	On your menu here it says sweet tea. Do you by chance serve a medley of sweet teas such as mint or perhaps persimmon?
WAITRESS:	Well, sweet tea is suga tea, suga.
NILES:	Very well, I'll take that as a no. And your chicken is that free-range?
WAITRESS:	It's $6.59. And sweetie, that's free enough.
NILES:	Alrighty then. Tell me, how is your couscous?
WAITRESS:	My what?!!
SFX:	A big, loud slap across the face.
ANNCR:	Folks, real food for real folks.
ANNOUNCER:	(tag #1 porterhouse/sweet potato chips) This fall at Folks we're featuring a new thick n' juicy, 12 oz. pork porterhouse. And to start things off, try sweet potato chips with a cinnamon marshmallow sauce for dipping. It's the perfect fall meal. And it's available at all seventeen Metro Folks locations.
	(tag #2 entrees) This fall at Folks we're offering chicken pot pie in a bread bowl, a 12 oz., thick n' juicy pork porterhouse and savory meatloaf made from a fantastic new recipe. They're the season's best entrees and they're available at all seventeen Metro Folks locations.
	(tag #3 entrees/holiday) This fall at Folks we have chicken pot pie in a bread bowl, a 12 oz., think n' juicy pork porterhouse and savory meatloaf. And for the holidays, we bring the feast to you. Just call our catering line at 404-874-5555 or one of our seventeen Metro Folks locations.

exhibit

20.2

Courtesy: Folks Restaurant
Management Group.

The radio commercial, like the TV commercial, has as its basic ingredient the promise of a significant and distinctive benefit or position. Once the promise has been determined, you are ready to use the arsenal of words and sounds to communicate your product. Ways to vitalize the copy include

● *Simplicity.* The key to producing a good radio commercial is to build around one central idea. Avoid confusing the listener with too many copy points. Use known words, short phrases, simple sentence structure. Keep in mind that the copy needs to be conversational. Write for the *ear,* not the eye. Get in the habit of reading your copy out loud.

- *Clarity.* Keep the train of thought on one straight track. Avoid side issues. Delete unnecessary words. (Test: Would the commercial be hurt if the words were deleted? If not, take them out.) Write from draft to draft until your script becomes unmistakably clear and concise. At the end of the commercial, your audience should understand exactly what you have tried to say. Despite having several facts in your commercial, make sure you have the big idea.

- *Coherence.* Be certain that your message flows in logical sequence from first word to last, using smooth transitional words and phrases for easier listening.

- *Rapport.* Remember, as far as your listeners are concerned, you are speaking only to them. Try to use a warm, personal tone, as if you were talking to one or two people. Make frequent use of the word *you.* Address the listeners in terms they would use themselves.

- *Pleasantness.* It is not necessary to entertain simply for the sake of entertaining, but there is no point in being dull or obnoxious. Strike a happy medium; talk as one friend to another about the product or service.

- *Believability.* Every product has its good points. Tell the truth about it. Avoid overstatements and obvious exaggerations; they are quickly spotted and defeat the whole purpose of the commercial. Be straightforward; you want to convey the impression of being a trusted friend.

- *Interest.* Nothing makes listeners indifferent faster than a boring commercial. Products and services are not fascinating in themselves; the way you present them makes them interesting. Try to give your customer some useful information as a reward for listening.

- *Distinctiveness.* Sound different from other commercials and set your product apart. Use every possible technique—a fresh approach, a musical phrase, a particular voice quality or sound effect—to give your commercial a distinct character.

Some Techniques

Basically a medium of words, radio—more than any other medium—relies heavily on the art of writing strong copy. However, just as print ads and TV commercials include pictures and graphics to add impact to the copy, radio creates mental pictures with other techniques. Radio copywriters can choose among many proven techniques to give more meaning to the copy, to help gain the attention of the busy target audience, and to hold that attention for the duration of the commercial. Some of these techniques parallel those used in television.

- *Humor.* Humor is an excellent technique for service and retail businesses. Consumers never relate an ad to the advertising agency that produced it; they only relate the spot to the advertiser. Therefore, humor can portray a company as friendly, likable, and easy when negotiating a sale.

    Many award-winning radio spots use humor. Tom Little, a creative director who has judged many award shows, once said humorous spots won awards because they stood out from the hundreds that he had to listen to. If that's true, then the same probably works for consumers. Of course, humor may be part of any writing technique we have discussed. The Sega Saturn "Woman" spot (Exhibit 20.3) starts very soft and feminine, but soon she says, "It gives me that just-dropped-a-tall-strong-man-on-my-knee-and-broke-his-spine feeling. And I like that." It goes from soft to forceful with humorous overtones. Humor is often appropriate for low-priced packaged products, products people buy for fun, products whose primary appeal is taste, or products or services in need of change-of-pace advertising because of strong competition. Be very careful about making fun of the product or the user or treat too lightly a situation that is not normally funny. Sprite successfully made fun of soft drink advertising and what the product will do for you in its appeal to generation Xers.

- *Emotion.* This is an effective method to use when the topic is indeed emotional. Family, health care, donations, mental care, security, and similar products and services use emotion to stimulate the targeted response.

Goodby, Silverstein & Partners
Sega Saturn
"Woman" :60 Radio
As Produced

SOFT WOMAN VO WITH SOFT MUSIC
UNDER

WOMAN:	I'm a woman. I like flowers, and kittens, and things that smell pretty. Sometimes, I need a little something to make me feel fresh, and feminine again. Which is why I like to use Virtua Fighter.
SFX:	BURST OF LOUD VIRTUA FIGHTER SOUNDS
WOMAN:	On the new Sega Saturn.
WOMAN:	(PRETTY MUSIC) It gives me that just-dropped-a-tall-strong-man-on-my-knee-and-broke-his-spine feeling. And I like that. Of course, sometimes, I feel more romantic. That's when I reach for Panzer Dragoon.
SFX:	BURST OF LOUD PANZER DRAGOON SOUNDS.
WOMAN:	It's loud, it's warlike, and I get to blast the living BEEEEP out of anything that moves.
LITTLE GIRL:	Mommy? Am I turning into a woman?
WOMAN:	Yes, you are. And I think it's time.
LITTLE GIRL:	Time for what?
WOMAN:	Time for Daytona USA.
SFX:	DAYTONA USA.
MALE VO:	Sega Saturn. So real, it's kinda scary.
SFX:	PRETTY MUSIC FLOURISH
WOMAN:	For that spring fresh feeling.
SEGA SCREAM:	SEGA SATURN!

- *Music/sound effects.* Music creates the mood and sound effects create the imagery in the consumer's mind. Jingles can be very memorable and effective when they relate directly to the product or service.
- *White space.* This is, of course, a term used in print advertising. However, white space in radio can be extremely compelling. A 60-second spot may start with music or sound effects with no copy for 45 seconds, bringing the consumers' curiosity into play and leaving them wide open to accept a provocative message.
- *Dialogue.* This is a great technique to use in many situations. Dialogue doesn't confront the consumer; it allows the listener to eavesdrop on the conversation. Dialogue is also very successful when the advertiser has a product that appeals to men and women. Dialogue between a man and a woman allows the commercial to play to both targets.
- *Sex.* It can sell very well.
- *Straight announcer.* Sometimes the simplest approach works best. In this commonly used and most direct of all techniques, an announcer or personality delivers the entire script. Success depends both on the copy and on the warmth and believability of the person performing the

commercial. Tom Bodet for Motel 6 was all of these things and one of the reasons the commercials were so popular. This approach works particularly well when a positive image has previously been established and a specific event is being promoted, such as a sale. Mindtrap (Exhibit 20.4) uses only a voice-over to get the idea across in its "brother-in-law" spot promoting Mindtrap as an interesting game. This award-winning radio commercial, written by Pirate Radio & Television in Toronto, is clever and uses wry humor to introduce the game to the listener. As you can see, there is one sound effect at the end. You might notice that it uses the name of the product four times in interesting ways to gain brand recognition.

- *Combination.* Radio techniques may be mixed in countless ways, as illustrated by the Marines spot in Exhibit 20.5 (combines music, sound effects, an announcer, and a person). To select the right technique for a particular assignment, follow the guidelines discussed in chapter 19 for selecting TV techniques.

TIMING OF COMMERCIALS

Time is the major constraint in producing a radio commercial. Most radio stations accept these maximum word lengths for live commercial scripts:

- 10 seconds, 25 words
- 20 seconds, 45 words
- 30 seconds, 65 words
- 60 seconds, 125 words

MINDTRAP
"Brother-in-law" :60

VO:	You probably know someone who thinks they're pretty smart.
	Chances are you're related to them. In fact, they're usually married to your sister.
	Yes, the brother-in-law. You know the one. Six-four, good looking, virile, vice president, stock options, won the lottery, bought low, sold high, your parents worship him, good hair.
	I hate him already. And I don't even know him.
	Yes, you've been paddling in his wake for years. Then suddenly, you discover Mindtrap, the game. The idea behind it is simple. Whoever answers the most brainteasing questions—wins. It's all a matter of lateral thinking. Thinking being the operative word. There's long questions, silly questions, murder mysteries, funny questions and short questions—like this: If the maker doesn't want it, the buyer doesn't use it, and the user never sees it, what is it?
	The answer is . . . a coffin. Try *that* on Mr. Good Hair.
VO:	The best thing about Mindtrap is you don't have to be a nuclear fusion expert to guess the answers—it's a level playing field. So invite Mr. Good Bone Structure over and kick some buttinski. Buy Mindtrap and just do what I did. Read all the cards and memorize the answers.
SFX:	TRAP SNAP!
	Mindtrap. It's a game of one-upmanship. And your ship just came in.

ZJWB-6017
Client: USMC
Job #: MC-ENP-764504
Campaign: National Paid Radio
Title: "Lily/Paid"
Media: Radio
Length: :60
Comments: AS PRODUCED

Elements	Audio
MUSIC SFX:	(Up & Under)
ESPARZA:	I remember that day when I was gonna leave . . .
	All these thoughts are going through my mind . . . like "What am I doing?" . . . "Why am I doing this?"
	When I got to the island, it was raining.
	Your heart is pounding so hard 'cause you don't know what to expect.
SFX:	(DI on bus: "Welcome to the island—get off my bus now!")
ESPARZA:	The obstacles—they're constantly there all through boot camp.
	You see a wall and you're like, "There's no way I'm getting over that wall."
	And I remember I was coming down, and I was practically in tears 'cause I was so scared.
	And I did it . . . and it was like, "Oh, I made it!" It's an awesome feeling.
	When you feel like quitting, you have to look deep inside into your heart and ask yourself, "Do you want to claim that title?"
	Because they make you go through hell and back just to be called a Marine.
	If you take Lily the day she got on that bus and take Lily now, we're two totally different people.
ANNCR:	Maybe you can be one of us. The Few. The Proud. The Marines. Call 1-800-MARINES.
ESPARZA:	I claimed the title Marine . . . you can too.
"PAID" TAG:	Paid for by the Marines.

exhibit

20.5

Courtesy: J. Walter Thompson, Atlanta.

In prerecorded commercials, of course, you may use any number of words you can fit within the time limit. However, if you use more than 125 words for a 60-second commercial, the commercial will have to be read so rapidly that it may sound unnatural or even unintelligible. Remember, if you insert sound effects, that will probably cut down on the number of words you can use. If you have footsteps running for five seconds, you are going to have to cut 10 to 12 words. You need to time the musical intros and endings or sound effects because each will affect the number of words allowable. It is not unusual to go into the recording studio with a script that is a couple of seconds short because the extra time allows the talents to sound more natural. Actors need some breathing room to sound sincere (see Exhibit 20.6).

MUSICAL COMMERCIALS

Music can be a powerful tool for getting your product remembered. As musical writer Steve Karman has said: "People don't hum the announcer."[1]

In writing musical commercials, you have to start with an earthquake, then build to something really big. In other words, there is no room for subtlety. The thought process and strategy are different from those in regular songwriting.

There are three main elements to writing commercial music:

- *Intro:* The beginning of the song. The tempo and lyrics may be established here.
- *Verse:* The middle of the song. This is where the message is developed. There may be several verses.
- *Theme or chorus:* May be the conclusion of the song.

Often you begin with the chorus to establish your theme, or you may repeat the theme throughout. The theme is what listeners remember. Some musical forms, such as blues, can be thought of as both verse and chorus. A theme may serve as a musical logotype for a product, lasting about 4 to 10 seconds. Copywriter David Rosen wrote a spot for Fila's Stack II shoe, named after basketball star Jerry Stackhouse. He explains that, "Stackhouse's first step and his agility is his big thing—but the lyrics are about his personality:

> *The way I feel,*
> *You know the love is real,*
> *With your leather and lace,*
> *You've got a tongue but not a face.*
> *Left and right,*
> *I like all the things you do.*
> *Just show me that you love me,*
> *'Cuz I love both of you.*
>
> Chorus: *Jerry loves his Fila shoes.*
> *I know I'm gonna score with you."*

And the off-beat chorus continues and ends with "I think the man is freaken' out, Ooh, I love it when you make that little squeaky noise."

Many commercials are composed especially for the advertiser or product. Others are simply adapted from a familiar song. A melody is in the public domain, available for use by anyone without cost, after its copyright has expired. Many old favorites and classics are in the public domain and have been used as advertising themes. That is one of their detriments: They may have been used by many others.

Popular tunes that are still protected by copyright are available only by (often costly) agreement with the copyright owner. An advertiser can also commission a composer to create an original tune, which becomes the advertiser's property and gives the product its own musical personality.

Do you have the talent to write a jingle? Does the typical copywriter have the ability to do so? In general, the job of writing such copy is left to the music experts.

---

[1] Bruce Bendinger, *The Copy Workshop Workbook* (Chicago: Bruce Bendinger Creative Communications, Inc., 1988), p. 214.

Goodby, Silverstein & Partners
Sega of America
"Surgery"
:60 Radio
As Produced

SFX:	DRILL. BEEP OF LIFE MACHINE UNDER THROUGHOUT.
DOC:	Ever had brain surgery, Jim? (SFX: CRUNCH)
JIM:	No . . . um, do I have to be awake?
DOC:	Just try to relax, Jim . . . all right . . . we'll just snip this away . . . (SFX: SNIPPING) . . . say, Jim, have you seen that new Sega Saturn?
JIM:	Uh, yeah, the 3-D graphics are cool.
DOC:	You know, it sounds very impressive. Better than your home stereo in fact.
JIM:	Oh, really?
DOC:	See the Sega Saturn's 24-bit surround sound processor sends out this, uh, sonic image, fooling your cerebral cortex . . . here . . . (SFX: POKE) . . . .
JIM:	Ooohhhh . . .
DOC:	. . . into thinking it's surrounded. This in turn activates the hypothalamus under here (SFX: RRRIP) . . .
JIM:	OUCH!
DOC:	. . . which in turn stimulates the pituitary behind here . . . (SFX: POKE) . . .
JIM:	OW! THAT HURTS!
DOC:	. . . sending hormones along your corpus collosum behind this gray thing . . . if I could just . . . (SFX: GRUNTS, STRAINS) . . .
JIM:	AAAAAAAH! OK! OK! I BELIEVE YOU! STOP IT!
DOC:	. . . get around this reticular formation I could show you . . .
JIM:	AAAAAIIIIEEE!!!!! STOP IT! STOP! OK! YOU MADE YOUR POINT! AAAAAHHH!
(SOUND MONTAGE)	
VO:	Sega Saturn. So real it's kind of scary.
DOC:	Okay. Jim, Let's try this: bark like a dog.
JIM:	I'm not gonna . . . (SFX: SQUISH) . . . Woof! Woof!
VO:	Sega Saturn!

Audio Technology

Over the past 10 years there has been a radical change in the way music and sound are recorded. A little more than a decade ago, the world of high-fidelity multitrack recording and sync-to-picture belonged solely to record companies, postproduction houses, and commercial ventures.

In 1988, Digidesign's Sound Tools system broke this barrier by offering a CD-quality digital stereo recording environment. Using a Macintosh, musicians and sound designers could then record mono or stereo digital masters, but it was still impossible to record one track while listening to another, and there was no way to play back MIDI (musical instrument digital interface) sequences simultaneously with audio.

In 1990, OSC released Deck software to fill this void. Deck was the first Macintosh software that allowed true four-track recording and simultaneous MIDI file playback. Deck's simple interface was based on the integrated *portable studio* metaphor and required no knowledge of MIDI. It looked and functioned like a four-track cassette mixer/recorder, but it turned any Macintosh with a Digidesign NuBus card into a CD-quality production environment. It has been used extensively in the past few years to produce albums and CDs and for basic sync work. In 1993, Deck II was produced. It uses a variety of hardware systems that turn a Macintosh into a true multitrack digital audio workstation.

You can record your basic ideas digitally from the very beginning, add and edit digital audio and MIDI tracks to your composition, and synchronize your elements to video decks or QuickTime video. You can then use the software to transfer that master digitally to a digital audio tape (DAT), and you can print your stereo/master directly to time-coded DAT. Every step in the multitrack production of digital audio is in the hands of the individual.

Musicians can use it as a composition environment, and produce CDs or CD-quality demos from the original tracks. Video postproduction sound designers can use it for typical audio sweetening. MIDI studios can use it to record final audio tracks over existing MIDI tracks.

METHODS OF DELIVERY

There are three ways a radio commercial can be delivered: live, by station announcer, and prerecorded.

The Live Commercial

A live commercial is delivered in person by the studio announcer, disc jockey, newscaster, or other station personality; or perhaps by a sports reporter from another location. Although generally read from a script prepared by the advertiser, the commercial is sometimes revised to complement the announcer's style. If time allows, the revised script should be approved in advance by the advertiser. Ad-libbing (extemporizing) from a fact sheet should be discouraged because the announcer may inadvertently omit key selling phrases or, in the case of regulated products such as drugs, fail to include certain mandatory phrases.

Some commercials are delivered partly live and partly prerecorded. The prerecorded jingle, for example, can be played over and over with live-announcer copy added. Sometimes the live part (the dealer "tie-up") is left open for the tie-in ad of the local distributor.

One advantage of the live commercial is that the announcer may have a popular following, and listeners tend to accept advice from someone they like. The other big advantage is cost: Station announcers usually do your commercials free of extra talent costs.

Station Announcer

For a campaign dealing with a retail offer that will change frequently, advertisers often use a station announcer reading copy written by the agency. This is recorded at the station at no charge to the client—sometimes even with the client's musical theme in the background. This type of delivery allows for frequent changes in copy at no cost.

The Prerecorded Commercial

Advertises undertaking a regional or national campaign will not know local announcers' capabilities. In any case, it would be impractical to write a separate script to fit each one's particular style. Commercials for these campaigns are therefore usually prerecorded. Not only does this assure advertisers that the commercial will be identical each time it is aired, but it also allows them to take advantage of myriad techniques that would be impractical in a live commercial. (Actually, in many instances, "live" commercials are recorded by the station so that they can run even when the announcer is not on duty.)

Talent and Unions

As with television, the use and payment to performers appearing in radio commercials is dictated by the AFTRA (American Federation of Television and Radio Artists) commercial contract. Talent is paid a session fee when the commercial is recorded. There are other requirements for payment based upon usage, including spot, network, dealer, demo and copy testing, and foreign use. It is another cost the advertiser must consider.

PRODUCING THE RADIO COMMERCIAL

Although there are certain broad similarities, producing radio commercials is far simpler and less costly than producing TV commercials. First, the agency or advertiser appoints a radio producer, who converts the script into a recording ready to go on the air. After preparing the cost estimate and getting budget approval, the producer selects a recording studio and a casting director, if necessary. If music is called for, the producer calls a music "house" that usually composes, arranges, and takes all steps necessary to get the finished music. If the music is not a big-budget item, the producer may call for **"stock" music** (prerecorded and used on a rental basis).

After the cast has been selected, it rehearses in a recording studio, which can be hired by the hour. However, because most commercials are made in short "takes" that are later joined in the editing, a formal rehearsal is usually unnecessary. When the producer feels the cast is ready, the commercial is acted out and recorded on tape. Music and sound are taped separately and then mixed with the vocal tape by the sound-recording studio. In fact, by double- and triple-tracking music and singers' voices, modern recording equipment can build small sounds into big ones. However, union rules require that musicians and singers be paid extra fees when their music is mechanically added to their original recording. After the last mix, the master tape of the commercial is prepared. When final approval has been obtained, duplicates are made on $\frac{1}{4}$-inch tape reels or audiocassettes for release to the list of stations.

Things to Remember during Production

Phil Cuttino has a bias against having the account executive or client at a recording session. He feels their presence creates too many problems, which can inhibit great production. Among these: the talent and engineer tighten up, and everyone is concerned about time instead of producing an effective spot. He suggests that you use a phone patch from the studio to play the spot for the account executive first. Then, with his or her blessing, call the client for the final approval. The engineer and talent should remain in the studio until the final approval is achieved. Cuttino also has some other production thoughts:

Stock music
Existing recorded music that may be purchased for use in a TV or radio commercial.

- *Call ahead.* Have the studio pull the music and sound effects selections.
- *Studio.* Find a studio that has several talented engineers that will quickly learn your style. Make sure the studio has a good SFX and music library and the latest technology.
- *Brain power.* During production, use everyone's brain to make the spot better. Ask for input from your engineer and voice talent. Remember, they probably have been involved in more spots in a week than you have in months.
- *Take your time.* Don't push the talent or engineer. Lead them to what you want.
- *Keep up with the technology.* New technology will always broaden your creative envelope.
- *Casting.* Acting professionals usually have the best and most believable voices because they are visualizing the scene. This is particularly true with dialogue or group scenes. Go to plays often to find new talent. Do not look at the people who are auditioning for a part in the spot . . . they will try to sell you with facial expression, body language, and hand motions . . . all worthless on radio. At first, allow talent to give you their own interpretation of the scene. You may be inspired by their rendition.

Steps in Radio Production

We may summarize the steps in producing a commercial as follows:

1. An agency or advertiser appoints a producer.
2. The producer prepares cost estimates.
3. The producer selects a recording studio.
4. With the aid of the casting director, if one is needed, the producer casts the commercial.
5. If music is to be included, the producer selects a musical director and chooses the music or selects stock music.
6. If necessary, a rehearsal is held.
7. The studio tapes music and sound separately.
8. The studio mixes music and sound with voices.
9. The producer sees that the master tape is prepared for distribution on either tape or cassettes and shipped to stations.

You are on the air!

SUMMARY

Radio can be visual, despite its lack of visuals. It has the listener's mind to paint a picture within and is truly the theater of the mind. Words, sound effects, and music are the tools of the radio copywriter. The biggest limitation is that the radio copywriter is always working against the clock.

It is the duty of the radio writer/producer to take control of the listener's imagery and guide it to a positive reaction that seeds the memory with the targeted message and leads to the proper response. The power of a radio commercial is the idea imagery.

There has been a radical change in the way music and sound are recorded. Using a Macintosh computer, musicians and sound designers can record digital masters. So the computer and its innovative software are other creative tools—this time for broadcast. Music can be a powerful tool for getting products remembered.

When developing a commercial, it is important to keep it simple and concentrate on one main idea. Repetition of the main selling ideas is considered necessary, but the main thing is to get the brand and message remembered. Some of the writing techniques and formats include straight announcer, slice-of-life, jingle-announcer, customer interview, and humor.

As with television, all performers appearing in national commercials are subject to union compensation agreements.

REVIEW

1. Why is radio the theater of the mind?
2. Briefly summarize the elements of good radio commercials.
3. What is white space in radio?
4. Name four radio station programming formats.
5. What are the three main elements to writing commercial music?
6. What are the steps in radio production?

TAKE IT TO THE NET

We invite you to visit the Russell/Lane page on the Prentice Hall Web site at **PHLIP** **http://www.prenhall.com/phbusiness** for the bimonthly Russell/Lane update and for this chapter's World Wide Web exercise.

21

TRADEMARKS AND PACKAGING

CHAPTER OBJECTIVES

PRODUCT NAMES AND TRADEMARKS ARE VERY IMPORTANT TO BRAND EQUITY AND THE MARKETING PROCESS. IN TODAY'S MARKET, ADVERTISING AND PACKAGING MUST SUPPORT EACH OTHER. AFTER READING THIS CHAPTER YOU WILL UNDERSTAND

- **what a trademark is**
- **protecting the trademark**
- **forms of trademarks**
- **general trademark rules**
- **the process for developing memorable names**
- **packaging and marketing**
- **packaging and research.**

In 1924, Joseph Sinel published the first book dedicated to trademarks, in which he outlined rules for corporate identity and recognized that a trademark established the character of a company and influenced the appearance of a product. Today, the corporate mark is still the cornerstone of an identity program. Partially due to technology and expanding avenues of communication, corporate identity has become an all-encompassing discipline that embodies the corporate personality, history, reputation, and vision.

All brands, like people, have a personality of one kind or another, but like the strongest individuals, the most powerful brands have more than personality—they have more character, more depth, more integrity. They stand out from the crowd, according to Ken Love, of Lippincott & Margulies, an international identity and image management firm.[1]

Today packaging is a very important part of the brand equity and integrated marketing equation. It has been labeled as the only truly international method of branding. A distinctive shape such as the Coca-Cola bottle or Johnson & Johnson's baby

---

[1]"The New Corporate Identity," *Graphic Design: USA,* October 1997, pp. 64–84.

lotion is instantly recognized anywhere. What we are talking about in this chapter is the power of a strong effective image—a name, a symbol, a package—to build brand equity. Today, it goes beyond these basics of corporate marks and typeface and must carry seamlessly across many media landscapes from traditional print and broadcast to internal and external Web sites to virtual reality and other not-yet-thought-of forms of communicating. Here we focus primarily on trademarks and packaging.

There are those that believe that in an age of 500 TV channels, the retail shelf will become the only true mass medium. That notion has already produced greater attention to packaging a brand banner, widespread use of contemporary colors, and more senior marketing people getting involved in packaging. It is a product of twin forces that rule most marketing decisions: time and money. Consumers have less time to shop in a leisurely manner, so marketers are seeking new methods to attract their attention. And marketers are spending more money on putting the message where consumers make a purchase. Strategic design firms are constantly being told that packaging has to communicate the entire brand strategy, whereas not too long ago, packaging was simply a necessary evil. Herb Meyers of Gerstman + Meyers says, "Packaging and advertising have to support each other, so people are putting more work into getting their brand message across and an increasing insistence by marketers on integrated campaigns."[2]

The brand is one of the most important assets of a company, and the trademark is the brand's asset. Consider the financial investment in the name and trademark of Coca-Cola since 1886, when it was first developed. Think of the corporate and financial loss if Coca-Cola lost the exclusive right to its trademark. It is not impossible for them to lose that right. It is for this reason they go to great lengths to protect their trademark. Exhibit 21.1 (p. 564) illustrates the complex job the Coca-Cola Company has in protecting packaging, logos, and so forth on a global scale. All companies face the same threat, which we talk about later in this chapter.

This need to protect the investment in a brand or company name and trademark has spawned a whole body of law. Getting legal protection is the province of the attorney; however, it begins with the creation of the trademark itself. We touch here on some of the ground rules.

WHAT IS A TRADEMARK?

We have said that brands are among the most valuable assets a marketer has. When a product is manufactured and a brand is created, it must be distinctive from the competition.

There are several types of company and product identifications. The **trademark,** also called a *brand name,* is the name by which people can speak of the product. Very often a trademark will include some pictorial or design element. If it does, the combination is called a **logotype** (or simply a **logo**).

Trademarks are proper terms that identify the products and services of a business and distinguish them from products and services of others. Specifically, a trademark is a word, design, or combination used by a company to identify its brand and to distinguish it from others, and it may be registered and protected by law. Trademark formats can include letters, numbers, slogans, geometric shapes, pictures, labels, color combinations, product and container shapes, vehicles, clothing, and even sound.

Trademarks can also be termed *service marks* when used to identify a service. In general, a trademark for goods appears on the product or its packaging, and a service mark is used in advertising to identify the services.

The logo design is an extremely important element in the successful marketing of a product. It is difficult to sell a product until a reasonable level of name recognition is

[2]Terry Lefton, "Packaging All They Can Get into What's on the Shelf," *BrandWeek,* October 3, 1994, pp. 34–35.

Trademark
Any device or word that identifies the origin of a product, telling who made it or who sold it. Not to be confused with *trade name.*

Logotype, or logo
A trademark or trade name embodied in the form of a distinctive lettering or design. Famous example: Coca-Cola.

Trade name

A name that applies to a business as a whole, not to an individual product.

achieved among consumers. In fact, the creation of a logo is so important that a number of firms have been established whose primary function is the design of logos, packages, and corporate identity. Most designers attempt to forge a compatible relationship among the package design, logo, and advertising for the product. A strong logo on the package and in product advertising creates an environment of recognition.

Clearly, the most successful packages are those that combine an intriguing design scheme with a provocative logotype. What we mean is a logo that is distinctive enough if it is extracted from the package that it will still project the visual personality of the product. After all, when pushing a shopping cart down a supermarket aisle, the consumer's first images will be recognizable brand names.

Trademarks should not be confused with **trade names,** which are corporate or business names. General Motors, for example, is the trade name of a company making automobiles whose trademark (not trade name) is Buick. The terms trademark and trade name are often confused. Trade names are proper nouns. Trade names can be used in the possessive form and do not require a generic form. Many companies, however, use their trade names as trademarks. For example, Reebok International Ltd. is the corporate name, and Reebok may be used as a trade name, as "Reebok's newest line of athletic shoes is for children." Reebok also is used as a trademark: "Are you wearing Reebok athletic shoes or another brand?"

If you're confused, think of yourself as a new product. Your surname is your *trade name* (e.g., Lane, Smith, Bevil). Your gender is the *product classification* (Female Lane, Female Smith, or Female Bevil). Your given name then is the *brand* (Lois Lane, Judy Smith, Sheri Bevil) because it distinguishes you from other family members.

Some personal names (as with product names) may sound the same but may have different spellings—Sherry, Sherri, or Sheri, or even Cheri (Kwik-Draw, Quick-Draw, Kwic, Kwik, Quick). Or they may simply be very familiar names—Jennifer, Jane, Jessica, Susan, Emily—or clearly distinctive, like Ruhanna. Yet, distinctive may appear difficult to read or pronounce. Companies and products have a similar problem. They want names that can easily become familiar to consumers, yet be easy to read and pronounce and be memorable.

General Electric has a simple procedure for developing trademarks for its brands. GE's branding strategy has a number of steps:[3]

1. *Pick a name.* General Electric, for example.
2. *Create a memorable trademark.* The GE monogram is recognized the world over.
3. *Make a promise.* For 60 years, GE promised better living through electricity, which became better living through technology, for the past 30 years.
4. *Effectively communicate the promise.* GE has always had highly imaginative and memorable work produced by its agencies.
5. *Be consistent.* Even as we grow and modify our business, we carefully manage the use of our identity worldwide.
6. *Don't get bored.* GE has kept the same strategic promise for 30 years.

If you follow this basic strategy, your brand should thrive.

For a firm to qualify for an exclusive trademark, several requirements must be met. If these criteria are not satisfied, the trademark is not legally protected and will be lost to the firm.

The use of a design in an ad does not make it a trademark, or does having it on a flag over the factory. The trademark must be used in connection with an actual product. It must be applied to the product itself or be on a label or container of that product. If that is not feasible, it must be affixed to the container or dispenser of the product, as on a gas pump at a service station.

The trademark must not be confusingly similar to trademarks on comparable goods. It must not be likely to cause buyers to be confused, mistaken, or deceived as to whose product they are purchasing. The trademark must be dissimilar in appearance, sound, and significance from others for similar goods. Of course, it is up to a court to decide these issues. The products involved need not be identical. Air-O was held in conflict with Arrow shirts. The marks will be held in conflict if the products are sold through the same trade channels or if the public might assume that a product made by a second company is a new product line of the first company. The product Big Boy! powder for soft drinks was held in confusion with Big Boy stick candy.

Trademarks must not be deceptive—that is, they must not indicate a quality the product does not possess. For instance, the word *Lemon* soap was barred because it contained no lemon; as was the word *Nylodon* for sleeping bags that contained no nylon.

Trademarks must not be merely descriptive. A baker can't say, people ask for fresh bread, so we will trademark our bread *Fresh*. When people ask for fresh bread, they are describing the kind of bread they want, not specifying the bread made by a particular baker. To prevent such misleading usage, the law does not protect trademarks that are merely descriptive and thus applicable to many other products.

---

[3]Richard A. Costello, "Focus on the Brand," *The Advertiser,* Spring 1993, pp. 11–18.

Trademark Protection

Because a trademark is so valuable, companies go to great lengths to protect their brand names. In recent years, there have been a number of court cases involving allegations that one company has infringed on the trademark of another.

In deciding where trademark infringement has taken place, several factors are considered by the courts:

1. the distinctiveness of the complainant's mark
2. the similarity of the marks
3. the proximity of the parties' products
4. the likelihood of the complainant's bridging the gap between noncompeting products
5. the similarity of the parties' trade channels and advertising methods
6. the quality of the alleged infringer's products
7. the sophistication of the particular customers

Recently, a federal judge ruled that an Ohio-based Internet company infringed on copyrights held by BellSouth Corp. The judge held that the RealPages Web site owned by Don Madey did not have the right to use RealPages as its identification or as part of its Internet address. BellSouth has held a trademark on the phrase Real Yellow Pages since 1984. The Web site also used the phrase "let your mouse do the walking," but agreed to stop using that phrase. BellSouth also owns the copyright to the phrase "let your fingers do the walking." The company said they had no choice but to protect their marks. The company filed suit only after trying to discuss the issue with the Web site company.[4]

Beware if your trademark is based on a common word. It will be considered legally weak, and difficult to protect. Police unpermitted use of your trademark vigorously, and don't let any competitor use your mark even briefly. And, if you want to start a trademark infringement suit, don't do it unless you keep detailed records and can document lost profits accurately.

Trademark Loss

In short, if you don't use a trademark properly you can lose the rights to it. What would happen to Pepsi if the courts ruled you or anyone could call a soft drink *Pepsi*. Some companies have seen the untimely demise of a trademark. That's right—untimely demise. Many familiar words today were once valid trademarks:

aspirin	cornflakes
yo-yo	nylon
escalator	thermos
lanolin	raisin bran
cellophane	linoleum

To protect a trademark, advertisers must use it with a generic classification so the trademark does not become the name of the product. Originally, Thermos was the trademark owned by the Aladdin Company, which introduced vacuum bottles. In time, people began asking, "What brand of thermos bottle do you carry?" The word "thermos" had come to represent all vacuum bottles, not just those made by Aladdin. The courts held that Thermos had become a descriptive word that any manufacturer of vacuum bottles could use because thermos (with a lowercase "t") was no longer the exclusive trademark of the originator.

---

[4]Michael E. Kannell, "Judge Sides with BellSouth on Copyright," *Atlanta Journal-Constitution,* September 10, 1997, p. C2.

Selecting Brand Names

A strong brand name will aid marketing objectives by helping create and support the brand image. There are several considerations in the brand name selection.[5]

- *The name should differentiate the product from the competition.* In some product categories, there is a limit to how different brand images can be. In fragrances there has traditionally been one basic image—romance. There is great similarity among brand names—Caleche, Cacharel, Chantilly. Consider more distinctive names such as Obsession, Charlie, Passion, Safari. In either direction, creation and support of the brand image—abstract promise rather than actual benefit—are the dominant factors in name selection.
- *The name should describe the product, if possible.* Brand names such as Post-it, Pudding Pops, and Eraser Mate are very descriptive. They communicate to consumers exactly what to expect.
- *The name should be compatible with the product.* The product should be compatible with the brand name. In other words, do not name a sleeping tablet "Awake."
- *The name should be memorable and easy to pronounce.* One-word, one-syllable brand names are often considered ideal—Fab, Tide, Dash, Bold, Surf, Coke, Tab. Even though short names may be more memorable, they may be limiting in identifying the type of product or its use.

Forms of Trademarks

Dictionary Words   Many trademarks consist of familiar dictionary words used in an arbitrary, innovative, or fanciful manner. Many common words have already been used, causing the advertiser to seek other methods to name a product: Apple computers, Verbatim data disks, Ivory soap, Dial soap, Whopper burgers, Glad plastic bags, Shell oil, Coach leather, Water Grabber plant water absorber, Pert shampoo. This type of trademark must be used in a merely descriptive sense to describe the nature, use, or virtue of the product: Look at the word "natural" and related names such as Natural Blend, Natural Brand, Natural Impressions, Natural Light, Natural Man, Natural Silk, Natural Smoothe, Natural Stretch, Natural Suede, Natural Sun, Natural Touch, Natural Woman, and Natural Wonder; or the prefix "opti" as used in Opti Fonts, Opti Free, Opti-Fry, Opti-Grip, Opti Heat, Opti Pure, Opti-Ray, Opti-Tears, and Opti Twist.

The possible advantage of using dictionary words is that consumers will easily recognize them. Of course, the task is to get people to associate the word(s) with the product. Just think what the following real product names using two dictionary words are about: Healthy Choice, Skin Bracer, Budget Rent-A-Car, Drug Emporium, Wonder Bra, Big Mac, Water Grabber, Action Plus.

At times, a name can be somewhat limiting. For instance, when Burger King moved into a breakfast menu, the name Burger King was a limitation because people do not think of burgers as breakfast.

Coined word
An original and arbitrary combination of syllables forming a word. Extensively used for trademarks, such as PoFolks, Mazola, Gro-Pup, Zerone. (Opposite of a dictionary word.)

Coined Words   When we run out of dictionary options, we sometimes make up words, such as Ticketron, Advil, Infiniti, Primerica, Kleenex, Xerox, NYNEX, UNUM, Norelco, Exxon, Delco, Keds, Kodak, Mazola, TransAir, or PoFolks. **Coined words** are made up of a new combination of consonants and vowels. The advantage of a coined word is that it is new; it can be made phonetically pleasing, pronounceable, and short. Coined words have a good chance of being legally protectable. The challenge is to create a trademark that is distinctive. Ocean Spray took the ingredients of cranberries and apples and created the name Cranapple, which is distinctive, descriptive, and relatively easy to pronounce. There is, however, a Cranberry Apple herb tea. Is this confusing? Probably not.

---

[5]Daniel L. Doden, "Selecting a Brand Name That Aids Marketing Objectives," *Advertising Age,* November 5, 1990, p. 34.

The simpler coined words are one syllable. It is common to coin trademark words that have a vowel next to a hard consonant or a vowel between two hard consonants, such as Keds. This structure can be expanded—Kodak, Crisco, or Tab.

Personal Names   These may be the names of real people, such as Calvin Klein, Anne Klein, Estee Lauder, Tommy Hilfiger, Perry Ellis, Pierre Cardin, Alexander Julian, Oscar de la Renta, and Sara Lee; fictional characters, such as Betty Crocker; historical characters, such as Lincoln cars; or mythological characters, such as Ajax cleanser. A surname alone is not valuable as a new trademark; others of that name may use it. Names such as Ford automobiles, Lipton teas, Heinz foods, and Campbell's soups have been in use for so long, however, that they have acquired what the law calls a "secondary meaning—that is, through usage the public has recognized them as representing the product of one company only. However, a new trademark has no such secondary meaning.

There are a lot of names that use Mrs.—Mrs. Fields, Mrs. Winner's, Mrs. Richardson's, Mrs. Allison's, Mrs. Smith's, Mrs. Dash, Mrs. Baird's, Mrs. Butterworth's, Mrs. Lane's, and Mrs. Paul's.

Foreign names have been successfully used to endow a product with an exotic quality. Of course, because the market is now global, they are more and more common. The argument against creating foreign names may be the problem of pronunciation or remembering. However, foreign names are part of the global landscape: Toyota, Feni, Gianfranco Ferre, Corneliani, Lubiam, Bertolucci, Giorgia Brutini, Shiseido, Gucci, Volkswagen, Fila, Ferrari, L'Aimant.

Geographical Names   A geographical name is really a place name: Nashua blankets, Utica sheets, Pittsburgh paints, Newport cigarettes. These names are old trademarks and have acquired secondary meaning. Often the word "brand" is offered after the geographical name. The law does not look with favor on giving one person or company the exclusive right to use a geographical name in connection with a new product, excluding others making similar goods in that area. However, if the name was chosen because of a fanciful connotation of a geographical setting, rather than to suggest that the product was made there, it may be eligible for protection, as with Bali bras. Exhibit 21.2 shows an appropriate geographical name usage.

Geographical names can be combined with dictionary words to create trademark names such as Maryland Club coffee and Carolina Treat barbecue sauce. The options are many: Georgia Coffee, Texas Instruments, Texas Trails, New York Woman, Florida Queen, Newport Harbor, Georgia-Pacific.

Initials and Numbers   Many fortunes and years have been spent in establishing trademarks such as IBM, IKEA furniture, RCA, GE, AC spark plugs, A&W root beer, J&B whiskey, and A.1. steak sauce. Hence, these are familiar. In general, however, initials and numbers are the most difficult form of trademark to remember and the easiest to confuse and imitate. How many of these sound familiar: STP, DKNY, S.O.S., AMF, M.O.M.S., S.A.V.E., A.S.A., A & P, 6-12, 666? There are also combinations of initials and numbers: WD-40 lubricant; numbers and words: 9-Lives cat food, 4 in 1, Formula 44, Formula 109, Formula 28, Formula 36, 4 Most; or dictionary words and initials: LA Gear.

Pictorial   Many advertisers use some artistic device, such as distinctive lettering style or a design, insignia, or picture. The combination, as mentioned before, is called a logotype, or logo. It is important for the advertiser to make sure that any symbol or design is distinctive and will reproduce clearly when used in a small size. Parkland Health & Hospital Systems and the Don Ce Sar Beach Resort & Spa (Exhibits 21.3a, p. 570, and b, p. 571) have distinctive symbols and designs.

exhibit

21.2

Carolina First is a geographical name. Their slogan even says "The bank that puts South Carolina first," a very appropriate name for a regional bank.

Courtesy: Greg & Greg Advertising.

The Successful Trademark

Whatever the form of a specific trademark, it will be successful only if it is distinctive and complements the manufacturer's product and image. As we mentioned earlier in this chapter, the trademark cannot be considered an isolated creative unit. In most cases, it must be adaptable to a package. It must also be adaptable to many different advertising campaigns, often over a period of many years. The longer a trademark is associated with a brand, the more people recognize it and the greater its value.

Global Trademarks

In Exhibit 21.1 we saw an example of a global ad in which the trademarks of the Coca-Cola Company were being used in Japan. Coca-Cola has to protect their marks all over the world. Many U.S. businesses operate on a global scale.

Since the 1870s, trademark law has been based on use of the marks in commerce. "No trade, no trademark" was the law's basic premise. Since 1946, U.S. trademark owners have been required to submit proof of prior use when they apply to register their marks at the Patent and Trademark Office. Recently, the law was changed to permit

exhibit

21.3a

This logo for Parkland
Health & Hospital
System is distinctive.

*Courtesy: Aydlotte &
Cartwright.*

companies to base trademark applications on an *intent* to use the mark. This change brought U.S. policy in harmony with worldwide standards.

The law permits an applicant with a bona fide intent to use a mark to apply to register it, for example, on January 1, and if the registration is issued eventually—say, on October 31—to trace its rights back to the application date. A registration is issued when the application is approved by the Patent and Trademark Office and confirmed when the applicant submits proof of use within six months of approval. As many as five six-month extensions may be granted, giving the company several years to actually market a product under a particular mark. The registration period has been reduced from 20 to 10 years, but may be renewed indefinitely. This 10-year term is more in keeping with international standards and allows for clearing the trademark register of "dead-wood." The law also includes prohibiting false statements in advertising about a competitor's product.[6]

---

[6]Vincent N. Palladino, "New Trademark Law Aids U.S. in Foreign Markets," *Marketing News,* February 13, 1989, p. 7.

When Thomas Rowe built The Don in 1928,
it was one of the most impressive hotels
in the world. Some things never change.

The Don has been a landmark on St. Pete Beach for over 68 years. It is known around the world for its unique
European elegance and service. The Pink Palace, as it is affectionately known, combines a rich
history with a modern outlook. Guests enjoy a private beach, 2 pools including one with an underwater sound
system, a world-class spa, a great Sunday brunch and Boardwalk at the The Don's unique boutiques and
eateries. It is the perfect place for a one-of-a-kind weekend for locals and visitors alike.

THE
Don Ce Sar
BEACH RESORT & SPA
3400 GULF BLVD, ST. PETE BEACH, FL 33706 · 813-360-1881 · 800-282-1116

exhibit

21.3b

This logo is both
verbal and pictorial.

Courtesy: The Zimmerman
Agency and Don Ce Sar Beach
Resort & Spa.

General Trademark Rules

Putting a lock on the ownership of a trademark requires taking the following steps:

1. Always be sure the trademark word is capitalized or set off in distinctive type. KLEENEX, *Kleenex*, **Kleenex**
2. Always follow the trademark with the generic name of the product, or by using the word "brand" after the mark: Glad disposable trash bags, Kleenex tissues, Apple computers, Tabasco brand pepper sauce.
3. Do not speak of the trademark word in the plural, as "three Kleenexes," but rather, "three Kleenex tissues."
4. Do not use the trademark name in a possessive form, unless the trademark itself is possessive, such as Levi's jeans (not "Kleenex's new features," but "the new features of Kleenex tissues"), or as a verb (not "Kleenex your eyeglasses," but "Wipe your eyeglasses with Kleenex tissues").

exhibit

21.4

**Guidelines on Use
of Teflon Trademark**

Courtesy: DuPont.

RULE 1: Show Registration.

Show registration status, by using the symbol "®" each and every time the trademark appears.

If there is no ® on a keyboard, as in some electronic mail systems, use parenthesis "R" parenthesis: (R). For countries where the registration symbol is not recognized, use an asterisk (*).

Acceptable	Unacceptable
Teflon® resin	No designation of registration status
Teflon(R) resin	
*Teflon**resin	*Teflon* resin

IMPORTANT: Regardless of whether "®", (R), or (*) is used, a footnote must be used at least once in each document. Examples of acceptable footnotes:

* *Teflon* is a registered trademark of DuPont.
Teflon® is a registered trademark of DuPont for its fluoropolymer resins.

RULE 2: Be Distinctive.

Make the trademark distinctive from the surrounding text each and every time.

Acceptable	Unacceptable
Initial Cap: *Teflon*® resin	Any instance where the trademark is not distinguished from surrounding text, such as: "gaskets with teflon"
All Caps: TEFLON® resin	
Bold: **Teflon**® resin	
Italics: *Teflon*® resin	
Color: Teflon® resin	

RULE 3: Use Correct Generics.

Use the correct generic (common name) for the trademark at least once per package. Generic is the term for the class of goods for which the mark is registered.

Acceptable	Unacceptable
Teflon® resins	*Teflon*® president, *Teflon*® gasket, *Teflon*® cookware, *Teflon*® business
Other acceptable generics: films, fibers, finishes, fabric protector, fluoropolymer, fluoroadditive, micropowder, coating, solutions, PTFE, PFA, FEP, ETFE	

NOTE: Although not generics, it is acceptable to refer to the *Teflon*® trademark and the *Teflon*® brand.

RULE 4: Keep It Simple.

The trademark is the trademark. Don't embellish upon it!

Acceptable	Unacceptable
Wear resistance of *Teflon*®	**Possessives:** *Teflon*®'s wear resistance
Coatings of *Teflon*®	**Hyphens:** *Teflon*®-coated
Fabrics using *Teflon*® wear longer	**Line Breaks:** Fabrics using *Teflon*® wear longer
Coat pans with *Teflon*®	**Verbs:** *Teflon*® your pans
Teflon®	**Coined Words:** *Teflon*® ized

It is the advertising person's responsibility to carry out these legal strictures in the ads, although most large advertisers will have each ad checked for legal requirements including trademark protection.

DuPont promotes the correct use of their Teflon trademark (see Exhibit 21.4). "Protecting the Teflon trademark is critical to the successful management of a very valuable asset. Improper use of the trademark, or allowing others to use it improperly, lowers its value and can ultimately turn a respected trademark into a common generic term."

Registration Notice

Legal departments at some companies go to great lengths to protect their valuable trademarks. Some common ways of indicating trademark registration follow.

- The "®" symbol after the trademark as a superscript. Example: Mrs. Winner's®
- A footnote referenced by an asterisk in the text.
  Example: McDonald's*
  *A registered trademark of McDonald's Corporation.
  or
  *Reg. U.S. Pat. Tm. Off.
  or
  Registered in the U.S. Patent and Trademark Office.
- A *notation* of the registration in the text or as a footnote on the same page.
- If a trademark is repeated frequently in an ad, some firms require the registration notice only on the first use.

Most companies require notice of unregistered but claimed words and/or symbols as their trademark, by using the "TM" symbol.

HOUSE MARKS

As mentioned earlier in this chapter, trademarks are used to identify specific products. However, many companies sell a number of products under several different trademarks. These companies often identify themselves with a **house mark** to denote the firm that produces these products. Kraft is a house mark, and its brand Miracle Whip is a trademark.

SERVICE MARKS, CERTIFICATION MARKS

A company that renders services, such as an insurance company, an airline, or even Weight Watchers, can protect its identification mark by registering it in Washington as a **service mark.** It is also possible to register certification marks, whereby a firm certifies that a user of its identifying device is doing so properly. Teflon is a material sold by DuPont to kitchenware makers for use in lining their pots and pans. Teflon is DuPont's registered trademark for its nonstick finish; Teflon II is DuPont's certification mark for Teflon-coated cookware that meets DuPont's standards. Advertisers of such products may use that mark. The Wool Bureau has a distinctive label design that it permits all manufacturers of pure-wool products to use (Exhibit 21.5). Certification marks have the same creative requirements as trademarks—most of all, that they be distinctive.

COMPANY AND PRODUCT NAMES

Corporate Name Changes

Over the years, thousands of companies have undergone corporate name and identity changes. During the first half of 1997, for example, there were 826 name changes. The largest number of changes in recent years was in 1988, when there were 931, according to Anspach Grossman Enterprise of WWP Group. Corporations can spend millions of dollars to complete the process. Costs include hiring consultants, advertising, and changing logos and designs on such items as stationery, uniforms, trucks, and planes.

House mark
A primary mark of a business concern, usually used with the trademark of its products. *General Mills* is a house mark; *Betty Crocker* is a trademark; *DuPont* is a house mark; *Teflon II* is a trademark.

Service mark
A word or name used in the sale of services, to identify the services of a firm and distinguish them from those of others, for example, Hertz Drive Yourself Service, Weight Watchers Diet Course. Comparable to trademarks for products.

exhibit

21.5

Certification Mark

Sometimes a company feels a need to distance itself from a name, as ValuJet did. The start-up airline was damaged from all the negative publicity surrounding the crash of one of its planes in the Florida Everglades in 1996. The newspaper ad announcing the name change said, "When ValuJet became AirTran, we decided to change everything (well almost)." In late 1997, the airline officially changed its name to AirTran Airways after a merger. For the most part, however, such changes are rarely based on a company's attempt to distance itself from a negative incident of image, according to Ruffell Meyer, a director of Landor Associates in San Francisco. Fueling the increase is a rise in mergers and acquisitions, new business formation, and further consolidations in industries such as telecommunications and banking.[7]

Another ad said, "After all these years, we think it's time you call us by our first name: Bayer. Today Miles becomes Bayer." The copy started: "You know us as Miles, one of America's largest companies. But in nearly 150 countries, our name is Bayer. Bayer is one of the biggest health care, chemical and imaging technology companies in the world. . . . You already know Bayer for aspirin."

Folks Restaurant Management Group decided it was time to remodel and freshen its restaurants in the Atlanta area. They had been the largest franchisee of PoFolks in the country, but felt the growing sophistication of the market had outgrown that concept. The restaurant design inside and out was changed, but the basic menu remained similar. To introduce their new name, they said, "We're 18 Years Old & We're Already Getting a Facelift! Folks. Cooking with a Southern Accent" (Exhibit 21.6). The copy read, "We're celebrating 18 years in Atlanta with a fresh, new look and a catchy new name. Our Southern heritage shows in every detail of our new decor. As comfortable and inviting as Grandma's house. And we've freshened up our name to go with our new look. Folks. Just plain Folks. Honest folks looking to serve you an unforgettable meal at a fair price along with our famous Southern hospitality."

Corporate name changes and accordingly, graphic identity programs have been on the rise since the mid-1990s, as reported by Interbrand Schechter, a subsidiary of the Omnicom Group, which looks at publicly traded companies on the New York, American, and NASDAQ stock exchanges. They found that a record 100 publicly listed companies changed their names during 1997. The study indicated that merger and acquisition activity continues to be the leading agent of change. For example, the merger of BayBank and the Bank of Boston created BankBoston, and the merger of First Alliance and Premier Bank created Premier Bancshares. The surprising fact was that the changes were predominantly with larger companies, a shift from past studies.[8] Among the new names:

Alaris Medical	FIRSTPLUS Financial
Arcadia Financial	Ikon Office Solutions
Avatex	JumboSports
Centris Group	Popular Inc.
Dynex Capital	

The Process for Developing Memorable Names

There probably isn't a single procedure everyone accepts for selecting names. Ruffell Meyer of Landor Associates says, "The misconception is that you have a couple of people sitting around over a pizza lunch. The first step is to meet with senior management to talk about the direction of the company, its values and image. Does it want to be known for speedy or reliable service or reliability? Later employees and customers may be included in the discussion."

---

[7] Shelia M. Poole, "What's in a Name? For Most Firms—Everything," *Atlanta Journal-Constitution*, October 4, 1997, p. E2.

[8] "Corporate Identity Snapshot: More and Bigger Companies Are Changing Their Names," *Graphic Design: USA*, August 1997, pp. 24–26.

Once the information is gathered, the brand identity staff begins the name-generation and image-making processes. The tools are likely to include software packages that can morph word combinations. Landor has a database with more than 50,000 names. A typical list of possibilities can exceed a thousand names. When AT&T spun off what is now known as Lucent Technologies, the short list contained some 700 names including acronyms, name and number combinations, and coined words. Lucent was chosen because it implies clarity of thought and action.

A basic legal search would be made of each name to see if someone else owns the rights to it. This process reduces the possibilities by about 80 percent. You again analyze the remaining names against the objective and reduce them to a list of about a

exhibit

21.7

Land O' Lakes is a
memorable name that
can be used on a
variety of packaging
and media.

Courtesy: Land O' Lakes, Inc.

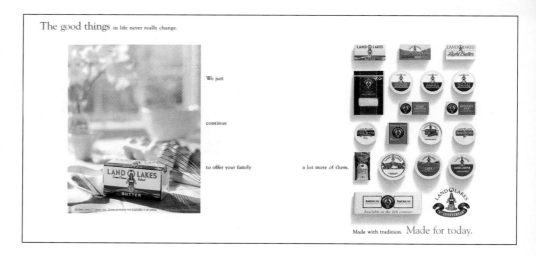

dozen or so. At this point, you would probably perform a linguistic analysis to determine what happens when the name is translated into foreign languages. Then you might test the names on consumers. You get the idea. Correctly done, the result is a memorable name that is adapted to a number of advertising formats (see Exhibit 21.7). Now let us look at the specific steps:

First, pull together the basic information:

- *Describe what you are naming.* In your description, include key features and characteristics, competitive advantages, and anything else that differentiates your company, product, or service from the rest of the field.
- *Summarize what you want your name to do.* Should it suggest an important product characteristic (e.g., Blokrot for treated lumber) or convey a particular image (e.g., Pandora's Secrets for an expensive perfume)? Write down the characteristics and images you want your name to convey.
- *Describe whom you are targeting with the name.* Identify your targets and their demographic and lifestyle characteristics. Would they react more positively to a traditional, conservative name or to a liberal, flashy one? List the name qualities you think would appeal to them (name length, sound, and image).
- *List names that you like and dislike.* Try to come up with a few dozen current names in both categories (include your competitors' names). Note words and roots that might work for your new name and jot them down.
- *Build a list of new name ideas.* Start with the list of names that you like and add to it by pulling ideas from a good thesaurus (e.g., *The Synonym Finder* by Jerome Rodale), a book of names (e.g., *The Trademark Register of the United States*), relevant trade journals, a book of root words (e.g., *Dictionary of English Word Roots* by Robert Smith), or other sources.
- *Combine name parts and words.* Take words, syllables, and existing name parts and recombine them to form new names.
- *Pick your favorites.* Select several names that meet all your criteria (just in case your top is unavailable or tests poorly).

Next, verify the name's availability and test your favorites:

- *Conduct a trademark search.* Check to make sure your names are not already in use. Thomson & Thomson in Boston, Corsearch, or Compu-Mark in Washington are companies that can help check state and U.S. patent and trademark records. The cost ranges from $300 to $800. The cost of having a lawyer do a search in the United States is $500 to $1,000 if you don't require a written opinion summarizing the findings, or $1,500 to $2,500 if you do. The search has to be analyzed for marks that are confusingly similar to your proposed name, and to make sure your proposed name doesn't dilute anyone else's trademark. *Dilution* refers to the injury to a trademark owner when a mark is used by another, even on goods that do not compete. There are state as well as federal statutes prohibiting dilution.[9]

● *Test your name before using it.* Regardless of how fond you are of the new name, others may have different opinions. Solicit reactions to your name from prospective customers, stockholders, and industry experts.

Coca-Cola ran into a controversy with Fruitopia's name. In 1991, students at Miami University in Ohio came up with a total marketing plan, which included a product name, for a sparkling water and juice drink in development for the Minute Maid brand at Coca-Cola Foods Canada. When they presented it to Coca-Cola, Coca-Cola thought the name Fruitopia was very "iffy." The product rolled out in the United States in 1994 with the Fruitopia name; although there was no question about the legal rights of ownership—Coca-Cola had paid the university a fee for all of the student's work—there was a question of who developed the name. Coca-Cola said that a marketing group, working independently with their advertising agency, came up with the name. This is a reason most companies don't take unsolicited proposals for new products, ads, or product names. If Coca-Cola had not paid for the rights for the students' work, there could have been a legal battle for the name Fruitopia.

Name Assistance   The naming of products may be developed by the advertiser or the advertising agency, working independently or together. There are companies and consultants that specialize in helping companies and agencies develop memorable names. The Namestormers uses software to help develop product and company names such as CarMax (used-car dealer network), Pyramis (medical systems), AutoSource (auto parts network), Spider's Silk (lingerie), CareStream (health-care company), and Wavemaker (notebook computer). Goldman & Young, Inc. uses Linguistic Architecture to define image strategy and positioning, then creates names such as Polaroid *Captiva*, Nissan *Pathfinder*, Oldsmobile *Achieva*, Clairol *Affluence*, Honda *Fourtrax atv*, and GMC *Yukon*. Namelab, another company that develops names, has used constructional linguistics to create the names Acura, Compaq, Geo, Lumina, and Zapmail.

Protect the Usage of Corporate Symbol

Earlier we indicated that companies should control how the trademark is used in writing ads, and so forth. Many companies provide departments and units with written guidelines instructing the use of trademarks. For example, Kodak has a 10-page document for proper use, with examples of incorrect usage, of their trademarks. This includes trademark printing instructions for black-and-white and color usage.

Blockbuster Corporation warns its employees, "Always use the exact registration or trademark form." You should never change the word or design; never change the upper and lowercase letters; never change the colors; never change the plural or singular form; never add the word "the" to the word or design; never add a design to the word or vice versa; and never make the mark a possessive noun.

PACKAGING

In the modern world of self-service marketing, the product package is much more than a container. The package must be designed to take several factors into account. First, it must protect the package contents; every other consideration is secondary to the function of the package as a utilitarian container. Second, the package must meet reasonable

---

[9]Maxine Lans Retsky, "Don't Change Your Name without Proper Clearance," *Marketing News,* October 27, 1997, p. 7.

cost standards. Because the product package is a major expense for most firms, steps must be taken to hold down costs as much as possible.

Once these two requirements of package protection and cost are satisfied, we move to the marketing issues involved in packaging. These include adopting a package that is conducive to getting shelf space at the retail level (see Exhibit 21.8). A unique package with strange dimensions or protruding extensions or nonflat surfaces is going to be rejected by many retailers. A package must be easy to handle, store, and stack. It should not take up more shelf room than any other product in that section, as a pyramid-shape bottle might. Odd shapes are suspect: Will they break easily? Tall packages are suspect: Will they keep falling over? The package should be soil-resistant. Does it have ample and convenient space for marking? The product should come in the full range of sizes and packaging common to the field.

For products bought upon inspection, such as men's shirts, the package needs transparent facing. The package can make the difference in whether a store stocks the item.

Small items are expected to be mounted on cards under plastic domes, called *blister cards*, to provide ease of handling and to prevent pilferage. Often these cards are mounted on a large card that can be hung on a wall, making profitable use of that space. Remember, the buyer working for the store judges how a product display will help the store, not the manufacturer.

Once we have considered the requirements of the retail trade, we can turn our attention to designing a container that is both practical and eye-catching. The package is, after all, the last chance to sell the consumer and the most practical form of point-

exhibit
21.8

Pizza usually is packaged in round or square packaging. Mama Mary's pizza crusts are packaged in a colorful box showing the crusts as finished, eatable pizzas.

Courtesy: Greg & Greg Advertising.

of-purchasing advertising. Therefore, it should be designed to achieve a maximum impact on the store shelf. Striving for distinctiveness is particularly critical in retail establishments such as grocery stores, where the consumer is choosing from hundreds of competing brands.

Changing Package Design and Marketing Strategies

Design firms redesign packages to suit changing market strategies for existing consumer products and develop new packaging concepts for product introductions. Several trends in package design can be cited. One is the increasing tendency to use packaging to shore up store brands. Another is the use of sophisticated design approaches or unique packaging to establish a high quality for upscale, private-label brands. There has also been a shift from packaging that suits the convenience of the manufacturer to packaging that is "consumer-friendly" in terms of opening and use, reclosing, and portions. In short, package design is responding to a more sophisticated, discerning consumer.

Today's package design firms do more than provide renderings for clients. They often act as adjunct marketing consultants, providing information on the retail environment and marketing trends, as well as expertise on the roles of positioning, timing, and brand equity in the success or failure of a product.

Design Can Be Weapon

Pepsi, Coca-Cola, Dr Pepper, and other soft-drink companies are keeping design firms busy. Packaging, according to Addis Group, is becoming the hub of the wheel because it is the one element that everyone sees. As a result, it isn't surprising to see so many soft-drink companies reviewing their graphic look. They are extremely aware of the importance of graphic design and innovation in packaging graphics and structure. Let us take a quick look at some soft-drink changes: Coca-Cola redesigned package graphics in early 1997. Later in the year, Pepsi moved toward a distinctively blue look. The scope of the project included new designs for cans, bottles, vending machines, soda fountains, and vehicles, which in turn also triggered the need for graphic changes in collateral and signs. The most apparent change is the heavier reliance on blue than in past Pepsi packaging in this country—a completely different package design in Europe has featured blue in recent years. Addis Group reports that the important thing for Pepsi is that the graphic design links up well with other elements in their marketing mix and positioning—the drink for a younger generation, or "Generation Next," as Pepsi's advertising claims—to send a consistent message. The design supports this in several ways: the italicized logo, the use of a background with lots of depth and two blues, and an abstract iced background for the Pepsi logo that gives a "visceral representation of refreshment."[10] In keeping with the trend, Diet Coke has new graphics that feature a silver background with the word "Diet" in black, and "Coke" appears in red with shadows. Research indicated that consumers found the redesign to better reflect the brand as "fun and exciting, great tasting and thirst quenching." Following the trend, Dr Pepper embarked on a new graphic identity campaign. The major focus was straightforward: to build a program and look that promotes brand equity. The resulting design strives to attract new customers while still appealing to current buyers through an "evolutionary" approach. The imagery represents an updated, more contemporary system without being a radical departure. The package retained its familiar background colors (maroon for regular, white for diet) and angled brand mark, although both were fine-tuned for greater legibility and impact. The biggest change is the addition of frosty graphics designed to simulate cold refreshment.

---

[10]"Cola Wars Bubble, Design Is More Valuable Weapon," *Graphic Design: USA*, April 1997, p. 1.

Packaging and Marketing

Until this century, the role of product packages was generally confined to protecting the product. Only the package label was linked with promotional activities. The Uneeda Biscuit package introduced in 1899 is generally considered to be the first that was utilized for promotion. However, few companies followed Uneeda's lead.

During the depression of the 1930s, the role of packaging as a promotional tool changed dramatically. Most companies had limited advertising funds during this period, so they resorted to using the package as an in-store means of promotion. So successful were their efforts that the role of packaging in the marketing mix became routinely accepted by manufacturers.

The package design for most products is developed in much the same way as an advertising campaign. Although each package is developed, designed, and promoted in a unique fashion, there are some common approaches to the successful use of a package as a marketing tool.

1. *The type of product and function of the package.* Is the product extremely fragile? Do consumers use the product directly from the package? Are there special storage or shipping problems associated with the product?
2. *The type of marketing channels to be used for the product.* If the product is sold in a variety of outlets, will this require some special packaging considerations? Will the package be displayed in some special way at the retail level? Are there special point-of-purchase opportunities for the product?
3. *The prime prospects for the product.* Are adults, children, upper-income families, or young singles most likely to buy the product? What package style would be most appealing to the target market?
4. *Promotion and advertising for the product and its package.* Will the package be used to complement other promotional efforts? Are on-pack coupons or premiums being considered? Can standard package-design ideas be adapted to any special promotional efforts being considered?
5. *The relationship to other packages in a product line.* Will the product be sold in different sizes? Is the product part of a product line that is promoted together? Does the product line use the same brand name and packaging style?
6. *The typical consumer use of the product.* Will the package be stored for long periods in the home? Does the product require refrigeration or freezing? Are only portions of the product from the package used?

Obviously, the answers to these and other questions can be obtained only through careful research. The package designer must strive for a balance between creativity and function.

Packaging and Color Influence

Advertisers are very much aware that colors work on people's subconscious and that each color produces a psychological reaction. Reactions to color can be pleasant or unpleasant. Color can inform consumers about the type of product inside the package and influence their perceptions of quality, value, and purity. Thus, color in packaging is an important tool in marketing communications.

What kind of consumer perceptions would you encounter if you brewed the same coffee in a blue coffeepot, a yellow pot, a brown pot, and a red pot? Would the perceptions of the coffee be the same? Probably not. Studies indicate that coffee from the blue pot would be perceived as having a mild aroma, coffee from the yellow pot would be thought a weaker blend, the brown pot's coffee would be judged too strong, and the red pot's coffee would be perceived as rich and full-bodied.

Exhibit 21.9 shows the Egg Beaters package using bright yellow and reds. Do people associate yellow with breakfast or the sun rising or both? What attracts your atten-

tion to CDs? Is it the illustration's color or the design? Obviously, the strategy in designing packaging for packaged goods and for CDs is similar but different (see Exhibit 21.10).

Package Research

Today, effective packaging is a vital part of marketing a product. The only absolute in testing a package design is to sell it in a test-market setting. There are several aspects of assessing a package design, including recognition, imagery, structure, and behavior.

- *Recognition.* A package must attract attention to itself so that the consumer can easily identify it in the retail environment. The recognition properties of a package can be measured. Research can determine how long it takes a consumer to recognize the package and what elements are most memorable.

- *Imagery.* The package must be easily recognized, but it must project a brand image compatible with the corporate brand-imagery objectives. A package can reinforce advertising, or it can negate it.
- *Structure.* The objective is to determine any structural problems consumers pinpoint that may inhibit repeat purchases. Is the package easy to open? Is it easy to close? Is it easy to handle? Is it easy to use?
- *Behavior.* This can be the most expensive means of researching packages. Often, this approach presents simulated shelf settings to groups of people and monitors whether they pick up or purchase a product.

Package Differentiation

Twelve suburban women sit around a focus group table, psyching themselves up to talk about cat food for two hours. Through the course of the evening, only two things really perk them up: the chance to describe their cats, and a vacuum-packed foil bag of cat food.

Even before they have examined the nuggets of cat food, most have said they would buy it, intrigued by the high-tech, brick-like bag they have come to expect to see in the coffee aisle, certainly, but never spotted before among the cans, boxes, and bags of pet food.

It is a point increasingly driven home to marketers of food, health and beauty product lines, and over-the-counter drugs: The package is the brand.

Marketers are paying more attention to package design because products are so much more at parity these days. When differentiation through taste, color, and other product elements has reached parity, packaging makes a critical difference.[11] A case in point is Pepsi-Cola's reaction to making their "plasticization" of the famous curved bottle. They couldn't duplicate the curved bottle, but they did create a stable of designs with monikers such as *Fast Break* or *Big Slam*. They found the bottles were a way to build excitement without changing the formula.

Brand Identity

Brand identity is a specific combination of visual and verbal elements that helps achieve the following attributes of a successful brand: create recognition; provide differentiation; shape the brand's imagery; link all brand communications to the brand; and—very important—be the proprietary, legal property of the company that owns the brand.

There are a surprisingly short number of components that make up a brand identity. These include name logos, which are the designed versions of a name; symbols; other graphic devices; color; package configuration (the physical structure of a package); and permanent support messages—slogans and jingles.[12]

Cotrends and Packaging

Cobranding, coadvertising, and *copackaging* are trends that enable companies with strong brand equities to team together to gain more market share at a lower cost. For example, Betty Crocker cobrands with Reese's Candy, Sunkist with Kraft, and Stayfree with Arm & Hammer. The challenge is to present the brand identities and brand communications in such a way that both brand names are strengthened by the visual association, while marketing costs are shared.

---

[11]Betsy Spethmann, "The Mystique of the Brand: Jarred, Bagged, Boxed, Canned," *BrandWeek,* June 27, 1994, p 25.

[12]Anita K. Hersh and John Lister, "Brand Identity," *The Advertiser,* Spring 1993, pp. 66–71.

Package Design

A product's package is more than a necessary production expense. Therefore, much care needs to be given to the role of packaging in integrated marketing, relationship marketing with its emphasis on quality, and interactive media. In its promotion function, the package does everything a medium should. At the point-of-purchase, it alone informs, attracts, and reminds the consumer. At the point-of-use, it reinforces the purchase decision. Quality and value are viewed as relatively new marketing concepts, yet some 15 years ago the Design and Market Research Laboratory showed that quality perception was one of the key criteria for packaging assessment. But quality and value have always been part of the marketing and packaging equation.

Because packaging is such an important weapon in the marketing arsenal, it should be approached as other marketing elements, with marketing research, specifically user research with target consumers.

Frank Tobolski, president of JTF Marketing/Studios, says research techniques measure the communication strengths and weaknesses of package graphics. They answer such questions as: Do the graphics communicate well? Do the graphics reinforce and enhance the image positioning? Do the products and package sell? He reports on a case where a toy company developed new packaging for a line of products. Perceptual and imagery evaluation in diagnostic laboratory tests were performed, indicating some problems and potential negative sales effects. To obtain behavioral sales data, test quantities of packages were produced for a balanced store test. For six weeks during the Christmas season, 18 stores stocked the new test design and 18 stocked the existing control design. Toy specialty, discount, department store, and mass merchandiser stores were used for the matched store pairings. The bottom line after six weeks found the existing control packages sold 63 percent more units than the test packages. Even after adjusting the test stores, the new designs sold 35 percent less.[13] A major loss in sales was diverted by testing. Imagine the loss if there had been a full new-package rollout.

Today's packaged-goods marketing managers constantly face the critical task of justifying expenditures in terms of the potential return on investment (ROI). Although most can instantly give you current sales figures, few know the yield on their latest shelf media, or, specifically, packaging design.

Why? There is growing evidence that packaging design has a much stronger impact on sales than is realized.

Two examples, redesigns of the popular Rice-A-Roni and Del Monte tomato product lines, illustrate how packaging design contributes to gains in market share and provides a significant ROI.

A packaging revitalization for Rice-A-Roni focused on the true personality of the product, unified the line, and added a dimension of quality and appetite appeal. When a freshened and updated Rice-A-Roni package hit the shelves, the brand experienced a 20 percent increase in sales compared with the previous year. The new design gave Rice-A-Roni considerably stronger shelf impact and clearly contributed to the strong sales increase.[14]

As any brand manager will tell you, packaging represents a substantial portion of brand equity. When the word "Coke" is uttered, it is more than likely that an image of the trademarked, hourglass-shaped bottle comes to mind.

A Package Value survey suggests that marketers should benchmark new packaging proposals against their own brand equity. The study interviewed a total of 251 men and women, all primary grocery shoppers. Those polled were shown a card with a brand

---

[13]Frank Tobolski, "Package Design Requires Research," *Marketing News,* June 6, 1994, p. 4.

[14]Michael Prone, "Package Design Has Stronger ROI Potential Than Many Believe," *Marketing News,* October 11, 1993, p. 13.

name printed on it and asked to rate the brand on a scale of 1 (agree strongly) to 5 (disagree strongly). Using "top box" methodology, only respondents who said they "agreed strongly" with all statements were included in the final results.

The subjects were then shown photos of actual packaging. The difference between the scores recorded when people were supplied with a brand name and when they were influenced by actual packaging is what makes the study intriguing. For example, when asked to rate the quality of Procter & Gamble's Tide, both the brand name and the packaging got scores of 61.[15]

Packaging and Color

Color has recently come to the forefront. The same contemporary colors that you can find in Saks Fifth Avenue can be found in the health and beauty aisles of the local supermarket or drug chain. In the past, packaged goods used to lag years behind the color trends. Today, marketers are more willing to experiment with such colors as teal or purple.

Package Look Alikes

Procter & Gamble sued the 124-store F & M drug chain over the chain's P&G look-alike packages. P&G said the look-alike products confused people and were a disservice to their customers. One of the products, for example, cloned P&G's Pantene, using the same color scheme with a swirl symbol in a small rectangle. Many of the private-label knockoff packaging was displayed next to the brand name products in the store.[16] P&G's move was like a warning shot to everyone with look-alike packages. Of course, the burden of proof lies with P&G proving that knockoff packaging causes consumer confusion. Attorney Maxine Lans says, "You can't stop a competitor from bringing out a similar product, but you can prevent the consumer from buying another product by accident because it looks so much like yours."

Design and Brand Identity Firms

Corporate identity, brand identity, packaging systems, research, brand equity management, naming, branded environments, retail design, and event branding—all of these often require firms that specialize in packaging and brand identity programs for corporations. Landor Associates is one of the firms that does all of these. These companies work with the agency or the corporation or both in developing packaging and may be involved with the total design concept of a corporation or brand. For example, when you think of McDonald's Corporation—the hamburger people—what comes to mind? Golden arches? Employee uniforms? Cup designs? Paper or box designs? Logo? Paper bags? Premiums? Letterheads? Publications? There are many elements that help identify McDonald's, and every element has its name or logo for starters. The corporate design people help the marketer and sometimes the agency develop strong corporate visual communications.

Packaging and Special Markets

Herb Meyers of the Gerstman + Meyers design firm believes how a product is packaged plays a critical role in how a market responds to brands. He points to the maturing baby boomers. The first of them turned 50 in 1996. They have always been the darling of the marketing community. Meyers notes that the percentage of Americans over age 65 has more than tripled since 1990; the most dramatic increase is expected from 2010 to 2030. The number of Americans over age 50 is estimated to soar over 80 percent, and the over-50 crowd will account for one-third of the population by the year

---

[15]Terry Lofton, "If Your Brand's Number Two, Get with the Package Program," *BrandWeek,* June 27, 1994, p. 26.

[16]Greg Erickson, "Seeing Double," *BrandWeek,* October 17, 1994, pp. 30–35.

2025. This segment has as much discretionary income—$150 billion—as all other age groups combined.

Gerstman & Meyers for eight years has been doing research in exploring the structural, graphic, and usage issues of packaging that impact this segment of the population. Their survey found typefaces to be a pivotal issue. Almost all mature consumers found it difficult to read small type. Respondents wanted packaging to clearly communicate, to provide information, and to present words in sharp contrast to the background color on labels. Furthermore, respondents looked for cues such as color and graphics with which they were familiar and had exposure to from advertising or purchasing habit. Consumers responded favorably to graphics, photographs, and illustrations as a representation of the package contents, and branding icons helped them find and differentiate the products they wanted.

Among the structural/ergonomic issues that influence packaging are seals. Respondents said that tamper-proof seals need to be balanced with accessibility. Price was important to them, but they were willing to pay more for packages they perceive to have added value, such as convenience of storage or ease in opening. They liked flip-top caps; freshness-preserving inner wraps for cookies and crackers; portion packs for coffee, tea, and baked goods; can lid opening rings that accommodate two fingers, and large handles on bottles. Unique features that do not solve problems, however, were considered an expensive frill: the toothpaste pump was singled out as one such item. These consumers preferred transparent packaging through which they could view the product. They also liked easy-to-pour products. Portion packages were considered to be a benefit for products not used frequently. The survey found that improvements driven by the needs and considerations of the aging market can be viewed as transgenerational packaging solutions.

Among those things the respondents didn't like were shrink wraps that are hard to open, tear tapes and tear tabs that are too small to grasp, gable-top milk and juice cartons that are difficult to open the first time, and heat-sealed cereal inner bags or potato chip bags that are difficult to open and reseal.[17]

SUMMARY

As we approach the millennium, packaging has become a very important part of the brand equity equation. It has been labeled as the only true method of international branding.

A product's trademark is like a person's name. It gives a product an identity and allows customers to be sure they are getting the same quality each time they purchase it. In addition, the trademark makes advertising and promotion activities possible. For established products, the trademark is one of the company's most valuable assets. It would be very difficult to estimate the value of trademarks such as Coca-Cola, Pepsi-Cola, IBM, or Mercedes. That is why companies take such pains to protect their trademarks.

The trademark can take the form of a word, a design, or a combination of both. Their formats can include letters, numbers, slogans, geometric shapes, color combinations, and so forth. When a trademark is a picture or other design, it is called a logotype. The same principle of trademark protection applies to logos as it does to brand names. Successful trademarks may take many forms; however, they should be easy to pronounce, have something in common with the product, and lend themselves to a variety of advertising and design formats.

The package design is developed in much the same way as an advertising campaign. Package research can help in assessing a number of factors, including recognition, imagery, structure, and behavior. Packaging is an important marketing tool and should be researched with target groups. Brand identity continues to be an important issue.

---

[17]"Aging Populace Shapes Package Design Needs, says Gerstman & Meyers Survey," *Graphic Design: USA,* March 1996, p. 21.

REVIEW

1. What is a trademark?
2. What is a service mark?
3. How can you lose a trademark?
4. What are the steps to putting a lock on the ownership of a trademark?
5. Name several marketing issues involved in packaging.

TAKE IT TO THE NET

We invite you to visit the Russell/Lane page on the Prentice Hall Web site at **PHLIP** **http://www.prenhall.com/phbusiness** for the bimonthly Russell/Lane update and for this chapter's World Wide Web exercise.

22

THE COMPLETE CAMPAIGN

CHAPTER OBJECTIVES

ADVERTISERS USUALLY CREATE CAMPAIGNS THAT FIT INTO AN INTEGRATED MARKETING COMMUNICATION PROGRAM. THEY DON'T CREATE JUST AN AD BY ITSELF. AFTER READING THIS CHAPTER YOU WILL UNDERSTAND

- **situation analysis**
- **creative objectives and strategy**
- **media objectives and strategy**
- **sales promotion plans**
- **research posttests.**

Today, many marketers think in terms of integrated marketing communication—that all of the communications from the company integrate or dovetail to support all other messages or impressions about the brand. These messages may include public relations, direct response, events, packaging, Web sites, and promotion among others. Jackie Reed, president and CEO of Fair Riley Call/Bozell, refers to thinking in terms of "media neutral." She defines this as the art and science of marketing communications that begins without a bias toward advertising or any other specific discipline, and systematically applies the right amount of each discipline to achieve the maximum return on investment. This may mean creating direct response or developing a Web site for a marketer, and not necessarily writing ads. Chapter 3 discussed a strategic marketing communication plan that could be applied to planning all marketing communications. Here we apply it specifically to advertising campaigns; *campaign,* as defined by Webster, being a "series of planned actions."

Earlier in the text, we talked about important components of the advertising process—development of strategy, media, research, print ads, and broadcast—all of which are extremely important. The truth is, we don't generally think in terms of individual ads because most brand advertising depends on a series of ads run over a period of time. In other words, a campaign. The ad campaign also doesn't work alone; it is integrated into the sales and marketing program. As a general rule, campaigns are designed to run over a longer period of time than an individual ad, although there are exceptions. The average length of a regional or national campaign is about 17 months, although it is not uncommon for a campaign to last three or four years, and a few campaigns have lasted much longer.

For example, in 1929 DuPont started using the campaign theme "Better Things for Better Living Through Chemistry." Fifty-five years later it was changed—"through chemistry" was dropped. That is building a lot of brand equity. Basically, the messages remained true to their original campaign premise. On the other hand, some campaigns need to change. "Pardon me, would you have any Grey Poupon?" worked too well in conveying a *premium* brand: consumers tended to reserve it for only special occasions and not for everyday eating. To change consumer habits meant going another direction and resulted in another campaign to get consumers to use it at ordinary meals. The older commercials, in which stuffy aristocrats pass the Grey Poupon through their Rolls-Royce windows, lasted a long time because of their appeal to both affluent and working consumers alike. The campaign said everybody could live the good life of the affluent when it comes to mustard. The simpler lifestyles of the mid-1990s diluted the impact and called for a broader approach to the product. The new direction asked consumers to "Poupon the potato salad" and "class up the cold cuts." The point is that advertisers must understand their product and consumers in a changing marketplace. There is no reason to change an advertising campaign for the sake of change.

Red Lobster, on the other hand, felt that their stores were aging and needed new life. Darden Restaurants, Inc., Red Lobster's parent company, invested more than $150 million over two years in remodeling the 700 outlets in the United States and Canada. It also cut prices, boosted promotion of its fresh fish entrees, and invested more in restaurant staffing. It closed older stores where business had slipped. As a result of these changes, there was a need for a new approach to their advertising. Darden spent $80 million on a new advertising campaign, which began during fall 1997, for positioning their restaurants as a tempting oasis from life's dry daily routine. The new theme for Red Lobster's advertising was "Life on Land Is Dry." This campaign replaced its long-running "Red Lobster—For the Seafood Lover in You." Due to the internal store and menu changes and new advertising, sales have increased. The question is, can they sustain sales over time in a highly competitive full-service restaurant market?[1]

There is never a guarantee that the next campaign will be as strong, let alone stronger, than the original. And some companies grope for a better campaign with little success. For example, in the mid-1970s, Burger King had perhaps its most famous campaign, "Have It Your Way," but decided it was time to change. So they followed with

America Loves Burgers, and We're America's Burger King
(November 1977–February 1978)

Who's Got the Best Darn Burger?
(February 1978–January 1980)

Make it Special. Make it Burger King.
(January 1980–January 1982)

Aren't You Hungry for Burger King Now?
(January 1982–September 1982)

Battle of the Burgers.
(September 1982–March 1983)

Broiling vs Frying.
(March 1983–September 1983)

---

[1] "Red Lobster Hopes its Ad Campaign Goes Swimmingly," *Atlanta Journal-Constitution*, October 15, 1997, p. C-3.

The Big Switch.

(September 1983–November 1985)

Search for Herb.

(November 1995–June 1986)

This Is a Burger King Town.

(June 1986–January 1987)

We Do It Like You Do It.

(April 1988–May 1989)

Sometimes You Gotta Break the Rules.

(October 1989–April 1991)

Your Way. Right Away.

(April 1991–October 1992)

BK Tee Vee: I Love This Place.

(1992–1994)

Get Your Burgers Worth.

(1994+)

Any campaign needs to bring together all of the advertising elements we have discussed into a unified campaign. This calls for an advertising plan. As we have emphasized, good advertising starts with a clear understanding of marketing goals, both short- and long-term. These goals are often expressed as sales or share-of-market objectives to be accomplished for a given budget and over a specific time period.

With our marketing goals in mind, we begin to build the advertising plan with a situation analysis.

SITUATION ANALYSIS

To plan and create future advertising, we need to establish a current benchmark or starting point—this is the role of the situation analysis. It has two time orientations: the past and the present. In other words, it asks two basic questions: Where are we today, and how did we get here? The rest of the advertising plan asks the third basic question: Where are we going in the future?

The situation analysis is the first step in developing a campaign. Exhibit 22.1 reminds us of the planning process discussed earlier in chapter 3. There are strategic steps that must be taken in the planning process. Campaigns are planned, they don't just happen.

exhibit

22.1

Planning Cycle

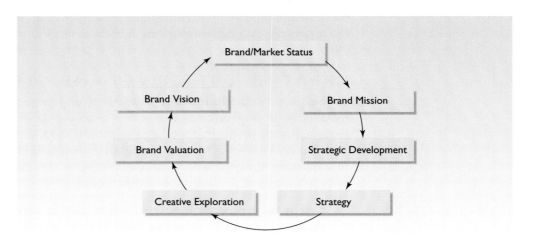

The Product

Successful advertising and marketing begin with a good product. At this point, we need to analyze our product's strengths and weaknesses objectively. Most product failures stem from an overly optimistic appraisal of a product. Among the questions usually asked are

1. What are the unique consumer benefits the product will deliver?
2. What is the value of the product relative to the proposed price?
3. Are adequate distribution channels available?
4. Can quality control be maintained?

Prime-Prospect Identification

The next step is to identify our prime prospects and determine if there are enough of them to market the product profitably. As discussed in chapter 4, there are a number of ways to identify the primary consumer of our product.

Who buys our product and what are their significant demographic and psychographic characteristics? Can we get a mental picture of the average consumer? Who are the heavy users of the product—the prime prospects? Remember the 80/20 rule; do we need to find those market segments that consume a disproportionate share of our product and determine what distinguishes them from the general population? Finally, we need to examine the prime prospect's problem. What are their needs and wants in the product or product type?

Competitive Atmosphere and Marketing Climate

We carefully review every aspect of the competition, including direct and indirect competitors. Which specific brand and products compete with your brand, and in what product categories or subcategories do they belong? Is Mountain Dew's competition 7-Up or Sprite, Mellow-Yellow or Crush, or does it extend to colas, iced tea, and milk? If so, to what extent in each case?

With what does Neon directly compete? Indirectly? Neon's competitive subcompact set includes Honda Civic, Ford Escort, Saturn, Nissan Sentra, Toyota Tercel, Toyota Corolla, Chevrolet Cavalier, Geo Prizm, Plymouth Sundance, and Dodge Shadow. When we examine the demographic competitive set, we find the typical subcompact buyers are 50 to 55 percent female, over half are married, they tend to be 35 to 40 years of age, and less than half have a college degree. Honda Civic and Saturn models attract the most distinguishable buyer profiles—typically better educated, earning more income, and younger. The psychographic profile is the competitive set. The greatest fluctuations in psychographic profiles for this set exist between import and domestic buyers. Domestic buyers tend to be motivated by style over engineering; they prefer roomier cars and greater performance. Import buyers prefer engineering over style; they like compact cars and believe imports offer higher quality overall. Now we're beginning to scratch the surface. As you can see there are numerous factors.

CREATIVE OBJECTIVES AND STRATEGY

At this point, we begin to select those advertising themes and selling appeals that are most likely to move our prime prospects to action. As discussed in chapter 16, advertising motivates people by appealing to their problems, desires, and goals—it is not creative if it does not sell. Once we establish the overall objectives of the copy, we are ready to implement the copy strategy by outlining how this creative plan will contribute to accomplishing our predetermined marketing goals:

1. Determine the specific claim that will be used in advertising copy. If there is more than one, the claims should be listed in order of priority.

2. Consider various advertising executions.

3. In the final stage of the creative process, develop the copy and production of advertising.

Creative Criteria for Campaigns

Most advertising experts agree on the need for *similarity* between one advertisement and another in developing successful advertising campaigns. Another term, *continuity,* is used to describe the relationship of one ad to another ad throughout a campaign. This similarity or continuity may be visual, verbal, aural, or attitudinal.[2]

Visual Similarity All print ads in a campaign should use the same typeface or virtually the same layout format so that consumers will learn to recognize the advertiser just by glancing at the ads. This may entail making illustrations about the same size in ad after ad and/or the headline about the same length in each ad. A number of ads in campaigns have appeared throughout this book (e.g., Healthtex, Snap-on Tools, egg beaters). Each illustration in the Electric Cooking ads (Exhibit 22.2, p. 592) is the same size, heads are visually treated in the same manner, the body copy is in two columns of about the same length, and there is a similar style illustration in the same location. For a different kind of client and reader, the Snap-on business-to-business ads (Exhibit 22.3, p. 593) use similar styles but not identical style illustrations and treatment of type; however, there is still definite continuity. You have the same visual feel from ad to ad. We are saying visual continuity—not sameness. These examples pertain to print, but the look could easily be carried over to television or direct marketing.

The Sun-Maid Raisins ads (Exhibit 22.4a, p. 594, and 22.4b, p. 595) show the relationship of print and television working together. There is no doubt about their being a part of the same campaign and reinforcing the same message and objectives. Another device is for all ads in a campaign to use the same spokesperson or continuing character in ad after ad. Still another way to achieve visual continuity is to use the same demonstration in ad after ad from one medium to the other.

Verbal Similarity It is not unusual for a campaign to use certain words or phrases in each ad to sum up the product's benefits. It is more than a catchy phrase. The proper objective is a set of words that illuminates the advertising, encapsulates the promise, and can be associated with one brand only.

Here are a few campaign phrases that have worked:

For hair so healthy it shines.

Pantene

Have you driven a Ford lately?

Ford

Where's your mustache?

Milk

From Sharp minds come Sharp products.

Sharp

From the French Alps.

evian

For the skin that just has to be touched.

Aveeno

---

[2]Kenneth Roman and Jane Maas, *The New How to Advertise* (New York: St. Martin's Press, 1992), pp. 71–78.

exhibit

22.2

These Electric Cooking ads are very similar, but definitely not the same.

Courtesy: Aydlotte & Cartwright.

Pepsi used the words "You're in the Pepsi Generation" to help position it among a younger audience and make Coca-Cola appear to be an old-fashioned brand. But it didn't limit all the upbeat, self-assuring benefits of membership of being part of the Pepsi Generation to people between 13 and 24 years of age; it opened it up to everybody—everybody wanted to be in the Pepsi Generation. It wasn't a point of *time* in years, it was a point of *view*. No matter what your age, you could be part of the Pepsi Generation. Great words and great strategy make great campaigns. Here are a few other words and *classic* campaign strategies:

Aren't you glad you use Dial?
Don't you wish everybody did?

You're in good hands with Allstate.

American Express. Don't leave home without it.

Have it your way at Burger King.

Is it true blondes have more fun?
Be a Lady Clairol blonde and see!

You deserve a break today, at McDonald's.

Nike. Just do it.

Never slow down.

Everyone needs energy. And everyone needs fast, easy ways
to get it. Which is probably why so many people
take this little red box along with them. Wherever they go.
Or why they sprinkle our raisins on so many of their
favorite dishes. Sun-Maid® Raisins. Fast fruit for
people who just don't have time to slow down. Ever.

Sun•Maid Raisins
Fast Fruit

© 1996 Sun-Maid Growers of California

exhibit

22.4b

Repeating the benefits, theme, and key copy points in ad after ad bestows continuity across all media and helps build brand personality.

We have shown a number of Healthtex ads throughout this text to give you a real taste of their campaign. These ads use visual, verbal, and attitude similarity. And we didn't include all the great ones from the beginning of this campaign:

When you're bald and toothless, you'd better wear cute clothes.

Why do babies put everything in their mouths until it's time to eat?

My head. A tight squeeze. Lots of labor:
Didn't we just go through this, Mom?

Joe Alexander, the copywriter on this campaign, comments on its success: "The best advertising is always personal. It relates to me or to something happening in my life. We understood what moms and dads wanted to know. We wanted to show kids as they really are." It just happens that three of the four members of the Healthtex creative team have children.

The Healthtex campaign is really about smart marketing. They do a lot of account planning. And conceptually, this enabled the agency to speak in a language that talks to mom. The campaign budget is generally around $5 million a year and runs primarily in parenting magazines. Over a two-year period, sales increased 42 percent and advertising awareness jumped up 35 percent. According to Alexander, Healthex positioned itself in a leadership position in a me-too market. This has been a great campaign.

Aural Similarity   You can create aural continuity in broadcast, if you desire. You may use the same music or jingle in commercial after commercial. Using the same announcer's voice in each ad also helps build continuity—"This is Tom Bodett for Motel 6." The same sound effect can make a campaign very distinctive. Avon used the sound of a doorbell for many years in its "Avon Calling" advertising. Maxwell House used the perking sound for its Master Blend commercials, giving an audible campaign signal.

Attitudinal Similarity   Each ad expresses a consistent attitude toward the product and the people using it. The commercial's attitude is an expression of brand personality. The Pepsi Generation campaign was more than words. It communicated an attitude to younger consumers and older consumers. Of course, we cannot leave out the Nike shoe campaign, which said, "Just Do It"—or their swoosh campaign.

Everyone agrees that Nike is one of the strongest brand names in the world, and not just because it sells great products. Its presence and identity are so strong that many people want to connect with the brand. It signifies status, glamour, competitive edge, and the myriad intricacies of cool. It is this description that is communicated in every message, no matter to whom it is directed. Their secret of success resides along a delicate and emotionally charged progression that connects the company, the consumers, and the abiding fantasies that are tethered to sports.[3] In true integrated marketing fashion, its personality is communicated to all—from employees, to stockholders, to consumers. It is conveyed through its corporate culture, as well as its advertising.

MEDIA OBJECTIVES

Although we have chosen to discuss creative strategy before media objectives, both functions are considered simultaneously in an advertising campaign. In fact, creative and media planning have the same foundations—marketing strategy and prospect identification—and cannot be isolated from each other. The media plan involves three primary areas.

Media Strategy

> **Media strategy**
> Planning of ad media buys, including identification of audience, selection of media vehicles, and determination of timing of a media schedule.

At the initial stages of media planning, the general approach and role of media in the finished campaign are determined:

1. *Prospect identification.* The prime prospect is of major importance in both the media and the creative strategy. However, the media planner has the additional burden of identifying prospects. The media strategy must match prospects for a product with users of specific media. This requires that prospects be identified in terms that are compatible with traditional media audience breakdowns. You will recall that this need for standardization has resulted in the 4A's standard demographic categories discussed in chapter 4.
2. *Timing.* All media, with the possible exception of direct mail, operate on their own schedule, not that of advertisers. The media planner must consider many aspects of timing, including media closing dates, production time required for ads and commercials, campaign length, and the number of exposures desired during the product-purchase cycle.
3. *Creative considerations.* The media and creative teams must accommodate each other. They must compromise between using those media that allow the most creative execution and those that are most efficient in reaching prospects.

Media Tactics

At this point, the media planner decides on media vehicles and the advertising weight each is to receive. The reach-versus-frequency question must be addressed and appropriate budget allocations made.

Media Scheduling

Finally, an actual media schedule and justification are developed, as described in the example in chapter 7.

---

[3]Lisa Siracuse, "Looks Aren't Everything: An Examination of Brand Personality," *Integrated Marketing Communications Research Journal,* Spring 1997, pp. 38–39.

The Sales Promotion Plan

As with any integrated communications planning, the sales-promotion plan for consumers is discussed very early, and its relationship to the advertising plan (and other communications activities) is determined. Sales-promotion activities may involve dealer displays, in-store promotions, premiums, cooperative advertising, and/or couponing offers.

Once a theme for communications has been established, creative work is begun on the sales-promotion material, which is presented along with the consumer advertising material for final approval. Naturally, advertising and sales-promotion materials would reinforce each other. Once the sales-promotion material is approved, the production is carefully planned so that all of the sales-promotion material will be ready before the consumer advertising breaks.

GETTING THE CAMPAIGN APPROVED

We now have a complete campaign: the ads, the media schedule, sales-promotion material, and costs for everything spelled out, ready for management's final approval. For that approval, it is wise to present a statement of the company's marketing goals. The objectives may be to launch a new product, to increase sales by x percent, to raise the firm's share of the market by z percent, or to promote a specific service of a firm. Next, the philosophy and strategy of the advertising are described, together with the reasons for believing that the proposed plan will help attain those objectives. Not until then are the ads or the commercials presented, along with the media proposal and the plans for coordinating the entire effort with that of the sales department.

What are the reasons for each recommendation in the program? On what basis were these dollar figures calculated? On what research were any decisions based? What were the results of preliminary tests, if any? What is the competition doing? What alternatives were considered? What is the total cost? Finally, how may the entire program contribute to the company's return on its investment? Those people who control the corporate purse strings like to have definite answers to such questions before they approve a total advertising program.

RESEARCH—POSTTESTS

The final part of the campaign entails testing its success. Posttesting falls into two related stages. In the first, the expected results are defined in specific and measurable terms. What do you expect the advertising campaign to accomplish? Typical goals of a campaign are to increase brand awareness by 10 percent or improve advertising recall by 25 percent.

In the second stage, the actual research is conducted to see if these goals were met. Regardless of what research technique is used (for example, test markets, consumer panels), the problem is separating the results of the advertising campaign from consumer behavior that would have occurred in any case. That is, if we find that 20 percent of the population recognizes our brand at the end of a campaign, the question arises as to what the recognition level would have been if no advertising took place. To answer this question, a research design is often used as a pretest. The pretest is intended not only to provide a benchmark for the campaign, but also to determine reasonable goals for future advertising.

A 10-year study by Information Resources Inc.'s BehaviorScan showed that advertising produces long-term growth even after a campaign ends. The study emphasized TV campaigns and concluded the following:

● Increased ad weight alone will not boost sales.
● Typically, advertising for new brands, line extensions, or little-known brands produced the best incremental sales results.

exhibit

22.5

These ads are targeted
to recruit nurses.

Courtesy: Aydlotte &
Cartwright.

- Campaigns in which the "message in the copy is new" or the media strategy had changed also produced good sales results.
- Results of copy recall and persuasion tests were unlikely to predict sales reliably.

The study also suggested that discounting results in "training customers to buy only on a deal," and the trade promotion actually worked against TV advertising. However, couponing often helped a brand message and spurred a sale.

The test was conducted in 10 markets with household panels of 3,000 respondents in each market. The commercials were transmitted to two equal groups of homes. This study compared purchase information obtained through scanners and a card encoded with demographic and other information that was presented at supermarket checkout stands.[4]

Campaign Portfolio

Health Care   Georgia Baptist Health Care System, as most hospital systems, has to compete to get the best nurses available. Exhibit 22.5 shows examples of their highly targeted campaign to recruit nurses.

Business-to-Business   Sawyer Riley Compton created a campaign with strong visual continuity for Snap-on Industrial Tools. You have seen examples in chapters 3 and 5. Exhibits 22.3a and 22.3b show how the campaign continued.

Global   You probably didn't know that the Coca-Cola Company distributes coffee in a can in Japan. They also were a sponsor of the 1998 Olympic Games in Nagano. Two promotional ads touting the Olympic Torch Relay are shown in Exhibit 22.6.

Jackie Hathiramani, Ogilvy & Mather Advertising/Singapore, created a clever visual campaign for Celebrity Oriental Restaurant featuring menu items (see Exhibits 22.7a, p. 600, and 22.7b, p. 601). The visual continuity is very obvious in these ads.

---

[4]Gary Levin, "Tracing Ads' Impact," *Advertising Age,* November 4, 1991, p. 49.

exhibit

22.6

Georgia Coffee's
promotional ads for
Olympic Torch Relay.

Courtesy: Coca-Cola (Japan)
Company, Limited.

SUMMARY

The steps in preparing a national campaign for a consumer product are

1. Situation analysis
   a. Product analysis
   b. Prime-prospect identification
   c. Prime-prospects' problem analysis
   d. Competitive atmosphere and market climate

exhibit

22.7a

Smart use of visual
continuity can be a
very important part of
a campaign portfolio.

Courtesy: Ogilvy & Mather
Advertising, Singapore.

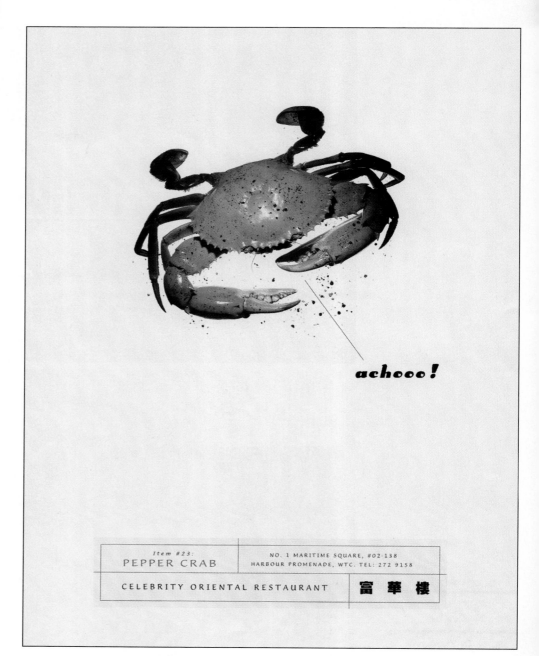

achooo!

Item #23:
PEPPER CRAB

NO. 1 MARITIME SQUARE, #02-138
HARBOUR PROMENADE, WTC. TEL: 272 9158

CELEBRITY ORIENTAL RESTAURANT 富華樓

2. Creative objectives and strategy
   a. Determine specific copy claims
   b. Consider various advertising executions
   c. Begin creation of ads and commercials (and other integrated communications)
3. Media objectives
   a. Media strategy—includes prospect identification, timing, and creative considerations
   b. Media tactics
   c. Media scheduling
4. The sales-promotion plan (and/or other integrated programs)
5. Getting the campaign approved
6. Research posttests

In general, advertising campaigns need to have similarity from ad to ad. It may be visual, verbal, aural, or attitudinal. Campaigns should be designed to last and not be changed simply because you are bored with them.

exhibit

22.7b

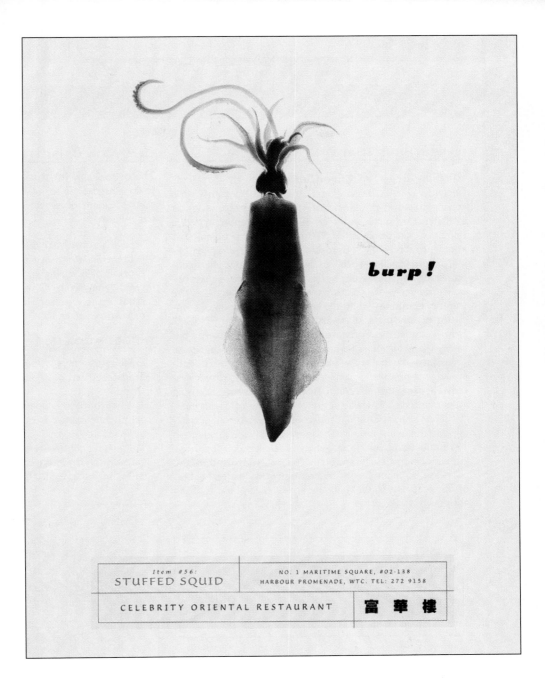

Item #56:
STUFFED SQUID

NO. 1 MARITIME SQUARE, #02-138
HARBOUR PROMENADE, WTC. TEL: 272 9158

CELEBRITY ORIENTAL RESTAURANT　富華樓

REVIEW

1. What is the basic purpose of an ad campaign?
2. What is ad continuity?
3. What is involved in the situation analysis?
4. What are some of the means of guaranteeing continuity in a campaign?

TAKE IT TO THE NET

We invite you to visit the Russell/Lane page on the Prentice Hall Web site at
PHLIP **http://www.prenhall.com/phbusiness** for the bimonthly
Russell/Lane update and for this chapter's World Wide Web exercise.

case
HISTORY

MARKETING SITUATION

"Trailing Edge" of Client Serve

Recently, Dun & Bradstreet Software had a tough time staying ahead in the world of information technology, as evidenced by three years of declining revenue. In 1995, sales revenue declined by $70 million. The problem that contributed to Dun & Bradstreet Software's image as being on the "trailing edge" of technology was their mainframe legacy. They were seen as a mainframe software–only provider—even among their own customers—as the trend in computing shifted to the decentralization of computing processing and toward the birth of "client/server." Dun & Bradstreet Software was not seen as a player because client/server software was not part of its heritage. Therefore, customers were under attack by more leading-edge competitors to migrate to their client/server systems. In fact, the retention rate for mainframe licensing agreements in 1994 was at an all-time low of 77 percent.

However, as Dun & Bradstreet Software was preparing to launch its own client/server software product in 1995, the client/server target market shifted from those innovators and early adopters (phase I) involved in the purchase of client/server technology in its earliest stages of development to what is now considered phase II of the adoption model.

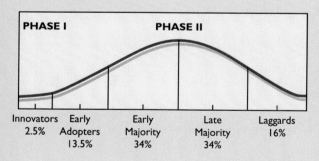

| PHASE I | | PHASE II | | |
| Innovators 2.5% | Early Adopters 13.5% | Early Majority 34% | Late Majority 34% | Laggards 16% |

These customers, considered as the early to late majority adopters on the adoption bell, were characterized as more conservative regarding the use of technology. Their foremost concern was finding solutions to business problems rather than employing technology for technology's sake. After hearing of or experiencing the problems of client/server computing, they weren't ready or willing to trash their mainframe investment in favor of client/server. Rather, as they considered their next move in information technology, they knew they wanted a software vendor who understood their needs by providing the right *business solutions* through the use of technology, *whether it be mainframe, client/server, or a combination of both.*

CAMPAIGN OBJECTIVES

The overall goal for the company was to stop the three-year sales decline in mainframe sales while doubling the sales of client/server software. Dun & Bradstreet's objectives were:

- Stop the three-year decline in company-wide revenue.
- Protect mainframe revenue by preventing further erosion of licensing revenue.
- Hold renewals at 77 percent.
- Double client/server software revenue from $40 million to $80 million.

TARGET AUDIENCE

- *Existing customers* who were unaware that Dun & Bradstreet was a player in the client/server software world.
- The *conservative early and late majority adopters* who use technology as a tool to help them make better business decisions.
- The *information technology and financial managers* who contribute to the purchase decision of enterprise-wide software.

Can't we all just get along?

Of course we can. The days when mainframe and client/server systems clashed with each other are gone. Dun & Bradstreet Software offers tools that give you an integrated view of business information, so you can make better decisions—whether you're using a mainframe, a client/server system, or a combination. Let's talk: call us at 1-800-290-7374, ext. 560, or reach us on the Internet at: solutions@dbsoftware.com.

Dun & Bradstreet Software

FINANCIALS   HUMAN RESOURCES   MANUFACTURING   DECISION SUPPORT

YOU'RE THE CLIENT.

WE'RE THE SERVER.

A simple statement of our philosophy.

It's how we go about business, whether you're using a mainframe, a client/server system, or a combination of both. We want to make your goals our own. So we're there with you, not just delivering software, but helping you use it to make better, faster decisions. Make us prove it — after all, you're the client. Call us at 1-800-290-7374, extension 760, or reach us on the Internet: solutions@dbsoftware.com.

Dun & Bradstreet Software

FINANCIALS   HUMAN RESOURCES   MANUFACTURING   DECISION SUPPORT

CREATIVE STRATEGY

Cutting a New "Leading Day"

Through research, it was discovered that Dun & Bradstreet Software had developed a "problem/solution" approach to addressing business needs versus the approach of their competitors, who simply talked about the products they had to sell. They saw this as an opportunity to take advantage of the market shift into a more advanced stage of the product adoption model, personified by the more conservative early and late majority prospects who considered the use of technology and their vendors as the tools to assist them in making better business decisions. This shift in not only who the target was but the buying mind-set allowed them to not only introduce the new Dun & Bradstreet Software client/server software product but to actually relaunch the positioning of Dun & Bradstreet Software as a company who considers the relationship between vendor and customer rather than simply the technology as the key ingredient in making these better business decisions.

Therefore, this philosophy was reflected in the first execution: "You're The Client, We're The Server."

This assertion positioned Dun & Bradstreet Software as a definite player in the client/server software world, while simultaneously stating their operating philosophy. Subsequent executions in the campaign were more product specific in addressing various relevant issues such as coexistence and flexibility of software systems, yet they remained focused on *you,* the customer, not *them* and their product.

MEDIA STRATEGY

Due to limited resources and the highly targeted market of enterprise-wide software publishers, Dun & Bradstreet needed to concentrate messages in just several I/T publications and one deputy financial officer targeted publication. However, because the kinds of companies they were targeting were not concentrated in any one particular geographical area, they had to choose rather broad-based tech books that were national in scale.

Primary vehicles were *Computerworld, Information Week,* and *PC Week* (executive edition). Advertising ran twice a month from March through December 1995, in each vehicle. Because of the secondary target, the top financial manager, they also ran a full monthly schedule in *CFO.*

RESULTS

The three-year decline in sales revenue was halted. Following the sales decline of $70 million in 1994, company-wide sales actually grew by $15 million in 1995. The turnaround in company sales revenue in less than a year's time was astounding. While the goal was to slow down the hemorrhaging of mainframe sales of the past several years, retention rate for mainframe customers was moved from 77 percent to 84 percent—a 9 percent improvement rate, *the highest in Dun & Bradstreet Software's history.* This improvement rate represented a +$20 million revenue impact, which resulted in a +$10 million additional contribution to profitability. Client/server sales were even more dramatic. Although perception and awareness levels of Dun & Bradstreet Software as a client/server software remained low, the goal for 1995 had been to double sales revenue. However, 1995 sales were up by 150 percent over 1994, moving from $40 million to $100 million. In fact, 1995 was the first time in history that Dun & Bradstreet Software experienced revenue growth and profitability every quarter of the year.

Courtesy: J. Walter Thompson.

part III

Other Environments of Advertising

THIS FINAL SECTION OF THE TEXT DEALS with some of the areas of advertising that are not considered in earlier chapters. Chapter 23 examines the fast-paced world of the retailer, in which advertising decisions and their results are known immediately and there is little time to consider past successes before the next marketing battle unfolds. The hectic pace of retailing is not for everyone, but those who enjoy being tested on a daily basis find it the most exciting area of advertising and marketing. The retail sector demands a sales-oriented approach, with price, customer service, and convenience being much more important than the subtleties of national advertising, which often seeks to build an image over time.

Going from one extreme to the other, we move from the local department store to the global advertisers on the multinational stage in chapter 24. In this arena, advertisers must be aware of such diverse considerations as language, culture, and product preference, unlike anything they deal with in domestic advertising. As these huge advertisers move from country to country, the elements of media placement, research, and product distribution are constantly changing. The local customer, whether in the United States or Korea, must be reached in a manner appropriate to the customs of that country. International marketers find that customers are largely unforgiving of offensive communication—even that which is unintended.

Chapters 25 and 26 deal with the legal, regulatory, and ethical environment in which advertisers must deal. In the last 25 years the public has become much more sophisticated about marketing and advertisers. Practices that might have been accepted or overlooked in earlier times can quickly bring major problems to companies. The combination of a vigilant public and increasing government intervention has made advertisers very wary of taking any action that has even the appearance of being improper. The advertising industry itself also has taken significant steps to strengthen the process of self-regulation. The formal system of self-regulation, best represented by the Council of Better Business Bureaus, has the dual responsibility of identifying misleading and deceptive advertising as well as providing the public with more confidence in the advertising they see and hear.

23

RETAIL ADVERTISING

BOTH RETAILERS AND CONSUMERS HAVE CHANGED AND ARE CHANGING THE WAY THEY DO BUSINESS AND SHOP. THE LOCAL MEDIA HAVE RESPONDED TO THESE CHANGES. AFTER READING THIS CHAPTER YOU WILL UNDERSTAND

- **retail trends**
- **changes in retailing**
- **differences in national and retail advertising**
- **media in retailing**
- **use of cooperative advertising.**

When someone mentions the word "retailer," you probably think of the kinds of stores found in or near regional shopping malls: major department stores such as Lord & Taylor, JCPenney, Neiman-Marcus, Rich's, Bloomingdale's, Nordstrom, Marshall Fields, Macy's, and Parisian; specialty stores such as Victoria's Secret, The Limited, Casual Corner, Pottery Barn, Crate & Barrel, GAP, the Disney Store; discounters such as Target, Kmart, Wal-Mart, Books-A-Million, Stein-Mart, Best Buys, Circuit City, and Toys "Я" Us; supermarkets such as Publix, Kroger, and A&P; and convenience stores such as 7-Eleven and Circle K. This is only scratching the surface. There are thousands of independent clothing, shoe, grocery, drug, camera, and specialty shops that also come to mind. You probably don't always think of warehouse clubs such as Sam's; service retailers such as banks, restaurants, quick-service restaurants, video stores, and beauty salons; or mail-order catalog stores such as Lands' End as retailers.

Retailing has been defined as all activities in selling goods or services directly to consumers for their personal use. Most retailing takes place in retail stores, of course, but don't forget that nonstore retailing—mail, telephone, door-to-door, vending machines, CD-ROM catalogs, and so on—has mushroomed, and Internet shopping is beginning to increase significantly.

Recently, a number of changes have taken place in retail. Consumers have new kinds of retail outlets—category killers (superstores), Internet, CD-ROM catalogs, outlet malls, interactive television—all in a battle with department stores, specialty shops, and mom-and-pop stores. Then there is the growth of brand-name retailers such as Warner Bros., Niketown, and the Disney Store, who are selling retail as entertainment. Printed catalogs and Web purchases are growing rapidly as consumers are finding they are pressed for time. It seems like retailing is "schizophrenic."

Despite the strength of discounters such as Wal-Mart and category killers such as Home Depot, Office Depot, and Toys "Я" Us, there hasn't been any sign of the demise of the small retailer, especially in such categories as consumer electronics, cameras, and home furnishings (see Exhibit 23.1), which account for significant employment and growth.

Now showing at four convenient locations.

See these feature attractions and more at our Rockville, Bethesda, Falls Church and Alexandria stores. T-cushion sofa with botanical print slipcover, reg. $1,328. SALE $999. T-cushion chair, reg. $599. SALE $499. Ottoman, reg. $299. SALE $249. Our distinguished sofa collection starts at $699. Gunmetal cocktail table, reg. $459. SALE $409. End table, reg. $309. SALE $259. Amish-made pine armoire, reg. $999. SALE $799. Other exciting attractions coming soon to a Storehouse near you.

storehouse®
HOME FURNISHINGS 25ᵗʰ ANNIVERSARY

Rockville, Congressional Plaza, 1625 Rockville Pike, (301) 231-7310, Bethesda, 6700 Wisconsin Avenue at Bradley Blvd., (301) 654-6829
Falls Church, 7505 Leesburg Pike (Idylwood Plaza next to Fresh Fields), (703) 821-5027
Alexandria, 809 S. Washington St., Old Town, (703) 548-6934

Atlanta • Austin • Birmingham • Charlotte • Columbia • Dallas • Ft. Worth/Arlington • Greensboro • Greenville • Houston • Knoxville • Nashville
New Orleans • Raleigh • San Antonio • Tulsa • Washington, D.C.

RETAIL BRANDING

National retail companies have refocused themselves to become more competitive and profitable or just to survive. Over a number of months, Montgomery Ward & Co. moved into federal bankruptcy protection; Woolworth Corp., long the heart of main street, closed its variety stores; and Levitz Furniture has filed for bankruptcy. Each had its specific problems, but common to all was a failure to brand effectively at a time when America is overpaved with too many stores. Sales per square foot at malls did not keep up with inflation in 1996.

Jack Sansolo, senior vice president–global brand direction at Spiegel's Eddie Bauer, says, "There are really too many choices and we are overstored. We are now in the same position as packaged goods. Retailers must rise above the marketplace clutter and go to the emotional relationship with the customer."[1] Some chains, including Banana Republic, Ralph Lauren, and Eddie Bauer have "connected" with their consumers by developing a lifestyle niche. Kohl's Corp., a Midwest department store, is predicted to increase total sales by 20 percent over the next few years because of their brand effort, themed "That's more like it." Retailers are beginning to understand that they can't tell consumers they have 40 percent off this week, and come back with the same message next week. JCPenney has developed a new formula to balance branding and sales by using a broadcast branding campaign supplemented by an increased use of radio to drive immediate sales. This can get expensive. Sears spent $588 million in 1996 to promote its "Softer Side." GAP's "Fall into GAP" raised its budget 72.6 percent.

If we mention JCPenney or Lord & Taylor ads, images of their ad formats probably come to mind. Retail advertising takes on all forms and involves all media. Exhibits 23.2 and 23.3 illustrate two different approaches: the local County Seat restaurant attempts to take the risk out of trying its new restaurant with a deal to enjoy Southern hospitality, and national retailer Charles David promotes the fashion aspect of shoes.

exhibit

23.2

Just snip out the coupon and come join us at County Seat Cafe. County Seat takes out part of the risk of sampling.

Courtesy: Folks Restaurant Management Group.

[1]Alice Z. Cuneo, "Shakeout Sends Stores Scurrying for a Niche," *Advertising Age,* September 29, 1997, p. s26.

exhibit

23.3

**Example of Retail
Ad Run in National
Magazines**

Courtesy: Lambesis.

Kisses, on occasion, begin at the toes.

charles david *by Nathalie M*

Retailers' Own Brands

A lot of retailers are making more room in their stores for their own branded lines of clothes. There is more profit from selling their own brands—2 percent to 8 percent more on average—because they cut out the middleman. These private labels are attempts by department stores to differentiate themselves from competitors:

Saks: The Works, Essentials, and Real Clothes
Carson Pirie Scott: Hasting & Smith, Great Lakes Recreation, and Architect
Federated: INC, Charter Club, Alfani, and Badge
JCPenney: Arizona
Barney's: New York Collection

"Private label is an important part of our strategy," says Joseph Feczko, senior vice president of marketing at Federated. "Before it was a commodity opportunity. Now, we are building brands with a personality. Five years ago only 5 percent of Federated's apparel was made up of its own brands, but that number is closer to 15 percent today."

Another factor in the equation is that many designer brands have opened their own stores in competition with department stores. Kurt Salmon Associates, a management consulting firm, says that every department store has Tommy Hilfiger and DKNY, and so there is no reason to go to Macy's over Bloomingdale's. The key is to make the private labels "branded." Advertising can help provide the proper image by evoking a certain mood or attitude. For example, the notion is that it will make wearers feel sexy (Calvin Klein) or sporty (Abercrombie & Fitch) or wealthy (Ralph Lauren). As Penney's vice president of brand development says, "You've got to get into people's head. You have to project an image." In 1990, JCPenney came up with the Arizona jeans line, which competes right next to Levi's. Sales have grown from $50 million a year to more than $1 billion. The number of consumers aware of the line increased from 32 percent in 1994 to 64 percent in 1997. Macy's INC woman is between 20-something and her mid-40s. She has a career, a hectic lifestyle, and may have a family. She is a forward-thinking working woman. To embody this woman in advertising, Federated booked the model Shalom Harlow, who recently satirized the out-to-lunch supermodel image with her role in the movie "In & Out."[2]

---

[2]Jennifer Steinhauer, "Strutting Their Own Stuff," *The New York Times,* September 27, 1997, p. B-1.

Most retailers admit that their bread and butter is still among the established brands. They will establish a significant percentage of private label, but the dominant factor will always be the so-called market brands.

Before we discuss the advertising, let us take a look at retail trends and the nature and scope of the business. Marketing research indicates continued change in supermarkets, discount department stores, traditional department stores, megastores, specialty apparel shops, and shopping centers:[3]

Supermarkets are the most-shopped type of retail store, which probably isn't surprising. Despite their success, supermarkets are beset with two main competitive alternatives: discount super centers (e.g., Super Kmart, Super Wal-Mart) and warehouse clubs (e.g., Sam's). Without more efficient operating procedures, supermarkets might be overtaken in the low-margin grocery business by wholesale clubs and super centers.

Discount department stores continue to attract more shoppers every year, as they have for 20 years. Elements that will contribute to their continued growth in the next decade include operating efficiencies due to extensive use of technologies, emphasis on low prices, wide selections, and service.

Traditional department stores have experienced a steady decline in shopping frequency since 1974. Stores are attempting to be more consumer-service oriented.

Wholesale clubs have attracted close to 20 percent of shoppers, but have recently stumbled. Basically, warehouse clubs have moved away from their original concepts by adding bakeries and perishables because of increased competition from expanded format supermarkets and combination superstores. There is a saturation of wholesale clubs.

Big-box destination retailers, or mega warehouses, continue to boom in almost every category: computers, office supplies, children's toys, building materials, pet supplies, sporting goods, baby supplies, books, crafts, and so forth. In each category there has been a rush of expansion and market share, followed by consolidation to establish format dominance.

Specialty apparel retailers have been losing customers for the past 20 years as demographics and shopping habits have changed. The result has been a significant decline in shopping frequency over these years. The future will bring closings and consolidation as competition for apparel specialists in outlet centers and power strip centers intensifies.

Shopping centers have seen sales per square foot decline over the past 25 years. Customer visits to shopping centers have declined since 1980, and the number of stores visited per trip also declined. Trips to regional malls are declining almost as rapidly as visits to downtown areas. The future is bright only for those with superior regional access, densely populated trade areas, and economically strong anchors.

Top Retail Companies' Revenues

Rank Brand	Revenue (millions)	Advertising (millions)
1 Wal-Mart	$99,826	$144.9
2 Sears	34,848	588.1
3 Kmart	30,378	240.8
4 Dayton Hudson Corp.	25,371	270.8
5 JCPenney	23,649	305.1
6 Federated Department Stores	15,229	405.0
7 May Department Stores	11,650	398.8
8 The Limited	8,645	20.6
9 Woolworth Corp.	8,090	47.1
10 TJM Cos.	6,689	54.5

Source: Advertising Age, September 29, 1997, p. s28.

---

[3]Howard L. Green, "New Consumer Realities for Retailers," *Marketing News,* April 25, 1994, p. 4.

Retailing's Future Environment

Let us look now at some retailing facts. According to the Bureau of Labor Statistics, retail employment in the United States stood at 21 million in 1995, which is 18 percent of all nonfarm wage and salary employment. Francesca Turchiano, president of In Fact, says retailers do a lot of really good customer satisfaction research, which results in decisions made about product mix, advertising, and even store layout and design. Unfortunately, it doesn't appear to have any effect on the customers' encounters at the store. Instead, much of a store's image derives from the impression customers have of its staff, which is a problem for most retailers. One of the problems is employees' low wages.[4]

- The average weekly wage of all U.S. retail workers in 1995 was $222, according to the Bureau of Labor Statistics, compared with $244 in 1986 (in 1995 dollars).
- The largest concentration of retail jobs is, and will remain, in the most populated cities. Chicago, Los Angeles, Boston, New York, and Washington, D.C. top the list. It is projected that Los Angeles may outrank Chicago by 2006, and fast-growing Atlanta may replace New York on the top-five list. These shopping areas not only have large populations to draw upon but also attract customers from hundreds of miles away due to the large range of stores and merchandise that smaller towns can't support.
- Retailing is just one place you see balkanization in today's society. On the one hand, most shoppers have high service expectations, and on the other, retail establishments don't spend the time and money to properly train staff to provide that level of service.
- Most retail business is still transacted the traditional way across countertops in a store; however, an increasing number of transactions are taking place through remote channels. The alternative section has grown from its mail-order origins to include TV, phone, and online shopping. In the future, service will remain an essential element of successful retailing, whether it is measured by attentiveness of a store clerk or the accurate and speedy delivery of a catalog order.

Millennium Trends

As we approach the millennium, retailing should continue to undergo massive structure changes as consumers increasingly demand reasonable prices. The rise of off-price and warehouse clubs as well as superstores has changed the way people shop. Many traditional retailers can expect to wither away if they do not learn to adapt to the new environment. Let us examine a few trends in retailing.

- *Traditional retailers.* There is little doubt that typical smaller stores and retailers will continue to feel pressure from high-volume deep-discount competitors. Many will not be able to compete on price, but they can build their reputations in specific areas—as JCPenney did with quality, value-priced goods. Traditional retailers should consider adopting new strategies that combine traditional retail business with mail-order, Web-site, or transactional television components. The direct-response option should inspire more interest in the retailer.
- *Restaurants.* Competition will intensify as many markets have reached saturation. It is predicted that there will be a continuing boom in *ethnic* chains and broader menus. Established chains from Pizza Hut to Taco Bell have been successful in the "Americanization" of Italian and Mexican fare. Current growth areas include Chinese and possibly Thai or Indian.
- *Grocery stores.* The future of local grocery stores and chains may well depend on their ability to create individual store personalities, making geodemographic targeting essential.
- *Home shopping.* The home shopping networks on cable television will continue to see sales climb. And as programming becomes more interactive, television shopping by category or department is a likely scenario.

---

[4]Diane Crispell, "Retailing's Next Decade," *American Demographics,* May 1997, pp. 4–10.

- *Fashion.* People will demand that clothing fit their style and lifestyle rather than fitting themselves into the latest styles. Office wear will continue the more functional and less formal trend. Evening wear will err on the side of simplicity and flexibility. This shift does not mean an abandonment of high style. But it will take less ornamentation to impress. Vanity will give way to value: A dress that goes to work should also be adaptable for dinner—either at home or on the town. The trend will favor clothing with lasting, go-anywhere, flexible, interchangeable lines, but distinction will not disappear.
- *Entertainment and freedom products.* The boom in home entertainment products will expand. The *electronic hearth* will be the center of fun and family recreation for the baby boomer generation. The millennium will bring *nomadic* products—the first of which was the Walkman—allowing consumers to bring their inside world to the outside and vice versa. The convenience these products give is their greatest selling point. Nomadic products empower consumers—or at least executives and professionals—by granting them control of the use of their time. Just think of the impact of cell phones and beepers.

Nontraditional Buying

It has been predicted that by the year 2010, more than half of all shopping will be done through nontraditional methods such as home television shopping, interactive shopping, Web shopping, and old-fashioned ordering by phone. Technological advances and consumers' increasing time pressures will be the catalysts.

More factories will customize mass-produced goods, and 60 percent of the merchandise will be shipped directly to consumers. Gateway 2000 was a leader in selling computers directly to consumers by phone orders, although they have recently opened retail centers. In the future, many stores will become pseudotheaters that display new merchandising ideas.

CONSUMER ATTITUDES

Truthfulness of Ads

A recent Better Business Bureau study found a high degree of skepticism about truthfulness of local retail and sale ads (Exhibit 23.4). Only 6.6 percent of respondents from midwestern cities said retail ads were truthful; only about 13 percent thought sale ads were very truthful.

Among consumers' objections:

- insults to one's intelligence
- false and exaggerated savings claims
- false and exaggerated product claims

exhibit

23.4

Consumers are skeptical about ads.

Source: Advertising Age,
November 19, 1991.

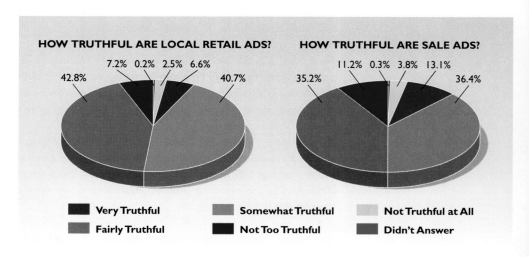

Consumers found car dealerships, appliance retailers, furniture dealers, and discount stores among those thought most guilty of deception.

Retail Satisfaction Profiles

Frequency Marketing, Inc. identifies the household member who does the most department store shopping by demographics, values and attitudes, and shopping behavior. The five classifications for women are as follows:[5]

- *Fashion Statements.* This is the most affluent and educated women's group. Because of their household incomes (average, $73,400), they have a high index of planned purchases and like being on the cutting edge of fashion. They account for 13.2 percent of primary department store shoppers.
- *Wanna-Buys.* This group has some of the same attitudes as the Fashion Statements, but don't have as much money (average, $40,600). They account for 18.6 percent of shoppers and buy on impulse.
- *Family Values.* This group accounts for one in six shoppers, and a large percentage have children living at home. Half have college degrees, and 9 in 10 are professionals. They are most likely to be planning to buy children's clothing, sporting goods, and a new washer or dryer.
- *Down to Basics.* This group has more children than the other groups (about 60 percent have children), a median age of 34, and an average household income of $32,600. Only 3 percent graduated from college. Despite having less money, they have attitudes similar to those in the Family Values group. They are careful spenders and buy little on credit. They check for sales and buy little other than for children. They account for roughly 16 percent of primary shoppers.
- *Matriarchs.* These are older women often living in retired households, and they are the most conservative group. Their favorite place to shop is in department stores; however, they have fewer planned purchases, and feel *things change too fast these days.*

Men fall into three classifications:

- *Patricians.* Just one in five in this group are married; they have the most money (average, $57,500) and are good targets for men's clothing, electronics, and sporting goods.
- *Practicals.* This group has an average income of $39,500. Members of this group are likely to be single. They prefer to pay with cash and are more likely to shop in discount stores. They are good targets for men's clothing, and even better for electronics and sporting goods.
- *Patriarchs.* This group is the lowest educated and has the lowest household incomes of male clusters. They are the oldest of the male clusters and buy primarily to replace worn-out items; however, they replace them with top-of-the-line items.

Integrated Marketing Includes P-O-P

Today's emphasis on integrated marketing and consistency of message means more involvement of point-of-purchase at the early stages of creative planning. A Point-of-Purchase Advertising Institute study of brand management found that 40 percent of all in-store media is purchased from or developed by sales promotion and advertising agencies. Ad agencies were responsible for recommending 36.8 percent of temporary P-O-P and 27.8 percent of permanent in-store programs.

A Kmart study found that P-O-P merchandising increased sales of coffee by 567 percent, paper towels by 773 percent, and toothpaste by 119 percent.

Retailers said in a 1997 trends survey that the greatest weaknesses of P-O-P displays provided by manufacturers include that they were inappropriate for the channel

---

[5]Susan Krafft, "How Shoppers Get Satisfaction," *American Demographics,* October 1993, pp. 13–16.

of trade (26.1 percent), the wrong size (22.6 percent), poorly built (19.2 percent), and unattractive (13.3 percent). The survey indicated that specialty stores, supermarkets, and department stores were the most receptive to P-O-P displays.[6]

RETAILING IN THE LATE 1990s

Frequency Marketing's director of customer relations research says, "Retailing in the 1990s is all about understanding customers and catering to their specific needs regarding merchandise, quality, value, and customer service."

The growth of discount retailing illustrates the changing value systems of today's shoppers. Shoppers can no longer be identified by a single value concept. They display multiple values. For example, consumers still prefer traditional department stores for adult fashions, but even the most upscale shoppers look to discount stores for children's clothing.[7]

NATIONAL AND RETAIL ADVERTISING

The primary difference between consumer product advertising and retail advertising is that product advertising is generally feature and benefit oriented, whereas much of retail advertising is price and availability oriented. As we said earlier in this chapter, more national retailers are running *image* advertising to develop the public's perceptions about the store as a brand, but the bulk of retail advertising features a number of products promoting price. In national advertising, the advertising says, *Buy this brand or product at any store.* In retail advertising, the ad says, *Buy this product here. Better come early.*

In national advertising, it is difficult to trace the sales effect of a single insertion of an ad. Even tracing the effect of a series of ads takes time and is difficult unless the series runs exclusively in one medium. In retail advertising, on the other hand, an advertiser can usually tell how effective it is by noon of the day after the ad appeared.

TYPES OF RETAIL ADVERTISING

Retail advertising is as diverse as the establishments that use it. However, there are certain patterns of retail advertising that reflect the character and goals of various retailers. The Newspaper Advertising Bureau has suggested six categories of retail advertising:[8]

1. *Promotional.* Here the emphasis is on sales and high sale volume at a reduced price. Discount stores such as Kmart are the primary users of this type of advertising.
2. *Semipromotional.* In this type of advertising, sale offerings are interspersed with many regular-priced items. Most department stores and supermarkets use this advertising strategy.
3. *Nonpromotional.* Many small shops and specialty stores adopt a no-sale advertising strategy. Their advertising plays down price and emphasizes dignified appeals featuring the quality of the merchandise and the expertise of their sales staffs.
4. *Assortment ads.* The intent of these ads is to show the large variety of products. The ads have an institutional aspect in that they promote the store as a place for one-stop shopping.
5. *Omnibus ads.* Similar to assortment ads, omnibus ads are usually more clearly sales oriented. These ads may feature related items or a variety of nonrelated items from several departments.

---

[6]"P-O-P 98 Trends," *P-O-P & Sign Design,* November/December 1997, p. 32.

[7]"Dayton's Is Top Retailer in Customer Satisfaction Survey," *Marketing News,* June 6, 1994, p. 8.

[8]*The I-Wonder-How-to-Set-Up-an-Advertising-Program-and-How-Much-to-Budget Book,* a publication of the Newspaper Advertising Bureau.

6. *Institutional ads.* Many stores use advertising that emphasizes their unique character. Institutional ads must be careful to tell a story of importance to a store's customers.

Retailer's Business Cycles

Retailers don't sell the same amount of merchandise every month. Selling cycles vary according to the product or service category. Exhibit 23.5 shows that August is the best month for restaurants, followed by July and June; new domestic auto dealers' best months are May and August; November is the month for carpet; December sales are double any other month for jewelry stores; November is tops for fabric and sewing stores; and May tops hardware store sales. Retailers use this information in planning their advertising and promotional efforts.

Special Promotion Times

It is no surprise that there are special promotions for Christmas, Mother's Day, President's Day, Memorial Day, and Father's Day (see Exhibit 23.6, p. 616). But there are many, many other promotional opportunities, including Boss's Day, National Singles Week, Pancake Day, National Stress Awareness Day, National Lingerie Week, Take Our Daughters to Work Day, National Hugging Day, National Library Week, Girl's Club Week, Jewish Heritage Month, Senior Citizens Month, National Pet Week, National Diabetes Month, National Pie Day, Better Sleep Month, National Decorating Month, National Barbecue Month, Nurse's Day, International Pickle Week, Chocolate Awareness Month, and National Anti-Boredom Month—you get the idea. There are lots of advertising and promotional opportunities.

In June alone, the promotional opportunities include

Bridal fairs/weddings	National Skin Safety Month
Belmont Stakes racing	National Fragrance Week
Summer begins	National Fishing Week
Adopt-A-Shelter Cat Month	Pet Appreciation Week
Dairy Month	National Little League Week
National Beef Steak Month	Flag Day
National Fresh Fruit/Vegetable Month	Father's Day
National Frozen Yogurt Month	Turkey Lover's Month
National Iced Tea Month	National Pest Control Month
National Rose Month	

exhibit

23.5

Advertisers' Seasonal Business Cycles

Courtesy: Radio Advertising Bureau.

	JAN	FEB	MAR	APR	MAY	JUN	JUL	AUG	SEP	OCT	NOV	DEC
All stores and services (%)	7.2	7.0	**8.2**	**8.1**	8.7	**8.5**	**8.4**	8.8	**8.2**	8.3	8.6	10.0
Appliance stores	7.2	6.6	7.7	7.7	8.6	8.7	8.9	**8.5**	7.7	8.3	9.1	10.9
Auto dealers (new domestic)	7.5	7.4	8.8	8.6	9.2	9.1	8.9	9.2	**8.5**	8.2	7.6	7.1
Auto dealers (new import)	7.4	7.2	9.0	8.6	9.3	9.1	8.8	9.6	**8.1**	8.2	7.4	7.3
Beer	7.7	7.3	**8.4**	**8.2**	9.2	9.3	9.4	9.6	**8.1**	8.3	7.6	7.0
Bookstores	**9.4**	6.4	6.5	6.4	6.9	6.9	6.9	10.0	10.1	7.9	8.6	14.0
Bridal market	5.0	5.8	6.4	7.6	9.8	11.4	9.3	10.5	9.6	9.0	7.7	8.0
Department stores	5.5	5.9	7.8	7.6	7.9	7.6	7.1	**8.5**	7.6	8.2	10.4	16.0
Discount stores	5.8	5.9	7.6	7.7	**8.2**	**8.1**	7.6	**8.4**	7.6	8.2	10.2	14.7
Drugstores	7.8	7.5	**8.2**	7.9	**8.3**	**8.1**	**8.0**	**8.4**	**8.0**	8.4	**8.5**	11.0
Fabric and sewing stores	7.5	7.2	**8.3**	7.7	7.7	7.2	7.9	**8.5**	**8.2**	10.0	10.6	9.2
Fast food	7.3	7.2	**8.3**	**8.2**	8.6	8.9	9.1	9.2	**8.3**	8.4	**8.1**	**8.4**
Jewelry stores	5.6	6.7	6.5	6.6	**8.5**	7.4	6.9	7.3	6.6	7.1	9.2	21.5
Restaurants	7.5	7.3	**8.2**	**8.3**	8.7	8.8	8.9	9.2	**8.3**	8.5	**8.1**	**8.2**
Shoe stores	6.4	6.1	8.8	**8.5**	**8.5**	**8.1**	7.6	9.9	**8.4**	7.9	8.6	11.2
Women's wear stores	6.3	6.1	**8.1**	**8.1**	**8.5**	7.8	7.7	**8.5**	**8.0**	8.3	9.4	13.1

exhibit

23.6

Mother's day is County Seat's best day of the year. This promotional ad features Father's day.

Courtesy: Folks Restaurant Management Group.

THE RETAIL ADVERTISING MIX

Like other styles of advertising, retail advertising must (1) determine overall goals and objectives to the marketing and advertising programs, (2) identify target markets, and (3) develop a copy and media strategy to reach these targets. But the way in which retail advertising strategy is carried out differs markedly from that in which national advertising (which we discussed earlier) is carried out.

exhibit

23.7

County Seat Cafe uses local outdoor to promote new store locations.

Courtesy: Folks Restaurant Management Group.

A retail advertising campaign usually includes media other than newspapers. Radio advertising is used frequently with great success because it is reasonable in cost and easy to produce, and it can be changed within hours if necessary. Television is also used more frequently now, although not as often as radio. Many successful campaigns use brochures and catalogs. Frequently, the catalogs are distributed with Sunday newspapers. Outdoor ads, such as for County Seat Cafe (Exhibit 23.7) are used as well.

Selecting local media is a "How best to . . .?" problem: how best to use newspapers, radio, television, direct mail—the chief media—alone or in combination to sell merchandise and attract store traffic.

Newspapers in Retailing

Newspapers are the primary local advertising vehicle, although they don't have the dominance among retailers they once enjoyed. Research indicates that consumers as well as retailers regard newspapers as the prime medium for local advertising. Exhibits 23.8a (p. 618) and 23.8b (p. 619) illustrate how County Seat restaurant uses newspaper to promote its burgers, baby-back ribs, liver and onions, and prime rib features.

Today's newspapers offer a retailer more than just retail advertising space. For example, the *Atlanta Journal-Constitution*'s services are typical of metro newspapers:

● *Preprinted inserts.* A *Zoned Area Preprints* program offers select or total market coverage. Advertising preprints are inserted directly into the newspaper and are distributed to subscribers and single-copy purchasers.

● *Direct mail.* The *ZIP* program allows advertisers to reach nonsubscribers by mailing their preprint to selected zip codes. This program enables advertisers to take advantage of less-expensive newspaper distribution to reach subscribers while using direct mail for nonsubscribers. Shared mail, solo mail, and a variety of targeting options are also available.

● *Extra editions.* Some seven extra community editions with 11 advertising zones cover the metro area, enabling advertisers to target primary market areas.

● *Ajc Direct.* The most desirable households are targeted with their own carrier program to deliver advertising, product samples, magazines, catalogs and other material targeted to some 350,000 upscale households. The paper can also merge the advertiser's customer names and credit card lists with the newspaper's subscriber list and eliminate any duplication.

As you can see, these newspaper services can be tailored to the advertiser's needs.

Starch Research found that the average adult newspaper ad-noted score for a full-page ad was 42 percent (men scored 34; women, 48); the half-page score was 34 percent (men, 32; women, 35); and the quarter-page score was 23 percent (men, 23; women, 29). The noted score for all ads was 28 percent (men, 24; women, 31). Remember that a *noted* score indicates the percentage of newspaper readers who reported *seeing* the ad being measured.

Exhibit 23.9 shows a chart indicating product categories. You can see that the noted scores vary by product category. To use this chart, choose the business type and move across the chart to the appropriate ad size. The numbers show the percentage of male and female adult newspaper readers seeing ads of that size and business category. By multiplying this percentage times the circulation of the newspaper, you can calculate how many newspaper readers will likely see an ad.

Furniture ads in general attract more women readers. The average noted score for a full page for women is 44 percent, and is less for men, but averages 37 percent. Advertising agency West & Vaughan faced a conundrum in promoting the early twentieth-century, modernist-style furniture of New York City dealer Palazzetti, Inc. The sofas and chairs are hardly inexpensive; they are exact reproductions of museum-quality

exhibit

23.8b

exhibit

23.9

Newspaper Ad Noted Scores

Product	Men (%)				Women (%)			
	1 Page	3/4 Page	1/2 Page	All Ads	1 Page	3/4 Page	1/2 Page	All Ads
Appliance	33	33	25	23	31	30	28	25
Department stores	31	32	26	26	58	55	47	48
Drugstores	40	41	34	27	56	51	47	39
Food stores	28	20	24	22	50	42	41	42
Lawn/garden	46	27	39	28	33	38	37	32
Shoe stores	28	—	22	18	56	—	59	36
Sporting goods	51	40	38	29	50	27	19	20

Source: Roper Starch.

designs by such influential artists as Mies van der Rohe and Le Corbusier. But advertising couldn't say so because, although the reproductions are totally authentic (all measurements, materials, colors, and craftsmanship), they are unsigned. It is an expensive distinction. The Palazzettis, lacking only a one-inch, engraved signature, go for about half what an otherwise identical, "authorized" replica sells for. Even so, a $3,837 day bed, for example, is not an impulse buy for most shoppers. Creative director Robert Shaw chose to showcase the products in museum-like, authentic modernist graphic design, treating them like artwork, with no room setting or accessories of any kind allowed to interfere (see Exhibit 23.10).

Radio in Retailing

Radio spot scheduling is very flexible. Promotions can easily be adapted to radio. Folks Restaurants has used radio-remote broadcasts for new store openings in the Atlanta area with great results, in addition to their regular radio schedule. Retailers often use radio to supplement ads in other media because it is a good reminder medium. As indicated earlier, radio is a segmented medium enabling a retailer to reach certain targeted consumers. On the negative side, in large markets a retailer may have to buy a number of different stations to reach their prospects because the share of audience of a single station is relatively small.

Television in Retailing

Television became a major force in retailing during the 1980s. Much of the retail advertising dollars spent has been a result of the growth of independent TV station and cable outlets with relatively low advertising rates. Spots on both independent stations and cable may be as low as $20 to $50.

Most major markets have more than one cable system, which means an advertiser with stores on one side of town can simply target prospects by buying only the cable system(s) that reach their prospective customers. At the same time, there are companies that will allow an advertiser to make one buy and reach multiple cable systems. Advertisers can buy cable networks such as CNN, ESPN, USA, CNN's Headline News, the Weather Channel, MTV, VH-1, and so forth because of the availability of time for local advertisers, usually at rates significantly lower than network stations in the same market. The audience is probably significantly smaller at any given time on a specific cable network than the number of households hooked to cable, which means a high cost per thousand, but the cost is within the budgets of even the smallest retail advertiser.

Database Marketing

Database-driven direct marketing can target specific consumers. Instead of targeting all teens, it may allow a marketer to target teens who have purchased a video game worth more than $50 in the last 90 days. That's much more specific, and much more useful if you want to sell computer games. Of the 96-million-plus households in the United States, 74 percent have a Sears relationship, and Sears is trying to make the most of it. Several years ago, Sears started a program to make better use of its customer database—typical of most major retailers. It has mailed as many as 16 million pieces per month to a selection of the database. Building customer loyalty through retention and upgrading of *most-valued customers* is a major item.

Measured marketing, a term used by supermarkets that issue plastic cards to their customers so they can build a database, permits the stores to identify their best customers and treat them differently. Customers in the top 10 percent group make 1.8 visits per week and spend $3,674 per year—double what the next best decile spends. The top 30 percent of the cardholders accounts for roughly 75 percent of the store's total sales.[9]

---

[9]Arthur Middleton Hughes, "The Real Truth about Supermarkets—and Customers," *DM News,* October 3, 1994, p. 40.

THE BEST OF TECHNOLOGY BOTH IN AND OUT OF THE CLASSROOM

● ●

 *PHLIP—Video/Video Case/Internet E*

New! An exciting array of information and exercises await you and your stud
Available from our comprehensive Web resource, PHLIP (www.prenhall.com
you will find biweekly updates from an extensive collection of periodicals. I
addition, you can access video cases (text and the video itself), together with
Internet exercise that relates to major parts of the text.

For example, you can access the GOT MILK? video case via PHLIP, view th
video, and assign your students an interesting Internet exercise that directs th
use the resources of various Web sites to come up with additional strategies f
campaign and explore useful information. The videos, video cases, and Inter
exercises are also available in hard copy from Prentice Hall.

www.prenhall.com/phbusiness

● ●

• • • •

ercise

nts.
phlip),

n

new
m to
r the
et

• • • •

Considering the original is guarded by a highly paid security staff at New York City's Museum of Modern Art, we will say, without reservation, that our Mies Day Bed is a good deal more comfortable. Palazzetti reproduces several of Ludwig Mies van der Rohe's classic designs. What's more, we do it at a price you can afford. After all, we would like you to visit a nice museum now and then.

PALAZZETTI®

The Only Thing More Satisfying Than Owning A $73,000 Mies Day Bed Is Watching Everyone Think It Is.

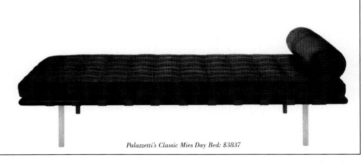

© Palazzetti Inc. 1-212-832-1199

Palazzetti's Classic Mies Day Bed: $3837

If you're looking for a Le Corbusier, you can visit New York City's Museum of Modern Art and look longingly at the originals on exhibit. Perhaps you could purchase an official "artiste" version at a boutique that's so incredibly expensive, you will need two credit checks before they let you inside. Then again, for only a mere $924, you could purchase a Palazzetti and never notice the difference.

PALAZZETTI®

Steal A Priceless Le Corbusier Without Setting Off The Alarm At The Museum Of Modern Art.

Palazzetti's Classic Corbu Club Chair: $924

Retail On-Line

Retail on-line success stories have been few and far between, says Greg Wester, with Yankee Group. Retail on-line has been successful for hardware and software companies with marketers such as Dell Computers reported to be doing $2 million a day in on-line sales. In late 1997, the Apple Store was created. For the first time, consumers could buy a Macintosh directly from Apple over the Internet, over the phone, or at a retail store. Their ad said, "We built the Apple Store with the same technology we used to build Dell's on-line store in 1996—only we used a more advanced version to make your shopping more rewarding. . . . We'll build one to your exact specifications. So, when you shop at the Apple Store, you can order your Macintosh the same way you order pizza—with just as much stuff on it as you like. (But no anchovies.) . . . saving time and money." Other commodity products that appeal to the Web's demographics, such as books and music, also have been successful. Ticketing and travel services routinely reach $1 million a week. Sellers of broad-based consumer goods have been slow to grow. GAP has had success with their Web site games and promotions and began developing a selling presence in 1997. They found that people stayed on their site 50 percent longer than the average site. An analyst commented that GAP had an excellent demographic fit with Web users, and many of their products, such as T-shirts and socks, don't usually require trying on for size.[10]

Cinema Commercials

Retailers, realizing that prospective customers frequently are nearby in a shopping center's adjoining cinema complexes, have moved into that medium.

Rod Eaton, Target's director of sales promotion, says that the idea should be a movie and not a commercial. Many advertisers are reluctant to enter the medium for that reason, because they believe messages should stick with soft sell, or risk incuring the ire of moviegoers.[11] Target has run spots in Screenvision Cinema Network consisting of 8,200 screens in 2,000 theaters. Target has run shorter versions of the cinema advertising on TV. Target, GAP, Sears, and food retailers such as McDonald's and Outback, have used cinema.

Outdoor

Retailers have always used outdoor advertising as a reminder or to tell consumers that a store is down the street. Often it is used in conjunction with other media. Exhibit 23.7 shows a message directing drivers to a new store location.

Cooperative Advertising

The simplest definition of *cooperative advertising* is a joint promotion of a national advertiser (manufacturer) and a local retailer on behalf of the manufacturer's product or service in the retail store. The Kodak ad in Exhibit 23.11 is prepared by Kodak and is available for the local merchant to advertise and have Kodak pay as much as 50 percent of the advertising cost. Therefore, a retailer that uses a lot of cooperative advertising could double its advertising budget.

Chief advantages:

- Cooperative advertising helps the buyer stretch his or her advertising capability.
- It may provide good artwork, with good copy of the product advertised—which is especially important to the small store (Exhibit 23.11).
- It helps the store earn a better volume discount for all its advertising.

---

[10]Alice Z. Cuneo, "The GAP Readies Electronic Commerce Plan for Web Site," *Advertising Age,* June 23, 1997, p. 18.

[11]Alice Z. Cuneo, "Now Playing: GAP, Target Take Retail to the Movies," *Advertising Age,* June 9, 1997, p. 18.

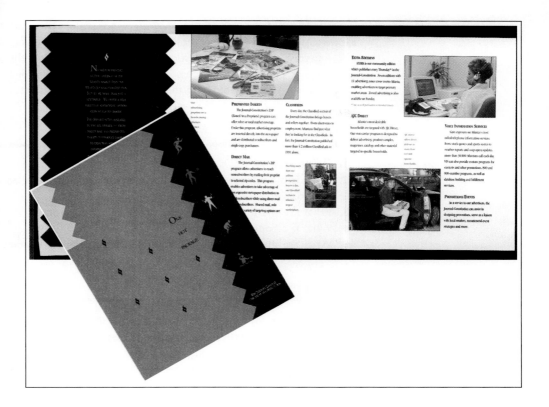
Cooperative advertising works best when the line is highly regarded and is either a style or some other kind of leader in its field.

Chief disadvantages:

● Although the store pays only 50 percent of the cost, that sum may be disproportionate for the amount of sales and profit the store realizes.
● Most manufacturers' ads emphasize the brand name at the expense of the store name.

Co-op requires a lot of paperwork. Most newspapers and some radio stations have co-op advertising departments that help retailers seek co-op allowances from manufacturers and supply affidavits and other documentation required by a manufacturer. Many small advertisers find the paperwork prohibitive, and the media try to make it easier in hope of getting their share of the advertising. In some cases, the retailer may have a business department inside their advertising department to make sure the store collects all the money due it.

SUMMARY

More retailers are turning to branding to compete with the competition. The media mix has expanded for retailers over recent years. Newspapers still account for the majority of retail advertising, but retailers use virtually every medium to promote their stores, products, and services. Consumers are looking for ways to save time and money. As a result, direct marketing and on-line buying is increasing. As with business in general, the retail business has been and is significantly changing. Part of the change is driven by the way consumers shop—from supermarkets, discount department stores, wholesale clubs, shopping centers, and malls, to big-box category killers—shopping patterns have changed.

These changes have given rise to sophisticated segmentation and niche marketers. Retail advertising is done by local merchants or service organizations to attract customers. Retailers use business-cycle information to decide when to advertise. Cooperative advertising offers retailers allowances from manufacturers that can actually double the advertising budgets.

As retailers get more sophisticated marketing information, the media have responded with services. For example, newspapers offer many extra services (direct mail, zones, research, and other services) to compete with the broadcast media and direct mail.

REVIEW

1. Define retailing.
2. What is the primary difference between consumer product advertising and retail advertising?
3. What are the three best months of sales for bookstores?
4. What is a zoned area preprint?
5. What are the advantages of cooperative advertising to a retailer?

TAKE IT TO THE NET

We invite you to visit the Russell/Lane page on the Prentice Hall Web site at **PHLIP** **http://www.prenhall.com/phbusiness** for the bimonthly Russell/Lane update and for this chapter's World Wide Web exercise.

BACKGROUND

Folks, Inc., a restaurant management group, operates some 20-plus restaurants in the Atlanta area. For 18 years they were the largest and most profitable franchisee of PoFolks, Inc., a regional chain in the family restaurant category. They also operate another restaurant concept under the County Seat Cafe name. In 1996, they decided that they needed to update the PoFolks concept and restaurants. As a result of extensive research, they decided to drop the PoFolks concept and name. Their task was to try and keep as many current customers and make the stores more inviting for new customers—quite a task. Sheri Bevil, marketing director, said "The family dining category is in a squeeze between the quick service restaurants and the casual dining restaurants. Our research indicated that we needed to move towards the casual category. As a result, we've created our own niche between the two, which we call casual family dining."

Over the years, Folks has occasionally used advertising agencies to supplement their own in-house agency. The introduction of the new name was orchestrated by their in-house agency. Most of their promotions and collateral advertising is created internally. Sheri Bevil is responsible for all marketing for both restaurant concepts. Bevil's job is to create, manage, and coordinate all integrated marketing functions. After the introduction of the new name, the Cole, Henderson & Drake advertising firm was hired to develop a branding campaign.

COMPETITION

The Atlanta market is one of the most competitive restaurant markets in the country. New competition opens literally weekly. The new Folks shifted from competing with the family dining restaurants such as Shoney's, Black-Eyed Pea, and Ryan's to competing with Chili's and Applebee's.

TARGET

Historically, each store pulls a different mix of consumers—some a little older, a little better educated, more ethnic, and so forth. Lunch attracts business and working people. Dinner attracts families—from young families to grandparents in the middle-income range. Extensive research indicated the need to target women 25 to 49 years of age.

MEDIA

Folks primarily uses radio, direct marketing, newspaper, outdoor, and a little television. Being a small chain, Folks isn't able to compete with the larger advertising budgets of many of their competitors. For this campaign, they didn't have the money to be heavy in television, but felt TV was necessary to help create the new image and branding effort. Television was used for three months followed by heavy radio flights and outdoor. They also used free-standing inserts and some direct mail. Because the restaurants aren't uniformly distributed through the Designated Market Area (DMA), a custom DMA was created by the agency from the zip codes housing the restaurants, and a ranker was run on this geography to determine which radio stations to use. Rankers were also run on the broader DMA because of its larger, more reliable sample size and because a number of the restaurant visitors come from the broader area.

TOTAL PROGRAM

The initial communications focused on image and name change. This became more focused as a branding effort followed by branding and promotions. The marketing and promotion efforts include more than just ads. The restaurant business demands a multitude of communications including quarterly promotions, menu designs, table tents, kids' coloring pieces, in-store promotions, employee motivation programs, public relations activities, and so on.

RESULTS

The transition from PoFolks to Folks has been successful. They did not lose their core customer in the transition and have successfully attracted new customers. Despite the increase in competition, Folks continues to grow steadily.

Courtesy: Folks Restaurant Management Group.

24

INTERNATIONAL ADVERTISING

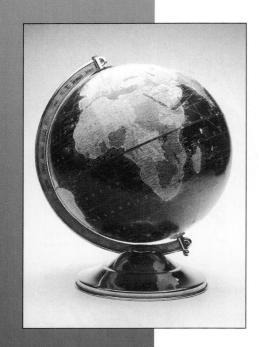

TWENTY-FIVE YEARS AGO THE GLOBAL VILLAGE WAS A CONCEPT; TODAY IT IS A REALITY. ADVERTISING ON A WORLDWIDE SCALE IS A MAJOR ELEMENT IN THE GROWTH OF THIS GLOBAL VILLAGE. AS MULTINATIONAL COMPANIES COMPETE ON AN INTERNATIONAL STAGE, WE SEE THE EFFECTS THROUGH THE DEVELOPMENT OF UNIVERSAL BRANDS AND EVEN A SIMILARITY OF PRODUCT USAGE AMONG PEOPLE IN DIVERSE CULTURES AND SOCIETIES. ADVERTISING HAS BECOME A PRIMARY TOOL TO GAIN BRAND AWARENESS IN BOTH DEVELOPED AND EMERGING COUNTRIES. AFTER READING THIS CHAPTER YOU WILL UNDERSTAND

- **the development of a global economy**
- **advantages and pitfalls of global marketing**
- **the relationship among economics, politics, and culture**
- **agency organization in a global economy**
- **unique advertising practices country by country.**

Advertising and marketing are truly worldwide, no longer dominated by American companies. Among the handful of companies with annual advertising budgets of more than $1 billion, seven are headquartered outside the United States. Led by giants such as Unilever, Nestlé, L'Oréal, Honda, and Sony, these companies challenge American companies on a global basis. The importance of the international market can also be seen in the advertising budgets of domestic firms. For example, more than 60 percent of the total advertising budgets of Coca-Cola and Colgate-Palmolive are allocated to international markets. The world's largest advertiser, Procter & Gamble, invests 48 percent of its advertising abroad, and Ford spends almost 40 percent in foreign countries.[1]

---

[1]Laurel Wentz and Kevin Brown, "Global Marketers," *Ad Age International,* November 1996, p. i15.

Regardless of the company or product category, more and more American marketers view the international marketplace as the best opportunity for future growth. As the markets of the United States and Canada, Japan, and Western Europe reach maturity, companies are hoping to expand into other parts of the world, especially the emerging nations of Asia, Africa, and South America. For example, when Procter & Gamble announced a 10-year plan to double sales, more than 25 percent of the increase was anticipated by expansion into these areas.[2]

Virtually every major U.S. marketer views international sales as part of their marketing strategy. For example, Neiman Marcus, long noted for its upscale Christmas catalog, launched its first overseas catalog in Japan. A Neiman Marcus executive said, "Japan offers an opportunity to expand internationally after good success and growth in the U.S." He went on to observe that international markets offer better prospects for growth than the company's mature domestic catalog business.[3]

Communications technology has become a method of bypassing historic governmental decisions about politics and economics. It has been suggested that we are seeing the evolution of *telecommunities* organized around ethnic and cultural identification rather than geographic location.[4]

One outcome of the growth of global markets is decentralization of management, including the advertising function, and a dispersion of major marketers throughout the world.

> We have come a long way since the days of the centrally produced, locally translated, one-ad-fits-all approach to global advertising. Brand ideas that can literally come from anywhere and travel anywhere have a new power—primarily because many so-called developing markets around the world have become as sophisticated and complex as the countries that used to send them advertising.[5]

As we see later in this chapter, international trade and communication have moved many companies to decentralize their marketing function. The reasons for the movement to decentralized control are twofold: (1) the sheer size and magnitude of the management task has made additional layers of management necessary, and (2) as companies move into more and more countries they find the political, cultural, and marketing structures demand local management that understands how multinational objectives can be translated to local markets.

It is clear that most companies will have to change dramatically their historic management structures to operate efficiently in a world market.

> If . . . responding to rapid changes in market conditions, customer needs and competitor activities [are] critical to effective execution—then we need a new model for management and managing change. The old "command and control" model of executive management—where the executive sat atop the organization, and information and instructions cascaded down the line and back up based on the assumption that sufficient intelligence to make the right decisions existed only at the top—is no longer sustainable.[6]

---

[2]"Procter & Gamble Betting on Brand-Name Oomph to Lift Sales," *Atlanta Journal-Constitution,* May 31, 1997, p. E5.

[3]Rebecca A. Fannin, "Neiman Marcus Is Looking Far East," *Advertising Age,* September 16, 1996, p. 16.

[4]"Communication Technology and National Sovereignty in the Global Economy," a report of the Annenberg Washington Program in Communications Policy Studies of Northwestern University, p. 3.

[5]Marcio M. Moreira, "The Idea's the Thing for Good Global Ads," *Advertising Age,* November 4, 1996, p. 34.

[6]Peter H. Fuchs and Terence V. Neil, "The New Execution Advantage," in *Outlook,* a publication of Andersen Consulting, p. 5.

In the future, we will see organizations, both companies and multinational advertising agencies, adopt management styles that emphasize information retrieval and data organization and interpretation rather than simply giving directives. Marketing employees of the future will be valued as much for the information and insights they provide top management as for the short-term skills they provide.

The major challenge of international marketing is dealing with a world that is expanding and simultaneously becoming more individualized.

> While marketing will be massive and global, it will also become more personal. In a sense, marketing will go back to selling door-to-door. The revolutionary difference is that the exchange will be computer-mediated instead of face-to-face. With network intelligence instead of gasoline and shoe leather, marketers and consumers will exchange custom-tailored information and even develop custom-tailored products.[7]

ADVERTISING, MARKETING, AND INTERNATIONAL SALES

American companies cannot maximize the potential of international markets by luck or by accident. It will require product development, research, and market planning that is quite different from what U.S. companies are accustomed to in domestic sales. For example, Lands' End executives thought their catalog was not fully tapping the Southern Hemisphere in countries such as Australia, Argentina, and Indonesia because the seasons were opposite those in the United States. They began to send seasonal catalogs appropriate to those countries. However, this expansion also meant that mailing houses were required to do separate mailings, print runs were increased, and most important, the company had to enlarge its warehouse capacity to stock both winter and summer merchandise.[8]

In some respects, advertising itself has a different role in many overseas countries compared to domestic promotions. A primary function of advertising is to introduce products and establish brand equity. In mature markets such as the United States, the majority of companies and brands are well known to most consumers. In established markets we are much more likely to see competition based on price and value-added promotions, with advertising playing a lesser role. However, in many foreign markets, American brands are largely unknown, and even some product categories may be unfamiliar to many consumers. In this introductory phase, advertising is often the most important part of the marketing plan. In fact, sometimes products that are available only in limited supplies are heavily advertised to create awareness in anticipation of later distribution.

It has only been since World War II that American companies have made international marketing a major part of their business strategy. Today, emerging markets around the world have become major battlefields for companies that know that firms that gain the first foothold will have a critical long-term advantage.

An interesting study in global marketing involves the ongoing fight between Coca-Cola and Pepsi for the world soft-drink market. The battle is important because the potential for increased soft-drink consumption globally is very high compared to that in the United States. For example, it is estimated that the per capita consumption of Coca-Cola in China is between one and two servings a year. Just think of the profitability to Coca-Cola if consumption were raised to only one bottle a month. The "cola wars" are just beginning in India and China and they are well under way in South America. In

---

[7]"FTC Holds Hearings in Global Marketplace," *Advertising Topics,* a publication of the Council of Better Business Bureaus, December 1995, p. 4.

[8]Barbara Drimmer, "Lands' End Debuts Counter-Seasonal Catalog," *DM News,* September 9, 1996, p. 1.

each case the eventual outcome will offer some interesting insight into how international marketing battles will be fought by U.S. business titans.[9]

The Coke–Pepsi fight is a high-profile battle between two of the world's best-known brands, and similar, albeit less publicized, fights are being waged by large and small companies in virtually every country. The marketing and advertising manager of the future will have to grasp the realities of the international market or be left far behind more innovative and aggressive competitors.

In addition to global marketing competition, the shift to an international emphasis has brought fundamental changes in the way advertising is conducted. The advertising agency is changing to meet the demands of international clients, and these changes have not come without stress. First, clients are demanding that their agencies become conversant with a menu of marketing and promotional techniques beyond the traditional expertise of many organizations. At the same time, agencies are asked to work efficiently in new and totally unfamiliar markets and situations.

In the remainder of this chapter, we discuss the complex world of international marketing and advertising. The changing environment of multinational marketing is uncertain. However, it is safe to predict that the advertising agency of the future will fall into one of two categories: (1) giant, full-service multinational agencies with offices and clients throughout the world, or (2) small agencies and boutiques serving primarily local firms. According to *Advertising Age,* the combined income of the top 10 international agencies is greater than that of the next 40 agencies.[10] Although there still will be opportunities for medium-sized agencies servicing regional and national accounts, such agencies will face competitive environment in gaining and keeping clients who are increasingly looking abroad for new markets.

GLOBAL MARKETING AND ADVERTISING

Multinational advertising

The coordination and execution of advertising campaigns that are directed to a number of countries.

Global marketing

Term that denotes the use of advertising and marketing strategies on an international basis.

One of the catch phrases of **multinational advertising** is **global marketing.** The term, attributed to Theodore Levitt of Harvard University, suggests that companies can develop worldwide advertising and marketing strategies for their products. At the heart of the concept is the assumption that consumers are basically alike all over the world and will respond to similar appeals regardless of their apparent differences. As one advertising executive observed, "The most difficult thing [about international advertising] is attaining a relevancy for your target audience while remaining faithful to the single message goal of the campaign. Talking specifically to differing cultures runs contradictory to this.[11]

To accommodate the demands of global marketing, multinational companies have begun to combine two marketing strategies that, at first examination, seem contradictory, but in fact work very well.

1. *Centralized management.* If global marketing is to work, it must be coordinated at top management levels. A number of companies have initiated very sophisticated control centers to market worldwide. Nestlé has long been viewed as a master of multinational marketing. From its headquarters in Vevey, Switzerland, it manages 10 worldwide corporate brands (e.g., Nestlé, Carnation, Perrier) and approximately 7,000 local brands (e.g., KitKat, Polo).
2. *Two-way flow of information.* Centralized management is usually looked upon as a manager dictating decisions from headquarters to far-flung branch offices around the world. This was certainly the former view of global marketing and centralized management.

---

[9]Chris Roush, "Coca-Cola Claims Victory in Russia," *The Atlanta Journal,* August 27, 1996, p. B1.

[10]"World's Top 50 Advertising Organizations," *Advertising Age,* April 21, 1997, p. s14.

[11]"Viewpoint," *Promo,* May 1997, p. 75.

Regardless of the approach used by a company for its international strategy, a key element is to maintain brand identity. The less standardization of product quality, advertising themes, and marketing tactics, the more difficult it is to establish a global personality. For example, Pizza Hut is one of the few truly global restaurant brands around the world. However, local menus featured everything from mashed potatoes to corn on the cob. To build a unique brand character, the company used the same television commercial throughout Europe featuring its stuffed-crust pizza—a single product, a single brand, a single identity.[12]

Three Models of International Marketing

When considering global marketing and advertising, companies and their agencies are faced with three basic options as to how to proceed.[13] As we discuss these alternatives, it is important to realize that each has a number of variations, and most companies will use some aspects of each in one or more countries or for particular products. There are few absolutes in the emerging field of international business.

1. *Standardization.* The strategy and execution of campaigns are handled globally with copy translated but no changes in creative or other elements of a campaign. Under this plan, one advertising agency is retained with centralized responsibility to interface with client counterparts at a central office. The strongest supporters of standardization take the view that "globalization will only be possible for companies that exploit a very specific and clearly-defined market sector, with practically no international differences."[14]

2. *Pattern standardization.* Under this plan, a global advertising agency controls overall strategy, general creative, and general campaign approaches; the execution is handled locally or regionally. Each country handles its own media selection and tailoring of campaigns. For example, Weight Watchers, having achieved a 50 percent share of market in the United States, moved into a number of international markets. The company found that it had to introduce new diets and weight-loss measures on a country-by-country basis.[15]

3. *Localization.* At the other end of the management spectrum from standardization is localization. Under this management philosophy, each country manages strategy and execution of campaigns with a local focus. Local advertising agencies tailor campaigns to each area's culture and needs. Organizational control is decidedly decentralized.

In fact, few companies would contemplate adopting a plan of full standardization or full localization. Marketers know that, with the exception of relatively small companies operating in only a few countries, a strict adherence to standardization will not work. Companies have to be flexible enough to deal with culture, language, the political system, and economic dissimilarities from one country to another. For example, advertising spending per capita in Japan and the United States is more than $300, whereas in China the figure is less than $5. On the other hand, the cost in time and money necessary to develop totally localized marketing and advertising programs for each country is not only unprofitable but impractical.

Research indicates most companies have two primary objectives for their global marketing strategies. The first is a single brand image. The second objective, related to the

[12]Laurel Wentz, "World Brands," *Ad Age International,* March 1997, p. i6.

[13]"Three Model Approaches," *Target Marketing,* February 1996, p. 12.

[14]Richard N. Miller, "Direct Marketing the World," *Target Marketing,* May 1996, p. 20.

[15]Rebecca A. Fannin, "Slimmer Pickings in U.S. Prompt Weight Watchers to Look Abroad," *Ad Age International,* February 1997, p. i4.

exhibit

24.1

Multinational firms usually develop marketing plans that represent a compromise between the needs of consumers and the firm.

use of a single brand, is to exploit cost efficiencies inherent in a single marketing and advertising strategy worldwide. As one international advertising executive pointed out, "Standardization seems to work best when the product is pragmatic or utilitarian and when it satisfies a universal physical need such as shaving or diapering babies. In such cases, the message is often informational . . . physical needs are what have made P&G such a global powerhouse with products like diapers, cleansers, toothpastes and detergents."[16]

With a few exceptions, it is unlikely that true global marketing will be available to multinational marketers. However, the general concept and its many variations become more practical each year. Satellite transmission and the popularity of television have permitted regional TV networks on every continent. At a minimum, these satellite systems permit multinational advertisers to gain a cost-effective foothold in every region of the world.

It is clear that technology is becoming more readily available to make the *idea* of international advertising and global marketing a reality. However, it is impossible to accommodate all the cultural and national differences in any single marketing strategy. Global marketing is such an appealing concept from a cost and efficiency standpoint that companies are tempted to adopt it even when it has obvious pitfalls. It can be argued that the misapplication of global marketing places the well-being of the firm ahead of the consumer. Exhibit 24.1 demonstrates the continuum of a one-strategy, one-execution global marketing approach versus a consumer-oriented marketing concept with a different-strategy, different-execution in each country approach.

As we saw in earlier examples of international marketing plans, the idea of a continuum of strategies is more common than an either/or notion of choosing between a strict interpretation of global marketing and the consumer orientation of the marketing concept. In most cases, companies develop a broad marketing and advertising plan. From this plan they then make necessary adaptations that consider the special cultural, economic, and language differences present in each country they enter.

Regardless of how much international companies would like to adopt a global strategy for their brands, the local marketplace dictates that local brands will continue to be a major force. For example, U.K.-based B.A.T. Industries markets 240 brands of cigarettes, but only 10, including Kent and Lucky Strike, are international. Likewise, Coca-Cola sells a host of local soft-drink brands including Thumbs Up, an Indian distributed cola; fruit-flavored Splash in Germany and Spain; and Beverly, an herbal drink sold in Italy.[17]

---

[16]Tom Duncan and Jyotika Ramaprasad, "Standardized Multinational Advertising: The Influencing Factors," *Journal of Advertising,* Fall 1995, pp. 61–62.

[17]Bill Britt, "For Multinationals, Value Lies in Eyes of Local Consumers," *Ad Age International,* May 1997, p. i18.

POLITICAL AND ECONOMIC MOVEMENTS TOWARD A WORLD ECONOMY

As discussed earlier, communication technology such as the Internet and satellites have made traditional political borders irrelevant in terms of government control of communication. The availability of information in formerly closed societies has created demand for products and services that only a few years ago would have been unknown in much of the world.

This new openness has created a demand that fosters international trade. Steps toward removing artificial barriers to commerce are in place or at the discussion stage throughout the world. The opening of China, Vietnam, and South Africa to trade with the United States is an example of multinational business that would have been considered unthinkable only a few years ago. In the following section, we briefly discuss three trade agreements that demonstrate the trend toward a more open environment for trade.

The North American Free Trade Agreement

North American Free Trade Agreement (NAFTA)
A treaty designed to eliminate trade barriers among the U.S., Mexico, and Canada.

In November 1993, Congress ratified the **North American Free Trade Agreement** (NAFTA), which is supposed to eliminate all trade barriers among the United States, Canada, and Mexico over the next 15 years. It is estimated that the agreement will create a market of 360 million people and goods totaling $6.7 *trillion*. Experts predict that NAFTA will have a larger impact on Mexico than the more developed economy of Canada. Presently, some of the provisions of NAFTA are still being refined. There remains skepticism in some quarters as to whether the long-term benefits will be equally shared among all three trade partners. Many opponents are apprehensive about the loss of U.S. industrial jobs to the Mexican labor force when all barriers are eventually removed. However, because Mexico is the third largest source of U.S. goods, following Canada and Japan, it represents a huge potential market for domestic goods.

The General Agreement on Tariffs and Trade

General Agreement on Tariffs and Trade (GATT)
A treaty designed to lower trade barriers among 117 nations.

Among the most far-reaching trade agreements is the **General Agreement on Tariffs and Trade** (GATT) signed by some 117 nations in 1993. Although not as all-inclusive as NAFTA, it takes a number of steps to reduce tariffs and import duties among the countries that are party to the agreement. It is estimated that GATT has the potential of adding $270 million to the world economy.

A major drawback to GATT is the number of countries and diverse cultures that are party to the agreement. Whereas price reductions will be a primary benefit to consumers in these countries, GATT cannot overcome cultural, language, and product-usage differences among nations.

The Economic Unification of Europe

European Community (EC)
The developing economic integration of Europe. Potentially a single market of over 300 million consumers in 1991.

Although it is too soon to judge the full implications of NAFTA and GATT, we can learn from the experiences of European nationals in attempting to create an environment for free trade. Since 1992, Europe has moved slowly toward a unified market consisting of most of the countries of the region. Called the **European Community** (EC), it represents the largest and most important experiment in bringing the concept of a global market to fruition. The idea of the EC is to eliminate most of the physical, tariff, and technical barriers to trade among the 15 nations of Western Europe.[18]

The proponents of the EC claim that when fully implemented it will provide a common trade area with 345 million people and a total value of $5 trillion. It will be 50 percent larger than the United States in population and 20 percent greater in sales potential. If all goes as planned, it will be the first demonstration that global marketing will work.

---

[18]The EC currently consists of Germany, Italy, Great Britain, France, Spain, The Netherlands, Belgium, Portugal, Greece, Denmark, Ireland, and Luxembourg; additional countries have applied for acceptance.

Obviously, an undertaking of this magnitude is a tremendous task. Countries that have been political and economic rivals for centuries are being asked to set aside their differences and make significant compromises for the common good. One of the major problems with the EC is how to control marketing efforts that originate outside the borders of a country. We have mentioned satellites and Internet communication; another area is telemarketing. A number of companies have set up pan-European calling centers. Telemarketers must be careful to adhere to the various regulations that apply to sales calls from country to country:

● In Germany it is illegal to make an unsolicited sales call to a private residence. A firm must have prior written permission from a person before engaging in telemarketing activities. However, business-to-business calls are permitted if they are related to the product or services of the company being called or if a prior contractual relationship exists.
● Great Britain has regulations similar to those in the United States. Calls must be made at reasonable times and the purpose of the call must be revealed at the outset. There are some major differences between Great Britain and the United States, however, such as (1) no random-dial techniques can be used, (2) unlisted numbers cannot be called, and (3) consumers cannot be called at work concerning nonbusiness products.
● In Switzerland, persons who do not wish to be solicited can have their telephone numbers removed from the public list of phone holders. In general, there are no specific rules governing telemarketing.
● Denmark is among the most restrictive countries in terms of telemarketing. No one can be called at home or at work without prior consent.

Telemarketing rules are just one of the hundreds of major and minor details still under negotiation among EC countries. They involve items as diverse as currency exchange to the manner in which products can be portrayed in television commercials. The detractors of the EC say that it will never be fully implemented because, in fact, there is no common European community. According to critics, to assume that geographic proximity can lead to economic cooperation on a scale suggested by the EC is impractical.

Like global marketing itself, the EC concept will probably find its final place somewhere between its strongest supporters and its harshest critics. There is ample evidence that nationalism among the EC countries will not be swept away overnight. It is a major challenge for marketers to overcome nationalistic tendencies in developing a fully integrated international market. Most companies that are involved in the EC and other multinational marketing find that they must immerse themselves in the total culture of a country to be successful.

The full implementation of the EC is many years in the future. However, it offers an excellent laboratory for multinational marketing. If developed countries, such as the ones that comprise the EC, are having difficulties, one can only imagine the problems implicit in the development of true worldwide marketing. However, it is the world, with all its inherent challenges, that offers the best future prospects for most American companies.

It is clear that, although there will always be differences in execution and approach to multinational advertising, the world market is growing closer. As one European advertising executive observed, "As a 'global village'—and one that is getting increasingly smaller—our various populations are all becoming highly adept at seeing and understanding messages from advertisements that come from other countries. Computer technology enables extremely rapid transfer of information, and it is no longer unusual for people everywhere to be exposed to advertising from around the world."[19] Ultimately, it may be that the familiarity with advertising from other countries may be a significant determinant in bringing global marketing to complete implementation.

---

[19]"British Self-Regulation System Similar to NAD," *Advertising Topics,* November 1995, p. 2.

THE MULTINATIONAL ADVERTISING AGENCY

As marketing has become a multinational enterprise, advertising has had to follow. In the 1940s and 1950s, when McCann-Erickson and J. Walter Thompson led American agencies into the international arena, they started foreign branches on a country-by-country basis. These branch agencies typically were responsible for the advertising of a few large U.S. clients in a limited number of countries.

This approach to international advertising was extremely expensive and did not guarantee that the foreign branches would adequately serve and coordinate the international marketing needs of their clients. During the 1970s, most U.S. agencies moved from ownership of foreign offices to some form of joint venture or minority ownership of existing foreign agencies. This plan overcame the long start-up time involved in beginning a new agency and provided advertising plans that reflected local business practices and culture. Joint ventures also recognized the growing expertise of local advertising talent and the fact that around the world new, young agencies were catching up with their older partners.

In the last decade, two major changes have significantly altered international advertising. The first is the manner in which clients and their agencies manage the advertising function, and the second is the manner in which they view their customers.

Management of the Advertising Function

Until fairly recently, it was necessary to manage global accounts on a decentralized basis. However, with the advent of Internet, fax, and other communication technology, it is now possible to have central management on a worldwide basis.

> Worldwide account directors have become the unsung heroes of the [advertising] business these days. . . . Clients are the ones driving the process. As the world becomes a more competitive marketplace, populated with multinational players seeking to grow beyond their own often mature turf . . . clients have scrambled to capitalize on the benefits of new global opportunities.[20]

The ability to manage multinational advertising is a key element in the success and profitability of most major advertising agencies. As clients have moved to consolidate accounts with single agencies, the complexity of serving these worldwide brands has become enormous. For example, McCann-Erickson creates advertising to run in 107 countries; Grey Advertising in 78 countries; and J. Walter Thompson in 67. Exhibit 24.2 lists major agencies and the number of their clients who advertise in at least 10 countries.

Unlike the early years of multinational expansion, centralization no longer means that a client's entire marketing operation is managed out of headquarters. Instead, huge multibrand conglomerates such as Unilever, Nestlé, or Procter & Gamble are organized as a number of business groups managing certain product categories. Advertising agencies serving these brands must develop a structure that emulates the organization of the client.

For example, when McCann-Erickson became the agency for Reckitt & Colman, a multinational package-goods manufacturer, it established account teams in those areas where the client had the greatest strength. Air-fresheners and sprays were directed out of England; toilet products from France; hard-surface cleaners in the United States; and insecticide products were managed out of Australia.[21]

A similar account management design was used by DMB&B when it won the Australian tourism business. The global strategy is defined by the lead account team in Syd-

---

[20]Noreen O'Leary, "World Tours Single Clients," *Adweek*, August 5, 1996, p. 34.

[21]M. H. Moore, "Going Global on a Small Scale," *Adweek*, August 5, 1996, p. 36.

Agency Growth from 1991 to 1996

Number of accounts each agency has in 10 or more countries, 1991 vs. 1996, and percentage of U.S.-based clients.

	1996	1991	U.S. Clients
Ammirati Puris Lintas	12	11	39%
BBDO Worldwide	23	18	50
Bates Worldwide	17	10	43
DDB Needham Worldwide	21	10	35
D'Arcy Masius Benton & Bowles	15	5	54
Grey Advertising	43	14	45
J. Walter Thompson Co.	25	19	57
Leo Burnett Co.	14	11	76
McCann-Erickson Worldwide	49	26	54
Ogilvy & Mather Worldwide	26	27	50
Saatchi & Saatchi Advertising Worldwide	21	23	43
Young & Rubicam Advertising	25	20	62

Source: Advertising Age International, agency reports.

exhibit

24.2

Multinational agencies have demonstrated significant growth in recent years.

Courtesy: Advertising Age.
Source: Ad Age International,
September 1996 p. i23.

ney. However, the various regional agencies were given responsibility for translating that basic strategy into local campaigns. For example, in planning for the 2000 Olympics, research indicated that Americans would be more likely to want an extended holiday taking in a number of Australian destinations, whereas the Japanese will be more likely only to attend the games.

Research and the Multinational Consumer

At one time, both clients and agencies tended to view their markets in terms of national boundaries in which they used more or less consistent advertising messages and marketing strategies to all customers in a particular country. Intuitively, this approach made as little sense as marketing products to the residents of California or Maine as if these states comprise homogeneous populations. However, a lack of valid marketing research in many countries left agencies with little choice.

Today, there is a great deal of research for multinational marketers in most countries. One of the most important approaches to international research is to study consumers on a regional rather than a national basis. In a landmark study, the Gallup Organization divided Latin American consumers into eight segments (see Exhibit 24.3, p. 638). The study was designed for companies to group consumers by demographic and psychographic characteristics rather than by national origin. As one marketer pointed out, "The approach is vital for strategic thinking. As a marketer, I won't look at countries anymore."[22]

Another primary category of international research is the brand audit. Brand audits are designed to gain consumer perspectives about a specific brand. The brand audit attempts to define what a brand means to consumers worldwide and then develop market strategies that will enhance the brand's future sales potential. Often a brand audit demonstrates that the perception that a company has of its brands doesn't match those of its customers.

For example, a brand audit for Polaroid showed that customers didn't view the camera as a conventional camera. Instead, they perceived Polaroid, by making pictures immediately available, as a social stimulant and catalyst providing fun moments. As a result of the audit, Polaroid advertising and promotions took on a decidedly lighter approach.

---

[22]Jeffery D. Zbar, "Gallup Offers New Take on Latin America," *Advertising Age,* November 13, 1995, p. 21.

Gallup's eight socioeconomic segments of Latin American consumers:

Emerging professional elite
14% of total; occupies top professional, executive positions:
- 51% graduated from university or technical college.
- 55% are married.
- 98% have color TV; 96%, VCR; 97%, car; 98%, credit card; 90%, vacuum cleaner.

Traditional elite
11%; almost half in top professional, executive positions:
- 53% finished secondary education.
* 54% married.
- All have color TV; 91%, VCR; 89%, car; 60%, credit card; 60%, vacuum cleaner.

Progressive upper middle class
13%; 36% in top or middle management:
- 75% studied beyond primary education, 30% studied beyond secondary school.
- 48% married.
- 99% have a color TV; 77%, VCR; 74%, car; 31%, credit card; 30% vacuum cleaner.

Self-made middle class
11%; skills gained through entrepreneurship:
- Most ended education with primary school, "virtually none" went beyond secondary school.
- Half married.
- 98% have color TV; 72%, VCR; 81%, car; 46%, credit card; 51%, vacuum cleaner.

Skilled middle class
9%; 45% have top operational jobs, 14% own small businesses:
- 60% completed secondary education, 18% completed university or technical college.
- Half married.
- 96% have color TV; 60%, VCR; 28%, car; 29%, credit card; 32%, vacuum cleaner.

Self-skilled lower middle class
13%; 58% employed in operational jobs:
- 42% went beyond primary school, 11% went beyond secondary education.
- Half married.
- 97% have color TV; 50%, VCR; 4%, car; 8%, credit card; none, vacuum cleaner.

Industrial working class
14%; a third are in skilled worker positions and another third in average operational jobs:
- 16% went beyond secondary school, 26% completed secondary school, 35% completed primary.
- 57% married.
- 92% have color TV; 13%, VCR; 5%, credit card; 15%, vacuum cleaner.

Struggling working class
15%; most in operational, skilled and unskilled jobs:
- 29% completed primary school, 24% completed secondary school.
- 53% married.
- 63% have color TV; no more than 10% have VCR, car, credit card or vacuum cleaner.

exhibit

24.3

International audiences cross country borders.

Courtesy: Advertising Age.
Source: Advertising Age,
November 13, 1995, p. 21.

In one television spot, a fan takes a picture of herself and throws it on stage during a rock concert. As a follow-up, Polaroid convinced a band in Hungary to take Polaroid photos of itself and toss them to fans. It also sponsored a contest on MTV Europe to have people send in Polaroid snapshots of themselves "living for the moment."[23]

Regardless of the function—creative, media, or research—agencies face two major problems in developing organizations that will meet the demands of clients. First, they are basically accommodating the organizational structure of clients. An agency with several multinational accounts often finds that the specific needs for account management

---

[23]Laurel Wentz, "Brand Audits Reshaping Images," *Ad Age International,* September 1996, p. i39.

will differ from one client to the other. In effect, some agencies find that they need different management organizations for each client.

The second major problem faced by multinational agencies is how to manage centrally and communicate locally. The adage, "think globally, act locally," is a dilemma for every agency. Agencies must translate broad client marketing strategies to the level of the individual customer in each country they serve. Despite the difficulties of centralized advertising management, there is little doubt that the trend will only become more prevalent in the future. The major advantages of centralized management are

1. Coordination offers cost savings in terms of client time and personnel and, to some extent, production costs.
2. It facilitates the sharing of experience: Lessons learned in one market can readily be applied in another.
3. It enables the effective control of the overall advertising budget so that funds are spent where and at the level they are needed.
4. The international importance of the account will ensure that it gets the benefit of the agency's top resources locally, regardless of the size of the budget for any particular market.
5. Most important, consistency of approach means that a positioning and image for a product can be built over time and across territory, a consideration of growing importance as internationally received media become more commonplace. Instead of being written off as a short-term tactical cost, advertising becomes an investment in an increasingly valuable international asset.

THE ADVERTISING FUNCTION IN INTERNATIONAL ADVERTISING

Although the basic functions of advertising are similar in all parts of the world, the specific execution and methods of operation vary widely. Consequently, it is difficult to discuss universal practices of international advertising. As you move from country to country, you will find that the use and receptivity of advertising as well as its objectives and basic goals demonstrate extraordinary diversity. As firms introduce products on a worldwide basis, their problems range from something as familiar as product category competition to the much more difficult problem of convincing buyers to change established habits or even reject previously held cultural taboos.

Regardless of the objective of a particular international campaign, advertisers must deal with a host of situations unique to each country.

Creative and Cultural Considerations

An American businessman newly assigned to Japan found he had to first learn the nuances of the culture of the country before meaningful business could be conducted. For example, he found that relationships and trust are central to Japanese business. The Japanese place a high priority on consensus, or *wa,* which means harmony. The process of gaining this environment of trust and good feelings may take several months, but once attained, execution of business matters goes relatively smoothly.

Likewise, business meetings are often surrounded by great ceremony where actions, taken for granted in the United States, are very formal. For example, the Japanese place great importance on the exchange of business cards (called *meishi*), and titles are extremely important in the way business is conducted. Japanese also are very literate and consume vast numbers of newspapers and magazines. Interestingly, some of the most popular publications are adult comic books, called *monga*. One reason for the popularity of print media is the long commute by Japanese workers, often as long as two hours one-way. Television viewing is very high, and quiz shows and variety programs, as well as sports and documentaries, are among the most popular programs.

Multiply the Japanese experience by the dozens of countries in which American companies have a major presence, and the scope of the problems of international business and marketing become apparent. Advertising, of course, is extremely dependent on culture, with its use of humor, puns, twists on familiar words, and an insider's knowledge of a society.

At one time, U.S.-based multinational advertisers routinely used word-for-word translations and exported American advertising around the world. Although this process might be quick and inexpensive, it also is almost always unsatisfactory. Today, a number of firms have been established to work with international agencies and their clients to develop advertising that takes into account not only language differences, but also the nuances of culture and the ways in which products are used and should be presented from one country to another.

Translation Management Direct Language Communications, Inc. (DLC) is a major **translation management** firm that works with a number of multinational companies. It deals with everything from traditional advertising to catalogs (see Exhibit 24.4). The translation process involves much more than just changing words from one lan-

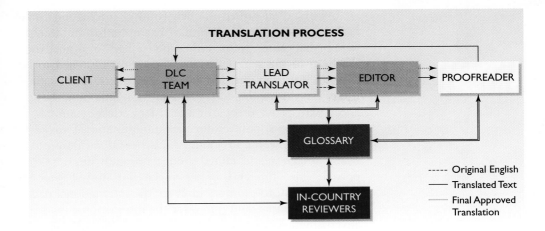

TRANSLATION PROCESS

CLIENT → DLC TEAM → LEAD TRANSLATOR → EDITOR → PROOFREADER

GLOSSARY

IN-COUNTRY REVIEWERS

----- Original English
——— Translated Text
········· Final Approved Translation

exhibit

24.5

Marketing translation involves much more than language.

Courtesy: Direct Language Communications, Inc.

guage to another. DLC has developed a system that includes checking and double checking all aspects of the translation, including working with in-country reviewers (see Exhibit 24.5).

Ideally, DLC begins the translation process during the design stage. At this point, DLC can offer a number of guidelines for multicultural communication. For example:

1. *Roman-based languages expand as much as 30 percent when translated.* Consideration must be given to spacing, layout, and the overall readability of the translated advertisement.
2. *Avoid excessive Americanisms.* Global copy and artwork are most easily transported from country to country if you avoid extensive use of American humor, acronyms, and satire. For example, "TGIF" would make no sense in most countries, and elements involving a woman driving a car would be inappropriate in Saudi Arabia.
3. *Be flexible in color design.* Colors carry distinctly different connotations in various countries. To Americans white is a symbol of purity, whereas in some countries it represents death.

Once the actual translation process begins, advertisers must be aware of both linguistic and cultural nuances. It is important that marketing communications provide product information in a manner that gives them credibility with their audiences. For example, Spanish-language advertisements targeted to an audience in Bogotá may be markedly different from advertising copy directed to customers in Madrid or Mexico City.

As part of the translation process, DLC assigns a native-language speaker from the appropriate country to work with the copy. The translator is familiar with the product category as well as the differences in languages. A Chinese advertisement suitable for a Taiwanese publication might miss the mark if published in a Chinese-language newspaper in San Francisco.

These nuances of advertising copy are really a reflection of the way a society views itself. As communication brings the world closer together, many long-standing traditions are being challenged by multinational marketing and advertising. "Let the marketplace drive how you position the client's products; define the demographics, what they read, watch, etc.; and then choose the most effective media plan. It only starts to fall apart when an office in a distant land tells you how to run a television ad from there, when it might not be the right choice for this market. Protection of a nation's sensibilities—and its products—takes many forms."[24]

---

[24]Jan Jaben, "Yanking the Welcome Mat," *Ad Age International,* October 16, 1995, p. i3.

As discussed earlier, the new form of international marketing tends to be centralized strategy and local execution. Examples for the necessity of this approach are endless. In Bangalore, India, armed police had to protect the local KFC restaurant when the head of the state farmers' association threatened to burn it down as a protest of Western intrusion into domestic farm markets. At the same time, India's Shiv Sena party leader was threatening to try to ban Coca-Cola from the country if the company moved ahead with plans to sponsor a Pakistani cricket team.[25]

Protectionist policies directed at multinational marketers are a problem throughout the world. However, in South Africa there is a widespread preference for foreign goods. Many foreign manufactured products proudly promote the fact that they are "fully imported." The "foreign is better" inclination moved Peter Stuyvesant cigarettes, a South African brand, to promote itself as "the international passport to smoking pleasure."[26]

The potential land mines for the international marketer are many. Companies and advertising agencies find that reliance on research and resident employees are the two primary means of avoiding the problems inherent in dealing with international consumers. It is clear that even the broadest advertising strategies must be translated to fit the local culture and customs. As we have discussed, the cost efficiencies of common creative themes, especially lower advertising production costs, make it important to try to develop creative campaigns that are exportable. More and more international campaigns seek to highlight similar consumer motivations and develop messages that emphasize the big idea rather than local differences among consumers.

MEDIA PLANNING: A GLOBAL PERSPECTIVE

Media buying is growing increasingly sophisticated among international advertisers. Media buys fall into one of four categories:

- *global buys,* in which every region carries some advertising
- *panregional buys,* in which buys are concentrated across a continent such as Europe, Asia, or North America
- *multicountry buys,* in which media placements are made in more than one country
- *local buys,* in which media is bought within only one country

Among large companies, local media buys are the exception; more and more companies are using at least multicountry media plans. Major media companies are aggressively moving into global competition for readers and viewers. For example, *The Asian Wall Street Journal* has shown double-digit circulation increases in Thailand, China, and Korea in recent years, and the Cartoon Channel reaches more than 30 million households in Europe.

Research shows that the growing household penetration of television sets, satellites, and cable is making it easier to do business on an international basis. "People around the world are more likely to have a television set than a washing machine or telephone, and are more than twice as likely to have a television set than a car."[27] Overall, a survey of 41 nations showed household television penetration at 96 percent. Likewise, cable television, which only a few years ago was a technology confined to the United States and a few other highly developed nations, is growing at a dramatic rate worldwide (see Exhibit 24.6).

---

[25]Mir Maqbool Alam Khan, "Values Clash as Economy Evolves," *Ad Age International,* October 16, 1995, p. i3.

[26]Jan Jaben, "Yanking the Welcome Mat," *Ad Age International,* October 16, 1995, p. i3.

[27]"Sixteen Numbers to Know," *The Public Pulse,* a publication of Roper Starch Worldwide, January 1996, p. 7.

exhibit

24.6

Television is making global advertising more practical.

Courtesy: Advertising Age.
Source: Ad Age International,
February 12, 1996, p. i12.

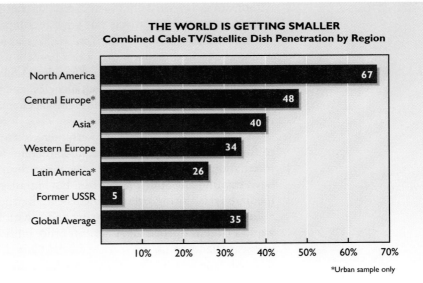

THE WORLD IS GETTING SMALLER
Combined Cable TV/Satellite Dish Penetration by Region

North America — 67
Central Europe* — 48
Asia* — 40
Western Europe — 34
Latin America* — 26
Former USSR — 5
Global Average — 35

10% 20% 30% 40% 50% 60% 70%

*Urban sample only

A number of factors have combined to create the current media environment. In addition to technology, particularly satellites, there has been unprecedented economic expansion in the former communist countries of Eastern Europe, much of Asia, and selected areas of Central and South America. Fueled in part by the communications technology, government controls of media and commerce have been relaxed in many parts of the world. Finally, a number of regimes recognize that it is in their self-interest to encourage foreign investment and the resulting rise in the domestic standard of living.

The combination of a world more receptive to international trade and the availability of communication to reach new markets presents the media planner with a tremendous array of options. The growth of international broadcasting and cable is truly an overnight phenomenon. In 1996, a survey of 17 European nations indicated that 46 percent of respondents said they subscribed to cable television. By 1998, that figure is estimated to be 63 percent.[28]

Nowhere is the expansion of media opportunities more obvious than in Asia. In one year, CNN International increased its household penetration by almost eight million. Daily newspapers in South Korea increased from 60 in 1988 to 125 in 1996. There are currently almost 300 newspapers in Taiwan. Rupert Murdoch, the Australian media tycoon, has saturated Asia with localized versions of his Star TV satellite system. His Hong Kong Star TV organization reaches 53 countries, and Murdoch's television operation in India controls 20 percent of all television advertising revenues in that country.

The growth of advertising in Asia is amazing. As recently as 1990, Japanese media revenues represented almost 80 percent of advertising dollars in the region (including Australia and New Zealand). Chinese advertising spending in that year was $243 million, or less than 1 percent of the total. By 1997, Chinese advertising accounted for $13 billion, or 15 percent of the regional total. During the same period, Korean advertising dollars increased more than 300 percent and Taiwan revenues more than doubled. Japan, where advertising revenues were constant at approximately $41 billion, saw its share of advertising decrease to less than 50 percent.[29] Similar figures are

---

[28]Juliana Koranteng, "EMS: Cable, Satellite Claim Places with Print," *Ad Age International,* May 1996, p. i24.
[29]"Asia Rising," *Adweek,* August 19, 1996, p. 22.

demonstrated in virtually every corner of the globe as mature economies such as the United States show relatively flat growth compared to dozens of emerging nations.

Like all advertising executives, media planners must take a multinational perspective as clients and media move across borders to add market share and audiences. During the last two decades, the international media-buying function has changed dramatically. Searching for cost efficiencies and recognizing the unique problems of international media buying, multinational clients have demanded special expertise from their agencies.

One by one, automobile, consumer electronics, and textile manufacturers moved to foreign countries, and American companies found themselves in a truly competitive international marketplace. In this new environment, a number of American companies have traditionally split their media-buying assignments between domestic and foreign media buyers, hiring overseas media-buying agencies to handle non-U.S. buys. Carat, a European media-buying company and—with billings of some $7 billion—one of the world's largest, opened an American office with the expressed purpose of convincing its overseas clients to use its services in the United States and at the same time recruit additional American multinationals for its international services.

This incursion by a foreign-based media-buying firm underscores the international competition facing American agencies. It also follows the pattern of international agencies actively (and often successfully) competing for the accounts of American multinational firms. U.S.-based media planners must compete aggressively with foreign agencies to retain the business of American-based clients such as Coca-Cola and Procter & Gamble, as well as to compete for foreign-based multinationals as future clients.

The Media and Marketing Translation Process

We earlier discussed the problems associated with translating creative messages from one country to another. Media planners also must deal with the process of **marketing translation** as they adapt marketing and media plans to the various countries in which they advertise. There are a number of areas that the media planner must consider as part of this translation process:

1. *Media availability.* In many countries, both print and broadcast media are severely limited, and nontraditional media such as direct mail may be unavailable or impractical. Some countries permit television commercials to be aired only in certain day parts, or they may be presented as blocks before or after programming.
2. *Legal requirements.* As in this country, products such as alcohol and tobacco, as well as other product categories, may be limited or excluded from all or certain media. There also are a number of restrictions about the way in which products can be presented from one country to another.
3. *Media and product usage.* Consumers in various countries demonstrate markedly different preferences for media and products. In Japan, daily television viewing averages more than eight hours per household; the figure is less than three hours in Great Britain.
4. *Research.* Reliable media and product usage data are just now becoming available in many countries. Media planners must be extremely careful in using research that may lack the degree of accuracy that is taken for granted in the United States.

Many media executives are predicting that, although regional and national adaptations are going to be needed for most media plans, television will soon change the process of international media planning. Satellites and cable are already offering programming and advertising that are simultaneously available in a number of countries. This development offers the potential for significant cost efficiencies in both international brand awareness and advertising.

Methods of Implementing the Media Function

Media planning is a tremendous challenge to multinational advertisers and their agencies. There are two major problems faced by agencies as they service clients on an international basis:

- variance of media usage levels from country to country
- different methods of media buying and availability of audience data

American advertisers find that media preferences, advertising availability, and costs of time and space differ markedly from those in the United States. However, as we have seen, television is fast becoming the medium of choice for both audiences and advertisers in most countries of the world. Most advertising executives view television as the most efficient means of achieving high audience penetration on a global basis. As set ownership and access to cable increase, these efficiencies will continue. In most respects, international media usage mirrors earlier trends in the United States. Television is growing in popularity in virtually every country in the world. This growth seems to be at the expense of print media, especially newspapers. In most of the world, television is the primary advertising medium, held back only by governmental advertising restrictions in several countries.

In addition to the differences in use of traditional media in various countries, media planners also must consider nontraditional media, which are very important in some areas of the world. For example, cinema advertising, regarded as a very minor medium in America, is a primary vehicle in Asia and parts of Europe. Out-of-home advertising is also extremely important in many countries.

One of the fastest-growing forms of advertising throughout the world is direct response. There are a number of advantages to international direct response. Direct mail can be translated into appropriate languages to reach segments within a multilingual country. It also can be targeted to special cultural or product usage markets. The problem with direct response is finding adequate mailing lists. In most Latin American countries, reliable mailing lists are very scarce, and in most of Asia there are a number of restrictions on the use of proprietary information about consumers, which makes building databases difficult.

Regardless of the media strategy adopted, advertisers must deal with the problems of developing and executing the plan. Media buying is so complex for large multinational buys that the media function is increasingly concentrated in buying combines or brokers that buy for a number of agencies. These combines can afford to hire highly trained personnel, conduct multinational audience research, and establish databases that would be beyond the financial reach of any single agency. The combines also can gain significant media discounts by buying as a group instead of on the basis of single agencies or brands. U.S. media generally give media discounts based on corporate media placement. However, in many parts of the world, media allow agencies to combine media placement for all their clients to establish discounts. Discounts based on total agency placement mean that the larger the broker, the greater the financial advantage to its clients.

INTERNATIONAL ADVERTISING LEGAL AND REGULATORY PROHIBITIONS

International advertisers are faced with an immense array of often conflicting laws and regulations as they move from country to country. However, the major areas of legislation are not that much different from those in the United States. Privacy issues, advertising to children, and restrictions on tobacco advertising are global topics of discussion. For example, Belgium bans all tobacco advertising, including that in imported magazines. Greece and Sweden have almost total prohibitions on children's advertising, and many countries have various exclusions concerning sharing personal data for commercial purposes.[30]

It is imperative that multinational marketers and their advertising agencies carefully monitor these individual situations. Controlling commercial communication has been made much more difficult by the advent of technology that has no regard for national borders. For example, as more companies establish Web sites for commercial purposes, increasingly difficult questions are arising. The U.S. Department of Transportation successfully fined Virgin Atlantic Airways, a British carrier, for an illegal promotion. The airline was in violation of U.S. advertising regulations, although it was in compliance in Great Britain. The courts ruled that because the promotion was easily obtained in the United States and applied to American flyers, it should have adhered to domestic regulations.

In a global economy, it is increasingly important for companies to make a concerted effort to have their advertising in compliance with local regulations. With multinational firms sometimes doing business in more than 100 countries, the monitoring process can be a difficult one. Fines and, in rare instances, product bans are possible if advertising fails to adhere to local ordinances.

As the Internet is used more and more for commercial purposes, executives suggest that—at least among major countries in which a firm does business—marketing communication should be cleared before any Internet advertising is initiated. When the number of countries make it impractical to get country-by-country clearances, these experts suggest that a disclaimer be made in the advertising that the offer is only for customers in a certain location.[31] Such a disclaimer may not relieve total responsibility for noncompliant advertising, but it probably would greatly mitigate any penalties.

ADVERTISING DIVERSITY IN THE UNITED STATES

To most of us, multinational advertising means American companies going abroad or overseas firms selling goods and services in this country. However, domestic advertisers in this country are not immune to the demands of an increasingly diversified society. A company that ignores the fact that significant changes are occurring in American culture does so at its own risk.

In broad terms, the three largest ethnic markets in the United States are African Americans, with a population of 33 million; Hispanics, at some 25 million; and Asian Americans totaling 8 million. It is projected that by the year 2050 these groups will make up half of the U.S. population, and the U.S. Census Bureau predicts that the Hispanic population will be the largest segment, with approximately 88 million people.[32]

Despite the huge potential market represented by these consumers, advertisers have historically failed to design advertising and products to accommodate the demands of these groups. Although much remains to be done, there is evidence that advertising agencies and their clients are moving to correct the underrepresentation of these groups in mainstream marketing plans (see Exhibit 24.7).

Hispanic advertisers are finding that assimilation among a majority of this market segment is a myth. As one Spanish-language television executive reported, "We are finding a continuing tie to the Spanish language and media through the second and third

---

[30]Paul Meller, "European Ad Rules Pulling Union in Many Directions," *Ad Age International,* October 1996, p. i17.

[31]John Feldman and Lewis Rose, "Advertising and the Law in Cyberspace," *Folio,* October 1, 1996, p. 47.

[32]Hallie Mummert, "Reaching Ethnic Markets," *Target Marketing,* November 1995, p. 14.

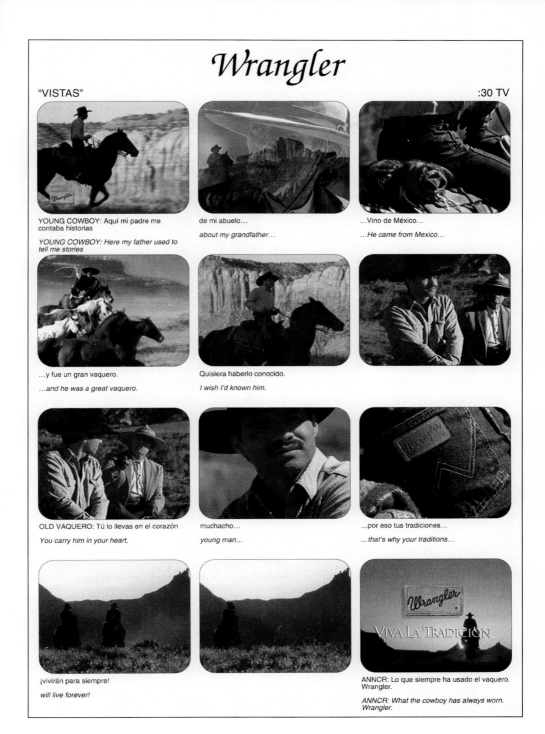

Wrangler

"VISTAS"
:30 TV

YOUNG COWBOY: Aquí mi padre me contaba historias

YOUNG COWBOY: Here my father used to tell me stories

de mi abuelo...

about my grandfather...

...Vino de México...

...He came from Mexico...

...y fue un gran vaquero.

...and he was a great vaquero.

Quisiera haberlo conocido.

I wish I'd known him.

OLD VAQUERO: Tú lo llevas en el corazón

You carry him in your heart,

muchacho...

young man...

...por eso tus tradiciones...

...that's why your traditions...

¡vivirán para siempre!

will live forever!

ANNCR: Lo que siempre ha usado el vaquero. Wrangler.

ANNCR: What the cowboy has always worn. Wrangler.

VIVA LA TRADICIÓN

exhibit

24.7

American advertising must reach a more diversified population.
Courtesy: Dieste & Partners.

generations going back 30 years, even among Hispanics who are today fully bilingual and whose English is without any trace of an accent. The presence of a critical population mass and a growing Spanish media base create an atmosphere of comfort that helps sustain the language."[33]

Several major companies have begun to reach out to these markets with specialized media and advertising messages. For example, in 1997 Sears launched its first African

---

[33]"Assimilation No Threat to Hispanic Media," *Advertising Age,* March 31, 1997, p. A2.

exhibit

24.8

Multilanguage advertising is becoming commonplace in many markets.

Courtesy: Ad Council.

TRANSLATION:
"Aaron Rodriguez"
Ballplayer in his first school-year
Little League coach in his second year
Dead in the third year of school.

If you don't stop someone from driving drunk, who will do it?
Do everything you can to stop them.

Don't permit your friends to drive drunk.

American–oriented advertising campaign. The $15 million campaign was intended to capitalize on the estimated $469 billion buying power of the African American community.[34]

Similar efforts are being directed to the Hispanic market. NationsBank aired commercials featuring a Spanish-speaking teller to make non–English speaking customers welcome. Discount broker Charles Schwab advertises its Spanish-language hotline for customers. In addition, public service advertising, such as that distributed by the Advertising Council, is often presented in Spanish language formats (see Exhibit 24.8).

Because the Hispanic market has been neglected for so long, consumers are often more receptive to commercial messages than the advertising-saturated mainstream market. "It's a rapidly growing market and one that's less saturated with advertising messages than the mass market. Dollars spent by advertisers in the Hispanic market may be more profitable than dollars spent in the general market."[35]

---

[34]Jim Kirk and Mary Ellen Podmolik, "Sears Tailors New Ad Campaign to Black Shoppers," *Chicago Sun Times Online Business,* May 5, 1997.
[35]Melanie Wells, "U.S. Advertisers Slowly Learn to Speak Spanish," *USA Today,* March 21, 1996, p. 1A.

Reaching the African American market is a much easier task for marketers than reaching either the Hispanic or Asian segments for two reasons:

- There is no language barrier to the African American community, so advertisers don't have to make decisions concerning English versus indigenous languages.
- Although there are differences of media and product preferences among African Americans, just as among the white majority, they represent a much more homogeneous market than either Asian or Hispanic consumers.

For example, among Hispanic residents of the United States, 60 percent are Mexican American, with the majority residing in the West and Southwest. The more than 10 percent of this group that are Puerto Rican by birth or heritage are concentrated in New York City and the Northeast. Cuban Americans make up approximately 8 percent of the total Hispanic population and are concentrated in South Florida. The remaining Hispanic population represents a number of Central and South American countries.

Reaching the Hispanic market represents a major challenge to advertisers. Less than half speak fluent English and approximately 75 percent prefer Spanish at home. In addition, the subsets of this market represent an array of customs and cultures that translate into a variety of product preferences. Currently, there are more than 1,500 media serving the Hispanic market.

The Asian American community is even more difficult to reach. Filipinos, who make up 21 percent of the U.S. Asian population, are the largest group. Two other segments, the Chinese (17 percent) and Vietnamese (16 percent), compose more than 10 percent of this market. Despite the difficulty of reaching this diverse market, Asians represent an extremely lucrative target market for many advertisers. They have a higher household income, a higher percentage of college graduates, and a higher level of personal savings than the general U.S. population.[36]

Not only is the Asian market a prime target for advertisers, Asians are increasingly becoming advertisers themselves. In part because of past discrimination, Hispanics and Asians have become independent entrepreneurs at a level significantly higher than the general population. By the year 2000, it is estimated that Hispanic-owned businesses will surpass two million. These emerging businesses advertise, and in so doing, they bring additional support to the many media vehicles catering to the diversified ethnic marketplace.

Whereas language differences and reaching ethnic minorities represent a challenge to advertisers, the real hurdle is communicating with sensitivity and understanding to people of diverse backgrounds and cultures. A number of major companies have attempted to reach out to these market segments with strategies that "include the recognition and understanding of ethnic holidays and religious, cultural and seasonal celebrations and by designing promotions around these rituals."[37] For example, McDonald's added fajitas to its menu in selected markets to recognize Cinco de Mayo, a holiday commemorating Mexico's defeat of France in 1862. Other marketers have recognized the African American celebration of Kwanzaa and Asian Americans' Chinese New Year.

The key to success in these markets is to reach them with a blend of the old and new. The more an advertiser is able to show a real understanding and insight for different cultures, the easier it is to build trust and consumer loyalty. Conversely, if advertisers commit major communication blunders, they would be better off sticking to "Americanized" advertising. The importance of the multicultural market is apparent in the growing number of foreign-language promotional messages seen across the United States in recent years.

---

[36]Jack Schmid, "Ethnic Niche Catalogs," *Target Marketing,* November 1995, p. 18.
[37]Carolyn Shea, "The New Face of America," *Promo,* January 1996, p. 57.

International advertising might better be described as multicultural advertising because it has long since transcended geographical boundaries. To one degree or another, the world has become the marketplace for most corporations, whether they are headquartered in the United States or overseas. However, the complexities of dealing in a global economy are testing the planning, research, and managerial abilities of companies as well as their agencies. The difficulties experienced by the European Community, a developed region with one of the highest standards of living in the world, reinforce the problems companies face as they introduce their products in the emerging nations.

Still, whether to develop an international position is no longer a subject of debate for most companies. The mature economies of the United States and Europe no longer offer the level of growth and expansion needed by large firms. In addition, sales in major developed countries are largely made at the expense of brand switching rather than resulting from real growth. The potential for foreign success offers rewards that will motivate companies to take significant risks.

Advertising will play a much larger role in most international markets compared to the U.S. market. The most successful brands will be those that establish the first beachhead in emerging markets. Recent marketing struggles between Pepsi and Coca-Cola underscore the importance of the international market. The common criteria for U.S. advertising—*CPMs*, cost-per-point, audited circulation, and verified ratings—are simply not applicable in many foreign markets. Instead, experience and judgment must be used to deal with the intricacies of international marketing.

Even those agencies who do not participate in multinational advertising will be faced with the challenges of ethnic diversity in this country. The growth of Hispanic, Asian, and other cultures within American society will increasingly require the creative use of media, promotion, and sales messages to reach this evolving market. Not just marketing expertise, but a sensitivity to the culture, language, and values of other peoples, will be a requirement in this new marketplace. However, for those willing to devote the time to learn how to operate in this diverse environment, the rewards will be great.

Clearly, multicultural advertising will continue to undergo a period of dramatic change throughout this decade. Many of these changes are unpredictable, but a number of future trends are apparent:

1. Overseas advertising growth will continue to increase at a greater rate than U.S. advertising investment. Non-U.S. advertising will increase as the largely untapped markets of Latin America and Asia are opened and commercial satellite television becomes more available in Europe.
2. Multinational advertising opportunities will continue to increase. Consumer demand for satellite and cable television are prompting governments to loosen current restrictions on commercial media, which creates additional advertising opportunities.
3. U.S. companies increasingly will find domestic competition stemming from international corporations operating in this country. In some cases, these competitors will compete in areas once dominated by American companies.
4. The number of multinational and global brands will continue to expand. As American, European, and Asian products seek expanded sales, the world will become their marketplace with resulting fierce competition in a number of countries.
5. In the future, marketing will be carried out on a regional basis with national boundaries less important than reaching select market segments within a number of countries.

R E V I E W

1. Why do U.S. companies increasingly look to overseas markets for expansion?
2. How might advertising's function differ in an emerging nation versus in the United States?
3. What is meant by the term "global marketing"?

4. How does developing an international advertising plan differ from developing a domestic one?

5. What is the role of translation management in global advertising?

6. What are some of the legal and regulatory considerations in international advertising?

7. Compare and contrast the approaches to advertising to African American and Hispanic populations in the United States.

TAKE IT TO THE NET

We invite you to visit the Russell/Lane page on the Prentice Hall Web site at **PHLIP** **http://www.prenhall.com/phbusiness** for the bimonthly Russell/Lane update and for this chapter's World Wide Web exercise.

25

LEGAL AND OTHER RESTRAINTS ON ADVERTISING

CHAPTER OBJECTIVES

FOR MORE THAN 50 YEARS, ADVERTISING HAS BEEN CONTROLLED AND MONITORED BY A NUMBER OF GOVERNMENT, INDUSTRY, AND PUBLIC POLICY ORGANIZATIONS. TODAY, ADVERTISING CONTINUES TO OPERATE IN AN ENVIRONMENT OF INCREASING REGULATION AND PUBLIC SCRUTINY. AFTER READING THIS CHAPTER YOU WILL UNDERSTAND

- **the historical context of advertising regulation**
- **the role of the FTC and other regulators**
- **First Amendment protection for advertising**
- **media's role in advertising clearance**
- **state and local regulation of advertising**
- **advertising self-regulation.**

The key to advertising regulation is to provide companies with enough latitude to create interesting messages that produce both sales and profits, while ensuring that these messages are presented in a manner that allows consumers to make informed purchase decisions. Accurate and factual information is an important ingredient in a free-market economy. When advertising is disseminated that is untrue or misleading, customers are unfairly induced to purchase unsatisfactory products. The implied relationship between the consumer and the firm creating the advertising is violated, creating *market failure*.

It is important that consumers be able to depend on advertising to present a full and reasonable disclosure of the product and its usage. When this pact between advertiser and consumer is broken, it is detrimental to the individual consumer and also to advertisers in general.

> Fraud by the producer or seller violates an implicit or explicit offer to provide, for a price, goods or services with particular attributes that have been advertised to attract consumer interest. When a seller induces the purchase of products or services that he or she knows, or should know, are unlikely

to perform as claimed or to meet the consumer's needs as promised, the seller perverts the system and causes injury.[1]

As discussed in chapter 1, the turn of the twentieth century marked a much-needed examination and "housecleaning" of flagrant advertising abuses. Today, most advertisers agree that those companies that create illegal or unethical advertising should be dealt with harshly. Not only is misleading advertising wrong, it is bad business. Most products depend on repeat business for their survival. When misleading advertising creates unreasonable customer expectations, it is unlikely that the product will enjoy future sales.

However, despite the fact that companies generally agree that consumer protection is a worthy objective, advertisers see in the current environment an overzealous attempt to control legitimate advertising. In particular, firms are frustrated by regulations implemented by agencies that, in their opinion, do not understand the role of advertising. For example, some regulators seem to take the position that advertising must include all relevant information, overlooking the fact that advertising is only one element in the sales process.

An illustration of this regulatory approach can be seen in the debate over disclosure of information in automobile leases. To fully comply with the original version of the Consumer Leasing Act, a 60-second radio ad would have had to include 50 seconds of lease requirements. Eventually, the act was modified so that a radio ad could refer listeners to a toll-free number or a print advertisement to get additional information. However, both television and newspapers argued that the time and space required to comply with the rule were unreasonable.

After lengthy negotiations, other revisions were implemented. However, to an advertising industry lobbyist the episode underlined "the importance of keeping on top of regulations in order to prevent disclaimer-mania in legislative and regulatory circles. Similar types of laws mandating use of certain language in ads for food products and warnings on alcoholic beverage spots have been introduced in the past."[2]

Whether advertisers think that some regulatory scrutiny is unfair is largely immaterial; the fact is that they must deal with the reality of an often hostile atmosphere. In this highly charged and controversial arena, it is imperative that advertisers avoid even the appearance of impropriety or deception. Advertisers must be extremely careful not to run afoul of the various laws and regulations applied to advertising.

There are three primary constraints on advertising:

1. laws and regulations of legally constituted bodies such as Congress and the Federal Trade Commission
2. control by the media through advertising acceptability guidelines
3. self-regulation by advertisers and agencies through various trade practice recommendations and codes of conduct (see Exhibit 25.1, p. 654).

You will notice that two of the three types of constraints are basically self-imposed. The typical advertiser is as concerned about misleading, false, or inappropriate advertising as any regulatory body. Advertising is not only a means of communicating with the public, but it also determines how the public perceives the companies, products, and services that advertise. Anything that damages the overall image of advertising hurts the efforts of every advertiser.

Prior to the twentieth century, commerce operated under the libertarian notion of **caveat emptor,** "let the buyer beware." This concept was based on the classical

Caveat emptor
Latin for "Let the buyer beware." Represents the notion that there should be no government interference in the marketplace.

---

[1]"Deceptive Advertising in a Free Market," *Advertising Topics,* a publication of the Council of Better Business Bureaus, Inc., May 1995, p. 2.

[2]Robyn Griggs, "A New Lease on Disclaimers," *Agency,* Winter 1996, p. 18.

Creative Code of the American Association of Advertising Agencies

ADOPTED APRIL 26, 1962

The members of the American Association of Advertising Agencies recognize:

1. That advertising bears a dual responsibility in the American economic system and way of life.

To the public it is a primary way of knowing about the goods and services that are the products of American free enterprise—goods and services that can be freely chosen to suit the desires and needs of the individual. The public is entitled to expect that advertising will be reliable in content and honest in presentation.

To the advertiser it is a primary way of persuading people to buy his goods or services, within the framework of a highly competitive economic system. He is entitled to regard advertising as a dynamic means of building his business and his profits.

2. That advertising enjoys a particularly intimate relationship to the American family.

It enters the home as an integral part of television and radio programs, to speak to the individual and often to the entire family. It shares the pages of favorite newspapers and magazines. It presents itself to travelers and to readers of the daily mails. In all these forms, it bears a special responsibility to respect the tastes and self-interest of the public.

3. That advertising is directed to sizable groups or to the public at large, which is made up of many interests and many tastes.

As is the case with all public enterprises, ranging from sports to education and even to religion, it is almost impossible to speak without finding someone in disagreement. Nonetheless, advertising people recognize their obligation to operate within the traditional American limitations: to serve the interests of the majority and to respect the rights of the minority.

Therefore we, the members of the American Association of Advertising Agencies, in addition to supporting and obeying the laws and legal regulations pertaining to advertising, undertake to extend and broaden the application of high ethical standards. Specifically, we will not knowingly produce advertising that contains:

    a. False or misleading statements or exaggerations, visual or verbal.
    b. Testimonials that do not reflect the real choice of a competent witness.
    c. Price claims that are misleading.
    d. Comparisons that unfairly disparage a competitive product or service.
    e. Claims insufficiently supported, or which distort the true meaning or practicable application of statements made by professional or scientific authority.
    f. Statements, suggestions, or pictures offensive to public decency.

We recognize that there are areas subject to honestly different interpretations and judgment. Taste is subjective and may even vary from time to time as well as from individual to individual. Frequency of seeing or hearing advertising messages will necessarily vary greatly from person to person.

However, we agree not to recommend to an advertiser and to discourage the use of advertising that is in poor or questionable taste or is deliberately irritating through content, presentation, or excessive repetition.

Clear and willful violations of this Code shall be referred to the Board of Directors of the American Association of Advertising Agencies for appropriate action, including possible annulment of membership as provided in Article IV, Section 5, of the Constitution and By-Laws.

Conscientious adherence to the letter and the spirit of this Code will strengthen advertising and the free enterprise system of which it is a part.

---

economic perception of a free marketplace of goods and ideas and perfect knowledge on the part of the participants in that marketplace. That is, buyers and sellers were presumed to have equal information, and it was assumed that both groups, being rational, would make correct economic choices without government interference into business transactions.

In the twentieth century, the complexities of the marketplace have led to the rejection of the principle of *caveat emptor.* It has been replaced by the idea that consumers cannot hope to have perfect knowledge of the marketplace and must be protected by legal guarantees of the authenticity of advertising claims. To shield the public from false and misleading advertising, numerous laws have been passed. Chief among these is the Federal Trade Commission Act, which we discuss here first.

THE FEDERAL TRADE COMMISSION (FTC)

**Federal Trade
Commission
(FTC)**
The agency of the
federal government
empowered to
prevent unfair
competition and to
prevent unfair
competition and to
prevent fraudulent,
misleading, or
deceptive advertising
in interstate
commerce.

The FTC is the agency with primary responsibility to oversee advertising. The original intent of the Federal Trade Commission Act, passed in 1914, was that "unfair methods of competition are hereby declared unlawful." At the outset, unfair methods of competition were largely regarded as those involving businesses. A primary goal of the FTC during this period was to protect local retailers from large chains that were just beginning to become a major factor in some retail categories, such as grocery stores.

During its early years, the FTC did not take action against a business unless it could be shown that competitors were being harmed by illegal trade practices. Business practices, including advertising, that injured the public were not considered within its jurisdiction. It was not until 1922, in *FTC* v. *Winsted Hosiery Company*, that the Supreme Court held that false advertising was an unfair trade practice. However, the FTC continued to function primarily as a means of protecting one business from another.

Then, in 1938, passage of the **Wheeler-Lea Amendments** broadened this interpretation to include the principle that the FTC could protect consumers from deceptive advertising. This law also gave the FTC specific authority over false advertising in the fields of food, drugs, therapeutic devices, and cosmetics. Today, the FTC has sweeping power over the advertising of all products sold or advertised across state lines.

Wheeler-Lea Amendments
Broadened the scope of the FTC to include consumer advertising.

The Role of the FTC

The FTC's role in regulating advertising is to ensure a free marketplace based on dissemination of complete, truthful, and nondeceptive advertising to the buying public. To accomplish this goal, the FTC tends to concentrate on those areas of concern deemed most important to the Commission at any particular time, such as telemarketing. Although the Commission may give special emphasis to a limited number of product categories or sales practices, at any time it is usually investigating a diverse group of complaints.

Testifying before a Congressional subcommittee, FTC Chairman Robert Pitofsky outlined some major initiatives of the Commission:

1. Eliminate unnecessary business burdens from the past by ensuring that outdated regulations or policies which are no longer beneficial are rescinded.
2. Focus the FTC's limited resources in areas of greatest significance and work through joint initiatives with states, businesses, and public groups whenever possible to gain greater leverage.
3. Prepare for the future by keeping abreast of and planning for the dramatic changes in the marketplace, due to rapid innovation, new technologies and globalization that may warrant new policies or enforcement strategies.[3]

Deceptive Advertising

One of the primary tasks of the FTC is to ensure that advertising is truthful and not misleading. It is important to distinguish between the fact that advertising messages can be literally true and still, taken in an overall context, mislead consumers. The key to FTC enforcement is the notion of substantiation of advertising claims. Advertisers must be prepared to prove, with objective and generally accepted evidence including scientific studies, that their claims are true. Often advertisers note in their advertising copy that some type of substantiation has taken place. Deceptive advertising has not been specifically defined by Congress, so the FTC operates through a series of guidelines developed over the years. Its judgment, in ruling an ad or claim deceptive, hinges on whether a consumer action was taken on the basis of advertising deception. In fact, general rules of deception are difficult to draft and must be considered on an ad-by-ad basis.

Currently, the FTC uses a three-part test to determine if an advertisement is deceptive or untruthful:

1. *There must be a representation, omission, or practice that is likely to mislead the consumer.* A statement does not have to be untrue to be deceptive. Sometimes advertisers will make a claim that is literally true but the total impression of the ad is misleading. For example, the FTC cited a comparison commercial for a window cleaner. The commercial showed the advertised product and a competing brand sprayed on half a window pane. The voice-over stated that the leading brand left streaks whereas the advertised brand was clear. The FTC found that although the

---

[3]"National Advertising and the Federal Trade Commission," *Advertising Topics,* a publication of the Council of Better Business Bureaus, July/August 1996, p. 1.

commercial was true, the spotting created by the leading cleaner would not have occurred if it had been wiped off immediately after spraying, as intended in normal use.

2. *The act or practice must be considered from the perspective of a consumer who is acting reasonably.* In other words, the advertiser is not responsible for every possible interpretation, no matter how far-fetched or unreasonable, that might be made by a consumer. However, when an advertisement provides a demonstration in an unusual manner, it may lead consumers to unique conclusions. In a plastic storage bag commercial, it was claimed that the one brand of plastic bag kept food fresher than a competing brand. To demonstrate the claim, the advertised brand and another brand, each containing a sandwich, were dipped into a tub of water. The other brand leaked, but the advertised brand stayed dry. The FTC ruled that although the demonstration may have been accurate, it did not prove one product was superior to another in maintaining freshness because freshness is determined by a number of factors.[4]

3. *The representation, omission, or practice must be material.* In other words, the claim, even if it is not true, must be judged to have had some influence over a consumer's decision. For example, the courts have ruled that using plastic ice cubes in a soft-drink commercial is not deceptive because no claims are being made about the ice cubes. Sometimes advertisers are tempted to substitute items in commercial demonstrations because the time and hot lights of television may change the perception of a product. When this is done, the consumer should be told or the advertiser should be certain that the changes will not be regarded as material to the message of the commercial.[5]

When the FTC decides that deception has indeed taken place, it can move quickly to stop the practice or advertising and severely penalize the company found guilty of the deception.

Methods of FTC Enforcement

The enforcement process of the FTC works in concert with the courts. In the ideal situation, the FTC will work with advertisers to validate a claim or to have advertisers end deceptive practices. However, if an advertiser refuses to stop running advertising that has been ruled deceptive, there is recourse in the courts for both parties.

1. The first step in the process is to file a claim of deceptive practices with the FTC. The complaint can come from consumers, competitors, or the FTC staff.
2. The FTC then begins its investigation. Normally, the investigation starts with a request for **substantiation** from the advertiser.
3. If the commission finds the practice to be unsubstantiated and therefore deceptive, a complaint is issued. At this point, the advertiser is asked to sign a **consent decree** in which the firm agrees to end the deceptive practice or advertising. Most complaints are settled in this manner. An advertiser who continues the practice after signing a consent decree is liable for a fine of $10,000 per day.
4. If an advertiser refuses to sign a consent decree, the commission issues a **cease and desist order.** Before such an order can become final, a hearing is held before an administrative law judge. The judge can dismiss the case and negate the cease and desist order. If it is upheld, however, the company may appeal the decision to the full commission.
5. Even if an advertiser agrees to abide by a cease and desist order, the FTC may find that simply stopping a particular practice does not repair past damage to consumers.

Substantiation
The key to FTC enforcement is that advertisers must be able to prove the claims made in their advertising.

Consent decree
Issued by the FTC. An advertiser signs the decree, stops the practice under investigation, but admits no guilt.

Cease and desist order
If an advertiser refuses to sign a consent decree, the FTC may issue a cease and desist order that can carry a $10,000-per-day fine.

---

[4]Stephen P. Durchslag, "Know the Rules When Using Product Demos," *Promo,* October 1995, p. 18.
[5]Don R. Pember, *Mass Media Law* (Dubuque, Iowa: Wm. C. Brown Publishers, 1990), pp. 488–491.

To counteract the residual effects of deceptive advertising, the FTC may require a firm to run corrective advertisements designed to "dissipate the effects of that deception." The FTC often stipulates several requirements for **corrective advertising** such as content, format, frequency, and even the media schedule. The commission normally requires corrective advertising when major advertising themes are the basis for consumers' choices. In one of the first cases of corrective advertising, Listerine was ordered to insert messages in $10 million worth of advertising that Listerine did not cure colds or lessen their severity, a long-running theme of its advertising.

6. If a company cannot reach agreement with the FTC, its next recourse is the Federal Courts, first to the Federal Court of Appeals and finally to the Supreme Court. It is extremely rare that a case would go beyond the cease and desist order. From a practical standpoint, most advertising campaigns have run their course by the time an advertiser would go to court. Equally important is the fact that few firms want the adverse publicity that surrounds a protracted court battle. However, in one case the FTC won a judgment against Geritol, 11 years after the original cease and desist order was issued.

Some Basic Rules of the Courts and the FTC

Because each advertising message is different, deception is largely determined on a case-by-case basis. However, the FTC often cites individual cases where they think there is the possibility that other advertisers may potentially be guilty of the same offense. In effect, the commission uses its enforcement authority to stop a current practice and at the same time preclude future violations by other advertisers. For example:

1. An egg producer was cited for making deceptive cholesterol-related claims in marketing its eggs. The settlement involved a $100,000 civil penalty. According to the FTC, the importance of the action was twofold: First, consumers are paying up to an additional dollar for these eggs, based on what the commission alleged were false and unsubstantiated claims, and consumers need truthful information about the health aspects of the foods they buy. Second, the case tells other advertisers making health claims that the agency takes these claims seriously and that failing to comply with an FTC order is a costly proposition.[6]

2. From time to time the FTC conducts hearings and workshops with advertisers to forestall misleading advertising. A case in point is the problem in determining what is meant by the term "Made in the U.S.A." During an FTC-sponsored meeting, a range of topics was discussed. For instance, what specific threshold for domestic content should a product have to meet to be considered "Made in the U.S.A."? There also were questions about consumer perceptions and understanding of these labels. Could terms such as "Assembled in the U.S.A." be used to denote a different level of domestic content than "Made in the U.S.A."?

As you can see from these examples, the responsibility of the FTC covers numerous business practices involving a variety of products and services. Unfortunately, some of these cases involve companies that may have knowingly violated FTC regulations. However, many advertisers run afoul of these regulations simply through ignorance or misunderstanding.

Over the years, the FTC has developed a number of industry guidelines or FTC rules that outline in some detail exactly what a business can and cannot do in terms of business practices. Examples of such FTC guidelines are the

- Recycled Oil Rule
- Telemarketing Sales Rule
- R-Value Rule (for home insulation products).

---

[6]"FTC Focus," *Advertising Topics,* a publication of the Council of Better Business Bureaus, March 1996, p. 6.

At the same time, the FTC constantly reviews its rules and rescinds those that address areas that no longer represent major consumer problems. For example, the Binocular Rule, which required a disclosure in any advertising or on packaging indicating the instrument was nonprismatic or partially prismatic, was deleted.

In the following section we discuss some of the common problems often faced by advertisers and how the FTC views them.

The Term "Free" in Advertising   The use of offers such as "buy one, get one free" or "two for one sale" have become so prevalent and their abuses so widespread that the FTC issued a four-page guide for nondeceptive usage of the term "free." The guide emphasizes that when the word "free" is used, a consumer has the right to believe that the merchant will not recoup any cost associated with the purchase of another item. A "two for one" deal requires that the first item is sold at regular price or the lowest price offered within the last 30 days. The commission also requires that any disclosure about the offer price must be made in a conspicuous manner in close conjunction with the offer. In other words, a fine-print footnote in an advertisement is not acceptable disclosure.[7]

Advertising as a Contract   One of the many gray areas of advertising is the degree to which an ad constitutes a binding, contractual agreement with consumers. For the most part, the courts and the FTC have ruled that it is unreasonable to expect an advertisement or commercial to contain all the details of a formal contract. The commission expects that such a contract will be part of the final sales negotiation, whereas advertising is normally the first step in the process of selling a product. To this end, the courts have been lenient on pricing errors in ads where no deception is intended.

However, under certain circumstances advertisements have been regarded as constituting binding offers. For example, when there is some language or commitment, no error in the ad, and the defendant has some control over potential liability, a court may find an obligation to provide a good or service at an advertised price. Because the issue is somewhat ill-defined, cautious advertisers would be well advised to treat every advertisement as if it were potentially a contract.

Fact versus Puffery   "Puffery consists of exaggerated opinions, usually at the highest degree of exaggeration, which means superlatives, such as 'the best' or 'superior.' You puff your product. . . . It can be the best tasting, best looking, best lasting . . . or just plain the best."[8] The use and boundaries of **puffery** are extremely controversial. Some critics categorize any statement that is not literally true as deceptive. However, the legal definition of puffery is that it is "an exaggeration or overstatement expressed in broad, vague, and commendatory language, and is *distinguishable* from misdescriptions or false representations of specific characteristics of a product and, as such, is not actionable." Advertisers must be wary of pushing the boundaries of puffery too far. It is easy to cross the line between humorous or creative messages and misleading claims.

Testimonials   At one time, testimonial advertising, especially celebrity endorsements, were viewed very liberally by regulators. It really didn't matter whether celebrities actually used the product they endorsed. However, in recent years, the FTC has taken the position that consumers can reasonably expect celebrities to be satisfied users of the products they endorse. To put teeth into this opinion, the courts have consistently held that endorsers who willfully engage in deception can be held liable along with the ad-

Puffery
Advertiser's opinion of a product that is considered a legitimate expression of biased opinion.

---

[7]Arthur Winston, "How to Define the Concept "Free" Via the FTC," *DM News,* June 24, 1996, p. 15.

[8]Ivan Preston, *The Tangled Web They Weave* (Madison: University of Wisconsin Press, 1994), p. 103.

vertiser for damages. This ruling gives many would-be endorsers pause before they jump into a commercial.

Lotteries Lotteries are schemes for the distribution of prizes won by chance. In most states, lotteries, except state-operated ones, are illegal if a person has to pay to enter them. Promotional sweepstakes are lotteries, but because they don't require an entry fee, they are not illegal. Both the U.S. Postal Service and the FTC will move against illegal lotteries that either use the mail or are advertised across state lines. In recent years, a number of states have started their own lotteries to augment tax revenues.

THE ROBINSON-PATMAN ACT AND COOPERATIVE ADVERTISING

The FTC, through its antitrust division, has responsibility for enforcing another law affecting marketing and advertising, the Robinson-Patman Act. The Robinson-Patman Act is part of a three-law "package" that evolved over a period of almost 50 years. These laws and their purposes are as follows:

1. *1890 Federal Sherman Antitrust Act.* This act was designed to prevent alliances of firms formed to restrict competition.
2. *1914 Clayton Antitrust Act.* This act amended the Sherman Act. It eliminated preferential price treatment when manufacturers sold merchandise to retailers.
3. *1936 Robinson-Patman Act.* In turn, this law amended the Clayton Act. It prevents manufacturers from providing a "promotional allowance" to one customer unless it is also offered to competitors on a proportionally equal basis. Prior to the **Robinson-Patman Act,** some manufacturers were using a loophole in the Clayton Act. They seemed to be charging all their customers equitable prices, but actually were giving money back to their bigger customers in the form of promotional allowances. For example, large retailers might be given co-op advertising allowances that were unavailable to small retailers, which, in effect, lowered the price of the goods sold to these large retailers. Thus, the promotional allowance was a device for under-the-table rebates.

The regulation of co-op allowances has evolved as the media environment has become more complex and the relationships between retailers and manufacturers have changed. At the time Robinson-Patman was passed, the vast majority of retail advertising dollars were placed in newspapers. Today, with the large number of retail advertising options, the FTC requires that alternative promotions must be offered in co-op programs. For example, a manufacturer may not limit co-op dollars to television, knowing that many retailers do not use television in a particular market. Such an offer is known as an *improperly structured program.*

The FTC also interprets Robinson-Patman as requiring that manufacturers assume the responsibility of developing equitable co-op programs even for retailers with whom they deal indirectly through independent distributors. "This [indirect responsibility] has posed some very real problems for many manufacturers in that they don't always know all the customers a distributor has. Nonetheless, they have had to put forth a legitimate effort at informing all customers. Some manufacturers have used trade advertising . . . and even gone as far as printing the [co-op] program on cartons to insure that it reaches everyone."[9] After almost 60 years, Robinson-Patman is still a strong deterrent to antitrust practices at the retail level.

Robinson-Patman Act
A federal law, enforced by the FTC. Requires a manufacturer to give proportionate discounts and advertising allowances to all competing dealers in a market. Purpose: to protect smaller merchants from unfair competition of larger buyers.

---

[9]Richard Bogash and Tom McGoldrick, *What Every Account Executive Should Know about Co-op Advertising,* a publication of the American Association of Advertising Agencies, 1990, p. 11.

THE FEDERAL FOOD, DRUG, AND COSMETIC ACT

In 1938, Congress passed the Federal Food, Drug, and Cosmetic Act, which established the FDA. The agency was given broad powers over the labeling and branding—as contrasted to the advertising—of foods, drugs, therapeutic devices, and cosmetics. It is due to this law that food and drug manufacturers must put their ingredients on labels.

The jurisdiction of the FDA to control and regulate labeling was enhanced with Congressional passage of the Nutritional Labeling and Education Act of 1990. After passage of this act, the FDA became much more aggressive in the enforcement of regulations dealing with health claims on labels and packaging. For example, if cosmetic or health food products imply that they "cure" some ailment or disorder, the FDA will require extensive substantiation and product testing before these claims are approved.

At the same time, the FDA moved to relax a number of restrictions to make the wording on food labeling more flexible. The agency recognized that within the spirit of the regulations, advertisers needed to use shortened versions of health claims, and it allowed the use of more understandable synonyms for nutrient content.

During most of its history, the FDA rarely became involved in the regulation of advertising. Although there was a cooperative relationship between its activities and those of the FTC, it was understood that the FTC had primary responsibility for advertising oversight. However, the role of the FDA changed dramatically in 1996.

In that year, the FDA, led by David Kessler, then head of the agency, asserted that cigarette and smokeless tobacco were delivery devices for nicotine and, as such, could be classified as drugs. Citing an immediate public health crisis, the FDA, with presidential support, issued broad-based restrictions on tobacco marketing. In a series of decisions, the courts ruled that the FDA had jurisdiction, in a limited manner, over tobacco advertising.

The FDA's aggressive stance against the tobacco industry led to an industry settlement that greatly restricted tobacco advertising and promotion and resulted in multibillion dollar payments by the industry. The originally agreed upon limitations on tobacco promotion largely ban premiums such as caps, jackets, and other merchandise with tobacco company logos; point-of-purchase displays; and outdoor boards, including those in sports arenas. They also significantly decrease or eliminate advertising in print media that might expose underage audiences to tobacco advertising. In April 1998, the tobacco industry announced that they were backing out of the agreement, and the issue remains unresolved. However, of more importance than the effects on one industry is the fact that advertisers have been put on notice that another extremely formidable agency has declared its intention to regulate some aspects of advertising.

OTHER FEDERAL CONTROLS OF ADVERTISING

Bureau of Alcohol, Tobacco, and Firearms

The liquor industry's advertising must conform to the basic regulatory and legal rules of all advertising. However, in addition, the industry is required to adhere to unique requirements administered by the Treasury Department through the Bureau of Alcohol, Tobacco, and Firearms (BATF), generally referred to as the ATF. For an interesting historical reason, the federal laws are under the jurisdiction of the Treasury Department. The first American excise tax was levied on alcoholic beverages under Secretary of the Treasury Alexander Hamilton. Enforcement of labeling, advertising, and other alcohol-related regulations are still under that department. Like the FTC, ATF enforces basic legislation through a number of guidelines and interpretations of the law.

ADVERTISING AND THE FIRST AMENDMENT

Americans have long looked to the First Amendment as a unique protection for free speech. It can be argued that the right of open expression guaranteed by the Constitution has been a primary factor in the development of our society. The value of the First Amendment is that it creates an open "marketplace of ideas" in which differing opinions compete and the strongest ideas win the support of the majority. However, advertisers and commercial speech have historically been denied the full protection of the First Amendment. Whereas noncommercial speech is offered the widest possible protection, advertising is held to a much stricter standard. In addition, the specific limits that can be placed on commercial speech are constantly changing and open to continuing interpretation by the courts.

A major frustration for many advertisers is that they consider that they are fighting for rights that they already possess. These proponents of advertising argue that the original writers of the Constitution made no distinction as to what type of speech would be granted constitutional protection. In the last 50 years, commercial speech has been afforded some First Amendment protection. However, the problem for advertisers is that judicial opinions supporting commercial speech have been uneven and contradictory with a consistent doctrine of commercial speech yet to be enunciated by the courts. In the past decade, the advertising community has been encouraged by some Supreme Court decisions that appear to offer stronger First Amendment protection to commercial speech.

To understand the legal protection afforded commercial speech, it is helpful to trace court opinions and attempts at regulation of commercial speech over the past several years.

The Development of the First Amendment and Advertising

For almost 60 years, the courts have offered a number of concessions to commercial speech protection. However, the move toward a more open interpretation of commercial communication has been anything but smooth. In a number of cases, advertisers thought they had seen a major breakthrough in a particular decision, only to have it withdrawn or weakened in a later one. To examine this issue, we need to take a brief look at the development of the status of advertising and the historical protection of commercial speech by the courts.[10]

1942 The Supreme Court ruled that advertising was not entitled to First Amendment protection. The Court ruled that there were *no* restrictions on government's right to prohibit commercial speech.

1964 The Court decided that an advertisement that expressed an opinion on a *public issue* was protected by the First Amendment, but only because it did not contain commercial speech.

1975 The Court gave advertising its first constitutional protection when it overturned a Virginia law making it a criminal offense to advertise out-of-state abortion clinics in Virginia newspapers. However, the ruling left open the question of protection for purely commercial speech that did not deal with opinion or some controversial public issue.

1976 In what many advertisers regard as the major breakthrough for commercially protected speech, the Court held in the case of *Virginia State Board of Pharmacy* v. *Virginia Citizens Consumer Council* that the state of Virginia could not prohibit the

---

[10]Stephen R. Bergerson, "Supreme Court Strikes a Blow for Commercial Speech," *American Advertising*, Summer 1993, p. 24.

advertising of prescription drug prices. It said, in effect, that society benefits from a free flow of commercial information just as it benefits from a free exchange of political ideas.

1979   Advertisers' optimism that they had finally achieved full constitutional protection was short-lived. In the case of *Friedman* v. *Rogers,* the Court upheld the right of the state of Texas to prevent an optometrist from using an "assumed name, corporate name, trade name or any other than the name under which he is licensed to practice optometry in Texas." In its decision, the Court said that First Amendment protection for commercial speech is not absolute and that regulation of commercial speech can be allowed even when the restrictions would be unconstitutional "in the realm of non-commercial expression."

1980   Until this year, the Courts seemingly ruled on each case involving commercial speech on a purely ad hoc basis. Advertisers were left with little if any guidance or precedent as to how the next case would be settled. However, in 1980 the court articulated a set of general guidelines concerning the limits of constitutional protection that would be afforded commercial speech. These guidelines were set forth in the case of *Central Hudson Gas & Electric* v. *Public Service Commission of New York.*

This case concerned a prohibition by the New York Public Service Commission against utility advertising. The state's rationale was that the ban was compatible with public concerns over energy conservation. In overturning the prohibition, the Court established a four-part test to determine when commercial speech is constitutionally protected and when regulation is permissible. These guidelines, known as the **Central Hudson Four-Part Test,** are

Central Hudson Four-Part Test
Supreme Court test to determine if specific commercial speech is protected under the Constitution.

1. *Is the commercial expression eligible for First Amendment protection?* That is, is it neither deceptive nor promoting an illegal activity? Obviously, no constitutional protection can be provided for commercial speech that fails this test.
2. *Is the government interest asserted in regulating the expression substantial?* This test requires that the stated reason for regulating the advertisement must be of primary interest to the state rather than of a trivial, arbitrary, or capricious nature.
3. *If the first two tests are met,* the Court then considers if *the regulation of advertising imposed advances the cause of the governmental interest asserted.* That is, if we assume that an activity is of legitimate government concern, will the prohibition of commercial speech further the government's goals?
4. *If the first three tests are met,* the Court must finally decide if *the regulation is more extensive than necessary to serve the government's interest.*

In the Central Hudson case, the Court ruled that the case met the first three guidelines, but that a total prohibition of utility advertising was more extensive than necessary. Thus, it failed the fourth part of the test and was ruled unconstitutional. The Central Hudson guidelines remain the foundation on which most commercial speech cases are considered.

1986   Most advertisers thought that Central Hudson had provided significant protection in limiting the rights of states to ban legitimate advertising. However, in the case of *Posadas de Puerto Rico Associates* v. *Tourism Company of Puerto Rico,* the Court seemed to once again strengthen the ability of states to regulate advertising. This case involved a Puerto Rican law banning advertising of gambling casinos to residents of Puerto Rico, even though casino gambling is legal there. In a 5 to 4 decision, the Court ruled that the ban met all four standards of the Central Hudson Test.

1988   Many legal scholars see 1988 as marking a significant change in the Court's attitude toward advertising and, just as important, a change in its interpretation of Central Hudson. *Board of Trustees of the State University of New York* v. *Fox* dealt with a college regulation that restricted "private commercial enterprises" on campus. Students challenged the regulation, arguing that at events such as "Tupperware parties" noncommercial subjects were discussed. Because the regulation had the effect of prohibiting both noncommercial and commercial speech, it was too broad, and therefore did not meet the fourth part of the Central Hudson test.

In upholding the regulation, the Court ruled that regulations must be "narrowly tailored," but not necessarily the "least restrictive" option available. Critics of the decision point out that the term "narrowly tailored" is vague and may eliminate the protections of Central Hudson.

1993 In *City of Cincinnati* v. *Discovery Network,* the Court seemed to offer a clear victory for proponents of First Amendment protection of commercial speech. In a 6 to 3 decision, the Court held that the Cincinnati City Council violated the First Amendment by banning newsracks for free promotional publications but allowing them for traditional newspapers. The Court ruled that because the ban was based solely on the content of the publications in the racks, it did not meet the "narrowly tailored" test. The case was widely seen as a victory for commercial speech.

1995 Alcohol has long represented a product category in which state and federal legislation was extremely strict and rigid. Laws controlling the sale and promotion of alcohol have been extremely restrictive. However, in 1995 the Supreme Court ruled in *Rubin* v. *Coors Brewing* that a federal law prohibiting alcohol content to appear on malt beverage container labels was unconstitutional. Although the case did not address advertising directly, it did open the question of whether some restrictions regarding alcohol were too narrow.

1996 Legal scholars predict that two cases heard in 1996 may provide a significant step in affording more complete constitutional protection to commercial speech. In *44 Liquormart, Inc* v. *Rhode Island,* the Court ruled that a Rhode Island ban on price advertising for alcoholic beverages was unconstitutional. The Court referred to the Central Hudson Case and ruled that the Rhode Island law failed to prove that the ban on price promotions advanced the state's interest in promoting temperance (that is, it failed the third test of Central Hudson). Furthermore, the legislation was more extensive than necessary to accomplish the goals of the state (here, it failed the fourth test of Central Hudson).

Writing for the majority of the Court, Justice John Paul Stevens said, "bans that target truthful, non-misleading commercial messages rarely protect consumers from such harms. Instead, such bans often serve only to obscure an 'underlying governmental policy' that could be implemented without regulating speech."[11] Commenting for the advertising industry, Wally Snyder, president of the American Advertising Federation, noted that "the Supreme Court ruling represented the strongest opinion to date protecting truthful advertising from government censorship."[12]

In a subsequent case in 1996, the Court underscored the Rhode Island decision by returning to the Fourth Circuit U.S. Court of Appeals a case involving a Baltimore ban on billboard advertising of alcoholic beverages. In *Anheuser-Busch, Inc.* v. *Schmoke,* the beermaker challenged the city ordinance on constitutional grounds of denial of the First Amendment right to free speech. However, demonstrating the unpredictability of advertising and the law, the Appeals Court upheld its original verdict, ruling that because alcoholic beverage companies had other avenues for their advertising, the ban was not as broad as the Rhode Island law and therefore was constitutional.

---

[11]"High Court's Hard Line on Ad Bans," *Advertising Age,* May 20, 1996, p. 57.
[12]"Advertising Alcoholic Beverages," *Advertising Topics,* a publication of the Council of Better Business Bureaus, May 1996, p. 2.

Corporate Speech and Advertising

In recent years, we have seen a tremendous growth in corporate advertising espousing some idea or corporate philosophy as contrasted to selling a product or service. Like all other forms of commercial speech, corporate advertising falls into a gray area. Similar to commercial speech, the Court has ruled that corporate advertising is protected under certain circumstances. In *First National Bank of Boston* v. *Bellotti,* the Court overturned a state law that prohibited national banks from using corporate funds to advocate voting against a state constitutional amendment that would allow the legislature to impose a graduated income tax.

Over the years, the Court has delineated several legal principles concerning corporate speech:[13]

1. Spending money to speak does not, in itself, result in the loss of First Amendment rights.
2. Speaking on commercial subjects does not entail loss of First Amendment rights.
3. Speaking for economic interests does not entail loss of First Amendment rights.

We should note that the Court is saying that a commercial aspect to speech does not *necessarily* remove that speech from the rights granted by the First Amendment. However, the converse of this view does not automatically grant these rights to either advertising or corporate speech.

Advertising and the Right of Publicity

A private individual is protected by right of privacy from having his or her likeness used in an advertisement without permission. Laws vary from state to state, but every state has some legislation that addresses the right of privacy of an individual. In many jurisdictions the use of a name or picture of a person without prior consent is a misdemeanor. However, civil liability, potentially involving significant judgments, is a much greater concern to advertisers.

Generally, the courts have ruled that public figures have far less protection than the general public in terms of their right to privacy. However, in recent years the courts have made it clear that this distinction of public versus private persons is related to news, not advertising or other commercial use. Legal precedent makes it clear that public figures are protected from commercial use of their name or likeness by a doctrine of the right of publicity.

In the past, most issues of privacy dealt only with living personalities. However, in recent years some states, notably California, have addressed the issue of deceased celebrities. With the use of new technology, deceased personalities can be integrated into commercials. John Wayne, Humphrey Bogart, and other stars from the past have been used in a number of commercials with the permission of their estates. Likewise, the courts have ruled against a number of advertisers who used impersonators in commercials without permission.

Because state laws vary widely, advertisers will normally be extremely prudent in using a personality's name or likeness. The normal course of action is that an advertiser or agency will never use a model, personality, or likeness without legal permission.

ADVERTISING OF PROFESSIONAL SERVICES

One of the most controversial areas of commercial speech involves advertising by professionals, especially attorneys and health-care providers. Until the mid-1970s virtually all forms of professional advertising were banned, often by trade associations such as

---

[13]Candiss Baksa Vibbert, "Freedom of Speech and Corporations: Supreme Court Strategies for the Extension of the First Amendment," *Communications,* vol. 12, 1990, p. 26.

state medical groups or bar associations. Critics of restrictions on legal advertising claim that one of the overriding concerns was to limit competition for established professionals and, in fact, constituted restraint of trade.

Research indicates that among doctors, those most likely to use advertising are those who have been in practice the least time, those who have smaller practices, and females.[14] In addition, the medical specialty most likely to advertise is plastic surgery. From a marketing perspective, the data indicate that, as with any business, health-care professions use advertising to gain market entry, increase market share, and gain patients (customers) in the most competitive market segments. For example, a majority of plastic surgery is elective.

Due in part to criticism that the bans constituted barriers to market entry, the absolute prohibition of attorney (and by extension most other professional) advertising was lifted in 1977 in the case of *Bates* v. *State Bar of Arizona.* The Supreme Court ruled that state laws forbidding advertising by attorneys was unconstitutional on First Amendment grounds. The fourth test of the Central Hudson case, not an issue in 1977, seems to reinforce the Bates decision. That is, most legal scholars think that the total prohibition of a class of advertising will generally not meet the fourth test because any such total ban will be considered broader than necessary. Bar associations and other professional groups still have regulatory powers over the accuracy and scope of their members' advertising, but they cannot prohibit their members from advertising.

In 1988, the Supreme Court extended the right of attorneys to advertise professional services. A Kentucky lawyer, Richard Shapero, was cited for violating a Kentucky law prohibiting targeted mail solicitations to people who were in need of legal services because of some special circumstance. In this case, Shapero had mailed an advertisement to homeowners facing foreclosures.

The Court ruled that although personal contact by an attorney could be prohibited, a letter posed no threat of undue influence to consumers who are under threat of legal action. In addition, the Court reasoned that a written proposal to a potential client could be more carefully regulated than a personal contact. The Shapero case had the immediate effect of lifting the ban on targeted letters in the 25 states that had previously prohibited them.

In 1993, the Court made an interesting distinction among various types of professional solicitations. The Florida board of accountancy banned personal solicitations for clients, either in person or by telephone. In *Edenfield* v. *Fane* the Court overturned the ban and, in doing so, made a clear distinction between lawyers and accountants. The Court held that, unlike lawyers, CPAs are not trained in the art of persuasion, are dealing with clients who probably have had a previous professional relationship with an accountant, and the client of a CPA is probably not under the stress that a lawyer's potential client might be. The Court found that it was unlikely that the potential clients of the CPA would be subject to "uninformed acquiescence," which might be the case for a lawyer's client.

These recent court rulings are related in many respects to the issue of advertising and First Amendment protection. Although the Court has eliminated sweeping bans against professional advertising, it has not given such promotion the status of other forms of speech. Furthermore, *Edenfield* v. *Fane* demonstrates again the difficulty of anticipating how the Court may rule in any particular case involving commercial expression.

A 1995 case demonstrated that the courts consider a number of circumstances in ruling on professional solicitations and they are not prepared to issue blanket denial of any state regulations. For example, the Court upheld a Florida Bar Association rule

---

[14]Boris Becker and Dennis O. Kaldenberg, "To Advertise or Not to Advertise? in Advertising Expenditures by Professionals," *Proceedings of the American Academy of Advertising, 1995,* ed. Charles S. Madden (Waco, Tex.: Baylor University, American Academy of Advertising, 1995).

prohibiting lawyers from sending direct mail to accident victims. The Court took the position that an accident victim is in a more vulnerable state of mind than a person facing foreclosure—the circumstance of those solicited by Shapero. Again, referring to the Central Hudson guideline, "The state had a substantial interest in protecting the integrity of its legal system."[15]

STATE AND LOCAL LAWS RELATING TO ADVERTISING

During the early years of the twentieth century, the advertising industry realized that something had to be done to prevent the charlatans and frauds that were preying on an unsuspecting public. Led by major media and leading advertisers and their agencies, national advertising moved successfully against the worst offenders. Unfortunately, little was done to stop local, fly-by-night operators.

Printers' Ink, a leading trade magazine, proposed state and local advertising regulations in 1911 to address the growing problem of false advertising. Basically, it sought to regulate "untrue, deceptive, or misleading advertising." Although *Printers' Ink* has long ago ceased publication, its model statute, in its original or modified form, has influenced local advertising in virtually every state (see Exhibit 25.2).

Until recently, the roles of state and federal jurisdictions in regulating advertising were clearly separated. At the national level, the FTC had primary responsibility for regulating advertising in interstate commerce, whereas individual states were involved in local consumer-protection legislation. State regulations usually dealt with retailers and smaller companies operating locally.

Currently, advertisers see a shift toward more local control. National advertisers argue that the cost of developing different campaigns, advertising appeals, and creative executions for each state would make national advertising impossible. Outdoor advertising, in particular, is concerned about local ordinances limiting the size of outdoor signs. Without consistent sizes, outdoor would cease to exist as a national medium. Both media and advertisers seek national regulations across states administered by an appropriate federal agency.

The National Association of Attorneys General (NAAG) has been at the forefront of local advertising regulation. The organization and the attorneys general in several

exhibit

25.2

Printers' Ink was a leader in the fight for truthful advertising.

THE *PRINTERS' INK* MODEL STATUTE FOR STATE LEGISLATION AGAINST FRAUDULENT ADVERTISING

Any person, firm, corporation, or association, who with intent to sell or in any wise dispose of merchandise, securities, service, or anything offered by such person, firm, corporation, or association, directly or indirectly, to the public for sale or distribution, or with intent to increase the consumption thereof, or to induce the public in any manner to enter into any obligation relating thereto, or to acquire title thereto, or an interest therein, makes, publishes, disseminates, circulates, or places before the public, or causes, directly or indirectly, to be made, published, disseminated, circulated, or placed before the public, in this state, in a newspaper or other publication, or in the form of a book, notice, handbill, poster, bill, circular, pamphlet, or letter, or in any other way, an advertisement of any sort regarding merchandise, securities, service, or anything so offered to the public, which advertisement contains assertions, representation, or statement of fact which is untrue, deceptive, or misleading shall be guilty of a misdemeanor.

---

[15]Rosalind C. Truitt, "The Cases for Commercial Speech," *Presstime,* March 1996, p. 31.

states have moved aggressively against a number of advertisers, even those that operate nationally. In recent years, questions have been raised about the extent that states will be allowed to go beyond or contradict national legislation. Although the question is far from settled, it appears that in most areas the federal courts are asserting the superiority of federal law when a question arises.

COMPARATIVE ADVERTISING

An often-used sales technique is to compare one brand with its competitors. There are a number of approaches to comparative advertising, each with its own risks and benefits. J. Sterling Getchell is generally credited with the first major use of comparative advertising. The Getchell Agency introduced the Chrysler car in the 1930s by inviting customers to "Try All Three." Ever since, it is rare that some automobile campaign does not feature comparative selling.

Despite the fact that advertisers have used comparative advertising for a number of years, many in the industry are not enthralled with it. For many years, conventional wisdom was that if you mentioned a competitor's name, you were giving away free advertising. However, when properly executed, comparative advertising is still an effective sales tool in competitive markets.

Comparative advertising became a major advertising theme after the FTC pushed for more comparative advertising in 1972. The Commission urged ABC and CBS to allow commercials that named competitors. Until then, only NBC had permitted such messages, whereas ABC and CBS would allow nothing but "brand X" comparisons. Given this regulatory stamp of approval, the instances of comparative advertising increased dramatically over the next few years.

Despite its popularity, comparative advertising still has its detractors. Critics of the technique think that a product should stand on its own benefits rather than on comparisons with other brands. Those who advocate comparative focuses argue that consumers make purchases on the basis of brand comparisons every day, and that such advertising is simply demonstrating marketplace reality. The controversial nature of comparative selling is demonstrated by the fact that a major category of competitor-initiated complaints directed to regulatory bodies involve comparative advertising.

Public Perception of Comparative Advertising

The detractors of comparative advertising point to two major problems of public perception with the use of the technique. First, as mentioned earlier, there is the problem of giving competitors recognition. By naming other brands by name, there is a risk that consumers will remember the advertising, but not necessarily the details of the comparison. If not carefully executed, an advertiser may simply build brand awareness for a competitor. Even in instances where consumers are not confused, they may regard the comparison as giving credibility to the competition. A consumer may legitimately ask, "Why would a company name another company's brand if they didn't see it as a threat?"

A second reason to be wary of comparative advertising is the danger that the public may perceive it as unfair. Unless it is carefully executed, comparative advertising can create a boomerang effect and gain support for the brand being disparaged. This boomerang effect is a potential danger if the comparison seems to be dealing with irrelevant or trivial points of contrast.

Legal Risks of Comparative Advertising

Beyond problems of public perception of comparative advertising, advertisers and their agencies may have legal problems if their advertising is ruled deceptive. The primary legal recourse open to companies involves several provisions of the Lanham Act. As amended in 1988, the Lanham Act allows an advertiser to sue if a competitor "misrepresents the nature, characteristics, qualities, or geographic origin of his or her or another person's goods, services, or commercial activities." Under the act, companies may sue to stop ads in which false claims are made either about the advertiser's products or about the plaintiff's. Naming competitors, either directly or by inference, is not without risk to both the agency and client. If a competitor can show damages (such as a decrease in market share) resulting from a dishonest or unfair comparison, it may collect multi-million dollar settlements under the act.

Courts have ruled that a competitor may sue if claims made in an ad were false or if the overall perception of a literally true ad was designed to create consumer confusion. For example, if your advertising claims that your product meets all tests for quality (which is true), but leaves the impression that competing products do not, then the advertising may be actionable.

By the same token the courts have ruled that if an advertisement refers to some specific and measurable standard of product performance (i.e., a motor oil leads to longer engine life) and leads consumers to believe that competing products do not, when they do, this is not acceptable puffery but must be substantiated in tests with other motor oils. Generally, the courts have taken a dim view of claims that advertising misstatements were acceptable because the "public knows that the message is simply advertising exaggeration."

Furthermore, advertisers are not protected from action under the Lanham Act just because a competitor is not named. In some cases, the courts have held that a company may have damaged a number of other firms by claiming some product superiority that is not unique to that brand even when no competing brand is named. In other cases, successful suits have been brought by companies claiming that any intelligent consumer would have been expected to know which unnamed brand was the topic of unfair comparison.

In summary, there are three primary standards against which unfair competition is measured:

1. *Confusion.* The most common form of unfair competition that the law recognizes as wrongful is the marketing of products or services in a way that may confuse buyers about identity, source, or sponsorship.
2. *Disparagement.* The disparagement of competitors is recognized by courts as an actionable wrong, but carries with it the onerous requirement that resulting lost business be proved. Although many advertising professionals think that any form of competitive disparagement is unprofessional, the Lanham Act is concerned only with disparaging statements that are factually untrue and injure a competitor's business in a demonstrable fashion.
3. *Misrepresentation.* Misrepresentation of the qualities of the advertised product or service, whether derogatory of competitive offerings or not, may be the basis for a lawsuit by competitors who can show that the misrepresentation has diverted or may divert business from them through deception of the public.[16]

Advertising clearance process
The internal process of clearing ads for publication and broadcast, conducted primarily by ad agencies and clients.

THE ADVERTISING CLEARANCE PROCESS

To this point, we have emphasized the legal and regulatory environment in which contemporary advertising must function. However, it would be a mistake to assume that most companies and agencies produce honest advertising only to avoid legal penalties or that there is little interest in truthful advertising beyond minimum legal standards.

---

[16] *What Every Account Executive Should Know about the Law and Advertising,* a publication of the American Association of Advertising Agencies, 1990, p. 20.

In fact, the vast majority of advertisers not only want to produce truthful advertising, but they are also equally interested in making sure that their peers do likewise. When consumers are misled by untruthful advertising, all advertisers pay a price.

The Media

The public has long expected the media to act on their behalf by prohibiting fraudulent and misleading advertising. For example, citing the importance of network advertising previewing, the chairman of the FTC said, "For years, the media, particularly the national media, have screened advertising before it is run as an important part of the network's efforts to control deceptive advertising. However, with the proliferation of media sources, the impact of the networks' screening has been eroded."[17]

As a reaction to this reduction in media vigilance of deceptive advertising, the FTC took several steps to encourage stronger media vigilance to misleading advertising, including

- bringing cases to the media's attention that illustrate how some advertising with clearly implausible claims is slipping through the cracks
- identifying, in some cases, the names of the media that ran the advertising
- discussing with a variety of media what they can do to improve their advertising screening programs.

As an *Advertising Age* editorial commented, "Any signs that media companies are willing to make tough decisions about accepting the ads that come their way should be good news for the hard-pressed FTC. . . . The benefit is public confidence, as well as the confidence—and dollars—of legitimate advertisers."[18]

It is important to remember that the standards, scope, and diligence exercised by the various media will vary a great deal.

> With the sole exception of broadcast advertising by a bona fide candidate for public office, no U.S. newspaper, magazine, radio, or television station or network must accept any advertising material it does not wish to publish or broadcast. Each vehicle imposes its own standards that advertisers must meet for the material to be acceptable: some vehicles accept virtually anything, many others limit their concerns to areas of potential legal liabilities. But each manager or owner is free to direct these standards based on his or her own assessments of the laws, the audience values and what is ethically right and proper.[19]

Just because a medium has wide latitude to accept or reject advertising does not mean it is without liability for the advertising it carries. Recent cases have placed the media in potential joint liability for the advertising they accept. If a statement in an advertisement or commercial is false or defamatory, the media can be sued along with the advertiser. From a practical standpoint, unless a medium knowingly accepts deceptive or libelous advertising, the legal liability is not that great. However, a more practical concern of the media is the loss of goodwill with their audiences if a deceptive ad is cleared for publication or broadcast. No responsible agency or medium would argue that deceptive advertising should be created or run.

---

[17]"National Advertising and Government Affairs," *Advertising Topics,* a publication of the Council of Better Business Bureaus, March 1996, p. 2.

[18]"Just Say No," *Advertising Age,* April 1, 1996, p. 28.

[19]Herbert J. Rotfeld, "Media Standards for Acceptable Advertising," in *Proceedings of the American Academy of Advertising, 1995,* ed. Charles S. Madden (Waco, Tex.: Baylor University, American Academy of Advertising, 1995), p. 238.

SELF-REGULATION BY INDUSTRYWIDE GROUPS

In addition to the efforts of individual advertising agencies and media to ensure that advertising is truthful, there are similar efforts by industrywide groups to review advertising on both a national and local basis. These efforts offer the public, competitors, and other interested parties a voluntary forum for negotiation without resorting to a formal legal or regulatory body for the adjudication of disagreements.

Industry self-regulation serves two important purposes beyond ensuring more informative and truthful advertising. First, it partially overcomes the relatively poor public perception of advertising by showing that there is a concerted attempt to foster responsible advertising. Second, strong self-regulation may ward off even stricter government control.

One of the ways in which the industry promotes better advertising is through various guidelines and codes of practice promoted by advertising agencies groups and media associations as well as trade and professional associations. One of the leading advertising groups promoting truthful and ethical advertising is the American Advertising Federation (AAF). A primary aim of the AAF is to foster truthful and fair advertising through local advertising clubs.

Despite the best efforts of federal regulatory agencies, the media, and individual advertisers, the opinion persists among a large group of consumers that advertising is either basically deceptive or does not provide sufficient information. Given the investment that companies are making in advertising, this perception is a major problem and one that needs to be addressed with a united front by all honest businesses. As we see in this section, the advertising industry is making substantial investments in moving against deceptive advertising.

Better Business Bureaus

One of the best-known, aggressive, and successful organizations in the fight for honest and truthful advertising is the national network of Better Business Bureaus (BBBs) coordinated by the Council of Better Business Bureaus, Inc. (CBBB). The forerunner of the modern BBBs dates to 1905, when various local advertising clubs formed a national association that today is known as the National Advertising Federation. In 1911, this association launched a campaign for truth in advertising coordinated by local vigilance committees. In 1916 these local committees adopted the name Better Business Bureaus and they became autonomous in 1926. Today, there are approximately 180 local bureaus in the United States and Canada.

Although the BBBs have no legal authority, they are a major influence on truth and accuracy in advertising. The BBBs are able to exert both the force of public opinion and peer pressure to set up voluntary efforts to address examples of misleading or deceptive advertising.

The NAD/NARB Self-Regulation Program

In 1971, in response to the many different consumer groups complaining about deceptive advertising, the major advertising organizations—the American Advertising Federation, the American Association of Advertising Agencies, and the Association of National Advertisers—joined with the CBBB to form the National Advertising Review Council (NARC). NARC's primary purpose was to "develop a structure which would effectively apply the persuasive capacities of peers to seek the voluntary elimination of national advertising which professionals would consider deceptive." Its objective was to sustain high standards of truth and accuracy in national advertising.

NARC established a number of units that actively review and present findings concerning the suitability of various advertisements (see Exhibit 25.3). The primary investigative unit is the active investigative unit, the **National Advertising Division** (NAD)

National Advertising Division (NAD)
The policy-making arm of the National Advertising Review Board.

exhibit

25.3

The NARC review
process is established
to ensure fairness.

Courtesy: National Advertising
Division.

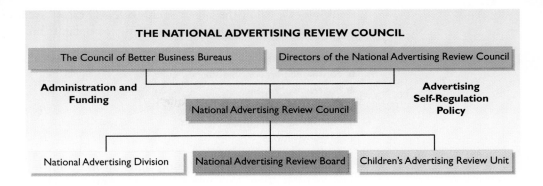

THE NATIONAL ADVERTISING REVIEW COUNCIL

The Council of Better Business Bureaus

Directors of the National Advertising Review Council

Administration and Funding

Advertising Self-Regulation Policy

National Advertising Review Council

National Advertising Division

National Advertising Review Board

Children's Advertising Review Unit

of the Council of Better Business Bureaus. The National Advertising Review Board (NARB) provides an advertiser with a jury of peers if it chooses to appeal an NAD decision. The NAD is staffed by full-time lawyers who respond to complaints from competitors and consumers and referrals from local BBBs. They also monitor national advertising. In 1974, the Children's Advertising Review Unit (CARU) was established to review the special advertising concerns of advertising directed at children. We discuss CARU in detail later in this section.

In recent years, many within the advertising industry have encouraged the NARC to further expand the scope of self-regulation. Specifically, it has been asked to consider guidelines for self-regulation of alcohol and tobacco advertising as well as advertising to teenagers. What form such self-regulation would take remains to be seen. However, the fact that a number of advertising executives look to the NARC emphasizes the important place that the organization occupies in the advertising industry.

After a complaint is received, the NAD determines the issues, collects and evaluates data, and makes an initial decision on whether the claims are substantiated. If the NAD finds that substantiation is satisfactory, it announces that fact. If the NAD finds that the substantiation is not adequate, it recommends that the advertiser modify or discontinue the offending claims. If the advertiser does not agree, it may appeal to the NARB. NAD decisions are released to the press and also are published in its monthly publication, *NAD Case Reports*.

The NARB comprises 70 members—40 representing advertisers, 20 representing advertising agencies, and 10 from the public sector. Five members in the same proportion are assigned to hear an appeal. If the panel thinks the NAD's decision is justified, but the advertiser still refuses to correct the deceptive element, the NARB may refer the advertising to the appropriate government agency.

Advertising complaints fall into a relatively small number of product categories (see Exhibit 25.4). Underscoring the competitive nature of advertising claims, competitor

exhibit

25.4

Complaints by Product Category for 1996

Courtesy: National Advertising
Division.

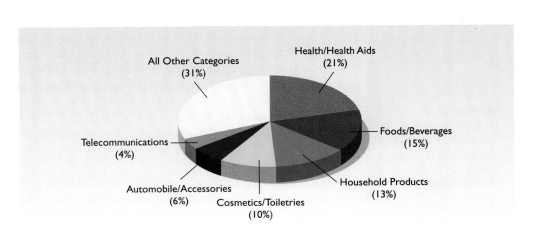

All Other Categories
(31%)

Health/Health Aids
(21%)

Foods/Beverages
(15%)

Household Products
(13%)

Cosmetics/Toiletries
(10%)

Automobile/Accessories
(6%)

Telecommunications
(4%)

challenges are by far the largest source of NAD cases. According to the NAD, there are six primary areas that provide most of the complaints brought to the organization:

- product testing
- consumer perception studies
- taste/sensory claims
- pricing
- testimonial/anecdotal evidences
- demonstrations

In a number of cases, the complaints involve comparative advertising. For example, a challenge is often made when product testing or product demonstrations involve other brands' alleged deficiencies in some area.

A summary of recent cases investigated by the NAD shows that only a small minority of cases are referred to some governmental agency. However, the number of cases turned over to the government has risen in recent years, a fact that is troublesome to some in the industry. Noting the increase in referred cases, one observer pointed out, "It might indicate some lack of respect for this organization [NAD] in the 1990s among members of the trade. However, the willingness of NAD/NARB to turn recalcitrant advertisers over to the government suggests a certain level of spine within the organization."[20]

In our examination of the NAD/NARB process, we should understand that it cannot

- order an advertiser to stop an ad
- impose a fine
- bar anyone from advertising
- boycott an advertiser or a product.

What it can do is bring to bear the judgment of an advertiser's peers that the company has produced advertising that is not truthful and is harmful to the industry, to the public, and to the offender. This judgment has great moral weight. It is reinforced by the knowledge that, if the results of an appeal to the NARB are not accepted, the whole matter will be referred to the appropriate government agency and at the same time will be released to the public. This step, unique in business self-regulation machinery, avoids any problem of violating antitrust laws, presents the entire matter to public view, and still leaves the advertiser subject to an FTC ruling on the advertising.

The Children's Advertising Review Unit of the NAD

It is estimated that the 33 million children under the age of 12 influence almost $180 billion in purchases and personally buy goods and services worth more than $10 billion. Given the level of purchasing power held by these children, it is no surprise that they are increasingly targeted by advertising messages developed especially for this market.

The classification of children as a discrete market has raised questions among a number of groups about the wisdom and ethics of advertising directed to this unsophisticated audience. Advertising claims that would be perfectly suitable for adults might be unacceptable for children, especially preteens. Because of this concern with children's advertising, the NAD, in cooperation with the advertising community founded the **Children's Advertising Review Unit** (CARU) in 1974.

Children's Advertising Review Unit (CARU)
The CARU functions much as the NAD to review complaints about advertising to children.

[20]Eric J. Zanot, "The Evolution of Advertising Self Regulation at the National Advertising Division and National Advertising Review Board," in *Proceedings of the American Academy of Advertising, 1995,* ed. Charles S. Madden (Waco, Tex.: Baylor University, American Academy of Advertising, 1995), p. 237.

The CARU mission is similar to that of the NAD except it considers the special circumstances of the younger audience reached by child-oriented advertising. "CARU works with the industry to ensure that advertising directed to kids is truthful, and above all, fair. By promoting adherence to self-regulatory guidelines, CARU seeks to maintain a balance between regulating the messages children receive from advertising, and promoting the dissemination of important information to children through advertising."[21]

In 1997, CARU issued its most recent *Self-Regulatory Guidelines for Children's Advertising.* The primary change between it and earlier versions is that it added a section on interactive and electronic media advertising to children. However, television remains by far the primary medium for reaching children, and it is the most important focus for CARU. Children's television is not only a major concern of CARU, but recent legislative and regulatory actions indicate that advertisers will not be allowed the latitude in advertising to children that they have with adults. Beginning October 1, 1991, the FCC mandated limits on children's program advertising to $10\frac{1}{2}$ minutes an hour on weekdays and 12 minutes on weekends. The action of the commission underscores the fact that children's television, both programming and advertising, is considered a separate category from that directed to general audiences.

Questions concerning children's advertising have few easy answers. Many critics think that no advertising should be directed to children. To these people only a total ban on such messages will be satisfactory. However, given the economic support of the media through advertising, it is unlikely that any such ban will ever be permitted. It is imperative that all parties involved (media, advertisers, parents, and special interest groups) work to ensure that children's advertising is appropriate for the audience to which it is intended. With public opinion running against them, advertisers must be extremely cautious about the content of all advertising messages directed to children.

SUMMARY

This chapter only begins to highlight some of the legal, self-regulatory, and public opinion constraints on advertising. The subject is far too complex to cover completely in a book, much less in a single chapter. However, from our discussion you should be able to gain an overview of the pitfalls that advertisers, even the most scrupulous, face. Advertisers are constantly at risk of running afoul of the many rules directed at advertising. In addition to formal laws and regulations directed toward advertising, companies also find that public opinion must be carefully considered.

Among major advertisers, there is little disagreement that advertising should be fair, truthful, and follow both the letter and the spirit of the law. In fact, honest advertisers are among the most aggressive groups in weeding out the charlatans who make it difficult for all advertisers by eroding public confidence. For the foreseeable future, it is clear that advertisers will have to contend with the numerous, sometimes conflicting, and constantly changing advertising regulations.

REVIEW

1. How did the concept of consumer protection change in the early years of the twentieth century?
2. Discuss the contemporary role of the Federal Trade Commission in regulating advertising. How does its function differ from the early years of the FTC?
3. Discuss the FTC's view of deceptive advertising and how the commission makes its judgments in this regard.

---

[21] *Advertising, Nutrition and Kids,* a publication of the Council of Better Business Bureaus, Inc.

4. What is the difference between a cease and desist order and a consent decree?
5. Compare and contrast fact, puffery, and deception.
6. In recent years, how has the role of the FDA changed in terms of advertising regulation?
7. Discuss the importance of the Central Hudson Four-Part Test in regulating advertising.
8. Discuss the role of the Lanham Act and comparative advertising.
9. Describe the roles of the NAD and NARC in the process of advertising self-regulation.

TAKE IT TO THE NET

We invite you to visit the Russell/Lane page on the Prentice Hall Web site at
PHLIP **http://www.prenhall.com/phbusiness** for the bimonthly
Russell/Lane update and for this chapter's World Wide Web exercise.

26

ECONOMIC AND SOCIAL EFFECTS OF ADVERTISING

CHAPTER OBJECTIVES

THROUGHOUT THE TEXT WE HAVE DISCUSSED THE MANY ROLES OF ADVERTISING AND ITS PLACE IN THE SOCIAL, CULTURAL, AND ECONOMIC ENVIRONMENT IN WHICH IT OPERATES. ADVERTISING HAS BOTH ECONOMIC AND SOCIAL CONSEQUENCES— SOME INTENDED AND SOME COINCIDENTAL. AFTER READING THIS CHAPTER YOU WILL UNDERSTAND

- the societal and economic roles of advertising
- good citizenship also is good business
- the role of advertising as a mirror of society
- advertising and cause-related marketing
- the inadvertent social role of advertising
- the Advertising Council as a social institution
- growing sensitivity of advertisers.

Research shows that Americans have a mixed reaction to advertising. A 1996 study conducted by the Cumming Center for Advertising Studies at the University of Illinois showed that overall 75 percent of consumers either liked or were neutral toward advertising. Slightly more than half of consumers indicated they look at most ads and almost 70 percent used advertising to make purchase decisions. On the negative side, consumers thought they were often misled by advertising, and almost half of consumers thought advertising insulted their intelligence. Generally, women are somewhat more likely to be positive toward advertising, as are younger adults and those with incomes below $35,000.

The primary aim of this text is to examine the techniques and business practices associated with the advertising industry. As pointed out in chapter 25, advertising, with its pervasive nature as a marketing communication tool, has a special responsibility to adhere to high ethical and honest business practices. By the same token, advertising continues to be a driving force in preserving and expanding the economy.

exhibit

26.1

Source: Study conducted by
DDB Needham Worldwide,
Chicago for Porter/Novelli,
cited in "Numbers for the
'90s," *Advertising Age,*
October 23, 1995, p. 3.

**Top Five Influences in Consumer
Buying Decisions**

Quality of product	95%
How a company handles complaints	85
How a company handles crisis when at fault	73
Government challenge about product safety	60
Accusations of illegal/unethical trading practices	59

As we see in this chapter, honest advertising and ethical business practices are not contradictory. In fact, sophisticated consumers increasingly reward with increased patronage those companies that engage in socially responsible behavior and forthright advertising. As Exhibit 26.1 indicates, consumers cite, as a major factor in purchasing a product, a company's behavior in terms of crisis management and history of product safety or issues of trade practices. It is unfortunate that because of advertising's high profile, it is often the target of unfair criticism that blames advertising for actions that are beyond its control.

Advertising, like most business functions, is simply a tool. It may be used for the best or the worst motives, and it is practiced by both those of high moral standards and charlatans. Effective advertising provides efficient and profitable communication for the firms that utilize it and reaches prospects with information that will aid consumers in making beneficial purchase decisions. However, to the extent that advertising has an important social component, advertisers have a special responsibility to the public.

One only has to examine the number of advertisements and commercials that advocate some special position to understand the important role that advertising plays beyond promoting sales. Companies use advertising to sway public opinion concerning controversial issues or to underscore their corporate citizenship. Charitable organizations are increasing their use of advertising, and we are seeing a growing number of advertising campaigns that join firms and charities in efforts to solve some social problem.

Advertising practitioners are sensitive to the dual role of balancing economic efficiency and social responsibility, and they work hard to fulfill both of these obligations. In the remainder of this chapter, we discuss how advertising endeavors to achieve both economic efficiency for sellers and social benefits for buyers.

The first step is to understand that the social and economic elements of advertising are not mutually exclusive. For example, businesses are part of society and benefit from attention to environmental issues, better education, and other relevant societal issues that are brought to the public's attention through advertising. By the same token, to the extent that advertising can contribute to ending economic recession and expanding the economy, the public will gain by a higher standard of living.

In this chapter, we examine two major roles of advertising. First, we discuss advertising's contribution to economic efficiency. That is, does advertising provide market information in a manner that could not be more effectively accomplished by other means? The second area of discussion is advertising's role in the social process as we examine the broad, noneconomic effects it has on society.

THE ECONOMIC ROLE OF ADVERTISING

One of the most controversial areas of advertising is the specific role it plays as part of the economy. To some, it is a vital and extremely efficient means of introducing new products and maintaining brand awareness. Numerous studies have indicated that a strong positive relationship exists between high brand awareness and market dominance.

For example, a number of studies have attempted to estimate the value of an established brand name. Although exact figures are difficult to estimate, most observers judge that brand names such as Coca-Cola, Sony, IBM, and Ford are worth billions of dollars not only in this country but worldwide. The causal relationship between brand awareness and sales is often difficult to track, but clearly advertising plays a major role in moving consumers from brand awareness to product preference to ultimate purchase.

To more precisely chart the financial return from advertising, the American Association of Advertising Agencies has launched a multiyear study to determine how much specific advertisers should be spending and where advertising budgets should be allocated. Dubbed MAX, short for Maximum Advertising Expenditure for Financial Performance, the study seeks to quantify the value of advertising.[1]

The MAX research seeks to solve one of the most perplexing problems facing advertising researchers—determining its precise economic contributions on both a macro- and microeconomic basis. It is extremely difficult to separate the value of advertising in the intricate matrix of consumer behavior. For example, why did you buy the shoes, belt, or T-shirt you are wearing today? To what degree did advertising, promotion, public relations, or personal selling enter into the steps that led to your purchase? For that matter, to what degree did marketing communication functions play a role in buying your last car or other high-ticket item?

Most of us would be hard pressed to identify a specific role that advertising played in any particular product purchase decision. Obviously, if we are unsure about the role of advertising in our own purchase behavior, it is even more difficult for companies to determine advertising's role in their overall sales. Despite the difficulty of determining the exact relationship between advertising and purchase behavior, overwhelming evidence exists that favorable product perception is important for sales success.

At least one study has traced the role of advertising at various stages of the marketing communication process. It found that those companies who not only used advertising, but were committed to its role in the marketing process tended to be more successful than other companies in the same product category. Among the findings were

I. Advertising is not a frill activity, but rather it is a necessary and important part of a business's marketing operations. Without advertising, the company misses a vital link in the process that starts with brand awareness and leads through a series of complex steps to increased sales, greater market share, and improved profitability (see Exhibits 26.2 and 26.3, p. 678).

(see Exhibits 26.2 and 26.3, p. 678).

e x h i b i t

26.2

How Advertising Affects the Perception of Quality Among Competing Products

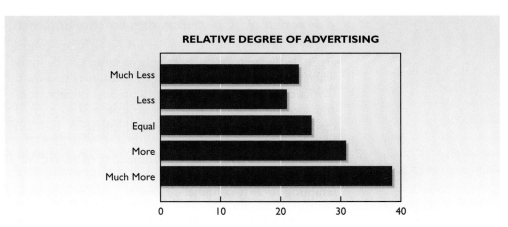

Here is another indication of the power of advertising to influence the perception of quality. The graph shows the quality ratings of competing products. The difference in the perception of quality is almost directly related to the level of advertising. The businesses that advertise the least have the lowest quality rating, whereas those that advertise the most have the highest quality rating.

[1] Laura Petrecca, "4A's Will Study Financial Return on Ad Spending," *Advertising Age,* April 7, 1997, p. 3.

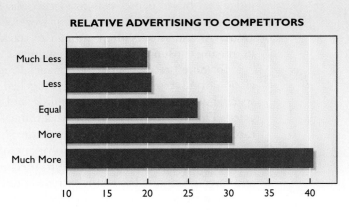

RELATIVE ADVERTISING TO COMPETITORS

We've just seen that market share is important. Now let's look at how advertising affects market share. This graph shows that businesses with low advertising activity generally have low market share and that market share increases as the level of advertising increases.

2. There is direct relationship between the amount of advertising a business does and its success in the marketplace. It isn't enough that a product is advertised. Of even greater importance is the amount of advertising. The businesses that advertise more than their competitors get better results. Token programs get token results.

3. Advertising enhances the way a product is perceived in the marketplace. To a large extent, the reputation that a product has for quality and for value are actually determined by the way and the degree to which the product is advertised, and quality is the single most important factor in making a sale.

4. Finally, the study showed that although advertising is an art, it is also a science. We know a great deal about the way it works, how it interacts with other aspects of the marketing operations of a business and the way it helps to build profitability.[2]

Simply put, effective advertising enhances the consumer's image of a product, which in turn increases the likelihood that the product will be purchased. Advertising's contribution to product enhancement will often lead to a significantly higher profit margin compared to products with lower customer esteem.

Advertising's Contributions to the Economy

There is anything but agreement on advertising's contributions to the economy. Some argue that advertising encourages consumers to be brand loyal and less price sensitive, whereas others claim that informed consumers become more price and value conscious. Critics claim that new entrants to a product category must overcome high-profile brands and spend proportionately more to gain market entry. Proponents of advertising contend that advertising's low cost and efficiency facilitates market entry of competing brands.

One of the basic economic functions of advertising is resource allocation. That is, as advertising seeks to build demand for one product or service, it is simultaneously attempting to shift customers, resources, and money away from other commodities.

> Any planet, any continent, any society, any city, home or individual, faces the problems of resource allocation. There is only so much time, so many raw materials, so much money. Decisions must be made and resources allocated appropriately. Advertising has been both criticized and championed as playing a significant role in this allocation process, either through rein-

[2] *How Advertising Drives Profitability,* Cahners Advertising Research Report, No. 2000.9, p. 6.

exhibit

26.3

How Advertising Affects Market Share

forcing existing values or, far more ominously, through altering the old and shaping the new."[3]

Advertising plays a number of roles for the overall economy, the financial well-being of specific firms, and, of course, for the individual consumer. Let us examine some of the major areas in which advertising makes a contribution to the economic well-being of firms.

Advertising as a Marketing Communications Tool   Advertising is only one of a number of marketing communications options available to marketing and promotion executives. For them to choose advertising as a part of the marketing communications mix, it must be an efficient part of the promotion process. Among the available promotional techniques, advertising is almost always the least expensive means of reaching a target audience. However, cost, although a major consideration in any choice, cannot be the only consideration in weighing whether advertising will be used and, if so, in what proportion relative to other means of marketing communication.

Marketers know that advertising, no matter how effective, will not ensure sales. Rather, it works within an extremely complex matrix of variables that ultimately determine purchase behavior. Product price, availability, service, and perceived quality all play roles in making advertising effective, and, in turn, they are affected by advertising. Different companies have unique problems associated with each of these factors, and advertising may play a greater or lesser role in addressing a particular issue. As discussed in chapter 2, when advertising is unsuccessful, it is very likely that it was used to solve a problem for which it was inappropriate.

Advertising is flexible enough to speak to a number of marketing issues. It is the role of marketing and advertising departments to make sure that goals and objectives for the advertising program are clearly and realistically spelled out. For example, companies sometimes make the mistake of assuming that aggressive brand promotion is the only legitimate goal of advertising. However, advertisers must remember that advertising operates on two levels. Exhibit 26.4 shows how advertising moves the consumer

[3]Clifford G. Christians, Kim B. Rotzoll, and Mark Fackler, *Media Ethics,* 3rd ed. (New York: Longman, 1991), p. 278.

exhibit

26.4

Effective advertising creates both brand and generic demand.

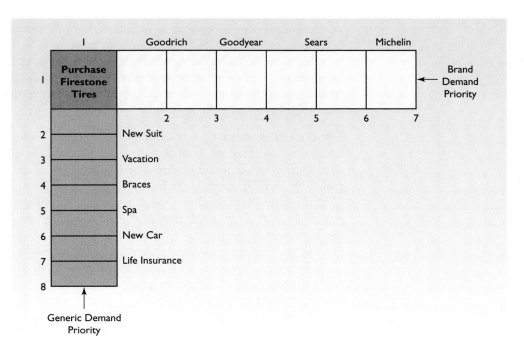

exhibit

26.5

At higher levels of brand awareness, a 1.0 percentage point increase in awareness converts to a larger increase in preference share.

Courtesy: Cahners Publishing Co., Cahners Advertising Research Report. No. 104.2.

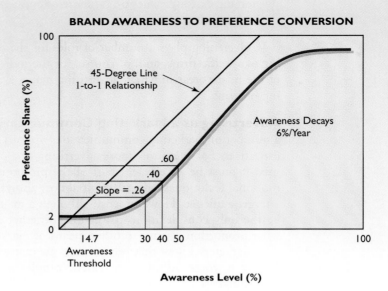

BRAND AWARENESS TO PREFERENCE CONVERSION

Generic demand
The demand demonstrated for a product class rather than a specific brand.

vertically (**generic demand**) and horizontally (brand demand). A firm with very high market share might well engage in a strategy of generic demand to increase product category spending. On the other hand, companies holding small shares of market will usually have to engage in determined brand advertising to maintain a competitive balance with larger firms.

As companies realize the importance of positive brand awareness to overall sales, more companies will increase the use of advertising. As discussed in chapter 14, firms realize the potential long-term damage to brand equity brought about by an overreliance on sales promotion, price cutting, and other "quick fixes." They also have found that strong brands can simultaneously work on both generic and brand demand levels, whereas most sales promotion is directed solely at brand demand.

Although sales promotion may be an ideal tool for maintaining and even increasing short-term sales, brand awareness and preference is normally a product of consistent and sustained advertising. As Exhibit 26.5 shows, there is a direct relationship between brand awareness and preference. A number of advertising executives predict a return to the importance of brand awareness and advertising as a means of achieving meaningful product differentiation.

Effects of Advertising on Corporate Profits

Advertising, like any form of marketing communication, is used only if firms conclude that it is making a significant contribution to corporate profits. The fact that advertisers are currently investing more than $150 billion is ample testimony to the value that companies place in advertising. A recent survey indicated that there has been a significant movement for companies to implement integrated marketing strategies. However, among these companies, advertising continues to be the most used technique for marketing communication, with 90 percent of companies indicating they use some form of advertising.[4]

Obviously, businesses would not spend more than $150 billion on advertising if it did not contribute to corporate profitability. However, the prudent advertiser knows that advertising is only a contributing factor to overall profits. Profitability depends on a good, reliable product that is perceived in that way; a reputation that is built by strong equity-oriented advertising; and a market rank that is built by advertising and enhanced

---

[4]John F. Yarbrough, "Putting the Pieces Together," *Sales & Marketing Management,* September 1996, p. 71.

by promotion. It is clear that profits are based on brand reputation, and reputation is determined in large measure by a combination of marketing communication techniques.

All but the most unreasonable critics of advertising acknowledge its place in modern selling. Increasingly, criticism of advertising is rightfully directed toward specific advertising rather than arguments concerning whether it has a place in the economic makeup. The value of advertising is best demonstrated by the dependency placed on advertising as a primary sales tool by so many firms.

Contributions of Advertising to the Overall Welfare of the Economy   Economic productivity must be viewed from the perspective of both the individual firm and the total economy. Clearly, single corporations must advertise to prevent brand share erosion even in the absence of overall sales increases in a particular industry. However, most economists are interested in advertising from a macroeconomic perspective. That is, does advertising contribute to the overall economic system as opposed to a specific firm? Does it efficiently introduce new products? Does it contribute to economic expansion and create new jobs?

Currently American advertising accounts for approximately 2.5 percent of the national gross national product (GNP).[5] Even though this figure is less than the comparable investment 50 years ago, it still represents a tremendous expenditure. Economists view advertising's contribution to the economy as falling into one of four categories:

1. *Counterproductive.* Advertising is counterproductive when it raises prices or in some other way creates dissatisfaction with products that still have utility, thus causing unnecessary consumption.
2. *Unproductive.* Unproductive advertising does not increase generic demand, but causes no harm. Advertising designed to create brand switching among present consumers would fall into this category.
3. *Somewhat productive.* Advertising in this category creates an increase in overall demand, but at a level lower than some other technique or at an unreasonably high cost.
4. *Most productive.* The most productive advertising produces the greatest economic well-being at the lowest cost. The implication of this category is that both buyer and seller are benefited equally.

It is difficult to deal in generalities when evaluating the economic value of advertising. Advertising's contribution to product sales is dependent on a host of circumstances unique to each product. The utility of advertising in a market for a relatively new product such as home computers is much different than for the beer or cigarette industries, which are characterized by flat sales and brand switching among present users. However, it is obvious that overall advertising does contribute to profitability or companies would not use it.

THE SOCIAL ROLE OF ADVERTISING

Whereas the economic contributions of advertising are typically the major concern of both companies and consumers, in recent years its social implications are coming under increasing scrutiny. There is little disagreement, even among advertising's harshest critics, that it serves a role in informing customers of new products, locations, prices, and distribution outlets. These are the economic functions of the institution of advertising. However, the social and cultural roles of advertising are much less clear, and are a topic of growing discussion in a number of quarters.

---

[5]GNP is the total market value of all goods and services produced in a country or other economic unit in one year.

Regardless of whether one is a supporter or critic of advertising, there is general agreement that advertising functions in two distinctive ways as a social force. First is the so-called **inadvertent social role of advertising.** Many observers point out that advertising is both a mirror and a shaper of public opinions, mores, and social standards. They claim that by the sheer weight of exposure, advertising sets a social agenda as to what is expected, what is fashionable, and what is tasteful for a significant number of people. This influence is particularly true for the young, the undereducated, and the impressionable. More important than the influence advertising may have on individuals, some people claim that the manner in which advertising portrays various segments of society—the elderly, minority groups, the young, for example—determines in some measure how these people will be treated by others.

The second social role of advertising is *overt.* When advertising champions the fight against child abuse, forest fires, or drugs, or when it promotes adult literacy or higher levels of voter turnout, it is being used in a social activist role. Exhibit 26.6 is an ex-

A little bit of this can go the wrong way.

Be smart, don't start.

Depression. Addiction. Disease. Heavy drinking, whether over a long period or in a single night, can cause serious health risks. If you have a drinking problem, help is available. Talk to a school counselor, a friend, a teacher, or a parent.
    Call the National Council on Alcoholism and Drug Dependence (NCADD) 1-800-475-HOPE.

Join Together:
A NATIONAL RESOURCE FOR COMMUNITIES FIGHTING SUBSTANCE ABUSE

ample of advertising used for an overtly social purpose. In the last decade, we have seen a significant growth in this type of advertising as more and more special interest groups have seen the value and efficiency of advertising in getting their messages before the public.

TYPES OF ADVERTISING CRITICISM

A review of contemporary advertising criticism points out the important role that social issues play in the debate concerning the value and propriety of modern advertising. Most criticism falls into one or more of the following four categories:

- the content of advertising
- the product being advertised
- excessive advertising exposure
- advertising's unwanted influences on society

The Content of Advertising

Currently, the majority of advertising criticism concerns the content of specific ads and commercials. Critics point to a spectrum of alleged abuses from the use of sexual themes, exaggerated product claims, debasement of language by using misspelled words and incorrect grammar, creation of stereotypes, and manipulation of children with unrealistic claims and promises. As discussed in chapter 25, the advertising industry is attempting to address the problem of children's advertising through the Children's Advertising Review Unit of the NARB, and the federal government has moved to mandate more educational programming for young viewers.

A major criticism of advertising content is its portrayal of some group in an unflattering or unrealistic manner. Advertisers have increasingly come to realize that a realistic portrayal of society in their advertising is morally correct and, just as important, it is good business. White-only and male-dominant depictions in a company's advertising often overlook the economic contributions that minorities and women are making to a firm's profits. Obviously, it is not good business to ignore a portion of your target market.

Clearly, advertising created only a few years ago would be considered insensitive or condescending today. During the 1990s, advertisers became more understanding of the roles of women and minorities. Despite advertising's heightened sensibility to women's issues and characterizations, studies show that many women remain unsatisfied with their depiction in advertising. One study found that women tend to judge advertising on two levels. Women are concerned about product and brand information. However, women are much more likely than men to judge an ad by the extent to which the advertiser seems to understand women and accurately reflect their lifestyle. An accurate portrayal will greatly increase the likelihood that the sales message will be accepted.

One female advertising executive stated that women "have gone through three decades of incredible change, and in the course of this their image of themselves has changed. Because these images have been in a state of flux, they look to advertising with heightened sensitivity."[6]

Fundamentally, the findings of this study show that women want to be realistically and fairly depicted in advertising. But it also underlines the changing nature of what is acceptable not only in advertising, but also in society in general. Astute advertisers understand that cultural issues and ethics change constantly and they make every effort to implement steps to stay abreast of these shifts.

---

[6]Jane L. Levere, "A Saatchi & Saatchi Survey Indicates Women Are Still Unhappy with How They Are Depicted in Ads," *The New York Times,* July 12, 1996, p. C5.

exhibit

26.7

The United States will demonstrate an even more diversified population in the next century.

Courtesy: Advertising Age.
Source: "Diversity," *Advertising Age*, February 17, 1997, p. S2.

A True Melting Pot

Projected U.S. population by race and percentage of total population by race (population in millions)

Year	White	Black	Hispanic	Asian	American Indian
1996	194.4 (73.3%)	32.0 (12.1%)	27.8 (10.5%)	9.1 (3.4%)	2.0 (0.7%)
2000	197.1 (71.8)	33.6 (12.2)	31.4 (11.4)	10.6 (3.9)	2.1 (0.7)
2010	202.4 (68.0)	37.5 (12.6)	41.1 (13.8)	14.4 (4.8)	2.3 (0.8)
2020	207.4 (64.3)	41.5 (12.9)	52.7 (16.3)	18.6 (5.7)	2.6 (0.8)
2030	210.0 (60.5)	45.4 (13.1)	65.6 (18.9)	23.0 (6.6)	2.9 (0.8)
2040	209.6 (56.7)	49.4 (13.3)	80.2 (21.7)	27.6 (7.5)	3.2 (0.9)
2050	207.9 (52.8)	53.6 (13.6)	96.5 (24.5)	32.4 (8.2)	3.5 (0.9)

Source: U.S. Census Bureau.

As discussed in chapter 24, minority groups have often felt slighted by mainstream advertisers. In the past, many minority groups claimed, with justification, that they were often ignored in most advertising, and when included, their roles were not equal to those of white models. This situation is slowly changing for two reasons. First, there is growing sensitivity to the issue by companies and advertising agencies. Second, faced with the changing demographics of American society, an advertiser would have to be extremely shortsighted to ignore minorities as potential target markets (see Exhibit 26.7). As minorities increase their proportion of the population, their inclusion in advertising and marketing decisions will become part of the planning of any company or institution. For example, the Marine Corps has done extensive promotion to encourage minorities to consider a career in its officer corps (see Exhibit 26.8).

The portrayal of minorities is changing for the better. A survey conducted by Minority Markets Alert showed that among the 13 most popular magazines, minorities comprised approximately 25 percent of all people shown in advertising. Automobile advertising was by far the most diverse in its depiction of various minority groups, followed by beauty aids and bank and insurance advertising.[7]

Another group that has historically been underrepresented in advertising is the elderly (over 65 years old). Only recently have advertisers moved from their concentration on the 18- to 49-year-old market segments to address the growing and very lucrative elderly market for many products. Currently, approximately 20 percent of the U.S. population is over the age of 65; by the year 2015, this figure will be more than 33 percent.

More important than the size of the market is its economic strength. Overall, the age 65 and older population of the next decade and beyond will have higher discretionary incomes, be more likely to own their own homes, control more assets, and be in better health than any elderly group before them.

In recent years, there has been some improvement in marketing techniques and promotion to reach the elderly. Senior citizen discounts at restaurants, more clothing designed for mature buyers, and portrayal of elderly people in advertising have all increased in recent years (see Exhibit 26.9, p. 686). It also is of interest to advertisers that studies show the elderly are extremely receptive to advertising. A significant majority indicate that they find commercials helpful in making product decisions and that advertising is a useful source of product information. Research also indicates that the elderly are willing to switch brands and experiment with new products.[8]

---

[7]"Mass Circulation Magazine Ads Reflect Population, Lifestyle Shifts," *The Pointcast Network*, April 1, 1997.

[8]Thomas E. Robinson, Rick Duet, Tommy V. Smith, "The Elderly in Advertising: A Content Analysis of Prime-Time Television Commercials," in *Proceedings for the American Academy of Advertising, 1995*, ed. Charles S. Madden (Waco, Tex.: Baylor University, American Academy of Advertising, 1995), pp. 1–2.

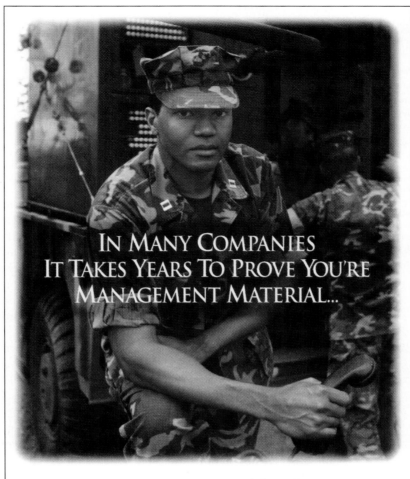

exhibit

26.8

Advertisers are reaching out to minorities.

Courtesy: J. Walter Thompson.

Another content-oriented criticism focuses on factors such as exaggeration and excessive puffery in advertising. Many critics charge that advertising is likely to provide misinformation that barely skirts basic legal requirements with negative appeals or, in some cases, outright falsehoods. As discussed in chapter 25, there is no business enterprise that undergoes more governmental and regulatory scrutiny than advertising. Apart from these formal constraints, advertisers know that it is bad business to mislead consumers. False or misleading advertising may influence a consumer to make an initial purchase, but rarely will an unsatisfied customer return. Putting aside the question of whether advertising is inherently less ethical than other business practices, we should at least give its practitioners credit for common sense.

exhibit

26.9

Some advertising categories are reaching out to elderly consumers.

Courtesy: American Academy of Advertising.
Source: Thomas E. Robinson, Rick Duet, Tommy V. Smith, "The Elderly in Advertising: A Content Analysis of Prime-Time Television Commercials," *Proceedings of the American Academy of Advertising*, 1995, Charles S. Madden, ed., p. 9.

Ads with Elderly by Product

Category	Number	Percent
Fast food restaurants	30	25
Food products	26	21
Retail advertising	17	14
Entertainment	14	12
Phone service	11	9
Auto dealers and related items	11	9
Other	12	10

The Product Being Advertised

Advertising and other forms of promotion are often the focal point of public policy arguments over the use of certain products. As discussed in chapter 25, federal government agencies have been involved in one degree or another in limiting the promotion of tobacco. Many observers, especially those within the tobacco industry, see the latest round of restrictions as another indicator that attempts will be made to expand the broadcast ban on tobacco advertising to a total prohibition on any form of tobacco promotion. Whether one agrees with these new restrictions or doesn't, it is obvious to most observers that advertising is being used as a means of promoting a more fundamental attack on the product itself.

Alcoholic beverage advertising is another category with many restrictions. Primarily through public pressure, industry prohibitions, and various media advertising policies, liquor advertising (as contrasted with beer and wine) has been largely banned from broadcast outlets. However, in 1996 the Distilled Spirits Council of the U.S. voted to drop its 60-year voluntary ban on broadcast advertising.

Criticism from the FCC and public interest groups such as Mothers Against Drunk Driving was quick to surface. The major television networks, network-owned stations, and other leading stations and cable outlets announced that they would not accept liquor advertising. However, with potential billings of several million dollars, it will be interesting to see which outlets begin to accept this advertising.[9]

However, a current battle being waged in the advertising community is how far government should go in eliminating advertising for legal products. Led by the American Advertising Federation, a major industry trade organization, a number of advertising organizations have joined to fight what they see as an infringement on the First Amendment rights of advertisers.

Their position is basically one of fighting against a policy that, if left unchecked, could lead to further censorship of truthful advertising. As they point out, "imagine having the right to sell a product, but no venue to communicate its availability. This is essentially the plight facing tobacco advertisers, their agencies, and the media today."[10]

Despite the philosophical questions involved in the ban of otherwise legal products such as tobacco, some in the industry still have serious reservations about the wisdom of defending such advertising. Rance Crain, editor-in-chief of *Advertising Age,* has long held the view that advertising trade associations should withdraw their support of cigarette companies' right to advertise.[11]

In part, the battle over cigarette advertising is being waged over whether advertising that is "offensive" should be limited in some way. Based on personal preferences, there are those who would limit personal hygiene items and other sensitive products.

---

[9]Ira Teinowitz and Michael Wilke, "Cable Net to Accept Spirits Ads," *Advertising Age,* November 11, 1996, p. 1.

[10]"Free Speech in America," *American Advertising,* Fall 1996, p. 12.

[11]Rance Crain, "Crain Gets Little Support for Anti-Cig Stance," *Advertising Age,* May 20, 1996, p. 32.

Even with the current AIDS epidemic, many television outlets prohibit the advertising of condoms, a position that many in the public-health community think is indefensible. Advertisers argue that public criticism of this type of advertising is unrealistic and tries to prevent society from gaining useful information about legitimate products.

Excessive Advertising Exposure

Another commonly heard criticism of advertising is that there is simply too much of it and it is often intrusive. Most of the criticism in this category is directed toward television because print ads are easily ignored by simply turning the page. As indicated in chapter 13, both direct mail and telemarketing are fighting a constant battle against those who wish to place legal restrictions against the use of these promotional techniques.

With the rapid introduction of new media technology, the fragmentation and interactive nature of future media vehicles will no doubt curtail a major portion of this criticism. Obviously, when interactive media allow consumers to seek out programming, advertising, or infomercials, there is little likelihood that advertising will be regarded as intrusive.

Advertising's Unwanted Influences on Society

Charges that advertising *makes* people buy things they don't want or need, lowers morals, and generally exploits the most susceptible segments of society are among the most common charges in this category of criticism. Most research shows that mass communication, especially overtly persuasive communication such as advertising, has a very difficult time making even small changes in behavioral intentions or attitudes (see Exhibit 26.10, p. 688). The idea that we see an ad and are compelled against our wishes to purchase a product is preposterous. Like any mass communication, there are going to be times when some reader or listener behaves in a manner totally contrary to the intent of the sender of the message.

It is interesting that the overwhelming criticism in this fourth category is designed to protect other people, not the critics themselves. That is, most critics take the view that although a particular advertising element will not fool them, they are duty bound to help those less intelligent who may be misled by some advertising ploy.

Advertising criticism is not a new phenomenon. A brief review of the history of advertising and its critics demonstrates that both have changed markedly over the last 130 years. Clearly, advertisers are asked to meet different standards than those of earlier years. The public view of advertising has changed over three major periods:

1. *The Era of Exaggerated Claims, 1865–1900.* During this period, most people accepted advertising as "buyer beware" communication; virtually any claim for a product was allowed. Some advertising claims, especially for patent medicine, were so outlandish that one wonders how anyone could have believed them.
2. *The Era of Public Awareness, 1900–1965.* By the turn of the twentieth century, legislation such as the Pure Food and Drug Act of 1906 demonstrated a recognition that the public was demanding a truthful portrayal of products and services. Many responsible advertisers feared for the very existence of the industry, as deceptive advertising became more and more prevalent during the closing years of the nineteenth century.
3. *The Era of Social Responsibility, 1965–present.* During the past 30 years or so, advertisers have come to realize that literal truth is not sufficient to meet the demands of many consumers. Advertisers know that they must meet a standard of **social responsibility** in addition to providing truthful advertising. The consumer movement of the 1960s, concerns with environmental safety, and a heightened awareness of social issues are reflected in modern advertising.

Social responsibility
The demand that advertising be aware of its responsibility to the public, i.e., it should do more than sell goods and services.

exhibit

26.10

Advertising cannot force a consumer to purchase a product.

Courtesy: American Association of Advertising Agencies.

Chapter 25 discussed the formal regulatory constraints on advertising. In addition to these organizations, there are a number of consumer and public policy groups that seek to constrain deceptive or misleading advertising through publicity. Among the most well known is the Center for Science in the Public Interest, which presents the annual Harlan Page Hubbard Memorial Award to those advertisers who have failed to serve the public interest. The award "honors" the nineteenth-century ad man who touted such products as Lydia Pinkham's Vegetable Compound, which promised cures for ailments from cancer to impotence. Meanwhile, organizations such as Mothers Against Drunk Driving publicize advertising they think appeals to underage drinkers and attempt to rouse public opinion against these companies.

These and dozens of other consumer advocacy groups have no official or legal authority. They do have the ability to muster negative public opinion and provide national scrutiny for dubious product advertising. No reputable company wants to receive this type of notoriety, and most will respond to these consumer organizations in a positive manner if they think the criticism is justified. For example, the American Lung Association names those television shows that the organization thinks glamorizes smoking and gives them a Phlemmy award.[12]

---

[12]"And Now, the Phlemmys," *The Atlanta Journal,* September 9, 1996, p. C7.

Advertisers and their agencies are particularly sensitive to public criticism of their product advertising or the programs and publications in which their messages appear. Some advertisers' policies are general in terms of media that cannot be used by their agencies and gain little attention except from the sales reps who are denied commissions. For example, General Motors will not allow advertising to be placed in racier men's magazines.

Occasionally, the debate over media content becomes a major issue among advertisers and the media. For example, during the past several years, a number of major advertisers have become alarmed at the content of some high-profile talk shows. In 1995, some leading daytime television advertisers, led by Procter & Gamble, reviewed individual episodes of talk shows and made decisions about whether their advertising will appear. In four cases, the general content of the programs was deemed so inappropriate that they were permanently taken off the P&G schedule.

The senior advertising vice president for P&G outlined the company's policy toward the shows:

> There are a lot of people concerned about talk TV, and rightly so. The content of daytime talk shows has become increasingly sensational, outrageous and—in many cases—outright offensive. . . . We encouraged the producers and distributors of all the talk shows we sponsor to raise their standards and improve content. We outlined what we consider to be appropriate content and we made it clear only those shows that live up to these standards will receive our advertising support.[13]

Although the major offenders among the talk shows will get few public defenders, there are those in the industry that have qualms about advertisers "working" with program producers concerning program content. In the same manner that a number of antismoking advertisers condemn the First Amendment ramifications of a ban on tobacco advertising, many have a problem with overt advertiser interference with program content, no matter how pure the motive. On the other hand, few question the right of an advertiser to exclude any program or publication from its advertising schedule, regardless of the reason.

INADVERTENT SOCIAL IMPLICATIONS OF ADVERTISING

Advertising operates on two levels: (1) the messages concerning products and services that convey information about brands and companies, and (2) largely unintended messages that, nevertheless, impart knowledge about society or some segment of the public and the way people behave. Advertising messages often function simultaneously on both levels. In providing product information, advertising can sometimes communicate messages about how society regards certain people or ideas.

In recent years, more research and attention have been devoted to these "secondary consequences" of advertising. Advertisers realize that people do react in positive or negative ways to the environment in which a product is shown and advertisers must be sensitive to these unintended cues. "Advertising thus does not work by creating values and attitudes out of nothing but by drawing upon and rechanneling concerns that the target audience (and the culture) already shares. . . . Advertising absorbs and fuses a variety of symbolic practices and discourses, it appropriates and distills from an unbounded range of cultural references."[14]

---

[13]R. L. Wehling, "A Positive Impact on TV Show Content," *Advertising Age,* November 20, 1995, p. 8.

[14]Sut Jhally, "Image-Based Culture," in Gail Dines and Jean M. Humez, *Gender, Race and Class in Media* (Thousand Oaks, Calif.: Sage, 1995), p. 80.

The implied, indirect communication conveyed by advertising is a topic advertisers will have to address increasingly in the future. Consumers are sophisticated in the way they view the media and advertising and are demanding more realistic and fair presentations of society. Addressing the problem is the first step in moving to solve a very complex issue. As one female advertising executive has pointed out, "It isn't completely clear why women are so displeased with most advertising. It's not that we're blatantly offending people. We're just not connecting with people. The texture of life is somehow missing."[15] It is this connection that advertisers are increasingly seeking with their audiences.

In addressing the controversy over advertising's societal role, some argue that Americans are too ready to jump on any misstep, no matter how innocuous, in the name of political correctness. Others view a healthy trend in which advertisers are becoming more sensitive to the potential harm done by inaccurate or unfair portrayals of people. The recent debate has brought to the forefront the matter of advertising's social role. This awareness of a dimension long ignored by most advertisers is perhaps the most positive element to come out of these recent controversies.

OVERT USE OF ADVERTISING FOR SOCIAL CAUSES

There is no question that advertising communicates a number of messages about society and culture apart from its intended messages. However, advertising also is used by a growing number of organizations, companies, and even individuals to convey messages about some social cause (see Exhibit 26.11). In this section, we discuss a number of reasons that we should expect to see an increasing amount of advertising of this nature.

The same characteristics that make advertising such a beneficial tool in marketing products and services are also used to move people to adopt various social causes and support for nonprofit organizations. For some time, advertising has been used to promote these organizations. However, the number of diverse organizations using advertising to promote social causes has dramatically increased in the last decade.

exhibit

26.11

Advertising is often used to communicate information concerning social causes.

Courtesy: Key-Ads.

---

[15]Sally Goll Beatty, "Women Dislike Their Reflection in Ads," *The Wall Street Journal,* December 12, 1995, p. 32.

In recent years, a number of civic, religious, and public-policy organizations have increasingly used advertising to disseminate their messages to the widest possible audiences. Advertising's low cost and the broad audiences it reaches will continue to make it a major means of circulating social messages. The most organized effort of social advocacy is the Advertising Council, mentioned briefly in chapter 1.

The Advertising Council[16]

From its inception in 1943 as the War Advertising Council to the present, the **Advertising Council** has contributed billions of dollars of advertising space and creative talent to solving a number of social ills. The War Advertising Council campaigns had the strident tone of war, but the success of the council during World War II showed that advertising could be a powerful tool for unifying the public and for effecting change in attitudes toward less clearly defined goals in peacetime.

In the years since turning to social and public awareness campaigns, the council has taken on a number of campaigns with great success. Campaigns such as those against drunk driving (see Exhibit 26.12) are credited with saving thousands of lives. The council also has addressed other issues, such as racial tolerance, equal rights, job and fair housing opportunities, and education (see Exhibit 26.13, p. 692).

The Advertising Council continues to select, define, and address some of the nation's most pressing problems. Familiar figures have become synonymous with its work:

Advertising Council

A non-profit network of agencies, media, and advertisers dedicated to promoting social programs through advertising.

e x h i b i t

26.12

Courtesy: Ad Council.

The "crashing glasses" for the U.S. Department of Transportation's drunk driving prevention campaign has become a symbol of the necessity of intervention in a problem that was once addressed with silence. The ads, created by Wells Rich Greene, encourage friends to take responsibility, even suggesting specific action— "Take the keys, call a cab, take a stand"—and have helped to decrease the incidence of fatalities on the nation's highways.

---

[16]Information in this section was provided by the Advertising Council.

Smokey Bear (see Exhibit 26.14), the Crying Indian who wept for a land once beautiful, and McGruff, the spokesdog for crime prevention, among others. The Advertising Council pioneered advertising to bring issues such as child abuse, understanding mental illness, and AIDS to the public's attention and in advocating actions people can take to prevent inhumanity, discrimination, and the spread of disease. Council programs will result in the donation of more than $1.5 billion worth of time and space this year.

Due in large measure to the efforts of the Advertising Council, the use of advertising to communicate social issues has been taken up by a number of other companies and organizations. Social institutions such as churches have turned to advertising, and advocacy advertising has also been used by corporations that think that media presentations of certain issues have been unfair and want to get their side of a story before the public. Although some people have reservations about the role of advertising in promoting certain social institutions and issues, proponents argue that there is no more effective or inexpensive means of getting their messages to the public.

In the future, we can expect this type of advertising to increase as people accept the legitimate role of the mass media as a forum for public debate as well as product information. The availability of media with narrowly defined audiences, such as cable and

Only You Can Prevent Forest Fires.
USDA Forest Service & Your State Forester

Perhaps the Advertising Council's most enduring—and endearing campaign, Smokey Bear was conceived by the agency Foote, Cone & Belding in the 1940s to help prevent what had become an increasing danger created by heavy use of national parks. In 1941, nearly 30 million acres per year were being destroyed by forest fires and nine in ten, the Forest Service reported, were caused by careless humans. Described 10 years later as "America's number one firefighter," Smokey was credited with a decrease of 10,000 forest fires per year, despite a 50 percent increase in park use.

exhibit

26.14

Courtesy: Ad Council.

specialized publications, will lead to even more, and perhaps franker, discussions of a host of nonproduct and sometimes controversial topics.

As the use of advocacy advertising has grown in recent years, so has the reluctance of some media to carry these ads. Media outlets sometimes think that carrying a particularly controversial ad will imply an endorsement of the position. In other cases, media have been reluctant to carry ads that attack major advertisers, fearing a loss of advertising revenue. The 4As has urged media to protect the flow of ideas by allowing wide latitude in accepting advocacy advertising. As it rightfully points out, advertising clearly identifies the sponsor of a message and therefore diminishes the chances of confusion between the views of the sponsor and those of the media carrying the message.

Advertising and Cause-Related Marketing

The days of companies supporting a number of charities with a check and photo opportunity are over. Today, large corporations are engaging in *strategic philanthropy,* by which they market their good works in the same way as they market their products. In a search for more value to their charitable work, companies seek to "own" a cause. They are making long-term commitments to one cause and building a type of benevolent brand equity and enhanced identification with their customers.[17]

In the previous section, we discussed the use of advertising primarily by nonprofit organizations to promote some socially beneficial action. Closely related to this type of advertising is **cause-related marketing,** or *social marketing.* Cause-related marketing

Cause-related marketing
Marketing strategies that attempt to link a company to some social or charitable cause.

---

[17]"Give and Thou Shall Receive," *Sales & Marketing Management,* March 1997, p. 75.

links companies with some worthy cause or organization. In so doing, it allows the company to build positive consumer attitudes toward the firm as a progressive company.

American Express is credited with introducing cause-related marketing in 1983 when it promised to make a donation to the renovation of the Statue of Liberty each time someone used its credit card. Cause-related marketing allows companies and their customers to help some organization, while the company increases sales and builds customer goodwill. Like most promotional techniques, cause-related marketing has grown because it has been shown to work.

There is always a danger that consumers will regard companies engaging in cause-related marketing as being more self-serving than socially motivated. However, a recent survey showed that only 21 percent of respondents questioned the motivation of companies engaged in cause-related marketing, down from 58 percent in 1993. More often, firms are becoming involved with charitable causes in which both the company and their employees have an inherent interest. This involvement, beyond money, no doubt is responsible for the public's more favorable attitude toward commercial related causes.[18]

Good deeds are noticed by consumers, and buyers support products sold by companies that are regarded as outstanding corporate citizens. However, a number of studies have indicated that consumers will not pay extra for products promoted through cause-related marketing. The technique is an excellent value added, but rarely should be the core strategy for selling a product. The most effective cause-related promotions are those that are based on long-term commitments to a single cause. Consumers grow to associate certain companies with specific concerns, such as the Ronald McDonald House, where families of hospitalized children can stay free of charge.

Environment Marketing

As mentioned earlier, environmental issues have become a major topic of cause-related marketing. A number of companies have developed relationships with a diverse group of environmentally aware organizations to promote good citizenship and save our natural resources. Environmental marketing takes many forms, but there are three primary areas in which environmental concerns are most prevalent:

1. *Social marketing linked to environmental organizations and causes.* Eddie Bauer and other companies have engaged in traditional cause-related marketing campaigns to promote environmental issues.
2. *Environmental citizenship campaigns.* As you get your bills from various companies, notice how many have some statement that they are prepared on recycled paper. Heavy users of paper, such as magazine and Yellow Pages publishers, also promote conservation through the responsible use of recycled paper and by encouraging consumers to dispose of these materials in a responsible manner. BellSouth encouraged customers to recycle telephone books by offering minor league baseball fans free or reduced admission to games if they brought their Yellow Pages directories to the gate.[19]
3. *The promotion of products as being safe for the environment.* As companies became aware of the importance many consumers attached to environmental issues, they jumped on the so-called "green bandwagon." That is, companies rushed to convince consumers that their products would have a beneficial effect on the environment and that their production methods were socially responsible.

Research showed that companies had every reason to worry about consumers and the environmental issue. A 1989 Gallup Poll indicated that 79 percent of consumers considered themselves environmentalists and many said they would pay more for prod-

---

[18] "'Strategic Philanthropy' a Hot Trend," *Chicago Tribune*, April 27, 1997, p. 1.
[19] "BellSouth Hits Home Run with Recycling Program," *Link,* July/August, 1996, p. 7.

ucts that protected the environment.[20] However, as more and more companies engaged in green marketing, many with dubious credentials, consumers became wary of many of these claims.

As is inevitably the case, when a sizable number of marketers act in an irresponsible fashion, it invites the introduction of government regulation. The environmental marketing situation was no exception. Since July 1995, the FTC has reviewed the situation, including demanding that advertisers follow strict guidelines in the use of common environmental terms in advertising such as "compostable" and "recyclable." The FTC stated that environmental claims must follow four principles:[21]

1. Qualifications and disclosures should be sufficiently clear and prominent to prevent deception.
2. Claims should make clear whether they apply to the product, the package, or a component of either.
3. Environmental claims should not be overstated or exaggerated.
4. Comparative claims should be sufficiently clear so that consumers know either the comparison is to a previous version of the advertiser's own product, or to a competitor's product.

For many product categories, marketers are finding that an environmental initiative is not an option. Consumers are increasingly demanding that some evidence of environmental responsibility be evident in a company's products or they will buy alternatives. However, paying lip service to the problem is not enough; words must be backed up with actions.

ADVERTISING AND INFLUENCE ON EDITORIAL CONSIDERATIONS

One of the long-standing criticisms of advertising is that it influences the media's treatment of the news. Critics point out that with 50 to 75 percent of the print media's revenue, and virtually 100 percent of broadcast support, coming from advertisers, it is unreasonable to expect that publishers and station owners will not be influenced by those who pay the bills.

The criticism of advertising influence of news is a serious charge because one of the positive features of an advertising-supported press system is that it allows the media to function without the constraints of either government or special-interest groups. However, a recurring theme among journalists is that "news media self-censor stories about advertisers or cave in to pressure exerted by their advertisers. When media don't self-censor or cave in to pressure, advertisers respond by withdrawing their advertising from offending media."[22]

The dilemma of separating advertising and editorial functions is not a new problem. It may have begun when the first advertiser met the first publisher. In 1911, the famous publisher and newspaper owner, E. W. Scripps, summed up the uneasy relationship with advertising, "The big advertiser is the mortal foe of honest journalism. I would rather go through a dark alley with a thug than to couple up, in a business way,

---

[20]Elizabeth Tucker, Bonnie B. Reece, and Nora J. Rifon, "Consumer Response to Eco-Ads: A Preliminary Test of an Integrated Model," in *Proceedings of the American Academy of Advertising, 1996,* ed. Gary B. Wilcox (University of Texas, American Academy of Advertising, 1996) p. 159.

[21]"FTC Focus," *Advertising Topics,* a publication of the Council of Better Business Bureaus, October 1995, Supplement 551, p. 3.

[22]Lawrence C. Soley and Robert L. Craig, "Advertising Pressures on Newspapers: A Survey," *Journal of Advertising,* December 1992, p. 7.

as a young newspaperman, with a big advertising patron." Scripps's views have been echoed by both broadcasters and print journalists throughout this century.

A troubling trend is the so-called *early warning* used most often by magazine editors to warn major advertisers of upcoming unfavorable stories. The idea is that by warning advertisers in advance, the magazine can allow companies to be prepared for any fallout and, perhaps, explain the magazine's editorial position prior to publication. However, it is a worrisome trend among many magazine editors. "The American Society of Magazine Editors board worries that some advertisers may mistake an early warning as an open invitation to pressure the publisher or editor to alter, or even kill, the article in question."[23]

Despite the fact that there are no ethical or economic reasons to have advertisers pressure the media to change or delete stories, the temptation to do so is great. In fact, the number of studies indicating that advertisers do attempt to influence news coverage are so consistent in their findings that the issue cannot be dismissed as rumor or mean-spirited gossip spread by critics of advertising. One newspaper study showed "about 90 percent of editors have been pressured by advertisers because of the type and content of stories carried by the paper. Seventy-seven percent said they were pressured to kill stories, and more than 90 percent of editors said advertisers withdrew advertising because of content disputes. More than one-third reported that advertisers succeeded in influencing news at their paper."[24]

This particular study dealt only with newspapers, but magazines and other media are not immune from advertiser pressure. For example, in 1997 Chrysler sent a letter to more than 100 magazines, claiming that it must be alerted in advance of any editorial content encompassing social, political, or sexual issues that could be perceived as offensive or provocative.[25] Obviously, knowing that certain story content may lose a major advertiser will have a chilling effect on all but the largest media outlets.

As one long-time newspaper executive pointed out, "the best thing you as a manager can do for advertisers is to establish your newspaper's creditability as a principled source of believable news and information that attracts and holds readers. Any advertising practice interfering with that is not in the long-term interests of either newspaper or advertiser."[26]

The Advertorial

Advertorial
The use of advertising to promote an idea rather than a product or service.

An ethical concern of many media executives is the growing use of the **advertorial,** and especially advertorial sections, often sponsored by a single company or organization. The idea of the advertorial is simple enough. A company, special interest group, or other organization places an ad to promote an idea rather than a product. The term "advertorial" suggests that the advertiser is placing a clearly identified message (or editorial) to bring some topic to the attention of readers or listeners. In principle, the idea is worthwhile and, some would argue, in the finest traditions of a free press.

Since the early 1980s, the use of the advertorial has changed dramatically, and its critics would say for the worst. Today, many advertorials are in the form of special sections that look very much like the editorial matter of the newspaper or magazine in which they appear. These special sections are devoted to topics such as lawn care or tips

---

[23]Constance L. Hayes, "Editors Urge Limits on Input by Advertisers," *The New York Times,* June 23, 1997, p. C7.

[24]Constance L. Hayes, "Editors Urge Limits on Input by Advertisers," *The New York Times,* June 23, 1997, p. C1.

[25]"Magazine Advertisers Demand Prior Notice of 'Offensive' Articles," *The Wall Street Journal,* April 30, 1997, p. 1.

[26]Conrad C. Fink, *Strategic Newspaper Management* (Boston: Allyn & Bacon, 1996), p. 486.

on purchasing automobiles. In the past, advertorials have been sponsored by foreign governments and have included lengthy pieces on economic and cultural issues. Sometimes the sections are liberally sprinkled with advertisements, giving the section the look of the rest of the publication. Advertorial sections, rather than being written by the editorial staff, are produced by advertising copywriters or public relations specialists. The "editorial" matter is an extension of the advertising and is totally dictated by the sponsor of the section.

It is obvious that the advertorial or feature advertising section is a permanent addition to the print landscape. In broadcasting, many would compare some of the talk-show format infomercials discussed in chapter 8 to the print advertorial. To protect the public from being misled by advertorials, both the American Society of Magazine Editors and individual newspapers have developed guidelines for their use. Some common rules for advertorial use are

1. Advertising supplements should not use the standard body type or headline type used by the news department.
2. The supplement's cover should carry clear identification that it is a sponsored piece, preferably above or below the nameplate.
3. The identification of the sponsor and who prepared the copy should be placed in a dominant position toward the front of the supplement.
4. Each page should be marked "Paid Advertising Supplement."

Despite these guidelines, research shows that more than one-third of advertorials were not properly labeled as advertisements. As one study of advertorial practices concluded, "Not only do readers need to be wary about the source of information in magazines, but magazine editors need to take stock of practices that might eventually alienate readers."[27]

Consumer Boycotts

A potential threat feared by every medium and advertiser is the consumer boycott. A number of religious and public-interest groups have singled out certain publications and programs and their advertisers with threats that continued advertising support will result in a boycott. The media often react more to the bad publicity of a threatened boycott than fear that they will lose substantial sales or audience.

Research indicates that few people agree that they would boycott an advertiser based on program violence or sexual content. Interestingly enough, respondents do indicate that they would boycott for environmental or political concerns. As one marketing executive commented, "Less than one percent of the population of this country said they would boycott for moral reasons. Will they boycott for tuna and dolphins? Absolutely. But for moral reasons? No."[28]

The problem is not as simple as it appears. Few media or advertisers will publicly admit they are pressured to change programming or advertising schedules because of boycott threats. However, few companies want to become embroiled in a nasty public relations dispute over the moral tone of the programs in which they advertise. As one media executive said, "They [advertisers] don't say they're going away; they just go away." It is difficult to measure the effects of boycott threats, but they are probably greater than either the media or advertisers would like to admit.

---

[27] Glen T. Cameron, Kuen-Hee Ju-Park, and Bong-Hyun Kim, "Advertorials in Magazines: Current Use and Compliance with Industry Guidelines," *Journalism and Mass Communication Quarterly*, Autumn 1996, p. 722.

[28] Jenny Pfalzgraf, "Boycott Phobia," *American Advertising*, Summer 1994, p. 18.

Advertising, like any business function, must operate within a complex environment of ethical, social, and economic considerations. In an increasingly complex business world, there are no easy answers to many of the questions raised by both critics and proponents of advertising. Advertisers, their agencies, and the media constantly wrestle with ethical problems of content, presentation, and the acceptability of a host of product categories, claims, and advertising practices. These problems do not have easy solutions and must be handled on a case-by-case basis.

The key to successful advertising is the concept of putting the consumer first. Advertisers that operate from the perspective of doing business in a manner that benefits the consumer will usually benefit themselves. Advertisers also realize that they cannot be held captive by every critic or criticism. In the end, advertisers will have to follow the advice of one industry executive who said that they must carefully consider all criticism, but follow their own conscience and sense of values.

Advertising industry leaders are increasingly concerned about the attacks made on legal and truthful advertising by critics who fail to see the economic and social value of unencumbered communication. As the president of the American Advertising Federation stated, "advertising powers the American economy and it protects and informs consumers. Advertising lays the foundation for a marketplace that leaves final choices up to the consumer."[29]

The future of advertising will be one of change and adaptation. The public interest will become an increasingly important part of the modern advertiser's agenda. It is very clear that advertising has reached a point of maturity where untruthful, misleading, and deceptive advertising is the great exception, practiced only by the short-termers and fastbuck artists. Contemporary advertising must incorporate the idea of social responsibility as routinely as it depends on a well-thought-out marketing plan for its success.

The future will be one of even more critical issues for the advertising industry. Technology will present advertisers with special problems and opportunities that are only now becoming apparent. For example, the issues of consumer privacy must be considered as our ability to gather more precise information about various target segments becomes more sophisticated. What is our responsibility in selling to children? Does advertising have a moral responsibility to refuse to sell produces that are of little, if any, social benefit, even if these products are legal? Where is the line between acceptable product puffery and exploitation and creative selling? These are all questions with no easy answers.

REVIEW

1. Briefly discuss some of the primary economic and social functions of modern advertising.
2. Discuss the concept of advertising's role in resource allocation.
3. In recent years, advertising has been used more and more for social causes. Why?
4. Briefly describe the inadvertent social role of advertising.
5. Describe the organization and function of the Advertising Council.
6. What are the primary benefits of cause-related marketing?
7. What are some arguments against editorial interference by advertisers?
8. What is the purpose of an advertorial?

TAKE IT TO THE NET

We invite you to visit the Russell/Lane page on the Prentice Hall Web site at
PHLIP **http://www.prenhall.com/phbusiness** for the bimonthly Russell/Lane update and for this chapter's World Wide Web exercise.

---

[29]Wally Snyder, "From the President," *American Advertising,* Winter 1994–95, p. 2.

GLOSSARY

A

Account planner. An outgrowth of British agency structure where a planner initiates and reviews research and participates in the creative process. In some agencies, the planner is considered a spokesperson for the consumer.

Advertising clearance process. The internal process of clearing ads for publication and broadcast, conducted primarily by ad agencies and clients.

Advertising Council. A non-profit network of agencies, media, and advertisers dedicated to promoting social programs through advertising.

Advertising goals. The communication objectives designed to accomplish certain tasks within the total marketing program.

Advertising objectives. Those specific outcomes that are to be accomplished through advertising.

Advertorial. The use of advertising to promote an idea rather than a product or service.

American Association of Advertising Agencies (AAAA, 4As). The national organization of advertising agencies.

Amplitude modulation (AM). Method of transmitting electromagnetic signals by varying the *amplitude* (size) of the electromagnetic wave, in contrast to varying its *frequency*. Quality is not as good as frequency modulation, but can be heard farther, especially at night. *See* Frequency modulation (FM).

Animation (TV). Making inanimate objects appear alive and moving by setting them before an animation camera and filming one frame at a time.

Appeal. The motive to which an ad is directed, it is designed to stir a person toward a goal the advertiser has set.

The Arbitron Company. Syndicated radio ratings company.

Audience fragmentation. The segmenting of mass-media audiences into smaller groups because of diversity of media outlets.

Audit Bureau of Circulations (ABC). The organization sponsored by publishers, agencies, and advertisers for securing accurate circulation statements.

Average quarter-hour estimates (AQHE). Manner in which ratio ratings are presented. Estimates include average number of people listening, rating, and metro share of audience.

B

Barter. Acquisition of broadcast time by an advertiser or an agency in exchange for operating capital or merchandise. No cash is involved.

Barter syndication. Station obtains a program at no charge. The program has presold national commercials and time is available for local station spots.

Bleed. Printed matter that runs over the edges of an outdoor board or of a page, leaving no margin.

Block programming. A series of television shows that appeals to the same general audience.

Bounce-back circular. An enclosure in the package of a product that has been ordered by mail. It offers other products of the same company and is effective in getting more business.

Brand. A name, term, sign, design, or a unifying combination of them, intended to identify and distinguish the product or service from competing products or services.

Brand development index (BDI). A method of allocating advertising budgets to those geographic areas that have the greatest sales potential.

Brand equity. The value of how such people as consumers, distributors, and salespeople think and feel about a brand relative to its competition over a period of time.

Brand loyalty. Degree to which a consumer purchases a certain brand without considering alternatives.

Brand name. The written or spoken part of a trademark, in contrast to the pictorial mark; a trademark word.

Brand positioning. Consumers' perceptions of specific brands relative to the various brands of goods or services currently available to them.

Brand preference. When all marketing conditions are equal, a consumer will choose a preferred brand over another.

Building block strategy. A media concept that buys the medium that reaches the most prospects first and works down to those that reach the smallest number of prospects.

Business-to-business advertising. Advertising that promotes goods through trade and industrial journals that are used in the manufacturing, distributing, or marketing of goods to the public.

C

Cable networks. Networks available only to cable subscribers. They are transmitted via satellite to local cable operators for redistribution either as part of basic service or at an extra cost charged to subscribers.

Cable television. TV signals that are carried to households by cable. Programs originate with cable operators through high antennas, satellite disks, or operator-initiated programming.

Category manager. A relatively new corporate position. This manager is responsible for all aspects of the brands in a specific product category for a company including research, manufacturing, sales, and advertising. Each product's advertising manager reports to the category manager. Example: Procter & Gamble's Tide and Cheer detergent report to a single category manager.

Cause-related marketing. Marketing strategies that attempt to link a company to some social or charitable cause.

Caveat emptor. Latin for "Let the buyer beware." Represents the notion that there should be no government interference in the marketplace.

Cease and desist orders. If an advertiser refuses to sign a consent decree, the FTC may issue a cease and desist order that can carry a $10,000-per-day fine.

Central Hudson Four-Part Test. Supreme Court test to determine if specific commercial speech is protected under the Constitution.

Children's Advertising Review Unit (CARU). The CARU functions much as the NAD to review complaints about advertising to children.

Classified advertising. Found in columns so labeled, published in sections of a newspaper or magazine set aside for certain classes of goods or services—for example, Help Wanted, Positions Wanted, Houses for Sale, Cars for Sale. The ads are limited in size and generally are without illustration.

Clearance. The percentage of network affiliates that carries a particular network program.

Closing date. Date when all advertising material must be submitted to a publication.

Clutter. Refers to a proliferation of commercials (in a medium) that reduces the impact of any single message.

Coined word. An original and arbitrary combination of syllables forming a word. Extensively used for trademarks, such as PoFolks, Mazola, Gro-Pup, Zerone. (Opposite of a dictionary word.)

Committee on Nationwide Television Audience Measurement (CONTAM). Industry-wide organization to improve the accuracy and reliability of television ratings.

Communications component. That portion of the media plan that considers the effectiveness of message delivery as contrasted to the efficiency of audience delivery.

Comparative advertising. It directly contrasts an advertiser's product with other named or identified products.

Compensation. The payment of clearance fees by a TV network to local stations carrying its shows.

Competitive stage. The advertising stage a product reaches when its general usefulness is recognized but its superiority over similar brands has to be established in order to gain preference. *See* Pioneering stage, Retentive stage.

Comprehensive. A layout accurate in size, color, scheme, and other necessary details to show how a final ad will look. For presentation only, never for reproduction.

Computer-generated imagery (CGI). Technology allowing computer operators to create multitudes of electronic effects for TV—to squash, stretch, or squeeze objects—much more quickly than earlier tools could. It can add layers of visuals simultaneously.

Concept testing. The target audience evaluation of (alternative) creative strategy. Testing attempts to separate good and bad ideas and provide insight into factors motivating acceptance or rejection.

Consent decree. Issued by the FTC. An advertiser signs the decree, stops the practice under investigation, but admits no guilt.

Consumer advertising. Directed to people who will use the product themselves, in contrast to trade advertising, industrial advertising, or professional advertising.

Consumer price index. Comparative index that charts what an urban family pays for a select group of goods including housing and transportation.

Contest. A promotion in which consumers compete for prizes and the winners are selected strictly on the basis of skill.

Continuity. A TV or radio script. Also refers to the length of time given media schedule runs.

Continuous tone. An unscreened photographic picture or image, on paper or film, that contains all gradations of tonal values from white to black.

Controlled circulation magazines. Sent without cost to people responsible for making buying decisions. To get on such lists, people must state their positions in companies; to stay on it, they must request it annually. Also known as *qualified-circulation publications.*

Cooperative advertising. Joint promotion of a national advertiser (manufacturer) and local retail outlet on behalf of the manufacturer's product on sale in the retail store.

Copy approach. The method of opening the text of an ad. Chief forms: factual approach, imaginative approach, emotional approach.

Copy testing. Measuring the effectiveness of ads.

Corrective advertising. To counteract the past residual effect of previous deceptive advertising, the FTC may require the advertiser to devote future space and time to disclosure of previous deception. Began around the late 1960s.

Cost per rating point (CCP). The cost per rating point is used to estimate the cost of TV advertising on several shows.

Cost per thousand (CPM). A method of comparing the cost for media of different circulations. Also weighted or demographic cost per thousand calculates the CPM using only that portion of a medium's audience falling into a prime-prospect category.

Coupon. Most popular type of sales-promotion technique.

Cross-media buys. Several media or vehicles that are packaged to be sold to advertisers to gain a synergistic communication effect and efficiencies in purchasing time or space.

D

Database marketing. A process of continually updating information about individual consumers. Popular techniques with direct-response sellers.

Direct houses. In specialty advertising, firms that combine the functions of supplier and distributor.

Direct marketing. Selling goods and services without the aid of wholesaler or retailer. Includes direct-response advertising and advertising for leads for sales people. Also direct door-to-door selling. Uses many media: direct mail, publications, TV, radio.

Direct Marketing Association (DMA). Organization to promote direct-mail and direct-response advertising.

Direct premium. A sales incentive given to customers at the time of purchase.

Direct-response advertising. Any form of advertising done in direct marketing. Uses all types of media: direct mail, TV, magazines, newspapers, radio. Term replaces *mail-order advertising. See* Direct marketing.

Drive time (radio). A term used to designate the time of day when people are going to, or coming from, work. Usually 6 A.M. to 10 A.M. and 3 P.M. to 7 P.M., but this varies from one community to another. The most costly time on the rate card.

E

Effective reach. The percentage of an audience that is exposed to a certain number of messages or has achieved a specific level of awareness.

Eight-sheet poster. Outdoor poster used in urban areas, about one-fourth the size of the standard 30-sheet poster. Also called *junior poster.*

End-product advertising. Building consumer demand by promoting ingredients in a product. For example, Teflon and Nutrasweet.

European Community (EC). The developing economic integration of Europe. Potentially a single market of some 300 million consumers in 1991.

Event marketing. A promotion sponsored in connection with some special event such as a sports contest or musical concert.

Everyday low pricing (EDLP). A marketing strategy that uses permanent price reductions instead of occasional sales promotion incentives.

Exclusionary zones (outdoor). Industry code of conduct that prohibits the advertising of products within 500 feet of churches, schools, or hospitals of any products that cannot be used legally by children.

Executional idea. It is a rendering in words, symbols, sounds, colors, shapes, forms, or any combination thereof, of an abstract answer to a perceived desire or need.

F

Family life cycle. Concept that demonstrates changing purchasing behavior as a person or a family matures.

Fast-close advertising. Some magazines offer short-notice ad deadlines, sometimes at a premium cost.

Federal Communications Commission (FCC). The federal authority empowered to license radio and TV stations and to assign wavelengths to stations "in the public interest."

Federal Trade Commission (FTC). The agency of the federal government empowered to prevent unfair competition and to prevent fraudulent, misleading, or deceptive advertising in interstate commerce.

Flat rate. A uniform charge for space in a medium, without regard to the amount of space used or the frequency of insertion. When flat rates do not prevail, *time discounts* or *quantity discounts* are offered.

Flighting. Flight is the length of time a broadcaster's campaign runs. Can be days, weeks, or months—but does not refer to a year. A flighting schedule alternates periods of activity with periods of inactivity.

Focus group. A qualitative research interviewing method using in-depth interviews with a group rather than with an individual.

Four-color process. The process for reproducing color illustrations by a set of plates, one that prints all the yellows, another the blues, a third the reds, and the fourth the blacks (sequence variable). The plates are referred to as *process plates.*

Free-standing inserts (FSI). Preprinted inserts distributed to newspaper publishers, where they are inserted and delivered with the newspaper.

Frequency. In media exposure the number of times an individual or household is exposed to a medium within a given period of time.

Frequency discounts. Discounts based on total time or space bought, usually within a year. Also called *bulk discounts.*

Frequency modulation (FM). A radio transmission wave that transmits by the variation in the frequency of its wave, rather than its size (as in amplitude modulation [AM]). An FM wave is twenty times the width of an AM wave, which is the source of its fine tone. To transmit such a wave, it has to be placed high on the electromagnetic spectrum, far from AM waves with their interference and static, hence its outstanding tone.

Fulfillment. The tasks of filling orders, shipping merchandise, and back in marketing.

Fulfillment firm. Company that handles the couponing process including receiving, verification, and payment. It also handles contests and sweepstake responses.

Full-run editions. An advertiser who buys the entire circulation of a publication is buying the full-run circulation.

Full-service agency. One that handles planning, creation, production, and placement of advertising for advertising clients. May also handle sales promotion and other related services as needed by client.

G

General Agreement on Tariffs and Trade (GATT). A treaty designed to lower trade barriers among 117 nations.

Generic demand. The demand demonstrated for a product class rather than a specific brand.

Global marketing. Term that denotes the use of advertising and marketing strategies on an international basis.

Gross rating points (GRP). Each rating point represents 1 percent of the universe being measured for the market. In TV it is 1 percent of the households having TV sets in that area.

H

Highway Beautification Act of 1965. Federal law that controls outdoor signs in noncommercial, nonindustrial areas.

Hoarding. First printed outdoor signs—the forerunner of modern outdoor advertising.

House mark. A primary mark of a business concern, usually used with the trademark of its products. *General Mills* is a house mark; *Betty Crocker* is a trademark; *DuPont* is a house mark; *Teflon II* is a trademark.

I

Idea advertising. Advertising used to promote an idea or cause rather than to sell a product or service.

Illuminated posters. Seventy to 80% of all outdoor posters are illuminated for 24-hour exposure.

Imagery transfer research. A technique that measures the ability of radio listeners to correctly describe the primary visual elements of related television commercials.

Inadvertent social role of advertising. Advertising sometimes communicates social messages unintended by the advertiser. Stereotyping and less-than-flattering portrayals of individuals and ethnic or social audience segments can lead to negative perceptions of advertising.

Incentives. Sales promotion directed at wholesalers, retailers, or a company's salesforce.

Independent delivery companies. Private companies that contract with magazine publishers to deliver their publications.

Industrial advertising. Addressed to manufacturers who buy machinery, equipment, raw materials, and the components needed to produce goods they sell.

Infomercial. Long form television advertising that promotes products within the context of a program-length commercial.

In-house agency. An arrangement whereby the advertiser handles the total agency function by buying individually, on a fee basis, the needed services (for example, creative, media services, and placement) under the direction of an assigned advertising director.

Institutional advertising. Advertising done by an organization speaking of its work, views, and problems as a whole, to gain public goodwill and support rather than to sell a specific product. Sometimes called *public-relations advertising.*

Integrated marketing communication (IMC). The joint planning, execution, and coordination of all areas of marketing communication.

Interconnects. A joint buying opportunity between two or more cable systems in the same market.

Internet. A worldwide system of computer links that provides instantaneous communication.

J

Jingle. A commercial or part of a commercial set to music, usually carrying the slogan or theme line of a campaign. May make a brand name and slogan more easily remembered.

Johann Gutenberg. Began the era of mass communication in 1438 with the invention of movable type.

L

Layout. A working drawing (may be computer developed) showing how an ad is to look. A printer's layout is a set of instructions accompanying a piece of copy showing how it is to be set up. There are also rough layouts, finished layouts, and mechanical layouts, representing various degrees of finish. The term *layout* is used also for the total design of an ad.

Letterpress. Printing from a relief, or raised, surface. The raised surface is inked and comes in direct contact with the paper, like a rubber stamp.

Lettershop. A firm that not only addresses the mailing envelope but also is mechanically equipped to insert material, seal and stamp envelopes, and deliver them to the post office according to mailing requirements.

Lifestyle segmentation. Identifying consumers by combining several demographics and lifestyles.

Lifetime value. An estimate of the long-term revenue that can be expected from a particular prospect.

List broker. In direct-mail advertising an agent who rents the prospect lists of one advertiser to another advertiser. The broker receives a commission from the seller for this service.

List manager. Promotes client's lists to potential renters and buyers.

Logotype, or logo. A trademark or trade name embodied in the form of a distinctive lettering or design. Famous example: Coca-Cola.

M

Magazine networks. Groups of magazines that can be purchased together using one insertion order and paying a single invoice.

Make-goods. When a medium falls short of some audience guarantee, advertisers are provided concessions in the form of make-goods. Most commonly used in television and magazines.

Market. A group of people who can be identified by some common characteristic, interest, or problem; use a certain product to advantage; afford to buy it; and be reached through some medium.

Marketing communication. The communication components of marketing, which include public relations, advertising, personal selling, and sales promotion.

Marketing concept. A management orientation that views the needs of consumers as primary to the success of a firm.

Marketing goals. The overall objectives that a company wishes to accomplish through its marketing program.

Marketing mix. Combination of marketing functions, including advertising, used to sell a product.

Marketing translation. The process of adapting a general marketing plan to multinational environments.

Market profile. A demographic and psychographic description of the people or the households of a product's market. It may also include economic and retailing information about a territory.

Market segmentation. The division of an entire market of consumers into groups whose similarity makes them a market for products serving their special needs.

Mass communication era. From the 1700s to the early decades of this century, advertisers were able to reach large segments of the population through the mass media.

MatchPrint. A high-quality color proof used for approvals prior to printing. Similar to a Signature print.

Media buyers. Execute and monitor the media schedule developed by media planners.

Media imperatives. Based on research by Simmons Media Studies, showed the importance of using both TV and magazines for full market coverage.

Media plan. The complete analysis and execution of the media component of a campaign.

Media planners. Media planners are responsible for the overall strategy of the media component of an advertising campaign.

Media schedule. The detailed plan or calendar showing when ads and commercials will be distributed and in what media vehicles they will appear.

Media strategy. Planning of ad media buys, including identification of audience, selection of media vehicles, and determination of timing of a media schedule.

Merge/purge (merge & purge). A system used to eliminate duplication by direct-response advertisers who use different mailing lists for the same mailing. Mailing lists are sent to a central merge/purge office that electronically picks out duplicate names. Saves mailing costs, especially important to firms that send out a million pieces in one mailing. Also avoids damage to the goodwill of the public.

Mergenthaler linotype. Ottmar Mergenthaler invented the linotype, which replaced hand-set type by automatically setting and distributing metal type.

Message management. Utilizes database information to offer different messages to various consumer categories.

Morphing. An electronic technique that allows you to transform one object into another object.

Multinational advertising. The coordination and execution of advertising campaigns that are directed to a number of countries.

N

National advertising. Advertising by a marketer of a trademarked product or service sold through different outlets, in contrast to *local advertising*.

National Advertising Division (NAD). The policy-making arm of the National Advertising Review Board.

Negative option direct response. Technique used by record and book clubs whereby a customer receives merchandise unless the seller is notified not to send it.

Networks. Interconnecting stations for the simultaneous transmission of TV or radio broadcasts.

Newspaper Association of America (NAA). The marketing and trade organization for the newspaper industry.

Newspaper networks. Groups of newspapers that allow advertisers to buy several papers simultaneously with one insertion order and one invoice.

Niche marketing. A combination of product and target market strategy. It is a flanking strategy that focuses on niches or comparatively narrow windows of opportunity within a broad product market or industry. Its guiding principle is to pit your strength against their weakness.

Nonwired networks. Groups of radio and TV stations whose advertising is sold simultaneously by station representatives.

North American Free Trade Agreement (NAFTA). A treaty designed to eliminate trade barriers among the United States, Mexico, and Canada.

North American Industrial Classification System. System that uses six-digit identification numbers for classifying manufacturing firms.

O

Off-network syndication. Syndicated programs that previously have been aired by a major network.

Offset lithography. A printing process by which originally an image was formed on special stone by a greasy material, the design then being transferred to the printing paper. Today the more frequently used process is *offset* lithography, in which a thin and flexible metal sheet replaces the stone. In this process the design is "offset" from the metal sheet to a rubber blanket, which then transfers the image to the printing paper.

On-line services. Refers to computer-accessed databases and information services for business and home use.

Open rate. In print, the highest advertising rate at which all discounts are placed.

Opticals. Visual effects that are put on a TV film in a laboratory, in contrast to those that are included as part of the original photography.

Outbound telemarketing. A technique that involves a seller calling prospects.

Outdoor Advertising Association of America (OAAA). Primary trade and lobbying organization for the outdoor industry.

Out-of-home. Outdoor and transportation advertising.

Outside producer. The production company person who is hired by the agency to create the commercial according to agency specifications.

P

Partial runs. When magazines offer less than their entire circulation to advertisers.

Partial runs include demographic, geographic, and split-run editions.

Pass-along readership. Readers who receive a publication from a primary buyer. In consumer publications, pass-along readers are considered inferior to the primary audience, but this is usually not the case with business publications.

Passive meters. Unobtrusive device that measures individual viewing habits through sensors keyed to household members.

Penny press. Forerunner of the mass newspaper in the United States. First appeared in the 1830s.

People meter. Device that measures TV set usage by individuals rather than by households.

Per inquiry (PI). Advertising time or space where medium is paid on a per response received basis.

Personal drive analysis (PDA). A technique used to uncover a consumer's individual psychological drives.

Pica. The unit for measuring width in printing. There are 6 picas to an inch. A page of type 24 picas wide is 4 inches wide.

Pioneering stage. The advertising stage of a product in which the need for such a product is not recognized and must be established or in which the need has been established but the success of a commodity in filling those requirements has to be established. *See* Competitive stage, Retentive stage.

Pixel. The smallest element of a computer image that can be separately addressed. It is an individual picture element.

Plant. In outdoor advertising the local company that arranges to lease, erect, and maintain the outdoor sign and to sell the advertising space on it.

Point (pt). The unit of measurement of type, about 1/72 inch in depth. Type is specified by its point size, as 8 pt., 12 pt., 24 pt., 48 pt. The unit for measuring thickness of paper, 0.001 inch.

Point-of-purchase advertising. Displays prepared by the manufacturer for use where the product is sold.

Positioning. Segmenting a market by creating a product to meet the needs of a select group or by using a distinctive advertising appeal to meet the needs of a specialized group, without making changes in the physical product.

Poster panel. A standard surface on which outdoor posters are placed. The posting surface is of sheet metal. An ornamental molding of standard green forms the frame. The standard poster panel is 12 feet high and 25 feet long (outside dimensions).

Potential rating index by ZIP market (PRIZM). A method of audience segmentation developed by the Claritas Corporation.

Premarketing era. The period from prehistoric times to the eighteenth century. During this time, buyers and sellers communicated in very primitive ways.

Premium. An item, other than the product itself, given to purchasers of a product as an inducement to buy. Can be free with a purchase (for example, on the package, in the package, or the container itself) or available upon proof of purchase and a payment (self-liquidating premium).

Printers' Ink **Model Statute (1911).** The act directed at fraudulent advertising, prepared and sponsored by *Printers' Ink,* which was the pioneer advertising magazine.

Product differentiation. Unique product attributes that set off one brand from another.

Product manager. In package goods, the person responsible for the profitability of a product (brand) or product line, including advertising decisions. Also called a brand manager.

Product user segmentation. Identifying consumers by the amount of product usage.

Professional advertising. Directed at those in professions such as medicine, law, or architecture, who are in a position to recommend the use of a particular product or service to their clients.

Psychographics. A description of a market based on factors such as attitudes, opinions, interests, perceptions, and lifestyles of consumers comprising that market.

Public relations. Communication with various internal and external publics to create an image for a product or corporation.

Puffery. Advertiser's opinion of a product that is considered a legitimate expression of biased opinion.

Q

Qualitative research. This involves finding out what people say they think or feel. It is usually exploratory or diagnostic in nature.

R

Radio Advertising Bureau (RAB). Association to promote the use of radio as an advertising medium.

Radio All Dimension Audience Research (RADAR). Service of Statistical Research, Inc., major source of network radio ratings.

Rate base. The circulation that magazines guarantee advertisers in computing advertising costs.

Rate differential. The controversial practice of newspapers charging significantly higher rates to national advertisers as compared to local accounts.

Rating point (TV). The percentage of TV households in a market a TV station reaches with a program. The percentage varies with the time of day. A station may have a 10 rating between 6:00 and 6:30 P.M. and a 20 rating between 9:00 and 9:30.

Rebate. The amount owed to an advertiser by a medium when the advertiser qualifies for a higher space discount.

Relationship marketing. A strategy that develops marketing plans from a consumer perspective.

Remnant space. Unsold advertising space in geographic or demographic editions. It is offered to advertisers at a significant discount.

Representative (rep). An individual or organization representing a medium selling time or space outside the city or origin.

Research era. In recent years advertisers increasingly have been able to identify narrowly defined audience segments through sophisticated research methods.

Residual. A sum paid to certain talent on a TV or radio commercial every time the commercial is run after 13 weeks, for the life of the commercial.

Response lists. Prospects who have previously responded to direct mail offers.

Retail advertising. Advertising by a merchant who sells directly to the consumer.

Retentive stage. The third advertising stage of a product, reached when its general usefulness is widely known, its individual qualities are thoroughly appreciated, and it is satisfied to retain its patronage merely on the strength of its past reputation. *See* Pioneering state, Competitive stage.

Reverse production timetable. Used in direct mail to schedule a job. The schedule starts with the date it is to reach customers and works backward to a starting date.

Ride-alongs. Direct-mail pieces that are sent with other mailings, such as bills.

Riding the boards. Inspecting an outdoor showing after posting.

Robinson-Patman Act. A federal law, enforced by the FTC. Requires a manufacturer to give proportionate discounts and advertising allowances to all competing dealers in a market. Purpose: to protect smaller merchants from unfair competition of larger buyers.

Rotary bulletins (outdoor). Movable painted bulletins that are moved from one fixed location to another one in the market at regular intervals. The locations are viewed and approved in advance by the advertiser.

Rotogravure. The method of printing in which the impression is produced by chemically etched cylinders and run on a rotary press; useful in long runs of pictorial effects.

S

Sales promotion. (1) Sales activities that supplement both personal selling and marketing, coordinate the two, and help to make them effective. For example, displays are sales promotions. (2) More loosely, the combination of personal selling, advertising, and all supplementary selling activities.

Sampling. The method of introducing and promoting merchandise by distributing a miniature or full-size trial package of the product free or at a reduced price.

Scatter plan. The use of announcements, over a variety of network programs and stations, to reach as many people as possible in a market.

Screen printing. A simple printing process that uses a stencil. It is economical but is limited in reproduction quality.

Secondary research. Research or data that is already gathered by someone else for another purpose.

Selective binding. Binding different material directed to various reader segments in a single issue of a magazine.

Self-liquidating premium. A premium offered to consumers for a fee that covers its cost plus handling.

Service advertising. Advertising that promotes a service rather than a product.

Service mark. A word or name used in the sale of services, to identify the services of a firm and distinguish them from those of others, for example, Hertz Drive Yourself Service, Weight Watchers Diet Course. Comparable to trademarks for products.

Share of audience. The percentage of households using TV tuned to a particular program.

Short rate. The balance advertisers have to pay if they estimated that they would run more ads in a year than they did and entered a contract to pay at a favorable rate. The short rate is figured at the end of the year or sooner if advertisers fall behind schedule. It is calculated at a higher rate for the fewer insertions.

Showing. Outdoor posters are bought by groups, referred to as *showings*. The size of a showing is referred to as a 100-GRP showing or a 75- or 50-GRP showing, depending on the gross rating points of the individual boards selected.

Simmons Market Research Bureau (SMRB). Firm that provides audience data for several media. Best known for magazine research.

Siquis. Handwritten posters in sixteenth- and seventeenth-century England— forerunners of modern advertising.

Situation analysis. The part of the advertising plan that answers the questions: Where are we today and how did we get here? It deals with the past and present.

Social responsibility. The demand that advertising be aware of its responsibility to the public, i.e., it should do more than sell goods and services.

Specialty advertising. A gift given to a consumer to encourage a purchase.

Spectacular. Outdoor sign built to order, designed to be conspicuous for its location, size, lights, motion, or action. The costliest form of outdoor advertising.

Spot television. Purchase of time from a local station, in contrast to purchasing from a network.

Standard Advertising Unit (SAU). Allows national advertisers to purchase newspaper advertising in standard units from one paper to another.

Standard Rate and Data Service (SRDS). SRDS publishes a number of directories giving media and production information.

Stock music. Existing recorded music that may be purchased for use in a TV or radio commercial.

Storyboard. Series of drawings used to present a proposed commercial. Consists of illustrations of key action (video), accompanied by the audio part. Used for getting advertiser approval and as a production guide.

Stripping. Scheduling a syndicated program on a five-day-per-week basis.

Substantiation. The key to FTC enforcement is that advertisers must be able to prove the claims made in their advertising.

Sweepstakes. A promotion in which prize winners are determined on the basis of chance alone. Not legal if purchaser must risk money to enter.

Sweep weeks. During these periods, ratings are taken for all television markets.

Syndicated TV program. A program that is sold or distributed to more than one local station by an independent organization outside the national network standard.

Synergistic effect. In media buying, combining a number of complementary media that create advertising awareness greater than the sum of each.

T

Target audience. That group that composes the present and potential prospects for a product or service.

Target marketing. Identifying and communicating with groups of prime prospects.

Telemarketing. Contacting prospective buyers over the telephone. Major area of direct marketing.

Theater of the mind. In radio, a writer paints pictures in the mind of the listener through the use of sound.

Time-shift viewing. Recording programs on a VCR for viewing at a later time.

Total concept. The combining of all elements of an ad—copy, headline, and illustrations—into a single idea.

Total market coverage (TMC). Where newspapers augment their circulation with direct mail or shoppers to deliver all households in a market.

Total survey area. The maximum coverage of a radio or television station's signal.

Trade advertising. Advertising directed to the wholesale or retail merchants or sales agencies through whom the product is sold.

Trademark. Any device or word that identifies the origin of a product, telling who made it or who sold it. Not to be confused with *trade name*.

Trade name. A name that applies to a business as a whole, not to an individual product.

Trade paper. A business publication directed to those who buy products for resale (wholesalers, jobbers, retailers).

Traffic Audit Bureau for Media Measurement (TAB). An organization designed to investigate how many people pass and may see a given outdoor sign, to establish a method of evaluating traffic measuring a market.

Traffic-building premium. A sales incentive to encourage customers to come to a store where a sale can be closed.

Translation management. The process of translating advertising from one culture to another.

TV director. The person who casts and rehearses a commercial and is the key person in the shooting of the commercial.

TvQ. A service of Marketing Evaluations that measures the popularity (opinion of audience rather than size of audience) of shows and personalities.

Typography. The art of using type effectively.

U

Up-front buy. Purchase of network TV time by national advertisers during the first offering by networks. Most expensive network advertising.

Up-selling. A telemarketing technique designed to sell additional merchandise to callers.

V

Values and Lifestyles System (VALS). Developed by SRI International to cluster consumers according to several variables in order to predict consumer behavior.

Vendor program. Special form of co-op advertising in which a retailer designs the program and approaches advertisers for support.

Vertical publications. Business publications dealing with the problems of a specific industry: for example, *Chain Store Age, National Petroleum News, Textile World.*

W

War Advertising Council. Founded in 1942 to promote World War II mobilization. It later evolved into the Advertising Council.

Wheeler-Lea Amendments. Broadened the scope of the FTC to include consumer advertising.

Y

Yield management. A product pricing strategy to control supply and demand.

Z

Zoning. Newspaper practice of offering advertisers partial coverage of a market, often accomplished with weekly inserts distributed to certain sections of that market.

A

AAAA. *See* American Association of Advertising Agencies (AAAA, 4As)
ABC (Audit Bureau of Circulations), 13, 276–78, 314–15, 402
ABC Coupon Distribution Verification Service, 402, 403
ABC television network, 207, 667
A/B split, 298–99
Accents, music for, 536
Accountability, 37
Account circles, 123, 125
Account planners, 135, 425–26
Account services department in agency, 121
Achievers (consumer group), 433
Action-oriented consumers, 434
Activities, interests and opinions (AIO), 96
Actualizers (consumer group), 432
Actual radio measurement (ARM), 246
Ad Council, 691
Addis Group, 579
Adhesive proof, 516, 517
Adnorm data, 443
Advertisers, marketing newspapers to, 262–63
Advertising, 2–21
 on cable television, 220–22
 classified, 267–68
 as contract, 658
 criticism of, 652–53, 683–89
 to diverse customer interests, 32–34
 history of
  1870–1900, 6–14
  beginnings of modern, 4–6
  in brief, 687
  no-rebate age (1918–1956), 117
  in twentieth century, 12–13
   1950–1975, 17–19
   advertising clubs and, 13
   Federal Trade Commmission Act (1914), 12–13, 654
   Pure Food and Drug Act (1906), 12, 688
   1920s, 14
   1980s, 19
   1930s Depression and, 14–16
   World War I, 13–14
   World War II, 16–17
  twenty-first century and, 20
  variations in importance of, 40–42
 as institution, 31–32
 in magazines, 290
 as marketing mix element, 26
 in marketing process, 42–43
 network television, 208–9
 roles of, 31–32
 sales promotion and, 389–91
 vs. sales promotion, 389–91
Advertising Age, 291
Advertising agencies. *See* Agencies, advertising
Advertising clearance process, 668–69
Advertising clubs, 13
Advertising Council, 16, 17, 282, 690–93
Advertising goals vs. marketing goals, 160–61, 177
Advertising mix, retail, 616–23
Advertising research, 436–37, 441–46
Advertising share of newspapers, 254
Advertising spiral, 62–80
 expanded, 68
 as management decision tool, 69
Advertorial, 696–97
Adweek Agency Directory, 113
Affidavit of performance, 412

African American press, 281
African Americans, 85
 in ads and commercials, 684–85
 campaigns targeting, 92–93
 marketing to, 97, 147–48, 646, 647–48, 649
AFTRA (American Federation of Television and Radio Artists), 559
Agencies, advertising, 112–39. *See also* Media strategy
 AAAA definition of, 113
 agency of record, 129
 clearance process and, 668–69
 compensation, 115, 117, 120, 133–35
 competing accounts, 128
 development of, 12, 113–18
  full-service agency, 118–20
  global, 126–28
  mega-agencies, 130–31
  multinational, 636–39
  networks, 130–31
  organization of, 120–23
  other services of, 135–37
 integrated marketing and, 27
 selection of, 158–60
 services in competition with, 131–33
Agency/client relationships, 115, 156–60
Agency media groups, 133
Agency of record, 129
Agency producer, 538–39
Agfa, 518
Agora Inc., 145
Agribusiness advertising, 325–27
AICP Bid and Specification Form, 537
Airline industry, 97
À la carte agency, 131
Alcoa, 320–21
Alcohol, advertising restrictions on, 663–64, 686
Aldus Pagemaker, 484
Ambiguity, avoiding, 467
Ambush marketing, 407
American Academy of Advertising, 682
American Advertising Federation (AAF), 13, 670, 686
American Association of Advertising Agencies (AAAA, 4As), 13, 113, 117, 235, 269, 670, 688
American Automobile Association (AAA), 138–39
American Dental Association, 100
American Express, 138–39, 467, 694
American Lung Association, 688
American Proteins, Inc., 149
American Society of Magazine Editors, 696
American Telephone and Telegraph. *See* AT&T
America Online, 227, 279
Ammirati Puris Lintas, 130, 156, 637
Amplification with body copy, 457
Amplitude modulation (AM), 239–40, 243
Analytics, advanced, 424–25
Ancillary promotional services, 322
Anheuser-Busch, Inc. v. Schmoke, 663
Animals, 468
Animatics, 441–42
Animation, 525–26
Anspach Grossman Enterprise of WWP Group, 573
Anthropology, advertising and, 427
Appeals, nature and use of, 448–51
Apple, 622
Aragon Consulting Group, 367
Arbitron Rating Company, The, 213, 224, 245–46, 250, 251
Area of dominant influence, 213
Arm & Hammer, 98
Arnold Communications, 147
Art director, 470, 486

Artist's medium, 486
Artwork
 sources of, 487–88
 in TV commercial, 525
Asian Americans, 85, 97, 147–48, 649
ASI Market Research, 425
Associated Advertising Clubs of the World (now American Advertising Federation), 13
Association of National Advertisers (ANA), 13, 160, 412, 670
Association of National Advertising Managers, 13
Associations with product attribute, developing, 100
Assortment ads, 614
ATI Grips, 88
Atlanta Journal and Constitution, 255, 279
AT&T, 14, 362, 575
Attention, attracting, 475–77
Attitudes, consumer, 612–14
Attitude segmentation, 96
Attitudinal similarity, 596
Audience
 business press, 317–18
 newspaper, 254
 radio, definitions of, 249–50
 share of, 203
 target, 105–7, 184–86, 295
Audience fragmentation
 newspaper, 19
 radio, 237–38
 television, 18
Audience measurement
 for magazines, 314–15
 for outdoor advertising, 344–45
Audience selectivity
 of magazines, 287, 290, 294–95, 369
 of outdoor, 335
Audio technology, 558
Audit Bureau of Circulation (ABC), 13, 276–78, 314–15, 402
Audit(s)
 brand equity, 74–77
 circulation, 314–15, 324–25
 of outdoor showing, 343
Aural similarity, 595
Austin Kelly Advertising, Inc., 173–74
Automated dialing recorded message programs (ADRMP), 363
Availability
 of network time, 209
 of outdoor, 335
Average quarter-hour estimates (AQHE), 248–50
Avis, 437
Avrett Free & Ginsberg, 78–79
Aydlotte & Cartwright, 114, 148, 154, 460, 476, 505, 507, 570, 598, 607
Ayer & Son, N.W., 13–14, 115

B

Baby boomers, 87
Babylonians, 4
Background music, 536
Balance, 479–80
Barbardier Motor Corporation of America, 165–67
Barter, 135
Barter syndication, 216
Bartle Bogle Hegarty, London, 446
BarzRadio, 550
Basic idea, 470–71
Basic (open) rate, 308–9
Bates v. State Bar of Arizona, 665

Bates Worldwide, 144, 637
Baxter, Gurian & Mazzei, 130
Bayer, 99, 574
BBDO, 129–30, 427, 434, 544, 637
  emotional measurement system, 442–43
BBDO West, 295
Beech-Nut, 98
Behavior, brand assets and, 72–74
BehaviorScan, 597–98
Believers (consumers), 432–33
BellSouth, 155, 267
Benefits segmentation, 96
Benson & Hedges, 467
Bernard Hodes Advertising, 130
Bernbach, 448
Betty Crocker, 582
Bidding process for TV commercial, 537
Big-box destination retailers, 610
Billboards, 331. *See also* Out-of-home advertising
Billing, agency, 120
Birth rate, 86
Black Box of Chicago, 518
Blacks. *See* African Americans
Bleed pages, 305
Bleed poster, 338
Blister cards, 578
Block programming, 175, 208
BMG Music Service, 373, 378, 379
*Board of Trustees of the State University of New York v.
  Fox*, 662–63
Bob Green Productions, 535
Body copy of ad. *See* Copy
Bolton Group, The, 36
Bombshell wipe, 534
Bonham Group, 408
Bookend spots, 526
Book-of-the-Month Club, 373
Book stocks, 384
Borders, Perrin & Norrander, 155–56
Bounce-back circulars, 370–71
Bound-in booklets, 305
Bozell, Jacobs, Kenyon & Eckhart, 34, 128
Bradford, William, 113–14
Brand awareness
  brand trial/awareness ratios, 437
Brand development index (BDI), 189–90
Brand equity, 72
  audit, 74–77
  global, 126
Brand identity, 582
Brand image, 355, 582
Brand management, 154–56
  integrated marketing, 143–47
Brand name, 33–34. *See also* Trademarks
Brand personality research, 428
Brand positioning, 76
Brand preference, 24
Brand(s), 3, 69–77, 563, 565
  accelerated life cycle of, 70
  basic elements of, 76
  brand asset valuator, 72–74
  consumer attitudes toward, 75–76
  consumers and, 70–72
  defined, 567
  integrated communications and, 72
  loyalty, 89–90
  origin of, 69–70
  retail, 608–12
Brand share, positioning to expand, 99–100
Brand switching, 393
Brand train, 347
Brand trial/awareness ratios, 437
Bridgestone Sports, 170, 173–74
Bruce hardwood floors, 36
Budget
  media, 195–96
  operations, setting, 148–52
Building-block strategy, 175
Bulk discount, 273
Bulldog Drummond, 88, 106, 466

Bureau of Alcohol, Tobacco, and Firearms (ATF),
  660
Bureau of Labor Statistics, 611
Bureau of Labor Statistics, Consumer Expenditure
  (CE) Survey, 86
Burger King, 588–89
Burrell Advertising, 156
Burrell Communications Group, 97
Business
  advertising's role in, 31–32
  advertising to, 46–48
Business cycles, retailer, 615–16
Business gifts, 399
Business press and business-to-business advertising,
  315–28
  agribusiness advertising, 325–27
  ancillary promotional services, 322
  business publications audit of circulation (BPA),
    324–25
  characteristics of, 317–19, 321
  consumer magazines compared to, 315–17
  expansion of services, 321–22
  forms of advertising, 46–48
  special features of advertising in, 323–25
  types of publications, 322–23
Business service teams, 123
Business-to-business campaign, 598
Bus wraps, 347, 349
Buyer, profile of, 102–3. *See also* Consumer(s)
Buyer's Guides, 345, 346

C

C. Donald Williams Advertising Inc., 348
Cable television, 199, 200, 204, 218–22
Cahners Advertising, 413
Cahners Advertising Performance Studies, 485
Cahners Publishing Co., 34, 303, 304, 316, 318, 319,
  375–76
Cains, 94
Calkins and Holden, 115
Camera directions, 532–34
Campaign, advertising, 587–603
  creative objectives and strategy for, 591–96
  getting approval for, 597
  media objectives for, 596–97
  portfolio, 598–99
  posttests of, 597–99
  situation analysis and, 589–90
Campaign evaluation research, 441
Campbell-Mithun-Esty, 134–35, 516
Campbell Soup Co., 147, 425
Capital Culture Center, 494
Captive audience, 549, 551
Card concept test, 442
Carolina First, 568
Catalogs, 371–73
Category killers, 607
Category manager, 143
Cause-related marketing, 693–94
Caveat emptor, 653–54
Caxton, William, 6
CBS, 207, 667
CD-ROM, 487–88
CDs, 558
Cease and desist order, 656
Celebrities, 459, 466, 523, 658–59, 664
Celebrity Oriental Restaurant, 509, 598, 600, 601
Census Bureau, 430–31
Census data (1990), 83–85
Center for Science in the Public Interest, 688
Central Carolina Bank, 113, 444, 479
Central Hudson Four-Part Test, 662
*Central Hudson Gas & Electric v. Public Service
  Commission of New York*, 662
Certification marks, 573
Chain-store ad, 15
Challengers (cohort group), 429
Charles David, 423, 609–10
Check-cashing cards, 435

Cheerwine, 94
Chick-fil-A, 342
Children, 468
  advertising to, 188, 671, 672–73, 683
  newspaper reading by, 261–62
Children's Advertising Review Unit (CARU), 671,
  672–73, 683
Christian Dior, 68
Chroma-keying, 541
Chrysler, 160, 544, 696
Chuck Blore Company, 550
Cigarette advertising, 18, 292, 336
Cinema commercials, 622
Circulars, bounce-back, 370–71
Circular wipe, 534
Circulation
  audits, 314–15, 324–25
  controlled, 324
  guaranteed, 312
  magazine, 312–14
  newspaper circulation analysis, 276–78
  paid, 312–13
  of weekly newspapers, 283–84
City magazines, 300–301
City of Cincinnati v. Discovery Network, 663
City zone, 278
Classified advertising, 254, 267–68
Classified display advertisements, 267
Clayton Antitrust Act (1914), 659
Clearance, in television broadcasting, 204
Clearance process, advertising, 668–69
Clear Choice Marketing, 394
Climate, analyzing marketing, 590
Clip art, 487–88
Clock wipe, 534
Close-ups, 524–25
Closing date, 297, 310, 496
Closing door wipe, 534
Clubs, advertising, 13
Clutter, 201
CMP Media, 356
CNN, 221
Coated paper, 384
Coca-Cola, 33, 127, 131, 134, 147, 159–60, 162,
  231, 396, 544, 562, 563, 564, 577, 598, 599,
  630–31
  new Coke, 424
Code of advertising practice (OAAA), 336
Cognition, 431
Cohort analysis, 428–29
Coined words as trademarks, 567–68
Cole, Henderson & Drake, 625
Color, 467
  as composing element, 480–82
  four-color process printing, 510–14, 511–14
  hiFi, 518
  in magazine advertising, 303–5
  in outdoor, 341
  in packaging, 580–81
  time schedule for ad production of, 496
Color Association of America, 481
Color management system (CMS), 518
Color Marketing Group (CMG), 481–82
Color proofing, 511
Color separation, 510, 518–19
Columbian Exhibition (1893), 8
Columbia Plantation General Hospital, 452, 453, 461
Combination of techniques, 526–27
Combination rates, 273
Comics, 280–81
Commercial art, trade practice in buying, 486–87
Commercials
  post production, 544
Commercials, test, 441–42. *See also* Radio commercial;
  Television commercial
Commission, agency, 115, 117, 120, 134
Committee of Public Information, Division of
  Advertising, 14
Committee on Nationwide Television Audience
  Measurement (CONTAM), 223–24

Communication(s)
  integrated. *See* Integrated marketing communication
  interactive, 118
  manager, 146
  in media plan, 188–89
  in nineteenth century, 7
Community at large, advertising to influence, 33
Company names, 573–74
Comparative advertising, 292–93, 462, 525, 667–68
Compensation, agency, 115, 117, 120, 133–35
Competition
  with agencies, services in, 131–33
  in business press, 318–19, 321
  for classified market, 267–68
  competing accounts, 128
  defined, 90–92
  intramedia, 292–93
  for local advertising, 268–69
  pressure of, 195
  product protection in TV advertising, 216
  unfair, 668
Competitive atmosphere, analyzing, 590
Competitive budgeting, 152
Competitive set, 423
Competitive stage, 59–60, 63–64
Comprehensive (mechanical) layout, 483
Compu-Mark, 576
Computer technology. *See also* Internet
  automatic dialing systems, 363
  in commercial post production, 544
  computer clip art, 487–88
  computer-generated imagery (CGI), 540–41
  digital advertising and production, 491–92
  digital scanners, 511
  fast-close advertising and, 297
  in homes, 58
  layout design, 483–85
  print production, 491–92
  production with, 496–97
Computer-to-plate (CTP) printing, 491–92
Concept, 471. *See also* Idea(s)
Concept testing, 442, 450
Condoms, 687
Confusion, unfair competition by, 668
Conocraft, 392
Consent decree, 117–18, 656
Consolidation, advertising in 1980s and, 19
Constraints on advertising, 653–54. *See also* Law(s);
  Regulation of advertising; Self-regulation
Consumer advocacy groups, 688
Consumer boycotts, 697
Consumer directories, 414–17
Consumerism, tactical, 153
Consumer Leasing Act, 653
Consumer magazine(s), 286–329
  as advertising medium, 294–97
  audience measurement, 312–14
  business press compared to, 315–17
  circulation, 314–15
  city magazines, 300–301
  costs of, 290–92, 297
  cross-media buys, 294
  elements of, 301–6
    ad color and size, 303–5
    bleed pages, 305
    inserts and multiple-page units, 305–6
    page size, 301
    position and space-buying designations, 302–3
  evolution of modern, 287, 290
  full-run edition, 298
  media competition and media imperatives (comparatives), 292–93
  partial-run edition, 296, 297–300
  psychographic research and, 301
  selective binding, 299–300
  selectivity of, 287, 290, 294–95
  selling space in, 306–12
    discounts, 308–9
    magazine dates, 297, 310
    magazine rate structure, 308

magazine short rate, 309–10
    placing order, 310
    rates, negotiation and merchandising, 306–8
    split-run editions, 298–99
Consumer-oriented perspective of newspapers, 254
Consumer Outdoor Recognition Study (CORS), 444
Consumer Price Index, 196
Consumer(s)
  advertising and, 31
  attitudes of, 612–14
  avoidance of unwanted solicitations, 357–58
  brands and, 70–72, 75–76
  fragmented consumer target, 152
  perceptions of, 35–36, 38–39, 57
Consumer sales promotion, 389–90
Contests, 408–10
Continuity, 190–93
Contract, advertising as, 658
Contrast, 467, 478–79
Controlled circulation, 324
Cooperative advertising, 271–72, 382, 410–13,
    622–23, 659
Cooperative Analyses of Broadcasting (CAB), 224
Copy, 446–69
  appeals, nature and use of, 448–51
  creative work plan, 464
  derivation of term, 451n
  design of, 468
  great advertising and, 448, 451–52
  outdoor, 341
  slogans, 462–64
  structure of advertisements, 452–59
    amplification with body copy, 457
    headline, 452–56
    proof, 457–59
    subheadline, 456–57
  style of, 459–62
Copy approach, 459
Copy testing, 438, 441
Corporate advertising, 47–48
Corporate branding, 33–34
Corporate profits, advertising and, 680–81
Corporate speech, 664
Corporate symbol, protecting usage of, 577
Corrective advertising, 18, 657
Corsearch, 576
Cost-based fee, 134
Cost control, 152
Cost per lead (CPL), 375
Cost per order (CPO), 375
Cost per rating point (CPP), 203
Cost per thousand (CPM), 185
  of consumer magazines, 297
  household costs, increase in, 208–9
  of insert, 305–6
  of magazines, 292
  of newspapers, 274
  of radio, 232
  ride-along, 382
  of shelter advertising, 349
  of transit advertising, 347
Cost-plus fee, 134
Cost(s)
  of consumer magazines, 290–92, 297
  of inserts, 305–6
  newspaper advertising, comparing, 274
  of outdoor, 338–39
  television, 199–201, 542–43
Cotrends, packaging and, 582
Council for Marketing and Opinion Research
    (CMOR) Respondent Cooperative Study, 424
Council of Better Business Bureaus (CBBB), 13, 670
  National Advertising Division (NAD) of, 670
County Seat Cafe, 404, 405
Coupons, 180, 391, 400–402
  redemption fraud, 402, 403
Coverage area, TV, 213–14
Cover date, magazine, 310
Cover of magazine, 302–3
Cover stocks, 384

CPM. *See* Cost per thousand (CPM)
Cramer-Krasselt, 304
Crayola, 391–92
Creative Artists Agency (CAA), 131
Creative department in agency, 121
Creative leap, 473–88
Creative research, testing, 441–46
Creative vision, 447
Creative work plan, 464
Creativity
  agency as creative center, 115
  in catalogs, 372
  creative options with magazines, 293–94
  creative strategy for campaign, 590–96
  in media plan, 188–89
  of newspapers, 254
  of outdoor, 335, 345
  radio, 237
Credibility of consumer magazines, 296
Credit, advertising in 1980s and, 19
Crest, 100, 101
Cromalin system, 516
Cronapress plates, 517
Cross-media buys, 294
CryoVein, 476
Cumming Center for Advertising Studies, 675
Cumulative or unduplicated audience (cume) estimates,
    249–50
Curiosity-invoking headlines, 455–56
Customer(s)
  advertising to diverse interests of, 32–34
  interviewing, 525
  lifetime value of, 360
  potential, 33
  as target market, 25
  value, 88
Custom X, 150
Cut, 532
Cutler-Hammer, 157
Cuttino Communications, 548, 550

D

Dailey & Associates, 130
Dailies, 539
D'Arcy Masius Benton & Bowles, 123, 516, 637
Darden Restaurants, Inc., 588
Database marketing, 358–60, 378, 620
  in retail advertising mix, 620
Databases, 372, 435
Dates, magazine, 297, 310
Dayparts, 215, 244
DDB Needham, 129, 637, 676
Dealer incentives, 417
Deals, 408
Deceptive advertising, FTC on, 655–56
Decoying, list, 381
Dell Computers, 622
Del Monte, 583
Demand, generic, 680
Demographics, 102–3, 208
  of newspaper readers, 255
  special magazine editions, 298
Demonstrations, 459, 524
Dentsu, 130
Department stores, 604
Depression of 1930s, 14–16
Design
  by computer, 483–85, 491–92
  firms, packaging, 584
  layout, 477–80, 482–83
  of outdoor advertising, 341–42
  package, 579, 583–84
Design and Market Research Laboratory, 583
Designated market area, 213
Desktop, in-house, 540–41
Diagonal wipe, 534
Dialogue, 553
Diamond screening, 518

Diary method, 224, 245–46
Dick Orkin's Radio Ranch, 549, 550
Dictionary words, trademarks using, 567
Dieste & Partners, 156, 157, 426, 542, 647
Differentiation
  package, 582
  product, 35–36, 355
Digidesign Sound Tools, 558
Digital advertising and production, 491–92
Digital audio tape (DAT), 558
Digital Domain, 544
Digital scanners, 511
Digital studios, 496
Direct-action short-term advertising, 42–43
Direct-digital printing, 519
Direct houses in specialty industry, 400
Direct Language Communications, Inc. (DLC), 640–41
Direct-mail advertising, 376–79, 617
  characteristics of, 377–78
  as competitor for local advertising, 268–69
  mailing list and, 379–82
  mail-production program, 382–85
  other techniques, 382
  planning direct-mail piece, 382–85
  production schedule for, 385
  selective binding and, 299
  testing, 378
Direct marketing, 352–87
  consumer complaints about, 356–57
  defined, 353–54
  direct mail for, 376–79
  telemarketing, 360–67
Direct Marketing Association (DMA), 355
Directories, 414–17
Direct premiums, 395–96
Direct response, 353–87. See also Direct-mail advertising; Direct marketing; Direct-response advertising
  benefits of, 354
  in business-to-business sector, 376
  database marketing and, 358–60, 378
  definition of terms in, 353–54
  image of, 356–58
  magazines and, 368–69
  modern direct-response industry, 354–55
  negative-option, 373
  offers, 370–74
  pros and cons of, 179–80
  radio and, 367
  use of videotapes, 223
Direct-response advertising, 18, 45–46, 352–87,
  364–65
  characteristics of successful, 369–70
  defined, 354
  growth of, 355–58
  magazines and, 368–69
  radio and, 367
  television and, 364–65
Direct sale offer, 370–74
  catalogs, 371–73
  fulfillment firm, 374
  negative options direct response, 373
  one-step purchase of specific product, 370–74
Discount department stores, 607, 610
Discounters, 607
Discounts
  magazine, 308–9
  newspaper, 273
Discretionary income, 86
Disparagement of competitors, 668
Display advertising, 268–70
Disposable diaper industry, 108
Disposable income, 86
Dissolve, 533
Distilled Spirits Council, 686
Distribution channel, 32
Distributors of specialty merchandise, 400
DMB & B, 636–37
Doctors, advertising by, 665
Don Ce Sar Beach Resort & Spa, 571
Double billing, 413

Down to Basic (consumer) group, 613
Drive time (radio), 244, 246
Drum scanner, 511
Dun & Bradstreet Software, 317, 602–5
Duotone, 510
DuPont, 44, 572, 588

E

Early warning, 696
Easton, 106
Economic role of advertising, 676–81
Economic unification of Europe, 634–35
Economist, The, 447
Edenfield v. Fane, 665–66
Editor, layout person as, 475
Editorial environment of consumer magazines, 296
Editorial fee, 543
Editorial process, advertising interference in, 695–97
Edsel, 424
Effective frequency, 192
Effective reach, 192
Efficiency/effectiveness balance, 190–93
Efficient consumer response (ECR), 154–55
Egg Beaters, 55–57, 63–64, 66–67, 73, 580–81
Egyptians, ancient, 4
Eight-Sheet Outdoor Advertising Association, 339, 340
Eight-sheet poster, 338–40
Elderly, advertising to, 684, 686
Electric Cooking, 591, 592
Electronic data interchange (EDI), 193
Electronic data processing, 19, 117
Electronic effects, 548
Electronic newspaper, 279
Electronic superhighway. See Internet
Electrotype, 517
Eller Media, 344
Em, 504
Emmerling Post Advertising, 493
Emotion, use of, 461–62, 552
Emotional measurement system, 442–43
Emphasis, 478
Employees
  advertising to influence, 32
  service advertising and, 50
End-product advertising, 44–45
English finish paper, 384
English newspapers, advertising in, 6
Entertainment products, 612
Environment, marketing, 152–54, 434–35
Environmentalism, 153, 694–95
Equity, brand. See Brand equity
ESPN, 221
Estrovite vitamins, 98
Ethics, advertising and, 3, 695–97
European Community (EC), 634–35
Evening newspaper, decline of, 258–59
Everyone's Racquet, 474
Exaggerated claims, era of (1865–1900), 687
Excessive advertising exposure, 687
Exclusionary zones (outdoor), 336
Executional idea, 472
Execution stage of advertising, 435
Exhibits, trade, 413–14
Experiencers (consumers), 434
Experimentation in brand management, 155–56
Eye-catching information, creating, 153

F

Factual approach, 459–61
Fact versus puffery, 658
Fade-in and fade-out, 533
Fads, 429
Fair Riley Call/Bozell, 156, 587
Fallon McElligott, 121
Family, trends involving, 153
Family life cycle, 430–31

Family Values group, 613
Fan wipe, 534
Farm press, 325–28
Fashion, 612
Fashion Statements (consumer classification), 613
Fast-close advertising, 297
Fast-food payout plan, 151
Federal Communications Commission (FCC), 199,
  214, 217, 243, 686
Federal controls of advertising, 654–59
Federal Food, Drug, and Cosmetic Act (1938), 16,
  660
Federal Trade Commission Act (1914), 12–13, 654
Federal Trade Commission (FTC), 12–13, 356–57,
  363–64, 462, 666
  basic rules of courts and, 657–59
  corrective advertising introduced by, 18
  on deceptive advertising, 655–56
  enforcement methods, 656–57
  environmental marketing, 695
  Robinson-Patman Act and, 659
  role of, 655
Fee arrangements, 134
Film clips, 544
Finish, halftone, 509
Finished commercial testing, 442
Finished print tests, 442
First cover, 302
First National Bank of Boston v. Bellotti, 664
First-run syndication, 217
Fitzgerald & Company, 288–89
Fixed fee, 134
Flame, 540, 541
Flatbed scanner, 511
Flat rate, 273
Flexibility
  of radio, 237
  of spot television, 213
Flighting, 194
Flip wipe, 534
Florida Board of Accountancy, 663
Florida Space Coast, 108
FM radio, 239–40, 243
Focus groups, 437–38, 450
Folks Restaurant Management Group, 131–32, 132,
  483, 484, 485, 506, 550, 551, 574, 575, 608, 616,
  617, 618, 619, 625–27
Food and Drug Administration (FDA), 292, 660
Foote, Cone & Belding (FCB), 128, 129, 448, 497,
  526–27
Ford, 140–41, 424
Foreign names, 569
Formal balance, 479
Four-color process printing, 510–14, 511–14
Fourth cover, 302
Fox network, 204, 207
Fragmentation, audience. See Audience fragmentation
Fragmented consumer target, 152
Fraud, 652
  co-op, 413
  coupon redemption, 402, 403
  in sales offers, 356–57
"Free" as advertising term, 658
Freedom products, 612
Free-standing insert (FSI), 401
Frequency, 190–93
  effective, 192
  of network radio and TV mix, 241–42
Frequency discounts, 273, 308–9
Frequency Marketing Inc., 613, 614
Frequency modulation (FM), 239–40, 243
Friedman v. Rogers, 662
Fruit of the Loom, 533
FTC v. Winsted Hosiery Company, 655
Fulfilleds, 432–33
Fulfillment, 374, 397
Full-line merchandise catalogs, 371
Full-run magazine edition, 297–98
Full-service agency, 118–20
FULLtone, 518

G

Gallagher Report, 149, 150
Gallup Organization, 637
Gamut Color, 518
Gannett Co., 259, 263
Gannett Outdoor, 342
Gatefolds, 305
General Agreement on Tariffs and Trade (GATT), 634
General Electric, 526, 565
General Motors, 564, 689
Generations, 87–88
Generation X, 87–88
Generic demand, 680
Generic terms, trademark loss due to, 566
Geographic segmentation, 93–95
Geography
 media plan and, 189–90
 and radio ratings patterns, 248
 special magazine editions, 294
 spot television targeting by, 213
 trademark names from, 569
Geomarketing, 427
Georgia Baptist Health Care System, 598
Georgia Department of Transportation (DOT), 256–58
Georgia Network, 269–70
Geritol, 657
Gerstman & Meyers, 563, 584–85
Gifts, business, 399
Gillette, 442, 478
Global advertising. See International advertising
Global marketing, 631–33
 strategies for, 632–33
 U.S. trademark law and, 569–70
Goals
 advertising, 160–61
 marketing, 23, 160–61
Going-off-the-card, 306
Gold'n Plump Poultry, 409
Golf GTI, 76
Goodby, Berlin & Silverstein, 448
Goodby, Silverstein & Partners, 130, 486, 557
Grapes of Wrath (Steinbeck), 14
Gravure duplicates, 517
Greeks, ancient, 4
Greg & Greg Advertising, 116, 495, 568, 578
Grey Advertising, 636, 637
Grey Poupon, 588
Grocery stores, 611
Gross impression (GI), 249
Gross rating points (GRPs), 201–3, 250
 of outdoor advertising, 342–43
Guaranteed circulation, 312
Guarantees, 458

H

Halftones, 507–11
Hal Riney & Partners, 58, 137
Hard sell slogans, 463
Harley-Davidson, 396
Harmony of design, 477–78
Harris Donovan Model for Outdoor Planning, 344
Harry (editing device), 541
Headlines, 452–56
Health care campaign, 598
Healthtex, 70–71, 430, 449, 451, 460, 461, 595
Hearst Corporation, 294, 307, 311
Heavy users, 102–3
Hewlett-Packard, 468
HiFi color, 518
Highway Beautification Act of 1965, 335
Hispanic Americans, 85
 marketing to, 97, 147–48, 157, 646–47, 648, 649
 press of, 281–83
 Sunday supplement for, 280
Hitachi, 468
Hoarding, 5
Home shopping, 366–67, 611
Honda, 427

Horizontal publications, 324
Horizontal rotation, 216
Horizontal wipe, 534
Household meter, 224
Households, 86
House lists, 381
House marks, 573
Howard Johnson's, 422–23
Hughes Advertising, 93, 107, 114, 181
Humor, use of, 449, 525, 552
Hungarian Radio, 550

I

Idea advertising, 49
Idea(s)
 attracting attention with, 475–77
 basic, 472–73
 creative leap and, 473–88
 creative team and, 472
 executional, 472
 layout of. See Layout
 visualization of, 473
Identity, brand, 582
Illinois Power, 148, 505, 507
Illuminated posters, 338
Illustration buyers, 494
Image, brand, 355, 582
Imagery transfer research, 238
Imaginative approach, 460–61
Immediately preemptible (IP) rate, 215
Imperatives, media, 292–93
Improperly structured program, 659
Inadvertent social role of advertising, 682, 689–90
Inbound telemarketing, 361–63
Incentives, 395, 417–18
Income, trends in, 86
Independent creative services, 131
Independent networks, magazine, 312
Industrial advertising, 47, 323
Industry self-regulation, 670–73
Infinity Broadcasting, 347
Infomercials, 364–66, 526
Informal balance, 479–80
Information Resources Inc., 597–98
Information technology, 20
Ingalls Advertising, 94, 119, 136, 491, 521–22
Ingredient manufacturer co-op, 411
In-group bias, 93
In-group bias theory, 93
In-house advertising, 131–33, 137
In-house services, 133, 541
Initials as trademarks, 569
Innovations
 new pioneering stage and, 68–69, 69
 timing of, 37–38
Inns, signs on seventeenth-century, 5
Insert(s)
 cards, 305
 free-standing (FSI), 401
 magazine, 305–6
 newspaper, 401, 617
 package, 382
Instant Coupon Machine, 402
Institute of Outdoor Advertising, 336, 338
Institutional advertising, 47–48, 615, 664
Institutional slogans, 462
In-store couponing, 402
Integrated brands, managing, 136
Integrated marketing brand management, 143–47
Integrated marketing communication, 26–27, 144–46
 brands and, 72
 point-of-purchase in, 613–14
Integrated Marketing Communications (Schultz), 145
Integrated services, 118
Integrated Services Digital Network (ISDN), 544
Interactive communications, 118
Interactive media, 188–89
Interactive voice response (IVR), 362–63
Inter•Act Promotion Network (IPN), 401

Interconnects, 221–22
Intermedia scheduling in market, 251
International advertising, 126–28, 628–51
 advertising diversity in U.S., 646–49
 advertising function in, 639–42
 creative considerations in, 639–42
 global advertising agency, 126–28
 global advertising campaign, 598
 global brand equity, 126
 global marketing and, 631–33
 legal and regulatory prohibitions, 645–46
 media planning and, 642–45
 multinational advertising agency, 636–39
 world economy and, 634–35
International Reciprocal Trade Association, 135
Internet, 20, 319
 advertising on, 268
 commercial use of, 226–27
 and introduction of new products, 58
 as media outlet, 175
 merchandising ties with magazines, 307
 for multinational marketers, 646
 newspapers on, 279
 pros and cons of, 183–84
 in retail advertising mix, 622
 as source for artwork, 493
 and television usage, 199
Interplak, 57
Interpublic Group, 130
Interview
 customer, 525
 recognition method, 443–44
Invasion of privacy, 357
Inventions, 7–10
IRI, 435
Iris wipe, 534

J

J. Walter Thompson Co., 16, 77–78, 126, 233–35, 317, 458, 555, 602–5, 636, 637
Jewish population, marketing to, 97–98
Jingles, 549
Joint liability of media for advertising, 669
Joint mail advertising, 382
JTF Marketing/Studios, 583
Junior (eight sheet) posters, 338–40
Justice Department, 235

K

KDKA, 14
Keebler, 396
Ketchum Public Relations, 28–30, 165–67
Key-Ads, 347, 690
Keying, 541
Kibbles 'n Bits, 406
Kimberly-Clark, 98
KISS principle, 464–65
Kleid Company, 377
Kmart, 613
Kodak Signature system, 516
Kraft, 97–98

L

Lady Bird Bill, 335
Lambesis, 423, 609–10
Land O' Lakes, 443, 576
Landor Associates, 574
Lands' End, 630
Languages, spoken in U.S. advertising diversity and, 646–49
Lanham Act, 667–68
Late night television, 210
Law(s). See also Regulation of advertising
 on comparative advertising, 667–68
 Federal Trade Commission Act, 12–13, 654
 First Amendment, 336
 on international advertising, 645–46

Robinson-Patman Act (1936), 15, 659
state and local, 666–67
trademark, 569–70
Lawyers, advertising by, 665–66
Layout, 474
basic design principles, 477–80
computer design, 483–85
other composing elements, 480–82
preparing, 482–83
test, 442
visual, 485
Layout person as editor, 475
Lead-getting direct response, 374–76
Leading, 505
Leading Independent Agency Network, 130
Learning, 431
Leo Burnett Co., 123, 128, 129, 143, 156, 171, 471,
533, 637
Letterpress duplicates, 517
Letterpress printing, 497, 498
Lettershop, 381
Lever Brothers, 471
Levi's, 526–27
Life cycle, family, 430–31
Life-stage research, 429–31
Lifestyle segmentation, 95–96. See also Psychographics
Line art, 505–7
Line color, 506–7
Line conversion, 509
Line spacing, 505
Linetint, 505–6
Linotype-Hell, 518
Lintas, 438, 464
Lippincott & Margulies, 562
44 Liquormart, Inc. v. Rhode Island, 663
List brokers, 380
List compilers, 380
List decoying, 381
Listeners per dollar (LPD), 249
List managers, 381
List protection, 381
Literary magazines, 9
Lithography, offset, 497, 498–99
Liveamatics, 442
Live radio commercial, 558
Living patterns, trends in, 86
L.L. Bean, 373, 374
LMC Group, 396
Local advertising, 44, 214–16, 268–69, 269. See also
Retail advertising
Local identity, spot television for, 211–13
Local laws, 666–67
Location shoots, 542
Logotype (logo), 563–64
Long Haymes Carr, 130
Longwater Advertising, Inc., 156
Lord Group, The, 472
Los Angeles Times, The, 259
Lotteries, 659
Lowe Group, The, 130
Loyalty, brand, 89–90
Lucent Technologies, 575
Lufthansa Airlines, 135

M

Machine finish paper, 384
Macintosh computer, 540, 541, 544, 558
Macon Magazine, 300
Magazine Publishers of America, 115, 292, 293, 294
Magazine(s), 18. See also Business press and business-
to-business advertising; Consumer magazine(s)
as advertising medium, 294–97
complementary use of TV and, 294
dates for, 297, 310
direct-response advertising and, 368–69
elements of, 301–6
features of advertising in, 297–301
partial run edition, 298–99
pros and cons of, 181–82

psychographic research and, 301
rate structure of, 308
selectivity of audiences, 369
nineteenth century, 9, 12
Magazine supplements, 280–81
Mailing list, 379–82
Mail order. See Direct marketing
Mail-order advertising. See Direct-response advertising
Mail preference service (MPS), 358
Mail-production program, 382–85
Majority fallacy, 90
Make-goods, 210–11
Makers (consumers), 434
Mama Mary's pizza crusts, 578
Management and finance department in agency, 123
Management publications, 323
Managers
category, 143
communications, 146
marcom, 145
product, 143
Manual effects, 548
Manufacturer to wholesaler co-op, 411
Marcom manager, 145
Margeotes/Fertitta & Weiss, 486
Marine Corps, 231, 233–35, 457, 458, 554
Market, 90
definition of, 75
profile of, 101–2
Market context, 74–75
Market failure, 652
Marketing, 23
ambush, 407
approach to visualization, 473
climate, 590
communication, 176–79, 389. See also Integrated
marketing communication
concept, 88–92
environment, 152–54, 434–35
global, 631–33
goals, 23, 160–61
integrated, 26–27
mix, 25–27
objectives
sweepstakes and contests, 410
packaging and, 579, 580
plan, 23
problem, analyzing, 118–19
process, 42–43
business and professional advertising and, 46–48
consumer advertising and, 43–46
nonproduct advertising and, 49–50
role of advertising in, 42–43
research. See Upfront (marketing) research
traditional vs. new five Ps of, 161–63
Marketing services department in agency, 122–23
Marketing-services system, 141–43
Marketing translation, 644
Market profile, 101–2
MarketSearch, 365
Market segmentation, 88, 92–96. See also Niche
marketing; Positioning
benefits and attitude segmentation, 96
by brand loyalty, 89–90
geographic segmentation, 93–95
lifestyle segmentation, 95–96
product differentiation and, 38–39
product-user segmentation, 95
risks in, 96
Market segmentation, PRIZM system, 186–88
Market share, 101
Markups, 134
Married couples, 86
MARTA, 347
Martin Agency, The, 130, 448–49
Mass communication era, 3
Mass production, 11–12
MatchPrint, 516
Matriarchs, 613
Matte, 533

Maximum Advertising Expenditure for Financial
Performance (MAX), 677
Maxwell House, 595
McCabe & Company, 441
McCann-Erickson, 124, 130, 131, 424–25, 436, 478,
636, 637
McDonald's, 33, 95, 97, 129, 188, 214, 584, 694
McRae Communications, 138–39
Measured marketing, 620
Mechanicals, 483
Media
advertising from 1870 to 1900 and, 8–10
clearance process and, 669
estimated advertising expenditures (1997), 172
expenditures, 172
interactive, 188–89
nontraditional, 175–76
out-of-home, 331
usage levels from country to country, 642
Media buyers, 133, 175
Media commissions, 134
Media mix, 206
Media Networks, 312
Media objectives, 596–97
Media planner, 170–71
Media Store, 135
Media strategy, 170–97, 596. See also specific media
budget, 195–96
competition and, pressure of, 195
media characteristics and, 177–84
media plan, 120, 174–75, 184–93
communication requirements and creative elements,
188–89
efficiency/effectiveness balance, 190–93
geography and, 189–90
international advertising and, 642–45
target audience and, 184–86
media schedule, 193–94
Media synergism, 294
Mega-agencies, 130–31
Men, retail classifications of, 613
Mercedes-Benz, 544
Merchandising (value-added) programs, 274, 307–8
Mergenthaler linotype, 7
Merge/purge (merge & purge), 381
Mergers, ad agency, 128
Meridith Corp., 492
Merkley Newman Harty, 130, 425
Message management, 378, 379
Metro rating area, 213
Metro survey area (MSA), 248
Meyers Research Center, 393
Michelob, 69
MIDI (musical instrument digital interface), 558
Miller, 161–62
Milline rate, 274 n
Mindtrap, 554
Minorities
marketing to, 147–48
Minority groups. See also African Americans; Asian
Americans; Hispanic Americans
changes in, 85
treatment in advertising, 684
Misrepresentation of competition, 668
3M MatchPrint, 516
Model State, Printers' Ink, 13
Moderation, 153
Money magazine, 299, 305
Montgomery Ward, 371
Mood imagery, 526
Moot Wood Turnings, 398
Morphing, 541
Mortise, 509
Morton Vardeman & Associates, 149, 441, 581
Motel 6, 595
Mothers Against Drunk Driving, 686, 688
Motivation, 431
Motivational research, 450–51
Mountain Dew, 428
Movement, music for, 536

MRI, 295–96
Mrs. Baird's Bagels, 426, 542
3M Scotchprints, 517
Multimedia schedule, 195
Multinational advertising agency, 636–39
Multinational selling, 631
Multiple-page advertising in consumer magazines, 305–6
Music
  for commercials, 535–36, 548–49, 556–58
  in radio commercials, 553
  stock, 559
Mutual Advertising Agency Network, 130

N

NAA. *See* Newspaper Association of America (NAA)
NAD/NARB self-regulation program, 670–72
Name assistance, 577
Name changes, 573–74
Names, company and product, 573–77. *See also*
  Trademarks
Namestormers, 577
National advertising, 10–11, 43–44, 160–61, 269–71,
  614
National Advertising Division (NAD) of Council of
  Better Business Bureaus, 670–72
  Children's Advertising Review Unit (CARU) of, 683
National Advertising Federation, 670
National Advertising Review Board (NARB), 670–72,
  683
National Advertising Review Council (NARC), 13,
  670–72
National Association of Attorneys General (NAAG),
  666–67
National Association of Broadcasters (NAB), 223
National-brand deal segment, 90
National-brand loyal segment, 89
National-brand switcher, 90
National Geographic, 294
National Infomercial Marketing Association, 526
National Jeweler, 321
National moods, 153–54
National Newspaper Association, 283
National newspapers, 258, 259–60
National Public Radio (NPR), 237–38
NBC, 14, 207, 229, 667
Need, consumer, 35–40, 70–72
Negative-option direct response, 373
Negotiation
  age of (1956–1990), 117–18
  for buying network time, 210
  in buying spot radio time, 247–48
  rate, 306
Neiman Marcus, 629
Network organizations, 88
Network radio, 241–42
Network(s)
  agency, 130–31
  magazine, 311–12
  newspaper, 270
  nonwired, 211
  outdoor, 344
  TV shopping, 366–67
Network television, 204, 207–11, 241
  buying network time, 209–10
  cost of advertising on, 200–201
  ownership of, 207
New pioneering stage, 67–69
  newest stage, 67–69
New products, 35–36, 42, 55–58, 63–64
Newspaper Advertising Bureau, 614
Newspaper Association of America (NAA), 259, 268,
  270, 682
Newspaper National Network, 271, 272
Newspaper(s), 253–85
  advertising in, 6, 266–75
    classified advertising, 254
    comparing costs of, 274

cooperative advertising, 271–72
  display advertising, 268–70
  rate card, 273–74
  rate structure of, 269–70, 272–73
  space contract, 275
African American and Hispanic press, 281–83
audience fragmentation, 19
circulation analysis, 276–78
consolidation of, 254–55, 258
magazine supplements in, 280–81
marketing of, 260–63
national, 258, 259–60
newspaper networks, 270
population shifts and, 18
pros and cons of, 177–78
radio advertising mix with, 251
in retail advertising mix, 617–20
technology and future of, 279–80
nineteenth century, 8–9
total market coverage (TMC), 266
weekly, 283–84
zoned editions, 264–66
Newsplan contract, 275
News stock, 384
New York Times, The, 259
Niche marketing, 96–98, 200
Nielsen Company, A.C., 210–11, 224
Nielsen Media Research, 213
Nielsen Station Index (NSI), 224
Nielsen Storage Instantaneous Audimeter, 224
Nielsen Television Index (NTI), 224
Nike, 79, 434, 596
Nissan, 162
Nonilluminated panels, 338
Nonpreemptible rate, 215–16
Nonproduct advertising, marketing process and, 49–50
Nonpromotional advertising, 614
Nontraditional buying trends, 612
Nonwired networks, 211
No-rebate age (1918–1956), 117
No-rebating provisions
  consent decrees against, 117–18
  Curtis no-rebating rule, 115
North American Advertising Agency Network, 156
North American Free Trade Agreement (NAFTA), 634
North Broward Medical Center, 455
Numbers as trademarks, 569
Nutritional Labeling and Education Act of 1990, 660

O

OAAA Marketing, 331
Objectives
  advertising, 24
  marketing, 23
Ocean Spray, 567
Offers, direct-response, 370–74
  direct sales, 370–74
  lead getting, 374–76
Off-network syndication, 217
Off-press proofs, 515
Offset duplicates, 517
Offset lithography, 497, 498–99
Ogilvy & Mather, 129, 156, 471, 509, 528, 598, 600,
  601, 637
  Creative Council of, 451–52
Oldies footage, 524
Olympic Games, 407, 598, 599
Omission of information, deception by, 656
Omnibus ads, 614
Omnicom Group, 130
On-line services, 20, 227
O & O (owned and operated) stations, 204
Open (basic) rate, 308–9
Open rate, 273
Operations, marketing/advertising, 140–67
  agency-client relationship, 115, 156–60
  agency selection, 158–60

brand management, 154–56
  integrated marketing, 143–47
budget, setting, 148–52
marketing environment and changing, 152–54
  nation's mood, 153–54
marketing-services system, 141–43
national advertising, appraising, 160–61
restructuring corporate, 147–48
Opportunities, outlining, 23
Opticals, 532–34
OSC, 558
Outbound telemarketing, 361–63
Outdoor advertising. *See under* Out-of-home advertising
Outdoor Advertising Association of America (OAAA),
  331, 332, 336, 341
Outdoor Systems, 344
Out-of-home advertising, 330–51, 622
  alcohol on, 663–64
  outdoor advertising, 5, 6, 182, 333–37
    advantages/disadvantages of, 182, 333–35
    billboards, 18
    buying, 342–43
    Consumer Outdoor Recognition Study (CORS), 444
    forms of, 337–41
    image of, 335–36, 345
    outdoor networks, 344
    overview of industry, 332
    plan, 336–37
    trends in, 345
    verifying, 343
  shelter advertising, 349–51
  transit advertising, 345, 347–49
  trends in, 345
Out-of-home media, 331
Output service bureaus, 497
Outside producer, 539
Overlay proofs, 516, 517
Overt social role of advertising, 682–83, 690–95

P

Package goods product payout plan, 151
Package inserts, 382
Package plans, radio, 246–47
Package rates, 216
Package Value survey, 583–84
Packaging, 562–86, 577–85
  brand identity and, 582
  color influence and, 580–81
  cotrends and, 582
  design firms for, 584
  marketing and, 579, 580
  package design, 583–84
  package differentiation, 582
  package research, 581–82
  unique designs for brand image, 582
Paid circulation, 312–13
Painkillers, 90–92
Painted bulletins, 340
Palmas Del Mar Resort, 75, 93, 106, 107, 181
Palmer, Volney B., 114
Pantone Color Institute, 481
Pantone Matching System (PMS), 507
Paper for direct-mail advertising, selecting, 384
Paradigm, 162
Paradox, 161–62
Parity performance, 152
Parkland Hospital, 154
Partial-run magazine editions, 296, 297–300
Pass-along readership, 313, 323–24
Passion, 163
Passive people meter, 225
Patent applications, 7
Patent-medicine advertising, 9–10, 12
Patriarchs (shopper group), 613
Patricians (shopper group), 613
Patrick Media, 344
Payout plan, 151–52
Pay-per-view movies, 223

Pediatric AIDS Foundation, 282
Penn, 437
Penny newspapers, 8–9
People meters, 225
PepsiCo, 147, 155–56, 214, 242, 462, 592, 596, 630–31
Pepto Bismol, 471
Percentage of sales method of budgeting, 150–51
Perception, consumer, 35–36, 38–39, 57
Performance fee, 134
Performer Q, 226
Per-inquiry (PI) advertising, 366
Personal drive analysis (PDA), 434
Personality types, matching media with, 294
Personal medium, radio as, 230
Personal message, direct response as, 354
Personal names as trademarks, 568–69
Personal responsibility, 153
Personal selling, 25
Perspective, 162
Persuasion, 163
Photography, 486
  sources, 488
Photomatics, 442
Photoshop, 484
Pica, 504
Pick-up rates, 274
Pictorial trademarks, 569, 570
Pioneering advertising stage, 55–58, 63–64
  newer and newest, 67–69
Pioneer Stereo, 427
Pirate Radio & Television, 554
Pixel, 483
Plan, media. See under Media strategy
Planning, 52–109
  advertising stages of product and, 55–62
    advertising spiral, 62–80, 68
    after retentive stage, 67–69
    competitive stage, 59–60, 63–64
    new pioneering stage, 67–69
    pioneering stage, 55–58, 63–64
    retentive stage, 60–62, 62
  of direct-mail piece, 382–85
  Lintas:Link and, 464
  outdoor advertising, 336–37
  print production, 491–92, 493–95
  TV commercial, 528–29
Plant operator, 337
Pocket people meter, 225
Point-of-purchase advertising, 391–97
Point-of-Purchase Advertising Institute, 392
Point-of-purchase merchandising, 613–14
Point (pt), 504
Polaroid, 637–38
Politics, television and, 18
Pollak Levitt Chalet, 320–21
Popular magazines, 9
Population
  growth from 1870 to 1900, advertising and, 7
  shifts, newspapers and, 18
  trends in, 84–85
Posada De Puerto Rico Associates v. Tourism Company of Puerto Rico, 662
Positioning, 98–102
  brand, 76
  defined, 588
  to expand brand share, 99–100
  how to approach problem of, 100
Position of advertising in consumer magazines, 302–3
Post, 526
Post-buy inspection, 337, 343
Poster panels, 337–39
Poster test, 442
Postproduction process for TV commercial, 537–38, 539
Posttests of advertising campaign, 597–99
Potential Rating Index by Zip Market (PRIZM) system, 186–88, 250, 301
Power consumption, 8
Power Master malt liquor, 92–93

Practicals (shopper group), 613
Predictive dialing, 363
Preemptible with two weeks' notice, 215
Preemption rate, 215–16
Preference, brand, 24
Preferred-position rates, 273
Premarketing era, 3
Premiums, 391, 395–97
Preprinted newspaper inserts, 617
Preproduction for TV commercial, 537–38
Prerecorded radio commercial, 559
Presses, sheet-fed vs. web-fed, 499
Press proofs, 515–17
Presstek/Heidelberg, 519
Pretesting, 435
Pretest research, 438–39
Pricing, 39–40
  everyday low (EDLP), 42, 400
  price competition, 34
Prime prospects, 83–88, 590
Primetime Access Rule, 217
Printer, selecting a, 384–85
Printer's Ink, 13
Printers' Ink Model Statutes (1911), 666
Printing buyers, 495
Print producers, 494
Print production, 490–520
  computer production, 491–92
  duplicate material, making, 517
  functions in, 494–95
  mechanical and artwork
    color proofing, 511
    halftones, 507–11
    press proofs, 515–17
  new technology, 517–19
  planning and scheduling, 496–97
  prepress process, 492–93
  production data, 495–96
  selecting printing process, 497–500
  typography, 493, 500–502
    measurement of type, 504–5
    reading and, 501–2
    typesetting methods, 505
Print testing example, 442–43
Privacy, invasion of, 357
Private-label deal segment, 90
Private-label loyal segment, 90
Private-label switcher, 90
PRIZM system, 186–88, 250, 301
Pro Balanced, 94
Problem solution techniques, 23, 526
Procter & Gamble, 98, 109, 140, 141, 171, 400, 448, 584, 629
Producer, TV commercial, 538–39
Product, 89–90
  analyzing, 590
  criticism of, 686
  definition of, 89–90
  for selected markets, creating, 99
Product advertising, stages of, 55–62
  advertising spiral, 62–80, 68
  after retentive stage, 67–69
  comparison of, 62–64
  competitive stage, 59–60, 63–64
  pioneering stage, 55–58, 63–64
    newer and newest, 67–69
  retentive stage, 60–62, 62
Product awareness, 35–36
Product classification, 565
Product differentiation, 38–39, 355
Product distribution, uneven, 213
Production
  1870–1900, 7–10
  mass, 11–12
Production commissions, 134
Production costs, TV, 201
Production/talent agencies, 131
Product manager, 143

Product names, 573–77
Product placement, 407–8
Product protection, 216
Product quality, 35–40
Product research, 437
Product timing, 37–38
Product-user segmentation, 95
Professional advertising, 47
Professional publications, 323
Professional services, advertising of, 663, 664–66
Profit margin, degree of advertising and, 40–41
Profit potential, 37
Profits, advertising and corporate, 680–81
Progressive proofs (progs), 515
Promotional Products Association International, 397–98, 399
Promotional retail advertising, 614
Promotion Decisions, 400–401
Proof, 457–59, 515–17
Prospect identification, 596
Prospect research, 436
Proximity to purchase, radios, 236
Prudential Security, 112
Psychographics, 103–9
  defined, 103
  research on, 301
  target audience, 105–7
  test marketing and, 107–9
Psychology, advertising and, 431–32
Public Awareness, Era of (1900–1965), 687
Public Broadcasting Magazine Network, 312
Publicity, advertising and right of, 664
Public relations, 26
Public-service campaigns, 347, 690–95
Puffery, fact vs., 658
Pure Food and Drug Act (1906), 12, 687
Purell Instant Hand Sanitizer, 58

Q

"Q" reports, 226
Quaker Oats, 147
Quaker State, 438
Qualitative characteristics of consumer magazines, 296
Qualitative ratings, 226
Qualitative research, 437
Quality
  product, 35–40
  service advertising, 50
Quark XPress, 484
QuickTime video, 558

R

Radio, 229–52
  advertising mix with newspapers, 251
  arrival of, 14, 117
  audience, definitions of, 249–50
  buying radio, 247–48
  as complement to other media, 231–32
  cost of, 232, 238
  direct-response advertising and, 367
  features and advantages of, 230–37
  limitations and challenges of, 237–39
  pervasiveness of, 230–31
  programming, types of, 244–45
  pros and cons of, 179, 180
  rate classifications, 246–47
  ratings, using, 248–51
  rating services, 245–46
  in retail advertising mix, 620
  scheduling for, 250–51
  selling radio commercial time, 240–45
    AM vs. FM as advertising medium, 243
    network radio, 241–42
    spot radio, 242–43, 246–47
    time classifications (dayparts), 244
  technical aspects of, 239–40
  television and, 18

Radio Advertising Bureau (RAB), 231, 232, 236, 250, 251, 412
Radio All Dimension Audience Research (RADAR), 246
Radio boutiques, 550
Radio commercial, 548–63
  creating, 548–49
  methods of delivery, 558–59
  musical commercials, 556–58
  nature of the medium, 548–49
  producing, 559–60
  script development, 549–50
  writing, 550–54
Radioland, 550
Radiosurgery software, 92
Radio waves, 239
Railroads, 7
Rand Corporation, 85
Raster Scan Graphics, 483
Rate base, 312–13
Rate cards, 273–74
Rates
  consumer magazine, 291–92, 308–9
  first rate directory, 115
  local/national rate differential, 269–70
  magazine, 308
  newspaper, 269–70, 272–73
  radio rate classifications, 246–47
Rating(s)
  methodologies, 224–26
  qualitative, 226
  radio, 248–51
  television rating-point system, 201–3, 226
Rating services
  radio, 245–46
  syndicated, 223–25
Reach, 190–93
  effective, 192
  of outdoor, 334
  of radio, 230–31, 231
  of television
    cable, 221
Reach Marketing, 147
Readership
  analysis, 443–44
  consumer magazines, 296, 313–14
  newspapers, 261–62
  pass-along, 313, 323–24
Reading, typography and, 501–2
RealFind USA, 268
Rebates, 275, 408
Recency, 193
Reckitt & Colman, 636
Recognition, package, 581
Recognition method of interviewing, 443–44
Recorded effects, 548
Recording and mixing, cost of, 543
Reddi-wip, 304
Red Lobster, 588
Red Roof Inn, 96–97
Reebok International Ltd., 434, 564–65
Reengineering of agency, 118, 123–25
Registration notice, trademark, 572–73
Regulation of advertising, 652–74. See also Law(s)
  Bureau of Alcohol, Tobacco, and Firearms (ATF), 660
  comparative advertising, 667–68
  Federal Trade Commission and, 654–59, 666, 667
  Food and Drug Administration and, 660
  for international advertising, 645–46
  outdoor advertising, 335–36
  self-regulation, 653, 668–69
  state and local, 666–67
  of telemarketing, 363–64
  U.S. Postal Service, 659
Relationship marketing, 263, 359
Release, 487
Religious publications, 9
Remnant space, discounts on, 309
RemoteWare ad, 475, 476
Repositioning strategy, 99–100, 100

Representatives (reps), television, 211
Reputation, 459
Research, 3, 4, 422–45
  advertising, 436–37
    testing creative research, 441–46
  brand personality, 428
  campaign evaluation, 441
  Consumer Outdoor Recognition Study (CORS), 444
  database marketing for, 360
  focus group, 437–38
  imagery transfer, 238
  as informational tool, 423
  life-stage, 429–31
  motivational, 450–51
  and multinational consumer, 637
  package, 581–82
  posttesting, 597–99
  pretest, 438–39
  prospect, 436
  on psychographics, 301
  qualitative, 437
  right kind of, 424
  secondary, 426
  services, 135–36
  strategic or account planners, 425–26
  syndicated magazine readership, 315
  telephone, 224
Research data
  on outdoor, 345
  on radio, difficulty of obtaining, 246
Research era, 4
Residuals, 543
Response lists, 381
Responsibility, personal, 153
Restructured brand management approach, 146
Restructuring corporate operations, 147–48
Retail advertising, 44, 606–27
  consumer attitudes and, 612–14
  mix, 616–23
  national advertising and, 614
  retail branding, 608–12
  retailer's business cycles and, 615–16
  retailing in 1990s and, 614
  retail trends and, 609–11
  special promotion times, 615–16
  types of, 614–16
Retail Advertising Bureau, 615
Retail catalogs, 371
Retailer control, 155
Retail on-line, 622
Retail satisfaction profiles, 613
Retentive advertising stage, 60–62, 62
Return on investment (ROI), 23–24
Revenues, 37
Reverse copy, 502
Rhino Records, 295
Rice-A-Roni, 583
Rick Lyon Music, 536
Ride-alongs, 382
Riding the boards, 337, 343
Ripamatics, 442
Risk in brand management, 155–56
Robinson-Patman Act (1936), 15, 659
Rock oldies, 536
Rolodex agency, 133
Roman merchants, ancient, 4
Roper Organization, 71, 153–54
Roper Reports, 521
Roper Starch, 198–99, 424
Rotary bulletin, 340
Rotation of a schedule, 216
Rotogravure, 497, 499
Rotoscope technique, 526
Rough layouts, 483
Royal Crown Cola, 68
Rubin v. Coors Brewing, 663
80/20 rule, 102–3
Run-of-paper (ROP) position rate, 273
Run of schedule (ROS), 216
Ruszel Woodworks, 393

S

Saatchi & Saatchi, 108, 130, 637
Sales, 37
Sales incentives, 417
Salesmen, space, 114
Sales promotion, 26, 388–419
  advertising and, 389–91
  consumer, 389–90
  defined, 388
  forms of, 391
    cooperative advertising, 271–72, 410–13, 659
    coupons, 400–402
    directories and Yellow Pages, 414–17
    event marketing, 406–8
    point-of-purchase advertising, 391–97
    premiums, 395–97
    product placement, 407–8
    sampling, 402, 404–6
    specialty advertising, 397–400
    sweepstakes and contests, 408–10
    trade incentives, 417–18
    trade shows and exhibits, 413–14
  plan, 597
Sampling, 402, 404–6, 458
Satellite transmission
  network radio and, 241–42
  television, 214
Saturn, 137, 162
Sawyer Riley Compton, 123, 125, 156, 598
Sawyer Riley Compton and Eaton, 511
Scanner reporting systems, 435
Scatter buying sessions, quarterly, 209–10
Scatter plans, 209–10
Schedule
  media, 193–94, 596
  multimedia, 195
  for print production, 496–97
  for radio, 250–51
  spot television, 215
Scientific American, 491
Scitex, 518
Screening, stochastic, 518–19
Screen printing, 500
Script
  radio commercial, 549–50
  TV commercial, 529–32
SEA·DOO, 165–67
Seals of approval, 458
Sears Roebuck & Co., 242, 371, 620
Secondary research, 426
Second cover, 302
Sega, 557
Segmentation. See Market segmentation
Selective binding, 299–300
Selective headlines, 456
Selectivity
  of consumer magazines, 287, 290, 294–95
  of direct mail, 378
  of radio, 545
Self-liquidating premiums, 396
Self-regulation, 653, 668–69
  advertising clearance process, 668–69
  by industrywide groups, 670–73
Semipromotional advertising, 614
Sequence, 478
Serials, 524
Service advertising, 49–50
Service bureaus, 381
Service marks, 542, 563, 573
Share of audience, 203
Sheet-fed presses, 499
Shelf space, slotting allowances for, 155
Shelter advertising, 349–50
Shelter Advertising Association, 332, 350
Sherwin-Williams, 361–62
Shooting TV commercial, 539
Shopping behavior, radio's influence on, 236

Shopping centers, 610
Shopping networks, TV, 366–67
Short rate, 275
Short-term advertising, direct-action, 42–43
Showings of outdoor advertising, 342–43
Siddall, Matus & Coughter, Inc., 256–58
Signal, radio, 239
Silhouette, 509
Silicon Graphics (SGI), 484
Similarity of ads in campaign, 595
Simmons Market Research Bureau, Inc. (SMRB), 315, 344
Singles, 86
Single-source data, 435
Siquis, 6
Situation analysis, 23, 92, 589–90
Situations (TV commercials), 525
Size of ad in consumer magazines, 303–5
Skepticism of retail and sales ads, 612–13
Slice-of-life technique, 525
Sliding fee, 134
Slogans, 462–64
Slotting allowances, 155
SLRS Advertising, 487
Smokey Bear, 692, 693
Snap, 477
Snap-on Tools, 59, 125, 591, 593, 598
Snapple, 57
Social class, 428
Social marketing, 693
Social Responsibility, Era of (1965–present), 687
Social role of advertising, 32, 675–98
   inadvertent, 682, 689–90
   overt, 682–83, 690–95
   unwanted influences on society, 687–89
Societal factors in growth of direct-response, 355
Sociology, advertising and, 427–31
Soft drink industry, 68–69, 92, 579, 590
   market demographics, 102
Sony, 33
Sound
   effects, 548, 553
   for radio commercial, 548
   similarity of in advertising, 595
Soundtrack for TV commercial, 534–35
Space-agers (cohort group), 429
Space-buying designations for magazines, 302–3
Space contract, 275, 310
Space order, consumer magazine, 310
Space salesmen, 114
Space wholesalers, 115
Special effects, 543
Special features, 216
Special promotion times, 615–16
Specialty apparel retailers, 610
Spectaculars, 340–41
Spiral, advertising. See Advertising spiral
Split-run magazine editions, 298–99
Split spot, 526
Spokesperson, 524
Sponsorship of events, 406–8, 598, 599
Sports Illustrated, 294
Spot radio, 242–43, 247–48
Spot television, 211–13
   buying and scheduling, 215
   preemption rate, 215–16
Square halftone, 509
SRI International, 95–96, 432
Standard Advertising Invoice (SAI), 268
Standard Advertising Register, 158
Standard Advertising Unit (SAU), 270
Standard agency commission, 115, 117
Standard Directory of Advertising Agencies (Agency Red Book), 113
Standardization of newspaper national advertising, 270, 272
Standard Rate and Data Service (SRDS), 323
   production source, 495–96
Starbucks, 79
Starch Advertisement Readership Service, 482

Starch Readership Award, 468
Starch Readership Service, 443–44
Starch Research, 459, 473, 618
Starch Tested Copy, 464
   guidelines for creating an ad, 464–68
State laws, 666–67
Statement stuffers, 382
Station announcer, delivery of commercial by, 559
Statistical Research, Inc. (SRI), 238, 246
Status-oriented consumers, 433
Stayfree, 582
Still photographs in TV commercial, 525
Stilson & Stilson, 365
Stochastic screening, 518–19
Stockholders, advertising to influence, 33
Stock music, 559
Stock photos, 488
Stolichnaya, 467
Stop motion, 526
Storyboard development for TV commercial, 531, 532, 533
Storyboards, video, 442–43
Straight announcer approach, 553–54
Strategic (marketing) planners, 425–26
Strategy, 119
   creating radio commercials from written, 549
   development, 435
   marketing, 23
      global, 632–33
   media. See Media strategy
   for nurturing brands, 33–34
   translating information into, 436
Stratification, 428
Stripping, 218
Strivers (consumer group), 433
Strugglers, 434
Studio shoots, 542
Study of Media Involvement VII, 296
Subheadline, 456–57
Substantiation, 656
Sunday supplements, 280
Sunkist, 393, 582
Sun-Maid Raisins, 591, 594–95
SuperGraphics, 332, 349
Supermarkets, 155, 610
Supers, 534
Suppliers of specialty merchandise, 400
Supreme Court, 655, 661
Surprint, 509
Surveys, 102–9, 424
Sweepstakes, 391, 409–10
Sweep weeks, 225
Sweet Factory, 453, 454
SWOP (Specifications for Web Offset Publications)/ GAA (Gravure Association of America) guidelines, 516
Synchographics, 377
Syndicated magazine readership research, 315
Syndicated rating services, 223–25
Syndicated TV programming, 216–18
Synergistic effect, 175, 188

T

Tack-up advertisements (siquis), 6
Taco Bell, 96
Tactical consumerism, 153
Tactics, media, 596
Talent, 543, 559
Talent/production agencies, 131
Tangibles in service advertising, 50
Target audience, 105–7, 184–86, 295
Targeted communication, direct response as, 354
Target marketing, 25, 82–109, 366
   defined, 83
   new marketing concept and, 88–92
   planning advertising, 92–98
      market segmentation, 92–96
      niche marketing, 96–98

positioning, 98–102
   profile of buyer, 102–3
   profile of market, 101–2
   prime prospects, defining, 590
   psychographics and, 103–9
Task method of budgeting, 152
Taster's Choice, 194
TBWA Chiat/Day, 121, 130, 156, 161
Team, creative, 472
Technicolor, 368
Technology. See also Computer technology
   advertising in 1980s and, 18
   audio, 558
   direct-response advertising and, 46
   future of newspapers and, 279–80
   information, 20
   new print production, 517–19
   new product innovations, 57–58
   TV, ratings problems due to, 224–25
   and Yellow Pages, 416–17
Teenagers, newspaper reading by, 261
Teflon, 44, 572
Telecommunications Act of 1996, 232
Telecommunications companies, 242
Telecommunities, 629
Teleflora, 492
Telemarketing, 180, 360–67
   international, 635
   sales rule, 358
900-telemarketing, 363
Telephone ad, 8
Telephone Consumer Protection Act (TCPA) (1992), 363–64
Telephone preference service (TPS), 358
Telephone research, 224
Television, 18, 198–228
   advent of, 117
   as advertising medium, 178–79, 199–201
   cable, 200, 207, 218–22
   as challenge to radio, 229
   costs of, 542–43
   director, 537
   direct-response advertising and, 364–65
   evolution of, 18
   forms of, 204, 207–16
      local TV advertising, 214–16
      network television, 204, 207–11, 241
      spot television, 211–13, 215–16
   fragmented audience of, 19
   future of, 222
   and newspaper share of advertising, 253–54
   ownership of, 199
   politics and, 18
   radio and, 19
   rating-point system, 201–3, 226
   in retail advertising mix, 620
   share of audience, 203
   shopping channels, 366–67
   shopping networks, 366–67
   syndicated rating services and, 223–25
   syndicated TV programming, 216–18
   talk shows, 689
   TV coverage area, defining, 213–14
   usage variance from country to country, 642–43
   videocassette recorders (VCRs) and, 222–23
Television Advertising Bureau, 225, 412
Television commercial, 521–45
   controlling cost of, 542–43
   copy development timetable sequence, 523
   creating, 523–36
      music, 535–36
      music video influence, 527
      opticals, 532–34
      planning, 528–29
      soundtrack, 534–35
      storyboard development, 531, 532, 533
      visual techniques, 523–27
      writing script, 529–32
   direct-response TV commercial, length of, 364–65

Television commercial (*continued*)
  producing, 537–38
    postproduction process, 539, 540–41
    preproduction, 537–38
    producer's role, 538–39
    shooting, 539
Test commercials, 441–42
Testimonials, 459, 523, 658–59
Testing creative research, 441–46
Testing direct-mail advertising, 378
Test marketing, 107–9
Theater of the Mind, 550
Third cover, 302
Thomas Howell Group, 460
Thomson & Thomson, 576
Thumbnail sketches, 482
Time, Inc., 294, 298, 492
Time banks, 135
Time control, 153
Time-shift viewing, 222
Timing
  media strategy and, 596
  product, 37–38
Titling, 543
Tobacco advertising, 18, 336, 686
Topologically Integrated Geographic Encoding and Referencing (Tiger), 83–84
Total audience plans (TAP), 246–47
Total concept, 470–89. *See also* Idea(s); Visual layout
Total market coverage (TMC), 266
Total plan, 120
Total Research Corp., 523
Total survey area (TSA), 213, 248
Town criers, 4
Toyota, 427
Trade advertising, 46–47
Trade incentives, 417–18
Trademarks, 562–86. *See also* Packaging
  brand name selection, 567
  certification marks, 573
  defined, 563–73
  forms of, 567–69
  general rules, 571–72
  house marks, 573
  law on, 569–70
  loss of, 566
  protecting, 566, 577
  registration notice, 572–73
  service marks, 563, 573
  successful, 569
Trademark search, 576
Trade name, 564–65
Trade papers, 322–23
Trade promotion, 390, 391
Trade publication. *See* Business press and business-to-business advertising
Trade shows and exhibits, 413–14
Traditionalists (cohort group), 429
Traffic Audit Bureau (TAB), 344
Traffic-building premiums, 395
Transit advertising, 345, 347–49
Transitioners (cohort group), 429
Transition music, 526
Translation, 640–42
  marketing, 644
Transportation, advertising from 1870 to 1900 and, 7
Transportation Displays Inc. (TDI), 347
TranStop, 332
Treasury Department, ATF Division of, 660
Trends, 153–54, 428
Trial offers, 458
Trone Advertising, 428
True North Communications, 128
TV. *See* Television

TV Guide, 492
TvQ, 226
Two-color halftone plates, 509–10
Type family, 502–4
Type font, 502–5
Typesetting, 505
Typography, 493, 500–502
  measurement of type, 504–5
  reading and, 501–2
  typefaces
    in outdoor, 342
  type fonts and families, 502–5
  typesetting methods, 505
Typography experts, 494

U

Unfair competition, 668
Unions, 559
Unique selling proposition (USP), 447
Unity of design, 477
Universal Product Code (UPC), 70, 435
University of Alberta, 342
Unwanted solicitations, consumer avoidance of, 357–58
Up-front buys, 209–10
Upfront (marketing) research
  anthropology and, 427
  marketing environment and, 435–36
  Personal Drive Analysis (PDA), 434
  psychology and, 431–33
  sociology and, 427–31
UPN, 204
Upper Deck survey, 96
Up-selling, 362
U.S. Department of Justice, 18, 117–18
U.S. Department of Transportation, 691
U.S. Postal Service, 356–57, 402, 659
USA Today, 259–60
Users, heavy, 102–3
User segmentation, 95

V

VALS and VALS 2, 95–96, 431–32
Value, 40
Value added by advertising, 23–24
Value-added (merchandising) programs, 274, 307–8
"Value gap," 40
Values and Life-Style 2 (VALS 2), 95–96, 431–32
ValuJet, 574
Vendor programs, 411
Venture Communications List Marketing, 359
Verbal similarity, 591–95
Verified Audit Circulation Company (VAC), 325, 326
Vertical publications, 324
Vertical rotation, 216
Vertical wipe, 534
Vice president of advertising, 149
Vice president of marketing, 149
Videocassette recorders (VCRs), 19, 222–23, 367
Videoconferencing focus groups, 438
Video direct marketing, 367
Video storyboards, 440–41
Video Storyboard Tests, 440–41, 528
Videotapes, 222–23
Vignettes (TV commercials), 525
Virginia State Board of Pharmacy v. Virginia Citizens Consumer Council, 661–62
Visa, 28–30
Visix Software, 60, 61
Visual element, radio's lack of, 238–39
Visualization of ideas, 473
Visual recall, 153

Visual similarity, 591
Visual techniques, 523–27
V-Mail, 17
Voice-It Personal Note Recorder, 288–89
Volume discounts, 308–9
Volume of sales, degree of advertising and, 40

W

Waggener & Associates, 345
Wall Street Journal, The, 259
Wal-Mart, 42–43, 140
Wanna-buys, 613
War Advertising Council, 16, 691
Warner-Lambert, 427
Warranties, 459
Washington Post, 259
Waterless printing, 518
Wavefront, 540
WB, 204
Weather Channel, 363
WebConnect, 356
Web-fed presses, 499
Weekly newspapers, 283–84
Weighted *CPM*, 185
Western Laser Graphics, 492
Westinghouse, 14
West & Vaughan, 60, 113, 444, 477, 479, 618, 620
Wheeler-Lea Act (1938), 16, 655
Whirlpool, 427
White space
  in print ads, 482
  in radio commercials, 553
Wholesale clubs, 610
Wholesalers, space, 115
Wieden & Kennedy, 448
Wipe, 534, 535
Women
  in ads and commercials, 683
  newspaper reading by, 261
  shifting priorities of, 154
  shopping classifications for, 613
Wool Bureau, 573
Work plan, creative, 464
Works Progress Administration (WPA), 14
Worldata, 356
World economy, movements toward, 634–35
World War I, advertising in, 13–14
World War II, advertising in, 16–17
World Wide Radio, 550
Wrangler, 157
Writing stocks, 384
WWP Group, 130

Y

Yamaha golf carts, 83, 84, 91
Yankee Group, 622
Yankelovich Monitor, 163
Yankelovich Partners, 357
Yellow Pages, 182–83, 267, 414–17
Yield management, 40
Young adults, newspaper reading by, 261
Young & Rubicam, 72–74, 464, 637

Z

Zimmerman Agency, The, 108, 452, 453, 455, 461, 474, 494, 571
ZIP codes, penetration by, 266
ZIP program, 617
Zoned editions, 264–66
Zones Area Preprint (ZAP) Program, 265–66, 617
Zoning, 264–66